understanding company law

HEAD OFFICE: 100 Harris Street PYRMONT NSW 2009
Tel: (02) 8587 7000 Fax: (02) 8587 7100
For all sales inquiries please ring 1800 650 522
(for calls within Australia only)

INTERNATIONAL AGENTS & DISTRIBUTORS

NORTH, CENTRAL & SOUTH AMERICA,
CARIBBEAN
Carswell Co
Ontario, Canada

HONG KONG
Sweet & Maxwell Asia
Hysan Avenue, Causeway Bay
Hong Kong

MALAYSIA
Sweet & Maxwell Asia
Petaling Jaya, Selangor

NEW ZEALAND, PACIFIC ISLANDS
Brooker's Ltd
Wellington

SINGAPORE
Sweet & Maxwell Asia
Battery Road

EUROPE, MIDDLE EAST AND AFRICA
ISM Europe, Middle East & Africa
Sweet & Maxwell Ltd
Andover, Hampshire

AUSTRALIA, PAPUA NEW GUINEA
Thomson Legal & Regulatory Ltd
Pyrmont, Sydney

JAPAN, KOREA, TAIWAN
ISM Asia Operations
Thomson Legal & Regulatory
Pyrmont, Sydney

understanding company law

Phillip Lipton

Senior Lecturer
Department of Business Law and Taxation,
Monash University

Abe Herzberg

Senior Lecturer
Department of Business Law and Taxation,
Monash University

thirteenth edition

LAWBOOK CO. 2006

Published in Sydney by
Lawbook Co.
100 Harris Street, Pyrmont, NSW

First edition	1984	Seventh edition	1998
Second edition	1986	Eighth edition	1999
Third edition	1988	Ninth edition	2000
Fourth edition	1991	Tenth edition	2001
second impression with supplementary chapter	1992	Eleventh edition	2003
Fifth edition	1993	Twelfth edition	2004
Sixth edition	1995	Thirteenth edition	2006

National Library of Australia
Cataloguing-in-Publication entry

Lipton, P (Phillip).
Understanding company law.

13th ed.
Bibliography.
Includes index.
For tertiary students.
ISBN 0 455 22243 6.

1. Corporation law - Australia. I. Herzberg, A (Abraham).
II. Title.

346.94066

This edition is up to date as of 1 November 2005.

Editors: Sue Jamieson and Corina Brooks
Product Manager: Adrian Burrell

Typeset in Univers 45 Light 8.5 on 12 point by Midland Typesetters, Australia

Printed by Ligare Pty Ltd, Riverwood, NSW

to

Ilana, Evelyn, Robert, Natalie and Jack
Nan, Jessica and Adam

preface

While there have not been many legislative changes since the twelfth edition, there are many items presently on the law reform agenda. In this edition we outline the key recommendations of the following CAMAC reports:

> Insider Trading report (November 2003); and
> Report on Rehabilitating Large and Complex Enterprises in Financial Difficulties (October 2004).

This edition also refers to the following CAMAC discussion papers and law reform references:

> Corporate Duties Below Board Level – discussion paper (May 2005);
> Personal Liability for Corporate Fault – discussion paper (May 2005);
> Corporate Social Responsibility – discussion paper (November 2005); and
> Long tail liabilities – reference (October 2005).

In October 2005 the government announced a detailed insolvency reform package which is its response to recommendations stemming from the Parliamentary Joint Committee on Corporations and Financial Services, *Corporate Insolvency Laws: A Stocktake* (June 2004), CAMAC's reports *Rehabilitating Large and Complex Enterprises in Financial Difficulties* (October 2004), *Corporate Groups* (May 2000) and *Corporate Voluntary Administration* (June 1998).

The *Corporations Amendment Act (No 1) 2005* which amended s 197 of the *Corporations Act* to overcome the decision in *Hanel v O'Neill* (2004) 22 ACLC 274 is discussed in Chapter 3 below. The exposure draft of the *Corporations Amendment Bill (No 2) 2005* to remove the "100 member rule" for calling shareholders' meetings is discussed in Chapter 14 below.

This edition incorporates the following important new directors' duty cases in Chapter 13:

> *ASIC v Vines* [2005] NSWSC 738;
> *Gold Ribbon (Accountants) Pty Ltd v Sheers* [2005] QSC 198;
> *Southern Cross Mine Management Pty Ltd v Ensham Resources Pty Ltd* [2005] QSC 233; and
> *ASIC v Vizard* [2005] FCA 1037.

Together with Corina Brooks and Adrian Burrell we have improved the layout and design of the book. A new feature is the use of margin notes to assist students to focus on the main points in the text. We have also introduced a design feature to better highlight our discussion of significant cases. The use of paragraph numbering will help readers to navigate their way through the book.

As with previous editions, we have continued cross-references to the Lipton-Herzberg website portal (**http://www.lipton-herzberg.com.au**). The website gives users easy access to a vast collection of corporate law Internet resources. *Pathways* – **http://www.lipton-herzberg.com.au/pathways.html** – is the centrepiece of the Lipton-Herzberg website portal and organises Internet links on a topic-by-topic basis. Access to *Pathways* is restricted to purchasers of this book. The necessary username and password are set out below.

We were privileged yet again to work with Corina Brooks, Senior Editor, Thomson Lawbook Co., who orchestrated the production of the 13th edition like the maestro that she is. Her usual unflappable, efficient style was apparent at all stages. We are grateful to Sue Jamieson who handled the flurry of digital paper work with consummate skill. We also acknowledge the coordinating role of Adrian Burrell, Product Manager, Thomson Lawbook Co.

We wish to thank Aashish Srivastava for his good work in updating the bibliographies at the end of each chapter and the Department of Business Law and Taxation, Monash University for providing research funding in relation to the bibliographies. Thanks again to Ellison Marks, Jason Harris and Graham Peirson who kindly maintain their interest in suggesting improvements to the text.

Many thanks to our webmaster, Rob Scherer of Green Eggs, for maintaining the Lipton-Herzberg website. Rob's skills have enabled the website to remain a user-friendly and valuable resource.

Last, but of course, not least we especially thank our families.

PHILLIP LIPTON
ABE HERZBERG

Melbourne
1 November 2005

To access Pathways:	http://www.lipton-herzberg.com.au/pathways.html
Username:	comein
Password:	spinner

acknowledgments

The following extracts attributed herein were reproduced with the kind permission of:

Auditing and Assurance Standards Board (by the CPA Australia): http://www.auasb.gov.au
> Auditing Standard AUS210: *The Auditor's Responsibility to Consider Fraud and Error in an Audit of a Financial Report.*

Australian Accounting Research Foundation (AARF): http://www.aarf.asn.au
> Discussion Paper, "Payment of Dividends under the Corporations Act 2001".

Australian Securities & Investments Commission (ASIC): http://www.asic.gov.au
> ASIC's OFFERlist database.
> ASIC Media Release (05-228).
> ASIC Practice Note 42.3: *Independence of Experts' Reports.*

Australian Stock Exchange (ASX): http://www.asx.com.au
> ASX Fact File 2004.
> ASX Corporate Governance Council, *Principles of Good Corporate Governance and Best Practice Recommendations. © Australian Stock Exchange Limited ABN 98 008 624 691 (ASX) – 2002. All rights reserved. No warranty of accuracy or reliability as to such information is given. To the extent permitted by law, ASX will not be liable for any loss or damage arising in any way from or in connection with this material. This document cannot be reproduced in whole or in part without the prior written permission of ASX.*

CCH (Australia): http://www.cch.com.au
> Australian Company Law Cases (ACLC).

Committee on Legal and Constitutional Affairs (by the Parliament of Australia): http://www.aph.gov.au
> House of Representatives Committee on Legal and Constitutional Affairs (the Griffiths Committee), *Fair Shares for All: Insider Trading in Australia* (November 1989).
> Senate Select Committee on Legal and Constitutional Affairs (the Cooney Committee), *Social and Fiduciary Duties and Obligations of Company Directors* (1989).

Corporations and Markets Advisory Committee (CAMAC) (formerly CASAC): http://www.camac.gov.au
> CASAC, *Corporate Groups Final Report* (May 2000).
> CASAC, *Shareholder Participation in the Modern Listed Public Company: Final Report.*

Council of Law Reporting for New South Wales:
> New South Wales Law Reports (NSWLR). *© Council of Law Reporting for New South Wales*
> Weekly Notes (New South Wales) (WN (NSW)). *© Council of Law Reporting for New South Wales*

Council of Law Reporting in Victoria (by the Consultative Council of Australian Law Reporting):
> Victorian Reports (VR).

Department of the Treasury: http://www.treasury.gov.au
> Insolvency Reform Package released by the Parliamentary Secretary to the Commonwealth Treasurer, October 2005; accessible from the Treasury website http://www.treasury.gov.au/contentitem.asp?NavId=&ContentID=1022

The Incorporated Council of Law Reporting for England & Wales: http://www.lawreports.co.uk
> Appeal Cases (AC).
> Chancery Division Reports (Ch D).
> King's Bench (KB).
> Queen's Bench (QB).

Lawbook Co., part of Thomson Legal and Regulatory Limited: http://www.thomson.com.au
> Commonwealth Law Reports (CLR).
> Federal Law Reports (FLR).
> State Reports of New South Wales (SR (NSW)).
> South Australian State Reports (SASR).

LexisNexis Butterworths, Australia: http://www.lexisnexis.com.au

- Australian Company Law Reports (ACLR).
- Australian Corporations and Securities Reports (ACSR).
- Australian Law Reports (ALR).
- New South Wales Reports (NSWR).

New Zealand Council of Law Reporting:

- New Zealand Law Reports (NZLR).

Organisation for Economic Co-operation and Development (OECD): http://www.oecd.org

- OECD, *Principles of Corporate Governance* (2004).

Parliamentary Joint Committee on Corporations and Financial Services (by the Parliament of Australia): http://www.aph.gov.au

- Parliamentary Joint Committee on Corporations and Securities, *Report on Aspects of the Regulation of Proprietary Companies* (March 2001).
- Parliamentary Joint Committee on Corporations and Financial Services, *Report on Corporate Insolvency Laws: A Stocktake* (June 2004).

Prentice-Hall (A Pearson Education Company): http://www.prenticehall.com

- F G Hilmer and R I Tricker, "An Effective Board" in R I Tricker, *International Corporate Governance, Text, Readings and Cases* (1994).

Takeovers Panel: http://www.takeovers.gov.au

- Guidance Note 1 — *Unacceptable Circumstances.*
- Guidance Note 4 — *Remedies and Enforcement.*
- Guidance Note 12 — *Frustrating Action.*

Thomson Lawbook Co. and the authors are grateful to the publishers, agents and authors who have allowed us to use extracts of their work in this book. While every care has been taken to establish and acknowledge copyright, Thomson Lawbook Co. tenders its apology for any accidental infringement. The publisher would be pleased to come to a suitable agreement with the rightful owners in each case.

table of contents

chapter one

regulatory framework

key points ...

- A company is an artificial entity recognised by the law as a legal person with its own rights and liabilities. It is regarded as an entity that is separate and distinct from its owners (its shareholders or members) and managers (its directors and officers).
- Company law is a combination of case law and legislation largely contained in the *Corporations Act 2001* (Cth). The Corporations Act scheme was developed to meet the need for uniform Australia-wide corporations legislation, administered by a single Commonwealth authority, the Australian Securities and Investments Commission (ASIC).
- Companies vary greatly in the scale of their businesses, their objectives and their numbers of shareholders. The largest companies in Australia choose to have their shares listed on the Australian Stock Exchange (ASX) which operates the largest Australian stock market in which shares of listed companies can be bought and sold. Listed companies must comply with detailed disclosure obligations imposed by the ASX listing rules and the *Corporations Act*.

what is a company?

A company is an artificial entity recognised by the law as a legal person with its own rights and liabilities.

[1.05] A company is an artificial entity recognised by the law as a legal person with its own rights and liabilities. The terms "company" and "corporation" are often interchangeable, however, the *Corporations Act 2001* (Cth) regards a company, or its predecessors, registered under that Act as one type of corporation. A corporation also includes other artificial legal entities such as trade unions and incorporated associations as well as entities formed in other countries.

A company is regarded as a separate entity distinct from its shareholders, its directors who control its management, and its officers and employees. The fact that a company is regarded as an entity separate from the people behind it means that the company may own property, enter into contracts and sue and be sued in its own name.

Limited liability is an important characteristic of companies.

The separate legal entity concept also means that a company has a potentially unlimited lifespan. Its directors and shareholders may change but this does not affect the company's existence as a legal person. Even though a company is an artificial entity, it has the same legal capacity and powers as a human being. It is therefore able to engage in any business or activity and may acquire and exercise rights in the same way as an individual.

Limited liability is an important characteristic of companies and is often one of the main reasons why people choose to form a company to conduct their businesses. Limited liability means that shareholders are not personally liable for their company's debts. The shareholders' liability is limited to paying the issue price of the shares that they own. The implications of a company being a separate legal entity and limited liability are discussed in Chapter 2 below. That chapter also contains a comparison of a company with a partnership and a trust, the other common forms of business organisations.

Transferability of shares is another significant characteristic.

Transferability of shares is another significant characteristic that distinguishes a company from a partnership. As a general rule, shareholders are able to transfer or sell their shares free of any restrictions. Unless a company's constitution says otherwise, shareholders who wish to sell their shares do not need to obtain approval from other shareholders or the company's directors. Free transferability of shares facilitates stock exchange share trading.

There are three main sources of rules that regulate companies:

> legislation, particularly the *Corporations Act 2001* which applies throughout Australia. Also important is the *Australian Securities & Investment Commission Act*, which establishing the Australian Securities and Investments Commission (ASIC) as the main government authority responsible for administering the *Corporations Act* and enforcing its compliance;
> case law, particularly those that establish contractual and fiduciary principles; and
> the constitution of each company sets out the rules that regulate their internal management. Company constitutions are discussed in Chapter 4 below.

Companies are the most popular form of business organisation. There are well over a million companies registered in Australia and they vary greatly in the size of their businesses and their number of shareholders. The overwhelming majority of companies operate small business enterprises and are typically controlled by an individual person or family.

Some companies, particularly those that operate large businesses, frequently organise their affairs in a corporate group structure with a holding company that controls one or more subsidiary companies within an economic entity. The separate entity concept, as well as limited liability, has interesting implications for corporate groups. This is discussed further in Chapter 2 below.

Company formation (also referred to as "registration" or "incorporation") is a relatively simple process that involves filing an application for registration with ASIC and paying the prescribed fee. Once ASIC registers the company it comes into existence as a legal entity and can operate anywhere in Australia. The procedures for registering a company are further discussed in Chapter 2 below.

The *Corporations Act* makes a formal distinction between ownership and control of companies. Companies are required to have shareholders (also called "members") who in a non-legal sense, are regarded as the owners of the company. The shareholders contribute capital by paying the issue price on their shares and may receive dividends if the company generates profits. The *Corporations Act* and company constitutions give shareholders significant rights. For example, they have the right to receive the company's audited financial reports and in the case of public companies, the right to attend, speak and vote at the company's annual general meetings. Financial reporting and auditors are discussed in Chapters 15 and 16 below. Shareholders' meetings are discussed in Chapter 14 below.

Companies are required to have shareholders (also called "members") who in a non-legal sense, are regarded as the owners of the company.

Every company must also have directors who are collectively referred to as a "board". Company constitutions usually give directors the exclusive power to control management of the company's business. Because directors control the management of the company they are subject to strict fiduciary and statutory duties. For example, directors are required to exercise their powers in the best interests of the company and its shareholders. Directors' fiduciary and statutory duties are discussed in Chapter 13 below.

Every company must also have directors who are collectively referred to as a "board".

As discussed in Chapter 3 below, the *Corporations Act* draws a distinction between public and proprietary companies. A company must be one or the other. Proprietary companies are more prevalent than public companies and their regulation is designed to suit the needs of companies with small numbers of shareholders. One-person proprietary companies are permitted. Proprietary companies are divided into two sub-categories: small and large proprietary companies. The distinction is based on the scale of the proprietary company's business. Most proprietary companies are small proprietary companies and are subject to minimum financial disclosure requirements. The legislation imposes more onerous obligations and greater public transparency on public companies because they are permitted to raise capital from the public and usually operate large-scale businesses with large numbers of shareholders. The fundraising rules are discussed in Chapter 7 below.

The *Corporations Act* draws a distinction between public and proprietary companies.

The largest public companies choose to list their shares on the Australian Stock Exchange (ASX) which operates the main Australian stock market in which shares of listed companies can be easily bought and sold. There are approximately 1,500 companies whose shares are listed on the ASX.

The largest public companies choose to list their shares on the ASX which operates the main Australian stock market in which shares of listed companies can be easily bought and sold.

Listed public companies must comply with detailed disclosure obligations imposed by the ASX listing rules as well as the *Corporations Act*. The ASX listing rules also provide greater shareholder protection mechanisms than the *Corporations Act*. Despite the more onerous regulation imposed on listed companies, there are significant advantages to being listed for both listed companies and their shareholders. An active stock market enables investors to easily trade listed shares and as a result listed companies have the ability to raise very large amounts of capital.

history of company law

earliest companies

[1.10] From medieval times there has been a need for the creation of incorporated bodies with characteristics of legal personality. The earliest such bodies in England were monasteries and local government boroughs. They required that ownership of property be conferred on a legal entity separate from individuals and that this legal entity continued to exist beyond the life span of individuals.

The first commercial organisations were the guilds that served the functions of trade union, club and benevolence society. The guilds required incorporation as a method of excluding outsiders from their particular trade. These medieval organisations were incorporated by Royal Charter and so represent the first corporations. The needs of commerce in enabling individuals to pool together their resources were recognised by law in the development of partnerships whereby each partner was an agent of the other partners with unlimited liability.

With the expansion of foreign trade, Royal Charters were conferred on trading companies with the objectives of conferring monopoly powers and facilitating administration over the territory conferred to the company. This was the origin of the great trading companies such as the East India Company and the Hudson Bay Company. This form of organisation eventually adopted the partnership characteristic of trading on joint account, which in turn led to the evolution of joint stock and marked the first stage in the development of the concept of a share. In the early stages of the East India Company, for example, the joint stock and profits from a particular voyage were divided after the completion of each venture.

By the end of the 17th century, the concept of a permanent joint stock was introduced. This development acknowledged the needs of large scale commercial ventures that required resources far in excess of the capabilities of individuals. The law allowed a small number of joint stock companies to trade for the profit of their members where this privilege was conferred by statute or Royal Charter.

Thus the first companies evolved out of partnerships with provision for the division of the undertaking into shares which were transferable to varying degrees. There were problems, however, in adapting partnerships so that they operated as joint stock companies. The common law regarded partnerships as being based on the law of contract and so there were difficulties in assigning rights by the transfer of shares. The end of the 17th century saw certain characteristics of companies established. They existed in perpetuity, could own property, could be parties to legal proceedings and by their common seal could enter contracts independently of their members. The concept of transferability of shares was still in doubt and the development of limited liability was to come later, although the debts of a company and of its members were already regarded as separate.

By the 18th century the trading companies declined as the state assumed their role of administering foreign territories. Companies that were concerned with infrastructure such as railways and domestic trade developed. This important development provided a mechanism which enabled investors to provide funds to entrepreneurs, thereby facilitating the growth of commerce. These companies were incorporated by statute, Royal Charter or developed from partnerships. It was the growth of the last of these that was resented by companies duly incorporated by Parliament and Royal Charter. At the instigation of the South Sea Company the *Bubble Act* was passed in 1719 to suppress speculation in company shares and the private development of joint stock companies. It had the objective of prohibiting the promotion and operation of "dangerous and mischievous undertakings and projects, wherein the undertakers and subscribers have presumed to act as if they were corporate bodies".

first companies legislation

[1.15] Although the *Bubble Act* remained until repealed in 1825, it had little effect in preventing the growth of joint stock companies. Despite the lack of legal recognition, these companies played an important role meeting the needs of business in satisfying the large appetite for capital which arose during the industrial revolution. The number of prosecutions under the Act was relatively small as the law largely turned a blind eye to this development. Early in the 19th century, as the industrial revolution gathered momentum, companies came to be tolerated by Parliament as the needs of commerce were increasingly recognised by the law. This tolerance became encouragement with the passing in 1844 in England of the first modern *Companies Act* which set out a procedure whereby companies could be incorporated without Royal Charter or special Act. A further development came in 1855 with the introduction of limited liability, whereby shareholders were liable only to the extent of the nominal value of their shares. Companies with this privilege had to use the word "Limited" after their names. The basis of modern company law was laid and these characteristics remain to this day. The various statutes dealing with companies were consolidated in the *English Companies Act 1862*. Most of the Australian colonies passed legislation modelled on the English statutes with some innovations. In Victoria the no liability company was introduced for mining companies in 1871. Indeed, Victoria became the pace setter in company legislation when, in 1896, it established the distinction between public and proprietary companies. Proprietary companies were seen to be most suited to small business ventures in which there were relatively few members. Such companies were not required to have their financial affairs audited, nor were they required to publish their financial statements.

case law and legislation

[1.20] The result of the history and development of company law both in England and Australia has been the interaction and interdependence of case and statute law. It is necessary for the study of company law to understand the interrelationship between cases and the *Corporations Act*, for each presumes the existence of the other. Over a long period of time the courts have been asked to interpret and define many aspects of the legislation. In turn, the Parliaments have amended the legislation over the years assuming the existence of common law principles which evolved from the cases. Thus the Australian corporations legislation does not purport to be a comprehensive code covering all aspects of company law. Rather, the sections of the legislation must be read in conjunction with case law, which gives the legislation greater meaning. This situation is to be contrasted with the law of contract, for example, where the legal principles largely come from cases through the doctrine of precedent with relatively little statute law.

development of Australian company law

constitutional position

[1.25] During the first half of the 20th century, Australian company law was characterised by a lack of uniformity from State to State because the Commonwealth Parliament was not given a clear power by the Australian Constitution to make laws with respect to all companies. The closest such power is s 51(xx) of the Constitution, which empowers the Commonwealth to make laws with respect to "foreign corporations, and trading and financial corporations formed within the limits of the Commonwealth".

In the early years of the Commonwealth, the High Court in *Huddart Parker & Co Pty Ltd v Moorehead* (1909) 8 CLR 330, adopted a narrow interpretation of the power in s 51(xx) so as to deny the Commonwealth the power to make laws with respect to the creation of companies. This conclusion was based on the strict interpretation of the word "formed", meaning already in existence. It was also regarded as questionable whether mining, investment and charitable companies were "foreign corporations, and trading or financial corporation".

The Commonwealth once had limited jurisdiction under the Constitution to make laws with respect to the incorporation and regulation of companies.

The result of this interpretation was that the Commonwealth had limited jurisdiction under the Constitution to make laws with respect to the incorporation and regulation of companies. This was historically largely a State matter. This approach to the interpretation of s 51(xx) was followed by the *High Court in New South Wales v Commonwealth* (1990) 8 ACLC 120. This case concerned a challenge by several States to the constitutional validity of certain sections of the Commonwealth *Corporations Act 1989* which provided, among other things, for the incorporation of trading and financial corporations. The High Court held that s 51(xx) did not empower the Commonwealth to make laws with respect to the incorporation of trading and financial corporations and consequently, provisions that related to incorporation were invalid. The basis of the majority judgment focused on the phrase "formed within the limits of the Commonwealth" in s 51(xx). The *Huddart Parker* case was followed to interpret this phrase as referring to corporations that have already been created in Australia and excludes the process of incorporation itself. In order to overcome the difficulties arising from these constitutional limitations, from the 1960s the Commonwealth and States entered into various agreements aimed at achieving greater uniformity in the regulation of companies throughout Australia.

Uniform Companies Acts

[1.30] The *Uniform Companies Acts 1961* largely achieved the aim of attaining uniform legislation throughout Australia. Each Australian State enacted essentially identical legislation. It was then possible to speak of a particular section and generally this was identical in the Companies Acts of each State. However, over time, various amendments were adopted in some States but not others, so that differences between States began to reappear.

As well as lack of uniformity in the respective Companies Acts, it was inconvenient for a company operating and raising funds throughout Australia to have to comply with all the applicable Companies Acts. For example, a company incorporated in one State was regarded as a "foreign" company in the other States and therefore had to comply with a series of laws and regulations applicable to such entities. Also, if a company sought to raise funds throughout Australia, it had to register a prospectus in each State. A further matter of concern related to the lack of adequate regulation and supervision of the stock exchanges. There was no single regulator or market operator with power to supervise the various State-based stock exchanges or interstate share trading.

As a result of a severe stock market crash in the early 1970s with associated allegations of improper practices, a Senate Select Committee (the Rae Committee) was set up to inquire into the securities industry. The main recommendation of the Rae Committee was that a national commission be established to regulate and oversee the activities of all the securities markets throughout Australia, thereby recognising the reality that the securities industry in Australia operated on a national basis.

Co-operative Scheme

[1.35] The Co-operative Scheme was developed in the 1980s to further establish a national regulatory scheme. The objectives of the Co-operative Scheme were to bring about uniformity in the law and in its administration. The Commonwealth passed legislation that applied only in the Australian Capital Territory and each State passed legislation applying the Commonwealth legislation as its own law. The legislative package of the Commonwealth Acts and State Application Acts was referred to as a "Code". For example, in Victoria the companies legislation was referred to as the *Companies (Victoria) Code*.

An important feature of the Co-operative Scheme was that it established the National Companies and Securities Commission (NCSC), a predecessor of ASIC, with the responsibility of formulating policy, administering company law and regulating the securities and futures industry. While the NCSC was a Commonwealth authority, it was required to delegate many of its significant responsibilities (such as the incorporation of companies and filing of documents) to the various State Corporate Affairs Commissions.

It was widely acknowledged that the Co-operative Scheme was a considerable improvement on previous legislative structures. It produced greater administrative efficiency by introducing the concept of "one-stop shopping". This concept meant that a company carrying on business in more than one State or Territory could lodge its various documents (such as annual returns or prospectuses) with the Corporate Affairs Commission in its home State without the need to file duplicates elsewhere.

During the late 1980s the Co-operative Scheme came under increasing criticism. This was partly related to its compromise nature which sought to balance national and State interests and partly due to the rapid changes taking place in the corporate and global financial environment. This increased the importance of collaboration between national regulatory bodies and resulted in more sophisticated corporate and market dealings.

The Co-operative Scheme structure also diffused political responsibility through the Ministerial Council for Corporations and Securities (MINCO) so that no single government or Minister was responsible for the legislation. Amendments to the legislation required the approval of MINCO. Because MINCO comprised Ministers representing each State and the Commonwealth, it was unwieldy from the point of view of reforming the law to take account of contemporary practices. This resulted in a tendency to produce "lowest common denominator" decision-making.

It was also considered that the relationship between the NCSC and the State Corporate Affairs Commissions resulted in administrative inefficiency. Each of the Corporate Affairs Commissions adopted its own interpretations of the law and rulings. The NCSC was not empowered to give directions to the State Corporate Affairs Commissions on administrative procedures or deployment of resources. This was critical because the NCSC itself operated on a very small budget.

corporations law scheme

the attempted Commonwealth takeover

[1.40] The deficiencies of the Co-operative Scheme led the Commonwealth to enact legislation in 1988 which had the effect of giving the Commonwealth sole control of companies and securities regulation. The main features of this legislation were the *Corporations Act 1989* (Cth), which largely amalgamated the provisions previously contained in the various separate Codes and the *Australian Securities Commission Act 1989* (Cth), which established the Australian Securities Commission (ASC) to replace both the NCSC and the respective State Corporate Affairs Commissions.

The Commonwealth's attempted takeover provoked intense political controversy. Several States were hostile to it and challenged the constitutional validity of the new scheme in the High Court. The States were concerned that as a consequence of the replacement of their Corporate Affairs Commissions by the ASC they would lose control over local companies as well as their ability to generate revenue from fees levied on companies.

High Court challenge

[1.45] The legislative package was passed in September 1989 but several States brought a High Court action against the Commonwealth alleging that the 1989 legislation was unconstitutional.

case note

In *New South Wales v Commonwealth* (1990) 8 ACLC 120, the parties all agreed that the only issue to be considered by the High Court was whether or not the provisions in the *Corporations Act 1989* (Cth) concerning the incorporation of companies were constitutionally valid. The High Court held that the Commonwealth did not have the power under s 51(xx) of the Constitution to pass laws providing for the incorporation of trading and financial corporations and therefore the Commonwealth did not have the power to completely take over corporate regulation in Australia.

key features of the scheme

[1.50] As a result of the decision in *New South Wales v Commonwealth* (1990) 8 ACLC 120 the Commonwealth needed the co-operation of the States in order to arrive at a structure that, on the one hand, addressed the deficiencies of the Co-operative Scheme and on the other, satisfied the respective governments. After the High Court case the Commonwealth and the States negotiated a new Corporations Agreement which set out the key features of the *Corporations Law* scheme.

The Corporations Agreement addressed the main deficiencies of the Co-operative Scheme by establishing a legislative framework of Commonwealth legislation applied as State law, in a similar manner as the previous Co-operative Scheme. The Commonwealth amended the *Corporations Act 1989* (Cth) so that it applied only in the Australian Capital Territory. The last section of the amended 1989 Act then stated "the *Corporations Law* is as follows". Technically, the *Corporations Law*, comprising over 2,000 sections and three Schedules, was contained in one section of the *Corporations Act 1989* (Cth). Each of the States and the Northern Territory passed their own legislation which applied the Commonwealth's *Corporations Law* as their own law.

The *Corporations Law* commenced operation on 1 January 1991. Each of the eight *Corporations Laws*, while technically legislation of a particular State or Territory, had the characteristics of, and were treated for all practical purposes as if they were, a Commonwealth rather than State law.

The essential difference between the Co-operative Scheme and the new legislative structure set up by the Corporations Agreement was the increased power and control over corporate regulation given to the Commonwealth. The Corporations Agreement achieved this in a number of ways. It provided for the establishment of the ASC, with regional offices in each capital city, as the sole regulatory authority to replace both the NCSC and the respective State and Territory Corporate Affairs Commissions. The ASC was to be accountable only to the Commonwealth Parliament with the Commonwealth Attorney-General as the responsible Minister. The ASC was renamed the Australian Securities and Investments Commission (ASIC) from July 1998 with the Commonwealth Treasurer as the responsible Minister. The role and functions of ASIC are further discussed below, para [1.65] and in Chapter 21.

To ensure uniformity of corporate regulation, the Corporations Agreement provided that federal bodies such as the ASC, the Commonwealth Director of Public Prosecutions (DPP) and the Australian Federal Police were the authorities responsible for investigation and prosecution of criminal offences under the legislation throughout Australia. Further, Commonwealth administrative laws were to be applied as the administrative laws of the respective States and Territory for purposes of the *Corporations Law* scheme.

Apart from establishing the *Corporations Law*, a complex legal framework to "federalise" the *Corporations Law* scheme was set up. For example, even though each of the eight Corporations Laws was technically a State or Territory law, the State and Commonwealth legislation provided that the *Corporations Law* was to be administered and enforced on a national basis, in the same way as if it were a law of the Commonwealth. Commonwealth administrative laws applied to the respective Corporations Laws with the result that Commonwealth administrative bodies such as the Commonwealth Administrative Appeals Tribunal and the Commonwealth Ombudsman were given jurisdiction to the exclusion of their State equivalents. The various Corporations Acts also federalised criminal law so that *Corporations Law* offences were treated as Commonwealth offences even though the *Corporations Law* was technically the law of a State. Further, criminal investigations and prosecutions of *Corporations Law* offences were carried out by federal authorities such as ASIC and the Commonwealth Director of Public Prosecutions (DPP).

As discussed below, the High Court in *Bond v R* (2000) 169 ALR 607 held that for constitutional reasons the Commonwealth DPP did not have the power to appeal against a criminal sentence imposed for breaching a *Corporations Law* offence. Until the High Court's decision in *Re Wakim* (1999) 17 ACLC 1055, discussed below, the Federal Court of Australia was the main court for hearing *Corporations Law* cases even though they were based on the *Corporations Law* of a particular State or Territory. This was achieved by the cross-vesting provisions of the State and Commonwealth Corporations Acts. Under this system the Federal Court, the Family Court and each State and Territory Supreme Court had jurisdiction to decide *Corporations Law* cases irrespective of which State or Territory the dispute arose in. The cross-vesting system also enabled one court to transfer cases to another court in appropriate situations.

constitutional crisis

[1.55] The constitutional validity of the federalised nature of the *Corporations Law* scheme was thrown into doubt in a number of High Court cases such as *Re Wakim* (1999) 17 ACLC 1055, *Bond v R* (2000) 169 ALR 607 and *R v Hughes* (2000) 171 ALR 155. The constitutional problems highlighted by these cases centred on the power of Commonwealth bodies to deal with issues arising under the *Corporations Laws* of the various States and the Northern Territory.

In *Re Wakim* (1999) 17 ACLC 1055 the High Court held that the cross-vesting provisions were unconstitutional and of no effect in so far as they purported to give the Federal Court jurisdiction to hear and decide cases arising under the *Corporations Law* of a State or the Northern Territory. The High Court held that under the Constitution the Federal Court did not have the power to decide matters that were exclusively within the jurisdiction of the States. Since the *Corporations Law* was legally State legislation this decision meant the Federal Court could not hear or decide *Corporations Law* cases.

In *Bond v R* (2000) 169 ALR 607 the High Court held that while the Commonwealth DPP had the power to initiate and institute prosecutions, it did not have the power to appeal against sentences. The powers of the Commonwealth DPP were also the main issue in *R v Hughes* (2000) 171 ALR 155. In that case the High Court recognised that it was only the peculiar circumstances of the case that prevented a successful constitutional challenge to the Commonwealth DPP's powers and called for prompt reform of the *Corporations Law* scheme. *R v Hughes* (2000) 171 ALR 155 caused significant concern about the constitutionality of other aspects of the *Corporations Law* scheme. The High Court made it clear in that a Commonwealth body that undertook a function under State law involving the exercise of a duty had constitutional powers in relation to State legislation only if the Constitution gave the Commonwealth Parliament power in relation to the matter. This raised the question of whether ASIC, the main regulator of the *Corporations Law* scheme and a Commonwealth authority, had the power to register companies. This was of major concern as ASIC had registered over 600,000 companies between 1991 and 2000. As discussed above, para [1.45], the High Court held in *New South Wales v Commonwealth* (1990) 8 ACLC 120 that the Constitution did not give the Commonwealth the power to makes laws dealing with the formation of companies. Clearly early resolution of the constitutional crisis was necessary.

Corporations Act 2001

[1.60] In August 2000, the States and the Northern Territory agreed in principle to resolve the constitutional crisis by referring to the Commonwealth the substance of the *Corporations Law* scheme together with the powers of Commonwealth authorities to carry out the scheme. Section 51(xxxvii) of the Constitution gives the Commonwealth this power in relation to any matter referred to it by the States. There was also agreement in principle for the States to refer to the Commonwealth the power to amend the legislation. The Commonwealth and the States also agreed that the referral would have a sunset clause to allow a State to terminate it after five years.

As a result of the enactment of the referral legislation by the States, the Commonwealth passed the *Corporations Act 2001* and the *ASIC Act 2001*. The *Corporations Act 2001* replaced the previous *Corporations Act 1989* (Cth), as well as the eight Corporations Laws of the various States and Territories. The *ASIC Act 2001* is discussed below, para [1.65].

The *Corporations Act 2001* became operative on 1 July 2001 and applies Australia-wide.

The *Corporations Act 2001* became operative on 1 July 2001 and applies Australia-wide. If one or more States terminate their reference, the *Corporations Act* will still apply in the remaining referring States. The *Corporations Act* is administered and enforced on a national basis by Commonwealth bodies, such as ASIC. In addition, existing Commonwealth legislation such as the *Crimes Act 1914*, the *Criminal Code Act 1995*, the *Director of Public Prosecutions Act 1983* and the *Acts Interpretation Act 1901* apply to the exclusion of equivalent State legislation. Part 9.6A of the *Corporations Act* reinstates the jurisdiction of the Federal Court and the integrated cross-vesting provisions in relation to civil matters and effectively overrules the decision of the High Court in *Re Wakim* (1999) 198 CLR 511.

The rules governing the interpretation of the various provisions of the *Corporations Act* are set out in the *Acts Interpretations Act 1901* (Cth): s 5C. For example, ss 15AA and 15AB of the *Acts Interpretation Act 1901* directs the courts, when interpreting a provision of the *Corporations Act*, to prefer a construction that would promote the purpose or object underlying the Act. When the meaning of a provision is ambiguous or obscure the courts are permitted to make use of extrinsic material such as an explanatory memorandum relating to the legislation, a report of a law reform agency or a report of a parliamentary committee. There have been numerous instances where the courts of the various States have adopted conflicting interpretations of the previous Corporations legislation. However, in *ASC v Marlborough Gold Mines Ltd* (1993) 11 ACLC 370 the High Court was of the opinion that this lack of uniformity in the interpretation of the legislation was undesirable. In their joint judgment Mason CJ, Brennan, Dawson, Toohey and Gaudron JJ stated:

> **< Uniformity of decision in the interpretation of uniform national legislation such as the [*Corporations Act*] is a sufficiently important consideration to require that an intermediate appellate court—and all the more so a single judge—should not depart from an interpretation placed on such legislation by another Australian intermediate appellate court unless convinced that that interpretation is plainly wrong. >**

Australian Securities and Investments Commission

ASIC is the main Commonwealth authority responsible for administering the *Corporations Act 2001*.

[1.65] The Australian Securities and Investments Commission (ASIC) is the main Commonwealth authority responsible for administering the *Corporations Act 2001*. Prior to 1998, ASIC was called the Australian Securities Commission (ASC). As well as changing the Commission's name, ASIC was given additional functions dealing with the consumer protection and market integrity aspects of insurance and superannuation regulation. This was in line with the main recommendations of the *1997 Financial System Inquiry Final Report* (Wallis Committee Report). These functions are outside the scope of this book.

The *Australian Securities and Investment Commission Act 2001* (Cth) (*ASIC Act*) was enacted at the same time as the *Corporations Act 2001* and largely re-enacted the previous package of ASIC legislation as a single Commonwealth law that operates in every State that referred its powers to the Commonwealth as well as the ACT and Northern Territory.

ASIC is a body corporate with between three and eight government-appointed members headed by a Chair: *ASIC Act*, ss 8–10. ASIC must have an office and employ a Regional Commissioner in each referring State and Territory: *ASIC Act*, ss 95 and 96. ASIC has also established other offices and business centres in most large Australian cities. These were set up so that ASIC may better serve the needs of the business communities in the various referring States and Territories. ASIC's website sets out vast amounts of valuable information and is linked to the Lipton-Herzberg Corporate Law Websites at **http://www.lipton-herzberg.com.au/corp-law-websites.html**

objectives of ASIC

[1.70] In performing its functions and exercising its powers, s 1(2) of the *ASIC Act* directs ASIC to strive to:

> **maintain, facilitate and improve the performance of the financial system and the entities within that system in the interests of commercial certainty, reducing business costs, and the efficiency and development of the economy;**
> **promote the confident and informed participation of investors and consumers in the financial system;**
> **administer the laws that confer functions and powers on it effectively and with a minimum of procedural requirements;**
> **receive, process and store, efficiently and quickly, the information given to the Commission under the laws that confer functions and powers on it;**
> **ensure that information is available as soon as practicable for access by the public; and**
> **take whatever action it can take, and is necessary, in order to enforce and give effect to the laws that confer functions and powers on it.**

functions and powers of ASIC

[1.75] Section 11(1) of the *ASIC Act* provides that ASIC has such functions and powers as are conferred on it by or under the corporations legislation. Section 5(1) defines the term "corporations legislation" to mean the *ASIC Act* and the *Corporations Act*. Under s 11(2) and (3) ASIC is given the following additional functions:

> **to provide such staff and support facilities to the Takeovers Panel, the Companies Auditors and Liquidators Disciplinary Board;**
> **to advise the Minister about any changes to the corporations legislation (other than the excluded provisions) that, in ASIC's opinion, are needed to overcome, or would assist in overcoming, any problems that ASIC has encountered in the course of performing or exercising any of its functions and powers; and**
> **to advise the Minister and make recommendations about corporate law reform proposals put forward by the Corporations and Markets Advisory Committee (CAMAC).**

ASIC's s 11 functions and powers do not apply to the "excluded provisions" of the corporations legislation. Section 5(1) defines this to mean the functions set out in s 12A of the *ASIC Act*. Section 12A gives ASIC certain functions and powers in relation to:

> **insurance and superannuation; and**
> **monitoring and promoting market integrity and consumer protection in relation to the Australian financial system as well as the payments system.**

ASIC's s 12A functions and powers are beyond the scope of this book.

ASIC is responsible to the Commonwealth Treasurer and therefore ultimately to the Commonwealth Parliament. Prior to 1996 the Commonwealth Attorney-General was the responsible Minister. This change was to reflect the role of corporations legislation in the economy. The Treasurer may give written directions to ASIC about the policies it should pursue and the priorities it should follow: s 12. Before giving ASIC a direction, the Minister must provide the chairman of ASIC the opportunity to discuss a proposed direction. To maintain the independence of ASIC from the executive arm of government, the Minister is not permitted to issue directions about particular cases.

registering companies

ASIC is the government authority that registers companies.

[1.80] ASIC is the government authority that registers companies. As discussed in Chapter 2 below, any person who wishes to register a company must lodge an application for registration with ASIC and pay the appropriate fee. ASIC registers the company and issues a certificate of registration. Once registered, a company is permitted to operate in every other Australian State or Territory.

ASCOT database

ASIC provides publicly accessible information on all Australian companies through its national corporate database, ASCOT.

[1.85] ASIC provides publicly accessible information on all Australian companies through its national corporate database, ASCOT. The ASCOT database contains public information about:

> **corporations, including their names, registered offices, particulars of directors and principal activities;**
> **registered charges granted by corporations; and**
> **licensed financial service providers (eg stockbrokers and investment advisers), registered auditors and liquidators.**

ASCOT also provides access to ASIC's document image system, DOCIMAGE. This has digitised copies of all documents that companies are required to lodge with ASIC, such as annual returns. Any person is able to search ASCOT to obtain publicly accessible information about companies. Corporation extracts from ASCOT or copies of DOCIMAGE documents provided by ASIC are regarded, in the absence of evidence to the contrary, as proof of the information contained in them and are admissible in court proceedings as evidence without formal certification of their accuracy: *Corporations Act*, s 1274B.

regulation of financial services and markets

ASIC is the main authority responsible for regulating financial products, financial services and financial markets.

[1.90] ASIC is the main authority responsible for regulating financial products, financial services and financial markets. For example, under Pt 7.2 of the *Corporations Act* operators of a financial market such as the ASX and the SFE must be licensed by ASIC. ASIC is also given the power to direct a market licensee to suspend dealings in particular securities on the Australian Stock Exchange (ASX) and to enforce compliance with the ASX's Listing Rules: ss 793C and 794D. Under Pt 7.6, financial service providers such as stockbrokers and investment advisers must be licensed by ASIC. ASIC also has broad powers to regulate fundraising by the issue of securities. For example, Ch 6D of the *Corporations Act* requires a disclosure document in relation to offers or issues of securities to be lodged with ASIC before they are issued to potential investors. Section 741 gives ASIC wide power to grant exemptions in relation to the fundraising provisions.

takeovers

[1.95] ASIC is also given an important role in regulating company takeovers. As discussed in Chapter 18 below, under Pt 6.5 of the *Corporations Act* takeover bidders must lodge a bidder's statement and offer document with ASIC containing prescribed information before an offer is sent to a target company's shareholders. In addition, takeover target companies are also required to lodge with ASIC a target's statement containing prescribed information. The purpose of the bidder's and target's statements is to ensure that shareholders of target companies receive adequate information so as to enable them to assess the merits of takeover offers. ASIC is also given broad powers to grant exemptions from, or modify the application of, the takeover provisions. To ensure both the spirit and the letter of the takeover provisions are complied with, Pt 6.10, Div 2 enables ASIC or any person (including the bidder or target) whose interests are affected by a decision of ASIC or unacceptable circumstances to apply to the Takeovers Panel for an order affecting a decision of ASIC or a declaration that unacceptable circumstances have occurred in relation to an acquisition of shares.

powers of investigation

[1.100] ASIC has the responsibility of ensuring compliance with the provisions of the *Corporations Act*. To this end, Pt 3 of the *ASIC Act* provides ASIC with wide investigatory and information-gathering powers where it has reason to suspect that a contravention of a national scheme law may have been committed. For example, s 19 of the *ASIC Act* gives ASIC the power to require any person to give reasonable assistance and answer questions on oath where it conducts an investigation. Under ss 28–39 of the *ASIC Act* it can compel persons to produce books and records in a wide range of circumstances. ASIC's investigations and information-gathering powers are further discussed in Chapter 21 below.

ASIC has the responsibility of ensuring compliance with the provisions of the *Corporations Act*.

powers to bring legal proceedings

[1.105] ASIC is given the power to initiate civil proceedings against a person where as a result of an investigation or examination it forms the opinion that it is in the public interest to do so: *ASIC Act*, s 50. The proceedings may, for example, be brought in the name of a company against its directors for the recovery of damages for fraud, negligence, default, breach of duty, or other misconduct. Section 50 also enables ASIC to initiate class actions for the recovery of damages on behalf of shareholders or other persons. In addition, under s 1330 of the *Corporations Act*, ASIC has the power to intervene in any legal proceedings initiated by others relating to a matter arising under the corporations legislation. ASIC may also bring a criminal prosecution where, as a result of an investigation, it forms the opinion that a person has committed an offence against the corporations legislation and ought to be prosecuted: *ASIC Act*, s 49. ASIC's powers to begin criminal prosecutions overlap with similar powers granted to the Commonwealth Director of Public Prosecutions (DPP). Because this overlap caused past tension between ASIC and the DPP, guidelines were established that require senior officers of ASIC and the DPP to meet regularly and review all investigations and prosecutions in which ASIC and the DPP have common interests. The guidelines also require ASIC to consult with the DPP before taking civil enforcement action in any case where criminal proceedings may also be available. Unresolved disputes between the two organisations must be referred to the Committee for Corporate Wrongdoing for determination.

ASIC is given the power to initiate civil proceedings.

education role

[1.110] ASIC also performs an important educative function. It releases policy statements, practice notes, information booklets and media releases so that both the public at large and the business community can more easily understand the operation of the *Corporations Act* and ASIC's interpretation of its provisions.

consumer protection

[1.115] ASIC has established Fido, a consumer webpage which aims to provide warnings of dishonest financial schemes and advice to investors and consumers. It also includes an annual award, "Pie in the Sky" for the "most outrageous financial scheme that is too good to be true". ASIC established the Consumer Advisory Panel in 1998 to advise on consumer protection issues and to give feedback on ASIC policies and activities.

the ASX

[1.120] The Australian Stock Exchange Limited (ASX) operates Australia's main financial markets for equities including shares, derivatives and fixed interest securities. The ASX was formed in 1987 when

The ASX operates Australia's main financial markets for equities including shares, derivatives and fixed interest securities.

the independent stock exchanges which operated in the various state capitals amalgamated. The ASX was then a mutual organisation of stockbrokers. It demutualised in 1998 and became a public company listed on its own exchange.

The major role of the ASX is to ensure the integrity of the market.

The major role of the ASX is to ensure the integrity of the market so that it operates in a fair, orderly and transparent manner.

The ASX operates a number of financial markets apart from its market in equity securities. It also operates markets in derivatives and interest rate securities.

The major responsibilities of the ASX include:

> **surveillance of its markets;**
> **supervising market participants (stockbrokers);**
> **admitting entities to its official list; and**
> **monitoring and enforcing compliance by listed entities with its listing rules.**

In carrying out these responsibilities, the ASX plays an important role in corporate governance regulation. The continuous disclosure regime incorporates both legislative regulation and ASX listing rule requirements. Under the continuous disclosure obligations, listed entities must inform the ASX of any information concerning the company of which it becomes aware which is not generally available and which a reasonable person would expect to have a material effect on the price of the company's securities. The continuous disclosure requirements play a key role in promoting an informed and transparent market. These requirements are discussed in Chapter 15 below.

The ASX formed a Corporate Governance Council comprising 21 interested organisations which issued its *Principles of Good Corporate Governance and Best Practice Recommendations* setting out recommended best practices which listed companies must either follow or explain to the market why they have not done so. These practices are discussed in Chapter 13.1 below.

There have been concerns expressed about the dual roles of the ASX as market supervisor and as a commercial entity listed on its own market. In response to these concerns, a subsidiary, ASX Supervisory Review Pty Ltd (ASXSR) was established with the roles of reviewing supervisory policy and procedures, providing assurance that the ASX complies with its supervisory responsibilities and overseeing supervision of listed entities where conflicts may arise because they are competitors of ASX or commercial partners.

The ASX website contains valuable information about the stock market and ASX listed companies and is linked to the Lipton-Herzberg Corporate Law Websites at **http://www.lipton-herzberg.com.au/corp-law-websites.html**

Trading in ASX listed securities is conducted electronically under the CHESS system. CHESS is discussed in Chapter 9 below.

Takeovers Panel

The Takeovers Panel replaces the courts as the main forum for resolving disputes about takeovers.

[1.125] The Takeovers Panel (called the Corporations and Securities Panel prior to March 2002) was established under the predecessor of the *ASIC Act 2001*. While a takeover bid is on foot the Takeovers Panel replaces the courts as the main forum for resolving disputes about takeovers.

The Panel was set up as the primary forum for dealing with takeover disputes to ensure such disputes could be resolved quickly by a specialist body and to prevent the various parties involved in a takeover from slowing up the process by initiating court litigation as either a defensive or aggressive takeover strategy. A person's right to commence court proceedings about a takeover bid is delayed until after the end of a takeover bid period. Only ASIC or another public authority has the power to commence court proceedings in relation to a takeover bid before the end of the bid period: s 659B.

The Takeovers Panel is a peer review body with members appointed by the government on the basis of their knowledge or experience in business, the financial markets, law, economics and accounting. This was done so that a specialist body comprised of takeover experts, attuned to the commercial realities and aware of market practices, could resolve takeover disputes.

The *Corporations Act* gives the Panel broad powers in relation to takeovers. In particular, it can declare circumstances in relation to a takeover, or to the control of a company, to be unacceptable circumstances: s 657A. Under s 657D the Panel can make a wide range of remedial orders to protect the rights of any person affected by the circumstances to ensure that a takeover bid proceeds the way that it would have proceeded if the unacceptable circumstances had not occurred. The Takeovers Panel also has the power to review certain decisions of ASIC to grant exemptions or modifications during the life of a takeover: s 656A.

The role of the Takeovers Panel is discussed further in Chapter 18 below. The Panel's website contains information about the Panel's guidance notes, media releases, decisions and rules and is linked to the Lipton-Herzberg Legislative Framework Pathway at **http://www.lipton-herzberg.com.au/secure/pathways-legislative-framework.html**

financial reporting system

[1.130] The financial reporting system was substantially reformed in 1999 and several further amendments were introduced in 2004 by the *Corporate Law Economic Reform Program (Audit Reform and Corporate Disclosure) Act 2004* (the CLERP 9 amendments).

The 1999 changes resulted in the establishment of new institutional arrangements for the Australian accounting standards-setting process and for the adoption of new procedures to be followed by the standard setter when making or formulating accounting standards. In particular, the current provisions provide for the establishment of the Financial Reporting Council (FRC). The FRC is an advisory body with responsibility for oversight over the process of setting Australian accounting and auditing standards. The 1999 amendments also reconstituted the Australian Accounting Standards Board (AASB). The changes are further discussed in Chapter 15 below.

The CLERP 9 amendments expanded the responsibilities of the FRC to also include oversight of the new auditor independence requirements and the auditing standard setting arrangements. The Auditing and Assurance Standards Board (AuASB) was reconstituted under a chair appointed by the Minister with a similar role in standard setting to that of the AASB. Both accounting and auditing standards have the force of law. The main objects of the financial reporting system as set out in s 224 of the *ASIC Act* are:

> **to facilitate the development of accounting standards that require the provision of financial information that—**
  - **— allows users to make and evaluate decisions about allocating scarce resources; and**
  - **— assists directors to discharge their obligations in relation to financial reporting; and**
  - **— is relevant to assessing performance, financial position, financing and investment; and**
  - **— is relevant and reliable, facilitates comparability and is readily understandable;**

> **to facilitate the development of auditing and assurance standards and related guidance materials that—**
  - **—provide Australian auditors with relevant and comprehensive guidance in forming an opinion about, and reporting on, whether financial reports comply with the requirements of the *Corporations Act*; and**
  - **— require the preparation of auditors' reports that are reliable and readily understandable by the users of the financial reports to which they relate;**

> **to facilitate the Australian economy by reducing the cost of capital, enabling Australian entities to compete effectively overseas and having accounting and auditing standards that are clearly stated and easy to understand; and**

> **to maintain investor confidence in the Australian economy (including its capital markets).**

Financial Reporting Council

FRC is an advisory body with responsibility for oversight of the process of setting Australian accounting standards, auditor independence requirements and auditing standard-setting arrangements.

[1.135] The FRC is an advisory body with responsibility for oversight of the process of setting Australian accounting standards, auditor independence requirements and auditing standard-setting arrangements. The FRC's functions and powers were designed to ensure that while it had broad oversight over the standard-setting process, it would not be able to determine the content of particular standards. For example, the FRC does not have any direct influence over technical deliberations of the AASB and cannot veto any accounting standard made by the AASB. This is also the case with the setting of auditing standards.

The FRC operates as a single oversight body for the key elements of the financial reporting framework. This aims to ensure that oversight is coherent and effective and in alignment with a common policy direction.

Under s 225(1), the FRC's general functions include:

> **providing broad oversight of the processes for setting accounting and auditing standards in Australia;**
> **monitoring the effectiveness of and advising on auditor independence requirements;**
> **giving reports and advice to the Minister; and**
> **establishing appropriate consultative mechanisms.**

The FRC appoints the members of AASB and AuASB, other than the chair and has responsibility to approve and monitor the AASB's and the AuASB's priorities, business plans and budgets. The CLERP 9 amendments and Commentary are linked to the Lipton-Herzberg Law Reform site at **http://www.lipton-herzberg.com.au/law_reform.htm**

Australian Accounting Standards Board

The AASB is the body that sets accounting standards.

[1.140] The AASB is the body that sets accounting standards. Its broad strategic plan and priorities are subject to FRC approval. In recent years its activities have concentrated on the implementation of the FRC directive that Australia should adopt International Accounting Standards and Interpretations commencing after 1 January 2005.

Under s 227(1) the functions of the AASB include:

> **developing a conceptual framework for the purpose of evaluating proposed accounting standards and international standards;**
> **making and formulating accounting standards; and**
> **participating in the development of a single set of accounting standards for worldwide use.**

In performing its functions, the AASB must follow the FRC's broad strategic and general policy directions: s 232. It must also take into account the advice and feedback on matters of general policy given by the FRC. Examples of a general policy direction include how quickly Australia should move towards greater adoption of international standards and/or market value accounting. However, the FRC does not have the power to direct the AASB in relation to the development or making of a particular standard, nor does it have the power to veto standards formulated and recommended by the AASB: s 225(5) and (6).

The AASB is a body corporate whose members, apart from the chair who is appointed by the Minister, are appointed by the FRC: s 236B. The AASB website contains information about the AASB, its media releases, newsletters and publications and is linked to the Lipton-Herzberg Legislative Framework Pathway at **http://www.lipton-herzberg.com.au/secure/pathways-legislative-framework.html**

Auditing and Assurance Standards Board

[1.145] The CLERP 9 amendments established the Auditing and Assurance Standards Board (AuASB) as a Commonwealth authority: *ASIC Act,* s 227A. Its functions and powers largely mirror those of the AASB. The main function of the AuASB is to make the auditing standards which are given legal effect by s 336 of the *Corporations Act.* The AuASB is also required to participate in and contribute to the development of a single set of auditing standards for world-wide use: *ASIC Act,* s 227B.

The main function of the AuASB is to make the auditing standards.

Registered company auditors, irrespective whether they are members of the accounting professional bodies, must use auditing standards when performing auditing work in accordance with the *Corporations Act*. Auditing standards are discussed in Chapter 16.

The AuASB is required to follow the broad strategic and general policy directions determined by the FRC and take into account the advice and feedback on matters of general policy given by the FRC: *ASIC Act,* s 234C. The FRC does not have the power to give directions on the development or making of or to veto a particular auditing standard: s 225(7) and (8).

The Minister can give the AuASB a direction about the role of international auditing standards in the Australian auditing standard-setting system after receiving and considering a report from the FRC about the desirability of giving the direction: s 234D.

As with the AASB, meetings of the AuASB which are concerned with the contents of auditing standards or international auditing standards must be held in public: s 236E(2).

The chair is appointed by the Minister and all other members are appointed by the FRC: s 236F.

Financial Reporting Panel

[1.150] The Financial Reporting Panel (FRP) was established to resolve disputes between ASIC and companies concerning accounting treatments in financial reports. The establishment of the FRP is an alternative to court proceedings which is less expensive and allows disputes to be heard by Panel members who possess accounting expertise. The FRP's hearings are informal and do not involve legal representation unless leave for representation is granted by the Panel. The FRP's findings are not binding and both ASIC and the company concerned can have the matter heard in court where the court may have regard to the findings of the FRP.

The FRP was established to resolve disputes between ASIC and companies concerning accounting treatments in financial reports.

Companies Auditors and Liquidators Disciplinary Board

[1.155] The Companies Auditors and Liquidators Disciplinary Board (CALDB), established under the *ASIC Act* is a disciplinary body which acts upon applications made to it by ASIC in respect of the conduct of registered auditors and liquidators. Its membership consists of persons selected by the government. As a result of changes introduced by the CLERP 9 amendments, hearings are conducted by Panels comprising a majority of non-accountants. These amendments were introduced to address the perception held regarding the previous structure of CALDB of a lack of sufficient independence from the professional accounting bodies.

The CALDB is a disciplinary body in respect of the conduct of registered auditors and liquidators.

Under s 1292 of the *Corporations Act* the CALDB may, on the application of ASIC, cancel or suspend the registration of a person as an auditor or a liquidator if, after conducting a hearing, it is satisfied that the person has failed to carry out adequately and properly her or his duties or is otherwise not a fit and proper person to remain registered. The CALDB also has the power to impose monetary penalties as an alternative to cancellation or suspension of registration.

Corporations and Markets Advisory Committee

[1.160] CAMAC (called the Companies and Securities Advisory Committee, or CASAC prior to March 2002) is the main corporate law reform advisory body of the *Corporations Act* scheme. Under s 148 of the *ASIC Act* CAMAC's primary function is to advise and make recommendations to the government on any matter connected with the operation, administration and reform of the corporations legislation. CAMAC can also make recommendations regarding the financial products industry and the financial services industry as well as proposals for improving the efficiency of the financial markets.

CAMAC's primary function is to advise and make recommendations to the government on any matter connected with the operation, administration and reform of the corporations legislation.

CAMAC and its predecessor, CASAC, have produced a large number of reports and issues papers dealing with a variety of topics. The Lipton-Herzberg Law Reform site at **http://www.lipton-herzberg.com.au/law_reform.htm** has links to these reports.

Parliamentary Joint Committee on Corporations and Financial Services

[1.165] Part 14 of the *ASIC Act* provides for the appointment of a Parliamentary Joint Committee on Corporations and Financial Services (PJC) at the commencement of the first session of each Parliament. Prior to March 2002, the PJC was called the Parliamentary Joint Committee on Corporations and Securities. The PJC consists of ten members of the Commonwealth Parliament, five of whom are senators appointed by the Senate and five who are members of the House of Representatives appointed by that House. The Commonwealth Treasurer is the Minister responsible for the political supervision of both ASIC and the corporations legislation. The purpose of the PJC is to add an additional level of parliamentary supervision over the *Corporations Act* scheme. According to s 243 of the *ASIC Act*, the duties of the PJC are to inquire and report into the operation of the corporations legislation generally, ASIC and the Takeovers Panel. The PJC website contains information about its role, current inquiries and recent reports and is linked to the Lipton-Herzberg Legislative Framework Pathway at **http://www.lipton-herzberg.com.au/secure/pathways-legislative-framework.html**

The purpose of the PJC is to add an additional level of parliamentary supervision over the *Corporations Act* scheme.

recent reforms

[1.170] In recent times the pace of law reform has considerably quickened and there have been numerous amendments to the legislation. This has occurred in order to modernise corporate regulation and is also in response to deficiencies which became apparent in light of several corporate collapses. There are several bodies which put forward corporate law reform proposals. These include ASIC, the Corporations and Markets Advisory Committee (CAMAC), the Parliamentary Joint Committee on Corporations and Financial Services (PJC) and the Australian Law Reform Commission (ALRC). Most of the recent corporate law reforms stem from the Corporate Law Economic Reform Program (CLERP) initiated in 1997. This program reflected the government's desire to implement corporate law reform in the context of a wider economic framework that includes such areas as taxation, competition laws, regulation of financial institutions and financial products. The primary objectives of CLERP are to:

> **promote the operation of informed markets by removing unnecessary obstacles to fundraising and thereby encouraging investment;**

> promote higher standards of corporate governance while encouraging directors to be more entrepreneurial and innovative;
> facilitate the development of accounting standards which ensure the maintenance of an informed and efficient capital market and which are responsive to the needs of the business community; and
> improve the market for corporate control and thereby provide incentives for greater corporate efficiency.

The Commonwealth Treasury's website sets out the objectives of CLERP. This is linked to the Lipton-Herzberg Legislative Framework Pathway at **http://www.lipton-herzberg.com.au/secure/pathways-legislative-framework.html**

The most recent significant reforms were contained in the *Corporate Law Economic Reform Program (Audit Reform and Corporate Disclosure) Act 2004* (CLERP 9 amendments) which came into effect on 1 July 2004. These amendments aimed to enhance audit regulation and the general corporate disclosure framework. They incorporated recommendations contained in the Ramsay Report, *Independence of Australian Company Auditors* (October 2001), the report of the Joint Committee of Public Accounts and Audits *Review of Independent Auditing by Registered Company Auditors* (September 2002), and the report of the HIH Royal Commission. This legislation, commentary and these reports are linked to the Lipton-Herzberg site at **http://www.lipton-herzberg.com.au**

The most recent significant reforms were contained in the CLERP 9 amendments.

The main features of these amendments include auditor independence requirements, strengthened obligations of auditors to report breaches of the law to ASIC, enhanced enforcement mechanisms in relation to continuous disclosure and the imposition of a duty on analysts to manage conflicts of interest.

pathways questions . . .

The following questions dealing with the legislative framework of the corporations legislation may best be answered by reading this Chapter and considering the Internet resources linked to the Lipton-Herzberg Legislative Framework Pathway at **http://www.lipton-herzberg.com.au/secure/pathways-legislative-framework.html**

1. Go to ASIC's website and look up its most recent Annual Report:
   (a) What were the main strategies and priorities implemented by ASIC during the year?
   (b) What are the corporate governance structures and practices of ASIC? In your answer consider matters such as how ASIC commissioners are appointed, how they carry out their responsibilities, how potential conflicts of interest are dealt with and how the commissioners are monitored.
   (c) What were the main activities of ASIC during the year in relation to:
   > enforcement; and
   > consumer protection?
   (d) List five examples of people successfully prosecuted by ASIC for criminal offences. Include the type of offence and the sentence imposed.
   (e) How many registered companies are there in Australia?
   (f) How many investigations were commenced by ASIC during the year referred to in the Annual Report?
   (g) Give three examples of interventions by ASIC where it believed the law had been breached in relation to the operation of securities and futures markets.

2. Outline some current areas of interest and concern to ASIC as indicated by recent speeches given by ASIC Commissioners and senior officers. Choose one of these speeches and describe the issues raised in it.

3. What is the purpose of ASIC's "Pie in the Sky Award"? Describe a scheme that won this award.

4. How can investors, creditors and others ascertain whether there have been changes to a company's documents lodged with ASIC?

5. What is the role and function of the Takeovers Panel? Describe a recent matter that came before the Takeovers Panel and the decision of the Panel.

6. Select one of CAMAC's latest reports or discussions papers and briefly describe the main issues raised in it.

7. What are the objectives and policies of CLERP? Explain how the CLERP 9 amendments seek to further these objectives and policies.

bibliography . . .

Bottomley, S "Where did the Law Go? The Delegation of Australian Corporate Regulation" (2003) 15 Aust Jnl of Corp Law 105.

Hetherington, Marion "Resolving the Company Law Crisis after the High Court's Decision in The Queen v Hughes" (2000) 28 ABLR 364.

Kingsford-Smith, D "Interpreting the Corporations Law: Purpose, Practical Reasoning and the Public Interest" (1999) 21 Syd LR 161.

McQueen, R "Company Law as Imperialism" (1995) 5 Aust Jnl of Corp Law 187.

McQueen, R "An Examination of Australian Corporate Law and Regulation 1901–1961" (1992) 15 UNSWLJ 1.

McQueen, R "Limited Liability Company Legislation: The Australian Experience" (1991) 1 Aust Jnl of Corp Law 22.

McQueen, R "Why High Court Judges Make Poor Historians: The Corporations Act Case and Early Attempts to Establish a National System of Company Regulation in Australia" (1990) 19 FL Rev 245.

Ramsay, I "Challenges to Australia's Federal Corporate Law", Uni of Melbourne, Centre for Corporate Law and Securities Regulation, Corporate Law Research Papers, **http://cclsr.law.unimelb.edu.au/research-papers/**

Rose, D "The Hughes Case: The Reasoning, Uncertainties and Solutions" (2000) 29 UWALR 180.

Whincop, M "Phoenix or Souffle? The Economics of the Rise, Fall and Second Rise of the NationalScheme". Papers presented at the conference "The Future of Corporate Regulation: Hughes & Wakim and the Referral of Powers" (3 November 2000) **http://cclsr.law.unimelb.edu.au/researchpapers/conf-papers.html**

Williams, G "Cooperative Federalism and the Revival of the Corporations Law: Wakim and Beyond" (2002) 20 C & SLJ 160.

revision questions on the material in this chapter ...

> Please see eQuiz at **http://www.thomson.com.au/academic** for multiple choice questions and answers.

> For further corporations law links and material please refer to the Lipton-Herzberg website at **http://www.lipton-herzberg.com.au**

chapter two

registration and its effects

key points ...

- Upon registration a company is regarded as a legal entity that is separate and distinct from its members/shareholders and directors. Even a one-person company is regarded as a separate legal entity distinct from that person.

- The fact that a company is a separate legal entity means that it may sue and be sued in its own name. Company property belongs to the company, not its members. A company continues to exist until it is deregistered, even if its members die.

- Limited liability is an important characteristic of companies and their shareholders. Most companies are registered on the basis that the liability of members is limited to the amount unpaid (if any) on the issue price of their shares. This encourages shareholder investment because the risk of the company's insolvency is largely transferred from its shareholders to its creditors.

- Occasionally, both the *Corporations Act* and case law lift the corporate veil to either disregard the fact that a company is a separate legal entity or remove the privilege of limited liability.

- The procedure for setting up a company involves lodging an application for registration with ASIC. This application must contain prescribed information. The *Corporations Act* imposes a number of post-registration requirements, such as the establishment of registers, financial records and minute books, which must be carried out soon after a company is registered.

characteristics of a company

Companies are abstract, artificial entities recognised by the law as legal persons with rights and liabilities separate from their shareholders or members.

[2.05] Companies are abstract, artificial entities recognised by the law as legal persons with rights and liabilities separate from their shareholders or members.This chapter discusses the legal implications which flow from this definition. Companies are used for a wide range of purposes and differ considerably in terms of size of business, number of shareholders, spread of shareholdings, nature of activities and value of assets held. Despite this diversity, the fundamental consequences of registration are the same for all registered companies.

[2.10] A company comes into existence as a body corporate at the beginning of the day on which it is registered with the name specified in its certificate of registration: s 119. This means that after the application for registration has been lodged with ASIC and a certificate of registration has been issued, a new legal entity is created. This legal entity is separate from its members. Thus, for example, the assets of the company are not the assets of its members and contracts entered into by the company will create rights and liabilities that vest in the company and not in its members.

effects of registration

[2.15] The powers and liabilities of a company are the direct consequence of its creation as a distinct legal entity. A company is distinguished from the members it may have from time to time. The legal capacity and powers of a company include the capacity and powers of an individual and a body corporate: s 124. Powers of an individual applicable to companies include the power to acquire and dispose of property and the right to sue.

The legal capacity and powers of a company include the capacity and powers of an individual and a body corporate.

Powers of a company as a body corporate are listed in s 124(1) and include the power to:

> **issue shares and debentures;**
> **grant options over unissued shares;**
> **distribute the company's property among its members;**
> **grant a floating charge or give security over uncalled capital; and**
> **do anything it is lawfully authorised to do.**

A body corporate is an incorporated legal entity created and recognised by the law. It is an artificial legal person as opposed to individuals, who are known as natural persons. The term "body corporate" is a general term used to describe any artificial legal person. The various types of body corporate are discussed in Chapter 3 below. Under the *Corporations Act* a body corporate is regarded as one type of "corporation": s 57A. A company registered under the *Corporations Act* is also a type of corporation.

Because a company is a separate legal entity it follows that it may enforce rights by suing and conversely it may incur liabilities and be sued by others. Once the common law rule in *Foss v Harbottle* did not allow shareholders or members to sue on behalf of their company. However, Pt 2F.1A (ss 236–242) may now permit a member or officer to bring legal proceedings in the company's name with prior leave of the court. Such proceedings are referred to as "statutory derivative actions" and are discussed in Chapter 17 below. The separate nature of a company is illustrated by the fact that a company may sue and be sued by its own members. This may be contrasted with the difficulties faced by unincorporated associations and their members seeking to enforce legal rights against each other.

Because a company is a separate legal entity it follows that it may enforce rights by suing and conversely it may incur liabilities and be sued by others.

A further consequence of the fact that a company is a separate legal entity is that a company may own property distinct from the property of its shareholders or members. This means that shareholders do not have a proprietary interest in the property of the company. This is illustrated by *Macaura v Northern Assurance Co Ltd* [1925] AC 619, discussed below para [2.45]. Shareholders only own shares in the company. The legal nature of shares is discussed in Chapter 8 below. A change in shareholder of a company will have no effect on the company's ownership of its assets.

A company may own property distinct from the property of its shareholders or members.

A company continues to exist until it is deregistered by ASIC: s 601AD(1). Its shareholders may come and go but this does not affect the continuing legal personality of the company. Even if all shareholders of a small company died, the company would still survive. A deceased shareholder's shares are transmitted to their personal representative, who will usually be the executor named in the deceased shareholder's will.

A company continues to exist until it is deregistered by ASIC.

Historically, one of the effects of registration was that a company could enter into a contract only if there was a contractual document bearing the impression of the company's seal. Section 126 now provides that the power of a company to make a contract may be exercised by an individual acting with the company's express or implied authority and on behalf of the company. This power may be exercised without the use of a common seal. The validity of the exercise of power by an individual to act on behalf of a company is determined by the law of agency and the assumptions in s 129. This is discussed in Chapter 5 below.

Prior to 1998, all companies were required to have a common seal. It is now optional for companies to have a common seal: s 123(1). Consequently, a company may execute a document without using a common seal: ss 127(1) and (3).

If a company chooses to have a common seal, its name and Australian Company Number (ACN) or Australian Business Number (ABN) must be set out on the seal: s 123(1). If a company has an ABN issued for goods and services tax purposes, it may use its ABN in place of its ACN provided that the ABN includes its nine-digit ACN. It is a strict liability offence to use or authorise the use of a seal in non-compliance with these requirements: s 123(3).

limited liability

reasons for limited liability

Limited liability means that shareholders of a company are not personally liable for their company's debts.

[2.20] Business enterprises with limited liability are a feature of all developed legal systems. Limited liability means that shareholders of a company are not personally liable for their company's debts. The extent of a shareholder's liability depends on the type of company, as provided by s 112. These various types of companies are discussed in Chapter 3 below. In any case, if a company has incurred obligations, it is primarily liable because its debts are separate from the debts of its shareholders. It is only when the company has insufficient assets to pay its debts that the issue of whether shareholders may be liable arises.

The liability of shareholders of a company limited by shares is limited to the amount, if any, unpaid on the issue price of their shares.

By far the most common type of company is a company limited by shares. The liability of shareholders of such a company is limited to the amount, if any, unpaid on the issue price of their shares: s 516. Shareholders who own fully paid shares have no further liability to pay further amounts to the company.

The effect of limited liability is that the risk of business failure is largely transferred from the company's shareholders to its creditors.

The effect of limited liability is that the risk of business failure is largely transferred from the company's shareholders to its creditors.

The arguments in favour of limited liability were stated by CASAC in para 1.52 of its *Corporate Groups Final Report* (May 2000):

> Limited liability achieves various economic goals:
>
> - **facilitating enterprise.** Limited liability facilitates investment and otherwise encourages economic activity by separating investment and management functions and shielding investors from any corporate loss in excess of their equity capital. This protection for investors reduces the costs of raising capital. Also, corporate controllers may be more willing to undertake entrepreneurial activity through their controlled companies, given that, as shareholders of those companies, they are shielded against unlimited liability for the debts of those companies
> - **reducing monitoring.** Limited liability decreases the need for shareholders to monitor the managers of companies in which they invest. The risk to those shareholders of a company's failure is confined to the loss of the equity invested
> - **promoting market efficiency.** Limited liability promotes the liquidity and efficient operation of securities markets, as the wealth of each shareholder of a public company is irrelevant to the trading price of its shares. This allows shares to be freely traded, as their price is set by factors other than their owners' wealth. The free transfer of shares may in turn promote efficient management, given that shares in a poorly managed company may trade at a discount, creating the climate for a takeover and the replacement of incumbent management
> - **encouraging equity diversity.** Limited liability permits investors to acquire shares in a number of companies. This might not be possible for particular investors if the principle of unlimited liability applied and they could lose all or most of their personal wealth through failure of one company in which they held equity.

CASAC's *Corporate Groups Final Report* is linked to the Lipton-Herzberg Effects of Registration Pathway at **http://www.lipton-herzberg.com.au/secure/pathways-effect-of-registration.html#Corporate_groups**

The argument in favour of limited liability is less compelling in the case of closely held small companies and subsidiaries within corporate groups.

limited liability and closely held companies

[2.25] The argument in favour of limited liability is less compelling in the case of closely held small companies and subsidiaries within corporate groups. These companies, usually registered as proprietary companies, have small numbers of shareholders who typically also function as, or nominate, the directors and managers. Within corporate groups, some of the benefits of limited liability, such as the reduction in monitoring costs, are irrelevant as it is usual for a controlling company to monitor its controlled companies.

Further, the benefit of promoting an efficient market for shares through limited liability is not applicable as there is no market for the shares of unlisted group companies. It is also arguable that limited liability is more likely to encourage excessive risk taking by parent companies, because the benefit of a business risk will accrue to the company while if the risk fails, the burden falls on creditors. In most cases, the main reason for incorporation of closely held companies is not to obtain the benefits of limited liability, but to minimise income tax.

Tax considerations are the main purpose behind the common practice of incorporating a company to act as trustee of a discretionary trust to operate a family business. Typically, such companies are established with a small paid up capital, usually $2. These companies, often referred to as "$2 companies", operate businesses and incur debts on behalf of the beneficiaries of the trusts but do not have any assets of their own. If trust assets are insufficient, trust creditors cannot look to the personal assets of the trustee's shareholders. Trustee companies are discussed in Chapter 3 below.

limited liability and contract creditors

[2.30] The impact of limited liability on creditors depends on the type of creditor. The risks in dealing with limited liability companies are often overcome by creditors such as banks and other financial institutions. Since such lenders usually have strong bargaining power they generally will not lend money to limited liability entities unless they receive security for their loans. The security may take the form of a debenture granting the lender a fixed or floating charge over company assets. It may also consist of a mortgage over the real estate or goods owned by the company. In the case of closely held companies, finance creditors commonly also insist on security in the form of personal guarantees from the directors and shareholders. As well as requiring security for loans, finance creditors often further protect themselves from the risk of business failure by insisting on the inclusion in loan agreements of terms that restrict the borrowing company's dividend policy, investment decisions that alter the risk characteristics of the company's earnings and the ability to raise further debt capital.

Trade creditors supply goods or services to a company on credit. Such creditors rarely insist on security before they supply on credit to a company. For this reason they bear a large part of the risk of the debtor company's insolvency. Trade creditors can reduce the risk of insolvency by charging a higher price for the goods or services supplied. In addition, trade creditors may take out insurance to protect themselves from bad debts. Further, because trade creditors, as a general rule, are creditors of more than one company, they effectively diversify the risk that one of their customers may become insolvent. Accordingly, their overall risk is often minimised.

The employees of a company are a special category of unsecured creditors adversely affected by limited liability. Unlike finance or trade creditors they rarely obtain security or diversify the risk of their employer's insolvency. Further, most employees have little information about their employer's financial condition. The *Corporations Act* to some extent recognises the difficulties that confront employees in the event of insolvency and seeks to provide some protection. Section 556 accords unpaid employee wages, holiday pay and long service leave preferential treatment in the event of the liquidation of their corporate employer. Part 5.8A also protects employees from agreements which have the purpose of defeating the recovery of their entitlements. These provisions are discussed in Chapter 25 below.

ASIC has published on its website an information paper, "Don't Get Burned", that suggests steps creditors should take to reduce their risk when dealing with limited liability companies. This paper is linked to the Lipton-Herzberg Effects of Registration Pathway at **http://www.lipton-herzberg.com.au/secure/pathways-effect-of-registration.html#Limited_liability**

limited liability and tort creditors

[2.35] While contract creditors bear some risk when they provide credit to a limited liability company, they generally enter into the contract voluntarily. This is not the case for a company's tort creditors who are generally involuntary creditors. Victims of torts, such as negligence, committed by a company bear an uncompensated and involuntary risk in the event of the company's insolvency, yet they are usually in a poor position to protect themselves against the risk of harm. This is especially so where a parent company seeks to quarantine tort liability in a subsidiary which has inadequate assets to meet all tort

While contract creditors bear some risk when they provide credit to a limited liability company, they generally enter into the contract voluntarily. This is not the case for a company's tort creditors who are generally involuntary creditors.

claims and the parent company then seeks the protection of limited liability to prevent tort creditors recovering compensation from the parent and other companies in the group.

Several arguments have been put forward in favour of limiting the operation of limited liability in relation to tort claims against members of a corporate group:

> **it is economically inefficient to leave involuntary tort creditors with the risk of uncompensated injuries because the party best able to take measures to avoid the risk, which is the holding company, should bear the liability;**
> **excessive risk-taking business behaviour is not deterred. One of the main objectives of tort law is to discourage unnecessarily harmful behaviour by the imposition of compensation liability on the person who commits a tort. This objective is undermined if the wrongdoer can avoid having to meet claims against it through reliance on the principle of limited liability. This is known as "externalising risk"; and**
> **it is unethical for companies to profit from business activities which cause harm without bearing the costs arising from death and injury caused by these activities.**

Similarly, there is little incentive for a limited liability entity to carry adequate negligence insurance since, in the event of default, shareholders can only lose their investment. It is not surprising, therefore, to note that many professionals, such as accountants, architects and engineers, incorporate their practices as limited liability companies to avoid potential liability for negligence. Even for those professionals, such as solicitors, who are not permitted to incorporate their practices in limited liability entities, it is not uncommon to find that they have shifted their other assets to limited liability companies.

The operation of limited liability in corporate groups was considered in the *Report of the Special Commission of Inquiry into the Medical Research and Compensation Foundation* (2004). This inquiry by David Jackson QC was into the circumstances of the restructuring of James Hardie Industries Limited. The Report includes a Discussion Paper "The Concept of Limited Liability—Existing Law and Rationale" by Counsel Assisting, John Sheahan SC. The Report and Discussion Paper are linked to the Lipton-Herzberg website at **http://www.lipton-herzberg.com.au**

company as separate legal entity

[2.40] The various reasons for the development of companies are discussed in Chapter 1 above. While the *Corporations Act* sets out the various characteristics described above, it is clear that the original companies legislation was drafted primarily to meet the needs of large-scale businesses with large numbers of investors. The attractiveness of incorporation for small partnerships and sole traders was not envisaged in the 1840s.

However, the benefits of incorporation were soon recognised by smaller enterprises, whose controllers increasingly decided to form companies as the structure by which to carry on their businesses. It was not until the late 19th century, in the famous case *Salomon v Salomon & Co Ltd* [1897] AC 22, that the full implications of the concept that a company is a separate legal entity were recognised—especially in relation to what was in reality a one-person company. This case established that as long as the necessary formalities of incorporation were satisfied, a new entity comes into existence that is separate and distinct from its directors and shareholders. This is so whether the company has a large number of shareholders or, as in Salomon's case (see below), is a company managed and controlled by one person.

case note

Salomon was a boot manufacturer who owned a large successful business that he operated as a sole trader. Several of his sons worked in the business and he wished to give them each a share. For this reason he formed a company, which was duly incorporated under the applicable English *Companies Act*. The company was at all times intended to be what would now be a proprietary company. No invitation was made to the public to take up shares. The subscribers to the memorandum were Salomon, his wife and five of his children. Each of them took up one share. Salomon and his two eldest sons were appointed directors. The company purchased Salomon's business for £39,000, which was an excessive price. The purchase price was paid as follows: 20,000 £1 fully paid shares and debentures worth £10,000 were issued to Salomon; £1,000 was paid in cash to Salomon and £8,000 went in discharge of the debts of the business.

After these transactions were completed, Salomon held 20,001 of the 20,007 issued shares in his company. Further, there was evidence that the other shareholders held their six shares as nominee for Salomon, so that Salomon & Co Ltd was in reality a "one man" company.

Largely as a result of strikes in the industry, the company experienced financial difficulties. In an attempt to maintain the company Salomon advanced it further funds from his own resources. When this proved insufficient he borrowed £5,000 from a lender, Broderip, which was then on-lent to the company. As security for Broderip's loan Salomon granted him a mortgage over his debentures and caused them to be reissued in Broderip's name.

Despite this infusion of funds the business continued to decline. The company defaulted on paying the interest due on the debentures and Broderip appointed a receiver to realise the security. Soon after, the company was compulsorily wound up due to its insolvency and a liquidator was appointed.

The liquidator found that the company's realisable assets amounted to about £6,000. This was sufficient to repay Broderip's claim of £5,000. The remaining £1,000 was claimed by Salomon as beneficial owner of the debentures. If these claims had been met, there would have been nothing left for payment of the unsecured creditors who were owed approximately £8,000.

The liquidator initially resisted Broderip's demand for repayment of the £5,000 and by way of defence counterclaimed against Salomon seeking to have the sale of business contract rescinded and the debentures cancelled. The liquidator argued that Salomon, as promoter of his company, had breached his fiduciary duties by selling his business to it for an excessive price. He also maintained that the formation of the company was a fraud on its unsecured creditors.

The case eventually was decided by the House of Lords: *Salomon v Salomon & Co Ltd* [1897] AC 22. By the time the hearing commenced, the liquidator had met Broderip's claim, so the case against Salomon was the sole question to be determined. The House of Lords unanimously decided in Salomon's favour and reversed the earlier decisions.

It held that, provided the formalities of incorporation were observed, it was not contrary to the intention of the *Companies Act 1862* (UK) for a trader to gain limited liability and obtain priority as a debenture-holder over other creditors. A person may sell a business to a limited liability company of which the person is virtually the only shareholder and director. The company was a separate legal entity distinct from its shareholders and directors. It therefore followed that the company could be a secured debtor of its shareholders, thereby enabling them to rank ahead of its unsecured creditors. Lord Macnaghten stated:

The company was a separate legal entity distinct from its shareholders and directors. It therefore followed that the company could be a secured debtor of its shareholders, thereby enabling them to rank ahead of its unsecured creditors.

> < When the memorandum is duly signed and registered, though there be only seven shares taken, the subscribers are a body corporate "capable forthwith" to use the words of the enactment, "of exercising all the functions of an incorporated company". Those are strong words. The company attains maturity on its birth. There is no period of minority—no interval of incapacity. I cannot understand how a body corporate thus made "capable" by statute can lose its individuality by issuing the bulk of its capital to one person, whether he be a subscriber to the memorandum or not. The company is at law a different person altogether from the subscribers to the memorandum; and, though it may be that after incorporation the business is precisely the same as it was before, and the same persons are managers, and the same hands receive the profits, the company is not in law the agent of the subscribers or trustee for them. Nor are the subscribers as members liable, in any shape or form, except to the extent and in the manner provided by the Act. That is, I think, the declared intention of the enactment. If the view of the learned judge were sound, it would follow that no common law partnership could register as a company limited by shares without remaining subject to unlimited liability. >

Upon incorporation a separate entity is created, even if all the company's issued shares are beneficially owned by the same person.

The House of Lords maintained that the fact that Salomon & Co Ltd was a "one man" company made no difference. Upon incorporation a separate entity is created, even if all the company's issued shares are beneficially owned by the same person. Lord Herschell explained the reasoning for this conclusion:

> < How does it concern the creditor whether the capital of the company is owned by seven persons in equal share, with the right to an equal share of the profits, or whether it is almost entirely owned by one person, who practically takes the whole of the profits? The creditor has notice that he is dealing with a company the liability of the members of which is limited, and the register of shareholders informs him how the shares are held, and that they are substantially in the hands of one person, if this be the fact. The creditors in the present case gave credit to, and contracted with, a limited company ...
>
> The Court of Appeal has declared that the formation of the respondent company and the agreement to take over the business of the appellant were a scheme "contrary to the true intent and meaning of the *Companies Act*". I know of no means of ascertaining what is the intent and meaning of the *Companies Act* except by examining its provisions and finding what regulations it has imposed as a condition of trading with limited liability ... The legislature, therefore, clearly sanctions a scheme by which all the shares except six are owned by a single individual, and these six are of a value little more than nominal. >

Lord Halsbury LC was of the opinion that the conclusion that the business was Salomon's business and that the company was his trustee or agent involved a logical contradiction.

> < Either the limited company was a legal entity or it was not. If it was, the business belonged to it and not to Mr Salomon. If it was not, there was no person and no thing to be an agent at all; and it is impossible to say at the same time that there is a company and there is not. >

Lord Watson made the point that the company was under no obligation to specifically inform its unsecured creditors of the existence of Salomon's debenture. They could have discovered this themselves by conducting searches of the records kept by the registering authority.

application of Salomon's case

[2.45] *Salomon's* case is significant because it was not until the House of Lords handed down its decision that a de facto one-person company was fully recognised as being a separate legal entity. The *Corporations Act* has taken this to its logical conclusion and now allows the formation of public or proprietary companies with a single shareholder: s 114. The principle in *Salomon's* case has been applied in many cases so that its operation has expanded to many situations which the House of Lords judges would not have anticipated. This is particularly so in the case of corporate groups discussed below.

Salomon's case is significant because it was not until the House of Lords handed down its decision that a de facto one-person company was fully recognised as being a separate legal entity.

case note

In *Lee v Lee's Air Farming Ltd* [1961] AC 12, Lee was a pilot who conducted an aerial top-dressing business. He formed a company to conduct the business. The capital of the company comprised 3,000 £1 shares, of which 2,999 were allotted to Lee. The remaining share was taken by his solicitor as nominee for Lee. Under the articles of association, Lee was governing director with very wide powers. Workers' compensation insurance was taken out, naming Lee as an employee.

Lee was killed when his aeroplane crashed while engaged in aerial top-dressing. His widow made a claim for payment under the *Workers' Compensation Act 1922* (NZ). Her claim was initially rejected on the ground that as Lee had full control of his company he could not be a "worker" within the meaning of that Act. "Worker" was defined under the *Workers' Compensation Act* as a person "who has entered into or works under a contract of service ... with an employer". The Privy Council rejected this argument. It held that as the company was a separate legal entity distinct from its founder, Lee, it could enter into a contract of employment with him. Lord Morris explained the rationale of this principle:

> < In their Lordships' view, it is a logical consequence of the decision in *Salomon v Salomon & Co Ltd* [1897] AC 22, that one person may function in dual capacities. There is no reason, therefore, to deny the possibility of a contractual relationship being created as between the deceased and the company. If this stage is reached, then their Lordships see no reason why the range of possible relationships should not include a contract for services, and if the deceased as agent for the respondent company, could negotiate a contract for services as between the company and himself there is no reason why a contract of service could not also be negotiated. >

The recognition of a company as a separate legal entity may also in some cases work against the person responsible for the formation of the company.

case note

In *Macaura v Northern Assurance Co Ltd* [1925] AC 619, Macaura owned land on which stood timber. He sold the land and timber to a company he formed and received as consideration all the fully paid shares. The company carried on the business of felling and milling timber. A fire destroyed all the timber that had been felled. Macaura had earlier insured the timber against loss by fire in his own name. He had not transferred the insurance policy to the company.

When Macaura made a claim his insurers refused to pay, arguing that he had no insurable interest in the timber. Only persons with a legal or equitable interest in property are regarded as having an insurable interest in it. The House of Lords agreed that the insurers were not liable. It was only Macaura's company, as owner of the timber, which had the requisite insurable interest in it. Only the company, and not Macaura, could insure its property against loss or damage. Shareholders, the court held, have no legal or equitable interest in their company's property. This is the case whether a company has only one or many shareholders.

Section 17 of the *Insurance Contracts Act 1984* (Cth) dispenses with the common law requirement of "insurable interest" and may now overcome the decision in *Macaura's* case. This provides that where an insured, under a general insurance contract, suffers a pecuniary or economic loss by reason of damage to or destruction of the insured property, the insurer is not relieved of liability just because the insured did not have a legal or equitable interest in the property.

This provision, however, raises the question whether a shareholder suffers a pecuniary or economic loss if the company's property is damaged. Most probably a shareholder in Macaura's position, holding all the shares in a company, would have a strong case for compensation by the insurer. The loss would arise by reason of the decline in the value of the shares as a consequence of the damage or destruction of the company's property. It is less clear whether there would be a quantifiable loss for the purposes of s 17 in the case of an insured who is a minority shareholder in respect of damage to property of the company, particularly where the property represents a relatively small proportion of the company's assets.

One consequence arising from the conclusion that shareholders have no legal or equitable interest in company property is that it is theoretically possible for a shareholder to be found guilty of stealing company property. This is the case even in one-person companies. In *MacLeod v The Queen* [2003] HCA 24 the High Court held that a person who was the sole director and shareholder could be convicted under s 173 of the *Crimes Act* of fraudulently applying property owned by the company for his own use. According to the High Court:

> **< The self-interested "consent" of the shareholder, given in furtherance of a crime against the company, cannot be said to represent the consent of the company. >**

Salomon's principle and corporate groups

An important use of companies is within corporate groups which are often controlled by a large listed company.

[2.50] An important use of companies is within corporate groups which are often controlled by a large listed company. A report by Ian Ramsay and Geoff Stapledon, *Corporate Groups in Australia*, Centre for Corporate Law and Securities Regulation, Faculty of Law (1998) found that:

> **89% of listed companies controlled other companies;**
> **the larger the listed company, the more companies it tended to control in a group. The average number of controlled companies in the study group was 28, however the average for the highest quartile was 72 controlled companies; and**
> **90% of controlled companies were wholly owned and of the partly owned companies, 90% were more than 50% owned.**

This paper is linked to the Lipton-Herzberg Law Reform page at **http://www.lipton-herzberg.com.au/law_reform.htm#ccls**

The CASAC *Corporate Groups Final Report* (May 2000) gave several reasons why corporate groups exist. These include:

> **Reducing risk or maximising returns by diversifying an enterprise's activities into various businesses each of which is operated by a separate group company.**

- Acquiring existing companies to expand an enterprise or increase market power. The acquired companies may possess recognised brands or goodwill. It is often more advantageous to acquire a company as a going concern than to acquire its assets.
- Equity may be attracted into part of a company's overall business by establishing a partly owned subsidiary with a minority shareholder.
- High-risk liability may be confined to particular subsidiaries and remaining group assets are thereby isolated from potential risk.
- Better security may be required by a lender through a transfer of some group assets to a particular company and conferring a charge over those assets.

The CASAC report noted that large enterprises often operate through a corporate group structure and considered whether the law based on the principle in *Salomon's* case properly accommodates such groups. This is further discussed below.

CASAC's *Corporate Groups Final Report* is linked to the Lipton-Herzberg Effects of Registration Pathway at **http://www.lipton-herzberg.com.au/secure/pathways-effect-of-registration.html#Corporate_groups**

The application of the principle in *Salomon's* case to corporate groups means that each company in a group is a separate legal entity distinct from other companies in the group. As a result of this, creditors of a company in a group can only enforce their rights against the debtor company, shareholders of each group company have limited liability and directors owe duties to the particular companies of which they are directors and not the group as a whole.

The application of the principle in *Salomon's* case to corporate groups means that each company in a group is a separate legal entity distinct from other companies in the group.

A strict application of *Salomon's* principle in this context may to some extent be contrary to commercial practice and expectations because parent companies are invariably in a position to give directions to other companies in the group and this is often the understanding upon which the group was created. Despite this, the controlling company or other companies in the group will not be liable for the debts of another group company. This problem is exacerbated where assets are moved between companies and the unsecured creditors of one company cannot claim assets which have been transferred to another company in the group. As discussed below, para [2.110], in order to alleviate some of these difficulties, the corporate veil may be lifted so that the parent company may sometimes be liable for the debts of a subsidiary.

case note

In *Walker v Wimborne* (1976) 137 CLR 1, the High Court had to consider the liability of directors of a number of associated companies. The directors had moved funds between the companies to enable various debts to be paid and used assets of one company as security for loans obtained by others. The companies went into liquidation and the liquidator brought an action under the predecessor of s 598 on the grounds that the directors had been guilty of fraud, negligence, default, breach of trust or breach of duty in relation to a corporation and the corporation had thereby suffered loss.

Mason J rejected the argument that where companies were associated in a group, directors could disregard their duties to individual companies in the group provided their actions were undertaken for the benefit of the group as a whole. He said:

> < Indeed, the emphasis given by the primary judge to the circumstance that the group derived a benefit from the transaction tended to obscure the fundamental principles that each of the companies was a separate and independent legal entity, and that it was the duty of the directors of Asiatic to consult its interests and its interests alone in deciding whether payments should be made to other companies. In this respect it should be emphasised that the directors of a company in discharging their duty to the company must take account of the interest of its shareholders and its creditors. Any

The directors of a company in discharging their duty to the company must take account of the interest of its shareholders and its creditors.

failure by the directors to take into account the interests of creditors will have adverse consequences for the company as well as for them. The creditor of a company, whether it be a member of a "group" of companies in the accepted sense of that term or not, must look to that company for payment. His interests may be prejudiced by the movement of funds between companies in the event that the companies become insolvent. >

In this case Mason J refused to recognise the group as a single entity and, for the purpose of determining the liability of directors, held that each company was a separate legal entity to each of which duties were owed.

In *Walker v Wimborne* the issue arose in the context of associated companies. The association existed because each company had the same persons as its directors and shareholders. They were not, however, related bodies corporate as defined in ss 46–50.

case note

In *Industrial Equity Ltd v Blackburn* (1977) 137 CLR 567 the consolidated accounts of a group of companies of which Industrial Equity was the holding company disclosed sufficient profits from which a dividend could be paid. These profits were actually made by the subsidiaries. Industrial Equity asserted that it could pay dividends to its own shareholders from the profits made by its subsidiaries notwithstanding that the subsidiaries had not paid dividends to the holding company. The High Court rejected this approach. It regarded each company within the group as a separate legal entity. A subsidiary's profits could not be regarded as the profits of its holding company available for payment of the holding company's dividend. The High Court asserted that merely because the group accounting requirements treated a group as a single entity to ensure that sufficient information of the group's financial position is provided, this did not mean that the corporate veil could be lifted for other purposes.

case note

Pioneer Concrete Services Ltd v Yelnah Pty Ltd (1987) 5 ACLC 467 concerned a complex marketing agreement involving the manufacture and supply of readymix concrete. The agreement, entered into in 1982, was between three independent parties: Pioneer Concrete Services Ltd, Hi-Quality Concrete (Holdings) Pty Ltd and its subsidiaries and interests associated with Yelnah Pty Ltd. One of the Hi-Quality Concrete subsidiaries was Hi-Quality Concrete (NSW) Pty Ltd. A clause of the agreement provided that Hi-Quality Concrete (NSW) Pty Ltd, the subsidiary, would at all times act in the best interests of Pioneer Concrete and other companies associated in the business and would not attempt to increase its interest in the venture at the expense of Pioneer. In 1985 Pioneer Concrete Services alleged that Hi-Quality Concrete (Holdings) Pty Ltd, the holding company, entered into a transaction with Yelnah Pty Ltd in breach of the agreement and sought an injunction to prevent its completion. The court decided that the holding company was not a party to this clause of the agreement. Rather, it was an undertaking given by its subsidiary, and the two were separate legal entities. It was impossible to infer an agency relationship between the holding and subsidiary companies in the circumstances.

The Lipton-Herzberg Effects of Registration Pathway at **http://www.lipton-herzberg.com.au/secure/pathways-effect-of-registration.html#Corporate_groups** contains links to the CASAC May 2000 *Corporate Groups Final Report*, as well as to journal articles that discuss the implications that *Salomon's* case has on regulating corporate groups.

lifting the veil of incorporation

[2.55] The recognition that a company is a separate legal entity distinct from its shareholders is often expressed as the "veil of incorporation". This is because, once a company is duly incorporated, the courts usually do not look behind the "veil" to inquire why the company was formed or who really controls it. Further, when the separate entity concept is coupled with limited liability, the corporate veil ensures that shareholders are not personally liable to creditors for their company's debts. In the case of a company limited by shares, their liability is limited to the amount, if any, unpaid on the nominal value of their shares: s 516.

The recognition that a company is a separate legal entity distinct from its shareholders is often expressed as the "veil of incorporation".

Ever since the House of Lords handed down its decision in *Salomon's* case it has been recognised that an inflexible application of the concepts of separate entity and limited liability, with all that they imply, can result in undesirable consequences. There are various statutory provisions that have the effect of lifting the corporate veil. In addition, the courts have sometimes sought ways to look behind the company form.

by statute

[2.60] directors' liability for insolvent trading. In some circumstances, directors may become personally liable for debts incurred by their company. This liability arises where directors breach the duty contained in s 588G by failing to prevent the company incurring debts when there are reasonable grounds for suspecting that it is insolvent. This is known as "insolvent trading".

In some circumstances, directors may become personally liable for debts incurred by their company.

Directors who breach this duty are liable to pay as compensation an amount equal to the loss or damage suffered by unsecured creditors in relation to the debts so incurred because of the company's insolvency: ss 588J, 588K and 588M. As a general rule, the compensation is payable to the company's liquidator who distributes it to the company's unsecured creditors. As well as a liability to pay compensation, contravention of the s 588G duty may also result in the imposition of a civil penalty order pursuant to Pt 9.4B of the *Corporations Act*. Directors may also commit a criminal offence under s 588G(3) if their failure to prevent the company incurring the debt was dishonest. The liability for failing to prevent insolvent trading is further discussed in Chapter 13.5 below.

[2.65] uncommercial transactions. There are provisions in the *Corporations Act* that lift the corporate veil for purposes of treating corporate insiders such as directors and other related entities of the company differently from others who have dealings with the company. The aim of clawing back uncommercial transactions is to ensure that such persons do not obtain preferential treatment from the company at the expense of the company's creditors.

For example, s 588FB is specifically aimed at preventing insolvent companies from disposing of assets prior to liquidation through uncommercial transactions which result in the recipient receiving a gift or obtaining a bargain of such magnitude that it could not be explained by normal commercial practice. The company's liquidator can set aside any uncommercial transaction entered into within two years of the commencement of winding up: s 588FE(3). If the recipient of an uncommercial transaction is a director or related entity of the company, the liquidator can avoid uncommercial transactions entered into within four years of the commencement of winding up. Uncommercial transactions are discussed further in Chapter 25 below.

[2.70] company officer charges. Section 267 also lifts the corporate veil. It regards company officers who lend their company funds secured by a charge over its assets differently from secured loans by arm's-length creditors. Under that section, an officer who has been granted a charge over company property is not, within six months of its creation, entitled to take any steps to enforce the charge without first obtaining the court's permission. Enforcing a charge means appointing a receiver or taking possession of property secured by the charge so that it can be sold to repay the secured debt. The court may, however, permit an officer to enforce the charge if it is satisfied that the company was solvent when it was granted and it is just and equitable for it to do so: s 267(3). Company charges are discussed in Chapter 11 below.

[2.75] financial assistance. In some situations the veil is pierced so as to render officers liable for civil penalties if they were involved in their company's contraventions of the *Corporations Act*. Where a company provides financial assistance for the acquisition of its own shares in contravention of s 260A, any person involved in the contravention breaches the section and may be liable under the civil penalty provisions. The company is not guilty of an offence: s 260D. The financial assistance prohibition is discussed in Chapter 8 below.

[2.80] taxation legislation. There are also other statutes, particularly revenue legislation, which provide for lifting of the corporate veil. For example, the *Income Tax Assessment Act 1997* (Cth) provides that directors may be liable to pay the company's unremitted group tax and other similar liabilities. They will be liable if, after receiving notice, they have not caused the company to pay the group tax owing or initiated an insolvency administration. This is discussed in Chapter 13.5 below.

at common law

Australian courts have, as a general rule, been reluctant to depart from the principle in *Salomon's* case and lift the corporate veil.

[2.85] In the absence of specific legislation, Australian courts have, as a general rule, been reluctant to depart from the principle in *Salomon's* case and lift the corporate veil. This has occurred only in relatively rare situations and it is not clear when the courts will do so.

[2.90] fraud. The courts have lifted the corporate veil where a company is used as a vehicle for fraud.

The courts have lifted the corporate veil where a company is used as a vehicle for fraud.

case note

In *Re Darby* [1911] 1 KB 95, Darby and Gyde formed a company of which they were sole directors and together with five nominees were the shareholders. The company purchased a licence to work a quarry and then floated another company, Welsh Slate Quarries Ltd, for the purpose of purchasing the licence at a substantial overvalue. The new company issued a prospectus and issued shares to the public. With the money thus obtained, Welsh Slate Quarries Ltd paid the company formed by Darby and Gyde for the licence. The profits were then divided between Darby and Gyde. Welsh Slate Quarries Ltd then failed and the liquidator claimed in the bankruptcy of Darby for the secret profit made by him. This claim was on the basis that Darby was in breach of duty as promoter of Welsh Slate Quarries Ltd. The duties of promoters are discussed in Chapter 6 below.

It was argued that the profit was made by the company formed by Darby and Gyde and not by Darby himself. This argument was rejected and Darby was ordered to disgorge his profit because the company he set up was a "dummy company" formed for the purpose of enabling him to perpetrate a fraud. Thus the court looked behind the façade of the legal entity.

The courts will lift the corporate veil if a company has been used as a sham so as to avoid a legal obligation under contract or statute.

[2.95] avoidance of legal obligations. The courts will also lift the corporate veil if a company has been used as a sham so as to avoid a legal obligation under contract or statute.

case note

In *Gilford Motor Co Ltd v Horne* [1933] Ch 935, Horne was appointed managing director of Gilford Motor Co Ltd for a term of six years. The service agreement provided that he was not to solicit or entice away from the company any of its customers during his appointment or after termination of his appointment. Some three years later, Horne resigned and started his own business in competition with the company. He then sent circulars to customers of the company seeking their business. Horne formed a company to conduct this business, the shareholders being his wife and an associate. Gilford Motor Co Ltd brought an action seeking to restrain Horne and the company he formed from soliciting their customers. The action was successful and an injunction was granted against both Horne and the company, even though the company was not a party to the contract with the plaintiff. Lord Hansworth MR considered that the company was a "mere cloak or sham" used as a device for enabling contractual obligations to be avoided.

case note

Similarly, in *Creasey v Breachwood Motors Ltd* (1992) 10 ACLC 3,052 the English Queen's Bench Division held that it was prepared to lift the corporate veil where a company was used to avoid a legal obligation to a creditor. In that case Creasey, a sacked employee of Welwyn Ltd, commenced legal proceedings for wrongful dismissal. Prior to the hearing of that case Welwyn's controllers caused it to cease operations and transferred its business and other assets to Breachwood Motors Ltd, another company they controlled. All debts to Welwyn's creditors were paid but no provision was made for Creasey's claim in the likely event of it succeeding. Creasey obtained judgment against Welwyn. However, because it had no assets, Welwyn was struck off the register as defunct and dissolved. The court lifted the corporate veil and held that Breachwood Motors Ltd was liable for Welwyn's debt to Creasey.

Directors owe a duty not to prejudice the interests of their company's creditors where the company is insolvent or in financial difficulties. Where directors seek to avoid legal obligations to creditors, they may breach their duties to the company: *Jeffree v NCSC* (1989) 7 ACLC 556. This is discussed in Chapter 13.5 below.

The High Court in *Ascot Investments Pty Ltd v Harper* (1981) 148 CLR 337 held that even if a company was not formed for the purpose of avoiding a legal obligation, it may lift the corporate veil if the company was a mere puppet of its controller.

The courts will lift the corporate veil if a company knowingly participates in a director's breach of fiduciary duties.

[2.100] involvement in directors' breach of duty. The courts will also lift the corporate veil if a company knowingly participates in a director's breach of fiduciary duties.

case note

This occurred in *Green v Bestobell Industries Ltd* [1982] WAR 1. Green, the Victorian manager of Bestobell Industries, became aware that Bestobell was preparing a tender for certain construction works. Without Bestobell's knowledge or consent, Green incorporated his own company, Clara Pty Ltd, and caused it to submit its own tender for the work. Clara's tender was successful and it was awarded the contract. When Bestobell discovered this it brought proceedings against both Green and Clara.

The Supreme Court of Western Australia held that Green, in tendering for the same project, had breached his fiduciary duty to Bestobell by placing himself in a position where his duty to it conflicted with his own interests. Further, because Clara knowingly and for its own benefit participated in Green's breach of duty, it was ordered to account to Bestobell Industries for the profit it derived.

[2.105] attributing mind and will of company. In some circumstances it is necessary to determine the purpose or intention of a company. Where this is the case the courts will look behind the veil of incorporation and attribute the purpose or intention of individuals behind the company to the company itself. However, this attribution is only made in respect of the persons who are regarded as the "directing mind and will" of a company rather than as mere employees: *Tesco Supermarkets Ltd v Nattrass* [1972] AC 153. This is discussed in Chapter 5 below.

lifting the corporate veil of group companies

Frequently, the courts have been requested to look behind the corporate veil in respect of companies associated as a group where, to all outward appearances, they seem to operate as a single entity.

[2.110] Frequently, the courts have been requested to look behind the corporate veil in respect of companies associated as a group where, to all outward appearances, they seem to operate as a single entity. The Australian courts, more than their English counterparts, have been reluctant to depart from the separate entity principle where there is no legislation requiring them to do so. This is illustrated by *Walker v Wimborne* (1976) 137 CLR 1 discussed above, para [2.50]. However, occasionally both the *Corporations Act* and the courts treat a group of companies as a single economic entity.

[2.115] holding company's liability for insolvent trading by subsidiary. Where companies operate as a group, the *Salomon* principle of separate personality prevents creditors of an insolvent company from gaining access to the funds of the other companies in the group for payment of their debts. This may not be appropriate where the business activity of a subsidiary has been directed or controlled by the holding company.

Sections 588V–588X lift the corporate veil of subsidiary companies by making holding companies liable for the debts incurred by their insolvent subsidiaries. Under these provisions, if a holding company fails to prevent one of its subsidiaries from incurring a debt while there were reasonable grounds to suspect that the subsidiary was insolvent, the subsidiary's liquidator may recover from the holding company amounts equal to the amount of loss or damage suffered by the subsidiary's unsecured creditors.

[2.120] the benefit of the group as a whole.

case note

The New South Wales Court of Appeal, in *Equiticorp Finance Ltd v Bank of New Zealand* (1993) 11 ACLC 952, agreed with the *Walker v Wimborne* principle that directors of associated companies owe separate duties to act in the best interests of each company. However, it recognised that in some circumstances a transaction that is entered into for the benefit of one or more companies in the group can have derivative benefits for other companies in the group.

A bank loan to one company was repaid after funds were transferred from other companies in the group. Upon liquidation of the Equiticorp group, the liquidator of the transferring companies sought to recover the funds from the bank. They claimed that the transfer of funds involved a breach of fiduciary duty by the directors to act in the best interests of those companies. The New South Wales Court of Appeal held that there was no breach of duty because, while the transaction benefited the group as a whole, it also indirectly benefited the transferring companies. Had the transactions not taken place, the companies would have lost the bank's support for their own funding arrangements.

[2.125] moving targets. Where companies within a group operate as a single commercial entity, it is often difficult for creditors to determine the actual legal entity they are dealing with. In *Qintex Australia Finance Ltd v Schroders Australia Ltd* (1991) 9 ACLC 109, the court thought that rigid legal distinctions between wholly owned subsidiaries and their holding company did not accord with commercial practice and created difficulties for creditors in insolvency situations. Rogers CJ believed it was desirable for Parliament to consider whether this distinction should be maintained in certain circumstances. He stated:

Where companies within a group operate as a single commercial entity, it is often difficult for creditors to determine the actual legal entity they are dealing with.

> < **As I see it, there is today a tension between the realities of commercial life and the applicable law in circumstances such as those in this case. In the everyday rush and bustle of commercial life in the last decade it was seldom that participants to transactions involving conglomerates with a large number of subsidiaries paused to consider which of the subsidiaries should become the contracting party ...**
>
> **Regularly, liquidators of subsidiaries, or of the holding company, come to court to argue as to which of their charges bears the liability ... As well creditors of failed companies encounter difficulty when they have to select from amongst the moving targets the company with which they consider they concluded a contract. The result has been unproductive expenditure on legal costs, a reduction in the amount available to creditors, a windfall for some, and an unfair loss to others. Fairness or equity seems to have little role to play.** >

[2.130] consolidated financial statements. The financial statements, and in particular the entity reporting requirements of the accounting standards, provide another instance where the *Corporations Act* disregards the corporate veil. As discussed in Chapter 15 below, s 296 requires a company's financial report to comply with accounting standards. Under AASB 127 *Consolidated and Separate Financial Statements*, a company that is a chief entity must prepare consolidated financial statements for the financial year of the economic entity constituted by the company and all the entities it controls. In this respect the *Corporations Act* and the accounting standards do not treat each entity in an economic entity as separate but recognise the reality that the members of an economic entity function as one organisation.

[2.135] taxation consolidation. Since 2003, corporate groups headed or controlled by an Australian company may elect to lodge a single consolidated tax return for the entire group. This enables intra group transactions to be ignored and permits pooling of losses and franking credits. In the same way as consolidated financial statements, this taxation regime allows a parent company to lift the corporate veil and treat the corporate group as a single taxpayer.

[2.140] subsidiaries as agents or partners. In some cases the corporate veil has been lifted where the court finds that a subsidiary has acted as an agent for its holding company.

In some cases the corporate veil has been lifted where the court finds that a subsidiary has acted as an agent for its holding company.

case note

In *Smith Stone & Knight Ltd v Birmingham Corporation* [1939] 4 All ER 116, the Birmingham Corporation, a local government authority, sought to compulsorily acquire some land owned by Smith Stone & Knight Ltd. To all outward appearances the land was occupied by, and the business conducted on it was operated by, Birmingham Waste Co Ltd, a wholly owned subsidiary of Smith Stone & Knight. The Birmingham Corporation refused a compensation claim for disturbance of business because the subsidiary's tenancy of the land from its parent company was for less than a year and hence under the relevant legislation it was not entitled to compensation. Smith Stone & Knight asserted that it in fact conducted the business on the land and was therefore entitled to compensation for the disturbance caused by the compulsory acquisition. It argued that the subsidiary conducted the business as agent for the holding company. This agency argument was upheld by the court because of the special circumstances that existed.

Atkinson J was careful to point out that the existence of an agency relationship was not always present between holding and subsidiary companies. He held that the following six requirements must be established before the *Salomon* principle could be disregarded to support a finding that a subsidiary carried on a business as agent for its holding company:

- the profits of the subsidiary must be treated as the profits of the holding company;
- the persons conducting the business must be appointed by the holding company;
- the holding company must be the head and brain of the trading venture;
- the holding company must govern the venture and decide what should be done and what capital should be embarked on it;
- the profits of the business must be made by the holding company's skill and direction; and
- the holding company must be in effectual and constant control.

In *Pioneer Concrete Services Ltd v Yelnah Pty Ltd* (1987) 5 ACLC 467, the court indicated that it would be prepared to disregard the corporate veil if there was evidence that companies in a group operated in partnership. Young J did not indicate what evidence would be sufficient to indicate a partnership between a holding company and its subsidiary. It would seem from the conclusion in the case that more is required than the mere fact that the companies operated as a group.

[2.145] tort liability. There are indications that Australian courts may be increasingly prepared to lift the veil of subsidiary companies and make the parent company liable for the subsidiaries' torts. This question has arisen in several asbestos injury cases.

case note

In *Briggs v James Hardie & Co Pty Ltd* (1989) 7 ACLC 841, Briggs suffered from asbestosis which he alleged he contracted while being employed by a subsidiary of James Hardie & Co Pty Ltd. In a negligence action against both his employer and the holding company, James Hardie & Co raised certain procedural matters including whether Briggs had a valid cause of action against it. In other words, Briggs argued that the corporate veil of the subsidiary could be lifted to make the holding company liable. The New South Wales Court of Appeal held that given the uncertainties of the law governing this point, lifting the corporate veil was a possibility and ordered that the issue should be determined at a trial of the negligence action.

Rogers AJA rejected as too simplistic the proposition that the corporate veil may be pierced where a holding company exercises complete dominion and control over a subsidiary. Nevertheless, he suggested that in deciding whether to lift the corporate veil in actions in tort different considerations should apply from the criteria applied to actions in contract, taxation or compensation cases. He stated:

< Generally speaking, a person suffering injury as a result of the tortious act of a corporation has no choice in the selection of the tortfeasor. The victim of the negligent act has no choice as to the corporation which will do him harm. In contrast, a contracting party may readily choose not to enter into a contract with a subsidiary of a wealthy parent. The contracting entity may inquire as to the amount of paid up capital and, generally speaking, as to the capacity of the other party to pay the proposed contract debt and may guard against the possibility that the subsidiary may be unable to pay ...

Control and dominance by a holding company of a subsidiary do not in themselves increase the risk of injury to tort victims ... I recognise that it is possible to argue that the proposed general tort considerations should not be applicable in cases where the injured person is an employee. It could be argued that such a person has equal opportunity with a contracting party in determining whether or not to enter into the employer-employee relationship out of which the injury arises. However, whilst the employee may be able to choose whether or not to be employed by the particular employer, generally speaking, he has no real input in determining how the business will be conducted and whether reasonable care will be taken for his safety. >

A controlling company may be held directly liable to an employee of its subsidiary on the basis that the controlling company itself owed a duty of care to the employee under the law of negligence. This duty may arise in the absence of a direct employment relationship and is most likely to arise where the controlling company exercises a high degree of control over the day-to-day activities of its subsidiary out of which the tort claim arose. This requires both foreseeability and a relationship of proximity between the parties with respect to both the relevant class of act or omission and the relevant kind of damage: *CSR Ltd v Wren* (1998) Aust Tort Reports 81-461. In this case, CSR owed a duty directly to Wren because even though he was employed by AP, a subsidiary of CSR, all the management staff who had operational responsibility for AP's enterprise and therefore Wren's work conditions were CSR staff. CSR failed in its duty to provide a safe system and place of work.

A controlling company may be held directly liable to an employee of its subsidiary on the basis that the controlling company itself owed a duty of care to the employee under the law of negligence.

case note

In *CSR Ltd v Young* (1998) Aust Tort Reports 81-468, the plaintiff was born in Wittenoom and was exposed to asbestos from birth to the age of 27 months. Her father was employed by ABA, a subsidiary of CSR as a draftsman and often returned home from work with asbestos fibres in his clothing. Tailings containing asbestos fibres were spread in areas in which children played. The plaintiff contracted malignant mesothelioma at 34 years of age and died soon after.

The court held that for the purposes of liability, CSR was in the same position as ABA as it conducted the overall operations at Wittenoom. CSR owed a duty of care to the people living in the town which was co-extensive with that owed by ABA as an employer. The degree of control of the controlling company over the activities of the subsidiary was sufficiently strong so that the controlling company itself effectively conducted those activities and the subsidiary was merely a conduit or facade.

case note

The New South Wales Court of Appeal (differently constituted) took a stricter view in *James Hardie & Co Pty Ltd v Hall* (1998) 43 NSWLR 554. In this case, the plaintiff was a New Zealand resident who contracted mesothelioma as a result of exposure to asbestos dust at the premises of his employer, a New Zealand subsidiary of James Hardie. The action was brought in New South Wales against New South Wales registered companies which supplied and exported asbestos to the plaintiff's employer because common law actions seeking damages were barred in New Zealand. The New South Wales Court of Appeal had to determine whether the tort was committed in New South Wales or New Zealand and whether the holding company owed a duty of care to the plaintiff who was employed by the New Zealand subsidiary.

The Court of Appeal held that the holding company was not responsible for workplace safety at the New Zealand plant. All that could be said was that the holding company was in a position to insist that proper workplace standards were maintained. This did not amount to a duty owed to the plaintiff when the holding company neither occupied the New Zealand premises nor employed those responsible for workplace safety.

In Chapter 4 of its *Corporate Groups Final Report* (May 2000), CASAC rejected the idea of making a parent company automatically liable for the torts of the companies in its group. It was of the opinion that the imposition of additional tort liability on parent companies of corporate groups should be left to specific statutes and general common law principles. CASAC's *Corporate Groups Final Report* is linked to the Lipton-Herzberg Effects of Registration Pathway at **http://www.lipton-herzberg.com.au/secure/pathways-effect-of-registration.html#Corporate_groups**

The deep concerns raised by the events surrounding James Hardie's restructuring and the payment of compensation to asbestos victims led to the establishment by the New South Wales government in 2004 of a Special Commission of Inquiry. John Sheahan SC, Senior Counsel Assisting the Commission, recommended "reform of the *Corporations Act* so as to restrict the application of the limited liability principle as regards liability for damages for personal injury or death caused by a company that is part of a corporate group, confining the benefit of limited liability to members of the ultimate holding company". This submission is appended to the Report of the Special Commission of Inquiry into the Medical Research and Compensation Foundation (2004) in a Discussion Paper Annexure T "The Concept of Limited Liability—Existing Law and Rationale". The Report and Discussion Paper are linked to the Lipton-Herzberg website at **http://www.lipton-herzberg.com.au**

law reform proposals

[2.150] One of the issues considered in CASAC's May 2000 *Corporate Groups Final Report* was whether the regulation of corporate groups should be based on:

> the separate entity approach, or
> the single enterprise approach, or
> a combination of these approaches.

CASAC recommended that the *Corporations Act* should permit a wholly owned corporate group to opt to be a consolidated corporate group for all or some of the group companies. Companies in a consolidated corporate group would be regulated by single enterprise principles, such as:

> the consolidated corporate group would be regarded as one legal structure;
> directors of group companies could act in the overall consolidated group interest;
> the parent company and each group company would be collectively liable for the contractual debts of all group companies; and
> group companies could merge merely at the discretion of the holding company's directors.

CASAC's *Corporate Groups Final Report* is linked to the Lipton-Herzberg Effects of Registration Pathway at **http://www.lipton-herzberg.com.au/secure/pathways-effect-of-registration.html#Corporate_groups**

pathways questions ...

The following questions dealing with the effect of registration may best be answered after reading this chapter and considering the Internet resources found on the Lipton-Herzberg Effects of Registration Pathway at http://www.lipton-herzberg.com.au/secure/pathways-effect-of-registration.html

1. **What impact has the decision in *Salomon's* case had on commercial practice?**
2. **Do you consider that the decision has proven to be commercially desirable?**
3. **To what extent have the consequences of *Salomon's* case been overruled or modified by statutory amendments?**
4. **Explain how the principle in *Salomon's* case operates in relation to corporate groups. What problems arise from the application of *Salomon's* principle in this context? Discuss how the *Corporations Act* has addressed these problems.**
5. **In light of the circumstances surrounding the James Hardie restructure, should parent companies be liable for tort claims against their subsidiaries? Consider the application of *Salomon's* principle and the operation of limited liability within corporate groups.**
6. **Outline the main changes recommended by CASAC in its *Corporate Groups Final Report* that relate to the separate legal entity principle.**

a company compared with partnership and trust

nature of the organisation

[2.155] Upon registration of a company an artificial legal entity is created that is separate and distinct from its members. Section 114 allows a company to be formed with one or more members. The *Corporations Act* does not require a company to be formed for any specific purpose, such as profit making. Its purpose or objects may be specified in its constitution if it chooses to have one.

A partnership, on the other hand, is defined as an association of two or more legal persons (they may be companies) carrying on business in common with a view of profit. This means that associations such as sports clubs and charitable organisations, for example, cannot be partnerships, as they generally do not carry on a business with the purpose of profit for their members. The relationship among partners is governed by the various State Partnership Acts and any partnership agreement and is based on contractual and fiduciary principles.

A trust is the relationship between a trustee and beneficiaries in respect of trust property. It commonly involves three parties:, the settlor, the trustee and the beneficiaries (also called a cestui que trust). A trust arises when the settlor, the creator of the trust, gives property to the trustee to hold or invest on behalf of the beneficiaries. The trustee is said to own the legal interest in the trust property and the beneficiaries own the equitable interest. The trustee's obligations are governed by rules of equity and are referred to as "fiduciary obligations". This means that a trustee is under a duty to act bona fide, in good faith, when dealing with trust property and the beneficiaries. This has some similarities to the duties owed by directors to their companies, which is discussed in Chapter 13 below.

separate legal identity

[2.160] We have seen that, in the case of a company, registration creates a separate legal person distinct from its shareholders. The company's property is owned by it and not by its shareholders. Further, the company's shareholders are generally not responsible for the debts of the company, although shareholders are fully liable in the case of unlimited companies. Indeed, as illustrated in *Salomon's* case, a shareholder of a company may also be a creditor of the company. A partnership, on the other hand, is not a legal entity separate from its members, the partners. This is so, even though the State Partnership Acts refer to partners collectively as a "firm". Each partner has an interest in the assets of the partnership.

A trust, too, is not an entity recognised as separate and distinct from its constituents. It cannot sue or be sued in its own name. The trustee holds the legal title to trust property on behalf of beneficiaries who hold the equitable interest. For example, parents frequently open bank accounts for their infant children. The parents act as trustees and the account is in their names. The children, however, are the persons who are ultimately entitled to the money in the account.

liability

[2.165] The liability of members of a company depends on the type of company. Section 112 allows the formation of four different types of companies according to the liability of their members:

> **companies limited by shares;**
> **companies limited by guarantee;**
> **unlimited companies limited by shares; and**
> **no liability companies.**

These are discussed in Chapter 3 below. By far the most common type of companies are companies limited by shares. The liability of shareholders is limited to the amount, if any, unpaid on their shares.

In the case of a partnership, since it is not an entity separate from the partners, each of the partners is personally liable to outside creditors to the full extent of the partnership debt. Further, each partner is an agent of all the others and in most cases the act of a partner binds the other partners, thereby making them all personally liable to the full extent of their assets. Partners cannot limit their liability to creditors of the partnership and are only entitled to a return from the partnership once all outside creditors are paid in full. In most Australian States partnership legislation permits the formation of limited partnerships where the liability of inactive partners is limited, with unlimited liability imposed only on the active partners.

In the case of a trust, two separate issues must be considered in determining liability to outside creditors; first, the trustee's liability and secondly, the liability of the beneficiaries. The trustee is personally liable in respect of all the costs and expenses involved in administering the trust. Trust creditors are entitled to look to the trustee for satisfaction of their debts and the trustee has unlimited liability. Provided the trustee has not breached obligations towards the beneficiaries, he or she is entitled to be reimbursed from trust assets in respect of any trust debts incurred. Indeed, the trustee is not required to pay trust creditors from personal assets and then seek reimbursement, but can pay trust debts directly from trust assets. These rights are referred to as a "trustee's right of indemnity". If the trust assets are insufficient to satisfy the trustee's right of indemnity, the trustee can look to the beneficiaries to make up the shortfall. If they are of full age, the beneficiaries are personally liable to the trustee to the extent of their interest in the trust.

enforcement of legal rights

[2.170] As a general rule, the rights of a company can only be enforced by the company itself. A shareholder of a company is generally not able to bring an action seeking to enforce rights accruing to the company. However, Pt 2F.1A (ss 236–242) of the *Corporations Act* permits a shareholder or an officer to bring legal proceedings on behalf of their company with prior court leave. This is discussed in Chapter 17 below.

A partner is able to bring an action enforcing rights of the partnership in the names of all the partners. This is because the relationship among partners is based on the law of agency. Difficulties that may be caused by requiring all partners to be parties to any legal action have been largely overcome by court rules which allow a partnership to sue and be sued in its firm name.

A trust, not being an entity recognised by the law as a legal person, is incapable of suing or being sued in its own name. Only the trustee on behalf of the trust has this power. A trustee who is in breach of her or his fiduciary obligations can be sued by the beneficiaries. Subject to the trustee carrying out her or his duties in a proper way, beneficiaries cannot direct the trustee as to the manner in which the trust should be administered.

duration of existence

[2.175] A company continues to exist after the death of its shareholders. The shares of a deceased shareholder are transmitted to someone else but the existence of the company is unaffected. There is no question of apportioning the company's assets to the estate of the deceased shareholder. If the estate wishes to realise the shares of the deceased, they must be sold and the purchaser becomes a member in place of the deceased shareholder.

A partnership may exist for a fixed term or for as long as the partners desire. A partnership automatically dissolves on the retirement, death or bankruptcy of a partner. This is subject to an agreement to the contrary by the partners.

A trust, however, is not permitted to continue indefinitely. The "rule against perpetuities" limits the duration of a trust to the life of some nominated person—"a life in being"—plus 21 years. In some States an alternative period of 80 years can apply. Any trust that contravenes this rule is void. The only exception to the rule against perpetuities concerns trusts established for charitable purposes, which may continue forever. The death of a beneficiary does not affect the existence of the trust. The precise nature of a beneficiary's interest in a trust determines whether that interest passes in the deceased beneficiary's estate. Often, a trustee is given power to reallocate a deceased beneficiary's interest in the capital of the trust to surviving beneficiaries. The death of the trustee, however, does affect the trust. A new trustee must be appointed. If the trustee does not appoint a successor, her or his executor or the beneficiaries or the courts can nominate a successor. Such difficulties are overcome in practice by the appointment of a company as trustee and, of course, a company cannot die.

transfer of interest

[2.180] Registration of a company allows its shareholders a high degree of freedom in the transferring of their shares. When shares are transferred, the transferor's place is taken by the transferee and the transferor generally ceases to be liable in any way. A company may impose restrictions on the transfer of its shares and in the case of a proprietary company, s 1072G provides for a replaceable rule that directors may refuse to register a transfer of shares in the company for any reason. In the absence of such restrictions in its constitution or applicable replaceable rules there is a presumption that shares are transferable free from any restrictions.

In a partnership, a partner can assign their share in the partnership but generally the consent of all other partners is necessary. Retiring partners remain liable for debts of the partnership incurred while they were partners, unless the creditors agree to release them.

Similarly, beneficiaries may assign their interest in a trust. The extent of their interest depends on what has been granted to them by the settlor—the person who created the trust.

formalities and expense

[2.185] Registration requires the lodgment of an application for registration with attendant expense. During the life of a company there are certain formalities related to the keeping of financial records, financial statements, registers and minutes that must be complied with. It may be necessary to appoint an auditor, which also involves expense. These expenses are especially significant in the case of a public company. A small proprietary company is not as expensive to form or operate. Winding up is generally a costly procedure, especially if the company is insolvent.

A partnership does not require any formality in its formation. It can even be formed by verbal agreement, although a partnership agreement is usually drawn up to clearly set out the relationship among the partners. The dissolution of a partnership is also a cheap and informal procedure in most cases.

Generally, a trust does not require any formality in formation. However, some types of trusts, such as trusts creating interests in land, do have to be evidenced in writing in order to be enforceable. The procedure for winding up a trust is usually set out in the document creating the trust—the trust deed. If the trust is not wound up, it nevertheless comes to an end at the expiration of the perpetuity period. The legal interest in the capital of the trust is then allocated among the beneficiaries.

disclosure of financial reports

[2.190] The *Corporations Act* requires public companies and large proprietary companies to lodge annual financial reports and other information with ASIC. This information is then available for inspection by anyone paying the appropriate search fee. Small proprietary companies are exempt from having to comply with this requirement.

Neither a partnership nor a trust need publish or disclose any financial reports. If, however, the trustee is a company, then it must disclose the extent of its right of indemnity.

audit

[2.195] Companies are required to appoint an independent auditor. Small proprietary companies are generally exempt from this requirement. They need only appoint an auditor in certain circumstances.

Neither a partnership nor a trust need appoint an auditor unless there is specific legislation to that effect. For example, a partnership of solicitors who conduct a trust account for their clients must have their accounts audited.

management and ownership

[2.200] The policy of the *Corporations Act* is to separate management and ownership. A company must appoint directors, whose task is to manage that company. The powers of directors are set out in the company's constitution or the replaceable rule in s 198A which provides that directors may exercise all the powers of the company subject to the *Corporations Act* or any constitution requirements. This generally allows wide powers of management.

Ownership of the company vests in its shareholders. Generally, shareholders do not have the power to participate in management of the company, although in most small companies the directors and shareholders are often the same persons. In such cases, those persons will sometimes act as directors and at other times as shareholders. Directors are appointed and usually removed by the shareholders.

Partnership law presumes that all partners take part in management of the partnership business. This is subject to the partnership agreement providing otherwise. While this presumption is realistic in the case of a partnership with relatively few partners, it would be totally unworkable in the case of a company with thousands of members. The management of the affairs of a trust is vested in the trustee. The beneficiaries cannot interfere unless the trustee exercises those powers improperly.

limits on size

[2.205] While there are no limits on the maximum number of shareholders of a public company, s 113 requires a proprietary company to have no more than 50 non-employee shareholders. Partnerships generally are limited to 20 partners. Some professional partnerships are allowed a greater number. For example, a partnership of accountants may consist of up to 1,000 partners and a partnership of solicitors may have up to 400 partners.

There are no limits as to the number of beneficiaries a trust can have. Indeed, the beneficiaries need not even be individually named. They may be described as a class of persons. In such cases the courts require that the class of beneficiaries be able to be identified with certainty so that it is possible to decide whether any person is or is not within the class of beneficiaries. Family trusts, for example, often describe a class of beneficiaries as the children of a named person.

raising capital

[2.210] A company is generally able to raise funds in much the same way as an individual, a partnership or a trust. This includes the power to borrow money. A company is also able to raise funds by the issue of shares and debentures. The *Corporations Act*, however, regulates the raising of funds. This aims to control fundraising by requiring public companies seeking funds to comply with the fundraising provisions in Ch 6D of the *Corporations Act*. As a general rule, the fundraising provisions require companies that seek to raise funds by the offer of their securities to provide investors with a disclosure document, a copy of which has been lodged with ASIC.

Section 727 prohibits a person from making an offer of securities or distributing an application form for an offer of securities that needs disclosure to investors under Pt 6D.2. Sections 706–708 specify when an offer of securities needs disclosure to investors under that Part. For example, under s 706 an offer of securities for issue needs disclosure to investors unless the offer comes within one of the numerous exceptions listed in s 708. The fundraising rules are discussed in Chapter 7 below.

Proprietary companies must not engage in any activity that would require disclosure to investors under Chapter 6D of the *Corporations Act*: s 113(3). A unique feature of companies is their ability to raise funds by the issue of debentures secured over their assets. Charges are discussed in Chapter 11 below.

A partnership commences with an initial capital contribution by partners. A partnership may raise further capital by the partners contributing further capital or making loans.

A trust initially gains its capital by means of a gift from the settlor. Trusts may raise funds from outsiders. A recent development is the operation of management trusts. They invite the public to purchase units in a unit trust which are tradeable or redeemable at short notice. Units are within the definition of "managed investment scheme" in s 9 and such invitations are regulated by Pt 5C. This is discussed in Chapter 20 below.

income tax

[2.215] Prior to 1 July 1987, the income of a company was taxed twice. The company was taxed at a fixed rate on its taxable income. When a dividend was paid this was included in the shareholders' assessable income and taxed at the appropriate marginal rate. This system of double taxation of company profits was altered by the imputation system of taxation of dividends. Under this system a company must still pay tax on its taxable income. The current rate is 30 per cent. However, if it pays dividends from profits that have been taxed (called "franked dividends"), Australian resident shareholders who receive them obtain a taxation credit (called "imputation credit") for the tax paid by the company. The imputation credit may then be offset against the tax liability on a shareholder's other sources of income. The effect of this system is to impute the tax paid by a company on its profits to shareholders who receive dividends. It means that shareholders are, to the extent of the imputation credits, no longer liable to pay tax on dividend income.

Partnerships are not taxed separately from their partners. A partnership return is lodged but this is for the purpose of ascertaining the share of the partnership profit or loss attributed to each partner. This share is then taken into account in determining each partner's taxable income from all sources. Limited partnerships are treated as companies for tax purposes.

A trust is also not recognised as a separate entity for income tax purposes. If a trust derives income which the trustee distributes to beneficiaries, that income is included in their assessable income. If no distribution is made, the trustee is personally liable to pay tax at penalty rates.

company registration

[2.220] In Chapter 1 above, we referred to the fact that a key feature of the *Corporations Act* is the provision for the registration of companies. There are now over one million companies registered in Australia. Here we outline the registration procedure for new companies. We deal first with the procedure for registration and then with the immediate post-registration requirements. Companies formed under the predecessors of the *Corporations Act* are taken to be registered under the *Corporations Act*.

The ASIC publication, *How to Register a Company*, is linked to the Lipton-Herzberg Registration Procedure Pathway at **http://www.lipton-herzberg.com.au/secure/pathways-registration-procedure.html**

Companies may also be registered electronically using ASIC's Electronic Company Registration (ECR) system. The system is linked to an electronic payment facility and uses digital signatures to authenticate information. ASIC's background paper, "Electronic Company Registration", is also linked to the Lipton-Herzberg Registration Procedure Pathway.

The *Corporations Act* does not directly specify who must incorporate. Rather, it prohibits the formation of certain partnerships or associations unless they are incorporated. Section 115 provides that a person must not participate in the formation of a partnership or association which has as an object gain for itself or any of its members and which has more than 20 members.

The *Corporations Regulations* may permit certain partnerships or associations to be formed with more than 20 members: s 115(2). Regulation 2A.1.01 specifies the following professional partnerships and their respective maximum memberships:

- **Accountants 1,000**
- **Legal practitioners 400**
- **Architects 100**
- **Pharmaceutical chemists 100**
- **Veterinary surgeons 100**
- **Actuaries 50**
- **Medical practitioners 50**
- **Patent attorneys 50**
- **Sharebrokers 50**
- **Stockbrokers 50**
- **Trademark attorneys 50**

company name

requirements

[2.225] The persons forming the company may choose the company name. A company name may be its Australian Company Number (ACN), which is a nine-digit number allocated by ASIC upon the company's registration: s 148(1).

There are certain requirements and restrictions regarding company names. A limited company must have the word "Limited" or the abbreviation "Ltd" as part of and at the end of its name and a limited proprietary company must have the words "Proprietary Limited" or its abbreviation "Pty Ltd" at the end of its name: s 148(2). A no liability company must have the words "No Liability" or the abbreviation "NL" as part of and at the end of its name: s 148(4).

The purpose of these requirements is to act as a warning to those dealing with the company that its members have limited liability. This is especially important in the case of companies limited by shares because shareholders of such companies have liability limited to the amount, if any, unpaid on their shares. Creditors and prospective creditors are warned of this every time they see the company name. Unlimited companies have no such requirements because members of such companies have unlimited liability. A person is prohibited from carrying on business under a name which includes "Limited" or "No Liability" unless it is allowed or required to do so under Australian law: s 156. Similarly, a public company must not use the word "Proprietary" unless it fulfils the legislative requirements of such companies: s 148(5).

availability of name

[2.230] Persons wishing to form a company with a name other than the ACN should ensure that the proposed name is available.

Under s 147(1) a name is available to a company unless:

> - **it is identical to a name that has already been reserved or registered;**
> - **it is identical to a name that is included on the national business names register in respect of another person; or**
> - **it is unacceptable.**

The *Corporations Regulations*, Sch 6, sets out rules for determining whether a name is identical and provides a number of instances where a name is unacceptable or restricted for the purposes of s 147(1). Schedule 6, Pt 2 excludes names that in the opinion of ASIC are undesirable or likely to be offensive or contain specified words or phrases which imply a connection with a government, the Royal family or Sir Donald Bradman. A name is also unacceptable if it implies that the members of an organisation are incapacitated if this is not the case. Schedule 6, Pt 3 lists restricted words or phrases which imply a purpose or status that would be misleading if they could be freely used. Examples of such restricted words are "executor", "stock exchange", "trust", "RSL" and "chartered".

Other sections also restrict the use of particular names. For example, s 923B restricts the use of the names "stock broker" or "share broker" to persons authorised to do so by a financial services licence held by them.

ASIC provides an Identical Names Check facility to check whether a proposed company name is identical to one already registered on the ASIC database. ASIC's National Names Index permits the making of electronic searches of all currently registered names. The Lipton-Herzberg Registration Procedure Pathway at **http://www.lipton-herzberg.com.au/secure/pathways-registration-procedure.html** provides a link to ASIC's information sheet on the Identical Names Check facility and the National Names Index.

reserving a name

[2.235] Reservation of a proposed name is optional. A person may lodge an application to reserve a specified name of an intended company: s 152(1). If the name is available, it must be reserved by ASIC for two months: s 152(2). The period of reservation may be extended by a further two months at the request of the applicant: s 152(2). A reservation must be cancelled by ASIC if requested by the applicant: s 152(3).

change of name

[2.240] A company may, by special resolution, change its name: s 157(1). The proposed new name must be available: s 157(3). An application and a copy of the special resolution approving the change of name must be lodged with ASIC: s 157(1) and (2). If the proposed name is available, ASIC must change the company's name by altering the details of the company's registration. The change of name takes effect after the company's registration details are altered: s 157(3).

A company cannot change its name after the commencement of winding up as the members lose their powers to pass a special resolution. Similarly, a company cannot apply for the reservation of a name after winding up has commenced. It can no longer act by its directors: *Re HDT Special Vehicles (Aust) Pty Ltd* (1991) 9 ACLC 1336.

omission of "Limited" from name

[2.245] Although limited companies are generally required to include the word "Limited" as part of their name, ASIC may authorise a company limited by guarantee to dispense with this requirement. Section 150(1) allows this if the constitution of the company:

> **requires the pursuit of charitable purposes only and application of its income in promoting those purposes;**
> **prohibits distributions to members and payment of fees to its directors; and**
> **requires the directors to approve all other payments made to directors.**

A licence granted under previous legislation that allowed a company to omit "Limited" from its name continues in force: s 151(1). Some of these companies are not companies limited by guarantee. ASIC may revoke a company's licence if it breaches the required provisions in its constitution: s 151(3).

The purpose of this section is to enable organisations of a charitable or socially useful nature, which do not seek to operate to the financial benefit of their members, to dispense with the appearance of being a commercial enterprise. This is seen as desirable by charitable organisations which still seek the benefit of being distinct legal entities.

publication and display of company name

[2.250] A company is required to set out its name followed by its ACN on its common seal and on all its public documents and negotiable instruments: ss 123(1) and 153(1). "Public document" is defined in s 88A as including "a business letter, statement of account, invoice, receipt, order for goods, order for services or official notice" of the company. It does not include documents of a non-contractual nature: *National Education Advancement Programs Pty Ltd v Ashton* (1996) 14 ACLC 30.

In Practice Note 47, ASIC sets out its understanding of the law governing the use and display of company names and numbers. For example, a company's name and ACN do not have to appear on advertisements as these are not generally "public documents". Further, ASIC does not require credit card vouchers issued by a company to contain its ACN. Section 123(1)(b) permits a company that has an Australian Business Number (ABN) for goods and services tax purposes, to use its ABN in place of its ACN provided that the ABN includes its nine-digit ACN.

The company name must also be prominently displayed at every place at which the company carries on business and that is open to the public: s 144(1). A public company must also display its name at its registered office: s 144(2). The company's ACN, while required on company documents, is not required to be displayed at the registered office.

misuse of identical or similar name

[2.255] passing off. The names provisions of the *Corporations Act* tries to ensure that companies will not be registered with identical or closely resembling names. Inevitably, however, this may occur. The common law also seeks to protect the owner of a business name from others using a similar name. It does so in circumstances where the purpose of using the similar name is to create the impression that the business is that of another and is thereby taking advantage of the reputation of an established business to its detriment. The existing business may bring an action in the tort of passing off and seek damages for loss of profits and loss of goodwill. The party passing off may be ordered to pay over profits made as a result of the passing off. An injunction may also be obtained restraining the defendant from continuing with its business or company name.

It is not necessary in establishing passing off to prove that the defendant intended to deceive. However, the defendant must carry on the same kind of business as the plaintiff. A person may, however, use a similar or identical name to someone else if the person is using her or his own name and does so honestly.

case note

In *Cameron Real Estate Pty Ltd v Cameron* (1985) 3 ACLC 83, the Supreme Court of the Australian Capital Territory granted an injunction to prevent the promoters of a company from proceeding with the registration of "Don and Mary Cameron Realty Pty Ltd". There was a real likelihood that the name could be confused with "Cameron Real Estate Pty Ltd", a registered company carrying on a business in the same industry and in the same locality.

[2.260] section 52 of the Trade Practices Act. Another remedy available in similar circumstances as passing off is under s 52 of the *Trade Practices Act 1974* (Cth). Section 52(1) prohibits a corporation, in trade or commerce, from engaging in misleading or deceptive conduct. This includes the misleading use of another's name.

A problem that arises occasionally is when a foreign company with an internationally known name wishes to set up operations in Australia, only to find that its name is unavailable here because a company with a similar name is already incorporated. Sometimes the only reason the local company has been formed is to enable its promoters to "sell" the name back to the foreign company. However, if the foreign company's name has become associated with it in Australia, the use of the name by the local company may amount to misleading or deceptive conduct for the purposes of s 52 of the *Trade Practices Act*.

case note

This question arose in *Aerospatiale Societe Nationale Industrielle v Aerospatiale Helicopters Pty Ltd* (1986) ATPR 40-700. The applicant was an internationally known French helicopter corporation and the name "Aerospatiale" was associated with it and its products. When it attempted to incorporate a company called Aerospatiale Helicopters Australia Pty Ltd to sell helicopters in Australia, it found that the name was unavailable because the respondent company was already formed with a similar name and with the object of engaging in a similar business. The Federal Court held that the local company breached s 52 and ordered it to change its name.

registration procedure

application for registration

[2.265] Figure 2.1 below illustrates the registration procedure. In order to register a company, a person must lodge an application with ASIC using the prescribed form (Form 201): s 117(1). The Lipton-Herzberg Registration Procedure Pathway at **http://www.lipton-herzberg.com.au/secure/pathways-registration-procedure.html#Forming_a_company** has a link to a blank application form.

In order to register a company, a person must lodge an application with ASIC using the prescribed form.

The application must state specified information: s 117(2). This includes:

> the type of company;
> the company's proposed name;
> names and addresses of persons consenting to be members;
> names, addresses and date and place of birth of persons consenting in writing to be directors and company secretary;
> address of registered office and hours of opening;
> address of principal place of business;

figure 2.1 registration procedure

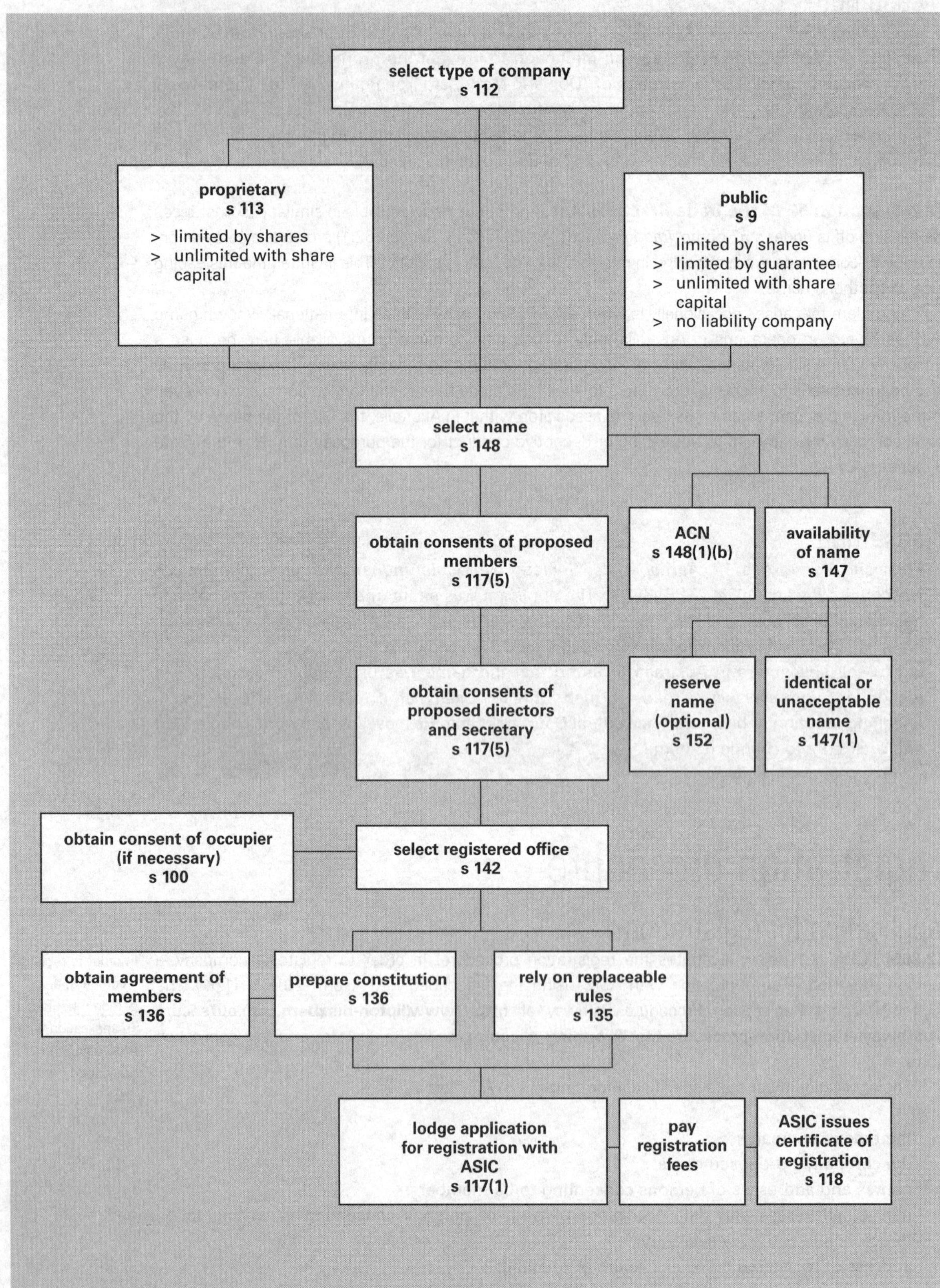

- details of issued shares including whether fully paid and beneficially owned by the member on registration;
- whether the company will have an ultimate holding company and if so, details of that ultimate holding company; and
- prescribed information regarding issues of shares for non-cash consideration by public companies.

An applicant must have the consents and agreements in respect of persons becoming directors, secretary or members when the application is lodged: s 117(5). After registration, these consents and agreements must be retained by the company. A proposed public company which is to have a constitution must lodge it together with the application for registration.

registered office

[2.270] A company must have a registered office in Australia to which communications and notices to the company may be addressed: s 142(1). A document is validly served on a company by posting it to, or leaving it at, the registered office: s 109X(1).

If the registered office is at premises not occupied by the company, the company may be required to show consent of the occupier to the address being used as the company's registered office: s 143(1). This commonly occurs where the registered office of a company is the place of business of the company's accountant.

A company must lodge a notice of change of address of its registered office within 14 days of the change: s 142(2). The company's name must be prominently displayed at its registered office together with the words "registered office": s 144(2).

The registered office of a public company must be open to the public for at least three hours during business hours each business day: s 145(1). The opening hours must be lodged with ASIC if they are not standard opening hours: s 145.

The address of the company's principal place of business (if it is not the registered office) must also be notified to ASIC: s 146.

replaceable rules and constitution

[2.275] The *Corporations Act* contains a set of basic rules that regulate the internal management of companies. These are called replaceable rules. New companies may choose to be governed by the replaceable rules, their constitution or by a combination of both: s 134.

shareholders and officers

[2.280] The persons named with their consent in the application for registration become members, directors and company secretary from the time of registration of the company: s 120(1). The shares stated in the application to be taken up by the members are taken to be issued on registration of the company: s 120(2). A share certificate must be issued within two months: s 1071H(1).

fees

[2.285] Together with lodgment of the application for registration, prescribed fees are payable for registration and reservation of name where this is sought. ASIC's information sheet "Fees for Commonly Lodged Documents" is linked to the Lipton-Herzberg Registration Procedure Pathway at **http://www.lipton-herzberg.com.au/secure/pathways-registration-procedure.html#Post_registration_requirements** The applicable fees as at 1 September 2005 are:

- application for registration if a company with a share capital: $800; and
- application for reservation of name: $40.

certificate of registration

[2.290] If an application for registration is lodged, ASIC may:

> allot the company an ACN;
> register the company; and
> issue a certificate stating the company's name, ACN and type of company. The certificate states the date of registration and that the company is registered under the *Corporations Law*: s 118(1).

While ASIC has a discretion whether to register a company, it will only refuse to register a company in unusual cases where registration would involve a breach of the *Corporations Act*. This could arise, for example, where a disqualified director is named in the application.

A certificate of registration is conclusive evidence that all requirements for registration have been complied with and the company was duly registered on the specified date: s 1274(7A).

post-registration requirements

[2.295] Figure 2.2 in para [2.310] below illustrates the post-registration requirements. ASIC's Checklist For Registered Companies and Their Officers, which summarises the document lodgment requirements of the *Corporations Act*, and ASIC's information sheet *What Books & Records Should My Company Keep?* are both linked to the Lipton-Herzberg Registration Procedures Pathway at **http://www.lipton-herzberg.com.au/secure/pathways-registration-procedure.html#Post_registration_requirements**

appointment of directors and secretary

[2.300] The initial directors and secretary are those persons named with their consent in the application for registration. Subsequent appointments of directors may be made in accordance with the replaceable rules contained in ss 201G and 201H or the company's constitution. Under the replaceable rules, a company may appoint a director by resolution passed at a general meeting or the other directors may appoint a person as a director. Where the other directors appoint a director, the appointment must be confirmed by the general meeting: s 201H(2) and (3). A public company must have at least one secretary: s 204A(2). As a result of changes made in 1999, a proprietary company need not have a secretary: s 204A(1). The directors appoint company secretaries: s 204D.

common seal

[2.305] As discussed in Chapter 5 below, it is no longer mandatory for a company to have a common seal. Where a company chooses to have a common seal, its name and ACN or ABN must be set out on the seal: s 123(1).

The common seal is affixed to certain formal documents, for example, share certificates and finance documentation.

registers

[2.310] Section 168 requires a company to set up and maintain the following registers:

> a register of members (this is discussed in Chapter 9 below);
> a register of option holders and copies of option documents if the company grants options over unissued shares (this is discussed in Chapter 8 below); and
> a register of debentures if the company issues debentures (this is discussed in Chapter 11 below).

figure 2.2 post-registration requirements

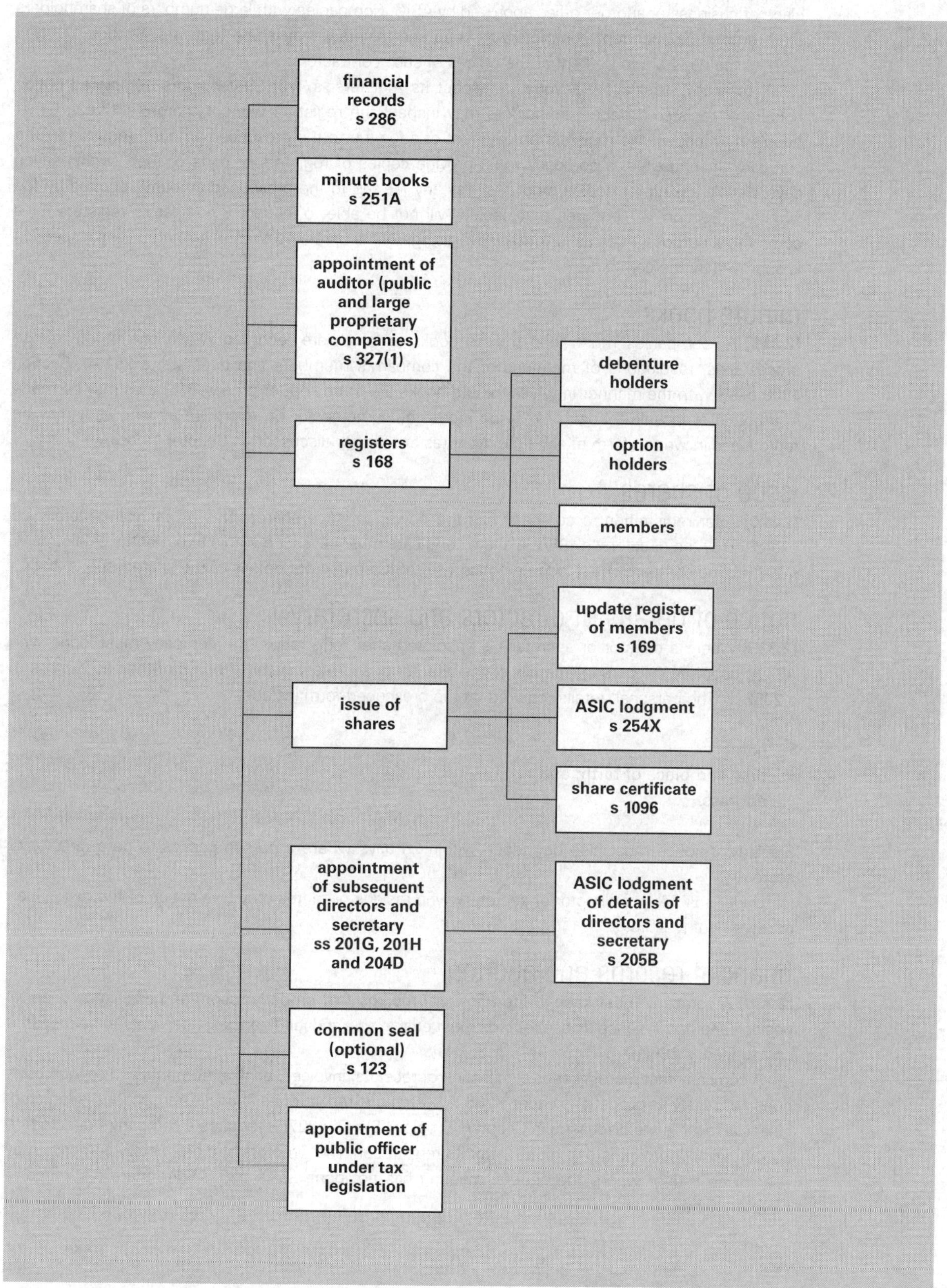

Under s 172 these registers must be kept in Australia at the company's registered office, principal place of business or another office approved by ASIC. Companies with large numbers of shareholders often employ independent contractors to keep and maintain their share registers. Section 172(1)(c) permits the registers to be kept at the offices of such contractors.

A company must allow anyone to inspect its registers: s 173. Shareholders, registered option holders or registered debenture-holders may inspect the registers without charge: s 173(2). Other people may inspect the registers on payment of a fee (up to the prescribed amount) required by the company. If requested, a company must provide copies of registers or parts of them within seven days. People asking for copies must first pay any fee (up to the prescribed amount) required by the company. Section 177 ensures that people will not be able to inspect a company's registers for a commercial purpose, such as junk mail advertising, that is unrelated to their holding unless inspection is approved by the company.

minute books

[2.315] All companies must keep minute books in which are recorded within one month of the proceedings, resolutions of meetings of the company's members and directors: s 251(A). Section 1306 deals with the manner in which minute books are to be kept or prepared. Entries may be made in a bound or looseleaf book or may be stored by computer or on microfilm as long as it may be reproduced in written form at any time. Minutes are further discussed in Chapter 14 below.

issue of shares

[2.320] After registration, a company has the power to issue shares. This power will generally be exercised by the directors: s 198A. A share certificate must be issued within two months of allotment: s 1071H. The company must lodge a notice with ASIC setting out details of the share issue: s 254X.

notice of details of directors and secretary

[2.325] Where a director or secretary is appointed after registration, the company must lodge with ASIC a notice of the personal details of the director or secretary within 28 days of their appointment: s 205B(1). The personal details required on the prescribed form include:

- **name;**
- **date and place of birth; and**
- **address.**

Similarly, a notice must also be lodged within 28 days where a person ceases to be a director or secretary.

Under s 205A(1), a director or secretary who resigns or retires may give notice of the resignation or retirement to ASIC.

financial records and auditor

[2.330] A company must keep written financial records that properly record and explain its financial position and performance. These records must enable true and fair financial statements to be prepared and audited: s 286(1).

A company that merely keeps a collection of receipts, invoices, bank statements and cheque butts does not satisfy its obligations under s 286. A systematic record of its financial transactions is required. Financial records are discussed in Chapter 15 below. Section 327(1) requires a company's directors to appoint an auditor within one month after its registration. The directors of a proprietary company may appoint an auditor where the general meeting has not done so: s 325. Auditors are discussed in Chapter 16 below.

use of name

[2.335] Section 144 obliges a company to display its name in a prominent position outside its registered office as well as outside premises where its business is being carried on and that is open to the public. The registered office of a public company must prominently bear the words "registered office" associated with the company name. Further, a company must ensure that its name and either its ACN or ABN appears on every public document and negotiable instrument: s 153(1). This includes letterheads, invoices, cheques and receipts.

public officer

[2.340] Every company is required to appoint a "public officer" within three months after commencing carrying on business. This is imposed by s 252 of the *Income Tax Assessment Act 1997* (Cth). The company's public officer is responsible for doing all things required to be done by the company under that Act.

bank account

[2.345] All companies ought to open a bank account. Such an account is used for the company's daily transactions as well as initially holding the paid up capital.

ASIC notifications

[2.350] Table 2.1 below, taken from the Small Business Guide contained in s 111J, sets out the various changes of which a company must notify ASIC.

table 2.1 notification requirements

	If ...	the company must notify ASIC of the change ...	see section ...
1	a company issues shares	within 28 days after the issue	254X
2	a company changes the location of a register	within 7 days after the change	172, 1302
3	a company changes the address of its registered office or principal place of business	within 28 days after the change	142, 146
4	a company changes its directors or company secretary	within 28 days after the change	205B
5	there is a change in the name or address of the company's directors or secretary	within 28 days after the change	205B
6	a company creates certain kinds of charges	within 45 days after the charge is created	263
7	a company has a new ultimate holding company, or details about the ultimate holding company change	within 28 days after the change happens	349A
8	any of the changes in items 1 to 7 means that: (a) the company must add or alter particulars in its member register kept under section 169; or (b) the company must add or alter particulars in its member register kept under section 169, and as a result, details about the number and class of shares on issue, or the amount paid and unpaid on the shares, alter.	within the time determined under the table in section 178D	178A 178C

shelf companies

[2.355] It is very common that those who wish to form a company acquire a "shelf company" instead of completing the company registration procedures described above. "Shelf company" is not a legal term. It describes a company that has not previously operated a business and has been formed specifically for the purpose of being sold. Lawyers and accountants often register shelf companies for sale to their clients when they need a registered company quickly.

Anyone who acquires a shelf company must go through certain steps to transfer ownership and control to themselves—such as transfers of shares and changes of directors and registered office. The purchasers of a shelf company must also notify ASIC of the changes so that the ASIC database can be updated. The following table describes the steps that must be undertaken and documents that must be lodged with ASIC to acquire a shelf company that relies on the replaceable rules.

table 2.2 **procedure to acquire a (replaceable rules) shelf company**

	Necessary steps	Lodgment of forms with ASIC
Original shareholders sell their shares in the shelf company to the purchaser	> Register transfer of shares: s 1071D and update share register: s 169. > Issue new share certificate to the purchasing shareholders: s 1071H(3) > Notify ASIC within 28 days (s 178A) and pay the prescribed fee	Form 484 Section C4
Appoint new directors	> Obtain signed consents to act as director: s 201D > Hold shareholders' meeting and pass ordinary resolution appointing directors: s 201G > Notify ASIC within 28 days (s 205B) and pay prescribed fee	Form 484 Section B2
Original directors resign	> Notify ASIC within 28 days of resignation: s 205B(5) and pay the prescribed fee	Form 484 Section B1
Change address of registered office	> Hold directors' meeting to approve change of address of registered office: s 198A > Notify ASIC within 28 days of change: s 142(2) and pay prescribed fee	Form 484 Section A1
If the shelf company purchasers wish to change name of the shelf company	> Check whether the proposed new name is available: s 157(3) > Hold shareholders' meeting and pass special resolution adopting new name: s 157(1)(a). > Lodge copy of resolution with ASIC within 14 days of passing of resolution (s 157(2)) and pay prescribed fee	Form 205

pathways questions ...

The following questions dealing with registration procedure may best be answered by reading this chapter and considering the Internet resources on the Lipton-Herzberg Registration Procedure Pathway at **http://www.lipton-herzberg.com.au/secure/pathways-registration-procedure.html**

1. Abe and Phillip would like to form a company to be called Vandalay Industries Pty Ltd. Is the name available?

2. Assume you wish to form a company.
   (a) Select an available name for your proposed company.
   (b) Fill in an application for registration form.
   (c) What is the fee for lodging an application for registration with ASIC?
   (d) What consents must be obtained before the application for registration can be lodged with ASIC?
   (e) Do you need to prepare a constitution for your proposed company?
   (f) Outline the books, records and registers that your company must establish after it is formed.
   (g) Can your company's invoices set out its ABN instead of its ACN?

bibliography ...

Barrett, R "Skirting the Corporate Veil" (1998) 72 ALJ 286.

Baxt, R & Lane, T "Developments in Relation to Corporate Groups and the Responsibilities of Directors: Some Insights and New Directions" (1998) 16 C & SLJ 628.

Blumberg, P "National Law and Transnational Groups and Transactions: Survey of the American Experience" (1995) 5 Aust Jnl of Corp Law 295.

Carroll, R "Corporate Parents and Tort Liability" in Gillooly, M (ed) *The Law Relating to Corporate Groups*. Federation Press, 1993, Ch 4.

Cassidy, J "Sexually Transmitted Debts: The Scope of Defences to Directors' Liability for Insolvent Trading" (2002) 20 C & SLJ 372.

Clarke, F, Dean, G & Houghton, E "Corporate Restructuring, Creditor's Rights, Crossguarantees and Group Behaviour" (1999) 17 C & SLJ 85.

Coburn, N "The Phoenix Reexamined" (1998) 8 Aust Jnl of Corp Law 321.

Lord Cooke of Thorndon "Corporate Identity" (1998) 16 C & SLJ 160.

Companies and Securities Advisory Committee, "Corporate Groups Final Report" (May 2000) **http://www.camac.gov.au/camac/camac.nsf./byHeadline/PDFFinal+Reports+2000/$file/Corporate_Groups_May_2000.pdf**

Corcoran, S "Living on the Edge: Utopia University Ltd" (1999) 27 FL Rev 265.

Cross, K & Webster J "Issues Facing Directors in Corporate Groups" (1997) 25 ABLR 436.

Dean, G, Clarke, F & Houghton, E "Corporate Restructuring, Creditors' Rights, Crossguarantees and Group Behaviour" (1999) 17 C & SLJ 85.

Dean, G & Clarke F, "Corporate officers' views on cross guarantees and other proposals to "lift the corporate veil" (2005) 23 C & SLJ 299.

Easterbrook, F & Fischel, D "Limited Liability and the Corporation" (1985) 52 UChiLR 89.

Farrar, J "Corporate Group Insolvencies, Reform and the United States Experience" (2000) 8 Insolv LJ 148.

Farrar, J "Frankenstein Incorporated or Fools' Parliament? Revisiting the Concept of the Corporation in Corporate Governance" (1998) 10 Bond LR 142.

Farrar, J "Legal Issues Involving Corporate Groups" (1998) 16 C & SLJ 184.

Gronow, M "Insolvent Corporate Groups and their Employees: The Case for Further Reform" (2003) 21 C & SLJ 188.

Halpern, P, Trebilcock, M & Turnbull, S "An Economic Analysis of Limited Liability in Corporations Law" (1980) 30 U of Toronto LJ 117.

Hansmann, H & Kraakman, R "Towards Unlimited Shareholder Liability for Corporate Torts" (1991) 100 Yale LJ 1879.

Harris, J "Lifting the corporate veil on the basis of an implied agency: A re-evaluation of Smith, Stone and Knight" (2005) 23 C & SLJ 7.

Hill, J "Cross-Guarantees in Corporate Groups" (1992) 10 C & SLJ 312.

McQueen, R "Life without Salomon" (1999) 27 FL Rev 181.

Murphy, D "Holding Company Liability for Debts of its Subsidiaries: Corporate Governance Implications" (1998) 10 Bond LR 241.

Noakes, D "Dogs on the Wharves: Corporate Groups and the Waterfront Dispute" (1999) 11 Aust Jnl of Corp Law 27.

Priskich V, "CASAC's Proposals for Reform of the Law Relating to Corporate Groups" (2001) 19 C & SLJ 360.

Ramsay, I M & Stapledon, G P "Corporate Groups in Australia" (2001) 29 ABLR 7.

Ramsay, I M & Noakes D B, "Piercing the Corporate Veil in Australia" (2001) 19 C & SLJ 250.

Schulte, R "The Future of Corporate Limited Liability in Australia" (1994) 6 Bond LR 64.

Sealy, L "Modern Insolvency Laws and Mr Salomon" (1998) 16 C & SLJ 176.

Spender, P "Resurrecting Mrs Salomon" (1999) 27 FL Rev 217.

Ville, S P "Judging Salomon: Corporate Personality and the Growth of British Capitalism in a Comparative Perspective" (1999) 27 FL Rev 203.

Watson, S "Who Hides Behind the Corporate Veil? Finding a Way Out of 'The Legal Quagmire'" (2002) 20 C & SLJ 198.

Whincop, M "Overcoming Corporate Law: Instrumentalism, Pragmatism and the Separate Legal Entity Concept" (1997) 15 C & SLJ 411.

revision questions on the material in this chapter …

> Please see eQuiz at **http://www.thomson.com.au/academic** for multiple choice questions and answers.

> For further corporations law links and material please refer to the Lipton-Herzberg website at **http://www.lipton-herzberg.com.au**

chapter three

types of companies

key points ....

- The *Corporations Act* classifies companies in several ways. Companies are classified according to the liability of members. A company limited by shares is the most common type of company. In such companies the liability of members (shareholders) is limited to the amount, if any, unpaid on the issue price of their shares. Therefore, shareholders who own fully paid shares have no further liability.

- Companies are also classified according to whether they are public or proprietary companies. The regulation of proprietary companies is generally less onerous than in the case of public companies, particularly in relation to disclosure obligations.

- A proprietary company must have no more than 50 shareholders and cannot issue shares or debentures in circumstances that would require disclosure to investors under the fundraising provisions of the *Corporations Act*. A company that does not comply with these prohibitions is classified as a public company.

- Proprietary companies are divided into two sub-classifications: large proprietary companies and small proprietary companies. Whether a proprietary company is large or small depends on criteria such as its gross operating revenue, value of its gross assets and number of employees.

- The *Corporations Act* imposes enhanced disclosure requirements on disclosing entities such as listed companies. A disclosing entity must prepare and lodge half-yearly financial reports as well as end-of-year financial reports. They are also subject to the continuous disclosure requirements.

- A holding company-subsidiary relationship arises where the holding company controls over half the issued capital of the subsidiary or controls the composition of its board of directors. A holding company, its subsidiaries and subsidiaries of subsidiaries are all referred to as "related" companies.

corporations and companies

[3.05] At common law the terms "body corporate" and "corporation" refer to any type of artificial legal entity. The *Corporations Act*, however, defines these terms differently. A corporation is defined in s 57A to include:

- a company; and
- any body corporate (whether incorporated in this jurisdiction or elsewhere); and
- an unincorporated body that under the law of its place of formation, may sue or be sued, or may hold property in the name of its secretary or of an officer of the body duly appointed for that purpose.

Excluded from the definition are:

- an exempt public authority. These are public authorities, instrumentalities or agencies of the Crown; and
- a corporation sole, for example the Public Trustee.

figure 3.1 types of bodies corporate

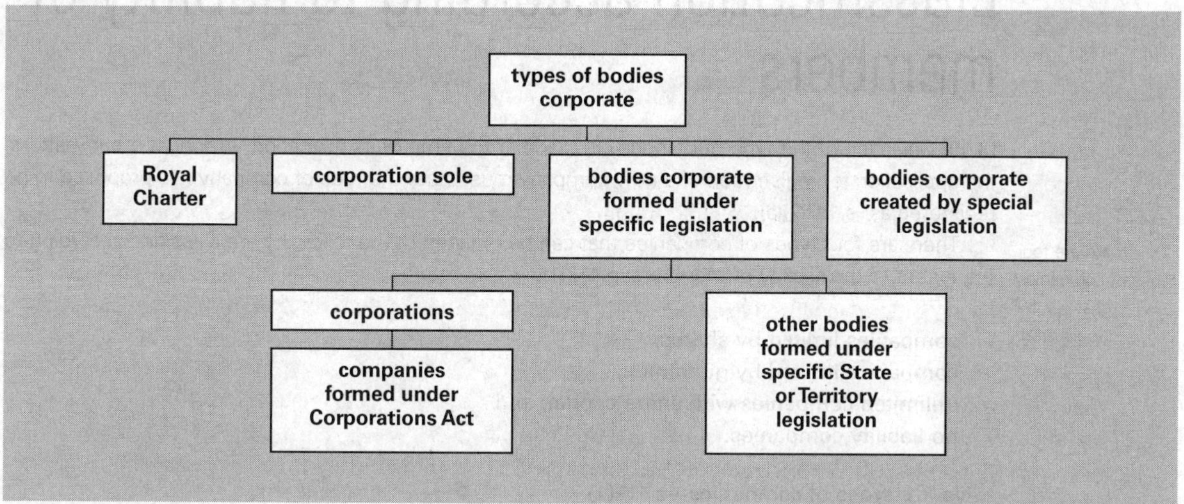

A company registered under the *Corporations Act* or its predecessors is one type of corporation: s 57A. In Chapter 1 above, we noted that the oldest form of incorporated entity is a body corporate established by Royal Charter. The Royal College of Surgeons is an example of such a body. There are also numerous instances where artificial entities have been formed by special legislation. Monash University is one example of such an entity. There are also some types of legal entities that come into existence under specific legislation. Trade unions are legal entities recognised under industrial legislation. Bodies corporate established under strata titles legislation are another instance of an artificial entity formed by special legislation.

In this book we are concerned mainly with companies registered under the *Corporations Act* and its predecessors. According to ASIC registration statistics, the number of companies registered in Australia as at July 2005 was:

NSW	VIC	QLD	SA	WA	TAS	NT	ACT	TOTAL
500,099	444,376	229,876	81,754	126,936	15,633	7,632	26,102	1,432,408

The *Corporations Act* also recognises certain bodies, such as building societies, credit unions and incorporated associations, formed under specific State or Territory legislation. These are referred to as "registrable Australian bodies" and do not have to be registered under the *Corporations Act* unless they do business outside their State or Territory of formation.

The *Corporations Act* classifies companies in a variety of ways. The more significant classifications are according to:

The *Corporations Act* classifies companies in a variety of ways.

> **the liability of members;**
> **their public status, that is public or proprietary companies;**
> **the size of proprietary companies;**
> **their relationship with other companies, that is holding companies, subsidiary companies, related bodies corporate and members of economic entities;**
> **whether or not they are disclosing entities;**
> **the place of formation, that is whether registered in Australia or foreign companies; and**
> **the type of business, such as mining companies, managed investment schemes and trustee companies.**

classification according to liability of members

[3.10] Selection of the type of company is made at the time of its formation. Amongst other matters, the application for registration of a new company must state the type of company it is proposed to be registered as: s 117(2)(a).

There are four types of companies that can be registered.

There are four types of companies that can be registered. The following are classified according to the extent of the liability of members: s 112(1).

> **companies limited by shares;**
> **companies limited by guarantee;**
> **unlimited companies with share capital; and**
> **no liability companies.**

table 3.1 types of companies—s 112(1)

Proprietary companies	Limited by shares Unlimited with share capital
Public companies	Limited by shares Limited by guarantee Unlimited with share capital No liability company

company limited by shares

[3.15] This is by far the most common type of company. Companies limited by shares comprise approximately 99 per cent of all companies registered in Australia. Such companies have the ability to raise funds (referred to as equity or share capital) by issuing shares to investors.

A company limited by shares is defined in s 9 as a company formed on the principle of having the liability of its members limited to the amount, if any, unpaid on the shares respectively held by them.

A company limited by shares is defined in s 9 as a company formed on the principle of having the liability of its members limited to the amount, if any, unpaid on the shares respectively held by them.

The issue price for a share is determined by agreement between the company and the investor. Shares may be issued on the basis that the investor pays the entire issue price in one instalment. Such shares are referred to as "fully paid shares". A shareholder who owns fully paid shares cannot be forced to contribute any further amounts to the company.

Shares may also be issued on the basis that the shareholder pays part of the issue price immediately. Such shares are referred to as "partly paid shares". A shareholder who owns partly paid shares is liable to pay the balance of the issue price of their partly paid shares if the company makes a call. If a company limited by shares goes into liquidation, partly-paid shareholders are liable to pay the unpaid amounts without a call having to be made.

Under s 515, a shareholder is liable to contribute to the company's property an amount sufficient to pay the company's debts and liabilities and the costs, charges and expenses of the winding up. However, a shareholder need not contribute more than the amount, if any, unpaid on the shares in respect of which the shareholder is liable as a member: s 516.

In some situations a past shareholder may also be liable to contribute to the company's property on a winding up. They need not contribute if they were not shareholders within one year of the commencement of winding up: s 521. Further, past shareholders are only liable if the court is satisfied that the existing shareholders are unable to satisfy the contributions they are liable to make: s 522. In any event, past shareholders will not be liable for any debt or liability of the company contracted after the past shareholder ceased to be a shareholder: s 520.

Because the shareholders of a company limited by shares have limited liability, creditors of such a company do not have access to the personal property of the shareholders in order to satisfy their debts. Therefore, s 148(2) requires a limited company to have the word "Limited" or its abbreviation "Ltd" as part of and at the end of its name. This is a warning to potential creditors that the liability of the shareholders is limited and debts of the company can only be satisfied from the assets of the company. The prudent creditor should ascertain whether the issued capital of the company is sufficiently large and the company holds sufficient assets to cover the debt. The prudent creditor may also seek a personal guarantee from the directors.

company limited by guarantee

[3.20] There are about 9,000 companies limited by guarantee. A company limited by guarantee is a company whose members have their liability limited to the amounts that they have undertaken to contribute to the property of the company in the event of it being wound up: s 9.

A company limited by guarantee is a company whose members have their liability limited to the amounts that they have undertaken to contribute to the property of the company in the event of it being wound up.

Such a company does not have a share capital. Members are not required to contribute capital while the company is operating. However, in the event of the company being wound up and its assets being insufficient to meet its liabilities, its members are liable to pay up to the amount specified as the members' guarantees. The guaranteed amount must be set out in the company's application for registration: s 117(2)(m).

The obvious drawback with this type of company is that it does not raise initial or working capital from its members. Accordingly, such companies are very rarely used for the purposes of trading. Nevertheless, this type of company may be convenient for clubs, charities and other non-trading companies whose capital needs can be met from outside sources, donations, subscriptions and social activities. An incorporated association formed under specific State legislation, such as the *Associations Incorporation Act 1981* (Vic) or the *Associations Incorporation Act 1984* (NSW), is an alternative to a company limited by guarantee for a non-profit association.

Guarantee companies still retain the advantages of being legal entities with the liability of their members limited to the amount of the guarantee. On winding up, s 517 provides that members at the time of commencement of winding up need not contribute more than the amount they have undertaken to contribute to the company's property if it is wound up. As is the case of a company limited by shares, the past members of a company limited by guarantee may also be liable if the assets of the company are insufficient and the present members are unable to meet the company's liabilities. Past members' liability to contribute arises only in respect to those persons who were members within the year prior to the commencement of winding up. They are not, of course, liable to contribute towards those company debts incurred after they ceased to be members.

Under s 150, ASIC may permit a company limited by guarantee that pursues charitable purposes to omit the word "Limited" from its name if certain requirements and prohibitions are set out in the company's constitution.

unlimited company

[3.25] An unlimited company is defined in s 9 as a company whose members have no limit placed on their liability. There are about 600 unlimited companies in Australia.

An unlimited company is a company whose members have no limit placed on their liability.

This is the oldest type of company. Unlimited companies formed prior to July 1998 were given the choice of whether to have a share capital. However, as a result of 1998 amendments, only unlimited companies with a share capital may now be registered.

Members of unlimited companies are liable in a winding up for the debts of the company without limit if the company has insufficient assets to meet its debts. In this respect, it is similar to a partnership. However, it has all the other characteristics of incorporation such as recognition as a separate legal entity.

Because limited liability is one of the most important reasons for forming a company, unlimited companies are rare in the case of trading companies. Some accountancy and solicitors' practices are conducted as unlimited companies because professional rules prohibit them from being conducted with limited liability, yet they still desire to obtain other advantages of incorporation.

no liability company

[3.30] Companies engaged in mining have always had a speculative character because of the nature of the industry. This has especially been the case in Australia. Victoria was the first Australian State to specially cater for such companies and introduced the no liability company in 1871. There are about 1,000 no liability companies in Australia.

A public company may be registered as a no liability company or convert into one under s 162. To be registered, a no liability company must:

> **have a share capital;**
> **state in its constitution that its sole objects are mining purposes; and**
> **have no contractual right under its constitution to recover calls made on its shares from a shareholder who fails to pay a call: s 112(2).**

A no liability company is prohibited from engaging in activities that are outside its mining purposes objective.

A no liability company is prohibited from engaging in activities that are outside its mining purposes objective: s 112(3). Directors of a no liability company must not let a mine or claim or enter into a contract for working any land over which it has a claim unless this is approved by a special resolution of the company's shareholders: s 112(4).

A no liability company must have the words "No Liability" or the abbreviation "NL" at the end of its name: s 148(4). Only no liability companies are able to use these words in their name: s 156.

A call on a share in a no liability company is not effective unless it is made payable more than 14 days after the call is made. Notice of details of the call must be given to shareholders at least seven days before the call is payable: s 254P(1) and (2).

The acceptance of shares in a no liability company does not constitute a contract by the shareholder to pay calls or contribute to the debts and liabilities of the company: s 254M(2).

A share in a no liability company is forfeited if a call is unpaid 14 days after it became payable: s 254Q(1). Forfeited shares must be offered for sale by advertised public auction within six weeks after the call becomes payable: s 254Q(2) and (3). The directors may fix a reserve price for the sale of forfeited shares of an amount no greater than the amount of the calls unpaid on the shares: s 254Q(7). If the reserve price is not reached at auction, the shares may be withdrawn from sale and held on trust for the company. The shares must then be disposed of in accordance with the company's constitution or resolution. Unless specifically otherwise provided by resolution, the shares must be offered to shareholders before being disposed of in any other way: s 254Q(9).

A shareholder whose shares have been forfeited may, at any time before the sale, redeem the shares by paying the calls due on the shares and a proportion of expenses incurred in the forfeiture on a pro rata basis: s 254R.

Shares in a no liability company are issued on the basis that if the company is wound up, any surplus must be distributed among the shareholders in proportion to the number of shares held by them irrespective of the amounts paid up. Where a shareholder is in arrears in payment of a call, the right to participate in the distribution in respect of those shares is lost until the amount owing is paid: s 254B(2).

In a winding up, shares issued for cash rank ahead of vendor and promoter shares issued for non-cash consideration: s 254B(3). The holders of vendor and promoter shares are not entitled to preference on winding up despite anything to the contrary in the company's constitution or terms of the issue: s 254B(4).

company limited both by shares and guarantee

[3.35] This type of company may no longer be registered as a result of 1998 amendments. Very few companies of this type were previously formed. Those still in existence are allowed to remain. Their essential feature is that a member of such a company need not contribute more than the aggregate of the following:

> **any sums unpaid on any shares held by the member; and**
> **the amount the member has undertaken to contribute to the company's property if the company is wound up.**

proprietary and public companies

[3.40] Companies vary greatly in size and objectives, from large companies listed on the stock exchange with many thousands of shareholders to small family companies carrying on a relatively small-scale business. The *Corporations Act* recognises that companies and their shareholders have different needs depending on their size and nature. For this reason the *Corporations Act* draws a distinction between public and proprietary companies. More onerous obligations are imposed on public companies because disclosure and investor protection are important concerns of the legislation where there may be large numbers of shareholders. Proprietary companies usually have a relatively small number of shareholders and so are less heavily regulated by the *Corporations Act*.

More onerous obligations are imposed on public companies.

Proprietary companies encompass a wide range of company organisations. Subsidiaries of public companies are often proprietary companies which may own very substantial assets. Some proprietary companies evolved from family businesses to very large companies but wish to restrict share ownership to a relatively small number of shareholders. Other proprietary companies evolved from sole traders or partnerships, perhaps for income tax and estate planning reasons. The managerial and ownership functions continue very much as they did prior to the formation of the company and the assets of such companies remain relatively small.

A distinction is made between large and small proprietary companies in recognition of the fact that many large proprietary companies are either subsidiaries of public companies, or operate large businesses with substantial numbers of employees. It is in the public interest to ensure that such

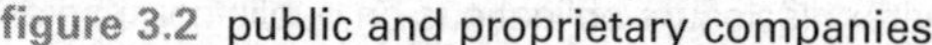
figure 3.2 public and proprietary companies

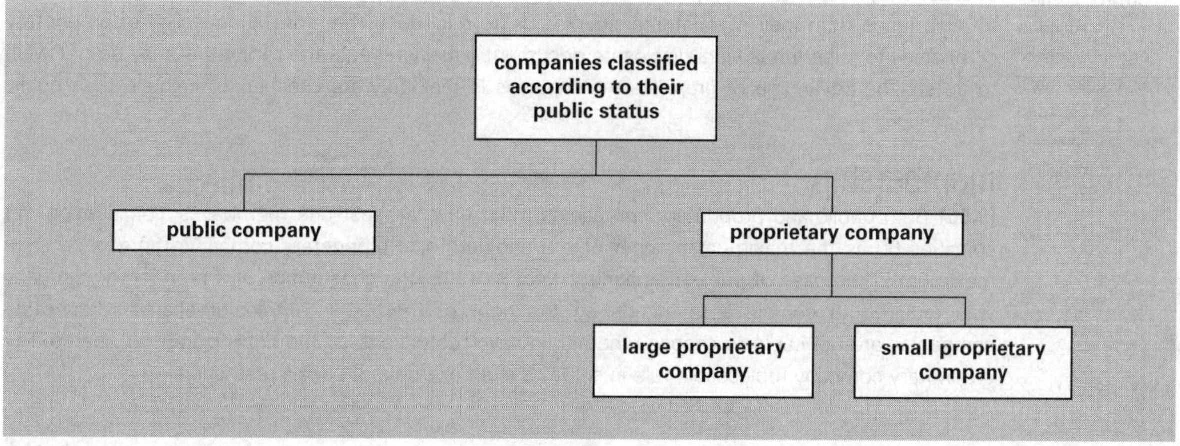

businesses have greater public transparency of their operations. As a result, the disclosure obligations applicable to large proprietary companies are more onerous than in the case of small proprietary companies.

The *Small Business Guide* contained in Pt 1.5 of the *Corporations Act* is written in plain English and summarises the main provisions of the legislation that are likely to be relevant to small companies. It is designed to help people who operate such companies to understand their rights and responsibilities.

definitions

[3.45] The definitions of public and proprietary company are mutually exclusive. All companies must be one or the other. A "public company" means a company other than a proprietary company: s 9.

A proprietary company must be either a company limited by shares or an unlimited company that has a share capital. Further, it must have no more than 50 non-employee shareholders.

Under s 112(1) a proprietary company must be either a company limited by shares or an unlimited company that has a share capital. Further, it must have no more than 50 non-employee shareholders: s 113(1). Joint holders of shares are counted as one person: s 113(2).

Proprietary companies must not engage in any activity that would require disclosure to investors under Ch 6D of the *Corporations Act*.

Proprietary companies must not engage in any activity, such as issuing shares or debentures, that would require disclosure to investors under Ch 6D of the *Corporations Act*, except for an offer of its shares to existing shareholders or employees of the company or of its subsidiary: s 113(3). An act or transaction is not invalid merely because of a contravention of s 113(3): s 113(4). Contravention is an offence of strict liability with a maximum five penalty unit fine: s 113(3A). In addition, ASIC may require a company that contravenes s 113 to convert to a public company: s 165.

It is not necessarily size that is characteristic of proprietary companies, but the restrictions and prohibitions of s 113. These ensure that members of the public cannot be members of proprietary companies.

public and proprietary companies compared

function

[3.50] Proprietary companies are by far the most popular type of company. They out-number public companies by a ratio of approximately 50:1.

Proprietary companies are particularly suited as the vehicle for carrying on a small- to medium-size business.

Public companies are more suited to large businesses which require many investors to participate in fundraising.

The reasons for the popularity of proprietary companies are readily apparent. They are particularly suited as the vehicle for carrying on a small- to medium-size business. Such businesses are usually family run or tightly held and consequently see no advantage in the ability to have large numbers of members or to raise capital through a prospectus issue. Public companies are more suited to large businesses which require many investors to participate in fundraising.

The policy of the *Corporations Act* is to impose greater disclosure obligations on public companies because they may raise money from large numbers of people. Family run businesses are usually able to raise funds from their own internal sources or from lenders. Therefore, the inability of proprietary companies to raise funds via a disclosure document usually reflects the reality that they do not wish to do so. The advantage of proprietary companies is that they are cheaper to maintain than public companies.

membership

[3.55] Both public and proprietary companies must have at least one member: s 114. Section 113 specifies 50 as the maximum number of shareholders of a proprietary company. There is no such maximum in the case of public companies. Prior to 1995, the constitution of a proprietary company was required to contain a restriction on the right of members to transfer shares. Proprietary companies are now able to choose whether to have restrictions on the right to transfer shares. The proprietary company replaceable rule in s 1072G is an example of such a restriction.

name

[3.60] All companies whose members have limited liability, except no liability companies, must have the word "Limited" or the abbreviation "Ltd" as part of and at the end of their name. Proprietary companies must in addition have the word "Proprietary" or the abbreviation "Pty" as part of their name inserted immediately before the word "Limited": s 148(2).

All companies whose members have limited liability, except no liability companies, must have the word "Limited" or the abbreviation "Ltd" as part of and at the end of their name.

An unlimited proprietary company need only have the word "Proprietary" at the end of its name: s 148(3).

replaceable rules and company constitution

[3.65] A company's internal management may be governed by provisions of the *Corporations Act* that apply to the company as replaceable rules, by a constitution, or by a combination of both: s 134. Some of the provisions are replaceable rules for proprietary companies and mandatory rules for public companies. For example, s 249X gives a shareholder the right to appoint a proxy. This is a replaceable rule for proprietary companies but a mandatory rule for public companies.

Single director/shareholder proprietary companies do not require comprehensive, formal rules. Such companies are not governed by the replaceable rules: s 135(1). The *Corporations Act* has several basic rules appropriate for single director/shareholder proprietary companies. These provide that a director may appoint another director by recording the decision and signing the record and may exercise all of the company's powers and is responsible for the management of the company's business: ss 198B, 201F and 202C.

Proprietary company constitutions usually give directors a discretion to refuse to register a transfer of shares. This is less common for public companies. There is a replaceable rule for proprietary companies in s 1072G which gives directors the power to refuse to register a transfer of shares for any reason.

The replaceable rules and constitution are discussed in Chapter 4 below.

directors

[3.70] Proprietary companies must have at least one director, while a public company must have at least three: s 201A. At least two of the directors of a public company, and one in the case of a proprietary company, must ordinarily reside in Australia.

Proprietary companies must have at least one director, while a public company must have at least three.

Prior to 2003 amendments, the appointment of directors of public companies of or over the age of 72 years was subject to certain requirements. These requirements have now been abolished.

Directors of public companies must be individually appointed unless a general meeting of members unanimously agrees to appoint two or more directors by a single resolution: s 201E(1).

Directors of a public company can only be removed by resolution of its members: ss 203D and 203E. The question of who can remove directors of a proprietary company is left to the company's constitution (if any). The proprietary company replaceable rule in s 203C gives this power to the general meeting of shareholders.

Chapter 2E of the *Corporations Act* prohibits public companies from giving financial benefits to directors or other related parties without prior shareholder approval: s 208. Shareholder approval is not required if the financial benefit falls within certain exceptions. This is discussed in Chapter 13.3 below. Public company directors who have a material personal interest in a matter that is being considered at board meetings are not permitted to attend or to vote: s 195.

secretary

[3.75] The *Corporations Act* does not require a proprietary company to have a secretary. If it chooses to appoint one or more secretaries, at least one must ordinarily reside in Australia: s 204A(1). A public company must have at least one secretary and at least one must ordinarily reside in Australia: s 204A(2).

raising funds

[3.80] Proprietary companies are prohibited by s 113(3) from engaging in any activity that would require disclosure to investors under Ch 6D of the *Corporations Act*. This means that a proprietary company cannot raise funds by offering its shares or debentures to a large number of people. Public companies are not so prohibited. However, public companies that wish to issue shares, debentures or other securities must comply with the fundraising provisions in Ch 6D of the *Corporations Act*. Unless one of the specific exceptions applies, a disclosure document must be prepared and lodged with ASIC. The fundraising provisions are discussed in Chapter 7 below.

AGM

[3.85] A public company is required to hold an annual general meeting (AGM) at least once a year unless it has only one member: s 250N. The first AGM must be held within 18 months of incorporation: s 250N(1). The main purpose of the AGM is to give shareholders an opportunity to consider the company's audited financial report. As a result of 1995 amendments, proprietary companies do not have to hold an AGM unless this is required by their constitution.

A proprietary company with more than one shareholder may pass a resolution without a general meeting being held if all the shareholders sign a document stating that they approve of the resolution set out in the document: s 249A. This is known as a "circulating resolution". This procedure cannot be used to pass a resolution to remove an auditor. Shareholder meetings are discussed in Chapter 14 below.

auditors

Public companies and large proprietary companies are required to appoint an independent auditor.

[3.90] Public companies and large proprietary companies are required to appoint an independent auditor to audit their financial reports. In some circumstances ASIC may relieve a large proprietary company from the requirement to appoint an auditor. This is discussed in Chapter 16 below. Small proprietary companies need only appoint an auditor to audit financial reports if requested by ASIC or shareholders holding at least 5 per cent of the voting shares.

As a result of the CLERP 9 amendments, auditors of public companies and large proprietary companies must satisfy the general requirement for auditor independence in ss 324CA–324CD as well as the specific independence requirements in ss 324CE–324CG. These requirements are discussed in Chapter 16 below. Prior to the CLERP 9 amendments, proprietary company auditors were permitted to be officers of the company. After the CLERP 9 amendments only small proprietary companies may appoint officers as their auditor: s 324CH.

registered office

All companies must have a registered office.

[3.95] While all companies must have a registered office, proprietary companies are not obliged to keep it open to the public. Public companies must keep their registered office open to the public during the opening hours specified in s 145. Public companies must also display their name and the words "registered office" prominently at their registered office: s 144.

large and small proprietary companies

[3.100] When the distinction between public and proprietary companies was originally introduced in 1896, proprietary companies were regarded as entities suitable for closely held small business enterprises. In order to protect members of the public who invested funds in public companies, such companies were required to prepare and lodge audited financial statements. All proprietary companies were once exempted from these disclosure requirements.

It soon became apparent that many public companies were reluctant to make detailed disclosure of their financial positions. The aims of the original legislation were easily avoided when public companies conducted their businesses through proprietary company subsidiaries that they controlled.

The only disclosure then required of the public company was an accounting entry showing dividends received from the subsidiary.

To overcome such avoidance practices the legislation was altered in two ways. First, as discussed in Chapter 15 below, accounting standard AASB 127 *Consolidated and Separate Financial Statements* requires a company that is a chief entity of an economic entity to prepare consolidated financial statements of all the entities it controls.

Secondly, proprietary companies are classified as either large or small proprietary companies. This distinction seeks to distinguish small, closely held companies conducting small-scale business enterprises, from large proprietary companies which are often subsidiaries of public companies. As discussed below, small proprietary companies have numerous advantages over large proprietary companies in terms of disclosure requirements and recurring costs.

Section 45A defines the terms "small proprietary company" and "large proprietary company". A proprietary company that does not come within the definition of small proprietary company is regarded as a large proprietary company.

Under s 45A(2) a proprietary company is regarded as a "small proprietary company" for a financial year if it satisfies at least two of the following three criteria:

> **the consolidated gross operating revenue for the financial year of the company and the entities it controls is less than $10 million;**
> **the value of the consolidated gross assets at the end of the financial year of the company and the entities it controls is less than $5 million; and**
> **the company and the entities it controls have fewer than 50 employees at the end of the financial year.**

"Consolidated gross operating revenue" and the value of "consolidated gross assets" are calculated in accordance with applicable accounting standards: s 45A(6). In counting employees for purposes of the s 45A definition, part-time employees are taken into account as an appropriate fraction of a full-time equivalent: s 45A(5). The question whether a proprietary company "controls" an entity is decided in accordance with accounting standards such as AASB 127: s 45A(4).

advantages of small proprietary companies

[3.105] The main advantages of small proprietary companies are that they are subject to fewer requirements in relation to preparation, lodgment and audit of financial reports.

The main advantages of small proprietary companies are that they are subject to fewer requirements in relation to preparation, lodgment and audit of financial reports.

Public companies and large proprietary companies are required to prepare financial reports: s 292. They are also required to have their financial reports audited: s 301. Copies of the financial report, directors' report and auditor's report must be sent to members: s 314. In addition, the financial reports and directors' reports must be lodged with ASIC: s 319.

Every company must keep and maintain sufficient financial records to allow true and fair financial statements to be prepared: s 286. However, a small proprietary company is not required to prepare annual financial reports or appoint an auditor unless directed to do so by:

> **shareholders holding 5 per cent or more of the voting shares: s 293; or**
> **ASIC: s 294.**

Written requests for financial reports by small proprietary company shareholders may be made at any time within 12 months after the end of the financial year concerned: s 293(2). Unless shareholders specify otherwise, the financial reports must be prepared in accordance with applicable accounting standards: s 293(3)(a). Shareholders of a small proprietary company may also request that the financial reports be audited: s 293(3)(c).

A small proprietary company is not required to prepare annual financial reports or appoint an auditor unless directed to do so.

The auditor of a small proprietary company is permitted to be employed as an officer of the company. This is not the case for auditors of public and large proprietary companies. As a result of the

CLERP 9 amendments, their auditors must satisfy the general requirement for auditor independence in ss 324CA–324CD as well as the specific independence requirements in ss 324CE–324CG.

Even though the *Corporations Act* does not require small proprietary companies to prepare annual financial statements, preparation of tax profit and loss statements are required for taxation purposes. In addition, banks and other financial institutions may insist on receiving financial reports before lending money to small proprietary companies.

law reform proposals

[3.110] In March 2001 the Parliamentary Joint Committee on Corporations and Securities (now called the Parliamentary Joint Committee on Corporations and Financial Services) released its *Report on Aspects of the Regulation of Proprietary Companies*. The Committee concluded that the distinction between large and small proprietary companies was not meeting the objectives of the financial reporting system.

> **< [There are] fundamental conceptual and practical problems with the new financial reporting system for proprietary companies. Because of these problems the new system has not achieved the objectives set for it. While the new system has eliminated reporting requirements under the *Corporations Law* for 99.4 per cent of all proprietary companies, small proprietary companies are still subject to the full requirements of the Accounting Standards if they meet the definition of a reporting entity as defined in the Standards. At the same time, small proprietary companies are less accountable in a public manner. On the other hand, proprietary companies which are classified as large according to the large/small test but are non-reporting entities can disregard the full requirements of the Standards. Other objectives of the system, such as reducing compliance costs and eliminating the complexity of the reporting rules, have not been met for the same reasons. >**

After canvassing a number of options the Committee recommended that:

> the previous distinction between exempt and non-exempt proprietary companies be reinstated to replace the large and small distinction in s 45A;
> all directors of proprietary companies be required to sign and lodge a declaration of solvency with their annual reports;
> in preparing financial statements, reporting and non-reporting entities apply all the recognition and measurement requirements of the Accounting Standards; and
> all company financial statements, which are required to be lodged with the ASIC, should be required to be audited.

A proprietary company may wish to convert to a public company as a preliminary step in an application for listing on the stock exchange.

conversion from proprietary to public company

[3.115] A proprietary company may wish to convert to a public company as a preliminary step in an application for listing on the stock exchange. The *Corporations Act* permits a proprietary company limited by shares to convert to a public company limited by shares by passing a special resolution to this effect and lodging an application with ASIC: ss 162 and 163. The company name must also be changed by omitting the word "Proprietary" from the company name. The company is then issued with an amended certificate of registration and becomes a public company. This does not create a new legal entity and does not affect any rights and liabilities of the company.

Under s 165, ASIC may direct a proprietary company to change to a public company if it is satisfied that the company has contravened s 113. This provision specifies the maximum membership of proprietary companies and prevents them from engaging in an activity that would require disclosure to investors under Ch 6D of the *Corporations Act*.

conversion from public to proprietary company

[3.120] A public company limited by shares may wish to convert to a proprietary company to reduce its financial disclosure obligations. The *Corporations Act* permits a public company to convert to a proprietary company by passing a special resolution and lodging an application to this effect with ASIC: ss 162 and 163. The special resolution must alter the company name so as to include "Proprietary" or the abbreviation "Pty".

A public company limited by shares may wish to convert to a proprietary company to reduce its financial disclosure obligations.

The company must also comply with s 113. That section requires proprietary companies to have a share capital and a maximum of 50 members. As in the case of conversion from a proprietary to a public company, an amended certificate of registration is issued. A change of type of company does not create a new legal entity, affect the company's rights or obligations or any legal proceedings involving the company: s 166(1).

asx listed companies

[3.125] The largest businesses in Australia are public companies that have chosen to have their shares listed on the Australian Stock Exchange Ltd (ASX) which operates a number of financial markets including Australia's main share market where the buying and selling of shares of listed companies takes place. The ASX website contains valuable information about the ASX and the ASX listed companies. This website is linked to the Lipton-Herzberg Corporate Law Websites at **http://www.lipton-herzberg.com.au/corp-law-websites.html**

The largest businesses in Australia are public companies that have chosen to have their shares listed on the ASX.

table 3.2 snapshot of ASX listed companies

	Year ended 31 December 2003
Market capitalisation ($ million)	1,098,801
Number of entities with equities quoted on ASX	1,471
Turnover – sequities	
Transactions (000s)	16,053
Volume (million shares)	222,539
Value ($ billion)	567,394

Source: ASX Fact File 2004

ASX listed companies are regulated by the *Corporations Act* and are also required to comply with the even more onerous disclosure and other obligations imposed by the ASX Listing Rules. These deal with such matters as admission to the list and disclosure of information. The Listing Rules are set out on the ASX website which is linked to the Lipton Herzberg Corporate Law Websites at **http://www.lipton-herzberg.com.au/corp-law-websites.html#Australian_Stock_Exchange**

ASX listed companies are regulated by the *Corporations Act* and are also required to comply with the even more onerous disclosure and other obligations imposed by the ASX Listing Rules.

The main reason public companies choose to be listed is that they have a greater ability to raise capital to grow a larger business. Being listed gives shareholders a better opportunity to sell their shares and enhances the ability of potential investors to acquire shares and thus broaden the company's shareholder base. Listed companies have a higher public profile with their customers and suppliers who often perceive listed companies as having financial strength.

To gain listing, a public company must satisfy the various requirements in ASX Listing Rule 1. These detailed requirements include a minimum shareholder requirement and a company size requirement. The minimum shareholder requirement seeks to make sure that there are enough shareholders to make a market for share trading and the company size requirement ensures that listed companies have a history of profits or have significant assets apart from cash.

There are two alternative minimum shareholder requirements that a company must meet. These are that the company has a minimum of:

- **500 shareholders each holding a parcel of shares with a value of at least $2,000; or**
- **400 shareholders each holding a parcel of shares with a value of at least $2,000, 25 per cent of whom are unrelated parties of the company.**

Listed public companies are "disclosing entities".

The company size requirement may be satisfied by either a profits test (aggregated profit from continuing operations for the last three financial years of at least $1 million) or an assets test (net tangible assets of at least $2 million).

The *Corporations Act* imposes additional requirements on listed companies. For example, under s 300A, the directors' report of listed companies must include specified information about remuneration of directors and senior management.

The *Corporations Act* requires disclosing entities to prepare and lodge half-year financial reports as well as annual financial reports.

Listed public companies are "disclosing entities" as defined in Part 1.2A of the *Corporations Act*. The definition of "disclosing entity" is complex but corresponds in most cases to listed entities. Under s 111AC a body is regarded as a disclosing entity if any of its securities (eg shares) are enhanced disclosure securities (ED securities). Securities are ED securities if they are securities of a body that is included in a licensed market's official list: s 111AE.

Disclosing entities are subject to the continuous disclosure requirements.

Disclosing entities are subject to enhanced disclosure requirements. The enhanced disclosure scheme has two main features:

- **periodic reporting; and**
- **continuous disclosure.**

The *Corporations Act* requires disclosing entities to prepare and lodge half-year financial reports as well as annual financial reports. In addition, listed companies must also comply with the periodic disclosure requirements in ASX Listing Rule 4. The periodic reporting requirements in the *Corporations Act* and ASX Listing Rule 4 are discussed in Chapter 15 below.

In addition, disclosing entities are subject to the continuous disclosure requirements of Ch 6CA of the *Corporations Act*. These provisions require disclosing entities to disclose information that a reasonable person could be taken to expect would have a material effect on the price or value of their securities. For example, ASX listed disclosing entities must comply with the continuous disclosure requirements in ASX Listing Rule 3.1: s 674. Under that listing rule, the continuous disclosure information must be provided to the ASX, which makes it available to the public. The continuous disclosure requirements are further discussed in Chapter 15 below.

Prospectuses issued by listed disclosing entities do not have to be as detailed as prospectuses of other corporations: s 713. This is because the enhanced disclosure scheme requires listed disclosing entities to disclose information to the ASX which would be likely to have a material effect on the price of their securities. Consequently, much of the information that would normally be required to be contained in prospectuses issued by listed disclosing entities is already known to potential investors. Prospectuses are discussed in Chapter 7 below.

The ASX Listing Rules also regulate the governance practices of listed companies.

The ASX Listing Rules also regulate the governance practices of listed companies. For example, under Listing Rule 4.10.3 the annual reports of listed companies must disclose the extent to which the company has followed the ASX Corporate Governance Council's *Principles of Good Corporate Governance and Best Practice Recommendations*. These are discussed in Chapter 13.1 below.

The ASX Listing Rules contain various enhanced shareholder protection mechanisms.

The ASX Listing Rules contain various enhanced shareholder protection mechanisms. For example, under ASX Listing Rule 7, significant changes in share capital and new issues require shareholder approval. Under ASX Listing Rule 10, shareholder approval is also required for significant company transactions with persons in a position of influence such as directors or major shareholders.

The definition of "disclosing entity" in the *Corporations Act* also covers certain unlisted companies as well as companies listed on the ASX. As a result of the complex definition of disclosing entity in ss 111AA–111AX, the term "disclosing entity" also includes entities whose securities have been:

> **issued to more than 100 people and a disclosure document has been lodged with ASIC: s 111AF; or**
> **issued to more than 100 people as consideration for an acquisition under an off-market takeover bid or Pt 5.1 compromise or arrangement: s 111AG.**

As is the case with listed disclosing entities, unlisted disclosing entities are also subject to periodic reporting and continuous disclosure requirements. While listed disclosing entities must comply with the continuous disclosure requirements of ASX Listing Rule 3.1 which requires the continuous disclosure information to be provided to the ASX, unlisted disclosing entities must lodge the information with ASIC: s 675.

holding and subsidiary companies–related bodies corporate

The *Corporations Act* classifies companies as holding and subsidiary companies.

[3.130] The *Corporations Act* classifies companies as holding and subsidiary companies. Prior to 1991, the main reason for this classification was for purposes of the financial reporting requirements. A holding company was once required to prepare consolidated financial statements for all the companies in the group. However, as discussed in Chapter 15 below, from 1992 onwards the *Corporations Act* departed from the concept of group reporting by a holding company and its subsidiaries and now requires entity-based reporting by a chief entity for all the entities comprising an economic entity.

Despite the 1992 amendments, the holding and subsidiary company classification still has some significance. For example:

> **under s 260A(1), a company may financially assist a person to acquire shares in itself or its holding company only if certain requirements are met;**
> **under ss 588V–588X, a holding company may be personally liable for debts incurred by its insolvent subsidiary if at the time the debts were incurred there were reasonable grounds for suspecting that the subsidiary was insolvent (this is discussed in Chapter 2 above); and**
> **under s 202B, a company must disclose the remuneration paid to each director of the company or a subsidiary by the company or by a controlled entity if directed to do so by members holding at least 5 per cent of voting shares or at least 100 members.**

definition of subsidiary

Sections 9 and 46 define whether a body corporate is a subsidiary of another body corporate (the holding company).

[3.135] The term "holding company" is not defined directly in the *Corporations Act*. Instead, ss 9 and 46 define whether a body corporate is a subsidiary of another body corporate (the holding company).

Under s 46(a), a body corporate is regarded as a subsidiary of another body corporate if, and only if, the other body:

- **controls the composition of the board of directors of the subsidiary (s 46(a)(i));**
- **is in a position to cast, or control the casting of, more than one-half of the maximum number of votes that might be cast at a general meeting of the subsidiary (s 46(a)(ii)); or**
- **holds more than one-half of the issued share capital of the subsidiary: s 46(a)(iii). Shares that carry no right to participate beyond a specified amount in a distribution of either profits or capital are not counted. Preference shares usually fall within this excluded category.**

The subsidiary of a holding company that is itself a subsidiary of another body corporate is regarded as a subsidiary of that other body corporate: s 46(b).

control of composition of board

[3.140] For purposes of s 46(a)(i), the composition of the board of directors is taken to be controlled by another body corporate if the other body can exercise a power to appoint or remove all or a majority of the directors: s 47. This power must be a legally enforceable power to control the composition of the board of directors and not practical or de facto control that arises by a significant shareholding in a company: *Mount Edon Gold Mines (Aust) Ltd v Burmine Ltd* (1994) 12 ACLC 185.

position to cast or control the casting majority of votes

[3.145] Section 46(a)(ii) has two alternate tests for determining whether a company is a subsidiary of another. A company is a subsidiary if another company:

- **is in the position to cast more than half the maximum number of votes that might be cast at a general meeting of the company; or**
- **controls the casting of more than half the maximum number of votes that might be cast at a general meeting of the company.**

The second test in s 46(a)(ii)—the "control" test—is satisfied if a company has a legally enforceable power to control the casting of the necessary number of votes required. However, according to *Bluebird Investments Pty Ltd v Graf Holdings Pty Ltd* (1994) 12 ACLC 724, certain arrangements falling short of control will satisfy the first test in s 46(a)(ii)—the "position to cast" test. For example, a company is in a position to cast the required percentage of votes if it has a present ability to cast the votes. This would be the case if the company held open proxies enabling it to cast more than 50 per cent of the votes at a general meeting of another company.

holding more than half issued capital

[3.150] Under s 46(a)(iii), a company is regarded as a subsidiary if another company holds more than half its issued capital. A company "holds" shares if it is a registered shareholder. Shares in a subsidiary held by a nominee in trust for the holding company are treated as being held by the holding company: s 48(3). On the other hand, where a company is merely holding the shares in a fiduciary capacity, such as a trustee, the shares are not treated as being held by a holding company: s 48(2).

deficiencies of definition

The s 46 definition of subsidiary company contains significant loopholes.

[3.155] The s 46 definition of subsidiary company contains significant loopholes. For example, a company may have de facto control over another without that other company falling within the s 46 definition of subsidiary company. Further, under s 46, only bodies corporate are capable of being classified as subsidiaries. Under the previous group accounting provisions, an unincorporated entity, such as a trust, could not be considered as a subsidiary even though it was controlled by the holding company. As a result, the trust's assets and liabilities did not have to be consolidated in the group's balance sheet. These "off-balance sheet" devices were widely abused with the result that shareholders and other users of accounts did not receive meaningful information of the "group's" overall financial position. This led to the introduction of entity-based reporting in the accounting standards which adopts the broader concept of control.

CASAC's *Corporate Groups Final Report* (May 2000) recommended that the existence of company groups should be determined by a single uniform "control" test based on s 50AA. This "control" test should replace the holding/subsidiary and related companies tests.

Section 50AA(1) provides that an entity controls a second entity if the first entity has the capacity to determine the outcome of decisions about the second entity's financial and operating policies. CASAC was of the opinion that the control test better identified "all forms of de facto control, as it is not limited to control through majority shareholding or control through composition of the board of directors".

ultimate holding company

[3.160] A body corporate is defined in s 9 as an ultimate holding company of another if:

> **that other body corporate is a subsidiary of that holding company; and**
> **the holding company is not itself a subsidiary of another.**

Where applicable, the annual return must give particulars of the company's ultimate holding company.

wholly-owned subsidiary

[3.165] A body corporate is a wholly-owned subsidiary if none of its members is a person other than:

> **its holding company;**
> **a nominee of its holding company;**
> **another wholly-owned subsidiary of the holding company; or**
> **a nominee of such a wholly-owned subsidiary.**

A director of a wholly-owned subsidiary is taken to act in good faith in the best interests of the subsidiary if the constitution authorises the director to act in the interests of the holding company, the director acts in good faith in the best interests of the holding company and the subsidiary remains solvent: s 187. The duty of directors to act in good faith in the interests of the company is discussed below in Chapter 13.2.

An issue or transfer of shares of a company to an entity it controls is void unless the transfer is by a wholly-owned subsidiary and the entity is also a wholly-owned subsidiary of the same body corporate: s 259C(1)(d).

related bodies corporate

[3.170] Under s 50 where a body corporate is:

> **a holding company of another body corporate;**
> **a subsidiary of another body corporate; or**
> **a subsidiary of a holding company of another body corporate**

all the companies are related to each other.

This is illustrated by Figure 3.3 below.

A disclosure document is not required where a body offers its securities to executive officers or a related body: s 708(11). This is discussed further in Chapter 7 below.

figure 3.3 related companies

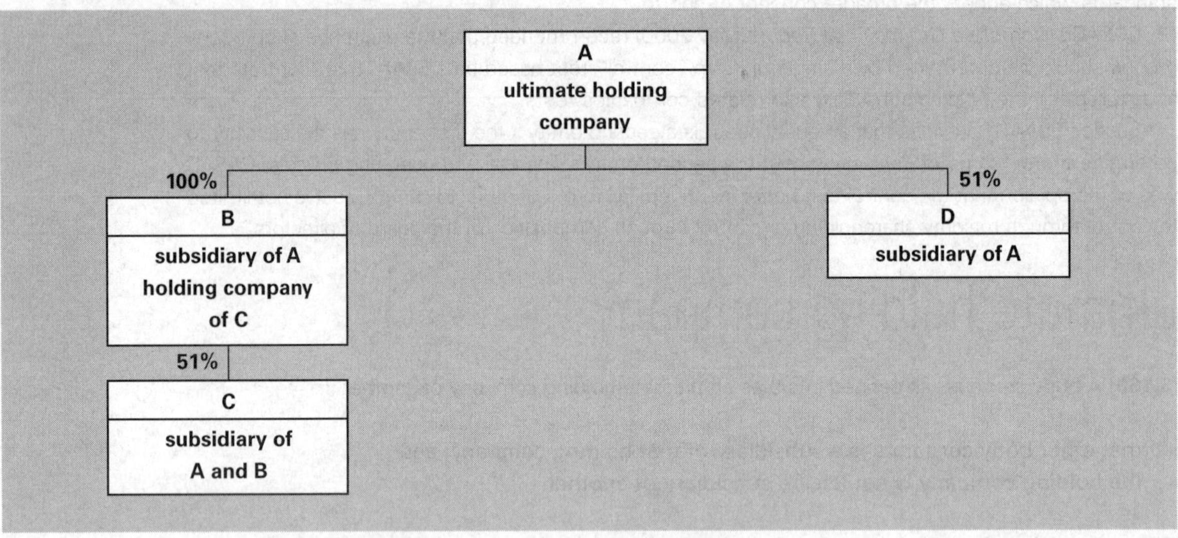

recognised and foreign companies

recognised companies

[3.175] Prior to 1 July 2001, a company was registered under the *Corporations Law* of a particular State or Territory which was its home jurisdiction. A company was able to carry on business in other jurisdictions where it was referred to as a recognised company.

The concept of recognised companies is no longer relevant as all companies are now registered under a single Commonwealth Act, the *Corporations Act*. This regulatory framework is discussed in Chapter 1 above.

Companies are still taken to be registered in the particular State or Territory specified in the application for registration lodged with ASIC. This is for the purpose of allowing certain State legislation, such as that dealing with stamp duty, to operate.

foreign companies

A body corporate incorporated outside Australia is referred to as a "foreign company" and is not permitted to carry on business in Australia unless it is registered with ASIC.

[3.180] A body corporate incorporated outside Australia is referred to as a "foreign company" and is not permitted to carry on business in Australia unless it is registered with ASIC: s 601CD. Once a foreign company is registered with ASIC it may carry on business in Australia without any additional requirements.

registrable Australian bodies

[3.185] Under s 57A, the term "corporation" includes bodies incorporated or formed under specific State or Territory legislation. These include incorporated associations, co-operatives, building societies and credit unions. Such bodies are referred to in s 9 as "registrable Australian bodies".

As long as a registrable Australian body carries on business exclusively in the State or Territory of its formation it need not become registered under the *Corporations Act*.

A registrable Australian body must not carry on business outside the State or Territory of its origin unless it is registered under Pt 5B.1.

In order to be registered, a registrable Australian body must lodge an application for registration with ASIC using the prescribed form. The application must be accompanied by the documents referred to in s 601CB.

trustee companies

types of trustee companies

[3.190] Trustee companies serve a variety of commercial purposes. For example, all the States and Territories have legislation that empowers a small number of companies to act as executors and personal representatives of deceased estates. These statutory trustee companies have a high degree of skill and experience in administering trusts. They are required by legislation to have substantial asset backing and in some States the liability of their shareholders is greater than in the case of ordinary companies limited by shares. Because of the nature of their activities they are entitled to charge fees for their services. Apart from acting as executors, statutory trustee companies often also administer other types of trusts. For example, they are eligible for appointment as trustees for debenture-holders: s 283AC(1). This is discussed in Chapter 11 below. In addition, because of their recognised integrity and skill, they are often appointed to act as trustees of public unit trusts and as responsible entities of managed investment schemes, discussed in Chapter 20 below.

Trustee companies serve a variety of commercial purposes.

Most banks and stockbrokers also operate associated trustee companies. These are not statutory trustee companies as described above. For a fee they hold investments, usually shares, as nominees for clients who for one reason or another wish to remain anonymous.

There are many proprietary companies formed with minimal issued capital, commonly referred to as "$2 companies". Typically, such companies are formed to act as trustees of trusts that own family investments or operate family businesses. The most popular type of family trust is the discretionary trust in which the trustee is given a discretion to distribute trust income and capital among a nominated class of beneficiaries. The trustee company's directors are able to control the trust through the exercise of the trustee's discretionary powers.

Discretionary trusts allow for greater flexibility for income-splitting than companies. Trustees of discretionary trusts are usually able to vary the amounts of trust income to be distributed to particular beneficiaries from year-to-year. While variable distributions of dividends to shareholders holding different classes of shares are possible, the *Income Tax Assessment Act* discourages the practice.

Companies are usually appointed to act as trustees of family discretionary trusts for several reasons. As explained in Chapter 2 above, companies continue to exist until deregistered by ASIC. This avoids the need to replace human trustees when they die. However, the more probably reason companies are selected is to ensure limited liability for trust debts.

trustees' right of indemnity

[3.195] According to trust law, trustees are personally liable to trust creditors for the debts and liabilities properly incurred in administering the trust investments or carrying on its business. If trustees pay trust debts or liabilities from their own personal resources, they are entitled to be reimbursed from the assets of the trust. In some situations trustees have the right to be reimbursed by the beneficiaries themselves: *J W Broomhead (Vic) Pty Ltd v J W Broomhead Pty Ltd* (1985) 3 ACLC 355. This right is referred to as a "right of reimbursement".

Trustees, however, are not required to pay trust creditors from their own resources and then reimburse themselves. They are permitted to pay trust debts and liabilities directly from trust assets. This right is referred to as a "right of exoneration".

A trustee's rights of reimbursement and exoneration are collectively known as a "trustee's right of indemnity". The right of indemnity is regarded as an asset of a trustee. Accordingly, if a trustee is a "$2 company", its right of indemnity will be the only meaningful asset it has to meet the claims of trust creditors.

liability of directors of trustee companies

[3.200] A trustee's right of indemnity is not always available. It is lost if the trustee breaches the trust while incurring debts or liabilities. For example, there will be a breach of trust if the trustee invests trust assets in unauthorised investments or if the trustee acts carelessly.

The loss of the right of indemnity due to a breach of trust can cause considerable hardship to trust creditors, particularly if the trustee has no other assets to meet the creditors' claims. This is usually the case with $2 companies. Trust creditors bear the loss despite the fact that they have no way of knowing that the trustee has breached the trust. The hardship to trust creditors has to some extent been alleviated by s 197. This section specifies that where a company, while acting as a trustee, incurs a liability that it has not itself discharged, and for any reason it is not entitled to be fully indemnified out of the assets of the trust in respect of the liability, then the persons who were its directors at the time the liability was incurred are jointly and severally liable with the company to discharge the liability. This is so even if the trust does not have enough assets to indemnify the trustee. The Full Court of the South Australian Supreme Court in *Hanel v O'Neill* (2004) 22 ACLC 274 interpreted s 197(1) so as to expand the potential liability of directors of corporate trusts. The majority held that liability may be imposed on directors under s 197 where the trust has insufficient assets to indemnify the trustee.

This interpretation represented an unexpected expansion of director liability and resulted in the *Corporation Amendment Act (No. 1) 2005*. This act amended s 197(1) by clarifying that it does not impose liability on a director merely because there are insufficient trust assets out of which the corporation can be indemnified. In such cases, however, directors may become personally liable if they contravene the duty in s 588G by failing to prevent the company incurring debts when there are reasonable grounds for suspecting it is insolvent. This is discussed in Chapter 13.5 below. The liquidation of trustee companies raises some particular issues and these are discussed in Chapter 25 below.

bibliography ...

Copper, J "Piercing the 'veil of obscurity'—the decision in Hanel v O' Neill" (2004) 22 C & SLJ 313.

Eisenberg, M A "Corporate Groups" in Gillooly, M (ed) *The Law Relating to Corporate Groups.* Federation Press, 1993, Ch 1.

Ford, H A J "Trading Trusts and Creditors' Rights" (1981) 13 MULR 1.

Sparold, G C "The Unit Trust—A Comparison with the Corporation" (1991) 3 Bond LR 249.

Parliamentary Joint Committee on Corporations and Securities, "Report on Aspects of the Regulation of Proprietary Companies" (March 2001).

revision questions on material in this chapter ...

> Please see eQuiz at **http://www.thomson.com.au/academic** for multiple choice questions and answers.

chapter four

constitution and replaceable rules

key points . . .

- A company's internal management may be governed by replaceable rules contained in the Corporations Act or by a constitution or by a combination of both.
- A company has the legal capacity and powers of an individual and a body corporate. The historical doctrine of ultra vires has been abolished. Acts of a company are not invalid merely because they are contrary to or beyond any objects stated in its constitution.
- According to s 140(1), a company's constitution (if any) and any applicable replaceable rules have effect as a contract between:
  - the company and each member; and
  - the company and each director and secretary; and
  - a member and each other member.
- Subject to certain restrictions, a company's constitution may be modified or repealed if its members pass a special resolution: s 136(2). A company that did not have a constitution when it was formed can displace or modify any or all of its replaceable rules if it adopts a constitution by special resolution: s 135(2).
- There are several limits on the right of a company to alter its constitution. The courts have struck down alterations that were beyond any purpose contemplated by the constitution or were oppressive. The courts have been particularly protective of members where an alteration is made for the purpose of expropriating or compulsorily acquiring a member's shares. The *Corporations Act* allows certain compulsory acquisitions provided specified procedures are followed.

[4.05] Companies have considerable flexibility in deciding the rules that govern their internal management. Typically, these rules deal with such matters as the powers of directors, meetings of directors and shareholders, rights of shareholders and the share transfer process. A company's internal management may be governed by replaceable rules contained in the *Corporations Act* or by a constitution or by a combination of both: s 134.

replaceable rules

The *Corporations Act* contains "replaceable rules" that govern the internal administration and management of companies.

[4.10] The *Corporations Act* contains a set of rules, called "replaceable rules" that govern the internal administration and management of companies. The replaceable rules, located throughout the *Corporations Act*, apply to companies formed after July 1998 and those companies formed before that date which have repealed their constitutions: s 135(1)(a)(i) and (ii). As the name suggests, the rules are replaceable. A company may be formed with a constitution that replaces or modifies any one or all of the replaceable rules: s 135(2).

The replaceable rules do not apply to a company formed prior to 1998 which retained its constitution. According to s 135(1)(a)(ii), they only apply to such a company if it has repealed its constitution and did not replace it with another. There is therefore no direct reference in the legislation to the position of a pre-1998 company which has repealed only part of its constitution. While it is not entirely clear, it would appear that in such a case the replaceable rules would not apply at all and the constitution of such a company would comprise the remaining provisions contained in its constitution (known as "articles of association" prior to 1998) and any gaps not so provided for are deemed to be governed by the provisions of Table A which have not been displaced or excluded. The historical effect of Table A and its repeal are discussed below, para [4.35].

The heading of a section in the *Corporations Act* specifies whether that section is a replaceable rule. The headings of relevant replaceable rule sections also indicate the type of company to which a particular replaceable rule applies. Most replaceable rules apply to both public and proprietary companies. However, according to s 135, some replaceable rules apply only to proprietary companies. For example s 194, which deals with proprietary company directors voting at board meetings on matters involving directors' personal interests, is a proprietary company rule. Other sections are regarded as replaceable rules for proprietary companies but are mandatory rules for public companies as ordinary provisions of the *Corporations Act*. For example, s 249X, which deals with the appointment of proxies, is a replaceable rule for proprietary companies but mandatory for public companies. A mandatory rule applies despite anything to the contrary in the public company's constitution.

The heading of a section in the *Corporations Act* specifies whether that section is a replaceable rule. The headings also indicate the type of company to which a particular replaceable rule applies.

According to s 135(3), a failure to comply with applicable replaceable rules is not of itself a contravention of the *Corporations Act*. As a result, the provisions in the *Corporations Act* regarding criminal liability, civil liability and statutory injunctions do not apply to breaches of the replaceable rules.

table of replaceable rules

[4.15] Section 141 contains the following table which indicates the provisions of the *Corporations Act* that apply as replaceable rules.

table 4.1 provisions that apply as replaceable rules

	OFFICERS AND EMPLOYEES	
1	Voting and completion of transactions—directors of proprietary companies	194
2	Powers of directors	198A
3	Negotiable instruments	198B
4	Managing director	198C
5	Company may appoint a director	201G
6	Directors may appoint other directors	201H
7	Appointment of managing directors	201J
8	Alternate directors	201K
9	Remuneration of directors	202A
10	Director may resign by giving written notice to company	203A
11	Removal by members—proprietary company	203C
12	Termination of appointment of managing director	203F
13	Terms and conditions of office for secretaries	204F
	INSPECTION OF BOOKS	
14	Company or directors may allow member to inspect books	247D

	DIRECTOR'S MEETINGS	
15	Circulating resolutions of companies with more than 1 director	248A
16	Calling directors' meetings	248C
17	Chairing directors' meetings	248E
18	Quorum at directors' meetings	248F
19	Passing of directors' resolutions	248G
	MEETINGS OF MEMBERS	
20	Calling of meetings of members by a director	249C
21	Notice to joint members	249J(2)
22	When notice by post or fax is given	249J(4)
22A	When notice under paragraph 249J(3)(cb) is given	249J(5)
23	Notice of adjourned meetings	249M
24	Quorum	249T
25	Chairing meetings of members	249U
26	Business at adjourned meetings	249W(2)
27	Who can appoint a proxy *[replaceable rule for proprietary companies only]*	*249X*
28	Proxy vote valid even if member dies, revokes appointment etc.	250C(2)
29	How many votes a member has	250E
30	Jointly held shares	250F
31	Objections to right to vote	250G
32	How voting is carried out	250J
33	When and how polls must be taken	250M
	SHARES	
33A	Pre-emption for existing shareholders on issue of shares in proprietary company	254D
33B	Other provisions about paying dividends	254U
34	Dividend rights for shares in proprietary companies	254W(2)
	TRANSFER OF SHARES	
35	Transmission of shares on death	1072A
36	Transmission of shares on bankruptcy	1072B
37	Transmission of shares on mental incapacity	1072D
38	Registration of transfers	1072F
39	Additional general discretion for directors of proprietary companies to refuse to register transfers	1072G

ne person proprietary companies

[4.20] The *Corporations Act* recognises that a proprietary company with a single shareholder who is also the sole director does not need formal rules governing its internal management. According to s 135(1), the replaceable rules do not apply to such companies. It is also unnecessary for these companies to have a constitution.

Instead of a constitution or replaceable rules, the *Corporations Act* has a number of basic rules that apply specifically to single director/shareholder proprietary companies. These include:

The *Corporations Act* has a number of basic rules that apply specifically to single director/shareholder proprietary companies.

> **the business of the company is to be managed by or under the direction of the director who may also exercise all the powers of the company such as the power to issue shares, borrow money and issue debentures (s 198E(1));**
> **the director may execute a negotiable instrument (s 198E(2));**
> **the director may appoint another director by recording the appointment and signing the record (s 201F); and**
> **the director is to be paid any remuneration for being a director that the company determines by resolution: s 202C.**

These rules apply only while the company is a single director/shareholder proprietary company. The replaceable rules become applicable as soon as the company issues shares to another person or appoints additional directors.

companies limited by guarantee

[4.25] Many replaceable rules, such as those that deal with dividends or transfer and transmission of shares, are inappropriate for a company limited by guarantee. Consequently, the internal management of these types of companies cannot be governed solely by the replaceable rules and such companies should have a constitution.

While companies limited by guarantee ought to have a constitution, their internal rules may be governed by a combination of both the rules in their constitution as well as selected replaceable rules.

no liability companies

[4.30] The internal management of a no liability company cannot be governed solely by the replaceable rules. Section 112(2) requires a no liability company to have a constitution that states that:

> **its sole objects are mining purposes; and**
> **the company has no contractual right to recover calls made on its shares from a shareholder who fails to pay them.**

While no liability companies must have a constitution, their internal rules may be governed by a combination of the rules in their constitution as well as selected replaceable rules.

repeal of Tables A and B

[4.35] Prior to 1998, companies other than companies limited by guarantee were deemed to have adopted the regulations in Table A of Sch 1 of the pre-1998 legislation as their articles unless they were specifically excluded or modified by their own constitution. Table B of Sch 1 of the previous legislation had the equivalent provisions for no liability companies.

The regulations in Tables A and B were repealed by 1998 amendments. Companies formed after 1998 are no longer deemed to have adopted those regulations as their default constitution. However, if a pre-1998 company adopted Table A or B articles, those regulations are still regarded as its constitution after 1 July 1998.

The replaceable rules have a number of advantages compared with the regulations in Table A. The replaceable rules are drafted in plain English and are easier to understand than equivalent Table A regulations. Unlike the Table A regulations, the replaceable rules cater for the use of modern communications technology, such as teleconferencing and video-conferencing in directors' and members' meetings: ss 248D and 249S. Table A did not cater for single director/shareholder proprietary companies and was therefore unsuitable for such companies which had to incur the additional expense of drafting their own constitutions.

The regulations in Table A changed over time. A company that adopted Table A had the regulations that were in Table A of the company legislation applicable at the time of its incorporation. The replaceable rules, on the other hand, are those that are in the *Corporations Act* as amended from time to time. This obviates the need for a company to change its internal regulations to keep up to date with changes in the *Corporations Act*.

the company's constitution

[4.40] Prior to July 1998, all companies were required to have a constitution consisting of two documents—the memorandum of association and the articles of association. Where a company has retained its memorandum and articles, these documents are still regarded as the company's constitution.

Companies formed after July 1998 have a choice regarding the rules governing their internal management. Under s 134 those rules may comprise a constitution specially drafted to suit a company's particular needs, or the replaceable rules in the *Corporations Act* or a combination of both. If a company decides to have a constitution, it consists of one document. The previous division of the constitution into two documents no longer applies. In particular, the requirement to have a memorandum of association has been abolished. Most of the information that previously was required to be contained in the memorandum is now set out in a company's application for registration. This is discussed in Chapter 2 above.

If a company decides to have a constitution, it consists of one document.

statutory requirements

[4.45] Companies can adopt a constitution in any one of the following three ways:

> **a new company is regarded as having adopted a constitution on registration if the persons named in the application for the company's registration as having consented to become members, agree in writing to the terms of the constitution before the application is lodged (s 136(1)(a)); or**

> **a company that is registered without a constitution can adopt one by passing a special resolution (s 136(1)(b)); or**

> **a court order is made under s 233 (the oppression remedy discussed in Chapter 17 below) that requires the company to adopt a constitution: s 136(1)(b).**

Public companies that have a constitution are required to lodge a copy with ASIC. A copy of the constitution and relevant special resolutions must be lodged within 14 days of the company adopting or modifying the constitution: s 136(5). If a member makes a written request, a company must send a copy of its constitution to that member within seven days: s 139.

In its October 1999 Report, *Matters Arising from the Company Law Review Act 1998*, the Parliamentary Joint Committee on Corporations and Financial Services (PJC) recommended that proprietary companies should also be required to lodge a copy of their constitutions with ASIC. This recommendation has not been adopted.

contents of constitution

[4.50] Except in the case of certain types of companies, the *Corporations Act* does not prescribe what information must be contained in a company's constitution. Typically, a constitution sets out the rules governing matters such as the rights of members, the conduct of members' and directors' meetings, powers of directors and their appointment and remuneration. The replaceable rules listed in para [4.15] serve as an indication of the type of rules that are usually contained in a company's constitution.

A constitution sets out the rules governing matters such as the rights of members, the conduct of members' and directors' meetings, powers of directors and their appointment and remuneration.

If a company limited by guarantee wishes to omit the word "Limited" in its name, s 150(1) insists that its constitution:

> **requires the company to pursue charitable purposes only and apply its income in promoting those purposes;**
> **prohibits the company making distributions to its members and paying fees to its directors; and**
> **requires the directors to approve all other payments the company makes to directors.**

In the case of a no liability company, s 112 requires its constitution to state that its sole objects are mining purposes and that the company has no contractual right to recover calls made on its shares from a shareholder who fails to pay them.

Listed companies must have a constitution that is consistent with the ASX listing rules: ASX LR 15.11. For example, a listed company's constitution must contain provisions that facilitate electronic share trading and the CHESS electronic settlement and transfer system that the ASX operates. This is discussed in Chapter 9 below. Other examples include provisions in a constitution that

> **the company has only one class of ordinary shares (ASX LR 6.2); and**
> **shareholders have one vote per share on a poll: ASX LR 6.9.**

objects clause

[4.55] A company's constitution may contain an objects clause that identifies and restricts the businesses and activities in which the company may engage: s 125(2).

A company's constitution may contain an objects clause that identifies and restricts the businesses and activities in which the company may engage.

Prior to 1984, all companies had to have an objects clause in their constitutions. After that date, this requirement became optional. Many companies formed after 1984 still choose to include objects in their constitutions. This is often because the company was formed for particular purposes and its members do not want the company to depart from these purposes. This is usually the case where a company is formed to carry out a joint venture or a social, cultural, charitable or non-commercial purpose.

While not compulsory, a statement of the company's objects in its constitution may serve a useful function. In many ways it is like a mission statement in that it indicates to shareholders the nature of the business activities to which their funds will be devoted.

legal capacity and powers of a company

[4.60] Historically, companies were regarded as having limited legal capacity in that they were legally capable of engaging only in those businesses and activities specified in the objects clause of their constitutions. Amendments in 1983 significantly affected the rules dealing with the legal capacity of companies. Companies now have the same legal capacity as a human being.

section 124

A company has the legal capacity and powers of an individual.

[4.65] A company has the legal capacity and powers of an individual: s 124(1). This means that it is able to engage in any business or activity and may acquire and exercise rights in the same way as a natural person.

Section 124(1) also gives a company certain powers that are inapplicable to humans.

Section 124(1) also gives a company certain powers that are inapplicable to humans. It has all the powers of a body corporate, including the power to:

> **issue and cancel shares (this power does not apply to a company limited by guarantee);**
> **issue debentures;**
> **grant options over unissued shares in the company;**
> **distribute any of the company's property among members, in kind or otherwise;**
> **give security by charging uncalled capital;**
> **grant a floating charge over the company's property;**
> **arrange for the company to be registered or recognised as a body corporate in any place outside Australia; and**
> **do anything that it is authorised to do by any other law (including the law of a foreign country).**

A company's legal capacity to do something is not affected by the fact that the company's interests are not served by doing a particular thing: s 124(2). This provision ensures that the effect of the English case, *Rolled Steel Products Ltd v British Steel Corp* [1986] Ch 246, does not apply in Australia. Section 124(2) aims to protect outsiders by enabling them to enforce contracts with a company even though the contract involved an abuse of power by the company's directors or controlling shareholders.

abolition of doctrine of ultra vires

Companies were once regarded as being legally capable of engaging only in those businesses and activities set out in the objects clause.

[4.70] Historically, a company's objects clause was regarded as the most important part of its memorandum of association—a key component of the constitution. Companies were once regarded as being legally capable of engaging only in those businesses and activities set out in the objects clause. Any company contract or transaction that was not within the scope of one of its objects was referred to as "ultra vires", or beyond the power of the company. The doctrine of ultra vires stated that such contracts or transactions were void and had no legal effect: *Ashbury Railway Carriage & Iron Co v Riche* (1875) LR 7 HL 653.

The doctrine of ultra vires operated together with the doctrine of "constructive notice". This meant that people dealing with a company were regarded as being aware of a company's objects merely because they were set out in its constitution, which was lodged with the registering authority and hence available for inspection by the public. The doctrine of constructive notice has been abolished by s 130(1). A person is not taken to have information about a company merely because the information is available to the public from ASIC.

The original purpose of the doctrine of ultra vires was to protect a company's shareholders and creditors. Shareholders were considered to have a right to expect that their capital would be used only for the objects specified in the company's constitution. The doctrine aimed to protect creditors by ensuring that their loans to the company would only be used for its stated objects. Despite these purposes, a strict application of the ultra vires doctrine often resulted in the intention of the parties to a contract being thwarted by the application of a technical, unrealistic rule. It enabled both the company and the other contracting party to avoid an ultra vires contract.

The doctrine of ultra vires has been abolished by the combined effect of ss 124 and 125. The doctrine could only have application to a company whose constitution contained an objects clause or other self-imposed restriction or prohibition on the exercise of its powers. The *Corporations Act* now does not require a company to have an objects clause in its constitution. Indeed, as a result of 1998 amendments, a company does not even need a constitution as the replaceable rules may govern its internal management. All companies have the legal capacity and powers of an individual: s 124(1).

The doctrine of ultra vires has been abolished by the combined effect of ss 124 and 125.

If a company has an objects clause, s 125(2) provides that an act is not invalid merely because it is contrary to or beyond any of its objects. Further, if a company's constitution contains an express restriction or prohibition on the exercise of any of its powers, s 125(1) states that the exercise of power is not invalid merely because it is contrary to such an express restriction or prohibition. Such contraventions of a company's constitution may have other consequences even though they cannot affect the validity of the company's contracts. Allegations that a company acted contrary to its objects or other restrictions or prohibitions in the company's constitution may be an element in a legal action against the company's directors for breach of duty. A failure to comply with the constitution may also be contrary to the interests of members as a whole or oppressive and allow a member to seek a remedy under s 233. It may also allow a member to obtain an order for the winding up of the company on a just and equitable ground: s 461(1)(k).

effect of constitution and replaceable rules

contractual effect

[4.75] Section 140(1) provides that a company's constitution (if any) and any replaceable rules that apply to a company have effect as a contract between:

> **the company and each member (s 140(1)(a)); and**
> **the company and each director and company secretary (s 140(1)(b)); and**
> **a member and each other member (s 140(1)(c));**

A company's constitution (if any) and any replaceable rules that apply to a company have effect as a contract.

under which each person agrees to observe and perform the constitution and rules as far as they apply to that person.

The s 140(1) statutory contracts have certain features that depart from ordinary principles of contract law. For example, normally, only parties to a contract are bound by it. Under the s 140(1)(a) contract, however, the provisions of the constitution have the effect of a contract not only between the company and the persons listed in the application for registration as the persons who gave written consent to be members and to be bound to the terms of the constitution, but also between the company and any person who became a member after the company was registered. Further, in the case of a company that is formed with only the replaceable rules, those rules have the effect of a contract between the company and its present and future members whether or not they consented to the replaceable rules.

Ordinarily, contracts cannot be altered without the consent of all the parties. This is not the case with the s 140(1) contracts. A company may modify or repeal its constitution, or a provision of its constitution, by special resolution: s 136(2). A special resolution is also required if a company wishes to adopt a constitution to modify or replace any replaceable rules that apply to it: s 136(2). Special resolutions are defined in s 9 as resolutions passed by at least 75 per cent of the votes cast by members entitled to vote on the resolution. This means that the terms of the s 140(1)(a) and (c) contracts are alterable and the alteration will bind even those members who voted against the modification. Similarly, the terms of the s 140(1)(b) contract can be altered by a special resolution of members and the alteration will bind the company's directors and secretary: *NRMA Ltd v Snodgrass* [2001] NSWSC 76.

The main purpose of s 140 is to provide a way for the parties to the statutory contracts to enforce compliance with a company's constitution (if any) and any replaceable rules that apply.

The main purpose of s 140 is to provide a way for the parties to the statutory contracts to enforce compliance with a company's constitution (if any) and any replaceable rules that apply. For example, members can assert a breach of the s 140(1)(a) contract if a company does not comply with provisions in its constitution that apply to members. While damages are the usual remedy sought for breach of contract, this is not the case with the s 140(1) contracts. The appropriate remedy is a court injunction or declaration to enforce compliance with the constitution or applicable replaceable rules.

The contractual rights under s 140(1) do not extend to by-laws made under a power conferred by the constitution: *Wilcox v Kogarah Golf Club Ltd* (1996) 14 ACLC 415. By-laws are detailed rules by which particular constitutional powers are implemented but do not have the same status under s 140(1) as the company's constitution.

contract between company and members

Section 140(1)(a) provides that a company's constitution (if any) and any applicable replaceable rules have effect as a contract between the company and each member.

[4.80] Section 140(1)(a) provides that a company's constitution (if any) and any applicable replaceable rules have effect as a contract between the company and each member. One consequence of this is that the company can take action against its members to force them to comply with the provisions in the constitution or applicable replaceable rules where they are unwilling to do so voluntarily.

case note

In *Hickman v Kent or Romney Marsh Sheep-Breeders' Assoc* [1915] 1 Ch 881, Hickman was a member of the Kent or Romney Marsh Sheep-Breeders' Association, an incorporated non-profit-making company. He began a court action complaining of various irregularities in the affairs of the association. Clause 49 of the association's constitution, however, provided that disputes between it and its members should be referred to arbitration. Relying on this clause, the association sought to prevent Hickman's court case from proceeding. The court upheld the association's case and stayed Hickman's court case. Astbury J held that by virtue of the statutory contract in the English equivalent of s 140(1)(a), cl 49 was binding on Hickman and he was therefore obliged to refer his disputes to arbitration.

enforcement of constitution by members

Members can enforce only those provisions that confer rights on members in their capacity as members.

[4.85] While *Hickman*'s case illustrates the situation where a company enforces provisions in its constitution against a member, s 140(1)(a) also clearly has contractual effect on the company. A member is able to require the company to comply with the provisions of its constitution. However, as Astbury J noted by way of obiter in *Hickman*'s case, not all provisions in a company's constitution have contractual effect. Members can enforce only those provisions that confer rights on members in their capacity as members. Section 140(1) expresses this limitation when it says that the persons referred to in s 140(1)(a), (b) and (c) agree to observe and perform the constitution and rules *so far as they apply to that person.*

The replaceable rule in s 250E is an example of a rule that applies to members. According to s 250E(1), at a meeting of members of a company with a share capital, each member has one vote on a show of hands, and on a poll, one vote for each share they hold.

It is sometimes difficult to ascertain precisely the types of provisions in a constitution that confer rights on members in their capacity as such and are therefore capable of being enforced by them against the company. Prior to 1999 amendments, this issue was complicated by the rule in *Foss v Harbottle*. The rule prevented members from challenging internal irregularities, such as breaches of a company's constitution, if those irregularities were capable of being ratified by an ordinary resolution. An exception to the rule arose where a member sought to enforce a personal right. As discussed in Chapter 17 below, Pt 2F.1A of the *Corporations Act* permits a member to bring legal proceedings on behalf of the company with prior leave of the court. Under s 239(1), the fact that members may have ratified an internal irregularity does not mean that a member is prevented from bringing the legal proceedings.

According to *Pender v Lushington* (1877) 6 Ch D 70, members have the right to enforce provisions in a constitution entitling them to have their votes counted at a general meeting. Similarly, they have the right to enforce payment of a declared dividend: *Wood v Odessa Waterworks Co* (1889) 42 Ch D 636.

Section 1322(2) reinforces this right of members to enforce the constitution. It enables the court to invalidate a procedural irregularity that causes substantial injustice. In *Chew Investments Pty Ltd v General Corp of Australia Ltd* (1988) 6 ACLC 87, the Supreme Court of Western Australia held that a rejection of a valid demand for a poll constituted appropriate circumstances to invalidate resolutions passed at the meeting under the predecessor of s 1322(2). This power of the court is discussed in Chapter 14 below.

In *Associated World Investments Pty Ltd v Aristocrat Leisure Ltd* (1998) 16 ACLC 455, it was held that a shareholder was bound by a provision in the company's constitution which allowed the directors to require a member to dispose of shares in circumstances where the company's business was endangered.

outside capacity

[4.90] Members cannot enforce provisions in the constitution that purport to give them rights in some other capacity than that of a member, such as a solicitor or promoter.

Members cannot enforce provisions in the constitution that purport to give them rights in some other capacity than that of a member.

case note

This point is illustrated in *Eley v Positive Government Security Life Assurance Co* (1875) 1 Ex D 20. The company's constitution, drafted by Eley, provided that he was to be its permanent solicitor and could only be dismissed for misconduct. He acted as solicitor for some time, though no separate employment contract was entered into. Eley also received an allotment of shares in consideration of the work he did in forming the company. Subsequently, the company ceased to employ him. Eley brought an action for breach of contract against the company but failed. It was held that the constitution conferred no rights on a member where the member seeks to enforce a right in a capacity other than as a member. Eley was seeking to assert a right in his capacity as solicitor of the company. In order to do so, he should have entered into a separate contract independent of the constitution.

Section 232, discussed in Chapter 17 below, has to some extent reduced the importance of determining whether members are enforcing rights in their capacity as members. Under that provision, members do not have to show that a breach of the constitution (if any) or applicable replaceable rules affects them in their capacity as members. A member need only prove that a breach is contrary to the interests of members as a whole, oppressive or unfair in order to gain a remedy under that section.

non-members

A constitution does not have the effect of an enforceable contract between a company and non-members.

[4.95] A constitution does not have the effect of an enforceable contract between a company and non-members even if a constitution purports to give them rights.

case note

In *Forbes v New South Wales Trotting Club Ltd* [1977] 2 NSWLR 515 a committee of the New South Wales Trotting Club decided to exclude Forbes, a professional punter, from admission to the racetracks controlled by the club. Forbes tried to overturn this exclusion on the basis that in making its decision the committee did not comply with procedures in the company's constitution for exclusion. The court held, however, that Forbes had no case on this ground. He could not force the Club to comply with its constitution, as he was not a member of the New South Wales Trotting Club Ltd. The only rights Forbes had were that of a spectator.

contract between members

The constitution has effect as a contract between a member and each other member.

[4.100] Section 140(1)(c) provides that the constitution has effect as a contract between a member and each other member.

The s 140(1)(c) contract assumes importance where a company's constitution contains a pre-emption clause. Such clauses give shareholders rights of first refusal to buy other shareholders' shares or to sell their own shares to the remaining shareholders. Registration of transfers of shares effected in breach of a pre-emption clause is void and the register may be corrected under s 175: *Carew-Reid v Public Trustee* (1996) 14 ACLC 1106.

case note

In *Re Caratti Holding Co Pty Ltd* [1975] 1 ACLR 87, one of the clauses in the company's constitution empowered the majority shareholder to compulsorily acquire the shares of a minority shareholder. The Western Australian Supreme Court held that there was a contractual right under the predecessor of s 140(1)(c) to enforce the compulsory acquisition. Further, that clause could be enforced against the minority shareholder by either the company or the majority shareholder himself. The compulsory acquisition, however, was ultimately disallowed for other reasons, including that it was oppressive. Oppression under s 232 is discussed in Chapter 17 below.

The proprietary company replaceable rule in s 254D contains another type of pre-emption clause. It gives pre-emption rights to existing shareholders on the issue of additional shares. Under s 254D(1), before issuing shares of a particular class, the directors of a proprietary company must offer them to existing holders of shares of that class. As far as practicable, the number of shares offered to each shareholder must be in proportion to the number of shares of that class that they already hold. Non-compliance with s 254D would be a breach of the s 140(1)(a) contract and not the s 140(1)(c) contract because the shares are issued by directors on the company's behalf.

As is the case with the s 140(1)(a) contract, only those provisions in the constitution (if any) or applicable replaceable rules that apply to members in their capacity as members have effect as a contract and are hence enforceable by them.

Some disputes between members, even if related to their respective obligations as members, may fall outside s 140.

case note

In *Andy Kala Pty Ltd v E J Doherty (Northcote) Pty Ltd* (1995) 13 ACLC 1630, a dispute between members of a professional body relating to unethical poaching of clients did not come within s 140(1)(c) so as to create a legally enforceable agreement constituted by the constitution of the professional body. The dispute did not involve issues concerning the nature or incidence of the members' relationships.

contract between the company and its directors and secretary

[4.105] Section 140(1)(b) provides that a company's constitution (if any) and any replaceable rules that apply to the company have effect as a contract between the company and each director and company secretary.

A company's constitution (if any) and any replaceable rules that apply to the company have effect as a contract between the company and each director and company secretary.

As is the case with the s 140(1)(a) and (c) contracts, not every replaceable rule or provision in a company's constitution has effect as a contract between the company and its directors and secretary. Only those provisions in a company's constitution that apply to such officers have effect as a contract under s 140(1)(b). The replaceable rules in ss 198A, 201G, 201H and 202A dealing with the appointment, powers and remuneration of directors are examples of rules that apply to directors and therefore have effect as a contract under s 140(1)(b). Similarly, the s 204F replaceable rule clearly applies to a company secretary and therefore has effect as a contract between the company and the secretary.

directors' contracts of service

[4.110] It is quite common for directors to enter into separate contracts of service that are independent of the company's constitution (if any) and applicable rules. Such contracts are most frequently made when a managing director or executive director is appointed.

The fact that a company cannot be prevented from altering its constitution or displacing applicable replaceable rules as long as the correct procedure is followed has an impact on the s 140(1)(b) contract between a company and each director and secretary. For example, if the constitution contains provisions for the appointment of a specific person as a director for a nominated period, this has the effect of a contract between the company and that director. There will be a breach if the company terminates the appointment if the correct removal procedures are not followed.

If the constitution does not adequately provide a procedure for removal, the members can resolve to alter it under s 136(1) without exposing the company to liability for wrongful dismissal.

case note

In *Shuttleworth v Cox Bros & Co (Maidenhead) Ltd* [1927] 2 KB 9, the company's constitution contained a provision that appointed a person director for life. Certain grounds for removal were specified. The company altered its constitution to add an additional ground for removal, enabling a director to be removed upon a written request signed by all other directors. Such a request was signed and the director dismissed. The court rejected the argument that the clause in the constitution appointing the director created a contract that could not be varied without his consent. The court held that the clause appointing him as a director for life was subject to the statutory power given to companies to alter their constitution. In this case, the director had no separate contract independent of the constitution.

The position is different if the director has entered into a separate contract with the company. The company cannot avoid its contractual obligations by altering its constitution: *Allen v Gold Reefs of West Africa Ltd* [1900] 1 Ch 656. Sections 203C and 203D confirm that while a company has the power to remove a director, this does not deprive the director of any rights to compensation or damages.

A difficult question of construction arises if the constitution and service agreement are subject to one another.

case note

In *Carrier Australasia Ltd v Hunt* (1939) 61 CLR 534, Hunt was appointed under a service agreement to act as the company's managing director for five years. The agreement provided that his appointment could be terminated if he ceased to be a director of the company. Further, the agreement was stated to be subject to the company's articles of association. One of the articles, on the other hand, provided:

> < Subject to the provisions of any agreement for the time being subsisting the company may by extraordinary resolution remove any director before the expiration of his period of office. >

After differences arose between Hunt and the company, it amended the above article by deleting the reference to any subsisting agreement. The company then removed Hunt from the office of director and terminated the service agreement. When he sued for wrongful dismissal, the Supreme Court of New South Wales held that the company had the power to alter its articles. Nevertheless, it was liable for damages for breach of contract. When the case went on appeal, the High Court was evenly divided and consequently the decision of the Supreme Court stood. Evatt and McTiernan JJ arrived at the same decision as the Supreme Court, holding the company liable in damages because it could not avoid contractual liability on the service agreement by altering its articles. Rich and Starke JJ, however, held that as the service agreement was subject to the articles, the company had the power to alter them and Hunt had no right to damages for breach of contract.

remedies

[4.115] One issue that arises concerns the appropriate remedy that can be obtained if the company breaches an employment contract constituted by a replaceable rule such as s 201G or a provision in the constitution. Ordinarily, an injunction or declaration is the appropriate remedy where the complaint involves breach of either the s 140(1)(a) or (c) contract. This is because the member seeks to have the constitution or replaceable rule observed. However, the equitable remedies of injunction and specific performance are not granted to enforce employment contracts on unwilling parties. If this is true under s 140(1)(b), it means that directors cannot prevent the company from terminating their appointment but can only obtain damages for wrongful dismissal.

In *Southern Foundries (1926) Ltd v Shirlaw* [1940] AC 701, Lord Porter stated:

> **A company cannot be precluded from altering its articles thereby giving itself power to act upon the provisions of the altered articles—but so to act may nevertheless be a breach of contract if it is contrary to a stipulation in a contract validly made before the alteration. Nor can an injunction be granted to prevent the adoption of the new articles, and in that sense they are binding on all and sundry, but for the company to act upon them will nevertheless render it liable in damages if such action is contrary to the previous engagements of the company.**

alteration of constitution and replaceable rules

statutory requirements

[4.120] Shareholder approval is required to alter a constitution or displace a replaceable rule. A company may displace or modify any one or more of the replaceable rules that applies to it by adopting a constitution: s 135(2). A company adopts a constitution if it passes a special resolution to that effect: s 136(1)(b). A special resolution is also required to modify or repeal a constitution or a provision of a constitution: s 136(2). If the entire constitution is repealed, the company's internal management is governed by the replaceable rules.

Shareholder approval is required to alter a constitution or displace a replaceable rule.

Section 9 defines a "special resolution" as a resolution passed by at least 75 per cent of the votes cast by members entitled to vote on the resolution. In addition, s 249L(c) requires the notice of the meeting at which a special resolution is proposed to set out an intention to propose the special resolution and state the resolution.

Unless a different date is specified, a special resolution adopting, modifying or repealing a company's constitution takes effect on the date the resolution is passed: s 137(a). There are different dates of effect of special resolutions to change a constitution that involve a change of name (s 157(3)), a change of company type (s 164(5)), or a variation or cancellation of class rights (s 246D).

Section 136(5) requires a public company to lodge with ASIC a copy of a special resolution adopting, modifying or repealing its constitution within 14 days after it is passed. In addition, if a special resolution of a public company:

- **displaces a replaceable rule with a constitution, it must also lodge a copy of the constitution with ASIC within that period; or**
- **modifies its constitution, it must also lodge a copy of that modification with ASIC within that period.**

ASIC may direct a company to lodge a consolidated copy of its constitution: s 138. This ensures that ASIC's database contains a complete and up to date constitution and enhances comprehension of a constitution where there have been numerous changes.

limits on right to alter constitution

[4.125] As discussed above, shareholders have the power to alter the replaceable rules and their company's constitution by passing a special resolution to that effect. This means that the s 140(1) contracts can be altered and this will be binding on those members who may have opposed the special resolution. While members can generally vote to alter the replaceable rules and the constitution in any way they see fit, their power to do so is not unlimited. Both the *Corporations Act* and the common law impose certain limits and restrictions that seek to protect individual members and ensure that the shareholders who voted in favour of the special resolution do not abuse their powers.

Both the *Corporations Act* and the common law impose certain limits and restrictions that seek to protect individual members and ensure that the shareholders who voted in favour of the special resolution do not abuse their powers.

under the Corporations Act

[4.130] entrenching provisions. Section 136(3) recognises that a company's constitution may contain provisions (sometimes referred to as "entrenched provisions") that restrict the company's ability to modify or repeal its constitution by imposing further requirements for such alterations over and above a special resolution. Examples of such further requirements include a greater majority than 75 per cent and obtaining the consent of a particular person. An entrenched provision may itself also be entrenched: s 136(4).

There may be a number of reasons why a constitution would contain entrenching provisions. For example, a person may wish to ensure control of a company. The constitution of such a company could contain an entrenching provision that confers weighted voting rights on a particular person or the holder of a particular class of shares.

[4.135] section 140(2). Under s 140(2), a member is not bound by a modification of the constitution made after becoming a member so far as the modification:

> **requires the member to take up additional shares; or**

> **increases the member's liability to contribute to the share capital of, or otherwise to pay money to, the company; or**

> **imposes or increases a restriction on the right to transfer the shares already held by the member.**

A member will be bound by a modification to the constitution where this is agreed in writing.

In *Gambotto v WCP Ltd* (1995) 13 ACLC 342, the High Court held that the predecessor of s 140(2)(c) did not apply to an alteration of a company's constitution that forced minority shareholders to sell their shares to the majority shareholder. Such an alteration did not impose or increase restrictions on the right to transfer the shares already held by the minority shareholders. This case is further discussed below.

[4.140] variation of class rights. A further limitation on the power to alter a company's constitution occurs when its share capital is divided into shares of different classes. Frequently, the rights attached to the various classes are set out in the company's constitution. For example, s 254A(2) states that a company can issue preference shares only if certain rights attached to those shares are set out in the company's constitution (if any) or have been otherwise approved by a special resolution. Sections 246B–246G, discussed in Chapter 8 below, are designed to restrict majority shareholders from varying or cancelling class rights. As a general rule, class rights can be varied or cancelled only with the approval of a special resolution of both the company and the holders of the affected class: s 246B.

[4.145] oppression remedy. Section 232 enables members to apply to the court for a remedy if the majority votes in favour of a resolution altering the constitution or replaceable rules that is contrary to the interests of the members as a whole, oppressive, unfairly prejudicial or unfairly discriminatory to members. Section 232 is discussed in Chapter 17 below.

common law

[4.150] why are restrictions imposed? The courts have also imposed restrictions on altering a constitution. In deciding where to draw the line between valid and invalid alterations of the constitution, the courts attempt to strike a balance between the interests of majority and minority shareholders. The High Court in *Gambotto v WCP Ltd* (1995) 13 ACLC 342 explained:

> **< On the one hand, the courts have recognised that the proprietary rights attaching to shares are subject to modification, even destruction, by a special resolution altering the articles and that the power to vote is exercisable by a shareholder to his or her own advantage. On the other hand, the courts have acknowledged that the power to alter the articles should not be exercised simply for the purpose of securing some personal gain which does not arise out of the contemplated objects of the power. >**

[4.155] alteration valid unless improper or oppressive. Early cases, such as *Allen v Gold Reefs of West Africa Ltd* [1900] 1 Ch 656, asserted an alteration of the constitution was valid unless the court was satisfied that it was not "bona fide for the benefit of the company as a whole". However, the High Court in *Gambotto v WCP Ltd* (1995) 13 ACLC 342 rejected "the benefit of the company as a whole" test and applied different tests depending on whether or not an alteration involved "an actual or effective expropriation of shares or of valuable rights attaching to shares". It was held that an alteration which did not involve an expropriation of shares was valid unless it was either beyond any purpose contemplated by the constitution or oppressive. The High Court provided no illustrations of how this test would apply.

[4.160] expropriation of shares. On registration, a company's constitution may provide for the expropriation or compulsory disposal of a member's shares. If this power is exercised reasonably, the shareholder's rights are limited by the constitution and the shareholder may not have the right to be heard: *Associated World Investments Pty Ltd v Aristocrat Leisure Ltd* (1998) 16 ACLC 455. The position is different where the expropriation of shares is to be achieved by means of an alteration to the constitution.

case note

In *Gambotto v WCP Ltd* (1995) 13 ACLC 342, after a successful takeover bid of WCP, the bidder acquired over 99 per cent of its share capital and sought to alter the company's constitution so as to allow any member entitled to over 90 per cent of the issued shares to compulsorily acquire all other issued shares. This alteration was justified by the bidder on the grounds of the potential taxation and administrative cost savings.

The High Court held that where an alteration of a constitution involved an expropriation of the shares owned by the minority the alteration was valid only if the majority of shareholders proved it is:

- for a proper purpose; and
- fair in all the circumstances.

The High Court was of the opinion that an expropriation to secure taxation and administrative advantages for the majority shareholders of WCP was not for a proper purpose in relation to the expropriation of Gambotto's shares. For this reason it held that the alteration of WCP's constitution was invalid.

The High Court decided that an expropriation of shares would be for a proper purpose if it prevented the company from suffering significant detriment or harm. For example, an expropriation may be justified in the case of a shareholder that is competing with the

An expropriation of shares would be for a proper purpose if it prevented the company from suffering significant detriment or harm.

company or where this is necessary to meet legislative requirements in relation to shareholders' maximum holdings.

case note

In *Grey Eisdell Timms v Combined Auctions Pty Ltd* (1995) 13 ACLC 965, the directors of Combined Auctions, a company that was an auction house for pawnbrokers, were concerned that Grey EisdellTimms (GET), a competitor, was trying to take over the company by buying shares from its non-pawnbroker members. They convened a shareholders' meeting and a special resolution was passed amending the company's constitution so as to limit shareholdings (apart from the managing director's shares) to no more than 10 per cent of the issued capital and to expropriate shares held by non-pawnbrokers. The court applied the decision in *Gambotto v WCP Ltd* (1995) 13 ACLC 342, and held that the expropriation would only be justified if the minority's continued shareholding would be detrimental to the company and expropriation was a reasonable means of eliminating this detriment. In the circumstances, the expropriation was not justified because the fact that significant numbers of current members were not pawnbrokers meant that the alteration was not needed to protect the company's business. Further, it was oppressive because it was a means of ensuring that the managing director obtained a controlling shareholding in the company.

An alteration of a constitution that involves an expropriation of shares must be fair as well as for a proper purpose.

[4.165] fairness. An alteration of a constitution that involves an expropriation of shares must be fair as well as for a proper purpose: *Gambotto v WCP Ltd* (1995) 13 ACLC 342. Fairness in this context involves two elements.

- **the process of the expropriation must be fair. This element requires the majority to disclose all relevant information leading up to the alteration. It also requires the shares to be valued by an independent expert; and**
- **the second element of fairness is concerned with the price to be paid to the expropriated shareholders. If the price is less than the market price, it is prima facie unfair. However, the current market price is not necessarily the sole criterion of fairness. A fair price should take into account a variety of factors, including assets, market value, dividends, and the nature of the corporation and its likely future.**

The *Gambotto* requirements regarding alteration of a constitution that involve expropriations of shares also apply to alterations that attempt to remove or restrict shareholders' voting rights: *Shears v Phosphate Co-operative Co of Australia Ltd* (1989) 7 ACLC 812.

The decision in *Gambotto*'s case creates significant obstacles for majority shareholders seeking to expropriate the shares of the minority and will be rarely satisfied in practice. It is arguable that a consequence of this case could be significant disincentive for company takeovers by enabling minority shareholders to extract excessive additional amounts from takeover bidders. This is sometimes referred to as "greenmail".

The compulsory acquisition provisions of Pts 6A.1 and 6A.2, inserted in 1999, strengthen the position of majority shareholders and now make it easier for compulsory acquisitions to occur in a takeover and other situations. These provisions are discussed in Chapters 17 and 18 below.

bibliography ...

Cilliers, J & Luiz, S "Comments on the Test Determining the Validity of an Alteration of Articles of Association" (1999) 11 Aust Jnl of Corp Law 89.

Colla, A "Eliminating Minority Shareholdings—Recent Developments" (2001) 19 C & SLJ 7.

Dharmananda, K "Ultra Vires Goes Ultra Violet" (1997) 71 ALJ 622.

Fisher, C "Corporate Gifts: Some Organising Principles" (1994) 9 JIBFL 288 & 345.

Mitchell, V "The High Court and Minority Shareholders" (1995) 7 Bond LR 58.

Mitchell, V "The US Approach Towards the Acquisition of Minority Shares: Have We Anything to Learn?" (1996) 14 C & SLJ 283.

Sealy, L S "The Enforcement of Partnership Agreements, Articles of Association and Shareholder Agreements" in Finn, P D (ed). *Equity and Commercial Relationships.* LawBook Company, Sydney, 1987, Ch 4.

Walton, R "Gambotto v WCP Ltd: A Justified Reassertion of Minority Shareholder Rights or Unwelcome Step Back in Time?" (2000) 12 Aust Jnl of Corp Law 20.

Whincop, M J "Gambotto v WCP Ltd: An Economic Analysis of Alterations to Article and Expropriation Articles" (1995) 23 ABLR 276.

revision questions on the material in this chapter ...

> Please see eQuiz at **http://www.thomson.com.au/academic** for multiple choice questions and answers.

chapter five

the company's relations with outsiders

key points ...

- Since a company is regarded as an artificial legal entity separate and distinct from its members and directors it can only be represented by, or act through, individuals, either by application of the organic theory or the law of agency.
- The organic theory identifies individuals who are the "directing mind and will of the company". Such persons are the "brains" of the company and have the power to act independently with full discretion to make decisions without relying on instructions from superiors. The knowledge or intentions of persons who represent the directing mind and will of the company are attributed to the company itself.
- Companies can enter into contracts only through the intervention of individuals. In some cases the company enters into a contract directly such as where its common seal is affixed to a document, but usually companies contract via an agent acting with the company's authority who makes contracts on the company's behalf.
- Whether a company is bound by a contract made on its behalf is determined by the law of agency and the *Corporations Act* assumptions of regularity based upon the common law rule in *Turquand's* case.
- Under the *Corporations Act*, a person who has dealings with a company is entitled to rely on one or more of seven assumptions of regularity of the dealings and the company is not permitted to assert that the assumptions are incorrect.
- A person who has dealings with a company cannot rely on an assumption if that person either knew or suspected that the assumption was incorrect.

A company can only be represented by, or act through, individuals.

[5.05] In Chapter 2 above, we saw that one of the effects of registration is the creation of an artificial legal entity separate and distinct from its members. Because of the abstract nature of the corporate personality, a company can only be represented by, or act through, individuals. This creates conceptual difficulties in the context of the company's relationship with outsiders.

In many situations, the law must interpret the company's state of mind. This is particularly important in determining a company's liability for a criminal offence. A successful prosecution for most serious criminal offences requires proof of criminal intent or mens rea. While a company cannot be imprisoned, it can be fined. How, then, does one establish the necessary mens rea or criminal intent of a company?

Companies are most usually formed to carry out business ventures. This inevitably requires the company to enter into contracts with outsiders. The question then arises as to which individuals are capable of entering into the contract for the company?

There are two ways of resolving such questions. The first involves the "organic theory" where the company contracts directly in its own name. The second and more usual means arises where an agent acts for the company. This involves the application of the principles of the law of agency.

Organic theory seeks to attribute to the company the actions, state of mind, knowledge or purpose of its senior officers. In Chapter 12 below, we see that a company is divided into two constituent parts or organs: the board of directors and the general meeting of members. Wide powers of management are conferred on the board of directors. This is typical of most companies. Accordingly, when the board exercises those powers, its acts are regarded as the acts of the company. In other instances, the acts of the members in general meeting are regarded as the acts of the company. Sometimes, the board of directors delegates some of its powers to particular individuals, such as the managing director or other senior officers.

In practice, outsiders rarely deal directly with the board of directors or the members in general meeting. More frequently, their relationship with the company involves dealings with its agents or employees. Companies are capable of being bound by the acts of their agents in the same way as natural persons: s 126. This involves the application of the principles of agency law, in particular the question whether those who purport to act on the company's behalf have the authority to do so. Agency law has several distinct features in its application to companies.

the directing mind and will of a company

organic theory

[5.10] A company can act through its agents provided they have the requisite authority. Where agents have actual or apparent authority, those actions within the scope of their authority bind the company. The courts, however, recognise that the organs of a company—the board of directors and the members in general meeting—are more than mere agents. When they act within the ambit of the powers conferred on them by the company's constitution or replaceable rules, they are treated as being the company itself. This is the "organic theory" of corporate personality. The acts of the organs of a company are the acts of the company itself and their state of mind is the state of mind of the company. The organ is regarded as the directing mind and will of the company: its ego.

The acts of the organs of a company are the acts of the company itself and their state of mind is the state of mind of the company.

This organic theory is an extension of the law of agency. The person who has actual or apparent authority in some cases may be regarded as not only an agent of the company but the company itself. In *Northside Developments Pty Ltd v Registrar-General* (1990) 8 ACLC 611, Dawson J stated:

> < **The organic theory, which was originated by Lord Haldane LC in *Lennard's Carrying Co Ltd v Asiatic Petroleum Co Ltd* [1915] AC 705 at 713–714 ... has been used to impose liability upon companies beyond that which could be imposed by the application of the principles of agency alone. It is an approach which has been particularly useful in criminal cases where the liability of a company has depended upon a mental element ... But the organic theory merely extends the scope of an agent's capacity to bind a company and there must first be authority, actual or apparent. It is only then that a person may be regarded not only as the agent of a company, but also as the company itself—an organic part of it—so that "the state of mind of [the agent] is the state of mind of the company": *H L Bolton (Engineering) Co Ltd v T J Graham & Sons Ltd* at 172 per Denning LJ.** >

The organic theory is a legal fiction that allows the company to be identified with the individuals who control it. This is not always applicable. According to the High Court in *Smorgon v Australia and New Zealand Banking Group Ltd* (1976) 134 CLR 475, the organic theory can only be applied "in areas in which the ends of justice have been thought to require the attribution of mental states to corporations".

The organic theory is a legal fiction that allows the company to be identified with the individuals who control it.

case note

The expression "directing mind and will of the company" stems from the judgment of Viscount Haldane LC in *Lennard's Carrying Co Ltd v Asiatic Petroleum Co Ltd* [1915] AC 705. In that case Lennard's Carrying Co Ltd owned a ship. Lennard was the active director of the company and took an active role in the management of the ship. The ship carried oil owned by Asiatic Petroleum and, because it was in an unseaworthy state, it caught fire and its cargo was destroyed. Under s 502 of the *Merchant Shipping Act 1894*, the owner of a British ship was not liable for "any loss or damage happening without his actual fault or privity". The company sought to avoid liability to Asiatic Petroleum under this provision claiming that the loss arose not from its default but rather the default of Lennard himself. The House of Lords rejected this argument and held that Lennard's default was attributed to the company and hence it could not rely on s 502 of the Act. Viscount Haldane LC described Lennard's position with the company in the following terms:

> < A corporation is an abstraction. It has no mind of its own any more than it has a body of its own; its active and directing will must consequently be sought in the person of somebody who for some purposes may be called an agent, but who is really the directing mind and will of the corporation, the very ego and centre of the personality of the corporation. That person may be under the direction of the shareholders in general meeting; that person may be the board of directors itself, or it may be, and in some companies it is so, that that person has an authority coordinate with the board of directors given to him under the articles of association, and is appointed by the general meeting of the company, and can only be removed by the general meeting of the company ... For if Mr Lennard was the directing mind of the company, then his action must, unless a corporation is not to be liable at all, have been an action which was the action of the company itself within the meaning of s 502. >

case note

In *Meridian Global Funds Management Asia Ltd v Securities Commission* (1995) 13 ACLC 3245, the Privy Council considered whether the knowledge of a company's chief investment officer was to be attributed to the company. Lord Hoffman stated that the emphasis in determining this question was on the purpose of the attribution. In this case, the company's chief investment officer caused the company to contravene the New Zealand substantial shareholder provisions and concealed this from the company's directors. It was held that because he had authority to enter into share transactions, his knowledge of the breach was attributed to the company. The Privy Council considered that this decision was in accordance with the policy of the legislation, as otherwise a company could claim lack of knowledge as a result of its failure to properly monitor its officers and employees.

By attributing the directing mind and will of individuals to companies, the courts, in effect, lift the corporate veil to examine who is behind the company.

who is the directing mind and will?

[5.15] Whether a particular person represents the directing mind and will of a company depends on the circumstances.

the "brains" of the company

[5.20] In *H L Bolton (Engineering) Co Ltd v T J Graham & Sons Ltd* [1957] 1 QB 159, Denning LJ drew an analogy between a company and the organs of a human body. In that case one of the issues raised was whether a company could be said to have formed an intention to occupy certain premises for its own business. The intentions of the general meeting or the board of directors could not be attributed to the company in this case as these organs had not formally met to consider the question. The company's business was, however, managed by various directors. The court held that their intention was in fact the intention of the company. Denning LJ explained:

> **< A company may in many ways be likened to a human being. It has a brain and nerve centre which controls what it does. It also has hands which hold the tools and act in accordance with directions from the centre. Some of the people in the company are mere servants and agents who are nothing more than hands to do the work and cannot be said to represent the mind or will. Others are directors and managers who represent the directing mind and will of the company, and control what it does. The state of mind of these managers is the state of mind of the company and is treated by the law as such ... So here the intention of the company can be derived from the intention of its officers and agents. Whether their intention is the company's intention depends on the nature of the matter under consideration, the relative position of the officer or agent and the other relevant facts and circumstances of the case. >**

A company may in many ways be likened to a human being. It has a brain and nerve centre which controls what it does. It also has hands which hold the tools and act in accordance with directions from the centre.

management

[5.25] Senior managers may be the directing mind and will of the company.

case note

In *Tesco Supermarkets Ltd v Nattrass* [1972] AC 153, the House of Lords indicated that the directing mind can be employees of the company to whom managerial powers have been delegated. However, only those managers who are entrusted with a significant degree of freedom from supervision of higher authority are so regarded.

In that case the company owned a chain of supermarkets. At one store, a large advertisement was displayed stating that a particular item was on sale at a reduced price. When the reduced-price items had all been sold, a shop assistant put out on display the same items marked at the normal, higher price. This was not reported to the store manager and the advertisement remained in the window. On the following day, a customer saw the advertisement and tried to buy the item at the reduced price. He was informed that there were none available at the reduced price, so he paid the normal price.

The company was prosecuted for breaching the English equivalent of s 75AZC(1)(g) of the *Trade Practices Act 1974* (Cth), which prohibits the making of false or misleading statements with respect to the price of goods. Under the English legislation the company had a defence and would therefore avoid criminal liability if it could show that:

- the commission of the offence was due to the act or default of another person, and
- it had taken all reasonable precautions and exercised all due diligence to avoid the commission of the offence.

The main issue in the case was whether the store manager was "another person" for purposes of the defence. The prosecution argued that the store manager was not. It asserted that in relation to pricing, the store manager was the directing mind of the company.

The House of Lords held that the store manager did not have the necessary responsibility or control of the company's operations to be identified as the controlling mind and will of the company. For this reason the company was not liable for the act or default of one of its subordinate managers after it had done all it could to implement a proper system.

Lord Reid said:

> < Normally the board of directors, the managing director and perhaps other superior officers of a company carry out the functions of management and speak and act as the company. Their subordinates do not. They carry out orders from above and it can make no difference that they are given some measure of discretion. But the board of directors may delegate some part of their functions of management giving to their delegate full discretion to act independently of instructions from them. I see no difficulty in holding that they have thereby put such a delegate in their place so that within the scope of the delegation he can act as the company. It may not always be easy to draw the line but there are cases in which the line must be drawn. *Lennard*'s case was one of them. >

The board of directors may delegate some part of their functions of management giving to their delegate full discretion to act independently of instructions from them.

[5.30] This case has been criticised because it takes a narrow approach in imposing criminal liability on companies. The *Criminal Code*, discussed below, para [5.55], seeks to impose greater responsibility on companies by attributing criminal liability where a company authorises or permits the commission of an offence. This may arise where the corporate culture led to the non-compliance with a particular statutory provision rather than having to attribute the requisite mind and will of an officer or someone in senior management to the company.

company secretary

[5.35] In some instances the secretary may be regarded as an organ of the company so that any acts of the secretary are regarded as acts of the company. A secretary is so regarded when what he or she does is referable to the company's day to day affairs and administration.

case note

In *Donato v Legion Cabs (Trading) Co-operative Soc Ltd* (1966) 85 WN (Pt 1) (NSW) 242, the company was successfully sued for defamation arising from an untrue statement, published by its secretary, that the plaintiff had been expelled from its membership.

change in control

[5.40] In some instances, where control of the company changes, the company may change its mind and adopt the intention and purpose of its new controllers.

case note

In *FCT v Whitfords Beach Pty Ltd* (1982) 12 ATR 692, a company was formed to acquire land for the recreational purposes of its shareholders. Several years later the company was taken over by developers who arranged for the company to develop and sell the land. Tax was assessed on the profits from the sale of the land. The High Court upheld the assessment on the basis that what was done constituted the carrying on of business and hence the proceeds should be included in the company's assessable income. In arriving at that conclusion, the court considered that it was relevant to consider the purposes of the actions of the company. These purposes changed when the company engaged in commercial activities because the purpose of a company is determined by the purpose of those who control it. The controllers represented the directing mind and will of the company and their state of mind was the state of mind of the company.

the mind and will of more than one person

[5.45] Ascertaining who is the directing mind and will of a large corporation is more difficult than in the case of a company with few directors and shareholders. In large corporations, control of the company's business is typically delegated to a relatively large number of executives and managers in an organisational hierarchy. The actions and intentions of senior management are relevant to determining the state of mind of a corporation and more than one person may be regarded as its directing mind and will.

The actions and intentions of senior management are relevant to determining the state of mind of a corporation and more than one person may be regarded as its directing mind and will.

case note

In *Brambles Holdings Ltd v Carey* (1976) 2 ACLR 176, the company was engaged in a carrying business. Responsibility for ensuring that the company's vehicles complied with the relevant legislation had been delegated to three employees: the company's main driver, the heavy haulage supervisor and the operations manager. The company was charged with offences relating to the maximum loads of its vehicles. These offences occurred when the main driver was on sick leave and replaced by another who had not been properly instructed by the operations manager.

The company raised the defence of honest and reasonable mistake. It claimed that it had reasonable grounds for believing that its vehicles had not breached the relevant legislation. This was based on evidence that its heavy haulage supervisor honestly believed the vehicles were correctly loaded. On the other hand, the company's operations manager knew, or ought to have known, that proper loading instructions had not been given to the drivers. The issue was therefore whose knowledge and belief could be attributed to the company. The court upheld the convictions and decided that in the circumstances, the operations manager was the directing mind of the company. Bray CJ stated:

> < ... in my view, it is a fallacy to say that any state of mind to be attributed to a corporation must always be the state of mind of one particular officer alone and that the corporation can never know or believe more than that one man knows or believes. This cannot be so when it is a case of successive holders of the office in question or of the holder of the office and his deputy or substitute during his absence. >

aggregated knowledge

[5.50] In some situations separate pieces of information known by several people can be aggregated and attributed to their company. In *Brambles Holdings Ltd v Carey* (1976) 2 ACLR 176, Bray CJ said:

In some situations separate pieces of information known by several people can be aggregated and attributed to their company.

> **< Let us suppose that a piece of information, x, is conveyed to one officer of the company, A. Then A goes on holidays and B takes his place and a further piece of**

> **information, y, is communicated to him. It is a fallacy to say that the company does not know both x and y because A only knows x and B only knows y. As a matter of fact, it may well be B's duty when he is told about y to find out about x ... I hasten to add that although I think a corporation has in a proper case the combined knowledge or belief possessed by more than one of its officers, that does not mean that it can know or believe two contradictory things at once. It is rational belief, not schizophrenia, which is to be attributed to it.** >

The knowledge of various company officers may not be aggregated where information has not been communicated to a company officer in the normal way. It may become important to ascertain precisely when the information is communicated within the company so that the company is taken to possess knowledge of the aggregated information.

case note

In *Re Chisum Services Pty Ltd* (1982) 1 ACLC 292, one of the issues was whether a bank had reason to suspect that a customer was insolvent at the time the customer repaid a bank loan. At the time of the payment the bank's branch manager was unaware of information published in *Dun's Gazette* that a petition to wind up the company had been presented. The branch manager was aware the company was experiencing financial difficulties but did not believe it was insolvent. However, the *Dun's Gazette* had been received by and noted by officers at the bank's head office. While they were unaware of the company's financial straits, the liquidator argued that the knowledge and beliefs of the branch manager and the officers at the head office could be combined and together indicated that the bank had the necessary suspicions. Separately, these pieces of information would not necessarily have amounted to a suspicion of insolvency.

The court held that there was no "super mind" identified with the legal personality of the bank that would allow the knowledge of its various officers to be aggregated for the purpose of ascertaining its state of mind. In a large company, like a bank, the proper approach was to follow the established lines of communication in order to ascertain when, and in what manner, information would in the normal course be disseminated to its various officers and thus be attributed to the company. If head office had information that it was required to communicate to its branches, the bank could only be said to be aware of it when, in the normal course of events, the information would have been received by the branch.

criminal liability of companies

Companies are subject to the criminal law in much the same way as individuals.

[5.55] Companies are subject to the criminal law in much the same way as individuals. At common law a company may be liable for criminal offences in either one of two ways. It may assume primary criminal liability where an offence is committed by its directing mind. This is an application of the organic theory discussed above. In such cases, the prosecution must prove that the illegal acts were committed and mens rea must be shown to exist. "Mens rea" means that the defendant had the intention to commit the criminal act, or had knowledge that the act was unlawful. Where the accused is a company, the mental state of those persons who control and manage it is attributed to the company. Consequently, if the directing mind of a company commits an unlawful act with the necessary criminal intention, the company will be guilty.

The common law principles relating to criminal offences have been replaced by the *Criminal Code*, contained in the Schedule of the *Criminal Code Act 1995*. The aim of the *Criminal Code* is to codify the principles of criminal responsibility under Commonwealth laws such as the *Corporations Act*.

Under s 12.1(2) of the *Criminal Code*, a body corporate may be found guilty of any offence, including one punishable by imprisonment. While a company cannot be imprisoned, it can be fined. Section 4B of the *Crimes Act 1914* enables a fine to be imposed for offences that only specify imprisonment as a penalty.

A body corporate may be found guilty of any offence, including one punishable by imprisonment.

The common law approach described above limited the criminal liability of companies to those actions which could be traced to highly placed persons whose mind and will could be attributed to the company. This is illustrated by the *Tesco Supermarket* case discussed above, para [5.20]. This approach was seen as too narrow and did not impose appropriate criminal responsibilities on companies.

Section 3.1(1) of the *Criminal Code* specifies that a criminal offence consists of physical elements (defined in ss 4.1–4.3) and fault elements (defined in ss 5.1–5.6). A physical element of an offence includes conduct or the result of conduct. A fault element for a particular physical element may be intention, knowledge, recklessness or negligence.

A criminal offence consists of physical elements and fault elements.

Under s 12.2 of the *Criminal Code*, a physical element of an offence is attributed to a company if it is committed by an employee, agent or officer of the company acting within the actual or apparent scope of their employment or within their actual or apparent authority. This is wider than the *Tesco Supermarket* directing mind and will principle which limited a company's liability where the physical element of a criminal offence was committed by a senior manager who is its directing mind and will.

A fault element in relation to a physical element of an offence must be attributed to a company that expressly, tacitly or impliedly authorised or permitted the commission of the offence: s 12.3(1). The means by which such authorisation or permission may be established are set out in s 12.3(2) and include:

> **proving that the board of directors or a high managerial agent intentionally, knowingly or recklessly carried out the relevant conduct or expressly, tacitly or impliedly authorised or permitted the commission of the offence. This does not apply if the body corporate can prove that it exercised due diligence to prevent the conduct, authorisation or permission of the high managerial agent;**
> **proving that a corporate culture existed within the body corporate that directed, encouraged, tolerated or led to non-compliance with the relevant provision; and**
> **proving that a body corporate failed to create and maintain a corporate culture that required compliance with the relevant provision.**

Section 12.3(6) of the *Criminal Code* defines the expressions "high managerial agent" and "corporate culture" used in s 12.3(2). "High managerial agent" is an employee, agent or officer with duties of such responsibility that their conduct may fairly be assumed to represent the body corporate's policy. "Corporate culture" means an attitude, policy, rule, course of conduct or practice existing within the body corporate generally or in that part of it in which the relevant activities take place.

Section 3.1(2) of the *Criminal Code* recognises that a law that creates an offence may provide that there is no fault element for one or more physical elements. This is the case of the *Corporations Act* which contains numerous offences that are characterised as either offences of strict liability or absolute liability.

A strict liability offence is one that has no fault elements for any of the physical elements: s 6.1(1)(a). The defence of mistake of fact under s 9.2 is available for strict liability offences: s 6.1(1)(b).

A strict liability offence is one that has no fault elements for any of the physical elements. The defence of mistake of fact is available for strict liability offences.

A mistake of fact defence arises if, at the time of the conduct constituting the physical element, the accused person was under a mistaken but reasonable belief about those facts and had those facts existed, the conduct would not have constituted an offence.

Under s 12.5(1) of the *Criminal Code* a company can only rely on the mistake of fact defence if:

> **the employee, agent or officer of the company who carried out the conduct was under a mistaken but reasonable belief about the facts that, had they existed, would have meant that the conduct would not have constituted an offence; and**

> **the company proves that it exercised due diligence to prevent the conduct. A failure to exercise due diligence may be evidenced by the fact that the prohibited conduct was substantially attributable to inadequate corporate management, control or supervision of the company's employees, agents or officers or the failure to provide adequate systems for conveying relevant information to relevant people in the company.**

An absolute liability offence is one that has no fault elements for any of the physical elements and the defence of mistake of fact is unavailable.

An absolute liability offence is one that has no fault elements for any of the physical elements and the defence of mistake of fact is unavailable: s 6.2(1).

liability of companies in tort

A company, like any employer, is vicariously liable for the torts committed by its employees in the course of their employment. Similarly, a company, as principal, is liable for the torts committed by its agents acting within the scope of their actual or apparent authority.

[5.60] A company, like any employer, is vicariously liable for the torts committed by its employees in the course of their employment. Similarly, a company, as principal, is liable for the torts committed by its agents acting within the scope of their actual or apparent authority: *Lloyd v Grace Smith & Co* [1912] AC 716. Thus, a company may be vicariously liable for the negligence or fraud of its employees, committed in the course of their employment. It is on this basis that companies are usually liable in tort.

Damages in favour of a company may be reduced on the grounds of contributory negligence by the company where its directors or management were negligent.

case note

In *Daniels v Anderson* (1995) 13 ACLC 614, a company was awarded damages arising from the negligence of its auditors. The auditors obtained a deduction of damages because of the company's contributory negligence. It was held that the negligent acts of management should be treated as acts of the company for the purposes of a finding of contributory negligence.

This conclusion was reached on two grounds. The company was vicariously liable for the negligence of its management. It was also liable because its directors almost wholly delegated the task of setting up and operating a foreign exchange operation to management and failed to monitor and control this operation.

Section 128(3) codifies the common law rule regarding the vicarious liability of companies for the fraudulent acts of their servants and agents. That section ensures that a company does not escape liability for the acts of its officers, agents or employees just because they have acted fraudulently, if the company would otherwise have been liable for their acts. Section 128(3) is discussed further below, para [5.210].

Unlike its vicarious liability for the criminal acts of its employees, there are no restrictions on the type of torts for which a company may be held vicariously liable. Because of this, the courts have not often found it necessary to apply the organic theory to the law of torts, though there is no reason in principle why the concept of the "directing mind" should not apply to such cases. Indeed, the *Lennard's Carrying Co Ltd v Asiatic Petroleum Co Ltd* [1915] AC 705 case is an instance of the company's primary liability in tort.

contracts with the company

[5.65] A company, being an abstract entity, can enter into contracts only through the intervention of humans. At common law, a company could only contract directly by affixing its common seal to a contract in accordance with its constitution. While entering a contract in this way is still permitted, s 123(1) indicates that it is optional for a company to have a common seal and under s 126(1), a company's power to make a contract may be exercised by an individual acting with the company's expressed or implied authority and on its behalf. This power may be exercised without using a common seal.

A company's power to make a contract may be exercised by an individual acting with the company's expressed or implied authority and on its behalf.

The rules of general agency law are applicable in cases where an agent acts on behalf of a company. However, because of the nature of companies, the law of agency is modified to take into account some specific problems that may arise in this context.

The rules of general agency law are applicable in cases where an agent acts on behalf of a company.

At common law, contracts made by an agent could only bind the company as principal if they were within the objects of the company as stated in its constitution. Contracts outside the scope of the company's objects are ultra vires and were once not binding on either the company or the other contracting party. Section 125(2), however, provides that an act of a company is not invalid merely because it is outside any objects in the company's constitution. This is discussed in Chapter 4 above.

Where the acts of an agent were carried out where the internal proceedings of a company had not been properly carried out, the common law rule in *Turquand's* case operated in favour of outsiders who were able to assume that the internal proceedings of a company had been properly carried out. This prevented a company from relying on an internal irregularity to avoid a contract. This rule was subject to certain exceptions where the outsider did not act bona fide.

The rule in *Turquand's* case has been largely replaced by the statutory assumptions an outsider is entitled to make under s 129. These assumptions are based on the common law rule and are subject to the limitations contained in s 128(4). These limitations are based upon the common law exceptions to the rule in *Turquand's* case but appear to differ in some respects.

execution of documents

[5.70] A company is able to enter into a contract directly by executing a contractual document. This involves directors or other authorised persons signing the document as an act of the company. In *195 Crown St Pty Ltd v Hoare* [1969] 1 NSWR 193, Asprey JA explained that:

A company is able to enter into a contract directly by executing a contractual document.

> < **The execution of a document by a company ... resembles the execution of a document by a natural person who cannot write except through the medium of someone else who signs the disabled person's name at his request and direction. An authorised signatory of a company's document when acting under this section is the company's amanuensis.** >

common seal

[5.75] Historically, a company could only execute a document by affixing its common seal in accordance with its constitution. As a result of 1998 amendments, common seals are optional.

Under s 127(2), a company with a common seal may execute a document by affixing its common seal to a document and the fixing of the seal is witnessed by the appropriate officers. These are:

Under s 127(2), a company with a common seal may execute a document by affixing its common seal to a document and the fixing of the seal is witnessed by the appropriate officers.

- two directors of the company; or
- a director and a company secretary; or
- for a proprietary company that has a sole director who is also the sole company secretary—that director.

In *Northside Developments Pty Ltd v Registrar-General* (1990) 8 ACLC 611, Mason CJ stated:

> < **The affixing of the seal to an instrument makes the instrument that of the company itself; the affixing of the seal is in that sense a corporate act, having effect similar to a signature by an individual, as I noted earlier. Thus, it may be said that a contract executed under the common seal evidences the assent of the corporation**

itself and such a contract is to be distinguished from one made by a director or officer on behalf of the company, that being a contract made by an agent on behalf of the company as principal. >

Company constitutions often set out provisions regarding the use of the company seal. Typically, a constitution will provide that the seal may be used only with the authority of the company's board of directors.

The common seal of a company must set out the company's name and its Australian Company Number (ACN) or its Australian Business Number (ABN): s 123(1).

If the company seal is affixed to a contract that does not have to be sealed and the affixing or witnessing of the seal is not in compliance with the constitution, the contract may still be binding on the company.

case note

In *MYT Engineering Pty Ltd v Mulcon Pty Ltd* (1999) 17 ACLC 861 the company seal was affixed to a deed of company arrangement and witnessed by one person although the constitution required the affixing of the seal to be signed by a director and countersigned by another director or secretary. The deed was validly executed by the company as the members of the company and members of the board authorised the director to do so and agreed the instrument should be executed.

A company may also have a duplicate common seal: s 123(2). This is useful where a company conducts business in various States.

The affixing of the seal may be void or unenforceable if the attesting directors or secretary act without authority. The circumstances where this may occur are discussed below, para [5.165].

execution without common seal

A company may also execute a document without using a common seal if two directors or a director and a company secretary sign the document.

[5.80] A company may also execute a document without using a common seal if two directors or a director and a company secretary sign the document: s 127(1).

one person proprietary companies

[5.85] A sole director may witness the fixing of the seal of a proprietary company that has only one director who is also the sole secretary: s 127(2). Similarly, under s 127(1), a proprietary company with a sole director who is also the sole secretary may execute a document without using a common seal by that person signing the document on the company's behalf.

As a result of changes made in 1999, a proprietary company is not required to have a secretary. A proprietary company may now be formed with just one director who is also the sole shareholder. Section 127 was not amended to deal with such companies and does not cover execution of documents by one person proprietary companies that do not have a secretary.

significance of s 127

Section 127(4) provides that a company can execute documents in other ways than those specified in s 127(1) and (2).

[5.90] Despite the fact that s 127(4) provides that a company can execute documents in other ways than those specified in s 127(1) and (2), executing documents in accordance with s 127(1) and (2) protects outsiders. If a company executes a document in accordance with s 127(1) or (2), persons dealing with the company are entitled to rely on s 129 (5) or (6) and assume that documents have been duly executed by the company, even if this is not true. The s 129(5) and (6) assumptions are discussed below, para [5.165].

contracts made by agents

[5.95] Section 126 allows a company to contract through an agent. When this is the case, the law of agency together with the overlapping rules in ss 128–130 govern the company's contractual rights and obligations. This may involve the important question of whether the agent had the requisite authority to bind the company.

Section 126 allows a company to contract through an agent.

A company will be bound by the acts of its agents in the same way as any other principal. The rules of agency law therefore apply to companies. Agency in the context of company contracts is discussed below at para [5.110].

An agent's acts bind the principal to a contract with an outsider in a number of ways. Those that concern us here are agency created by:

> **actual authority; and**
> **apparent or ostensible authority.**

Agency created by ratification of contracts made before registration is discussed in Chapter 6 below.

actual authority

[5.100] An agent who enters into a contract on the principal's behalf binds the principal to the contract with an outsider if the contract is within the scope of the agent's actual authority, whether express or implied. In this situation there are two relationships—the agency relationship between the principal and the agent, and a contract between the principal and outsider. There is no contractual relationship between the agent and the outsider. Having brought the principal and outsider into a contractual relationship, the agent drops out of the picture.

An agent who enters into a contract on the principal's behalf binds the principal to the contract with an outsider if the contract is within the scope of the agent's actual authority,

An agent's actual authority may derive from a principal expressly giving the agent authority to enter into particular contracts on the principal's behalf. This type of authority is referred to as express actual authority. A common example of an agent with such authority is a person to whom a power of attorney has been granted. A power of attorney is the appointment of an agent by deed. The extent of the attorney's actual authority is usually set out in the document that creates the power.

An agent may also have implied actual authority. The extent of this authority, though actual, is not expressly agreed upon as between the agent and the principal. The authority is implied from the conduct of the parties and the circumstances. Implied actual authority most frequently arises when an agent is placed in a particular position by the principal. For example, an agent who is appointed to manage a business has implied authority to make all those contracts that a manager in such a position customarily has: *Hely-Hutchinson v Brayhead Ltd* [1968] 1 QB 549.

In *Brick and Pipe Industries Ltd v Occidental Life Nominees Pty Ltd* (1992) 10 ACLC 253, a director was taken to have implied actual authority to act as the company in the circumstances because he held a controlling shareholding and assumed the role of managing director with the acquiescence of the other directors. Transactions were generally entered into without prior reference to the board and no attempt was made to interfere with this assertion of control.

Kirby P in a dissenting judgment in *Equiticorp Finance Ltd v Bank of New Zealand* (1993) 11 ACLC 952, suggested that the scope of an agent's implied actual authority should be restricted to making contracts that are apparently in the best interests of the company and not detrimental to it.

apparent or ostensible authority

[5.105] An agent's apparent or ostensible authority (the terms "apparent" and "ostensible" authority have the same meaning) arises if a principal gives the impression that an agent has authority to act on the principal's behalf. It does not depend on any agreement between principal and agent.

An agent's apparent or ostensible authority arises if a principal gives the impression that an agent has authority to act on the principal's behalf.

It is quite rare for an outsider to know whether an agent has actual authority and the extent of that authority. Usually, all the outsider relies on is the appearance of authority. Depending on the circumstances, the extent of an agent's apparent authority may be the same as the agent's actual authority or it may exceed the scope of the agent's actual authority. In some situations a person may have apparent authority to enter contracts for a principal even though that person does not have actual authority to contract.

If an agent's apparent authority can be proved it creates an agency by estoppel.

If an agent's apparent authority can be proved it creates an agency by estoppel. This means that as between principal and outsider, the principal is prevented (or estopped) from asserting that the agent lacked authority. An agency by estoppel creates a contract between the principal and outsider in the same way as a contract is created by an agent with actual authority.

Apparent authority arises when:

> **the principal represents or holds out to the outsider that the agent has the requisite authority to make particular contracts on the principal's behalf; and**
> **the outsider relies on the principal's representation to enter into the contract with the agent who is purportedly acting on the principal's behalf.**

The principal must make the representation of the agent's authority to the outsider. A principal is not liable merely on the representations of the agent.

The principal must make the representation of the agent's authority to the outsider. A principal is not liable merely on the representations of the agent.

The principal may expressly make the representation to the outsider. It is more usual for the representation to arise by the principal's conduct. A representation by conduct may take either one of two forms:

> **It may arise when the principal permits the agent to occupy a particular position. In such cases the principal represents or holds out that the agent has the customary authority of a person in such a position. In this respect it is similar to an agent with implied actual authority resulting from the position occupied.**
> **It may also arise when the principal's conduct permits the agent to carry out particular tasks on the principal's behalf that are beyond the scope of the agent's customary authority. For example, a bookkeeper in an accounting firm would act beyond the job's customary authority by purchasing office equipment. But if the employer holds out to the equipment supplier that the bookkeeper had such authority, the employer would be liable as principal in respect of such purchases.**

authority of the company's agents

A company may enter into a contract either through an organ such as its board of directors or by means of an authorised agent such as an officer or employee.

[5.110] A company may enter into a contract either through an organ such as its board of directors or by means of an authorised agent such as an officer or employee. Where a contract is entered into directly by the board and the constitution or replaceable rules authorise the board to act in this way, questions of authority of the board to enter into the contract may arise if there was an irregularity such as a failure to comply with the constitution or replaceable rules. This may occur if, for example, the particular meeting of the board was not properly convened, a quorum was not present, members of the board were not properly appointed or the required officers did not attest the company seal.

Where such irregularities occur, a balance of interests arises. An outsider dealing with a company is generally protected where an irregularity arises which is internal to the company. However, in some cases such protection may unduly facilitate fraud at the expense of innocent shareholders and creditors of the company.

Where the board has delegated its powers to a managing director, a committee of directors or another officer or agent, a question may arise whether the particular contract was within the authority of the person to whom the power was delegated.

the doctrine of constructive notice

[5.115] The constitutions of public companies must be lodged with ASIC: s 136(5). One consequence of this requirement is that the constitution is available for public inspection. If the constitution contains a limitation on the authority of the company's organs, officers or agents, the common law deemed this limitation to be known by an outsider dealing with the company. This was known as "the doctrine of constructive notice".

The doctrine of constructive notice has now largely been abolished by s 130(1). It now applies only with respect to documents relating to registrable company charges: s 130(2). This is discussed in Chapter 11 below.

the rule in Turquand's case

The rule in *Turquand*'s case states that even though persons dealing with a company are taken to have constructive notice of the contents of the company's public documents, they need not go further to ensure that the internal proceedings of the company have been properly carried out and can assume that these proceedings were properly carried out.

[5.120] At common law, the doctrine of constructive notice imposed difficulties on outsiders dealing with companies. However, under the rule in *Turquand*'s case this doctrine did not operate where the directors or other agents of a company acted outside their authority but this was not apparent from the constitution or other public documents of the company. The rule in *Turquand*'s case states that even though persons dealing with a company are taken to have constructive notice of the contents of the company's public documents, they need not go further to ensure that the internal proceedings of the company have been properly carried out and can assume that these proceedings were properly carried out.

The company cannot rely upon the rule as its purpose is to protect outsiders, not the company: *Hughes v NM Superannuation Pty Ltd* (1993) 11 ACLC 923. According to Lord Simonds in *Morris v Kanssen* [1946] AC 459, the rule is "designed for the protection of those who are entitled to assume, just because they cannot know, that the person with whom they deal has the authority which he claims".

case note

In *Royal British Bank v Turquand* (1856) 6 E & B 327; 119 ER 886, the deed of settlement (the equivalent of the constitution of a company) empowered the board of directors to borrow such sums as were authorised by a resolution of the general meeting of the shareholders. The company borrowed money from a bank on the authority of two of its directors who authenticated the company's common seal. There was no authority given by the general meeting. The company refused to repay the loan and argued that the bank had constructive notice of the constitution and should have been aware of the lack of authority. It was held that an outsider need not inquire into whether such a resolution had in fact been passed. The company was still bound to the bank because the passing of the resolution was a matter internal to the company.

The rule in *Turquand*'s case protects an outsider where, for example, there is an irregularity concerning the proper holding of a meeting. A quorum may not have been present, inadequate notice may have been given or a voting irregularity may have occurred. The rule also operates in situations where the common seal is not affixed in accordance with the constitution or the board is not properly constituted. In these cases, an outsider can assume the constitution has been complied with and hold the company liable.

The rule in *Turquand*'s case has been adopted by s 129(1), which entitles outsiders to assume that the constitution of a company and any applicable replaceable rules have been complied with. Aspects of the rule in *Turquand*'s case also form the basis of the other statutory assumptions contained in s 129. The exception contained in s 128(4) is worded differently to the common law exceptions to the rule in *Turquand*'s case although in many cases it has a similar operation.

exceptions to the rule in Turquand's case

The rule in *Turquand*'s case is subject to several exceptions.

[5.125] The rule in *Turquand*'s case is subject to several exceptions. The most significant of these arise where the outsider has actual knowledge of the irregularity or is put upon inquiry by the circumstances of the case and fails to make inquiries. Where these exceptions apply, the outsider loses the protection of the rule.

Mason CJ considered the reasons behind the rule in *Turquand's* case and its exceptions in *Northside Developments Pty Ltd v Registrar-General* (1990) 8 ACLC 611.

> **< What is important is that the principle and the criterion which the rule in *Turquand's* case presents for application give sufficient protection to innocent lenders and other persons dealing with companies, thereby promoting business convenience and leading to just outcomes. The precise formulation and application of that rule calls for a fine balance between competing interests. On the one hand, the rule has been developed to protect and promote business convenience which would be at hazard if persons dealing with companies were under the necessity of investigating their internal proceedings in order to satisfy themselves about the actual authority of officers and the validity of instruments. On the other hand, an over-extensive application of the rule may facilitate the commission of fraud and unjustly favour those who deal with companies at the expense of innocent creditors and shareholders who are the victims of unscrupulous persons acting or purporting to act on behalf of companies. >**

case note

The operation of the rule in *Turquand's* case and the inquiry exception was applied by the High Court in *Northside Developments Pty Ltd v Registrar-General* (1990) 8 ACLC 611. The common seal of Northside was affixed to a mortgage document that secured a loan from Barclays to a company controlled by Sturgess, a director and shareholder of Northside. The mortgage was over land owned by Northside which was its only major asset. The common seal was affixed and signed by Sturgess as director and by his son who purported to sign as the company secretary. The son had not been appointed under the constitution although lodged documents named him as the company secretary. The other two directors, who were also the remaining shareholders, did not know of or authorise the execution of the mortgage, nor did they know of the purported appointment of the secretary. They had no interest in the borrowing company and Northside derived no benefit from the transactions.

The High Court considered the validity of the mortgage. This depended upon whether it had been executed by Northside. The case was decided under the common law rules because the mortgage was purportedly executed in 1979, prior to the inclusion of the predecessors of ss 128–130 into the legislation.

The High Court held that Northside was not bound by the mortgage because the affixing of the common seal was invalid. Although the rule in *Turquand's* case enabled Barclays to assume that the common seal was properly affixed and the internal proceedings of the company had been properly carried out in accordance with its constitution, the circumstances of the case should have put Barclays upon inquiry. Because Barclays failed to make further inquiries as to whether the common seal was properly affixed it was unable to rely on the rule in *Turquand's* case and Northside was not bound by the mortgage.

The circumstance that put Barclays upon inquiry was that the mortgage secured Northside's major asset where the transactions were outside its usual business and not for its benefit. Barclays was prevented from relying on the rule in *Turquand's* case because it ought to have suspected an irregularity. Barclays did not have to have actual knowledge of the lack of authority of Sturgess and his son to affix the company seal.

actual authority of company agents

[5.130] Where an outsider contracts with an agent of a company, the company is bound if the agent has actual authority in the same way as any other principal is bound. An agent's actual authority may arise expressly or by implication. It arises by implication when the company appoints the agent to occupy a particular office. Unless expressly limited, the agent's implied actual authority extends to all those acts that are customarily done by persons occupying that office. For example, the replaceable rule contained in s 201J permits the directors to appoint a managing director for the period, and on the terms (including remuneration) as they see fit. In addition, under the replaceable rule in s 198C the directors may confer on a managing director any of the powers that the directors can exercise. The express actual authority of a managing director will consist of the powers conferred on that person by the board. A managing director's implied actual authority will also consist of the customary powers and authority of persons occupying the office of managing director provided those customary powers are not inconsistent with the managing director's express actual authority.

Unless expressly limited, the agent's implied actual authority extends to all those acts that are customarily done by persons occupying that office.

The customary authority of managing directors and other officers of a company is discussed below, para [5.175].

In some cases, the courts will regard a de facto managing director as having actual authority to manage the business of the company. This may arise where a dominant director acts with the acquiescence of the board. In such a case the mind and will of the director is attributed to the company. Such a person could then bind the company and hold out as the company that someone else had apparent authority in relation to a particular dealing. This conferral of authority may be informal and based on previous dealings between the parties: *Brick and Pipe Industries Ltd v Occidental Life Nominees Pty Ltd* (1992) 10 ACLC 253. Just because a director acts in a dominant way, does not necessarily mean that actual authority is conferred, especially in the absence of knowledge or acquiescence of the board regarding the director's activities or where the constitution has not been complied with.

case note

In *National Australia Bank Ltd v Sparrow Green Pty Ltd* (1999) 17 ACLC 1665, a finance agreement and a debenture deed were executed by the only active director of a company. He signed the documents as a sole director and company secretary. The other director had agreed to step aside from management before the negotiations leading to the finance agreements began. The company's constitution provided for at least two directors and the affixing of the company seal required the signatures of two directors or a director and secretary. A copy of the constitution was provided to the bank. Soon after the company went into liquidation and the liquidator claimed that the company was not bound by the finance agreements.

It was held that the remaining director did not have actual or apparent authority to bind the company. Actual authority could only be conferred through the constitution or by resolution of the board. In this case, the management of the company vested in the board, not a single director.

apparent authority of company agents

[5.135] Outsiders, however, are rarely aware of the extent of an agent's actual authority but they rely on the agent's apparent or ostensible authority. Where the agent acts within the scope of this authority, the company is also bound by the agent's actions. We saw earlier that for apparent authority to arise, the principal must represent or hold out to the outsider that the agent had authority in relation to the contract and the outsider was induced by this representation of authority to enter into the contract.

The rules relating to apparent authority have special features when the principal is a company. This stems from the fact that the company is an artificial entity that can only act through humans. The question arises: who can hold out for the company by making representations of authority to outsiders on the company's behalf so as to bind the company?

The rules relating to apparent authority have special features when the principal is a company.

Where full management powers are bestowed on the board of directors by the constitution or replaceable rules, the board is the organ that is capable of making the necessary representations of authority. Outsiders, however, rarely negotiate contracts with the board. They usually deal with persons to whom the board has delegated the necessary authority, for example the managing director. When this is the case, the managing director possesses actual authority to do those things concerned with management, and also has apparent authority to bind the company to contracts within the scope of the management powers. The representation by the company, through its organ, the board of directors, is established by the fact that the company has appointed a person to occupy the position of managing director with all the customary powers that accompany that office.

In some instances an outsider may deal with a person who acts as a managing director but who has either not actually been appointed to that position or whose appointment is defective in some way. The defect in the appointment may arise because the resolution of the board making the purported appointment is invalid for any number of reasons, such as there was no quorum present. The defect may also arise if the board fails to formally appoint at all, or the term of appointment has expired and a person is allowed to continue to act as the managing director.

case note

In *Freeman and Lockyer v Buckhurst Park Properties (Mangal) Ltd* [1964] 2 QB 480, Kapoor and Hoon formed a company for the purpose of developing a property. They each held half the issued shares and together with a nominee of each, comprised the board of directors. The quorum of the board was four, but at all material times, Hoon was overseas. Kapoor acted as managing director with the approval of the board, although he had not actually been appointed to that position.

Kapoor engaged a firm of architects and surveyors on behalf of the company. The firm brought an action claiming payment for work carried out when the company refused to pay its fees. It was held that the company had held out that Kapoor was its managing director and was therefore bound by his actions. He had apparent authority to employ the architects because this was within the customary authority of a managing director. Because the outsiders had relied on the apparent authority of the managing director, they did not have to examine the company's constitution or inquire whether the managing director had been properly appointed.

Diplock LJ examined the law of agency as it applies to contracts with companies where the agent does not have actual authority. He concluded:

It must be shown that a representation that the agent had authority to enter on behalf of the company into a contract was made by a person or persons who had "actual" authority to manage the business of the company either generally or in respect of those matters to which the contract relates.

> < If the foregoing analysis of the relevant law is correct, it can be summarised by stating four conditions which must be fulfilled to entitle a contractor to enforce against a company a contract entered into on behalf of the company by an agent who had no actual authority to do so. It must be shown: (a) that a representation that the agent had authority to enter on behalf of the company into a contract of the kind sought to be enforced was made to the contractor; (b) that such representation was made by a person or persons who had "actual" authority to manage the business of the company either generally or in respect of those matters to which the contract relates; (c) that he (the contractor) was induced by such representation to enter into the contract, that is, that he in fact relied on it; and (d) that under its memorandum or articles of association the company was not deprived of the capacity either to enter into a contract of the kind sought to be enforced or to delegate authority to enter into a contract of that kind to the agent. (Condition (d) does not apply in Australia: s 125(2).) >

In *Freeman and Lockyer* the representation that Kapoor had authority was made by the board, which had actual authority to manage the affairs of the company. This was so, even though the board had made no formal decision to that effect. The representation arose because the board failed to prevent him from acting as if he were the company's managing director.

In some instances such a representation may be made by a person who lacks actual authority. The representation then may not be sufficient to create an agent's apparent authority.

case note

In *Crabtree-Vickers Pty Ltd v Australian Direct Mail Advertising & Addressing Co Pty Ltd* (1976) 50 ALJR 203, Australian Direct Mail (ADM) was a family company. Its directors were Bruce McWilliam Senior, his son, Bruce McWilliam Junior, and their wives. The wives, however, took no active role in the company's affairs. Another son, Peter McWilliam, was employed by the company but was not a director. A committee consisting of Bruce Senior, Bruce Junior and Peter, collectively managed the company's affairs. The company's constitution provided for the appointment of a managing director by the board. While Bruce Junior was given that title, he had never been formally appointed. It was found that he had no actual authority to manage the company's business, despite his title.

Peter negotiated a contract to buy machinery from Crabtree-Vickers. ADM's own order form was used and signed by Peter on Bruce Junior's behalf. ADM, however, refused to go ahead with the contract and argued that while Peter had authority to obtain quotations he was not authorised to finalise the agreement on the company's behalf. There was evidence that Bruce Junior had held out to the other contracting party that Peter had the necessary authority to finalise the contract for their company.

The High Court applied the reasoning of Diplock LJ in *Freeman and Lockyer* and held that as Peter had no actual authority to finalise the contract, the outsider could only succeed if it could establish that he had apparent authority to do this. This it could not do. The representation of Peter's authority came from his brother, Bruce Junior, who himself lacked actual authority. At most, Bruce Junior had apparent authority to do those things concerned with management arising from the fact that the board held him out as managing director.

The High Court held that an agent who merely has apparent authority is not capable of making representations for the company. The only persons who had actual authority to make the necessary representation in the *Crabtree-Vickers* case were either the three-man committee or the full board itself and there was no evidence that either had made any representations to the outsider. This decision can be criticised on the basis that it does not give due regard to commercial practice. It is almost impossible for an outsider in the position of Crabtree-Vickers to discover who has actual authority to make representations for the company.

It is anomalous that a company is bound by a contract entered into by a de facto managing director but not bound by representations of the de facto managing director that someone else has apparent authority.

A similar approach was adopted in *National Australia Bank Ltd v Sparrow Green Pty Ltd* (1999) 17 ACLC 1665, the facts of which are described above, para [5.130]. The director concerned did not have actual or apparent authority to bind the company. The director did not have apparent authority because a representation as to authority had to be made by someone with actual authority, such as the board. A person cannot confer authority on themselves by their own acts.

A company will not be bound by contracts made by officers or agents who exceed their customary authority unless the holding out extends their customary authority.

A company may hold out that a person occupies a particular position in the company. The extent of that person's authority will be limited to the customary authority of a person occupying such a position. A company will not be bound by contracts made by officers or agents who exceed their customary authority unless the holding out extends their customary authority. The customary authority of directors and secretaries is discussed below.

the statutory assumptions: s 129

A person dealing with a company is entitled to make certain assumptions of regularity in relation to those dealings.

[5.140] A person dealing with a company is entitled to make certain assumptions of regularity in relation to those dealings. These assumptions are set out in s 129 and are binding on the company which is not able to assert that any of the assumptions are incorrect: s 128(1). The right to make these assumptions is lost where a person knew or suspected that the assumptions were incorrect: s 128(4). The purpose behind the s 129 assumptions is to protect outsiders who deal in good faith with persons who can reasonably be expected to have authority to act for the company.

The purpose behind the s 129 assumptions is to protect outsiders who deal in good faith with persons who can reasonably be expected to have authority to act for the company.

To a large extent, the assumptions codify and clarify the rule in *Turquand's* case. In particular, the entitlement to make the assumptions together with the limitations in s 128(4) attempt to clarify the balance of competing interests referred to by Mason CJ in *Northside Developments Pty Ltd v Registrar-General* (1990) 8 ACLC 611, extracted above, para [5.125].

The s 129 assumptions apply in relation to "dealings" with a company. Despite the use of the plural "dealings" in s 128, the section also applies to a single transaction: *Advance Bank Australia Ltd v Fleetwood Star Pty Ltd* (1992) 10 ACLC 703. In *Story v Advance Bank Australia Ltd* (1993) 11 ACLC 629, it was held that the concept of having dealings with a company extends beyond dealing with someone who has actual authority and includes situations where a document is forged. It extends to purported dealings.

Each of the s 129 assumptions is separate and discrete: *Brick and Pipe Industries Ltd v Occidental Life Nominees Pty Ltd* (1992) 10 ACLC 253. This means that if an outsider cannot rely on one assumption, they may still rely on any of the other assumptions. While the assumptions are discrete, they may overlap and an outsider may rely upon more than one assumption: *Bank of New Zealand v Fiberi Pty Ltd* (1994) 12 ACLC 48. The effect of s 129(8) is to give cumulative operation to the assumptions. For example, a person may assume that an officer properly performs their duties under s 129(4) and in order to make this assumption may rely on the assumption under s 129(3) that the officer has been duly appointed and has the authority to perform those duties. It is not necessary for an outsider to have actually made these assumptions in order to rely upon them: *Lyford v Media Portfolio Ltd* (1989) 7 ACLC 271.

In *Australian Capital Television Pty Ltd v Minister for Transport and Communications* (1989) 7 ACLC 525, it was held that a predecessor of s 128(1) allowed the s 129 assumptions to be made only in relation to assertions by the company that they are not correct. Where an assertion of non-compliance with the constitution is made by a third party, the rule in *Turquand's* case and its limitations will still apply.

compliance with the constitution

A person may assume, in relation to dealings with a company, that its constitution and any applicable replaceable rules have been complied with.

[5.145] A person may assume, in relation to dealings with a company, that its constitution and any applicable replaceable rules have been complied with: s 129(1). Under s 128(4), a person is not entitled to make this assumption if at the time of the dealing he or she knew or suspected that there had been non-compliance with the constitution or replaceable rules. Section 128(4) is discussed below, para [5.200].

This assumption is a restatement of the rule in *Turquand's* case. However, it appears to have a wider operation. As discussed above, the rule in *Turquand's* case protected an outsider only where a breach of the constitution was not apparent from reading it. However, the s 129(1) assumption applies even though an irregularity may have been apparent to the outsider had the constitution been read. For example, if the constitution contains a restriction on the power of the board to borrow in excess of a certain sum, an outsider who has not read the constitution is not taken to know of this restriction. In fact, the outsider can assume that the board has the power to borrow an amount greater than the specified amount.

figure 5.1 section 129 assumptions

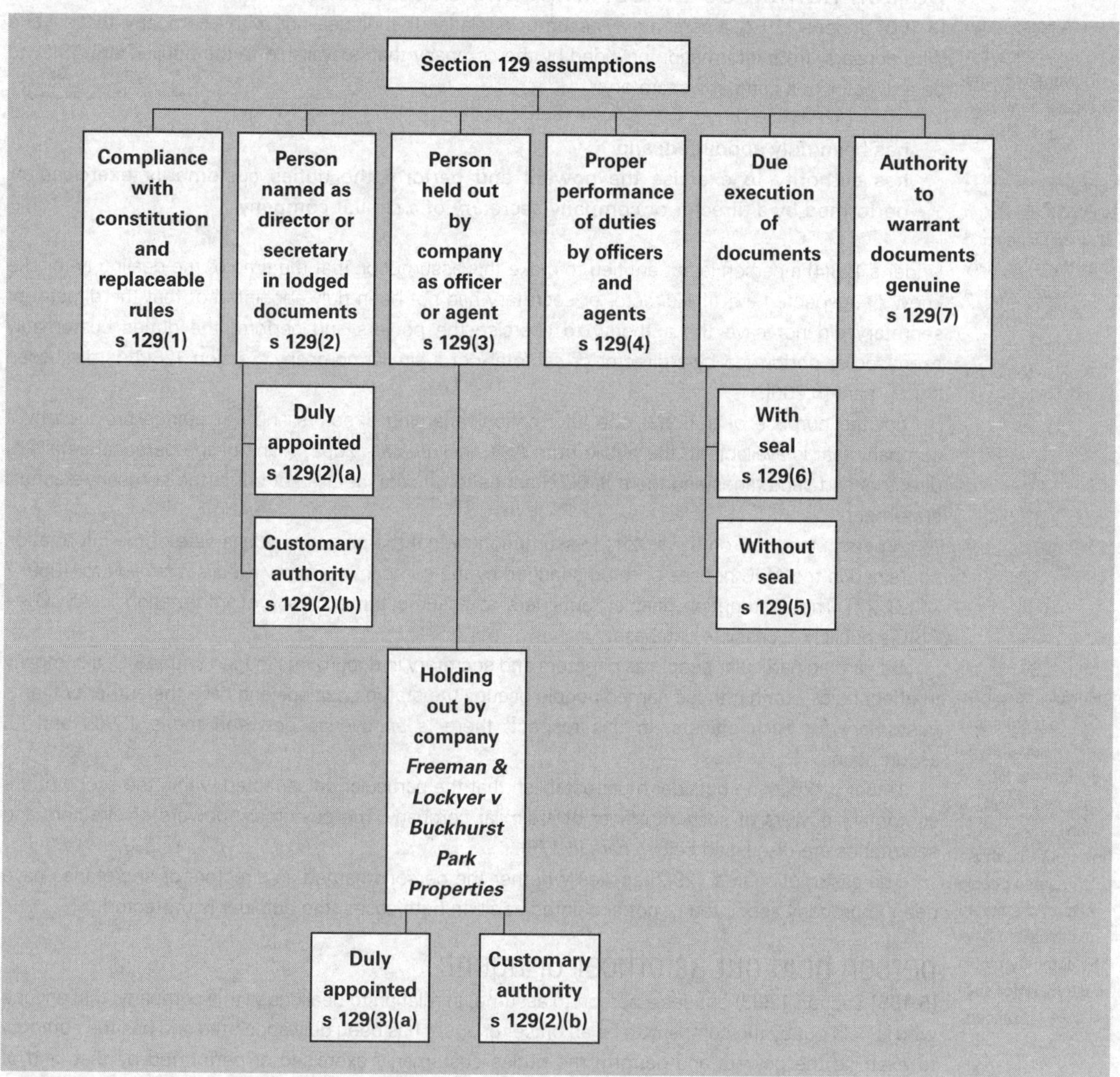

case note

In *Bank of New Zealand v Fiberi Pty Ltd* (1994) 12 ACLC 48, a company seal was affixed to a mortgage in breach of its constitution. The company's constitution required authorisation for use of the seal by the directors and attestation by a director and secretary. In fact, no authorisation was given and the person purporting to sign as secretary had not been appointed in accordance with the company's constitution. Kirby P held that the mortgagee was entitled to rely on the predecessor of s 129(1) and could assume that the relevant provisions of the company's constitution had been complied with. These included provisions that required the seal to be kept in safe custody and only be used with proper authority and be properly attested by officers of the company. However, on the facts of the case, the limitations contained in the predecessor of s 128(4) prevented reliance on the assumption.

person named as officer in public documents

A person may assume that anyone who the company names as a director or secretary in documents lodged with ASIC has been duly appointed and has the customary authority of a director or secretary of a similar company.

[5.150] Under s 129(2), a person may assume, in relation to their dealings with a company, that anyone who appears, from information provided by the company that is available to the public from ASIC, to be a director or a company secretary:

> **has been duly appointed; and**
> **has authority to exercise the powers and perform the duties customarily exercised or performed by a director or company secretary of a similar company.**

Under s 128(4) a person is not entitled to make this assumption if at the time of the dealing he or she knew or suspected that the director or secretary had not been duly appointed or that the director or secretary did not have the authority to exercise the powers and perform the duties customarily exercised or performed by a director or secretary of a similar company. Section 128(4) is discussed below, para [5.200].

For the purpose of s 129(2), the information regarding directors and secretaries provided by a company that is available to the public from ASIC includes a s 205B notice of the personal details of directors and secretaries and the s 346C changes to officers' details set out in the company's annual statement.

A person may rely on the s 129(2) assumption even if the person was unaware of the information contained in the ASIC notices or returns lodged by the company: *Lyford v Media Portfolio Ltd* (1989) 7 ACLC 271. The assumption enables outsiders to assume the accuracy of information in ASCOT—ASIC's publicly accessible database.

By naming particular people as directors and secretary in documents lodged with ASIC, a company in effect holds out that those named people occupy the stated positions and have the authority that is customary for such officers.

By naming particular people as directors and secretary in documents lodged with ASIC, a company in effect holds out that those named people occupy the stated positions and have the authority that is customary for such officers. In this respect, there is an overlap between the s 129(2) and (3) assumptions.

Under s 129(2), an outsider must establish that the particular officer acted within the scope of the customary powers of such an officer of a similar company. The customary powers of directors and secretaries are discussed below, para [5.175].

The assumption in s 129(2) applies whether the persons named as directors or secretaries have been improperly appointed or not appointed at all. In both cases, the outsider is protected.

person held out as officer or agent

Section 129(3) entitles a person to assume that anyone who is held out by the company to be an officer or agent has been duly appointed and has the authority to exercise the powers and perform the duties customarily exercised or performed by that kind of officer or agent of a similar company.

[5.155] Section 129(3) entitles a person to assume, in relation to dealings with a company, that anyone who is held out by the company to be an officer or agent has been duly appointed and has the authority to exercise the powers and perform the duties customarily exercised or performed by that kind of officer or agent of a similar company. Under s 128(4) a person is not entitled to make this assumption if at the time of the dealing he or she knew or suspected that the officer or agent had not been duly appointed or that the officer or agent did not have the authority to exercise the powers and perform the duties customarily exercised or performed by that kind of officer or agent of a similar company. Section 128(4) is discussed below, para [5.200].

The term "officer" is defined in s 9 and includes directors and secretaries, as well as persons who participate in making decisions that affect the whole or a substantial part of the business of a corporation. Persons who have the capacity to affect significantly the corporation's financial standing also come within the definition.

A person dealing with a company has the onus of proving each element of s 129(3) before being entitled to rely on the assumption contained in it. This means that where there is a dispute regarding the authority of a company's officer or agent in relation to dealings with a company, the outsider must establish two things:

> **a holding out by the company that a person is an officer or agent; and**

> **that the particular power exercised by the person so held out is within the scope of the powers customarily exercised or performed by an officer or agent of a similar company.**

Where a company has held out that a person is an officer or agent, persons dealing with the company need not establish that the officer or agent has in fact been appointed. Section 129(3) allows them to assume that this is the case even if it is not true. In this respect, there is no difference between a defective appointment and a non-existent appointment.

Where a company has held out that a person is an officer or agent, persons dealing with the company need not establish that the officer or agent has in fact been appointed.

Section 129(3) requires proof that a company has held out a particular person to be an officer or agent. This raises the same question as arises in connection with the general agency rules of apparent authority. Who can make a holding out for the company? Section 129(3) restates the agency rules in this respect. As discussed above, para [5.135], a holding out by the company can be made only by a person who has actual authority "to manage the business of the company either generally or in respect of those matters to which the contract relates": *Freeman and Lockyer v Buckhurst Park Properties (Mangal) Ltd* [1964] 2 QB 480.

A holding out by the company can be made only by a person who has actual authority.

case note

In *Australia and New Zealand Banking Group Ltd v Australian Glass and Mirrors Pty Ltd* (1991) 9 ACLC 702, it was held that a company had held out two persons to be a director and secretary respectively. The holding out had occurred because lodged documents named the two persons as its directors and they had previously conducted negotiations and signed documents as if they were directors.

case note

Similarly, in *Re Madi Pty Ltd* (1987) 5 ACLC 847, a company held out a person as its secretary by naming that person as its secretary in a document lodged with ASIC. The company was bound by the act of this person even though he had not been appointed at the time.

Re Madi Pty Ltd indicates that s 129(3) modifies the normal agency rules of apparent authority as stated in *Freeman and Lockyer*. One of the common law requirements for the existence of apparent authority is that the outsider relies on the representation made by the company. In *Re Madi Pty Ltd*, there was no suggestion that the creditor was aware of the information contained in the company's return and so could not be said to have relied on the information contained in it.

Under s 129(3) the person entitled to make the assumption must also establish that the disputed power exercised by the "held out" officer or agent is within the ambit of those powers customarily exercised or performed by an officer or agent of a similar company. The customary powers of officers or agents vary depending on the type of position the person occupies. While the courts have laid down some broad guidelines as to the customary powers of directors and secretaries there are no such guidelines in relation to other officers and agents of a company. The extent of their customary powers is a question of fact determined on a case-by-case basis. The customary powers of directors and secretaries are discussed below, para [5.175].

officers and agents properly perform their duties

[5.160] A person may assume, in relation to dealings with a company, that the officers and agents of the company properly perform their duties to the company: s 129(4). Under s 128(4), a person is not entitled to make this assumption if at the time of the dealing he or she knew or suspected that the officer or agent did not properly perform their duties to the company. Section 128(4) is discussed below, para [5.200].

A person may assume, in relation to dealings with a company, that the officers and agents of the company properly perform their duties to the company.

The s 129(4) assumption restates the common law rule established in *Richard Brady Franks Ltd v Price* (1937) 58 CLR 112. Under this rule, a company has cannot avoid a contract entered into on its behalf by an officer who has breached her or his fiduciary duty where the outsider acts in good faith without notice of the breach of duty.

The s 129(4) assumption is unclear as to the type of duties to which it refers. The duties may refer to one or more of the following duties:

> **fiduciary and statutory duties of officers and agents;**
> **administrative or statutory tasks delegated to officers or agents under the company's constitution or legislation; and**
> **other tasks delegated by the board.**

The decision in *Chew v R* (1992) 10 ACLC 816 appears to support the argument that the reference to proper performance of duties in s 129(4) covers both the fiduciary duties as well as acting with authority. In that case the High Court considered the meaning of the word "improper" in the predecessor of s 182 which prohibits officers and employees improperly using their position. It was held that a person might act improperly under the predecessor of s 182 if that person knowingly abuses her or his powers as an officer or agent. They may also act improperly if they do something that they are not authorised to do.

In the context of the fiduciary duties of directors, the situation may be governed by both the fiduciary and equitable principles and the s 129(4) assumption and its exceptions. Where a director acts in breach of fiduciary duties and an outsider was involved in the breach of duty and acquires property, the company may recover the property from the outsider on the basis that the outsider was holding the property as a constructive trustee for the company. If the interpretation of "duties" in s 129(4) encompasses the fiduciary duties, it may mean that the relationship of a company and outsiders would be governed by both the statutory assumptions and their exceptions and the equitable principles of constructive trusts. An outsider may be liable as a constructive trustee where the trust property was received with knowledge of the breach of duties by the directors or the outsider participated in the breaches of duties. The circumstances where an outsider may be liable or the company may recover property under these equitable principles may be different to those where the statutory assumptions and their exceptions are applied. It is unclear whether the statutory rules displace the equitable principles or whether they operate in addition to other rules of common law and equity. The legislation does not expressly address this question. The constructive trust remedy is discussed below in Chapter 13.6.

In some cases, this may result in different consequences. For example, as discussed in Chapter 13.2 below, if directors issue shares for an improper purpose, they breach their fiduciary duties and the company may have the share issue declared void. However, under s 129(4), the person to whom the shares have been issued may assume that the directors have properly performed their duties with the result that the share issue is valid.

A company may execute a document with or without fixing its common seal to the document.

document duly executed

A person may assume, in relation to dealings with a company, that a document has been duly executed by the company if the document appears to have been signed in accordance with s 127(1).

[5.165] A company may execute a document with or without fixing its common seal to the document. Section 129 has two provisions that contain assumptions regarding the due execution of company documents to cover both situations. Section 129(5) sets out an assumption of due execution where a document is executed without a seal and s 129(6) sets out the equivalent assumption of due execution where a document is executed with a seal. A person is not entitled to make an assumption under either s 129(5) or (6) if he or she knew or suspected that the assumption was incorrect: s 128(4).

Section 129(5) provides that a person may assume, in relation to dealings with a company, that a document has been duly executed by the company if the document appears to have been signed in accordance with s 127(1). A person may also assume under s 129(5) that anyone who signs the document and states next to their signature that they are the sole director and secretary of the company, occupies both offices.

As discussed above, para [5.80], s 127(1) provides that a company may execute a document without using its common seal if two directors or a director and company secretary sign the document. In the case of a proprietary company that has a sole director who is also the sole company secretary, a company may execute a document if that director signs it.

Under s 129(6) a person may also assume that a document has been duly executed if:

A person may assume that a document has been duly executed if: the company's common seal appears to have been fixed to the document in accordance with s 127(2); and the fixing of the common seal appears to have been witnessed in accordance with s 127(2).

> **the company's common seal appears to have been fixed to the document in accordance with s 127(2); and**
> **the fixing of the common seal appears to have been witnessed in accordance with s 127(2).**

A person may also assume that anyone who witnesses the fixing of the common seal and states next to their signature that they are the sole director and secretary of the company occupies both offices: s 129(6).

A person may assume that a company has duly executed a document if it "appears" to have been signed in accordance with s 127(1) or the fixing of the company's common seal "appears" to have been witnessed in accordance with s 127(2). A document will "appear" to have been signed or witnessed in accordance with s 127(1) and (2) if the appropriate officer signs or witnesses the document and states next to their signature that they are either:

> **a director or secretary; or**
> **in the case of a one-person proprietary company, the sole director and the sole company secretary.**

The s 129(5) or (6) assumptions may apply even if the officer who signs or witnesses a document does not occupy the designated position.

case note

This occurred in *Brick & Pipe Industries Ltd v Occidental Life Nominees Pty Ltd* (1992) 10 ACLC 253 where a company fixed its seal to a guarantee witnessed by two directors, one of whom was incorrectly described as the company secretary. However, that person had not been appointed as secretary. It was held that under a predecessor of s 129(6) the other party to the guarantee could assume the guarantee was duly executed notwithstanding the incorrect designation. The court also held that the guarantor company had held out that the director who incorrectly signed as secretary was the secretary.

Even though s 129(6) is worded differently from its predecessor, it is arguable that the *Brick & Pipe* case would have been decided in the same way if s 129(6) had applied although for different reasons. Since the witnesses to fixing Brick & Pipe's seal to the guarantee were designated as a director and secretary, the document "appears" to have been witnessed in accordance with s 127(2)(b). The wrong designation of the post of one of the witnesses would still entitle the other party to the guarantee to assume it was duly executed. However, if that person knew or suspected that the witness did not occupy the designated position, then under s 128(4) he or she could not rely on the due sealing assumption.

case note

In *MYT Engineering Pty Ltd v Mulcon Pty Ltd* (1999) 17 ACLC 861, the company purported to execute a deed of company arrangement for the purposes of Pt 5.3A of the *Corporations Act*. A director, who purported to witness as both a director and secretary, attested the fixing

of its common seal to the deed. The High Court held that a person would not have been able to assume that the document had been duly sealed under the predecessor of s 129(6) because the previous provision did not contemplate execution by sole director/sole secretary proprietary companies.

Arguably, the same result would have been reached in the *MYT Engineering* case if s 129(6) had applied though for different reasons. While s 129(6) now recognises execution of documents by one-person companies, a document executed by such a company will "appear" to be executed in accordance with s 127(2) only if the company is a proprietary company and the signatory states next to their signature that they are the sole director and sole company secretary.

case note

In *Myers v Aquarell Pty Ltd* [2000] VSC 429 the Victorian Supreme Court held that a person was entitled to assume that a mortgage was duly executed under s 129(6) as the company seal was affixed in the presence of its sole director and secretary in compliance with s 127(2), even though the company's constitution required that the company should have a minimum of two directors and that fixing the seal was to be witnessed by at least one director and countersigned by the company secretary.

The s 129(5) and (6) assumptions appear to strengthen the position of persons dealing with a company compared with their position prior to the 1998 amendments. The now repealed s 164(3)(e) assumption of valid sealing could only be made if the persons witnessing the fixing of the company seal appeared to be directors or director and secretary by virtue of having been held out by the company as the relevant officers or named as such in the company's lodged documents. Under the assumptions contained in s 129(5) and (6), there is no requirement that the persons signing the document or witnessing the fixing of the seal need to be held out or named by the company as relevant officers. It is sufficient if the document appears on its face to have been signed, or the company seal witnessed, by the required officers.

Section 129(5) and (6) only addresses whether it may be assumed that the formal requirements of execution have been met. Ramsay, Stapledon and Fong, in their article "Affixing of the Company Seal and the Effect of the Statutory Assumption in the Corporations Law" (1999) 10 *Journal of Banking Law & Practice* 38 suggest that in order for an executed document to bind the company it must also be shown that the signatories were authorised to commit the company to the transaction. This may be established by applying the general rules of agency or the statutory assumptions, particularly s 129(2) and (3) which are discussed above. The basis of this argument is that an outsider must show that an agent has authority conferred by a principal in cases of contracts which do not involve an executed document. This requirement should not be removed just because the contract involves an executed document.

warranting documents genuine

A person may assume that an officer or agent of the company who has authority to issue a document or certified copy of a document on its behalf also has authority to warrant that the document is genuine.

[5.170] Under s 129(7), a person, in relation to dealings with a company, may assume that an officer or agent of the company who has authority to issue a document or certified copy of a document on its behalf also has authority to warrant that the document is genuine or is a true copy. Therefore, a company secretary may be assumed to have the requisite authority to warrant that a share certificate is genuine. At common law it was doubtful whether a company secretary had authority to do this.

case note

Section 129(7) overrules a principle stated in *Ruben v Great Fingall Consolidated* [1906] AC 439. In that case, a company secretary forged a share certificate and purported to issue it on behalf of the company. The share certificate appeared to have been validly issued, however the company seal had been affixed without authority. Two directors' signatures had been forged and the company secretary countersigned the certificate without authority. The secretary then lodged the certificate as security for a loan to himself. After the secretary defaulted, the lender was refused registration as owner of the shares and sued the company. He argued that the rule in *Turquand's* case operated so that he could assume that the internal proceedings of the company regarding the issue of share certificates were properly carried out.

The House of Lords held that the forged certificate did not bind the company. It had not held out that the secretary had the authority to do more than merely deliver valid certificates. Therefore, the lender was not the true owner of the shares.

While the authority of a company secretary has been considerably broadened since this case, the authority of a secretary to warrant that a document that he or she has issued is genuine has not been expressly considered by the courts. The s 129(7) assumption specifically clarifies this situation. The customary authority of a company secretary is discussed below, para [5.195].

customary authority of officers

[5.175] We saw earlier that under s 129(2) and (3), an officer or agent of a company only binds the company to contracts with outsiders if he or she exercises the powers and performs the duties customarily exercised or performed by an officer or agent of a similar company. The question then arises: what are the customary powers and duties of particular officers or what is their customary authority?

individual directors

[5.180] We see in Chapter 12 below that the constitution or replaceable rules usually confer powers of management on the directors collectively as a board. However, frequently individual directors are given the power to:

> **witness the fixing of the company's common seal (s 127(2)); and**
> **sign the company's negotiable instruments, including cheques: s 198B.**

An individual director does not have customary authority to contracts on the company's behalf. In *Northside Developments Pty Ltd v Registrar-General* (1990) 8 ACLC 611, Dawson J stated:

An individual director does not have customary authority to contracts on the company's behalf.

< **The position of director does not carry with it an ostensible authority to act on behalf of the company. Directors can act only collectively as a board and the function of an individual director is to participate in decisions of the board. In the absence of some representation made by the company, a director has no ostensible authority to bind it.** >

While the customary authority of individual directors is limited, they will nevertheless bind their company if they have actual authority or have been held out as having greater authority than is customary for individual directors. This may often arise in the case of a small proprietary company where management is effectively conducted by a particular director with the acquiescence of the other director or directors.

In *Brick and Pipe Industries Ltd v Occidental Life Nominees Pty Ltd* (1992) 10 ACLC 253, a dominant director was taken to represent the mind and will of the company and have the authority of a managing director where the other directors acquiesced to this and did not involve themselves in transactions entered into by the dominant director.

In the absence of acquiescence of other directors, an individual director does not have customary authority to represent that someone else has been appointed as secretary: *Bank of New Zealand v Fiberi Pty Ltd* (1994) 12 ACLC 48.

managing director

A managing director has the customary authority to make any contracts related to the day to day management of the company's business.

[5.185] A managing director has the customary authority to make any contracts related to the day to day management of the company's business. This includes engaging persons to do work for the company (*Freeman and Lockyer v Buckhurst Park Properties (Mangal) Ltd* [1964] 2 QB 480) and borrowing money on the company's behalf: *British Thomson-Houston Co Ltd v Federated European Bank Ltd* [1932] 2 KB 176. A managing director's customary authority may not include a purported sale of the entire business of the company.

In *Re Tummon Investments Pty Ltd* (1993) 11 ACLC 1139, it was held that a managing director did not have customary authority to enter into a loan contract that was not in the ordinary course of the company's business as the loan was not for the benefit of the company.

In *Re Qintex Ltd* (1990) 8 ACLC 811, it was held that a managing director did not have the customary authority to make "critical" decisions following the presentation of an application to wind up the company. In that case, the managing director did not have authority to appoint solicitors to oppose the application.

chair

The chair does not have the customary authority to contract on the company's behalf.

[5.190] The chair has the same customary authority as any other individual director and consequently does not have the customary authority to contract on the company's behalf: *Hely-Hutchinson v Brayhead Ltd* [1968] 1 QB 549.

secretary

[5.195] The status of a secretary has, in the eyes of the courts, changed over the past century. So, too, has the secretary's customary authority. The early cases held that a secretary had no customary authority to bind a company.

case note

The present position with respect to a secretary's customary authority is illustrated in *Panorama Developments (Guildford) Ltd v Fidelis Furnishing Fabrics Ltd* [1971] 2 QB 711. In that case the secretary of Fidelis, without authority, hired cars from Panorama, which he stated were for the purpose of carrying his company's important customers. The secretary, however, used the cars for his own purposes. When he failed to pay the hire charges Panorama sued his company, arguing that the secretary had apparent authority to enter into that contract. The court upheld Panorama's claim and decided that a company secretary has the customary authority to enter into contracts connected to the administrative side of the company's affairs.

A company secretary has the customary authority to enter into contracts connected to the administrative side of the company's affairs.

The customary authority of a company secretary is not as wide as that of a director. This role is limited to matters of an administrative, internal nature required for day to day running of the company's affairs such as employing staff, and ordering cars. The customary powers of a secretary do not include authority to mortgage the company's land: *Northside Developments Pty Ltd v Registrar-General* (1990) 8 ACLC 611.

limitations to the statutory assumptions: s 128(4)

[5.200] A person cannot rely on any of the assumptions set out in s 129 if the person knew or suspected that a particular assumption was incorrect at the time of the dealings: s 128(4). This provision contains two elements in relation to the state of mind of the person dealing with a company. That person either:

A person cannot rely on any of the assumptions set out in s 129 if the person knew or suspected that a particular assumption was incorrect at the time of the dealings.

- knew; or
- suspected;

that the assumption was incorrect.

To some extent, s 128(4) adopts the general law limits to the rule in *Turquand*'s case. However, the general law limits are expressed in different words. The common law rule could not be relied upon where the outsiders actually knew of the irregularity or the circumstances were such that they were put on inquiry: *Northside Developments Pty Ltd v Registrar-General* (1990) 8 ACLC 611.

figure 5.2 section 129 assumptions

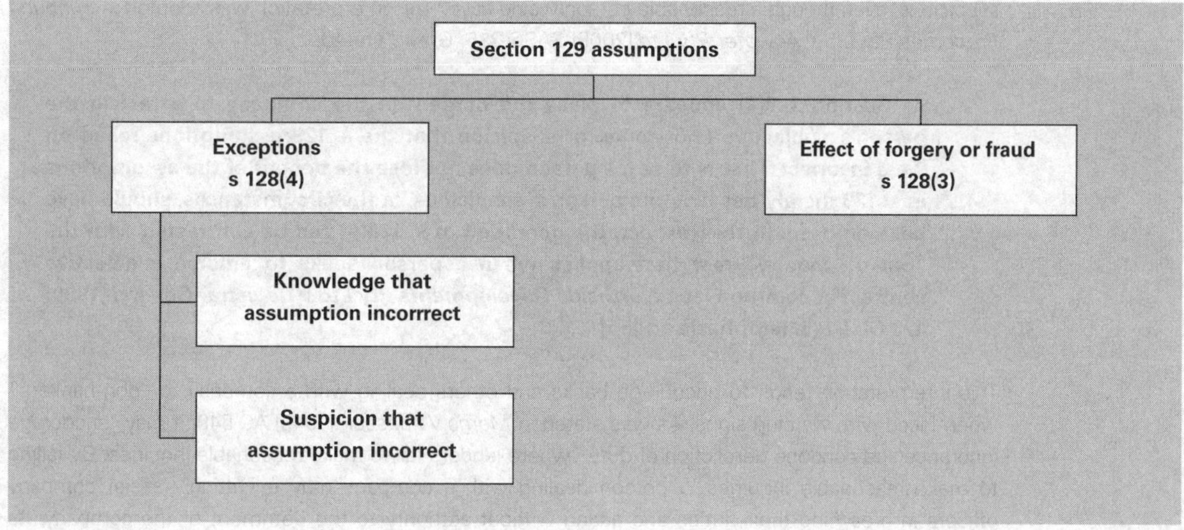

knew assumption incorrect

[5.205] Under s 128(4), a person is not entitled to make an assumption in s 129 if at the time of the dealing he or she knew that the assumption was incorrect. This exception is worded differently from its predecessor which prevented a person from making an assumption if he or she had "actual knowledge" that it was incorrect. It is possible that the word "knew" in s 128(4) means the same thing as "actual knowledge".

A person is not entitled to make an assumption in s 129 if at the time of the dealing he or she knew that the assumption was incorrect.

In *Brick and Pipe Industries Ltd v Occidental Life Nominees Pty Ltd* (1992) 10 ACLC 253, the Full Court of the Victorian Supreme Court thought that the expression "actual knowledge" meant what it said and did not lend itself to definition or elaboration. However, it still depended on the facts and circumstances in a particular case and the inferences they allow. In this case the court indicated that it might be prepared to impute to the lender, the actual knowledge of its solicitor. This means that the knowledge of an agent may be taken to represent the actual knowledge of the outsider.

It is unclear whether a person is taken to know that an assumption was incorrect where the person was aware of various facts but failed to appreciate their combined significance or where a person wilfully shut her or his eyes to the surrounding circumstances. A literal interpretation of what a person "knew" may result in an outsider receiving the benefit of the s 129 assumptions even though conclusions were not drawn, nor inquiries made, when the circumstances clearly warranted them.

On a broader interpretation, a person may be taken to have known that an assumption was incorrect for the purpose of the s 128(4) limitations where the person is wilfully blind in the face of facts which obviously lead to a conclusion that there had been a breach of duty or fraud by officers of the company.

Where the outsider is a company, the question may arise as to what it knew in relation to an assumption being incorrect. As discussed above, para [5.10], the company is regarded as having the knowledge of its directing mind and will.

Sometimes, a company and the outsider have common directors. This raises the question whether the outsider is taken to have the knowledge possessed by the shared directors.

suspected assumption incorrect

A person cannot rely on the s 129 assumptions if at the time of the dealing they suspected that the assumption was incorrect.

[5.210] A person cannot rely on the s 129 assumptions if at the time of the dealing they suspected that the assumption was incorrect: s 128(4).

There are at least two possible interpretations of the suspicion exception in s 128(4). On one interpretation, s 128(4) prevents a person from making a s 129 assumption only if circumstances surrounding the dealing result in the person actually suspecting the assumption is incorrect. Consequently, a person could rely on a s 129 assumption if the person did not in fact form such suspicions, even though a reasonable person would have. This interpretation was adopted in *Sunburst Properties Pty Ltd v Agwater Pty Ltd* [2005] SASC 335. Gray J stated:

> < **Section 128(4) appears to place the burden on the company to establish the person's subjective knowledge or suspicion that the s 129 assumptions relied on were incorrect. That is to say, a person does not lose the benefit of the assumptions in s 129 merely because the person's suspicions, in the circumstances, should have been aroused. In this respect, the operation of s 128(4) can be contrasted with the "put on inquiry" test that applies when a person seeks to enforce a defective contract at common law: *Northside Developments Pty Ltd v Registrar-General* (1990) 170 CLR 146. (emphasis added)** >

This interpretation tends to encourage banks and others dealing with a company to "don blinkers" when faced with warning signs. As was stated in *Morris v Kanssen* [1946] AC 549, it may "encourage ignorance and condone dereliction of duty" where lenders fail to make reasonable inquiries. By failing to make reasonable inquiries, a person dealing with a company may unwittingly assist company officers in breaching their duties and acting without authority to the detriment of the company, its innocent shareholders and creditors.

Another possible interpretation of the suspicion exception in s 128(4) is that it prevents a person from making a s 129 assumption if the circumstances surrounding the dealing would result in a reasonable person suspecting the assumption is incorrect. Under this interpretation, the test of whether there are suspicions is objective and would prevent a person from relying on a s 129 assumption if the person failed to act reasonably in the face of suspicious circumstances.

The explanatory memorandum to the 1998 amending legislation that inserted s 128(4) is unhelpful in deciding which of the above interpretations were intended. It stated that the test of whether a person suspected an assumption was incorrect under s 128(4) was objective and stricter than the replaced s 164(4)(b) exception. Further, the wording of s 128(4) is intended to make it clear that the common law "put on inquiry" test does not apply to the s 129 assumptions. This explanation raises several difficulties in the interpretation of the provision. It indicates that an objective assessment should be made in order to determine whether a person suspected that an assumption was incorrect. This is not apparent from a reading of s 128(4) which adopts subjective wording.

the effect of fraud or forgery

[5.215] A person may rely on the assumptions in s 129 even if an officer or agent of the company acts fraudulently or forges a document in connection with the dealings: s 128(3). Section 128(3) covers the situation where a company seal or signatures attesting its application are not genuine but are forged: *Story v Advance Bank Australia Ltd* (1993) 11 ACLC 629.

A person may rely on the assumptions in s 129 even if an officer or agent of the company acts fraudulently or forges a document in connection with the dealings.

This provision restates the common law rule that a company or employer is liable for the fraudulent acts of its officers, agents or employees where they have acted within their actual or apparent authority. It also overrules a principle stated in *Ruben v Great Fingall Consolidated* [1906] AC 439 that a forgery is a nullity and cannot bind a company. The facts of this case are described above, para [5.170].

bibliography ...

Brand, V "Legislating for Moral Propriety in Corporations? The Criminal Code Amendment (Bribery of Foreign Public Officials) Act 1999" (2000) 18 C & SLJ 476.

Carroll, R "Proper Performance of Duties by Company Officers: The Statutory Assumption in s 164(3)(f) of the Corporations Law" (1995) 69 ALJ 200.

Chapple, L & Lipton, P "Corporate Authority and Dealings with Officers and Agents" Centre for Corporate Law and Securities Regulation, 2002.

Lord Cooke of Thorndon "Corporate Identity" (1998) 16 C & SLJ 160. Edwards, R "Corporate Killers" (2001) 13 Aust Jnl of Corp Law 231.

Edwards, R "The Application of the Statutory Internal Management Rule to Cheques" (2000) 18 C & SLJ 242.

Grantham, R "Attributing Responsibility to Corporate Entities: A Doctrinal Approach" (2001) 19 C & SLJ 168.

Hammond, C "Put Upon Inquiry Has Been Put to Rest Under Section 128(4) of the Corporations Law, But Have Third Parties Dealing With Companies Been Placed in a Stronger Position?—A Question of Statutory Interpretation" (1998) 16 C & SLJ 562.

Hodges, C "Manslaughter by Corporations" (1994) 22 ABLR 81.

Law, L & Pascoe, J "Financiers and Corporate Borrowers: Protection Versus Liability" (2000) 11 Aust Jnl of Corp Law 219.

Lipton, P "The Unauthorised Use of the Company Seal: Alarm Bells for Bankers" (1995) 3 *Current Commercial Law* 105.

Loxton, D "One Step Forward, One Step Back: The Effect of Corporate Law Reform on Procedures in Dealing with Companies Borrowing or Giving Guarantees" (1999) 10 JBFLP 24.

Ramsay, I, Stapledon, G & Fong K "Affixing of the Company Seal and the Effect of the Statutory Assumption in the Corporations Law" (1999) 10 JBFLP 38.

Wheelwright, K "Prosecuting corporations and officers for industrial manslaughter—recent Australian developments" (2004) 32 ABLR 239.

Zakrzewski, R "The Law Relating to Single Director and Single Shareholder Companies" (1999) 17 C & SLJ 156.

revision questions on the material in this chapter ...

> Please see eQuiz at **http://www.thomson.com.au/academic** for multiple choice questions and answers.

chapter six

promoters and pre-registration contracts

key points ...

- A promoter is a person who is involved, actively or passively, in forming a company, raising its capital and establishing its business.
- Promoters owe fiduciary duties to their company. These duties require the promoter to act in the best interests of the company, disclose their interests in contracts with the company and not make undisclosed profits.
- The nature and extent of a promoter's interests in the company's formation and any property acquired by it must also be disclosed in a prospectus if the company seeks to raise capital from the public.
- Pre-registration contracts may be enforced by the outside contracting party against the company after its registration or against a person who entered into the contract for the company.

A promoter is a person involved in the formation of a company.

[6.05] The term "promoter" has at least two meanings depending on the context in which it is used and the relationship the law is seeking to govern. A promoter is a person involved in the formation of a company. The common law imposes fiduciary duties on persons involved in the setting up or floating of companies. A person who enters into a contract on behalf of a company before it is registered is sometimes also referred to as a promoter. Pre-registration contracts are discussed in paras [6.65–6.80] below.

promoters

who is a promoter?

[6.10] The question: *who is a promoter?* has not been precisely defined by the courts. The term "promoter" encompasses a very wide range of persons. In *Twycross v Grant* (1877) 2 CPD 469, Cockburn CJ stated:

> < **A promoter, I apprehend, is one who undertakes to form a company with reference to a given project and to set it going, and who takes the necessary steps to accomplish that purpose.** >

active promoters

The person who actively undertakes the formation of a company by carrying out the procedure necessary for incorporation is a promoter.

[6.15] The person who actively undertakes the formation of a company by carrying out the procedure necessary for incorporation is a promoter. Incorporation includes, among other things, registration of the company, payment of registration and legal fees, preparation of the company's constitution, obtaining directors and shareholders, raising capital, negotiation of preliminary agreements and preparation of a prospectus. The persons who undertake these activities include a person who forms a proprietary company to purchase a business previously run by a sole trader. This is a very common occurrence and an example is found in *Salomon's* case.

A person who forms a company with the objective of selling particular property to the company and arranging for the shares of the company to be taken up by others is also a promoter. This would be so even if such a person held neither shares nor any managerial position in the company. In this type of case there is the possibility that the promoter may abuse the position for personal profit, to the detriment of the company and its shareholders.

While persons who actively take the required steps to incorporate a company are promoters, those acting merely in a professional capacity to incorporate the company on behalf of a promoter are not. This excludes solicitors and accountants who do no more than carry out the instructions of the person seeking to incorporate the company and take no further part in the enterprise. Similarly, where a company becomes a promoter due to the activities of an officer, the officer does not become a promoter because they do not stand to personally gain from the promotion. An officer who can be said to represent the directing mind and will of the promoter company may also be regarded as a promoter: *Aequitas v AEFC* (2001) 19 ACLC 1006.

passive promoters

[6.20] A person who takes no active part in the incorporation of a company and the raising of its share capital, but leaves this to others on the understanding that they will profit from the enterprise, may also be a promoter.

A person who takes no active part in the incorporation of a company and the raising of its share capital, but leaves this to others on the understanding that they will profit from the enterprise, may also be a promoter.

case note

In *Tracy v Mandalay Pty Ltd* (1953) 88 CLR 215, the High Court considered the question of who is a promoter. A company purchased land on which it intended to construct a block of flats. The land was then sold at a profit to a new company, Mandalay Pty Ltd. Mandalay advertised and attracted many applicants for parcels of shares, each of which entitled the owner to sole use of a flat. The flats were never built and Mandalay brought an action against the promoters and vendor of the land to recover the moneys paid by its shareholders. Various shareholders of the company that initially purchased the land took part in this scheme and were held to be promoters. Some were actively involved, others took no active part but stood to profit and allowed the other promoters to act on their behalf. Some others were held to be promoters even though they had fallen out with the active promoters and stood only to recover their original contributions after commencing litigation.

duties of promoters

fiduciary duties

[6.25] Because promoters are often able to abuse their position by making a profit for themselves at the expense of the company, the courts, in a series of late 19th century cases, laid down the principle that a promoter has a fiduciary relationship with the company and is therefore under an obligation to the promoted company to act bona fide (in good faith) and to avoid conflicts of interest with the company. The fiduciary obligations arise automatically once a person is identified as a promoter. It is not necessary to find a specific undertaking of a kind that would constitute a fiduciary relationship in the specific circumstances: *Aequitas v AEFC* (2001) 19 ACLC 1006. These fiduciary duties also apply to directors in relation to their companies. If a promoter becomes a director, their duties as a promoter overlap with their duties as director. Directors' duties are discussed in Chapter 13 below.

A promoter has a fiduciary relationship with the company and is therefore under an obligation to the promoted company to act bona fide (in good faith) and to avoid conflicts of interest with the company.

The fiduciary duties of promoters are owed for the entire period during which a person is a promoter. It is a question of fact in each case precisely when a person becomes or ceases to be a promoter. The person may become a promoter before the incorporation of the company. That person remains a promoter for as long as the formation of the company continues. This could include the issue of a prospectus, the raising of funds from the public and the performance of contracts imposed upon the company by the promoters. A person may continue to be a promoter even after the appointment of the board of directors where the directors are passive and act in the interests of the promoters: *Twycross v Grant* (1877) 2 CPD 469.

disclosure of interests in a contract

A promoter must ensure that full disclosure is made of their interest in any contract entered into by the company.

[6.30] In the context of a promoter's fiduciary obligations to a company, a promoter must ensure that full disclosure is made of their interest in any contract entered into by the company. Non-disclosure is a breach of the promoter's duty towards the company. This is so whether or not the promoter was acting honestly or even whether they made a profit or not.

case note

An illustration is provided by *Erlanger v New Sombrero Phosphate Co* (1878) 3 App Cas 1218. A syndicate purchased an island which it was hoped would prove to contain valuable minerals. A company was formed for the purpose of purchasing the island from the syndicate. The head of the syndicate nominated the directors of this company and, at its first meeting, the company adopted the contract. It turned out that the island was worth considerably less than the purchase price the company had paid. In this way the promoters made a profit to the detriment of the company and its shareholders. The House of Lords held that the company could rescind the contract with the result that the purchase money was returned to it and the island transferred back to the syndicate. The promoters were under a duty when forming the company to provide it with an independent board of directors to whom full disclosure of the promoters' interests in contracts with the company must be made. The directors are then able to exercise an independent and reasoned judgment on the transaction.

undisclosed profits

[6.35] In addition to disclosing their interest in a contract with the company, promoters also have a duty to disclose personal profits that may arise from their position.

case note

In *Gluckstein v Barnes* [1900] AC 240, the House of Lords held that the promoters were under a duty to disclose all profits made and that disclosure to a board of directors comprised of other members of the syndicate formed for the purpose of making that profit was insufficient. There had been no disclosure to an independent board of directors or to the ultimate shareholders of the company. In that case, a syndicate was formed to purchase a particular property being sold by a liquidator. The syndicate first repaid a debt owing to mortgagees of the property at a discount of £20,000. The freehold was then purchased for £140,000. A company was formed for the purpose of buying the land, which was sold to it by the syndicate for £180,000 subject to the charge given to the syndicate. The profit of £40,000 was revealed but no mention was made of the profit of £20,000 representing the discount on the mortgage. The company sought to recover this sum from the syndicate. It was held that all the promoters who shared the secret profit were severally liable for the full amount, with a right of contribution from their co-promoters. This is analogous to the liability of partners.

These cases illustrate that the promoter should make disclosure to an independent board of directors. In many cases, however, where a small company is incorporated to purchase the assets of its promoter, it is inappropriate to speak of an independent board of directors. On the other hand, as stated in *Gluckstein v Barnes*, it is insufficient for a promoter merely to disclose to others also involved in the venture who happen to be directors. Therefore, a promoter should make full disclosure to an independent board if this is possible. If this is not practicable, full disclosure should be made to the shareholders. It may also be necessary to make disclosure to potential shareholders in a disclosure document under Ch 6D. The fundraising requirements are discussed in Chapter 7 below.

The obligation not to make secret profits is only one instance of the broad duty of a promoter to avoid conflicts of interest. There is also the obligation not to disclose confidential information. A promoter must also avoid taking up a contract or opportunity that in equity belongs to the company. Promoters will breach this duty if, during the course of a promotion, they purchase property that ought to have been acquired by the company. A breach also occurs if, during the promotion, promoters buy property with the intention of selling it to the company at a profit.

fundraising disclosure

[6.40] The fundraising provisions in Ch 6D of the *Corporations Act* require companies that seek to raise funds by the offer of their securities to provide investors with a disclosure document, a copy of which has been lodged with ASIC. A prospectus is the main type of disclosure document that is required: s 709. Among other matters, s 711(2) requires a prospectus to set out the nature and extent of the interests that a promoter had in:

> **the formation or promotion of the company; or**
> **property acquired or proposed to be acquired by the company in connection with its formation or promotion or the offer of securities; or**
> **the offer of the securities.**

The prospectus must also set out the amount paid or agreed to be paid for the promoter's services in connection with the formation or promotion of the company or the offer of securities: s 711(3).

remedies for breach of duties

[6.45] The remedies for breach of a promoter's fiduciary duty are available to the company and not its shareholders. In circumstances where promoters control the company, whether through control of the board of directors or the general meeting, the company will not usually wish to exercise any rights available to it against the promoters. In such instances minority shareholders may have rights, as discussed in Chapter 17 below.

The remedies for breach of a promoter's fiduciary duty are available to the company and not its shareholders.

rescission

[6.50] If a promoter breaches the fiduciary duties owed to the company, for example, because of failure to disclose a personal interest in a contract with the company, the most important remedy is rescission of the contract. It is irrelevant that the promoter made no profit or had no dishonest motive in respect of the contract. Under contract law, however, the right to rescind is unavailable if:

> **the company does not rescind reasonably promptly after becoming aware of the misrepresentation;**
> **the company, after becoming aware of the misrepresentation, does something which indicates that it has affirmed the contract;**
> **restitutio in integrum is impossible, that is, it is not possible to restore the parties to their original positions. For example, if the property purchased from the promoter has undergone a substantial alteration in the hands of the company, it could not be said that the return of that property to the promoter restores her or him to her or his pre-contract position; or**
> **prior to the rescission of the contract, innocent third parties acquire some interest in the property.**

If the right to rescind is properly exercised, the result is that the promoter must return any consideration received and the company must return the property. This happened in *Erlanger v New Sombrero Phosphate Co.*

If the misrepresentation is fraudulent as opposed to innocent, the company may obtain damages as well as rescind the contract. In *Re Leeds and Hanley Theatres of Varieties Ltd* [1902] 2 Ch 809, it was held that the promoters had fraudulently omitted to disclose a profit made by them on the sale of property to the company. The appropriate measure of damages was the promoter's profit on the sale.

In some cases equitable compensation may be combined with an order for rescission. In *Tracy v Mandalay Pty Ltd* (1953) 88 CLR 215, the order for rescission was accompanied by orders which enabled the company to recover various costs such as taxes, rates and other losses which were ancillary to the primary remedy of rescission and which ensure that restitution occurs.

If a promoter sells property to the company that was acquired by the promoter prior to becoming a promoter and the company elects not to rescind but to proceed with the contract with the promoter, it is not permitted to recover the secret profit made by the promoter: *Tracy v Mandalay Pty Ltd* (1953) 88 CLR 215. In cases where the right to rescind is lost in relation to prior acquired property, it is unclear whether other remedies such as account of profits and equitable compensation are available. Austin J suggested that these remedies should be available in order to prevent injustice: *Aequitas v AEFC* (2001) 19 ACLC 1006.

recovery of secret profits and constructive trust order

[6.55] In some cases the secret profit may be separate from the contract price. *Gluckstein v Barnes* [1900] AC 240 is an illustration of such a situation. There, the court ordered that the company could recover the secret profit even though it chose not to rescind the contract. The liability of promoters is joint and several. A promoter who is found liable may recover contributions from the other promoters.

Where the promoter during the course of promotion acquires property for personal gain instead of for the company, the company may obtain a constructive trust order and require the promoter to hand it over at cost. This is because a promoter is taken to have acquired the property for the benefit of the company, which gains an equitable interest in it.

Where the promoter during the course of promotion acquires property for personal gain instead of for the company, the company may obtain a constructive trust order and require the promoter to hand it over at cost.

liability under Corporations Act

[6.60] In certain circumstances, promoters in breach of their fiduciary duties may incur statutory liability. For example, s 711(2) and (3) require a prospectus to set out certain information with respect to a promoter's interest in the formation, promotion or property acquired by the company. Omission of that information contravenes s 728(1). If a promoter is involved in that contravention, then any person who suffers loss or damage may recover that loss or damage from the promoter under s 729. The fundraising provisions are discussed in Chapter 7 below.

Promoters are within the definition of "related entity" in s 9. Consequently, a promoter may be liable to a liquidator under the antecedent transaction provisions. These are discussed in Chapter 25 below.

Promoters in breach of their fiduciary duties may incur statutory liability.

pre-registration contracts

common law position

[6.65] Prior to its registration, a company does not exist as a legal person. This proposition resulted in the common law rule that a company cannot enter into a binding contract until it is registered. As discussed below, s 131 changes the common law rule.

This common law rule meant that a person could not make legally binding contracts in the name of a company in anticipation of it being registered: *Newborne v Sensolid (Great Britain)* Ltd [1954] 1 QB 45. A company was also not bound by a pre-registration contract made on its behalf by a person who purported to act as its agent. A company could not have an agent before it was registered because the law of agency presumes the existence of a principal at the time the agent entered the contract.

As a consequence of the common law rule, pre-registration contracts caused difficulties for the other contracting party. The company was not bound by a contract made prior to its registration. In addition, except in exceptional circumstances, the person who purported to make the pre-registration contract was also not personally bound by the contract: *Black v Smallwood* (1966) 117 CLR 52. A person who made a contract for a company prior to its registration could be personally bound only if that person intended to contract as a principal: *Kelner v Baxter* (1866) LR 2 CP 174.

At common law, a company was also incapable of ratifying a pre-registration contract after it was registered: *Kelner v Baxter* (1866) LR 2 CP 174. This was because under the law of agency, ratification has retrospective effect and the contract was regarded as being made at the time it was entered into by the agent when the company was not in existence.

The only way a company could be liable on a pre-registration contract was by novation. This occurred where a company entered into a fresh contract on the same terms as the pre-registration contract after it was registered.

impact of s 131

[6.70] The difficulties that arise at common law with respect to pre-registration contracts have been overcome by s 131, which puts an innocent outsider in a far more certain position. Section 131 replaces the common law rules with respect to pre-registration contracts: s 133.

Section 131 enables the outsider to enforce a pre-registration contract against the company if it ratifies the contract after it is registered. However, if registration does not occur or the company does not ratify the pre-registration contract, the person who entered the contract on its behalf becomes personally liable to pay damages to the other contracting party.

Section 131 enables the outsider to enforce a pre-registration contract against the company if it ratifies the contract after it is registered. If registration does not occur or the company does not ratify the pre-registration contract, the person who entered the contract on its behalf becomes personally liable to pay damages to the other contracting party.

Section 131 only applies to contracts made before a company is registered. It does not apply where a company was registered at the time a contract was made and later changed its name: *Commonwealth Bank of Australia v Australian Solar Information Pty Ltd* (1987) 5 ACLC 124.

ratification after registration

[6.75] Section 131(1) changes the common law rule that a company cannot ratify a pre-registration contract. Under that section, a company becomes bound by and is entitled to the benefit of a pre-registration contract entered into on its behalf or for its benefit if the company is registered and ratifies the contract within either an agreed time or within a reasonable time after the contract is entered into.

case note

In *Aztech Science Pty Ltd v Atlanta Aerospace (Woy Woy) Pty Ltd* [2004] NSWSC 967, prior to its registration Aztech's promoter entered into a contract on Aztech's behalf with Atlanta under which Atlanta, for a specified fee, agreed to provide certain services for Aztech once it was formed. It was agreed that the contract would come to an end if Aztech was not registered or failed to ratify the pre-registration contract within 60 days of the contract and that notwithstanding s 131, the contracting parties would not have any further rights against each other to require performance of the contract or to claim damages for its breach. Atlanta failed to provide the services and Aztech, which was registered three days after the designated date, sued it for breach of contract.

It was held that the parties acted with express regard for s 131 and had agreed upon a time as contemplated by s 131(1)(a). As neither registration nor ratification occurred within the agreed time, there was no contract created under s 131.

Ratification means that a company has adopted or confirmed the pre-registration contract.

Ratification means that a company has adopted or confirmed the pre-registration contract. Its meaning in s 131 derives from agency law as modified by that provision. For example, a company ratifies a contract if it signs a document to that effect or its directors pass a resolution ratifying the contract. Under s 126(1) a company's power to ratify may also be exercised by an individual acting within the company's express or implied authority and on behalf of the company. This power may be exercised without using a common seal. Ratification may also be implied from the company's conduct. For example, if a pre-registration contract involved a purchase of goods, then payment of the purchase price or use of the goods by the company after it is registered would constitute evidence that it has ratified the contract.

Section 131(1) applies where a person enters into a contract "on behalf of" a company before it is registered. This covers situations where a person enters a contract as agent or trustee of a company before it is registered. By using the expression "for the benefit of", s 131(1) also applies where a person enters a pre-registration contract in the name of a company.

In some situations, the name of the proposed company, in whose name a pre-registration contract is entered into, may not be the actual name of the company when it is registered. For example, the proposed company name may be unavailable. Section 131(1) still applies in such cases as long as the company that is registered is reasonably identifiable with the one identified in the pre-registration contract.

liability where company not registered or fails to ratify

The person who enters into a pre-registration contract is liable to pay damages to the other contracting party if the company is not registered within either an agreed time or a reasonable time after the contract is entered into.

[6.80] Under s 131(2), the person who enters into a pre-registration contract is liable to pay damages to the other contracting party if the company is not registered within either an agreed time or a reasonable time after the contract is entered into. That person is also liable if the company is registered but does not ratify the contract or does not enter into a substitute contract within this time period. The person who enters into a pre-registration contract will not bear a liability for damages if the other contracting party signs a release to that effect: s 132(1).

The amount of damages for which a person may be liable under s 131(2) is the amount the company would be liable to pay if it had ratified the contract but did not perform it at all. This includes any lost profits the other contracting party expected to make on the contract as well as wasted expenditure incurred in reliance of the contract being performed.

Section 131(2) imposes a liability for damages only on the person who enters into the pre-registration contract on behalf of a company even though that person may have acted on behalf of others.

Section 131(2) imposes a liability for damages only on the person who enters into the pre-registration contract on behalf of a company even though that person may have acted on behalf of others. For example, in *Bay v Illawarra Stationery Supplies Pty Ltd* (1986) 4 ACLC 429, an accountant, who was one of four promoters of a company, entered into a pre-registration contract for office supplies on behalf of a proposed company. When the company failed to ratify the contract the supplier sued all four promoters under a predecessor of s 131(2). The Supreme Court of New South Wales held that only the accountant was liable, as he was the only one who signed the contract. The court noted, however, that the accountant would have a separate right to claim against the other promoters if he acted as their agent in relation to the contract.

If it were not for s 132(2), a person who enters into a pre-registration contract as trustee for a proposed company may, under the rules of equity, have a right to be indemnified by the company for that person's liability for damages under s 131(2). Clearly, this would be contrary to the intention of s 131. For this reason, s 132(2) removes the right of indemnity against the company for such a liability despite any rule of law or equity.

Section 131(4) gives additional protection to outsiders who contract with non-existent companies. Under that section, if the company ratifies the pre-registration contract but fails to perform all or part of it, the court may order the person who entered into the contract to pay all or part of the damages that the company is ordered to pay. This section is designed to prevent a person from deliberately setting up an assetless company to ratify a pre-registration contract and therefore avoiding a liability for damages under s 131(2).

A company may bear some liability to an outsider even if it does not ratify a pre-registration contract. Under s 131(3), if a person is sued for damages under s 131(2) because the company is registered but does not ratify the pre-registration contract or enter into a substitute for it, the court may do anything that it considers appropriate in the circumstances, including ordering the company to do one or more of the following:

> pay all or part of the s 131(2) damages;
> transfer to the other contracting party property that the company received because of the contract; or
> pay an amount to a party to the contract.

revision questions on the material in this chapter ...

> Please see eQuiz at **http://www.thomson.com.au/academic** for multiple choice questions and answers.

chapter seven
fundraising

key points . . .

- The fundraising provisions of the *Corporations Act* aim to balance the need for investor protection against the need to facilitate an efficient and credible capital market that enables companies to raise capital without excessive regulatory requirements and costs.
- Offers of securities need disclosure to investors of relevant accurate information unless an offer comes within a specific exemption. The exemptions recognise that not all investors need protection and in some situations it would be commercially unrealistic to impose costly disclosure requirements. Some investors are financially sophisticated and do not need legislative protection. They are able to obtain their own information to make an informed choice about the securities they are being offered.
- Where an offer of securities needs disclosure to investors, the fundraising provisions require the offer and any application form for the securities to be accompanied by a disclosure document. In addition, a copy of the disclosure document must be lodged with ASIC before it is given to investors.
- The information that must be disclosed to investors depends on the type of disclosure document that is applicable to the fundraising. There are four different types of disclosure documents:
  - a prospectus;
  - a short form prospectus;
  - a profile statement; and
  - an offer information statement.
- A prospectus contains more detailed information than the other types of disclosure documents. A prospectus must satisfy a general disclosure test as well as contain specified information.
- The fundraising provisions aim to ensure that a disclosure document does not contain misleading or deceptive statements or omits material information. This is achieved by imposing both criminal liability as well as a personal liability to pay compensation on the various people involved in preparing a disclosure document.

The fundraising provisions protect investors by requiring a corporation that seeks to raise funds by issuing securities to disclose relevant information to enable investors to make informed investment decisions.

[7.05] The most important feature of large companies, especially those listed on stock exchanges, is that they provide a mechanism for the pooling of funds from many investors who wish to participate in particular business ventures. A significant objective of the *Corporations Act* is to encourage such investment and to protect members of the investing public by requiring full and accurate disclosure of relevant information concerning the activities of public companies.

In this chapter we consider the fundraising provisions of Ch 6D (ss 700–741) of the *Corporations Act*. The fundraising provisions protect investors by requiring a corporation that seeks to raise funds by issuing securities to disclose relevant information to enable investors to make informed investment decisions.

Shares and debentures of a body are included in the definition of securities: ss 700(1) and 761A. Options to acquire, by way of issue, shares or debentures are also included in the definition. As discussed in Chapter 19 below, Pt 7.9 of the *Corporations Act* sets out similar disclosure requirements in relation to issues of other types of financial products.

The Centre for Corporate Law & Securities Regulation published a 2003 research report. I Ramsay,

Use of Prospectuses by Investors and their Professional Advisors. This research report discusses how prospectuses are used by recipients and their views on the utility of prospectuses. The report is posted on the Centre's website at **http://cclsr.law.unimelb.edu.au** and is linked to the Lipton-Herzberg Law Reform site at **http://www.lipton-herzberg.com.au/law_reform.htm#other**

overview of fundraising provisions

[7.10] The aim of the fundraising provisions is to balance the needs for investor protection with an efficient and credible capital market. The investor protection objective aims to ensure that a minimum amount of relevant, accurate information is disclosed to financially unsophisticated retail investors so as to enable them to make an informed decision whether or not to accept an offer of securities. The information must be disclosed in a clear, concise and effective manner. The extent of the disclosure depends on the type of disclosure document. These are:

The aim of the fundraising provisions is to balance the needs for investor protection with an efficient and credible capital market.

- a prospectus;
- a short form prospectus;
- a profile statement; and
- an offer information statement.

The general prospectus content rule requires disclosure of all information that investors and their professional advisers would both reasonably require and reasonably expect to find in the prospectus to make an informed investment decision. This allows a prospectus to be tailored to meet the needs of the targeted investors. In addition, the *Corporations Act* specifies further specific prospectus content requirements. The body issuing a disclosure document, its directors and advisers have the responsibility of ensuring that the disclosure document contains the required information.

Section 717 contains the following table that summarises what a person who wants to offer securities must do to make an offer of securities that needs disclosure to investors.

table 7.1 offering securities (disclosure documents and procedure)

	Action required	Sections	Comments and related sections
1	Prepare disclosure document, making sure that it: — sets out all the information required — does not contain any misleading or deceptive statements — is dated and that the directors consent to the disclosure document.	710 711 712 713 714 715 716	Section 728 prohibits offering securities under a disclosure document that is materially deficient. Section 729 deals with the liability for breaches of this prohibition. Sections 731, 732 and 733 set out defences.
2	Lodge the disclosure document with ASIC	718	Subsection 727(3) prohibits processing applications for non-quoted securities for 7 days after the disclosure document is lodged.
3	Offer the securities, making sure that the offer and any application form is either included in or accompanies: — the disclosure document; or — a profile statement if ASIC has approved the use of a profile statement for offers of that kind.	721	Sections 727 and 728 make it an offence to: — offer securities without a disclosure document — offer securities if the disclosure document is materially deficient. Subsection 729(3) deals with liability on the prospectus if a profile statement is used. The securities hawking provisions (section 736) restrict the way in which the securities can be offered.

	Action required	Sections	Comments and related sections
4	If it is found that the disclosure document lodged was deficient or a significant new matter arises, either: — lodge a supplementary or replacement document under section 719; or — return money to applicants under section 724.	719 724	Section 728 prohibits making offers after becoming aware of a material deficiency in the disclosure document or a significant new matter. Section 730 requires people liable on the disclosure document to inform the person making the offer about material deficiencies and new matters.
5	Hold application money received on trust until the securities are issued or transferred or the money returned.	722	Investors may have a right to have their money returned if certain events occur (see sections 724, 737 and 738).
6	Issue or transfer the securities, making sure that: — the investor used an application form distributed with the disclosure document; and — the disclosure document is current and not materially deficient; and any minimum subscription condition has been satisfied.	723	Section 721 says which disclosure document must be distributed with the application form. Section 729 identifies the people who may be liable if: — securities are issued in response to an improper application form; or — the disclosure document is not current or is materially deficient. Sections 731, 732 and 733 provide defences for the contraventions. Section 737 provides remedies for an investor.

types of disclosure documents

[7.15] One of the main criticisms of the previous fundraising rules was that prospectuses were often too long and complicated and obscured information of interest to investors, particularly retail investors. The present fundraising provisions addressed these criticisms by recognising four different types of disclosure documents. The reforms were designed to minimise the costs of fundraising while maintaining investor protection.

Section 9 defines a disclosure document for an offer of securities as:

> **a prospectus; or**
> **a profile statement; or**
> **an offer information statement.**

The table in s 705 shows what disclosure documents to use if an offer of securities needs disclosure to investors.

table 7.2 types of disclosure documents—s 705

	Type	Sections
1	**Prospectus** The standard full disclosure document	Content [710, 711, 713] Procedure [717] Liability [728 and 729] Defences [731, 733]

	Type	Sections
2	**Short form prospectus** May be used for any offer. Section 712 allows a prospectus to refer to material lodged with ASIC instead of setting it out. Investors are entitled to a copy of this material if they ask for it.	Content [712]
3	**Profile statement** Section 721 allows a brief profile statement (rather than the prospectus) to be sent out with offers with ASIC approval. The prospectus must still be prepared and lodged with ASIC. Investors are entitled to a copy of the prospectus if they ask for it.	Content [714] Procedure [717] Liability [728 and 729] Defences [732, 733]
4	**Offer information statement** Section 709 allows an offer information statement to be used instead of a prospectus for an offer to issue securities if the amount raised from issues of securities is $5 million or less.	Content [715] Procedure [717] Liability [728 and 729] Defences [732, 733]

The following table indicates the number and types of disclosure documents in relation to equity (shares) fundraisings that were lodged with ASIC for the year ending 30 June 2004.

table 7.3 disclosure documents for equities lodged with ASIC 1 July 2003 to 30 June 2004

Type of disclosure document		Number lodged
Prospectuses		
Unquoted securities	426	
Quoted securities	206	632
Short form prospectuses		
Unquoted securities	55	
Quoted securities	63	118
Offer Information Statements		61
Total		811

Source: ASIC's OFFERlist database

when is disclosure to investors needed?

[7.20] The *Corporations Act* requires disclosure to investors in certain circumstances where an offer of securities is made. This is determined by means of a general rule in either s 706 or s 707. Section 708 contains specific exemptions that stipulate the offers of securities that do not need disclosure to investors.

The fundraising provisions apply to offers of securities of public companies. A proprietary company must not engage in any activity that would require disclosure to investors under Ch 6D of the *Corporations Act* except for an offer of its shares to existing shareholders or employees: s 113(3). ASIC may require a proprietary company to convert to a public company if it breaches the s 113(3) prohibition: s 165.

general rule

[7.25] The *Corporations Act* sets out different disclosure rules for issue offers of securities (primary issues) and sale offers of securities (secondary trading). The disclosure requirements in relation to secondary trading are discussed below, para [7.155].

An offer of securities for issue needs disclosure to investors unless one of the exemptions in s 708 says otherwise.

Under s 706 an offer of securities for issue needs disclosure to investors unless one of the exemptions in s 708 says otherwise. While s 706 refers to "offering securities for issue", s 700(2)(a) makes it clear that this includes inviting applications for the issue of securities.

The prohibitions in s 727 complement s 706. A person is prohibited from making an offer of securities or distributing an application form for an offer of securities that needs disclosure unless a disclosure document for the offer has been lodged with ASIC: s 727(1). Further, under s 727(2) offers of securities that need disclosure to investors must be included in the appropriate disclosure document or accompanied by a copy of the disclosure document. Section 726 imposes a similar prohibition against offering securities in an unformed body or an unregistered managed investment scheme that needs to be registered.

Offers of securities that need disclosure to investors must be included in the appropriate disclosure document or accompanied by a copy of the disclosure document.

Contravention of ss 726 and 727 is a criminal offence punishable by a fine of 200 penalty units or five years imprisonment or both: s 1311 and Sch 3.

In *ASIC v Australian Investors Forum Pty Ltd* (*No 2*) [2005] NSWSC 267, Palmer J considered that:

> < **The circumstances in which particular offers of securities are made for the purposes of ss 727(1) and 708(10) will vary infinitely but the indicia of the making of such an offer will generally include:**
>
> > **Identification of the company in which the securities are offered;**
> > **What is the general nature of the securities offered;**
> > **The price for which the securities may be acquired;**
> > **The suggestion that the securities are available for acquisition by the person to whom the information is conveyed;**
> > **The suggestion that the securities may be acquired now or at some specified future time, by the requisite payment.** >

The general rule in s 706 applies to offers of securities that emanate from Australia. With the increasing popularity of the Internet it is relatively easy for Australian investors to be offered overseas shares or other investments. Such offers do not have to comply with the stringent disclosure requirements of the *Corporations Act* and consequently there is a danger that investors may not have adequate information to properly assess the merits of overseas offers. ASIC has several publications on its website that warn prospective investors of the dangers associated with Internet fundraising. These publications are linked to the Lipton-Herzberg Fundraising Pathway at **http://www.lipton-herzberg.com.au/secure/pathways-fundraising.html**

ASIC Policy Statement 141 sets out ASIC's policies regarding offers of securities on the Internet. Among other things, the policy statement discusses when ASIC will regulate such Internet offers. The Lipton-Herzberg Fundraising Pathway has a link to Policy Statement 141.

offers that do not need disclosure

Financially sophisticated wholesale investors have the ability to look after their own interests and take steps to inform themselves about the merits of an offer of securities.

[7.30] The fundraising provisions recognise that financially sophisticated wholesale investors have the ability to look after their own interests and take steps to inform themselves about the merits of an offer of securities. Such investors do not rely upon the fundraising provisions to as great an extent as smaller investors. In the case of small offerings, it would be commercially unrealistic to impose costly disclosure requirements. Section 708 lists situations where offers of securities do not need disclosure to investors. These are set out in Table 7.4 below.

table 7.4 offers that do not need disclosure — s 708

Small scale offerings	708(1)–(7)
Sophisticated investors Large offers Offers to wealthy investors Offers to experienced investors	 708(8)(a) and (b) 708(8)(c) 708(10)
Professional investors	708(11)
Executive officers	708(12)
Existing security holders	708(13) and (14)
No consideration	708(15) and (16)
Compromise or arrangement	708(17)
Takeovers	708(18)
Debentures	708(19)
Offers by exempt bodies	708(20)
Exempt public authority	708(21)

small scale offerings

[7.35] Section 708(1)–(7) contains the exemption for small scale offerings of securities. The exemption focuses on the number of issues of securities in a 12-month period, and not the number of offers made. It also focuses on the amount raised from investors in a 12-month period.

Under s 708(1) "personal" offers of securities do not need disclosure to investors if none of the offers results in a breach of the "20 investors ceiling" and the "$2 million ceiling". It is an offence to issue securities without disclosure to investors if this results in a breach of either the 20 investors ceiling or the $2 million ceiling: s 727(4).

Under s 708(1) "personal" offers of securities do not need disclosure to investors if none of the offers results in a breach of the "20 investors ceiling" and the "$2 million ceiling".

[7.40] Personal offers. The small scale offerings exclusion is limited to "personal" offers of securities. This limitation is designed to prevent offers being made to investors at large without an appropriate disclosure document. Under s 708(2) a personal offer is one that:

> **may only be accepted by the person to whom it was made; and**
> **is made to a person who is likely to be interested in the offer as a result of previous contact, professional or other connection with the offeror, or statements or action by the investor that indicate they are interested in offers of that kind.**

[7.45] The 20 investors ceiling is breached if an offer to issue securities results in the number of people to whom securities have been issued exceeding 20 in any 12-month period: s 708(3)(a).

[7.50] The $2 million ceiling is breached if an offer to issue securities results in the amount raised by the issuing body exceeding $2 million in any 12-month period: s 708(3)(b). For purposes of the $2 million ceiling, s 708(7) requires the following amounts to be included in calculating the amount of money raised:

> **the amount payable for the securities at the time when they are issued;**
> **amounts payable at a future time if a call is made where the securities are partly paid shares;**
> **amounts payable on the exercise of an option where the security is an option; and**
> **amounts payable on the exercise of a conversion right where the securities are convertible into other securities.**

Securities issued and amounts raised as a result of offers under other s 708 exemptions are disregarded in counting the 20 investors ceiling and the $2 million ceiling: s 708(5). Issues made under a disclosure document are also not counted.

Section 734(1) prohibits advertising or publicity for offers covered by the small scale offerings exception in s 708(1).

sophisticated investors

Sections 708(8) and (10) contain several exemptions from the disclosure requirements in relation to offers of securities to experienced, financially sophisticated or wealthy investors.

[7.55] Sections 708(8) and (10) contain several exemptions from the disclosure requirements in relation to offers of securities to experienced, financially sophisticated or wealthy investors. The *Corporations Act* takes the view that such investors have sufficient means to obtain their own investment advice or have the bargaining power over the issuing body to obtain the necessary information without the *Corporations Act* assisting by requiring mandatory disclosure documents.

[7.60] large offers. Section 708(8)(a) deals with large offers of securities. Under that section an offer of securities does not need disclosure to investors if the minimum amount payable for the securities on acceptance of the offer is $500,000 or more. Further, under s 708(8)(b), disclosure to investors is not required in the case of an investor who either accepts an offer of securities for at least $500,000 payable by instalments over a period of time or tops up a previously accepted large offer. In calculating the amount payable or paid for securities under s 708(8)(a) or (b), any amount lent by the person offering the securities or their associate is disregarded: s 708(9).

The large offer exemptions are based on the assumption that people who invest such large amounts are presumed to have the ability to demand the disclosure of information necessary to decide whether or not to invest.

[7.65] offers to wealthy investors. Offers of securities made to "wealthy" investors do not need disclosure to investors: s 708(8)(c). An offer comes within this exemption if a qualified accountant certifies that the investor had either a gross income over each of the previous two financial years of at least the amount specified in the *Corporations Regulations* ($250,000) or had net assets of at least the amount specified in the *Corporations Regulations* ($2.5 million). A qualified accountant is defined in s 9 as a member of a professional body that is approved by ASIC for the purposes of s 708(8)(c). In Policy Statement 154, ASIC states that it has approved members of CPA Australia, the Institute of Chartered Accountants in Australia and the National Institute of Accountants who comply with the continuing professional educational requirements of those organisations. ASIC Policy Statements are linked to the Lipton-Herzberg Fundraising Pathway at **http://www.lipton-herzberg.com.au/secure/pathways-fundraising.html**

[7.70] offers to experienced investors. Offers of securities made to "experienced" investors do not need disclosure to investors: s 708(10). An offer comes within this exemption if it is made through a financial services licensee: s 708(10)(a). Under s 708(10)(b), the licensee must be satisfied on reasonable grounds that the investor has previous experience in investing in securities that allows them to assess such matters as the merits of the offer, the value of the securities, the risks involved in accepting the offer and the adequacy of the information given by the person making the offer. The investor must sign a written acknowledgment that the licensee has not given them a disclosure document in relation to the offer: s 708(10)(d).

[7.75] offers to professional investors. An offer of securities does not need disclosure to investors if it is made to a "professional investor". Section 9 defines a professional investor to include a financial services licensee, a body regulated by APRA and a trustee of a superannuation fund that has net assets of at least $10 million.

executive officers

[7.80] An offer of securities does not need disclosure to investors if it is made to a senior manager of the body or a related body or their spouse, parent, child, brother or sister: s 708(12). "Senior manager" is defined in s 9 to mean a person (other than a director or secretary) who makes, or participates in making, decisions that affect the whole, or a substantial part, of the business of the corporation. Section 708(12) also exempts offers of securities to a body corporate controlled by senior managers or their relatives.

existing security holders

[7.85] Offers of securities to present holders of securities for issue do not need disclosure to investors if they are offers of fully paid shares to existing shareholders under a dividend reinvestment plan or bonus share plan: s 708(13). Disclosure to investors is also not required in the case of offers of a disclosing entity's debentures for issue to existing debenture-holders: s 708(14).

lodgment of disclosure documents

[7.90] A disclosure document used for an offer of securities must be lodged with ASIC: s 718. Further, s 727(1) makes it an offence for a person to offer securities or distribute an application form for an offer of securities that needs disclosure to investors unless the disclosure document for the offer has been lodged with ASIC.

A disclosure document used for an offer of securities must be lodged with ASIC.

ASIC Policy Statement 152 sets out ASIC's policies regarding lodgment of disclosure documents. The Policy Statement explains the obligations of the fundraiser as well as ASIC's approach to scrutiny of disclosure documents lodged with it. Policy Statement 152 is linked to the Lipton-Herzberg Fundraising Pathway at **http://www.lipton-herzberg.com.au/secure/pathways-fundraising.html**

Disclosure documents may be given to potential investors immediately after they have been lodged with ASIC. However, in the case of offers of non-quoted securities, s 727(3) imposes a seven-day waiting period after ASIC lodgment before applications for the non-quoted securities can be accepted. ASIC may extend the period to a maximum of 14 days.

The waiting period is designed to give ASIC and other interested parties an opportunity to consider the contents of the disclosure document before the non-quoted securities are processed. If the disclosure document is found to be deficient, ASIC or aggrieved parties have the ability to apply for injunctions to halt the fundraising. There is no waiting period for offers of quoted securities because they already have an established market price and are subject to ASX continuous disclosure obligations.

Under s 720 directors must give their consent to the lodgment of the disclosure document with ASIC.

ASIC maintains a database called "OFFERlist" that contains a list of all disclosure documents for fundraising offers lodged with ASIC. OFFERlist, which is accessible on the Internet, aims to facilitate access to these offer documents during the required exposure period of seven days. Information about OFFERlist and the ability to search OFFERlist can be found on the ASIC website which is linked to the Lipton-Herzberg Fundraising Pathway at **http://www.lipton-herzberg.com.au/secure/pathways-fundraising.html**

contents of disclosure documents

The *Corporations Act* has different content requirements for the various types of disclosure documents.

[7.95] The *Corporations Act* has different content requirements for the various types of disclosure documents. More detailed information must be set out in a prospectus, which is regarded as a full disclosure document, than in the other types of disclosure documents. Section 715A, inserted by the 2004 amendments, requires the information in a disclosure document to be worded and presented in a clear, concise and effective manner.

Examples of current prospectuses are available on the Lipton-Herzberg Fundraising Pathway at **http://www.lipton-herzberg.com.au/secure/pathways-fundraising.html** which has a link to the "Upcoming Floats" heading on the ASX website. Companies seeking to float on the ASX often make their prospectuses available on the ASX website.

The Lipton-Herzberg Fundraising Pathway also has a link to an ASIC issues paper, *Multimedia Prospectuses and Other Offer Documents*, by Dr Elizabeth Boros, published on the ASIC website. The paper examines the issues raised by multimedia prospectuses under three broad headings:

> **equality of access;**
> **the relevance of lodgment to dissemination; and**
> **multimedia information that is not reducible to text.**

prospectuses

[7.100] The *Corporations Act* imposes a general disclosure test for the contents of a prospectus as well as specific disclosure obligations.

general disclosure test

A prospectus must contain all the information that investors and their professional advisers would reasonably require to make an informed assessment.

[7.105] Under s 710(1), a prospectus must contain all the information that investors and their professional advisers would reasonably require to make an informed assessment of the matters set out in the table in that section. A prospectus must contain this information:

> **only to the extent to which it is reasonable for investors and their professional advisers to expect to find the information in the prospectus; and**
> **only if the information is actually known or in the circumstances ought reasonably to have been obtained by making inquiries.**

Section s 710(1) contains a table which specifies the following information which must be disclosed in relation to an offer to issue shares, debentures or interests in a managed investment scheme. This includes:

> **the rights and liabilities attaching to the securities offered; and**
> **the assets and liabilities, financial position and performance, profits and losses and prospects of the body that is to issue the shares, debentures or interests.**

In deciding what information should be included under the general disclosure test, s 710(2) specifies that regard must be had to such matters as the nature of the securities and the matters that likely investors may reasonably be expected to know.

In *Fraser v NRMA Holdings Ltd* (1995) 13 ACLC 132, which dealt with a prospectus issued as part of a restructuring of the company's business, the Federal Court held that the prospectus should have discussed the disadvantages of the proposed restructuring of which the directors were aware.

A person who omits information required by the s 710 general disclosure test contravenes s 728(1). This is a criminal offence if the omission is materially adverse from the point of view of an investor: s 728(3). In addition, if an investor suffers loss or damage because of the omission they can recover compensation from the people listed in the table in s 729. This is discussed below.

forecasts

[7.110] Profit, dividend and other financial forecasts in a prospectus can significantly influence a person's decision whether or not to invest. Among other things, the general disclosure test in s 710(1) requires a prospectus to disclose information regarding the financial performance and prospects of the body that is issuing securities. These requirements do not necessarily mean that a prospectus must include forward-looking statements such as financial forecasts. The decision whether or not to include forward-looking statements is left to the body issuing the prospectus.

Because predictions about the future are uncertain, there is always the possibility that forecasts and other forward-looking statements contained in a prospectus may not eventuate. A disclosure document that contains a forward-looking statement is regarded as being misleading for purposes of the liability provisions if the person making it does not have reasonable grounds for making the statement: s 728(2). Prior to the changes made by 1999 amendments, the predecessor of s 728(2) put the onus of proving the existence of reasonable grounds on the person making the statement. The 1999 amendments removed this reverse onus of proof to encourage the inclusion of material of potential use to investors without exposing issuers to liability for legitimate forecasting.

A disclosure document that contains a forward-looking statement is regarded as being misleading for purposes of the liability provisions if the person making it does not have reasonable grounds for making the statement.

ASIC Policy Statement (PS 170), *Prospective Financial Information,* outlines ASIC's views on when prospective financial information can or should be disclosed and what are reasonable grounds for prospective financial information. This Policy Statement is linked to the Lipton-Herzberg Fundraising Pathway at **http://www.lipton-herzberg.com.au/secure/pathways-fundraising.html**

alternative disclosure test

[7.115] The general disclosure test for prospectuses of listed companies is not as stringent as the general disclosure test for unlisted companies. Listed companies are subject to the continuous disclosure requirements of the *Corporations Act* and ASX Listing Rules. Continuous disclosure is discussed in Chapter 15 below. Since listed companies are required, on a continuing basis, to disclose information to the ASX that would be likely to have a material effect on the price of their securities, much of the information that s 710(1) would normally require to be included in a prospectus is already known to the market.

As a consequence, s 713 sets out an alternative general disclosure test in the case of a prospectus for an offer of continuously quoted securities of a body. Continuously quoted securities are securities that are in a class of securities that were quoted ED (enhanced disclosure) securities at all times in the 12 months before the date of the prospectus: s 9. Under s 713(2), such prospectuses must contain all the information investors and their professional advisers would reasonably require in order to make an informed assessment of such matters as the effect of the offer on the body and the rights and liabilities attaching to the securities offered.

The alternative general disclosure test does not require the prospectus to contain information regarding the assets and liabilities, financial position and performance, profits and losses and prospects of the issuing body. The market should already know this information because of the continuous disclosure and periodic reporting requirements imposed on listed disclosing entities.

specific disclosures

[7.120] Section 711 lists certain basic information that must be contained in every prospectus. Table 7.5 below highlights the specific prospectus disclosures required by s 711.

table 7.5 specific prospectus disclosures — s 711

Terms and conditions of the offer	711(1)
Disclosure of interests, fees and benefits of certain people involved in the offer	711(2)–(4)
Quotation of securities	711(5)
Expiry date	711(6)
Lodgment with ASIC	711(7)
Information prescribed by the regulations	711(8)

short form prospectuses

[7.125] One of the complaints made of the previous prospectus provisions was that prospectuses were often lengthy and overly complex documents. This was a particular concern for retail investors not experienced in reading and comprehending technical information. This concern has been addressed by the current fundraising provisions, which facilitate the use of short form prospectuses.

A short form prospectus is a disclosure document that refers to material in documents lodged with ASIC instead of that information being included in the prospectus.

A short form prospectus is a disclosure document that refers to material in documents lodged with ASIC instead of that information being included in the prospectus. This is permitted by s 712(1). Referred documents are regarded as being part of the prospectus: s 712(3). The reference must identify the lodged document that contains the information and inform people of their right to obtain a copy free of charge on request. If the information is primarily of interest to people such as professional analysts, the reference must say so and include a description of the contents of the document.

profile statements

[7.130] Section 709(2) permits fundraisers to prepare a profile statement in relation to an offer in addition to a prospectus if ASIC has approved the use of profile statements in the making of offers of that kind. An approved profile statement may be sent to investors instead of the full prospectus: s 721(2). However, a free copy of the prospectus must be provided to an investor on request: s 721(3).

Section 714 sets out the contents of profile statements. Among other things, they must:

> **identify the issuing body and the nature of the securities;**
> **state the nature of the risks involved in investing in the securities;**
> **give details of all amounts payable in respect of the securities (including fees, commissions or charges);**
> **state that a copy of the prospectus is available free of charge; and**
> **give any other information required by the Regulations or by ASIC.**

As a result of the amendments made by the *Financial Services Reform Act 2001*, profile statements are now rarely used in practice. They were originally intended to facilitate offers of interests in selected managed investment schemes such as units in cash management trusts and property trusts. As a result of the 2001 amendments, offers of such financial products are now regulated by the financial product disclosure regime contained in Pt 7.9 of the *Corporations Act*.

offer information statements

[7.135] Amendments made in 1999 introduced the use of an offer information statement (OIS) as a new type of disclosure document for relatively small fundraisings. An OIS, disclosing minimal information, may be used instead of a prospectus if the amount of money to be raised by the issuer, when added to all amounts previously raised by it, its related bodies or controlled entities, is $5 million or less: s 709(4).

An OIS, disclosing minimal information, may be used instead of a prospectus if the amount of money to be raised by the issuer, when added to all amounts previously raised by it, its related bodies or controlled entities, is $5 million or less.

The cost of preparing an OIS is considerably cheaper than a prospectus. This is because the OIS disclosure obligations do not require extensive due diligence inquiries to be made. Section 715 sets out the contents of an OIS. Among other things, an OIS must:

> **identify the issuing body and the nature of the securities;**
> **describe the body's business and what the funds sought to be raised are to be used for;**
> **state the nature of the risks involved in investing in the securities;**
> **give details of all amounts payable in respect of the securities; and**
> **state that the OIS has a lower level of disclosure requirements than a prospectus and that investors should obtain professional advice before investing.**

Section 715(1)(i) also requires an OIS to include a copy of the body's financial report. The financial report must be prepared in accordance with accounting standards, be audited and be for a 12-month period with a balance date that occurred within six months before the securities were first offered under the OIS: s 715(2).

ASIC Policy Statement 157 sets out ASIC's policies regarding the financial reports that must accompany an OIS. The Lipton-Herzberg Fundraising Pathway at **http://www.lipton-herzberg.com.au/secure/pathways-fundraising.html** has a link to this Policy Statement.

restrictions on issue of securities

minimum subscription

[7.140] If a disclosure document states that the securities will not be issued unless applications for a minimum number of securities are received or a minimum amount is raised, the person making the offer must not issue any of the shares until that minimum subscription condition is satisfied: s 723(2). Application money received from investors must be held in trust until the minimum subscription condition is fulfilled and the securities are issued: s 722.

The purpose of s 723 is to protect early subscribers where the company is unable to raise the minimum amount it needs to be a viable concern. Otherwise, preliminary expenses would be met by a relatively small number of investors without any real future prospects.

Under s 724, if the minimum subscription condition is not satisfied within four months after the date of the disclosure document, the company must either:

> **repay the money received from the applicants; or**
> **give the applicants a supplementary or replacement disclosure document that changes the terms of the offer and one month to withdraw their application and be repaid; or**
> **issue the securities to the applicants and give them a supplementary or replacement disclosure document that changes the terms of the offer and one month to return the securities and be repaid.**

stock exchange listing

[7.145] It is of great importance to prospective investors that their securities will be listed on a stock exchange. This gives their investment a much greater degree of marketability. In addition, ASX listing requirements afford additional protection to securities holders. Therefore, if a corporation states in a disclosure document that it has applied or will apply for stock exchange listing of the securities, it should take all possible steps to become listed. If the securities are not listed within the prescribed period, the issue is void and the corporation must repay the money received by it pursuant to the disclosure document: s 723(3).

If a corporation states in a disclosure document that it has applied or will apply for stock exchange listing of the securities, it should take all possible steps to become listed.

expiration of disclosure document

[7.150] Disclosure documents expire 13 months after their date: ss 711(6), 714(2) and 715(3). The securities may be issued to the applicant if the application was received on or before the expiry date: s 725(2). However, if the application is received after the expiry date, the company must, under s 725(3), either:

Disclosure documents expire 13 months after their date.

> **repay the money received from the applicants; or**
> **give the applicants a supplementary or replacement disclosure document that changes the terms of the offer and one month to withdraw their application and be repaid; or**
> **issue the securities to the applicants and give them a supplementary or replacement disclosure document that changes the terms of the offer and one month to return the securities and be repaid.**

secondary trading

[7.155] The fundraising provisions of the *Corporations Act* are largely directed at offers of securities for issue (primary issues) and have limited application to the subsequent sale of securities (secondary trading). Only some sales of securities need disclosure to investors. As a general rule, secondary trading of listed securities quoted on the stock exchange does not require disclosure to investors. Section 707 specifies when sales of securities need disclosure.

Only some sales of securities need disclosure to investors.

sales by controller

[7.160] Under s 707(2) an offer of securities for sale needs disclosure to investors if the person making the offer controls the body whose securities are being offered and the securities are not quoted. Where the securities offered for sale by a controller are quoted securities, s 707(2) also requires disclosure to investors if the securities are not offered for sale in the ordinary course of trading on a relevant financial market (eg the ASX).

Section 50AA defines when a person controls a body. The s 50AA definition is similar to the definition of "control" in the accounting standards. Under s 50AA, an entity controls a second entity if the first entity has the capacity to determine the outcome of decisions about the second entity's financial and operating policies.

Section 707(5), which is designed to prevent avoidance of s 707(2), requires disclosure to investors where a sale offer of securities of a body amounts to an indirect sale by the person who controlled the body. Section 707(5) applies to both a sale offer of unquoted securities and off-market sale offers within 12 months after their sale by a controller. Such offers require disclosure to investors if the controller sold the securities without disclosure to investors and either the controller sold them with the purpose of the buyer on-selling the securities (s 707(5)(c)(i)); or the buyer acquired the securities with the purpose of on-selling the securities: s 707(5)(c)(ii).

A controller is taken to have sold the securities and a buyer is taken to have acquired the securities, for the s 707(5)(c)(i) and (ii) purposes if any of the securities are subsequently sold, or offered for sale, within 12 months after their sale by the controller unless it is proved that the circumstances of the initial sale and the subsequent sale are not such as to give rise to reasonable grounds for concluding that the securities were sold with that purpose: s 707(6).

The exception for small scale offers in s 708(1) does not apply to sales amounting to indirect off-market sales by the controller under s 707(5).

sale amounting to indirect issue

[7.165] Section 707(3) is another anti-avoidance provision. It aims to ensure that a body issuing securities cannot avoid disclosure to investors by issuing securities to an investor under one of the s 708 exemptions in circumstances where either the issuer or the investor had the purpose of securities being on-sold to others. In such circumstances the issue needs disclosure to investors.

Under s 707(4), securities are taken to have been issued or acquired with the purpose of on-sale if any of the securities are subsequently sold, or offered for sale, within 12 months after their issue unless it is proved that the circumstances of the issue and the subsequent sale are not such as to give rise to reasonable grounds for concluding that the securities were issued or acquired with that purpose.

Section 708A, inserted by the CLERP 9 amendments, exempts the issuer from the requirement to make disclosure to investors under s 707(3) if investors already have access to prospectus-type information. The information can be available because:

> **a prospectus for a retail issue has already been issued at about the same time as the private placement: ss 708A(11) and (12); or**
> **the issuer by a notice to the market verifies that it has complied with all its continuous disclosure and reporting obligations: s 708A(5) and (6). The notice must also set out information that is excluded from the continuous disclosure to ensure that investors receive prospectus-like disclosure: s 708A(7).**

securities hawking

[7.170] The secondary trading disclosure requirements of s 707 are reinforced by the securities hawking prohibition in s 736(1). The aim of this prohibition is to prevent high pressure selling of financial products to retail clients by means of unsolicited meetings or telephone "cold calling".

Section 736 prohibits a person from making unsolicited offers of securities for issue or sale in the course of a meeting or telephone call with a prospective investor.

The prohibition does not apply if the offer:

> **does not need a disclosure document because of the sophisticated investor exemptions in ss 708(8) or (10); or**
> **does not need a disclosure document because of the professional investor exemption in s 708(11); or**
> **is an offer of listed securities made by telephone by a licensed securities dealer; or**
> **is made to an established client by a licensed securities dealer.**

If securities are issued or transferred to an investor in contravention of the securities hawking prohibition, s 738 gives the investor the right to return the securities within one month after the issue or transfer and obtain a refund of the amount paid for the securities.

There are equivalent hawking prohibitions in relation to managed investments (s 992AA) and other financial products such as superannuation, life and general insurance and derivatives: s 992A.

ASIC has issued a guidance paper, *The Hawking Prohibitions: An ASIC Guide (July 2002)*, to assist the financial services industry in complying with this legislation. This paper is linked to the Lipton-Herzberg Fundraising Pathway at **http://www.lipton-herzberg.com.au/secure/pathways-fundraising.html**

advertising restrictions

[7.175] The primary aim of the fundraising provisions is investor protection through compulsory disclosure of relevant information. While the *Corporations Act* cannot oblige investors to read a disclosure document, it seeks to ensure that they have the disclosure document at hand prior to applying for the securities. This is achieved by s 727(2), which requires application forms for securities to be included with or accompanied by a disclosure document.

The aim of the fundraising provisions would be easily thwarted if a company could freely advertise or publicise its intention to issue securities. For this reason, the *Corporations Act* regulates advertising issues of securities.

The *Corporations Act* regulates advertising issues of securities.

Amendments made in 1999 relaxed the former pre-prospectus advertising and publicity restrictions. Under the previous provisions, advertising was allowed only after a prospectus had been lodged.

Different advertising restrictions apply for listed and unlisted securities. In the case of securities of a class already listed on the ASX, s 734(5)(a) permits advertising before lodgment of a disclosure document if the advertising includes a statement indicating that a disclosure document will be made available and that an application form in the disclosure document must be completed to acquire the securities.

Advertising unlisted securities prior to lodgment of a disclosure document is limited by s 734(5)(b) to the following:

> **a statement identifying the offer or the securities;**
> **a statement that a disclosure document will be made available when the securities are offered;**
> **a statement that investors will have to complete an application form in or attached to a disclosure document; or**
> **optionally, a statement of how to receive a copy of the disclosure document.**

Image advertising that forms part of the normal advertising of a body's products or services and is genuinely directed at maintaining its existing customers or attracting new customers for those products or services is not subject to the fundraising advertising restrictions: s 734(3).

Sending draft disclosure documents to persons covered by the sophisticated investors or professional investor exemptions in s 708(8), (10) and (11) is not regarded as contravening the pre-lodgment advertising restrictions: s 734(9).

After a disclosure document has been lodged with ASIC, s 734(6) requires advertisements to include a statement that:

> **the offers of securities will be made in, or accompanied by, a copy of the disclosure document; and**
> **anyone wishing to acquire the securities will need to complete the application form that will be in or will accompany the disclosure document.**

Section 734(7) specifically permits certain advertisements and publications. These include advertising or publicity that:

> consists solely of a notice or report of a general meeting of the body; and
> is a news report or is genuine comment in the media relating to the lodgment of a disclosure document or the information in such a document. News reports and genuine media comment are not permitted if anyone gives consideration or another benefit for publishing the report.

Section 1041H, which is based on s 52 of the *Trade Practices Act 1974* (Cth), has potential application to advertising in relation to securities. That section prohibits a person from engaging in misleading or deceptive conduct in connection with a notice published in relation to a financial product: s 1041H(2)(b)(ii). A security is a type of a financial product: s 764A(1). Contravention of s 1041H is not a criminal offence: s 1041H(3).

In addition, ASIC or any person whose interests are affected may apply for an injunction under s 1324 to halt misleading or deceptive advertising or other notices in relation to securities.

ASIC's power to exempt and modify

[7.180] The *Corporations Act* recognises that in some situations strict compliance with the fundraising provisions is either too onerous or inappropriate. Section 741(1) gives ASIC the power to exempt a person from a particular provision of the fundraising provisions. That section also gives ASIC the power to modify or vary any of the fundraising provisions.

misstatements and omissions

stop orders

[7.185] Section 728 prohibits a person from offering securities under a disclosure document if it contains a misleading or deceptive statement or omits information required by the fundraising provisions. Where ASIC is satisfied that a lodged disclosure document would contravene s 728, ASIC has the power under s 739(1) to make a stop order that prevents any further offers, issues, sales or transfer of the securities from being made. ASIC can also issue a stop order if it is satisfied that the information in a disclosure document is not worded and presented in a clear, concise and effective manner as required by s 715A.

Before issuing a stop order, ASIC must hold a hearing at which any interested person is given an opportunity to make representations about whether a stop order should be made: s 739(2). ASIC may make an interim stop order pending the holding of a hearing if it considers that any delay in making the order would be prejudicial to the public interest: s 739(3). An interim stop order has effect for 21 days.

The power of ASIC to make a stop order in respect of an offer of securities extends beyond the closing date of offers: *Thompson v ASIC* (2002) 20 ACLC 826.

supplementary and replacement documents

[7.190] Section 728 makes it an offence to continue making offers after a person has become aware that a disclosure document contains misleading or deceptive statements, has omitted required information or new circumstances have arisen since lodgment that are materially adverse from the point of view of an investor. In such cases, s 719 requires the lodgment of either a supplementary or replacement document to correct the deficiency in the original disclosure document. A supplementary or replacement disclosure document may also be lodged if the person making the offer becomes aware that the information in the disclosure documents is not worded and presented in a clear, concise and effective manner: s 719(1A).

Once a supplementary or replacement document has been lodged with ASIC, both the original disclosure document and the supplementary or replacement document must accompany subsequent offers of securities: s 719(4) and (5).

The s 719 requirement to lodge a supplementary or replacement document aims to ensure that a disclosure document contains accurate, adequate and up to date information prior to the expiration of the disclosure document.

liability for misstatements or omissions

table 7.6 people liable on disclosure document

People liable on disclosure document		[operative]
These people ...		Are liable for loss or damage caused by ...
1	the person making the offer	any contravention of subsection 728(1) in relation to the disclosure document
2	each director of the body making the offer if the offer is made by a body	any contravention of subsection 728(1) in relation to the disclosure document
People liable on disclosure document		[operative]
3	a person named in the disclosure document with their consent as a proposed director of the body whose securities are being offered	any contravention of subsection 728(1) in relation to the disclosure document
4	an underwriter (but not a sub-underwriter) to the issue or sale named in the disclosure document with their consent	any contravention of subsection 728(1) in relation to the disclosure document
5	a person named in the disclosure document with their consent as having made a statement: (a) that is included in the disclosure document; or (b) on which a statement made in the disclosure document is based	the inclusion of the statement in the disclosure document
6	a person who contravenes, or is involved in the contravention of, subsection 728(1)	that contravention

Section 728(1) is the key provision that prohibits a person from offering securities under a disclosure document if there is a misleading or deceptive statement in, or an omission from, a disclosure document.

The right to compensation requires proof that the loss or damage was suffered because of the misleading or deceptive statement in or omission from a disclosure document.

[7.195] Section 728(1) is the key provision that prohibits a person from offering securities under a disclosure document if there is a misleading or deceptive statement in, or an omission from, a disclosure document. Contravention of s 728(1) is a criminal offence only if the misleading or deceptive statement or omission is materially adverse from the point of view of an investor: s 728(3).

Section 729 deals with the right to recover compensation for loss or damage resulting from a contravention of s 728(1). Under s 729(1), the right to compensation requires proof that the loss or damage was suffered because of the misleading or deceptive statement in or omission from a disclosure document. Section 729 sets out, in Table 7.6 above, the range of people potentially liable for compensation and the extent of their liability. The issuer of a disclosure document, its directors and under-writers are responsible for the disclosure document as a whole. Other people (such as experts) named with their consent in the disclosure document are liable only for their own statements in the disclosure document.

case note

In *Reiffel v ACN 075 839 226 Ltd* [2003] FCA 194, Pannel Kerr Forster Consulting Australia (PKFCA), an independent expert, reviewed profit and other financial forecasts contained in a prospectus. The review report, which was also in the prospectus, contained PKFCA's negative assurance that nothing had come to their attention which caused them to believe the forecasts were not reasonable. PKFCA's review report also stated that it had reviewed the sensitivity analysis and that the underlying assumptions on which the forecasts were based were reasonable. After a number of investors acquired the securities issued pursuant to the prospectus, it was discovered that the actual profitability of the business was substantially below the forecasts. The investors commenced a class action against the promoter as well as PKFCA. In the case of PKFCA it was alleged that the negative assurance was misleading and deceptive for purposes of the predecessor of s 728. The court held that in giving a "negative assurance", PKFCA was in effect saying that based upon what it knew, the directors' assumptions provided a reasonable basis for the forecasts in the prospectus. It was implicit that PKFCA would exercise an appropriate degree of care, skill and judgment in informing itself and expressing the opinion. In the circumstances it was misleading and deceptive for PKFCA to express the opinions in its review report without qualification.

Under s 730, a person referred to in the s 729 table must notify the person making the offer as soon as practicable if they become aware that:

> **a material statement in the disclosure document is misleading or deceptive; or**
> **there is a material omission from the disclosure document of required material; or**
> **a material new circumstance has arisen since lodgment of the disclosure document that would have been required to be included if it had arisen before the disclosure document was lodged.**

Sections 731–733 set out the defences in relation to both criminal actions and compensation claims. Section 731 furnishes a due diligence defence in relation to a prospectus. Under s 731, there is a defence if the person made all reasonable inquiries and believed on reasonable grounds that the statement was not misleading or deceptive or that there was no omission.

Under s 731, there is a defence if the person made all reasonable inquiries and believed on reasonable grounds that the statement was not misleading or deceptive or that there was no omission.

Section 732, which applies to misleading or deceptive statements and omissions in an OIS and a profile statement, provides a defence if the person proves he or she did not know the statement was misleading or deceptive or that there was an omission.

Section 733(1) establishes a general reliance defence applicable to all disclosure documents under which there is no liability if the person proves he or she reasonably relied on information given by someone else. For the reliance defence to succeed, the person relied upon must be someone other than a director, employee or agent: s 733(1). A person is not regarded as an agent for purposes of the reasonable reliance defence in s 733(1) merely because he or she performs a particular professional or advisory function: s 733(2).

Under s 733(3), there is a defence in relation to misleading or deceptive statements and omissions for proposed directors, underwriters or makers of statements in disclosure documents if they publicly withdrew their consent to being named in a disclosure document.

pathways questions ...

The following questions dealing with fundraising may best be answered by reading this chapter and considering the Internet resources on the Lipton-Herzberg Fundraising Pathway at http://www.lipton-herzberg.com.au/secure/pathways-fundraising.html

1. Refer to a prospectus of a company seeking to float on the ASX in the near future.
   (a) What are the purposes of raising the capital?
   (b) Describe the company's history, business/es and business environment.
   (c) What are the stated strategies and future directions the company intends to pursue?
   (d) Does the prospectus refer to growth prospects?
   (e) Does the company propose to acquire a business? If so, from whom?
   (f) What is the minimum subscription (if any)?
   (g) What information is contained in the independent accountant's report?
   (h) Outline the main risk factors prospective investors should consider.
   (i) Describe any material or significant contracts entered into by the company.

2. Under s 709, an offer information statement may be used in certain situations.
   (a) What are ASIC's policies regarding offer information statements?
   (b) When may an offer information statement be used?
   (c) What information must be included?

3. Refer to the ASIC discussion paper *Multi Media Prospectuses and other Offer Documents* by Professor Boros.
   (a) How does the *Corporations Act* facilitate the use of electronic prospectuses?
   (b) What are ASIC's main policies with regard to electronic prospectuses?
   (c) Outline the main advantages and disadvantages arising from the use of electronic prospectuses.
   (d) Describe the approaches taken in Canada and the United States to the inclusion of multimedia material in prospectuses.

4. How has ASIC sought to protect investors who participate in online fundraising?

bibliography ...

Boros, E "The Online Corporation: Electronic Corporate Communications" Uni of Melbourne, Centre for Corporate Law and Securities Regulation, Corporate Law Research Papers, **http://cclsr.law.unimelb.edu.au/research-papers/**

Boros, E & ASIC "Multimedia Prospectuses and Other Offer Documents" Uni of Melbourne, Centre for Corporate Law and Securities Regulation, Corporate Law Research Papers, **http://cclsr.law.unimelb.edu.au/research-papers/**

Calleja, N "Current Issues Relating to Prospectus Advertising and Securities Hawking" (2000) 18 C & SLJ 23.

Coburn, N "Emergence of Global Fraud: Tracing and Returning Funds of Fraudulent Investment Schemes" (2000) 18 C & SLJ 542.

Farrar, J "Good Faith and Dealing with Dissent in Prospectuses" (1999) 1(1) Uni of Notre Dame Australia LR 27.

Grose, C "Will the Small Business Fundraising Reforms Proposed by CLERP Really Make it Easier for SMEs to Raise Capital in Australia?" (1998) 16 C & SLJ 297.

Hone, F "Fundraising and Prospectuses—The CLERP Proposals" (1998) 16 C & SLJ 311.

Karl, A, Kazakoff, A & Chapple, L "Market Response to Offer Information Systems" (2003) 21 C & SLJ 231.

Kyrwood, T "Disclosure Forecasts in Prospectuses" (1998) 16 C & SLJ 350.

Minns, S & Golding, G "Prospectus Due Diligence—A Focused Approach" (1993) 11 C & SLJ 542.

Morrison, D & Quirk, P "Beer, Shares and the Internet" (1997) 5 *Current Commercial Law* 15.

Sim, D "Electronic Fundraising: Cyberfloating the Australian Corporation" (1998) Aust Jnl of Corp Law 158.

Whincop, M "Promoters, Prospectuses and Pragmatism: Updating Fiduciary Duties in a Time of Economic Reform" (1998) 24 Mon Uni LR 454.

revision questions on the material in this chapter ...

> Please see eQuiz at **http://www.thomson.com.au/academic** for multiple choice questions and answers.

> For further corporations law links and material please refer to the Lipton-Herzberg website at **http://www.lipton-herzberg.com.au**

chapter eight

share capital

key points ...

- A share is an item of intangible property also known as a "chose in action". Ownership of a share gives the investor proprietary rights as defined by the company's constitution and the law.
- A company issues shares to investors to raise funds for operating its business activities. The issue price of a share is determined by contractual agreement between the company and the investor. Usually, the issue price is paid in the form of cash, although non-cash consideration is also permitted.
- An investor who pays the full issue price for their shares has no further liability to contribute capital to the company. Shares may also be issued partly paid. A shareholder who owns partly paid shares is liable to pay calls up to the amount of the issue price.
- A company may issue different classes of shares with differing rights attached. Ordinary and preference shares are share classes that are most frequently issued. Preference shares are a class of shares whose holders are usually given a right to be paid dividends at a fixed rate in priority to ordinary shareholders.
- Holders of classes of shares are protected from variations of class rights made without their approval. Such rights may only be varied in accordance with the constitution or a procedure set out in the *Corporations Act* which requires approval of at least 75 per cent of the votes of the affected class as well as a special resolution of the company.
- The *Corporations Act* regulates various types of share capital transactions such as share capital reductions, share buy-backs, indirect self-acquisitions and financial assistance to enable investors to acquire shares in the company. The common aim of this legislation is to ensure that the transactions do not materially prejudice the interests of the company, its shareholders or the ability of the company to pay its creditors.

Share capital is the total amount of money or other property that investors provide to the company in consideration for the shares issued to them.

[8.05] Issuing shares to investors is one of the main sources of funds for a company limited by shares. Share capital (sometimes also referred to as "equity capital") is the total amount of money or other property that investors provide to the company in consideration for the shares issued to them. Directors usually have the power to issue shares and raise equity capital for a company. Directors' fiduciary duty to issue shares for a proper purpose is discussed in Chapter 13.2 below. Share issues are regulated partly by the company's constitution or applicable replaceable rules and partly by the *Corporations Act*. ASX Listing Rules also regulate share issues by listed companies.

The fundraising provisions of the *Corporations Act* require companies that offer shares to disclose relevant and accurate information to potential investors so that they can make an informed decision whether or not to take up the shares. The fundraising rules are discussed in Chapter 7 above.

When shares are issued they are allotted to the holders who become members after their names are entered in the register of members. The rules regarding the issue of shares are discussed below in this chapter and the process for becoming a member is discussed in Chapter 9.

A company may also wish to issue shares that carry rights and obligations that differ from those of other shares. In such a case, the company may issue different classes of shares.

Historically, the issued share capital of a company was accorded great significance. In particular, in the case of companies limited by shares, its creditors were seen as being entitled to rely on the issued capital as the source of payment of their debts. Hence, there is an obligation imposed on companies to maintain their share capital. This is known as the rule in *Trevor v Whitworth*, which has been modified by the *Corporations Act*.

nature of shares

[8.10] A share is an item of intangible property also known as a "chose in action". Ownership of a share gives the shareholder proprietary rights as defined by the company's constitution and the law. Shares may be bought and sold, bequeathed and given as security for loans. In *Pilmer v The Duke Group* (2001) 19 ACLC 1172, the High Court said that:

A share is an item of intangible property also known as a "chose in action". Ownership of a share gives the shareholder proprietary rights as defined by the company's constitution and the law.

> **< Once issued, a share comprises a collection of rights and obligations relating to an interest in a company of an economic and proprietary character, but not constituting a debt. >**

The law also recognises that ownership of a share is capable of being divided into legal and equitable interests: s 1070A(3). Generally, the same person holds both the legal and equitable interest in a share. However, in some cases, they may be held by different persons. When shares are held on trust, the trustee has the legal interest and the beneficiary holds the equitable interest. This also occurs when shares are sold. When the contract of sale is made the purchaser first acquires an equitable interest. The vendor retains the legal interest in the shares. The purchaser obtains the legal interest when the transfer of shares is registered by the company. This is discussed in Chapter 9 below.

A share is a proportionate interest of a shareholder in the net worth of a company. A share's value is that proportion of the total net worth of the company's enterprise. The net asset backing of shares is based upon the balance sheet value of net assets. The market value of listed company shares takes into account various considerations such as market perceptions of the value of net assets, present and estimated future earnings, and prospects of the industry in which the company operates.

share options

[8.15] There are a number of different types of share options. One form of share option arises when a company agrees to issue shares to a person (the "option holder") at a future date. If the option holder agrees to take up the shares, they are said to exercise the option and can require the company to allot the shares. As with any other contract, an option requires the option holder to provide consideration for being granted the share option.

There are a number of different types of share options.

Another form of option arises when a person, other than the company, grants someone else an option in relation to shares. The option may be either a "put" or "call" option. The ASX conducts an options market for the shares of certain listed companies.

An option holder is not a member of the company until the option is exercised.

A convertible debenture or note has similarities to a share option because it entitles the holder to convert a loan to the company into shares at a future date. The issue of convertible debentures or convertible notes involves a company borrowing money on terms whereby the loan may be redeemed by a later issue of shares. The debenture, or note, holder in effect has an option to take up shares in the company at a future date. Convertible debentures and convertible notes are discussed in Chapter 11 below.

ASX Listing Rule 7.1 regulates the issue of options to take up shares in the future. Amongst other things, this rule requires a listed company to obtain shareholder approval when granting options which, if exercised, would result in an issue of shares exceeding 15 per cent of the company's capital. The ASX Listing Rules may be viewed on the ASX website which is linked to the Lipton-Herzberg Corporate Law Website page at **http://www.lipton-herzberg.com.au/corp-law-websites.html#Australian_Stock_Exchange**

To ensure disclosure of future capital commitments, s 170 requires companies to maintain a register of option holders and copies of option documents containing the required particulars.

Companies often grant share options to their directors and executives as part of their remuneration.

Companies often grant share options to their directors and executives as part of their remuneration. Typically, the options may only be exercised if the company, its directors and its executives satisfy defined performance conditions. Options with appropriate performance conditions are a feature of good corporate governance because they can help ensure the interests of shareholders are aligned with the personal interests of the company's management.

The *Corporations Act* ensures that shareholders receive information about options the company grants to its directors and senior officers. Disclosure of particulars regarding options granted to directors as part of their remuneration must also be made in an unlisted company's annual directors' report under s 300 and in the financial reports of the company. Similar disclosure is required of options granted to the five most highly remunerated officers other than directors: s 300(1). There are greater disclosure requirements regarding share options that a listed company grants to its directors and its five most highly remunerated executives as part of their remuneration: s 300A(1). The disclosure includes the value of options granted to those people as part of their remuneration as well as the value of options that they exercised during the financial year: s 300A(1)(e)(ii) and (iii).

stock

[8.20] Stock is a collection of shares expressed in units of money. Stock has the characteristic that, unlike a share, a holder can freely divide stock into amounts of any value. Each unit of stock can then be sold individually. Companies are prohibited from issuing stock or converting shares into stock: s 254F. Foreign corporations may have stock.

bearer shares

[8.25] Section 254F prohibits a company issuing bearer shares. Bearer shares or share warrants are documents sealed by a company which state that the bearer is entitled to specified shares. A bearer share is a negotiable instrument, which means it is transferable by delivery and a person who takes it for value without notice takes it free of any defect in title of the person from whom it is taken.

The term "share warrant" is now also used in a different sense. It is similar to an option over shares in a company. However, the right is granted by a third person and not the company. Such share warrants are not included within the s 254F prohibition and are actively traded on the ASX.

paid up capital

authorised share capital abolished

Amendments made in 1998 abolished the rule that required a company limited by shares to state in its constitution the amount of authorised or nominal capital with which it was registered and the division of this capital into shares of a fixed amount, called the "par" or "nominal" value of the shares.

[8.30] Amendments made in 1998 abolished the rule that required a company limited by shares to state in its constitution the amount of authorised or nominal capital with which it was registered and the division of this capital into shares of a fixed amount, called the "par" or "nominal" value of the shares. An allotment of shares in excess of the authorised capital was void: *Bank of Hindustan China & Japan Ltd v Alison* (1871) LR 6 CP 222.

However, it is open to a company to provide in its constitution that directors may not issue shares in excess of a stated limit. Such a restriction may be desirable where shareholders seek to prevent their holdings being diluted or new members acquiring shares without the consent of existing shareholders.

The concept of authorised capital was originally intended to allow a company's creditors to assess the size of the company. The requirement to specify the authorised capital did not serve a useful purpose because:

> the authorised capital did not have to be issued and the issued capital was of greater significance because it represented or approximated the amount received by the company from the issue of its shares;
> a company could raise funds by borrowing and this was unrelated to its authorised capital; and
> authorised capital could be increased or decreased by ordinary resolution without notice to creditors.

The issued capital of a company is of much greater importance. In particular, creditors of companies limited by shares have a general right to expect that issued capital will not be returned to shareholders in circumstances where the prospects of payment to creditors may be diminished. The principle that requires companies to maintain their share capital is discussed below, para [8.165] and following.

no par value

[8.35] A company may issue shares for any amount that it chooses without being restricted to a predetermined par or nominal value as specified in its constitution.

A company may issue shares for any amount that it chooses.

Amendments made in 1998 abolished the concept of "par value shares". Section 254C provides that shares no longer have a par value even if issued before the 1998 amendments became operative.

The abolition of the concept of par value recognised that it no longer served a useful commercial purpose and its continued existence added unnecessary complexity to the law dealing with share capital. Par value was an arbitrary amount stated in the constitution that did not usually bear any resemblance to the real value of its shares. In some cases, the par value of a share could be misleading to unsophisticated investors.

The removal of the concept of par value has resulted in significant simplification of various aspects of the share capital provisions. It is now not possible for companies to issue shares at a premium or discount because this presupposes that the shares have a par value.

fully and partly paid shares

[8.40] A company may issue fully paid shares or partly paid shares: s 254A(1)(c). Issuing fully paid shares means that the investor has paid the entire issue price of the shares. Shareholders who own fully paid shares have no obligation to contribute further money to the company. A person who holds partly paid shares is liable to pay calls on the shares unless the company is a no liability company: s 254M.

Shareholders who own fully paid shares have no obligation to contribute further money to the company. A person who holds partly paid shares is liable to pay calls on the shares.

On a winding up, a member is liable to contribute to the company's property to an amount sufficient to pay the company's debts and the costs of the winding up: s 515. A shareholder need not contribute more than the amount (if any) unpaid on the shares: s 516. A liquidator has the power to make a call: s 477(2)(ca). A liquidator can make calls whether or not calls are permitted by the company's constitution: *Wright v Mansell* [2001] FCA 1519.

The issue of partly paid shares presupposes an obligation to pay a call because to reduce the liability of a shareholder in respect of unpaid capital amounts to a reduction of capital. The requirements for permitted capital reductions are discussed below, para [8.185]. The amount unpaid on partly paid shares is called "reserve capital" or "uncalled capital".

The issued share capital of a company comprises paid up capital and reserve capital. A company may give security over its uncalled capital: s 124(1)(e). A company's shareholders may pass a special resolution that has the effect of restricting the company's right to make calls to situations where the company becomes insolvent and goes into a form of external administration such as voluntary administration or liquidation: s 254N. The amount unpaid on shares, if any, must be stated in the register of members: s 169(3)(f).

The issued share capital of a company comprises paid up capital and reserve capital.

issue of shares
contractual rules

offer and acceptance

Usually, an investor makes an offer for a share issue by sending the company an application form and paying the issue price.

[8.45] The normal rules of contract law apply to share issues. Usually, an investor makes an offer for a share issue by sending the company an application form and paying the issue price. This offer is accepted when the company, through its directors, decides to allot the shares and sends the notice of allotment. As these communications are usually by post, acceptance by post is deemed effective when posted: *Byrne v Van Tienhoven* (1880) 5 CPD 344. For example, in *Household Fire & Carriage Accident Insurance Co v Grant* (1879) 4 Ex D 216, a notice of allotment sent by the company was lost in the mail. The applicant was held to be a member and therefore liable on a call even though he did not receive communication of acceptance. The requirement of communication of acceptance was impliedly dispensed with by the offeror in using the post.

Under the law of contract, an offer lapses if not accepted within a reasonable time. In *Ramsgate Victoria Hotel Co v Montefiore* (1866) LR 1 Exch 109, it was held that an investor's offer to take up a share issue lapsed after a period of five months after being sent to the company. Therefore, the application for shares was no longer capable of acceptance by the company when it purported to allot the shares.

rights issues

A rights issue involves a company offering to issue shares to existing shareholders in proportion to shares held. A contract is formed when the shareholder accepts the company's offer.

[8.50] A rights issue involves a company offering to issue shares to existing shareholders in proportion to shares held. A contract is formed when the shareholder accepts the company's offer. Usually, the company specifies a closing date after which its offer lapses. From the date of the offer until the closing date the shareholder owns rights.

A distinction is made between a renounceable rights issue and a non-renounceable rights issue. A renounceable rights issue is one that gives the shareholder the power to sell her or his rights prior to the closing date. The company agrees to issue shares to any person who owns the rights and accepts the offer. Renounceable rights are often listed on the ASX and are marketable in the same way as listed shares.

issue of fewer shares than applied for

[8.55] Application forms for share issues usually provide that the applicant agrees to take the number of shares applied for or any lesser number that is allotted. This prevents problems arising where the number of shares applied for exceeds the number the company proposes to issue. An allotment of a lesser number than that applied for would otherwise constitute a counter-offer because the terms of the offer and acceptance are not identical. The effect of a counter-offer is to destroy the original offer. By requiring an applicant to make an offer for a certain number of shares or a lesser number at the discretion of the company, this awkward result is avoided, and the contract is complete when the shares are issued.

allotment and issue of shares

[8.60] The expressions, "allotment of shares" and "issue of shares" are sometimes used interchangeably, although there is a distinction. In *Commonwealth Homes & Investment Co Ltd v Smith* (1937) 59 CLR 443, Dixon J stated:

> **But an "allotment" of shares really bears a double aspect. In the formation of a contract of membership it may be the acceptance of the offer constituted by the application or the making or authorisation of an offer or counter-offer accepted by the subsequent assent of the allottee. But it is also the appropriation of a given**

number of shares to the allottee. Shares are personal property. Allotment, entry in the share register and the sealing and delivery of share certificates are matters of fact which constitute the issue of shares, considered as a form of property. >

It follows that allotment is one step in the broader process of an issue of shares. The various ways in which a person can become a member of a company are considered in Chapter 9 below.

restrictions on allotment

[8.65] There are several provisions in the *Corporations Act* that prohibit or make it an offence to issue securities in certain circumstances where conditions set out in a disclosure document are not met. This aims to protect shareholders. Disclosure documents and the fundraising provisions of the *Corporations Act* are discussed in Chapter 7 above.

minimum subscription

[8.70] If a disclosure document states that the securities will not be issued unless applications for a minimum number of securities are received or a minimum amount is raised, the person making the offer must not issue any of the shares until that minimum subscription condition is satisfied: s 723(2). Application money received from investors must be held in trust until the minimum subscription condition is fulfilled and the securities are issued: s 722.

If a disclosure document states that the securities will not be issued unless applications for a minimum number of securities are received or a minimum amount is raised, the person making the offer must not issue any of the shares until that minimum subscription condition is satisfied.

The purpose of s 723 is to protect early subscribers where the company is unable to raise the minimum amount it needs to be a viable concern. Otherwise, preliminary expenses would be met by a relatively small number of investors without any real future prospects.

Under s 724, if the minimum subscription condition is not satisfied within four months after the date of the disclosure document, the company must:

- **repay the money received from the applicants; or**
- **give the applicants a supplementary or replacement disclosure document that changes the terms of the offer and one month to withdraw their application and be repaid; or**
- **issue the securities to the applicants and give them a supplementary or replacement disclosure document that changes the terms of the offer and one month to return the securities and be repaid.**

If securities are issued in contravention of s 724, applicants have the right to return the securities and have their application money repaid. This right applies even where the company is being wound up and therefore confers a priority on applicants in liquidation: s 737(1).

Applicants may exercise this right by written notice to the company within one month after the date of the issue: s 737(2). The directors of the company are personally liable to repay the application money if it is not repaid by the company: s 737(3).

financial market quotation

[8.75] A disclosure document for an offer of securities may state or imply that the securities are to be quoted on a financial market (eg the ASX), whether in Australia or elsewhere. In such a case, unless an application for listing is made within seven days after the date of the disclosure document and the securities are listed within three months of that date, any issue or transfer of the securities in response to an application under the disclosure document is void. The offeror must return money received from applicants as soon as practicable: s 723(3). The offeror must also act in accordance with s 724(2). This is discussed above.

A disclosure document for an offer of securities may state or imply that the securities are to be quoted on the ASX.

Applicants have the right to have their application money repaid on the giving of notice under s 737.

expiration of disclosure document

A disclosure document must state that no securities will be issued on the basis of the document after the specified expiry date. This date must be no later than 13 months after the date of the disclosure document.

[8.80] A disclosure document must state that no securities will be issued on the basis of the document after the specified expiry date. This date must be no later than 13 months after the date of the disclosure document: ss 711(6), 714(2) and 715(3).

If an application for securities is received by the company after the expiry date, under s 725(3) the company must either:

> **return application money received; or**
> **give the applicants one month to withdraw their application or return the securities that have been issued.**

validation of improper issue of shares

The court has wide powers to validate or confirm a purported issue of shares which is invalid for any reason.

[8.85] The court has wide powers to validate or confirm a purported issue of shares which is invalid for any reason or in which the terms of the issue are inconsistent with or unauthorised by any law or the company's constitution: s 254E. The company, a shareholder or creditor of the company or any other person whose interests are affected by the share issue may make an application for validation. This section prevents a shareholder or creditor being adversely affected in certain circumstances if the company has made an improper share issue that would otherwise be void.

case note

The operation of a predecessor to s 254E was considered in *Re Swan Brewery Co Ltd (No 2)* (1976) 3 ACLR 168. There, the company issued substantial numbers of shares to several other companies. The holders of these shares had, for several years after they were entered on the register of members, been paid dividends, allotted bonus shares and generally treated as members. It was eventually discovered that these companies were at all material times subsidiaries of the Swan Brewery Co Ltd. The allotments to them were consequently void under a provision corresponding to s 259C which prohibited a subsidiary holding shares in its holding company. The companies sought to have the allotments validated by the court. Gillard J held that in the exceptional circumstances of the case it was "just and equitable" to validate the allotments so as to assist a large number of innocent people who would otherwise be victims of invalid allotments.

case note

In *Kokotovich Constructions Pty Ltd v Wallington* (1995) 13 ACLC 1113, the New South Wales Court of Appeal validated an allotment of shares because the parties had proceeded for 20 years on the basis that shares had been properly issued and an order validating the issue was just and equitable. The court rejected the argument that its discretion under the predecessor of s 254E should only be exercised where the validation was uncontentious.

consideration for share issue

[8.90] An investor must pay the company the issue price of the shares. This is the investor's consideration for the share issue. In most cases, the consideration is cash. However, companies may issue shares for a non-cash consideration: *Re Wragg Ltd* [1897] 1 Ch 796. The payment of a non-cash consideration for a share issue often occurs when a partnership or sole tradership evolve into a proprietary company. The partners or sole trader may sell their property to a newly formed company that they control and in return it allots them shares. This occurred in *Salomon's* case discussed in Chapter 2 above.

An investor must pay the company the issue price of the shares. This is the investor's consideration for the share issue.

The policy of the *Corporations Act* is to ensure that the issued capital of a company is a meaningful indicator of the funds available to its creditors. Therefore, a company cannot issue shares gratuitously. The non-cash consideration must be consideration recognised by the law of contract. Hence the issue of shares in consideration of past services is past consideration and is not permitted. The company may require the allottee in such circumstances to later pay the full value of the shares in cash.

The non-cash consideration must be consideration recognised by the law of contract.

In *Re White Star Line Ltd* [1938] 1 All ER 607, it was held that the value of the consideration for an allotment of shares must be more than "sufficient" consideration required under the law of contract. It must represent money's worth for the allotment.

The consideration for an allotment of shares must be more than "sufficient" consideration required under the law of contract. It must represent money's worth for the allotment.

The application for registration of a company limited by shares must, among other things, set out the amount (if any) each member agrees in writing to pay for each share: s 117(2)(k)(ii). Further, the application for registration of a public company that is limited by shares must set out the prescribed particulars about the share issue if shares will be issued for a non-cash consideration: s 117(2)(l). This is not required if the shares will be issued under a written contract and a copy of the contract is lodged with the application. Section 254X requires a company to lodge a notice of share issue with ASIC. This includes a copy or particulars of any contract whereby shares are issued by a public company for non-cash consideration. In addition, under s 254X(2) the company must also lodge with ASIC a certificate stating that payable stamp duty has been paid.

It is common for a company to issue shares for non-cash consideration to its promoters or directors. This is open to abuse if the company acquires overvalued assets. Promoters or directors are usually able to control the management of the company and so there may be no opportunity for an independent assessment of the value of the acquired asset. Promoters and directors in such cases may breach their fiduciary duties. This is discussed in Chapter 6 above and Chapter 13 below.

Where a company acquires overvalued assets, this may be detrimental to shareholders and creditors. Section 711(2) requires a prospectus to set out details of interests held by directors, promoters and others connected with the prospectus or the offer that relate to the promotion of the company and property acquired by it. A lesser degree of disclosure is required in other types of disclosure documents: ss 714(1)(c) and 715(1)(e).

classes of shares

[8.95] A company may wish to issue different classes of shares for various reasons.

A company may wish to issue different classes of shares for various reasons.

> **It may wish to raise share capital on terms similar to borrowing from external creditors. This can be done by issuing shares that carry a stated rate of dividend but with limited voting rights and no rights to participation in distribution of surplus assets on winding up.**
> **Small family companies may wish to concentrate control of the company in the hands of the holders of a particular class of shares. Such shares often have weighted voting rights.**
> **Some taxation minimisation schemes involve the issue of different classes of shares.**
> **A home unit company may own a building and issue different classes of shares, each of which entitles the shareholder to certain rights in respect of a particular unit in the building to the exclusion of the holders of other classes of shares.**

The most common ways in which different classes of shares differ are as follows:

> **entitlement to dividend;**
> **right to priority in payment of dividend;**
> **voting rights;**
> **right to priority of repayment of capital on winding up; and**
> **right to participate in a distribution of surplus assets on winding up.**

The creation of different classes of shares is regarded as a matter for the company to determine because it does not affect creditors or other outsiders. If a company wishes to differentiate between the rights of different classes of shares, these should be clearly set out in the constitution or the share issue contract.

The application for registration of a company must include the class of shares that the persons who consent to be members agree in writing to take up: s 117(2)(k). A company must lodge a notice with ASIC setting out particulars of any division of shares into classes if the shares were not previously so divided or the shares were converted into shares in another class: s 246F(1). A public company must lodge (within 14 days) with ASIC a copy of each document or resolution that attaches rights or varies or cancels rights attaching to issued or unissued shares: s 246F(3).

preference shares

The most common classes of shares are ordinary and preference shares.

[8.100] The most common classes of shares are ordinary and preference shares. Holders of preference shares have preferential rights to receive dividends ahead of ordinary shareholders. Preference shareholders usually have the right to receive dividends at a fixed percentage of the issue price of their shares. As a general rule, the dividend entitlements of ordinary shareholders are not expressed in terms of a fixed percentage of the issue price of their shares. Ordinary shareholders receive dividends if the company has surplus profits after payment of preference shareholders' dividends. Usually, the preference shareholders also have preferential rights ahead of ordinary shareholders to be repaid their capital if the company is wound up.

If a company has a profitable year, the ordinary shareholders may receive a larger dividend than preference shareholders. On the other hand, if the company does not operate profitably, the ordinary shareholders may receive a smaller or even no dividend while the preference shareholders usually still receive their fixed rate of dividend subject to the dividend payment rules discussed in Chapter 10 below. Therefore, the returns on investment to ordinary shareholders are usually more closely tied to the fortunes of the company. Preference shares normally only carry restricted voting rights. These characteristics of preference shares reflect that preference shareholders are commercially seen as being similar to external creditors.

participating preference shares

Preference shares may be participating or non-participating.

[8.105] Preference shares may be participating or non-participating. They are referred to as "participating preference shares" if the preference shareholders have the right to receive additional dividends as well as their preferential dividend entitlements. If the company is wound up, participating preference shareholders are presumed at common law to be entitled to receive surplus capital after the repayment of their capital contribution: *Re Plashett Pastoral Co Pty Ltd* (1969) 90 WN (Pt 1) (NSW) 295. Preference shares are presumed to be non-participating where this entitlement is not expressly stated in the company's constitution: *Will v United Lankat Plantations Co Ltd* [1914] AC 11. This reflects the commercial attitude that preference shareholders are similar to creditors who lend at a fixed rate of return.

cumulative preference shares

[8.110] Preference shares may be cumulative or non-cumulative. If a company does not pay dividends in a particular year, cumulative preference shareholders have the right to be paid arrears of dividends in subsequent years ahead of ordinary shareholders. Preference shares are presumed to be cumulative if the company constitution is silent on the matter: *Webb v Earle* (1875) 20 Eq 556.

Preference shares may be cumulative or non-cumulative.

deferred shares

[8.115] Shares are sometimes also classified as deferred or founder's shares. The holders of these shares only have rights to dividends if a prescribed amount has been paid to ordinary shareholders. Accordingly, the relationship between deferred and ordinary shares is similar to that between ordinary and preference shares.

voting rights

[8.120] Preference shareholders usually have limited voting rights. Examples of limited voting rights are rights to vote only:

> **during a period when dividends are in arrears;**
> **on a proposal for reduction of capital; or**
> **on a proposal to wind up the company.**

setting out preference shareholder rights

[8.125] Certain important rights attaching to preference shares must be set out in the company's constitution. Sections 254A(2) and 254G(2) require a company that issues preference shares or converts ordinary shares into preference shares to set out in its constitution or otherwise approve by special resolution the rights of preference shareholders with respect to the following:

Certain important rights attaching to preference shares must be set out in the company's constitution.

> **repayment of capital;**
> **participation in surplus assets and profits;**
> **cumulative or non-cumulative dividends;**
> **voting; and**
> **priority of payment of capital and dividends in relation to other shares or other classes of preference shares.**

This enables prospective and existing preference shareholders to easily ascertain the rights attaching to their shares. It also seeks to ensure that the rights attaching to preference shares are more entrenched than they would be if contained in an ordinary resolution of the company or board of directors. It is still open for a company to provide in its constitution that the directors retain a discretion to determine the amount of dividends or the rate of redemption of redeemable preference shares. The exercise of such a power would not contravene ss 254A(2) and 254G(2).

consequences of failure to set out preference shareholders' rights

[8.130] Sections 254A(2) and 254G(2) require a company to set out in its constitution the rights of preference shareholders in relation to certain important matters. However, at common law certain presumptions can be made regarding the rights of preference shareholders where the constitution is silent on the matter. It is unclear what effect a contravention of ss 254A(2) and 254G(2) has on those common law presumptions. It is also uncertain whether there are any civil consequences where the provisions are contravened. There are several possibilities.

For example, it may be that contravention of these provisions only constitutes an offence by the company and officers in default and does not otherwise alter preference shareholders' presumed common law rights.

On the other hand, a contravention may mean that the issue to preference shareholders is illegal. Under the law of contract where a contract is illegal because it is prohibited by a statute, the courts will not permit either party to enforce it. Such an interpretation would have dire consequences for preference shareholders who may not even be able to obtain a refund of their investment. However, there may be an exception that assists the preference shareholders in this situation. The courts do allow actions for recovery of money paid under an illegal contract by parties who are not in pari delicto (equal fault). A party to an illegal contract is not in pari delicto if the purpose of the statutory prohibition is to protect persons in such a position. It is probable that this applies to these statutory requirements that are intended to provide protection for preference shareholders, by requiring companies to specify their rights. Preference shareholders may also apply to the court under s 254E for an order validating the improper issue to them.

Sections 254A(2) and 254G(2) prohibit the issue of or conversion into preference shares only if the rights are not set out in the constitution or otherwise approved by special resolution. There is nothing to prohibit the deletion of such rights after the shares are issued. In *Simon v HPM Industries Pty Ltd* (1989) 7 ACLC 770, Hodgson J refrained from implying such a prohibition in a predecessor of s 254A(2). In such a case, the holders of a class of shares are left with statutory rights preventing variation of their class rights, as discussed below.

redeemable preference shares

A feature of redeemable preference shares is that the company can pay back the issue price of the shares to the shareholder.

[8.135] A company may issue redeemable preference shares: s 254A(1)(b). A feature of redeemable preference shares is that the company can pay back the issue price of the shares to the shareholder. This is referred to as the company "redeeming" its shares. Redeemable preference shares may be redeemed at a fixed time or at the option of the company or shareholder: s 254A(3). Redeemable preference shares may be redeemed only on the terms on which they were issued: s 254J(1).

There is a great similarity between an issue of redeemable preference shares and borrowing money. In both cases the company pays a set rate of return and is repaid at an agreed future time. The issue of redeemable preference shares has certain advantages over borrowing from the company's point of view. The company is under no legal obligation to declare dividends, however there is a contractual obligation to meet interest payments. Consequently, the rights of lenders in the case of default are far stronger than the rights of shareholders. There are some disadvantages. For example, if the company borrows money, interest paid is deductible for taxation purposes as are expenses incurred in procuring the loan. Dividends, however, are paid after the taxable income of a company is ascertained.

The *Corporations Act* imposes restrictions on the redemption of redeemable preference shares to ensure that the rights of the company's creditors are not adversely affected. Under s 254K a company may only redeem redeemable preference shares:

> **if they are fully paid (s 254K(a)); and**
> **out of profits or the proceeds of a new share issue made for the purpose of the redemption: s 254K(b).**

If a company does not redeem redeemable preference shares out of profits, the redemption involves a reduction of capital and the requirements of ss 256B and 256C must be complied with. These are discussed below at para [8.185]. In addition, the company's directors may contravene the insolvent trading provision in s 588G and be personally liable under s 588M if the company becomes insolvent when it redeems any redeemable preference shares. Insolvent trading is discussed in Chapter 13.5 below.

variation of class rights

statutory provisions

[8.140] The class rights provisions in ss 246B–246G are designed to protect the rights of holders of particular classes of shares against attempts by the directors or controlling shareholders to vary or cancel those rights. Section 246B is the key provision. It aims to ensure that holders of a class of shares approve any proposal to vary the rights attaching to their class of shares.

The class rights provisions in ss 246B–246G are designed to protect the rights of holders of particular classes of shares against attempts by the directors or controlling shareholders to vary or cancel those rights.

Section 246B deals with two situations: varying and cancelling class rights:

table 8.1 varying and cancelling class rights—section 246B

If constitution sets out the procedure for varying and cancelling class rights	Rights may be varied or cancelled only where the procedure in the constitution is followed: s 246B(1).
If company does not have a constitution or the constitution does not set out the procedure for varying and cancelling class rights	Rights may be varied or cancelled only — by special resolution of the company; and — by special resolution passed at a meeting of the holders of the affected class; or — with the written consent of members with at least 75% of the votes of the affected class: s 246B(2)

Members of companies are assisted in determining what rights are attached to their shares. As discussed above in para [8.125], ss 254A(2) and 254G(2) require a company that issues preference shares or converts ordinary shares into preference shares to set out in its constitution or otherwise approve by special resolution certain specified rights of preference shareholders. Further, the company must lodge, within 14 days, a notice with ASIC setting out particulars of any division of shares into classes or conversion of shares from one class to another: s 246F(1). A public company must also lodge, within 14 days, a copy of a document or resolution that affects rights attaching to issued or unissued shares or binds a class of members: s 246F(3). A member may request a copy of the document or resolution from the company: s 246G(1).

application to set aside variation

[8.145] Section 246D(1) gives members of a class the right to apply to the court to set aside a variation or cancellation of their rights or a modification of the constitution to allow their rights to be varied or cancelled, if the members in a class do not all agree to the variation, cancellation or modification.

Section 246D(1) gives members of a class the right to apply to the court to set aside a variation or cancellation of their rights.

The application must be made by members with at least 10 per cent of the votes of the class concerned and, under s 246D(2), must be made within one month after the variation, cancellation or modification is made. The members of the class who want to have the variation, cancellation or modification set aside may appoint one or more of themselves to make the application on their behalf: s 246D(4). To enable a member to bring an application, the company must give written notice of the variation to members of the class within seven days after the variation is made: s 246B(3).

A variation, cancellation or modification takes effect one month after it is made. However, if an application is made to set it aside, it takes effect when the application is withdrawn or determined: s 246D(3). If all the members in a class agree to a variation, cancellation or modification, it takes effect on the date of the resolution or consent or on a later specified date: s 246E.

remedies

[8.150] After hearing a s 246D(1) application, the court may set aside the variation, cancellation or modification if it is satisfied that it would unfairly prejudice the applicants: s 246D(5).

The court may set aside the variation, cancellation or modification if it is satisfied that it would unfairly prejudice the applicants.

While s 246D(1) only allows members holding at least 10 per cent of the votes in the class of shares concerned to apply to set aside a variation, cancellation or modification, the *Corporations Act* provides a number of other remedies that can be pursued by members including members with fewer than 10 per cent of the votes. If the company does not comply with the procedures in its constitution for varying or cancelling class rights, this constitutes a breach of the s 140(1)(a) contract between the company and its members. As discussed in Chapter 4 above, affected members of the class can apply for an injunction to force the company to comply with its constitution.

In addition, if a company attempts to vary or cancel class rights in contravention of either s 246B(1) or (2), affected members of the class can apply for an injunction under s 1324 to prevent the contravention. A single member of a class may also apply for a remedy under s 232 if the variation, cancellation or modification is oppressive or unfair. Sections 232 and 1324 are discussed in Chapter 17 below.

A special resolution to vary or cancel a class right contained in a company's constitution may be invalid if the alteration is beyond any purpose contemplated by the constitution or is oppressive: *Gambotto v WCP Ltd* (1995) 13 ACLC 342. This is discussed in Chapter 4 above.

what is a variation of class rights?

[8.155] While ss 246B and 246D give a degree of protection to the holders of classes of shares against variation of their rights without their consent these protections apply only if conduct constitutes a variation or cancellation of rights.

Both s 246C and the common law regard certain actions as varying class rights.

Both s 246C and the common law regard certain actions as varying class rights. Table 8.2 below sets out the situations that s 246C regards as variations of class rights. For example, s 246C(6) regards new issues of equally ranking preference shares as varying the class rights of existing preference shareholders. It appears anomalous to protect holders of existing preference shares from later issues that rank equally while withholding protection where the later issue ranks ahead of existing preference shares. However, if a new issue of preference shares ranking ahead of existing preference shareholders involves a division of the preference shares into further classes, s 246C(1) takes this to be a variation of rights of the class existing before the division.

At common law, a variation of class rights is a variation that affects the strict legal rights of the member of the class.

The common law meaning of a variation of class rights is extremely narrow. At common law, a variation of class rights is a variation that affects the strict legal rights of the member of the class. A variation that merely affects the value of the shares of a class member is not regarded as a variation of class rights and consequently the provisions of ss 246B–246G do not apply. Examples of the strict legal rights of a class include the right to a specified rate of dividend and the right to appoint directors to represent a particular class of shareholders.

case note

The nature of a variation of class rights was considered in *Greenhalgh v Arderne Cinemas Ltd* [1946] 1 All ER 512. A company issued 21,000 preference shares of 10s each and 31,000 ordinary shares of 10s each. Under the articles, each share carried one vote. The company also had the power to subdivide its existing shares. When the company fell into financial difficulties it entered into an agreement with Greenhalgh by which he lent it £11,000 secured by a debenture. He was also issued with 10s ordinary shares subdivided into 2s shares. Each 2s share was to have the same voting rights as the issued ordinary 10s shares. After differences arose between the parties, the company resolved at a general meeting to subdivide all existing 10s shares into 2s shares ranking equally with the subdivided shares held by Greenhalgh. The effect of this was to diminish the proportion of votes that Greenhalgh previously had and meant that he no longer held sufficient shares to block the passing of special resolutions. Greenhalgh argued that the voting rights attached to his shares were varied without the consent of the holders of those shares as required by the articles. It was held that the voting rights were not varied even though they were affected in a business sense.

table 8.2 variation of class rights under s 246C

Company with share capital	If the shares in a class are divided into further classes and after the division the rights attached to all those shares are not the same.	The division is taken to vary the rights attached to every share in the class existing before the division: s 246C(1)(a).
	If the rights attached to some of the shares in a class are varied.	The variation is taken to vary the rights attached to every other share that was in the class before the variation: s 246C(2)(a).
Company without share capital	If the members in a class are divided into further classes and after the division the rights of all those members are not the same.	The division is taken to vary the rights of every member in the class existing before the division: s 246C(3)(a)
	If the rights of some of the members in a class are varied.	The variation is taken to vary the rights of every other member who was in the class before the variation: s 246C(4)(a).
Company with one class of shares	If new shares are issued.	Under s 246C(5) the issue is taken to vary the rights attached to the shares already issued if: — the rights attaching the new shares are not the same as the rights attached to shares already issued; and — those rights are not provided for in the company's constitution (if any) or a notice, document or resolution lodged with ASIC.
Preference shares	If new preference shares are issued that rank equally with existing preference shares.	Under s 246C(6) the issue is taken to vary the rights attached to the existing preference shares unless the issue is authorised by: — terms of the issue of the existing preference shares; or — the company's constitution (if any) as in force when the existing preference shares were issued.

This narrow interpretation given to the expression "variation of class rights" was also applied in *White v Bristol Aeroplane Co* [1953] Ch 65. In that case, a bonus issue to holders of ordinary shares only was held not to "affect, modify, vary, deal with or abrogate" the rights of existing preference shareholders. While the bonus issue had the effect of diluting the percentage of votes of preference shareholders at shareholders' meetings, this did not affect preference shareholders' strict legal rights. They continued to have the right to vote one vote per preference share.

A return of capital to preference shareholders is a satisfaction of their rights and does not constitute a variation of class rights: *House of Fraser Plc v ACGE Investments Ltd* [1987] 2 WLR 1083.

Whether the share capital of a company is comprised of different classes of shares depends on whether there is a commonality of interest between shareholders of a particular class.

what is a class of shares?

[8.160] Whether the share capital of a company is comprised of different classes of shares depends on whether there is a commonality of interest between shareholders of a particular class.

case note

The question "what constitutes a class of shares?" arose in *Crumpton v Morrine Hall Pty Ltd* [1965] NSWR 240. Crumpton owned shares in a home unit company that entitled her to certain rights in respect of one of six units in the building owned by the company. The company altered its constitution so as to restrict the right of shareholders to lease the units and to allow determinations of the right to occupy in certain circumstances. Crumpton argued that these alterations constituted a variation of her class rights and hence the procedure for class consent set out in terms similar to s 246B(2) should have been followed. It was held that the shares were divided into different classes despite the fact that the constitution did not refer to the groups of shares as classes. They were classes of shares because one group had quite different rights to another group.

A company's share capital may be divided into classes of shares even though there is only one holder of a particular class of shares. In such a case, a class meeting would be comprised of a single shareholder: *Buckland v Johnstone* (1991) 9 ACLC 1193.

share capital transactions

[8.165] Earlier in this chapter it was noted that generally companies must receive cash or its equivalent when they issue shares to members. The funds raised in this way constitute the company's issued capital. A company's creditors can only look to the issued capital, and the way in which it has been applied, for payment in the event of a winding up. Similarly, the company's members are entitled to expect that the issued capital will be employed by the company for the objects (if any) set out in the company's constitution.

In order to protect creditors and shareholders a general rule was developed that limited liability companies must maintain their issued share capital. This rule is known as "the rule in *Trevor v Whitworth*", (1887) 12 App Cas 409, and it prohibits a company from reducing its issued share capital. A clear way in which a company may reduce its capital is to purchase its shares from a shareholder.

The *Corporations Act* provides detailed procedures and requirements that must be complied with where a company engages in various share capital transactions. These provisions stem from the rule in *Trevor v Whitworth*. However, depending on the transaction, the rule has been modified in various respects. Reforms in 1998 streamlined the procedures for share capital transactions and removed several restrictions while attempting to provide for creditor and shareholder protection.

The *Corporations Act* deals with the following transactions:

- **share capital reductions;**
- **share buy-backs;**
- **self-acquisition and control of shares; and**
- **financial assistance.**

The rule in *Trevor v Whitworth* means that a company is generally prohibited from reducing its issued share capital because a reduction in capital would prejudice the rights of creditors.

the rule in Trevor v Whitworth

[8.170] The rule in *Trevor v Whitworth* means that a company is generally prohibited from reducing its issued share capital because a reduction in capital would prejudice the rights of creditors. The reduction would in effect diminish the pool of funds available to the company to pay its creditors.

case note

In *Trevor v Whitworth* (1887) 12 App Cas 409, the executors of Whitworth, a deceased shareholder in James Schofield & Son Ltd, sold Whitworth's shares in the company back to the company. Payment was to be by two instalments. Prior to the payment of the second instalment the company went into liquidation. The executors claimed this sum from the company's liquidator, Trevor. While the company's memorandum did not authorise it to purchase its own shares, its articles did. The House of Lords held that a company had no power to purchase its own shares even if its articles permitted such an acquisition. Hence, as the purchase was void, Whitworth's claim for the balance failed. This decision was based on the principle that the capital of a limited liability company should remain available to creditors. Creditors take the risk that the company's capital may be diminished in the course of the company's business. However, the law does not expect that capital will be returned to shareholders ahead of creditors.

The requirement that a company maintain its capital is also reflected in s 254T, which provides that a dividend may only be paid out of the profits of the company. This provision is designed to prevent a reduction in capital being disguised as a payment of dividends out of a company's issued capital. Dividends are discussed in Chapter 10 below.

While companies cannot generally acquire their own shares, a seemingly analogous situation arises when shares are forfeited as a result of non-payment of a call by a shareholder. The circumstances in which a shareholder may forfeit shares are discussed in Chapter 9 below. In some respects, a forfeiture of shares has similarities to a reduction of capital. However, the cancellation of forfeited shares is permitted under s 258D by resolution passed at a general meeting. Forfeiture is not usually detrimental to the interests of creditors because it does not result in the company providing any consideration for the shares.

A reduction of capital that involves a return of capital to holders of one class of share is not a variation of the class rights of other classes of shareholders: *Re Fowlers Vacola Manufacturing Co Ltd* [1966] VR 97. This means that the protective provisions applicable to variation of class rights discussed above, para [8.140], do not apply to reductions of capital which differentiate between the classes of shares.

self-acquisition prohibition: s 259A

[8.175] The rule in *Trevor v Whitworth* has been incorporated into the *Corporations Act*. Under s 259A, a company must not acquire shares in itself except in any one of the following circumstances:

The rule in *Trevor v Whitworth* has been incorporated into the *Corporations Act*.

- **in buying back shares under s 257A. Permitted share buy-backs are discussed below, para [8.185];**
- **in acquiring an interest in its fully-paid shares if no consideration is given by the company or an entity it controls;**
- **under a court order; and**
- **in circumstances covered by s 259B(2) and (3). These provisions deal with the situation where a company takes security over its shares under an approved employee share scheme or the security is taken in the ordinary course of business of a lender.**

A company that contravenes the s 259A self-acquisition prohibition is not guilty of a criminal offence: s 259F(1). In addition, a contravention does not affect the validity of the acquisition. However, any person who is involved in a company's contravention of s 259A is in breach of s 259F(2) and subject to the civil penalty provisions. A person commits an offence if they are involved in a contravention of s 259A and the involvement is dishonest: s 259F(3).

taking security over own shares

[8.180] The self-acquisition prohibition has been extended to prevent a company from taking security over its shares or the shares of a company that controls it: s 259B(1). This prohibition recognises that where a company takes security over its own shares, the enforcement of the security would result in the company acquiring shares in itself with the same effect as a breach of the prohibition in s 259A. Exceptions to this prohibition arise where the security is under an approved employee share scheme or is taken by a financial institution in the ordinary course of its business: s 259B(2) and (3).

Contravention of s 259B is treated in the same way as a contravention of the s 259A self-acquisition prohibition.

permitted share capital reductions

[8.185] Share capital reductions and share buy-backs are covered by ss 256A–258F of the *Corporations Act*. According to s 256A, the purpose of these provisions is to protect the interests of shareholders and creditors by:

- **addressing the risk that the transactions may lead to the company's insolvency;**
- **seeking to ensure fairness between the company's shareholders; and**
- **requiring the company to disclose all material information.**

A company must not reduce its capital unless it complies with the requirements set out in s 256B(1).

A company must not reduce its capital unless it complies with the requirements set out in s 256B(1): s 256D(1).

Under s 256B(1), a company may reduce its share capital if the reduction:

- **is fair and reasonable to the shareholders as a whole; and**
- **does not materially prejudice the company's ability to pay its creditors; and**
- **is approved by shareholders under s 256C.**

Share capital reductions may take a number of forms. A company reduces its share capital if it makes a payment to its shareholders that does not come from profits. The payment to shareholders may involve a return of the shares to the company which then cancels some or all of the shares. Such capital reductions have a similar effect to share buy-backs.

A reduction of capital also occurs when a company cancels any paid-up share capital that is lost or is not represented by available assets. This is referred to as "a loss reduction" and is specifically permitted by s 258F provided it does not involve a cancellation of shares. A share capital reduction may also involve cancelling or reducing the amount unpaid on partly-paid shares.

Various capital reductions are authorised in ss 258A–258E and therefore fall outside the s 256B(1) requirements. These include:

- **share capital reductions by unlimited companies (s 258A);**
- **where a company has the right to grant a lease or right of occupancy under a company-title home unit scheme. This enables a person to gain occupancy rights over an apartment by means of acquiring particular shares in the company that owns the building. Should the building be converted into strata title, the shares are surrendered in return for the transfer of strata title over the apartment. This surrender is a capital reduction authorised by s 258B;**
- **payment of brokerage or commission paid to a share underwriter with no restriction on amount: s 258C. The brokerage is a payment made out of issued capital;**
- **cancellations of shares forfeited under the terms on which they were issued. The cancellation must be by resolution of the general meeting (s 258D);**

> redemptions of redeemable preference shares out of the proceeds of a new issue of shares made for this purpose: s 258E(1)(a). This is governed by s 254K;
> share buy-backs under ss 257A–257J where the shares are paid for out of share capital; and
> cancellation of paid up share capital that is lost or not represented by available assets: s 258F. This reduction does not apply in the case of trading losses incurred in the ordinary course of business but applies to unusual losses.

fair and reasonable to shareholders

[8.190] A permitted reduction of capital must be fair and reasonable to the company's shareholders as a whole: s 256B(1)(a). A shareholder who alleges that a reduction of capital is not fair and reasonable has the right to apply for a s 1324 injunction to restrain the contravention of s 256B(1)(a) and prevent the implementation of the reduction. At the hearing of the s 1324 injunction, the company, not the shareholder, has the onus of proving that the reduction is fair and reasonable: s 1324(1B).

A permitted reduction of capital must be fair and reasonable to the company's shareholders as a whole.

The explanatory memorandum to the 1998 legislation that inserted the current reduction of capital provisions identified the following factors that might be relevant to determining whether a capital reduction was fair and reasonable to shareholders as a whole:

> the adequacy of the consideration paid to shareholders;
> whether the reduction would have the practical effect of depriving some shareholders of their rights (for example, by stripping the company of funds that would otherwise be available for distribution to preference shareholders);
> whether the reduction was being used to effect a takeover and avoid the takeover provisions; or
> whether the reduction involved an arrangement that should more properly proceed as a scheme of arrangement.

The explanatory memorandum also noted that as the s 256A(1)(a) requirement focused on whether a capital reduction was fair and reasonable to shareholders "as a whole", it was possible to satisfy the requirement even though a reduction was not fair and reasonable for every individual shareholder.

case note

The "fair and reasonable" requirement was considered by the New South Wales Court of Appeal in *Winpar Holdings Ltd v Goldfields Kalgoorlie Ltd* [2001] NSWCA 427. In that case Goldfields Kalgoorlie Ltd (GKL) called a shareholders' meeting to approve a selective reduction of capital that involved the cancellation of the shares held by GKL's minority shareholders in consideration of a payment to them of 55 cents per share. This was 8 cents in excess of the amount determined by an independent expert as a fair and reasonable price per share. The effect of the capital reduction was to give GKL's majority shareholder 100 per cent ownership of the company. Winpar, one of the minority shareholders, argued that the capital reduction was not fair and reasonable because it gave the majority shareholder a "special benefit" consisting of both a reduction in the level of head office costs as well as other synergy benefits from future rationalisation of operations. According to Winpar, the value of this "special benefit" should be allocated entirely to the minority shareholders. The New South Wales Court of Appeal rejected Winpar's argument. It noted that the capital reduction gave benefits to both the majority and minority shareholders that they would not otherwise have received. The majority shareholder obtained a benefit arising from 100 per cent ownership. However, the minority shareholders also obtained an enhanced price for their shares.

case note

In *Re Fowlers Vacola Manufacturing Co Ltd* [1966] VR 97, decided under the previous share capital reduction provisions, it was held that a reduction of capital that involved a payment only to the company's ordinary shareholders was not fair to the company's preference shareholders. Fairness required at least equal treatment between the ordinary and preference shareholders in the reduction of capital because the company's constitution gave the preference shareholders a priority to a return of capital in the case of a winding up.

ability to pay creditors

A reduction of capital is permitted if it does not materially prejudice the company's ability to pay its creditors.

[8.195] A reduction of capital is permitted if it does not materially prejudice the company's ability to pay its creditors: s 256B(1)(b). Creditor protection is a key rationale underlying the share capital reduction rules.

Section 1324(1A) expressly gives creditors standing to apply for an injunction to prevent a reduction of capital if the company's insolvency is an element of a contravention of s 256B(1)(b). At the hearing of the s 1324 injunction, the company has the onus of proving that the reduction does not prejudice its ability to pay creditors: s 1324(1B). Section 256C(5) requires a company to lodge details relating to a proposed capital reduction with ASIC to assist creditors in discovering the details of a proposed capital reduction. This information, available to creditors and others through ASIC's Alert system, assists creditors in deciding whether they should apply for the s 1324 injunction to stop the capital reduction.

A reduction of capital that involves a cancellation of shares for no consideration does not require consideration of creditors' interests as the company's financial position remains unaltered.

Section 256B(1)(c) permits a capital reduction if it is approved by shareholders under s 256C.

shareholder approval

[8.200] Section 256B(1)(c) permits a capital reduction if it is approved by shareholders under s 256C. The shareholder approval requirements vary depending on whether the reduction is an equal or selective reduction. There are more onerous shareholder approval requirements for selective reductions because of their potential for unfair discrimination against shareholders.

An equal reduction of capital must be approved by ordinary resolution passed at a general meeting of the company. A selective reduction must be approved by special resolution.

An equal reduction relates only to ordinary shares and is required to have the same terms for each ordinary shareholder and applies to each shareholder in proportion to the number of ordinary shares held. In other cases, it is a selective reduction: s 256B(2). Certain differences in the terms of the reduction may be ignored for the purposes of determining whether the reduction is an equal reduction. Under s 256B(3), these include differences that are attributable to the shares having different dividend entitlements or unpaid amounts. These differences would not result in any inequity in the treatment of shareholders and so are disregarded for the purposes of determining the type of shareholder approval.

An equal reduction of capital must be approved by ordinary resolution passed at a general meeting of the company: s 256C(1). Under s 256C(2), a selective reduction must be approved by special resolution. No votes in favour of the reduction may be cast by any person or their associates who would receive payment or other consideration as part of the reduction or whose liability to pay unpaid amounts on their shares is to be reduced. Alternatively, all ordinary shareholders may agree to the selective reduction by resolution at a general meeting.

A selective reduction that involves a cancellation of shares must also be approved by special resolution passed at a class meeting of the shareholders whose shares are to be cancelled, as well as the special resolution passed at the general meeting.

Section 256C(2) gives additional protection to minority shareholders where a selective reduction involves a cancellation of shares. This recognises the rights of shareholders to prevent their shares from being expropriated against their wishes. A selective reduction that involves a cancellation of shares must also be approved by special resolution passed at a class meeting of the shareholders whose shares are to be cancelled, as well as the special resolution passed at the general meeting: s 256C(2). In *Winpar Holdings Ltd v Goldfields Kalgoorlie Ltd* [2001] NSWCA 427, the New South Wales Court of Appeal held that s 256C(2) required the class approval for a selective reduction involving a cancellation to be obtained at a separate class meeting, distinct from the general meeting at which the special resolution was passed.

The shareholders' meeting that considers a proposed reduction of capital must comply with the usual notice requirements. These are discussed in Chapter 14 below. In addition, the company must provide a statement with the notice of the shareholders' meeting, setting out all known information that is material to the decision on how to vote on the resolution to approve the capital reduction: s 256C(4). The company need not disclose information that would be unreasonable to provide because it had previously disclosed the information to shareholders.

It would not be unreasonable for a company to repeat previously disclosed information if that information had been disclosed in a different context and its relevance to shareholders voting on a reduction would not be apparent to them.

Information that is material to the decision of shareholders in considering how to vote on the resolution includes:

- **the effect of the reduction on particular shareholders and other shareholders;**
- **the interests of directors in the reduction; and**
- **correction of any misapprehensions that shareholders may have arising from accompanying reports or statements.**

The company must lodge with ASIC the notice of the meeting and any accompanying documents before the notice is sent to shareholders: s 256C(5). Any resolution approving the reduction must be lodged within 14 days after it is passed and the company cannot make the reduction until 14 days after lodgment: s 256C(3).

If the reduction involves a share cancellation, a prescribed notice must be lodged with ASIC setting out the number of shares cancelled, the class of share and the consideration paid by the company on the cancellation: s 254Y.

These notice requirements are aimed at giving creditors and members advance notice of proposed reductions so that they may exercise their rights to oppose the reduction.

failure to comply with reduction requirements

[8.205] A capital reduction must comply with the requirements set out in s 256B(1): s 256D(1). If these requirements are not complied with, the contravention does not affect the validity of the reduction or any connected transaction: s 256D(2). The company is not guilty of any offence as the legislation is concerned to protect shareholders and creditors and this would not be achieved if the company were made liable for an offence. Any person who is involved in a contravention by a company breaches the legislation and may be liable under the civil penalty provisions by virtue of s 1317E: s 256D(3). A person commits an offence if they are involved in a company's contravention of s 256B and the involvement is dishonest: s 256D(4).

Section 1324 specifically encompasses reductions of capital made in contravention of s 256B where the reduction is not fair and reasonable to the company's shareholders as a whole or prejudices the ability of the company to pay its creditors. Under s 1324, the court may grant an injunction to prevent a person from contravening the *Corporations Act*. A person affected by the contravention may bring the application and this includes a member or creditor of the company if the insolvency of the company is an element of the contravention: s 1324(1A)(b).

Where an application is brought under s 1324 in relation to a contravention involving a reduction of capital, the onus of proof is on the company or any other person who allegedly acted in contravention of s 256B(1) to prove that there was no contravention: s 1324(1B).

The application brought under s 1324 may also seek damages: s 1324(10). Statutory injunctions are also discussed in Chapter 17 below.

While a person may apply for a s 1324 injunction to stop a capital reduction from taking place that contravenes the s 256B(1) requirements, the effect of s 256D(2) is that the reduction is regarded as valid and cannot be reversed once it is made: *Winpar Holdings Ltd v Goldfields Kalgoorlie Ltd* [2001] NSWCA 427.

The insolvent trading section contained in s 588G deems a reduction of share capital as the incurring of a debt by the company when the reduction takes effect.

The insolvent trading section contained in s 588G deems a reduction of share capital as the incurring of a debt by the company when the reduction takes effect: s 588G(1A). Therefore, if the reduction of capital of a company takes effect when the company was insolvent or it became insolvent because of the reduction, the directors may be liable under s 588M. An action under s 588M may be brought against the directors by the liquidator of the company or proceedings may be brought under the civil penalty provisions that apply to a contravention of s 588G: s 1317E. Insolvent trading and the civil penalty provisions are discussed in Chapter 13.5 below.

Section 256E lists various provisions that may be relevant to share capital reductions. These include:

> **Ch 6CA which requires disclosure of information by a disclosing entity about its securities which is material and not generally available. A listed company must disclose information regarding a reduction so as to keep the market informed. This is discussed in Chapter 15 below;**
> **Ch 2E dealing with financial benefits to directors and related parties may require approval of the general meeting. A reduction may confer a financial benefit on directors. This is discussed in Chapter 13.3 below;**
> **s 125 allows a company's constitution to restrict the exercise of the company's powers and this may include the power to reduce share capital. This is discussed in Chapter 4 above; and**
> **ss 246B–246G protect holders of classes of shares from a variation of their class rights. This is discussed above.**

share buy-backs

[8.210] One way in which a company may reduce its share capital is by buying back its shares from a shareholder. Prior to 1989, the rule in *Trevor v Whitworth* and legislative adoptions of this rule prohibited share buy-backs. It became increasingly apparent that the prohibition against share buy-backs was largely ineffective in its primary aim of protecting creditors.

Section 257A permits a company to buy back its own shares.

Section 257A now permits a company to buy back its own shares if:

> **the buy-back does not materially prejudice the company's ability to pay its creditors; and**
> **the company follows the procedures laid down in ss 257A–257J.**

The purposes of the share buy-back rules as stated in s 256A are the same as for reductions of share capital. They are to protect the interests of shareholders and creditors by:

> **addressing the risk of these transactions leading to the company's insolvency;**
> **seeking to ensure fairness between the company's shareholders; and**
> **requiring the company to disclose all material information.**

reasons for permitting share buy-backs

[8.215] Share buy-backs have become increasingly common and may provide valuable benefits to the shareholders who sell their shares as well as for those who choose not to sell. This reflects the tax-driven preference of some investors to receive capital gains rather than dividends. Many buy-backs combine a purchase of shares together with a fully franked dividend. The Companies and Securities Law Review Committee in its 1987 report, *A Company's Purchase of its Own Shares*, considered the following to be valid reasons for allowing share buy-backs to occur.

> **In an increasingly internationalised financial market, Australian companies may be disadvantaged relative to other companies that enjoy the flexibility of being able to exercise greater control over their equity. In nearly all other countries, companies are permitted to**

buy back their own shares. The prohibition of this practice could also discourage foreign companies from incorporating in Australia.

> Increased capital mobility whereby capital returns to shareholders may be redirected into more efficient investments. This encourages the retirement of capital that is no longer needed and may result in a more efficient allocation of resources.
> Self-purchases as a takeover defence may create a more competitive price environment and thereby benefit shareholders.
> A self-purchase may represent the best investment by a company when it perceives that its shares are undervalued. This may also add depth to the securities market and enable market price to more accurately reflect underlying values. A self-purchase proposal may act as a signal to the market that a company's shares are undervalued and thereby lead to a better informed market.
> Employee share schemes could be encouraged by providing a mechanism to enable a company to acquire the shares of a departing employee.
> Efficiency and harmony within a company may be enhanced by the purchase of dissident members' shares.
> An appropriate financial restructuring may require a reduction in a company's equity base and consequent increase in its gearing ratio.

permitted share buy-backs

[8.220] The *Corporations Act* recognises the following five types of buy-backs:

The *Corporations Act* recognises five types of buy-backs.

> equal access schemes;
> selective buy-backs;
> on-market buy-backs;
> employee share scheme buy-backs; and
> minimum holding buy-backs.

Section 257B contains a table that indicates the procedural requirements for each type of buy-back. See Table 8.3 below.

table 8.3 procedures applicable to buy-backs — s 257B

		Employee share scheme		On-market		Equal access scheme		
Procedures (and sections applied)	**Min holding**	**within 10/12 limit**	**over 10/12 limit**	**within 10/12 limit**	**over 10/12 limit**	**within 10/12 limit**	**over 10/12 limit**	**Selective buy-back**
ordinary resolution s 257C	–	–	yes	–	yes	–	yes	–
special/ unanimous resolution s 257D	–	–	–	–	–	–	–	yes
lodge offer documents with ASIC s 257E	–	–	–	–	–	yes	yes	yes

Procedures (and sections applied)	Min holding	Employee share scheme: within 10/12 limit	Employee share scheme: over 10/12 limit	On-market: within 10/12 limit	On-market: over 10/12 limit	Equal access scheme: within 10/12 limit	Equal access scheme: over 10/12 limit	Selective buy-back
14 days notice to ASIC s 257F	–	yes	yes	yes	yes	yes	yes	yes
disclosure relevant information when offer made s 257G	–	–	–	–	–	yes	yes	yes
cancel shares s 257H	yes	yes	yes	yes	yes	yes	yes	yes
notify ASIC of cancellation s 254Y	yes	yes	yes	yes	yes	yes	yes	yes

As a general rule, companies are able to buy back up to 10 per cent of their shares within a 12-month period (the 10/12 limit) without shareholder approval and with minimum procedural requirements. This general rule does not apply to selective buy-backs.

As a general rule, companies are able to buy back up to 10 per cent of their shares within a 12-month period (the 10/12 limit) without shareholder approval and with minimum procedural requirements. This general rule does not apply to selective buy-backs.

The 10/12 limit refers to 10 per cent of the smallest number of votes attaching to voting shares during the last 12 months: s 257B(4). In determining whether this limit has been exceeded, previous buy-backs that occurred in the last 12 months and the voting shares that are subject to the proposed buy-back are taken into account: s 257B(5). The reference to the smallest number of votes attaching to voting shares on issue in s 257B(4) is aimed at preventing companies from issuing shares so as to increase the permitted share buy-back limit.

Once a buy-back agreement has been entered into, all rights attaching to the shares bought back are suspended. This means that the shares no longer carry voting rights and the company cannot deal in the shares. Upon registration of the transfer to the company, the shares must be cancelled: s 257H.

Within one month after the shares are cancelled, the company must lodge a notice with ASIC stating the number and class of shares transferred and the consideration paid: s 254Y.

equal access scheme

An equal access scheme requires offers to be made only to ordinary shareholders to buy back the same percentage of shares from each and every shareholder.

[8.225] An equal access scheme is defined in s 257B(2) and (3) and requires offers to be made only to ordinary shareholders to buy back the same percentage of shares from each and every shareholder. All offers must have the same terms and all ordinary shareholders must have a reasonable opportunity to accept the offers made to them. The buy-back agreements are not entered into until a specified time for acceptances has closed.

Certain differences in the terms of the offers are permissible in cases such as where the shares have different accrued dividend entitlements and the shares are paid up to different amounts: s 257B(3).

Where the 10/12 limit is exceeded, an ordinary resolution of the general meeting must approve the terms of the buy-back agreement before it is entered into or the agreement must be conditional on such an approval: s 257C(1). The notice of meeting must include all material information known to the company and not previously disclosed, to enable the shareholders to decide whether to vote in favour of the resolution: ss 257C(2) and 257G. Notice of an intended buy-back setting out the terms of the offer and any accompanying documents must be lodged with ASIC irrespective of whether the 10/12 limit is exceeded: s 257F.

selective buy-backs

[8.230] These are defined in s 9 to mean a buy-back not included in the other four types. Selective buy-backs are buy-back offers made to particular shareholders to the exclusion of others or offers made to holders of shares other than ordinary shares. Because of the possibility of differential treatment, the *Corporations Act* imposes more stringent procedural requirements than for other types of buy-backs. The shareholders must approve the selective buy-back either unanimously or by special resolution.

Selective buy-backs are buy-back offers made to particular shareholders to the exclusion of others.

Selling shareholders or their associates cannot vote in favour of this resolution: s 257D(1). Material information must accompany the notice of meeting in the same way as in the case of an equal access scheme: ss 257D(2) and 257G. The documents must also be lodged with ASIC: s 257D(3). ASIC has the power to exempt a company from the operation of s 257D: s 257D(4). ASIC must be notified at prescribed times both before and after the buy-back: ss 257E, 257F and 254Y.

on-market buy-backs

[8.235] A buy-back is an on-market buy-back if it results from an offer made by a listed corporation on a prescribed financial market (eg the ASX) in the ordinary course of trading on that market: s 257B(6). Shareholder approval by ordinary resolution is necessary only where the buy-back exceeds the 10/12 limit. Notice must be lodged with ASIC before the buy-back is entered into (s 257F) and after cancellation of the shares: s 254Y. ASX Listing Rules 7.29 and 7.33 regulate on-market buy-backs. ASX Listing Rule 7.33 provides that a company may only buy back shares under an on-market buy-back at a price which is not more than 5 per cent above the average of the market price for shares in that class.

A buy-back is an on-market buy-back if it results from an offer made by a listed corporation on a prescribed financial market (eg the ASX) in the ordinary course of trading on that market.

employee share scheme buy-backs

[8.240] "Employee share scheme buy-back" is defined in s 9 and has as its purpose the acquisition of shares in a company by or on behalf of employees or directors who hold salaried employment in the company or a related body corporate. The required procedure is identical to that of on-market buy-backs.

"Employee share scheme buy-back" has as its purpose the acquisition of shares in a company by or on behalf of employees or directors who hold salaried employment in the company or a related body corporate.

minimum holding buy-backs

[8.245] This type of buy-back is defined in s 9 as a buy-back of all of a holder's shares in a listed corporation if the shares are less than a marketable parcel. The only applicable procedural requirement is that ASIC is notified of the cancellation.

Prior to changes made to ASX Listing Rules in 1995, people could generally only buy or sell marketable parcels of listed shares. Small numbers of shares less than a marketable parcel were referred to as "odd lots" and could only be traded through an odd-lot broker. With the introduction of the CHESS settlement system in 1995 the ASX eliminated the requirement for trading in marketable parcels of shares.

other relevant provisions

[8.250] Section 257J sets out signposts to other provisions that are relevant to buy-backs. These include the insolvent trading section contained in s 588G and the statutory injunction provision in s 1324. Other provisions relevant to share capital reductions listed in s 256E are also applicable to share buy-backs. These are set out above, para [8.205].

A company that buys back its shares is deemed to have incurred a debt at the time the buy-back agreement is entered into: s 588G(1A). This may result in a director being made personally liable for insolvent trading, discussed below in Chapter 13.5.

Where a buy-back causes a company to become insolvent, the liquidator of the company may seek a court order to recover the consideration paid to vendor shareholders for the buy-back as a voidable transaction: s 588FF. This is discussed below in Chapter 25.

Where the company goes into liquidation, and at the time it has not paid the selling shareholders in full, the shareholders may claim as creditors for the debt but rank after other creditors: ss 553AA and 563AA. The priorities of unsecured creditors are discussed below in Chapter 25.

Where a share buy-back constitutes a contravention of the *Corporations Act*, it is deemed to affect the interests of creditors and shareholders if the insolvency of the company is an element of the contravention: s 1324(1A). This enables a creditor or member to apply to the court for an injunction or damages under s 1324(1) and (10).

indirect self-acquisitions

A company may indirectly acquire control of its own shares by gaining control of an entity that holds those shares.

[8.255] A company may indirectly acquire control of its own shares by gaining control of an entity that holds those shares. Such cross-shareholding arrangements amount to indirect self-acquisitions and could enable de facto share buy-backs to occur outside the regulation of the share buy-back and capital reduction provisions thereby defeating the policy behind the rule in *Trevor v Whitworth* and related statutory prohibitions in ss 256B and 257A. Indirect self-acquisitions are regulated by ss 259C and 259D.

Indirect self-acquisitions are regulated.

The issue or transfer of shares of a company to an entity it controls is void: s 259C(1). The controlled entity may be a partnership, trust or other company. This prohibition is subject to several exceptions. These include where:

> **the issue or transfer is to the entity as trustee and neither the company nor the entity has a beneficial interest in the trust (s 259C(1)(b));**
>
> **the issue is made as a result of an offer to all holders of the class of shares being issued and does not discriminate unfairly in favour of the entity (s 259C(1)(c)); and**
>
> **the transfer to the entity is by a wholly-owned subsidiary of a body corporate and the entity is also a wholly-owned subsidiary of that body corporate: s 259C(1)(d).**

ASIC may exempt a company from the operation of the s 259C prohibition: s 259C(2). Issues or transfers in the situations covered by s 259C(1)(c) and (d) must be disposed of within 12 months of acquisition or the company must cease to control the entity: s 259D(1). ASIC may extend the 12-month period.

A company may also gain indirect control over its shares by gaining or increasing control over an entity that already holds shares in the company. In such cases, s 259D(1) applies so that the entity must cease holding the shares or the company must cease to control the entity within 12 months after the company gains control of the entity. During the period when the company controls the entity, voting rights attaching to the shares cannot be exercised: s 259D(3).

If voting rights are exercised in contravention of s 259D(3), the resolution on which the voting rights were exercised will be invalidated by the court only if it is of the opinion that a substantial injustice has been caused that cannot be otherwise remedied: s 1322(3B). If the company still controls the entity at the end of the 12-month period and the entity continues to hold the company's shares, the company commits an offence for each day during which the situation continues: s 259D(4). However, a contravention of s 259D does not affect the validity of any transaction: s 259D(6). Under s 259D(5) the requirements under s 259D(1) do not apply where the entity holds the shares as a personal representative or trustee where neither the entity nor the company have a beneficial interest in the trust.

the meaning of "control"

A company is regarded as being in control of an entity that holds shares in the company if the company has the capacity to determine the outcome of decisions about the entity's financial and operating policies.

[8.260] A company is regarded as being in control of an entity that holds shares in the company if the company has the capacity to determine the outcome of decisions about the entity's financial and operating policies: s 259E(1). This definition of control is similar to the definition of "control" in Accounting Standard AASB 127, *Consolidated and Separate Financial Statements*. In determining whether a company has this capacity, the practical influence the company can exert is considered rather than the legal rights it can enforce. It is also relevant to consider existing practice or patterns of behaviour affecting the entity's financial or operating policies: s 259E(2).

A company is not taken to control an entity merely because the company and an unrelated entity jointly have the capacity to determine the outcome of decisions about another entity's financial and operating policies: s 259E(3). This may arise under a joint venture agreement. Control of an entity also does not arise merely because of a capacity that a company is under a legal obligation to exercise for the benefit of someone other than its shareholders: s 259E(4). Such a situation may arise if a company holds shares as a trustee.

financial assistance

[8.265] A company could indirectly reduce its capital if it financially assists a person to acquire shares in the company. Such financial assistance is regarded as offending the spirit of the rule in *Trevor v Whitworth*.

Prior to the 1998 amendments, the *Corporations Act* prohibited a company providing a person with financial assistance in connection with or for the purpose of an acquisition of its shares. While the financial assistance prohibition was subject to a number of exceptions, such as shareholder approval, it was regarded as excessively complex and covered many transactions that had no potential to harm the interests of a company's shareholders or creditors.

The present financial assistance provisions in ss 260A–260D seek to maintain shareholder and creditor protection where appropriate, without imposing unnecessary restrictions on companies. Further, the requirements for giving financial assistance have been brought into line with the requirements for capital reductions.

Section 260A, prohibits a company from financially assisting a person to acquire shares in the company or its holding company unless certain conditions are satisfied. These are that:

Section 260A, prohibits a company from financially assisting a person to acquire shares in the company or its holding company unless certain conditions are satisfied.

> **giving the assistance does not materially prejudice the interests of the company, its shareholders or the company's ability to pay its creditors (s 260A(1)(a)); or**
> **the assistance is approved by shareholders under s 260B; or**
> **the assistance is exempted under s 260C.**

what is financial assistance?

[8.270] "Financial assistance" is not defined in the *Corporations Act*. The previous financial assistance provisions gave several examples of financial assistance. These included:

> **the company lending a person money to be used to acquire shares in the company;**
> **the company guaranteeing a person's loan where the proceeds of the loan are used to acquire shares in the company; and**
> **the company providing its own assets as security for a person's loan where the proceeds of the loan are used to acquire shares in the company.**

Under s 260A(2) financial assistance may be given before or after the acquisition of shares and it may take the form of paying a dividend.

case note

ASIC v Adler [2002] NSWSC 171 is an example of a subsidiary company giving financial assistance to assist with the acquisition of shares in its holding company in contravention of s 260A(1)(a). In that case, HIH Casualty & General Insurance Co Ltd (HIHC), a subsidiary of HIH Insurance Ltd (HIH) provided an unsecured $10 million loan to Pacific Eagle Equity Pty Ltd (PEE), a company controlled by Adler. At the time Adler was also a non-executive director and, through Adler Corporation Ltd, a substantial shareholder of HIH. PEE used about $4 million of the $10 million to buy HIH shares on the stock market. PEE later sold its HIH shares at a $2 million loss. PEE's purchase of HIH shares was designed to give the stock market the false impression that Adler was supporting HIH's falling share price by personally buying its shares. The Court found that Adler did not intend PEE to make a quick profit on the purchase and resale of HIH shares. His true intention was to shore up the HIH share price for the benefit of Adler Corporation Ltd's substantial shareholding in HIH. This was evidenced by the fact that when PEE sold its HIH shares it was only after Adler had caused Adler Corporation first to sell its HIH shareholding, accentuating the loss for PEE.

The New South Wales Supreme Court held that the substance of the transaction was that HIHC gave PEE financial assistance to acquire shares in HIH, HIHC's holding company. According to Santow J both HIHC and HIH suffered material prejudice as the result of the financial assistance and therefore s 260A was contravened. HIHC was materially prejudiced by the fact that it initially exchanged $10 million cash for either an unsecured loan to PEE or from the equitable rights it obtained against PEE which were of less value than the cash handed over. Both HIHC and HIH suffered material prejudice because of the lack of safeguards and disadvantageous terms of the AEUT investment. It was also held that the $10 million transaction involved multiple breaches of directors' duties. These are discussed in Chapter 13.2 below.

The following cases provide additional examples of financial assistance.

case note

In *Hunters Products Group Ltd v Kindley Products Pty Ltd* (1996) 14 ACLC 826, a shareholder of Hunters Products Group Ltd (Hunters) agreed to buy the shares owned by Hunters' other shareholder. Part of the purchase price came from Hunters' bank account. The Supreme Court of Victoria held that this amounted to Hunters providing financial assistance for the purchase of its shares and was prohibited under a predecessor of s 260A.

case note

In *Independent Steels Pty Ltd v Ryan* (1989) 7 ACLC 804, the shareholders of Marlon Australia Pty Ltd (Marlon) agreed to sell their shares to another company. Under the sale agreement the vendor shareholders were to be paid part of the purchase price from the gross turnover of Independent Steels Pty Ltd, a wholly-owned subsidiary of Marlon. The Supreme Court of Victoria held that this payment resulted in a subsidiary providing prohibited financial assistance for the purchase of shares in its holding company.

case note

The complex facts in *Darvall v North Sydney Brick & Tile Co Ltd* (1989) 7 ACLC 659 illustrate the giving of indirect financial assistance in the context of takeover defensive tactics. In that case, Darvall made a takeover offer for the shares in North Sydney Brick & Tile Co Ltd (Norbrick), whose most valuable asset was a large parcel of undeveloped land. The directors of Norbrick opposed the offer in the belief that the offer price was grossly inadequate. In response, they arranged for Norbrick to sell the land to a wholly-owned subsidiary, Norwest. The subsidiary then entered into a joint venture with Chase Corporation Ltd

(Chase) to develop the land. Norbrick's managing director, Lanceley, was the principal negotiator of the joint venture scheme on its behalf. Unknown to the other Norbrick directors, another aspect of the scheme also involved Chase providing Lanceley with a loan, on very favourable terms. This enabled Lanceley to make his own takeover offer for Norbrick at a higher price than Darvall's offer. Darvall applied to the court to set aside the joint venture on the grounds that the Norbrick directors breached their fiduciary duties by approving the joint venture and that the scheme involved the giving of prohibited financial assistance. The directors' duties aspect of this case is discussed in Chapter 13.2 below. Hodgson J, at first instance, decided that Chase gave financial assistance to Lanceley for the purpose of enabling him to acquire shares in Norbrick. Chase only provided this assistance because Norbrick caused its subsidiary to enter into the land development joint venture. In effect, this meant that Norbrick and Norwest indirectly provided financial assistance to Lanceley to acquire Norbrick shares in breach of a predecessor of s 260A. On appeal, the majority in the New South Wales Court of Appeal mainly dealt with the directors' duties aspect of the case and assumed that financial assistance had been given, without deciding the issue.

case note

ZBB (Aust) Ltd v Allen (1991) 9 ACLC 687 provides another illustration of indirect financial assistance. In that case Duke Securities Ltd, a member of the Duke group of companies, agreed to underwrite an issue of ZBB's shares to the public. In order to induce Duke Securities to enter into the underwriting agreement, ZBB agreed that it would deposit subscription moneys paid by Duke Securities as a result of a shortfall of the public share issue with a nominated member of the Duke group. The deposit would be treated as a loan to that company repayable on call. As a consequence of the October 1987 stock market crash, ZBB's share issue did not attract public support and Duke Securities, as underwriter, became liable to take up the shortfall of about $2 million. As Duke Securities was technically insolvent, it arranged for Duke Pacific Finance Ltd, another member of the Duke group, to pay the $2 million to ZBB on its behalf. On the same day ZBB, pursuant to the underwriting agreement, deposited the $2 million into Duke Pacific's account. Subsequently, all members of the Duke group of companies were placed in liquidation.

The New South Wales Supreme Court held that ZBB gave indirect financial assistance to Duke Securities to acquire its shares in contravention of the *Companies Code* equivalent of s 260A. By depositing with Duke Pacific the full amount of the subscription moneys received on behalf of Duke Securities, ZBB was in effect, making a loan.

shareholder approval

[8.275] According to s 260A(1)(b), a company may financially assist a person to acquire shares in the company or its holding company if the assistance is approved by shareholders under s 260B. Shareholder approval for financial assistance must be given by special resolution passed at the general meeting or by resolution agreed to by all ordinary shareholders. The person acquiring the shares or an associate may not cast votes in favour of the resolution: s 260B(1).

A company may financially assist a person to acquire shares in the company or its holding company if the assistance is approved by shareholders.

If the company that gives the financial assistance becomes a subsidiary of an Australian holding company immediately after the person acquires its shares, the financial assistance must also be approved by a special resolution passed at a general meeting of that holding company: ss 260B(2) and (3).

Where meetings are convened for the purpose of passing a special resolution under s 260B, a statement must accompany the notice of meeting that sets out all known information material to the decision on how to vote on the resolution. Previously disclosed information which it would be unreasonable to require to be disclosed again need not be sent to members: s 260B(4).

The notice of meeting and accompanying documents must be lodged with ASIC before being sent to members: s 260B(5). A special resolution approving the financial assistance must also be lodged with ASIC within 14 days of being passed: s 260B(7).

exempted financial assistance

A company may financially assist a person to acquire shares in the company or its holding company if the assistance is exempted under s 260C.

[8.280] Under s 260A(1)(c) a company may also financially assist a person to acquire shares in the company or its holding company if the assistance is exempted under s 260C. The table below highlights the various s 260C exemptions.

table 8.4 exempted financial assistance — section 260C

Financial assistance given in the ordinary course of commercial dealing consisting of: — acquiring or creating a lien on partly-paid shares — entering into an agreement under which a person may make payments to the company on shares by instalments	 260C(1)(a) 260C(1)(b)
Financial assistance given in the ordinary course of business of financial institutions and on ordinary commercial terms	260C(2)
Financial assistance in the form of a guarantee or other security given by a subsidiary of a borrower in relation to debentures in the ordinary course of commercial dealing	260C(3)
Financial assistance given under an employee share scheme that has been approved by the general meeting of the company and if it is a subsidiary, the approval of the general meeting of the holding company	260C(4)
Other exemptions: — a permitted reduction of share capital — a permitted share buy-back — assistance given under court order — a discharge on ordinary commercial terms of a liability incurred by the company in relation to a transaction entered into on ordinary commercial terms	 260C(5)(a) 260C(5)(b) 260C(5)(c) 260C(5)(d)

consequences of failing to comply with s 260A

Section 260A is a civil penalty provision and therefore any person who is involved in a company's contravention is subject to the civil penalty provisions.

[8.285] As is the case with contraventions of the reduction of capital provisions, s 260D provides that a contravention of s 260A does not affect the validity of the transactions concerned and the company is not guilty of an offence. Section 260A is a civil penalty provision and therefore any person who is involved in a company's contravention of s 260A is subject to the civil penalty provisions by virtue of s 1317E. The civil penalty provisions are discussed in Chapter 13.6 below.

bibliography ...

Dharmawan, G & Mitchell, J "The Legislative Framework of Share Buy-backs: A Comparison on the 'Old' and 'Existing' Requirements" (1999) 18(2) U Tas LR 283.

Edmundson, P "Indirect Self-Acquisition: The Search for Appropriate Concepts of Control" (1997) 15 C & SLJ 264.

Fletcher, K "Re-baiting the Financial Assistance Trap" (2000) 11 Aust Jnl of Corp Law 119.

Fletcher, K "F A after 75 years" (2005) 17 Aust Jnl of Corp Law 323.

Goldwasser, V "Differential Voting Rights and the Super Share" (1995) 7 *Corporate and Business Law Journal* 203.

Lamba, A S & Ramsay, I M, "Comparing share buybacks in highly regulated and less regulated market environments" (2005) 17 Aust Jnl of Corp Law 261.
McLaughlin B & Balazs, J "Corporate privatization by selective capital reductions: The Third Way" (2005) 23 C & SLJ 347.
Mannolini, J "The Brave New World of No Par Value Shares" (1999) 17 C & SLJ 30.
Robson, K "Share Buy-backs and Treasury Stock" (1999) 73 ALJ 446.

revision questions on the material in this chapter ...

> Please see eQuiz at **http://www.thomson.com.au/academic** for multiple choice questions and answers.

chapter nine

membership

key points ...

- There are various ways in which a person may become a member of a company. Generally, a person must agree to become a member and be registered.
- The register of members is proof of the matters shown in it in the absence of evidence to the contrary. A person may apply to the court to have the register corrected.
- A company must generally issue a share certificate where shares are issued or a transfer of shares has been lodged. A share certificate is evidence of the title of a member to the shares specified.
- A share certificate may be relied upon and if it contains incorrect information, the company is liable for any loss arising from the error.
- A transfer of shares occurs on a sale or gift and passes ownership from one shareholder to another. Shares are presumed to be freely transferable although proprietary companies in particular will usually restrict the transfer of shares by provision in the constitution that allows directors to refuse to register a transfer.
- The procedure for transfers of shares requires delivery to the company of an instrument of transfer signed by the transferor and transferee and the share certificate held by the transferor.
- The constitutions of companies often give directors the right to refuse to register a transfer of shares and they need not give reasons for a refusal unless required to do so. Directors must exercise their discretion in accordance with their fiduciary duties. The court may intervene where a refusal to register a transfer is without just cause or is oppressive.
- CHESS is the electronic settlement system used in the Australian Stock Exchange (ASX) trading. It replaced the traditional procedure of paper transfers for share market transactions.
- Shares may pass from a shareholder to another by operation of law. This occurs upon the death or bankruptcy of a member and involves a transmission of shares to an executor or other personal representative or the trustee in bankruptcy, respectively.

[9.05] The members of a company limited by shares are its shareholders. To become a shareholder of such a company it is first necessary to become a member. The members of a company limited by guarantee are not shareholders because the company does not have a share capital. Similarly, as an unlimited company could previously be formed without a share capital, its members are not necessarily shareholders.

The *Corporations Act* prescribes the minimum number of members a company may have. A company need only have one member: s 114. Section 113 sets 50 as the maximum number of non-employee shareholders of a proprietary company. There is no upper limit on the membership of public companies.

Various rights and obligations are incidental to membership. The determination of whether a person is a member of a company is significant for a number of reasons:

- **only members or their proxies are entitled to vote at general meetings. This is discussed in Chapter 14 below;**

> **only members are entitled to receive dividends. This is discussed in Chapter 10 below;**
> **members are liable to pay calls made by a company other than a no liability company if their shares are partly paid (s 254M(1));**
> **if the company is in the process of being wound up, the members may be liable to contribute towards the payments of its debts (ss 514–529); and**
> **members, as contributories, are generally entitled to share in the company's surplus assets on a winding up: s 485.**

While a company can generally hold shares in another company, a company cannot hold shares in itself or, if it is a subsidiary, it cannot hold shares in its holding company. These prohibitions are applications of the principle that a company must maintain its share capital, discussed in Chapter 8 above.

becoming a member

[9.10] As discussed in Chapter 8 above, the relationship between a company and its members is based on contract law. This means that there must be an agreement between the company and the member. Members must agree to become members and have their names entered on the register of members: s 231(b). A person may become a member in several ways:

A person may become a member in several ways.

> **being a member on the registration of the company (s 231(a));**
> **arising from conversion of a company from one limited by guarantee to one limited by shares (s 231(c));**
> **applying for and receiving an issue of shares. This is discussed in Chapter 8 above;**
> **accepting a transfer of shares from a present member;**
> **receiving shares by transmission on the death or bankruptcy of a member;**
> **exercising an option over shares and requiring the company to issue the shares;**
> **buying shares at the strike price under a call warrant. Warrants are discussed in Chapter 8 above; and**
> **holders of convertible notes may exercise their right to convert them into shares in the company. Convertible notes are discussed in Chapter 11 below.**

consenting to membership in application for registration

[9.15] The application for registration of a company must state the names and addresses of each person who consents to become a member: s 117(2)(c). Those persons become members on registration of the company, being issued with the specified number of shares: s 120. The persons' names must be entered in the register of members: s 169.

The application for registration of a company must state the names and addresses of each person who consents to become a member.

register of members

[9.20] In nearly all other cases, a person must agree to become a member and to have their name entered in the register of members before the person becomes a member: s 231(b). The only exception occurs when a member dies, becomes bankrupt or is otherwise incapable of administering their own affairs. The member's personal representative may then become a member of the company.

required information

All companies must set up and maintain a register of members (also called a "share register") containing prescribed information about the shareholders and the shares they own.

[9.25] All companies must set up and maintain a register of members (also called a "share register") containing prescribed information about the shareholders and the shares they own: ss 168(1)(a) and 169. The information includes:

> **names and addresses of the members;**
> **the date at which the name of the member was entered;**
> **if the company has more than 50 members, an up-to-date index of members' names. The index must be convenient to use; however, a separate index is not required if the register itself is kept in alphabetical order;**
> **the dates on which allotments took place, the number of shares in each allotment, the shares held by each member, the class of shares, the share or certificate numbers (if any) and the amounts paid on the shares;**
> **indications of any shares in non-listed companies that a member does not hold beneficially; and**
> **name and details of each person who stopped being a member of the company within the last seven years and the date of ceasing to be a member. This information must be kept separately from the rest of the register.**

location

[9.30] The register of members must be kept at the registered office, the principal place of business, the place where the work involved in maintaining the register is done or a place approved by ASIC. The place must be in Australia: s 172(1). The address at which the register is kept must be notified to ASIC within seven days after it is established or moved from its registered office or principal place of business: s 172(2).

Companies were formerly permitted to maintain branch registers. A company may now only keep a branch register of members at a place outside Australia. An overseas branch register must be kept in the same manner as is required of the principal register. The details of the branch register must be included in the principal register: s 178.

right of inspection

A company must allow anyone to inspect its share register.

[9.35] A company must allow anyone to inspect its share register: s 173(1). Shareholders may inspect the register without charge: s 173(2). The company may require other people who wish to inspect the register to pay a fee up to a prescribed amount. A person may request a company to give a copy of part or all of a register upon payment of a fee up to a prescribed amount. The company is not required to disclose share certificate numbers: s 173(5).

prohibited use of register information

The *Corporations Act* attempts to balance two competing policies. On the one hand, the public has a right to know the identity of a company's shareholders. On the other hand, shareholders are entitled to have their privacy protected.

[9.40] The *Corporations Act* attempts to balance two competing policies. On the one hand, the public has a right to know the identity of a company's shareholders. On the other hand, shareholders are entitled to have their privacy protected. The public's right to know is achieved by s 173(1), discussed above. The competing privacy policy consideration is achieved by s 177(1) and (1A).

Under s 177(1), a person must not use or disclose information obtained from a register to contact shareholders or send material to shareholders. A note to s 177(1) says that putting a shareholder's name and address (obtained from the register) on a mailing list for advertising material is an example of using information obtained from a register to contact or send material to a member and is not permitted.

Contravention of s 177(1) is an offence of strict liability: s 177(1B). A person who contravenes s 177(1) is also liable to compensate anyone who suffers loss or damage as a result of the contravention: s 177(2). In addition, the company can claim any profits made by a person as a result of a contravention: s 177(3) and (4).

Section 177(1A) creates two exceptions to the prohibition in s 177(1). A person can use information obtained from a register to contact or send material to shareholders if the use or disclosure of the information is:

> relevant to the holding of the shares recorded in the register or the exercise of the rights attaching to them; or
> approved by the company.

According to the explanatory memorandum accompanying the predecessor of s 177(1A), a person may use register information for purposes such as contacting shareholders in relation to takeovers or in order to influence company management about the operation of the company.

case note

In *IMF (Aust) Ltd v Sons of Gwalia Ltd* [2005] FCAFC 75, a company in the business of commercial funding of litigation sought to rely on the exemption in s 177(1A). IMF obtained a copy of the share register of Sons of Gwalia, a company that was in voluntary administration. IMF sought a declaration from the court that s 177(1A) permitted it to use the register to contact past and present Sons of Gwalia shareholders and invite them to participate in a class action against their company and its directors. The legal costs of the class action would be funded by a loan from IMF. It was alleged that many investors had acquired shares as a result of misleading information about the company's financial position. The court refused to make the declaration and held that use of the share register information for this purpose was not permitted by s 177(1A). IMF's proposed use of the information in the register was in effect an attempt to market its services. The invitation to join the proposed litigation was not connected with the "holding of the shares recorded in the register or the exercise of the rights attaching to them" as required by s 177(1A). Rather, the proposed litigation was connected with the circumstances in which investors became members of Sons of Gwalia by purchasing shares.

Section 177(1A) permits a person to use a share register to obtain shareholders' names and addresses so as to send them offers to buy their shares. The use of the register for this purpose may, however, be abused.

case note

For example, in *National Exchange Pty Ltd v ASIC* [2004] FCAFC 90, National Exchange used Onesteel Ltd's share register to find out the names and addresses of shareholders holding small parcels of shares. National Exchange then sent them offers to buy their shares at market value. It was held that National Exchange engaged in misleading and deceptive conduct under s 1041H because the overall impression of offer letters suggested that the total price for the shares was payable in full immediately on acceptance of the offer, when in fact it would be paid over 15 years in equal annual instalments.

After this case was decided the *Corporations Act* was amended with effect from 2004. As discussed in Chapter 19 below, ss 1019C–1019K now regulate unsolicited offers to purchase shares in listed companies off-market. Under these provisions, such unsolicited offers, must set out in a clear, concise and effective manner, information about the offer price and the market price of the shares.

significance of register

A register is proof of the matters shown in it.

[9.45] In the absence of evidence to the contrary, a register is proof of the matters shown in it: s 176.

case note

In *Re Clifton Springs Hotel Ltd* [1939] VLR 27, Pask made application for shares and forwarded payment to the company. His name was entered in the register of members but no notice of allotment or acceptance was sent to him. He denied receiving any communication from the company other than notice of an extraordinary meeting. The company subsequently went into liquidation and the liquidator included Pask on a list of contributories as a holder of partly paid shares even though there were no minutes recording an allotment of shares to him. Pask applied to the court to have the register rectified by removal of his name and an order for the return of the allotment money paid by him. The court refused and Pask was held to be a member because his name was entered in the register.

In *Maddocks v DJE Constructions Pty Ltd* (1982) 148 CLR 104, the High Court held that a person does not become a member until the person's name is entered in the share register. It was irrelevant that the company had not maintained a register.

However, where the register is altered in contravention of the constitution, the entry in the register is void and the transferor remains the legal owner of the shares.

case note

In *Sung Li Holdings Ltd v Medicom Finance Pty Ltd* (1995) 13 ACLC 952, the company's constitution provided that a transfer of shares was only to be registered if authorised by the board. The board did not meet to approve the transfer, but the transferee's name was registered. It was held that the transferee could not be recognised as the owner of the shares until the board approved of the transfer.

A company need only deal with those persons named in the register and cannot have regard to the interests that those persons may create over their shares in favour of others. No notice of a trust is entered on the register: s 1072E(10).

Only a person registered as a member can gain rights under provisions of the *Corporations Act* applicable to members. In *BWN Industries Pty Ltd v Downey* (1993) 11 ACLC 1191, a mortgagee with security rights over shares was unable to requisition a meeting of members under the predecessor of s 249D through notice given by a receiver manager. An applicant seeking a remedy under s 232 must also generally be a registered member. This is discussed below in Chapter 17.

A contravention of the company registers provisions is an offence with the prescribed penalties under Sch 3 of the *Corporations Act*.

correction of register

A company or a person aggrieved may apply to the court to correct a register kept by the company.

[9.50] Under s 175(1), a company or a person aggrieved may apply to the court to correct a register kept by the company. A member is the most obvious example of an aggrieved person where a register is incorrect. The court may order the company that the register be corrected and also that the company compensate the applicant for loss or damage suffered: s 175(2). Where a register is corrected by order of the court, the company must lodge notice of the correction with ASIC: s 175(3).

Although s 175 allows an applicant to obtain a remedy of a procedural nature, it may require the court to examine various issues relating to share ownership. An application for correction of the register may involve the resolution of a dispute between members or between an alleged member and the company but the court may, because of the summary nature of the hearing, require the plaintiff to bring an ordinary legal action where there are complex issues to resolve.

case note

An example of where the court ordered correction of the register is provided by *McLaughlin v Daily Telegraph Newspaper Co (No 2)* (1904) 1 CLR 243. McLaughlin became incapable of managing his business affairs because of mental illness. He executed a power of attorney authorising his wife to deal with his property. Exercising this power, his wife sold shares in the company, standing in his name. She signed the transfer, which was then registered by the company. Neither the company nor transferee had notice of McLaughlin's insanity.

Some time later McLaughlin recovered so as to be able to manage his affairs. In the meantime the value of the shares had substantially increased and the company had made a share issue to existing shareholders. Large dividends had also been declared. He applied to the court for rectification of the register of the company, claiming that he did not know that he was executing a power of attorney and his wife was aware of this. The court found that this was so and therefore the power of attorney was void. As a result, the purported transfer executed by McLaughlin's wife was also void. The company was ordered to rectify its register so as to enter McLaughlin as the owner of the shares sold, together with the new shares subsequently issued by the company and to pay all dividends declared on those shares to him. McLaughlin, however, was ordered to pay over to the company the proceeds from the sale of shares received by his wife.

case note

In *Bothranch Pty Ltd v Monitronix Ltd* (1987) 7 ACLC 443, the register of a company was corrected under a predecessor of s 175. The capital of the company had been altered in an irregular manner because its directors had not been properly appointed. This resulted in purported allotments of shares being invalid. As the company's register was fundamentally flawed, the first remedial step was to rectify the register in order to ascertain who the members were.

Correction of the register is an appropriate remedy sought by a member who can show that the directors were exercising powers for an improper purpose by issuing shares in breach of their fiduciary duties. A court order that the allotment was invalid would then require a supplementary order to correct the register.

The register may also be corrected where a transfer of shares occurs in breach of the constitution or replaceable rules, for example where a pre-emption clause is not complied with: *Carew-Reid v Public Trustee* (1996) 14 ACLC 1106.

In *Homestake Gold of Australia Ltd v Peninsula Gold Pty Ltd* (1996) 14 ACLC 903, transfers of shares to minors were held to be ineffective and the transferor was restored to the register. The transfers were voidable and the order for correction of the register dated from the order and not the transfers.

minors as members

A contract under which a minor acquires shares is an example of a voidable contract.

[9.55] Minors, that is persons under 18 years of age, may be shareholders of companies. A contract under which a minor acquires shares is an example of a voidable contract. This is because the minor acquires an interest in a subject of a permanent nature under which continuous or recurring obligations arise. Such contracts are voidable in that they are valid and binding on the minor unless and until the minor repudiates the contract before attaining 18 years of age or within a reasonable time thereafter. Thus minor shareholders are liable to pay calls, if the calls are made prior to repudiation, but they are not liable to pay calls made after they repudiate.

While a minor may avoid further obligations after repudiation of the contract, generally, money paid for the shares is irrecoverable. In order to recover money paid, the minor must show total failure of consideration.

case note

In *Steinberg v Scala (Leeds) Ltd* [1923] 2 Ch 452, a minor applied for shares which she was duly allotted. She paid the amount due on allotment and the first call. She did not receive any dividends and did not exercise any rights attaching to the shares. While still a minor, she repudiated the contract and sought to recover the money she had paid. This claim was unsuccessful. There had not been total failure of consideration. She had paid for the shares and they had been duly allotted to her. She obtained what she had bargained for despite the fact that she had obtained no tangible benefit as a result of being a shareholder.

In *Homestake Gold of Australia Ltd v Peninsula Gold Pty Ltd* (1996) 14 ACLC 903, deeds that provided for the transfer of shares to minors and were signed by each minor's guardian were held to be ineffective. Under the *Minors (Property and Contracts) Act 1970* (NSW), the deeds would only be binding on the minors if they had participated in their execution and they were beneficial to them.

list of members in extract of particulars

[9.60] As discussed in Chapter 1 above, ASIC maintains ASCOT, a publicly accessible database of information on all Australian companies. Among other things, this information includes shareholders' names and addresses. ASIC obtains this information from the companies themselves. As discussed in Chapter 15 below, s 346A requires ASIC to send a company, within two weeks of its review date, an annual extract of particulars that contains the information prescribed by reg 2N.2.01 of the *Corporations Regulations*. The prescribed information includes details, as at the review date, of the names and addresses of all members in the case of companies with no more than 20 members. For companies with more than 20 members, the information includes the names and addresses of the top 20 members in each class of shares. If the information in a company's extract of particulars is incorrect, s 346C requires the company to respond and give ASIC the correct information.

disclosure of interests in shares

As a general rule, the *Corporations Act* does not require a person who holds shares as a trustee to disclose that fact to the company or to disclose the identity of the beneficiaries.

[9.65] A person may hold shares as a trustee for a particular beneficiary. This is often the case when a shareholder dies or becomes bankrupt. On death, the deceased's executor or trustee becomes entitled to the legal interest in the deceased's shares. On bankruptcy, the bankrupt's shares vest in the trustee of bankruptcy on behalf of the bankrupt's creditors. Similarly, trustees of superannuation funds that own shares, hold those shares on behalf of members of the fund.

As a general rule, the *Corporations Act* does not require a person who holds shares as a trustee to disclose that fact to the company or to disclose the identity of the beneficiaries. As regards the register of members, s 1072E(10) provides, except as provided by that section, no notice of a trust must be entered on a register and the company is not regarded as recognising the existence of any trust. Section 1072E(10) is primarily for the convenience of public companies. A company may, however, consent to marking its register in such a way as to identify that the shares are held by a trustee: s 1072E(9).

In the case of proprietary companies, a person who holds shares as a trustee for a body corporate must notify the proprietary company of that fact: s 1072E(11).

The substantial shareholding provisions and the tracing beneficial ownership provisions of the *Corporations Act* are exceptions to the general rule and may require a person who holds shares in a listed company as a trustee to disclose that fact to the company or to disclose the identity of the beneficiaries.

The substantial shareholding provisions and the tracing beneficial ownership provisions of the *Corporations Act* are exceptions to the general rule and may require a person who holds shares in a listed company as a trustee to disclose that fact to the company or to disclose the identity of the beneficiaries.

The substantial shareholding provisions, ss 671B–671C, aim to promote an informed market for shares of listed companies. The provisions oblige persons entitled to not less than five per cent of the voting shares of a listed company to disclose to the company full particulars of their entitlement in the shares. Disclosure of substantial shareholdings enables both a company and the market to know who controls significant shareholdings. The filing of a substantial shareholder notice is often the first indication of an impending takeover bid.

Sections 672A–672F complement the substantial shareholding provisions. They enable the company or ASIC to obtain information not only as to the identity of persons who control voting shares or a "relevant interest" in those shares, but also the nature and extent of their interest.

These disclosure requirements are closely related and complementary to other aspects of disclosure required under the takeover provisions of the *Corporations Act* and are discussed in Chapter 18 below.

share certificates

statutory requirements

[9.70] A share certificate is prima facie evidence of the title of a member to the number of shares specified: s 1070C(2). Where a share certificate has been duly issued but the shareholder's name has not been entered in the register of members, the shareholder may be a member for the purposes of an application under s 232. This is despite the operation of s 176 which states that the register is prima facie evidence of the matters contained therein: *Re Independent Quarries Pty Ltd* (1994) 12 ACLC 159.

A share certificate is prima facie evidence of the title of a member to the number of shares specified.

Share certificates also enable the company to identify its members and as discussed below, para [9.95], a company will generally require production of the certificate before registering a transfer or transmission of shares.

Under s 1070C(1), a share certificate must state:

> **the name of the company and its jurisdiction of registration;**
> **the class of shares; and**
> **the amount unpaid on the shares.**

A company is required by s 1071H(1) and (2) to complete and have ready for delivery a share certificate within two months of an allotment of shares or within one month after a transfer of shares is lodged with the company. Non-compliance with these requirements is an offence. Application may be made to the court for an order compelling the company to issue a share certificate: s 1071H(6).

A company need not issue a share certificate where it is entitled not to do so. It will be so entitled if it refuses to register a transfer (s 1071H(3)), or where the conditions of allotment provide that a certificate need not be issued: s 1071H(1).

Under s 1071H(2), a company also need not issue a share certificate if the operating rules of CHESS apply. This is designed to facilitate electronic stock exchange transactions.

liability of company for issue of incorrect share certificate

[9.75] A share certificate is not a contractual document but merely a certification by the company of the information contained. As discussed above, para [9.45], the legal rights and liabilities of members depend on their names being entered in the register of members. However, because a share certificate is prima facie evidence of the title of the member to the shares, the company is liable at common law for any loss arising from an error in the share certificate. The purpose of a share certificate is to enable people to rely on the information it contains. Once a share certificate has been issued by the company and someone changes position in reliance on it, the company is estopped, or prevented from denying the truth of its contents.

Once a share certificate has been issued by the company and someone changes position in reliance on it, the company is estopped or prevented from denying the truth of its contents.

case note

In *Re Bahia and San Francisco Rail Co* (1868) LR 3 QB 584, B relied on a share certificate that stated A was the owner of a certain number of shares and purchased those shares from him. After B became registered as the holder, it transpired that A was not the true owner. He had forged the signature of the true owner, C, on a transfer and had forwarded this forged transfer together with a stolen share certificate made out in C's name to the company. The company, without negligence or fraud, then issued the certificate to A.

The court held that C, as true owner, was entitled to have his name restored to the register. B could not acquire better title than the defective title of A. As a result, B's name was removed from the register. B obviously had rights against A based on A's fraud. The company was held liable to B for damages because it was estopped from denying to him that A was the true owner. The company could not deny to B that which it had earlier certified. While it could not register B as the holder of the shares because of its duty to C, the company could only compensate B by paying damages, being the value of the shares at the time the company refused to register B or when B's name was removed from the register.

Estoppel may arise where a purported transfer of shares is later found to be invalid.

case note

In *Daily Telegraph Co v Cohen* (1905) 5 SR (NSW) 520, shares were sold under a purported exercise of a power of attorney. The power of attorney and associated transfer of shares were later held to be void. The original owner's name was therefore restored to the register. In the meantime, the transferee had in turn transferred the shares to Cohen. Cohen's name was removed from the register, but the company was held liable in damages to him because it was estopped from denying that his transferor was the true owner as it had previously certified.

If a certificate states that a shareholder has fully paid shares when in fact they are partly paid, the company is also estopped from denying that they are fully paid. This means that the company is unable to make a call on the shares: *Burkinshaw v Nicholls* (1878) 3 App Cas 1004.

Estoppel operates against a company only where someone has changed position in reliance on the certificate. It therefore cannot be used by anyone who has knowledge of the truth. It is rare for a person to whom a false certificate is first issued to be able to rely on estoppel. Generally, that person knows the true situation and has not changed her or his position in reliance on the certificate.

The position of an outsider who relies on a share certificate issued by a company is further strengthened by the assumptions contained in s 129. In particular, the outsider may assume that an officer or agent of the company who has authority to issue a document or certified copy of a document on behalf of the company also has authority to warrant that the document or certified copy is genuine: s 129(7).

A company is not liable to someone who has put forward a forged transfer. This is so even if the person did not know of the forgery. In fact a person who presents a transfer to the company impliedly warrants that the transfer is genuine and will be held liable to the company even though acting innocently.

forged certificates

[9.80] While a company cannot deny the truth of information contained in its valid share certificates, it is generally not liable if the certificate is forged. However, if the forgery is the result of fraudulent acts of an officer, agent or employee of the company, the assumptions in s 129 permit an outsider to assume that the certificate is validly executed and is otherwise genuine: s 128(3). In such a case, the company is bound by the share certificate even though it has been forged. This overcomes the decision in *Ruben v Great Fingall Consolidated* [1906] AC 439, discussed in Chapter 5 above.

transfer of shares

transferability of shares

[9.85] A transfer of shares occurs when ownership of shares passes from one shareholder to another. This results in the transferee becoming a member of the company after the name of the transferee is entered in the register of members. The transferor ceases to be a member if the entire shareholding is transferred. As a general rule, shares in a company are presumed to be transferable without restrictions. This is an important characteristic of listed companies and is necessary for stock exchange trading.

As a general rule, shares in a company are presumed to be transferable without restrictions.

Section 1070A(1) provides that shares are transferable as provided by the company's constitution. Proprietary companies were once required to restrict the transfer of shares. The constitutions of many proprietary companies still contain restrictions on the transfer of shares because the shareholders have an expectation that their approval will be required before a new person can become a shareholder. It is the nature of closely held companies that the identity of members is important and membership is restricted to known or approved persons. The proprietary company replaceable rule in s 1072G is an example of a typical restriction on the transfer of shares. Section 1072G gives directors of proprietary companies a discretion to refuse to register a transfer for any reason.

The ASX Listing Rules prohibit listed public companies from including restrictions on the transfer of shares in their constitutions in other than exceptional circumstances. This is because the existence of such restrictions would prevent the operation of a free market in the company's shares as a purchaser would be uncertain of gaining registration as a shareholder.

instrument of transfer

An "instrument of transfer" documents the transfer of ownership of shares from a member to another person.

[9.90] A sale of shares is similar to a sale of land since, in addition to a contract of sale, further steps are necessary to complete the transaction. A contract for the sale of shares is not complete until the shares are transferred and the name of the transferee is entered in the register of members.

Section 1071B(2) prohibits a company, notwithstanding anything in its constitution, from registering a transfer unless a "proper" instrument of transfer has been delivered to the company. An "instrument of transfer" documents the transfer of ownership of shares from a member to another person. There is no specific requirement in the *Corporations Act* as to the form of the transfer. The instrument of transfer is usually signed by the transferor and the transferee. The seller (transferor) delivers a signed transfer, together with the relevant share certificates, to the buyer (transferee). Some Australian states impose a tax called "stamp duty" on transfers of shares in unlisted companies. Stamp duty on transfers of shares in listed companies was abolished in 2001.

The replaceable rule in s 1072F(2) provides that the directors are not required to register a transfer unless the transfer and any share certificate has been lodged at the company's registered office. The directors may also reasonably require any further information to establish whether the transferor has the right to transfer the shares. Lodgment is usually done by the transferee. The transferor remains the holder of the shares and a member until the transfer is registered and the name of the transferee is entered in the register of members: s 1072F(1). This is important where the shares are partly paid because the transferor remains liable for calls until the transfer is registered. For this reason, provision is made by s 1071D(1) for the transferor to require the company to register the transfer in the same manner as if the application had been made by the transferee.

The CHESS system allows the shares of listed companies to be transferred electronically without the use of transfer documentation and share certificates. This system is discussed below, para [9.125].

procedure for transfer of shares

To complete a share transaction in an unlisted company, a share transfer must be executed and delivered to the registered office of the company, together with the share certificate.

[9.95] To complete a share transaction in an unlisted company, a share transfer must be executed and delivered to the registered office of the company, together with the share certificate: s 1072F(2). Any other requirement set out in the constitution, such as approval of directors, must also be met: *Poliwka v Heven Holdings Pty Ltd* (1992) 10 ACLC 1759.

The procedure for transfer of shares is relatively straightforward where all the shares specified in the share certificate are sold to one buyer. A seller who is selling only part of the shares will generally be reluctant to hand over the share certificate to the buyer. In other cases, the transferor can forward the share certificate to the company with the request that it certificate the instrument of transfer. If this is done, the company notes on the instrument of transfer that it holds the transferor's share certificate.

Under s 1071G(4), an instrument of transfer is deemed to be certified if it bears the words "certificate lodged" or words to that effect. The certification constitutes a representation by the company to any person acting on the faith of it that such documents as on the face of them show prima facie title to the shares to the transferor named in the instrument of transfer, have been produced to it: s 1071G(1). The certification is not, however, a representation that the transferor has any title to the shares.

unregistered transfers

[9.100] As discussed above, for a sale of shares to be complete, several steps must be taken. Usually there is a contract between the transferor and transferee. The transferor then hands over the duly executed transfer and share certificate to the transferee. The transferee lodges the completed transfer and certificate with the company. To complete the process, the company registers the name of the transferee in the register of members and issues a new share certificate in the transferee's name.

A problem arises where the transferor and transferee enter into a contract for sale of shares but for some reason the share transfer is not registered by the company. From the company's point of view, the transfer is incomplete or inchoate. As discussed above, para [9.65], under s 1072E(10) the company need only recognise legal interests in shares and is not affected by notice of any trusts. This is also often set out in the constitution. The effect of this is that the company recognises the transferor as holder of the shares until her or his name is removed from the register and replaced by the name of the transferee. This is important if, for example, the company makes a call before the transfer is registered. In such a case the transferor is still liable. Similarly, the company is entitled to send notice of meetings to the transferor and it is the transferor who is entitled to vote in respect of the shares: *Re Fernlake Pty Ltd* (1994) 12 ACLC 453.

With regard to the transferor and transferee, property in the shares passes at the time the transferor hands over the signed transfer and share certificate. The transferee becomes the beneficial owner as soon as the contract is made. From this time on, the seller holds the shares as trustee for the buyer. The buyer is said to have an equitable interest: *Niord Pty Ltd v Adelaide Petroleum NL* (1990) 8 ACLC 684. Thus the seller must account to the buyer for any dividends the company may pay to the seller and the buyer must indemnify the seller for any obligations incurred after the contract date.

The unregistered buyer is entitled to direct the seller how to exercise voting rights. If the seller fails to obey the directions of the buyer, that vote is valid in terms of the company but the buyer can bring an action against the seller either for breach of contract or breach of trust: *Re Fernlake Pty Ltd* (1994) 12 ACLC 453.

As with the sale of land, registration of transfers of shares is of great importance. If an unscrupulous shareholder enters into a contract to sell the same shares to two buyers, the buyer who first obtains registration becomes the holder of the shares. This is an application of a legal principle, which also applies to sale of land. Where the equities are equal, the first to register a valid transfer acquires priority. In this way the claim of the first buyer may be defeated by the second buyer if the second buyer obtains registration first, without notice of the previous contract. The first buyer only has an action against the seller: *Shropshire Union Railway v The Queen* (1875) 7 HL 496. This situation is very unlikely if the first buyer obtains the share certificate. This would usually be effective in precluding the second buyer obtaining registration.

Where neither buyer obtains registration, the first to acquire an interest under the contract will prevail. This may occur where the directors properly exercise a power to refuse to register a transfer.

restrictions on transfer of shares

[9.105] There are two conflicting legal principles governing transfer of shares. The owner of property, including a shareholder, is presumed to have the right to transfer personal property. Application of this principle prevents a shareholder being locked into a company unwillingly. Transferability of shares was an important feature in the development of companies. On the other hand, companies are permitted to restrict the transfer of shares. Section 140(2) prevents modifications of the constitution to increase or impose restrictions on the right to transfer shares without a member's consent in writing.

As shareholders are presumed to have a prima facie right to transfer their shares, any restriction contained in the company's constitution must be clear and unambiguous: *Greenhalgh v Mallard* [1943] 2 All ER 234. A restriction will not be implied in a particular case and where possible, the restriction will be construed narrowly rather than broadly.

As shareholders are presumed to have a prima facie right to transfer their shares, any restriction contained in the company's constitution must be clear and unambiguous.

The most usual form of restriction on transfer of shares confers a discretion on the directors under the articles to refuse to register a transfer.

It was held in *Andco Nominees Pty Ltd v Lestato Pty Ltd* (1995) 13 ACLC 835 that a restriction on the transfer of shares in the constitution did not apply:

> **to a transmission of shares on the death or bankruptcy of a shareholder;**
> **to a compulsory transfer of shares by court order; or**
> **to a transfer of shares from a retiring trustee to a new trustee.**

refusal to register transfer or transmission of shares

[9.110] The proprietary company replaceable rule in s 1072G provides that directors of a proprietary company have the power to refuse to register a transfer of shares for any reason. The replaceable rule in s 1072F(3) is applicable to all companies and allows directors to refuse to register a transfer of shares if the shares are not fully paid up or the company has a lien over the shares.

If a company refuses to register a transfer, it must send the transferee notice of the refusal within two months after the transfer was lodged with it: s 1071E. Breach of this requirement is an offence. It may also result in the company losing the right to deny registration to the transferee: *Re Swaledale Cleaners Ltd* [1968] 1 WLR 1710.

Where the company's constitution gives directors a discretion to refuse to register a transfer, they must exercise this power in good faith in the best interests of the company. This is one aspect of the fiduciary duty owed by directors to the company and is further discussed in Chapter 13.2 below.

reasons for refusal

[9.115] If the company's constitution does not require the directors to disclose grounds or reasons for a refusal to register a transfer, it is extremely difficult to challenge such a refusal. The person wishing to challenge the refusal must prove that the directors acted in bad faith or for improper purposes. As the directors are not bound to disclose their grounds or reasons, it is difficult to discharge the onus of proof resting on the plaintiff.

case note

In *Re Smith and Fawcett Ltd* [1942] Ch 304, the company's constitution provided that "the directors may at any time in their absolute and uncontrolled discretion refuse to register any transfer of shares". The father of the applicant was the holder of 4,001 shares in the company at the time of his death. The applicant, as executor of his father's estate, sought to be registered as the holder of those shares. The directors refused to register the transfer unless 2,000 of the shares were sold to a certain director at a stated price, in which case they would register a transfer of the remaining shares. It was held that the directors had an unfettered discretion that had only to be exercised bona fide in the interests of the company as seen by them. The applicant failed as he could not prove that the directors had acted in bad faith.

In *Roberts v Coussens* (1991) 9 ACLC 1403, an executor sought registration of a transmission of a share to him. The directors refused to register the transmission as permitted under the constitution. They were not required to assign any reason for such a refusal. Once the directors give a reason, it could be scrutinised by the court where an application is sought under s 1071F. This is discussed below.

Where the directors are only permitted to refuse to register a transfer on certain specified grounds and it can be shown that the refusal was on other grounds, the courts may order that the transfer be registered. However, in *Berry and Stewart v Tottenham Hotspur Football Co* [1935] Ch 718 where the constitution provided that directors need not specify the grounds upon which a registration of transfer is refused, the court did not require the directors to disclose reasons or grounds for refusal.

Where the constitution of a company empowers it to refuse to register a transfer of shares in some particular circumstances, the courts will strictly examine the provisions in the constitution in order to determine whether the refusal was authorised or not.

case note

In *Equiticorp Industries Ltd v ACI International Ltd* (1987) 5 ACLC 237, ACI refused to register transfers of shares to Equiticorp. The constitution provided that the directors could refuse to register a transfer if it would result in a foreign person controlling more than 15 per cent of the voting shares. It was held that Equiticorp was not a foreign person and ACI was required to register the transfers.

Where the constitution requires the directors to pass a resolution refusing to register a transfer, the transferee is entitled to registration unless the directors actually resolve as a board to reject registration. In *Moodie v W & J Shepherd Ltd* [1949] 2 All ER 1044, the two directors of the company disagreed and neither had a casting vote. In such circumstances, the court held that the transferee was entitled to be registered.

without just cause

[9.120] If the directors refuse to register a transfer of shares, the transferee may apply to the court and if the court is satisfied that the refusal to register the transfer was without just cause, the court may order that the transfer be registered or make such order as it thinks just and reasonable, including an order providing for the purchase of the shares by a specified member or by the company itself: s 1071F. The constitutions of some companies require a particular person, other than the board of directors, to approve the registration of a transfer of shares. Section 1071F also gives the transferee a remedy if that person refuses to register the transfer without just cause.

If the directors refuse to register a transfer of shares, the transferee may apply to the court and if the court is satisfied that the refusal to register the transfer was without just cause, the court may order that the transfer be registered or make such order as it thinks just and reasonable.

Section 1071F gives effect to the general right of shareholders to transfer their shares. Its purpose is to provide transferees with an easier procedure than correcting the register under s 175. The court has a wide discretion to balance the interests of the parties. Section 1071F applies to a transmission of shares as well as a transfer of shares. Transmission of shares is discussed below, para [9.145].

Section 232 probably enables members to apply for a remedy in cases where directors fail to register a transfer of shares and this failure constitutes "oppression or conduct which is unfairly prejudicial to, or unfairly discriminatory against" the members. This may now enable a member to obtain a remedy in cases such as *Re Smith and Fawcett Ltd* [1942] 1 All ER 542.

case note

In *Re Winmardun Pty Ltd* (1991) 9 ACLC 238, a shareholder of a family company entered into a deed of arrangement under Pt X of the *Bankruptcy Act* and Waters was appointed as the trustee of the deed. Under the deed, the shareholder's property vested in the trustee. Waters sought registration from the directors of a transmission of the shares to him. While the directors did not formally refuse to register the transmission, they indicated that they would not register the transmission to Waters on the grounds that he was not a family member. The directors argued that this was not in the company's best interests. Waters applied under a predecessor of s 1071F for an order that the company acquire the shares.

The court held that the reasons given by the directors for the refusal to register the transmission did not provide a foundation for the formation of a bona fide opinion by them that it would not be in the company's best interests to register Waters as a shareholder. For this reason their failure to register the transmission was without just cause. The court, however, refused to order that the company purchase the shares and instead ordered that Waters be registered as a shareholder of the company.

CHESS

[9.125] The Clearing House Electronic Subregister System (CHESS) is the electronic settlement and transfer system operated by the ASX and for listed companies it has replaced the traditional share transfer procedure involving the lodgment of instruments of transfer and issue of paper share certificates. Under CHESS, shares and other securities are electronically transferred and the subregister is automatically updated to reflect the change in ownership.

CHESS is the electronic settlement and transfer system operated by the ASX and for listed companies it has replaced the traditional share transfer procedure involving the lodgment of instruments of transfer and issue of paper share certificates.

The ASX has published the following papers on its website:

> CHESS: An Overview; and
> How ASX Clearing and Settlement Works.

These publications are linked to the Lipton-Herzberg Corporate Law Websites at **http://www.lipton-herzberg.com.au/corp-law-websites-main.html#Australian_Stock_Exchange**

purpose of CHESS

[9.130] The purpose of CHESS is to enable the ASX to compete effectively with overseas stock exchanges by offering an efficient settlement system. This system complements the computerised securities trading system SEATS (Stock Exchange Automated Trading System). The aims of CHESS include:

> **faster settlement with reduced risk;**
> **predictability of settlement obligations within a fixed time;**
> **more efficient settlement at times when market volumes are high; and**
> **cost savings for market participants.**

These aims are achieved by enabling both transactions and settlement to take place electronically.

sponsorship

[9.135] Stockbrokers and institutional investors are referred to as clearing and settlement (CS) facility "participants" as they have direct access to the settlement process. These participants are able to sponsor their clients who enter into a sponsorship agreement with a broker. The client's shareholdings are registered on the sponsor's own electronic register. Brokers are deemed to have warranted that a transferor has good title, the information contained in the transfer document is accurate and the broker was authorised to effect the transfer: *Corporations Regulations*, reg 7.11.17.

Some companies offer "issuer sponsorship" which enables a shareholder to choose the company as sponsor rather than a broker. In such a case, the holding is registered on the company's register. This register, together with the CS subregister, comprises a particular listed company's register of members.

Clearing and Settlement operating rules

[9.140] The Clearing and Settlement operating rules are binding on issuers, participants and the CS facility itself as if contracts under seal: s 822B. The rules may be enforced by the court: s 822C.

The operating rules override the constitution of a company in respect of CS transfers: s 1070A(1). The CS facility is entitled to assume that its operating rules have been complied with: *Corporations Regulations*, reg 7.11.34.

transmission of shares

Transmission of shares occurs by operation of law if a shareholder dies, becomes incapable through mental or physical incapacity or becomes a bankrupt.

[9.145] Transmission of shares occurs by operation of law if a shareholder dies, becomes incapable through mental or physical incapacity or becomes a bankrupt. In such cases, the shares vest in the deceased shareholder's personal representative or the trustee in bankruptcy. The procedure for transfer of shares does not apply.

Where the shareholder dies leaving a will, the executor named in the will becomes the deceased's personal representative. If there is no will, the shares vest in the Public Trustee and on the granting of administration they vest in the administrator who is usually the deceased's next of kin. The personal representative becomes legal owner of the shares even though not registered as a member. Proof of the personal representative's status must be furnished to the company. Sufficient evidence of this is a document evidencing a grant of probate or letters of administration: s 1071B(13).

The replaceable rule in s 1072A deals with the transmission of shares on the death of a shareholder. If the shares were owned solely by the deceased shareholder, the company will only recognise the personal representative as being entitled to the deceased shareholder's interest in the shares: s 1072A(1). If the personal representative provides the information the directors reasonably require to establish the representative's entitlement to be registered as a shareholder, the personal representative may elect to be registered or may, by completing a share transfer, transfer the shares to another person. The personal representative has the same rights as the deceased shareholder, whether or not registered as the holder of shares: s 1072A(2)(b). If the personal representative chooses to be registered, the company must register the representative as a shareholder: s 1072A(3). If the personal representative elects to transfer the shares, the transfer is subject to the rules applicable to transfers generally: s 1072A(4).

Where a deceased shareholder owned shares jointly, the company will recognise only the survivor as being entitled to the deceased shareholder's interest in the shares. The estate of the deceased shareholder is not released from any liability in respect of the shares: s 1072A(5). This is applicable to calls made on partly paid shares.

Section 1072E(2) provides that a personal representative may choose to be registered in a representative capacity as the holder of the shares registered in the name of the deceased. The personal representative is then subject to the same liabilities as if the shares had remained registered in the name of the deceased. This provision is subject to provisions to the contrary in the company's constitution. For example, the directors could refuse to register the personal representative if empowered to do so.

The administrator of the estate of a shareholder who has become incapable through mental or physical infirmity stands in a similar position to a personal representative: s 1072E(4).

A personal representative may, however, choose not to become registered as a member and merely execute a transfer to another. Section 1071B(5) and (6) allows the personal representative to do this even though not registered. Again, this is subject to provisions to the contrary in the company's constitution.

For the purpose of seeking a remedy under s 232, a person to whom a share in the company has been transmitted by will or by operation of law is taken to be a member and may therefore bring an action whether or not he or she is registered as a member where the requisite oppression or unfairness can be shown. This is discussed in Chapter 17 below.

If a shareholder becomes bankrupt the *Bankruptcy Act 1966* (Cth) provides that their property vests in the trustee in bankruptcy. Under s 1072E(6) the trustee in bankruptcy may be registered as the holder of the shares. However, usually registration is not sought because adequate powers are conferred by the *Bankruptcy Act* to carry out the trustee's functions without registration. The bankrupt usually remains a member.

Section 1072B provides for a replaceable rule dealing with transmission of shares on the bankruptcy of a shareholder. Similar to the situation of transmission on the death of a shareholder, the trustee may be required by the directors to establish entitlement to be registered. Upon doing so, the trustee may choose to be registered or to transfer the shares to another person: s 1072B(1). The company must then register the trustee as holder of the shares or transfer the shares in accordance with the rules applicable to transfers generally: s 1072B(2) and (3). This replaceable rule is subject to the *Bankruptcy Act 1966*: s 1072B(4).

Where an insolvent person enters into a deed of arrangement under the *Bankruptcy Act*, the shares held by the insolvent also pass to the trustee by operation of law and is a transmission of shares: *Re Winmardun* (1991) 9 ACLC 238.

liability of members

The liability of members of a company limited by shares is limited to the amount, if any, unpaid on their shares.

[9.150] As discussed in Chapter 3 above, the liabilities of members depends upon the type of company. The liability of members of a company limited by shares is limited to the amount, if any, unpaid on their shares: s 516. If a company has issued partly paid shares, members are liable to pay calls on the shares in accordance with the terms on which the shares are on issue: s 254M(1). Directors usually have the power to make calls. Where a call is not paid by a member holding partly paid shares, the shares may be forfeited as discussed below, para [9.160].

On the winding up of a company, s 515 provides that every present and past member is liable to contribute to the property of the company to an amount sufficient for payment of its debts, costs of winding up and adjustment of rights as between its contributories. This broad statement is then subject to several qualifications. A past member who has ceased to be a member for more than one year prior to commencement of winding up is not liable to contribute: s 521. This period is extended to three years in the case of an unlimited company having converted to a limited company during that period: s 523. A past member is not liable to contribute in respect of any debts or liabilities incurred after he or she ceased to be a member (s 520), only being liable to contribute where it appears to the court that the existing members are unable to satisfy the company's debts: s 522.

The liability of a member of a company limited by guarantee is limited to the amount undertaken to be contributed by the member to the property of the company in the event of its being wound up: s 517. In the case of an unlimited company, members are liable to contribute to the full extent of the debts and liabilities of the company. The liability of past members is subject to the same qualifications as in the case of companies limited by shares.

The liability of contributories is of the nature of a debt under a deed at the time their liability commenced but payable from the time calls are made enforcing the liability: s 527.

A "contributory" is any person who is liable to contribute to the property of a company on winding up. Its meaning is extended by s 9 to include members holding fully paid shares even though they have no further liability, and past members who are liable to contribute under s 516.

Contributories have the right to apply to the court for a compulsory winding up under s 462(2)(c). This is discussed in Chapter 25 below.

Although members are contractually bound by the company's constitution and any replaceable rules under s 140(1), they are not bound by a modification of the constitution made after they became members where the modification requires them to take more shares or increases their liability to the company. This is subject to their agreement in writing: s 140(2).

cessation of membership

[9.155] In discussing the ways in which a person may become a member we have indirectly looked at some ways by which a person ceases to be a member. Where shares are transferred and the transfer is duly registered, the transferor ceases to be a member. The death of a member also results in cessation of membership. The deceased's shares are transmitted to her or his personal representative.

A person may cease to be a member where that person's shares are compulsorily acquired. This may occur by way of a selective reduction of capital under ss 256B and 256C, as part of a scheme of arrangement (s 414) or under the compulsory acquisitions provisions in Chapter 6A.

All persons cease to be members on the dissolution of the company, discussed in Chapter 25 below.

forfeiture on non-payment of calls

[9.160] As discussed in Chapter 8 above, shares may be issued partly paid. The unpaid amount may be called up in whole or in part by the company or by the liquidator. The power to make calls is usually exercised by the directors under the general powers conferred by the replaceable rule contained in s 198A. Where a company issues partly paid shares, the shareholder is liable to pay calls on the shares in accordance with the terms of the share issue: s 254M(1). A shareholder of a no liability company is not under a contractual obligation to pay calls or any contribution to the debts and liabilities of the company: s 254M(2).

Section 254Q sets out a procedure that confers a power of forfeiture on a no liability company where a call is not paid. It provides for immediate forfeiture without the need for a resolution of the directors. In *Diversified Mineral Resources NL v Amusmet Investments Pty Ltd* (1991) 9 ACLC 1047, shares in a no liability company were automatically forfeited 14 days after the date of a call. This was despite the existence of substantive litigation that involved a dispute over whether the shares were fully paid or not at the time of the call.

A forfeiture of shares is similar to a reduction of capital but is allowed as long as the forfeiture is as a result of non-payment of a call. Further, s 254Q requires a no liability company to sell forfeited shares. This is an exception to the prohibition on a company dealing in its own shares because forfeiture does not involve any payment by the company: *Trevor v Whitworth* (1887) 12 App Cas 409.

surrender of shares

[9.165] A shareholder cannot surrender partly paid shares because this would breach the principle that a company must maintain its share capital. It would constitute an indirect way for a company to hold shares in itself and would result in part of the issued capital being extinguished. It is even doubtful whether a company can accept a surrender of fully paid shares. A valid surrender of shares may only occur where they are liable to be validly forfeited: *Trevor v Whitworth* (1887) 12 App Cas 409.

the company's power of lien

[9.170] Similar to the power of a company to forfeit and sell shares after non-payment of a call is a company's right of lien over partly paid shares for all money called or payable at a fixed time in respect of that share. This right is often set out in a company's constitution and usually extends to all dividends payable on the shares.

A lien is the right to hold property of another as security for payment of a debt. The company may then sell the shares over which it has a lien. In this way, the shareholder ceases to be a member. Any surplus proceeds from the sale after the debt has been met are payable to the shareholder.

Where the constitution is expressed in broad terms to confer a lien over all shares and not just partly paid shares, the lien may secure any debts of the shareholder and is not restricted to debts relating to the shares: *Chase Corp (Aust) Pty Ltd v North Sydney Brick and Tile Co Ltd* (1994) 12 ACLC 997.

---

bibliography ...

Ali, P "Alphabet Soup: An Overview of Exotic Convertible Securities" (2000) 18 C & SLJ 579.
Lipton, J "Security over Electronically Registered Shares" (1995) 6 JBFLP 165.
Rees, S "Rectification of the Share Register—Damage and Compensation" (1990) 8 C & SLJ 149.

revision questions on the material in this chapter …

> Please see eQuiz at **http://www.thomson.com.au/academic** for multiple choice questions and answers.

chapter ten

dividends

key points ...

> The rules governing the procedure for payment of dividends are contained in either the replaceable rules or in a company's constitution (if any).

> Under the replaceable rules, directors have the power to pay dividends. If a company provides for declaration of dividends in its constitution, the directors usually have the power to recommend that a dividend be paid and the shareholders can only declare a dividend up to the recommended amount. Shareholders cannot override the powers of the directors even where there are available profits.

> Dividends may only be paid out of profits as otherwise the payment results in a reduction of capital.

> The meaning of "profits" has been given a wide interpretation and dividends may be paid in some circumstances where there would be no profits according to accepted accounting practice.

> A payment of dividends other than out of profits may result in civil penalty orders against the directors because of a breach of the reduction of capital or insolvent trading provisions. Directors may also breach their fiduciary duties, especially where creditors are adversely affected.

A company's profits may be distributed to shareholders. Such distributions are called "dividends".

[10.05] A company's profits may be distributed to shareholders. Such distributions are called "dividends" and represent a return on the shareholder's investment in the company. Section 124(1)(d) expressly gives companies the power to distribute property among its members, in kind or otherwise. This power includes the power to pay dividends. In some exceptional cases, however, a company's constitution may exclude the power. For example, a company limited by guarantee may be registered without "Limited" in its name if, among other things, its constitution prohibits the company making distributions to its members: s 150.

payment of dividends

The rules governing the procedure for payment of dividends are contained in either the replaceable rules or the dividend provisions in a company's constitution (if any).

[10.10] The rules governing the procedure for payment of dividends are contained in either the replaceable rules (ss 254U and 254W(2)) or the dividend provisions in a company's constitution (if any). Dividends may be paid in a number of ways. While a cash payment is the most common form of dividend, a company may also pay dividends by an issue of shares. Such dividends are referred to as "bonus shares". Many listed companies have dividend reinvestment plans that give shareholders the option of foregoing a cash dividend in exchange for the issue of new shares. Other methods of paying dividends include the grant of share options and the transfer of assets. Dividends may also be applied to paying up any amount unpaid on partly paid shares.

declaration

The replaceable rule in s 254U(1) gives directors the power to pay a dividend.

[10.15] The replaceable rule in s 254U(1) gives directors the power to pay a dividend without the need for a prior dividend declaration by shareholders. This rule enables directors to determine that a dividend is payable and fix the amount, time for payment and method of payment.

A company must comply with its constitution if it contains rules that displace or modify s 254U. The constitutions of many companies formed prior to 1998 amendments consist of the Table A articles.

For such companies, a dividend can only be paid if it is declared by shareholders at a general meeting on the recommendation of the directors.

As a general rule, shareholders cannot force a company to pay dividends even though it has available profits: *Burland v Earle* [1902] AC 83. However, in exceptional circumstances a refusal by a profitable company to pay dividends may amount to oppressive or unfair conduct for purposes of a remedy under s 232: *Sanford v Sanford Courier Service Pty Ltd* (1986) 5 ACLC 394. This is discussed in Chapter 17 below.

As a general rule, shareholders cannot force a company to pay dividends even though it has available profits.

final and interim dividends

[10.20] It is quite common for a company's constitution to draw a distinction between the payment of interim and final dividends. This allows dividend payments to be staggered through the course of a year.

It is quite common for a company's constitution to draw a distinction between the payment of interim and final dividends.

Prior to 1998, a decision to pay a final dividend could not be revoked or amended after declaration but only before it was paid. The final dividend, once declared, was regarded as a debt due by the company to its shareholders and could be enforced in the same way as any other contractual debt. This was not the case with interim dividends. These could be revoked or amended before the dividend was paid: *Brookton Co-operative Soc Ltd v FCT* (1981) 147 CLR 441.

Amendments made in 1998 changed the rules regarding final dividends and treats them in the same way as interim dividends. Under s 254V(1), a company does not incur a debt merely by fixing the amount or time for payment of a dividend. The debt arises only when the time fixed for payment arrives and the decision to pay the dividend may be revoked at any time before then. However, if a company has a constitution that provides for the declaration of dividends, the company incurs a debt when the dividend is declared: s 254V(2).

dividend rights

[10.25] Dividends are payable to the people entered on the company's share register as members at the time the dividend is declared. In many companies, the shares may be divided into different classes. In the case of public companies, s 254W(1) specifies that each share has the same dividend rights unless the company has a constitution that provides for the shares to have different dividend rights or different dividend rights are provided for by special resolution of the company.

Dividends are payable to the people entered on the company's share register as members at the time the dividend is declared.

In the case of proprietary companies, s 254W(2) contains a replaceable rule that allows directors to pay dividends as they see fit. This is subject to the terms on which the shares were issued.

Section 254W(3) and (4) sets out special rules for no liability companies. A shareholder of a no liability company is not entitled to a dividend if a call has been made on the share that is due and unpaid. Further, subject to provisions to the contrary in a no liability company's constitution, dividends are payable in proportion to the number of shares held, irrespective of the amount paid up on them.

payment out of profits

[10.30] A dividend may only be paid out of profits of the company: s 254T. The profits must exist at the time fixed for payment of the dividend. The consequences of improper dividend payments—payments other than out of profits—are discussed below, para [10.70].

A dividend may only be paid out of profits of the company: s 254T. The profits must exist at the time fixed for payment of the dividend.

In its April 2002 Discussion Paper, *Payment of Dividends under the Corporations Act 2001*, the Legislation Review Board of the Australian Accounting Research Foundation (AARF) suggested that dividend provisions of the *Corporations Act* were "outdated" and the law should be changed. AARF noted that the dividend rules had not been brought into line with 1998 amendments that introduced the present share capital rules. As discussed in Chapter 8 above, the share capital provisions are based on the concept of solvency. For example, one of the key requirements of the share buy-back provisions and the reduction of capital provisions is that the buy-back or reduction does not materially prejudice the company's ability to pay its creditors: ss 256B(1)(b) and 257A(a). To ensure consistency, AARF suggested that the dividend rules should also explicitly use a solvency test. The AARF Discussion Paper is linked to the Law Reform page on the Lipton-Herzberg website at **http://www.lipton-herzberg.com.au/law_reform.htm**

definition of profits

The term "profits" is not defined in the *Corporations Act*.

[10.35] The difficulty with s 254T is that the term "profits" is not defined in the *Corporations Act*. Where the definition of "profits" has been considered in cases, the courts have generally indicated a reluctance to define the word precisely. They generally regard this as a matter of internal management of a company.

The meaning of "profit" was considered in *Re Spanish Prospecting Co Ltd* [1911] 1 Ch 92. Fletcher Moulton LJ stated:

> **< "Profits" implies a comparison between the state of a business at two specific dates usually separated by an interval of a year. The fundamental meaning is the amount of gain made by the business during the year. This can only be ascertained by a comparison of the assets of the business at the two dates ... If the total assets of the business at the two dates be compared, the increase which they show at the later date as compared with the earlier date (due allowance of course being made for any capital introduced into or taken out of the business in the meanwhile) represents in strictness the profits of the business during the period in question. >**

relevance of accounting standards

[10.40] As discussed in Chapter 15 below, public and large proprietary companies must prepare a financial report for each financial year: s 292. Among other things, the financial report consists of the financial statements for the year: s 295(1)(a). A profit and loss statement is one of the components of the financial statement: s 295(2)(a). The financial report must comply with the accounting standards and the financial statements must give a true and fair view of the financial position and performance of the company: ss 296 and 297.

It is unclear to what extent a profit disclosed by a profit and loss statement that complies with the accounting standards is the same as the legal definition of profits. In *QBE Insurance Group Ltd v ASC* (1992) 10 ACLC 1490, Lockhart J stated:

> **< The meaning of the word "profits" is for the courts to determine. But the identification of what in relation to the affairs of a particular company constitute its profits is determined by the courts with close regards to the views of the accountancy profession. The courts are influenced by professional accountancy bodies and men of business and the evidence of accountants is given great weight by the courts. >**

distinction between fixed and circulating assets

[10.45] The definition of profits in *Re Spanish Prospecting* does not distinguish between increases in the value of fixed and circulating assets in an accounting period. Increases in circulating capital are profits derived from dealings in the normal course of carrying on a company's business. Increases in fixed capital are profits from the sale or revaluation of a company's fixed assets such as plant and equipment and buildings.

Whether particular assets of a company are classified as fixed or circulating depends on the nature of its business. In *QBE Insurance Group Ltd v ASC* (1992) 10 ACLC 1490, the Federal Court held that in the case of banks and insurance companies, their investments constituted circulating assets. As a consequence, under the accounting standards, they were obliged to include in their profit and loss statements any unrealised gains or losses in the value of these investments.

profits from circulating assets

[10.50] A company's circulating assets are assets, such as trading stock, which a company deals with in the normal course of its business. Profits available for payment of dividends include the difference between a company's receipts from the disposal of circulating assets and the expenditure incurred in producing them. The calculation of profits also includes the increase in the value of a company's circulating assets held at the end of the accounting period compared to the value of similar assets held at the beginning of that accounting period. Such profits are also referred to as "revenue profits".

Profits available for payment of dividends include the difference between a company's receipts from the disposal of circulating assets and the expenditure incurred in producing them.

Dividends may be paid out of current year revenue profits even if the company had losses in prior years: *Ammonia Soda Co Ltd v Chamberlain* [1918] 1 Ch 266. Each accounting period is treated in isolation and not as part of a continuous process. A company is not obliged to make good prior year revenue losses. The AARF Discussion Paper, *Payment of Dividends under the Corporations Act 2001*, noted that this was a deficiency in the law because the rules regarding payment of dividends may allow such payments even though the solvency of the company could be in some doubt. AARF pointed out:

Dividends may be paid out of current year revenue profits even if the company had losses in prior years.

> **< There is also no requirement that a company must make a profit in a given period before being able to authorise and pay a dividend so long as the dividend is paid out of the profits, which may have been achieved in some previous period(s). A company can therefore pay dividends even though it is making losses or has made losses and subsequent profits have yet to extinguish accumulated losses. >**

The AARF Discussion Paper is linked to the Law Reform page on the Lipton-Herzberg website at **http://www.lipton-herzberg.com.au/law_reform.htm**

realised profits from fixed assets

[10.55] The profit available for dividend purposes may include realised profits from the disposal of fixed assets such as plant and equipment and buildings.

The profit available for dividend purposes may include realised profits from the disposal of fixed assets such as plant and equipment and buildings.

case note

In *Lee v Neuchatel Asphalte Co* (1889) 41 Ch D 1, the company owned a concession to operate asphalt mines which by their nature were wasting. As the mine was worked it became less valuable. Further, as the concession was only for a limited period, its value also declined with the passing of time. The company declared a dividend but in calculating its profit made no allowance for the decline in the value of the concession or the mines. The court authorised the payment of the dividend notwithstanding the decline in value of the company's assets.

Lee's case established that when calculating profits for purposes of determining whether a dividend could be paid, the proper approach was to ascertain whether there was an excess of current earnings over current expenses. In *Verner v General & Commercial Investment Trust Ltd* [1894] 2 Ch 239, the court applied the decision in *Lee's* case. It drew the distinction between fixed and circulating capital. Fixed capital could not be returned to shareholders because it represents the assets purchased by the subscribed capital. Profits were regarded as the increase in circulating capital in a period. This amount could be distributed as dividends even though there may be a considerable loss in the value of fixed assets.

This rule, however, has been qualified by the requirement that the whole of the assets be taken into account before the declaration of a dividend: *Foster v New Trinidad Lake Asphalte Co Ltd* [1901] 1 Ch 208. In that case, the company proposed to pay a dividend from the repayment to it of debts that had previously been regarded as valueless. The company treated the payment of the debts as a realised increase in its fixed assets even though the debts had never appeared as assets in the company's balance sheet. The court refused to sanction the payment of the dividend. It held that it was improper to include in the dividend fund a realised accretion of only one fixed asset.

case note

The requirement that the whole of the assets be taken into account was also accepted by the High Court in *Australasian Oil Exploration Ltd v Lachberg* (1958) 101 CLR 119. The company, which had lost most of its fixed assets, proposed to declare a dividend from the sale of its most valuable asset. The court held that this could not be done.

> < [A] company has no capital profits available for dividend purposes unless upon a balance of account it appears that there has been an accretion to the paid up capital. >

The proper approach to be taken if a company wishes to pay a dividend from realised increases to its fixed assets is to revalue all its fixed assets. If, after this is done, there is a surplus over paid up capital it may be included in its profits and distributed by way of dividend.

unrealised profits from fixed assets

[10.60] A profit for dividend purposes may include a profit arising from the revaluation of fixed assets.

The profit arising from a revaluation may be capitalised and a dividend in the form of bonus shares paid to shareholders.

It is common accounting practice for a company periodically to revalue its fixed assets. This is done in order to comply with Accounting Standard AASB 116 *Property, Plant and Equipment*. It is also accepted accounting practice that the profit arising from a revaluation may be capitalised and a dividend in the form of bonus shares paid to shareholders. The capitalisation of profits means that profits otherwise available for distribution as cash dividends are credited to shareholders in the form of bonus shares or in paying up partly paid shares. This is permitted by the replaceable rule in s 254S.

Once profits have been capitalised they can no longer be transferred back to the profit and loss appropriation account for distribution as dividends. This would amount to an improper reduction of capital. This treatment of unrealised gains does not adversely affect creditors. The pool of cash available to meet their claims does not diminish by the issue of bonus shares.

There are conflicting authorities on the question of whether a cash dividend may be paid from the profit arising from the revaluation of fixed assets. In *Westburn Sugar Refineries Ltd v Inland Revenue Cmmrs* [1960] TR 105, it was held that a profit arising from the revaluation of fixed assets cannot be distributed as a cash dividend. On the other hand, *Dimbula Valley (Ceylon) Tea Co Ltd v Laurie* [1961] Ch 353, held that under certain conditions it could. The revaluation must be carried out in good faith by competent valuers and should not be subject to short term fluctuations. Buckley J said:

There are conflicting authorities on the question of whether a cash dividend may be paid from the profit arising from the revaluation of fixed assets.

> **< It has, I think, long been the generally accepted view of the law in this country (though not established by judicial authority) that, if the surplus on capital account results from a valuation made in good faith by competent valuers and is not likely to be liable to short-term fluctuations, it may properly be capitalised: see *Inland Revenue Commission v Thornton Kelley & Co Ltd* [1957] 1 WLR 482. Indeed, as I have pointed out, this was actually done by Westburn Sugar Refineries Ltd. For myself, I can see no reason why, if the valuation is not open to criticism, this should not be so or even why, in any case in which the regulations of the company permit the distribution by way of dividend of profit on capital account, a surplus so ascertained should not be distributed in that manner. After all, every profit and loss account of a trading concern which opens and closes with a stock figure necessarily embodies an element of estimate. The difference between ascertaining trading profits by, amongst other things, estimating the value of the stock in hand at the beginning and end of the accounting period and ascertaining capital profits by comparing an estimated value of the assets with their book value appears to me to be a difference of degree but not of principle. Moreover, if a company has fluid assets available for payment of a dividend, I can see nothing wrong in its using those assets for payment of a dividend and at the same time as a matter of account treating that dividend as paid out of a capital surplus resulting from an appreciation in value of unrealised fixed assets. The proper balance of the company's balance sheet would not be disturbed by such a course of action. The company would be left with assets of sufficient value to meet the commitments shown on the liabilities side of its balance sheet, including paid up share capital. >**

The view taken by Buckley J in *Dimbula Valley (Ceylon) Tea Co Ltd v Laurie* that cash dividends can be paid from unrealised gains in fixed assets is contrary to accepted accounting practice. Indeed, Buckley J himself conceded that the declaration of dividends from such a profit is an unwise commercial practice. In any case, a dividend can only be paid from the profit arising from a revaluation of fixed assets if the paid up capital is intact: *Australasian Oil Exploration Ltd v Lachberg* (1958) 101 CLR 119. It is also subject to the rule that the company does not become insolvent.

A dividend can only be paid from the profit arising from a revaluation of fixed assets if the paid up capital is intact.

profits of subsidiaries

[10.65] A holding company cannot pay a dividend arising from the profits made by a subsidiary.

case note

This rule was established by the High Court in *Industrial Equity Ltd v Blackburn* (1977) 137 CLR 567. The holding company had insufficient profits of its own to enable it to pay a

dividend. One of its subsidiaries, however, did have enough profits. The subsidiary could have paid a dividend to its parent, which in turn could then have paid its own dividend. This step, however, was not taken. The holding company argued that as the *Uniform Companies Act* required consolidated accounts of the group, this meant that the group ought to be regarded as a single entity.

The High Court rejected this approach. It regarded each company in the group as a separate legal entity distinct from its members. This is an application of the rule in *Salomon's* case discussed in Chapter 2 above. The High Court was not prepared to lift the corporate veil to examine the commercial realities. It held that a company could not declare dividends from anticipated profits. In cases such as this the holding company must actually receive the dividends from its profitable subsidiary. This dividend then forms part of the holding company's profit from which its dividend may be declared.

remedies for improper dividend payments

unauthorised reduction of capital

Dividends that are paid other than out of profits involve a reduction of capital.

[10.70] Dividends that are paid other than out of profits involve a reduction of capital. If the reduction is not authorised by s 256B, the company contravenes s 256D. While the contravention does not invalidate the dividend payment, any director involved may be liable for a civil penalty order: s 256D(2) and (3). Reductions of capital are further discussed in Chapter 8 above.

insolvent trading

[10.75] As discussed in Chapter 13.5 below, directors contravene s 588G if they fail to prevent their company from incurring debts when there are reasonable grounds for suspecting that the company is insolvent. This is called "insolvent trading". Under s 588G(1A), a company is regarded as having incurred a debt when a dividend is paid or, if the company has a constitution that provides for the declaration of dividends, when the dividend is declared.

When the company is wound up, directors who contravened s 588G may be personally liable to either the company's liquidator or particular unsecured creditors for any loss or damage suffered because of the company's insolvency: s 588M. Section 588G is also a civil penalty provision and the court may make civil penalty orders against directors who contravene the section: ss 1317E and 1317G.

A dividend should not be paid if the company is insolvent or the payment results in the company becoming insolvent. The payment of dividends in such circumstances prejudices the interests of the company's creditors.

breach of fiduciary duties

[10.80] A company may have profits available for dividends even though it is insolvent and cannot pay its debts as they fall due. For example, as discussed above, para [10.50], a company may pay dividends out of current year profits even though it has accumulated prior year losses.

A dividend should not be paid if the company is insolvent or the payment results in the company becoming insolvent. The payment of dividends in such circumstances prejudices the interests of the company's creditors. Directors who authorise the dividend payment breach their fiduciary duties and may be held personally liable to repay the amount of the dividend to the company: *Hilton International Ltd v Hilton* (1988) 4 NZCLC 96–265.

injunction to restrain dividend payment

[10.85] A company contravenes s 254T if it pays dividends other than out of profits. Section 1324 gives the company's shareholders and creditors the right to apply for an injunction to restrain the company from contravening s 254T if the company's insolvency is an element of the contravention. Section 1324 injunctions are further discussed in Chapter 17 below.

taxation of dividends

[10.90] The imputation system for the taxation of company dividends was introduced in 1987 to eliminate double taxation of company profits. Under the imputation system, the tax paid by a company is imputed to shareholders by means of imputation credits attached to the dividends they receive (called "franked dividends"). The current company tax rate is 30 per cent.

Franked dividends plus an amount equal to the imputation credits attaching to them are included in a shareholder's assessable income. Australian resident shareholders, however, are entitled to a tax offset in the form of a rebate of the imputation credit applicable to those dividends. The imputation credit is 30/70ths of a dividend.

The operation of the imputation system is illustrated by the following example:

Taxable income of company	$1,000
less: company tax	$300
After tax income paid as dividend	$700
Dividend received by shareholder	$700
plus: imputation credit	$300
Assessable income of shareholder	$1,000
Tax on shareholder's income including the Medicare levy (assuming shareholder is at top marginal rate (48.5%))	$485
less: rebate for imputation credit	$300
Tax payable	$185

As a general rule a company must frank a dividend to the extent of the credit or surplus balance in its franking account at the time the dividend is paid. Credits to a franking account arise when a company pays a tax instalment. They also arise when a company receives a franked dividend from another company. Franked dividends paid by a company to its shareholders are debited from its franking account.

A company must provide a dividend statement in an approved form when it pays dividends to its shareholders. This tells shareholders the extent to which their dividends are franked and the amount of the imputation credit attaching to them.

To the extent that a dividend is unfranked there are no imputation credits attached. Such dividends are included in the assessable income of shareholders and are taxed at their marginal rates.

bibliography ...

Arjunan, K & Low, C K "Dividends: A Comparative Analysis of the Provisions in Hong Kong & Australia" (1995) 5 Aust Jnl of Corp Law 295.

Legislation Review Board, AARF, "Payments of Dividends under the Corporations Act 2001" **http://www.aarf.asn.au/docs/Dividends.pdf**

Routledge, J & Slade, "The Company Dividend Restriction: Does it Promote Good Corporate Governance?" (2003) 21 C & SLJ 447.

Yamey, B S "Aspects of the Law Relating to Company Dividends" (1941) 4 MLR 273.

revision questions on the material in this chapter . . .

> Please see eQuiz at **http://www.thomson.com.au/academic** for multiple choice questions and answers.

chapter eleven

debentures and loan capital

key points ...

- A company may raise capital by borrowing. This is often done by the company issuing debentures. A debenture involves an undertaking by the company to repay a debt. It often includes a charge over the company's assets to secure the debt. Debentures may be issued to a large number of investors or to a single creditor—such as a bank or other financier.
- An offer of debentures to investors attracts the operation of the fundraising provisions in the same way as offers of shares. In addition, a borrowing company must enter into a trust deed with certain required terms and appoint a trustee.
- A borrowing company may grant a fixed or floating charge as security to the debenture-holder. A floating charge allows the borrower to deal with the charged assets in the ordinary course of its business. If the debenture terms are breached, the floating charge crystallises and attaches to the secured category of assets.
- A charge may be invalidated for various reasons. For example, it may constitute an unfair preference or an uncommercial transaction. Charges in favour of officers may also be invalid where the officer takes steps to enforce the charge within six months of its creation without obtaining prior court leave.
- ASIC maintains a publicly accessible database called the Australian Register of Company Charges that enables those dealing with a company to find out details of charges it has granted over its property. Members of the public have constructive notice of the information contained in this database whether they have inspected it or not.
- Where a company creates a charge, notice of the charge containing prescribed details must be lodged with ASIC within 45 days after the charge's creation. The notice is then entered onto the Australian Register of Company Charges. Only the types of charges specifically listed in s 262(1) are registrable in this way.
- Registrable charges over the same property are ranked in order of priority. The general rule is that registered charges have priority according to the time they were registered. This rule is subject to several exceptions. The *Corporations Act* and property law determines priorities between competing unregistrable charges or between unregistrable and registrable charges.
- The time of registration is also significant because if a notice of charge is not lodged by the 45-day deadline and the company goes into voluntary administration or a liquidator is appointed within six months of the creation of the charge, the charge is void against the liquidator or administrator.

distinction between share capital and loan capital

[11.05] We saw in Chapter 8 above that one of the ways in which a company may raise funds is by the issue of share capital. The other important method by which a company may raise funds is by borrowing from lenders. This is called loan capital or loan finance. It is part of the management function of the board of directors to determine the extent to which the financial needs of a company are to be met by a raising of share capital or loan capital. This decision may involve a consideration of many factors.

The basic distinction between share capital and loan capital is that a shareholder is a member of the company, whereas a lender is an external creditor. We also saw in Chapter 8 above that there are rules dealing with the raising and maintenance of share capital. These rules do not apply to loan capital. For example, interest on a loan can be paid from the company's capital while dividends can only be paid from profits.

The basic distinction between share capital and loan capital is that a shareholder is a member of the company, whereas a lender is an external creditor.

While this distinction between the nature of shareholders and lenders seems clear cut in most cases, their respective rights are sometimes very similar. Chapter 8 above further revealed that preference shares and, in particular, redeemable preference shares, usually give redeemable preference shareholders rights that are very similar to the rights of external creditors. Their role in the company may be viewed as similar to that of lenders. Nevertheless, the holders of such shares are still members of the company. This is important in the event that the company is wound up because a company's creditors have priority in repayment over all members. In considering whether to raise funds from an issue of shares or from borrowing, the directors of a company may take into account whether the issue of further shares will result in a dilution of their or another member's shareholding. This is particularly important where the directors wish to prevent control of the company passing to others.

gearing

[11.10] The extent to which the company has previously borrowed is often relevant. The ratio of borrowed funds to issued share capital is described as the "gearing" of a company. If the company has borrowed a large amount relative to its issued share capital, it is said to be "highly geared". On the other hand, if it has borrowed relatively little compared to its issued share capital, the company is said to have a "low gearing" ratio. The effect of a high gearing ratio is to make the return on shareholders' funds relatively volatile. If the company operates profitably and thereby uses its borrowed funds to obtain a return greater than interest paid on the loans, the return on shareholders' funds will be relatively high. If, however, the company operates at a loss, the loss on shareholders' funds will be relatively greater than if the company had borrowed less. If the company records a relatively low profit, the effect of payment of interest on the borrowed funds results in a relatively low return on shareholders' funds.

The optimum gearing of a company depends on several considerations. For example, the nature of the industry in which the company operates is relevant. By their nature, banks utilise borrowed funds to a large degree and therefore have a very high gearing. The receptiveness of the capital market to an issue of shares is relevant to large companies seeking to raise large amounts. The anticipated inflation rate or foreign exchange rates also affect the decision whether to borrow or issue further share capital. When a company seeks to borrow large amounts, it must be sure that it will be able to meet the interest payments. Interest must be paid irrespective of whether the company makes a profit in a particular year or not. On the other hand, as discussed in Chapter 10 above, there is generally no obligation on a company to declare and pay a dividend. In fact, a company is prohibited from paying a dividend otherwise than from profits.

taxation

[11.15] Income tax legislation confers certain advantages on the raising of loan finance compared with the issue of share capital. The payment of interest on a loan and other associated expenses, such as procurement fees, are allowable deductions that reduce the taxable income of companies. Of course, interest received by lenders is assessable income in their hands. Dividends paid by a company, together with expenses incurred in issuing share capital, are not deductible. In fact, dividends are only paid from profits *after* tax is paid by the company. As discussed in Chapter 10 above, under the imputation system where a company pays dividends from profits that have been taxed ("franked dividends") Australian resident shareholders who receive these obtain a taxation credit ("imputation credit") for the tax paid by the company. The imputation credit may then be offset against shareholders' tax liability on the dividend and, if there is any excess, from other sources of income.

borrowing powers of companies

A company has the power to borrow in the same way as an individual. It also has specific power to issue debentures and give security for loans by charging uncalled capital and granting floating charges over its property.

[11.20] A company has the power to borrow in the same way as an individual. It also has specific power to issue debentures and give security for loans by charging uncalled capital and granting floating charges over its property: s 124(1). This is despite any express restriction or prohibition contained in the company's constitution, if it has one: s 125(1).

Another matter of concern to lenders is whether the persons acting for the company have the requisite authority to borrow on behalf of the company. The power to borrow is usually conferred on the directors. The replaceable rule in s 198A gives directors the power to manage the company's business. This includes the power to borrow. In rare cases this may not be so, or the directors may have a limit imposed by the company's constitution on their borrowing powers. In such a case, an outsider is protected by s 129(1) and may assume that the constitution has been complied with. This is discussed in Chapter 5 above.

debentures

definitions

[11.25] A company may borrow funds in much the same ways as individuals. Thus, a company may borrow from a bank or other money lender with or without security. An indirect method of borrowing available to both companies and individuals is to delay payments to trade creditors.

The term "debenture" has a number of meanings.

A further important method of borrowing unique to companies is the issue of debentures. The term "debenture" has a number of meanings. At the common law, a debenture is a document that acknowledges the indebtedness of the company. The debt is often secured by a charge over the property of the company but this is not necessary. Under the *Corporations Act*, "debenture" has a broader meaning than the common law meaning. Section 9 says a debenture means a chose in action that includes an undertaking by a body to repay as a debt, money deposited with or lent to the body. The chose in action may (but need not) include a charge over the property of the body to secure repayment of the money.

Certain undertakings to repay money deposited or lent are excluded from the s 9 definition. The exclusions include undertakings:

> **by an Australian ADI (authorised deposit-taking institution) to repay money deposited with it or lent to it in the ordinary course of its banking business; and**
> **to pay money under a cheque or bill of exchange.**

The *Corporations Act* restricts how borrowers may describe or refer to debentures.

While the s 9 definition of debenture specifically notes that a debenture may (but need not) be secured by a charge over the body's property, this does not accord with the public's understanding of the word. For this reason, the *Corporations Act* restricts how borrowers may describe or refer to debentures: s 283BH. The appropriate description depends on whether a charge has been granted as security for the borrowing and if so, the type of charge.

A borrower may describe a debenture in any one of the following three ways:

table 11.1 how debentures may be described

Description	When description may be used
Mortgage debenture	Only if the circumstances in s 283BH(2) are satisfied. These circumstances include where repayment of the borrowings is secured by a first mortgage given to the trustee for debenture-holders over land vested in the borrower or in any of the guarantors: s 283BH(2)(a).
Debenture	Only if the circumstances in ss 283BH(2) and (3) are satisfied. These circumstances include where repayment of the borrowings is secured by a charge in favour of the trustee for debenture-holders over the tangible property of the borrower or guarantors: s 283BH(3)(a).
Unsecured note or unsecured deposit note	In any other case.

The relationship between the borrowing company and a debenture-holder is governed by the law of contract and, if the debenture is secured, also by property law. The debenture provisions in Ch 2L (ss 283AA–283I) of the *Corporations Act* also regulate the borrowing companies that issue debentures.

convertible debentures or notes

[11.30] A borrowing company may issue convertible debentures or convertible notes to lenders. These provide the holders a right that allows them to convert the debentures into shares. In this way, the holders obtain the advantages of being debenture-holders with a secure, regular return and after a period they may exercise their right to become a shareholder and thereby participate more fully in the success of the company. This is particularly advantageous if the market value of the shares increases significantly over their issue price. It thereby affords the holder a hedge against inflation. From the company's point of view, if its future prospects are attractive, it may find its convertible debentures marketable at a relatively low interest rate. Holders may be prepared to accept a low interest rate in exchange for the prospect of converting the debentures into shares with a relatively high market value. The company may also be able to avoid having to raise funds to redeem the debentures if the holders elect to convert them into shares.

Section 727 prohibits a person making offers of debentures or distributing application forms for debenture offers unless a disclosure document for the offer has been lodged with ASIC.

application of fundraising provisions

[11.35] As the term "debenture" comes within the s 92 definition of "securities", s 727 prohibits a person making offers of debentures or distributing application forms for debenture offers unless a disclosure document for the offer has been lodged with ASIC. The fundraising provisions are discussed in Chapter 7 above. In addition, the provisions of Ch 2L apply specifically to offers of debentures that need disclosure under the fundraising provisions of Ch 6D of the *Corporations Act*: s 283AA(1)(a).

In some situations, the *Corporations Act* requires a borrowing company that proposes to offer its debentures to appoint a trustee for the debenture-holders and prepare a trust deed.

requirement for trust deed and trustee

[11.40] In some situations, the *Corporations Act* requires a borrowing company that proposes to offer its debentures to appoint a trustee for the debenture-holders and prepare a trust deed. The provisions of Pt 2L.1 set out the requirements for a trust deed and trustee for debenture-holders.

Under s 283AA, a body must enter into a trust deed and appoint a trustee before the body:

> makes an offer of debentures that needs disclosure to investors under Ch 6D of the *Corporations Act*; or
> makes an offer of debentures as consideration for the acquisition of securities under an off-market takeover bid; or
> issues debentures under an approved compromise or arrangement under Pt 5.1.

Section 283AB requires the trust deed to provide that the following are held in trust by the trustee for the benefit of the debenture-holders:

> the right to enforce the borrower's duty to repay;
> any charge or security for repayment; and
> the right to enforce any other duties that the borrower and guarantor have under the terms of the debentures, the provisions of the trust deed, or Ch 2L of the *Corporations Act*.

Section 283AC restricts the range of entities that are eligible to act as a trustee for debenture-holders. They include:

> the Public Trustee of any State or Territory;
> an authorised trustee company that is permitted under State or Territory law to take a grant of probate of a will of a deceased person;
> a body corporate registered under the *Life Insurance Act 1995*;
> an Australian ADI (authorised deposit-taking institution) such as a bank; and
> a body corporate approved by ASIC under s 283GB.

In order to ensure the trustee is independent of the borrower, s 283AC(2) specifies that a person may only be appointed or act as trustee if the appointment will not result in a conflict of interest or duty.

borrower's and guarantor's duties

The *Corporations Act* imposes a number of statutory duties on a borrower.

[11.45] The *Corporations Act* imposes a number of statutory duties on a borrower including a requirement to enter into a trust deed under s 283AA. The term "borrower" in relation to a debenture means the body that is, or will be, liable to repay money under the debenture: s 9. Under s 283BB, the general duties of a borrower include the duty to:

> carry on and conduct its business in a proper and efficient manner; and
> make all its financial and other records available for inspection by the trustee and give the trustee any information, explanations or other assistance required about the matters relating to those reports.

Sections 283BC–283BF impose a number of specific duties on borrowers. They have a duty to:

> notify ASIC of the name of the trustee (s 283BC);
> replace the trustee if this becomes necessary (s 283BD);
> inform the trustee about any charges it creates (s 283BE); and
> give the trustee and ASIC quarterly reports about certain specific matters: s 283BF.

A guarantor in relation to a debenture means a body that has guaranteed the repayment of any money deposited or lent to the borrower under the debenture: s 9. Under ss 283CB and 283CC, a guarantor is under a duty to carry on and conduct its business in a proper and efficient manner, to make its financial records available for inspection by the trustee, and to notify the trustee about any charges it creates.

A borrower and guarantor commit a criminal offence if they intentionally or recklessly contravene any of the statutory duties imposed upon them: ss 283BI and 283CE.

trustee's duties

[11.50] The trustee is subject to a range of duties listed in s 283DA. For example, a trustee must exercise reasonable diligence to ascertain whether the property of the borrower and of each guarantor will be sufficient to repay the amount deposited or lent when it becomes due: s 283DA(a). A trustee must also exercise reasonable diligence to ascertain whether the borrower or any guarantor has committed any breach of the terms of the debentures, the provisions of the trust deed, or Ch 2L of the *Corporations Act*.

statutory rights of debenture-holders

[11.55] The *Corporations Act* confers several rights on the debenture-holders or their trustee. Under s 318, a borrower in relation to debentures must give the trustee a copy of its annual financial report, directors' report and auditor's report by the deadline for the financial year set by s 315. In addition, a borrower's auditor must give the trustee for debenture-holders a copy of the auditor's report within seven days after providing the original to the company or its members: s 313(1). The auditor must also provide a report on any matters prejudicial to debenture-holders' interests within seven days of the auditor becoming aware of the matter: s 313(2).

Section 283EA gives debenture-holders who hold 10 per cent or more of the nominal value of the issued debentures the power to direct the borrower to call a meeting of debenture-holders. The trustee may also call a meeting of debenture-holders if the borrower or guarantor has failed to remedy any breach of the terms of the debentures, provisions of the trust deed or Ch 2L of the *Corporations Act*: s 283EB(1). The purpose of this meeting is to enable the trustee to inform the debenture-holders of the failure, submit proposals for protection of the debenture-holders' interests and to ask for directions in relation to the matter.

register of debenture-holders

[11.60] A company that issues debentures is required to set up and maintain a register of debenture-holders: s 168(1)(c). Under s 171, the register of debenture-holders must contain the following information about each holder of a debenture:

A company that issues debentures is required to set up and maintain a register of debenture-holders.

> **the debenture-holder's name and address; and**
> **the amount of the debentures held.**

company charges

what is a charge?

A charge involves a borrowing company giving a lender security over some or all of its property for repayment of the debt.

[11.65] In its broadest sense a charge involves a borrowing company giving a lender security over some or all of its property for repayment of the debt. The lender is a secured creditor, also known as a "chargee" and the assets over which security is given are said to be "charged" or "secured". If the borrowing company that has granted a charge defaults under the loan agreement, the secured creditor is entitled to take possession of the secured property and sell it. The secured creditor can use the proceeds from the sale of the secured property to repay the debt owed to it. The enforcement of a charge is often carried out by a receiver appointed by the chargee. Receiverships are discussed in Chapter 23 below.

A charge can involve a number of different types of securities. For example, a borrowing company may give a secured lender a mortgage over its land as well as a charge over the company's plant and equipment. A company has the power to grant floating charges over its property: s 124(1)(f). It may also give security by charging its uncalled capital: s 124(1)(e).

While, in a strict legal sense, there is a difference between a mortgage and a charge, s 9 defines the word "charge" in very broad terms. It means a charge created in any way and includes a mortgage.

fixed and floating charges

A borrowing company can grant the lender a fixed or floating charge over its property as security for a loan.

[11.70] A borrowing company can grant the lender a fixed or floating charge over its property as security for a loan.

A fixed charge attaches to specific property owned by the borrower.

A fixed charge attaches to specific property owned by the borrower. This property may or may not be owned by the company at the time the charge is created. In fact, it need not necessarily be in existence at the time the charge is given. The courts of equity also recognise fixed charges over future property. Because of the nature of a fixed charge, the company is unable to dispose of the charged assets without the lender's consent.

Floating charges are charges that float above specified categories of property such as inventory.

Floating charges are charges that float above specified categories of property such as inventory. The company is free to dispose of these assets in the normal course of business and to replace them by acquiring the same category of assets in the future. When a specified event occurs, such as the company defaulting or going into liquidation, the debenture-holders may enforce the charge, usually by appointing a receiver. From this time, the charge ceases to float and drops down to attach itself to the specified categories of assets then owned by the company. On default, the floating charge is said to "crystallise" and becomes, in effect, a fixed charge over the assets of the company held at the time of crystallisation or acquired afterwards.

A floating charge provides a very practical device for companies to secure debts. A company may already have granted a mortgage over specific assets, or it may not own land or other assets suitable for a fixed charge. However, its other assets, particularly its trading stock, may be of considerable value. Such assets are acquired for the purpose of resale or manufacture and it is not practical for the company to retain such assets or seek the consent of the debenture-holders every time trading stock is sold. A floating charge enables a company to dispose of its trading stock in the ordinary course of business, while still giving the debenture-holders a good security by floating over any trading stock that may be acquired. Similarly, a floating charge may also be conferred over book debts.

distinction between fixed and floating charges

[11.75] The distinction between fixed and floating charges was made by Buckley LJ in *Evans v Rival Granite Quarries Ltd* [1910] 2 KB 979. He said:

> < **A floating security is not a future security; it is a present security, which presently affects all the assets of the company expressed to be included in it. On the other hand, it is not a specific security; the holder cannot affirm that the assets are specifically mortgaged to him. The assets are mortgaged in such a way that the mortgagor can deal with them without the concurrence of the mortgagee. A floating security is not a specific mortgage of the assets, plus a licence to the mortgagor to dispose of them in the course of his business, but is a floating mortgage applying to every item comprised in the security, but not specifically affecting any item until**

some event occurs or some act on the part of the mortgagee is done which causes it to crystallise into a fixed security. >

This distinction between fixed and floating charges indicates that the holder of a floating charge has no legal or equitable interest in specific property of the company while the charge is floating and the company may dispose of assets subject to the charge in the ordinary course of its business.

In *United Builders Pty Ltd v Mutual Acceptance Ltd* (1980) 144 CLR 673, the High Court held that whether a charge is a fixed or floating charge depends on the intention of the parties. A charge is a floating charge if:

> it is a charge on a class of assets of a company—present and future;
> that class is one that in the ordinary course of the company's business would be changing from time-to-time; and
> it is contemplated that, until some future step is taken by or on behalf of those interested in the charge, the company may carry on its business in the ordinary way as far as concerns the particular class of assets.

It is sometimes important to determine whether a charge is fixed or floating because floating charges are subject to certain priorities in receivership under s 433 (discussed below in Chapter 23) and in a liquidation under s 561 (discussed in Chapter 25 below). This means that holders of fixed charges stand in a stronger position than floating charge holders. Floating charges are also required to be registered under s 262(1) as discussed below, para [11.120]. This distinction has created difficulties, especially in relation to book debts which by their nature are usually subject to floating charges. In several cases lenders have sought to create a fixed charge over book debts.

case note

In *Whitton v ACN 003 266 886* (1996) 14 ACLC 1799, it was held that a charge over book debts was a fixed charge where the company was prohibited from dealing with or disposing of its book debts. Such a prohibition was inconsistent with a fundamental characteristic feature of a floating charge.

case note

On the other hand, in *National Westminster Bank plc v Spectrum Plus Ltd* [2005] UKHL 41, a charge described as a fixed charge was granted over book debts. Under the terms of the charge, the chargee did not take control of the account into which the proceeds of the book debts were paid as the chargor company retained the right to access and draw on the money in the account. The House of Lords held that this was a floating charge despite the description of the charge as "fixed".

While these cases appear inconsistent, the main question revolves around the degree of control exercisable by the chargee. If the debtor company is obliged to pay proceeds from debts into a designated account and can only draw on the account with the consent of the chargee, the charge is more likely to be a fixed charge.

In *US Trust Co of New York v ANZ Banking Group Ltd* (1995) 13 ACLC 1225, the New South Wales Court of Appeal held that a subordination agreement between various creditors of a company was not a floating charge and hence did not have to be registered under s 262(1).

disposal in ordinary course of business

A floating charge enables the borrowing company to dispose of the charged property in the ordinary course of its business without obtaining the lender's consent.

[11.80] A floating charge enables the borrowing company to dispose of the charged property in the ordinary course of its business without obtaining the lender's consent. What dealings are in the ordinary course of business?

case note

In *Reynolds Bros (Motors) Pty Ltd v Esanda Ltd* (1983) 1 ACLC 1333, the New South Wales Court of Appeal held that transactions are within the ordinary course of business if they are made for the purpose of carrying on the business. This is so even where a particular transaction is exceptional in nature provided its purpose is to maintain the company as a going concern. In that case Reynolds, a dealer in agricultural equipment, entered into an agreement in 1980 with Esanda. The agreement provided that Reynolds had possession of certain tractors as bailee for Esanda. This enabled it to sell the tractors as Esanda's agent and earn a commission. Reynolds also owned a number of its own tractors. In 1981, Reynolds granted the State Bank of New South Wales a floating charge over all its assets. In 1982, Reynolds breached its agreement with Esanda when it sold Esanda's tractors and failed to account for the proceeds. In order to reduce this debt, Reynolds transferred ownership of 10 of its own tractors to Esanda. The State Bank treated this as a breach of the terms of its floating charge and appointed a receiver and manager who challenged the validity of the transaction with Esanda.

The court held that the transfer of the tractors to Esanda was within Reynolds' ordinary course of business. This was because it enabled Reynolds to maintain itself as a going concern and meant that the tractors were not covered by the State Bank's floating charge.

case note

A transaction held to be not "in the ordinary course of the ordinary business" of a company is seen in *Fire Nymph Products Ltd v The Heating Centre Pty Ltd* (1992) 10 ACLC 629. A distributor of heating units, The Heating Centre Pty Ltd (THC), entered into an agreement with its major supplier, Fire Nymph Products Ltd (FNP), whereby FNP agreed to take back all units previously supplied by it. It was acknowledged that FNP had full title to the goods and THC retained possession as a bailee of FNP. THC was authorised to sell the goods at cost price with proceeds of sales to be paid into FNP's account. A finance company, AGC, had previously loaned money to THC secured by a floating charge over the whole of its assets. THC defaulted and AGC appointed receivers to THC who sold a number of heaters. FNP sought to recover the proceeds of these sales under the agreement.

It was held that the agreement with FNP was not in the "ordinary course of the ordinary business" of THC. The agreement was a means by which FNP attempted to recover money from an insolvent debtor by return of stock and use of THC's sale facilities. This resulted in AGC's floating charge automatically crystallising immediately before the agreement came into effect and title did not pass to FNP.

It is also within the ordinary course of business for a company to grant a later fixed charge over specific assets that has priority over a prior floating charge covering that category of assets. Priorities are discussed below, para [11.90]. A disposal of a company's business in its entirety as a preliminary step in ceasing business would not be in the ordinary course of business.

crystallisation of floating charges

[11.85] As discussed above, a feature of a floating charge is that the secured property consists of a class of property owned by a borrowing company. The floating charge creditor does not have security over any specific items within the class. The borrowing company may dispose of those items in the ordinary course of business. A floating charge is said to crystallise when a floating charge transforms into a fixed charge that attaches to those items of property in the class that are owned by the borrowing company at the time of crystallisation. From the time of crystallisation, the borrowing company loses the ability to dispose of the items of property covered by the floating charge in the ordinary course of business.

A floating charge is said to crystallise when a floating charge transforms into a fixed charge that attaches to those items of property in the class that are owned by the borrowing company at the time of crystallisation.

The loan agreement usually specifies the circumstances in which a floating charge crystallises. The most common situation that will trigger crystallisation occurs when the borrowing company defaults in paying interest or repaying the principal sum and the creditor gives notice that it intends to take steps to enforce the charge by taking possession of the secured property. The creditor may do this personally or appoint a receiver. Debentures and debenture trust deeds usually confer on the debenture-holders, or the trustee for the debenture-holders, the power to appoint a receiver on the occurrence of default by the company. Receivers are discussed in Chapter 23 below.

A floating charge also crystallises when the borrowing company is wound up or ceases to carry on business. This is because it is an implied condition of a floating charge that the company continues to carry on business.

Floating charge loan agreements often make provision for automatic crystallisation on certain stated events. These include where the borrowing company:

> **defaults in payment of interest for a specified period;**
> **breaches restrictions on future borrowings;**
> **allows the value of charged assets to decline below a minimum amount; or**
> **ceases to deal with charged assets in the ordinary course of its business.**

Automatic crystallisation occurs upon the happening of a specified event when the charge becomes fixed without any further action being required by the chargee. Automatic crystallisation can result in commercial difficulties. A charge may crystallise without anyone being aware of it and both the borrower and lender may continue to act as though the charge is still floating. The borrower continues to trade normally and the lender takes no steps to enforce its rights. This can cause problems in determining competing rights to property if the borrower continues to dispose of assets to third parties in the ordinary course of business.

For this reason, the Australian Law Reform Commission in its *General Insolvency Inquiry (1987)* recommended that crystallisation of floating charges take place only in one of two situations:

> **when a public act has occurred such as the entry into possession of property of the company by a receiver or the appointment of a liquidator; or**
> **when a notice to the effect that the charge has crystallised and therefore becomes fixed has been lodged with the Commission.**

This recommendation has not been adopted.

priorities between floating charges and later fixed charges

[11.90] Where a borrowing company grants a floating charge and later purports to grant further charges to other lenders over the same property, important questions of priority arise as between the different lenders. A company that has given a floating charge may grant a later fixed charge on assets already covered by the floating charge because this is regarded as being within the ordinary course of the company's business. In such a case, a later fixed charge ranks ahead of a floating charge, as long as it was given before the floating charge crystallised. This is so, even if the later chargee had notice of the existence of the earlier floating charge: *Re Hamilton's Windsor Ironworks* (1879) 12 Ch D 707. This is subject to a provision preventing the creation of later, prior-ranking charges contained in the debenture or debenture trust deed or other instrument creating the floating charge.

A later fixed charge ranks ahead of a floating charge, as long as it was given before the floating charge crystallised.

Even if the debenture creating the floating charge restricts the power of the company to grant later fixed charges, the later mortgagee may still have priority if the mortgage is a legal mortgage as opposed to an equitable mortgage and the later mortgagee did not have notice of the earlier floating charge and the restriction contained in it. This rule makes it important for debenture-holders secured by a floating charge to give notice of restrictions on future borrowings by the company. Where a company creates a floating charge, it must lodge with ASIC a notice including particulars of restrictions on the creation of later charges: s 263(1)(a)(iii). Lodging this notice constitutes constructive notice to the world so as to prevent a later chargee taking priority over the prior holders of a floating charge: s 130(2).

If the company creates a later equitable mortgage or charge, the mortgagee or chargee may take priority over the holders of the earlier charge if the prior chargee has permitted the company to represent that it is free to deal with unencumbered assets. This may occur where the company is able to retain possession of title deeds: *Re Castell & Brown Ltd* [1898] 1 Ch 315. A prudent trustee for debenture-holders or chargee consequently takes possession of title deeds over the secured property of the company. The question of priorities of registrable charges is discussed further below, para [11.140].

negative pledges

A "negative pledge" is a contractual promise given by a borrowing company that it will not grant charges in favour of other creditors without the prior consent of a lender.

[11.95] A "negative pledge" is a contractual promise given by a borrowing company that it will not grant charges in favour of other creditors without the prior consent of a lender. The terms of a loan containing a negative pledge will usually provide for repayment of principal and other enforcement procedures if the negative pledge is breached. If a debtor company grants a later charge to another creditor in breach of an existing negative pledge agreement, the later chargee is able to enforce the charge provided the later chargee did not have notice of the prior negative pledge and provided valuable consideration for the later charge. A later chargee who had had notice of a prior negative pledge agreement may not be able to enforce the charge, however, the law is unsettled on this point.

In the case of a registered floating charge that includes a negative pledge, later chargees are taken to have constructive notice of particulars contained in the register of charges: s 130(2). Therefore, any later chargee would be subject to the priority of the original chargee who gave notice of the negative pledge in the register of charges.

retention of title clauses

A "retention of title clause" is a term in the contract between a buyer and seller of goods which provides that ownership of the goods does not pass to the buyer until the goods are paid for.

[11.100] A "retention of title clause" is a term in the contract between a buyer and seller of goods which provides that ownership of the goods does not pass to the buyer until the goods are paid for. Such clauses seek to protect the seller during the time between delivery of goods to the buyer on credit and payment of the purchase price by the buyer. This protection arises because title to the goods remains with the seller, whereas title usually passes on delivery. Where the buyer becomes insolvent before payment, the seller is able to regain possession of the goods as the owner. In the absence of a retention of title clause, the seller would stand in line as a creditor with no rights to the goods.

case note

Retention of title clauses are sometimes referred to as "Romalpa" clauses from the case *Aluminium Industries Vaassen BV v Romalpa Aluminium Ltd* [1976] 2 All ER 552, the first case to deal with the question. A retention of title clause was contained in a contract for the sale of aluminium foil. Some of the foil was sold by the buyer to third parties. It kept the remainder in its possession. The price for the goods remained unpaid when a receiver was appointed by the holder of a floating charge granted by the buyer. There was no dispute that the unsold foil retained by the buyer could be repossessed by the seller. But an issue arose between the seller and the receiver as to who was entitled to the proceeds of the sale of the foil that had been sold. The court held that the effect of the retention of title clause was to make the buyer a bailee of the foil until payment took place. As a result, the buyer had a fiduciary obligation to account to the seller for the proceeds of the sales.

Retention of title clauses are sometimes referred to as "Romalpa" clauses.

Vendors have sought to include increasingly wider retention of title clauses in contracts for the supply of goods. These may include a provision that enables an unpaid vendor, who is unable to identify particular unpaid goods, to claim ownership of all goods supplied to the purchaser until the particular goods are paid for. This is known as a "current account" or "all debts" clause. This type of clause is helpful to suppliers of homogeneous goods who would find it difficult to associate particular invoices with specific goods.

A vendor may also provide for an entitlement to recover the proceeds of resale of goods that were in the purchaser's possession, where the purchaser defaults in payment for the goods to the vendor. This tracing of proceeds clause requires the existence of a fiduciary relationship between the vendor and purchaser. In *Chattis Nominees Pty Ltd v Norman Ross Homeworks Pty Ltd* (1992) 28 NSWLR 338, it was held that a fiduciary relationship which permits tracing only arises where the purchaser is required to keep the proceeds of sale separate from other funds. This requirement will generally not be implied. The intention of the provision was that the purchaser was indebted to the supplier for the relevant amount.

case note

In *Associated Alloys Pty Ltd v ACN 001 452 106 Pty Ltd* (2000) 18 ACLC 509, the High Court considered a retention of title clause that provided that if the goods were used in a manufacturing process, the buyer was to hold the proceeds from the sale of the finished goods in trust for the seller. It was held by the majority that this clause was an agreement to constitute a trust of future acquired property and was not a charge on a book debt that required registration under s 262(1). The charge was therefore not void against the administrator appointed over the buyer company under s 266(1). However, the claim of the seller failed because it was unable to identify that any payments made by a third party to the buyer were related to the goods supplied by the seller under any particular invoice. The seller was therefore unable to establish the existence of any trust constituted under the retention of title clause.

This case opens the possibility of a seller successfully drafting a retention of title clause whereby the proceeds of the on-sale of products containing the original goods may be traced by a claim that the proceeds are held on trust for the original seller. The seller must be able to relate particular proceeds from the sale of finished goods with the supply of particular deliveries of the original goods. This may often present difficulties. The enforcement of a retention of title clause in these circumstances will usually be detrimental to other creditors, especially financial institutions seeking to enforce security over the buyer's assets.

An unpaid vendor may be unable to claim goods under a retention of title clause where the goods are affixed to land and become fixtures. In such a case, ownership of the goods passes to the owner of the land: *Trust Bank Central Ltd v Southdown Properties Ltd* (1992) ANZ Conv R 257.

The effectiveness of a retention of title clause is also limited where an administrator is appointed to the purchaser. The unpaid vendor is an owner of goods being used by, or in the possession of, the company and is bound by the moratorium provisions and by the deed of company arrangement. Voluntary administrations are discussed in Chapter 24 below.

invalidation of charges

There are a number of provisions in the *Corporations Act* that invalidate charges granted by a company.

[11.105] There are a number of provisions in the *Corporations Act* that invalidate charges granted by a company. As discussed below, para [11.155], a charge may be invalidated where notification of details of a charge is not lodged with ASIC and the company granting it is placed in liquidation or voluntary administration within six months of its creation: s 266.

Several sections also invalidate charges granted by an insolvent company. As discussed in Chapter 25 below, ss 588FA–588FJ permit the liquidator of an insolvent company to avoid certain antecedent transactions. These are transactions entered into by a company prior to the commencement of its winding up in insolvency. The antecedent transactions provisions apply, inter alia, to a charge that is:

- **an unfair preference under s 588FA; or**
- **an uncommercial transaction under s 588FB; or**
- **an unfair loan under s 588FD.**

Unfair preferences and uncommercial transactions are referred to as "insolvent transactions" if the company was insolvent when they were entered into: s 588FC. Under s 588FE, insolvent transactions and unfair loans entered into during specified periods prior to the "relation-back day" are voidable transactions. The relation-back day is the date of the application for winding up: s 9. An unfair preference is voidable under s 588FE(2) if it was entered into during or after the six months ending on the relation-back day. An uncommercial transaction is voidable if it was entered into during or after two years ending on the relation-back day. Unfair loans to the company are voidable whenever made: s 588FE(6).

The company's liquidator may apply to the court for a variety of orders under s 588FF in relation to voidable transactions. The orders include an order declaring the agreement constituting the transaction to be void: s 588FF(1)(h).

Section 588FJ deals specifically with the invalidation of floating charges. Under s 588FJ(2), a floating charge created during the six months ending on the relation-back day is void as against the company's liquidator, except so far as it secures:

- **an advance paid to the company, or at its direction, at or after that time and as consideration for the charge; or**
- **interest on such advance; or**
- **the amount of a liability under a guarantee or other obligation undertaken at or after that time on behalf of, or for the benefit of, the company; or**
- **an amount payable for property or services supplied to the company at or after that time; or**
- **interest on an amount so payable.**

Section 588FJ(1) does not apply if it is proved that the company was solvent immediately after the creation of the floating charge.

case note

In *Cuthbertson & Richard Sawmills Pty Ltd v Thomas* (1999) 17 ACLC 670, the Federal Court considered whether a charge was valid on the grounds that it was part of an undertaking on behalf of or for the benefit of the company for purposes of s 588FJ(2)(c). It was held that the test was an objective one and the Court took into account that two directors had given security over their homes and transferred proceeds to the company. This led to the conclusion that the whole of the funding transactions, including the charge, were undertaken for and on behalf of the company.

charge in favour of officers

[11.110] Where a company creates a charge in favour of an officer or an associate and the officer takes steps to enforce the charge within six months of its creation, the charge is void unless the leave of the court is obtained to enforce it: s 267(1). Leave of the court may be granted if the company was solvent at the time of creation of the charge and it is just and equitable to enforce the charge: s 267(3).

Where a company creates a charge in favour of an officer or an associate and the officer takes steps to enforce the charge within six months of its creation, the charge is void unless the leave of the court is obtained to enforce it.

This section supplements the unfair preference provisions and is aimed at situations where insolvent companies grant charges or debentures to directors shortly before going into liquidation. This enables the director whose loan is secured to gain an advantage over other creditors and to appoint a receiver under the charge who obtains control of the company's books. This presents difficulties for the liquidator who must apply to the court to set aside the charge as an unfair preference.

The enforcement of a charge within the meaning of the section requires the taking of control or exercise of dominion over the charged assets. This may occur by the appointment of a receiver (s 267(2)(a)) or the institution of legal proceedings.

case note

In *Re The 21st Century Sign Co Pty Ltd* (1993) 11 ACLC 161, the secretary of a company who had advanced money to it was granted a floating charge over the company's assets in lieu of payment. About four months later the secretary demanded payment. When the company failed to comply, the secretary gave notice that the charge had crystallised and appointed a receiver. The company was subsequently wound up. The Supreme Court of Queensland held that the notice was a step in enforcing the charge for purposes of s 267(2) and the charge was void because prior leave of the court had not been obtained under s 267(1).

Where an officer who is entitled to enforce a charge exercises the right under s 436C to appoint an administrator, this is not enforcing a charge for the purposes of s 267(1). The appointment of an administrator may result in the chargee being unable to enforce the charge at all: *Australian Innovation Ltd v Dean-Willcocks* [2001] NSWSC 1204. A letter threatening to take legal proceedings or seeking an undertaking about future action and advising another party of a claim of an interest in property also does not constitute enforcement of a charge: *400 Lonsdale Nominees Pty Ltd v Southern Cross Airlines Holdings Ltd* (1993) 11 ACLC 744.

case note

The power of the court under s 267 was considered in *Abalcheck Pty Ltd v Pullen* (1990) 8 ACLC 1078. The directors and shareholders of Abalcheck agreed to sell all their shares to a purchaser, Powell. A deposit was paid and the balance was payable by instalments. It was agreed that the balance was to be secured by a charge granted by the company over its assets. After the charge was executed the vendor shareholders resigned their directorships and the purchaser was appointed to the board. Within six months of the creation of the charge, the purchaser defaulted in paying an instalment and the former directors purported to appoint receivers pursuant to the charge notwithstanding that the purchaser had offered to pay the arrears within two weeks. Since the directors had not obtained leave of the court as required by s 267, the charge was void. When the significance of s 267 was appreciated by the former directors they applied for leave under the predecessor of s 267(3), arguing that the company was solvent at the time of creation of the charge. They also sought an extension of time for the obtaining of such leave under the predecessor of s 1322(4)(a) which allows the court to validate procedural irregularities. The company opposed this, arguing that the purported appointment of receivers had damaged the company's business.

The court refused to grant leave because granting leave would mean that the company would not be entitled to sue for damages caused by the invalid appointment of the receivers. Even if the application for leave had been made in time, it was by no means clear that the court would have granted it, having regard to the drastic nature of the remedy of appointment of receivers, the likelihood that unsecured creditors would not be paid in full if the charge were validated, and the existence of the offer to make good the arrears within two weeks by the purchaser. The court also held that s 1322(4)(a) did not give it the power to grant leave retrospectively.

Section 267 also applies where a company creates a charge in favour of a person associated with an officer: s 267(7).

case note

In *IPT Systems Ltd v MTIC Corporate Pty Ltd* (2001) 19 ACLC 386, IPT Systems Ltd (IPT) held 80 per cent of the shares in MTIC Corporate Pty Ltd (MTIC). MTIC granted IPT a floating charge which IPT sought to enforce. Leave of the court was required under s 267(1) if IPT was a "relevant person" under s 267(7) in that it was associated with an officer of MITC. Both companies had a common director but this in itself did not make IPT an associate of the director. IPT would be an associate if it acted in concert with the director under s 15(1)(a). This required that a common purpose was decided upon between IPT and a director of MTIC which had a "base or pejorative" element to avoid the letter or spirit of the legislation. The court held that it was inappropriate to draw such an inference and s 267 did not apply.

registration of charges

The *Corporations Act* provides for a system of registration of company charges with ASIC.

[11.115] The *Corporations Act* provides for a system of registration of company charges with ASIC. ASIC is required by s 265(1) to keep a publicly accessible database—the Australian Register of Company Charges. The main purpose of the database is to enable a potential creditor of a company, who proposes to lend money on security of particular property, to find out whether the company has already given a charge over that property to another creditor. It also enables an unsecured creditor to determine the extent to which the assets of a company have been charged, and thereby ascertain the rights of secured creditors who rank ahead of an unsecured creditor in priority of payment. Further provisions also determine the priorities of registrable charges as against each other.

Persons dealing with a company are taken to have constructive notice of the information contained in the Australian Register of Company Charges maintained by ASIC: s 130(2).

Persons dealing with a company are taken to have constructive notice of the information contained in the Australian Register of Company Charges maintained by ASIC.

registrable charges

[11.120] Section 262 sets out the charges (whether legal or equitable) that must be registered. The charges required to be registered under s 262(1) constitute an exhaustive list. The following types of charges must be registered with ASIC:

- a floating charge on the whole or a part of the property, business or undertaking of the company. Under s 9, a floating charge includes one that has crystallised and thus becomes a fixed charge;
- a charge on uncalled capital;
- a charge on a call on shares made but not paid;
- a charge on a personal chattel, including personal chattels that are unascertained or to be acquired in the future (s 262(3) defines "personal chattel" to include any article capable of complete transfer by delivery after the creation of the charge and a fixture or growing crop that is charged separately from the land);
- a charge on goodwill, a patent, a trademark, a copyright or a registered design;
- a charge on a book debt ("book debts" are defined in s 262(4) to include a debt due or to become due to the company in connection with its business. It need not actually be entered in a book and includes debts of the same nature incurred in the future. Excluded are debts in respect of mortgages and charges of land);
- a charge on a marketable security ("marketable security" is defined in s 9 to include debentures, shares or bonds of any corporation or government body, options and any interest in a managed investment scheme. Excluded from "marketable securities" are deposits of title to the marketable security such as share certificates. This excludes the situation where a lender takes possession of a share certificate and acknowledges this in writing or where a transfer of the shares is registered in the lender's name: s 262(6));
- a lien or charge on a crop, a lien on wool or a stock mortgage; and
- a charge on a negotiable instrument other than a marketable security (this includes bills of exchange, cheques and promissory notes).

Only those charges specifically mentioned in s 262 must be registered with ASIC. There are certain charges that do not need to be registered. Therefore, a potential lender to a company may not be able to ascertain the full extent to which the assets of the company are encumbered.

Only those charges specifically mentioned in s 262 must be registered with ASIC.

Fixed charges over partnership interests and commercial contracts do not require registration.

case note

For example, in *United Builders Pty Ltd v Mutual Acceptance Ltd* (1980) 144 CLR 673, the company gave a charge over its share in a partnership. This charge was held to be a fixed charge and therefore not required to be registered under the predecessor to s 262(1). While the underlying partnership property may continually change in nature and value, a partner's interest in the partnership is fixed and definite. The company then gave a later floating charge that was duly registered. It was held that the registered floating charge was subject to the priority of the earlier fixed charge even though it was not registered.

Charges on land are specifically excluded and do not have to be registered with ASIC: s 262. This is because there is already provision for the registration of interests in land in the Titles Office registers of the various States. Charges that would otherwise have been required to be registered under various State Bills of Sale legislation need only be registered under s 262(1): s 273. This avoids duplication by automatically giving effect to the State legislation.

The operation of s 273 also extends to the registration of crop liens, wool liens and stock mortgages. These need no longer be separately registered under the Bills of Sale legislation in the Australian Capital Territory and Victoria.

procedure for lodgment and registration of charges

notification of details

A company that creates a charge must ensure that a notification of details of a charge is lodged with ASIC.

[11.125] A company that creates a charge must ensure that a notification of details of a charge is lodged with ASIC: s 263(1). In practice, the lender usually lodges the ASIC notification. The prescribed form is *Corporations Regulations*, Sch 2, Form 309, which requires particulars of:

> **the date the charge was created;**
> **whether the charge is created or evidenced by a resolution, an instrument, a deposit or conduct;**
> **whether it is a fixed charge, a floating charge or both a fixed and floating charge;**
> **if the charge is a floating charge, a statement whether there are restrictions on the creation of subsequent charges;**
> **a description of the liability secured by the charge;**
> **a description of the property charged;**
> **if the charge is constituted by the issue of debentures, the name of the trustee for the debenture-holders (if any);**
> **if there is no trustee for debenture-holders, the name of the chargee; and**
> **the amounts of payment made or discount allowed to persons, in connection with the issue of debentures: s 263(7).**

Together with this notice, the company must lodge a copy of the document creating the charge, or a copy of the debenture or the first debenture if there is a series, or a statement in writing verifying the execution of the first debenture or document creating or evidencing the charge: s 263(1) and (2).

The time for lodgment is within 45 days after the creation of the charge.

The time for lodgment is within 45 days after the creation of the charge (s 263(1)), or acquisition of property subject to a charge: s 264. A charge is created on the date of execution of the instrument of charge and not the date when the money is actually advanced: *Esberger & Son Ltd v Capital & Counties Bank* [1913] 2 Ch 366.

The time and date of lodgment of a notice of charge, together with the main particulars, are entered in the Australian Register of Company Charges kept by ASIC: s 265(2). From this time, the charge is deemed to be registered: s 265(3).

extension of time for lodgment

The time limit for lodging a notice of charge may be extended by the court.

[11.130] The time limit for lodging a notice of charge may be extended by the court under s 266(4). Any interested person, usually the chargee, or the company may apply to the court for such an order. The court may exercise its discretion where the failure to lodge within the prescribed time was accidental, due to inadvertence or not of a nature to prejudice the position of creditors or shareholders. The discretion of the court may also be exercised on other grounds where it is just and equitable to extend the time for lodgment.

In exercising its discretion, the court is reluctant to interfere with the rights of creditors after winding up has commenced or the company's solvency is in question: *J J Leonard Properties Pty Ltd v Leonard (WA) Pty Ltd* (1988) 6 ACLC 247.

provisional entry in Register

[11.135] To encourage and facilitate early lodgment of charges, s 265 provides for provisional entry in the Register. This enables charges to be registered despite the fact that stamp duty may not have yet been paid or the notice is in some respects defective.

A notice of charge may be entered in the Register and marked "provisional" if it contains at least the name of the company that created the charge and the name of the trustee for debenture-holders or the chargee, as the case may be. If the company then provides the required further particulars within a prescribed period of time, these are recorded in the Register and the word "provisional" is deleted. The charge is then deemed to have been registered from the date of the provisional entry: s 265(9). If the company does not provide the required further particulars within the prescribed time, the charge is deemed to have been registered only on the date when the information is entered in the Register: s 265(7). A charge may also be lodged for provisional entry in the Register where stamp duty has not been paid on the applicable document: s 265(4). In such a case, evidence of proper payment of stamp duty must be forwarded to ASIC within 30 days: s 265(5).

priorities of registrable charges

time of registration

[11.140] The time of registration is important because it determines priorities among different registered charges over the same property. The question of priority of charges arises when a company borrows from two or more lenders and purports to give each of them security over the same property. If the company then defaults in payment to the lenders, the question arises as to which lender has priority in enforcing the security. Sections 279–282 set out a system of priorities between the holders of competing registrable charges over the same property. The general rule is that registered charges have priority according to the time they were registered. This rule is subject to a number of qualifications discussed below.

The time of registration is important because it determines priorities among different registered charges over the same property.

The *Corporations Act* only determines priorities as between holders of charges that are registrable under s 262. Priorities of competing unregistrable charges or between unregistrable and registrable charges are determined according to the general law. This is discussed below, para [11.145].

exceptions to time of registration rule

[11.145] The order of priorities of registrable charges as set out in ss 280–282 is subject to any express or implied consent given by the holder of a charge that would otherwise be entitled to priority, or any agreement between chargees, varying the priorities of the charges: s 279(2).

The holder of a registered floating charge is deemed to have consented to a subsequently registered fixed charge gaining priority where the fixed charge was created before the floating charge crystallises. This is so unless there was breach of a provision in the document creating the floating charge which prohibited or restricted the creation of future charges and notice of this provision was lodged with ASIC before the creation of the subsequent registered fixed charge: s 279(3). The prescribed form of notification of details of a charge, Form 309, includes a statement whether or not the creation of subsequent charges is restricted or prohibited by the floating charge. This is a negative pledge and is discussed above, para [11.95]. It is therefore important for holders of floating charges to ensure that the notice is accurate and complete.

The following rules determine priorities in relation to registered charges:

- **Registered charges generally have priority in order of the time and date when they were entered in the Register.**
- **A prior-registered charge, however, loses priority over a subsequently-registered charge where the subsequently-registered charge was created before the prior registered charge and the holder of the prior-registered charge is proved to have had actual or constructive notice of**

the subsequently-registered charge at the time the prior-registered charge was created: s 280(1)(a). Therefore, if charge A is registered on 1 June and charge B is registered on 3 June, charge A is a prior charge and as a general rule has priority over charge B, which is a subsequent charge. However, if charge B was created first and the chargee of A had notice of charge B when charge A was created, charge B has priority over charge A.

> A registered charge generally has priority over an unregistered charge unless the unregistered charge was created first and the holder of the registered charge can be proven to have had actual or constructive notice at the time of the creation of the registered charge of the existence of the unregistered charge: s 280(1)(b). "Unregistered charge" is defined in s 278(1) and means a charge that is one of the categories of registrable charges under s 262 but has not been registered. Therefore, if charge A is registered and charge B is unregistered, generally charge A has priority over charge B. However, if charge B was created first and the chargee of A had notice of charge B when charge A was created, charge B has priority over charge A.

> Unregistered charges take priority according to their time of creation: s 281(b).

present and prospective liabilities

Section 282 sets out a system of priorities in a situation where a charge secures a present liability and also secures further advances by the holder of the charge.

[11.150] Section 282 sets out a system of priorities in a situation where a charge secures a present liability and also secures further advances by the holder of the charge. The question arises as to the extent to which such a charge has priority over a later charge given over the same property. A common form of borrowing by a company is the fixing of a charge to a bank as security for an overdraft. The amount of the overdraft may fluctuate over time. If the company then charges the same property to another creditor, to what extent does the bank have priority over the later chargee?

For the purposes of determining priorities in such situations, s 282 uses the terms "present liability" and "prospective liability". These are defined in s 261(1). "Present liability" is a liability that has arisen and the amount of which is fixed and capable of being ascertained. "Prospective liability" is any liability that may arise in the future but does not include a present liability. The prescribed form of notification of details of a charge provides for a description of whether the liability is present or prospective.

> As a general rule, priority accorded to a charge over another charge only extends to a present liability under that charge as at the priority time: s 282(1). "Priority time" means the time and date on which the charge was entered in the Register: s 278(1).

> Where a prior-registered charge secures a prospective or future liability up to a specified maximum amount, and that amount and the nature of the prospective liability are specified in the lodged notice of charge, the prior-registered charge has priority over subsequently-registered charges up to the specified amount of the prospective liability. This is irrespective of whether the further advances are made before or after registration of the subsequent charge or whether or not the prior chargee knew of the later charge: s 282(3).

> Where the lodged notice of charge does not specify the maximum amount secured by the registered charge, together with the nature of the prospective liability, the prior charge has priority only with respect to further advances made by the prior chargee up to the time he or she first obtained actual notice of the subsequent charge: s 282(4)(c). Section 282(2) has similar effect where the registered charge secures a prospective liability of an unspecified amount.

> Where the terms of the registered charge require the chargee to make further advances, all such further advances will have the same priority as the charge itself, even where the chargee had actual notice of the existence of later charges at the time when the further advances were made: s 282(4)(d).

The provisions of s 282 determine priority of charges on the basis of the actual knowledge rather than the constructive knowledge of the prior chargee. This means that the prior chargee is under no obligation to search the Register before making further advances under the security. However, in order to gain protection against later chargees, the prior chargee should be careful to specify the maximum amount and the nature of the prospective liability in the notification of details of a charge.

effect of failure to lodge notice of charge

[11.155] A charge on the property of a company is not invalid by reason only of the failure to lodge a notice of the charge with ASIC: s 262(11). However, as discussed above, para [11.140], the system of priorities provides incentive to chargees to ensure that notice of charges are lodged and registered.

A further reason for chargees to ensure that notice of their charges are lodged is provided by s 266. This section provides that if a notice of charge is not lodged within the prescribed 45-day period and the company goes into liquidation or has an administrator appointed or executes a deed of company arrangement within six months, the charge will be void as against the liquidator, company administrator or the deed's administrator: s 266. The policy behind this section is to prevent a person avoiding disclosure of the existence of a charge until just before the company goes into liquidation and then at the last moment registering the charge and acquiring its benefits.

If a notice of charge is not lodged within the prescribed 45-day period and the company goes into liquidation or has an administrator appointed or executes a deed of company arrangement within six months, the charge will be void as against the liquidator, company administrator or the deed's administrator.

The requirement of lodgment means that the charge need not be actually registered. It is sufficient to lodge a notice that gains only provisional entry in the Register, even if this entry is subsequently deleted: *Wilson v Dunn* (1994) 12 ACLC 922. Section 266 similarly applies to situations where property is acquired subject to a charge, or a charge is assigned or varied. The time limit is subject to any extension ordered by the court under s 266(4).

The operation of s 266 means that failure to lodge a notice of a charge does not automatically render the charge void against a liquidator or administrator. It merely exposes the chargee to that risk, if winding up is commenced or an administrator is appointed within six months of eventual lodgment. A charge is valid against a liquidator or administrator even though notice of the charge is lodged after the commencement of winding up or appointment of an administrator, as long as it is lodged within 45 days of the creation of the charge.

Where the charge is void against a liquidator or administrator, the chargee remains a creditor of the company, but without security. The chargee's position is thereby weakened as he or she becomes merely an unsecured creditor.

assignment and variation of charges

[11.160] In order to keep the Register accurate and up-to-date, s 268 provides for notice to be given to ASIC within 45 days of assignments and variations of charges. Notice of an assignment of a charge must also be sent to the company.

A notice of variation of a charge must be lodged together with a copy of the instrument of variation if there is a variation in the terms of the charge having the effect of increasing the amount of the debt or the present or prospective liabilities secured by the charge, or prohibiting or restricting the creation of subsequent charges on the property charged: s 268(2). Where a charge secures a debt of an unspecified amount and an advance is paid under the terms of the charge, this is not taken as a variation of the charge: s 268(3).

satisfaction and release of property from charge

[11.165] Where the debt secured by the charge has been paid in whole or in part or the property charged has been partly or wholly released from the charge, the holder of the charge must forward to the company within 14 days after receipt of a request from the company, a memorandum acknowledging payment of the debt or release of the property: *Corporations Regulations*, Sch 2, Form 312. The company may then lodge this memorandum with ASIC for entry in the Register: s 269.

case note

In *J J Leonard Properties Pty Ltd v Leonard (WA) Pty Ltd* (1988) 6 ACLC 247, a charge was lodged that inadvertently left out the charging clause which identified the property to be charged. The chargor went into liquidation and the chargee was notified that it was an unsecured creditor. The chargee applied for an order under the equivalent of s 274 that the debenture be rectified to include the charge clause as it had appeared in an earlier debenture.

The court declined to rectify the register because to do so would prejudice the rights of unsecured creditors by displacing the right they had obtained at the commencement of winding up. This would offend against a clear principle that upon commencement of winding up, the court should not assist one creditor to improve its position relative to other creditors.

Section 270 enables notices to be lodged with ASIC by any interested person, including the chargee.

lodgment of notices by chargee

[11.170] We saw that ss 262 and 263 require a company to ensure that notices with respect to charges on its property are lodged with ASIC. Failure to lodge the proper notices may adversely affect the rights of chargees by affecting the priority of charges. For this reason, s 270 enables notices to be lodged with ASIC by any interested person, including the chargee. Failure to lodge a notice is an offence by the company and any defaulting officers: s 270(2).

rectification of register

[11.175] Application may be made to the court under s 274 for an order that an omission or misstatement in the register be rectified. This power of the court is exercisable in similar circumstances as where the court will grant an extension of time for lodging a notice of charge under s 266(4).

company's register of charges

Details of charges are required to be entered in a register of charges kept by the company.

[11.180] Details of charges, including those that do not need to be registered under s 262(1), are required to be entered in a register of charges kept by the company: s 271(2). The company must keep the register open for inspection by creditors, members and others. Breach of s 271 constitutes an offence by the company and any defaulting officer. It does not, however, affect the validity of any charge not entered in the register.

law reform proposals

[11.185] The report of the Australian Law Reform Commission (ALRC) on *Personal Property Securities* (January 1995) recommended significant changes to the law dealing with charges. It proposed a single legal regime for all Australian jurisdictions for the regulation of priorities between competing claims for personal property security interests. The implementation of such a regime would require uniform legislation and a national register. The securities subject to the new scheme would cover all personal property security interests that have the commercial effect of providing financial accommodation. This includes security interests such as mortgages, liens, charges, financing leases, hire-purchase and retention of title agreements. These securities are presently regulated by a range of Commonwealth and State legislation according to form rather than substance and effect.

The ALRC report also considered that the existing rules for determining priorities were unsatisfactory and sometimes an inconsistent mix of statute, common law and equity. It recommended new rules based on three rules:

> **a registered security prevails over an unregistered one;**
> **an earlier registered security prevails over one registered later; and**
> **an unregistered but registrable security for which value is given earlier in time prevails over an unregistered security for which value is given later in time.**

The proposed new rules would not have regard to notice of a prior unregistered charge in the absence of fraud by the security holder.

bibliography ...

Ali, P "Alphabet Soup: An Overview of Exotic Convertible Securities" (2000) 18 C & SLJ 579.

Australian Law Reform Commission, "Personal Property Securities". Final Report No 64. **http://www.austlii.edu.au/au/other/alrc/publications/reports/64/**

Burns, F R "Automatic Crystallisation of Company Charges: Contractual Creativity or Confusion" (1992) 20 ABLR 125.

Cameron, I "Company Charges and the Australian Law Reform Commission: Scrutinising the Department of Utter Confusion" (1994) 12 C & SLJ 357.

Carlin, T "Associated Alloys Pty Ltd v Can 001 452 106 Pty Ltd: A Commentary and Analysis" (2002) 30 ABLR 106.

Chandler, J "The Modern Floating Charge" in Gillooly, M (ed) *Securities over Personalty*. Federation Press, 1994, Ch 1.

Collier, B "Enforcement of Company Charges by Directors and Other 'Relevant Persons' Under Section 267 of the Corporations Law" (1995) 3 Insolv LJ 168.

Corney, G "Registration and Validity of Company Charges—Some Problem Areas" (1992) 4 Bond LR 21.

Edwards, R "Taking a Fixed Charge Over Book Debts" (1998) 6 *Current Commercial Law* 21.

Finch, A "Security Over Shares" (1995) 13 C & SLJ 292.

Fisher, S "Romalpa Clause as Security Interests: Problems, Pitfalls and Solutions" (1993) 8 JIBFL 119.

Hamilton, G "Provisions which Avoid Charges Under the Corporations Law: The Effect on Secured Creditors and Receivers" (1998) 16 C & SLJ 333.

Harris, G "The Current Account Romalpa Clause Held to Effectively Retain Title and Permit Tracing" (1991) 9 C & SLJ 390.

Keay, A "The Power to Extend Time to Lodge Notice of Corporate Charges" (1996) 14 C & SLJ 136.

Lipton, J D "Security over Electronically Registered Shares and s 47 of the Trade Practices Act 1974 (Cth)" (1994) 22 ABLR 426.

McGrath, T "The Floating Charge and Void and Voidable Transactions" (2002) 10 Insolv LJ 37.

Nash, L & Collier, B "Fixed Charges over Book Debts after Agnew v Commissioner of Inland Revenue" (2001) 9 Insolv LJ 116.

Nkala, J C "Some Aspects of the Jurisprudence of the Floating Charge" (1993) 11 C & SLJ 301.

Ong, D S K "Romalpa Clauses" (1992) 4 Bond LR 186.
Powers, L "Legal Rights and Commercial Realities: The Position of the Unpaid Seller When Insolvency Intervenes" (1995) 13 C & SLJ 178.
Purcell, D "Automatic Crystallisation of Floating Charges" (1989) 7 C & SLJ 131.
Sneddon, M "Automatic Crystallisation of Floating Charges Catching a Disposition which Triggers the Crystallisation" (1993) 21 ABLR 152.
Spagnole, J A "Security Interests US Style: A Device for Financing Small Businessmen and Protecting Yourself in Liquidation" (1992) 4 Bond LR 115.
Taylor, L "What a Company Charge Does Not Reveal—The Financier's Perspective" (1992) 10 C & SLJ 396.
Worthington, S "Pledges as the New Security Device" (1993) 11 C & SLJ 43.
Young, M "Floating Charge Restrictive Clauses and Unsecured Negative Pledge Covenants in Australian Corporate Debt Financing" (1999) 10 JBFLP 205.

revision questions on the material in this chapter ...

> Please see eQuiz at **http://www.thomson.com.au/academic** for multiple choice questions and answers.

chapter twelve

directors

key points ...

> Directors exercise their powers collectively at board meetings. Generally, the directors determine how board meetings are to be conducted. Because the legal rights of shareholders may be affected, board meetings must be held in compliance with some basic procedural rules in order to pass valid resolutions.

> The definition of "director" is broad and includes persons appointed to that position as well as de facto and shadow directors. There are different types of directors reflecting the different roles directors may play on a board. A board may form committees to which particular areas of responsibility are delegated.

> The two organs of a company are the board of directors and the general meeting of shareholders. The constitution, replaceable rules, *Corporations Act* and the ASX Listing Rules determine the respective powers of the board and the general meeting. The board nearly always has the power of management of the business of the company as well as a number of ancillary powers.

> The power of management is very broad and the general meeting cannot interfere with the exercise of this power. Shareholders can only remove directors of whom they disapprove.

> Directors are generally appointed by resolution of the general meeting.

> A person may be disqualified from acting as a director for the purpose of protecting the public from directors who have committed certain offences or been involved with insolvent companies.

> Directors may only be removed in accordance with the constitution and, in the case of public companies, by resolution of the general meeting.

> The company secretary is the company's chief administrative officer with responsibility over the company's internal administration and compliance matters.

All companies must have directors. The directors are collectively referred to as a "board of directors".

[12.05] All companies must have directors. The directors are collectively referred to as a "board of directors". Proprietary companies need only have one director: s 201A(1). Public companies must have at least three directors: s 201A(2). The initial directors are those persons named with their consent in the application for registration of the company: s 120(1). Subsequent appointments of directors may be made in accordance with the replaceable rules contained in ss 201G and 201H or the company's constitution (if any).

A company consists of two components or organs:

> **the board of directors; and**
> **the members in general meeting.**

The ability of either of these organs to act as the company depends on the division of power between the board of directors and the members in general meeting and the extent of authority bestowed on them by the replaceable rules, the company's constitution (if any) or the *Corporations Act*.

who is a director?

section 9 definition

[12.10] A director of a company is defined in s 9 as a person who is appointed to the position of a director or alternate director regardless of the name given to their position. The s 9 definition also regards certain persons to be directors even though they are not validly appointed.

A director is a person who is appointed to the position.

Unless the contrary intention appears, a person who is not validly appointed as a director is also regarded as a director if:

> **they act in the position of a director ("de facto director"); or**
> **the directors are accustomed to act in accordance with the person's instructions or wishes ("shadow director").**

According to the note in the s 9 definition of director, the following provisions of the *Corporations Act* are examples of a contrary intention where a de facto director or shadow director would not be included in the term "director":

> **s 249C (power to call meetings of a company's members);**
> **s 251A(3) (signing minutes of meetings); and**
> **s 205B (notice to ASIC of change of address).**

ASIC may ask a person to inform it whether he or she is a director or secretary of a particular company: s 205E. Where the person has ceased to be a director or secretary, ASIC may ask the date when this occurred.

de facto directors

[12.15] A director includes persons who act in the position of a director even though they have not been appointed to that position: s 9. Such people are referred to as "de facto" directors.

A director includes persons who act in the position of a director even though they have not been appointed to that position. Such people are referred to as "de facto" directors.

In *DFC of T v Austin* (1998) 16 ACLC 1555, Madgwick J said that it is not practicable to formulate a general statement as to what constitutes acting as a director. This often involves a question of degree requiring a consideration of the duties performed in the context of the operations and circumstances of the company. A necessary condition of acting as a director is that the person exercised top level management functions. In the case of a small company, where a person has acted as the company in relation to important matters, this may indicate the person has acted in the capacity of a director. In the case of a large company, many important matters are delegated to employees and the exercise of such discretions does not necessarily indicate that the person is a director. It is also relevant to consider how the person claimed to be a director is perceived by outsiders who deal with the company where the person has been held out to be a director.

A person may be regarded as a de facto director if the person is the driving force behind the company business despite not having been appointed to that position, or continues to participate in the management of the company after the expiration of the term of appointment as a director as if still a director: *Corporate Affairs Commission v Drysdale* (1978) 141 CLR 236.

shadow directors

"Shadow" directors are persons whose instructions or wishes are customarily followed by the directors of a company.

[12.20] As noted above, the s 9 definition of director also includes persons who act as "shadow" directors. These are persons whose instructions or wishes are customarily followed by the directors of a company. A person is not regarded as a director merely because the directors act on advice given by the person in the performance of functions attaching to the person's professional capacity, or the person's business relationship with the directors.

A holding company may be a "shadow" director of a subsidiary if the directors of the subsidiary are nominee directors who customarily follow the holding company's directions or instructions. This is discussed in Chapter 13.2 below.

types of directors

managing directors

Many companies have a managing director or CEO who is put in charge of managing the company's daily business.

[12.25] Many companies have a managing director or chief executive officer (CEO) who is put in charge of managing the company's daily business. The replaceable rules allow the directors to appoint one or more of themselves to the office of managing director: s 201J. A managing director may be conferred with any of the powers that the directors can exercise: s 198C.

A managing director performs a vital role in large companies. Because of the scale of the company's business it is usually impracticable for the board to actively carry out daily management and so it delegates its management function to the managing director who is accountable to the board. The managing director is in charge of and responsible for the senior executives employed to manage the company. The respective functions and roles and relationship of the board and managing director are important corporate governance issues. Corporate governance best practice is discussed in Chapter 13.1 below.

As part of the managing director's management role, it is usual that wide customary authority to bind the company is conferred. The customary authority of a managing director is discussed in Chapter 5 above.

chair of directors

[12.30] The *Corporations Act* and replaceable rules provide that the directors may appoint a director to chair directors' meetings (s 248E) and an individual may be elected by the directors to chair meetings of the company's members: s 249U. Minutes must be signed by the chair of the meeting or the chair of the next meeting: s 251A(2). The chairman has a casting vote at directors' meetings: s 248G(2). Typically, company constitutions make little further mention of the chair.

The essence of chairmanship is exercising procedural control over a meeting.

The essence of chairmanship is exercising procedural control over a meeting: *Woonda Nominees Pty Ltd v Chng* (2000) 18 ACLC 558. The exercise of procedural control over meetings includes nominating who is to speak, dealing with the order of business, putting questions to the meeting, declaring resolutions to be carried or defeated, asking for general business and closing the meeting: *Kelly v Wolstenholme* (1991) 9 ACLC 785. In exercising procedural control over a general meeting, the chair must act honestly and bona fide.

case note

The significance of the chair is illustrated in *Colorado Constructions Pty Ltd v Platus* [1966] 2 NSWR 598. A board meeting had been convened but arguments developed as to who was to assume the chair. Two of the directors left after a brawl developed. The remaining directors continued and purported to pass a resolution. When this was challenged the court held that as no chair had been appointed, no valid meeting passing the resolution had occurred. Street J considered the role of chair:

< It is an indispensable part of any meeting that a chairman should be appointed and occupy the chair. In the absence of some person (by whatever title he be described) exercising procedural control over a meeting the meeting is unable to proceed to business. This may perhaps require some qualification if all present are unanimous. And, in a small meeting, procedural control may pass from person to person according to who for the time being is allowed by the acquiescence of those present to have such control. But there must be some person expressly or by acquiescence permitted by those present to put motions to the meeting so as to enable the wish or decision of the meeting to be ascertained. >

In practice, the chair is often given special powers which go beyond the supervision of meetings and in listed public companies the position carries important corporate governance responsibilities. These are discussed in Chapter 13.1 below. Rogers CJ, in *AWA Ltd v Daniels* (1992) 10 ACLC 933, described the responsibilities of the chair:

The chair is often given special powers which go beyond the supervision of meetings.

< The chairman is responsible to a greater extent than any other director for the performance of the board as a whole and each member of it. The chairman has the primary responsibility of selecting matters and documents to be brought to the board's attention, for formulating the policy of the board and promoting the position of the company. >

In *ASIC v Rich* [2003] NSWSC 85, Austin J thought it appropriate to consider corporate governance literature and best practice in determining the special responsibilities of the chair for the purposes of determining whether a chair had breached a duty of care. This duty is discussed in Chapter 13.4 below. These sources indicate that among other things, a chair of a listed company is responsible to a greater extent than any other director for ensuring that the board is properly informed, familiar with the financial circumstances of the company and the board properly meets its supervisory duties.

executive and non-executive directors

[12.35] Executive directors are full-time employees of the company. Their main role is to take part in the daily management of the company's business. In this respect they comprise the senior management of the company under the leadership of the chief executive officer. In the case of large listed companies, the style and complexity of business means that the board of directors must delegate substantial control of the company's activities to its management.

Executive directors are full-time employees of the company.

Non-executive directors are not directly involved in the daily management of the company's business. They have a part-time involvement in the company and participate in board meetings or meetings of board committees. Non-executive directors have an important role to play in monitoring the activities of the management team headed by the CEO and bringing an independent view and judgment and often an outside or broad perspective to the board's deliberations. Their role is to consider the interests of the company as a whole and the general body of shareholders.

Non-executive directors are not directly involved in the daily management of the company's business.

A crucial aspect of best practice corporate governance is that boards of listed companies comprise a majority of non-executive directors who are independent of management, substantial shareholders and material suppliers or customers of the company. The effectiveness of company boards as monitors of management is enhanced by the appointment of a significant number of independent non-executive directors.

Non-executive directors can also play an important role in sensitive areas such as where conflicts of interests arise or where the interests of management and the company as a whole diverge. This may occur in relation to remuneration, related party transactions and succession planning. Corporate governance best practice provides for these types of issues and the functions of internal control and accountability to be delegated to board committees controlled by a majority of independent non-executive directors. The most important of these committees is the audit committee. The corporate governance role of independent non-executive directors is discussed in Chapter 13.1 below.

alternate directors

[12.40] Company constitutions often provide for the appointment of alternate directors. For example, the replaceable rule in s 201K(1) provides that a director may, with the approval of the other directors, appoint an alternate to exercise some or all of the director's powers. The appointment of an alternate allows for a replacement where a director is unable to attend board meetings or otherwise exercise powers as a director. ASIC must be given notice of the appointment and termination of appointment of an alternate director: s 205B(2) and (5). Where an alternate director exercises a director's powers, this exercise of powers is as effective as if exercised by the director: s 201K(3).

The alternate director has no legal status whenever the director for whom the alternate acts is present at a board meeting.

In *Markwell Bros Pty Ltd v CPN Diesels (Qld) Pty Ltd* (1982) 7 ACLR 425, it was held that alternate directors were within the definition of "director" and subject to the same fiduciary and statutory duties a director owes to her or his company. Directors' duties are discussed in Chapter 13 below. In *Playcorp Pty Ltd v Shaw* (1993) 11 ACLC 641, an alternate director who had not been called upon to act as such and had never attended any board or management meetings was not liable under the insolvent trading predecessor of s 588G. An alternate director is not merely an agent of his appointor: *Anaray Pty Ltd v Sydney Futures Exchange Ltd* (1988) 6 ACLC 27.

nominee directors

[12.45] Sometimes a director is appointed to represent the interests of a particular shareholder or creditor on the board of directors. Such directors are sometimes referred to as "nominee directors".

A holding company usually has power to appoint directors to the board of its subsidiary companies. In such cases, the subsidiary's directors may be nominees of the holding company. In the case of companies formed to carry out a joint venture, it is usual for each of the parties to have the right to nominate a specified number of nominees as directors. Where directors are appointed to represent sectional interests, a question may arise as to whom they primarily owe duties—the company or the person who appointed them. The duties of nominee directors are discussed in Chapter 13.2 below.

functions and powers of the board

[12.50] The board plays a crucial corporate governance role by setting the direction of the company and holding its management accountable. The powers of the board are determined by the replaceable rules, the company's constitution (if any) and the *Corporations Act*. Usually, the board is given a broad power of management. The shareholders typically have the power to appoint or replace the directors.

functions of the board

The essential functions of the board are "to provide strategic guidance for the company and effective oversight of management".

[12.55] Principle 1 of the ASX Corporate Governance Council's *Principles of Good Corporate Governance and Best Practice Recommendations* (2003) states that the essential functions of the board are "to provide strategic guidance for the company and effective oversight of management". The precise responsibilities of the board will depend on matters such as the size and ownership structure of the company and the skills of its directors and management and these will vary between different companies. However, in carrying out its key functions, the board usually has the following responsibilities:

> oversight of the company including its control and accountability systems;
> appointing and removing the CEO or managing director;
> ratifying the appointment and removal of the chief financial officer and company secretary;
> input into and final approval of management's development of corporate strategy and performance objectives;
> reviewing and ratifying systems of risk management and internal compliance and control, codes of conduct and legal compliance;
> monitoring senior management's performance and implementation of strategy and ensuring appropriate resources are available;
> approving and monitoring the progress of major capital expenditure, capital management and acquisitions and divestitures; and
> approving and monitoring financial and other reporting.

The ASX Corporate Governance Council's *Principles of Good Corporate Governance and Best Practice Recommendations* (2003) may be accessed on the ASX website which is linked to the Lipton-Herzberg Corporate Governance Pathway at **http://www.lipton-herzberg.com.au/secure/pathways-corporate-governance.html** Corporate governance is discussed in Chapter 13.1 below.

diagram 12.1 an effective board

	Short term	Long term
External	**Accountability** **Reporting to shareholders** **Ensuring statutory/regulatory compliance** **Reviewing audit reports**	**Strategic thinking** **Reviewing and initiating strategic analysis** **Formulating strategy** **Setting corporate direction**
	Appointment and rewarding Chief executive	
Internal	**Supervision** **Review key executive performance** **Reviewing business results** **Monitoring budgetary control and corrective action**	**Corporate policy** **Approving budgets** **Determining compensation policy for senior executives** **Creating corporate culture**

Source: FG Hilmer and RI Tricker "An Effective Board" in *International Corporate Governance , Text, Readings and Cases* RI Tricker Prentice-Hall 1994 at page 287

In Diagram 12.1 above, Hilmer and Tricker compartmentalise the important functions performed by the board according to whether they are of a long-term or short-term nature and whether they have an internal or external objective. Therefore, long-term concerns include setting strategy which has an external focus, and creating a corporate culture or formulating policies which are concerned with internal matters. Short-term matters include monitoring and supervision of management and ensuring the organisation is accountable to external stakeholders. The function of the board which is generally regarded as the most important of all is the appointment of the chief executive officer. This appointment has major implications for all the other board functions.

The function of the board which is generally regarded as the most important of all is the appointment of the chief executive officer.

Hilmer and Tricker also distinguish between board functions which are concerned with conformance and performance. The conformance functions are generally of a short-term nature while the performance functions are more long-term. Different boards may choose to emphasise either conformance or performance functions depending on what is seen as appropriate at the time.

the power of management

The replaceable rule in s 198A states that the business of a company is to be managed by, or under the direction of, its directors.

[12.60] The replaceable rule in s 198A states that the business of a company is to be managed by, or under the direction of, its directors who may exercise all the company's powers except any powers that the *Corporations Act* or the company's constitution (if any) requires the company to exercise in general meeting. The constitutions of most companies give the directors similar wide management powers.

The scope of the management power in s 198A is extremely broad. It includes changing the direction of the company or selling the only business carried on by it. Directors do not have to obtain shareholder approval to sell the company's only business: *Strong v J Brough & Son (Strathfield) Pty Ltd* (1991) 9 ACLC 1018.

The constitutions of most companies give the directors similar wide management powers.

ASX Listing Rules give shareholders of listed companies a role in significant management decisions. For example, under Listing Rule 11.1, the ASX may require shareholder approval if a listed company proposes to make a significant change to the nature or scale of its activities. Further, Listing Rule 11.2 requires shareholder approval if the significant change involves the company disposing of its main undertaking.

The constitutions of some companies permit management of the company's business to be delegated to a management company. In its 1990 report, *Company Directors and Officers: Indemnification, Relief and Insurance*, the Companies and Securities Law Review Committee was of the opinion that this was undesirable and recommended that it should be compulsory for directors to have full management powers. This recommendation has not been implemented.

table 12.1 powers of the board

Management	The replaceable rule in s 198A(1) gives the directors the power to manage the business of the company. It is extremely common for directors to be given similar broad management powers in a company's constitution.
Company's powers	The replaceable rule in s 198A(2) provides that directors may exercise all the powers of the company except any powers that the *Corporations Act* or the company's constitution requires the company to exercise in general meeting. For example, directors may issue shares or debentures and borrow money on the company's behalf. They may also make calls on partly-paid shares.
Delegation of powers	Section 198D provides that unless the company's constitution provides otherwise, the directors may delegate any of their powers to a committee of directors, a director, an employee or any other person. In addition, the replaceable rule in s 198C gives the directors the power to confer any of their powers on a managing director.
Registration of transfers of shares	As discussed in Chapter 9 above, a person transferring shares remains the holder of the shares until the transfer is registered and the name of the transferee is entered in the company's share register. The replaceable rule in s 1072F gives directors the power to register transfers of shares.

table 12.1 (continued)

	Under s 1072F(3) they may refuse to register a transfer of shares if the shares are not fully paid or the company has a lien on the shares. The replaceable rule in s 1072G, which applies to proprietary companies, enables directors to refuse to register a transfer of shares for any reason. Directors may also suspend registration of transfers of shares for periods not exceeding 30 days in any one calendar year: s 1072F(4).
Calling meetings	The replaceable rules set out the requirements for convening directors' and members' meetings. Section 248C allows a director to call a directors' meeting by giving reasonable notice individually to every other director. A director may also call a meeting of the company's members: s 249C. Members' meetings are discussed in Chapter 14 below.
Dividends	The replaceable rule in s 254U gives directors the power to determine that a dividend is payable. They may also fix amount, the time for payment and the method of payment. Dividends are discussed in Chapter 10 above.
Execute documents	Under s 127(1) a company may execute a document without using a common seal if the document is signed by: — two directors; or — a director and a company secretary; or — in the case of a proprietary company that has a sole director who is also the sole secretary—that director. A company with a common seal may execute a document if the seal is affixed to the document and the fixing is witnessed by the people listed above: s 127(2). People will be able to assume that a document executed in accordance with either s 127(1) or (2) is properly executed even if the signatories do not have authority to sign: s 129(5) and (6). The s 129 assumptions are discussed in Chapter 5 above.
Negotiable instruments	According to the replaceable rule in s 198B any two directors of a company that has two or more directors, or the director of a proprietary company that has only one director, may sign, draw, accept, endorse or otherwise execute negotiable instruments such as company cheques and bills of exchange.

The replaceable rules and the constitution (if any) also usually confer various specific powers on the board of directors which complement, or are incidental to, the power of management. Table 12.1 above, sets out the important powers of the board. These powers are conferred on the directors as a board and not on individual directors.

shareholders cannot override management decisions

[12.65] If the board has full management powers, shareholders cannot override the directors and involve themselves in the management of their company.

Shareholders cannot override the directors and involve themselves in the management of their company.

case note

In *Automatic Self-Cleansing Filter Syndicate Co v Cuninghame* [1906] 2 Ch 34, the directors were ordered by a general meeting to sell the company's property. The directors refused to do this, relying on a provision in the constitution similar to s 198A. The members argued that the constitution was subject to the overriding rule that the directors, as agents of the company, were obliged to follow the instructions of their principal, the company; the will of the company being a resolution of the general meeting. The Court of Appeal rejected this argument. It held that the directions of the general meeting were a nullity that could be ignored by the directors. The constitution gave management powers to the board of directors, which included the power to sell the company's property. The members could not interfere with the directors in this respect as they were contractually bound by the constitution.

case note

This principle was applied in *John Shaw & Sons (Salford) Ltd v Shaw* [1935] 2 KB 113 to prevent the general meeting attempting to override a decision of the board to bring legal actions against some of the directors. The court held that the board of directors was properly exercising the powers of management vested in it by the constitution and the general meeting could not usurp this power. If the directors purport to exercise a power that should properly have been exercised by the general meeting, their action can be ratified by an ordinary resolution of the general meeting and the improper exercise of power becomes valid. The power of the general meeting to ratify the actions of the directors is discussed in Chapter 17 below.

separation of ownership and management

The conferral of wide powers of management on the board of directors results in the separation of management and ownership.

[12.70] The conferral of wide powers of management on the board of directors results in the separation of management and ownership. Ownership, in an economic sense, vests in the shareholders. This separation of functions is an important difference between companies and partnerships. Partnership law presumes that all partners have a right to participate in management.

In the case of large, public companies it is essential that management vests in the board of directors. Where there is a large number of shareholders, it would quickly become unworkable if the general meeting had the power to manage the company.

In the case of small proprietary companies, there is no such difficulty. These may have evolved from sole traders or partnerships and even after incorporation they continue to function in a similar manner as before. The directors and shareholders of such companies are often the same people and in practice there is no separation of management and ownership. However, to meet the requirements of the legislation, the distinction between members in general meeting and directors is maintained even if in many cases it is a fictitious distinction. The *Corporations Act* recognises the existence of proprietary companies with a single director who is also the sole shareholder. Further, proprietary companies are not required to hold an AGM.

The separation of ownership and control raises the possibility that management will act in its own interests in ways which may not be in the interests of the shareholders.

The separation of ownership and control raises the possibility that management will act in its own interests in ways which may not be in the interests of the shareholders. For example, management may have an interest in maximising their remuneration while this may not be in the shareholders' interests. The development of increased interest in corporate governance reflects higher expectations by the public and investment community that greater efforts be made by listed public companies to develop structures and procedures to ensure management is effective and acts in the interests of shareholders and adopts appropriate standards of corporate behaviour. Corporate governance is discussed in Chapter 13.1 below.

board procedure

directors' meetings

[12.75] Directors exercise their powers by making decisions and passing resolutions at board meetings. The rules governing directors' meetings are set out in the replaceable rules or the constitution (if any) or are determined by the board itself. There are also common law rules dealing with the conduct of meetings. The courts generally require adherence to these rules because resolutions of the board may affect the legal rights of members, directors and the company. In order to be valid, board meetings require broad compliance with procedural rules which aim to ensure that the meeting is fairly conducted.

Directors exercise their powers by making decisions.

A board meeting of a company with more than one director requires more than the directors meeting together informally to discuss the company's affairs. According to *Petsch v Kennedy* [1971] 1 NSWLR 494, a discussion between directors will not amount to an effective directors' meeting unless the directors are aware, before proceeding to business, that the occasion is to be a directors' meeting. In *Poliwka v Heven Holdings Pty Ltd* (1992) 10 ACLC 641, a meeting at a cafe of two persons who were the directors of a company was held not to be a meeting of directors.

Directors do not have to be physically present at the one place. For example, a directors' meeting can take place using teleconferencing or video-conferencing facilities. Section 248D permits a directors' meeting to be called or held using any technology consented to by all directors. The consent may be a standing one. A director may only withdraw her or his consent within a reasonable period before the meeting.

resolutions

[12.80] Directors make decisions at board meetings by passing resolutions. The replaceable rule in s 248G provides that a directors' resolution must be passed by a majority of the votes cast by directors entitled to vote on the resolution. The chair has a casting vote if necessary, in addition to any vote they have in their capacity as a director: s 248G(2).

Directors make decisions at board meetings by passing resolutions.

resolutions without meetings

[12.85] Directors may pass resolutions without a meeting being held by passing a circulating resolution. According to the replaceable rule in s 248A, a resolution of directors can be passed if all the directors entitled to vote on the resolution sign a document containing a statement that they are in favour of the resolution set out in the document. The resolution is passed when the last director signs: s 248A(3). Separate documents may be used for signing by directors if the wording of the resolution and statement is identical in each copy: s 248A(2).

Directors may pass resolutions without a meeting being held by passing a circulating resolution.

A single director proprietary company obviously does not have directors' meetings. Under s 248B, the sole director may pass a resolution by recording it and signing the record.

notice of board meetings

[12.90] As a general rule all directors must receive notice that a board meeting has been convened: *Petsch v Kennedy* [1971] 1 NSWLR 494. The replaceable rules and constitution (if any) specify the notice requirements. The replaceable rule in s 248C permits a directors' meeting to be called by a director giving reasonable notice individually to every other director. The frequency of board meetings is usually a matter for the directors to decide. However, it is common practice for companies to hold board meetings at regular fixed dates.

As a general rule all directors must receive notice that a board meeting has been convened.

Notice to a director may be dispensed with if the director is not "within reach of notice". This is determined by having regard to modern means of rapid communication. Notice of each meeting is not, however, necessary if the constitution or the directors set regular fixed meetings.

The amount of notice must be in accordance with the constitution (if any) or be fair and reasonable in light of the practice of the directors of the particular company: *Toole v Flexihire Pty Ltd* (1992) 10 ACLC 190.

In relation to the contents of notice of a board meeting, the requirements correspond to those applicable to notices of general meetings. As discussed in Chapter 14 below, a notice of meeting must contain a clear and full summary of the business to be dealt with. This is to enable recipients of notice to decide whether they should attend: *Devereaux Holdings Pty Ltd v Pelsart Resources NL* (1986) 4 ACLC 12. In *Jenashare Pty Ltd v Lemrib Pty Ltd* (1993) 11 ACLC 768, the proceedings of a board meeting were void because the notice of meeting made no mention of business considered by the meeting.

If notice of a board meeting is required but is not given, the meeting is irregular. The irregularity, however, does not prejudice outsiders. A person dealing with the company may presume that the internal rules of the company have been properly obeyed: s 129(1). This is discussed in Chapter 5 above.

quorum

A quorum is the minimum number of directors required for a valid meeting.

[12.95] A quorum is the minimum number of directors required for a valid meeting. The replaceable rules and constitution (if any) specify how many directors constitute a quorum for a valid board meeting. The replaceable rule in s 248F provides that the quorum is two directors unless the directors determine otherwise. The quorum must be present at all times during the meeting.

case note

In *Mancini v Mancini* (1999) 17 ACLC 1570, a divorced husband and wife were the only directors of three companies. The wife sought to remove the husband as a director at meetings of the directors of the companies, at which the husband was not present. The resolutions removing the director were invalid for a number of reasons, including the lack of a quorum. The constitutions of the companies provided for a quorum of two. This requirement was not satisfied by the presence of one director who also purported to act as a delegate of another.

The directors constituting the quorum must be entitled to vote on the matters discussed at board meetings. Thus, if the meeting is to consider whether the company should enter into a contract in which a particular director has an interest, that director is ineligible to vote and accordingly is not counted for the purpose of making up the quorum: *Re Austplat Minerals NL* (1990) 8 ACLC 720.

Section 195 prohibits a public company director from being present and voting at board meetings where a matter in which the director has a material personal interest is considered. The interested director does not count for the purpose of a quorum.

minutes

Proceedings and resolutions of directors' meetings (including meetings of a committee of directors) must be recorded in the company's minute book.

[12.100] Proceedings and resolutions of directors' meetings (including meetings of a committee of directors) must be recorded in the company's minute book: s 251A(1)(b). The minute book should also record circulating and other resolutions passed by directors without a meeting: s 251A(1)(d). The chair must sign the minutes within a reasonable time after the meeting: s 251A(2). A minute that is recorded and signed is evidence of the proceeding or resolution to which it relates, unless the contrary is proved: s 251A(6). Minutes of shareholders' meetings are discussed in Chapter 14 below.

committees of the board

Companies often delegate various board functions to committees of directors.

[12.105] Companies often delegate various board functions to committees of directors. Section 198D allows the directors to delegate any of their powers to a committee of directors. A committee must exercise the powers delegated to it in accordance with any directions of the board. The effect of the committee exercising a power in this way is the same as if the board exercised it. Delegations to a committee must be recorded in the company's minute book: s 251A.

The main reasons for the establishment of board committees are to ensure that important matters are given full attention, the workload of the board is effectively distributed and non-executive directors make effective contributions in areas requiring independent judgment. For this reason committees will often comprise at least a majority of independent non-executive directors. The most common committees are the audit committee, remuneration and nomination committees. In particular industries, it may be appropriate to establish committees which deal with important issues for that industry. This may include an environmental or risk management committee.

The most common committees are the audit committee, remuneration and nomination committees.

Audit committees are very common in listed companies and those included in the S&P/ASX All Ordinaries Index are required to have an audit committee by Listing Rule 12.7. An audit committee is regarded as an important part of corporate governance best practice as it enables the board to carry out its fundamental role to present a clear and accurate assessment of the company's financial position and to ensure that the audit is effective. An audit committee should deal directly and independently with the company's external and internal auditors. It should review areas of financial risk and systems of internal control that have been put in place. It should also consider the accounts policies and any significant transactions of an unusual nature.

Committees of the board play an important role in corporate governance. This is discussed in Chapter 13.1 below.

appointment of directors

[12.110] Section 201A requires a proprietary company to have at least one director and a public company must have three directors. The first directors are the people named as such in the application for registration of a company: s 120(1).

who may be appointed?

[12.115] Persons under the age of 18 years cannot be appointed as directors: s 201B(1). A director cannot be a body corporate but must be a natural person. A holding company that does not formally hold office as a director of its subsidiary may nevertheless be regarded as a "shadow" director for the purpose of owing duties to the subsidiary.

At least two directors of a public company must ordinarily reside in Australia. In the case of a proprietary company, at least one must reside in Australia: s 201A(1) and (2). A person may be a director of more than one company. The same person may be both a director and secretary of a company.

consent

[12.120] A director must consent in writing to being appointed to the position. The company must keep a copy of the consent but it does not have to be lodged with ASIC. The applicant for registration of a new company must have the consent when the application is lodged with ASIC: s 117(5). A company contravenes s 201D if a person does not give the company a signed consent to act as a director before being appointed.

lodgment of directors' names and details

[12.125] The application for registration of a new company must set out the name, address, date and place of birth of each person who consents in writing to become a director: s 117(2)(d) and (f). A company must lodge a notice with ASIC, in the prescribed form, of the personal details of new directors within 28 days after they are appointed: s 205B(1). The personal details include the director's name, address, date and place of birth: s 205B(3). A person's address is normally her or his usual residential address unless they are entitled to have an alternative residential address: s 205D. A company must also lodge notices with ASIC within 28 days if a director's personal details change or a person stops being a director: s 205B(4) and (5).

appointment by general meeting

[12.130] According to the replaceable rule in s 201G, subsequent appointments of directors may be made by a shareholders' resolution passed in general meeting. A person who has consented to be a candidate for election as a director cannot withdraw their candidacy between the commencement of the ballot and the declaration of the result: *Hedges v New South Wales Harness Racing Club Ltd* (1991) 9 ACLC 1025.

In some companies, such as joint ventures, certain shareholders have the power under the constitution to appoint a number of their nominees as directors. This ensures representation on the board commensurate with the extent of their shareholding or to represent their interests as shareholders.

In the case of public companies, where appointment of directors is by the general meeting, each director must be individually appointed by separate resolution: s 201E. More than one director may be appointed by a single resolution if the general meeting has first unanimously agreed to a resolution to that effect: s 201E(1). This section prevents the voting in of a director who is on a joint ticket with another who may have strong support. The appointment of a director in contravention of this section is void.

casual vacancies

[12.135] The replaceable rule in s 201H makes provision for the directors to appoint other directors to fill a casual vacancy. A casual vacancy is any vacancy in the office of director arising otherwise than by retirement at the end of the term. This occurs if a director dies, resigns or is otherwise unable to continue to act as a director. In the case of a proprietary company, the appointment of a director by the other directors must be confirmed by resolution of the shareholders within two months after the appointment is made: s 201H(2). If the company is a public company, the appointment by the directors must be confirmed by the members at the company's next AGM: s 201H(3).

appointment by sole director/shareholder

[12.140] A single director/shareholder of a proprietary company may appoint another director by recording the appointment and signing the record: s 201F.

If a sole director/shareholder of a proprietary company dies, becomes mentally incapable or becomes bankrupt, her or his personal representative or trustee may appoint a person as a director of the company: s 201F(2) and (3). The person so appointed holds that office as if he or she had been properly appointed in the usual way.

share qualification of directors

[12.145] The constitution of a company may require a director to hold a minimum number of shares in the company. This required number of shares is called the "director's share qualification". A share qualification serves two purposes. It provides directors with an added incentive to ensure the financial success of their company. It is also attractive to shareholders to see that directors are risking their own money as well as that of the members.

disqualification from managing a corporation

[12.150] Part 2D.6 of the *Corporations Act* contains a number of provisions under which a person may be disqualified from managing corporations.

Part 2D.6 of the *Corporations Act* contains a number of provisions under which a person may be disqualified from managing corporations.

Section 206B automatically disqualifies a person from managing corporations if the person is convicted of serious criminal offences or becomes bankrupt. The court also has the power to disqualify a person from managing corporations:

> **for contravention of civil penalty provision (s 206C);**
> **if the person was an officer of two or more failed companies (s 206D); or**
> **if the person repeatedly contravened the *Corporations Act*: s 206E.**

ASIC has the power to disqualify a person from managing corporations if the person was an officer of two or more companies that became insolvent: s 206F.

A person who is disqualified from managing corporations under Pt 2D.6 may only be appointed as a director of a company if the appointment is made with ASIC's permission under s 206F(5) or with court leave granted under s 206G: s 201B(2).

Section 1274AA requires ASIC to keep a register of persons disqualified from managing corporations. This register is available for public inspection.

purpose of disqualification provisions

[12.155] In *Rich v ASIC* [2004] 50 ACSR 242, the High Court held there are three main purposes of the disqualification provisions in the *Corporations Act*. Disqualification aims to:

> **protect a company's shareholders against further abuse;**
> **punish an offender; and**
> **generally deter improper behaviour.**

managing a corporation

[12.160] The meaning of "managing corporations" for the purposes of Pt 2D.6 is explained in s 206A. Under that provision, a person who is disqualified from managing corporations commits an offence if they:

> **make, or participate in making, decisions that affect the whole or a substantial part of the corporation's business; or**

> exercise the capacity to affect significantly the corporation's financial standing; or
> communicate instructions or wishes to the directors knowing that they are accustomed to act in accordance with those instructions or wishes or intending that the directors will act in accordance with those instructions or wishes.

case note

In *Commissioner for Corporate Affairs v Bracht* (1989) 7 ACLC 40, the Victorian Supreme Court held that a bankrupt participated in making decisions that affected a substantial part of the company's business and was therefore involved in managing a corporation under the predecessor of s 206B(3) in the following circumstances. The person negotiated credit facilities with a company's suppliers, a rent increase with a lessor of the factory leased to the company and held discussions with the company's bank manager regarding the obtaining of bank guarantees. "Managing a corporation" involves more than performing merely clerical or administrative acts. While it requires the exercise of some responsibilities, it need not involve the exercise of control.

automatic disqualification

convicted person

A person is automatically disqualified from managing corporations if they are convicted of certain criminal offences.

[12.165] Under s 206B(1), a person is automatically disqualified from managing corporations if they are convicted of certain criminal offences that:

> concern the making of decisions that affect the business of the corporation or concerns an act that has the capacity to affect significantly the corporation's financial standing (s 206B(1)(a)); or
> are a contravention of the *Corporations Act* that is punishable by imprisonment for a period greater than 12 months or other offence involving dishonesty that is punishable by imprisonment for at least three months: s 206B(1)(b).

If the person is imprisoned, the period of disqualification is five years from their release from prison and five years from the date of conviction if they did not serve a term of imprisonment: s 206B(2). ASIC may apply to the court before the expiration of the first year of automatic disqualification to extend the disqualification period for up to a further 15 years: s 206BA.

Section 206B(3) automatically disqualifies a person from managing corporations if he or she is an undischarged bankrupt.

undischarged bankrupt

[12.170] Section 206B(3) automatically disqualifies a person from managing corporations if he or she is an undischarged bankrupt. Similar automatic disqualification applies to persons who executed deeds of arrangement under Pt X of the *Bankruptcy Act* that have not been fully complied with or whose creditors accepted compositions and final payment has not been made: s 206B(4).

Section 206C(1) gives the court the power to disqualify a person from managing corporations where that person contravened a civil penalty provision.

disqualification by court order

contravention of civil penalty provision

[12.175] Section 206C(1) gives the court the power to disqualify a person from managing corporations where a court has declared under s 1317E that the person contravened a civil penalty provision.

Applications for a disqualification order under s 206C can only be made by ASIC. Disqualification under s 206C is further discussed in Chapter 13.6 below.

The court must be satisfied that a disqualification order is justified. In determining whether this is the case, s 206C(2) directs the court to have regard to the person's conduct in relation to the management, business or property of any corporation and any other matters considered appropriate.

Unlike automatic disqualification under s 206B, there is no fixed duration of the disqualification for contravention of a civil penalty provision. Under s 206C(1) disqualification is for a period that the court considers appropriate.

case note

McHugh J in *Rich v ASIC* (2004) 50 ACSR 242, commented that the approach of the courts in determining the period of disqualification is similar to that adopted in sentencing in criminal cases:

> Elements of retribution, deterrence, reformation and mitigation as well as the objective of the protection of the public inhere in the orders and periods of disqualification made under the legislation ... They take into account factors such as the size of any losses suffered by the corporation, its creditors and consumers, legislative objectives of personal and general deterrence, contrition on the part of the defendant, the gravity of the misconduct, the defendant's previous good character, prejudice to the defendant's business interests, personal hardship and the willingness of the defendant to render assistance to statutory authorities and administrators.

failed companies

[12.180] Section 206D(1) gives the court the power to disqualify a person from managing corporations for up to 20 years if, within the last seven years, the person has been an officer of two or more failed companies and the court is satisfied that the manner in which the corporation was managed was responsible for it failing. Applications for a disqualification order under s 206D can only be made by ASIC.

Section 206D(1) gives the court the power to disqualify a person from managing corporations if the person has been an officer of two or more failed companies.

Under s 206D(2), a corporation is regarded as having failed if, for example, it is compulsorily wound up on grounds of its insolvency or it enters voluntary administration and its creditors are unlikely to be fully paid.

The court must be satisfied that a disqualification order is justified. In determining whether this is the case, s 206D(3) directs the court to have regard to the person's conduct in relation to the management, business or property of any corporation and any other matters considered appropriate.

repeated contraventions of the Corporations Act

[12.185] Section 206E(1) gives the court the power to disqualify a person from managing corporations if the person has *at least twice*:

- been an officer of a body corporate that has contravened the *Corporations Act* and each time the person failed to take reasonable steps to prevent the contravention; or
- contravened the *Corporations Act* while he or she was an officer.

Applications for a disqualification order under s 206E can only be made by ASIC. The court must be satisfied that a disqualification order is justified. In determining whether this is the case, s 206E(2) directs the court to have regard to the person's conduct in relation to the management, business or property of any corporation and any other matters considered appropriate.

There is no fixed duration of the disqualification under s 206E. Disqualification is for a period that the court considers appropriate.

ASIC's power of disqualification

Section 206F gives ASIC the power to disqualify a person from managing corporations for up to five years.

[12.190] Section 206F gives ASIC the power to disqualify a person from managing corporations for up to five years. In order to exercise that power, ASIC must give the person a "show cause" notice requiring the person to demonstrate why they should not be disqualified and an opportunity to be heard on the question: s 206F(1)(b).

ASIC may give notice under s 206F to a person if within the last seven years he or she has been an officer of two or more companies that were wound up and whose liquidators lodged reports under s 533(1) about their inability to pay debts. As discussed in Chapter 25 below, s 533 requires liquidators to lodge reports with ASIC if the company is unable to pay its unsecured creditors more than 50 cents in the dollar.

If ASIC disqualifies a person from managing corporations under s 206F, it must serve a notice on the person advising her or him of the disqualification which takes effect from the time the notice is served.

While the grounds for disqualification under s 206F are similar to the court's power to disqualify a person under s 206D, s 206F disqualifications have a number of advantages for ASIC. ASIC must make an application to the court for an order to disqualify a person from managing corporations under s 206D and ASIC has the onus of satisfying the court that disqualification is justified. However, s 206F proceedings do not require ASIC to apply to the court for a disqualification order and the person served with the "show cause" notice has the onus of demonstrating why they should not be disqualified.

An order may be made against a person under s 206F without the need to show breaches of commercial morality or gross incompetence. It need only be shown that the director was the subject of two or more reports that were lodged by a liquidator under s 533: *Laycock v Forbes and ASC* (1997) 15 ACLC 1814.

In *Nicholas v Commissioner for Corporate Affairs* (1987) 5 ACLC 673, the Supreme Court of Victoria stated that the object of the section was to protect the public and past events were only relevant to indicate present fitness to act as a director. There are no penalties provided by the section for the past conduct.

case note

In *Cullen v Corporate Affairs Commission* (1989) 7 ACLC 121, the Supreme Court of New South Wales held that it was appropriate to disqualify a person under the predecessor of s 206F. The evidence established that a director of four failed companies had not met the standards that the community expects a director to reach. He did not remit group tax, failed to take appropriate action to minimise losses and intermingled the affairs of different companies. The period of disqualification was fixed for two years. The maximum period of five years is reserved for the worst cases involving dishonesty or a large number of defaults.

case note

A disqualification of two and a half years was imposed in *Delgona v ASC* (1995) 13 ACLC 246. Matters taken into account were that the transgressions were serious and the director showed a lack of understanding of the way a company should operate. This included a lack of knowledge of accounts requirements, failure to hand over books to the liquidator and lack of knowledge that a company of which the person was a director, was insolvent.

leave to manage

[12.195] Under s 206G(1), a person who is disqualified from managing corporations may apply to the court for leave to manage corporations or a particular corporation. The person must lodge a notice with ASIC at least 21 days before applying for court leave: s 206G(2). The order granting leave may be expressed to be subject to exceptions and conditions determined by the court. If leave is granted, the person may be appointed as a director or secretary of a company.

A person who is disqualified from managing corporations may apply to the court for leave to manage corporations or a particular corporation.

Where ASIC has disqualified a person from managing corporations, s 206F(5) allows ASIC to give the disqualified person written permission to manage a particular corporation or corporations. The permission may be expressed to be subject to exceptions and conditions determined by ASIC.

managing a corporation while disqualified

[12.200] A person who manages a corporation while disqualified commits an offence: s 206A(1). In addition, s 588Z enables a liquidator to apply to the court for an order that a person who contravened s 206A be made personally liable for a specified part of the company's liabilities: s 588Z. A person may be liable under this section if they managed a corporation within four years of the relation-back day, usually the day of filing the application for a winding up order. In exercising its discretion whether to impose liability on the disqualified person, the court should consider whether there is some relevant connection between the debts and liabilities of the company and the role of the person in the management of the company: *Nilant v Shenton* [2001] WASCA 421.

A person who manages a corporation while disqualified commits an offence.

termination of appointment as director

[12.205] A director may be appointed for such a term as is provided by the constitution. To meet the needs of particular companies, the constitution may allow directors to be appointed for life, for an indefinite term or for a certain prescribed term. If a director is appointed for a particular term, the appointment terminates at the expiration of that term.

A director may also resign from office. Under the replaceable rule in s 203A, a director may resign by giving a written notice of resignation to the company at its registered office.

removal of directors

[12.210] The rules that regulate removal of directors are different for public companies and proprietary companies. Removing proprietary company directors is regulated by the proprietary company's constitution or replaceable rules. The *Corporations Act* regulates removal of public company directors.

Removing proprietary company directors is regulated by the proprietary company's constitution or replaceable rules. The *Corporations Act* regulates removal of public company directors.

[12.215] proprietary company directors. Proprietary company shareholders can remove a director only if they are given that right in the replaceable rules or constitution (if any). While most proprietary company constitutions give shareholders this power, such a requirement is not compulsory. Indeed, some proprietary company constitutions may permit a director to be removed from office by a majority vote of the other directors. The proprietary company replaceable rule in s 203C permits the shareholders to remove a director and appoint another person by resolution.

The removal of directors contrary to a provision in the replaceable rules or constitution (if any) may result in the company breaching the statutory contract contained in s 140(1)(b) or an outside contract. This is discussed in Chapter 4 above.

Removing a public company director can only be done by resolution of the public company's shareholders.

[12.220] public company directors. Removing a public company director can only be done by resolution of the public company's shareholders even if there are contrary provisions in either the public company's constitution or a separate agreement between the director and the company: s 203D. The office of director becomes vacant on the passing of the resolution. This is not the case if the director was appointed to represent the interests of a particular class of shareholders or debenture-holders. In such a case, the resolution to remove the director does not take effect until a successor has been appointed: s 203D(1). This ensures that the particular class of shareholders or debenture-holders is represented by a director at all times.

Section 203D gives shareholders of public companies control over the composition of the board of directors. It prevents a majority of public company directors from removing a director unless the shareholders agree. A director of a public company cannot be removed by the other directors notwithstanding anything in the constitution or any agreement to that effect: s 203E.

A director of a public company cannot be removed by the other directors notwithstanding anything in the constitution or any agreement to that effect.

Notice of the intention to move the resolution removing a public company director must be given to the company at least two months before the meeting is to be held: s 203D(2). A copy of the notice must also be given to the director concerned who is given the right to put her or his case to members: s 203D(3) and (4). The director is entitled to put their case to members by giving the company a written statement for circulation to members and speaking to the motion at the meeting whether or not the director is a member of the company: s 203D(4). The director's statement does not have to be circulated to members if it is more than 1,000 words long or defamatory: s 203D(6).

It has been suggested that where a shareholders' meeting has been called to consider a resolution to remove a director, the board is placed in a caretaker role so that it is subject to restrictions on its powers to make fundamental or significant decisions, act outside the ordinary course of the company's business or alter the balance of voting power. This caretaker principle may extend beyond situations where there is a controlling shareholder and the decision of the general meeting is not in doubt: *Woonda Nominees v Chng* (2000) 18 ACLC 627.

Section 203D permits a public company in general meeting to remove all appointed directors, despite its reference to a singular director. This would not result in a breach of s 201A(2), which requires public companies to have at least three directors, where it is proposed to immediately replace the removed directors: *Claremont Petroleum NL v Indosuez Nominees Pty Ltd* (1986) 4 ACLC 315.

Where a director is removed prior to the expiry of their term, the question arises whether the director can restrain the company from so acting or obtain damages for wrongful dismissal. A director cannot prevent the company from exercising its right of removal. The equitable remedies of injunction and specific performance are not granted to enforce personal relations on unwilling parties: *Atlas Steels (Aust) Pty Ltd v Atlas Steels Ltd* (1948) 49 SR (NSW) 157.

payment and disclosure of remuneration and other benefits

fixing remuneration

[12.225] In Chapter 13 below, we discuss the fact that directors have a fiduciary relationship with their company. One consequence of this is that they are not entitled to receive any remuneration from the company unless this is specifically permitted by the shareholders, the replaceable rules or the company's constitution: *Re George Newman & Co* [1895] 1 Ch 674.

The replaceable rule in s 202A provides that the directors are to be paid the remuneration that the company determines by resolution. That replaceable rule also sanctions the payment of travelling and other expenses properly incurred by the directors in connection with the company's business.

It is common for constitutions to provide that the remuneration of a managing director or executive directors employed by the company will be fixed by the board of directors under a contract of employment. It is contrary to good corporate governance practice but not in breach of the law to provide in the constitution that the directors may fix their own remuneration: *Sali v SPC Ltd* (1991) 9 ACLC 1511. This practice may lead to a conflict of interests.

Corporate governance best practice in relation to remuneration is discussed in Chapter 13.1 below.

In *Guinness Plc v Saunders* (1990) 8 ACLC 3061, a director was paid by the company an amount approved by a member of a board committee. The House of Lords held that the company was entitled to return of the payment because, under the constitution, only the board could authorise special remuneration to a director. This could not be done by a committee of the board of directors or the chief executive.

The payment of excessive remuneration to directors may constitute oppressive or unfair conduct under s 232, especially where dividends are either not paid or reduced to a small amount. This may be oppressive or unfairly detrimental to a shareholder who is prevented from being a director. This is discussed in Chapter 17 below. In addition, s 588FE(6A) provides that unreasonable director-related transactions entered into during the four years prior to a company's winding are voidable. The company's liquidator can apply for a court order requiring repayment of these unreasonable amounts. An unreasonable director-related transaction includes unreasonable payments to directors or their close associates: s 588FDA. Such transactions are discussed in Chapter 25 below.

disclosure of remuneration and other benefits

[12.230] Shareholders have a right to know the remuneration and other benefits paid to directors. With this information they can better ascertain whether there are links between the company's performance and directors' pay. For this reason, the *Corporations Act* and accounting standards require details of directors' remuneration to be disclosed in the company's annual financial report. The amount and quality of the remuneration disclosures vary depending on whether the company is listed on a stock exchange or is unlisted. There are greater and more detailed remuneration disclosures for listed companies.

Shareholders have a right to know the remuneration and other benefits paid to directors.

unlisted companies

[12.235] AASB 124 *Related party disclosures* governs the remuneration disclosures that must be set out in the financial statements of unlisted companies. That accounting standard requires disclosure of the aggregate remuneration of a company's "key management personnel" broken down into the following five categories:

> **short-term employee benefits;**
> **post-employment benefits;**
> **other long-term benefits;**
> **termination benefits; and**
> **share-based benefits.**

The term "key management personnel" is defined as those persons having authority and responsibility for planning, directing and controlling the activities of the entity, directly or indirectly, including any director (whether executive or otherwise) of that entity.

listed companies

[12.240] Section 300A requires the directors' report of a listed company to disclose in a separate and clearly identified section of the report ("the remuneration report") the following information:

> **discussion of broad policy for determining the nature and amount of remuneration of directors, secretaries and senior managers of the company;**

- **discussion of the relationship between such policy and the company's performance; and**
- **prescribed details in relation to the nature and amount of remuneration of each director and each of the five named company executives receiving the highest remuneration.**

The disclosure of remuneration of directors and executives of disclosing entities such as listed companies is also governed by Accounting Standard AASB 1046: *Director and Executive Disclosures by Disclosing Entities.* Under that Accounting Standard, the financial statements of a listed company must disclose the remuneration of all directors and at least the five non-director executives with the greatest authority. The specified directors and executives must be individually named and each component of their remuneration disclosed. The components are in four categories:

- **primary;**
- **post-employment;**
- **equity compensation; and**
- **other benefits.**

The aggregate remuneration, as well as each component, must be disclosed together with comparative figures for the preceding reporting period. AASB 1046 also requires disclosure of the aggregate of loans to specified directors and executives and on an individual basis where indebtedness exceeds $100,000.

In May 2005, the government released for public comment an amendment to the *Corporations Regulations* that will exempt listed companies from making AASB 1046 disclosures in their annual financial reports on the condition that those disclosures are included in the annual directors' report and are audited. This change is intended to avoid duplication of the same remuneration disclosures in a listed company's remuneration report and its financial statements.

Section 300(1)(d) requires the company's annual directors' report to include details of options over unissued shares granted to any of the directors or any of the five most highly remunerated officers of the company as part of their remuneration. The annual reports of listed companies must also include details of contracts to which directors are a party or under which directors are entitled to a benefit: s 300(11).

Shareholders of listed companies have a greater capacity to express an opinion on remuneration policies.

As a result of the CLERP 9 amendments shareholders of listed companies have a greater capacity to express an opinion on, and hold directors accountable for, their remuneration policies by introducing a requirement that the chair allow reasonable opportunity for discussion by shareholders of the remuneration section of the directors' report at the AGM: s 250SA. In addition, a listed company must put and allow shareholders to vote on a non-binding resolution as to whether the shareholders adopt the remuneration report: s 250R(2). The notice of meeting must inform shareholders that such a resolution will be put: s 250L(2).

Several ASX Listing Rules affect executive remuneration in listed companies. Remuneration agreements may constitute price-sensitive information for the purposes of the continuous disclosure obligations set out in Listing Rule 3.1. The ASX has indicated that it regards the remuneration details of the contract of appointment of a new CEO as being information which a reasonable person could expect to have a material effect on the price of the company's securities and the key terms and conditions of the contract should be disclosed. The continuous disclosure regime is discussed in Chapter 15 below.

Listing Rule 4.10.3 requires companies to include in their annual report a statement disclosing their corporate governance practices and the extent to which the best practice recommendations of the Corporate Governance Council have been followed. The Council made several recommendations in relation to executive remuneration which are discussed in Chapter 13.1 below.

The issue of equity securities to directors generally requires member approval under Listing Rule 10.11 and there are restrictions on increasing directors' fees and conferring of termination benefits without shareholder approval under Listing Rules 10.17, 10.18 and 10.19.

other remuneration disclosures

[12.245] Shareholders with at least five per cent of the votes that may be cast at a general meeting or at least 100 members are given the right under s 202B to demand disclosure of the remuneration paid to each director of the company or its subsidiaries. The company must disclose all remuneration paid to the directors regardless of whether it is paid to the directors in their capacity as directors or another capacity. The statement must be audited, sent to the members and laid before the next general meeting: s 202B(2).

Certain other payments and financial benefits given to directors and related parties by public companies and their related entities are regulated by Pt 2E. These provisions require such financial benefits that could diminish or endanger the company's resources to be disclosed to and approved by the general meeting before they are given. These provisions are in addition to the fiduciary and statutory duties of officers. This is discussed in Chapter 13.3 below.

termination payments and benefits

[12.250] Termination payments to directors are a significant corporate governance issue. If termination payments are too high they can be regarded as a reward for failure and by their nature they do not link remuneration to performance. For this reason certain termination payments require shareholder approval.

Termination payments to directors are a significant corporate governance issue.

Sections 200A–200J regulate the circumstances in which shareholder approval is required before a benefit may be given to a person in connection with their retirement or termination from the board or managerial office in a company. Under s 200B(1), such payments cannot be made unless prior shareholder approval is obtained. The general meeting must approve the giving of the benefit on the basis of full disclosure as specified in s 200E. The value of the benefit must be stated or an estimate made of its value. The s 200B shareholder approval requirements apply to benefits given by company, an associate of a company, or a superannuation fund.

Certain benefits are excluded from the operation of s 200B(1) and therefore do not need shareholder approval. These are defined as "exempt benefits" in s 200F(1) and include payments or other benefits:

> **that are genuine payments by way of damages for breach of contract;**
> **given under an agreement before the director took up office, as part of the consideration for agreeing to hold office; and**
> **that are payments made in respect of leave of absence under an industrial award.**

Under s 200F(2), where a payment is made pursuant to one of the s 200F(1) exemptions, shareholder approval is still required if the payment exceeds an amount calculated in accordance with a formula specified in s 200F(3) or exceeds the value of one year's remuneration—whichever is the greatest.

Shareholder approval is also not required for genuine payments by way of pension or lump sum payments in respect of past services and superannuation payments up to a maximum amount determined by a formula set out in s 200G(3).

Section 200C also prohibits the giving of benefits to a director in connection with the transfer of the whole or any part of the undertaking or property of a company. This prohibition seeks to ensure that sales of a company's property are not improperly influenced by the making of payments to directors, relatives or associates. The prohibition is subject to shareholder approval; however, this approval does not relieve a director of any of the duties owed to the company in connection with the giving of the benefits: s 200E(2). Directors must act bona fide in the best interests of the company.

ASX Listing Rules also require a listed company to obtain shareholder approval for officers' termination benefits if the total of all officers' termination benefits would exceed five per cent of total share capital and reserves.

the company secretary

[12.255] A public company must have at least one secretary. If it has more secretaries, at least one of them must ordinarily reside in Australia: s 204A(2). A proprietary company is not required to have a secretary, but if it does have one or more secretaries, at least one of them must ordinarily reside in Australia: s 204A(1).

The term "secretary" is not defined in the *Corporations Act*. However, a secretary of a corporation is included within the s 9 definition of "officer" and is subject to the statutory duties of officers and employees in Ch 2D of the *Corporations Act*. This is discussed in Chapter 13 below.

appointment of secretaries

[12.260] The first secretary of a company is the person specified in the company's application for registration with her or his consent as the proposed company secretary: s 120.

The secretary's term of office and conditions of employment are usually determined by the board of directors.

Section 204D requires the subsequent secretaries to be appointed by the directors. The secretary's term of office and conditions of employment are usually determined by the board of directors. The replaceable rule in s 204F provides that a secretary holds office on the terms and conditions (including as to remuneration) that the directors determine.

A company contravenes s 204C if it is not given a signed consent to be secretary before the person is appointed. The company must keep the consent. A director of a company may also be its secretary.

Neither the *Corporations Act* nor the replaceable rules specify who has the power to dismiss the secretary, though this power is probably within the board's management powers. A secretary may normally resign on reasonable notice to the board of directors. In *Northside Developments Pty Ltd v Registrar-General* (1987) 5 ACLC 642, resignation notified to a de facto managing director without authority to accept it was held to be invalid.

Section 205B requires a company to lodge a notice of the personal details of the secretary within 28 days after they are appointed. This does not apply to the first secretary named in the application for registration of the company. Further notices must be lodged within 28 days of a change.

who may be appointed?

[12.265] Only an individual who is at least 18 years of age may be appointed as a secretary: s 204B(1). A person who is disqualified from managing corporations under Pt 2D.6 may only be appointed as a secretary with permission of either ASIC or the court under ss 206F and 206G. The secretary, or if there is more than one, each of them, must ordinarily reside in Australia: s 204A.

As is the case with directors, the *Corporations Act* does not require the secretary to have any special skills or qualifications. However, secretaries often have accounting or legal qualifications.

administrative role of secretary

[12.270] Secretaries were once regarded as persons of low status and authority in the company. This is no longer the present view. The company secretary, particularly in large companies, is now regarded as a position of importance with significant responsibilities and influence. Salmon LJ in *Panorama Developments (Guildford) Ltd v Fidelis Furnishing Fabrics Ltd* [1971] 2 QB 711, described a secretary as the company's chief administrative officer.

The company secretary, particularly in large companies, is regarded as the company's chief administrative officer.

A company secretary is now also seen as having customary authority to make contracts connected with the administration of the company. A secretary also has the power to be co-witness to the affixation of the company seal pursuant to a resolution of the board of directors. This is discussed in Chapter 5 above.

The nature of the secretary's duties varies from company to company. Responsibilities are imposed upon the secretary by the *Corporations Act*, the constitution or the appointing board of directors.

statutory responsibilities

[12.275] Section 188(1) makes a secretary of a company responsible for the following matters:

> **the s 142 requirement for the company to have a registered office;**
> **the s 145 requirement for a public company's registered office to be open to the public;**
> **the s 346C requirement to respond to an extract of particulars;**
> **the s 348D requirement to respond to a return of particulars;**
> **the lodgment of the various notices with ASIC under ss 146, 178A, 178B, 178C, 205B 254X and 349A; and**
> **the lodgment of financial reports with ASIC under s 319A(1).**

A secretary who contravenes the s 188(1) responsibilities commits a strict liability offence: s 188(2A). Section 188(3) gives the secretary a defence if the secretary took all reasonable steps to ensure that the company complied with the section.

If a proprietary company does not have a secretary, s 188(2) makes each of its directors responsible for ensuring compliance with the matters listed in s 188(1).

The secretary is also ordinarily responsible for keeping minutes of meetings of the general meeting and the board of directors.

defective appointments

[12.280] The *Corporations Act*, the replaceable rules and the company's constitution (if any) impose formal requirements with respect to the appointment and qualification of directors. These requirements are discussed above, para [12.110]. In some cases, directors or secretaries may act despite the fact that there is a technical defect in their appointment.

Sections 201M and 204E deal with the effectiveness of acts done by invalidly appointed directors and secretaries. According to those provisions, an act done by a director or secretary is effective even if their appointment is invalid because the company, the director or secretary did not comply with the company's constitution (if any) or a provision of the *Corporations Act*.

According to the notes to these sections, the kinds of acts that they validate are those that are only legally effective if the person doing them is either a director or secretary. For example, s 249C allows a director to call a meeting of the company's members. If the person who called the meeting was not validly appointed as a director, s 201M says the act of calling the meeting is still effective.

Sections 201M and 204E do not deal with the question whether an effective act by a director or secretary binds the company in its dealings with other people or makes the company liable to another person. Such matters are dealt with by ss 128–130 which contain rules about assumptions people are entitled to make when dealing with a company and its officers. These assumptions are discussed in Chapter 5 above.

---

bibliography ...

Agardy, P "Who wants to be a deemed director?" (2004) 12 Insolv LJ 104.

Ballinger, S "Women and the Public Company Director of Corporate Law" (1998) 9 Aust Jnl of Corp Law 81.

Brooks, A, Chalmers, Keryn, Oliver, J & Veljanovski, A "Issues Associated with Chief Executive Officer Remuneration: Shareholders' Perspectives" (1999) 17 C & SLJ 360.

Defina, A, Harris, T C & Ramsay, I M "What is Reasonable Remuneration for Corporate Officers?" (1994) 12 C & SLJ 341.

Demott, D "Shareholder Challenges to Executive Remuneration" (2000) 74 ALJ 576.

duPlessis, J "Some Peculiarities Regarding the Removal of Company Directors" (1999) 27 ABLR 6.

duPlessis, J & McConvill, J "Removal of Company Directors in a Climate of Corporate Collapses" (2003) 31 ABLR 251.

Fox, M & Walker, G "Boards of Directors and Board Committees in New Zealand: International Comparisons" (1998) 10 Bond LR 341.

Hill, J "'What Reward Have Ye?' Disclosure of Director and Executive Remuneration in Australia" (1996) 14 C & SLJ 232.

Middleton, T "The High Court's decision in Rich v ASIC [2004] HCA 42 and its potential impact upon ASIC's disqualification orders, banning orders and oral examinations" (2005) 23 C & SLJ 248.

revision questions on the material in this chapter ...

> Please see eQuiz at **http://www.thomson.com.au/academic** for multiple choice questions and answers.
> For further corporations law links and material please refer to the Lipton-Herzberg website at **http://www.lipton-herzberg.com.au**

chapter thirteen

corporate governance and duties of directors

overview

[13.0.05] The expression "corporate governance" is not a legal term and has no precise definition. The ASX Corporate Governance Council's *Principles of Good Corporate Governance and Best Practice Recommendations* provides an explanation of the concept.

> < **Corporate governance is the system by which companies are directed and managed. It influences how the objectives of the company are set and achieved, how risk is monitored and assessed, and how performance is optimised.** >

Corporate governance is regulated by a mix of legal regulation and self-regulation. The self-regulatory aspects of "best practice" corporate governance are discussed in Chapter 13.1 below.

Legal regulation is the core of corporate governance. The law, particularly by means of the fiduciary and *Corporations Law* duties of directors, in effect, imposes minimum corporate governance requirements. These legal requirements and the consequences of a breach of duty form the subject of Chapters 13.2 to 13.7

the nature of fiduciary duties

[13.0.10] Directors have a fiduciary relationship with their company and owe various fiduciary duties to it. Senior managers of a company are also regarded as having a similar fiduciary relationship. The relationship between directors and their company is one example of a fiduciary relationship. Other examples of fiduciary relationships are trustees and beneficiaries of the trust and partners with one another. In *Hospital Products Ltd v United States Surgical Corp* (1984) 156 CLR 41 Mason J described critical features of a fiduciary relationship in the following terms:

> < **The accepted fiduciary relationships are sometimes referred to as relationships of trust and confidence or confidential relations viz, trustee and beneficiary, agent and principal, solicitor and client, employee and employer, director and company, and partners. The critical feature of these relationships is that the fiduciary undertakes or agrees to act for or on behalf of or in the interests of another person in the exercise of a power or discretion which will affect the interests of that other person in a legal or practical sense. The relationship is therefore one which gives the fiduciary a special opportunity to exercise the power or discretion to the detriment of that other person who is accordingly vulnerable to abuse by the fiduciary of his position ...**
>
> **It is partly because the fiduciary's exercise of the power or discretion can adversely affect the interests of the person to whom the duty is owed and because the latter is at the mercy of the former that the fiduciary comes under a duty to exercise his power or discretion in the interests of the person to whom it is owed.** >

Directors and senior managers owe fiduciary duties to their company which includes a duty of loyalty.

Directors and senior managers owe fiduciary duties to their company which includes a duty of loyalty. The concept of "loyalty" has a number of different aspects. In *Bristol & West Building Society v Mothew* [1998], Ch 1 Millett LJ explained:

> < **The distinguishing obligation of a fiduciary is the obligation of loyalty. The principal is entitled to the singleminded loyalty of his fiduciary. This core liability has several facets. A fiduciary must act in good faith; he must not make a profit out of his trust; he must not place himself in a position where his duty and his interest may conflict; he may not act for his own benefit or for the benefit of a third person without the informed consent of his principal.** >

fiduciary and Corporations Act duties

[13.0.15] In the various parts of this Chapter we discuss the fiduciary duties of directors to:

> **act in good faith in the best interests of the company;**
> **exercise their powers for proper purposes;**
> **retain their discretionary powers; and**
> **avoid undisclosed conflicts of interest.**

Directors also owe a duty of care to their company.

The fiduciary duties stem from equitable principles developed through case law. The fiduciary duties are supplemented by various statutory duties contained in the *Corporations Act*. The most important of these duties are contained in Chapter 2D—ss 180–183—which largely restate but do not replace or override the fiduciary duties. The Chapter 2D duties have effect in addition to the fiduciary duties owed to a corporation: s 185.

The fiduciary duties are supplemented by various statutory duties which largely restate but do not replace or override the fiduciary duties.

In Chapter 13.2 below, we discuss the fiduciary duties of directors of a company to act in good faith in the best interests of the company and to exercise their powers for proper purposes. Section 181, which imposes concurrent statutory duties on directors and other officers, is also discussed in Chapter 13.2 below.

Directors' fiduciary duties to avoid undisclosed conflicts between their personal interests and the interests of their company are complemented by ss 182 and 183. These provisions prohibit improper use of position and improper use of information respectively. The fiduciary and statutory duties in relation to conflicts of interest and disclosure obligations are discussed in Chapter 13.3 below.

Directors also owe a duty at common law and under s 180(1) to exercise reasonable care, skill and diligence. This duty is concerned with questions such as whether a director exhibited appropriate levels of skill and judgment in matters such as making business decisions, gaining knowledge of the company's business and financial position, making inquiries where necessary and relying on others. This duty is discussed in Chapter 13.4.

Chapter 13.5 discusses the duties of directors of insolvent companies. When a company becomes insolvent or experiences financial difficulties, its best interests increasingly correspond to the interests of creditors rather than its shareholders. The interests of creditors become paramount because there is little likelihood that there will be company assets left beyond the claims of creditors. If the company goes into liquidation, the liquidator is conferred with wide powers to bring actions against directors on behalf of the company for the benefit of its creditors. Directors prejudice the interests of the company's creditors if they give away company assets or otherwise dispose of them for less than market value. Chapter 13.5 also considers directors' liability for insolvent trading. Section 588G imposes a statutory duty on directors to prevent their company incurring debts when there are reasonable grounds to suspect that it is insolvent.

The company has a range of remedies if directors breach their fiduciary duties. The various Chapter 2D duties and other statutory duties are designated civil penalty provisions. Under Pt 9.4B, ASIC may apply to the court for an order to impose one or more of the three types of civil penalty orders against directors and others who either contravene or are involved in a contravention of a civil penalty provision. Criminal liability can also be imposed if dishonesty was an element in a contravention of certain civil penalty provisions. The remedies and penalties for breach of duty are discussed in Chapter 13.6 below.

Chapter 13.7 discusses the power of shareholders to exonerate breaches of directors' duties. This sub-chapter also looks at directors' and officers' insurance.

who owes Corporations Act duties?

The obligations in Chapter 2D of the *Corporations Act* are imposed on both directors as well as officers of a corporation.

[13.0.20] The obligations in Chapter 2D of the *Corporations Act* are imposed on both directors as well as officers of a corporation. The s 9 definition of director is discussed in Chapter 12 above. Under that definition a director is a person who has been appointed to the position of director. However, a director is also a person who has not been validly appointed but acts in the position of director (a de facto director) as well as a person on whose instructions or wishes the directors of a company are accustomed to act (a shadow director).

The term "officer" is defined in s 9 to include a director and secretary. It also includes a person:

> **who makes or participates in making decisions that affect the whole or a substantial part of a company's business; or**
> **who has the capacity to affect significantly the company's financial standing; or**
> **in accordance with whose instructions or wishes the directors are accustomed to act.**

Certain other persons involved in managing a company in an insolvency context, such as a receiver, administrator and liquidator, are also included in the definition of officer.

case note

ASIC v Adler [2002] NSWSC 171 (the facts of which are set out in Chapter 13.2 below) provides an example of a person who was held to be an officer under the s 9 definition even though that person was not appointed to that position. In that case the court held that Adler was an officer of a wholly-owned HIH subsidiary even though Adler had not been appointed a director or officer of the subsidiary. Adler role as an HIH director and a member of HIH's investment committee indicated that he participated in making decisions that affected the whole or a substantial part of the subsidiary's business. Adler also had the capacity to affect significantly the subsidiary's financial standing because of his role on HIH's board and investment committee.

The CAMAC Discussion Paper, *Corporate Duties Below Board Level* (May 2005), considered whether the classes of persons subject to the *Corporations Act* duties should be broadened. It noted that it was unclear whether the following categories of persons who could be involved in corporate decision making were subject to the statutory duties:

> **middle-level managers;**
> **persons other than employees such as consultants and independent contractors; and**
> **group executives who may not have been appointed officers of a subsidiary.**

These issues were raised by Justice Owen in the HIH Royal Commission Report (April 2003). He recommended that the present definition of the persons upon whom duties are imposed should be repealed and replaced with a definition that:

< would focus on the function performed by the relevant person—not the classification of their legal relationship to the corporate entity... >

The CAMAC Discussion Paper, *Corporate Duties Below Board Level* (May 2005), is linked to the Lipton-Herzberg website at **http://www.lipton-herzberg.com.au/law_reform.htm**

The HIH Royal Commission Report is linked to the Lipton-Herzberg website at **http://www.lipton-herzberg.com.au/hih.htm**

chapter thirteen.one

corporate governance

key points ...

- Corporate governance describes the practices and procedures used by a board to ensure that it operates effectively and makes management accountable so that it acts in the interests of shareholders.
- The ASX Listing Rules require the annual report of a listed company to state the extent to which the company complied with the ASX Corporate Governance Council's Principles of Good Corporate Governance and Best Practice Recommendations.

[13.1.05] "Corporate governance" is not a legal term and is used to describe the rules and practices put in place within a company to align the interests of management with the interests of shareholders and other stakeholders. In large organisations, especially listed companies, these interests may diverge because of the separation of ownership and control and the different interests of managers and shareholders. Corporate governance deals with the wide range of checks and incentives which are put in place to ensure that managers act in the interests of shareholders.

As discussed in Chapter 12 above, the board of directors usually has a broad power of management with which shareholders are generally unable to interfere. In the case of large companies with complex businesses, it is not practicable for boards to engage in daily management. The board usually appoints a managing director or chief executive officer (CEO) with responsibility for conducting the business of the company. The law provides little guidance as to the specific roles of the board and management. Various principles of corporate governance practice have evolved which address the roles, functions and structures of the board and its relationship to management.

Interest in corporate governance has recently grown because of a combination of various factors that include dramatic corporate collapses in Australia and overseas, increasing statutory obligations imposed on companies and their directors as well as increasing shareholder activism, particularly by institutional investors.

what is corporate governance?

Corporate governance mechanisms aim to ensure that the board is accountable to stakeholders, especially shareholders, and that management is accountable to the board.

[13.1.10] "Corporate governance" has different meanings and is a term used in different contexts. In general terms it is concerned with how corporations are controlled and the accountability and control mechanisms to which they are subjected. These mechanisms aim to ensure that the board is accountable to stakeholders, especially shareholders, and that management is accountable to the board. Corporate governance therefore describes the system by which companies are directed and controlled. This involves determining how the objectives and policies of the company are set and achieved, how risk is monitored and assessed and how performance is optimised. It is helpful to an understanding of corporate governance to appreciate that it is concerned with how corporate entities are governed as distinct from the way the businesses within those entities are managed. Governance relates to where the company is going. Management is concerned with getting the company there. This distinction is central in determining the role and function of the board.

why is good corporate governance important?

[13.1.15] The Preamble of the OECD *Principles of Corporate Governance* (2004) stated why corporate governance was an important global issue.

> < **Good corporate governance should provide proper incentives for the board and management to pursue objectives that are in the interests of the company and its shareholders and should facilitate effective monitoring. The presence of an effective corporate governance system, within an individual company and across an economy as a whole, helps to provide a degree of confidence that is necessary for the proper functioning of a market economy. As a result, the cost of capital is lower and firms are encouraged to use resources more efficiently, thereby underpinning growth.** >

According to the ASX Corporate Governance Council *Principles of Good Corporate Governance and Best Practice Recommendations* March 2003:

> < **Good corporate governance structures encourage companies to create value (through entrepreneurism, innovation, development and exploration) and provide accountability and control systems commensurate with the risks involved.** >

The OECD Principles and the *Principles of Good Corporate Governance and Best Practice Recommendations* are linked to the Australian Corporate Governance website at **http://www.australian-corporate-governance.com.au/corp_gov_codes.htm**

the regulation of corporate governance

[13.1.20] The regulation of corporate governance is a mix of legal regulation and self-regulation. The main regulatory elements are:

The regulation of corporate governance is a mix of legal regulation and self-regulation.

- legal obligations largely imposed by the *Corporations Act* and fiduciary duties;
- requirements which have legislative recognition and the force of law such as the ASX Listing Rules and accounting and auditing standards; and
- codes of corporate governance best practice such as the ASX Corporate Governance Council's Principles of Good Corporate Governance and Best Practice Recommendations which are not mandatory but are voluntarily adopted.

ASIC has responsibility for legal regulation and enforcement while, for listed companies, the ASX plays a significant role in corporate governance regulation through the administration of its Listing Rules. The *Corporations Act* deals with a wide variety of corporate governance issues. These include:

- directors' duties (discussed in the following parts of Chapter 13);
- shareholders' meetings, rights and remedies (discussed in Chapters 14 and 17);
- the continuous and periodic disclosure obligations (discussed in Chapter 15);
- the requirement for and regulation of auditors (discussed in Chapter 16); and
- the regulation of takeovers (discussed in Chapter 18).

Legal regulation prescribes minimum standards which if breached may result in civil and, in worst cases, criminal liability. However, legal regulation alone has been found to be insufficient in promoting corporate governance best practice. For listed companies this is best achieved by self-regulation and disclosure of corporate governance practices to the market under the ASX Listing Rules.

The focus of corporate governance is usually on the role and function of the board of directors. A board's functions falls into two distinct and separate categories: *supervisory* and *strategic*. The separation of these roles has led to several recommended corporate governance practices such as separation of the roles of chair and CEO, the appointment of independent directors and the use of board committees—especially in the areas where management may act in its own interests and not in the interests of shareholders. The features of corporate governance best practice are discussed below.

ASX corporate governance listing rule

[13.1.25] Since 1996, the ASX Listing Rules have required listed companies to disclose in their annual reports the main corporate governance practices that they had in place during the year. The initial approach did not require specific corporate governance practices to be adopted by all listed companies nor were they required to comment upon why certain practices were not adopted. Rather, there was a list of indicative practices and it was up to individual companies to establish their own governance practices and disclose what they were to the market.

The aftermath of the Enron collapse and developments in the US and other international markets led to strong questioning of the "indicative" ASX approach. A widespread perception arose that the ASX was falling behind other stock exchanges which adopted a more assertive approach of endorsing best practice principles for their listed companies. This criticism prompted the ASX to establish the ASX Corporate Governance Council in August 2002. This body comprised representatives of 21 interested groups including financial institutions, director organisations, business interest groups and professional organisations.

The main aim of the Council was to develop a suitable framework for corporate governance which reflected international best practice and could provide a practical guide for listed companies, investors and other interested persons. In March 2003, the Council released its *Principles of Good Corporate Governance and Best Practice Recommendations* which set out 10 essential corporate governance principles with best practice recommendations on how these principles should be implemented. The *Principles of Good Corporate Governance and Best Practice Recommendations* are linked to the Australian Corporate Governance website at **http://www.australian-corporate-governance.com.au**

ASX Listing Rule 4.10.3 requires listed companies to disclose in their annual reports the extent to which they have followed the best practice recommendations in *Principles of Good Corporate Governance and Best Practice Recommendations.*

ASX Listing Rule 4.10.3 requires listed companies to disclose in their annual reports the extent to which they have followed the best practice recommendations in *Principles of Good Corporate Governance and Best Practice Recommendations.* While there is recognition of the varying needs of different companies depending on their size, complexity and other considerations, there is an obligation on companies to explain to investors why an alternative approach has been adopted where there has been departure from the Best Practice Recommendations—the "if not, why not?" approach. According to the ASX, this approach puts emphasis on disclosure rather than compliance with prescribed practices, thereby allowing for greater flexibility and adaptation to changes as corporate governance principles evolve.

corporate governance principles and best practice

[13.1.30] The ASX Corporate Governance Council *Principles of Good Corporate Governance and Best Practice Recommendations* set out the following 10 principles:

1. **lay solid foundations for management and oversight.** Recognise and publish the respective roles and responsibilities of board and management.
2. **structure the board to add value.** Have a board of an effective composition, size and commitment to adequately discharge its responsibilities and duties.
3. **promote ethical and responsible decision-making.** Actively promote ethical and responsible decision-making.
4. **safeguard integrity in financial reporting.** Have a structure to independently verify and safeguard the integrity of the company's financial reporting.
5. **make timely and balanced disclosure.** Promote timely and balanced disclosure of all material matters concerning the company.
6. **respect the rights of shareholders.** Respect the rights of shareholders and facilitate the effective exercise of those rights.
7. **recognise and manage risk.** Establish a sound system of risk oversight and management and internal control.
8. **encourage enhanced performance.** Fairly review and actively encourage enhanced board and management effectiveness.
9. **remunerate fairly and responsibly.** Ensure that the level and composition of remuneration is sufficient and reasonable and that its relationship to corporate and individual performance is defined.
10. **recognise the legitimate interests of stakeholders.** Recognise legal and other obligations to all legitimate stakeholders.

Each principle has recommendations setting out how best practice may be achieved. These recommendations are described as guidelines to be used by companies as a focus for re-examining their corporate governance practices and represent the most authoritative statement of Australian current best practice. The most important best practice recommendations include the following.

roles and functions of the board and management

[13.1.35] Recommendation 1.1 states that the board should adopt a formal board charter that details the board's functions and responsibilities and the division of roles and responsibilities between the board and management. This should include an explanation of the balance of responsibility between the chair and chief executive officer.

The board should adopt a formal board charter that details the board's functions and responsibilities and the division of roles and responsibilities between the board and management.

The responsibilities of the board usually include:

> **oversight of the company including its control and accountability systems;**
> **appointing and removing the CEO;**
> **input into and final approval of corporate strategy and performance objectives;**
> **reviewing and ratifying systems of risk management, internal compliance and control, codes of conduct and legal compliance;**

> **monitoring performance of senior management;**
> **approving and monitoring major capital transactions; and**
> **approving and monitoring financial and other reporting.**

Directors should clearly understand what is expected of them. This is best achieved by setting out these expectations in a formal letter of appointment containing key terms and conditions such as time commitment envisaged, expected committee work, requirement to disclose conflicts of interest, company policies such as those relating to trading in the company's shares and other securities, induction training and access to outside legal advice.

structure and composition of the board

A majority of the board should be independent directors.

[13.1.40] A majority of the board should be independent directors in the sense that they are non-executive directors, independent of management and not in any business or other relationship that could materially interfere with, or be reasonably perceived as interfering with, their independent judgment. In assessing the independence of directors, the Recommendations set out the criteria of independence which include: not being a substantial shareholder, employee or professional adviser within the last three years or supplier or customer of the company or a board member for a long period of time: Recommendation 2.1.

To facilitate directors bringing independent judgment to bear in decision-making, there should be an agreed procedure for directors to take independent professional advice if necessary, at the company's expense. Non-executive directors should consider the practice of regular sessions at which management are not present.

chair

[13.1.45] The responsibilities of the chair are to:

> **provide leadership for the board;**
> **ensure the efficient organisation of the board and conduct of its functions;**
> **brief all directors on issues arising at board meetings; and**
> **facilitate effective contributions by all directors and promote constructive and respectful relations among board members and between board and management.**

These responsibilities were expressed in greater detail by Austin J in *ASIC v Rich* [2003] NSWSC 85. He summarised the chair's responsibilities as being concerned with:

> **the general performance of the board;**
> **the flow of financial information to the board (including information about cash reserves, actual segment performance and key transactions);**
> **the establishment and maintenance of systems for information flow to the board;**
> **the employment of a finance director;**
> **the public announcement of information;**
> **the maintenance of cash reserves and group solvency; and**
> **making recommendations to the board as to prudent management of the group.**

The roles of chair and CEO should not be exercised by the same person.

These responsibilities are generally best carried out by an independent chair: Recommendation 2.2. The proper carrying out of these responsibilities is time-consuming so other positions held and their time commitments should be considered. The roles of chair and CEO should not be exercised by the same person: Recommendation 2.3. The separation of these roles makes it clear that there is a division of responsibility at the head of the company and the two roles are quite distinct. This increases accountability and recognises that to combine the roles in one person may give rise to an undesirable concentration of power and lead to conflicts of interest. In some cases, it may be necessary to remove the CEO and this may best be done where the roles are separated. The independence of the chair is compromised if the CEO goes on to become chair of the same company.

nomination to the board

[13.1.50] The board, especially of larger companies, should establish a nomination committee as an efficient means of determining board selection and appointment practices which best meet the needs of the company: Recommendation 2.4.

The board should establish a nomination committee.

The nomination committee should consist of a majority of independent directors, one of whom should be chair. Its role, responsibilities, structure and composition should be clearly set out in a charter.

The responsibilities of the nomination committee should include:

> **assessment of the necessary and desirable competencies of board members;**
> **review of board succession plans;**
> **evaluation of board performance; and**
> **recommendations for the appointment and removal of directors.**

The selection and appointment of new directors should involve a formal and transparent procedure including an evaluation of the skills, experience and expertise on the board and any possible gaps, before a candidate is recommended for appointment.

code of conduct

[13.1.55] The company should clarify the standards of ethical behaviour required of directors and senior executives and encourage observance of those standards. The company should publish its rules regarding directors' and executives' trading in the company's securities and associated derivatives.

The company should clarify the standards of ethical behaviour required of directors and senior executives and encourage observance of those standards.

A code of conduct should be established to guide directors and senior executives as to practices necessary to maintain confidence in the company's integrity and the responsibility and accountability of individuals for reporting and investigating reports of unethical practices: Recommendation 3.1.

audit committees

[13.1.60] The board should establish an audit committee for the purpose of focusing on verifying and safeguarding the integrity of the company's financial reporting and the independence of the external auditor: Recommendation 4.2. The existence of an independent audit committee is widely recognised as an important corporate governance practice.

The board should establish an audit committee.

All entities included in the S&P/ASX All Ordinaries Index (top 500 Australian listed companies) at the beginning of the entity's financial year are required to have an audit committee under ASX Listing Rule 12.7. The recommendations dealing with composition, operation and responsibilities of the audit committee must be complied with. The structure of the audit committee should consist of:

> **only non-executive directors;**
> **a majority of independent directors (as defined in Recommendation 2.1);**
> **an independent chair who is not chair of the board; and**
> **at least three members.**

It is vital that the audit committee exercises independent judgment. For this reason it has been suggested that best practice requires that only independent directors sit on the audit committee. The ASX Corporate Governance Council encourages companies to move towards this stance over the next three years.

The members of an audit committee should all be financially literate, able to read and understand financial statements. At least one member should possess financial expertise (either a qualified accountant or experienced financial professional). Some members should possess relevant industry understanding.

The audit committee should have a formal charter which clearly sets out the committee's role and responsibilities, composition, structure and membership requirements: Recommendation 4.4. To carry out its tasks, the committee should have necessary powers and resources such as access to management and both internal and external auditors without the presence of management and rights to seek further information and explanations.

The audit committee should meet as often as is necessary to carry out its role effectively. It should keep minutes of its meetings which should be included in the board papers for the next board meeting.

The audit committee should report to the board on all matters relevant to its role and responsibilities. The main issues will generally include:

> **assessment of whether external reporting is consistent with committee members' knowledge and is adequate for shareholders' needs;**
> **assessment of the management processes supporting external reporting;**
> **procedures for the appointment of the external auditor and rotation of external auditor partners;**
> **recommendations for appointment and removal of the auditor;**
> **assessment of the performance and independence of the external auditor and whether the committee is satisfied that the independence of the auditor has been maintained, especially having regard to non-audit services provided by the audit firm;**
> **assessment of the performance and objectivity of the internal audit function; and**
> **report on review of risk management and internal compliance and control systems. This matter is dealt with further in Principle 7.**

timely disclosure

The company must put in place policies and procedures to ensure compliance with ASX Listing Rule 3.1 dealing with continuous disclosure.

[13.1.65] The company must put in place policies and procedures to ensure compliance with ASX Listing Rule 3.1 dealing with continuous disclosure: Recommendation 5.1. This Listing Rule is aimed at ensuring the market has equal and timely access to material information concerning the company including information about the company's financial position, performance, ownership and governance. Information should be presented in a timely, factual, clear and balanced way disclosing both positive and negative news so as to enable investors to assess the impact of the information when making investment decisions. Continuous disclosure is discussed in Chapter 15 below.

Written policies and procedures should be established to ensure compliance with the Listing Rule and accountability for that compliance.

risk management and internal control

It is part of the board's role to oversee the establishment and implementation of the risk management system.

[13.1.70] It is part of the board's role to oversee the establishment and implementation of the risk management system and to review its effectiveness at least annually. Especially for larger companies, it may be more efficient for these policies to be established by an internal committee such as an audit committee or a risk management committee: Recommendation 7.1. This function includes analysing the effectiveness of the company's risk management and internal compliance and control system and the effectiveness of their implementation.

Risk management involves establishing and implementing a system for identifying, assessing, monitoring and managing material risk throughout the organisation. Larger companies in particular should have an internal audit function.

Recommendation 7.2 requires that the CEO and CFO should state in writing to the board that:

> **the statement regarding the integrity of the financial statements (best practice Recommendation 4.1) is based upon a sound system of risk management and internal compliance and control which implements board policies; and**
> **the company's risk management and internal compliance and control system is operating efficiently and effectively in all material respects.**

The purpose of this requirement is to encourage management accountability in the integrity of the company's financial reporting, risk management and internal control.

board performance evaluation

[13.1.75] The performance of the board, its committees, individual directors and senior executives should be regularly reviewed against both measurable and qualitative indicators. The processes for performance evaluation should be disclosed. The responsibility for evaluating board performance is generally with the nomination committee: Recommendation 8.1.

The performance of the board, its committees, individual directors and senior executives should be regularly reviewed.

remuneration

[13.1.80] As discussed in Chapter 12 above, the directors' report of listed companies is required to include a remuneration report in a separate section. The remuneration report must disclose the information specified under s 300A. This information includes broad policies for determining the nature and amounts of remuneration, the relationship of such policy and the company's performance and details of the nature and amount of each element of the remuneration packages of each director and the five highest paid officers of the company.

Companies should adopt remuneration policies which ensure that the level and composition of remuneration is sufficient and reasonable to attract quality directors and employees and is related in a defined way to corporate and individual performance: Recommendation 9.1.

Disclosure of the remuneration policy is a fundamental requirement for remuneration reporting. It should be transparent and readily understandable so as to enhance investor confidence by enabling investors to understand the costs and benefits of those policies and the link between remuneration paid to directors and key executives and corporate performance.

The underlying principle is that the level and form of remuneration should not be determined by the recipients but should be approved by independent persons acting in the interests of the shareholders. The board, particularly of larger companies, should establish a remuneration committee to focus on appropriate remuneration policies designed to enhance individual and corporate performance: Recommendation 9.2.

The board should establish a remuneration committee.

Membership of the remuneration committee should comprise a minimum of three, the majority being independent. The chair should be independent. The committee should have a formal charter that sets out its role and responsibilities, composition, structure and membership requirements.

Executive remuneration packages should involve a balance between fixed and incentive pay which reflect short- and long-term performance objectives appropriate to the company. A proportion of executive directors' remuneration should be structured so as to link rewards to corporate and individual performance.

The major issue which has emerged both in Australia and the US has been the practice of incorporating share and option schemes in executive remuneration packages. Until recently, such schemes were seen as desirable because they aligned the interests of executives with those of shareholders as they provided incentive to lift the share price which was in the shareholders' interests.

Recent corporate collapses in Australia and the US highlighted the dangers of providing executives large numbers of options without suitable performance hurdles. In several cases this has provided incentives for strategies which push up the share price in the short term but may disadvantage the longer term viability of the company and encouraged the use of fraudulent or misleading accounting practices to overstate profits. Stock options were also not expensed and therefore did not reduce stated profits. The adoption of standards issued by the International Accounting Standards Board will require Australian companies to value and expense share options. The widespread use of options, particularly in the US, was also criticised because it had the effect of diluting other shareholdings. The Corporate Governance Council Recommendations urge companies to voluntarily and fully disclose the existence and conditions of all share and option schemes and performance hurdles.

Non-executive directors' remuneration should be treated differently to that of executives:

- **their remuneration should normally be by way of fees and not involve participation in schemes designed for executive remuneration;**
- **they should not receive options or bonus payments; and**
- **they should not receive retirement benefits apart from statutory superannuation: Recommendation 9.3.**

The remuneration of non-executive directors should be fully disclosed to and approved by shareholders. Where there is a retirement benefit scheme for non-executive directors other than statutory superannuation, its existence and terms should be included in the corporate governance section of the annual report. Such schemes have been criticised because they provide incentive for non-executive directors to remain in office for long periods of time and discourage an independent approach in challenging board and management decisions.

pathways questions . . .

The following questions dealing with corporate governance may be answered after reading this chapter and considering the Internet resources found on the Australian Corporate Governance website at http://www.australian-corporate-governance.com.au

1. **Refer to the report of the HIH Royal Commission into the collapse of HIH, especially Vol 1, Pt 3. What deficiencies in the system of corporate governance of HIH became apparent to the Royal Commission? What lessons can be learned from this case study?**

2. **Refer to the APRA *Report into Irregular Currency Options Trading at the National Australia Bank* (NAB). What circumstances led to this report? To what extent was the board and its committees responsible for the resulting losses? Describe the corporate governance practices that contributed to the problems faced by the company. In the light of the APRA report and the ASX Corporate Governance Council's Principles and Recommendations, what steps should the NAB board take to prevent such losses in the future?**

3. **ASX Listing Rule 4.10.3 requires the annual report of a listed company to set the extent to which it complies with best corporate governance practices. Choose three listed company annual reports (try to include a large and a small company) which may be found by looking at the websites of companies. You can find many company websites by looking at the ASX**

top listed companies on the Lipton-Herzberg website at **http://www.lipton-herzberg.com.au/asx_listed_companies.htm** Compare the corporate governance statements contained in the annual reports that you have chosen in respect of the following matters:
(a) amount of detail contained;
(b) composition of the board;
(c) responsibilities and functions of the board;
(d) types of committees and their responsibilities; and
(e) any matter that is addressed in one annual report that is not mentioned in the others.

4. Provide an overview of the OECD Principles of Corporate Governance. To what extent have these principles been incorporated into Australian legislation or practice?

5. Select three codes or principles such as the ASX Corporate Governance Council Recommendations, the New York Stock Exchange Corporate Governance Standards and Combined Code (UK) and compile a comparative table showing:
(a) how each deals with particular issues; and
(b) highlighting any significant differences.

6. What is the role of institutional investors in corporate governance?

7. What are the main features of the *US Sarbanes-Oxley Act 2002* and how do these corporate governance requirements compare to requirements in Australia?

bibliography . . .

Ablen, D "Remunerating 'Fairly and Responsibly' The 'Principles of Good Corporate Governance and Best Practice Recommendations' of the ASX Corporate Governance Council" (2003) 25 Syd LR 555.

Acquaah-Gaisie, G "Towards more effective corporate governance mechanisms" (2005) 18 Aust Jnl of Corp Law 1.

Armstrong, A "Corporate governance standards: intangibles and their tangible value" (2004) 17 Aust Jnl of Corp Law 97.

Baxt, B "Corporate Governance—Is this the Answer to Corporate Failures?" (2003) 29 Mon ULR 234.

Bird, H "The Rise and Fall of the Independent Director" (1995) 5 Aust Jnl of Corp Law 235.

Brooks, A, Chalmers, Keryn, Oliver, J & Veljanovski, A "Issues Associated with Chief Executive Officer Remuneration: Shareholders' Perspectives" (1999) 17 C & SLJ 360.

Calleja, N "To Delegate or not to Delegate: Board Committees and Corporate Performance in Australia's Top 100 Companies" (1999) 21 Syd LR 5.

Carson, E "The Development of Board Sub-Committees" (2000) 18 C & SLJ 415.

Cassidy, A & Chapple, L "Australia's Corporate Disclosure Regime: Lessons from the US Model" (2003) 15 Aust Jnl of Corp Law 81.

Cassidy, D "The Role of Monitoring and Morality In Corporate Law: A Criticism" (1997) 7 Aust Jnl of Corp Law 343.

Chang, M, Hillman, R & Watson, I "Are corporate governance mechanisms effective in reducing insider trading profits?" (2005) 23 C & SLJ 165.

Clarke, A "The Relative Position of Employees in the Corporate Governance Context: An International Comparison" (2004) 32 ABLR 111.

Clarke, A "The Business Judgment Rule: Good Corporate Governance or Not?" (2000) 12 Aust Jnl of Corp Law 85.

Clarke, A "Australia's corporate governance: Balancing historic, regional and free trade paradigms" (2005) 18 Aust Jnl of Corp Law 103.

Clarke, A "The relative position of employees in corporate governance context: an international comparison" (2004) 32 ABLR 111.

Clyne, S "Modern Corporate Governance" (2000) 11 Aust Jnl of Corp Law 276.

Corbett, A "A Proposal for a More Responsive Approach to the Regulation of Corporate Governance" (1995) 23 FL Rev 277.

Corfield, A "The Stakeholder Theory and its Future in Australian Corporate Governance: A Preliminary Analysis" (1998) 10 Bond LR 213.

Demott, D "Shareholder Challenges to Executive Remuneration" (2000) 74 ALJ 576.

Dignam, A & Galanis, M "Australia Inside-Out: The Corporate Governance System of the Australian Listed Market Corporate Law and Labour Law" Centre for Corporate Law & Securities Regulation, Corporate Law Research Papers Website **http://cclsr.law.unimelb.edu.au/research-papers/index.html**

Dignam A & Galanis, M "Australia inside-out: the corporate governance system of the Australian listed market" (2004) 28 Melbourne University Law Review 623.

Duffy, M "Shareholder Democracy or Shareholder Plutocracy? Corporate Governance and the Plight of Small Shareholders" (2002) 25 UNSWLJ 434.

DuPlessis, J "Reverberations after HIH and other Recent Australian Corporate Collapses: The Role of ASIC" (2003) 15 Aust Jnl of Corp Law 225.

Farrar, J "A Brief Thematic History of Corporate Governance" (1999) 11 Bond LR 259.

Farrer, J "In Pursuit of an Appropriate Theoretical Perspective and Methodology for Comparative Corporate Governance" (2001) 13 Aust Jnl of Corp Law 1.

Fong, K, Ramsay, I & Stapledon, G P "Corporate Governance: The Perspective of Australian Institutional Shareholders" (2000) 18 C & SLJ 110.

Fox, M & Walker, G "Boards of Directors and Board Committees in New Zealand: International Comparisons" (1998) 10 Bond LR 341.

Fridman, S "Conflict of Interest, Accountability and Corporate Governance: The Case of the IOC and SOCOG" (1999) 22 UNSWLJ 781.

Grantham, R "The governance of government owned corporations" (2005) C & SLJ 181.

Hill, J "Deconstructing Sunbeam—Contemporary Issues in Corporate Governance" (1999) 17 C & SLJ 288.

Keeves, J S "Directors' Duties—ASIC v Rich—Landmark or Beacon?" (2004) 22 C & SLJ 181.

Lessing, J "Institutional Investors: Will We See Greater Cooperation Between Them Regarding Corporate Governance?" (1998) 10 Bond LR 376.

Loke, A "A (Behavioural) Law and Economics Approach to Reforming Asian Corporate Governance" (2002) 20 C & SLJ 252.

Luck, K "The End of History for Corporate Governance or Just Another Moment in Time" (2001) 19 C & SLJ 305.

Lumsden, A "Audit Committee Membership and its Consequences" (2002) 20 C & SLJ 340.

Lumsden, A "The Role and Responsibilities of Directors on Board Sub-Committees" Centre for Corporate Law & Securities Regulation, Corporate Law Research Papers Website **http://cclsr.law.unimelb.edu.au/research-papers/index.html**

McConvill, J & Bingham, J "Comply or Comply: The Illusion of Voluntary Corporate Governance in Australia" (2004) 22 C & SLJ 208.

McConvill, M & Bagaric, M "Towards mandatory shareholder committees in Australian companies" (2004) 28 *Melbourne University Law Review* 125.

McMurray, S "Corporate Compliance with Human Rights" (2003) 31 ABLR 265.

Mitchell, R, O'Donnell, A & Ramsay, I "Shareholder Value and Employee Interests: Intersections Between Corporate Governance, Corporate Law and Labour Law" Centre for Corporate Law & Securities Regulation, Corporate Law Research Papers Website **http://cclsr.law.unimelb.edu.au/research-papers/index.html**

Nicoll, G "Recognition of Proprietorial Interests in Management and Corporate Governance" (1996) 7 Aust Jnl of Corp Law 80.

Quin, M "The Unchangeables: Director and Executive Remuneration Disclosure in Australia" (1999) 10 Aust Jnl of Corp Law 89.

Stapledon, G "Directors' Duties and Corporate Governance: Should Institutional Shareholders be Required to Exercise Their Voting Rights?" (1999) 17 C & SLJ 332.

Stapledon, G "Disincentives to Activism by Institutional Investors in Listed Companies" (1996) 18 Syd LR 152.

Stapledon, G & Lawrence, J "Board Composition Structure and Independence in Australia's Listed Companies" (1997) 21 MULR 150.

Svoboda, K "Corporate Governance Issues Arising from the 1998-1999 AMP-GIO Takeover" (2000) 18 C & SLJ 395.

Tomasic, R "Good Corporate Governance: The International Challenge" (2000) 12 Aust Jnl Corp Law 142.

Veasey, E N "The Defining Tension in Corporate Governance In America" (1997) 7 Aust Jnl of Corp Law 143.

Von Nessen, P "Corporate Governance in Australia: Converging with International Developments" (2003) 15 Aust Jnl of Corp Law 189.

Wei, Y "A Chinese Perspective on Corporate Governance" (1998) 10 Bond LR 363.

revision questions on the material in this chapter ...

> Please see eQuiz at **http://www.thomson.com.au/academic** for multiple choice questions and answers.

> For further corporations law links and material please refer to the Lipton-Herzberg website at **http://www.lipton-herzberg.com.au**

chapter thirteen.two

good faith and proper purpose

key points ...

- Directors are under both a *fiduciary* and *statutory* duty to act in good faith and in the best interests of the company.
- The duty to act in good faith in the best interests of the company means that directors must act in the interests of the general body of shareholders. This includes an obligation to act fairly across different classes of shareholders.
- The duty to act in the best interests of the company may cause difficulties for nominee directors and directors of a company that is a member of a larger corporate group. In both cases it may be difficult for a director to reconcile acting in the best interests of the company with acting in the best interests of the nominee director's appointor.
- Directors have a fiduciary and statutory duty to exercise their powers for a proper purpose and not for the purpose of conferring an advantage on themselves or someone else. This duty may be breached where directors issue shares for the purpose of preventing a takeover or altering the balance of power among shareholders.
- Directors who have mixed purposes (proper and improper) for exercising a particular power will breach their duty if the motivating purpose was improper.
- Shareholders have the power to ratify improper exercises of power by directors.

duty to act in good faith in the best interests of the company

Directors are under a fiduciary duty to act in good faith and in the best interests of the company.

[13.2.05] Directors are under a fiduciary duty to act in good faith and in the best interests of the company. Section 181(1)(a), which requires a director or other officer to exercise their powers and discharge their duties in good faith and in the best interests of the corporation, sets out the same requirements as the fiduciary duty. Section 181(1)(a) is discussed below, para [13.2.100].

The good faith aspect of both the fiduciary and statutory duties requires directors to genuinely believe that they are acting in the best interests of the company. Directors will not comply with their duty merely because they have an honest belief that their actions are in the best interests of the company. The duty also has an objective element. It is breached if a director acts in a way that no reasonable director would have considered to be in the best interests of the company: *ASIC v Adler* [2002] NSWSC 171. Bowen LJ explained the reason for this in *Hutton v West Cork Railway Co* (1883) 23 Ch D 654:

> **< Bona fides (good faith) cannot be the sole test, otherwise you might have a lunatic conducting the affairs of the company, and paying its money with both hands in a manner perfectly bona fide yet perfectly irrational. >**

Directors are presumed to have acted in good faith and in the best interests of their company and those persons alleging a breach of duty bear the onus of proving that this is in fact not the case.

best interests of the company

present and future shareholders

[13.2.10] A difficult question arises as to what is meant by the phrase "the best interests of the company". As discussed in Chapter 2 above, a company is regarded as a legal entity separate and distinct from its shareholders. Despite this, the courts take the view that the duty to act in good faith in the best interests of the company means that the directors must act in the best interests of the shareholders as a collective group. Evershed MR, in *Greenhalgh v Arderne Cinemas Ltd* [1951] Ch 286, stated:

The duty to act in good faith in the best interests of the company means that the directors must act in the best interests of the shareholders as a collective group.

> < **[T]he phrase, "the company as a whole", does not (at any rate in such a case as the present) mean the company as a commercial entity distinct from the corporators: it means the corporators as a general body.** >

As long as the company is solvent, the interests of the company are the interests of its shareholders. However, as discussed in Chapter 13.5 below, where the company is in financial difficulties, the company's creditors' interests become increasingly important.

In *Darvall v North Sydney Brick & Tile Co Ltd* (1988) 6 ACLC 154, Hodgson J, at first instance, considered that directors should have regard to both the interests of present and future shareholders as well as the interests of the company as a commercial entity. He stated:

> < **In my view, it is proper to have regard to the interests of the members of the company, as well as having regard to the interests of the company as a commercial entity. Indeed, it is proper also to have regard to the interests of creditors of the company. I think it is proper to have regard to the interests of present and future members of the company, on the footing that it would be continued as a going concern.** >

Hodgson J also held that directors may act in what they consider to be the best interests of the company as a commercial entity even though this may not be in the short-term interests of shareholders.

In most situations the interests of the company as a commercial entity and the interests of its shareholders coincide. As a general rule, shareholders' interests are paramount. Mahoney JA, in the Court of Appeal of the Supreme Court of New South Wales in *Darvall v North Sydney Brick & Tile Co Ltd* (1989) 16 NSWLR 260, asserted that a company has a legitimate interest in matters which extend beyond the company's business and the security of its assets. These may include who its shareholders are, the price of its shares and achieving a proper understanding of the company's business in the investment community.

individual shareholders

[13.2.15] Directors' duty to act in good faith in the best interests of the shareholders does not mean that they owe duties to particular shareholders.

Directors' duty to act in good faith in the best interests of the shareholders does not mean that they owe duties to particular shareholders.

case note

In *Percival v Wright* [1902] 2 Ch 421, a director of a company was approached by a shareholder wishing to sell his shares. The director agreed to buy them but did not disclose that there was an impending takeover bid at a substantially higher price. The shareholder afterwards sought to rescind the contract for the sale of his shares on the basis that the director breached his fiduciary duty to him by failing to disclose the information concerning the impending takeover even though it did not eventuate. The court rejected the shareholder's claim. It held that directors only owe fiduciary duties to the company as a whole and not to individual shareholders.

In some special circumstances, a director may owe fiduciary duties to an individual shareholder. For such circumstances to arise, the director must have been in direct and close contact with the individual member so that the director caused the member to act in a certain way which turned out to be detrimental to them: *Peskin v Anderson* (2001) 19 ACLC 3001.

case note

Such special circumstances arose in the New Zealand case *Coleman v Myers* [1977] 2 NZLR 225. The managing director of a family company arranged for the company to be taken over at an under-value by a new company controlled by him. It was held that the managing director breached fiduciary duties owed to the minority shareholders of the family company. The managing director failed to disclose material information concerning his potential profits and misled the shareholders as to the true value of the company's assets. Woodhouse J noted the factors that would give rise to a fiduciary duty to individual shareholders:

> < They include, I think, dependence upon information and advice, the existence of a relationship of confidence, the significance of some particular transaction for the parties and, of course, the extent of any positive action taken by or on behalf of the director or directors to promote it. >

case note

The New South Wales Court of Appeal held that there were special circumstances in *Brunninghausen v Glavanics* (1999) 17 ACLC 1247 which justified a departure from the general rule that a director does not owe a fiduciary duty to act in the best interests of particular shareholders. In that case, the company had two shareholders who were also its only directors. Glavanics, the minority shareholder, despite being a director, was not involved in the company's management and had no access to its financial records. After a falling out, Brunninghausen, the majority shareholder and managing director, entered into negotiations to buy Glavanics' shares. However, unknown to Glavanics, another person approached Brunninghausen offering to buy all the shares in the company. Eventually Glavanics agreed to sell his shares to Brunninghausen, who subsequently sold all the shares to the third party for a higher price. When Glavanics became aware of this, he sued Brunninghausen for breach of fiduciary duty and claimed equitable compensation.

The Court of Appeal held that while a director's fiduciary duties were generally owed to the company and not individual shareholders, the nature of a transaction may give rise to a director owing fiduciary duties to a shareholder. Brunninghausen possessed special knowledge acquired while managing the company which provided an opportunity to sell the company's business advantageously. This opportunity belonged to the company. Handley JA said:

> < A fiduciary duty owed by directors to the shareholders where there are negotiations for a takeover or an acquisition of the company's undertaking would require the directors to loyally promote the joint interests of all shareholders. >

beneficiaries of a trust

[13.2.20] Where a company acts as a trustee, directors of the trustee company may owe a duty to act in the best interests of the beneficiaries of the trust.

case note

In *Hurley v BGH Nominees Pty Ltd (No 2)* (1984) 2 ACLC 497, the South Australian Supreme Court considered whether the directors of a trustee company breached their duties to beneficiaries. The trust carried on business at leased premises. It was argued that the directors breached their duty by acquiring the freehold of the premises for themselves. Walters J approved of the decision in *Coleman v Myers* and held that it was incorrect to say that directors of a company are entitled in all circumstances to act as though they owe no duty to individual shareholders. In appropriate circumstances, directors of companies that act as trustees owe duties not only to individual shareholders but also to the beneficiaries of the trusts.

different classes of shareholders

[13.2.25] The task of ascertaining what constitutes the interests of the company as a whole is particularly difficult where its shares are divided into different classes. In such a case, the exercise of a power by the directors may benefit one class to the detriment of others.

In *Mills v Mills* (1938) 60 CLR 150, Latham CJ held that the test of whether a director is acting in the interests of the company is not appropriate in such circumstances. Rather, it involves the question of what is fair as between the classes of shareholders. He also stressed that while directors are required to act in the interests of the company, the law does not require them to "live in an unreal region of detached altruism". If they are also shareholders, they cannot reasonably be expected to disregard their own interests.

As discussed in Chapter 17 below, s 232 enables a member to obtain a remedy if the court is of the opinion that a resolution of a class of members was contrary to the interests of the members as a whole, oppressive or unfairly prejudicial or unfairly discriminatory. This may apply where directors exercise their voting rights as holders of a class of shares in a way that is detrimental to holders of other classes of shares.

nominee directors

[13.2.30] Nominee directors are appointed to represent sectional interests. They are often appointed to represent the interests of individual shareholders in a joint venture company or they may also be appointed to represent a majority shareholder, a class of shareholders, creditors, a holding company, employees or a government body. The position of directors within groups of companies is discussed below, para [13.2.35]. Typically, nominee directors are expected to act in the interests of their appointors rather than the company's shareholders generally.

Although nominee directors play an important role in a wide variety of situations, the inherent difficulties in determining the extent of nominee directors' fiduciary duties have not been fully resolved by the courts. The duties of nominee directors are discussed by R P Austin (now Justice Austin of the New South Wales Supreme Court) in an article published in *Bond Law Review*, "Representatives and Fiduciary Responsibilities–Notes on Nominee Directorships and Like Arrangements" (1995) 7 Bond LR 19. This article is linked to the Lipton-Herzberg Directors' Duties Good Faith and Proper Purposes Pathway at **http://www.lipton-herzberg.com.au/secure/pathways-directors-duties-good-faith-and-proper-purposes.html**

The fiduciary and statutory duties to act in good faith in the best interests of the company as a whole requires directors to act in the best interests of the shareholders as a collective group. However, difficulties arise in situations where a nominee director is appointed to represent the interests of particular persons. In such cases there may be problems in reconciling the nominee director's duty to act in the interests of the appointor and the director's duty to act in the interests of the company as a whole.

Nominee directors are permitted to act in the interests of their appointor provided that they honestly and reasonably believe that there is no conflict between the interests of their appointor and the interests of the company.

Nominee directors are permitted to act in the interests of their appointor provided that they honestly and reasonably believe that there is no conflict between the interests of their appointor and the interests of the company.

case note

For example, in *Re Broadcasting Station 2GB Pty Ltd* [1964–1965] NSWR 1648, a newspaper publishing company, Fairfax, gained control of Broadcasting Station 2GB Pty Ltd, a company that owned a radio station. The newspaper publishing company appointed a number of directors to the board of 2GB to represent its interests. One of the independent directors, who was also a shareholder, sought a remedy under a predecessor of s 232 alleging that the affairs of 2GB were being conducted in an oppressive manner. The alleged oppression concerned the appointment of the nominees to act solely in the interests of Fairfax and their conduct in withholding information from fellow directors concerning negotiations carried on by Fairfax in seeking the continuation of the radio station's broadcasting licence.

The court held that there was no oppressive conduct. Jacobs J found that the Fairfax nominee directors would be likely to act, and were expected by Fairfax to act, in accordance with its wishes without close personal analysis of the issues. However, there was no evidence that the nominee directors believed that the interests of Fairfax diverged from the interests of the company as a whole. While nominee directors may breach their duties if they act in a way that is not in the best interests of the company, this conclusion is not lightly reached. It is unrealistic to expect directors to approach each company problem with a completely open mind. This would put a nominee director in an impossible position.

A company's constitution or a shareholders' agreement may specifically permit the appointment of nominee directors to represent the interests of a particular shareholder or creditor.

case note

In *Levin v Clark* [1962] NSWR 686, Levin purchased the majority shareholding in a company and simultaneously mortgaged the shares to the vendor to secure payment of the purchase price. The company's constitution named Clark and Rappaport as the governing directors with wide powers.

They were appointed to represent the interests of the vendor and mortgagee. Under the sale agreement the constitution was amended so as to allow Clark and Rappaport to exercise their powers as governing directors only in the event of default in payment of the loan to Levin. In this way they were able to protect the interests of the mortgagee/vendor. Levin defaulted and Clark and Rappaport proceeded to exercise their powers to enforce the mortgage. Levin challenged this exercise of power on the basis that as governing directors, Clark and Rappaport's primary obligation was to the company and not to the mortgagee. The court held that the extent of the fiduciary duties of directors depends on the circumstances and these may include the fact that the constitution provided for the appointment of nominee directors. In this case it was implied that the nominee directors, Clark and

Rappaport, were expected to protect the mortgagee's interests in the event of default by the mortgagor. The fiduciary duties of Clark and Rappaport took into account the agreement of the shareholders even though this was not expressly stated.

Nominee directors breach their duty where there is a clear conflict between the interests of the company and their appointor and the company's interests are sacrificed. The duties of nominee directors of non-wholly owned subsidiaries was considered by the English Court of Appeal in *Scottish Co-operative Wholesale Soc Ltd v Meyer* [1958] 3 All ER 66. Lord Denning held that where the interests of a holding company and the subsidiary's minority shareholders do not coincide, nominee directors appointed by the holding company are bound to put the interests of the subsidiary's shareholders ahead of the interests of the majority shareholder.

Nominee directors breach their duty where there is a clear conflict between the interests of the company and their appointor and the company's interests are sacrificed.

case note

In *Scottish Co-operative Wholesale Soc Ltd v Meyer* [1958] 3 All ER 66, the company was a subsidiary of the Scottish Co-operative Wholesale Society. Minority shareholders held slightly less than half the issued shares in the subsidiary. Three directors of the subsidiary were appointed as nominees of the holding company and the other two represented the minority shareholders. The subsidiary operated a profitable textile manufacturing business using yarn purchased from its holding company. After a time, the Scottish Co-operative Wholesale Society decided to operate its own textile manufacturing business and stopped supplying yarn to its subsidiary. As a result, the subsidiary's activities were severely curtailed. The action of the holding company had the effect of preventing the subsidiary's minority shareholders from participating in the profits of the textile manufacturing business.

It was held that the subsidiary's directors appointed by the holding company acted contrary to the interests of the shareholders as a whole by failing to defend it from the actions of the holding company. Their failure to act, coupled with the holding company's conduct, was regarded as oppressive under the English equivalent of s 232. This is discussed in Chapter 17 below.

This approach was also taken by Street J in *Bennetts v Board of Fire Commissioners of New South Wales* (1967) 87 WN (Pt 1) (NSW) 307, where he stated categorically that a nominee director must put the interests of the company ahead of the interests of the appointor whenever a conflict arises.

company groups

[13.2.35] A holding company will usually appoint its nominees as directors of subsidiaries. In practice, nominee directors on the board of a subsidiary are required by the holding company to act in the best interests of the group of companies. In most cases, the interests of the holding company and the interests of a wholly-owned subsidiary will generally correspond. However, if there is a conflict between the interests of a subsidiary and the group, nominee directors must act in the subsidiary's best interests and not in the interests of the group as a whole: *Walker v Wimborne* (1976) 137 CLR 1.

If there is a conflict between the interests of a subsidiary and the group, nominee directors must act in the subsidiary's best interests and not in the interests of the group as a whole.

A holding company's nominees on the board of a non-wholly owned subsidiary are in a more delicate position. They must balance the interests of the group with the interests of the subsidiary's shareholders generally, including the minority shareholders. In most situations, the interests of a non-wholly owned subsidiary company and the wider interests of the group coincide. This may not, however, be the case where the various companies in the group are in financial difficulties. The movement of funds from one company to another group member may prejudice the interests of creditors of the transferring company. The duty of directors to creditors is discussed in Chapter 13.5 below.

It may be detrimental to the interests of minority shareholders if directors fail to act in the interests of a particular company and instead treat the company as part of a group.

case note

In *Re Spargos Mining NL* (1990) 8 ACLC 1218 and *Jenkins v Enterprise Gold Mines NL* (1992) 10 ACLC 136, a minority shareholder, Jenkins, obtained remedies under the equivalent of s 232 on the grounds that the directors of Spargos and Enterprise Gold Mines had diverted substantial assets that were used for the benefit of other companies in the group. This caused considerable losses to the shareholders not interested in the other companies because the transactions were of no commercial benefit to Spargos and Enterprise Gold Mines and their shareholders. These cases are discussed in Chapter 17 below.

A transaction undertaken for the benefit of the group or some other member of the group may be permitted if it is for the benefit of a particular company that assistance is given to other companies in the group.

case note

In *Equiticorp Finance Ltd v BNZ* (1993) 11 ACLC 952, funds were transferred from two companies in a group to satisfy the debt of a related company. The New South Wales Court of Appeal held that the dominant director of the group was justified in considering that the welfare of the group was intimately tied up with the welfare of the individual companies. The interests of the two companies were considered because provision was made for compensating them for the loss of the funds. The transactions were justified because the holding company of the group had guaranteed the debt which was repaid. The alternative was possible disaster for the whole group, including the two companies.

Section 187 assists directors who serve on the boards of wholly-owned subsidiaries.

Section 187, introduced by 1999 amendments, assists directors who serve on the boards of wholly-owned subsidiaries. Under this provision, a director of a wholly-owned subsidiary will be taken to act in good faith in the best interests of the subsidiary where:

> **the constitution of the subsidiary expressly authorises the director to act in the best interests of the holding company; and**

> **the director in fact acted in good faith in the best interests of the holding company.**

In order to protect the interests of the subsidiary's creditors, the operation of s 187 is limited to situations where the subsidiary is solvent at the time the director acts and does not become insolvent because of the director's action.

The Companies and Securities Advisory Committee (CASAC) issued its *Corporate Groups Final Report* in May 2000. It recommended that s 187 be extended so that directors of a solvent partly-owned group company should be permitted to act in the interests of the parent company if authorised by the minority shareholders of the partly-owned company. Where that authorisation is given, all minority shareholders who did not vote in favour of the resolution should have the right to be bought out. This report may be viewed on the CAMAC website, which is linked to the Lipton-Herzberg Directors' Duties Good Faith and Proper Purposes Pathway at **http://www.lipton-herzberg.com.au/secure/pathways-directors-duties-good-faith-and-proper-purposes.html**

employees

[13.2.40] Directors should not consider the interests of employees ahead of the interests of the company's shareholders.

case note

In *Parke v Daily News Ltd* [1962] Ch 927, a company that controlled two newspapers sold one of them. The directors intended to distribute surplus proceeds from the sale among its employees by way of compensation for dismissal. A shareholder brought an action to prevent these payments. It was held that the proposed payments were not reasonably incidental to the carrying on of the company's business. They were gratuitous payments to the detriment of shareholders and the company as a whole.

In most cases, a payment to employees will be in the interests of the company where their employment continues because its industrial relations may be improved. This did not arise in *Parke v Daily News Ltd* because the company was in fact selling that part of its business operations.

The employee entitlements provisions contained in Pt 5.8A of the *Corporations Act* require directors to consider the interests of employees in certain situations. These provisions were introduced in 2000 to protect employees by preventing directors of employer companies stripping the companies' assets and making the companies insolvent so as to prevent employees enforcing their entitlements. These provisions are discussed in Chapter 13.5 and Chapter 25 below.

The United Kingdom's company legislation requires directors to have regard to the interests of the company's employees in general as well as the interests of its members. The Senate Standing Committee on Legal and Constitutional Affairs (in its 1989 Report, *Social and Fiduciary Duties and Obligations of Company Directors*) recommended that a similar requirement should be included in the Australian legislation. This suggestion has not been adopted.

creditors

[13.2.45] As discussed above at para [13.2.05], directors are subject to a fiduciary duty to exercise their powers in good faith and in the best interests of their company. When the company is solvent, the best interests of the company correspond with the best interests of its shareholders as a collective group. Different considerations apply if the company is insolvent or in financial difficulties. In such circumstances, the interests of the company are those of its creditors. Directors have a duty to exercise their powers in a way that does not prejudice the company's ability to pay its creditors. Directors' duties not to prejudice their company's creditors are discussed in Chapter 13.5 below.

directors' duties and corporate social responsibility

[13.2.50] The traditional view is that directors' duty to act in the best interests of the company means that they are required to consider the interests of the shareholders and in insolvency situations, the company's creditors. There has been increasing concern that this view is too narrow and that companies also have wider social responsibilities. Consequently, directors may be required to consider the interests of other important stakeholders apart from shareholders when making business decisions. Other stakeholders who have a legitimate interest in a company's activities include:

Companies have wider social responsibilities. Consequently, directors may be required to consider the interests of other important stakeholders apart from shareholders when making business decisions.

> the company's employees;
> the company's customers and suppliers;
> the environment;
> regulators and other government agencies; and
> the broader community.

In March 2005, the Parliamentary Secretary to the Treasurer issued a reference to CAMAC to report on the following questions:

> Should the *Corporations Act* be revised to clarify the extent to which directors may take into account the interests of specific classes of stakeholders or the broader community when making corporate decisions?
> Should the *Corporations Act* be revised to require directors to take into account the interests of specific classes of stakeholders or the broader community when making corporate decisions?
> Should Australian companies be encouraged to adopt socially and environmentally responsible business practices and if so, how?
> Should the *Corporations Act* require certain types of companies to report on the social and environmental impact of their activities?

duty to exercise powers for proper purposes

[13.2.55] In Chapter 12 above we saw that certain powers are conferred on the board of directors by the replaceable rules and constitution (if any). These generally include broad powers of management. Examples of specific powers conferred on directors include the power to issue shares and to refuse to register transfers of shares.

The fiduciary duty of directors requires them to exercise their powers for proper purposes.

The fiduciary duty of directors requires them to exercise their powers for proper purposes. Directors may breach this duty even if they honestly believe their actions are in the best interests of the company as a whole.

In cases where it is alleged that the directors have exercised their powers for improper purposes, the courts consider two matters: the objective purpose for which the power was granted and the purpose which actually motivated the exercise of the power. The onus of establishing that the directors acted improperly rests with those alleging the breach of duty: *Australian Metropolitan Life Assurance Co Ltd v Ure* (1923) 33 CLR 199. The courts are generally reluctant to interfere in the internal management of a company unless improper purposes are clearly demonstrated.

A director may be in breach of the duty to exercise powers for a proper purpose even though not involved in a particular transaction. The duty is breached if the director disclosed a conflict of interest and abstained from voting but knew of the improper purpose of the other directors and failed to take steps to prevent the transaction from proceeding. In such a case, the director is under a positive duty to take steps to protect the company's interests: *Permanent Building Society v Wheeler* (1994) 12 ACLC 674.

Under s 181, directors and other officers are under a duty to act in good faith in the best interests of the corporation and for a proper purpose. Breach of this duty to exercise powers for a proper purpose attracts the civil penalty provisions and possibly criminal liability where dishonesty is involved. The civil penalty provisions are discussed in Chapter 13.6 below.

issue of shares

[13.2.60] While the duty to act for proper purposes may arise in a large variety of situations, most of the cases involving allegations of breach of directors' duty to act for proper purposes have concerned the issue of shares by directors. The power to issue shares is ordinarily conferred for the purpose of raising capital for the company. Shares may also be properly issued for purposes other than raising capital for the company. For example, companies often issue shares as consideration for the purchase of property. Share issues are also a means of remunerating employees of a company.

The power to issue shares is ordinarily conferred for the purpose of raising capital for the company.

Directors breach their fiduciary and statutory duties to exercise their powers for a proper purpose if they issue shares to:

> **maintain control of the company's management or majority shareholding;**
> **defeat a takeover bid; or**
> **create or destroy the voting power of majority shareholders.**

The company has a number of remedies if directors issue shares for improper purposes. The main remedy is to rescind the share issue. A shareholder may apply for court leave under s 236 to sue the directors in the name of the company if it is unwilling to take such action against its directors. Issuing shares for an improper purpose may also constitute oppressive or unfair conduct and enable a shareholder to obtain a remedy under s 232. Sections 232 and 236 are discussed in Chapter 17 below.

If directors suspect that a share issue may result in them breaching their fiduciary duty they should obtain shareholder approval at a general meeting. Shareholders may ratify an improper share issue. Shareholder ratification of directors' breaches of duty is discussed in Chapter 13.7 below.

Shareholders may ratify an improper share issue.

To a large extent, the ASX Listing Rules ensure that directors of listed companies do not make significant share issues without obtaining shareholder approval. Under Listing Rule 7.1 share issues exceeding 15 per cent of a listed company's issued capital in a 12-month period require shareholder approval. In addition, Listing Rule 10.11 requires shareholder approval for share issues to related parties of a listed company such as directors.

shares issued to maintain control

[13.2.65] Directors who issue shares for the purpose of maintaining their position of control of the company breach their fiduciary duty and the share issue may be invalidated.

Directors who issue shares for the purpose of maintaining their position of control of the company breach their fiduciary duty.

In *Ngurli Ltd v McCann* (1953) 90 CLR 425, Williams ACJ, Fullagar and Kitto JJ in a joint High Court judgment stated:

> **< The power must be used bona fide for the purpose for which it was conferred, that is to say, to raise sufficient capital for the benefit of the company as a whole. It must not be used under the cloak of such a purpose for the real purpose of benefiting some shareholders or their friends at the expense of other shareholders or so that some shareholders or their friends will wrest control of the company from the other shareholders. >**

creating or destroying a majority of voting power

[13.2.70] In *Howard Smith Ltd v Ampol Petroleum Ltd* [1974] AC 821, the Privy Council held that directors may act for improper purposes even where a share issue is not motivated by self-interest. Directors breach their duty to act for proper purposes if they use their power to issue shares for the purpose of creating a new majority shareholder or to manipulate control within the company. This is even where the directors may honestly believe their actions are in the best overall interests of the shareholders.

Directors breach their duty if they issue shares for the purpose of creating a new majority shareholder or to manipulate control within the company.

case note

The *Howard Smith Ltd v Ampol Petroleum Ltd* case arose out of a takeover battle for control of R W Miller (Holdings) Ltd. Its major shareholders were two independent companies, Ampol Petroleum and Bulkships Ltd, which between them controlled 55 per cent of Miller's issued capital. Ampol and Bulkships decided to combine their holdings and made a joint takeover bid for all the other Miller shares. Soon after, Howard Smith, a company friendly to Miller's board, made its own takeover bid offering a higher price. To give Howard Smith's takeover bid a chance of success, Miller's directors issued sufficient shares to it so as to reduce the Ampol-Bulkships majority shareholding to a minority position. When Ampol and Bulkships challenged the validity of the share issue, Miller's directors argued that they were primarily motivated by the fact that their company was in urgent need of funds to finance tankers then under construction and to ease other existing financial problems.

The Privy Council held that Miller's directors had breached their duty and invalidated the share issue to Howard Smith. It did not believe the directors' explanation of their reasons for the share issue. The directors were motivated primarily to reduce the combined majority shareholding of Ampol and Bulkships to a minority position in order to promote the Howard Smith takeover bid. This was improper even though a successful bid by Howard Smith meant that shareholders would have been able to obtain a higher price for their shares. Although Miller was in a position of tight liquidity, its financial position had improved at the time of the share issue partly by it pursuing a policy of raising loan capital.

case note

In *Whitehouse v Carlton Hotel Pty Ltd* (1987) 5 ACLC 421, the facts are unusual in that the decision of the court to invalidate a share issue operated to the advantage of the director who issued the shares and had changed his mind. Carlton Hotel was a family company controlled by the father who was its governing director. Under the articles, this position gave the father the sole power to issue shares. The company's capital was divided into three classes of shares. The father held "A" class shares. His wife owned "B" class shares and his two sons and four daughters each owned "C" class shares, which had no voting rights. While the father was alive only "A" class shares had voting rights. His wife's "B" class shares were given voting rights upon his death.

In 1973, the parents divorced. The daughters sided with their mother and the sons with their father. To ensure that his ex-wife and daughters would not gain control of the company after his death, the father purported to allot further "B" class shares to his sons. This allotment was made without the knowledge of the wife and was not recorded in the company's share register but was noted in several annual returns. In 1980, the father fell out with his sons and purported to annul the allotment of shares to them. The sons brought an action to have the share register rectified so as to reflect the allotment. The company argued that the issue of the "B" class shares was invalid because the father, as governing director, had issued them for the improper purpose of realigning the relative shareholdings upon his death.

By a majority of three to two, the High Court confirmed the company's argument and held that the allotment was invalid as a result of the governing director's breach of duty. Mason CJ, Deane and Dawson JJ, in a joint judgment, stated the general rule derived from *Howard Smith Ltd v Ampol Petroleum Ltd* [1974] AC 821:

> < The reason why, as a general rule, it is impermissible for the directors of a company to exercise a fiduciary power to allot shares for the purpose of destroying or creating a

majority of voting power was identified by the Privy Council in *Howard Smith v Ampol Petroleum*. It lies essentially in the distinction between indirect proprietorship and ultimate control of the shareholders on the one hand and the powers of management entrusted to the directors on the other. It is simply no part of the function of the directors as such to favour one shareholder or group of shareholders by exercising a fiduciary power to allot shares for the purpose of diluting the voting power attaching to the issued shares held by some other shareholder or group of shareholders ...

... it is unavailing that Mr Whitehouse was not motivated by purely selfish considerations in that he believed that the manipulation of voting power in favour of his sons at the expense of his former wife was in the interests of the company in that it would ensure that the management of the company after his death was in the hands of those whom he favoured. Indeed, in the ordinary case of a purported allotment of shares for such an impermissible purpose, it is likely that the directors will genuinely believe that what they are doing to manipulate voting power is in the overall interests of the particular company ... In this as in other areas involving the exercise of fiduciary power, the exercise of a power for an ulterior purpose or impermissible purpose is bad notwithstanding that the motives of the donee of the power in so exercising it are substantially altruistic. >

mixed purposes and the "but for" test

Where there is more than one purpose for a share issue, the "but for" test is applied.

[13.2.75] When directors exercise their powers to issue shares, they may be motivated by a number of purposes. This is particularly the case when the directors are themselves shareholders in the company. They must exercise their power in the interests of their company, but in doing so they may also promote their own interests as shareholders to the detriment of other shareholders. In such cases the courts will not intervene unless it is established that their motivating purpose is improper. This is so, even if the directors are also motivated by some subsidiary proper purpose.

In *Whitehouse v Carlton Hotel Pty Ltd* (1987) 5 ACLC 421, the High Court explained that where there was more than one purpose for a share issue, the "but for" test should be applied to work out whether the directors breached their duty and issued the shares for an improper purpose. An allotment of shares will be invalidated if the impermissible purpose is causative in the sense that, *but for* its presence, no allotment would have been made. Mason CJ, Deane and Dawson JJ stated:

> **< As a matter of logic and principle, the preferable view would seem to be that, regardless of whether the impermissible purpose was the dominant one or but one of a number of significantly contributing causes, the allotment will be invalidated if the impermissible purpose was causative in the sense that, but for its presence, "the power would not have been exercised":** ***Mills v Mills*** **(1938) 60 CLR 150 at 186 per Dixon J. >**

case note

In *Hannes v MJH Pty Ltd* (1992) 10 ACLC 400, it was held that the motivating purpose and the real reason for a governing director's actions to issue shares to himself and enter into a service agreement was self-interest and the desire to derive additional personal benefits. These motives overshadowed the director's duties to act in the interests of the company. The director breached his duty to act for a proper purpose.

case note

Similarly, in *Kokotovich Constructions Pty Ltd v Wallington* (1995) 13 ACLC 1113, the New South Wales Court of Appeal applied the "but for" test and held that an issue of shares by a governing director to his children was invalid even though one of the purposes of the issue was to raise capital. On the evidence, the court concluded that but for the governing director's improper purpose of manipulating voting power, the share issue would not have been made.

defending hostile takeovers

Defensive measures aimed at defeating a hostile takeover bid raise the possibility that the directors may be motivated by a desire to retain control of their company at the expense of their shareholders' interests.

[13.2.80] The question of whether directors have exercised their powers for a proper purpose has often arisen in the context of defensive measures aimed at defeating a hostile takeover bid. Such measures raise the possibility that the directors may be motivated by a desire to retain control of their company at the expense of their shareholders' interests. However, directors of target companies are not rendered impotent in the face of an inadequate takeover bid. They will not breach their fiduciary duties if they engage in defensive measures designed either to maximise the value of members' shares or advance the commercial interests of the company.

A 1986 NCSC discussion paper, *Defensive Schemes and the Duties of Directors*, observed that shareholders have the right to determine the composition of their company's board and that directors should not use their powers to block a takeover substantially as a means of retaining management. On the other hand, defensive measures may be desirable where the effect is to facilitate an auction for the company's shares, thereby maximising the return to shareholders, or to force compliance with disclosure or other legal requirements imposed on bidders.

While the discussion paper did not draw any final conclusions, it noted that the motive of directors was critical. This raises a number of difficulties of proof. The directors' motives must be shown to be incompatible with their duties to shareholders. This is especially difficult to prove in the case of complex business decisions that may involve a number of considerations. This discussion paper is further discussed in Chapter 18 below and may be accessed on the Takeovers Panel website which is linked to Lipton-Herzberg Corporate Law website at **http://www.lipton-herzberg.com.au/corp-law-websites.html#Regulatory_bodies**

Actions by target company directors which have the effect of frustrating a takeover bid may result in a declaration of unacceptable circumstances being made by the Takeovers Panel. The situations where this may arise are discussed below in Chapter 18.

use of company funds to promote re-election of directors

Directors may exercise their powers for an improper purpose where they use company funds to promote their own re-election against other candidates.

[13.2.85] Directors may exercise their powers for an improper purpose where they use company funds to promote their own re-election against other candidates.

case note

In *Advance Bank Australia Ltd v FAI Insurances Ltd* (1987) 5 ACLC 725, the New South Wales Court of Appeal held that while there was no absolute prohibition on the expenditure of company funds in an election for directors, such expenditure should be kept to a minimum and be confined to providing information that promotes an informed decision by shareholders. Self-praise and irrelevant personality issues should be avoided.

The directors breached their duty even though they honestly believed they were acting in the company's best interests because they resolved to form a campaign committee that used company funds to promote the re-election of certain directors and to secure the defeat of candidates nominated by FAI, a substantial shareholder. The information supplied by the committee to shareholders was emotional and misleading.

exercise of management powers

[13.2.90] Directors may breach their duty where management powers are exercised for an improper purpose.

case note

In *Permanent Building Society v Wheeler* (1994) 12 ACLC 674 the board of a building society caused the society to purchase land at an over-value. The purpose of this transaction was to provide the vendor with money to meet obligations to a company in which the majority of the society's directors had personal interests. The court held that the directors acted for an improper purpose. One of the directors who did not participate in the negotiations was held to have also acted for an improper purpose because he knew of the improper purpose of the other directors and failed to prevent the transaction from proceeding. The court ordered that the directors in breach of duty compensate the society for its losses.

In *Bishopsgate Investment Management Ltd v Maxwell* (1993) 11 ACLC 3128, a director was held to have used his powers as a director for an improper purpose where he gave away the company's assets to a family company for no consideration.

directors' refusal to register a transfer

[13.2.95] The right of a member to transfer shares to another is a feature that distinguishes companies from partnerships. This right may be restricted by the constitution or the replaceable rules. For example, under the replaceable rule in s 1072F directors may refuse to register a transfer of shares if the shares are not fully paid or the company has a lien on the shares: s 1072F(3). In the case of proprietary companies, the replaceable rule in s 1072G gives directors the power to refuse to register a transfer of shares for any reason.

Directors must exercise their discretion to refuse to register transfers of shares in good faith and in the best interests of the company and not for improper purposes. In *Australian Metropolitan Life Assurance Co Ltd v Ure* (1923) 33 CLR 199, Isaacs J discussed this discretionary power. He thought that if directors act honestly upon business considerations such as whether the transferee is solvent and maintaining the reputation of the company, the directors act within their power. Where they are not moved by a legitimate consideration but act upon an extraneous reason, the court would direct the transfer be registered. As discussed in Chapter 9 above, s 1071F provides that where directors refuse to register a transfer of shares without just cause, the transferee may apply to the court for an order that the transfer be registered.

Directors must exercise their discretion to refuse to register transfers of shares in good faith and in the best interests of the company and not for improper purposes.

A member may also obtain a remedy under s 232 by showing that a refusal to register a transfer of shares is part of conduct that is contrary to the interests of members as a whole, oppressive, unfairly prejudicial or unfairly discriminatory. This is further discussed in Chapter 17 below.

statutory duty to act in good faith and for a proper purpose: s 181

Section 181 is essentially the same as the fiduciary duty to act in good faith and in the best interests of the company.

[13.2.100] A director or other officer of a corporation must exercise their powers and discharge their duties in good faith in the best interests of the corporation and for a proper purpose: s 181(1). Section 181 is essentially the same as the fiduciary duty to act in good faith and in the best interests of the company. Consequently the legal principles discussed above dealing with the obligation to act in good faith and exercise powers for a proper purpose are applicable to the operation of s 181.

Like the fiduciary duty, the s 181(1) duty to act in good faith and for a proper purpose may be contravened even if directors believe they are acting in the company's best interests if no reasonable director could have reached that conclusion. This is particularly so where directors promote their personal interests in a situation where their personal interests conflict with the interests of the company.

The statutory duties contained in Ch 2D (ss 180–183) overlap. A director who causes a company to enter into an agreement which confers unreasonable personal benefits on the director and fails to make adequate disclosure of the conflict of interest acts "improperly" for the purposes of s 182 and also lacks good faith for the purposes of s 181. Section 182 is discussed below in Chapter 13.3.

case note

In *ASIC v Adler* [2002] NSWSC 171 (confirmed on appeal [2003] NSWCA 131), HIH Casualty & General Insurance Co Ltd (HIHC), a subsidiary of HIH Insurance Ltd (HIH) provided an undocumented, unsecured $10 million loan to Pacific Eagle Equity Pty Ltd (PEE), a company controlled by Adler. At the time, Adler was also a non-executive director and, through Adler Corporation Ltd, a substantial shareholder of HIH. After the loan, PEE became trustee of Australian Equities Unit Trust (AEUT) which was controlled by Adler Corporation Ltd. HIHC's $10 million loan to PEE was then applied to HIHC's subscription for $10 million worth of AEUT units. Under the trust, Adler was entitled to 10 per cent of the trust's income even though the $10 million was contributed by HIH. PEE used the $10 million in the following transactions:

- about $4 million was used to buy HIH shares on the stock market. PEE later sold its HIH shares at a $2 million loss. PEE's purchase of HIH shares was designed to give the stock market the false impression that Adler was supporting HIH's falling share price by personally buying its shares;
- nearly $4 million was used to purchase various unlisted shares in technology and communications companies from Adler Corporation. These shares were purchased at cost even though the stock market for such investments had collapsed and no independent assessment of their value was made. A total loss was made on these investments; and
- $2 million was loaned by the trust to Adler and associated interests. These loans were unsecured and not documented.

It was held that Adler breached his duties as an officer of HIH and HIHC under s 181 by reason of all these transactions. There was evidence of a consciousness of impropriety on

Adler's part because the normal investment safeguards put in place by HIH, such as the establishment of an Investment Committee, were by-passed in a semi-covert way. The s 181 duty may be breached where the interests of the company are put at risk by contraventions of other statutory provisions such as those dealing with related party transactions (s 208) and the financial assistance prohibition: s 260A. A contravention of s 181 does not require the director to gain a benefit from the conduct. It is sufficient to establish that the conduct was carried out in order to gain an advantage.

The *Adler* case involved the breach of several duties and is discussed in a number of places in this book. Financial assistance is discussed in Chapter 8, giving a financial benefit under Ch 2E and the duties not to improperly use position (s 182) and information (s 183) are discussed in Chapter 13.3, the duty of care and diligence is discussed in Chapter 13.4 and the civil penalty provisions are discussed in Chapter 13.6.

Section 181 is a designated civil penalty provision: s 1317E. The court has the power to impose a civil penalty order on any person who is involved in a contravention of s 181(1). A person is involved in a contravention in the circumstances described in s 79. Involvement in a contravention may arise where a person aids and abets, induces or is knowingly concerned in, or party to the contravention.

Section 181 is a designated civil penalty provision.

The civil penalty provisions are discussed in Chapter 13.6 below.

Criminal liability may be imposed under s 184(1) if a director or other officer of a corporation is reckless or intentionally dishonest and fails to exercise their powers and discharge their duties in good faith in the best interests of the corporation or for a proper purpose. This implies that conduct which falls short of the s 184 criminal liability requirements may constitute a breach of s 181 even though the director possessed the subjective belief that they were acting for proper purposes: *ASIC v Adler* [2002] NSWSC 171.

The statutory duty to act in good faith and for a proper purpose is discussed in several articles linked to the Lipton-Herzberg Directors' Duties Good Faith and Proper Purposes Pathway at **http://www.lipton-herzberg.com.au/secure/pathways-directors-duties-good-faith-and-proper-purposes.html**

duty to retain discretion

[13.2.105] Directors have a fiduciary duty to retain their discretionary powers. They will breach this duty if they enter into an agreement with outsiders that they will vote in a certain way at future board meetings. Such a contract is ineffective even if the directors are not otherwise in breach of their duties such as acting for an improper purpose.

Directors have a fiduciary duty to retain their discretionary powers.

However, directors may enter into contracts on behalf of the company, whereby they agree to vote in favour of a particular course of action if they properly consider this to be in the interests of the company at the time the agreement is entered into: *Thorby v Goldberg* (1964) 112 CLR 597.

A nominee director may be appointed to represent the interests and act on the instructions of the appointor. In such cases, the nominee director's discretion may be fettered, especially where the constitution allows the appointor to remove the nominee. The position of nominee directors is discussed above, para [13.2.30].

The replaceable rules and constitution (if any) may authorise the directors to delegate their powers. For example, the replaceable rule in s 201J empowers directors to appoint a managing director. However, the board may at any time revoke the delegation: s 203F.

pathways questions ...

The following questions dealing with directors' duties to act in good faith and for a proper purpose may best be answered by reading this sub-chapter and considering the Internet resources found on the Lipton-Herzberg Directors' Duties Good Faith and Proper Purposes Pathway at **http://www.lipton-herzberg.com.au/secure/pathways-directors-duties-good-faith-and-proper-purposes.html**

1. (a) Have the courts in Australia adopted a different approach to the English courts in dealing with the duties of nominee directors?
   (b) To what extent is a nominee director entitled to pass on information to the appointor?
2. In what circumstances may a person be liable as a shadow director?
3. What were the main reforms suggested by CASAC in relation to directors' duties in the context of corporate groups? Explain how these recommendations would improve the current law.
4. Does s 181 significantly add to the fiduciary duties of directors?
5. In what circumstances may a holding company and its directors be regarded and held liable as directors of a subsidiary?

bibliography ...

Austin, R "Representatives and Fiduciary Responsibilities: Notes on Nominee Directorships and Life Arrangements" (1995) 7 Bond LR 19.

Austin, R "Problems for Directors within Corporate Groups" in Gillooly M (ed) *The Law Relating to Corporate Groups*. Federation Press 1993, Ch 6.

Austin, R P "Fiduciary Accountability for Business Opportunities" in Finn, P D (ed) *Equity and Commercial Relationships*. LawBook Co, Sydney 1987, Ch 6.

Baxt, R & Lane, T "Developments in Relation to Corporate Groups and the Responsibilities of Directors" (1998) 16 C & SLJ 628.

Bostock, T "To Whom are the Duties of a Company Director Owed?" Uni of Melbourne, Centre for Corporate Law and Securities Regulation, Corporate Law Research Papers, **http://cclsr.law.unimelb.edu.au/research-papers/**

Carroll, R "Keeping Out of the Shadows: Lenders and Advisers as Shadow Directors" (1997) 5 *Current Commercial Law* 53.

Chan, S H & Law, L "Interests of the Company as a Whole: an Economic Appraisal of Fiduciary Controls" (1999) 20 U Qld LJ 186.

Cilliers, J "Directors' Duties in Corporate Groups–Does the Green Light for the Enterprise Approach Signal the End of the Road for Walker v Wimborne?" (2001) 13 Aust Jnl of Corp Law 109.

Companies and Securities Law Review Committee. "Nominee Directors and Alternate Directors" Report No 8. March 1989. **http://www.takeovers.gov.au/Content/Resources/CASES/07**

Cross, K & Webster, J "Issues Facing Directors in Corporate Groups" (1997) 25 ABLR 436.

Davies, P "Enlightened Shareholder Value and the New Responsibilities of Directors" Centre for Corporate Law & Securities Regulation, Corporate Law Research Papers Website **http://cclsr.law.unimelb.edu.au/research-papers/index.html**

Farrer, J "Reforming Australia's Takeover Defence Laws: What Role for Target Directors?" (1997) 8 Aust Jnl of Corp Law 1.

Friedman, S "An Analysis of the Proper Purpose Rule" (1998) 10 Bond LR 164.

Greenwood, A "Directors' Duties in the Light of CLERP and Recent Legal Developments" Uni of Melbourne, Centre for Corporate Law and Securities Regulation, Corporate Law Research Papers, **http://cclsr.law.unimelb.edu.au/research-papers/**

Haddy, S "A Comparative Analysis of Directors' Duties in a Range of Corporate Group Structures" (2002) 20 C & SLJ 138.

Heydon, J D "Directors' Duties and Company's Interests" in Finn, P D (ed) *Equity and Commercial Relationships*. LawBook Co, Sydney, 1987, Ch 5.

Hobson, M "The Law of Shadow Directorships" (1998) 10 Bond LR 184.

Kluver, J "Sections 181 & 189 of the Corporations Law and Directors of Corporate Group Companies" Uni of Melbourne, Centre for Corporate Law and Securities Regulation, Corporate Law Research Papers, **http://cclsr.law.unimelb.edu.au/research-papers/**

Langton, R & Trotman, L "Defining 'the Best Interests of the Corporation': Some Australian Reform Proposals" (1999) 3 Flinders J of Law Reform 163.

Lawrence, J "The Coleman v Myers Fiduciary Relationship: An Australian Resurgence?" (1996) 14 C & SLJ 428.

McCabe, B "The Roles and Responsibilities of Directors in a Takeover" (1994) 4 Aust Jnl of Corp Law 36.

McConvill, J & Joy, M "The Interaction of Directors' Duties and Sustainable Development in Australia: Setting Off on the Uncharted Road" (2003) 27 MULR 116.

Markovic, M "Banks and Shadow Directorships: Not an Almost Entirely Imaginary Risk in Australia" (1998) 9 JBFLP 284.

Mayanja, J "Standing to Challenge the Implementation of Improper Defensive Measures" (1995) 5 Aust Jnl of Corp Law 66.

NCSC Defensive Schemes and the Duties of Directors. October 1986. **http://www.takeovers.gov.au/display.asp?ContentID=505**

Nicoll, G "The Changing Face of 'The Company as a Whole' and Directors' Responsibilities to Members in the Exercise of Management Powers" (1994) 4 Aust Jnl of Corp Law 287.

Noakes, D "Corporate Groups and the Duties of Directors: Protecting the Employee or the Insolvent Employer?" (2001) 29 ABLR 124.

Pizer, J "Holding an Appointor Vicariously Liable for its Nominee Director's Wrongdoing–An Australian Roadmap" (1997) 15 C & SLJ 81.

Ramsay, I & Stapledon, G "Corporate Groups in Australia" (2001) 29 ABLR 7.

Santow, G "Codification of Directors' Duties" (1999) 73 ALJ 336.

Sealy, L S "Bona Fides and Proper Purposes in Corporate Decisions" (1989) 15 Mon LR 365.

Sievers, A S "Finding the Right Balance; The 2GB Case Revisited" (1993) 3 Aust Jnl of Corp Law 1.

Steele, T "Defensive Tactics in Company Takeovers" (1986) 4 C & SLJ 30.

Valentine, R "The Director-Shareholder Fiduciary Relationship: Issues and Implications" (2001) 19 C & SLJ 92.

Zakrewski, R "The Law Relating to Single Director and Single Shareholder Companies" (1999) 17 C & SLJ 156.

revision questions on the material in this chapter ...

- Please see eQuiz at **http://www.thomson.com.au/academic** for multiple choice questions and answers.
- For further corporations law links and material please refer to the Lipton-Herzberg website at **http://www.lipton-herzberg.com.au**

chapter thirteen.three

conflicts of interest and disclosure

key points ...

- Directors are under both *fiduciary* and *statutory* duties to avoid undisclosed conflicts between their personal interests and the interests of the company.
- The duty to avoid conflicts of interests is breached where directors fail to disclose their material personal interests in transactions with the company. The *Corporations Act* also imposes disclosure requirements. These disclosure requirements vary depending upon whether the company is a public or proprietary company.
- At common law, directors avoid breaching their duties if full disclosure is made to the company and approval given. This is generally taken to mean disclosure to and approval of the general meeting.
- Under the *Corporations Act*, disclosure of a material personal interest must be made to the other directors. A public company that gives a financial benefit to a director or other related party is required to obtain the approval of members in accordance with a specified procedure. Exceptions arise where the financial benefit is given on arm's length terms or is reasonable remuneration.
- The fiduciary duty to avoid conflicts of interests also requires directors not to make undisclosed personal profits arising from acting as director, not to take up corporate opportunities or misuse confidential company information.
- There are corresponding statutory duties that prohibit officers or employees from making improper use of their position and improper use of information gained while acting in their position.

Fiduciaries are under a duty to avoid conflict of interests situations.

[13.3.05] All fiduciaries are under a duty to avoid conflict of interests situations. This means that they must not allow a situation to develop where there is a conflict between their duties to the person for whose benefit they act and their personal interests. This is another aspect of the fiduciary duties owed by directors to their company.

The obligation to avoid conflict of interests aims to prevent directors improperly making a profit from their office. However, it goes further than this to prevent directors from putting themselves in a position where it appears that they may act in their own interests. In such a case, directors cannot avoid liability by claiming they did not make a profit, their company did not suffer any loss or that the contract was a fair one.

case note

In *Aberdeen Railway Co v Blaikie Bros* (1854) 1 Macq 461, a railway company entered into a contract with a partnership for the supply of a large quantity of iron seats. The company sought to avoid the contract on several grounds, including that at the time the contract was entered into, one of the partners was a director of the company. The House of Lords held that the company could avoid the contract even though its terms were fair.

The duty of directors to avoid a conflict of interests is strictly applied. The duty is imposed because of the recognition of the frailty of human nature. The duty is breached whether or not the directors had fraudulent motives.

A conflict of interest occurs where a director has a personal interest of a contractual nature. It does not arise where there is a mere unenforceable expectation: *Baker v Palm Bay Island Resort Pty Ltd* [1970] Qd R 210.

The strict fiduciary duty to avoid conflict of interests has been applied in various circumstances and these are categorised below. The common feature in all cases in which a breach of the duty has been established is that the directors placed themselves in a position where they put or may have put their own interests ahead of the interests of the company. The duty to avoid conflict of interest, however, is not confined to these defined situations. In *Phipps v Boardman* [1967] 2 AC 46, Lord Upjohn stated:

> **< Rules of equity have to be applied to such a diversity of circumstances that they can be stated only in the most general terms and applied with particular attention to the exact circumstances of each case. >**

The duty to avoid conflict of interests is also governed by the *Corporations Act*, especially ss 181–183. The duty under s 181 is breached when an officer fails to act in good faith in the best interests of the company or for a proper purpose. Section 181 is discussed in Chapter 13.2 above. More specific duties may be breached where the officer makes improper use of position or improper use of information within ss 182 and 183. These are discussed below, paras [13.3.80] and [13.3.130], respectively. Chapter 2E, discussed below, para [13.3.15], also regulates certain conflicts of interest transactions.

self-interested transactions with the company

fiduciary duties

[13.3.10] Directors breach their fiduciary duty if they have undisclosed interests in transactions with their company because they are then in a position where their personal interests conflict or may conflict with the company's interests. Directors should act in the interests of the company and not be seen to put themselves in a position where they may further their own interests. A company has a variety of different remedies available if directors breach their fiduciary duty by having an undisclosed interest in a transaction with their company. These remedies are discussed in Chapter 13.6 below. Rescission of contracts is the usual remedy in such circumstances. Directors can avoid liability for breaching their fiduciary duty if they make full disclosure of their personal interest in a transaction and obtain shareholder approval. Disclosure of interests is discussed below, para [13.3.155]. Shareholder approval (also referred to as "ratification") is discussed in Chapter 13.7 below.

Directors breach their fiduciary duty if they have undisclosed interests in transactions with their company.

The fiduciary duty regarding undisclosed self-interested transactions overlaps with both the fiduciary duty of good faith and best interest of the company (discussed in Chapter 13.2 above) as well as the statutory duties in ss 181 (discussed in Chapter 13.2 above), 182 and 183 (discussed below, paras [13.3.80] and [13.3.130], respectively).

A breach of the fiduciary duty arises whether the director's undisclosed interest in the contract is direct or indirect. A director who contracts personally with the company has a direct interest. An indirect interest in a contract arises when the director is a director or shareholder of another company that contracts with the company.

case note

This is illustrated in *Transvaal Lands Co v New Belgium (Transvaal) Land & Development Co* [1914] 2 Ch 488. In that case, Samuel and Harvey were two of the directors of Transvaal

Lands. Samuel was also a director of New Belgium. They both owned shares in New Belgium. Samuel's shares were held in his own right while Harvey held the New Belgium shares as trustee under a will. At the instigation of Samuel, Transvaal Land's board agreed to purchase certain shares owned by New Belgium. After the purchase was finalised, Transvaal Lands for the first time discovered Samuel and Harvey's interests in New Belgium and sought to have the contract rescinded.

The court held that Samuel's interests as both director and shareholder of New Belgium conflicted with his duty to act in the best interests of Transvaal Lands. He breached his fiduciary duty to that company even though he did not vote on the board's resolution that agreed to the contract. Harvey was also held to have conflicting interests even though his shareholding in New Belgium was only as a trustee. He was under a duty to Transvaal Lands to make the best bargain he could for it in relation to the transaction. This conflicted with his duty to make the best bargain he could for the beneficiaries of the trust.

case note

In *South Australia v Clark* (1996) 14 ACLC 1019, the Supreme Court of South Australia held that Clark, the managing director of the State Bank of South Australia, had a conflict of interest when he arranged for the bank to enter into a contract that indirectly benefited another company in which Clark was a director and shareholder. The court also held that the circumstances surrounding the contract indicated that Clark had breached his duty of care. This aspect of the case is discussed in Chapter 13.4 below.

A person who is a director of two companies that do business with one another may owe fiduciary duties to both companies. In *R v Byrnes* (1995) 13 ACLC 1488, the High Court stated:

> < **Being a fiduciary, the director of the first company must not exercise his or her power for the benefit or gain of the second company without clearly disclosing the second company's interest to the first and obtaining the first company's consent. Nor, of course, can the director exercise those powers for the director's own benefit or gain without clearly disclosing his or her interest and obtaining the company's consent.** >

Directors breach their fiduciary duty only if their undisclosed self-interested transaction is a material interest.

Directors breach their fiduciary duty only if their undisclosed self-interested transaction is a material interest. For example, a director of a proprietary company who owns a relatively small parcel of shares in a large public company does not have a material interest in any contract between the companies merely because of that shareholding.

The fiduciary duty regarding undisclosed self-interested transactions raises two important questions:

- **to whom must directors disclose their material interest; and**
- **what information must directors disclose?**

These issues are discussed below at para [13.3.155].

Directors satisfy their fiduciary duty if they disclose to the company's shareholders their material interest in a transaction with the company. They must also comply with the disclosure requirements in s 191.

Directors satisfy their fiduciary duty if they disclose to the company's shareholders their material interest in a transaction with the company. They must also comply with the disclosure requirements in s 191. These disclosure requirements are discussed below at para [13.3.155].

A company's constitution or the replaceable rules (if applicable) may however, modify the strict fiduciary requirement to disclose to shareholders by merely insisting on disclosure to the other directors: *Woolworths Ltd v Kelly* (1991) 9 ACLC 539. For example, under the proprietary company replaceable rule in s 194, a proprietary company director may retain the benefit of a self-interested transaction if the director discloses that interest to the other directors pursuant to s 191 and abstains from taking part in the board's decision on the matter.

Mere disclosure of a conflict and abstaining from voting may be insufficient to satisfy a director's fiduciary duty if the director has a position of power and influence over the board. The director may also be under a positive duty to take steps to protect the company's interest such as by using their power and influence to prevent the transaction going ahead: *ASIC v Adler* [2002] NSWSC 171.

It is not sufficient for directors merely to disclose that they have a material interest in a transaction with the company without giving details of it. They must make full disclosure of all relevant facts known to them about the matter so that the shareholders can assess whether or not they will consent to the transaction.

financial benefits to directors of public companies: Ch 2E

[13.3.15] Chapter 2E of the *Corporations Act* was introduced in 1992 and is designed to protect shareholders of a public company by requiring prior shareholder approval before the public company gives financial benefits to directors and other related parties: s 207.

The Explanatory Memorandum accompanying the 1992 amendments explained the purpose of the legislation:

> **< The Part is intended to protect shareholders of public companies against the possibility that the value of their investment will be eroded by a related party arranging for the company to enter into a transaction which gives a benefit to the related party. The Part will not prevent a public company from entering into full value, commercial transactions with related parties. The proposed Pt 3.2A (now Chapter 2E) will prevent only "uncommercial" transactions, as these are the kinds of transactions which have a potential to adversely affect shareholders' interests. And even in this case, [Ch 2E] will allow any transaction that has been agreed to by a majority of the public company's disinterested shareholders, provided they have been fully informed about the transaction and its likely impact upon the company. >**

Chapter 2E is intended to protect shareholders of public companies against the possibility that the value of their investment will be eroded by a related party arranging for the company to enter into a transaction which gives a benefit to the related party.

Directors are not relieved of any of their duties under the *Corporations Act* or fiduciary duties merely because a transaction is authorised or approved by members under Ch 2E: s 230. Uncommercial transactions that improperly benefit a director of a public company may also involve a breach of the general duties owed by a director as they may result in a conflict of interest.

shareholder approval needed for financial benefit

[13.3.20] Section 208 is the key provision of Ch 2E and applies to public companies as well as entities controlled by public companies. Under s 208(1)(a)(i), a public company may give a financial benefit to a related party if it obtains the approval of its shareholders in accordance with ss 217–227. Shareholder approval must be obtained no more than15 months before the public company gives the financial benefit: s 208(1)(a)(ii). Under s 208(1), public company shareholder approval is also required where an entity controlled by a public company gives a financial benefit to a related party of the public company.

Under s 208(1) a public company may give a financial benefit to a related party if it obtains the approval of its shareholders.

The detailed shareholder approval requirements in ss 217–227 seek to ensure that where a public company gives a financial benefit to related parties, it is agreed to by a majority vote of disinterested shareholders who are fully informed about the financial benefit and its impact on the company.

A financial benefit to a related party does not need approval of the public company's shareholders if the financial benefit falls within an exception set out in ss 210–216: s 208(1)(b).

financial benefit

The expression "giving a financial benefit" is defined in s 229.

[13.3.25] The expression "giving a financial benefit" is defined in s 229. Section 229(1) requires a broad interpretation in determining whether a financial benefit has been given, even if criminal and civil penalties may be involved. The commercial substance of the transaction prevails over its legal form and any consideration is to be disregarded even if it is adequate. According to s 229(2), a financial benefit may be given indirectly through interposed entities or by informal or unenforceable agreement. It may also comprise the conferring of a financial advantage that does not involve payment of money.

Examples of giving a financial benefit are provided in s 229(3).

Examples of giving a financial benefit are provided in s 229(3). They include:

> **giving or providing finance or property;**
> **buying or selling an asset;**
> **leasing an asset;**
> **supplying or receiving services;**
> **issuing securities or granting an option; and**
> **taking up or releasing an obligation.**

related parties

Section 228 defines the term "related party".

[13.3.30] Section 228 defines the term "related party". A related party of a public company can be an individual as well as an "entity". The word "entity" includes a company, a partnership as well as the trustee of a trust: s 9.

According to s 228, the following people are regarded as related parties of a public company:

> **directors of the public company (s 228(2)(a));**
> **the spouses, de facto spouses, parents and children of public company director (s 228(2)(d) and (3)); and**
> **directors of an entity that controls the public company as well as the spouses, de facto spouses, parents and children of the controlling entity's directors: s 228(2) (b) and (3).**

The following entities are related parties of a public company:

> **an entity that controls the public company (s 228(1));**
> **an entity controlled by a related party referred to in ss 228(1), (2) or (3) (s 228(4));**
> **an entity that was a related party of the kind referred to in ss 228(1), (2) or (3) during the previous six months (s 228(5)); or**
> **an entity that acts in concert with a related party of a public company on the understanding that the related party will receive a financial benefit if the public company gives the entity a financial benefit: s 228(7).**

As noted above, an entity controlled by a related party referred to in ss 228(1), (2) or (3) is regarded as a related party of a public company. Under s 50AA, "control" is the capacity of a person or entity to determine the outcome of decisions about a second entity's financial and operating policies.

when shareholder approval not required

Shareholder approval for the giving of a financial benefit is not required if any one of the exceptions in ss 210–216 apply.

[13.3.35] Shareholder approval for the giving of a financial benefit is not required if any one of the exceptions in ss 210–216 apply. If an exception applies the public company's directors control whether or not to give the financial benefit to the related party.

The exceptions include:

> **transactions that would be reasonable in the circumstances if the parties were dealing at arm's length or the terms were less favourable to the related party than arm's length terms (s 210);**

> reasonable remuneration as an officer or employee of the public company or an entity that controls or is controlled by the public company (s 211(1));
> repayment of expenses incurred by a related party in performing duties as an officer or employee of the public company or a controlling or controlled entity (s 211(2));
> payment of reasonable insurance premiums in respect of a liability incurred as an officer of the public company (s 212(1));
> payments in respect of legal costs incurred by an officer in defending an action involving a liability incurred as an officer of the public company (s 212(2));
> amounts of money given to a director or spouse of less than $2,000 (s 213);
> financial benefits to or by a closely held subsidiary (s 214); and
> benefits given to the related party as a member of the public company where the benefits do not discriminate unfairly against the other members: s 215.

approval meeting

[13.3.40] The public company must call a shareholders' meeting to consider a resolution to approve giving the financial benefit. The company must lodge with ASIC the notice convening the meeting of members and other accompanying documents at least 14 days before the notice is given to members: s 218(1). ASIC may approve a lesser time: s 218(2).

To ensure members are fully informed about the proposed financial benefit, an explanatory statement must accompany the notice convening the meeting: s 221(b). The explanatory statement must set out full details of the circumstances surrounding the proposed resolution in accordance with s 219. The explanatory statement must include all the information known to the company or any of its directors that is reasonably required by members in order to decide whether or not it is in the company's interests to pass the proposed resolution to approve giving the financial benefit.

To ensure members are fully informed about the proposed financial benefit, an explanatory statement must accompany the notice convening the meeting.

Section 219(2) provides examples of the kind of information that should be disclosed. The explanatory statement should state from an economic and commercial point of view the true potential costs and detriment of giving the financial benefits including opportunity costs, taxation consequences and benefits forgone.

Within 14 days after lodgment of the materials to be put to members, ASIC may give to the company written comments on those documents but not on whether the proposed resolution is in the company's best interests: s 220. Any comments by ASIC must be included in the documents sent to members with the notice convening the meeting: s 221(d).

In August 2004, ASIC announced a campaign to crack down on related party disclosure documents to ensure that shareholders receive sufficient information to make a decision about whether to grant related party benefits. ASIC observed that there were a number of common defects in related party documentation supplied to shareholders. The most common defect was not adequately valuing the financial benefit. According to ASIC, an adequate valuation requires disclosure of the basis of the valuation and the principal assumptions behind it. Another common defect was the failure to explain the reason for giving the financial benefit.

interested related parties cannot vote

[13.3.45] A related party or associate to whom the proposed resolution would permit a financial benefit to be given, cannot cast a vote on the resolution: s 224(1). ASIC may allow the related party to vote where it is satisfied that this would not cause unfair prejudice to the interests of any member of the company: s 224(4). A vote may be cast by a person as a proxy for someone who is not an interested related party: s 224(2). It is an offence to cast a vote in contravention of s 224(1) whether or not the resolution is passed: s 224(6). A contravention of s 224 does not generally affect the validity of a resolution: s 224(8).

A related party cannot cast a vote on the resolution.

A notice setting out the resolution must be lodged with ASIC within 14 days after it is passed: s 226.

consequences of breach

[13.3.50] A contravention of the s 208 requirement does not affect the validity of any contract or transaction connected with the giving of the benefit. The public company or entity that it controls is not guilty of an offence: s 209(1)(b).

A person who is involved in a contravention of s 208 by a public company contravenes s 209(2). This is a civil penalty provision.

A person who is involved in a contravention of s 208 by a public company contravenes s 209(2). This is a civil penalty provision: s 1317E. The civil penalty provisions are discussed in Chapter 13.6 below. A person commits a criminal offence if their involvement in the contravention of s 208 is dishonest: s 209(3).

A proposed benefit to a related party that contravenes s 208 may be stopped by the court where an application for an injunction is brought under s 1324. Injunctions under s 1324 are discussed in Chapter 17 below.

case note

In *Adler v ASIC* [2003] NSWCA 131, the facts of which are set out in Chapter 13.2 above, the Court of Appeal held that the payment of $10 million by HIHC (an entity controlled by a public company, HIH) to PEE was an interest-free unsecured loan. This amounted to HIHC giving a financial benefit to each of PEE, Adler Corporation and Adler within the meaning of s 229. PEE, Adler Corporation and Adler were all related parties of HIH. Further, the terms of the loan were unreasonable and therefore not on arm's length terms within the meaning of s 210. As there was no shareholder approval, it followed that both HIH and its controlled entity, HIHC, both contravened s 208. The court also held that there was no question that

figure 13.1 related party transactions—Chapter 2E Corporations Act

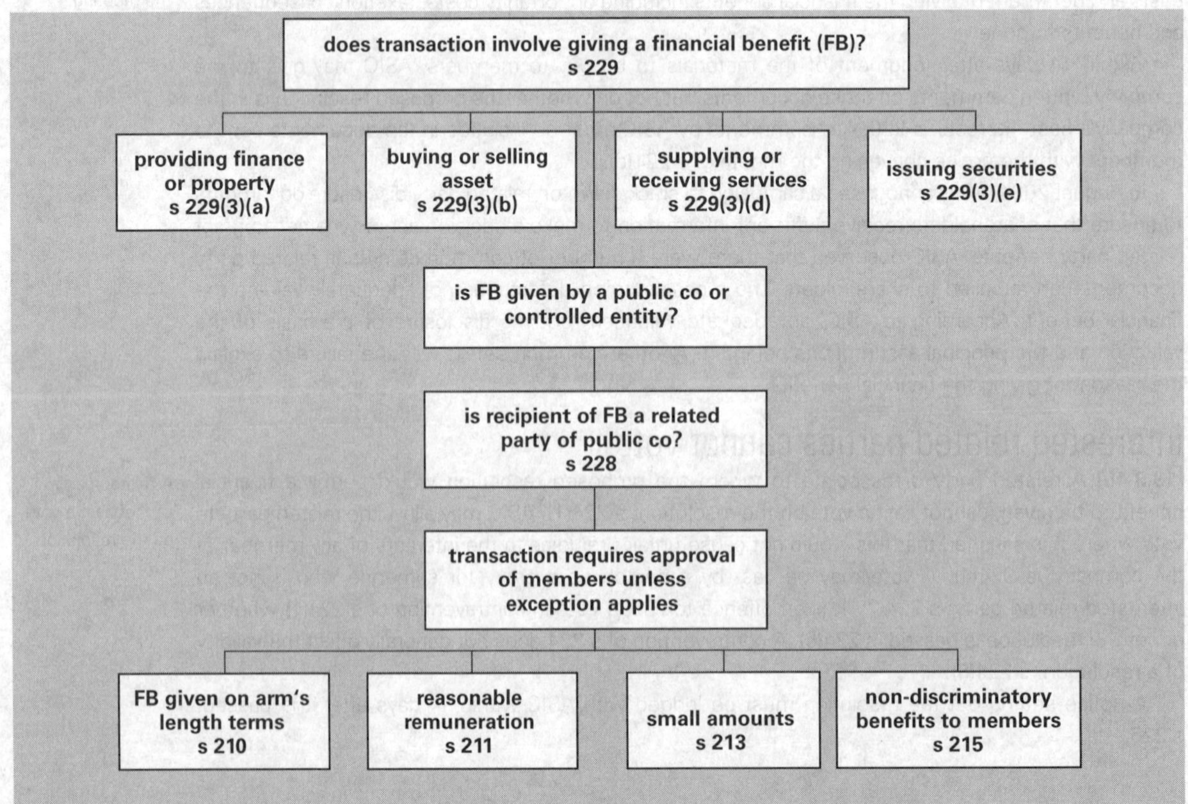

both Adler and Williams were involved in the contravention. Adler was fully aware that the $10 million loan was not on reasonable arm's length terms, having instigated it. Williams was also involved in the contravention because he authorised the payment knowing that Adler controlled PEE. Williams also ensured that the transaction was not brought to the attention of HIH's other directors or its Investment Committee. Fodera was also involved in the contravention because he had sufficient knowledge of the essential factual elements constituting the contravention even though he did not know every detail of it.

entitlement of interested director to vote

public companies

[13.3.55] Under s 195(1), a director of a public company who has a material personal interest in a matter before the board is prohibited from voting on the matter and must not be present while the matter is being considered by the board meeting.

A director of a public company who has a material personal interest in a matter before the board is prohibited from voting on the matter and must not be present while the matter is being considered by the board meeting.

This prohibition does not apply where the non-interested directors pass a resolution stating that they are satisfied that the interest should not disqualify the director from voting or being present. This resolution must also identify the director, the nature and extent of the director's interest and its relation to the affairs of the company: s 195(2). The prohibition on being present and voting does not apply where the interest does not need to be disclosed to the board under s 191: s 195(1)(d). The s 191 disclosure requirements are discussed below, para [13.3.170].

ASIC may declare that a director of a public company may be present and/or vote despite having a material personal interest. A declaration may only be made if the number of directors entitled to be present and vote would be less than a quorum and the matter needs to be dealt with urgently or there is some other compelling reason for the matter to be dealt with at a directors' meeting rather than by the general meeting: s 196(1). Section 195(4) provides for the general meeting to deal with matters where there are not enough directors entitled to be present and vote to form a quorum.

proprietary companies

[13.3.60] The *Corporations Act* does not prohibit an interested proprietary company director from voting at a directors' meeting that is considering matters that relate to the interest. This is left to the company's constitution (if any) or the proprietary company replaceable rule in s 194.

Section 194 provides that if the director makes disclosure to the board under s 191, then the director can vote, related transactions may proceed, the director may retain benefits under the transaction and the company cannot avoid the transaction merely because of the existence of the interest.

remuneration

[13.3.65] Remuneration is probably the most obvious situation where directors have a material self-interested transaction with the company and is a critical corporate governance issue. Remuneration packages often consist of a variety of components including fixed salaries, performance-based payments such as bonuses and equity related remuneration in the form of shares or options issued to directors. Termination payments on retirement or resignation also give rise to potential conflicts between directors' personal interests and the interests of the company.

Remuneration is probably the most obvious situation where directors have a material self-interested transaction with the company and is a critical corporate governance issue.

Because of the obvious potential for conflicts of interests in relation to remuneration of directors and senior officers of listed companies, there are detailed requirements for disclosure of remuneration payments contained in the *Corporations Act.* As discussed in Chapter 12 above, the main thrust of the

Corporations Act requirements in relation to remuneration of listed company directors and senior managers is disclosure of the remuneration in the company's financial reports and in some situations the requirement for shareholder approval.

ASX Listing Rules contain additional shareholder approval requirements in relation to remuneration packages for directors and senior officers of listed companies. In addition, the ASX Corporate Governance Council's *Principles of Good Corporate Governance and Best Practice Recommendations*, discussed in Chapter 13.1 above, also set out best practice recommendations for listed companies in relation to remuneration. These focus on the best practice internal processes for determining directors' and senior officers' remuneration packages. For example, under Recommendation 9.2, remuneration policies and practices of listed companies should be determined by a remuneration committee of the board consisting of a majority of independent directors.

related party disclosures in financial statements

[13.3.70] Accounting Standard AASB 124 *Related Party Disclosures*, imposes various disclosure requirements in relation to benefits received by directors and other related parties. Under AASB 124, the financial statements must disclose the value of all benefits to related parties including such matters as transactions where a director or other related entity is a customer of, or supplier to, the company. Directors' transactions as shareholders must also be disclosed.

Section 300A and AASB1046 *Director and Executive Disclosures by Disclosing Entities* apply to listed companies and detail the disclosure of directors and senior executive remuneration. Directors' remuneration is discussed in Chapter 12 above.

personal profits arising from acting as director

Directors are under a fiduciary duty not to make undisclosed personal profits while acting in their position.

[13.3.75] The directors' duty to avoid undisclosed conflicts of interests applies not just to self-interested transactions with the company. Directors are also under a fiduciary duty not to make undisclosed personal profits while acting in their position. This attempts to ensure that when acting for the company, directors are not tempted by the prospect of deriving private benefits for themselves or for others. This equitable principle applies even where the company has not suffered any loss, indeed it may even have benefited. Further, there is a breach of duty even if the transaction was fair from the company's point of view. Directors must be seen to act in good faith. Directors cannot place themselves in a position where it may appear that they are motivated by considerations other than what is in the best interests of the company.

case note

In *Regal (Hastings) Ltd v Gulliver* [1967] 2 AC 134n, Regal (Hastings) Ltd owned a cinema in Hastings. The directors wished to lease two other cinemas in the town and sell the whole business of the company as a going concern. A subsidiary company was formed for this purpose, with a capital of 5,000 £1 shares because the lessor of the two cinemas required the directors to guarantee payment of the rent unless the paid up capital of the subsidiary was £5,000. It was originally intended that Regal (Hastings) Ltd would own all the shares in the subsidiary; however, it was only able to contribute £2,000. At board meetings of the two companies, it was decided that the balance would be allotted to the four directors, the company solicitor and persons nominated by the chairman of directors. They were allotted 500 shares each in the subsidiary. The chairman, Gulliver, held the shares as trustee for two companies and one individual. He was a director as well as minority shareholder in both of these companies.

It was decided that instead of selling the business, the purchasers would buy all the shares in both Regal (Hastings) Ltd and its subsidiary. The shareholders of the subsidiary thereby acquired a profit of nearly £3 per share. The purchasers of the shares appointed new directors of the companies and then caused Regal (Hastings) Ltd to bring an action against the former directors and the solicitor seeking to recover the profit they had made. It was found as a fact that all the transactions were honestly made; nevertheless, the House of Lords held that the four directors were liable to repay the profits they had made on the sale of the shares. Lord Russell of Killowen stated:

> < The rule of equity which insists on those, who by use of a fiduciary position make a profit, being liable to account for that profit, in no way depends on fraud, or absence of bona fides; or upon such questions or consideration as whether the profit would or should otherwise have gone to the plaintiff, or whether the profiteer was under a duty to obtain the source of the profit for the plaintiff, or whether he took a risk or acted as he did for the benefit of the plaintiff, or whether the plaintiff has in fact been damaged or benefited by his action. The liability arises from the mere fact of a profit having, in the stated circumstances, been made. The profiteer, however honest and well-intentioned, cannot escape the risk of being called upon to account ...
>
> Let me now consider whether the essential matters, which the plaintiff (Regal Hastings Ltd) must prove, have been established in the present case. As to the profit being in fact made there can be no doubt ... Did such of the first five respondents as acquired these very profitable shares acquire them by reason and in the course of their office of directors of Regal? In my opinion, when the facts are examined and appreciated, the answer can only be that they did ...
>
> In the result, I am of the opinion that the directors standing in a fiduciary relationship to Regal in regard to the exercise of their powers as directors, and having obtained these shares by reason and only by reason of the fact that they were directors of Regal and in the course of execution of that office, are accountable for the profits they have made out of them. >

The House of Lords, however, considered that the positions of the chairman and solicitor were different from that of the other directors. While the solicitor had profited from the sale of the shares, he was not a director and had disclosed his profit to the appropriate organ of the company, the board of directors. Indeed, he only acquired the shares in the first place on their request. Gulliver, Regal's chairman, was also found not to have breached his duty to the company. The court accepted that he held the shares in the subsidiary as a trustee for others and consequently he derived no personal profit from the transaction.

Regal (Hastings) Ltd v Gulliver illustrates the far-reaching implications of the equitable principle that directors cannot make an undisclosed personal profit arising from acting in their position as directors. The directors, who personally profited, acted in good faith and the company had not been deprived of a business opportunity because it did not have the required funds. In fact, the company benefited as a result of the other shareholders taking up shares in the subsidiary. In addition, the successful action only benefited the purchasers of Regal (Hastings) Ltd who had contracted to pay an agreed price. The return of the profits to Regal (Hastings) Ltd meant that they succeeded in obtaining a reduction from the contracted purchase price. Directors in similar circumstances may now be able to avail themselves of s 1318. This section permits the court to relieve an officer from any liability for negligence, default, breach of trust or breach of duty if it appears that he acted honestly and having regard to the circumstances of the case, he or she ought fairly to be excused.

improper use of position: s 182

Section 182 prohibits officers or employees of a corporation from improperly using their position to gain an advantage for themselves or for any other person or to cause detriment to the corporation.

[13.3.80] Section 182 prohibits officers or employees of a corporation from improperly using their position to gain an advantage for themselves or for any other person or to cause detriment to the corporation.

Section 182 is the statutory version of the fiduciary principle applied in *Regal (Hastings) Ltd v Gulliver* that directors are under a duty not to make undisclosed personal profits arising from their position. However, s 182 is wider in that it applies to employees as well as officers. Further, s 182 is breached if officers or employees improperly use their position to gain an advantage for others. It appears that this would extend to a person in the chairman's position in *Regal (Hastings) Ltd v Gulliver* since a profit was made by him as trustee for others.

The directors' duty not to improperly use their position in s 182 overlaps with both their fiduciary duty to act in good faith in the best interests of the company as well as s 181. These obligations are discussed in Chapter 13.2 above. In *Southern Real Estate Pty Ltd v Dellow* [2003] SASC 318, Debelle J referred to the relationship between the duty to act in the best interests of the company and s 182:

> **< [Section 182] plainly flows from and might be regarded as one aspect of the duty to act in good faith in the best interests of the company. The duty spells out the obligations of a director not to allow personal interests to conflict with a duty to the company. That obligation stems from the fact that a director is a fiduciary. >**

Section 182 is a designated civil penalty provision.

Section 182 is a designated civil penalty provision: s 1317E. Any person who is involved in a contravention of s 182 also contravenes a civil penalty provision: s 182(2). The civil penalty provisions are discussed in Chapter 13.6 below.

meaning of "improper"

[13.3.85] The term "improper" means a number of things. It refers to conduct that is inconsistent with the "proper" discharge of the duties, obligations and responsibilities of an officer: *Grove v Flavel* (1986) 4 ACLC 654. In other words, directors improperly use their position if they breach their fiduciary duties. In *Chew v R* (1992) 10 ACLC 816, the High Court held that a director may act improperly even though the director considered they were acting in the best interests of the company as a whole and did not intend to act dishonestly.

Directors improperly use their position if they breach their fiduciary duties.

Directors may also improperly use their position if they act without authority.

case note

In *R v Byrnes* (1995) 13 ACLC 1488, two directors of Magnacrete Ltd, without authority of the board, arranged for their company's seal to be affixed to a guarantee and other documents that provided security for a loan to another company they controlled. It was held that the directors breached a predecessor of s 182 even though they reasonably but mistakenly believed that executing these documents was in the interests of Magnacrete. Brennan, Deane, Toohey and Gaudron JJ stated:

< Impropriety does not depend on an alleged offender's consciousness of impropriety. Impropriety consists in a breach of the standards of conduct that would be expected of a person in the position of the alleged offender by reasonable persons with knowledge of the duties, powers and authority of the position and the circumstances of the case. When impropriety is said to consist in an abuse of power, the state of mind of the alleged offender is important: the alleged offender's knowledge or means of knowledge of the circumstances in which the power is exercised and their purpose or intention in exercising the power are important factors in determining the question whether the power has been abused. But impropriety is not restricted to abuse of power. It may consist in the doing of an act which a director or officer knows or ought to know that they have no authority to do. >

case note

The principles in *R v Byrnes* were applied in *R v Cook* (1996) 14 ACLC 947. In that case the chairman of a company was held to have improperly used his position to gain an advantage for himself when he arranged, without authority of the board, for the company to transfer $199,000 from its bank account to a joint account he held with his wife. The court rejected the director's argument that the transfer was in the best interests of the company and not improper because he was concerned that the company's bank account might be frozen by the predecessor of ASIC.

case note

In *ASIC v Adler* [2002] NSWSC 171 (confirmed on appeal [2003] NSWCA 131), the facts of which are set out in Chapter 13.2 above, the court decided that Adler contravened s 182 when he arranged for part of HIHC's $10 million loan to PEE to be used to acquire HIH shares on the stock exchange. This acquisition was intended to support the HIH share price and enable Adler Corporation to sell its own HIH shares ahead of the sale of PEE's HIH shares. It was held that as a result of this transaction, Adler improperly used his position as a director of HIH and officer of HIHC and director of PEE to gain an advantage for Adler Corporation. The court held that Williams also breached his s 182 duty not to improperly use his position as a director of both HIH and HIHC to gain an advantage for Adler. He also improperly used his position to cause detriment to HIH and HIHC in authorising the $10 million payment without proper safeguards and without approval from HIH's investment committee as required by HIH's investment guidelines.

The court held that Adler also improperly used his position as a director in relation to PEE's acquisition of a number of unlisted venture capital companies from Adler Corporation at their cost price and without obtaining independent valuations. These acquisitions enabled Adler to extricate himself and Adler Corporation from commercially unviable business ventures. Adler knew that each of these companies had major cash flow difficulties and that there was a significant risk that they would fail. Adler failed to disclose his personal interest in these acquisitions to HIH's board other than Williams and Fodera.

A predecessor of s 182 has also been applied in an insolvency context.

case note

In *Jeffree v NCSC* (1989) 7 ACLC 556, the facts of which are discussed in Chapter 13.5 below, the Supreme Court of Western Australia held that a director improperly used his position in breach of the section when he sold all the company's business to another company he controlled without obtaining payment for goodwill. This sale, which left the company as a dormant shell, was entered into to defeat the claim of a contingent creditor. The director acted contrary to the interests of the company's future creditors.

to gain an advantage or to cause detriment

To contravene s 182, a director, officer or employee must not only improperly use their position but must also do so "to gain an advantage for themselves or for another person or to cause detriment to the corporation".

[13.3.90] To contravene s 182, a director, officer or employee must not only improperly use their position but must also do so "to gain an advantage for themselves or for another person or to cause detriment to the corporation".

A majority of the High Court in *Chew v R* (1992) 10 ACLC 816 interpreted the predecessor of s 182 as being purposive. This means an officer breaches the section if improper use is made of their office in order to gain advantage or to cause detriment. It is not necessary that the accrual of an advantage or suffering of a detriment actually occur. In their majority judgment, Mason CJ, Brennan, Gaudron and McHugh JJ said:

> < **... it is necessary to establish not merely that the accused intended that a result should ensue, but also that the accused believed that the intended result would be an advantage for himself or herself or for some other person or a detriment to the corporation.** >

The High Court in *Chew v R* suggested that the predecessor of s 183 should also be interpreted as being purposive in the same way as s 182.

case note

In *R v Donald* (1993) 11 ACLC 712, Donald was managing director and owned half the shares of Ardina Pty Ltd. The company entered into contracts with two other companies that he controlled. The invoices for payment to the two companies were passed directly to Donald for payment instead of being checked by employees of Ardina Pty Ltd, as was the usual practice. Some invoices were falsely made out. Donald did not disclose his interest in the two companies and was charged with a breach of the predecessor of s 182. The Queensland Court of Appeal applied the purposive test adopted in *Chew v R*. It held that the equivalent of s 182 was breached even though some payments were due under the contracts. The companies that received payment were still gaining an advantage and it was not necessary for them to gain a profit. This advantage was gained because the payments were made without the usual checking and scrutiny.

bribes and other undisclosed benefits

[13.3.95] An obvious example of making an undisclosed personal profit arising from acting in the position of director occurs when a director is paid a bribe or secret commission in order to procure a particular course of action by the company or to influence the director in a particular way. The receipt of the payment would also amount to a breach of the duty to act in good faith in the best interests of the company as well as ss 181 and 182.

An obvious example of making an undisclosed personal profit arising from acting in the position of director occurs when a director is paid a bribe or secret commission in order to procure a particular course of action by the company or to influence the director in a particular way.

case note

In *Boston Deep Sea Fishing & Ice Co v Ansell* (1888) 39 Ch D 339, Ansell was the managing director of the company and organised the construction of fishing boats on its behalf. However, unknown to his company, he was paid a commission by the shipbuilders. The company was also unaware that Ansell was a shareholder in an ice supplying company and a fish carrying company. These companies paid bonuses to shareholders who employed their services. Ansell contracted with the two companies in respect of Boston's fishing business. The court held that Ansell's personal interests conflicted with his fiduciary duty to Boston in respect of both the commission received from the shipbuilders as well as the bonuses received from the two companies of which he was a shareholder.

Directors who derive an undisclosed personal benefit breach their fiduciary and statutory duties irrespective of whether the company suffered loss as a result. In such cases, the director can be ordered to account to the company for the personal benefit derived. The various remedies for breach of directors' fiduciary and statutory duties are discussed in Chapter 13.6 below.

case note

In *Furs Ltd v Tomkies* (1936) 54 CLR 583, Furs Ltd carried on the business of processing furs for the manufacture of coats. Tomkies was its managing director and had special knowledge of the tanning, dyeing and dressing operations of the business, including secret formulae, which were of considerable value. Tomkies suggested that a separate company be formed to conduct this aspect of the business, or it be sold. A purchaser was found and Tomkies negotiated a price for the business, including the value of the formulae. The purchaser told Tomkies that he required his services for a new company that he proposed to form to conduct the business. This was disclosed to the chairman of directors of Furs Ltd who stated that Furs Ltd could not afford to continue to employ Tomkies and advised him to make the best arrangements for himself. Tomkies and the purchaser of the business concluded an arrangement whereby Tomkies was to be employed for three years at a particular salary and he was to be paid an additional amount to be satisfied by an issue of shares in the new company and by promissory notes. The sale of the business was concluded but the other directors and shareholders of Furs Ltd were not told of the payments to Tomkies. Furs Ltd successfully brought an action seeking to recover from Tomkies the amount of profit he made by reason of his breach of duty.

The court held that there was a clear conflict of interests because Tomkies failed to put the company first and the breach of duty was not dependent on the company suffering any detriment.

misuse of company funds

Directors are under a fiduciary duty to use the company funds for its legitimate business purposes and must not mix the company's funds with their own.

[13.3.100] Directors are under a fiduciary duty to act in their company's interests with respect to the use of the company's funds which must be used for the company's legitimate business purposes. Directors are also under a duty not to mix the company's funds with their own. In some instances this may also amount to theft or embezzlement.

A conflict of interests arises whether the company's funds are mixed with the director's personal funds or with the funds of another company in which the director has an interest.

case note

This is illustrated in *Totex-Adon Pty Ltd v Marco* (1982) 1 ACLC 228. Marco was a director of Totex-Adon which was formed to conduct a joint venture between Totex (Aust) Pty Ltd which carried on a trading business in New South Wales, and Adon Pty Ltd, a Queensland company. Marco was also a director and shareholder of Adon. Under the terms of the joint venture agreement, Totex-Adon was to purchase goods from Totex and then sell them in Queensland. Totex-Adon commenced proceedings against Marco under a predecessor of s 181, when it was discovered that Marco had failed to account to it for the proceeds of the sale of its goods. The evidence disclosed that Marco had failed to open a separate bank account for the plaintiff in Queensland and all its receipts and payments were deposited in and came from Adon's own account. The court held that Marco had clearly breached his fiduciary duty owed to Totex-Adon when he mixed its funds with that of his other company.

If directors, without proper disclosure, obtain funds from the company for their personal use, it is no defence for them to assert that the funds obtained were lent to them.

case note

This is illustrated in *Paul A Davies (Aust) Pty Ltd v Davies* (1983) 1 ACLC 1091. In that case the company carried on business as a car dealer. Because of a downturn in this business the directors decided to enter into a new venture. They purchased a freehold property that included a boarding house and restaurant business. This purchase was made in the directors' own names. However, it was financed partly from company funds in the form of interest-free loans to the directors. The balance of purchase money came from a bank loan to the directors. The company encountered financial difficulties and was eventually placed in voluntary liquidation. The liquidator commenced proceedings against the directors arguing that they had acted in breach of their fiduciary duty in that they used company funds without shareholder approval for their own private purposes and not for any purpose of the company. This claim was upheld and the Supreme Court of New South Wales ordered that the directors hold the property as constructive trustees for the company. It was no defence for them to assert that the moneys were lent to them.

taking up corporate opportunity

A director breaches the duty to avoid a conflict of interests where the director, without appropriate disclosure or approval, takes up an opportunity that should have been taken up by the company.

[13.3.105] A director breaches the duty to avoid a conflict of interests where the director, without appropriate disclosure or approval, takes up an opportunity that should have been taken up by the company. In such cases, the director may be liable to account to the company for any profit. The company may instead seek a constructive trust order, the effect of which is that the company takes the business opportunity for itself. Directors who take up a corporate opportunity in breach of their fiduciary duty will also breach their fiduciary duty to act in good faith in the best interests of the company as well as ss 181 and 182. The various remedies for breach of directors' fiduciary and statutory duties are discussed in Chapter 13.6 below.

diversion of contract

[13.3.110] A breach of the fiduciary duty regarding corporate opportunities occurs where a director, while negotiating a contract for the company, without appropriate disclosure and approval, arranges for the contract to be diverted from the company to the director personally or to another company in which the director is involved.

case note

In *Cook v Deeks* [1916] 1 AC 554, Toronto Construction Co was formed to engage in railway construction work on contract with the Canadian Pacific Railway. Its shares were held by four contractors in nearly equal proportions. They were also the directors. The company successfully completed several contracts of considerable value. Disagreements arose between three of the directors and the fourth, Cook. The three directors, G S Deeks, G M Deeks and Hinds, then negotiated a further contract on behalf of Toronto Construction Co. Towards the end of negotiations, Deeks, Deeks and Hinds indicated that the contract was for them and not for the company. The three directors formed a new company to carry out this contract. When Cook protested, resolutions were passed by the three as shareholders of Toronto Construction, approving the sale of part of its plant to the newly formed company, declaring that Toronto Construction Co had no interest in the new contract and authorising the directors to defend any action brought by Cook. Cook then brought a derivative action on behalf of Toronto Construction Co seeking an order that the contract and benefit of the contract belonged in equity to that company. The Privy Council held that the three directors breached their duty to Toronto Construction Co by diverting the contract to their newly formed company and consequently they held the contract as trustees for Toronto Construction Co.

The Privy Council also held that the resolution passed by the general meeting declaring that Toronto Construction Co had no interest in the contract was invalid as it constituted a fraud on the minority shareholder, Cook. The rights of a member to bring a legal action in the name of a company and to seek an order under the oppression remedy are discussed in Chapter 17 below.

A breach of the fiduciary duty regarding corporate opportunities also occurs where a director who is involved in a business that competes with the company arranges for the company to shut down its own business. The effect of this is that the company loses the benefit of its business.

case note

In *Mordecai v Mordecai* (1988) 12 NSWLR 58, three brothers, Joseph, David and Meyer, were directors of Morpack Packaging Pty Ltd. Joseph and David each held 50 per cent of the shares. Joseph separated from his wife. Later, he died and in his will deliberately excluded his wife and left his shares to his brothers as trustees for his infant son. His brothers caused Morpack to cease business. They set up a rival company that took over all Morpack's customers. Joseph's wife, on her son's behalf, claimed damages from David and Meyer alleging that they had breached their duty both as her son's trustees and as directors by disposing of Morpack's business in such a way as to reduce the value of her late husband's estate.

The Supreme Court of New South Wales agreed that David and Meyer had breached their duties as directors. They did more than merely set up a rival business in competition with Morpack—they deliberately closed down Morpack's business purely for their own private benefit. They improperly depreciated the value of the business by asking Morpack's customers to cease to deal with it and to deal with them instead.

company consent where director takes up opportunity

Directors who take up a corporate opportunity avoid breaching their fiduciary duty if they make full disclosure and the company gives its approval or consent.

[13.3.115] Directors who take up a corporate opportunity avoid breaching their fiduciary duty if they make full disclosure and the company gives its approval or consent. Directors who fail to make full disclosure and obtain consent cannot defend themselves by asserting that they acted honestly and that they benefited the company by taking up the opportunity or that the company did not have the means to take up the opportunity itself. In *Regal (Hastings) Ltd v Gulliver* [1967] 2 AC 134n, the facts of which are discussed above at para [13.3.75], the House of Lords noted that it was irrelevant that the company could not take up the opportunity to acquire shares in the subsidiary. The directors were in breach of duty despite appearing to act honestly and the company not having suffered any loss.

Directors satisfy their fiduciary duty if they make full disclosure to the company's shareholders and obtain their approval or consent. Section 191 also requires directors to make full disclosure to the board. The s 191 disclosure requirements are discussed below at para [13.3.170].

In both *Furs Ltd v Tomkies* (1936) 54 CLR 583 and *Regal (Hastings) Ltd v Gulliver* [1967] 2 AC 134n, the respective courts indicated that disclosure by a director must be made to the general meeting of shareholders. However, in some circumstances, particularly in closely held companies, it may not be necessary to call a general meeting as long as shareholders are kept fully informed of the relevant circumstances and give their informed consent. This is discussed in Chapter 13.7 below.

case note

In *Queensland Mines Ltd v Hudson* (1978) 52 ALJR 399, the managing director of the company, Hudson, took up mining exploration licences in circumstances where the company was financially unable to do so. Hudson made full disclosure of his intention to personally take up the licences and then resigned as managing director. He met all expenses and ran all risks until he proved the existence of valuable deposits. The rights were then sold to an American company with Hudson being entitled to royalties. When control of Queensland Mines changed, the company took proceedings against Hudson alleging breach of duty.

The Privy Council held that the opportunity to earn the royalties arose from the use Hudson made of his position as managing director. But he fully informed Queensland Mines shareholders as to his interest in the licence, and the company renounced its interest and assented to Hudson proceeding with the venture alone. Queensland Mines failed in its action for an account of the past and future profits from the royalties payable to Hudson.

The Privy Council also held that the disclosure by Hudson to the board of directors, who were nominees of the respective shareholders, was sufficient.

case note

In *Peso Silver Mines v Cropper* (1966) 58 DLR (2d) 1, the Supreme Court of Canada came to a similar conclusion. A mining claim was offered to Peso by a prospector. This offer was rejected after the directors acted in good faith, in the interests of the company and with sound business reasons. Soon after, the managing director, Cropper, was privately approached to take up the claims together with two others. Mayo Silver Mines was incorporated for this purpose. Peso merged with Charter Oil and after disagreements between Charter Oil's chairman and Cropper, Peso sought a declaration that Cropper's shares in Mayo were held by him in trust for Peso. It also sought an order requiring Cropper's shares in Mayo to be delivered to Peso or an account of the proceeds. It was held that the circumstances of the case differed from *Regal (Hastings) Ltd v Gulliver* as Cropper had been approached to take up the claims in his capacity as an individual member of the public and not as a director of Peso.

Directors have the onus of proving that the shareholders consented to them taking the opportunity after full and frank disclosure of all material information. The directors breach their duty if the information they disclose is misleading or inadequate.

case note

In *Southern Cross Mine Management Pty Ltd v Ensham Resources Pty Ltd* [2005] QSC 233, Ensham operated and managed an open-cut coal mine on behalf of its shareholders who were involved as joint venturers. Foots, Ensham's CEO, convinced the joint venturers that Ensham needed an additional dragline, a machine used in open-cut coal mining, for its operations. Foots advised that he had formed a company, Southern Cross Mine Management, which would buy a dragline and lease it to Ensham. Ensham's board consented to this arrangement and entered into a lease agreement with Southern Cross Mine Management which acquired the dragline from its original owner. The court found that Foots induced Ensham's consent by a number of misrepresentations. He falsely claimed that:

- the original owner of the dragline would not sell it to Ensham because it had already sold it to Southern Cross Mine Management; and
- it was significantly cheaper for Ensham to hire the dragline from Southern Cross Mine Management than to buy it outright.

Foots also failed to disclose to Ensham that Southern Cross Mine Management anticipated profits from the dragline lease would provide it with a return of more than 400 per cent on its investment.

It was held that because he was Ensham's CEO, he owed it a fiduciary duty in relation to dealings with the dragline. He learned of the opportunity to acquire the dragline because of his position as Ensham's CEO. It was Foots' duty to acquire the dragline for Ensham. As Ensham's fiduciary, Foots could be relieved of this duty and acquire the dragline himself only if Ensham consented after Foots disclosed all relevant information. While Foots disclosed his interest in Southern Cross Mine Management, his misrepresentations meant that Ensham's consent was not fully informed of all relevant information. The court described Foots' conduct as "disgraceful" and that the object of the arrangement was to "swindle Ensham of the profits from the dragline". Since Southern Cross Mine Management and Foots were regarded as indistinguishable, the court held that it knowingly participated in Foots' breach of fiduciary duty. The court declared that Southern Cross Mine Management held the dragline on a constructive trust for Ensham. A company's constructive trust remedy is discussed in Chapter 13.6 below.

company need not suffer loss

[13.3.120] A company need not suffer any loss to establish a breach of duty. This is illustrated in *Green v Bestobell Industries Pty Ltd* [1982] WAR 1. In that case, Green used information arising from his former position as Victorian manager of a company to prepare a building construction tender. His tender, which was submitted by a company he formed for the purpose, was successful. Bestobell Industries also tendered for the same project but came third. The court held that Green breached his duties and ordered an account of profits to Bestobell even though it would not have won the tender in any event.

misuse of confidential information

Directors have a fiduciary duty not to misuse confidential company information for their own benefit without appropriate disclosure and approval.

[13.3.125] Directors have a fiduciary duty not to misuse confidential company information for their own benefit without appropriate disclosure and approval. This principle includes the misuse of trade secrets, and lists of customers for the use of competitors and other confidential information. The duty overlaps in many instances with the duty not to take up a corporate opportunity, discussed above. The fiduciary duty regarding the misuse of confidential information is an aspect of the wider fiduciary and statutory duty to act in good faith in the best interests of the company. It also overlaps with the duty not to compete with the company, discussed below, para [13.3.150].

The duty not to misuse confidential information often arises when a director leaves one company to commence work for a competitor. A director or an employee after ceasing employment is not permitted to use confidential information obtained in the course of that employment for the purpose of competing with their former employer: *Facenda Chicken Ltd v Fowler* [1987] 1 Ch 117.

Confidential information includes trade secrets, customer lists and pricing information.

Confidential information includes trade secrets, customer lists and pricing information. In *Wright v Gasweld Pty Ltd* (1991) 22 NSWLR 317, Kirby P listed the following five factors to be considered in deciding whether information was confidential:

> **the skill and effort expended to acquire the information;**
> **the degree to which the information is jealously guarded by the employer, is not readily made available to employees and could not, without considerable effort or risk, be acquired by others;**
> **whether it was plainly known to the employee that the material was regarded by the employer as confidential;**
> **the usages and practices of the industry; and**
> **whether the employee in question has been permitted to share the information only by reason of their seniority or high responsibility within the employer's organisation.**

case note

In *Thomas Marshall (Exporters) Ltd v Guinle* [1978] 3 WLR 116, Guinle was managing director of a company that carried on an importing business. It imported goods from Eastern Europe and the Orient which it later resold in England. Without his company's knowledge, Guinle began to trade on his own account in competition with his company. When this was discovered his company sought an injunction to restrain him from dealing with the company's customers and suppliers. It also sought an injunction to prevent him from disclosing or using the company's confidential information or trade secrets. The court granted the injunctions after deciding that Guinle had breached his fiduciary duties.

case note

In *Riteway Express Pty Ltd v Clayton* (1987) 10 NSWLR 238, the company carried on a freight business. Clayton was an executive director of Riteway Express and the second defendant was its New South Wales state manager. In 1987 the company entered into a marketing agreement with Riteway Marketing, a company formed by Clayton and the second defendant. Riteway Marketing was granted the exclusive right to sell freight for Riteway Express. Clayton and the second defendant ceased their full-time employment with Riteway Express, though Clayton remained on its board as a non-executive director. After disputes arose between the two companies, Riteway Express terminated the marketing agreement and was granted an injunction to prevent Riteway Marketing and its directors from disclosing confidential information concerning Riteway Express business. The confidential information concerned the names and requirements of the clients of Riteway Express as well as the prices it customarily charged those clients.

case note

In *Forkserve Pty Ltd v Jack & Aussie Forklift Repairs Pty Ltd* [2000] NSWSC 1064 the Supreme Court of New South Wales held that the fiduciary duty regarding misuse of confidential information was breached when a former employee who was a *de facto* director set up his own business and began, prior to ceasing his employment, soliciting his former company's customers using the company's teledex book containing customers' names and telephone numbers. The teledex book could be classified as a customer list even though it could not be classified as confidential. Taking the teledex book for use in the future to compete with the employer would, but for the employer's consent, have amounted to a breach of duty by the employee. Santow J stated:

> < It is long settled that during a period of employment an employee and/or a director may not solicit customers for a future time when the employment has ceased and the employee or director has established his or her own business. However, once the employment has ceased, in the absence of special stipulation, the employee may canvass the customers of the late employer and may send a circular to every customer. Further, during the course of employment an employee is not able to make or copy a list of the employer's customers but cannot be restrained from sending circulars to customers whose names the employee remembers. >

improper use of information: s 183

Under s 183, a person who obtains information because they are or have been a director, officer or employee of a corporation must not improperly use the information to make a gain for themselves or any other person or to cause detriment to the corporation.

[13.3.130] Section 183 supplements the fiduciary duty regarding the misuse of confidential information. It is wider than the fiduciary duty in that it also applies to employees. Under s 183, a person who obtains information because they are or have been a director, officer or employee of a corporation must not improperly use the information to make a gain for themselves or any other person or to cause detriment to the corporation. It is clear that s 183 applies to former directors, officers and employees as well as current directors, officer and employees.

meaning of "information"

[13.3.135] While s 183 prohibits improper use of "information", the section does not use the word "confidential". The cases are divided as to whether confidentiality is an element of s 183. In *Es-me Pty Ltd v Parker* [1972] WAR 52, the Supreme Court of Western Australia made it clear that for the purposes of the fiduciary duties and a predecessor of s 183, the information need not necessarily be secret but must be confidential information possessed by the company.

There is some doubt as to the correctness of the proposition in *Es-me Pty Ltd v Parker* that the information used by officers must be confidential. In *McNamara v Flavel* (1988) 6 ACLC 802, the South Australian Supreme Court held that for purposes of a predecessor of s 183 a breach depended on how the information was acquired and not whether it was confidential. If a plaintiff must prove that the information was at least confidential, breach of this duty would be more difficult to prove than the broader duty under s 181 or the fiduciary duty not to make undisclosed profits.

Young J, in *Rosetex Co Pty Ltd v Licata* (1994) 12 ACLC 269, interpreted "information" as referring to that type of information that equity would restrict the director from using to his personal profit. Section 183 also may include a situation where an employee sets up in competition and makes improper use of information after leaving the company, even though there is no restraint of trade clause in the employee's contract with the company.

A director may improperly use confidential information to gain personal profits by obtaining inside information regarding the company's affairs and then trading in the company's shares. In such cases, the other trading party has no rights to a remedy under s 183 but may have rights under the insider trading provisions contained in ss 1042A–1043O. Insider trading is discussed in Chapter 19 below.

case note

In *ASIC v Vizard* [2005] FCA 1037, ASIC brought civil penalty proceedings against Vizard after he confessed to being involved in contraventions of the predecessors of s 183 in relation to three share transactions that were made as a result of confidential information he gained as a non-executive director of Telstra. To keep his involvement in the share trading secret, Vizard set up a share trading company, Creative Technology Investments Pty Ltd (CTI) of which his accountant was the sole director and shareholder. Vizard also controlled another company, Brigham Pty Ltd (Brigham), which was trustee of the Vizard family trust. Brigham lent money to CTI to fund its share trading activities. The loan agreement provided that CTI would pay Brigham 90 per cent of the proceeds derived from the sale of any shares.

Through his membership of Teltra's board, Vizard became aware of the following confidential information:

> In 2000, Telstra was involved in confidential merger discussions in which it was proposed that two other listed companies, Sausage Software Ltd and Solution 6 Holdings Ltd, would merge and that Telstra would acquire a substantial holding in the

merged entity. Guessing that once the proposed merger became public there would be a significant increase in the share price of Sausage Software, Vizard caused CTI to buy shares in Sausage Software. Vizard's guess was correct and following the public announcement of the merger, Sausage Software's share price rose substantially giving CTI an immediate paper profit on its acquisition. CTI subsequently sold its Sausage Software shares.

> Telstra owned a substantial interest in another listed company, Computershare Ltd. Telstra's board decided that it would sell its shares in Computershare to raise funds to help pay for its interest in the Sausage-Solution 6 merger. Telstra's proposed sale was kept confidential until the sale was completed. As CTI owned shares in Computershare, Vizard correctly reasoned that the market price of shares in that company would fall after the public announcement of Telstra's sale of its holding. Vizard caused CTI to sell its shares in Computershare ahead of Telstra's sale.

> In 2000, Telstra's board secretly proposed that the company should acquire a 51 per cent interest in Keycorp Ltd, a listed company. Vizard, realising that this would mean that Keycorp's share price would rise after the announcement of Telstra's acquisition, caused CTI to buy some shares in Keycorp ahead of Telstra. CTI later sold its Keycorp shares at a profit.

It was held that as a result of the above transactions, Vizard was involved in a contravention of the predecessors of s 183. In each instance he acquired confidential information by reason of his position as a non-executive director of Telstra. He made improper use of the information when he caused CTI to buy or sell shares. Vizard improperly used the information to gain an advantage for CTI, Brigham and ultimately for himself personally. The Court ordered that Vizard pay a pecuniary civil penalty as well as making a disqualification order. These remedies are discussed in Chapter 13.6 below.

relationship between ss 181 and 183

[13.3.140] The fiduciary and statutory duties regarding the misuse of information are an instance of the wider duty to act in good faith in the best interests of the company: *Southern Real Estate Pty Ltd v Dellow* [2003] SASC 318. A director who contravenes s 183 may in the same circumstances also contravene s 181.

A director who contravenes s 183 may in the same circumstances also contravene s 181.

case note

The overlapping operation of ss 181 and 183 is illustrated by *Marson Pty Ltd v Pressbank Pty Ltd* (1989) 7 ACLC 733. Pressbank was a joint venture company whose shareholders were companies controlled by Mr and Mrs Margolis on the one hand and Mr and Mrs Urban on the other. Mr and Mrs Urban were Pressbank's only directors. The company was formed to acquire land and a business. A deposit of $50,000 was due to the vendor. Pressbank raised this amount by borrowing $30,000 from the Urbans' company and $20,000 from the Margolis' company, Marson Pty Ltd.

When Mr and Mrs Margolis experienced trouble raising their share of the balance of the money required to settle the purchase it was agreed that the joint venture would be abandoned and that the Urbans would proceed with it themselves. It was accepted that Pressbank owed Marson $20,000 and would eventually repay this debt. When the Urbans told the vendor that Pressbank was unable to settle the purchase, the contract was rescinded and the deposit forfeited to the vendor. Because the vendor was anxious to settle the sale as quickly as possible he agreed that if Urban could find a new purchaser the vendor would refund $30,000 of the forfeited deposit.

The Urbans formed another company that settled the contract with the vendor for the same price. Mr Urban convinced the vendor to credit the new company with $30,000 of the total deposit paid by Pressbank. The remaining $20,000 remained forfeited to the vendor. When Margolis learned of this he caused his company to bring an action against the Urbans arguing that they were liable to Pressbank for breach of both their statutory and fiduciary duties as directors.

The Supreme Court of Queensland held that the directors had breached their duties under the predecessors of ss 181 and 183. The court found that it was only because of the Urbans' connection with Pressbank that they were able to negotiate what was in effect a reduction in price for their new company. Their actions indicated that they lacked honesty for purposes of the previous s 232(2). This may now indicate a lack of good faith and a failure to exercise powers for a proper purpose within the meaning of s 181(1). They also made improper use of information acquired by them as directors of Pressbank to gain an advantage for themselves and their company; the information being their awareness that the vendor would agree to a credit of $30,000 to a purchaser connected with Pressbank.

The court noted that the Urbans would not have breached their duties if they had arranged for their own company to conclude the contract with the vendor at the same price but with the $30,000 refund being credited to Pressbank. That would have left Pressbank with sufficient funds to repay the debt due to the Margolis' company.

misuse of information about a company's insolvency

Directors may contravene s 183 if they make improper use of information that their companies are in financial difficulties to gain an advantage for themselves over the company's creditors.

[13.3.145] Directors may contravene s 183 if they make improper use of information that their companies are in financial difficulties to gain an advantage for themselves over the company's creditors.

case note

In *Grove v Flavel* (1986) 4 ACLC 654, a director was convicted under a predecessor of s 183. The internal indebtedness within a group of companies was rearranged after the director acquired information that a company within the group was close to insolvency. A "round robin" of cheques resulted in the director, and the financially secure companies of which he was also a director, ceasing to be creditors of the company experiencing financial difficulties. Other companies of the group ceased being debtors of the troubled company and the danger of a liquidator calling up the debts was thereby removed.

It was held that the director had made improper use of information acquired by virtue of his position as an officer. The information led him to believe that the company faced a risk of liquidation which was real and not remote. He acted to protect himself and other companies of which he was a director from the consequences of a liquidation. This was detrimental to the creditors of the company in financial difficulties.

In *McNamara v Flavel* (1988) 6 ACLC 802, a director transferred for no consideration a valuable asset owned by his insolvent company to another company that he controlled. This was detrimental to the creditors of the first company. The extent to which directors owe duties to creditors is discussed in Chapter 13.5 below.

competing with the company

[13.3.150] As a general rule, fiduciaries are not permitted to enter into competition with the persons for whom they act. Trustees cannot compete with their beneficiaries and partners cannot compete with their partnerships. Despite the similarities of the duties of directors to the duties arising in these other relationships, it is not entirely settled that directors breach their fiduciary duty merely by being involved in a business that competes with their company. The courts draw a distinction between executive and non-executive directors.

In *Bell v Lever Bros Ltd* [1932] AC 161, the court held that non-executive directors of a company cannot be prevented from acting as a director of a competing company. While they are permitted to compete they cannot divulge confidential information obtained by them as director of one company to the other company or use for their own purposes information entrusted to them while acting as a director: *Markwell Bros Pty Ltd v CPN Diesels (Qld) Pty Ltd* (1982) 7 ACLR 425.

A company may provide in its constitution or in a service agreement entered into with a director that the director shall only engage in work related to the business of the company during normal office hours. Such a provision prevents the director from working for anyone else during those hours, whether or not they are engaged in a competing business.

case note

In *Hivac Ltd v Park Royal Scientific Instruments Ltd* [1946] 1 All ER 350, a company employed two employees who engaged in highly skilled, technical work. At least one of the employees had access to the company's manufacturing data. In their spare time they were employed by a rival company in similar work and also persuaded other employees to work for the rival company in their spare time. There was no evidence that the employees had revealed any confidential information to the rival company. It was held by the Court of Appeal, that an employee owes a duty of fidelity (good faith and no undisclosed conflicts) to the employer. An employee may work for another employer in their spare time. This is so in the case of a manual worker: what is done in their spare time is a private concern. However, a contract of employment may contain an express or implied term that an employee will not work for a competitor.

Hivac's case appears to suggest that an executive director employed under a service agreement at least owes an employees' duty of fidelity. This prevents the employee competing with the employer, the company.

While directors may sit on the boards of rival companies, they are not permitted to use or disclose the confidential information of one company to the rival company.

While directors may sit on the boards of rival companies, they are not permitted to use or disclose the confidential information of one company to the rival company.

case note

In *Riteway Express Pty Ltd v Clayton* (1987) 10 NSWLR 238, the Supreme Court of New South Wales noted that the law permits former employees of a company to compete with their company and use or disclose certain categories of information gained in the course of their employment. Former employees may, after leaving the company, legitimately use or disclose information that they have memorised. They can also use all their skills and experience acquired in the course of their previous employment.

Ex-employees, however, are not permitted to use or disclose trade secrets of their former employer. The court decided that the information in the present case fell into the permitted use category so that had Clayton merely been in the position of a former employee of the company he would have been permitted to use and disclose it. The court held, however, that because Clayton was still a non-executive director of Riteway Express he was not permitted to use the information. The court granted the injunction but made it subject to certain conditions. It would be lifted if either a general meeting of the company consented to Clayton carrying on a competing business or he ceased to be a director.

A director who forms an undisclosed intention to resign and set up a competing business is not permitted to actively solicit the company's customers for the competing business prior to the resignation or for a reasonable period of time thereafter: *Southern Real Estate Pty Ltd v Dellow* [2003] SASC 318. Directors are also not allowed to compete with their company where this involves them closing down the company's business and operating it for themselves: *Mordecai v Mordecai* (1988) 12 NSWLR 58.

disclosure of interests

[13.3.155] Directors who enter into a self-interested transaction with the company or otherwise put themselves in a conflict of interest situation which amounts to a breach of their fiduciary duty must disclose the details of their personal interest and obtain the company's fully informed consent if they are to avoid liability for the breach. Examples of such conflict of interest situations include where a director:

> **makes a personal profit that arises from their position:**
> **diverts an opportunity from their company: or**
> **misuses confidential company information.**

A key issue in relation to disclosure of interests is to whom directors must disclose their interests.

A key issue in relation to disclosure of interests is to whom directors must disclose their interests. As a general rule, directors' fiduciary obligations require them to make full disclosure of their potential conflicts of interest to the company's shareholders at a general meeting and obtain their consent (also referred to as "ratification"). However, as discussed below, a company's constitution may relax the obligation to disclose conflicts of interest to shareholders and allow disclosure to be made to the board. The *Corporations Act* also imposes disclosure and approval requirements. For example, as discussed above at para [13.3.15], s 208 requires prior shareholder approval if a public company provides a financial benefit to a related party. In addition, under s 191 directors who have a material interest in a matter that relates to the affairs of the company have a duty to disclose that to the other directors. Section 191 is discussed below, para [13.3.170].

under constitution and replaceable rules

A company's constitution may require a director's material interest to be disclosed to and approved by the company's directors instead of the general meeting of shareholders.

[13.3.160] A company's constitution may require a director's material interest to be disclosed to and approved by the company's directors instead of the general meeting of shareholders: *Woolworths Ltd v Kelly* (1991) 9 ACLC 539. The effect of such a provision in a company's constitution is to relax the strict fiduciary obligation to disclose conflicts of interest to shareholders. Even though such provisions are relatively common, companies recognise the possibility of the potential for conflicts of interest and their constitutions often provide that directors must disclose their personal interests and refrain from voting on the matter at directors' meetings. This is the case with the replaceable rule in s 194.

The proprietary company replaceable rule in s 194 permits directors of proprietary companies to have an interest in contracts with the company provided certain conditions are satisfied. The director must disclose the nature and extent of the interest at a directors' meeting. The rule also permits proprietary company directors to vote on whether the company enters into the contract if the director discloses the nature and extent of the interest at a directors' meeting: s 194(c).

The proprietary company replaceable rule in s 194 permits directors of proprietary companies to have an interest in contracts with the company provided certain conditions are satisfied.

While a company's constitution may prohibit an interested director from voting, such prohibitions only apply to voting at directors' meetings. A director who is also a shareholder is generally not disqualified from voting at a general meeting of members on matters affecting her or his personal interests as a shareholder: *North-West Transportation Co v Beatty* (1887) 12 App Cas 589. In some cases though, members may seek a remedy. This is discussed in Chapter 17 below.

at common law

[13.3.165] Directors' fiduciary obligations require them to make full disclosure of their potential conflicts of interest to the company's shareholders at a general meeting and obtain their consent (also referred to as "ratification"). Ratification by the general meeting of acts that constitute breach of directors' fiduciary duties is further discussed in Chapter 13.7 below.

As a general rule, the appropriate organ of the company to whom disclosure must be made is the general meeting of shareholders.

As a general rule, the appropriate organ of the company to whom disclosure must be made is the general meeting of shareholders.

case note

In *Furs Ltd v Tomkies* (1936) 54 CLR 83, discussed at para [13.3.95] above, the director defended his actions on the basis that he had disclosed his interest in a contract to his company's chairman of directors. The High Court rejected this defence on the basis that neither the chairman of directors nor the whole board were empowered to authorise him to disregard the interests of the company in pursuing his own interests.

case note

In *Regal (Hastings) Ltd v Gulliver* [1967] 2 AC 134n, the House of Lords took a similar view when it held that the directors could have protected themselves by making full disclosure to, and having their actions ratified by, the general meeting. This would have been a mere formality because the directors controlled the voting of the general meeting.

case note

A less strict approach was taken by the Privy Council in *Queensland Mines Ltd v Hudson* (1978) 52 ALJR 399, the facts of which are outlined above, para [13.3.115]. The company, after a change in control, brought an action claiming that Hudson had breached his duty as its managing director by taking up a corporate opportunity and making a profit for himself and that his profits should be accounted to the company. This argument was rejected by the Privy Council on the ground that Hudson had kept the boards of two companies, which originally controlled Queensland Mines Ltd, fully informed of his dealings. They permitted him to take up a mining licence himself, because the company had insufficient funds to utilise the opportunity itself. The two companies had very few shareholders and the respective boards were their nominees so that board approval was effectively the same as shareholder approval. Hudson was thus not in breach of his duty even though no formal disclosure had been made to the company's general meeting and it had not ratified his actions.

case note

In *Southern Cross Mine Management Pty Ltd v Ensham* [2005] QSC 233, the facts of which are discussed at para [13.3.115], it was held that the CEO had breached his fiduciary duty even though he had the company's shareholders' consent to his taking a corporate opportunity. As he had misrepresented important information, he had not satisfied his fiduciary obligation to make full disclosure. His misrepresentations meant that the shareholders' consent was not fully informed and therefore invalid.

under the Corporations Act

disclosure to other directors

Section 191(1) requires a director who has a material personal interest in a matter that relates to the affairs of the company to give notice of the interest to the other directors.

[13.3.170] Section 191(1) requires a director who has a material personal interest in a matter that relates to the affairs of the company to give notice of the interest to the other directors. Directors must make disclosure to both the shareholders and to the board as s 191 has effect in addition to and not in derogation of any general law rule about conflicts of interest and any applicable provision in the company's constitution: s 193.

Directors of proprietary companies who have a material personal interest in a matter relating to the affairs of the company are subject to the replaceable rule set out in s 194. It provides that if a director gives notice in accordance with s 191, the company cannot avoid the transaction merely because of the existence of the interest. The director may retain benefits under the transaction and can vote on matters that relate to the interest.

The notice required by s 191(1) must give details of the nature and extent of the interest and the relation of the interest to the affairs of the company: s 191(3)(a). It must be given at a directors' meeting as soon as practicable after the director becomes aware of their interest in the matter: s 191(3)(b).

The requirement to give notice under s 191(1) does not apply in the circumstances specified in s 191(2). For example, a director does not have to give notice of an interest if it is part of the director's remuneration or it relates to a proposed contract of the company that is subject to member approval and does not impose any obligation on the company if member approval is not obtained: s 191(2)(ii) and (iii).

Section 191 also does not apply to a proprietary company that has only one director: s 192(5).

A director may give standing notice to the other directors of the nature and extent of the director's interest in a matter: s 192(1). The details required to be disclosed correspond to the disclosure requirements set out in s 191 and it must also be minuted. The standing notice ceases to have effect when a new director is appointed until notice is given to the new director: s 192(5). It also ceases to have effect if the nature or extent of the interest materially increases above that disclosed in the notice: s 192(6). Standing notice is often given by directors who are on the boards of companies that may have frequent dealings with each other.

A contravention of ss 191 or 192 does not affect the validity of any act or transaction: ss 191(4) and 192(7). However, a breach constitutes an offence.

disclosure to the ASX

[13.3.175] Under s 205G, directors of listed companies must notify the ASX of relevant interests they hold in securities of the company or a related body corporate. They must also disclose any rights or options. Any changes in these holdings must be notified within 14 days. ASX Listing Rule 3.19A requires disclosure by a listed company of this information within five business days of a director acquiring a security holding or changing an existing holding. The information required to be given to the ASX includes details of relevant interests in securities which are indirectly held through interposed entities.

bibliography ...

Austin, R P "Fiduciary Accountability for Business Opportunities" in Finn, P D (ed) Equity and Commercial Relationships. LawBook Co, Sydney, 1987, Ch 6.

Baker, J "Are the Objects Stated in Section 243A of the Corporations Law Achieved by Part 3.2A?" (1997) 15 C & SLJ 471.

Brooks, A, Chalmers, K, Oliver, J & Veljanovski, A "Issues Associated with Chief Executive Officer Remuneration: Shareholders' Perspectives" (1999) 17 C & SLJ 360.

Farrer, J "A Note Dealing with Self Interested Transactions by Directors" (2000) 12 Bond LR 106.

Friedman, S "Conflict of Interest, Accountability and Corporate Governance: The Case of the IOC and SOCOG" (1999) 22 UNSWLJ 781.

Green, J M "Fuzzy Law–A Better Way to Stop Snouts in the Trough?" (1991) 9 C & SLJ 144.

Greenwood, A "Directors' Duties in the Light of CLERP and Recent Legal Developments" Uni of Melbourne, Centre for Corporate Law and Securities Regulation, Corporate Law Research Papers, **http://cclsr.law.unimelb.edu.au/research-papers/**

Hill, J "'What Reward Have Ye?' Disclosure of Director and Executive Remuneration in Australia" (1996) 14 C & SLJ 232.

Kearney, J B "Accounting for a Fiduciary's Gains in Commercial Contexts" in Finn, P D (ed) *Equity and Commercial Relationships*. LawBook Co, Sydney, 1987, Ch 7.

Kirby, J "The history and development of the conflict and profit rules in corporate law—A review" (2004) 22 C & SLJ 259.

Lipton, P "Has the 'Interested Director Cloud Been Lifted? A Comparison Between the US and Australian Approaches" (1994) 4 Aust Jnl of Corp Law 239.

McConvill, J & Bagaric, M "Related Party Transactions under Pt 2E of the Corporations Act: Time for Reconsideration" (2002) 15 Aust Jnl of Corp Law 19.

Ramsay, I "Corporate Disclosure of Loans to Directors: Reports of an Empirical Study" (1991) 9 C & SLJ 80.

revision questions on the material in this chapter ...

- Please see eQuiz at **http://www.thomson.com.au/academic** for multiple choice questions and answers.
- For further corporations law links and material please refer to the Lipton-Herzberg website at **http://www.lipton-herzberg.com.au**

chapter thirteen.four

duties of care, skill and diligence

key points ...

- Directors are under both common law and statutory duties to exercise their powers and discharge their duties with a reasonable degree of care and diligence, which a reasonable person would exercise if they were a director in the corporation's circumstances and had the same responsibilities as the directors.
- Directors are now expected to meet higher standards of care and diligence than was previously required. Directors are expected to make inquiries and be informed so as to monitor management and satisfy themselves that the company is properly run.
- The statutory duty of care imposes an objective standard of a reasonable director in the corporation's circumstances and in the director's position. Breach of this duty gives rise to civil and not criminal liability.
- The business judgment rule was introduced as a defence for directors against claims arising from breaches of the duty of care. To gain the protection of this rule, directors must show their judgment was made in good faith and for a proper purpose, they had no material personal interest, they were informed and they rationally believed their judgment was in the company's best interests.
- Directors may rely upon information or advice provided by others. Directors may also delegate their powers to others provided they are properly informed and the reliance or delegation is reasonable in the circumstances.

Directors and other officers are under a duty to exercise a reasonable degree of care and diligence. These duties are imposed by s 180(1) as well as the common law tort of negligence and the equitable duty of care.

[13.4.05] Directors and other officers are under a duty to exercise a reasonable degree of care and diligence. These duties are imposed by s 180(1) as well as the common law tort of negligence and the equitable duty of care. The substance of these duties is the same. Whatever the source of the law, it is recognised that directors are involved in managing a business with its attendant risks and uncertainties. As a consequence, the law allows directors great flexibility in how they exercise their management functions and shareholders are taken to accept this.

Amendments made in 1999 inserted a number of other provisions that are allied to the statutory duty of care:

- **s 180(2) contains a business judgment rule defence against actions for breaches of the duty of care and diligence;**
- **s 189 explains when directors are entitled to rely on information or advice; and**
- **s 190 deals with directors' responsibility for the actions of their delegates.**

changing attitudes and expectations

In the past, the law applied a very lenient approach in determining the standards expected of directors.

[13.4.10] In the past, the law applied a very lenient approach in determining the standards expected of directors. The rules governing directors' standards of care, skill and diligence were established in a series of English cases in the late 19th and early 20th centuries. In those days there were relatively few companies and their boards largely comprised part-time, non-executive directors who were regarded as figureheads and who were often appointed because of their title or reputation and not because of their business abilities.

Determining whether or not directors breach their general law duties of care, skill and diligence requires an assessment of the standards that must be observed by them. The early cases, such as *Re City Equitable Fire Insurance Co Ltd* [1925] Ch 407, held that the standard of care was measured by reference to the care an ordinary person might be expected to take on their own behalf. According to *Overend & Gurney & Co v Gibb* (1872) LR 56 HL 480, directors would only breach this standard if:

> **< they were cognisant of circumstances of such a character, so plain, so manifest, and so simple of appreciation, that no men with any ordinary degree of prudence, acting on their own behalf, would have entered into such a transaction as they entered into. >**

The effect of these cases was that directors would only be regarded as having breached their duty of care if they were grossly negligent.

The old cases also did not require directors to possess minimum levels of skill. Standards of skill were measured subjectively by reference to the particular director's knowledge and experience. In *Re City Equitable Fire Insurance Co Ltd* [1925] Ch 407, it was held that a director need not exhibit a greater degree of skill than may reasonably be expected from someone of their knowledge and experience. For example, a director of a life insurance company was not required to have the skills of an actuary. The implications of this were that the less knowledge and experience possessed by a director, the lower the standard of care. Conversely, a director with considerable business experience and knowledge was required to exercise a higher degree of care and skill. The courts were generally reluctant to override matters involving directors' business judgments and took the view that if shareholders elected incompetent amateurs they had only themselves to blame.

In the past, the courts took a very lenient view of directors' duty of diligence. In *Re City Equitable Fire Insurance Co Ltd* [1925] Ch 407, Romer J stated that a director:

> **< is not bound to give continuous attention to the affairs of the company. His duties are of an intermittent nature to be performed at periodical board meetings, and at meetings of any committee of the board upon which he happens to be placed. He is not, however, bound to attend all such meetings, though he ought to attend whenever, in the circumstances, he is reasonably able to do so. >**

Community attitudes and expectations concerning directors' standards of care, skill and diligence have changed since those early cases were decided. In its 1989 report, *Social and Fiduciary Duties and Obligations of Company Directors*, the Senate Select Committee on Legal and Constitutional Affairs (the Cooney Committee) recommended changes in the legislation to impose elements of an objective standard of care. It commented:

Community attitudes and expectations concerning directors' standards of care, skill and diligence have changed.

> **< The case law has developed the company director's general duty of care in this way because it has been recognised that her or his role involves a degree of risk taking and uncertainty. The courts have been concerned to allow flexibility and not to hamper entrepreneurs unduly. The standards laid down, however, barely meet the requirements of contemporary business and fall far short of the standards required of other professions. >**

There is no objective common law standard of the reasonably competent director, as there are objective standards for other professions. It is not an easy task to determine uniform minimum standards of behaviour for company directors. The activities of companies are diverse and consequently a range of skill and experience is useful on boards but, if the modern company directors want professional status, then professional standards of care ought to apply.

The changed judicial attitudes were initially reflected in a number of insolvent trading cases decided in the early 1990s such as *Statewide Tobacco Services Ltd v Morley* (1990) 8 ACLC 827 and *Commonwealth Bank of Australia v Friedrich* (1991) 9 ACLC 946. These cases required all directors to make inquiries about their company's financial position and to have the skills to understand a balance sheet and profit and loss statement. As Tadgell J observed in *Commonwealth Bank of Australia v Friedrich* (1991) 9 ACLC 946:

> **< As the complexity of commerce has gradually intensified (for better or for worse) the community has of necessity come to expect more than formerly from directors whose task it is to govern the affairs of companies to which large sums of money are committed by way of equity capital or loan. In response, the parliaments and the courts have found it necessary in legislation and litigation to refer to the demands made on directors in more exacting terms than formerly; and the standard of capability required of them has correspondingly increased. In particular, the stage has been reached when a director is expected to be capable of understanding his company's affairs to the extent of actually reaching a reasonably informed opinion of its financial capacity. >**

A speech by Justice Kirby of the High Court, contained on the High Court website, considers these changes in attitude in an historical context. This speech is linked to the Lipton-Herzberg Directors' Duties of Care, Diligence and Skill Pathway at **http://www.lipton-herzberg.com.au/secure/pathways-directors-duties-care-diligence-and-skill.html**

current standards of care, skill and diligence

[13.4.15] Directors and other officers owe duties of care, skill and diligence. These duties are imposed by s 180(1) as well as the common law tort of negligence and the equitable duty of care. The present standards of care, skill and diligence that directors and other officers must exercise is expressed in s 180(1) which was inserted by the 1999 amendments and was intended to reflect increasing expectations and to be consistent with recent case law on the common law duty of care.

Section 180(1) provides that a director or other officer of a corporation must exercise their power and discharge their duties with the degree of care and diligence that a reasonable person would exercise if they:

- **were a director or officer of a corporation in the corporation's circumstances; and**
- **occupied the office held by, and had the same responsibilities within the corporation as, the director or officer.**

The common law and s 180(1) both impose an objective "reasonable person" standard.

The common law and s 180(1) both impose an objective "reasonable person" standard. However, it is recognised that the precise degree or standard of care and diligence which a reasonable person would exercise in a particular case varies depending on the corporation's circumstances as well as the office and responsibilities held by the director or officer in question. Even though the standard of care is variable, the leading cases, such as *Daniels v Anderson* (1995) 13 ACLC 614 (the *AWA Case*), discussed below, para [13.4.30], make it clear that the law imposes minimum standards of care and diligence on directors.

General law tort law principles apply in determining how careful a reasonable director or officer should be when making decisions that involve a risk of harm: *ASIC v Vines* [2005] NSWSC 738. According to those principles, the standard of care that would be exercised by a reasonable person when making business decisions that involve risk is determined by weighing up the following factors:

- **the magnitude of the risk of harm and the probability of it occurring;**
- **the seriousness of the loss that would result if the harm occurs; and**
- **the expense, difficulty and inconvenience of taking alleviating action.**

corporation's circumstances

[13.4.20] Section 180(1)(a) recognises that a corporation's circumstances are one of the factors to be taken into account when deciding the degree of care and diligence which a reasonable person would exercise in a particular case. The reference to the "corporation's circumstances" was inserted by 1992 amending legislation. The explanatory paper explained the purpose of including these words.

A corporation's circumstances are one of the factors to be taken into account when deciding the degree of care and diligence which a reasonable person would exercise in a particular case.

> **< What constitutes the proper performance of the duties of the director of a particular company will be dictated by a host of circumstances, including no doubt the type of the company, the size and nature of its enterprise, the provisions of its articles of association, the composition of its board and the distribution of work between the board and other officers (*Commonwealth Bank of Australia v Friedrich* (1991) 9 ACLC 946, at 955 for Tadgell J; see also Explanatory Memorandum to the Corporate Law Reform Bill 1992, paragraph 86, which specifically mentions the state of the corporation's financial affairs and the urgency and magnitude of any problem). >**

case note

The rapidly deteriorating state of the financial circumstances of the One.Tel group of companies was regarded as relevant for purposes of determining whether the group's chairman contravened s 180(1) in *ASIC v Rich* [2003] NSWSC 85. While the case dealt only with the adequacies of ASIC's pleadings against One.Tel's chairman, it was noted that the One.Tel group's financial position and performance progressively deteriorated in the months prior to its May 2001 collapse. It required an immediate cash injection of about $270 million by the end of February 2001 if it was to continue its existing operations and meet current and reasonably foreseeable liabilities. Amongst other things, ASIC argued that a reasonable chairman of a company in One.Tel's circumstances would have known about the group's financial position and performance and would have ensured that the board was informed about this on a month-by-month basis. ASIC also argued that a reasonable chairman of a company in One.Tel's circumstances would have promptly recommended to the board that the group cease trading or appoint an administrator unless a cash injection of about $270 million was obtained.

director's office and responsibilities

[13.4.25] Section 180(1)(b) makes it clear that the office held by a director or officer and their responsibilities in the corporation are relevant factors in deciding the degree of care and diligence which a reasonable person would exercise in a particular case. This requirement recognises that the standard of care, skill and diligence that a reasonable person would exercise may vary from company to company depending on the type of office a particular director occupies and their responsibilities.

The office held by a director or officer and their responsibilities in the corporation are relevant factors in deciding the degree of care and diligence which a reasonable person would exercise in a particular case.

For example, as discussed in Chapter 12 above, one of the directors will be appointed to the position of the chair of the board with the special responsibilities attaching to that position. The boards of many companies consist of both executive directors, such as the managing director and chief financial officer, and non-executive directors. In some companies, directors may be on a board committee and be given particular committee responsibilities or may be appointed to the board because they have particular skills or experience.

In *ASIC v Rich* [2003] NSWSC 85, it was held that the word "responsibilities" in s 180(1)(b) refers to the factual arrangements operating within the company and affecting the director in question and is not limited to legal duties. This means that a director's responsibilities involve a consideration of the specific tasks delegated to the director by the company's constitution or the board, and the way in which work is actually distributed within the company as well as the particular director's experience and skills. Austin J stated:

A director's responsibilities involve a consideration of the specific tasks delegated to the director by the company's constitution or the board, and the way in which work is actually distributed within the company as well as the particular director's experience and skills.

> < **(T)he word "responsibilities" was intended to direct attention to the factual arrangements operating within the company and affecting the director in question—as opposed to the legal duty of care, implying specific legal duties in particular circumstances. The content of those specific duties would be affected by the factual matters specified in the section, relating to the corporation's circumstances, the nature of the director's office, and the director's responsibilities. The director's responsibilities would include arrangements flowing from the experience and skills that the director brought to his or her office, and also any arrangements within the board or between the director and executive management affecting the work that the director would be expected to carry out. The precise duty of care flowing from these arrangements would be subject, of course, to a minimum standard of care and diligence set by the statute in reflection of the common law position.** >

non-executive directors

[13.4.30] The boards of large listed companies usually consist of both non-executive and executive directors. The ASX Corporate Governance Council's *Principles of Good Corporate Governance and Best Practice Recommendations* recommend that the boards of listed companies should consist of a majority of independent non-executive directors.

Non-executive directors are not directly involved in the daily management of the company's business. Of necessity, non-executive directors of large companies must rely on management led by the company's managing director or chief executive officer to properly carry out their roles as directors.

The standard of care of non-executive directors recognises that their duties are of an intermittent nature.

The standard of care of non-executive directors recognises that their duties are of an intermittent nature to be performed at periodic board meetings and at meetings of any committee of the board to which the director has been appointed: *AWA Ltd v Daniels* (1992) 10 ACLC 933. While non-executive directors do not expect to be informed of the minute details of how the company is managed, they expect to be informed of anything untoward or anything appropriate for consideration by the board.

Even though the law does not require non-executive directors to have any particular educational qualifications or business experience, reflecting changing community attitudes and expectations of the modern directors' duty of care cases such as *Daniels v Anderson* (1995) 13 ACLC 614 set out minimum standards of care and diligence applicable to non-executive directors of listed public companies.

case note

In *Daniels v Anderson* (1995) 13 ACLC 614 AWA, a large listed company, incurred large losses from foreign exchange transactions carried out by one of its middle level managers. The foreign exchange dealings were not adequately supervised by senior AWA executives who did not put in place adequate internal controls to monitor foreign exchange activities. Nor did they ensure that there were adequate records kept of the numerous foreign currency dealings. While the unsupervised foreign exchange dealings were extremely profitable initially, during 1986 and 1987 there were large losses.

For a time, the foreign exchange manager concealed these losses from senior executives when he arranged unauthorised foreign currency borrowings from a number of banks. AWA's auditor failed to detect the unauthorised foreign currency borrowings.

However, he warned AWA senior executives of the inadequacies of the company's internal controls. The auditor failed to inform AWA's board of the full extent of the inadequacies even though he knew that the senior executives had not acted on his warnings. In December 1986, the auditor wrote to the company's chairman and chief executive officer suggesting improvements to the company's internal audit procedures but did not specifically mention the problems with the foreign exchange operations or stress the urgency of the matter. The board did not become aware of the full extent of the unsupervised foreign exchange deals and the unauthorised loans until the end of March 1987.

AWA sued its auditors for negligence, who then alleged contributory negligence on the part of AWA and instituted a cross-claim against all the AWA directors seeking contribution. In the cross-claim the auditors argued that AWA's directors had breached their duty of care. The New South Wales Court of Appeal held that the auditors were negligent but that AWA's contributory negligence reduced the audit firm's liability. AWA's contributory negligence arose because both its senior executives and chief executive officer were held to have been negligent and this was attributed to AWA.

The NSW Court of Appeal held that directors of listed companies are required to take reasonable steps to place themselves in a position to guide and monitor the management of a company. In particular:

Directors are required to take reasonable steps to place themselves in a position to guide and monitor the management of a company.

- directors must become familiar with the company's business when they join the board;
- while directors need not have equal knowledge and experience of every aspect of the company's activities, they are under a continuing obligation to make inquiries and keep themselves informed about all aspects of the company's business operations. "A director is not an ornament, but an essential component of corporate governance. Consequently, a director cannot protect himself behind a paper shield bearing the motto dummy director: *Francis v United Jersey Bank* 432 A 2d 814 (1981)";
- directors must also be familiar with their company's financial position by regularly reviewing its financial statements as they will be unable to avoid liability for insolvent trading by claiming that they do not know how to read financial statements: *Commonwealth Bank of Australia v Friedrich* (1991) 9 ACLC 946;
- directors who are appointed because they have special skills or experience in an aspect of the company's business must also pay attention to other aspects of the company's business which might reasonably be expected to attract inquiry even if this is outside their area of expertise. They must ensure that the board has the means to monitor management so as to satisfy themselves that the company is being properly run;
- directors are allowed to make business judgments and take commercial risks. However, they cannot safely proceed on the basis that ignorance and a failure to inquire are protection against liability for negligence; and
- directors cannot shut their eyes to corporate misconduct and then claim that they did not see the misconduct and did not have a duty to look. "The sentinel asleep at his post contributes nothing to the enterprise he is charged to protect."

It was held that AWA's non-executive directors did not breach their standard of care because on the facts of the case they had made inquiries and requested information about the foreign exchange dealings from senior management and the auditor but the full details were concealed from them.

case note

In *Sheahan v Verco* [2001] SASC 91, the Supreme Court of South Australia applied similar minimum standards to the non-executive directors of a much smaller company. In that case two investors became non-executive directors of an established company after they invested in a share issue. Their investment, together with a secured bank loan, enabled the company to expand its business. On becoming directors, they told the company's managing director and major shareholder, that they did not want to be involved in managing the company's business and expected to be treated as "sleeping partners".

The managing director misled the non-executive directors as to the company's financial position, falsely representing that it was profitable when in fact it owed a large amount to its bank as a consequence of previous unsuccessful business ventures. While the company's businesses themselves operated profitably, the company was incurring losses because of its high interest payments on its bank loans and inadequate deduction for amortisation and depreciation. The company was reliant on the continuing support of its banks and did not have the capacity to meet its obligations under the bank loans in the event of being asked to repay them. Eventually, the bank appointed a receiver because of non-payment of interest and instalments of principal. The company was subsequently placed in liquidation and the liquidator sued the non-executive directors alleging that they were negligent and responsible for the losses incurred by the company from the time of their appointment until the bank's receiver was appointed.

The court held that the non-executive directors breached their common law and statutory duties of care. When they became directors they did not ask to see even the basic financial statements for previous years which would have revealed the company's substantial bank debt. Neither of them sought any information as to how the business expansion had been financed or its capacity to meet any such financial obligations. They did not become familiar with the business and how it was conducted so that they could form a sound judgment about whether it was being properly run. They did not take reasonable steps to place themselves in a position to monitor and guide the company but were content to leave the management of the company entirely to the company's managing director. Even though the non-executive directors breached their common law and statutory duties of care, they were not liable for damages as their breach did not cause the company's losses. The losses stemmed from its continuing inability to meet the interest payments on bank loans which were taken out before the non-executive directors joined the company.

case note

In *ASIC v Adler* [2002] NSWSC 171 (approved on appeal in *Adler v ASIC* [2003] NSWCA 131), the facts of which are set out in Chapter 13.2 above, it was held that Adler breached s 180(1) because a reasonably careful and diligent director of HIH and HIHC in the position of Adler would not have caused or procured the $10 million payment by HIHC to PEE, part of which was applied in purchasing HIH shares. Further, Adler's failure to ensure that HIH and HIHC followed authorised investment practices which he was familiar with and his failure to safeguard HIH and HIHC's interests also fell well short of the standard of a reasonably competent person in his category of appointment.

A non-executive director who has special skills or experience in the company's business has a duty to give the company the benefit of that skill or experience. Such a director cannot avoid liability for negligence simply by asserting that they relied on the company's executive directors and officers.

case note

This is illustrated in *Gold Ribbon (Accountants) Pty Ltd v Sheers* [2005] QSC 198. In that case Dunn was a non-executive director of Gold Ribbon and was the only director on the five-man board with extensive lending experience. Together with the other directors, Dunn assisted the company in setting up a scheme that involved Gold Ribbon lending money to practising accountants or their associated service companies. The loans were at high interest rates and unsecured. Gold Ribbon's directors delegated the administration of the scheme to another company, Austide Holdings Pty Ltd, which was required to make "due diligence" inquiries about prospective borrowers' professional fees and their capacity to service their loans. Gold Ribbon's lending scheme effectively ceased when its bank, which had funded its lending activities, terminated its loan facility and demanded that Gold Ribbon repay its bank loan. Gold Ribbon in turn called up the loans it had made to borrowing accountants, however, five of the accountant borrowers defaulted under their respective loan agreements leaving Gold Ribbon with bad debts of over $3 million. Gold Ribbon went into liquidation and its liquidator commenced legal proceedings against Dunn alleging that he had breached his duty of care in relation to both the setting up of the lending scheme and the scheme's operation.

It was held that Dunn breached his duty of care in a number of respects. By its nature, Gold Ribbon's business was a high risk venture that was only likely to attract accountants who had had difficulties in borrowing money from other sources. Being the only person on Gold Ribbon's board with extensive lending experience, Dunn failed to ensure that the scheme was set up to comply with "accepted lending practice" to minimise the risk of borrowers' defaults. A reasonable director with Dunn's background and experience would have ensured that the company had appropriate procedures for making due diligence inquiries to ensure loan applicants had the financial capacity to service and repay their loans. Dunn breached his duty of care by failing to monitor Austide's administration of the scheme in circumstances where a director with his lending experience would have identified obvious deficiencies. Dunn also breached his duty of care because he failed to ensure that Austide's managers had the capacity to administer the scheme properly. He also failed to advise the other directors that Austide should be replaced as scheme administrator when it became apparent that it was incompetent.

A non-executive director who has special skills or experience in the company's business has a duty to give the company the benefit of that skill or experience.

chair

[13.4.35] The chair of a listed company has special responsibilities and therefore is subject to a higher standard of care and diligence than is applicable to non-executive directors discussed above.

The chair of a listed company has special responsibilities and therefore is subject to a higher standard of care and diligence than is applicable to non-executive directors.

case note

In *ASIC v Rich* [2003] NSWSC 85, ASIC brought civil penalty proceedings against Greaves, the chairman of One.Tel, alleging that he contravened s 180(1). The court did not make a decision on whether Greaves breached s 180(1) but dealt only with the preliminary issue of whether Greave's position as chairman and his skills and experience came within the meaning of "responsibilities" for purposes of s 180(1)(b).

ASIC's statement of claim alleged that Greaves had special responsibilities beyond those of the other non-executive directors by reason of his position as chairman of the board and its finance and audit committee and also because of his high qualifications, experience and expertise relative to the other directors. ASIC argued that these special responsibilities meant that Greaves had a higher standard of care which he failed to meet in the circumstances. In particular, ASIC's case was that a reasonable person occupying the offices occupied by Greaves and having Greaves' responsibilities would have known One.Tel's financial circumstances, would have promptly ensured that the board was informed and would have recommended that the company cease trading or appoint an administrator unless a significant cash injection was obtained. ASIC asserted that Greaves' responsibilities as a chairman of the board and chairman of its audit committee included the following:

> the general performance of the board;
> the flow of financial information to the board (including information about cash reserves, actual segment performance and key transactions);
> the establishment and maintenance of systems for information flow to the board;
> the employment of a finance director;
> the public announcement of information;
> the maintenance of cash reserves and group solvency; and
> making recommendations to the board as to prudent management of the One.Tel group.

Greaves argued that whether he had discharged his "responsibilities" for purposes of s 180(1) should turn only on the specific tasks that had been delegated to him by the company's constitution or by the board. Greaves noted that under One.Tel's constitution, the chairman's responsibilities were of a ceremonial or procedural nature concerned with chairing board meetings or shareholders' meetings.

The court rejected Greave's argument and held that the factual responsibilities of chairman of a listed company were more than "ceremonial or procedural matters" relating to chairing board meetings or shareholders' meetings. The court accepted the analysis of Rogers J in *AWA Ltd v Daniels* (1992) 7 ACSR 759 who asserted that a chairman has the primary responsibility of selecting matters and documents to be brought to the board's attention, in formulating the policy of the board and in promoting the position of the company. The court thought it would be appropriate for ASIC to provide expert opinion evidence of responsibilities ordinarily undertaken by chairmen of listed public companies in Australia as well as corporate governance literature describing the customary responsibilities and the role of chairman of a listed public company.

executive directors and officers

[13.4.40] All directors, whether executive or non-executive, must take reasonable steps to place themselves in a position to guide and monitor the management of a company: *Daniels v Anderson* (1995) 13 ACLC 614. Executive directors not only occupy a position on the board, they are also full-time employees of the company to whom the board has delegated particular managerial responsibilities. Their involvement in management means that executive directors have special responsibilities commensurate with their positions and have a greater knowledge of the daily operations of the company. They are therefore subject to higher standards than non-executive directors. Non-director officers are in a similar position in relation to their duty of care as executive directors.

Executive directors have special responsibilities commensurate with their positions. They are therefore subject to higher standards than non-executive directors.

Executive directors and other officers who are appointed to positions requiring the exercise of skill are also subject to objective standards of skill even though s 180(1) does not use the word "skill": *ASIC v Vines* [2003] NSWSC 1116.

case note

In *Daniels v Anderson* (1995) 13 ACLC 614, the facts of which are outlined above, para [13.4.30], the court held the AWA's chief executive officer breached his duty to act with reasonable care because he failed to make inquiries of the company's senior executives that would have led to a better appreciation of the risks and dangers of the foreign exchange dealings. As the company's chief executive officer, he was under a continuing obligation to supervise management and seek satisfactory explanations regarding the deficiencies of the foreign exchange trading system and procedures.

case note

In *ASIC v Adler* [2002] NSWSC 171, the facts of which are set out in Chapter 13.2 above, it was held that Williams, the managing director of both HIH and HIHC, breached s 180(1) because he failed to make sure that there were proper safeguards in place before HIHC lent $10 million to PEE, a company controlled by Adler. For example, Williams failed to ensure that there was an independent appraisal of the proposed investment and failed to ensure that there were appropriate safeguards to avoid investments being made in breach of the *Corporations Act*. The court also held that Fodera (HIH's finance director) also breached s 180 because he failed to submit the proposal to lend PEE $10 million to HIH's Investment Committee or board for approval.

case note

In *Circle Petroleum (Qld) Pty Ltd v Greenslade* (1998) 16 ACLC 1577, it was held that a highly experienced managing director of a petroleum supplier breached his duty to exercise a reasonable degree of care under a predecessor of s 180(1) when he allowed a customer to exceed its credit limits in a substantial departure from normal industry practice and in defiance of a resolution of the board. The managing director knew that the customer had been a difficult trade debtor and was not in a position to meet its obligations.

case note

In *South Australia v Clark* (1996) 14 ACLC 1019, the South Australian Supreme Court held that Clark, the managing director of the State Bank of South Australia, breached his duty of care to the bank. He arranged for the bank to acquire a subsidiary of APA Holdings Ltd for considerably more than its true value in the knowledge that APA would use the proceeds to repay a loan due to Equiticorp Holdings Ltd. Further, notwithstanding this was an unusually large transaction for the bank, Clark did not ensure that the bank carried out the usual due diligence inquiries and did not obtain an independent valuation of the subsidiary. Clark did not disclose to the other directors that he was indirectly benefiting from the transaction because he was also a director of Equiticorp Holdings Ltd and his family owned a large parcel of its shares.

Perry J commented on the degree of skill expected of Clark as the chief executive officer and managing director of a bank:

> < As the chief executive officer and managing director of a large bank, he was obliged to bring to bear an appropriate level of skill having regard to the responsibilities which that office entailed. No doubt, as is the case with all large corporations, it was necessary for him to delegate responsibility for the operation of different functions of the bank, in the circumstances where no further oversight could be expected. But he must unquestionably be regarded as responsible for the overall control of the operations of the bank, both in a day to day sense and in giving effect to the broader policies spelt out in the State Bank of South Australia Act and by the board of directors.
>
> Furthermore, it is clear that the board of directors looked to him and relied upon him not only to provide the board full and accurate information as to all of the matters which it was proper for the board to consider, but to see to it that any specific decisions of the board were implemented in a way which did not expose the bank to unnecessary risk. >

case note

In *Mistmorn Pty Ltd v Yasseen* (1996) 14 ACLC 1387, a de facto managing director of a family company was held to have breached both his statutory and common law duty of care when he arranged for his company to buy large quantities of stock for the company's shop which he knew was unnecessary. The stock was uninsured even though there had been previous burglaries.

case note

In *Permanent Building Society v Wheeler* (1994) 12 ACLC 674, a managing director was held to have breached his duty of care when he failed to make inquiries into an unusual transaction that was capable of causing harm to the company. The managing director had a responsibility to ensure that the other directors were made aware of the potential harm. The managing director breached his duty even though he declared a conflict of interest and did not vote on the board resolution in relation to the transaction.

case note

In *ASIC v Vines* [2005] NSWSC 738, ASIC brought civil penalty proceedings against Vines, Robertson and Fox, officers of GIO Australia Holdings Ltd, alleging that they breached their respective statutory duties of care and diligence under the predecessor of s 180(1) in relation to their involvement in preparing a profit forecast for their company. In 2000, AMP made a takeover offer for GIO, another listed insurance company. GIO's directors were of the opinion that AMP's takeover bid was inadequate and took vigorous defensive measures to defeat it. As required by the takeover provisions, GIO's directors responded to AMP's takeover bid by giving a target's statement (then called a "Part B statement") to their shareholders. A target's statement must include all the information that shareholders would reasonably require to make an informed assessment whether to accept the takeover offer: s 638(1). GIO's Part B statement included a profit forecast which indicated that GIO was "well on track to achieve a significant profit". The forecasted profit did not eventuate because it did not take into account material underwriting losses arising from a hurricane which occurred shortly before the forecast was finalised.

Vines was GIO's chief financial officer (CFO) and in addition to his CFO's role he had a prominent role in relation to GIO's Part B profit forecast and provided an unqualified assurance of its reliability. While the precise extent of GIO's hurricane liabilities were not certain at the time the profit forecast was being prepared, Vines was aware of further information which made it clear that the forecasted profits were unlikely to eventuate. The court held that Vines breached his duty of care in relation to the forecast because a reasonable CFO with his special responsibilities would have exercised care and diligence to ensure that the board was informed that the achievement of the forecast was improbable. Vines ought to have suggested the forecast should be redrafted.

Robertson and Fox were also officers of GIO and were in charge of its reinsurance business which was directly affected by the hurricane. Their particular responsibilities included formulating and supervising the preparation of the profit projections for the reinsurance business for inclusion in the profit forecast. Both Robertson and Fox also expressed unqualified satisfaction with the reliability of the profit forecast. The court held that they also breached their duty of care because they failed to obtain up-to-date information about the level of hurricane claims being made against GIO in circumstances when they should have done so. Despite the fact that they were aware that the level of claims would make the profit forecast improbable, they did not inform other senior GIO managers of this. Austin J stated:

< When [Vines, Robertson and Fox] provided information for the purposes of the Part B statement ... their standard of care and diligence was influenced by the circumstance that the information was provided within the framework of a due diligence process that was designed to ensure adequate and materially complete disclosure to GIO shareholders in compliance with the law and in a fashion that would protect those involved in the process from liability should a defect later be discovered in the document. These circumstances made it necessary for the defendants to take particular care in providing information. Moreover it was or should have been clear ... that it would not be enough for them not to confine their attention to what they knew, in circumstances where they could uncover material information by appropriate inquiries. >

consequences of contravention

[13.4.45] While common law and statutory duties and standard of care are essentially the same, different consequences result if there is a breach. Since the common law duty of care is owed to the company it can sue a director or officer for damages if their breach of the common law standard of care causes loss. Shareholders may bring proceedings in the name of the company under s 236 if they obtain prior leave of the court. This is discussed further in Chapter 17 below.

While common law and statutory duties and standard of care are essentially the same, different consequences result if there is a breach.

Contravention of the s 180(1) duty of care and diligence has different consequences. Section 180(1) is a designated civil penalty provision under s 1317E. As discussed in Chapter 13.6 below, a person who contravenes a civil penalty provision may be ordered to pay a pecuniary penalty of up to $200,000 under s 1317G; compensation to the corporation for damage suffered by it under s 1317H; or be disqualified from management under s 206C.

As a result of 1999 amendments, contravention of s 180(1) is not a criminal offence. The Explanatory Memorandum to the 1999 amending legislation considered that criminal liability required the existence of dishonesty—an active awareness of wrongdoing. Since the concepts of negligence and failure to exercise sufficient care and diligence do not involve dishonesty, contravention of s 180(1) was deliberately excluded from s 184, which provides for criminal offences where other directors' duties are breached dishonestly.

the business judgment rule

The business judgment rule provides a defence against actions for breaches of the duty of care in s 180(1), under the common law or equity.

[13.4.50] The business judgment rule was introduced as a result of 1999 amendments. It provides a defence against actions for breaches of the duty of care in s 180(1), under the common law or equity. The business judgment rule provides directors with a "safe harbour" from personal liability in relation to informed, rational business decisions made in good faith and in the best interests of the company.

The business judgment rule is contained in s 180(2) and adopts the US concept, which was developed so as to acknowledge that directors should not be liable for business decisions that may have turned out badly but were made in an honest, informed and rational way.

In some respects, Australian case law had developed principles that presumed that directors' decisions in relation to business judgments were valid and not subject to review by the courts. This reflected a broad attitude by judges that it was inappropriate for them to view the merits of business judgments in a risk-taking environment with the benefit of hindsight as to how particular decisions turned out.

The main arguments in favour of the business judgment rule defence are:

> **risk-taking and entrepreneurial activities will be encouraged because directors are assured by specific legislation that if they act honestly, they will not be personally liable as a result of adverse judicial review;**

> **better business decisions will be made as a result of the removal of uncertainty of liability under the statutory duty of care; and**

> **shareholder interests are better served by encouraging risk-taking. To make directors liable for mere errors of judgment promotes risk-averse decision-making with adverse effects on the economy.**

Section 180(2) provides that a director or other officer who makes a business judgment will not be liable in respect of the judgment under the statutory, common law or equitable duties of care and diligence where all of the following elements can be shown:

> **the judgment was made in good faith and for a proper purpose;**

> **there was no material personal interest in the subject matter of the judgment;**

> **the directors and officers informed themselves about the subject matter of the judgment to the extent they reasonably believed to be appropriate; and**

> **the judgment was rationally believed to be in the best interests of the corporation. Such a belief is regarded as rational unless the belief is one that no reasonable person in the officer's position would hold.**

If directors or other officers fulfil these requirements, they have an explicit safe harbour, being effectively shielded from liability for any breach of their duty of care and diligence. The merits of their business judgments are not subject to review by the courts.

"Business judgment" is defined to mean any decision to take or not take action in respect of a matter relevant to the business operations of the corporation: s 180(3). This definition is confined to decisions relevant to business operations and does not appear to include decisions made in the exercise of directors' powers such as the power to issue shares or pay dividends.

case note

As discussed above, para [13.4.40], in *ASIC v Adler* [2002] NSWSC 171 (affirmed on appeal in *Adler v ASIC* [2003] NSWCA 113), it was held that Adler, Williams and Fodera all breached their statutory duty of care in s 180(1). They could not rely on the business judgment rule as a defence.

The business judgment rule did not apply to Adler because he could not satisfy the s 180(2)(b) requirement as he had a clear conflict of interest in relation to the decision to invest HIHC's $10 million in PEE.

The business judgment rule did not apply to Williams because his failure to ensure that proper safeguards were implemented was not a business judgment for purposes of s 180(3). Even if this was a business judgment, as he was a major HIH shareholder, he had a "material personal interest" for purposes of s 180(2)(b). Williams also failed to present evidence that indicated that his judgment was made in good faith for a proper purpose as required by s 180(2)(a). Finally, there was no basis for concluding that Williams was properly informed under s 180(2)(c) as he had not obtained proper independent advice regarding appropriate safeguards that ought to have applied to the $10 million investment.

Fodera could not rely on the business judgment rule because his failure to refer the PEE transaction to HIH's board or the company's investment committee was not a business judgment for purposes of s 180(3).

As indicated in the note to s 180(2), the business judgment rule protects directors and officers against liability for breaches of the statutory duty of care and common law equivalent; it does not operate in relation to breaches of other duties such as the s 181(1) duty to act in good faith and for a proper purpose or the s 588G duty to prevent insolvent trading.

The business judgment rule does not operate in relation to breaches of other duties.

The Explanatory Memorandum to the 1999 amending legislation cites a decision to undertake a particular kind of business activity promoted in a prospectus as an example of a business judgment that would come within the scope of s 180(2). However, the rule would not apply to a failure to comply with the fundraising provisions. This is subject to its own liability regime with its own specific defences.

A speech by Justice Kirby contained on the High Court website describes the considerations behind the introduction of the business judgment rule. This speech is linked to the Lipton-Herzberg Directors' Duties of Care, Diligence and Skill Pathway at **http://www.lipton-herzberg.com.au/secure/pathways-directors-duties-care-diligence-and-skill.html**

reliance on others: s 189

[13.4.55] There is considerable uncertainty in the case law on the extent to which directors may rely on information and advice provided by others. In its 1989 report, *Social and Fiduciary Duties and Obligations of Company Directors*, the Cooney Committee noted:

> **< The entitlement to rely on others is not set down in the companies legislation. The limits of reliance are not firm and are worked out on a case-by-case basis. There is no requirement that directors actively supervise delegates or positively believe an official, on whom reliance is placed, is trustworthy. >**

In *AWA Ltd v Daniels* (1992) ACSR 759, Rogers J was of the opinion that directors were entitled to rely without verification on the judgment, information and advice of senior management. The right of reliance would be removed only where a director was aware of circumstances that were so obvious that no person with any degree of prudence would have relied on the particular judgment, information and advice.

On appeal in *Daniels v Anderson* (1995) 13 ACLC 614, the majority of the New South Wales Court of Appeal disagreed with the observations of Rogers J in relation to reliance. They thought that directors are under a positive obligation to keep informed about corporate activities and satisfy themselves that the person they are relying upon is competent and reliable.

Directors are under a positive obligation to keep informed about corporate activities and satisfy themselves that the person they are relying upon is competent and reliable.

case note

In *Duke Group Ltd v Pilmer* (1999) 17 ACLC 1329, the court thought that directors who are informed and experienced businesspeople are expected to be able to make sound estimates of share and company valuations. They cannot simply accept an expert's advice without question where this involves disregarding their own knowledge and suspending judgment. This failure by the directors was attributed to the company which therefore failed to take reasonable care for its own protection. As a result, the liability of the expert arising from the misstatement regarding the fairness of the share price was reduced by the extent of the company's contributory negligence.

Section 189 clarifies when directors may rely on others. Section 189 provides that a director may rely upon information or advice provided by:

> an employee whom the director believes on reasonable grounds to be reliable and competent in relation to the matters concerned (s 189(a)(i)); or
> a professional adviser or expert in relation to matters that the director believes on reasonable grounds to be within the person's professional or expert competence (s 189(a)(ii)); or
> another director or officer in relation to matters within the director's or officer's authority (s 189(a)(iii)); or
> a committee of directors on which the director did not serve in relation to matters within the committee's authority: s 189(a)(iv).

Under s 189(b), the reliance must be made in good faith and after making an independent assessment of the information or advice, having regard to the director's knowledge of the corporation and the complexity of its structure and operations.

For purposes of s 189, a director's reliance on information or advice is taken to be reasonable unless the contrary is proved. This means that the onus of proof rests upon the person asserting that the director's reliance was not reasonable.

The protection afforded to directors who reasonably rely on information or advice arises in proceedings to determine whether the directors have breached their duties under the *Corporations Act* Pt 2D or an equivalent general law duty: s 189(c).

case note

In *Sheahan v Verco* [2001] SASC 91, the facts of which are outlined above, para [13.4.30], the court held that the extent to which the non-executive directors were justified in trusting and relying on the company's managing director depended on the nature and circumstances of the company as they existed, not as the non-executive directors thought them to exist. This was so because of their failure to inform themselves about the affairs of the company. Had they done so and found it to be financially healthy and well-managed with appropriate procedures for reporting through the managing director to the board of directors, it may be expected that the non-executive directors could have left many matters to the managing director without being in breach of their duties as directors. However, the non-executive

directors were content to leave the management of the company entirely to the managing director without having made any relevant inquiries about the company, including its financial position, management structure and business.

responsibility for actions of delegates: s 190

[13.4.60] Section 190 complements s 189, the reliance provision, and makes it clear when directors are permitted to delegate tasks to others. That section also explains directors' responsibilities for the actions of their delegates. Section 190(1) states the general rule that if directors delegate a power under s 198D, they are responsible for the exercise of power by the delegate as if the power had been exercised by the directors themselves.

Section 198D authorises the directors of a company to delegate any of their powers to:

> **a committee of directors;**
> **a director;**
> **an employee of the company; or**
> **any other person.**

The delegation must be recorded in the company's minute book in accordance with s 251A. This power is subject to contrary provision in the company's constitution. The exercise of the power by the delegate is as effective as if the directors had exercised it themselves: s 198D(3).

Under s 190(2), a director avoids responsibility if the director believed on reasonable grounds that the delegate would exercise the power in conformity with the duties imposed on directors by the *Corporations Act* and company's constitution, in good faith, after making proper inquiry if the circumstances indicated the need for inquiry and the delegate was reliable and competent in relation to the power delegated and would exercise the power in conformity with the duties imposed on the directors by the *Corporations Act*.

If the s 190(2) requirements are satisfied, a director will not be responsible for the acts of a delegate if the delegate acts fraudulently, negligently or outside the scope of their delegation.

In *ASIC v Adler* [2002] NSWSC 171, Santow J summarised the various factors that should be taken into account in deciding whether a director's decision to rely on a delegate was reasonable for purposes of either ss 189(c) or 190(2):

> **the function that has been delegated is such that "it may properly be left to such officers" (*Re City Equitable Fire Insurance Co Ltd* [1925] Ch 407);**
> **the extent to which the director is put on inquiry, or given the facts of a case, should have been put on inquiry (*Re Property Force Consultants Pty Ltd* (1995) 13 ACLC 1051);**
> **the relationship between the director and delegate must be such that the director honestly holds the belief that the delegate is trustworthy, competent and someone on whom reliance can be placed. Knowledge that the delegate is dishonest or incompetent will make reliance unreasonable (*Biala Pty Ltd v Mallina Holdings Ltd* (1994) 15 ACSR 1);**
> **the risk involved in the transaction and the nature of the transaction (*Permanent Building Society v Wheeler* (1994) 14 ACSR 109);**
> **the extent of steps taken by the director, for example, inquiries made or other circumstances engendering "trust"; and**
> **whether the position of the director is executive or non-executive.**

frequency of board meetings and attendance

[13.4.65] Judicial attitudes regarding directors' attendance at board meetings and the frequency of such meetings have changed over the years. The old cases took an extremely lenient view. Non-executive directors were not required to give continuous attention to the affairs of their company. According to *Re City Equitable Fire Insurance Co Ltd* [1925] Ch 407, non-executive directors' duties were regarded as of an intermittent nature to be performed at periodical board meetings. Directors were not, however, bound to attend all such meetings.

An extreme example of non-attendance occurred in *Re Cardiff Bank; Marquis of Bute's Case* [1892] 2 Ch 100. In that case the Marquis of Bute was appointed president of a bank at the age of six months. Losses arose from irregularities in the bank's operations but the Marquis was not held liable despite having attended only one board meeting in 38 years.

The modern cases take a more stringent approach.

The obligation to attend board meetings is an aspect of a director's duty of care.

The obligation to attend board meetings is an aspect of a director's duty of care. Unless directors regularly attend board meetings they will be unable to participate in the governance of the company and therefore fulfil one of their prime responsibilities: *Gold Ribbon (Accountants) Pty Ltd v Sheers* [2005] QSC 198. The *Corporations Act* does not prescribe how many board meetings a company should have. This is generally left to the board itself to decide. Directors should meet as often as is necessary in order to fulfil their obligation to monitor management: *Daniels v Anderson* (1995) 13 ACLC 614. Directors are expected to attend all board meetings unless exceptional circumstances, such as illness or absence from the State, prevent them doing so: *Vrisakis v ASC* (1993) 11 ACLC 763.

Directors are expected to attend all board meetings unless exceptional circumstances, such as illness or absence from the State, prevent them doing so.

To assist shareholders in knowing the extent of directors' attendance at board meetings, s 300(10) requires a public company's directors' report to include details of the number of board meetings (including committee meetings) held in the financial year and each director's attendance at the meetings.

pathways questions ...

The following questions dealing with directors' duties of care, skill and diligence may best be answered by reading this sub-chapter and considering the Internet resources found on the Lipton-Herzberg Directors' Duties of Care, Diligence and Skill Pathway at http://www.lipton-herzberg.com.au/secure/pathways-directors-duties-care-diligence-and-skill.html

1. In what ways have recent cases reflected a change in community expectations as to directors' duty of care?

2. Why was the introduction of a business judgment rule welcomed by sections of the business community such as the Australian Institute of Company Directors?

3. Have the decisions in the AWA cases gone too far in discouraging directors from taking necessary risks?

bibliography ...

Baxt, R "One 'AWA' Case is Not Enough: The Turning of the Screws for Directors" (1995) 12 C & SLJ 414.

Berkahn, M "A Statutory Business Judgment" (1999) 3 Southern Cross Uni LR 215.

Bird, J "The Duty of Care and the CLERP Reforms" (1999) 17 C & SLJ 141.

Cassidy, J "Standards of Conduct and Standards of Care: Divergence of the Duty of Care in the United States and Australia" (2000) 28 ABLR 180.

Cassidy, J "An Evaluation of Corporations Law s 232(4) and the Directors' Duty of Care, Skill and Diligence" (1995) 23 ABLR 184.

Clarke, A "The Business Judgment Rule–Good Corporate Governance or Not?" (2000) 12 Aust Jnl of Corp Law 85.

Comerford, A & Law, L "Directors' Duty of Care and the Extent of 'Reasonable' Reliance and Delegation" (1998) 16 C & SLJ 103.

DeMott, D A "Shareholders Challenges to Executive Remuneration" (2000) 74 ALJ 576.

DeMott, D A "Directors' Duty of Care and the Business Judgment Rule: American Precedents and Australian Choices" (1992) 4 Bond LR 133.

Farrar, J "Towards a Statutory Business Judgment Rule in Australia" (1998) 8 Aust Jnl of Corp Law 327.

Finlay, A "CLERP: Non-Executive Directors' Duty of Care, Monitoring and the Business Judgment Rule" (1999) 27 ABLR 98.

Flint, G "Non-Executive Directors' General Law Duty of Care and Delegation of Duty—But Do We Need a Common Law Duty of Care?" (1997) 9 Bond LR 198.

Greenhow, A "The Statutory Business Judgment Rule: Putting the Wind into Director's Sails" (1999) 11 Bond LR 33.

Keeves, J S "Directors' Duties—ASIC v Rich—Landmark or Beacon?" (2004) 22 C & SLJ 181.

Keller, B "Australia's Proposed Statutory Business Judgment Rule: A Reversal of a Rising Standard in Corporate Governance" (1999–2000) 4 Deakin LR 125.

Kluver, J "Sections 181 & 189 of the Corporations Law and Directors of Corporate Group Companies" Uni of Melbourne, Centre for Corporate Law and Securities Regulation, Corporate Law Research Papers, **http://cclsr.law.unimelb.edu.au/research-papers/**

Law, L "The Business Judgment Rule in Australia: A Reappraisal Since the AWA Case" (1997) 15 C & SLJ 174.

Law, L "Company Directors: A Duty to Take Risks" (1996) 4 *Current Commercial Law* 89.

Lumsden, A "The Role and Responsibilities of Directors on Board Sub-Committees", Centre for Corporate Law & Securities Regulation, Corporate Law Research Papers Website **http://cclsr.law.unimelb.edu.au/research-papers/index.html**

Priskich, V "A Statutory Business Judgment Rule in Australia: Proposals and Policy" (1999) 27 ABLR 38.

Redmond, P "Safe Harbours or Sleepy Hollows: Does Australia Need a Statutory Business Judgment Rule?" in Ramsay, I M (ed) *Corporate Governance and Duties of Directors*. Centre for Corporate Law and Securities Regulation, University of Melbourne, 1997.

Riley, C "The Company Director's Duty of Care and Skill: The Case for an Onerous but Subjective Standard" (1999) 62 Mod L Rev 697.

Sievers, A S "Directors' Duty of Care: What is the New Standard?" (1997) 15 C & SLJ 392.

Sievers, A S "Farewell to the Sleeping Director—The Modern Judicial and Legislative Approach to Directors' Duties of Care, Skill and Diligence—Further Developments" (1993) 21 ABLR 111.

Tan, D "Delivering the Judgement on a Statutory Business Rule in Australia" (1995) 5 Aust Jnl of Corp Law 442.

revision questions on the material in this chapter ...

- Please see eQuiz at **http://www.thomson.com.au/academic** for multiple choice questions and answers.
- For further corporations law links and material please refer to the Lipton-Herzberg website at **http://www.lipton-herzberg.com.au**

chapter thirteen.five

directors of insolvent companies

key points ...

> Directors owe a duty not to prejudice the interests of their company's creditors where the company is insolvent or in financial difficulties.

> The *Corporations Act* imposes a duty on directors to avoid insolvent trading. This requires directors to prevent their company incurring debts when there are reasonable grounds to suspect that the company is insolvent.

> An insolvent trading action is usually brought by the liquidator seeking compensation from the directors. Amounts recovered from directors are primarily available to meet the claims of unsecured creditors.

[13.5.05] Creditors, especially unsecured creditors, take a risk when they lend money to a limited liability company. Shareholders are not personally liable for their company's debts. Consequently, if the company becomes insolvent, its creditors will be unable to fully recover their debts because it will not have sufficient funds to repay its outstanding debts in full. When the insolvent company is wound up, a liquidator is appointed, sells its property and divides the proceeds among unsecured creditors who are entitled to an equal proportionate share.

Directors of an insolvent company prejudice the interests of the company's creditors if they permit the company to give away its property or otherwise dispose of its assets at less than commercial values. Such actions prejudice the interests of the existing creditors of an insolvent company because the pool of assets available to pay the company's outstanding debts is diminished or assets are put out of the reach of the company's liquidator and cannot therefore be distributed to its creditors.

Directors of companies in financial difficulties are subject to a fiduciary duty not to engage in activities that prejudice creditors' interests.

The law regards arrangements that have the effect of putting valuable property out of the reach of an insolvent company's creditors as improper behaviour by directors. For this reason, directors of companies in financial difficulties are subject to a fiduciary duty not to engage in activities that prejudice creditors' interests. This duty is an aspect of directors' fiduciary duty to act in good faith in the best interests of the company. As discussed in Chapter 13.2 above, where the company is solvent, the best interests of the company means acting in the long term interests of its shareholders as a collective group. However, where the company is in financial difficulties, shareholders cease to be the key stakeholders and the duty to act in the best interests of the company means directors must not prejudice the interests of the company's creditors. Directors who prejudice creditors' interests may also breach their statutory duties in ss 181 (best interests of the company), 182 (improper use of position) and 183 (improper use of information).

As discussed in Chapter 25 below, the following provisions supplement directors' fiduciary and statutory duties not to prejudice creditors' interests:

> the provisions in s 588FE(5) which deal with company transactions that have the purpose of defeating the rights of creditors on a winding up;
> the uncommercial transaction provisions in s 588FB which allow a liquidator to recover company gifts and other uncommercial transactions from the other party to the transaction; and
> the unreasonable director-related provisions in 588FE(6A) which allow a liquidator to recover unreasonable bonuses or other remuneration paid to directors.

Directors may also adversely affect creditors if they fail to prevent their company incurring debts when there are reasonable grounds to suspect that the company is insolvent. This is because the continuation of trading after the onset of insolvency often increases the extent of the insolvency and so reduces the amount available to creditors in the liquidation. As discussed below at para [13.5.40], directors contravene s 588G if they fail to prevent their company incurring debts when there are reasonable grounds to suspect that it is insolvent. This is referred to as "insolvent trading".

interests of creditors

duty not to prejudice creditors' interests

[13.5.10] We noted in Chapter 13.2 above that directors are under a fiduciary obligation to exercise their powers in good faith in the best interests of the company. Directors owe similar duties under s 181.

When the company is solvent, the company's interests correspond with the interests of its shareholders. Different considerations apply when a company is in financial difficulties and directors must act in the interests of the company's creditors. Directors prejudice creditors' interests if they cause their company to enter into arrangements that reduce the pool of company assets that would otherwise be available to be shared among creditors when the company is wound up.

Directors prejudice creditors' interests if they cause their company to enter into arrangements that reduce the pool of company assets that would otherwise be available to be shared among creditors when the company is wound up.

case note

In *Walker v Wimborne* (1976) 137 CLR 1, the liquidator of an insolvent company, which was one of a group of associated companies, brought an action against its directors under a predecessor of s 598 to recover money disposed of by the company prior to its winding up. The directors caused the company to make loans to other companies in the group in circumstances where there was no prospect of repayment. They used the company's funds to pay wages of the employees of associated companies and to pay the associated companies for work that they had not in fact carried out. The High Court held that the directors were liable. Mason J stated:

> < The directors of a company in discharging their duty to the company must take account of the interests of its shareholders and its creditors. Any failure by the directors to take into account the interests of creditors will have adverse consequences for the company as well as for them. The creditor of a company ... must look to that company for payment. His interests may be prejudiced by the movement of funds between companies in the event that the companies become insolvent. >

case note

The New South Wales Supreme Court in *Ring v Sutton* (1979) 5 ACLR 546 followed *Walker v Wimborne*. The court held that directors breached their duty and disregarded the interests of creditors when they caused their company to lend money at less than market rates. They were in breach even though the company was solvent at the time the loan was made.

The directors' duty not to prejudice creditors' interests also arises in the context of corporate groups, particularly where the companies in a group enter into business transactions with one another.

The directors' duty not to prejudice creditors' interests also arises in the context of corporate groups, particularly where the companies in a group enter into business transactions with one another. For example, one company in a group may lend money to another company in the same group. This occurred in both *Walker v Wimborne* (1976) 137 CLR 1 and *Ring v Sutton* (1979) 5 ACLR 546. If the lending company is in financial difficulties, its directors prejudice the interests of the lending company's creditors if the interest rate on the loan is not on commercial terms or if the borrowing company is, or becomes, insolvent and cannot repay.

It is common commercial practice for companies in a group to enter into cross-guarantees to secure borrowings by other group companies. For example, a wholly-owned subsidiary may be asked by a bank to guarantee a bank loan to its holding company. Directors of the wholly-owned subsidiary who allow the subsidiary to guarantee the loan are taken to have acted it its best interests if doing so is in the best interests of the holding company—provided the subsidiary is solvent: s 187. However, if the subsidiary is in financial difficulties, s 187 does not apply and its directors must not allow it to enter into the guarantee if that would prejudice the interests of the subsidiary and its creditors.

case note

In *ANZ Executors & Trustee Co Ltd v Qintex Australia Ltd* (1990) 8 ACLC 980, Qintex raised $185 million during 1988 and 1989 by an unsecured debenture issue and executed a deed with ANZ acting as the trustee for the debenture-holders. To secure the borrowings, the deed provided that Qintex would arrange for its wholly-owned subsidiaries to guarantee its indebtedness. The subsidiaries were not parties to the deed. When Qintex defaulted, ANZ sought an order for specific performance requiring the subsidiaries to execute guarantees. At the time of the hearing the subsidiaries were insolvent.

The Supreme Court of Queensland refused to grant the order for specific performance. The effect of such an order would be that the subsidiaries would be making a gift of their assets to the detriment of their creditors. McPherson J stated:

> < For a commercial or trading company confronting insolvency to make a gift of its assets in derogation of the interests of creditors is not to use powers for their corporate purposes but to do so for a non-corporate purpose. For a subsidiary now to execute an instrument rendering it liable for an indebtedness in the order of $110 million cannot possibly be for its benefit. No doubt it may be for the benefit of solvent companies within a group to guarantee the liabilities of a holding company in order to benefit the guarantor companies as well as other members of the group ... The position is different if the guarantee is not for the purposes of a company's business or otherwise for its benefit. >

The duty of care may be breached where directors act contrary to the interests of creditors.

The duty of care may be breached where directors act contrary to the interests of creditors.

case note

In the New Zealand case *Hilton International Ltd v Hilton* (1988) 4 NZLC 96-265, Mr and Mrs Hilton, the directors and shareholders of Hilton International Ltd, owed the company considerable amounts. The company was experiencing financial difficulties and its bank insisted that the directors' loans be repaid. To this end, the company's factory was sold on a sale and lease-back basis and a dividend was declared and paid from capital profits. This dividend was used to repay the Hiltons' loans. When the company was placed in liquidation, the liquidator sought to recover the dividend arguing that it was paid contrary to law. Alternatively, he asserted that the Hiltons as directors acted carelessly in recommending the dividend and were liable to make good the loss.

The court upheld both of the liquidator's assertions. Tipping J held that directors breach their duty of care if, when recommending a dividend, they fail to have before them a proper set of accounts.

when are creditors' interests paramount?

[13.5.15] The courts have been deliberately vague as to precisely when creditors' interests become paramount. Directors must take creditors' interests into account if the company is insolvent or of doubtful solvency.

Directors must take creditors' interests into account if the company is insolvent or of doubtful solvency.

This issue was examined by the New Zealand Court of Appeal in *Nicholson v Permakraft (NZ) Ltd* [1985] 1 NZLR 172. Cooke J held, by way of obiter, that directors must take creditors' interests into account:

> **< if the company is insolvent, or of doubtful solvency, or if a contemplated payment or other course of action would jeopardise its solvency ...**
>
> **In my opinion, a payment made to the prejudice of current and continuing creditors when a likelihood of loss to them ought to have been made known is capable of constituting misfeasance by the directors; and hence they may be made liable for it. >**

The Supreme Court of New South Wales in *Kinsela v Russell Kinsela Pty Ltd* (1986) 4 NSWLR 722, (the facts of which are set out below, para [13.5.30]) cited with approval the statements of Cooke J in the *Permakraft* case. Street CJ accepted that a company's financial instability raised the directors' duties to act in the interests of the creditors. However, he declined to formulate a general test of the degree of financial instability that would have to be established.

phoenix companies

[13.5.20] "Phoenix company" is not a legal term. It describes a company that operates a business and incurs debts that are not paid. When creditors threaten to liquidate the company because of its insolvency, the directors form a new company and transfer to it the old company's business and its most valuable assets for little or no consideration. The old company is left an assetless shell and may be wound up by its creditors who receive very little in the liquidation. The new company, like the mythical phoenix, rises from the ashes of the failed company.

"Phoenix company"describes a company that operates a business and incurs debts that are not paid. When creditors threaten to liquidate the company because of its insolvency, the directors form a new company and transfer to it the old company's business and its most valuable assets for little or no consideration. The old company is left an assetless shell and may be wound up by its creditors who receive very little in the liquidation.

The Parliamentary Joint Committee on Corporations and Financial Services, in its report, *Corporate Insolvency Laws: a Stocktake* (2004), considered the problem of phoenix companies and expressed particular concerns with people who repeatedly set up such companies.

> **< Of more serious concern are careerist offenders who purposely structure their operations in order to engage in phoenix activity, avoid detection and exploit loopholes in insolvency laws. Certain creditors are targeted: the ATO, State payroll and workers compensation premium authorities and employees owed entitlements such as superannuation and long service leave. The timing of implementation of the arrangements is leveraged to ensure the maximum amount of debt is accumulated in the old company. The new phoenix company is established at the last possible moment. Assets are transferred to it for no consideration or at a value significantly below the market cost of the assets in question. The new company has the potential to repeat the pattern of failure, with similar consequences for employees with outstanding entitlements, subcontractors and the ATO and State and Territory revenue bodies. >**

This report is linked to the Lipton-Herzberg website at **http://www.lipton-herzberg.com.au/law_reform.htm#par**

Liquidators of phoenix companies face a major practical problem in prosecuting the directors for breach of duty. Because a phoenix company is usually stripped of all its valuable property, its liquidator rarely has enough funds to launch legal proceedings against its directors. This inevitably means that ASIC prosecutions of directors for breach of their statutory duties are the only avenue for dealing with such improper behaviour. In October 2005, the government released details of a package of reforms to improve the operation of Australia's insolvency laws. In outlining new measures for dealing with assetless phoenix companies, the government announced:

> **< ASIC will be provided with additional funding to establish an enforcement programme targeting misconduct by the officers of assetless companies. This programme will focus on disqualifying directors of assetless companies who are involved in repeat phoenix activity. It will address the perception that such conduct can be engaged in with impunity provided the amounts involved are low enough to 'fly below ASIC's radar'. >**

case examples of phoenix companies

[13.5.25] The following cases provide examples of how directors of phoenix companies may breach their duty to take into account creditors' interest.

case note

In *Jeffree v NCSC* (1989) 7 ACLC 556, Jeffree was a director of a company that operated a business as trustee for a family trust. When a dispute between the company and one of its customers was referred to arbitration, Jeffree, fearing an adverse award that the company could not meet, formed a new trustee company which bought all the tangible assets of the old company and took over the business but did not pay anything for goodwill. Only part of the purchase price was paid to the old company. This was used to pay the debts due to the old company's existing creditors. When the customer won the arbitration, the old company was a "dormant shell" and its only asset was the debt due from Jeffree's new company. This could have been recovered if the old company was wound up, however, the customer was unwilling to spend further amounts to apply for its liquidation. The NCSC, a predecessor of ASIC, sought to make Jeffree criminally liable for breach of a predecessor of s 182 alleging that Jeffree had made improper use of his position as a director.

Directors owe duties to their company's creditors, present and future, to ensure that corporate assets are not dissipated or exploited to their prejudice.

The Western Australian Supreme Court upheld Jeffree's conviction. It held that directors owe duties to their company's creditors, present and future, to ensure that corporate assets are not dissipated or exploited to their prejudice. Jeffree's action in transferring the assets to his new company was improper because he not only failed to take into account the interests of the customer, a contingent creditor, he acted positively against them. Full value for the transfer of assets had not been provided by the new company. There was no amount included for goodwill and part of the purchase price was never paid. It was no defence for Jeffree to assert that the balance of the purchase price could have been recovered had the customer taken the expensive step of placing the company in liquidation.

case note

In *Grove v Flavel* (1986) 4 ACLC 654, the South Australian Supreme Court applied s 183 to a director of a financially troubled company who acted improperly when he made improper use of information that the company faced a real risk of liquidation. The court held that the director acted improperly for the purposes of a predecessor of s 183 as the company's most valuable assets were debts due by associated companies and the director arranged for these debts to be transferred to himself and other companies in the group. This adversely affected creditors' interests because it decreased the amount that otherwise would have been available to them on liquidation.

case note

In *McNamara v Flavel* (1988) 6 ACLC 802 a director of an insolvent company arranged for it to cease trading and allowed its business name to be used by another company he controlled without payment for goodwill attaching to the name. The South Australian Supreme Court held that the director breached the equivalent of s 184(3) and was guilty of a criminal offence. The director made improper use of information that the company was in financial difficulties when he transferred the business name to the advantage of his other company. It was no defence for the director to assert that this information was not confidential to the company. The company's creditors suffered detriment. The director's actions deprived them of any value attaching to the goodwill associated with the company's name.

case note

In *Castrisios v McManus* (1991) 9 ACLC 287, a director became aware that the liquidation of the company was imminent. He sought to protect himself and his associates by diverting funds belonging to the company to discharge debts owed by himself and his associates. These debts had been incurred so that the borrowed money could be on-lent to the company. The diverting of company funds was to the detriment of creditors of the company and the director was convicted of making improper use of knowledge acquired as a director under the predecessor of s 184(3).

shareholders cannot ratify breach of duty

[13.5.30] Shareholders cannot ratify a directors' breach of duty that involves prejudicing the interests of creditors.

Shareholders cannot ratify a directors' breach of duty that involves prejudicing the interests of creditors.

case note

In the *Kinsela* case, the directors of a family company in financial difficulties arranged for the company to transfer its business and lease its building to themselves on advantageous terms. This meant that when the company went into liquidation the directors could continue to carry on the family business but the company could not easily sell the property. The court held that the liquidator could invalidate the lease because the directors had breached their duty. The company's shareholders had no power to ratify the directors' breach of duty since it involved their failure to take account of the creditors' interests. Street J stated:

> < It is, to my mind, legally and logically acceptable to recognise that, where directors are involved in a breach of their duty to the company affecting the interests of shareholders, then shareholders can either authorise that breach in prospect or ratify it in retrospect. Where, however, the interests at risk are those of the creditors I see no reason in law or in logic to recognise that the shareholders can authorise the breach. Once it is accepted, as in my view it must be, that the directors' duty to a company as a whole extends in an insolvency context to not prejudicing the interests of creditors, the shareholders do not have the power or authority to absolve the directors from that breach. >

right to bring legal action

Creditors cannot themselves bring a civil action against the directors to recover their losses.

[13.5.35] As discussed above, directors who fail to take into account the interests of their insolvent company's creditors may breach both their fiduciary and the statutory duties in Ch 2D of the *Corporations Act*. Nevertheless, creditors cannot themselves bring a civil action against the directors to recover their losses: *Spies v R* (2000) 18 ACLC 727. Creditors have indirect rights. The fiduciary duties are owed to the company and consequently, it is only the company that has the right to sue directors who act in breach of their duties. However, when the company is wound up, its liquidator can take action against directors in breach of duty and any amount recovered from them is available for distribution to creditors. In *Re New World Alliance Pty Ltd* (1994) 122 ALR 531, Gummow J described the duty not to prejudice creditors' interests as "a duty of imperfect obligation owed to creditors, one which creditors cannot enforce save to the extent that the company acts on its own motion or through a liquidator".

Breach of the statutory duties in Ch 2D of the *Corporations Act* attracts the civil penalty provisions of Pt 9.4B. Under these provisions, ASIC may apply for a civil penalty order including an order for compensation. The civil penalty provisions also enable the company to apply for a compensation order whether or not ASIC has applied for a civil penalty order: s 1317J(2).

duty to prevent insolvent trading

A director is under a duty to prevent the company incurring debts if there are reasonable grounds for suspecting that it is insolvent. This is referred to as "insolvent trading".

[13.5.40] A director is under a duty to prevent the company incurring debts if there are reasonable grounds for suspecting that it is insolvent: s 588G. This is referred to as "insolvent trading". Subject to four alternative defences set out in s 588H, contravening directors are liable to pay compensation to the company of an amount equal to the loss or damage suffered by unsecured creditors in relation to the debts so incurred because of the company's insolvency: ss 588J, 588K and 588M. In addition, contravention of s 588G may result in directors being liable for a civil penalty order pursuant to Pt 9.4B or a criminal offence under s 588G(3).

In *Hawkins v Bank of China* (1992) 26 NSWLR 562, Kirby P explained the legislative purpose of insolvent trading legislation in the following terms:

> **< The whole purpose or object of [a predecessor of s 588G] was to discourage officers of corporations from improvidently committing the corporation to obligations to pay money as a debt when they have reasonable grounds for supposing that their corporation is (or will, upon incurring the debt in question) become insolvent. >**

There have been relatively few insolvent trading cases since 1993 when s 588G was introduced into the *Corporations Act*. This may be due to the increasing use of the voluntary administration procedure, which encourages directors to appoint an administrator rather than continue in business and incur debts. This is discussed by A Herzberg in an article "Is Section 588G a Paper Tiger?". ASIC has published advice for directors of insolvent companies on its website. Both these resources may be found on the Lipton-Herzberg Duties of Directors of Insolvent Companies Pathway at **http://www.lipton-herzberg.com.au/secure/pathways-directors-duties-directors-of-insolvent-companies.html**

section 588G

who is liable?

[13.5.45] The duty to prevent insolvent trading applies to a person who is a director at the time when the company incurs the relevant debt: s 588G(1)(a). The duty is imposed only on directors because they control overall management of the company and have the ultimate power to prevent debts being incurred. Imposing the duty on directors is also consistent with s 295(4)(c) which obliges directors, in a declaration attached to the company's financial statements, to declare whether or not there are reasonable grounds to believe that the company will be able to pay its debts as and when they become due and payable.

The duty to prevent insolvent trading applies to a person who is a director.

Persons not formally appointed as directors but who act as either "de facto" or "shadow" directors are also subject to the duty because of the wide definition of "director" in s 9. A discussion of several cases that consider the liability of a shadow director is contained in an article in *Bond Law Review* by M D Hobson "The Law of Shadow Directorships" (1998) 10 *Bond Law Review* 184. This article is linked to the Lipton-Herzberg Duties of Directors of Insolvent Companies Pathway at **http://www.lipton-herzberg.com.au/secure/pathways-directors-duties-good-faith-and-proper-purposes.html**

incurring a debt

[13.5.50] An essential element in establishing a contravention of s 588G is the requirement that a company incurs a debt. According to the dictionary definition, a debt is an obligation by one person to pay a sum of money to another: *Powell v Fryer* [2001] SASC 59. A debt is incurred when a company "so acts to expose itself contractually to an obligation to make a future payment of a sum of money as a debt": *Hawkins v Bank of China* (1992) 26 NSWLR 562.

A debt is incurred when a company "so acts to expose itself contractually to an obligation to make a future payment of a sum of money as a debt".

Most reported insolvent trading cases involve a company contracting with a supplier to buy goods or services on credit terms. The debt is the obligation to pay the purchase price at the agreed time for payment. A debt is also incurred if a company:

> **borrows money from a bank or other lender: *Commonwealth Bank of Australia v Friedrich* (1991) 9 ACLC 946; or**
> **leases business premises from a landlord: *Russell Halpern Nominees Pty Ltd v Martin* (1986) 4 ACLC 393.**

In *Hawkins v Bank of China* (1992) 10 ACLC 588, the NSW Court of Appeal noted that the expression "incurs a debt" was capable of a number of meanings and the appropriate meaning depended on the context and the statutory purposes of the legislation. It was held that the word "debt" included a contingent debt such as a guarantee and the word "incurs" included "the undertaking of an engagement to pay a sum of money at a future time, even if the engagement is conditional and the amount involved is uncertain". These interpretations best advanced the purpose of the legislation.

The expression "incurs a debt" also covers situations that do not necessarily involve contracts under which a company exposes itself to an obligation to make a future payment of a sum of money as a debt. For example, in *Powell v Fryer* [2001] SASC 59 it was held debts included statutory obligations to pay taxes, assessed penalties for non-payment of taxes, statutory levies for workers' compensation insurance and assessed penalties for non-payment of such levies.

In *Jelin Pty Ltd v Johnson* (1987) 5 ACLC 463, it was held that a "debt" was a claim for an ascertained amount and did not include unliquidated claims for damages for fraudulent misrepresentation. However, in *Hawkins v Bank of China* (1992) 10 ACLC 588, Gleeson CJ left open the possibility that incurring a debt included incurring a liability for damages.

Section 588G(1A) gives an expanded meaning to the expression "incurs a debt". That section contains a table (see Table 13.5.1 below) which indicates that if a company takes any of the seven actions set out in column 2, it incurs a debt at the time set out in column 3. For example, under s 588G(1A), a company incurs a debt if it pays a dividend, buys back its shares or enters into an uncommercial transaction as defined in s 588FB.

table 13.5.1 when debts are incurred

Action of a company	When debt is incurred
1. paying a dividend	when the dividend is paid or, if the company has a constitution that provides for the declaration of dividends, when the dividend is declared
2. making a reduction of share capital to which Div 1 of Pt 2J.1 applies (other than a reduction that consists only of the cancellation of a share or shares for no consideration)	when the reduction takes effect
3. buying back shares (even if the consideration is not a sum certain in money)	when the buy-back agreement is entered into
4. redeeming redeemable preference shares that are redeemable at its option	when the company exercises the option
5. issuing redeemable preference shares that are redeemable otherwise than at its option	when the shares are issued
6. financially assisting a person to acquire shares (or units of shares) in itself or a holding company	when the agreement to provide the assistance is entered into or, if there is no agreement, when the assistance is provided
7. entering into an uncommercial transaction (within the meaning of s 588FB) other than one that a court orders or a prescribed agency directs, the company enter into	when the transaction is entered into

when is a debt incurred?

The time when a debt is incurred depends on the terms of the agreement between the parties and when, in "substance and commercial reality", the company is exposed to the unavoidable liability to pay the debt for which it otherwise would not have been liable.

[13.5.55] It is important to ascertain the time when a debt is incurred because s 588G(1)(b) requires proof that the company was insolvent at the time the debt was incurred or became insolvent by incurring that debt.

The time when a debt is incurred depends on the terms of the agreement between the parties and when, in "substance and commercial reality", the company is exposed to the unavoidable liability to pay the debt for which it otherwise would not have been liable: *Leigh-Mardon Pty Ltd v Wawn* (1995) 17 ACSR 741. This is usually at the time the contract is entered into but this may not always be the case.

case note

In *Hawkins v Bank of China* (1992) 10 ACLC 588, Gleeson CJ held that a debt is incurred when, by its conduct or operations, a company has necessarily subjected itself to a conditional, but unavoidable, obligation to pay a sum of money at a future time. In that case, a company guaranteed the pre-existing debts that two other companies in the same group owed to the Bank of China. At the time of the guarantee, the borrowing companies were unable to repay their loans because they were insolvent. It was held that the guarantor company incurred a debt to the bank when the guarantee was executed because after that date the company's obligation to the bank under the guarantee was unavoidable by any action of its own.

In *ASIC v Plymin* [2003] VSC 123, it was held that a debt can be incurred when the contract giving rise to the debt is entered into, even if contingencies affect the debt or the debt is a future debt. In the case of a future debt, it may be incurred at the time of entering the contract if it is then an ascertained or ascertainable amount. For example, in *Russell Halpern Nominees Pty Ltd v Martin* (1986) 4 ACLC 393, it was held that a debt for rent was incurred when the tenant executed the agreement to lease and not on the days when rent was due but not paid. On those days the tenant company merely accrued a liability for an amount. Similarly, in *John Graham Reprographics Pty Ltd v Steffens* (1987) 5 ACLC 904, a debt for interest under a loan agreement was on the date of execution of the agreement incurred not on the days interest became due and payable.

case note

In some situations a company may incur a debt in "substance and commercial reality" after the contract giving rise to it is entered into. For example, in *ASIC v Plymin* [2003] VSC 123, the company contracted to buy raw materials for its business from a large number of suppliers. The contract with one of the suppliers provided that the company could place orders for the raw materials from time-to-time and payment was to be made 30 days after delivery. The court held that the debt for a particular order was incurred, in "substance and commercial reality", when the company made the delivery order. A contract with another supplier related to the sale of a quantity of wheat which was to be stored by the supplier and delivered to the company as required. In this case, it was held that the debt was incurred when the contract was made and not when the deliveries were ordered. The company also had a contract for the supply of electricity. It was held that as a matter of substance and commercial reality, the debt for the supply of electricity was incurred when the electricity was used and not the date of the contract with the electricity supplier.

insolvency

[13.5.60] Section 588G(1)(b) requires proof that the company was insolvent at the time the debt was incurred or became insolvent by incurring that debt. The s 95A definition of insolvency has regard to the company's inability to pay its debts as and when they become due and payable. A person is solvent if, and only if, the person is able to pay all her or his debts, as and when they become due and payable: s 95A(1). A person who is not solvent is regarded as being insolvent: s 95A(2).

Section 588G(1)(b) requires proof that the company was insolvent at the time the debt was incurred or became insolvent by incurring that debt.

Whether or not a company is able to pay its debts when they become due is based on a cash flow test and is not determined simply on the basis of a surplus of assets over liabilities. In *Powell v Fryer* [2001] 159 FLR 433; [2001] SASC 59, Olsson J stated:

The conclusion of insolvency ought not to be drawn simply from evidence of a temporary lack of liquidity.

> < **The conclusion of insolvency must be derived from a proper consideration of the Company's financial position, in its entirety, based on commercial reality. Generally speaking, it ought not to be drawn simply from evidence of a temporary lack of liquidity. Regard should be had not only to the Company's cash resources**

> **immediately available, but also to moneys which it can procure by realization by sale, or borrowing against the security of its assets, or otherwise reasonably raise from those associated with, or supportive of, it. It is the inability, utilizing such resources as are available through the use of assets or which may otherwise realistically be raised to meet debts as they fall due which indicates insolvency. >**

In *ASIC v Plymin* [2003] VSC 123, the Victorian Supreme Court thought that the following 14 indicators were common features in insolvency situations:

1. Continuing losses.
2. Liquidity ratios below 1.
3. Overdue Commonwealth and State taxes.
4. Poor relationship with present Bank, including inability to borrow further funds.
5. No access to alternative finance.
6. Inability to raise further equity capital.
7. Suppliers placing [company] on COD, or otherwise demanding special payments before resuming supply.
8. Creditors unpaid outside trading terms.
9. Issuing of post-dated cheques.
10. Dishonoured cheques.
11. Special arrangements with selected creditors.
12. Solicitors' letters, summons[es], judgments or warrants issued against the company.
13. Payments to creditors of rounded sums which are not reconcilable to specific invoices.
14. Inability to produce timely and accurate financial information to display the company's trading performance and financial position, and make reliable forecasts.

The meaning of "insolvency" is further discussed in Chapter 25 below.

presumptions of insolvency

Two presumptions of insolvency assist in proving that a company was insolvent at the relevant time.

[13.5.65] Two presumptions of insolvency are available under s 588E to assist in proving that a company was insolvent at the relevant time. The presumptions do not apply in connection with criminal proceedings for contravention of s 588G. The presumptions may be rebutted by evidence to the contrary: s 588E(9).

Under s 588E(3), there is a presumption of continuing insolvency. If it can be proved that a company was insolvent at a particular time during the 12 months ending on the "relation-back day", it is presumed that the company remained insolvent thereafter. The relation-back day in the case of a compulsory winding up is the date of filing the application: s 9. Consequently, where a company incurs debts at different times within the 12-month period prior to the relation-back day, this presumption obviates the need to prove that it was insolvent on each occasion.

Under s 588E(4) there is also a presumption of insolvency where the company has for a time contravened either s 286(1) or (2) by failing to keep or retain adequate financial records. In such cases, it must be presumed that the company is insolvent during the period of contravention. This presumption seeks to overcome difficulties of proving insolvency in the absence of proper accounting records. It does not apply to a minor or technical contravention of s 286: s 588E(5). Nor does it apply if the s 286 contravention is due solely to someone other than the director destroying, concealing or removing the company's accounting records: s 588E(6).

In *Kenna & Brown Pty Ltd v Kenna* [1999] NSWSC 533, a company was presumed to be insolvent under s 588E(4) because its financial records had been falsified in contravention of the predecessor of s 289.

reasonable grounds for suspecting

[13.5.70] Directors do not contravene s 588G merely because the company is insolvent at the time a debt is incurred. Section 588G(1)(c) requires that there must be reasonable grounds for suspecting that the company was insolvent at the time the debt was incurred. This section involves two separate issues. What is meant by the word "reasonable" and what are suspicions of insolvency?

In *ASIC v Plymin* [2003] VSC 123, it was held that the word "reasonable" imported the standard of reasonableness appropriate to non-executive directors of reasonable competence and diligence, seeking to perform their duties as imposed by law and capable of reaching a reasonably informed opinion as to the company's financial capacity. Reasonable grounds for suspecting insolvency arise when a reasonably competent and diligent director would have had grounds for suspecting insolvency in the circumstances. It is not necessary for a plaintiff to prove that the director actually suspected insolvency. This case considered a number of aspects of the insolvent trading provisions. The decision of Mandie J in *ASIC v Plymin* [2003] VSC 123 was affirmed by the Supreme Court of Victoria Court of Appeal in *Elliott v ASIC* [2004] VSCA 54.

Reasonable grounds for suspecting insolvency arise when a reasonably competent and diligent director would have had grounds for suspecting insolvency in the circumstances.

Under the predecessor of s 588G, proof was required that a director had reasonable grounds to expect insolvency. A suspicion of insolvency is different to an expectation of insolvency. In *Queensland Bacon Pty Ltd v Rees* (1966) 115 CLR 266, the High Court held that a "suspicion" requires a degree of satisfaction, not necessarily amounting to actual belief but extending beyond speculation. An "expectation" of insolvency, on the other hand, involves a higher probability of insolvency than a "suspicion" of insolvency. Consequently, it is easier to prove a suspicion of insolvency than an expectation of insolvency.

The Harmer Report observed that the change from expecting insolvency to suspecting insolvency was more than an exercise in semantics. It was intended to impose a higher obligation on directors to act and to be more rigorous in monitoring the company's financial position.

failure to prevent incurring of debt

[13.5.75] Section 588G(2) requires proof that a director failed to prevent the company incurring the debt. According to *ASIC v Plymin* [2003] VSC 123, the expression "failing to prevent" covers inactivity or the failure to attempt to prevent the company from incurring the debt. A director fails to prevent the company incurring a debt if the director acquiesced in the company continuing to incur all such debts as it would incur in the ordinary course of business. It is not necessary for a plaintiff to prove that a director had the power to prevent the company incurring debts or continuing to trade. Nor is it necessary to prove that an individual director failed in his or her duty to take a particular step which would have been effective to prevent the company incurring the debt: *Elliott v ASIC* [2004] VSCA 54.

Section 588G(2) requires proof that a director failed to prevent the company incurring the debt.

A director contravenes s 588G by failing to prevent the company incurring the debt if the director is aware that at the time the debt is incurred there are reasonable grounds for suspecting the company's insolvency: s 588G(2)(a).

In *ASIC v Plymin* [2003] VSC 123, it was held that s 588G(2)(a) requires proof that the director is aware that there are reasonable grounds for suspecting the company's insolvency. It is not necessary to prove that the director had an actual suspicion that the company was insolvent. It is sufficient if the director was aware of facts which would cause a reasonably competent non-executive director to suspect that the company was insolvent at the time it incurred a debt.

A director also contravenes s 588G by failing to prevent the company incurring the debt if a reasonable person in a like position in a company in the company's circumstances would be aware of reasonable grounds for suspecting insolvency: s 588G(2)(b). This corresponds to the duty of care and diligence under s 180(1) and covers situations where a director was unaware of the facts or circumstances constituting reasonable grounds for suspecting insolvency because the director failed to ascertain them, but a reasonable person in a like position in a company in the company's circumstances would or ought to have ascertained those facts and circumstances: *Powell v Fryer* [2001] SASC 59.

defences

[13.5.80] Section 588H, sets out four alternative defences available to directors who otherwise contravene s 588G. In addition, s 1317JA gives the court discretionary power to relieve a director, either wholly or in part, from a liability for contravention of s 588G.

According to the Explanatory Memorandum to the 1992 amendments that introduced ss 588G and 588H:

> **< [The s 588H defences are designed to assist a director who has] acted diligently and has actively participated in management, but has nevertheless been unable to prevent the incurring of the crucial debt. >**

reasonable grounds to expect solvency

It is a defence if the director proves that, at the time when the debt was incurred, the director had reasonable grounds to expect, and did expect, that the company was solvent.

[13.5.85] Under s 588H(2) it is a defence if the director proves that, at the time when the debt was incurred, the director had reasonable grounds to expect, and did expect, that the company was solvent at that time and would remain solvent even if it incurred that debt and any other debts that it incurred at that time.

The 588H(2) defence refers to reasonable grounds to expect the company's solvency whereas contravention of s 588G requires proof of reasonable grounds to suspect insolvency. According to the Federal Court in *Metropolitan Fire Systems Pty Ltd v Miller* (1997) 23 ASCR 699:

> **< to "suspect" something requires a lower threshold of knowledge or awareness than to "expect" it. It implies a measure of confidence that the company is solvent. The directors must have reasonable grounds for regarding it as likely that the company would at the relevant date have been able to pay its debts as and when they fall due. >**

In that case the court held that the company's three directors could not prove the s 588H(2) defence. Their expectations of solvency were based on optimism regarding the company's future. These expectations were based on hope and were not objectively reasonable expectations.

As noted above, a company that experiences a temporary lack of liquidity is not regarded as being insolvent. Directors may seek to rely on expectations of additional external financial support from the company's bank or major creditors to demonstrate that they had reasonable grounds to expect that the company was solvent for purposes of the s 588H(2) defence. However, a director's expectations of additional financial support must be objectively reasonable in the circumstances.

A director does not establish the s 588H(2) defence by showing that they were completely unaware of the company's financial position.

A director does not establish the s 588H(2) defence by showing that they were completely unaware of the company's financial position.

case note

In *Tourprint International Pty Ltd v Bott* (1999) 17 ACLC 1543, Bott was a director for less than one year before the company went into voluntary administration and ultimately liquidation. Bott was held liable under s 588G(1) as he did not inform himself of the true financial position of the company either before becoming a director or while a director. He made no inquiries of the accountant or other director and did not inspect the company's books. Bott therefore did not have reasonable grounds to expect that the company was solvent at the time the debts were incurred for the purposes of s 588H(2).

Austin J stated:

> < Expectation, as required by s 588H(2), means a higher degree of certainty than mere hope or possibility or suspecting: *3M Australia Pty Ltd v Kemish* (1986) 4 ACLC 185, 192;

Dunn v Shapowloff [1978] 2 NSWLR 235, 249. The defence requires an actual expectation that the company was and would continue to be solvent, and that the grounds for so expecting are reasonable. A director cannot rely on a complete ignorance of or neglect of duty (*Metal Manufacturers Ltd v Lewis* (1986) 4 ACLC 739, 749) and cannot hide behind ignorance of the company's affairs which is of their own making or, if not entirely of their own making, has been contributed to by their own failure to make further necessary inquiries (*Morley v Statewide Tobacco Services Ltd* (1990) 8 ACLC 825, 847). >

delegation and reliance on others

[13.5.90] The s 588H(3) defence applies to a director who has delegated the monitoring of the company's financial position to others upon whom the director relies. This defence is based on a recommendation in the Harmer Report which explained that such a defence was necessary for directors of larger companies. For such companies it could not be expected that directors have control over every action taken in the conduct of the company's business. In addition, it thought that a defence of this nature could encourage a proper system of financial management.

The s 588H(3) defence applies to a director who has delegated the monitoring of the company's financial position to others upon whom the director relies.

A director must establish a number of matters before being able to rely on the defence in s 588H(3). First, the director must prove that at the time when the debt was incurred, the director had reasonable grounds to believe, and did believe, that a competent and reliable person was responsible for providing the director with adequate information about whether the company was solvent and that the other person was fulfilling that responsibility: s 588H(3)(a).

case note

In *ASIC v Plymin* [2003] VSC 123, it was held that Elliott, a non-executive director, could not rely on this defence. Elliott argued that he relied on information about the company's financial position provided to him by its managing director, Plymin, and the company's management. The court was not satisfied that Elliott believed that Plymin and management were competent and reliable persons who were fulfilling the responsibility to provide him with adequate information about whether the company was solvent.

The court held that a reasonable person would not have regarded that Plymin and management were competent and reliable persons who were fulfilling their responsibilities including that of providing adequate information about the company's solvency. The evidence disclosed that Plymin did not comply with board requirements for financial information. The court was not satisfied that Elliott, an experienced businessman and an astute intelligent individual, did not know that he could and should have obtained from management regular lists of debtors and creditors by age and amount, regular profit and loss and cash flow statements and reports on negotiation with creditors whose debts were outside trading terms. The court thought that Elliott turned a blind eye to the details of the company's liquidity crisis in the hope that "something would turn up".

In order to make out the s 588H(3) defence, the director must also prove that the director expected, on the basis of information provided to the director by the other person, that the company was solvent and would remain solvent even if it incurred that debt and any other debts that it incurred at that time. A director cannot be said to have expected that the company was solvent under s 588H(3)(b) if the director does not obtain any information about the company's solvency from a competent and reliable person.

A director cannot be said to have expected that the company was solvent if the director does not obtain any information about the company's solvency from a competent and reliable person.

case note

In *Metropolitan Fire Systems Pty Ltd v Miller* (1997) 23 ACSR 699, two directors of a company asserted that they had relied on the third director who had the responsibility for running the company and for providing them with all necessary information about its finances and that as far as they were aware, the third director was fulfilling those responsibilities. It was held the s 588H(3) defence did not apply in the circumstances. The evidence indicated that the two directors made no inquiries of the third director as to the state of the company's finances. Consequently, their belief that the company was solvent was not based on information provided by the third director. The court held that directors are under an obligation to take an interest in and demand information on the financial state of their company. They will not be able to rely on s 588H(3) if they fail to demand information when suspicions about the company's financial viability and survival should and would have been aroused.

absence from management

Section 588H(4) provides a defence for a director who was absent from management because of illness or for some other good reason.

[13.5.95] Section 588H(4) provides a defence for a director who was absent from management because of illness or for some other good reason at the time when the company incurs the debt in question.

A director may have a good reason for being absent from management at the time a debt was incurred if the director did not take part in the board decision on the matter because the director had a material personal interest. There may be other situations where a director may have a good reason for being absent from management. In *ACCC v ASIC* [2000] NSWSC 316, the ACCC applied to the court to reinstate a deregistered company so that the ACCC could join the company as a defendant in other court proceedings alleging various breaches of the *Trade Practices Act*. In granting the ACCC's application, the court noted that on reinstatement the company's directors would resume office. However, they would have no power to manage its affairs and so would have a s 588H(4) defence to any liability for insolvent trading.

A director does not have a "good reason" for being absent from management merely by not participating in managing the company's business.

At first sight, s 588H(4) appears to provide a complete defence for a passive director who fails to be involved in the company's management. This is not how the courts have interpreted s 588H(4). In *Tourprint International Pty Ltd v Bott* (1999) 17 ACLC 1543, it was held that a director does not have a "good reason" for being absent from management merely by not participating in managing the company's business. The policy underlying the insolvent trading provisions requires directors to have a "necessary commitment to an involvement with the management of a company in financial difficulties".

case note

Similarly, in *Deputy Commissioner of Taxation v Clark* [2003] NSWCA 91, the New South Wales Court of Appeal, overturning the decision at first instance (*Southern Cross Interiors Pty Ltd v Deputy Commissioner of Taxation* [2001] NSWSC 621), held that a married woman director of a family company run by her husband who took no part in its management could not assert that she had good cause for being absent from management because she deferred to her husband, the managing director. The court held that the legislative policy underpinning s 588G was that a person should not become a director unless they were prepared to assume the obligations and duties of such an office.

all reasonable steps to prevent debt being incurred

[13.5.100] Under s 588H(5), it is a defence if the director proves that they took all reasonable steps to prevent the company from incurring the debt. The Explanatory Paper accompanying the exposure draft of the 1992 Bill that inserted that defence indicated that s 588H(5) requires directors to take "unequivocal action".

Under s 588H(5), it is a defence if the director proves that they took all reasonable steps to prevent the company from incurring the debt.

To take advantage of s 588H(5), a court might require unequivocal action on the part of those directors seeking to rely on the defence to exercise what powers and functions they possess, either to prevent the incurring of the debt directly or to bring the matter to the attention, either of an officer with the necessary authority to prevent the incurring of the debt or to the board of directors where that is required.

In *Byron v Southern Star Group Pty Ltd* (1997) 15 ACLC 191, the New South Wales Court of Appeal held that an executive director could not avoid personal liability under a predecessor of s 588G simply by telling the company's managing director that he had reservations and did not agree with the company incurring further debts. If a director cannot prevent the debt being incurred, Ormiston J in *Statewide Tobacco Services Ltd v Morley* (1990) 8 ACLC 827 indicated that the director should seek to have the company wound up or resign.

Section 588H(6) encourages directors to make prompt use of the voluntary administration provisions. This is discussed in Chapter 24 below. In determining whether a defence under s 588H(5) has been proved, s 588H(6) directs the court to have regard to matters including any action the director took with a view to appointing an administrator of the company, when that action was taken and the results of that action.

consequences of contravention

[13.5.105] Several consequences may flow from a contravention of s 588G. The court may order the director to pay compensation. In addition, since s 588G is a civil penalty provision, contravention may also result in the imposition of a pecuniary penalty order under s 1317G or disqualification from managing corporations under s 206C. Further, under s 588G(3) contravention is a criminal offence, punishable by a fine or imprisonment (or both) if a director's failure to prevent the company incurring the debt in breach of s 588G was dishonest.

Several consequences may flow from a contravention of s 588G.

compensation

[13.5.110] The court can make a compensation order against a director who contravenes s 588G in a number of circumstances. Compensation orders can be made in the context of an application for civil penalty orders and as part of proceedings for the criminal offence: ss 588J and 588K. Compensation orders can be made whether or not the court imposes a civil penalty order or a criminal penalty. Compensation orders under either ss 588J or 588K may be made whether not the company is in liquidation.

If the company that incurred the debt has been placed in liquidation, s 588M gives the liquidator the ability to seek compensation from a director who contravenes s 588G. Liquidators are permitted to mount compensation recovery proceedings whether or not ASIC has commenced an application for a civil penalty order or criminal proceedings: s 588M(1)(e) and (f). For liquidators, the advantage of the compensation procedures in ss 588J and 588K is that ASIC initiates the proceedings and bears the legal costs in mounting actions for contravention of s 588G as part of the application for a civil penalty order or criminal proceedings.

If the company that incurred the debt has been placed in liquidation, s 588M gives the liquidator the ability to seek compensation from a director.

Unsecured creditors are also given a limited right to initiate their own compensation claims against directors: s 588M(3). They may only do this if the company's liquidator fails to launch an action or the

Unsecured creditors are also given a limited right to initiate their own compensation claims against directors.

liquidator consents to the creditor's action. In *Metropolitan Fire Systems Pty Ltd v Miller* (1997) 23 ACSR 699, a creditor began an s 588G case with the liquidator's consent.

Sections 588R–588U set out a regime for creditor-initiated compensation recovery actions. These provisions ensure that liquidators have sufficient time to consider whether to mount their own compensation claims. They require unsecured creditors to wait at least six months after the beginning of winding up and then apply for the liquidator's consent to the individual creditor's action. Where creditors initiate their own action they, of course, bear the onus of proving that the director has contravened s 588G.

Section 588S sets out the procedure for gaining a liquidator's consent. It requires the creditor to give the company's liquidator written notice of the creditor's intention to bring proceedings under s 588M. The notice can be given only after the end of six months from the beginning of winding up. In the notice the creditor must ask the liquidator to give consent to the creditor beginning the proceedings or to state the reasons why those proceedings should not be initiated. The liquidator has three months to respond to the notice. If the liquidator consents, a creditor may begin proceedings under s 588M in relation to the incurring by the company of an unsecured debt that is owed to the creditor: s 588R(1). Where, however, the liquidator has not consented to the creditor's action by the end of the three-month notice period, the creditor must apply for leave of the court to begin the proceedings: s 588T(2)(b).

Section 588U(1) ensures that in some circumstances creditors are not permitted to begin direct proceedings against a director. Creditors cannot begin their own proceedings if the liquidator has:

> **applied under the antecedent transactions provisions of s 588FF (discussed in Chapter 25 below) in relation to the debt, or in relation to a transaction under which the debt was incurred; or**
> **begun proceedings under s 588M in relation to the incurring of the debt; or**
> **intervened in an application for a civil penalty order against the director in relation to a contravention of s 588G in relation to the incurring of the debt.**

amount of compensation

[13.5.115] Under ss 588J, 588K and 588M, directors are liable to pay compensation equal to the amount of loss or damage suffered by all unsecured creditors whose debts were incurred in contravention of s 588G because of the company's insolvency. However, in the case of creditor-initiated actions, under s 588M(3), the amount recoverable is the amount of loss or damage suffered by the individual creditor.

As a general rule, the amount of "loss or damage suffered" by a creditor is the amount of the unpaid debt.

As a general rule, the amount of "loss or damage suffered" by a creditor is the amount of the unpaid debt: *Powell v Fryer* [2001] SASC 59. However, in *ASIC v Plymin* [2003] VSC 123, the court accepted that the amount of loss or damage recoverable from directors could be reduced by the amount of actual or expected dividends distributed to creditors. Where a deed of company arrangement is entered into by creditors and an administrator, the loss or damage suffered by creditors for the purposes of s 588J is the amount representing the shortfall between what was received under the deed and the amount of the debt. This is despite the fact that the remaining debt may have been extinguished under the terms of the deed: *Elliott v ASIC* [2004] VSCA 54. Deeds of company arrangement are discussed in Chapter 24 below.

The amount recoverable from directors is restricted to the loss or damage suffered by creditors in relation to debts that are wholly or partly unsecured: ss 588J(1)(b), 588K(1)(b)(i) and 588M(1)(c). In *Metropolitan Fire Systems Pty Ltd v Miller* (1997) ACSR 699, the Federal Court held that a creditor whose debt was secured by a retention of title clause was still an unsecured creditor. In this case the creditor had made no claim under the retention of title clause. If, however, a secured creditor proves for the debt as an unsecured creditor, s 588D regards the debt as unsecured.

who receives the benefit of compensation?

[13.5.120] Prior to the 1992 amendments, directors were liable to compensate only the particular creditor who took action. This offends the notion of equal sharing in insolvency. Under the current provisions, however, an amount recovered from directors pursuant to an application for a civil penalty order, a criminal proceeding or a liquidator-initiated proceeding is payable to the company and is available for distribution to all unsecured creditors including those creditors whose debts were incurred before reasonable suspicions of insolvency arose. In the case of creditor-initiated actions, however, the amount recovered is payable to the unsecured creditor who initiated the action.

An amount recovered from directors is payable to the company and is available for distribution to all unsecured creditors including those creditors whose debts were incurred before reasonable suspicions of insolvency arose.

Amounts recovered are not available to pay a secured debt of the company unless all the company's unsecured debts have been paid in full: s 588Y(1). Section 588Y stems from an ALRC recommendation that amounts recovered from directors should only be available for unsecured creditors because insolvent trading has a major impact on them.

Further, under s 588Y(2) the court has power to order that compensation recovered is not available to pay the debt of a creditor who, at the time the debt was incurred, knew that the company was insolvent, unless all the company's other unsecured debts have been paid in full. This may mean that a director who is an unsecured creditor of the company is unable to share in the proceeds of the compensation. The power to exclude creditors from participating in the amount recovered does not, by virtue of s 588Y(3), apply in relation to creditor-initiated proceedings.

court relief

[13.5.125] Pursuant to s 1317S(2), the court may relieve a person, either wholly or partly, from a liability for contravention of s 588G if it appears that the person has acted honestly and having regard to all the circumstances of the case ought fairly to be excused. Section 1317JA(3) reiterates s 588H(6) when it explains that in determining whether a person ought fairly to be excused, the matters to which regard is to be had include any action the person took, with a view to appointing an administrator of the company, when that action was taken and the results of that action.

National Insolvent Trading Program

[13.5.130] ASIC established the National Insolvent Trading Program in July 2003 to deal with possible insolvent trading before it occurs. Under the program, ASIC identifies specific companies that are financially stressed and reviews them for purposes of ensuring compliance by directors of their duties to prevent insolvent trading. In the review, ASIC discusses the company's financial position with its directors and reviews both their historical and current financial records and forecasts.

ASIC established the National Insolvent Trading Program in July 2003 to deal with possible insolvent trading before it occurs.

According to ASIC, the program aims to:

- **make company directors aware of their company's financial position;**
- **make directors of potentially insolvent companies aware of their responsibilities and the implications of continued trading if they know they're insolvent;**
- **encourage directors to seek external advice from accountants and lawyers on restructuring; and**
- **encourage directors to seek advice from insolvency professionals where appropriate, and to take action to appoint a voluntary administrator or liquidator where necessary.**

In a media release (05-228), ASIC Commissioner Berna Collier commented:

> **Through the program, ASIC aims to have company directors actively manage their company's financial position and seek early advice when financial difficulties arise. As well as reducing the risk of insolvent trading, with its potentially serious impact on creditors and the business community, active engagement by directors in financial difficulties their company is experiencing can improve the company's overall performance.**

Through the program, ASIC aims to have company directors actively manage their company's financial position and seek early advice when financial difficulties arise.

ASIC's media release also provided the following statistics that indicate the impact of the National Insolvent Trading Program.

table 13.5.2 insolvent trading program statistics for the 12 months to 30 June 2005

	NSW	QLD	VIC	WA	SA	TOTAL
Surveillance visits of companies	119	119	107	129	14	488
Companies that had an External Administrator appointed after an ASIC visit	20	13	13	16	1	63
Companies ASIC sought to appoint an External Administrator to, after a visit	5	1	3	1	0	10

liability for unremitted taxation

[13.5.135] Income tax legislation requires employer companies to deduct employees' taxation contributions from their wages and salaries. These amounts of tax must be remitted to the Commissioner of Taxation. There are similar requirements for companies that collect Goods and Services Tax (GST) from sales to remit the GST.

In some situations directors may become personally liable for unremitted amounts if their company fails to remit them. Under the provisions of the tax legislation, the Commissioner of Taxation must give 14 days' notice to the directors setting out details of the unpaid amount and the penalty. Directors will not be penalised if one of the following occurs:

> **the company pays the unremitted amount;**
> **the company enters an agreement relating to the unremitted amount;**
> **an administrator is appointed; or**
> **the company goes into liquidation.**

Directors who may be liable are those who were in office on or before the due date for payment of the deducted amount and any persons who became directors after this date. Any amount paid to discharge the liability of either the company or a director discharges other liabilities to the extent of that amount.

Directors subject to recovery proceedings by the Commissioner have available two defences:

> **the director, because of illness or other reason, took no part in management of the company at the time when one of the four prescribed courses of action should have been taken; or**
> **the director took all reasonable steps to ensure deductions were paid or the company complied with the four alternative courses of action by the due date or there were no steps that the director could have taken.**

Directors may be liable not only for actual unremitted amounts but also for amounts estimated as being liable.

employee entitlements

[13.5.140] The *Corporations Law Amendment (Employee Entitlements) Act 2000* introduced amendments which were aimed at assisting employees of insolvent companies to recover their entitlements. The amendments introduced the following main features into the *Corporations Act*:

> the insolvent trading provisions were extended to include uncommercial transactions. These include disposing of assets in a way that is detrimental to creditors but would previously not have involved incurring a debt. A liquidator now has greater scope to pursue such claims against individual directors. Uncommercial transactions are discussed in Chapter 25 below;
> a new offence that penalises persons who deliberately enter into agreements and transactions for the purpose of avoiding employee entitlements: s 596AB. This provision was a response to situations where assets were stripped from employer companies resulting in employees being unable to enforce their entitlements while related entities held substantial assets; and
> in addition to the criminal offence, s 596AC provides for payment of compensation.

Compensation may be payable even in the absence of a conviction as the burden of proof is lower than in the case of a criminal offence. Generally, the liquidator may bring an action seeking compensation and effectively lift the corporate veil so as to make anyone involved in the agreement or transaction liable to compensate the employees for otherwise lost entitlements. In some cases the employees may bring the action where the liquidator does not do so.

The *Corporations Law Amendment (Employee Entitlements) Act 2000*, together with the accompanying Explanatory Memorandum, can be found on the SCALEplus website and is linked to the Lipton-Herzberg Duties of Directors of Insolvent Companies Pathway at **http://www.lipton-herzberg.com.au/secure/pathways-directors-duties-directors-of-insolvent-companies.html**

fraudulent conduct

[13.5.145] It is an offence under s 592(6) for any person to be knowingly concerned in the doing of an act by a company with the intent of defrauding creditors of the company or any other person or for any other fraudulent purpose. Where a person has been convicted of an offence under s 592(6), the court may, on application by the Commission, creditors or members, order that that person be personally liable to the company without limitation of liability for an amount up to the whole of its debts as the court thinks proper: s 593(2). Creditors benefit because the insolvent company is then in a better position to pay its debts.

It is an offence for any person to be knowingly concerned in the doing of an act by a company with the intent of defrauding creditors of the company.

The ALRC, in its *General Insolvency Inquiry Report*, recommended that creditors should be able to take action without waiting for the conviction of a person for the criminal offence.

Creditors may be defrauded under s 592(6) where the intention is to defraud only some creditors and not all. It is not necessary, in order to establish an offence under s 592(6), to show that creditors were in fact defrauded. An intention to defraud is sufficient. An intent to defraud is an intent to deprive creditors, or some creditors, of an economic advantage or inflict upon them some economic loss: *Coleman v R* (1987) 5 ACLC 766.

pathways questions . . .

The following questions dealing with directors of insolvent companies may best be answered by reading this sub-chapter and considering the Internet resources found on the Lipton-Herzberg Duties of Directors of Insolvent Companies Pathway at **http://www.lipton-herzberg.com.au/secure/pathways-directors-duties-directors-of-insolvent-companies.html**

1. (a) To what extent is it true to say that directors owe a duty to creditors?
   (b) When must directors take into account the interests of creditors? Give examples of how directors may breach their duties by disregarding the interests of creditors.

2. How does ASIC's National Insolvent Trading Program prevent insolvent trading?
3. What impact does voluntary administration have on directors' insolvent trading liability?
4. What should directors do after they realise that their company is insolvent?

bibliography ...

Anderson, C & Morrison, D "Should directors be pursued for insolvent trading where a company has entered into a Deed of Company Arrangement" (2005) 13 Insolv LJ 163.

Anderson, H "Director's Personal Liability to Creditors: Theory vs Tradition" (2003) 18 Deakin LR 209.

Anderson, H "The Theory of the Corporation and its Relevance to Directors' Tortious Liability to Creditors" (2004) 16 Aust Jnl of Corp Law 73.

Berkahn, M "Directors Duties to The Company and to Creditors: Spies v The Queen" (2001) 6 Deakin LR 10 **http://www.austlii.edu.au/au/journals/DLR/2001/10.html**

Broderick, M & Lenicka, M "Uncommercial Transactions—Corporate Governance for Insolvent Companies" (2004) 22 C & SLJ 7.

Byrne, M "An Economic Analysis of Directors' Duties in Favour of Creditors" (1994) 4 Aust Jnl of Corp Law 275.

Cassidy, J "'Sexually Transmitted Debts': The Scope of Defences to Directors' Liability for Insolvent Trading" (2002) 20 C & SLJ 372.

Clarke, F, Dean, G & Houghton, E "Corporate Restructuring, Creditor's Rights, Cross-guarantees and Group Behaviour" (1999) 17 C & SLJ 85.

Coburn, N "The Phoenix Reexamined" (1998) 8 Aust Jnl of Corp Law 321.

Goldman, D B "Directors beware! Creditors protection from insolvent trading" (2005) 23 C & SLJ 216.

Grawehr, P "A Comparison Between Australian and European Insolvent Trading Laws" (1996) 14 C & SLJ 16.

Hargovan, A "Directors' Duties to Creditors in Australia after Spies v The Queen—Is the Development of an Independent Fiduciary Duty Dead or Alive?" (2003) 21 C & SLJ 350.

Hargovan, A "Geneva Finance and the 'duty' of directors to creditors: imperfect obligation and technique" (2004) 12 Insolv LJ 134.

Herzberg, A "Why are There So Few Insolvent Trading Cases?" (1998) 6 Insolv LJ 77.

James, P, Ramsay, I & Siva, P "Insolvent trading—An empirical study" (2004) 12 Insolv LJ 210.

Keay, A "Directors Duty to Take Into Account the Interests of Creditors" (2001) 25 MULR 315.

McConvill, J "Directors' Duties to Creditors in Australia after Spies v The Queen" (2002) 20 C & SLJ 4.

McNee, S "Why Women Should Love, Honour and Obey—An Attempt to Make the Wife's Special Equity a Statutory Defence" (2003) 11 Insolv LJ 147.

McPherson, B H "The Liability of Directors for Company Debts" (1993) 1 Insolv LJ 133.

Mosley, J "Insolvent Trading: What is a Debt and When is One Incurred?" (1996) 4 Insolv LJ 155.

Morrison, D "When is a Company Insolvent?" (2002) 10 Insolv LJ 4.

Morrison, D "The Addition of Uncommercial Transactions to s 588G and its Implications for Phoenix Activities" (2002) 10 Insolv LJ 229.

Noakes, D "Corporate Groups and the Duties of Directors: Protecting the Employee or the Insolvent Employer?" (2001) 29 ABLR 124.

Noakes, D "Dogs on the Wharves: Corporate Groups and the Waterfront Dispute" (1999) 11 Aust Jnl of Corp Law 27.

O'Donovan, J "Corporate Benefit in Relation to Guarantees and Third Party Mortgages" (1996) 24 ABLR 126.

Pascoe, J & Anderson, H "Personal Recovery Actions by Creditors against Company Directors" (2002) 11 Insolv LJ 205.

Pearlie, K "Shadow Director, Shadow Director, Who Art Thou?" (1996) 14 C & SLJ 340.

Purcell, J "A Public Policy Analysis of the Interaction between Insolvent Trading and Part 5.3A Administrations" (2000) 8 Insolv LJ 202.

Reynolds, M "The Corporations Law Amendment (Employee Entitlements) Act" [2001] QUT LJ 134.

Sealy, L S "Directors' Wider Responsibilities" (1987) 13 Mon LR 164.

Stoney, M "Borrower Companies Approaching Insolvency—The Potential Liability of the Lender as a De Facto Director" (2000) 8 Insolv LJ 192.

Su-King Hii "Directors' Duties to Prevent Insolvent Trading" (1999) 27 ABLR 224.

Vann, V "Another Way of Dealing with Phoenix Companies" (1997) 10 Corp & Bus LJ 141.

Yeo, V C S & Lee Suet Lin, J "Insolvent Trading—A Comparative and Economic Approach" (1999) 10 Aust Jnl of Corp Law 216.

revision questions on the material in this chapter ...

> Please see eQuiz at **http://www.thomson.com.au/academic** for multiple choice questions and answers.

> For further corporations law links and material please refer to the Lipton-Herzberg website at **http://www.lipton-herzberg.com.au**

chapter thirteen.six

remedies and penalties for breach of duty

key points ...

> Directors' duties are owed to the company and therefore the company is generally the proper plaintiff. The main remedies are compensation and account of profits.

> The *Corporations Act* provides civil penalties where certain statutory duties are breached.

> ASIC may seek a pecuniary penalty order or disqualification order. In such proceedings, the burden of proof is the civil burden, on balance of probabilities.

> Criminal liability may arise in relation to breaches of statutory duty involving dishonesty.

A breach of directors' duty may harm the company, its shareholders or creditors.

[13.6.05] A breach of directors' duty may harm the company, its shareholders or creditors. For example, directors who make undisclosed profits from the misuse of their position may deprive the company of profits to which it would otherwise be entitled. This indirectly affects the members because the value of their investment in the company is thereby reduced.

In other circumstances, a breach of duty may affect members directly. This can occur when the directors improperly refuse to register a transfer of shares.

When the company is in financial difficulties, creditors may also be adversely affected by improper use of the company's assets by its directors. Such acts may diminish the value of assets available for distribution to creditors on a winding up.

As a general rule, the company is the proper plaintiff to remedy wrongs done to it by the directors.

As a general rule, the company is the proper plaintiff to remedy wrongs done to it by the directors. This is because the duties are owed to the company and it is regarded as a legal entity separate from its members. If the company is in liquidation, its liquidator can bring an action in the name of the company against present or former directors. Under Pt 2F.1A of the *Corporations Act,* members have the right, with prior court leave, to bring legal proceedings against directors on behalf of the company. This is discussed in Chapter 17 below.

ASIC may bring proceedings in the name of a company to recover damages or property from directors who breach their duty or engage in misconduct: *AISC Act*, s 50.

A breach of various sections specified in s 1317E(1) attracts the civil penalty provisions of Pt 9.4B of the *Corporations Act.* The statutory duties which trigger the civil penalty provisions include:

- **care and diligence (s 180);**
- **good faith and proper purpose (s 181);**
- **improperly using position (s 182); and**
- **improperly using information: s 183.**

The consequences of breaching civil penalty provisions are discussed below. Under s 184, contravening the above duties is regarded as a criminal offence if the director or other officer did so dishonestly.

company's remedies

If director or officer breaches any of their fiduciary duties, the company has a variety of remedies available.

[13.6.10] If director or officer breaches any of their fiduciary duties, the company has a variety of remedies available. The appropriate remedy depends on the circumstances. In some cases, a company may have more than one remedy available and it may choose the remedy that achieves the best result from its point of view.

case note

In *Tavistock Holdings Pty Ltd v Saulsman* (1991) 9 ACLC 450, the facts of which are set out in Chapter 13.3 above, a director who breached his fiduciary duties was ordered to account for an overpayment made by a company to him and another company controlled by him. A manager of the company also breached his duties because he actively assisted the director to obtain payment. The court awarded equitable compensation to relieve the company against loss arising from the breach of fiduciary duty. The manager was liable to compensate the company to the extent it was unable to recover its losses from the director and his company.

A company also has similar remedies against outsiders who knowingly participate in an director's breach of duty.

case note

For example, in *Green v Bestobell Industries Ltd* [1982] WAR 1, Bestobell's Victorian manager, Green, breached his duty to avoid a conflict of interests when he incorporated his own company to obtain a contract that rightfully belonged to Bestobell. The court held that Green's company knowingly participated in the breach and ordered that it account to Bestobell for the profits made under the contract. This case is an example of the court lifting the corporate veil where a company is formed to assist someone in his breach of duty.

Occasionally, the person who derives a benefit from a breach of duty by a director may not knowingly be concerned in the breach. The company bears the onus of proving that the person had knowledge of the essential facts constituting the breach before property may be recovered. In this sense, "knowledge" may be actual knowledge, wilful shutting of the eyes to the obvious or knowledge of the circumstances which an honest and reasonable person would recognise as improper: *Abeles v P A (Holdings) Pty Ltd* (2000) 18 ACLC 867.

damages or compensation

[13.6.15] If a director breaches the fiduciary duties owed to the company and it suffers loss as a result, the company may apply for the equitable remedy of compensation. This is similar to the common law remedy of damages. If the officer is fraudulent, the company has a common law action for the tort of deceit and may recover damages. If the breach of duty arises from a failure to exercise reasonable care, the company has an action for negligence and can recover damages for any loss that results.

If a director breaches the fiduciary duties owed to the company and it suffers loss as a result, the company may apply for the equitable remedy of compensation.

The object of compensation or damages is to place the company, as near as possible, in the position it would have occupied had the breach of duty not occurred. All directors who participate in the breach of duty are jointly and severally liable. This means that the company can sue any one of several directors in breach of duty for the full amount of the damages or compensation. That director then has a right to seek contribution from the others who participated in the breach of duty.

The object of compensation or damages is to place the company, as near as possible, in the position it would have occupied had the breach of duty not occurred.

case note

In *Markwell Bros Pty Ltd v CPN Diesels (Qld) Pty Ltd* (1982) 7 ACLR 425, Markwell Bros Pty Ltd held a franchise to distribute marine engines manufactured by a Japanese supplier. The relationship between Markwell and the Japanese supplier deteriorated and the franchise was withdrawn and acquired by CPN Diesels (Qld) Pty Ltd. CPN was a company formed by two of Markwell's former directors and employees. After the loss of the franchise, Markwell agreed to purchase engines from CPN at landed cost plus 10 per cent. Two years later, it was discovered that CPN had sold engines to Markwell based on a price greater than the actual landed cost with the result that Markwell had been overcharged approximately $23,000. Markwell brought an action against CPN and its former directors seeking equitable damages or compensation for breach of fiduciary duty.

The Queensland Supreme Court held that the former directors breached their duties and were liable to compensate the company. The measure of compensation was the same whether the breach was of a contractual nature or of fiduciary duty. It was also held that CPN was liable for damages resulting from breach of duty by the directors as it knowingly participated in the breaches of duty. As discussed below, para [13.6.20], CPN may also have been liable to account for profits as a constructive trustee.

Where a company is entitled to compensation it may recover for the loss of the use of the money of which it has been deprived. This enables the company to be awarded compound interest at the bank overdraft rate paid by it. Overdraft interest rates are not appropriate where the company seeks an order for an account of secret profits paid by someone else because the company had not been deprived of the use of this money.

A person who has contravened a civil penalty provision, may be ordered by the court to pay compensation to the company for any loss suffered by the company.

A person who has contravened a civil penalty provision, such as ss 180–183, may be ordered by the court to pay compensation to the company for any loss suffered by the company: s 1317H. A company may apply for a civil penalty compensation order regardless of whether a declaration had been made. The civil penalty provisions are discussed below, para [13.6.35].

account of profits

[13.6.20] An officer's fiduciary duty to the company is breached when the officer makes undisclosed profits arising from a conflict of interests situation. In such circumstances, compensation may not be a satisfactory remedy for the company, since the breach can arise even if the company suffers no loss. The company may obtain an order that the officer hand over the profit made in breach of duty to the company. This is called "an account of profits". For example, in *Regal (Hastings) Ltd v Gulliver* [1967] 2 AC 134n, the directors breached their duty when they profited from the sale of shares in the company's subsidiary. They were in breach even though their company suffered no loss because it could not afford to acquire the subsidiary's shares itself. The directors were still ordered to disgorge the profits they had made.

A company may obtain an order that an officer hand over the profit made in breach of duty to the company. This is called "an account of profits

case note

In *Tavistock Holdings Pty Ltd v Saulsman* (1991) 9 ACLC 450, a manager breached his fiduciary duties by taking a management fee without the authority of the company. He was held liable to repay the money; however, he did provide services that benefited the company and was entitled to a just allowance for these.

A company may apply to the court for a compensation order against a person who contravenes a civil penalty provision: s 1317H. The amount of compensation that may be awarded includes any profits made by the person resulting from the contravention: s 1317H(2). The civil penalty provisions are discussed below, para [13.6.35].

rescission of contract

[13.6.25] Directors breach their duties if they have an undisclosed interest in a contract with the company. Subject to the company's constitution, the company may, at its option, rescind the contract. This enables the company to avoid an unfavourable contract to which the company no longer wishes to be bound. The aim of rescission is to put both parties to the contract in the position they would have been in had no contract been made. Thus, any money paid or property transferred is returned.

The aim of rescission is to put both parties to the contract in the position they would have been in had no contract been made.

case note

In *Kinsela v Russell Kinsela Pty Ltd* (1986) 4 NSWLR 722, the facts of which are set out in Chapter 13.5 above, a liquidator successfully sought a declaration that a lease was voidable at the company's option. This lease was granted by an insolvent company to its directors in breach of their duty to take into account the interests of the company's creditors.

If the directors profited from the contract, they are liable to account for the profit, irrespective of whether the company exercises its right to rescind.

A company's right to rescind may be lost if it is no longer possible to restore the parties to their original positions, if outsiders have bona fide acquired rights in the subject matter of the contract, or if the company fails to rescind within a reasonable time.

A company may also lose the right to rescind a contract if the person dealing with it is able to rely on the assumption in s 129(4). This allows persons who have dealings with a company to assume that company officers and agents properly perform their duties to the company. However, in most circumstances, directors who have dealings with their company will not be permitted to rely on this assumption because of the operation of s 128(4). The entitlement to make assumptions is discussed in Chapter 5 above.

return of property and constructive trusts

[13.6.30] Where a director acquires property as a consequence of a breach of duty, the company may seek a declaration that the director holds the property on constructive or resulting trust for the company with the effect that the property is returned to the company. This remedy is most appropriate where the director misappropriates property or misapplies money belonging to the company for their own purposes.

The company may seek a declaration that the director holds the property on constructive or resulting trust for the company with the effect that the property is returned to the company.

case note

For example, in *O'Brien v Walker* (1982) 1 ACLC 59, one of the directors of the Nugan Hand group of companies, misapplied funds from one of the companies in the group to purchase a house in his own name. After the director died and the companies went into liquidation, the liquidator obtained an order that the director's estate held the house on a constructive or resulting trust for the company. The company was then entitled to have the house registered in its own name. A similar remedy was obtained in *Cook v Deeks* [1916] 1 AC 554, discussed in Chapter 13.3 above.

case note

In *Paul A Davies (Aust) Pty Ltd v Davies* (1983) 1 ACLC 1091, the facts of which are discussed in Chapter 13.3 above, it was held that as the property acquired in breach of duty had not been sold, the directors held the entire property on a constructive trust for the company and in the circumstances any funds raised by way of mortgage to finance the acquisition of the property was not regarded as having come from the directors' own funds. Consequently, they were only entitled to be indemnified for debts incurred in the acquiring and running of the property and to be provided with reasonable remuneration associated with running the business.

Law of constructive trusts enables a company to recover assets that have come into the hands of third parties as a result of a breach of duty by a director.

The law of constructive trusts enables a company to recover assets that have come into the hands of third parties as a result of a breach of duty by a director. The third party may be compelled to return the property to the company if the property was received with knowledge of the breach of duty. This doctrine was developed in the context of breaches of duty by trustees and also operates in relation to directors: *Barnes v Addy* (1874) LR 9 Ch App 244 and *Consul Development Pty Ltd v DPC Estates Pty Ltd* (1975) 132 CLR 373.

The meaning of "knowledge" for the purpose of the law of constructive trusts is very broad and includes constructive knowledge such as where the third party failed to make reasonable inquiries where the circumstances required inquiries to be made.

civil penalties

what are civil penalty provisions?

[13.6.35] The civil penalty provisions in Pt 9.4B implement recommendations of the Senate Standing Committee on Legal and Constitutional Affairs report, *Social and Fiduciary Duties and Obligations of Company Directors* (1989) (the Cooney Committee). The Committee took the view that it was inappropriate to treat all contraventions of the *Corporations Act* as criminal offences because it was too difficult to successfully bring prosecutions for contraventions while having to prove the case on the criminal burden of proof beyond reasonable doubt. It recommended that civil penalties should be imposed for breaches of the *Corporations Act* to sanction misconduct that falls short of a criminal offence. Criminal sanctions should be applied only in cases genuinely criminal in nature where dishonesty was an element of the contravention.

Part 9.4B provides for three types of civil penalties to punish people who contravene designated civil penalty provisions.

Part 9.4B provides for three types of civil penalties to punish people who contravene designated civil penalty provisions:

> **a pecuniary penalty of up to $200,000 (s 1317G);**
> **disqualification from management (s 206C); and**
> **compensation for damage suffered: s 1317H.**

Section 1317E(1) lists the civil penalty provisions.

table 13.6.1 civil penalty provisions

Section	Topic	Discussed in
180(1), 181(1) and (2), 182(1) and (2), 183(1) and (2)	Officers' duties	Chapter 13.2–13.4
209(2)	Related parties rules	Chapter 13.3
254L(2), 256D(3), 259F(2) and 260D(2)	Share capital transactions	Chapter 8
344(1)	Requirements for financial reports	Chapter 15
588G(2)	Insolvent trading	Chapter 13.5
601FC(1), 601FD(3), 601FE(3), 601FG(2), 601JD(3)	Managed investment schemes	Chapter 20
674(2) or 675(2)	Continuous disclosure	Chapter 15
1041A	Market manipulation	Chapter 19
1041B(1) and 1041C(1)	False trading and market rigging	Chapter 19
1041D	Dissemination of information about illegal transactions	Chapter 19
1043A(1) and (2)	Insider trading	Chapter 19

case note

In *ASIC v Vizard* [2005] FCA 1037, the facts of which are set out in Chapter 13.3 above, Finklestein J made the following observations for determining the punishment which should be imposed under the civil penalty provisions:

- **the main consideration is the nature of the offence rather than the character of the defendant and the likelihood of further offences in the future;**
- **it is irrelevant whether or not a profit was made;**
- **the aim of the orders is to act as a general deterrence to improper commercial conduct;**
- **shaming is not a substitute for formal punishment imposed by the courts; and**
- **early acknowledgement of wrongdoing and co-operation with regulatory authorities entitles the defendant to a reduction of penalties.**

The civil penalty provisions are grouped into two broad categories, corporations/scheme civil penalty provisions and financial services civil penalty provisions. Sections 1041A, 1041B(1), 1041C(1), 1041D, 1043A(1) and (2) are classified as financial services civil penalty provisions: s 1317DA. The other civil penalty provisions listed in s 1317E(1) are corporations/scheme civil penalty provisions.

The pecuniary penalties for contravention of financial services civil penalty provisions are higher than those for contravention of the corporations/scheme civil penalty provisions.

The reason for these two classifications is because the pecuniary penalties for contravention of financial services civil penalty provisions are higher than those for contravention of the corporations/scheme civil penalty provisions. In addition, the compensation orders for contravention of financial services civil penalty provisions are slightly different from those that apply to contraventions of the corporations/scheme civil penalty provisions which are classified as corporations/scheme civil penalty provisions. Contravention of the financial services civil penalty provisions is discussed in Chapter 19 below.

As noted above, ss 180–183 are designated corporations/scheme civil penalty provisions. Directors and officers who contravene these provisions are liable to civil penalty orders. In addition, these all provide that any person who is involved in the contravention also contravenes the relevant section: ss 181(2), 182(2) and 183(2). Under s 79 a person is "involved" in a contravention if the person has:

> **aided, abetted, counselled or procured the contravention;**
> **induced the contravention;**
> **been in any way, by act or omission, knowingly concerned in or party to the contravention; or**
> **conspired with others to effect the contravention.**

For a person to be involved in a contravention they must have actual knowledge of the essential, material factual ingredients of the contravention. Knowledge may be inferred from the fact of exposure to the obvious where the person has wilfully remained ignorant and failed to make appropriate inquiry: *ASIC v Adler* [2002] NSWSC 171.

declaration of contravention

If a court is satisfied that a person contravened a designated civil penalty provision, it must make a declaration of contravention.

[13.6.40] If a court is satisfied that a person contravened a designated civil penalty provision, it must make a declaration of contravention under s 1317E(1). A declaration of contravention must specify the matters set out in s 1317E(2). These matters include identification of the conduct which constituted the contravention and the section contravened.

The rules of evidence and procedure for civil matters apply in relation to hearings for a declaration of contravention or pecuniary penalty order: s 1317L. This means that the burden of proof is the civil burden (on balance of probabilities) and not the criminal standard (beyond reasonable doubt): *ASIC v Plymin* [2003] VSC 123.

ASIC has the power to initiate civil penalty proceedings by applying to a court for a declaration of contravention, a pecuniary penalty order or a compensation order.

ASIC has the power to initiate civil penalty proceedings by applying to a court for a declaration of contravention, a pecuniary penalty order or a compensation order: s 1317J(1). If the court makes a declaration of contravention, ASIC can then seek a disqualification order under s 206C. A corporation also has the power to apply to the court for a compensation order: s 1317J(2). A corporation may also intervene in an application for a declaration of contravention or a pecuniary penalty order and is entitled to be heard on all matters other than whether the declaration or order should be made: s 1317J(3).

pecuniary penalty orders

The court may order a person to pay a pecuniary penalty.

[13.6.45] Under s 1317G(1), the court may order a person to pay a pecuniary penalty to the Commonwealth of up to $200,000 if the contravention of a corporations/scheme civil penalty provision is serious or materially prejudices the corporation's ability to pay its creditors. A pecuniary penalty is regarded as a civil debt payable to ASIC on the Commonwealth's behalf and may be enforced as if it were an order made in civil debt recovery proceedings: s 1317G(2).

The CLERP 9 amendments increased the maximum pecuniary penalty payable in relation to a contravention of a financial services civil penalty provision. The maximum for a body corporate was increased to $1 million: s 1317G(1B)(b). The maximum for an individual was unaltered and remains $200,000: s 1317G(1B)(a).

The purpose of a pecuniary penalty is to act as a personal and general deterrent against failure to comply with appropriate standards of commercial conduct in the management of corporations. The penalty should be no greater than is necessary to achieve this purpose and is at the discretion of the court. In exercising its discretion, the court will consider factors such as the amounts involved, whether efforts were made to repay misappropriated funds, whether actions involved dishonesty or negligence and carelessness, whether there were expressions of contrition or a likelihood of further contraventions and previous good character: *ASC v Donovan* (1998) 28 ACSR 583. In assessing a pecuniary penalty order, it is relevant to consider the consequences of an associated disqualification order. If these consequences are significant, a lesser penalty may be appropriate: *ASIC v Adler* [2002] NSWSC 171.

disqualification orders

[13.6.50] An important consequence of a declaration under s 1317E that a person has contravened a civil penalty provision is that ASIC may seek an order disqualifying that person from being a director or managing a corporation. The court may make such an order if it is satisfied that the disqualification is justified and for such period as the court considers appropriate: s 206C(1). The meaning of "managing a corporation" is discussed in Chapter 12 above.

ASIC may seek an order disqualifying a person from being a director or managing a corporation.

In determining whether disqualification is justified, s 206C(2) directs the court to have regard to the person's conduct in relation to the management, business or property of any corporation and any other matters considered appropriate. The policy behind the disqualification provisions was stated in *ASIC v Adler (No 5)* (2002) 20 ACLC 1146 as being for the purposes of protecting the public from harmful use of corporations and from use which is contrary to proper commercial standards. The public is protected from persons who are unsuitable to be directors. A disqualification order aims at personal and general deterrence but is not intended to inflict punishment.

There is no fixed duration of the disqualification under s 206C. Disqualification is for a period that the court considers appropriate. In *ASIC v Adler* [2002] NSWSC 171, Santow J considered the following factors in determining an appropriate period of disqualification. Longer periods of disqualification are appropriate for contraventions which are of a serious nature, such as where dishonesty is involved; the contraventions are recurring and large financial losses have occurred; and there is a likelihood of similar conduct in the future which is likely to be harmful to the public. A mitigating factor is where contrition is shown and there is a likelihood of the disqualified person reforming.

Part 2D.6 of the *Corporations Act* contains a number of other provisions under which a person may be disqualified. These are discussed above in Chapter 12.

compensation orders

[13.6.55] The court has the power to order a person who contravenes a corporations/scheme civil penalty provision to compensate a corporation for the damage that resulted from the contravention: s 1317H. The order must specify the amount of compensation. Applications for corporations/scheme compensation orders may be made by ASIC or the corporation: s 1317J. The CLERP 9 amendments made it clear that a company can apply to the court for a compensation order regardless of whether ASIC has obtained a declaration of contravention. The damage suffered by a corporation for purposes of a compensation order includes any profits made by any person resulting from the contravention: s 1317H(2).

The court has the power to order a person who contravenes a corporations/ scheme civil penalty provision to compensate a corporation for the damage that resulted from the contravention.

Where a compensation order is made against several defendants, the court has a discretion whether or not to make a compensation order against a particular defendant. However, the court should not differentiate between defendants in the apportionment of compensation as this is not authorised by the legislation and would not be in accord with the principles of joint and several liability applicable to multiple tortfeasors. Such issues should be determined in separate contribution proceedings involving the defendants: *ASIC v Adler* [2002] NSWSC 483.

A company can apply to the court for a compensation order regardless of whether ASIC has obtained a declaration of contravention.

Under s 1317S, a person may be relieved from liability for contravention of a civil penalty provision if the court is satisfied that the person acted honestly and ought fairly to be excused for the contravention. This power of the court operates in conjunction with a similar general power contained in s 1318. This provision is discussed in Chapter 13.7 below.

criminal penalties

relationship between civil penalties and criminal penalties

[13.6.60] Prior to 1999 amendments, the civil penalty provisions of Pt 9.4B also created criminal offences where a civil penalty provision was contravened dishonestly. The 1999 amendments relocated the criminal offences from Pt 9.4B and moved them to the relevant substantive provisions in the *Corporations Act*. Section 184 provides that if the civil penalty provisions contained in ss 181–183 are contravened, this may result in criminal offences if a director or officer was reckless or intentionally dishonest. Contravention of the statutory duty of care and diligence cannot give rise to criminal penalties.

If the civil penalty provisions contained in ss 181–183 are contravened, this may result in criminal offences if a director or officer was reckless or intentionally dishonest.

Criminal proceedings may be started against a person even though a civil penalty order has been made against that person: s 1317P. The rights of a defendant are protected to some extent by s 1317Q, which makes evidence previously given in civil proceedings inadmissible in a prosecution for a criminal offence involving substantially similar conduct.

A court hearing a criminal prosecution cannot make a pecuniary penalty order if the defendant is found not guilty: s 1317N. This makes it necessary for ASIC to begin fresh civil proceedings if it wishes to pursue civil remedies following an unsuccessful criminal prosecution.

Criminal proceedings may be started against a person even though a civil penalty order has been made against that person.

criminal offences

[13.6.65] There are numerous provisions in the *Corporations Act* that expressly state that contravention is a criminal offence. For example, under s 184(1) a director or officer commits a criminal offence if they are reckless or intentionally dishonest and fail to exercise their powers in good faith in the best interests of the corporation.

Section 1311(1) creates an offence even where a section of the *Corporations Act* does not expressly state that contravention is a criminal offence. Under s 1311(1) a person is guilty of an offence if they:

> **do something that the person is forbidden to do by a provision of the *Corporations Act*; or**
> **fail to do something that the person is required to do by a provision of the *Corporations Act*; or**
> **otherwise contravene a provision of the *Corporations Act*.**

Section 1311(1A) makes it clear that contraventions of certain provisions of the *Corporations Act* are not criminal offences unless the provision is included in the list of penalties set out in Sch 3 of the *Corporations Act*. For example, contraventions of the provisions of Chs 2A, 2B and 2C, which deal with registering a company, basic features of a company and company registers, are not offences unless included in the Sch 3 list.

application of the Criminal Code

[13.6.70] Chapter 2 of the *Criminal Code* sets out the general principles of criminal responsibility that apply to criminal offences under the *Corporations Act*. Section 3.1(1) of the *Criminal Code* specifies that an offence consists of physical elements (defined in ss 4.1–4.3) and fault elements (defined in ss 5.1–5.6). A physical element of an offence includes conduct or the result of conduct. A fault element for a particular physical element may be intention, knowledge, recklessness or negligence.

Section 3.1(2) of the *Criminal Code* recognises that a law that creates an offence may provide that there is no fault element for one or more physical elements. This is the case of the *Corporations Act* which contains numerous offences that are characterised as either offences of strict liability or absolute liability.

A "strict liability" offence is one that has no fault elements for any of the physical elements: s 6.1(1)(a). The defence of mistake of fact under s 9.2 is available for strict liability offences: s 6.1(1)(b). A mistake of fact defence arises if at the time of the conduct constituting the physical element, the accused person was under a mistaken but reasonable belief about those facts and had those facts existed, the conduct would not have constituted an offence.

An "absolute liability" offence is one that has no fault elements for any of the physical elements and the defence of mistake of fact is unavailable: s 6.2(1).

consequences of conviction

[13.6.75] A person who is guilty of an offence under the *Corporations Act* is punishable on conviction by a penalty not exceeding the penalty applicable to the offence: s 1311(2). If the section that creates the offence is included in the Sch 3 list then the maximum penalty is the penalty mentioned in that Schedule: s 1311(3). If a provision sets out its own penalty, then that is the maximum penalty on conviction: s 1311(4). Where a penalty is not otherwise provided, then the applicable penalty is 5 penalty units ($500): s 1311(5).

penalty notices

[13.6.80] Minor offences under the *Corporations Act* incur an "on the spot" fine under s 1313. ASIC is able to serve a penalty notice if it has reason to believe that a person has committed a prescribed offence. Payment of the penalty and remedying the contravention precludes further criminal proceedings. The prescribed penalty for offences under s 1311(5) is 5 penalty units ($500) for natural persons.

Minor offences under the *Corporations Act* incur an "on the spot" fine.

protection for whistleblowers

[13.6.85] The CLERP 9 amendments inserted a new Part into the *Corporations Act*—Pt 9.4AAA, ss 1317AA–1317AD. These provisions establish a framework designed to encourage officers, employees and others (commonly referred to as "whistleblowers") to report suspected breaches of the *Corporations Act* to ASIC, the company's auditor or other appropriate senior people within the company such as a director, secretary or senior manager.

Whistleblowers who disclose suspected breaches of the legislation by the company, its officers or employees in good faith are protected in a number of ways. For example, a whistleblower cannot be subjected to civil or criminal liability for making the disclosure: s 1317AB(1)(a). Whistleblowers are not, however, protected from liability for illegal conduct in which they have been involved. They have qualified privilege in relation to their disclosures and therefore have no liability for defamation: s 1317AB(2). Whistleblowers are also protected from being victimised because of their disclosures: s 1317AC.

Whistleblowers who disclose suspected breaches of the legislation by the company, its officers or employees in good faith are protected in a number of ways.

pathways questions . . .

The following questions dealing with liability of directors may best be answered by reading this sub-chapter and considering the Internet resources found on the Lipton-Herzberg Duties of Directors of Insolvent Companies Pathway at **http://www.lipton-herzberg.com.au/secure/pathways_dd_remedies.htm**

1. What are the purposes of the civil penalty provisions and how effective have these provisions been?

2. What is a constructive trust and how may this be used as a remedy where directors have breached their duties?

bibliography . . .

Andrews, N "If the Dog Catches the Mice: the Civil Settlement of Criminal Conduct Under the Corporations Act and the Australian Securities and Investments Commission" (2003) 15 Aust Jnl of Corp Law 137.

Bagaric, M & duPlessis, J "Expanding Criminal Sanctions for Corporate Crimes—Deprivation of Right to Work and Cancellation of Educational Qualifications" (2003) 21 C & SLJ 7.

Bird, H "The Problematic Nature of Civil Penalties in the Corporations Law" (1996) 14 C & SLJ 405.

Broderick, M "Equitable compensation—its place in the remedial sphere" (2005) 33 ABLR 369.

Gething, M "Do We Really Need Criminal and Civil Penalties for Contraventions of Directors' Duties?" (1996) 24 ABLR 375.

Gilligan, G, Bird, H and Ramsay, I "Civil Penalties and the Enforcement of Directors' Duties" (1999) 22 UNSWLJ 417.

Griggs, L "Equitable Compensation, Common Law Damages and the Director's Duty in Tort" (1997) 10 Corp & Bus LJ 207.

Lodge, M "Barnes v Addy: The Requirement of Knowledge" (1995) 23 ABLR 25.

Middleton, T "The Difficulties of Applying Civil Evidence and Procedure Rules in ASIC's Civil Penalty Proceedings under the Corporations Act" (2003) 21 C & SLJ 507.

Moodie, G & Ramsay, I "The Expansion of Civil Penalties Under the *Corporations Act*" (2002) 30 ABLR 61.

Ong, D "Breach of Fiduciary Duty: The Alternative Remedies" (1999) 11 Bond LR 336.

Pascoe, J "Remedial Constructive Trusts and Corporate Insolvency: An Australian Perspective" (2002) 8 *Current Commercial Law eZine* **http://www.lawbookco.com.au/academic/ccl-ezine/pdf/vol8issue1_RemedialTrusts.pdf**

Pascoe, J "Equitable Remedies in Cases of Misapplied Company Funds: Recent Developments" (1996) 14 C & SLJ 393.

Streets, S "Prosecuting Directors and Managers in Australia: A Brave New Response to an Old Problem?" (1998) 22 MULR 693.

Tomasic, R "Sanctioning Corporate Crime and Misconduct: Beyond Draconian and Decriminalisation Solutions" (1992) 2 Aust Jnl of Corp Law 82.

Welsh, M "The Corporations Law Civil Penalty Provisions and the Lessons that can be Learnt from the Trade Practices Act 1974" (2000) 11 Aust Jnl of Corp Law 298.

Welsh, M "Corporate Law Enforcement: Are Civil Penalty Provisions Acceptable?" (2002) 8 *Current Commercial Law eZine* **http://www.lawbookco.com.au/academic/ccl-ezine/pdf/vol8issue1_CorporateEnforcement.pdf**

Welsh, M "The Civil Penalty Provisions and the CLERP Bill 1998" (1999) 6 CCL 89.
Welsh, M "Eleven years on—An examination of ASIC's use of an expanding civil penalty regime" (2004) 17 Aust Jnl of Corp Law 175.
Whincop, M "An Economic Analysis of Criminalisation and Content of Directors' Duties" (1996) 24 ABLR 273.

revision questions on the material in this chapter ...

> Please see eQuiz at **http://www.thomson.com.au/academic** for multiple choice questions and answers.
> For further corporations law links and material please refer to the Lipton-Herzberg website at **http://www.lipton-herzberg.com.au**

chapter thirteen.seven

exoneration and relief for breach of duty

key points ...

> The general meeting has broad power to excuse directors who act in breach of duty.

> There are restrictions on a company in its constitution exempting a director from liability or providing an indemnity against liability arising from breach of duty.

> The court may order that a person be relieved from liability in any proceedings involving breach of duty where the person acted honestly.

exoneration by the company

general power of ratification of shareholders

Directors who breach their fiduciary duties to a solvent company may be excused from liability if shareholders pass an ordinary resolution to ratify their actions.

[13.7.05] Directors who breach their fiduciary duties to a solvent company may be excused from liability if shareholders pass an ordinary resolution to ratify their actions. Ratification may be either prospective or retrospective. The directors must also fully disclose all relevant circumstances to the shareholders and have acted in good faith. If the directors are also shareholders, they are permitted to vote as shareholders in favour of ratifying their own breach of duty.

However, ratification may be ineffective if it amounts to oppressive or unfair conduct for purposes of a remedy under s 232: *Hannes v MJH Pty Ltd* (1992) 10 ACLC 400. This will be the case if the directors who breach their duty control the majority of votes at the general meeting and vote in favour of their own ratification. Further, as discussed in Chapter 17 below, Pt 2F.1A of the *Corporations Act* now gives members, with prior court leave, the right to bring legal proceedings against directors in the name of the company. According to s 239(1), merely because conduct has been ratified or approved by a general meeting does not mean that a person cannot bring the legal proceedings or apply for court leave to do so under Pt 2F.1A. Under s 239(2), however, the court may take the ratification or approval into account in deciding what order or judgment to make.

It is unclear whether shareholders are able to ratify a breach of directors' statutory duties under Ch 2D of the *Corporations Act*. However, in *Pascoe Ltd v Lucas* (1998) 16 ACLC 1247, the court noted:

> **< There is a nice question whether shareholders can relieve a director from a breach of his statutory duties. But as the statutory duties reflect the duties of a director at common law and in equity, I do not think that there is any impediment to the shareholder excusing a breach of a statutory duty. If it were necessary to do so, I would invoke [s 1318] only for the purpose of enabling [the director] to have the benefit of the approval of [the shareholder] to the acts he performed at [the shareholder's] behest. >**

Shareholders are unable to ratify breaches of duty where directors fail to take into account the interests of creditors.

no ratification where company insolvent

[13.7.10] In *Kinsela v Russell Kinsela Pty Ltd* (1986) 4 NSWLR 722, the shareholders purported to excuse directors from a breach of duty. This was held to be invalid because the company was insolvent or near insolvency at the time. Shareholders are unable to ratify breaches of duty where directors fail to take into account the interests of creditors. Street CJ stated:

> **It is, to my mind, legally and logically acceptable to recognise that, where directors are involved in a breach of their duty to the company affecting the interests of shareholders, then shareholders can either authorise that breach in prospect or ratify it in retrospect. Where, however, the interests at risk are those of creditors I see no reason in law or in logic to recognise that the shareholders can authorise the breach. Once it is accepted, as in my view it must be, that the directors' duty to a company as a whole extends in an insolvency context to not prejudicing the interests of creditors the shareholders do not have the power or authority to absolve the directors from that breach.**

ratification by board

[13.7.15] In *Queensland Mines Ltd v Hudson* (1978) 52 ALJR 399, the Privy Council held that in the circumstances of that case, disclosure to the board of directors and its assent was sufficient to enable a director to retain his profits. It is unclear whether the board has a power to ratify a breach of duty by one of its number or whether the board relinquished the rights of the company to exploit a particular opportunity.

exemption from liability and indemnification

by the company

[13.7.20] At common law it was possible for a company to provide in its constitution that directors were exempt from liability for loss caused by negligent but honest acts or omissions. This is no longer the case. A company or related body corporate must not exempt an officer or auditor, directly or through an interposed entity, from liability to the company: s 199A(1). Similarly, a company or related body corporate must not indemnify an officer or auditor against a liability owed to the company, under a civil penalty order or owed to someone else and which did not arise out of conduct in good faith: s 199A(2).

A company or related body corporate must not exempt an officer or auditor, directly or through an interposed entity, from liability to the company.

Indemnity of legal costs incurred in defending an action for a liability incurred as an officer or auditor is generally permitted unless:

- **the person is found in the proceedings to have a liability for which the company is prohibited from indemnifying that person under s 199A(2);**
- **the person is found guilty in criminal proceedings;**
- **the court grants an order in proceedings brought by ASIC or a liquidator; or**
- **the court denies relief in proceedings where this is sought by the officer or auditor.**

Legal costs incurred in relation to actions taken by ASIC or a liquidator as part of an investigation before commencing proceedings for a court order may be indemnified even if ASIC or the liquidator are later successful in court proceedings: s 199A(3).

A company is able to give an officer a loan in respect of legal costs. Depending on the outcome of the legal proceedings, the officer may pay back the loan if an indemnity is not allowed or may retain the loan money as the indemnity to which the officer is entitled: s 212. This addresses a concern that arose under the previous legislation, which did not allow an officer to receive an indemnity for legal costs until after the outcome of the court proceedings was known. This could impose a substantial burden where the court proceedings are lengthy and complex.

Amendments in 1999 inserted Pt 2D.2 which rewrote the law dealing with restrictions on a company exempting, indemnifying or paying premiums for insurance in relation to liability of officers or auditors.

by the court

Officers may be relieved from liability if in any civil proceedings against them for negligence, default, breach of trust or breach of duty, it appears to the court that they acted honestly and ought fairly to be excused.

[13.7.25] Officers of a corporation and certain other persons specified in s 1318(4) may be relieved from liability if in any civil proceedings against them for negligence, default, breach of trust or breach of duty, it appears to the court that they acted honestly and ought fairly to be excused either wholly or partly: s 1318(1). Where the court grants relief to an officer, or auditor, he or she may be indemnified under the constitution for legal costs in relation to the proceedings: s 199A(3). The court also has power to grant partial relief.

There is a similar corresponding power of the court to grant relief from liability under s 1317S where a civil penalty provision is contravened. This power does not include proceedings for an offence except so far as the proceedings relate to the question whether the court should make an order for compensation under ss 588K or 1317H. In determining whether a person ought fairly to be excused under s 1317S for a contravention of s 588G (insolvent trading), the court should consider any action the person took with a view to appointing an administrator of the company, when that action was taken and the results of that action: s 1317S(3). Section 1317S does not limit, nor is limited by, s 1318: s 1317S(7).

In *Daniels v Anderson* (1995) 13 ACLC 614, the court stated that:

> **< the purpose of the section is to excuse company officers from liability in situations where it would be unjust and oppressive not to do so, recognising that such officers are businessmen and women who act in an environment involving risk in commercial decision making. >**

Generally, the court before which proceedings to enforce the liability have been taken has the power to grant relief. Provision is also made for an application for relief where it is anticipated that an action may be brought for negligence, default, breach of trust or breach of duty (s 1318(2)) or contravention of a civil penalty provision: s 1317S(4).

In *ASIC v Adler (No 5)* [2002] NSWSC 483, Santow J considered that just because a court was not prepared to make a finding that a person was dishonest, does not mean that it is satisfied that the person has acted honestly for the purposes of granting relief from liability under ss 1317S and 1318.

case note

In *Advance Bank Australia Ltd v FAI Insurances Ltd* (1987) 5 ACLC 725, the directors of Advance Bank spent company funds in an election campaign for the company's directors. Their primary purpose was to secure the re-election of retiring directors and defeat candidates proposed by a large shareholder. Although they acted honestly and bona fide in what they considered the best interests of the company, they failed to exercise their powers for a proper purpose. The New South Wales Court of Appeal refused to grant the Advance Bank directors relief under a predecessor of s 1318. The court held that the section requires the directors to act honestly with reference to all the circumstances of the case. Notwithstanding that they acted honestly, the way in which the default or breach occurred was not one in which the directors were entitled to relief. The information sent to shareholders contained misleading and prejudicial information so that the bank ought not to bear the costs improperly incurred by the directors.

case note

The effect of a predecessor of s 1318 was considered in *Commonwealth Bank of Australia v Friedrich* (1991) 9 ACLC 946. In that case Eise, the chairman of the National Safety Council, applied for relief from a $97 million liability to the bank under the insolvent trading provisions. The Victorian Supreme Court did not grant relief in the circumstances of the case. Tadgell J considered that Eise's conduct in signing the company's directors' statement and directors' report in 1988 falsely represented that the directors had considered the company's 1987 accounts. This involved "some moral turpitude" and was a clear and flagrant breach of both the letter and intent of the legislation.

directors' and officers' insurance

[13.7.30] A company is prohibited from paying premiums insuring directors and officers against liability arising out of conduct involving a wilful breach of duty in relation to the company or improper use of their position or information under ss 182 and 183. This restriction applies irrespective whether the premiums were paid directly or through an interposed entity: s 199B.

A company is prohibited from paying premiums insuring directors and officers against liability arising out of conduct involving a wilful breach of duty.

The restrictions set out in ss 199A and 199B do not authorise anything that would otherwise be unlawful: s 199C(1). Where an indemnity or payment of an insurance premium contravenes ss 199A or 199B, it is void to the extent of the contravention: s 199C(2).

bibliography ...

Ansell, S "Directors' and Officers' Liability Insurance—Recent Reforms and Developments in Australia and New Zealand" (1995) 23 ABLR 164.

Fridman, S "Ratification of Directors' Breaches" (1992) 10 C & SLJ 252.

Kyrou, E "Directors' Duties, Defences, Indemnities, Access to Board Papers and D&O Insurance Post CLERPA" (2000) 18 C & SLJ 555.

Yeung, K "Disentangling the Tangled Skein: The Ratification of Directors' Actions" (1992) 66 ALJ 343.

revision questions on the material in this chapter ...

- Please see eQuiz at **http://www.thomson.com.au/academic** for multiple choice questions and answers.
- For further corporations law links and material please refer to the Lipton-Herzberg website at **http://www.lipton-herzberg.com.au**

chapter fourteen

shareholders' meetings

key points ...

- Shareholders make decisions by passing resolutions at meetings. The calling and conduct of shareholders' meetings is governed by the *Corporations Act* as well as a company's constitution (if any) and applicable replaceable rules. The ASX Listing Rules impose additional requirements for shareholders' meetings of listed companies.
- Public companies must hold an AGM at least once in every calendar year and within five months after the end of their financial year. A proprietary company need only hold an AGM if this is required by its constitution.
- An AGM enables shareholders to obtain information and gives them the opportunity to ask questions and make comments regarding management of the company. To facilitate this, a public company's financial report, directors' report and auditor's report must be laid before its AGM. The usual business of an AGM is to enable shareholders to consider these reports, elect directors and appoint the auditor and fix the auditor's remuneration.
- While only public companies are required to hold an AGM, all companies may hold other general meetings of shareholders. Such meetings are often referred to as "extraordinary general meetings".
- A company's constitution (if any) and applicable replaceable rules specify who has the power to call a general meeting. In most cases, this power is given to the board of directors. The *Corporations Act* gives a single director of a listed Australian company the right to call a general meeting. The *Corporations Act* also allows a general meeting to be called at the request of shareholders.
- Shareholders must be given at least 21 days' notice of a meeting (28 days in the case of a listed Australian company). The notice must include the general nature of the meeting's business and details of proposed special resolutions. Shareholders also have a right to give the company notice of a resolution they propose to move at a general meeting.
- Shareholders' meetings must be held at a reasonable time and place. The company may hold a meeting at more than one venue by using any technology that gives shareholders a reasonable opportunity to participate.
- Voting on resolutions is carried out by a show of hands or by a poll. Unless the company's constitution says otherwise, each shareholder has one vote on a show of hands and one vote per share on a poll. Shareholders may personally attend and vote at a meeting or appoint a proxy to attend and vote on their behalf.
- There are two types of resolutions that can be passed at a shareholders' meeting: ordinary resolutions and special resolutions. An ordinary resolution is passed by a simple majority vote of the shareholders voting in person or by proxy. The *Corporations Act* requires certain types of decisions, such as changing the constitution, to be passed by a special resolution. This is passed by at least 75 per cent of the votes cast by shareholders entitled to vote on the resolution.

Shareholders make decisions by passing resolutions at general meetings.

[14.05] The division of powers within a company was discussed in Chapter 12 above. The two organs of a company are the board of directors and the general meeting of shareholders. Shareholders make decisions by passing resolutions at general meetings. The calling and conduct of meetings is part of the internal regulation of companies and is governed by the replaceable rules and the company's constitution. In addition, the *Corporations Act* sets out additional requirements that must be followed.

The *Corporations Act*, replaceable rules and sometimes the company's constitution expect that shareholders will participate in the affairs of a company and confer various rights on the general meeting. However, as discussed in Chapter 12 above, the board of directors usually has very wide powers of management. In addition, the board is usually able to control the calling of meetings, the matters discussed and to some extent the voting at meetings. The provisions of the *Corporations Act* regarding meetings are primarily aimed at ensuring that the will of the shareholders is reflected in the running of the company and that they have certain opportunities to acquire information regarding the affairs of the company. A meeting of a company's shareholders must be held for a proper purpose: s 249Q. A meeting of shareholders must be held at a reasonable time and place: s 249R.

ASX Listing Rules also impose requirements for the holding of general meetings in certain situations. Shareholders of listed companies must approve large share placements and major asset acquisitions and sales.

In its June 2000 publication, *Shareholder Participation in the Modern Listed Public Company: Final Report*, CASAC (renamed CAMAC in March 2002) made a number of recommendations regarding the calling and conduct of shareholder meetings of listed public companies. The report is linked to the Lipton-Herzberg Meetings Pathway at **http://www.lipton-herzberg.com.au/secure/pathways-chapter-14-meetings.html**

types of meetings

annual general meetings

requirement to hold AGM

[14.10] A public company must hold its first annual general meeting (AGM) within 18 months after its registration: s 250N(1). Thereafter, an AGM must be held at least once in every calendar year and within five months after the end of a company's financial year: s 250N(2). Default in holding an AGM is an offence of strict liability: s 250N(2A).

A public company AGM must be held at least once in every calendar year and within five months after the end of a company's financial year.

The requirement to hold an AGM in each year must be met even if other meetings are held in that year: s 250N(3). A public company that has only one shareholder is not required to hold an AGM: s 250N(4). Proprietary companies are not obliged to hold an AGM unless this is required by their constitution.

Proprietary companies are not obliged to hold an AGM unless this is required by their constitution.

A company may apply to ASIC for an extension of the period within which an AGM must be held: s 250P(1). The application must be made before the expiration of time during which the AGM was required to be held: s 250P(2). ASIC may extend the time for holding the AGM for a specified period and may impose conditions: s 250P(2) and (4). An extension will only be granted if, on balance, there is good cause to postpone an important right of shareholders to expect that an AGM will be held within the required times: *Exicom Ltd v Futuris Corp Ltd* (1996) 14 ACLC 39.

The court may also order that a general meeting be called if it is otherwise impracticable to call the meeting in any other way on the application of any director or shareholder entitled to vote: s 249G. The court may exercise its discretion by making any further orders it deems expedient: s 1319. These may include an order that one shareholder constitutes the quorum at the AGM and a minority shareholder will not be removed as a director: *Limnios v Tambu Pty Ltd* (1995) 13 ACLC 278.

business of AGM

[14.15] The AGM is usually the only meeting of shareholders held by a public company. It gives shareholders the opportunity to obtain information about the company's past performance and future plans. An AGM also enables shareholders to question the directors regarding the affairs of the company and question the auditor about the content of the auditor's report or the conduct of the audit.

The AGM gives shareholders the opportunity to obtain information about the company's past performance and future plans.

Section 250R(1) provides that the business of an AGM may include any of the following matters even if these items are not referred to in the notice of meeting:

> **consideration of the annual financial report, directors' report and auditor's report;**
> **election of directors; and**
> **appointment of the auditor and fixing of the auditor's remuneration.**

The directors' report of a listed company must contain a remuneration report. A non-binding shareholders' resolution on the remuneration report must be put to a vote at a listed company's AGM.

As a result of the CLERP 9 amendments, the directors' report of a listed company must contain a remuneration report that sets out prescribed information about the remuneration paid to the directors and top five executives. A non-binding shareholders' resolution on the remuneration report must be put to a vote at a listed company's AGM: s 250R(2) and (3). The notice of meeting must inform shareholders that this resolution will be put at the AGM: s 249L(2). The remuneration report is discussed further in Chapter 12 above.

According to s 317 the directors of a public company that is required to hold an AGM must lay the following reports before the AGM:

> **the financial report;**
> **the directors' report; and**
> **the auditor's report for the last financial year.**

The contents of these reports are described in Chapter 15 below.

The chair of an AGM must allow a reasonable opportunity for the shareholders as a whole at the meeting to ask questions or make comments regarding the management of the company.

The chair of an AGM must allow a reasonable opportunity for the shareholders as a whole at the meeting to ask questions or make comments regarding the management of the company: s 250S. At a listed company's AGM, the chair must also allow a reasonable opportunity for shareholders to ask questions about or make comments on the remuneration report: s 250SA.

Section 250T also gives shareholders a reasonable opportunity to direct questions to the auditor on matters relevant to the audit and auditor's report. The CLERP 9 amendments provide an additional mechanism for questioning a listed company's auditor. Under s 250PA, shareholders of a listed company (even if they do not attend the AGM) are able to submit written questions to the auditor about the content of the auditor's report or the conduct of the audit. These questions must be given to the listed company no later than five business days before the AGM. The company is required to forward all the questions it has received to the auditor who must prepare a list of questions submitted that the auditor considers are relevant to the content of the auditor's report or the conduct of the audit. The company must make this list available to shareholders who attend the AGM. Making the list available at the AGM highlights to shareholders possible areas of concern and may prompt them to ask further questions at the AGM. Under s 250T(1)(b), the chair of the AGM must allow a reasonable opportunity for the auditor or their representative to answer the written questions submitted under s 250PA.

An AGM may also deal with any other business allowed by the *Corporations Act* and the company's constitution.

Usually, directors set the agenda for a company's AGM and other general meetings. However, under s 249N, shareholders are given the right to require a company to put resolutions to be considered at a general meeting. This is discussed below, para [14.135].

extraordinary general meetings

[14.20] While the *Corporations Act* requires only public companies to hold an AGM, all companies may hold other general meetings. A general meeting other than an AGM is often referred to as an "extraordinary general meeting".

Chapter 3 of the December 1999 ASIC discussion paper, *The Online Corporation: Electronic Corporate Communications* by Dr Elizabeth Boros, examined the potential for electronic communications in calling meetings. The discussion paper is linked to the Lipton-Herzberg Meetings Pathway at **http://www.lipton-herzberg.com.au/secure/pathways-chapter-14-meetings.html**

class meetings

[14.25] Where a company issues different classes of shares, provision is made under the *Corporations Act* for the calling of meetings of classes of shareholders in certain circumstances. As discussed in Chapter 8 above, the rights attaching to a class of shares may only be varied with the consent of the holders of three-quarters of the issued shares of that class. Usually, class meetings are held separately from general meetings of all shareholders: *Re Australian Consolidated Press Ltd* (1994) 12 ACLC 879. Meetings of classes of shareholders may be called to initiate and approve a scheme of arrangement under s 411. A scheme may involve a reorganisation of share capital that affects the rights of holders of classes of shares in different ways. Schemes of arrangement are discussed in Chapter 22 below.

adjourned meetings

[14.30] Directors generally have the power to adjourn general meetings but not postpone them: *Smith v Paringa Mines Ltd* [1906] 2 Ch 193.

Notice need not generally be given of adjourned meetings unless required by the company's constitution. Section 249M, however, requires new notice to be given where a meeting is adjourned for more than one month. Further, unless permitted by the constitution, once a notice of meeting has been sent specifying a particular time and place for the meeting, the meeting cannot be cancelled and another called in its place: *Bell Resources Ltd v Turnbridge Pty Ltd* (1988) 6 ACLC 970. The correct procedure in such cases is to convene the meeting on the date specified in the notice and then adjourn it.

A resolution passed at a meeting resumed after an adjournment is passed on the day it is passed and is not taken to have been passed on the date of the adjourned meeting: s 249W(1). A replaceable rule set out in s 249W(2) provides that only unfinished business is to be transacted at a meeting resumed after an adjournment.

calling meetings

by directors

[14.35] The replaceable rules permit any director to call a meeting of the company's shareholders: s 249C. Company constitutions usually give this power to the board of directors. An individual director of a listed Australian company has the right to call a shareholders' meeting despite anything in the company's constitution: s 249CA.

The Parliamentary Joint Committee on Corporations and Financial Services (PJC) "Report in Relation to Matters Arising from the Company Law Review Act 1998" recommended that s 249CA be repealed because it could be inappropriately used as leverage in board discussions and have the effect of dissuading directors from exercising their commercial judgment. It was also considered that a single director whose views were not acceptable at board discussions was unlikely to fare any better at a shareholders' meeting. This recommendation has not been adopted.

The Report of the PJC is linked to the Lipton-Herzberg Corporate Law Website at **http://www.lipton-herzberg.com.au/law_reform.htm#par**

at shareholders' request

The directors of a company must call and arrange to hold a general meeting on the request of shareholders holding at least 5 per cent of the voting shares or of at least 100 shareholders who are entitled to vote at the general meeting.

[14.40] The directors of a company must call and arrange to hold a general meeting on the request of shareholders holding at least 5 per cent of the voting shares or of at least 100 shareholders who are entitled to vote at the general meeting: s 249D(1). The regulations may prescribe a different number:

s 249D(1A). The request must state any resolution to be proposed at the meeting and must be signed by the shareholders making the request: s 249D(2).

The directors must call the meeting within 21 days after the request is given to the company and the meeting must be held not later than two months after the request: s 249D(5). If the directors fail to call a meeting within 21 days after the request is given to the company, shareholders holding more than 50 per cent of the votes of all shareholders who made the request may call and arrange to hold a general meeting: s 249E(1). The meeting must be held within three months after the request is given to the company: s 249E(2).

The company must assist shareholders to call the meeting by providing a copy of the register of shareholders to the shareholders requesting the meeting: s 249E(3). The company must pay reasonable expenses incurred by the shareholders in calling and arranging the meeting: s 249E(4). The amount of these expenses may be recovered by the company from the directors. A director is not liable where it can be shown that reasonable steps were taken to comply with s 249D: s 249E(5).

As noted above, s 249D gives a minimum of 100 voting shareholders the right to requisition the calling of an extraordinary general meeting even though they may hold only a tiny proportion of the votes and have no prospect of their resolutions being passed. The company must bear the cost of arranging the meeting and in large listed companies with many thousands of shareholders these expenses are significant.

Chapter 2 of CASAC's publication, "*Shareholder Participation in the Modern Listed Public Company: Final Report*", discusses the appropriate prerequisites for permitting shareholders to requisition an extraordinary general meeting. CASAC recommended that in the case of a listed company, the current 100-shareholder threshold for requisitioning meetings should be abolished and that the *Corporations Act* should provide that only shareholders who, collectively, have at least 5 per cent of the votes should have that right. This report is linked to the Lipton-Herzberg Meetings Pathway at **http://www.lipton-herzberg.com.au/secure/pathways-chapter-14-meetings.html**

In February 2005, the government released for public comment an exposure draft of the *Corporations Amendment Bill (No 2)* 2005. Amongst other things, the Bill proposes to amend s 249D to remove the ability of 100 members to requisition a general meeting at the expense of the company (the "100 member rule"). The Bill will retain the "5 per cent rule" in s 249D(1) which enables shareholders with at least 5 per cent of the votes to request the calling of a general meeting. The Explanatory Memorandum to the Bill criticised the "100 member rule":

> **< ... for giving disproportionate influence to minority shareholders, failing to recognise the substantial size differences between companies and for being out of step with comparative laws in other countries. >**

A meeting of shareholders must be held for a proper purpose.

A meeting of shareholders must be held for a proper purpose: s 249Q. If the purpose of the request to hold a meeting is to consider and if thought fit, to pass a resolution, this is a proper purpose and it is not relevant that the shareholder requesting the meeting is motivated by ill-will or self-interest: *NRMA v Scandrett* [2002] NSWSC 1123. Directors may validly refuse to call a general meeting requested by shareholders if the purpose of calling the meeting is to harass the company and its directors: *Humes Ltd v Unity APA Ltd* (1987) 5 ACLC 15. However, in the *Humes* case, the court held that a meeting is not called for an improper purpose just because a proposed resolution is likely to be defeated causing inconvenience and expense to the company, its directors and majority shareholders.

Directors may validly refuse to call a meeting requested by shareholders if its sole purpose is to pass a resolution that interferes with the directors' exclusive power to manage the company's business.

Directors may also validly refuse to call a meeting requested by shareholders if its sole purpose is to pass a resolution that interferes with the directors' exclusive power to manage the company's business.

case note

In *NRMA v Parker* (1986) 4 ACLC 609, a member requested the calling of a general meeting. The proposed resolution purported to direct the board over a matter that NRMA's constitution exclusively vested in the directors. As this resolution could not effectively be passed by the members and this was the sole object of the meeting, it was held that the directors were entitled to refuse to act on the request.

by shareholders

[14.45] Shareholders with at least 5 per cent of voting shares may also call a general meeting without first requesting the directors to call the meeting: s 249F. This right is rarely invoked in practice because the shareholders calling the meeting must pay the incurred expenses.

Shareholders with at least 5 per cent of voting shares may also call a general meeting without first requesting the directors to call the meeting.

Once a shareholder exercises the right to call a general meeting under s 249F, the procedural rules set out in the *Corporations Act* and the company's constitution apply. The directors may postpone the meeting in accordance with the company's constitution where they act in good faith: *Pinnacle VRB Ltd v Ronay Investments Pty Ltd* (2000) 18 ACLC 733.

by court order

[14.50] The court has power to order that a meeting be called if it is impracticable to call a meeting in any other way. The application may be made by any director or shareholder entitled to vote: s 249G.

The court has power to order that a meeting be called if it is impracticable to call a meeting in any other way.

case note

The power of the court to order that a meeting of the company be called is illustrated in *Re Totex-Adon Pty Ltd and the Companies Act* [1980] 1 NSWLR 605. In this case, it was held to be "impracticable" to call a meeting because one of the two shareholders entitled to vote at meetings refused to co-operate in calling a meeting. It was ordered that a meeting be called and that the presence of one shareholder holding voting shares would constitute a quorum despite a provision in the constitution that required a quorum of two shareholders.

The court will not normally exercise its discretion to call a meeting under s 249G where the procedure for calling a meeting in the ordinary course is set out in the replaceable rules and the company's constitution. Mere speculation as to what may occur at a meeting does not constitute impracticability: *Jenashare Pty Ltd v Lemrib Pty Ltd* (1993) 11 ACLC 768.

notice of meetings

[14.55] Shareholders must be given written notice of a forthcoming meeting. The purpose of the notice is to enable shareholders to know what business will be considered at the meeting so that they can decide whether or not to attend and how to vote. Where notice is given that particular business will be transacted at a meeting, no other business can be proceeded with unless all the shareholders are present and consent. A genuine amendment that comes within the scope of the business stated in the notice may be properly considered: *Efstathis v Greek Orthodox Community of St George* (1988) 6 ACLC 706.

Shareholders must be given written notice of a forthcoming meeting to enable shareholders to know what business will be considered at the meeting so that they can decide whether or not to attend and how to vote.

Failure to give notice is a procedural irregularity. Under s 1322, such irregularities are not invalidated unless a substantial injustice is caused. This is discussed below, para [14.145].

amount of notice

As a general rule, notice of at least 21 days must be given of a meeting of a company's shareholders. Listed Australian companies must give 28 days' notice of shareholders' meetings.

[14.60] As a general rule, notice of at least 21 days must be given of a meeting of a company's shareholders: s 249H. The constitution of a company may specify a longer minimum period of notice. Despite anything in the company's constitution, listed Australian companies must give 28 days' notice of shareholders' meetings: s 249HA.

The Parliamentary Joint Committee on Corporations and Financial Services (PJC) issued a report *Matters Arising from the Company Law Review Act 1998* which recommended that the notice period for both listed and unlisted companies should be 21 days. This recommendation has not been adopted. The Report of the PJC is linked to the Lipton-Herzberg Corporate Law Website at **http://www.lipton-herzberg.com.au/law_reform.htm#par**

Notice of the intention to move a resolution to remove a director or auditor under ss 203D and 329, respectively, must be given to the company at least two months before the meeting is to be held. However, if the company calls a meeting after the notice of intention is given, the resolution may be passed even though the meeting is held less than two months after the notice is given: ss 203D(2) and 329(1A).

who must receive notice?

Written notice of a meeting of shareholders must be given individually to each shareholder entitled to vote and to each director.

[14.65] Written notice of a meeting of shareholders must be given individually to each shareholder entitled to vote and to each director: s 249J(1). The replaceable rule in s 249J(2) provides that notice to joint shareholders must be given to the joint shareholder named first in the register of shareholders. An auditor is entitled to the same notice and any other related communications as a shareholder is entitled to receive: s 249K.

Notice may be given personally, by post, fax or email or any other means permitted by the company's constitution.

Notice may be given personally, by post, fax or email or any other means permitted by the company's constitution: s 249J(3). The replaceable rule in s 249J(4) provides that notice by post is taken to be given three days after posting. Notice by fax or email is taken to be given on the business day after it is sent. Shareholders have the option of nominating an electronic means of being notified that notices of meetings are available: s 249J(3A). This enables the company to distribute a notice of meeting by sending shareholders an email advising them that a notice of meeting is available for viewing or download from the company's website. Under the replaceable rule in s 249J(5), notice is taken to be given under this new facility on the business day after the notice is made available.

shorter notice

[14.70] A company may call a meeting on shorter notice than 21 days if it obtains shareholder approval for this. Section 249H(2) provides that if the meeting is an AGM, all shareholders entitled to attend and vote at the AGM must agree to the shorter notice beforehand, while in the case of other general meetings, the holders of at least 95 per cent of votes must agree beforehand.

Shorter notice is not allowed where the meeting is to consider a resolution to remove a director or appoint a replacement: s 249H(3). Similarly, shorter notice is not allowed where the meeting is to consider a resolution to remove an auditor: s 249H(4).

content of notice

[14.75] A notice of meeting of shareholders must include specified information under s 249L. This includes:

A notice of meeting of shareholders must include specified information under s 249L.

> **place, date and time of meeting and the technology used to facilitate a meeting that is to be held at two or more places;**
> **the general nature of the meeting's business;**
> **the intention to propose a stated special resolution, if any; and**
> **if a shareholder has a right to appoint a proxy, this must be stated as well as whether the proxy must be a shareholder. A shareholder must also be informed of the right to appoint two proxies and to specify the proportion of votes each proxy is appointed to exercise.**

Section 249L(3), inserted by the CLERP 9 amendments, provides that the information contained in the notice must be worded and presented in a clear, concise and effective manner. In the past, notices often contained large amounts of information which made it difficult for shareholders to determine the essential business of the meeting.

The information contained in the notice must be worded and presented in a clear, concise and effective manner.

misleading information

[14.80] Directors have an obligation to ensure that the content of notices of meetings and accompanying explanatory documents sent to shareholders are not misleading. They must present full and true disclosure of all relevant information. Where the information is misleading, the holding of the meeting may be restrained: *Chequepoint Securities Ltd v Claremont Petroleum NL* (1986) 4 ACLC 711. If the meeting is held, resolutions passed may be overturned.

Directors have an obligation to ensure that the content of notices of meetings and accompanying explanatory documents sent to shareholders are not misleading.

The courts do not take a legalistic approach in determining whether the information is misleading. They judge it from the perspective of an ordinary shareholder who scans the documents quickly: *Deveraux Holdings Pty Ltd v Pelsart Resources NL* (1986) 4 ACLC 12.

Sometimes, the need to make full and fair disclosure must be balanced against the need to avoid confusing the typical shareholders to whom it is directed.

case note

In *Fraser v NRMA Holdings Ltd* (1995) 13 ACLC 132, a complex proposal about which there were difficult questions of commercial judgment was put to a large number of shareholders, many of whom had little experience in dealing with shares or corporate reorganisations. The Full Federal Court considered that it was appropriate for the information provided to be selective and confined to matters that were realistically useful in the circumstances.

Where a notice of meeting is accompanied by information that is false or misleading in a material respect or has omitted information that makes it misleading, an officer who furnishes the information may be guilty of an offence under s 1309.

Where directors issue a statement or furnish information in circumstances where opposing or dissenting directors are not given an opportunity to express their views or comments, a heavy onus is cast on the directors to ensure that the information is fair: *Browne v Panga Pty Ltd* (1995) 13 ACLC 853.

While directors are not generally required to circulate the views of dissentient directors to shareholders, this may sometimes be an appropriate means of providing full information to shareholders to enable them to make a properly informed judgment: *Fraser v NRMA Holdings Ltd* (1994) 12 ACLC 855.

proceedings at meetings

use of technology

[14.85] Companies with large numbers of shareholders may be unable to accommodate all attending shareholders at a general meeting in the one venue. It may also be desirable to hold a general meeting where shareholders attend simultaneously at different places.

A company may hold a meeting of its shareholders at two or more venues using any technology that gives the shareholders as a whole a reasonable opportunity to participate.

A company may hold a meeting of its shareholders at two or more venues using any technology that gives the shareholders as a whole a reasonable opportunity to participate: s 249S. This contemplates the use of video-conferencing and electronic communication and requires that all those present be able to hear and be heard. If a shareholder does not have a reasonable opportunity to participate in a meeting of shareholders held in two or more venues, the meeting will only be invalid on that ground if the court declares the meeting, or part of it, invalid. Such a declaration will only be made if a substantial injustice has been caused and it cannot be otherwise remedied: s 1322(3A).

Chapter 3 of the December 1999 ASIC discussion paper, *The Online Corporation: Electronic Corporate Communications* by Dr Elizabeth Boros also examines the potential for use of electronic communications in holding meetings, particularly online meetings. The discussion paper is linked to the Lipton-Herzberg Meetings Pathway at **http://www.lipton-herzberg.com.au/secure/pathways-chapter-14-meetings.html**

quorum

A quorum is the minimum number of shareholders whose presence is necessary for a meeting to be able to validly transact business.

[14.90] A quorum is the minimum number of shareholders whose presence is necessary for a meeting to be able to validly transact business. The quorum for shareholders meetings is set out in the company's constitution (if any) or the replaceable rules.

Under the replaceable rules, the quorum for a meeting of a company's shareholders is two and the quorum must be present at all times during the meeting: s 249T(1). Resolutions of single shareholder companies may be passed by the shareholder recording it and signing the record: s 249B.

In determining whether a quorum is present, proxies and body corporate representatives are counted. However, if a shareholder has appointed more than one proxy or personal representative, only one of them is counted: s 249T(2).

If a quorum is not present within half an hour after the appointed time of the meeting, it is adjourned to the time and place determined by the directors. If the directors make no such determination, the meeting is adjourned for one week at the same time and place: s 249T(3). If there is no quorum at the resumed meeting, the meeting is dissolved: s 249T(4).

chairing meetings

The "chair" is the person in charge of the meeting, with responsibility for ensuring that the meeting is properly conducted.

[14.95] The "chair" is the person in charge of the meeting, with responsibility for ensuring that the meeting is properly conducted. Under the replaceable rules, the directors may elect an individual to chair shareholders' meetings: s 249U(1). The directors at a meeting must elect a person to chair the meeting if they have not previously done so prior to the meeting or the previously elected person is not available for the meeting: s 249U(2). If the directors do not elect a chair for the shareholders' meeting, or the chair is unavailable, this must be done by the shareholders: s 249U(3). The replaceable rule in s 250E gives the chair a casting vote as well as any vote they have in their capacity as a shareholder.

case note

In *Kelly v Wolstenholme* (1991) 9 ACLC 785, the Supreme Court of New South Wales held that a chairman is a person who has control of a meeting. A person cannot merely say at a meeting that "I am the chairman" without actually exercising procedural control over it. Procedural control over the meeting involves nominating who is to speak, dealing with the order of business, putting questions to the meeting, declaring resolutions carried or not carried, asking for any general business and declaring the meeting closed.

In *AWA Ltd v Daniels* (1992) 10 ACLC 933, Rodgers CJ made the following comments on the role of the chair of directors:

> < **The chairman is responsible to a greater extent than any other director for the performance of the board as a whole and each member of it. The chairman has the primary responsibility of selecting matters and documents to be brought to the board's attention, for formulating the policy of the board and promoting the position of the company. In discharging his or her responsibilities the chairman will co-operate with the managing director if the two positions are separate or otherwise with senior management.** >

The chair of the meeting or the next meeting is required to sign the minutes of the meeting: s 251A(2).

case note

In *Corpique (No 20) Pty Ltd v Eastcourt Ltd* (1989) 7 ACLC 794, the chair of the general meeting closed the meeting on legal advice that the proposed resolutions were not in compliance with the company's articles. The resolutions sought to remove two directors, including the chair, and appoint two directors in their place. After closing the meeting, the chair and some other shareholders left the meeting, which then purported to pass the resolutions. It was held that the chair was wrong in stating that he did not have the power to put the resolutions. However, he acted honestly and bona fide and was entitled to accept the legal advice given to him. In these circumstances it was not open to some of the shareholders to continue the meeting after other shareholders had left in reliance upon the decision of the chair.

Shareholders may continue a meeting against the ruling of a chair if a lack of bona fides on the chair's part can be shown. This may arguably be the case where a chair disregards a motion of dissent or a no confidence motion. A chair cannot stop a meeting just because proceedings have developed in a way that the chair opposes.

voting

[14.100] Voting at a general meeting may be decided by a show of hands or by a poll. Generally, on a show of hands each shareholder has one vote and on a poll, each shareholder has one vote for each share held: s 250E(1). Shareholders of a company that does not have a share capital have one vote per person both on a show of hands or a poll. This is subject to any rights or restrictions contained in the company's constitution, which may confer weighted voting rights or diminished voting rights on certain shareholders.

Voting at a general meeting may be decided by a show of hands or by a poll.

Under the replaceable rules, a resolution put at a general meeting must first be decided on a show of hands unless a poll is demanded: s 250J(1). A declaration by the chair is conclusive evidence of the result of voting on a show of hands: s 250J(2).

A poll may be demanded on any resolution; however, the company's constitution may provide that a poll cannot be demanded on any resolution concerning election of the meeting chair or adjournment of a meeting: s 250K. A poll may be demanded by at least five shareholders entitled to vote, shareholders with at least 5 per cent of votes, or the chair: s 250L(1). A proxy may join in a demand for a poll: s 249Y(1)(c).

A replaceable rule gives the chair the power to determine when and how the poll must be taken; however, a poll on the election of a chair or on the question of an adjournment must be taken immediately: s 250M.

Shareholders are generally entitled to exercise their voting rights in their own interests. This is subject to certain statutory rights conferred on shareholders. These are discussed in Chapter 17 below. Further, shareholders may enter into agreements whereby they bind themselves to vote in accordance with the directions of another person.

The potential for electronic voting at meetings is examined in Chapter 3 of the December 1999 ASIC discussion paper, *The Online Corporation: Electronic Corporate Communications*, by Dr Elizabeth Boros. The discussion paper is linked to the Lipton-Herzberg Meetings Pathway at **http://www.lipton-herzberg.com.au/secure/pathways-chapter-14-meetings.html**

proxies

A "proxy" is a person authorised to vote on behalf of the appointing shareholder.

[14.105] Shareholders may wish to exercise their voting rights at general meetings even if they are unable to attend personally. A shareholder can do this by appointing a proxy. A "proxy" is a person authorised to vote on behalf of the appointing shareholder. A proxy may be an individual or a body corporate: s 249X(1A). Shareholders of listed companies often appoint the chair or one of the other directors as their proxy.

The rules regarding who can appoint a proxy are replaceable rules for proprietary companies and mandatory rules for a public company under s 249X. Under s 249X(1), a shareholder who is entitled to vote may appoint a proxy to attend and vote for the shareholder at the meeting. The appointment may specify the proportion or number of votes that the proxy may exercise: s 249X(2). A shareholder holding two or more voting shares may appoint two proxies who may each exercise half the votes if the appointment does not specify the proportion of votes each proxy may exercise: s 249X(3).

A company must send out, with the notice of meeting to shareholders entitled to appoint a proxy, a statement that the shareholder is entitled to appoint one or two proxies and if two are appointed, to specify the proportion of votes each proxy is appointed to exercise: s 249L(d).

A proxy has the rights of the appointing shareholder to speak at the meeting, to vote in accordance with the appointment and to join in the demand for a poll: s 249Y(1). The company's constitution may provide that a proxy is not entitled to vote on a show of hands: s 249Y(2). A proxy's authority to speak and vote at a meeting is suspended while the shareholder is present at the meeting. This can be made subject to a provision in the company's constitution that provides for the effect that a shareholder's presence has on the authority of the proxy: s 249Y(3).

If a company sends a shareholder a proxy appointment form for a meeting, it must send the form to all shareholders entitled to appoint a proxy: s 249Z.

To be valid, a proxy appointment form must be signed by the appointing shareholder and state the proxy's name or position and the meetings at which the proxy may be used: s 250A(1). An appointment does not need to be witnessed: s 250A(6).

A proxy's appointment must be received by the company at least 48 hours before the meeting: s 250B. The company's constitution may reduce this period: s 250B(5). An appointment authority may be sent to the company's registered office by post or fax or to the company's electronic address: s 250B(3). As a result of CLERP 9 amendments, a company can offer other electronic means for submission of proxy appointment forms. A company may specify in the notice of meeting that an appointment of a proxy is ineffective if the transmission to a fax number or electronic address is not verified in a particular way or the appointment authority is not produced at the meeting: s 250B(4).

The notice of meeting of a listed Australian company must specify the company's fax number and electronic address for purposes of proxy appointments: s 250BA.

A person who is not entitled to vote as a shareholder may vote as a proxy for another shareholder in accordance with the appointment: s 250C(1).

When appointing a proxy, a shareholder may direct how the proxy should vote. This is referred to as a "directed proxy". A shareholder may also appoint a proxy without specific voting instructions. This is referred to as an "open proxy". If a shareholder specifies the way the proxy is to vote on particular resolutions:

When appointing a proxy, a shareholder may direct how the proxy should vote. This is referred to as a "directed proxy". A shareholder may also appoint a proxy without specific voting instructions. This is referred to as an "open proxy".

- **the proxy need not vote on a show of hands, but if the proxy votes, they must vote as instructed (s 250A(4)(a));**
- **if the proxy is the chair, the proxy must vote on a poll and must vote as instructed (s 250A(4)(c)); and**
- **if the proxy is not the chair, voting on a poll is optional, but if they do vote, the proxy must vote as instructed: s 250A(4)(d).**

case note

In *Whitlam v ASIC* [2003] NSWCA 183, about 4,000 shareholders of NRMA Ltd appointed Whitlam, NRMA's chair, as their proxy with instructions to vote against a proposed resolution to increase the directors' remuneration. The rules applicable to the meeting required the proxy to sign the poll paper to constitute a valid vote. Whitlam omitted to sign the poll papers which resulted in disenfranchising the shareholders who appointed him their proxy to vote against the proposed resolution. The NSW Court of Appeal held that despite this, Whitlam did not contravene s 250A(4)(c). There was insufficient evidence to conclude beyond reasonable doubt that Whitlam's omission to sign was deliberate. Further, filling out and lodging poll papers was still a vote for the purposes of s 250A(4)(c) even though the papers were unsigned. A director who acts as a proxy for members is not necessarily exercising a director's powers or discharging a director's duties. As a consequence, a contravention of s 250A(4)(c) does not mean that the director also breached the statutory duties under ss 181 or 182.

The s 250A(4)(c) requirement to vote as instructed applies only if the proxy is the chair. Other proxy holders do not have similar obligations and are not obliged to vote. Further, s 250A(4)(d) allows a non-chair proxy holder to "cherry pick". This means that a proxy holder, with directed proxies from different shareholders, chooses to vote only those proxies with whose directions they agree. This effectively disenfranchises some shareholders and may influence the outcome of voting. The exposure draft of the *Corporations Amendment Bill (No 2) 2005* proposes to change s 250A(4)(d). While non-chair proxy holders will not be obliged to vote, if they do vote on a poll, they must vote each and every share over which they have a valid proxy and vote them as directed.

The s 250A(4)(c) requirement to vote as instructed applies only if the proxy is the chair. Other proxy holders do not have similar obligations and are not obliged to vote.

Under a replaceable rule, a vote cast by a proxy will be valid even if the appointing shareholder has died, the appointment was revoked, or the shareholder transferred the shares in respect of which the proxy was given. The validity of the proxy vote in these circumstances is subject to the company receiving written notice of the matter before the meeting: s 250C(2).

A listed company must record in the minutes of a meeting, the total number of proxy votes exercisable by all proxies validly appointed and the number of proxy votes for, against and abstained on each resolution: s 251AA(1).

The potential for authentication of electronically submitted proxies is examined in Chapter 3 of the December 1999 ASIC discussion paper, *The Online Corporation: Electronic Corporate Communications*, by Dr Elizabeth Boros. The discussion paper is linked to the Lipton-Herzberg Meetings Pathway at **http://www.lipton-herzberg.com.au/secure/pathways-chapter-14-meetings.html**

corporate representatives

[14.110] A body corporate that owns shares may appoint a corporate representative to exercise all the powers the body corporate could exercise at meetings of the shareholders, creditors, debenture-holders or relating to circulating resolutions or resolutions of one shareholder companies: s 250D(1).

The appointment may set out restrictions on the representative's powers: s 250D(2). While more than one representative may be appointed, only one may exercise the powers of the body corporate at any one time: s 250D(3).

These provisions allow a corporation shareholder to have a physical presence at a meeting of shareholders. It is placed in the position of a natural person and this implies that only single appointments of a representative can be made: *Atkins v St Barbara Mines Ltd* (1996) 14 ACLC 1777. In this case on appeal, (1997) 15 ACLC 800, Ipp J distinguished between a proxy and corporate representative. A representative "is really a statutory example of an official acting as an organ of the company rather than as a mere agent". A proxy is an agent of the corporate shareholder. This distinction may be significant where documents appointing a proxy must be given to the company at least 48 hours before the meeting under s 250B(1) and (2). Representatives cannot be required to notify their appointments before the meeting.

Resolutions that require a simple majority vote in favour to be passed are called "ordinary resolutions".

resolutions

ordinary and special resolutions

[14.115] There are different types of resolutions which reflect the importance of the motions being voted upon. Resolutions that require a simple majority vote in favour to be passed are called "ordinary resolutions". Ordinary resolutions are passed by a majority of shareholders who are present and voting (in person or by proxy) at the particular meeting.

Other matters may be more important and a resolution with respect to these matters may require a majority greater than a simple majority. A special resolution must be passed by at least 75 per cent of the votes cast by shareholders entitled to vote on the resolution: s 9. It also requires notice specifying the intention to propose the special resolution and stating the resolution: s 249L(c). The holders of at least 95 per cent of the issued shares with the right to vote may agree to pass a special resolution with less than 21 days' notice being given. An AGM may be called on shorter notice only if all shareholders entitled to vote agree beforehand: s 249H(2).

The *Corporations Act* requires a company to pass a special resolution in certain circumstances such as where it seeks to modify or repeal its constitution under s 136(2) or it wishes to reduce its capital by selective reduction: s 256C(2).

Certain resolutions must be lodged by a public company with ASIC within 14 days of their passing. These include documents or resolutions that vary or attach rights to shares: s 246F(3).

A special resolution must be passed by at least 75 per cent of the votes cast by shareholders entitled to vote on the resolution. It also requires notice specifying the intention to propose the special resolution and stating the resolution.

A special resolution of a class of shareholders also requires 21 days' notice. A special resolution of a class of shareholders must be passed before the rights of the holders of that class can be varied: s 246B.

The constitution of a company may provide that a special resolution is necessary in certain cases even though this is not required by the *Corporations Act*. In other cases, it is not open to a company to provide for a majority other than that specified in the legislation. For example, a company cannot alter its constitution by ordinary resolution in contravention of s 136(2).

Further, the constitution of a company or rules of an association may provide for a majority in excess of a simple majority other than a three-quarters majority. An example of this is *Edwards v Halliwell* [1950] 2 All ER 1064, where the rules of a trade union provided for an increase in subscriptions if a resolution to that effect was passed by a two-thirds majority.

resolutions without meetings

[14.120] proprietary company circulating resolutions. A proprietary company with more than one shareholder may pass a resolution without holding a general meeting if all shareholders entitled to vote on the resolution sign a document containing a statement that they are in favour of the resolution: s 249A(2). This is referred to as a "circulating resolution". Shareholders may sign separate copies of the document if the wording of the resolution and statement is identical in each copy: s 249A(3). The resolution is passed when the last shareholder signs: s 249A(4). Circulating resolutions cannot be used for resolutions to remove an auditor: s 329.

[14.125] one shareholder companies. A company with only one shareholder passes a resolution if the shareholder records the resolution and signs the record: s 249B. Resolutions passed in this way must be recorded in the company's minute books: s 251A.

the Duomatic principle

[14.130] This procedure recognises that in some cases, if all shareholders are in agreement, business may be transacted without the formalities of calling a meeting and passing a resolution. A rule known as "the Duomatic principle" states that where all shareholders entitled to attend and vote at a general meeting of a company assent with full knowledge and consent to some matter that could have been carried into effect at a general meeting, that assent is as binding as a resolution in a general meeting would have been. It is open to all the shareholders to agree to disregard the formalities associated with the calling of a meeting.

This doctrine does not operate where substantial rights are varied or where shareholders are not fully aware of the effect of the matter agreed to on their rights: *Herrman v Simon* (1990) 8 ACLC 1094. In *Parker and Cooper Ltd v Reading* [1926] Ch 975, the shareholders of a company informally ratified a debenture granted by the directors that was beyond their powers. The company was held bound by the unanimous ratification of the shareholders because the transaction was intra vires the company and was honest and for the benefit of the company. Only the consent of voting shareholders is required for such informal meetings: *Re Duomatic Ltd* [1969] 2 Ch 365.

shareholders' resolutions and statements

[14.135] A company's board of directors usually sets the agenda for its AGMs and other general meetings. However, the *Corporations Act* recognises that minority shareholders also have the right to require the company to circulate their own proposed resolutions and statements.

In *Shareholder Participation in the Modern Listed Public Company: Final Report*, CASAC explained that:

> **< This gives them the opportunity to bring a matter to the attention of other shareholders and seek their support before they decide whether to attend the meeting or how to complete their proxies. This shareholder right may also act as a counterbalance to the right of the directors to circulate their views to shareholders at the company's expense. >**

Section 249N gives shareholders the right to require a company to put resolutions to be considered at a general meeting. Shareholders with at least 5 per cent of the votes that may be cast or at least 100 shareholders entitled to vote may give a company notice of a resolution that they propose to move at a general meeting: s 249N(1). The exposure draft of the *Corporations Amendment Bill (No 2) 2005* proposes to change the "100 member" rule in s 249N(1)(b) to enable 20 members to put resolutions to a general meeting.

Section 249N gives shareholders the right to require a company to put resolutions to be considered at a general meeting.

Members' resolutions must be considered at the next general meeting occurring more than two months after the notice is given: s 249O(1). Notice of the resolution must be given to shareholders in the same way as notice of a meeting is given: s 249O(2).

A prescribed number of shareholders may request their company to distribute a statement to all shareholders about a proposed resolution to be moved at a general meeting or about any other matter that may properly be considered at a general meeting.

Under s 249P(1), a prescribed number of shareholders may request their company to distribute a statement to all shareholders about a proposed resolution to be moved at a general meeting or about any other matter that may properly be considered at a general meeting. Such statements are often used by shareholders' associations and trade unions to solicit shareholders for proxies at company AGMs.

The company must distribute a copy of the statement to all shareholders in the same way as it gives notice of a general meeting: s 249P(6). The company is responsible for the cost of distributing the statement to shareholders if it receives the statement in time to send it out to shareholders with the notice of meeting.

Under s 249P(2), the request to distribute a statement may be made by shareholders with at least 5 per cent of the votes that may be cast on a resolution or at least 100 shareholders who are entitled to vote at the meeting. A company need not comply with a request if the statement is more than 1,000 words long or defamatory.

The exposure draft of the *Corporations Amendment Bill (No 2) 2005* proposes to change s 249P(2)(b) and reduce the minimum number of members that may request a company to distribute a statement to members with the notice of meeting from 100 to 20.

minutes

A company must keep minute books in which it records proceedings and resolutions of meetings of the company's shareholders and directors, including meetings of committees of directors.

[14.140] A company must keep minute books in which it records proceedings and resolutions of meetings of the company's shareholders and directors, including meetings of committees of directors: s 251A(1). Resolutions passed by shareholders or directors without a meeting must also be recorded. This includes resolutions of one shareholder companies and circulating resolutions. The minutes of listed Australian companies must also record details about votes cast by proxies: s 251AA.

Minutes must be recorded within one month and be signed within a reasonable time after the meeting by the chair of the meeting or the chair of the next meeting: s 251A(2). Where a resolution is passed without a meeting, the minutes must be signed by a director: s 251A(3).

The minute books must be kept at the company's registered office, principal place of business or another place approved by ASIC: s 251A(5). The recording and signing of a minute is evidence of the resolution or proceeding to which it relates unless the contrary is proved: s 251A(6).

Shareholders are entitled to inspect and request copies of the minutes of meetings of shareholders and the resolutions of shareholders passed without meetings: s 251B(1) and (2).

irregularities

[14.145] Procedural irregularities are not invalidated unless the court is of the opinion that the irregularity has caused or may cause substantial injustice which may not otherwise be remedied by order of the court. In such cases, the court has power to declare the proceedings invalid: s 1322(2).

Examples of procedural irregularities include absence of a quorum and deficiency of notice or time: s 1322(1)(f).

case note

In *Bell Resources Ltd v Turnbridge Pty Ltd* (1988) 6 ACLC 970, a resolution was passed reducing the number of directors. This was held to be a procedural irregularity because it had not been approved by the directors, the required notice had not been given and the nature of this item had not been specified in the notice as required by the articles. This caused substantial injustice because it deprived shareholders of notice of important and fundamental resolutions. The resolution was declared invalid under the equivalent of s 1322(2).

The purpose of s 1322 is to enable the court to make orders in cases where the rights of shareholders or creditors are interfered with. The court must balance the real prejudice suffered by a shareholder against the prejudice to the company and other shareholders in considering whether or not to declare the proceedings invalid. The injustice must be real and not theoretical or insubstantial: *Re Compaction Systems Pty Ltd* [1976] 2 NSWLR 477.

Although "procedural irregularity" is given wide meaning, it does not extend to a failure to give notice to half the shareholders of a proposal to amend the company's constitution and to resolving to amend the constitution without the knowledge of those shareholders. The court could not validate such procedures under s 1322: *Jordan v Avram* (1998) 16 ACLC 867.

case note

In *Chew Investment Australia Pty Ltd v General Corp of Australia Ltd* (1988) 6 ACLC 87, General Corp of Australia Ltd (GCA) called an extraordinary general meeting to consider resolutions required under ASX Listing Rules. Peppinck held proxies for 10 shareholders including Chew Investment Australia Pty Ltd (CIA). His demand for a poll was rejected by the chair in contravention of the articles. It appeared that the resolutions would have been defeated on a poll. CIA sought orders under the equivalent of s 1322(2) declaring that the resolutions passed by the general meeting be declared invalid as there was an entitlement under the articles to a poll. The court granted the application as there was a clear injustice that prevented the exercise of voting rights. This was particularly so because of the Listing Rule that required the resolutions to be passed and the fact that a poll would have resulted in the defeat of the resolutions.

The procedure for a nomination of a person for election as a director at a general meeting of a company is not "a proceeding" within the meaning of s 1322(2). It is not a necessary part of an annual general meeting to require nominations in advance: *Wesgo Ltd v Gabriel* (1991) 9 ACLC 1087.

Where a company accidentally omits to give notice to a person entitled to attend a meeting and the meeting is required to be held under the *Corporations Act*, or the legislation prescribes that particular notice must be given, or a shareholder does not have a reasonable opportunity to participate at a meeting held in more than one venue, the meeting is not invalidated unless the court so declares. An application for such an order may be brought by a shareholder who did not receive notice or by ASIC: s 1322(3) and (3A). These provisions enable minor irregularities to be disregarded.

Any interested person may apply to the court for an order declaring that any act or proceeding is not invalid by reason of a contravention of the *Corporations Act* or a provision of the corporation's constitution: s 1322(4)(a).

The court may validate proceedings at meetings if the irregularity is essentially of a procedural nature and the parties to the contravention acted honestly. An order validating proceedings cannot be made unless it is in the public interest: s 1322(6).

It has been suggested that an order validating an irregularity will not be made where it involves a breach of the *Corporations Act* that constitutes a nullity and is rendered void. Irregularities will only be validated where the proceeding is voidable. This distinction depends on interpretation of the relevant section breached: *Harman v Energy Research Group Australia* (1985) 3 ACLC 536.

A broader approach was taken in *Abalcheck Pty Ltd v Pullen* (1990) 8 ACLC 1078, which held that s 1322 grants power "to validate something which otherwise would be completely and utterly void". This approach gives a wider operation to s 1322 which provides its own criteria in s 1322(6) rather than to look at the particular section which has been contravened: *Re Vanfox Pty Ltd* (1994) 12 ACLC 357.

pathways questions . . .

The following questions dealing with shareholders' meetings may best be answered by reading this chapter and considering the Internet resources on the Lipton-Herzberg Meetings Pathway at **http://www.lipton-herzberg.com.au/secure/pathways-chapter-14-meetings.html**

1. Refer to the ASIC discussion paper, *The Online Corporation: Electronic Corporate Communications*, by Dr Elizabeth Boros.
   (a) In what respect have recent amendments to the *Corporations Act* encouraged greater use of electronic communications by companies?
   (b) What are the major issues that can arise where electronic communications are used in relation to the calling and conduct of general meetings?
   (c) Can meetings be held online and, if so, which matters need to be addressed?
   (d) Is electronic voting and appointment of proxies feasible now? What are some of the main issues that need to be addressed?

2. Refer to CASAC's publication, *Shareholder Participation in the Modern Listed Public Company: The Final Report.*
   (a) Is it appropriate for 100 shareholders of a large, listed public company to have the power to requisition a meeting of the company or move a resolution?
   (b) Should proxy voting details be disclosed?
   (c) Should companies be permitted to allow voting by shareholders who are not present at a meeting?
   (d) What recommendations are made in the report to facilitate the adoption by companies of transparent procedures for the election of directors?

3. What amendments were put forward by CLERP 9 to facilitate improved shareholder participation?

4. What are the main issues to consider in deciding to hold a general meeting in more than one venue?

bibliography . . .

Bonollo, F "Electronic Meetings" (2002) 14 Aust Jnl of Corp Law 95.

Boros, E "The Online Corporation: Electronic Corporate Communications" Uni of Melbourne, Centre for Corporate Law and Securities Regulation, Corporate Law Research Papers, **http://cclsr.law.unimelb.edu.au/research-papers/**

Boros, E "Corporations Online" (2001) 19 C & SLJ 492.

Boros, E "Virtual shareholder meetings: who decides how companies make decisions?" (2004) 28 *Melbourne University Law Review* 265.

Darvas, P "Section 249D and the 'Activist' Shareholder: Court Jester or Conscience of the Corporation?" (2002) 20 C & SLJ 390.

Duffy, M "Shareholder Democracy or Shareholder Plutocracy? Corporate Governance and the Plight of Small Shareholders" (2002) 25 UNSWLJ 434.

McCombe, J "Shareholder Meetings: Key Issues and Developments" Centre for Corporate Law & Securities Regulation, Corporate Law Research Papers Website **http://cclsr.law.unimelb.edu.au/research-papers/index.html**

McConvill, J "The Obligation of Proxies to Vote as Directed: The Present State of Play and the Need for a Resolution" (2003) 21 C & SLJ 248.

Magner, E S "Notice of Purpose of Company General Meetings: The Common Law Requirement, the Fiduciary Duty" (1987) 5 C & SLJ 92.

Pathak, N & Lauritsen, H "A shareholder's right to call general meetings—a sharp word for the disgruntled shareholders or just a blunt instrument" (2005) 23 C & SLJ 283.

Shand, M "The Postponement by the Directors of Meetings Convened by a Member under s 249F of the Corporations Law" (2001) 19 C & SLJ 160.

Simmonds, R "Shareholder Democracy or a Banana Republic: The CASAC Proposals for Reform" (Dec 2000) 7(4) E Law (Murdoch Uni) **http://www.murdoch.edu.au/elaw**

Simmonds, R "Why Must we Meet? Thinking About Why Shareholder Meetings Are Required" (2001) 19 C & SLJ 506.

Zakrewski, R "The Law Relating to Single Director and Single Shareholder Companies" (1999) 17 C & SLJ 156.

revision questions on the material in this chapter ...

- Please see eQuiz at **http://www.thomson.com.au/academic** for multiple choice questions and answers.
- For further corporations law links and material please refer to the Lipton-Herzberg website at **http://www.lipton-herzberg.com.au**

chapter fifteen

financial reporting and disclosure

key points ...

> All companies must keep written financial records such as invoices, receipts and other documents of prime entry. A company's directors and its auditor are entitled to full access to the company's financial records so as to enable them to properly discharge their duties. ASIC also has the power to inspect the books and records of any company. Members do not have an automatic right to inspect a company's books and financial records.

> Companies other than small proprietary companies must prepare a financial report and a directors' report for each financial year. A small proprietary company has to prepare such reports only if its shareholders or ASIC direct it to do so. Disclosing entities are also required to prepare half-year financial reports and directors' reports as well as annual reports.

> The financial report consists of the financial statements, notes to the financial statements and the directors' declaration about the statements and notes.

> The financial statements must comply with accounting standards and give a true and fair view of the financial position and performance of the company and comprise a profit and loss statement, a balance sheet and a statement of cash flows.

> The directors' report must include general information about the company's operations and activities as well as the specific information prescribed by the *Corporations Act*.

> Listed entities must comply with continuous disclosure listing rules which require a notification to the ASX of any information concerning the company which could reasonably be expected to have a material effect on the company's share price.

> Companies other than small proprietary companies must send copies of their annual financial report, directors' report and auditor's report to their members by the prescribed deadline. These reports must also be lodged with ASIC.

The main aim of the financial reporting requirements is to force companies to disclose prescribed information about their affairs and financial position.

[15.05] In this chapter, we consider the financial reporting requirements of the *Corporations Act*. The audit requirements are discussed in Chapter 16 below. The main aim of the financial reporting requirements is to force companies to disclose prescribed information about their affairs and financial position. Disclosure of such information enables a company's members, potential investors and creditors to make rational and informed decisions in relation to the company.

The financial reporting requirements of the *Corporations Act* vary depending on the type of company. Disclosing entities such as listed companies are subject to more onerous financial reporting obligations than other types of companies. Public and large proprietary companies are subject to greater financial reporting obligations than small proprietary companies. ASX listing rules impose additional disclosure obligations on listed companies.

This chapter deals with the financial reporting and disclosure requirements of the *Corporations Act*. There are various other provisions that also have the effect of requiring companies to disclose financial information in particular situations. For example:

> **the fundraising provisions discussed in Chapter 7 above require a company to disclose certain financial information if it offers its securities for issue; and**

> **under the takeovers provisions (discussed in Chapter 18 below), both the bidder and the target must issue statements containing prescribed information.**

reasons for disclosure of financial information

[15.10] The disclosure of financial information by a company is primarily for the benefit of the members. By receiving full, accurate information regarding the financial affairs of a company, its members are able to assess the performance of the company's management. This is recognised by s 314(1) which requires companies, other than small proprietary companies, to report to members for a financial year by sending copies of the following:

> **the financial report for the year;**
> **the directors' report for the year; and**
> **the auditor's report on the financial report.**

Small proprietary companies are not required to prepare or provide members with the above reports unless shareholders with at least 5 per cent of the votes direct the company to do so: s 293.

[15.15] Other parties who may have an interest in disclosure of financial information include creditors, who may be concerned that a debtor company will be able to repay its debts and its financial position may be crucial in this regard. Potential members and potential creditors often consider the financial position of a company before deciding whether to invest in, lend or extend credit to a company. A sound disclosure regime serves the purpose of protecting members of the public from unduly risky investments made on the basis of inaccurate or incomplete information. In broader terms, it is desirable for investment decisions, whereby scarce resources are allocated to or withdrawn from businesses, to be made on the basis of accurate information. Others who may be interested in the disclosure of financial information by a company include competitors, customers, security analysts, trade unions, wage-fixing bodies, stock exchanges, taxation authorities and various other government bodies.

Each of these users seeks different information in the financial reports and there is considerable variance in the expertise they bring to bear upon their interpretation. This makes the task of formulating a single set of requirements very difficult. However, certain core information is of value to diverse interest groups.

financial records

duty to keep financial records

[15.20] Under s 286(1) a company, registered scheme or disclosing entity must keep written financial records that:

A company must keep written financial records.

> **correctly record and explain its transactions and financial position and performance; and**
> **would enable true and fair financial statements to be prepared and audited.**

The term "financial records" is defined in s 9 and includes invoices, receipts, documents of prime entry, working papers and other documents needed to explain the methods by which financial statements are made up.

The obligation to keep financial records requires more than simply keeping the source materials such as cashbooks, journals and ledgers from which a set of documents of prime entry might be written up. The minimum books of account required by s 286 are a general ledger and general journal. Company transactions can only be properly explained by appropriate journal entries with clear explanatory narratives: *Van Reesema v Flavel* (1992) 10 ACLC 291.

ASIC's website has an information leaflet, *What Books and Records Should My Company Keep?*, that provides guidance to directors of small proprietary companies about the financial records requirements. This publication is linked to the Lipton-Herzberg Registration Procedure Pathway under the "post-registration requirements" heading at **http://www.lipton-herzberg.com.au/secure/pathways-registration-procedure.html**

The financial records must be retained by the company for at least seven years after the transactions covered by the records are completed.

The financial records must be retained by the company for at least seven years after the transactions covered by the records are completed: s 286(2). While the financial records may be kept in any language, if they are not kept in English, an English translation must be made available within a reasonable time to a person who is entitled to inspect the records and asks for the translation: s 287. If the financial records are kept in electronic form, they must be convertible into hard copy: s 288.

The financial records may be kept in whatever location the company chooses: s 289(1). If financial records about particular matters are kept outside Australia, sufficient written information about those matters must be kept in Australia to enable true and fair financial statements to be prepared and ASIC must be notified of the place where the information is kept: s 289(2). ASIC may direct a company to produce specified financial records kept outside Australia: s 289(3).

consequences of non-compliance

Directors are responsible for ensuring that the company complies with the financial records and financial reporting provisions.

[15.25] Directors are responsible for ensuring that the company complies with the financial records and financial reporting provisions of Pts 2M.1 and 2M.2 of the *Corporations Act*. Contravention of s 286 is a strict liability offence and directors who fail to take all reasonable steps to comply with Pts 2M.1 and 2M.2 contravene s 344(1), a designated civil penalty provision under Pt 9.4B of the *Corporations Act*. Contravention of a civil penalty provision may result in a civil penalty order being imposed on the contravening director. The civil penalty provisions are discussed in Chapter 13.6 above.

A director will be regarded as having taken all reasonable steps to comply with the financial records provisions by ensuring the company employs competent staff and has appropriate procedures in place that define what the staff are required to do: *ASC v Fairlie* (1993) 11 ACLC 669.

Section 588E(4) provides that a company that fails to keep and retain financial records as required by s 286(1) or (2) is presumed to be insolvent for purposes of:

> **the s 588G director's duty to prevent insolvent trading; and**
> **the antecedent transactions provisions of ss 588FA–588FG.**

These are discussed in Chapters 13.5 and 25, respectively.

As a general rule, shareholders have limited access rights to the company's books and financial records.

access to books and financial records

[15.30] As a general rule, shareholders have limited access rights to the company's books and financial records. The replaceable rule in s 247D provides that the directors may authorise a member to inspect the company's books. Members may also obtain authorisation by a resolution passed at a general meeting. As discussed in Chapter 17 below, a member may apply to the court under s 247A for an order to inspect the books of the company. The court will only grant such an order if it is satisfied that the applicant is acting in good faith and the inspection is to be made for a proper purpose.

In order to ensure that directors are fully informed so as to be able to discharge their duties properly, s 290(1) gives them a right of access to the financial records at all reasonable times.

In order to ensure that directors are fully informed so as to be able to discharge their duties properly, s 290(1) gives them a right of access to the financial records at all reasonable times. A director may be restrained from exercising this right of access only if it is affirmatively established that the director intended either to misuse the information or that inspection would materially harm the company: *Deluge Holdings Pty Ltd v Bowlay* (1991) 9 ACLC 1486.

A director may also apply to the court for an order authorising a person acting for the director to inspect the financial records of the company: s 290(2). Under s 290(4), the court may limit the use that a person may make of information obtained during the inspection. This provision reflects the confidential nature of the financial records of a company and prevents such information being used against the interests of the company by competitors.

The common law right of directors to have the right of access to the company's books and financial records was to enable them to discharge their duties: *South Australia v Barrett* (1995) 13 ACLC 1369. It was unclear whether directors had access to this information after they had retired or where they were being sued by the company for breach of duty.

Section 198F changes the common law rule and gives current directors a right to inspect the company's books (other than its financial records) at all reasonable times for the purposes of a legal proceeding to which a director is a party: s 198F(1). Former directors have similar inspection rights. Their inspection rights continue for seven years after they cease to be a director: s 198F(2). Section 290, discussed above, restricts the right to inspect the company's financial records to current directors.

Both the company's auditor and receiver also have a right of access to the company's financial records: ss 310 and 431. Auditors and receivers are discussed in Chapters 16 and 23, respectively. Sections 28–39A of the *ASIC Act* give ASIC the power to inspect a company's books and financial records.

annual financial reports

overview

[15.35] The table in s 285(1) provides an overview of annual financial reporting obligations.

The table in s 285(1) provides an overview of annual financial reporting obligations.

table 15.1 overview of annual financial reporting obligations

	Steps	Sections	Comments
1.	prepare financial report	295	The financial report includes — financial statements — disclosures and notes — directors' declaration
2.	prepare directors' report	298	The report has both a general component (s 299) and a specific component (s 300)
3.	have the financial report audited and obtain auditor's report	301, 307, 308	A small proprietary company preparing a financial report in response to a shareholder direction under s 293 only has to have an audit if the direction asks for it. Under s 312, officers must assist the auditor in the conduct of the audit. ASIC may use its exemption powers under ss 340 and 341 to relieve large proprietary companies from the audit requirements in appropriate cases (s 342(2) and (3)).
4.	send the financial report, directors' report and auditor's report to members	314	A concise financial report may be sent to members instead of the full financial statements (s 314(1)–(2)). For deadline see s 315(1)–(4).
5.	lodge the financial report, directors' report and auditor's report with ASIC	319	For deadline see s 319(3). Companies that have the benefit of the grandfathering in s 319(4) do not have to lodge.
6.	[public companies only] lay financial report, director's report and auditor's report before AGM	317	For the AGM deadline see s 250N.

obligation to prepare annual financial report

Section 292(1) requires a financial report and a directors' report to be prepared for each financial year.

[15.40] Section 292(1) requires a financial report and a directors' report to be prepared for each financial year by:

> - disclosing entities;
> - public companies;
> - large proprietary companies; and
> - registered schemes.

A small proprietary company has to prepare the financial report only if it is directed to do so.

A small proprietary company has to prepare the financial report only if it is directed to do so by shareholders with at least 5 per cent of the votes: ss 292(2) and 293(1). The direction must be signed by the shareholders giving the direction: s 293(2)(a). A shareholders' direction must be made no later than 12 months after the end of the financial year concerned: s 293(2)(b). Under s 293(3), the direction may specify:

> - that the financial report does not have to comply with some or all of the accounting standards;
> - that the directors' report or a part of the report need not be prepared; and
> - that the financial report is to be audited.

A small proprietary company must also prepare a financial report if ASIC directs it to comply with the annual financial reporting requirements: ss 292(2) and 294(1). ASIC's direction may be general or may specify the particular requirements that the company must comply with: s 294(2). ASIC's direction must specify the financial year concerned and the date by which the documents have to be prepared, sent or lodged: s 294(2) and (3).

A financial report and directors' report must also be prepared by a small proprietary company if it is controlled by a foreign company and it is not consolidated in the financial statements lodged with ASIC by a registered foreign company, a company, registered scheme or disclosing entity: s 292(2)(b).

contents

[15.45] According to s 295(1), a financial report for a financial year consists of:

> - the financial statements for the year;
> - the notes to the financial statements; and
> - the directors' declaration about the statements and notes.

financial statements

[15.50] Section 295(2) specifies that the financial statements consist of:

> - a profit and loss statement for the year;
> - a balance sheet as at the end of the year; and
> - a statement of cash flows for the year.

As discussed below, the accounting standards govern the form and content of the various components of the financial statements and the notes to the financial statements. In the case of listed companies, the ASX Listing Rules also prescribe additional form and content requirements.

consolidated financial statements

[15.55] If required by the accounting standards, the financial statement must consist of a consolidated profit and loss statement, a balance sheet and a statement of cash flows: s 295(2)(d). Accounting standard AASB 127, *Consolidated and Separate Financial Statements*, requires an entity that is a parent of a group that is a reporting entity to present consolidated financial statements in which it consolidates its investments in subsidiaries. AASB 127 defines "control" as the power to govern the financial and operating policies of an entity so as to obtain benefits from its activities.

If required by the accounting standards, the financial statement must consist of a consolidated profit and loss statement, a balance sheet and a statement of cash flows.

Section 323 requires directors and officers of a controlled entity to supply all information that is necessary to prepare the consolidated financial statements and notes.

notes to financial statements

[15.60] Section 295(3) specifies that the notes to the financial statements are:

> disclosures required by the regulations;
> notes required by the accounting standards; and
> any other information necessary to give a true and fair view.

directors' declaration

[15.65] The directors' declaration required by s 295(4) is a declaration:

> that the financial statements and the notes comply with the accounting standards;
> that the financial statements and the notes give a true and fair view;
> whether, in the directors' opinion, there are reasonable grounds to believe that the company will be able to pay its debts as and when they become due and payable;
> whether, in the directors' opinion, the financial statements and the notes are in accordance with the *Corporations Act*, including whether they comply with accounting standards and give a true and fair view; and
> in the case of a listed company, whether the directors have been given the written and signed declarations by each of the CEO and CFO required under s 295A.

Section 295A was introduced by the CLERP 9 amendments and requires the CEO and CFO of a listed company to declare whether in their opinion the financial records have been properly maintained in accordance with s 286 and the financial statements and notes comply with the accounting standards and give a true and fair view. Generally, two declarations must be made unless the one person occupies both positions. The CEO and CFO declarations do not derogate from the primary responsibility of directors to ensure the financial statements comply with the legislation.

Section 295A requires the CEO and CFO of a listed company to declare whether in their opinion the financial records have been properly maintained in accordance with s 286 and the financial statements and notes comply with the accounting standards and give a true and fair view.

The directors' declaration must be signed by the directors and be made in accordance with a resolution of the directors and specify on which date the declaration is made: s 295(5).

Australian financial reporting system

[15.70] The Australian financial reporting system was substantially revised in 1999. These changes resulted in the establishment of the Financial Reporting Council (FRC). The FRC is an advisory body with responsibility for the oversight of the process of setting Australian accounting standards. The CLERP 9 amendments expanded the role of the FRC to include oversight of the auditor independence requirements and the auditing standard-setting process. These aspects of the FRC's role are discussed in Chapter 16 below. The Australian Accounting Standards Board (AASB) was also reconstituted as a result of the 1999 amendments. These changes are further discussed below.

The accounting standards provisions have three main objectives. According to s 224 of the *ASIC Act*, the objectives are:

1. to facilitate the development of accounting standards that require the provision of financial information that:
   > allows users to make and evaluate decisions about allocating scarce resources; and
   > assists directors to discharge their obligations in relation to financial reporting; and
   > is relevant to assessing performance, financial position, financing and investment; and
   > is relevant and reliable, facilitates comparability and is readily understandable;
2. to facilitate the Australian economy by reducing the cost of capital, enabling Australian entities to compete effectively overseas and having accounting standards that are clearly stated and easy to understand; and
3. to maintain investor confidence in the Australian economy (including its capital markets).

Financial Reporting Council

The FRC is an advisory body with responsibility for the oversight of the Australian accounting standards setting process.

[15.75] The FRC is an advisory body with responsibility for the oversight of the Australian accounting standards setting process. According to the Explanatory Memorandum to the 1999 amending legislation that established the FRC, the FRC's functions and powers were deliberately designed to ensure that while it had broad oversight of the standard-setting process, it would not be able to determine the content of particular standards. For example, the FRC does not have any direct influence over technical deliberation of the AASB and cannot veto any accounting standard made by the AASB.

Under s 225(2) of the *ASIC Act*, the FRC's functions include:

> providing broad oversight of the accounting standard-setting process and giving the Minister reports and advice on the process;
> appointing the members of the AASB, other than the AASB Chair (who is appointed by the Minister);
> approving and monitoring the AASB's priorities, business plan, budget and staffing arrangements;
> determining the AASB's broad strategic direction and giving the AASB directions, advice or feedback on matters of general policy and the AASB's procedures;
> monitoring the development of international accounting standards and the accounting standards that apply in major international financial centres; and
> monitoring the operation of accounting standards to assess their continued relevance and effectiveness in achieving their objectives in respect of both the public and private sectors of the Australian economy.

Under s 235A, FRC members are appointed by the Minister from nominations made by the following groups:

> professional accounting bodies;
> users, preparers and analysts of financial statements;
> government and public sector entities; and
> regulatory agencies, such as ASIC and the ASX.

Australian Accounting Standards Board

The AASB is the body that formulates Australian accounting standards.

[15.80] The AASB is the body that formulates Australian accounting standards. Apart from the chair, who is appointed by the Minister, AASB members are appointed by the FRC: s 236B.

Under s 227(1) of the *ASIC Act*, the functions of the AASB include:

> **developing a conceptual framework for the purpose of evaluating proposed accounting standards and international standards;**
> **making and formulating accounting standards; and**
> **participating in the development of a single set of accounting standards for worldwide use.**

In performing its functions, the AASB must follow the FRC's broad strategic and general policy directions: s 232. It must also take into account the advice and feedback on matters of general policy given by the FRC. Examples of a general policy direction include how quickly Australia should move towards greater adoption of international standards and/or market value accounting. However, the FRC does not have the power to direct the AASB in relation to the development or making of a particular standard, nor does it have the power to veto standards formulated and recommended by the AASB: s 225(5) and (6). Further, when evaluating proposed accounting standards, the AASB must have regard to the interests of Australian corporations that raise or propose to raise capital in major international financial centres: s 227(1A).

In performing its functions, the AASB must follow the FRC's broad strategic and general policy directions.

standards-setting framework

[15.85] Section 334 of the *Corporations Act* gives the AASB the power to make accounting standards for the purposes of the *Corporations Act*. The AASB also has the power to formulate accounting standards for other purposes, such as the public sector and non-Corporations *Act* entities: s 227(1)(c) of the *ASIC Act*. Accounting standards made by the AASB prior to the 1999 amendments continue in operation as if they were made by the reconstituted AASB.

Section 334 of the *Corporations Act* gives the AASB the power to make accounting standards for the purposes of the *Corporations Act*.

Section 227(3) of the *ASIC Act* also gives the AASB the power to make or formulate an accounting standard by issuing the text of an international accounting standard. The text of the international accounting standard may be modified to the extent necessary to ensure that any disclosure and transparency provisions in the standard are appropriate to the Australian legal or institutional environment.

Accounting standards are to be interpreted in a manner that promotes the s 224 objectives: s 228. An accounting standard may be of general or limited application: s 229(1). When making or formulating accounting standards, the AASB must have regard to the suitability of a proposed standard for different types of entities: s 229(2)(a). The AASB must also ensure that there are appropriate accounting standards for each type of entity that must comply with accounting standards: s 229(2)(c).

Before making or formulating a standard, s 231(1) requires the AASB to carry out a cost/benefit analysis of the impact of a proposed accounting standard. A cost/benefit analysis is not required where the standard is being made or formulated by issuing the text of an international standard. The AASB is required to give the Minister details of a cost/benefit analysis, if it is directed to do so: s 231(4).

The Minister may, after receiving a report from the FRC, give the AASB a direction about the role of international accounting standards in the Australian accounting standards-setting system: s 233. According to the Explanatory Memorandum to the 1999 amendments, the FRC's report to the Minister would be expected to have regard to the following issues:

> **whether the standards made by the international standard-setter had been endorsed by the International Organisation of Securities Commissions for cross-border raisings and listings;**
> **the level of acceptance of international accounting standards in the world's major capital markets; and**
> **whether the adoption of international accounting standards would be in Australia's best interests.**

Section 233 enables the Minister, upon advice of the FRC, to require the AASB to move towards greater adoption of international standards if the AASB has not done so of its own accord.

Financial Reporting Panel

[15.90] The CLERP 9 amendments established a Financial Reporting Panel (FRP) under s 239AA of the *ASIC Act* to resolve disputes between ASIC and companies regarding the application of accounting standards and the true and fair view requirement in financial reports. The FRP replaces the courts as the forum for such disputes so that matters may be dealt with quicker, with less formality and expense and by persons with financial and accounting expertise.

Australian accounting standards

The financial report of a company must comply with the accounting standards made by the AASB.

[15.95] Accounting standards are given legislative backing. The financial report of a company must comply with the accounting standards made by the AASB: s 296. A small proprietary company's financial report does not have to comply with particular accounting standards if the report is prepared in response to a shareholder director under s 293 and the direction specifies that compliance is not necessary.

true and fair view

The annual financial statements and notes must give a true and fair view of the financial position and performance of the company.

[15.100] Under s 297, the annual financial statements and notes must give a true and fair view of the financial position and performance of the company. If consolidated financial statements are required, these must also give a true and fair view of the financial position and performance of the consolidated entity. Section 297 does not affect the obligation for a financial report to comply with accounting standards. Additional information must be included in the notes to the financial statements if the financial statements and notes prepared in accordance with the accounting standards would not give a true and fair view: s 295(3)(c).

The term "true and fair view" does not have a precise meaning. This has largely been left to the accounting profession. It is generally accepted that financial statements provide a true and fair view if they have been prepared in accordance with widely accepted contemporary accounting methods.

directors' reports

[15.105] Section 298(1) requires a company to prepare a directors' report for each financial year. The directors' report must include both general information about the company's operations and activities as required by s 299, as well as the specific information required by s 300. Listed companies must also meet the requirements of ss 299A and 300A.

general information

[15.110] Section 299(1) requires the directors' report to set out the following information for a financial year:

> a review of the company's operations and the results of those operations;
> details of any significant changes in the company's state of affairs;
> the company's principal activities and any significant changes in the nature of those activities;
> details of any post-balance date matter or circumstance that has significantly affected, or may significantly affect, the company's operations, results or state of affairs in future financial years;
> a reference to likely developments in the company's operations and expected results in future financial years; and

> if the company's operations are subject to any particular and significant environmental regulation, details of the company's performance in relation to environmental regulation.

The CLERP 9 amendments included a further requirement that the directors' report of a listed company or disclosing entity must contain an operating and financial review to enable members of the company to make an informed assessment of its operations, financial position, business strategies and future prospects: s 299A. An operating and financial review is seen as an integral part of good corporate governance and financial reporting because it provides users of the financial reports with the directors' analysis of the company's business.

The directors' report of a listed company or disclosing entity must contain an operating and financial review.

Best practice guidance to CFOs as to the content of an operating and financial review was published by Group of 100, the professional association of CFOs. This guide is linked to the Lipton-Herzberg Disclosure Pathway at **http://www.lipton-herzberg.com.au/secure/pathways_disclosure.htm**

specific information

[15.115] Section 300(1)–(9) requires the directors' report to set out a range of specific information for a financial year. Public companies, listed companies and registered schemes must include the additional specific information listed in s 300(10)–(13) and 301A. Table 15.2 highlights the specific information required.

table 15.2 specific information required

Dividends or distributions to members	300(1)(a) and (b)
Directors' names	300(1)(c)
Options over unissued shares	300(1)(d), (1)(e), (1)(f), (3), (5), (6) and (7)
Indemnities given and insurance premiums paid to officers or auditors	300(1)(g), (8) and (9)
Public companies — directors' qualifications, experience and special responsibilities — attendance at board meetings — attendance at committee meetings	300(10)
Listed companies — directors' relevant interests in shares etc — directors' rights or options over shares etc — directors' contracts to call for shares etc	300(11)
Listed registered schemes — directors' relevant interests in scheme interests — directors' rights or options over scheme interests — directors' contracts to call for scheme interests	300(12)
Registered schemes — fees paid to responsible entity — interests held by responsible entity — issued interests — withdrawals — value of assets — number of interests	300(13)
Australian listed companies — discussion of board policy for determining emoluments of directors and senior executives — discussion of relationship between such policy and company performance — details of emolument of directors and 5 highest paid officers	300A

continuous disclosure and disclosing entities

Corporations and other entities that come within the definition of a "disclosing entity" are subject to an enhanced disclosure scheme.

[15.120] Corporations and other entities that come within the definition of a "disclosing entity" are subject to an enhanced disclosure scheme. The basic aim of the scheme is to ensure that investors can make informed decisions about their investments in listed companies and other disclosing entities.

There are two main features of the enhanced disclosure scheme.

There are two main features of the enhanced disclosure scheme. There is a regime for ongoing or continuous disclosure of information that a reasonable person could be taken to expect would have a material effect on the price or value of a disclosing entity's securities. In addition, the enhanced disclosure scheme implements a system of periodic reporting under which disclosing entities are required to prepare and lodge half-year financial reports as well as end-of-year financial reports.

The implementation of the enhanced disclosure scheme relaxed the prospectus requirements for disclosing entities that satisfy certain criteria concerning their disclosure of information. The prospectus requirements are discussed above in Chapter 7.

what is a disclosing entity?

The enhanced disclosure scheme applies to disclosing entities.

[15.125] The enhanced disclosure scheme applies to disclosing entities. These include entities whose securities are listed on a financial market such as the ASX. A complex definition of "disclosing entity" is contained in Pt 1.2A, ss 111AA–111AX. The effect of these provisions is that the following are also regarded as disclosing entities:

> **entities that raise funds pursuant to a disclosure document lodged with ASIC under Ch 6D of the *Corporations Act*;**
> **entities that offer securities other than debentures as consideration for an acquisition of securities in a target company under an off-market takeover bid; and**
> **entities whose securities are issued under a compromise or scheme of arrangement.**

The securities of such entities are referred to as ED securities (short for "enhanced disclosure securities").

half-year financial report and directors' report

[15.130] Disclosing entities are required to prepare annual financial reports and directors' reports: s 292(1)(a). In addition, a disclosing entity must prepare half-year financial reports and half-year directors' reports: s 302. The half-year financial reports must be audited or reviewed. Copies of the half-year reports must be lodged with ASIC.

The half-year financial report consists of the half-year financial statements, notes to the financial statements and the directors' declaration about the statements and notes: s 303(1). As is the case for annual financial reports, a half-year financial report must comply with accounting standards and the financial statements must give a true and fair view: ss 304 and 305. The information that must be contained in the half-year directors' report is not as extensive as is required for the annual directors' report. Section 306 requires it to name the directors and provide a review of the entity's operations during the half-year and the results of those operations.

continuous disclosure

[15.135] A disclosing entity is subject to the continuous disclosure provisions in Ch 6CA of the *Corporations Act*: ss 674–678. The continuous disclosure framework is designed to ensure that the market is fully informed at all times and that all investors have equitable access to material information. These provisions impose different disclosure requirements depending on whether the disclosing entity is a listed or unlisted disclosing entity. This is determined with reference to whether its securities are listed on a prescribed financial market: ss 111AL and 111AM.

A disclosing entity is subject to the continuous disclosure provisions in Ch 6CA of the *Corporations Act*.

listed disclosing entities

[15.140] Section 674(1) requires a listed disclosing entity to comply with the listing rules of a listing market which require the entity to notify the market operator of information about specified events or matters as they arise for the purpose of the operator making that information available to participants in the market. In the Australian context, this generally refers to the listing rules of the ASX.

In the case of ASX-listed disclosing entities, s 674(2) requires compliance with the continuous disclosure obligations of ASX Listing Rule 3.1. This rule provides that a listed company must immediately notify the ASX of any information concerning the company of which it is or becomes aware which is not generally available and which a reasonable person would expect to have a material effect on the price or value of the company's securities.

In the case of ASX-listed disclosing entities, s 674(2) requires compliance with the continuous disclosure obligations of ASX Listing Rule 3.1.

Under Listing Rule 3.1B, companies may also be required to respond to media comment or market speculation when the ASX considers that these may create a false market in the company's securities.

Under Listing Rule 3.1A, there is no obligation to comply with Listing Rule 3.1 if all of the following are satisfied:

> **a reasonable person would not expect the information to be disclosed;**
> **the information is confidential and the ASX has not formed the view that the information has ceased to be confidential; or**
> **one or more of the following applies:**
  - **it would be a breach of a law to disclose the information;**
  - **the information is, or is part of, an incomplete proposal or negotiation;**
  - **the information comprises matters of supposition or is insufficiently definite to warrant disclosure;**
  - **the information is generated for the internal management purposes of the company; or**
  - **the information is a trade secret.**

The ASX has issued Guidance Note 8 to assist companies in complying with Listing Rule 3.1. Price-sensitive information should be released through the ASX before being disclosed to analysts. The ASX considers that companies should make immediate disclosure upon becoming aware that there will be a material change in revenue and profit for a financial period compared with the previous corresponding period, forecast projections in a prospectus or information previously provided to the market or consensus estimates made by analysts. The ASX recommends that companies place relevant information on their websites after disclosure to the ASX. ASIC and the ASX released guidance principles, *Better Disclosure for Investors* (August 2000), upon which Guidance Note 8 was based.

Both these documents are linked to Lipton-Herzberg Disclosure Pathway at **http://www.lipton-herzberg.com.au/secure/pathways_disclosure.htm**

Section 676 explains when information is generally available for the purposes of ss 674 and 675. Information is generally available if:

> **it consists of readily observable matter; or**
> **it has been made known in a manner that would or would be likely to bring it to the attention**

of persons who commonly invest in securities of a kind whose price or value might be affected by the information; and

- **since it was so made known, a reasonable period for it to be disseminated among such persons has elapsed; or**
- **it consists of deductions, conclusions or inferences made or drawn from the above information.**

Section 677 sets out when a reasonable person will be taken to expect information to have a material effect on the price or value of securities for purposes of ss 674 and 675. This occurs if the information would, or would be likely to, influence persons who commonly invest in securities in deciding whether or not to acquire or dispose of the securities in question.

A failure to comply with Listing Rule 3.1 is a criminal offence under s 674(2) to which the *Criminal Code* applies. Section 674(2) is also a civil penalty provision. The civil penalty provisions are discussed in Chapter 13.6 above. The CLERP 9 amendments extended civil liability for contraventions of the continuous disclosure regime by disclosing entities to any other persons involved in the contravention: ss 674(2A) and 675(2A). This enables ASIC to seek civil penalty orders against persons such as directors, executives and advisers who participated in and had actual knowledge of a contravention.

The CLERP 9 amendments also introduced an infringement notice mechanism which enables ASIC to issue a notice containing a financial penalty to a disclosing entity which ASIC believes has contravened the continuous disclosure provisions. An infringement notice is issued in cases involving less serious contraventions and prevents such cases being pursued in the courts. ASIC must first notify the entity of the nature of the case against it and the entity may give evidence and make submissions at a hearing. If, following the hearing, ASIC issues an infringement notice, the disclosing entity is required to pay the penalty of up to $100,000 and remedy the inadequate disclosure. The financial penalty specified in an infringement notice is significantly less than the maximum penalty which can be sought under the civil penalty provisions. Compliance with the infringement notice means that the entity is not subject to further civil or criminal proceedings in relation to the contravention. Where the entity fails to comply with the infringement notice, ASIC may bring civil proceedings.

CLERP 9 is linked to the Lipton-Herzberg Law Reform site at **http://www.lipton-herzberg.com.au/law_reform.htm** Latest developments regarding the implementation of the CLERP 9 proposals into the *Corporations Act* are also contained on the Lipton-Herzberg website.

unlisted and other disclosing entities

[15.145] Section 675(2) requires an unlisted disclosing entity that becomes aware of price-sensitive information that is not generally available and which is not required to be included in a supplementary or replacement disclosure document to lodge a document containing the information with ASIC. This section also applies to listed disclosing entities which are listed on markets which do not have a continuous disclosure listing rule corresponding to ASX Listing Rule 3.1. Failure to comply with this provision is an offence. This section is also a civil penalty provision and the *Criminal Code* applies to an offence under the section: s 678.

ASX Listing Rules and periodic disclosure

ASX listed companies must also comply with the requirements for periodic disclosure set out in Ch 4 of the Listing Rules.

[15.150] ASX listed companies must also comply with the requirements for periodic disclosure set out in Ch 4 of the Listing Rules. ASX Listing Rule 4.10 sets out requirements in relation to the annual reports of listed companies that are additional to the *Corporations Act* requirements. These requirements include:

> a statement of all material differences between the information in the entity's half-yearly/preliminary final report (Appendix 4B) and the information in the accounts in its annual report including the amounts and reasons for the differences;
> whether the company had an audit committee (if it did not, it must explain);
> a statement of the main corporate governance practices that the entity had in place (these are discussed in Chapter 13.1 above);
> the names of substantial shareholders and the number of securities in which each has an interest;
> the number of holders of each class of shares and the voting rights attaching to each class; and
> the names of the 20 largest holders of each class of shares and the number and percentage of capital held by each of them.

Listed companies are regarded as listed disclosing entities under s 111AL. As a result, they are required to prepare and lodge half-year financial reports with ASIC. In addition, ASX Listing Rule 4.1 requires listed companies to lodge half-year financial reports containing prescribed information with the ASX no later than 75 days after the end of a half-year period. Listed mining companies are required to lodge quarterly reports with the ASX.

As discussed in Chapter 19 below, compliance with the Listing Rules may be enforced by the courts.

The ASX Listing Rules may be accessed from the ASX website which is linked to the Lipton-Herzberg Corporate Law Websites at **http://www.lipton-herzberg.com.au/corp-law-websites.html#Australian_Stock_Exchange**

annual financial reporting to members

duty to report to members

[15.155] Section 314 requires a company, registered scheme or disclosing entity to report to members by sending them copies of:

Section 314 requires a company to report to members.

> the annual financial report;
> the annual directors' report; and
> the auditor's report on the financial report.

As an alternative to the above reports, members may be sent a concise report: s 314(1)(b). The concise report is intended to provide members with a summary of the company's financial position and prospects in a form that is more comprehensible to the average investor.

Under s 314(2), a concise report consists of a concise annual financial report drawn up in accordance with accounting standards and the full annual directors' report. A concise report must also include the auditor's statement that the financial report has been audited and the auditor's opinion on whether the concise financial report complies with relevant accounting standards. It must also include a copy of any qualification and emphasis of matter section of the auditor's report on the financial report.

Members who receive concise reports may request that they be sent, free of charge, the full financial report, directors' report and auditor's report: s 316(1)(b). The concise report must indicate that members have this right: s 314(2)(e). Full or concise reports need not be sent if members so request: s 316(1)(a). Members' 316(1) requests may be standing requests or for a particular financial year: s 316(2).

Directors of a public company that is required to hold an AGM must lay the s 314 reports before its AGM: s 317. Public companies with only one member are not required to hold an AGM: s 250N. Section 318, which applies to borrowers in relation to debentures, requires copies of the reports to be sent to the trustee for debenture-holders before the deadline.

deadline for reporting to members

There are different deadlines for sending members the annual financial reports depending upon the type of company or other entity.

[15.160] There are different deadlines for sending members the annual financial reports depending upon the type of company or other entity. The following table highlights the various deadlines.

table 15.3 deadlines for sending members annual financial reports

Type of entity	Deadlines	Section
Public companies and disclosing entities that are not registered schemes	The earlier of: — 21 days before the next AGM after the end of the financial year; or — 4 months after the end of the financial year.	315(1)
Small proprietary companies directed to report by shareholders under s 293	The later of: — 2 months after the date of the direction; or — 4 months after the end of the financial year.	315(2)
Registered schemes	3 months after the end of the financial year.	315(3)
Large proprietary companies	4 months after the end of the financial year	315(4)

ASIC lodgment of reports

Companies must lodge reports with ASIC.

[15.165] Companies, registered schemes or disclosing entities that are required to prepare or obtain reports under s 314 must lodge those reports with ASIC: s 319(1). This obligation also extends to concise reports.

Small proprietary companies that prepare reports in response to a direction from their shareholders or ASIC under ss 293 or 294 are not required to lodge those reports: s 319(2). Certain large proprietary companies that were once classified as exempt proprietary companies are also not required to lodge their reports with ASIC: s 319(4).

Companies must lodge their reports with ASIC within four months after the end of the financial year: s 319(3)(b). Disclosing entities and registered schemes must lodge their reports with ASIC within three months after the end of the financial year: s 319(3)(a).

Half-year reports of disclosing entities must be lodged with ASIC within 75 days after the end of the half-year: s 320.

updating ASIC database

[15.170] Amendments made in 2002 (CLERP 7 amendments) reduced the regulatory burdens on business by simplifying the document lodgment and compliance procedures. The CLERP 7 amendments abolished the previous requirement for companies to prepare and lodge an annual return with ASIC and replaced it with an Annual Statement provided by ASIC on the review date of each company. The Annual Statement includes an Extract of Particulars and review fee invoice.

The Extract of Particulars includes details recorded on ASIC's database such as:

> **names and addresses of the company's officers;**
> **details of shares and options; and**
> **addresses of registered office and principal place of business.**

The review date is generally the anniversary of registration of the company: s 345A. A company may apply to ASIC to change its review date: s 345B. If the information in the Extract of Particulars is correct, the company is required to pay the annual review fee ($200) within two months of the review date. It does not need to lodge further documents. This change recognised that the vast majority of annual returns formerly lodged with ASIC repeated the information already on the ASIC database and therefore imposed unnecessary compliance and administrative burdens on companies and ASIC.

changes to company details

[15.175] Where changes have occurred that are not reflected in the Extract of Particulars, the company or its directors must notify ASIC of changes to the information within 28 days after the issue date of the Annual Statement: s 346C. Changes to company details must be notified to ASIC on Form 484 when they occur. ASIC forms may be accessed from the ASIC website which is linked to the Lipton-Herzberg Registration Procedure Pathway at **http://www.lipton-herzberg.com.au/secure/pathways-registration-procedure.html**

return of particulars

[15.180] ASIC may issue a Return of Particulars in certain circumstances: s 348A. These include where the review fee has not been paid on time, ASIC suspects the information on its database is incorrect, or documents have not been lodged for more than a year.

solvency resolution

[15.185] A company's directors must pass a solvency resolution within two months of the review date unless the company lodged its financial report and directors' report with ASIC in the 12 months before the review date: s 347A. Where directors pass a solvency resolution, notification to ASIC is not required. Where a negative solvency resolution is passed or no solvency resolution is passed, ASIC must be notified by Form 485: s 347B.

A company's directors must pass a solvency resolution.

Payment of the review fee is taken to mean that the company has represented to ASIC that it is solvent as at the end of the two-month period after its review date: s 347C.

notification of proprietary company changes

[15.190] Proprietary companies must notify ASIC within 28 days of changes to:

> **issued shares including total number, classes of shares and amounts paid and unpaid (s 178C);**
> **the particulars in the register of members regarding the top 20 members including name and address, increase or decrease in the number of shares held and any new members (ss 178A and 178B); and**
> **their ultimate holding company: ss 349A–349D.**

ASIC exemptions and modifications

[15.195] Sections 340 and 341 give ASIC the power to make specific exemption orders and class orders relieving a specific company or class of companies from compliance with the financial records and financial reporting requirements of Pts 2M.2, 2M.3 and 2M.4 of the *Corporations Act*. Such orders can be made on the application of the directors, the company or its auditor. Before making an order, s 342(1) specifies that ASIC must be satisfied that compliance with the relevant provisions would:

> **make the financial report or other reports misleading;**
> **be inappropriate in the circumstances; or**
> **impose unreasonable burdens.**

consequences of contravention

[15.200] Directors contravene s 344(1) if they fail to take reasonable steps to comply with or secure compliance with the financial records and financial reporting provisions of Pts 2M.2 and 2M.3 of the *Corporations Act*. Section 344(1) is a designated civil penalty provision and the provisions of Pt 9.4B of the *Corporations Act* apply and provide for civil penalty consequences of breaching the section. Contravention of s 344(1) is a criminal offence if the contravention is dishonest: s 344(2). The consequences of contravening the civil penalty provisions are discussed in Chapter 13.6 above.

bibliography ...

Blanchard, J "CLERP Information Reforms: Tinkering at the Edges" (2000) 4 Flinders J of Law Reform 157.

Blanchard, J "Corporate Social Reporting: A Case for Mandatory Disclosure Rules" (1998) 23 Alt LJ 172.

Blanchard, J "Corporate Accountability and Information" (1997) 7 Aust Jnl of Corp Law 326.

Boros, E "Disclosure of Information on Company Websites" (1999) 17 C & SLJ 522.

Boros, E "Corporations Online" (2001) 19 C & SLJ 492.

Cassidy, A & Chapple, L "Australia's Corporate Disclosure Regime: Lessons from the US Model" (2003) 15 Aust Jnl of Corp Law 81.

Dean, G & Clarke, F "Creative Accounting, Compliance and Financial Commonsense" (1997) 7 Aust Jnl of Corp Law 366.

George, G "Accounting, Auditing and Auditors—What is to be Done?" (2002) 14 Aust Jnl of Corp Law 51.

Golden, G & Kalfus, N "The continuous evolution of Australia's continuous disclosure laws" (2004) 22 C & SLJ 385.

Goodwin, J "Financial Reporting and Auditing Obligations of Proprietary Companies with Foreign Company Shareholders" (1998) 16 C & SLJ 451.

Koeck, W "Continuous Disclosure" (1995) 13 C & SLJ 485.

Little, P "The Policy Underlying Financial Disclosure by Corporations and its Effect Upon Legal Liability" (1991) 1 Aust Jnl of Corp Law 87.

McGregor-Lowndes, G "Corporate Disclosure, the Internet and the Australian Securities Commission" (1996) 14 C & SLJ 219.

Purcell, "The Contrasting Approach of Law and Accounting to the Defining of Solvency and Associated Directors' Declarations" (2002) 10 Insolv LJ 192.

Quinn, M "The Unchangeables: Director and Executive Remuneration Disclosure in Australia" (1999) 10 Aust Jnl of Corp Law 89.

Topalov, A "Environmental Reporting by Australian Corporations" (1999) 8 Griffith LR 411.

revision questions on the material in this chapter ...

> Please see eQuiz at **http://www.thomson.com.au/academic** for multiple choice questions and answers.

> For further corporations law links and material please refer to the Lipton-Herzberg website at **http://www.lipton-herzberg.com.au**

chapter sixteen

auditors

key points …

- The function of an auditor is to carry out an audit of a financial report which expresses an opinion as to whether it was prepared in accordance with appropriate financial reporting standards.
- Public companies and large proprietary companies are generally required to appoint an auditor. This is required to be done by the members at an annual general meeting.
- The CLERP 9 amendments significantly strengthened the requirements for auditor independence.
- An auditor's duties to a company arise under the contract of appointment and various provisions of the *Corporations Act*. The main duties of an auditor include duties to:
  - detect and report defects and irregularities;
  - be independent; and
  - use reasonable care and skill.
- An auditor may be liable in negligence to users of the audited accounts including shareholders and creditors. The extent of this liability has been restricted to certain situations where there is a relationship of proximity between the auditor and third party.

function of auditors

The function of an auditor is to carry out an audit and present a reliable, independent report on the accounts and financial position of a company.

An audit provides users of the financial reports with an assurance as to the reliability of the information provided.

[16.05] The function of an auditor is to carry out an audit and present a reliable, independent report on the accounts and financial position of a company. An auditor's report contains a professional opinion based on the audit of the company's financial reports.

An audit enhances the credibility of a company's financial reports prepared by its directors. An audit or review provides users of the financial reports with an assurance as to the reliability of the information provided. An audit is the main external check on the integrity of the financial statements. In a broad sense, this independent verification of the financial statements enhances the efficiency of the capital markets by providing better quality information and reducing information risk. The report "Independence of Australian Company Auditors" (October 2001) (The Ramsay Report) stated that "audited financial statements are an important part of the financial information that is available to the capital markets and an important part of effective corporate governance".

The *Corporations Act* has several provisions aimed at ensuring that the functions of an auditor are properly carried out. Section 310(a) gives the auditor a right of access at all reasonable times to the company's books. An auditor may require any officer to give the auditor information, explanations or other assistance for the purpose of the audit or review: s 310(b). An auditor who audits or reviews a financial report that includes consolidated financial statements has similar rights of access and assistance in relation to the books and officers of any controlled entity: ss 323A and 323B.

when must an auditor be appointed?

statutory requirements

[16.10] Directors of public companies are required to appoint an auditor within one month after the company is incorporated unless the members have appointed one at a general meeting: s 327A(1).

Under s 327A(2), the initial auditor holds office until the company's first AGM. A public company must appoint an auditor at its first AGM: s 327B(1)(a). A public company must also appoint an auditor to fill any vacancy in the office of auditor at each subsequent AGM: s 327B(1)(b). Auditors appointed at an AGM hold office until death, removal or resignation: s 327B(2).

The directors of a proprietary company may appoint an auditor if one has not been appointed by the company in general meeting: s 325. Small proprietary companies are generally not required to appoint an auditor unless either ASIC or shareholders holding at least 5 per cent of the votes direct the company to prepare an audited financial report: ss 293(3)(c) and 294.

audit relief for large proprietary companies

[16.15] ASIC may make specific exemption orders or class orders in respect of a specific company or specified class of companies relieving them of the need to comply with certain financial reports and audit requirements contained in Chapter 2M. ASIC Policy Statement 115: *Audit Relief for Proprietary Companies Chapter 2M and s 342(1) and (2)* sets out the circumstances where ASIC will give class order relief and specific company relief to large proprietary companies from the requirement to appoint an auditor and to lodge audited financial statements.

who may be an auditor?

registration requirements

[16.20] Prior to the CLERP 9 amendments, only an individual or a partnership could be an auditor. Now, a company auditor may be an individual, a partnership firm or a company: s 324AA. The *Corporations Act* tries to ensure that auditors are competent by requiring them to meet certain education and practical experience requirements before they can be registered as company auditors. Persons cannot act as auditors unless they are registered company auditors: s 324BA. Equivalent registration requirements in the cases of audit firms and companies are set out in ss 324BB and 324BC. An application to ASIC must be made for registration under s 1279. The applicant, if suitably qualified, attains registration unless ASIC is satisfied that the applicant is not a fit and proper person to be registered as an auditor.

A company auditor may be an individual, a partnership firm or a company.

Persons cannot act as auditors unless they are registered company auditors.

The education requirements for a person seeking registration as a company auditor are set out in s 1280(2A) and (2B). The applicant is required to:

> **hold a degree, diploma or certificate from a prescribed university or another prescribed institution in Australia and have passed examinations in subjects comprising a course of study in accountancy (including auditing) of not less than three years' duration and in commercial law (including company law) of not less than two years' duration; and**
> **have satisfactorily completed a specialist, prescribed course in auditing; or**
> **have in the opinion of ASIC, other equivalent qualifications and experience.**

The practical experience requirements may be met where ASIC is satisfied that the applicant has satisfied all the components of an auditing competency standard approved under s 1280A or has had prescribed practical experience. Applications for approval of auditing competency standards are expected to be made by accounting professional bodies but other organisations or firms may also seek approval.

ASIC must also be satisfied that the applicant is capable of performing the duties of an auditor and is otherwise a fit and proper person to be registered as an auditor.

authorised audit companies

[16.25] The CLERP 9 amendments introduced a procedure for the registration of authorised audit companies. This was done in recognition of concerns expressed by the auditing profession relating to professional liability and also to give accounting firms greater scope in the ways they structure their businesses.

A company may apply to ASIC for registration as an authorised audit company: s 1299A. A company is eligible for registration as an authorised audit company if the following requirements contained in s 1299B are met:

> **each of the directors is a registered company auditor not disqualified from managing a corporation;**
> **each share is held and beneficially owned by an individual or legal personal representative of an individual;**
> **registered company auditors must hold a majority of voting shares;**
> **ASIC is satisfied that the company has adequate and appropriate professional indemnity insurance to meet claims in relation to its audit activities; and**
> **the company is not under external administration.**

lodgment of annual statement

[16.30] Registered company auditors must lodge an annual statement with ASIC setting out prescribed information: s 1287A. The required information includes the auditor's personal particulars and details of the nature and complexity of major audit work undertaken by the auditor.

cancellation and suspension of registration

[16.35] The cancellation and suspension of registration of auditors and liquidators is governed by ss 1290–1298. Under these provisions, the Companies Auditors and Liquidators Disciplinary Board (CALDB), on an application by ASIC, has the power to hold hearings and decide whether to cancel or suspend the registration of an auditor.

CALDB, on an application by ASIC, has the power to hold hearings and decide whether to cancel or suspend the registration of an auditor.

Section 1292(1) sets out the grounds for cancellation or suspension of the registration of auditors. These include failing to lodge an annual statement under s 1287A, failing to properly carry out the duties of auditor or ceasing to have the necessary practical experience where audit work had not been carried out in the previous five years.

CALDB also has the power to impose penalties in addition to or as an alternative to cancellation or suspension of registration: s 1292(9). These additional penalties include:

> **admonishment or reprimand; and**
> **requiring the auditor to give an undertaking to engage in, or refrain from engaging in, specified conduct.**

disqualification

[16.40] Persons who are disqualified from managing corporations under Pt 2D.6 of the *Corporations Act* cannot obtain registration as an auditor: s 1280(3). Part 2D.6 of the *Corporations Act* is discussed in Chapter 12 above. Further, under s 1287, registered auditors must provide ASIC with particulars of the circumstances by reason of which they were disqualified from managing corporations under Pt 2D.6.

auditor independence

[16.45] Auditor independence became a major corporate governance issue in the wake of several recent corporate collapses in Australia and the US. The report, "Independence of Australian Company Auditors" (October 2001) (The Ramsay Report), considered that the independence requirements of auditors had not kept pace with developments such as the growth of the large international accounting firms and the growth of non-audit services provided by them. This report made several recommendations concerned with strengthening auditor independence, including a considerable expansion of the circumstances which were indicative of a lack of independence. These recommendations formed the basis of the CLERP 9 amendments. The Ramsay Report is linked to the Lipton-Herzberg website at **http://www.lipton-herzberg.com.au/law_reform.htm**

The Explanatory Memorandum accompanying the CLERP 9 amendments commented on the importance of auditor independence:

< 4.8 Audited financial statements are an important part of the financial information that is available to the capital markets and an essential element of effective corporate governance. Auditor independence is fundamental to the credibility and reliability of auditors' reports and in turn independent audits perform an important function in terms of capital market efficiency. There has been widespread concern about the efficacy of the audit function, including the independence of auditors as a result of major corporate collapses in Australia and overseas, including HIH.

4.9 The sound operation of Australia's financial markets is dependent upon parties such as auditors providing information or services to investors free from any bias, undue influence or conflict of interest. Auditor independence is concerned with the auditor's capacity, including the perception of that capacity, to exercise objective and impartial judgement in relation to the conduct of an audit.

Auditor independence is fundamental to the credibility and reliability of auditors' reports and in turn independent audits perform an important function in terms of capital market efficiency.

4.12 Over recent years there have been a number of corporate collapses which have called into question the degree of independence of auditors. These cases have demonstrated that while a company's actual financial position may have been poor, the financial statements and audit report did not reflect the true condition of the company. This has impaired the ability of shareholders and the market more generally to adequately assess the financial health of their investment. The proposals to promote independence will improve the quality and reliability of information provided to the market. >

The CLERP 9 amendments and accompanying Explanatory Memorandum are linked to the Lipton-Herzberg website at **http://www.lipton-herzberg.com.au/clerp9.htm**

The main elements of the auditor independence reforms introduced by the CLERP 9 amendments are:

- a general auditor independence requirement;
- a requirement that auditors make an annual declaration that the independence requirements of the *Corporations Act* and professional conduct codes have been complied with;
- restrictions on specific employment and financial relationships between auditors and their clients;
- the imposition of mandatory waiting periods before auditors may join an audit client as a director or senior manager;
- compulsory rotation of auditors, generally after five years;
- the assumption of responsibility by the Financial Reporting Council to oversee the auditor independence requirements; and

> **a requirement for listed companies to disclose in their directors' report the fees paid to the auditor for non-audit services and the nature of such services. Directors must also state whether they are satisfied that the provision of such services does not compromise auditor independence.**

general independence requirement

Section 324CA(1) states the general rule requiring auditor independence.

[16.50] Section 324CA(1) states the general rule requiring auditor independence. The general requirement also applies to members of an audit firm and directors of audit companies: ss 324CB and 324CC. The purpose behind these provisions is to encourage a culture of compliance by the whole audit firm or company and encourage the establishment and maintenance of adequate internal control systems so as to prevent a breach of the independence requirements.

An individual auditor, an audit firm or an audit company are prohibited from engaging in audit activity if a conflict of interest situation exists in relation to the audited body and the auditor is aware that the conflict of interest situation.

An individual auditor, an audit firm or an audit company are prohibited from engaging in audit activity in relation to an audited body at a particular time, if at that time, a conflict of interest situation exists in relation to the audited body and the auditor is aware that the conflict of interest situation. This provision is also contravened where the auditor becomes aware that a conflict of interest situation exists and does not take all reasonable steps to ensure that the conflict of interests ceases as soon as possible.

A "conflict of interest situation" is taken to exist in relation to an audited body if circumstances exist that:

> **the auditor, or a professional member of the audit team, is not capable of exercising objective and impartial judgment in relation to the conduct of the audit of the audited body; or**

> **a reasonable person, with full knowledge of all relevant facts and circumstances, would conclude that the auditor, or a professional member of the audit team, is not capable of exercising objective and impartial judgment in relation to the conduct of the audit of the audited body: s 324CD(1).**

In determining whether a conflict of interest situation exists, regard must be had to circumstances arising from any relationship between the auditor and audited entity. This provision extends to include an individual auditor, audit firm or any current or former member of the firm or audit company or any current or former director or person currently or formerly involved in management of the audit company: s 324CD(2).

A contravention also occurs where a conflict of interest situation exists even though an individual auditor, audit firm or audit company was not aware of the existence of the conflict of interest situation but they would have been aware had a quality control system been in place which was reasonably capable of making them aware of the existence of the conflict of interest: s 324CA(2), (4) and (5).

The obligations imposed by s 324CA are in addition to any other obligations imposed by other provisions of the *Corporations Act* or code of professional conduct: s 324CA(6).

specific independence requirements

[16.55] There are further detailed specific requirements for auditor independence applicable to individual auditors (s 324CE), audit firms (s 324CF) and audit companies (s 324CG). Each of these sections includes a table which identifies the specific auditor independence requirements applicable to each of the persons listed in the table. These tables refer to a list of relevant relationships between an auditor and the audited body set out in s 324CH(1). The impermissible relationships are determined by reference to these various tables.

The effect of this complex legislative scheme is to restrict specific employment and financial relationships between an auditor and audit client.

Examples where the auditor independence requirements are contravened include where:

- **an individual auditor is an officer or audit-critical employee of the audited body, being in a position to affect the efficacy or the conduct of the audit;**
- **a service company or trust acting on behalf of an individual auditor holds an investment in an audited company; or**
- **a person who is a non-audit services provider has significant investments in the audited body.**

The auditor independence restrictions extend to a former owner of the individual auditor's business or former professional employee of an auditor. Similar legislative frameworks apply to audit firms and audit companies whereby the relevant impermissible relationships set out in the table in s 324CH(1) are incorporated as applicable into ss 324CF and 324CG, respectively. These relationships fall into the two broad categories of employment (items 1 to 9) and financial (items 10 to 19) relationships. The restrictions on employment relationships do not apply to small proprietary companies.

Items 10 to 14 prevent an auditor from holding, or otherwise having an interest in, an investment in the audited body. Items 15 to 19 prevent an auditor being a significant debtor of the audited body or a related or controlled entity unless the debt is owed under a housing loan or a loan made in the ordinary course of business: s 324CH(5) and (6). Also prohibited are loans made to and from audited bodies and guarantees involving the auditor and audited body. An ordinary course of business exclusion also operates in relation to loans and guarantees: s 324CH(7) and (8).

The effect of this complex legislative scheme is to restrict specific employment and financial relationships between an auditor and audit client.

prohibition on retiring partners becoming officers

[16.60] Section 324CI implements a recommendation of the HIH Royal Commission which found that former partners of HIH's auditor became directors of the company soon after leaving the audit firm. This was seen as compromising the independence of the auditor engaged in the audit of a company of which former partners were directors or senior officers and could be seen as exerting some influence over members of the audit team.

A person who was a partner of an audit firm or director of an audit company which was engaged in an audit of an audited body is prohibited from becoming an officer of the audited body for a period of two years after ceasing to be a partner or director if that person was a professional member of the audit team: s 324CI. A similar two-year waiting period restriction also applies to any person who was a professional employee of an audit company engaged in an audit of an audited body if that person was a lead auditor or review auditor for the audit: s 324CJ.

Where a person becomes an officer of a company and that person was a partner in an audit firm or director of an audit company at the time that it was the auditor of the company, details must be disclosed in the directors' report: s 300(1)(ca).

A person who was a partner of an audit firm or director of an audit company which was engaged in an audit of an audited body is prohibited from becoming an officer of the audited body for a period of two years after ceasing to be a partner or director if that person was a professional member of the audit team.

prohibition on multiple partners becoming directors

[16.65] Section 324CK prohibits any more than one former partner of an audit firm or director of an audit company being an officer of an audited body or related entity. This provision adopts a recommendation of the HIH Royal Commission which found that several former audit partners had become officers of HIH and this resulted in a perception that the auditor was not independent of HIH. This provision does not apply where the audited body is a small proprietary company.

auditor independence declaration

An auditor must sign and give to the directors of the audited entity a written declaration that the auditor and each professional member of the audit team has complied with the auditor independence requirements of the *Corporations Act* and any applicable codes of professional conduct.

[16.70] An auditor must sign and give to the directors of the audited entity a written declaration that the auditor and each professional member of the audit team has complied with the auditor independence requirements of the *Corporations Act* and any applicable codes of professional conduct: s 307C(1). This declaration must be signed and given to the directors together with the audit report: s 307C(3). Where the auditor is a firm or company, the lead auditor must sign and give the auditor's independence declaration: s 307C(2). A copy of the declaration made under s 307C must be included in the annual directors' report and half-year report: ss 298(1)(c) and 306(2).

rotation requirements

Where a person has played a significant role in the audit of a listed company for a period of five successive financial years, that person cannot play a significant role in the audit of that company for at least another two successive financial years.

[16.75] The Ramsay Report recommended that auditors of listed companies should be required to rotate. This recommendation has been implemented in ss 324DA–324DD. Where a person has played a significant role in the audit of a listed company as defined in s 9 for a period of five successive financial years, that person cannot play a significant role in the audit of that company for at least another two successive financial years: s 324DA(1). A person may not play a significant role as auditor for more than five out of any seven successive financial years: s 324DA(2). This prevents an auditor circumventing the prohibition by standing down after four years and resuming the role the following year. It also recognises that independence may be compromised where an audit is not carried out by the same auditor over five successive years, but where the same auditor is involved over a long period of time with occasional breaks.

The rotation requirements also apply to audit firms and audit companies: ss 324DC and 324DD. In both cases, the rotation obligation is placed on the lead and review auditors as defined in s 324AF. Where an individual plays a significant role in an audit of a listed company in contravention of the rotation requirements, the audit firm contravenes the legislation if another member of the firm becomes aware that the individual is ineligible to play a significant role in the audit of the listed company and the firm fails to take the necessary steps as soon as possible, either to resign as auditor or ensure the individual ceases to act as lead or review auditor: s 324DC(1). Where an audit firm contravenes this section, each member of the firm commits a strict liability offence: s 324DC(2) and (3).

A member of an audit firm has defences where the member did not know of the circumstances which constituted the contravention by the firm or took all reasonable steps to correct the contravention as soon as possible after becoming aware of the circumstances: s 324DC(4). This approach to liability of members of a firm is consistent with the liability imposed in other cases of contravention of the auditor independence obligations. Responsibility is imposed on all members of the firm in order to encourage a culture of compliance with the legislation. The individual auditor who breaches the rotation requirements also commits an offence under s 324DB. Where the auditor is an audit company, contraventions of the rotation requirements are treated in much the same way as in the case of an audit firm except that the audit company also commits an offence: s 324DD.

disclosure of non-audit services

[16.80] The HIH Royal Commission recommended that boards of listed companies should be required to state all non-audit services provided by the audit firm and the fees applicable to those services. This recommendation was implemented by s 300(11B) which requires disclosure of the following information in the annual directors' report:

> details of the amount paid to the auditor for non-audit services during the year;
> a statement whether the directors are satisfied that the provision of non-audit services by the auditor is compatible with the general standard of independence for auditors imposed by the legislation; and
> a statement of the directors' reasons for being satisfied that the provision of the non-audit services by the auditor did not compromise the auditor independence requirements of the legislation.

The required statements must be made in accordance with advice provided by the company's audit committee or by resolution of the board of directors if there is no audit committee. Companies included in the ASX All Ordinaries Index must make the required statements in accordance with the advice provided by their audit committees: s 300(11D).

ASIC's power to modify rotation requirements

[16.85] ASIC has power to modify the operation of the auditor rotation requirements within the terms of s 342A. The conferring of this power introduces some flexibility into the rotation requirements recognising that these may sometimes impose an unreasonable burden on auditors and listed companies. This could arise in the circumstances stated in s 342A(7) where the listed company engages in activities which require specialist knowledge to properly carry out the audit or there are few available auditors to provide satisfactory audit services for the listed company.

ASIC has power to modify the operation of the auditor rotation requirements.

Where an auditor acts in reliance on an ASIC declaration under s 342A, the company must receive written notice of the declaration: s 342B. The annual directors' report must include details of the declaration: s 300(11A).

auditing standards

[16.90] Auditing standards are given legislative backing as a result of the CLERP 9 amendments. An audit or an audit review must be conducted in accordance with auditing standards and an auditor's report must include any statement or disclosures required by the auditing standards: ss 307A, 308A and 309A.

An audit or an audit review must be conducted in accordance with auditing standards and an auditor's report must include any statement or disclosures required by the auditing standards.

The CLERP 9 amendments also reconstituted the Auditing and Assurance Standards Board (AUASB) which was formerly a board of the Australian Accounting Research Foundation (AARF). Section 227A(1) of the *ASIC Act* establishes the AUASB and s 227B gives it the power to make auditing standards under s 336 of the *Corporations Act*. Transitional provisions ensure that specified auditing standards made by the pre-CLERP 9 AUASB have interim legal backing until July 2006.

The CLERP 9 amendments also expanded the functions of the Financial Reporting Council (FRC) to monitor the reconstituted AUASB. This is similar to the FRC's oversight of the AASB.

appointment of auditors

[16.95] As a general rule, the auditor is appointed by the members at an AGM. In the case of a newly-formed public company, the first auditor must be appointed by the directors within one month after incorporation of a company: s 327A(1). The duration of the first appointment is, however, only until the first AGM of the company: s 327A(2). At the first AGM, an auditor is appointed by the members and any vacancy in the office of auditor is to be filled at subsequent AGMs: s 327B.

An auditor holds office until death, removal, resignation or otherwise ceasing to be an auditor:

s 327B(2). An individual auditor, an audit firm or an audit company ceases to be an auditor of a company if they inform ASIC of a conflict of interest situation in relation to the company: s 327B(2A), (2B) and (2C). An auditor also ceases to hold office after a company goes into liquidation: s 330.

Where a vacancy occurs in the office of auditor, other than a vacancy caused by the removal of the auditor, the directors must fill the vacancy within one month: s 327C(1). In such cases, the auditor holds office until the next AGM (s 327C(2)) and must then be appointed by the general meeting.

If a company does not appoint an auditor when required by the *Corporations Act*, an application may be made by a member to ASIC for the appointment of an auditor: s 327E. The auditor so appointed also holds office until the next AGM: s 327E(6).

A person, audit firm or audit company may only be appointed to act as auditor of a company if they have consented in writing before the appointment: s 328A. Appointment without such consent is of no effect and constitutes an offence by the company and any officer in default: s 328A(4). A company is not entitled to appoint a person or firm as auditor at its AGM unless prior notice of nomination is given to the company by a member: s 328B(1).

removal and resignation

[16.100] The provisions restricting the removal of an auditor have the effect of strengthening the auditor's independence. Directors cannot remove an auditor who qualifies the financial statements. Auditors can only be removed by the shareholders subject to the additional requirements that special notice must be given and the auditor must be given the opportunity to explain the circumstances.

An auditor may be removed from office only by resolution of the company at a general meeting.

An auditor may be removed from office only by resolution of the company at a general meeting. At least 21 days' notice must be given to members of a meeting at which a resolution will be moved to remove an auditor: s 249H(4). Where the resolution is proposed by members, notice of intention to move the removal resolution must be given to the company at least two months before the meeting is to be held: s 329(1A). However, if the company calls a meeting after the notice of intention is given, the meeting may pass the resolution even though the meeting is held less than two months after the notice of intention is given.

When a company receives notice of a resolution to remove an auditor, it must send a copy of the notice to the auditor and lodge a copy with ASIC: s 329(2). The auditor is then given the opportunity to make representations in writing and may request that copies of the representations be sent by the company to all members entitled to attend the meeting: s 329(3). The company must send a copy of the representations to members in accordance with the auditor's request and the representations may be read out at the meeting: s 329(4). An auditor has a right to be heard at general meetings: s 249V.

Where an auditor is removed from office at a general meeting, the company may appoint another auditor at that meeting by a resolution passed by at least a three-quarters majority: s 327(10). If such a resolution is not passed or a notice of nomination has not been sent to the auditor under s 328, the auditor may be appointed at an adjourned meeting by ordinary resolution.

Auditors who wish to resign must apply to ASIC for consent to resign, stating their reasons.

Auditors who wish to resign must apply to ASIC for consent to resign, stating their reasons. The company must be notified in writing of the application and if ASIC gives its consent, the auditor may resign after giving written notice to the company: s 329(6). The resignation of an auditor of a proprietary company does not require ASIC's consent: s 329(9).

Protection is afforded by s 329(7) to an auditor who intends to resign. This section provides that statements made by an auditor in relation to her or his application to ASIC for consent to resign are not admissible in evidence in any proceedings, nor may they be made the ground of any action against the auditor.

Where an auditor resigns or is removed, notice of the resignation or removal must be lodged with ASIC within 14 days and a copy of the notice must also be sent to the trustee for the holders of debentures if one has been appointed: s 329(11).

duties to the company

[16.105] By accepting an appointment, an auditor enters into a contractual relationship with the company. There are express or implied terms in such contracts that the auditor will:

By accepting an appointment, an auditor enters into a contractual relationship with the company.

> **carry out an audit;**
> **report to members an opinion, based on the audit, whether the financial statements are properly drawn up in accordance with the *Corporations Act*—including their compliance with accounting standards and whether they present a true and fair view;**
> **be independent of the company; and**
> **exercise a reasonable degree of care and skill.**

In addition, the *Corporations Act* imposes specific statutory duties.

statutory duties of auditors

reporting to members

[16.110] Auditors have a statutory duty to report to members. An auditor who audits the annual financial report must report to members whether their opinion that the annual financial report is in accordance with the *Corporations Act*, including ss 296 and 297—the provisions dealing with compliance with accounting standards and true and fair view: s 308(1).

Auditors have a statutory duty to report to members.

An auditor of a disclosing entity must carry out either an audit or review of the disclosing entity's half-year financial reports: s 302(b). If it is audited, the auditor must report to members whether the auditor is of the opinion that the report is in accordance with the *Corporations Act*, including ss 304 and 305—the half-year provisions dealing with compliance with accounting standards and true and fair view: s 309(1).

An auditor who reviews the financial report for a half-year must report to members on whether the auditor becomes aware of any matter in the course of the review that makes the auditor believe that the financial report does not comply with the half-year financial reporting requirements of the *Corporations Act*: s 309(4).

Companies, registered schemes and disclosing entities must send the auditor's report to members together with the annual financial report and directors' report for the year: s 314(1). Alternatively, members may be sent a concise financial report. A concise financial report includes a statement by the auditor that the financial report has been audited and the auditor's opinion of whether the concise financial report complies with the accounting standards: s 314(2)(c). The concise financial report must also include a copy of any qualification in the auditor's report: s 314(2)(e).

Auditors of listed companies, or their representatives, must attend the company's AGM at which the auditor's report is to be considered.

auditors and AGMs

[16.115] As a result of the CLERP 9 amendments, auditors of listed companies, or their representatives, must attend the company's AGM at which the auditor's report is to be considered: s 250RA(1) and (2). Prior to these amendments, it was not compulsory for the auditor of a listed company to attend the AGM.

Auditors of non-listed companies are entitled to attend any general meeting and be heard at the meeting on any business that concerns the auditor in their capacity as auditor, however, their attendance is not compulsory: s 249V. If the auditor or representative attends a company's AGM, the chair must allow a reasonable opportunity for the members as a whole to ask questions relevant to the conduct of the audit and the preparation and content of the auditor's report: s 250T(1)(a).

If the auditor or representative attends a company's AGM, the chair must allow a reasonable opportunity for the members as a whole to ask questions relevant to the conduct of the audit and the preparation and content of the auditor's report.

An auditor has qualified privilege under s 1289 in respect of any statement made in the course of the auditor's duties as auditor. This includes answering questions at the AGM and providing answers to questions put in writing under s 250PA. Qualified privilege also applies to responses to requests for information by the Financial Reporting Council. Section 1289 protects the auditor from actions of defamation and thereby encourages candid responses to questions.

auditors of debenture issuers

[16.120] The auditor of a borrower in relation to debentures must give the trustee for debenture-holders a copy of the auditor's report within seven days of giving the originals to the borrowing corporation: s 313(1). In addition, an auditor of a borrowing corporation must give the borrower or guarantor a written report about any matter that, in the auditor's opinion, is likely to be prejudicial to the interests of debenture-holders and is relevant to the exercise of the powers of the trustee for debenture-holders: s 313(2).

reporting to ASIC

Auditors have a statutory duty to report to ASIC if they have reasonable grounds to suspect that a significant contravention of the *Corporations Act* has occurred.

[16.125] Auditors have a statutory duty to report to ASIC if they have reasonable grounds to suspect that a significant contravention of the *Corporations Act* has occurred, an attempt has been made to unduly influence, coerce, manipulate or mislead a person involved in the conduct of an audit or otherwise interfere with the proper conduct of the audit. Auditors who have such suspicions must notify ASIC as soon as practicable and in any case within 28 days after becoming aware of the circumstances: s 311(1) and (2).

The types of contraventions which may be considered as significant are indicated by s 311(4). These may include insolvent trading, breach of financial reporting provisions and the effect the contravention has on the financial position of the company.

contents of auditor's report

[16.130] Tables 16.1 and 16.2 highlight the matters that must be included in an auditor's report and auditor's review.

table 16.1 auditor's report

		Annual financial report	Half-year financial report
Auditor's opinion	Whether financial report is in accordance with the *Corporations Act*, including:	308(1)	309(1)
	— compliance with accounting standards; and	296	304
	— true and fair view. If the auditor is not of this opinion, the report must state why.	297	305
Non-compliance with accounting standards	Quantify the effect of non-compliance to the extent it is practicable to do so.	308(1)	309(2)
Description of any defects or irregularities		308(3)(a)	309(3)(a)
Description of any deficiencies, failures or shortcomings	In respect of whether: — auditor given all information, explanation and assistance necessary for the conduct of the audit; — sufficient financial records have been kept; and — other required records and registers have been kept.	308(3)(b)	309(3)(b)
Date report made		308(4)	309(6

table 16.2 auditor's review of half-year financial report

Auditor's awareness	Whether any matter that makes the auditor believe that the financial report does not comply with the *Corporations Act*'s half-year financial reporting requirements.	309(4)
Description of non-compliance		309(5)(a)
Reasons why auditor believes that financial report does not comply		309(5)(b)

duty to carry out audit

[16.135] An audit must be carried out in accordance with auditing standards before an auditor can form an opinion on whether or not the financial reports are properly drawn up in the manner required by s 308(1).

An audit must be carried out in accordance with auditing standards.

In carrying out an audit, particularly where the company's accounts are complex, an auditor is required to devise procedures and a program to assist in the detection of errors or fraud: *Pacific Acceptance Corp Ltd v Forsyth* (1970) 92 WN (NSW) 29.

Auditors are entitled to seek assistance from the company's directors, accountants and other employees in carrying out their functions. Auditors, however, breach their duty if they rely on them for information on which they are required to form their own independent opinion.

case note

This is illustrated in *Dominion Freeholders Ltd v Aird* [1966] 2 NSWR 293 where an auditor prepared an erroneous report. The company brought an action against Aird for breach of his contractual duty of care and he sought to join the company accountant as a co-defendant. This was on the basis that the accountant had supplied him with incorrect information and was in breach of duty owed to him. The application by the auditor was rejected because he was not entitled to rely on the information provided by the accountant. Such reliance was a breach of duty to the company as the auditor was required to come to an independent conclusion. The auditor could not shed responsibility by holding the accountant liable.

duty to detect and report fraud and irregularities

[16.140] An auditor is appointed to safeguard the interests of the members. As discussed earlier, the auditor must provide a report that is sent to members. Among other matters, the auditor's report must describe any defect or irregularity in the financial reports: s 308(3)(a).

Among other matters, the auditor's report must describe any defect or irregularity in the financial reports.

Auditing Standard AUS 210, *The Auditor's Responsibility to Consider Fraud and Error in an Audit of a Financial Report*, states that the primary responsibility for the prevention and detection of fraud and error rests with those charged with the governance and management of an entity (para .13).

In *Arthur Young & Co v WA Chip & Pulp Co Pty Ltd* (1989) 7 ACLC 496, it was held that an auditor will breach their duty of care if, having detected a possible irregularity not amounting to a suspicion of fraud, the auditor fails to investigate further and report the matter to the appropriate officers of the company. There will be a breach even if the amount involved was immaterial.

An auditor who detects an irregularity, regardless of materiality, has a duty to promptly report that finding to the board of directors or to an appropriate level of management.

An auditor who detects an irregularity, regardless of materiality, has a duty to promptly report that finding to the board of directors or to an appropriate level of management. In addition, under s 311, if an auditor has reasonable grounds to suspect that there has been a contravention of the *Corporations Act* and the circumstances are such that the matter has not been or will not be adequately dealt with by comment in the auditor's report or by bringing the matter to the notice of the directors, the auditor is required to report the matter to ASIC.

Auditing Standard AUS 210 states:

> < **When the auditor has obtained evidence that fraud exists or may exist, it is important that the matter be brought to the attention of the appropriate level of management as soon as practicable. This is so even if the matter might be considered inconsequential (for example, a minor defalcation by an employee at a low level in the entity's organisation). The determination of which level of management is the appropriate one is a matter of professional judgement and is affected by such factors as the likelihood of collusion and the nature and magnitude of the suspected fraud. Ordinarily, the appropriate level of management is at least one level above the persons who appear to be involved with the suspected fraud [.94].** >

case note

The question as to which level of management an auditor must report defects or irregularities was considered by the New South Wales Court of Appeal in *Daniels v Anderson* (1995) 13 ACLC 614 which held that the auditors breached their duty to report to the company's management the absence of proper accounting records and the weaknesses in internal controls. If the management did not take prompt action, the auditors should report the deficiencies to the board of directors. The court's decision on the contributory negligence of AWA and its directors is discussed below, para [16.165].

Corporate governance best practice considers that it is part of the role of an audit committee, comprising at least a majority of independent non-executive directors, to oversee a company's internal control and to have access to the external auditor without the presence of management. The adoption of these practices seeks to ensure that the board is made aware of any concerns the auditor may have regarding information discovered during the audit and the process of the audit itself such as any disagreements between the auditor and management. Audit committees are further discussed in Chapter 13.1 above.

duty to use reasonable care and skill

An auditor is under a contractual obligation to use reasonable care and skill in carrying out the audit and in forming an opinion on the company's financial report.

[16.145] An auditor is under a contractual obligation to use reasonable care and skill in carrying out the audit and in forming an opinion on the company's financial report. A failure to exercise reasonable care and skill renders an auditor liable to the company in damages for breach of contract.

An auditor may also be liable to the company in negligence. It has long been held that professionals owe a duty of care to their clients. However, from a plaintiff's point of view, damages for breach of contract in some circumstances provide a better remedy than damages from a negligence action. Further, if a company proceeds against an auditor on the basis of breach of contract, there is a divergence of judicial opinion on whether an auditor can raise a defence of contributory negligence by the company to reduce liability. Contributory negligence is discussed below, para [16.165]. An auditor who exercises less than the required degree of care and skill is liable to the company for any loss suffered as a result, but is not liable just because of failure to detect errors or frauds.

standard of care and skill

[16.150] A high standard of care and skill is expected from auditors. This is in line with the public's high expectations of the competence of auditors. An auditor must use a reasonable degree of care. The standards of reasonableness depend on the circumstances and are affected by changed expectations.

A high standard of care and skill is expected from auditors.

In *Pacific Acceptance Corp Ltd v Forsyth* (1970) 92 WN (NSW) 29, it was held that in determining what was reasonable care and skill expected of an auditor, the court should be guided by accepted auditing standards. Moffit J said:

> < **Reasonable skill and care calls for changed standards to meet changed conditions or changed understanding of dangers and in this sense standards are more exacting today than in 1896... However, now as formerly, standards and practices adopted by the profession to meet current circumstances provide a sound guide to the court in determining what is reasonable. The changes in accepted auditing standards are evidenced in that now, for some decades, in appropriate cases the auditor, after due inquiry and testing, relies on the company's system of internal control and by this method may avoid the time and cost involved in endless "surface" checking of all transactions in favour of checking samples "in depth". While this approach dispenses with some of the plodding and mechanical checks by audit clerks of former years, it calls for some care, skill and experience as the inquiries regarding the system and the selection, and to some degree the following through of appropriate samples, require an appreciation of the purpose of the procedures in relation to the company's system of carrying out its activities and documenting its dealings. In this sense it might be said that the modern procedures call for more sophistication and higher standards on the part of those who perform the work. By way of further example, it would seem that due skill and care calls for a more searching and critical approach today on matters of stock and provision for bad and doubtful debts than it did 50 years ago, and to some extent even ten years ago.** >

case note

In *Daniels v Anderson* (1995) 13 ACLC 614, the facts of which are outlined in Chapter 13.4 above, the New South Wales Court of Appeal held that the auditor failed to exercise reasonable care and skill in a number of respects. The court found that the auditor was aware that:

- while the company changed its record-keeping system, no proper accounting records in relation to foreign exchange trading were being kept;
- senior managers had not heeded the auditor's warnings that the company's internal controls in relation to foreign exchange trading were inadequate;
- the foreign exchange trading was not tied into the company's computerised accounts;
- foreign exchange trading was both a high audit risk area and a high commercial risk;
- foreign exchange trading was an area where internal controls are critical; and
- the company's exposure to foreign exchange losses was high.

Given the auditor's awareness of the above matters, his failure to promptly warn the company's directors of the deficiencies in the accounting records and inadequate internal controls meant that he breached his duty to exercise reasonable care and skill and was negligent.

causation and damage

If an auditor breaches a contractual duty to exercise reasonable care and skill, the auditor will be liable to pay damages to the company.

Before damages are awarded it must be shown that the breach of duty caused the loss.

[16.155] If an auditor breaches a contractual duty to exercise reasonable care and skill, the auditor will be liable to pay damages to the company. The aim of an award of damages for breach of contract is to put the company in the position it would have been in had the contract been properly performed. However, before damages are awarded it must be shown that the breach of duty caused the loss. In determining whether a breach of contract causes a loss, the courts usually adopt a "but for" test—would the loss have occurred *but for* the breach? Even if a breach caused a loss, damages will not be awarded if the loss is too remote. A loss is regarded as being too remote if the loss is outside the contemplation of the parties to the contract at the time they contracted.

case note

In *Alexander v Cambridge Credit Corp Ltd* (1987) 5 ACLC 587, it was held that while an audit had been negligently conducted, this was not the cause of the loss suffered by the company on the basis of the "but for" test. One significant factor causing its disastrous losses was the dramatic change in economic conditions in Australia between 1972 and 1974.

case note

Causation was also an important issue in *Daniels v Anderson* (1995) 13 ACLC 614. In that case, the New South Wales Court of Appeal held that the auditor's negligence had caused loss. As a result of the failure to promptly report deficiencies in the accounting records and internal control procedures, AWA lost the chance to take steps to avoid losses in foreign exchange dealings. AWA also lost the chance to take remedial action. However, as discussed below, the Court of Appeal held that AWA was also negligent and contributed to the losses suffered.

case note

In *Segenhoe Ltd v Akins* (1990) 8 ACLC 263, a company sued its auditors for negligence in that there was an overstatement of profits in the accounts due to an under-provision for taxation. As a result, the company paid dividends out of capital. It was held that the payments to shareholders were made due to the negligence of the auditors. Payment of dividends out of capital is a loss to the company. Although the company could bring a legal action to recover the payments made to shareholders, this was complicated and difficult litigation. Therefore, the auditors were liable to the company for the full payment out of capital. Even though the company was obliged to mitigate its losses, it was not required to bring actions to recover the dividend payments from its shareholders.

indemnification from liability

[16.160] Under s 199A(1) and (2), a company or related body corporate must not exempt or indemnify an officer or auditor from liability to the company incurred as an officer or auditor, or liability under the civil penalty provisions. The members in general meeting may, however, ratify an auditor's breach of duty. Companies can indemnify auditors against any costs incurred by them in successfully defending any civil or criminal action or where relief is granted to them by the court under s 1318. The power of the court to grant relief to officers and auditors is discussed in Chapter 13.7 above.

defences

contributory negligence

[16.165] Auditors who are sued by a company for the tort of negligence may seek to reduce their liability for damages by raising the defence of contributory negligence by the company. The apportionment of damages for contributory negligence is permitted by legislation such as s 26 of the *Wrongs Act 1958* (Vic) and s 10 of the *Law Reform (Miscellaneous Provisions) Act 1965* (NSW). In order to establish contributory negligence, an auditor must prove that the loss suffered by a company was partly due to its own negligence. For example, contributory negligence will arise if the loss suffered by the company is partly due to the negligence of its officers and their negligent actions are imputed to their company.

Auditors who are sued by a company for the tort of negligence may seek to reduce their liability for damages by raising the defence of contributory negligence by the company.

While it is clear that the defence of contributory negligence can be relied on where an auditor is sued for the tort of negligence, until quite recently the cases, both in Australia and overseas, were divided on whether that defence can be used if the auditor is sued for breaching the contractual duty of care.

case note

In *Daniels v Anderson* (1995) 13 ACLC 614, the New South Wales Court of Appeal was of the opinion that contributory negligence was a valid defence for breach of contract and AWA was guilty of contributory negligence because of the negligence of its board of directors and management.

The court held that AWA's management were negligent in that:

> they failed to establish an adequate system of internal controls in relation to foreign exchange operations;
> they failed to maintain an adequate system of records of contracts, books and accounts for those operations;
> they failed to adequately supervise the activities of Koval, AWA's foreign exchange manager;
> nor did they heed the auditor's warnings on the inadequacies of the internal controls; and
> the board of directors, as a collective unit, was also negligent in that the board permitted a grossly negligent management to persevere with foreign exchange dealings in an entirely unsatisfactory manner.

For these reasons the Court of Appeal reduced the damages payable by the auditor by one-third.

contribution

[16.170] The loss suffered by a victim of negligence may be caused by the concurrent but independent acts or omissions of two or more people (joint tortfeasors). For example, the loss suffered by a company may have been caused by the negligence of its auditor as well as the company's directors and managers. In such circumstances, State legislation provided that all joint tortfeasors were jointly and severally liable to pay damages to the company. Further, where the company sues only the auditor, they have a right of contribution against the negligent directors.

Many States have passed legislation that replaces the joint and several liability of joint tortfeasors with proportionate liability.

As a result of recent reviews of tort laws, many States have either passed legislation or intend to pass legislation that replaces the joint and several liability of joint tortfeasors with proportionate liability. The effect of this is that if an auditor's negligence causes only a proportion of the loss suffered by a company, the amount of damages the auditor will have to pay will be limited to that proportion. The CLERP 9 amendments introduced a proportionate liability regime for damages claims under s 82 of the *Trade Practices Act.* As result of this change, the right of contribution by joint tortfeasors has become less relevant.

liability of auditors to particular shareholders and outsiders

negligence

Shareholders, creditors and other users of the audited accounts may be able to sue auditors in an action for the tort of negligence if they can establish that the auditors owe them a duty of care.

[16.175] An auditor has a contractual relationship with the company. If an auditor breaches her or his contractual duty of care it is only the company that can sue the auditor. Shareholders, creditors and other users of the audited accounts may be able to sue auditors in an action for the tort of negligence if they can establish that the auditors owe them a duty of care in carrying out the audit and in making their report.

It was once thought that professionals owed a duty of care only to their clients and not to other people who rely on their statements. For example, in *Candler v Crane Christmas & Co Ltd* [1951] 2 KB 164, it was held that a firm of accountants was not liable in negligence to an outside investor who had relied on a negligently prepared report. This was because there was no contract between the accountants and the outsider and they were under no duty of care.

Since the decision in *Candler v Crane Christmas & Co Ltd*, the law of negligence with respect to negligent misstatements has developed significantly.

In a case that did not concern auditors, the High Court in *Shaddock & Assoc Pty Ltd v Parramatta City Council* (1981) 150 CLR 225, held that the duty to take reasonable care arises:

> **< Whenever a person gives information or advice to another upon a serious matter in circumstances where the speaker realises, or ought to realise, that he is being trusted to give the best of his information or advice as a basis for action on the part of the other party and it is reasonable in the circumstances for the other party to act on that information or advice — the speaker comes under a duty to exercise reasonable care in the provision of the information or advice he chooses to give. >**

The courts have restricted the range of people to whom auditors owe duties of care.

Until recently, the courts have been divided as to the extent to which auditors owe a duty of care to people other than their clients. Some courts have been particularly concerned to ensure that auditors should not be subject to "liability in an indeterminate amount for an indeterminate time to an indeterminate class": *Ultramares Corp v Touche* (1931) 174 NE 441. For this reason the courts have restricted the range of people to whom auditors owe duties of care.

case note

The question of whether or not an auditor owes a duty of care to a third party has been finally settled in Australia as a result of the High Court's decision in *Esanda Finance Corp Ltd v Peat Marwick Hungerfords* (1997) 15 ACLC 483. In that case, Excel Pty Ltd (Excel) guaranteed loans provided by Esanda Finance Corp Ltd (Esanda) to companies associated with Excel. Esanda relied on the unqualified audit report on the company's 1989 financial statements supplied to it by Excel and prepared by Peat Marwick Hungerfords (PMH). These financial statements did not disclose Excel's true financial position. When Excel was subsequently put in receivership, Esanda brought an action against PMH alleging that the auditors had been negligent.

PMH applied to strike out Esanda's statement of claim on the basis that it did not allege facts that in law were capable of founding a duty of care by PMH to Esanda. The statement of claim alleging that PMH owed a duty of care to Esanda was based on the fact that as PMH was a member of the Institute of Chartered Accountants, it was obliged to comply with its accounting standards, particularly AAS5. This standard provides a test of materiality in financial statements and requires, among other things, consideration of prime users, such as present and potential providers of equity and loan capital and creditors. Therefore, PMH ought reasonably to have foreseen that Esanda might rely on the audited financial statements because it was a creditor of Excel.

The High Court unanimously, though for slightly different reasons, struck out Esanda's statement of claim. The court asserted that in order to establish whether an auditor does owes a duty of care to third parties in negligent misstatement cases, it was not sufficient for a plaintiff merely to allege that it was reasonably foreseeable that a third party might rely on audited financial statements.

Brennan CJ proposed the following test and held that an auditor will owe a duty of care to a third party if it is alleged and can be proved that:

- the auditor knew or ought reasonably to have known that the auditor's report on the financial statements would be communicated to the third party, either individually or as a member of an identified class; and
- the audited financial statements would be so communicated for a purpose that would be very likely to lead the third party to enter into a transaction of the kind that the third party did enter into; and
- it would be very likely that the third party would enter into such a transaction in reliance on the audited financial statements and thereby risk the incurring of economic loss.

Dawson J held that in negligent misstatement cases claiming damages for pure economic loss, a third party must also establish a relationship of proximity between the maker of the statement and the third party. Such a relationship could arise if the negligent misstatement was supplied at the request of the third party. It could also arise if the maker of the statement intended to induce the third party to act on the statement. In this case, there was no suggestion in the statement of claim of a request for the audited financial information by Esanda or an intention by PMH to induce it to act. Dawson J left open the possibility that the statutory scheme governing auditors' duties may be relevant in determining whether an auditor's report is made with the intention to induce a particular person to act on it in a particular way.

Toohey and Gaudron JJ, in a joint judgment, observed that there was nothing in the circumstances of the case to suggest that it was reasonable for Esanda to act on the audited report without further inquiry. Esanda was able to have its own accountants ascertain Excel's financial position as a condition of granting the loan.

McHugh and Gummow JJ both relied on public policy considerations to support the auditor's appeal. McHugh J could find no good reason for extending the liability of auditors to those members of a class whom the auditor knows or ought to know will rely on the audit where the auditor has not assumed responsibility to those members or intended to induce them to rely on the audit. He found it difficult to accept that giving third parties unqualified rights against auditors would serve the public interest by raising auditors' standard of care any higher than is presently the case. Extending the liability of auditors will possibly result in a reduction in the number of auditors willing to act for high-risk businesses. It may also lead to the reduction in demand for auditors because increasing negligence insurance premiums will result in increased audit fees. In this case, Esanda was a well-informed creditor and could have taken steps to avoid the risk of loss. There was no good reason to extend auditor's liability to such third parties.

misleading and deceptive conduct

Section 52 of the *Trade Practices Act* may provide third parties with an alternative and simpler basis for suing auditors.

[16.180] Section 52 of the *Trade Practices Act 1974* (Cth) may provide third parties with an alternative and simpler basis for suing auditors. This section prohibits a corporation from engaging in misleading or deceptive conduct. Contravention of s 52 provides a plaintiff with a wide range of remedies against the corporation including damages: *Trade Practices Act 1974* (Cth), s 82. A natural person, such as an auditor, may be regarded as a corporation for purposes of s 52 in certain circumstances: *Trade Practices Act 1974* (Cth), s 6(2). Even if those circumstances do not apply, an auditor could also be liable under State Fair Trading Acts. This prohibits any person, in trade or commerce, from engaging in misleading or deceptive conduct. Not qualifying accounts when they should be qualified may amount to misleading or deceptive conduct. No intention to mislead or deceive is required. As discussed below, the CLERP 9 amendments introduced a proportionate liability regime which was incorporated into the *Trade Practices Act* as well as the *Corporations Act* and the *ASIC Act*.

proportionate liability of auditors

[16.185] Prior to the introduction of the CLERP 9 amendments, auditors were subject to joint and several liability in conjunction with other parties, such as company directors, for economic loss caused by negligence or misleading and deceptive conduct. This system raised increasing concern that professionals such as auditors were usually targeted by plaintiffs because they were seen as having "deep pockets". This was largely because they were invariably covered by professional indemnity insurance with the result that insured professionals bore a disproportionate burden of claims in comparison with uninsured co-defendants. It therefore became increasingly difficult for professionals to obtain insurance and premiums rose rapidly. It is important that professionals have ready access to insurance so as to protect consumers by enabling them to recover damages in the event of negligent provision of professional services.

The CLERP 9 amendments addressed these concerns by introducing a proportionate liability system to improve the availability and affordability of professional indemnity insurance for professional service providers such as auditors. These amendments apply the proportionate liability regime to the *ASIC Act*: (s 12GF(1)), the *Corporations Act*: (s 1041) and the *Trade Practices Act*: s 52. Many States have either passed legislation or intend to pass similar proportionate liability legislation. The basis of this system is that a defendant can only be liable for that portion of the damage for which that defendant was responsible. This involves a court determining the respective responsibilities of wrongdoers who are not parties to the proceedings. A defendant to a claim to which proportionate liability may apply is required to notify the plaintiff of any other persons who have contributed to the plaintiff's loss. The contributory negligence of a plaintiff is taken into account in apportioning liability.

Intentional torts, claims involving fraud, the liability of partners and a principal for the acts of an agent are excluded from the proportionate liability system.

---

bibliography ...

Anderson, H "A Different Solution to the Auditor's Liability Dilemma" (1996) 8 Bond LR 72.

Anderson, H "Auditors' Liability Headache: Is Proportionate Liability the Cure?" (1996) 4 *Current Commercial Law* 110.

Anderson, H "Reliance and Assumption of Responsibility in Establishing an Auditor's Duty of Care" (1996) 14 C & SLJ 374.

Anderson, H "Auditors' Liability: Is Misleading or Deceptive Conduct an Alternative to Negligence?" (1999) 17 C & SLJ 350.

Anderson, H "Liability Trends in the USA and their Relevance for Australian Auditors" (2001) 13 Aust Jnl of Corp Law 19.

Brooks, A, Chalmers, K, Oliver, J & Veljanovski A, "Auditor independence reforms: Audit committee members' views" (2005) 23 C & SLJ 151.

Companies and Securities Law Review Committee, Report to the Ministerial Council on the Civil Liability of Company Auditors (1986) **http://www.takeovers.gov.au/Content/Resources/CASES/04-CSLRC_CivilLiability.asp**

Emma, L "The auditor as the Gatekeeper for the investing public: Auditor Independence and the CLERP reforms—a comparative analysis" (2005) 23 C & SLJ 413.

Gay, G E & Pound, G D "The Role of the Auditor in Fraud Detection and Reporting" (1989) 7 C & SLJ 116.

George, G "Accounting, Auditing and Auditors—What is to be Done?" (2002) 14 Aust Jnl of Corp Law 51.

Gibson, R & Simnett, R "Objects of an Auditor's Duty of Care" (1994) Aust Jnl of Corp Law 54.

Martinez, C "What do Auditors do About Fraud and Other Illegal Acts?" (1995) 13 C & SLJ 537.

Stapledon, G "The AWA Case and the Availability to Auditors of the 'Defence' of Contributory Negligence" (1995) 13 C & SLJ 513.

Tomasic, R "Auditors and the Reporting of Illegality and Financial Fraud" (1992) 20 ABLR 198.

revision questions on the material in this chapter ...

> Please see eQuiz at **http://www.thomson.com.au/academic** for multiple choice questions and answers.

> For further corporations law links and material please refer to the Lipton-Herzberg website at **http://www.lipton-herzberg.com.au**

chapter seventeen

members' remedies

key points . . .

> There are various ways in which members may seek a remedy where the controllers of a company act unfairly. This usually arises where the members are no longer able to properly work together.

> Several statutory remedies aim to provide a more effective means for enabling minority members to bring an action. These largely replace the common law rules, which imposed greater difficulties on minority members.

> The oppression remedy allows for a flexible range of remedies that the court thinks appropriate in the circumstances. The court may make an order where the affairs of the company are conducted contrary to the interests of the members as a whole, oppressively or in a manner unfairly prejudicial or discriminatory against members.

> A statutory derivative action has been introduced that enables an individual shareholder to bring legal proceedings on behalf of a company where the company fails to do so. This action may often involve the enforcement of rights against directors who breach their duties to the company. A company will rarely bring such an action because the directors who breached their duties usually control the company.

> Other statutory remedies allow a member to seek an injunction to prevent conduct that contravenes the *Corporations Act* and to apply to wind up the company.

> To assist a member to bring a legal action, members may apply to the court for the right to inspect the company's books where it can be shown that they act in good faith and the inspection is for a proper purpose.

> A member may also enforce personal rights at common law. These include rights conferred by the *Corporations Act* and constitution, voting rights and protection against expropriation of their shares. The law has developed various remedies where the majority act unfairly or oppressively in order to protect the interests of the company and its members. The common law remedies that stemmed from the rule in *Foss v Harbottle* and its exceptions were complex and placed substantial difficulties upon members who complained of unfair treatment, particularly where this involved breaches of duty by directors.

[17.05] The *Corporations Act* provides more effective procedures than the common law to enable members to obtain remedies in circumstances where the controllers of a company act oppressively or unfairly towards them. The most significant of these remedies discussed in this chapter are:

> s 232, which provides a remedy where the affairs of a company are conducted in a manner that is contrary to the interests of the members as a whole, oppressive, unfairly discriminatory or unfairly prejudicial;

> ss 236–242, which enable members and officers to bring proceedings on behalf of a company where the company fails to do so;

> s 461(1)(e), which permits the court to wind up a company where the directors have acted in the affairs of the company in their own interests rather than in the interests of the members as a whole, or in any other manner that appears to be unfair or unjust to other members;

> s 461(1)(f) and (g), which permits the court to wind up a company where the grounds set out in s 232 are established;
> s 461(1)(k), which permits the court to wind up a company where it is of the opinion that it is just and equitable to do so; and
> s 1324, which allows the court to restrain contraventions of the *Corporations Act*.

The common law remedies are no longer important, especially as a result of s 236(3), which was introduced by 1999 amendments. This provision abolishes the right of a person at general law to bring, or intervene in, proceedings on behalf of a company. The common law remedies available to members are still significant where members seek to enforce personal rights.

The position of minority shareholders has also been strengthened by ss 247A–247D. These sections enable a member to apply to the court for an order enabling the member or other person acting on her or his behalf to inspect the books of the company. A successful application enables a member to gain access to information that may be helpful in establishing the necessary grounds for the remedies outlined above.

ASIC may initiate an investigation where it has reason to suspect that a contravention of the *Corporations Act* has been committed and it may cause civil proceedings to be brought in the name of a member, the company or other person: *ASIC Act*, s 50. This is discussed in Chapter 21 below. A person whom ASIC thinks appropriate may apply for an order under s 232 where ASIC has conducted investigations into the company's affairs: s 234(1)(e). This is discussed below.

statutory remedies

[17.10] There are various statutory rights that allow members to seek a wide range of remedies in circumstances where the controllers of companies unfairly misuse their positions of power or breach their duties. To assist in bringing these actions, members have enhanced rights of access to inspect the company's books.

oppressive or unfair conduct

Section 232 allows the court to provide members with a wide range of remedies if they can show that the conduct of a company's affairs is contrary to the interests of the members as a whole, oppressive, unfairly prejudicial or unfairly discriminatory.

[17.15] Section 232 allows the court to provide members with a wide range of remedies if they can show that the conduct of a company's affairs is contrary to the interests of the members as a whole, oppressive, unfairly prejudicial or unfairly discriminatory. The conduct may affect members in their capacity as members or in any other capacity. The conduct of the company's affairs may comprise an actual or proposed act, or omission by or on behalf of the company, or a resolution or proposed resolution of members or a class of members of a company.

Section 232 covers a very broad range of conduct including aspects of the just and equitable ground for winding up under s 461(1)(k). The requirements of s 232 also constitute grounds for winding up under s 461(1)(f) and (g). An important effect of s 232 is its use as a bargaining counter to force controllers of companies to consider the interests of minority shareholders.

In most cases, the member seeking an s 232 remedy will be a shareholder in a small, tightly held company who is unable to continue a workable relationship with other shareholders. In such circumstances, there is a great risk that the minority shareholder becomes "locked-in". It is more unusual for this to occur in the case of a listed public company. Where there is a market for a company's shares, aggrieved shareholders will usually sell their shares rather than incur considerable costs in attempting to enforce legal rights.

Proprietary companies offer more scope for the majority to abuse their positions. Listed companies must comply with ASX Listing Rules. These force listed companies to gain shareholder approval where they seek to make certain structural changes. The affairs of listed companies are also under closer public scrutiny. Nevertheless, there have been several cases involving listed companies where the oppression remedy has been used as a means of challenging actions of directors that involved a breach of duty.

In the case of partly-owned subsidiaries, the majority shareholders may disregard the interests of minority shareholders while acting in the interests of the controlling shareholder. CASAC's *Corporate Groups Final Report* considers amendments to the *Corporations Act* to assist directors of corporate group companies to effectively perform their duties and also to adequately protect shareholders and outsiders. Chapter 3 of this report deals with minority shareholders of partly-owned group companies. This report may be accessed on the CAMAC website and is linked to the Lipton-Herzberg Law Reform site at **http://www.lipton-herzberg.com.au/law_reform.htm**

Another type of company where recourse may be found in s 232 is a joint venture company. This is where investors, who may themselves be incorporated, form together in a venture where each of the participants contributes equity, expertise, rights or goods and services. Companies formed for joint ventures are similar in many respects to small, tightly held companies even though the joint venture may involve a large scale business operation. They are closely held and without public listing, therefore the possibility exists that a party may be locked in, unfairly treated or "squeezed out".

who may apply?

Section 234 sets out who may apply for an order under s 232.

[17.20] Section 234 sets out who may apply for an order under s 232. The accepted applicants are:

- **a member of the company even though the application relates to an act or omission that is against the member in a capacity other than as a member: s 234(a). The application may also relate to an act or omission that is against another member in their capacity as a member;**
- **a person removed from the register of members because of a selective reduction (s 234(b));**
- **a past member if the application relates to the circumstances in which they ceased to be a member (s 234(c));**
- **a person to whom a share in the company has been transmitted by will or by operation of law (s 234(d)); or**
- **a person whom ASIC thinks appropriate having regard to investigations it is conducting, or has conducted, into the company's affairs or matters connected with the company's affairs: s 234(e).**

It is unclear whether an applicant must be registered as a member for the purposes of s 234(a).

case note

In *Niord Pty Ltd v Adelaide Petroleum NL* (1990) 8 ACLC 684, a purchaser of shares in a company had not been registered as a member at the time when it instituted proceedings under a predecessor of s 232. It was held that an applicant must be registered in order to complain of oppressive conduct. An equitable interest as an unregistered transferee is insufficient.

case note

However, registration as a member was not seen as decisive in *Re Independent Quarries Pty Ltd* (1994) 12 ACLC 159 where a company was considered to be a member for the purposes of the predecessor of s 232 even though its name was not entered in the register of members. A share certificate had been duly issued but the transfer had not been registered because the register was under the control of the controlling shareholder and the directors were unable to rectify the matter.

If a member's name is removed from the register pursuant to some power in the constitution, before seeking relief under s 232, the member must first apply for correction of the register under s 175: *Re M Dalley & Co Pty Ltd* (1968) 1 ACLR 489.

The conduct of which members complain may affect them in their capacity as a member or in any other capacity: s 234(a)(i). Therefore, a remedy can be sought under s 232 even though the applicant is complaining of conduct such as removal as a director or employee of the company. A member also has standing to seek a remedy even where the person is not a member of the particular group of aggrieved members. This is as long as the application relates to an act or omission that is against the other member in their capacity as a member: s 234(a)(ii).

The conduct of which members complain may affect them in their capacity as a member or in any other capacity.

In *Re Spargos Mining NL* (1990) 8 ACLC 1218, the Supreme Court of Western Australia held that a member had standing to apply for a remedy even though that person was not a member at the time the oppressive or unfair conduct took place. Further, s 232 makes it clear that the right to apply for a remedy extends to a person to whom a share in the company has been transmitted by will or operation of law. Such a person does not have to be registered as a member.

conduct where a remedy may be sought

[17.25] company's affairs. Under s 232, an applicant must allege that the conduct of a "company's affairs" is contrary to the interests of the members as a whole, oppressive, unfairly prejudicial or unfairly discriminatory. The "company's affairs" includes conduct of the directors, majority shareholders, substantial shareholders as well as the company itself. According to the s 53 definition, "company's affairs" also includes a reference to:

The "company's affairs" includes conduct of the directors, majority shareholders, substantial shareholders as well as the company itself.

> **the promotion, formation, membership, control, business, trading, transaction and dealings, property, liabilities, profits and the income, receipts, losses, outgoings and expenditure;**
> **the internal management and proceedings; and**
> **the power of persons to exercise, or to control the exercise of, the rights to vote attached to shares in the body corporate or to dispose of, or to exercise control over the disposal of, such shares.**

Several cases have considered whether or not conduct of a "company's affairs" includes conduct of a subsidiary company so as to permit a shareholder of a particular company in a corporate group to seek a remedy where the oppressive or unfair conduct occurred in other companies in the group.

case note

In *Morgan v 45 Flers Avenue Pty Ltd* (1987) 5 ACLC 222 a company, Metal Recyclers (NSW) Pty Ltd, conducted a joint venture business controlled by two sets of brothers—the Morgan brothers and the Richards brothers. 45 Flers Avenue Pty Ltd, a company controlled by the Morgan brothers, owned 45 per cent of the shares in Metal Recyclers. The two Morgan brothers were appointed directors of Metal Recyclers as nominees of 45 Flers Avenue Pty Ltd. The two Richards brothers owned 45 per cent of the shares in Metal Recyclers in their own names and were also directors of Metal Recyclers. After disputes arose between the Morgan brothers, one of them resigned his directorship of Metal Recyclers and became the manager of a rival business. The board of Metal Recyclers resolved to distribute its profits in the form of large bonuses and fees to its remaining directors and declared low dividends to its shareholders. The decision effectively denied the brother, who had resigned, from participating in the profits of the joint venture company. He sought an order under the predecessor of s 232 for the compulsory purchase of his shares in 45 Flers Avenue. One of the arguments raised by the applicant was that his brother, in voting on the board of Metal Recyclers for the large bonuses and fees, acted in the affairs of 45 Flers Avenue, which had appointed him to that position, and this was oppressive and unfair to the applicant. The

Supreme Court of New South Wales refused to grant the order. Young J held that a nominee director, by participating in board decisions, could not be said to be acting in the affairs of the appointor company. This was so, according to the court, because nominee directors have an overriding duty to the company on whose board they sit in preference to the interests of their appointors.

case note

A wider interpretation of "company's affairs" was adopted by the Supreme Court of Queensland in *Re Norvabron Pty Ltd* (1987) 5 ACLC 184. A shareholder of a holding company applied for a remedy under a predecessor of s 232 alleging that one of its subsidiaries had awarded a contract to a company associated with some of its directors at a price that was considerably higher than a competitor's tender. Derrington J rejected as "artificial in the extreme" the holding company's argument that the conduct on which the applicant relied was conduct of the subsidiary and not the holding company. The directors of the holding company knew what was happening in the subsidiary because they were also the subsidiary's directors. Their failure to take action as directors of the holding company to prevent their own conduct as directors of the subsidiary constituted an omission that was oppressive and unfair conduct for purposes of the predecessor of s 232.

A refusal by directors to allow shareholders to inspect the financial records of a company and its subsidiaries was not "conduct" in the affairs of the company. Inactivity or negative action can only be regarded as "conduct" where there is a duty at law or in equity to act in a positive way: *Re Dernacourt Investments Pty Ltd* (1990) 8 ACLC 900.

[17.30] acts or proposed acts. Under s 232(b), a single act by or on behalf of a company may constitute conduct that is contrary to the interests of the members as a whole, oppressive, unfairly prejudicial or unfairly discriminatory. For example, in *Wayde v NSW Rugby League Ltd* (1985) 3 ACLC 799, the High Court held that a single resolution of the board of directors could be an oppressive or unfair act on behalf of the company. The conduct may also consist of an act that is merely proposed and has not yet occurred: s 232(b).

Conduct of the company's affairs may also take the form of a resolution or proposed resolution of members or a class of members.

[17.35] resolutions or proposed resolutions. Under s 232(c), conduct of the company's affairs may also take the form of a resolution or proposed resolution of members or a class of members. This modifies the general law principle that shareholders are able to exercise their voting rights in their own interests: *North-West Transportation Co v Beatty* (1887) 12 App Cas 589.

As discussed below, s 232 provides class members with a wider range of remedies than is the case for contraventions of the variation of class rights provisions in s 246B.

Section 232(b) also applies to omissions or proposed omissions.

[17.40] omissions. Section 232(b) also applies to omissions or proposed omissions. This may enable a member to obtain a remedy where a company with sufficient profits persistently refuses to pay dividends: *Sanford v Sanford Courier Service Pty Ltd* (1986) 5 ACLC 394.

A remedy may also be available under s 232(b) where the omission or proposed omission is a refusal by the directors to register a transfer of shares and this refusal is oppressive or unfairly prejudices or unfairly discriminates against a member. The reference to omissions or proposed omissions may mean that a member will be able to obtain a remedy under s 232 in circumstances similar to *Re Smith and Fawcett Ltd* [1942] Ch 304, the facts of which are set out in Chapter 9 above.

meaning of oppressive and unfair

[17.45] A statutory remedy for oppressive conduct has been part of Australian company legislation since the mid-1950s. These earlier provisions, based on English legislation, provided a remedy where there was "oppressive conduct".

This expression was interpreted narrowly and focused on the nature of the conduct rather than its effect on the minority shareholder. According to *Scottish Co-operative Wholesale Soc Ltd v Meyer* [1959] AC 324, "oppressive conduct" is conduct that is "burdensome, harsh and wrongful". In *Re Jermyn Street Turkish Bath Ltd* [1971] 1 WLR 1042, the English Court of Appeal added the additional requirement that oppression involves "some overbearing act or attitude on the part of the oppressor". The effect of these narrow interpretations was that the oppression remedy was not available except in the more extreme circumstances where the controllers of a company deliberately abused their powers.

"Oppressive conduct" is conduct that is "burdensome, harsh and wrongful".

The provision was extended to cover not only oppressive acts and conduct, but also conduct that is unfairly discriminatory, unfairly prejudicial or is contrary to the interests of the members as a whole. In *Morgan v 45 Flers Avenue Pty Ltd* (1987) 5 ACLC 222, the Supreme Court of New South Wales held that it is inappropriate to focus on each of the individual elements of s 232. The correct approach is to regard them as a "composite whole". The individual elements:

Oppression involves "some overbearing act or attitude on the part of the oppressor".

> **< should be considered merely as different aspects of the essential criterion, namely commercial unfairness. >**

Unfairness, in this sense, is determined objectively. For example, a director's conduct may be regarded as oppressive or unfair if no reasonable director would have acted in that way. As Brennan J stated in *Wayde v NSW Rugby League Ltd* (1985) 3 ACLC 799:

> **< The operation of [s 232] may be attracted to a decision made by directors which is made in good faith for a purpose within the directors' powers but which reasonable directors would think to be unfair. >**

case note

In *Wayde v NSW Rugby League Ltd* (1985) 3 ACLC 799, the NSW Rugby League sought to remove a club, Wests, from its competition to reduce the number of clubs to 12. Wests brought an application for a remedy under the equivalent of s 232 to restrain the League from proceeding with the exclusion. The High Court held that the League was entitled to exclude Wests. The decision was taken by the League's directors honestly in pursuit of the object of fostering the game of rugby league and serving its best interests. While the decision was harsh on Wests, it was one that a reasonable board could have made. Wests could not show that the actions of the League were oppressive, unfairly prejudicial or unfairly discriminatory. The court adopted a cautious approach in order to avoid unduly assuming a role of management of the company. The majority noted that it had not been shown that the board's decisions were such that no board acting reasonably could have made them.

The reference to "conduct contrary to the interests of the members as a whole" may broaden the operation of s 232 even further than situations of "commercial unfairness".

In *Re Spargos Mining NL* (1990) 8 ACLC 1218, Murray J suggested that the reference to "conduct contrary to the interests of the members as a whole" may broaden the operation of s 232 even further than situations of "commercial unfairness".

A court must balance the conflicting interests of majority and minority shareholders. This balance is achieved by examining the background of a company and the reasonable expectations of its shareholders.

In determining whether or not conduct is oppressive or unfair a court must balance the conflicting interests of majority and minority shareholders. This balance is achieved by examining the background of a company and the reasonable expectations of its shareholders. It is not necessarily oppressive or unfair just because the controllers of a company are pursuing management or dividend policies with which a minority shareholder disagrees. It is also not necessarily unfair if the majority shareholders refuse to buy the minority's shares: *Re G Jeffrey (Mens Store) Pty Ltd* (1984) 2 ACLC 421.

case note

In the New Zealand case *Re H W Thomas Ltd* (1984) 2 ACLC 610, a minority shareholder failed in his application because he could not show that the affairs of the company were conducted in a manner which was oppressive, unfairly prejudicial or unfairly discriminatory. The company was a family company in which it was accepted by all members, except the minority shareholder, that the company should continue to operate in the financially conservative way it always had. It was also understood that the company would be a source of employment for its shareholders and not merely a means of providing dividends. In such circumstances, the minority shareholder was not unfairly prejudiced by being required to abide by the decision of the majority of shareholders.

case note

A different approach was taken by the court in *Roberts v Walter Developments Pty Ltd* (1997) 15 ACLC 882. A member of a quasi-partnership company took a decision to remove himself from the "partnership" after disputes and this was recognised by the majority in that they excluded him from management. Wheeler J took the view that the majority failed to recognise that the change in the relationship imposed upon them a duty to take account of the minority members' interests. He was no longer effectively a partner in the enterprise but a minority shareholder.

examples of oppressive and unfair conduct

Section 232 provides a remedy for minority shareholders if the majority shareholders divert a corporate opportunity to themselves or their associates.

[17.50] diversion of corporate opportunity. Section 232 provides a remedy for minority shareholders if the majority shareholders divert a corporate opportunity to themselves or their associates: *Cook v Deeks* [1916] AC 554.

case note

In *Scottish Co-operative Wholesale Soc Ltd v Meyer* [1959] AC 324, a company was formed for the purposes of purchasing yarn and selling material. The majority shareholders, who also controlled the board of directors, owned a mill that wove the yarn and then sold the material to the company. The majority shareholders themselves proceeded to engage in the activities of the company and stopped selling material to it, with the result that the company's activities were severely curtailed. The House of Lords held that this constituted oppressive conduct under the English equivalent of s 232 and ordered that the majority buy the shares of the minority.

case note

In *Re Bright Pine Mills Pty Ltd* [1969] VR 1002, a company was engaged in the sawmilling business. Its shareholders were Swallow, who held 5,500 shares, Denton who held 1,250 shares and another who held 250 shares. The three shareholders were also its directors. Denton was voted off the board and replaced by the company's solicitor. A partnership consisting of Swallow's relatives and associates was established to utilise the waste from the sawmilling business. Both Denton and the company itself were excluded from this profitable business. The operations of the partnership were conducted on the company's premises, used the labour of the company's employees and were managed by the company's manager. The company also resolved to allow the partnership the benefit of a lucrative licence for the peeling of logs, which had been negotiated by the company. Denton brought an action under a predecessor of s 232 complaining that both these lucrative businesses should have been undertaken by the company but that the majority shareholders sought to deprive him, as a shareholder, from participating in the profits derived from the businesses. It was held that Swallow, as the person in control of the company, was conducting its affairs in such a way as to benefit himself and others of his choice and to harm Denton. This conduct decreased the value of the assets of the company. Swallow's conduct was "burdensome, harsh and wrongful" so that the affairs of the company were being conducted in a manner oppressive to Denton.

case note

In *Fexuto Pty Ltd v Bosnjak Holdings Pty Ltd* [2001] NSWCA 97 Bosnjak Holdings, a family company, operated the largest private bus company in Australia. Two of its three directors successfully tendered for a contract for additional bus services to be provided by a company in which they were the only shareholders. It was held that the directors breached their fiduciary duties and engaged in oppressive conduct, as the bus services contract was a corporate opportunity that belonged to Bosnjak Holdings. The New South Wales Court of Appeal held that while the third director consented to the acquisition, his consent was not fully informed, as he had not been told that Bosnjak Holdings' resources had been used in making the tender.

[17.55] diversion of profits. It is very common to find in companies that are in essence "quasi partnerships" that the reasonable expectations of shareholders are that profits of the business are divided up among themselves in accordance with the number of shares held. The majority may act oppressively or unfairly where minority shareholders are excluded from being directors and a significant proportion of the profits are paid in the form of high directors' fees and low dividends to shareholders.

The majority may act oppressively or unfairly where minority shareholders are excluded from being directors and a significant proportion of the profits are paid in the form of high directors' fees and low dividends to shareholders.

case note

In *Sanford v Sanford Courier Service Pty Ltd* (1986) 5 ACLC 394, a shareholder brought an action under the equivalent of s 232. The court ordered that the other shareholders purchase his shares. The majority shareholders acted oppressively towards the minority shareholder because they excluded him from the profits of Sanford Courier Service. This was done by diverting business away from the company to another company of which the majority shareholders were the sole directors and shareholders. This was also done by payment of high salaries, provision of motor vehicles and retirement benefits while refusing to pay dividends. This meant that a distribution of a significant part of the profits was made to the majority shareholders while the minority shareholder was excluded after he no longer remained as a director. In these circumstances, a refusal to pay dividends was part of oppressive conduct.

case note

However, in *Morgan v 45 Flers Avenue Pty Ltd* (1987) 5 ACLC 222, the Supreme Court of New South Wales held that the mere fact that dividends were not as high as they could have been is not necessarily an indication of unfairness. Further, of itself, a decision by the directors to pay themselves large bonuses and fees is not oppressive or unfair if the company's profitability had increased significantly because of their enterprise.

The mere fact that dividends were not as high as they could have been is not necessarily an indication of unfairness.

case note

Similarly, in *Dosike Pty Ltd v Johnson* (1997) 15 ACLC 181 the Supreme Court of Western Australia held that there was no oppressive or unfair conduct if the company only paid salaries to directors who worked in the business and not to a director who did nothing.

case note

In *Shamsallah Holdings Pty Ltd v CBD Refrigeration & Airconditioning Services Pty Ltd* [2001] WASC 8, the company had a policy of restricting dividends to 50 per cent of net profits after tax. This policy had not been reviewed for a number of years even though its profits had quintupled and it had substantial cash reserves that were surplus to its needs. The Supreme Court of Western Australia held that the directors' failure to review the dividend policy in light of the company's changing and improving circumstances is oppressive, especially when at the same time the directors are increasing their own remuneration.

Directors' failure to review the dividend policy in light of the company's changing and improving circumstances is oppressive, especially when at the same time the directors are increasing their own remuneration.

[17.60] exclusion from management. In companies that run a family business, it may be oppressive or unfair to exclude a particular family member from the company's management. Family companies are often run as if they were family partnerships with family members having a reasonable expectation of participating in the management of the family company's business.

In companies that run a family business, it may be oppressive or unfair to exclude a particular family member from the company's management.

case note

In *Fexuto Pty Ltd v Bosnjak Holdings Pty Ltd* [2001] NSWCA 97 Bosnjak Holdings Pty Ltd, a family company controlled by various members of the Bosnjak family had three directors: two brothers, Bob and Jim Bosnjak, and Carol, the wife of their deceased brother John. Fexuto Pty Ltd, Bob's family company which owned two-sevenths of the Bosnjak Holdings shares, sought a remedy under a predecessor of s 232. The New South Wales Court of Appeal held that even though Bob remained a director, the practice of the other directors of excluding Bob from involvement in the company's decision-making process was one of the relevant factors in their conclusion that there was oppressive and unfairly prejudicial conduct. The court found that, in essence, Bosnjak Holdings was a family partnership which had taken a corporate form. It was established to provide for the economic well-being of the Bosnjak family. In the circumstances, there was a legitimate expectation that Bob, as one of the senior members of the family, would be involved in the company's management.

case note

Similarly, in *GFS Management Services Pty Ltd v Ground & Foundation Supports Pty Ltd* [2001] WASC 143, the managing director of a company controlled 30 per cent of its shares. The other two directors each owned 35 per cent. As a result of a disagreement about the managing director's salary package, a board meeting was held and the other two directors resolved to terminate the managing director's position as managing director. He subsequently resigned his directorship and set up a competing business. It was held that the controlling directors had acted oppressively and unfairly as they had not given the former managing director notice of the resolution to terminate his position. They had also not given him the opportunity to put his case.

[17.65] directors' failure to act in the interests of the company. Minority shareholders may apply for a remedy under s 232 where directors breach their fiduciary duties by failing to act in the company's best interests and do not permit the company to take action against them.

Minority shareholders may apply for a remedy under s 232 where directors breach their fiduciary duties by failing to act in the company's best interests and do not permit the company to take action against them.

case note

In *Re Spargos Mining NL* (1990) 8 ACLC 1218, the company was, together with Enterprise Gold Mines NL, a member of the Independent Resources Ltd group. The court found that the affairs of the company were conducted in a manner that was oppressive and unfair. The directors exhibited "an endemic incapacity" to deal with the company's affairs by giving sole attention to its interests. There were clear cases of conflicts of interest that were detrimental to the company, its shareholders generally and the minority shareholders not otherwise interested in other companies for whose benefit the transactions were undertaken. The transactions were almost entirely devoid of any commercial benefit to the company.

case note

In *Jenkins v Enterprise Gold Mines NL* (1992) 10 ACLC 136 Enterprise Gold Mines NL (EGM), a listed company, was a member of a group of companies controlled by persons who also controlled Independent Resources Ltd (IRL). At all relevant times, EGM and IRL had common directors. Over the space of about two years, EGM was involved in a number of transactions with other companies in the IRL group resulting in considerable losses to the company. These transactions were entered into and carried out by its directors without adequate disclosure to the shareholders or independent directors and in breach of their fiduciary duty to avoid a conflict of interest. In relation to these transactions the directors of EGM had disregarded their duty to act in the best interests of that company and acted in the interests of other companies in the IRL group. It was held there was oppression or unfairness where the controlling directors pursued a course of conduct designed by them to further their own interests or the interests of others to the detriment of the company or to the detriment of the minority shareholders. The court ordered that a receiver and manager with power to investigate breaches of directors' duties be appointed to take control of the company because it thought independent, outside management was necessary in the circumstances.

case note

In *Re Overton Holdings Pty Ltd* (1984) 2 ACLC 777 Faye, Overton's managing director and majority shareholder, arranged for the company to lend money to two other companies controlled by him. These loans were made without the knowledge of Overton's other director and minority shareholder. The Supreme Court of Western Australia held that Faye had breached his duty because there appeared to be no commercial advantage to Overton in lending the money. The loans were unsecured and the borrowing companies were in financial difficulties. It was held that this conduct was oppressive because it was unlikely that the board would take action against Faye where the circumstances indicated it had a reasonable cause of action.

case note

In *Dynasty Pty Ltd v Coombs* (1995) 13 ACLC 1290, directors arranged for Dynasty to guarantee the debts of another company controlled by one of its directors and majority shareholder. The Federal Court held that because there was no commercial benefit to Dynasty in acting as guarantor, the directors breached their fiduciary duty and consequently acted oppressively and unfairly for purposes of the predecessor of s 232.

If the directors who breached their duty are also the majority shareholders, they will act oppressively or unfairly if, as shareholders, they vote to ratify their improper actions.

[17.70] improper share issue. As discussed in Chapter 13.2 above, directors breach their fiduciary duties if they issue shares for improper purposes. If the directors who breached their duty are also the majority shareholders, they will act oppressively or unfairly if, as shareholders, they vote to ratify their improper actions.

case note

In *Hannes v MJH Pty Ltd* (1992) 10 ACLC 400, Hannes was the governing director and controlling shareholder of a family company. The constitution gave him total control of management as well as control of the majority of votes at the general meeting. Without disclosure to, or approval of, the other shareholders, Hannes and another director resolved to issue additional shares to himself. They also agreed that Hannes be employed under a service contract which provided for a large termination payment. They also decided to establish a superannuation fund for Hannes. When the other shareholders discovered this they applied for a remedy under a predecessor of s 232 arguing that the board's decisions were oppressive or unfairly prejudicial or discriminatory. The New South Wales Court of Appeal granted the remedy and ordered that the company's constitution be changed to remove Hannes' absolute control over the voting at shareholders' meetings. The court held that Hannes' dominant motive in relation to the share allotment and service contract was self-interest. He sought to provide himself with additional financial benefits at a time when his relationship with the other shareholders was deteriorating. The court further decided that in the circumstances, Hannes as majority shareholder could not ratify his own breaches of duty. This would be oppressive or unfair. The particular decisions made by the directors could only be ratified by the disinterested shareholders.

case note

In *Re Dalkeith Investments Pty Ltd* (1985) 3 ACLC 74, Smith and his wife each held a third of the shares of a company, the remaining shares being held by Inglis and his wife. Smith was chairman and a director, his wife being the other director. Smith and his wife separated and the affairs of the company were conducted in an atmosphere of animosity. Smith arrived late at a general meeting of the company and in his absence Inglis took the chair and together with his wife was appointed a director of the company. Control thereby passed to Inglis and his wife with the acquiescence of Smith's wife. The directors then resolved to issue shares to all members. This resulted in Smith having a choice of either investing more money in a company whose shareholders were hostile to his interests or allowing his shareholding to be diluted. It was also resolved that the company would acquire land from Inglis, the purchase price being paid partly in cash and partly by allotment of shares in the company. Smith brought an action seeking that the company be wound up or alternatively, that his shares be purchased at valuation. It was held that the actions of Inglis, his wife and Smith's wife were taken for the purpose of diluting Smith's shareholding and were not in the interests of the company as a whole. The directors acted oppressively by excluding Smith from an opportunity to participate in, or oppose, their decisions. The conduct also resulted in giving control of the company to one of the three groups of shareholders. This was unfairly prejudicial to, or discriminatory against, Smith in his capacity as a member and the court ordered that his shares be purchased at an appropriate valuation.

remedies

[17.75] The court has wide powers to make any order it considers appropriate if shareholders can prove that the conduct of a company's affairs is contrary to the interests of the members as a whole, oppressive, unfairly prejudicial or unfairly discriminatory: s 233(1). Examples of orders that may be appropriate are set out in this section. These include orders:

The court has wide powers to make any order it considers appropriate.

- that the company be wound up (s 233(1)(a));
- that the existing constitution be modified or repealed (s 233(1)(b));
- regulating the future conduct of the company's affairs (s 233(1)(c));
- for the purchase of the shares of any member by other members or a person to whom a share has been transmitted by will or by operation of law: s 233(1)(d). This is the most common order made;
- for the purchase of the shares with an appropriate reduction of the company's share capital (s 233(1)(e));
- that the company institute or defend legal proceedings or authorise a member to institute or defend legal proceedings in the name of the company: s 233(1)(f) and (g). Such an order would be appropriate in cases where a company ratifies a breach of duty by directors or if it fails to bring an action against a director for breach of duty in circumstances where the ratification or failure is oppressive or unfairly prejudicial or unfairly discriminatory to one or more members;
- appointing a receiver or a receiver and manager (s 233(1)(h));
- restraining a person from engaging in specified conduct or from doing a specified act: s 233(1)(i). Such an order would be appropriate where an act or conduct that is oppressive, unfairly prejudicial or discriminatory has not yet been carried out but has merely been proposed. It is also appropriate where the conduct is of an ongoing nature; and
- requiring a person to do a specified act: s 233(i)(j). This remedy enables omissions to be rectified.

The policy behind ss 232 and 233 is to enable an oppressed member to be released from the company in the circumstances set out in s 232: *Fedorovitch v St Aubins Pty Ltd* (1999) 17 ACLC 1558. A remedy under s 233 should not include an element of compensation. This excludes matters such as the incurring of capital gains tax and legal costs incurred in the transfer of assets.

Where an order is made under s 233, the applicant must lodge a copy of the order with ASIC within 14 days after it is made: s 235.

The most common remedy sought by minority shareholders is an order that the majority shareholders buy their shares.

[17.80] share buy-out. The most common remedy sought by minority shareholders in s 232 cases is an order that the majority shareholders buy their shares: s 233(1)(d).

The court also has a wide discretion in determining a valuation for the purposes of a purchase of shares of members by other members or by the company. For example, in *Scottish Co-operative Wholesale Soc Ltd v Meyer* [1959] AC 324, the court ordered that the majority shareholders purchase the shares of the minority members at a price based on the value the shares would have had, had the oppressive conduct not taken place.

case note

In *Re Bagot Well Pastoral Co* (1993) 11 ACLC 1, a number of considerations were taken into account in determining a valuation of shares. The shares were valued at the date of lodging the application under the predecessor of s 232. The valuation took into account the minority share-holder's disadvantageous position under the constitution. The majority shareholder had a right to require further shares to be issued and sole right to participate in distribution of surplus assets on a winding up. The assessment was based on revised annual accounts which assumed proper commercial arrangements between the company and interests associated with the majority shareholder. The annual accounts were also revised to take into account the position that would have occurred, had the directors paid reasonable dividends. The advantage to the majority shareholder of gaining full control was also a relevant factor.

[17.85] replacement of directors. The court has the power to replace directors.

case note

In *Re Spargos Mining NL* (1990) 8 ACLC 1218, Murray J in the Supreme Court of Western Australia ordered that two directors of the company be replaced by a newly constituted board, comprising people who were independent of the controlling shareholders. The new board was ordered to investigate certain transactions entered into by the company and cause the company to commence proceedings against the former directors if that was appropriate.

The court has the power to appoint a receiver to safeguard the company's assets and investigate alleged breaches of directors' duties.

[17.90] appointment of receiver. In appropriate circumstances, the court has the power to appoint a receiver to safeguard the company's assets and investigate alleged breaches of directors' duties.

case note

In *Jenkins v Enterprise Gold Mines NL* (1992) 10 ACLC 136, the Full Court of the Supreme Court of Western Australia ordered the appointment of a receiver and manager with powers to investigate the transactions involving apparent breaches of directors' fiduciary duties and where necessary, institute proceedings against them. The Full Court was of the opinion that this was the most suitable order to deal with the oppressive and unfair conduct. The court thought that the order made by Murray J at first instance in the case, *Re Enterprise Gold Mines NL* (1991) 9 ACLC 168, was inappropriate. Murray J ordered that as new directors had been appointed, the company should remain under the control of the board but that shareholder approval be required in relation to the disposal of assets to directors, and associated companies. The Full Court held that this order would not overcome any unfairness to minority shareholders, nor would it facilitate investigation and prosecution of transactions involving conflicts of interest by former directors of the company.

[17.95] authorisation of legal action. The court may permit an oppressed or unfairly treated shareholder to bring a legal action against directors in the name of the company.

The court may permit an oppressed or unfairly treated shareholder to bring a legal action against directors in the name of the company.

case note

In *Re Overton Holdings Pty Ltd* (1984) 2 ACLC 777, the Supreme Court of Western Australia granted an order authorising a member to institute legal proceedings on behalf of the company under the equivalent of s 233(1)(g) against the managing director and his associated companies for breach of their duties to Overton Holdings. The court, in effect, allowed a derivative action to be brought. This type of action is now primarily governed under Pt 2F.1A, which allows proceedings to be brought on behalf of a company by its members. This procedure is discussed below.

[17.100] director not to participate in management. A director may be ordered not to interfere with the company's management.

A director may be ordered not to interfere with the company's management.

case note

In *Re H R Harmer Ltd* [1958] 3 All ER 689; [1959] 1 WLR 62, a father and two sons were the directors of a family company. The father was chairman and governing director; however, the company's constitution did not confer any special powers upon him. Together with his wife, he controlled more than three-quarters of the shares and generally regarded the business of the company as his own. He ignored the wishes of the other directors and disregarded resolutions of the board. It was held that this conduct amounted to oppression. An order was made that the father, the company's governing director, should not interfere with valid decisions of the board of directors and that he enter into a contract with the company as a consultant at a specified salary.

[17.105] alteration of constitution. The court has the power to order the company to alter its constitution.

The court has the power to order the company to alter its constitution.

case note

In *Hannes v MJH Pty Ltd* (1992) 10 ACLC 400, the facts of which are set out above, para [17.115], the court ordered that the share issue and service agreement be set aside. In addition, it ordered that the company's constitution be altered so as to give the other shareholders a right to appoint their representative to the board, a role in relation to alteration of the company's constitution and director's remuneration, and advance notice of further issues of shares.

If the court orders that the constitution of the company be repealed or modified, the company cannot make any further alterations inconsistent with the order unless permitted by the order or with the leave of the court: s 233(3).

The courts are generally reluctant to wind up a solvent company.

[17.110] winding up. The courts are generally reluctant to wind up a solvent company as an alternative remedy will usually be of greater benefit to members. Where an order to wind up is made, the *Corporations Act* provisions apply as if the winding up was ordered under s 461: s 233(2).

proceedings on behalf of a company: Part 2F.1A

Part 2F.1A provides for a statutory derivative action which enables shareholders and other eligible applicants to bring legal proceedings on behalf of a company where the company is unwilling or unable to do so itself.

[17.115] Part 2F.1A of the *Corporations Act* was inserted as a result of 1999 amendments and provides for a statutory derivative action which enables shareholders and other eligible applicants to bring legal proceedings on behalf of a company where the company is unwilling or unable to do so itself. The aim of Pt 2F.1A is to strengthen shareholders' rights and thereby provide more effective internal mechanisms to encourage appropriate corporate governance practices by directors.

In order to better reflect the nature of the proceedings involved, the expression "proceedings on behalf of a company" is used instead of "statutory derivative action". In order to promote certainty regarding the nature of the action and avoid confusion, shareholders' common law rights to bring derivative actions under the exceptions to the proper plaintiff rule in *Foss v Harbottle* are abolished: s 236(3).

The *Corporations Act* recognises that a consequence of making it easier for shareholders to bring an action is that directors may be unnecessarily inconvenienced by inappropriate legal actions detrimental to the company, brought by disgruntled shareholders. Part 2F1.A therefore requires the leave of the court to be obtained for the legal action to proceed. Such leave is only granted where the court is satisfied that the action is appropriate.

Commentary on statutory derivative actions may be seen in several articles linked to the Lipton-Herzberg Members' Remedies Pathway at **http://www.lipton-herzberg.com.au/secure/pathways-chapter-17-members-remedies.html**

application to bring proceedings

[17.120] Under s 236(1), the following persons may bring proceedings on behalf of a company:

> **a member, former member or person entitled to be registered as a member of the company or of a related body corporate; or**
> **present or former directors and officers of the company.**

Eligible applicants must obtain leave from the court before commencing a proceeding on behalf of a company.

To ensure that company management is not undermined by vexatious litigation, eligible applicants must obtain leave from the court before commencing a proceeding on behalf of a company or intervening in proceedings to which the company is a party: s 236(1)(b).

The court must grant an application for leave if it is satisfied that each of the requirements in s 237(2) is met.

The court must grant an application for leave if it is satisfied that each of the requirements in s 237(2) is met. These are:

> **it is probable that the company will not itself bring the proceedings (s 237(2)(a));**
> **the applicant is acting in good faith (s 237(2)(b));**
> **it is in the best interests of the company that the applicant be granted leave (s 237(2)(c));**
> **there is a serious question to be tried (s 237(2)(d)); and**
> **the applicant gave notice to the company at least 14 days before making the application of the intention to apply for leave and the reasons for applying, or it is appropriate to grant leave even though notice was not given: s 237(2)(e).**

case note

In *Charlton v Baber* [2003] NSWSC 745, it was held that a shareholder satisfied the s 237(2) requirements and was granted leave to bring proceedings in the name of a company in liquidation against one of its directors. The shareholder alleged that prior to the company's liquidation, the director breached his fiduciary duty in a number of respects. It was alleged that the director arranged for the company to lend money on uncommercial terms, paid excessive wages and other benefits to the director's wife, caused the company to make improper dividend payments contrary to the company's constitution to the director's wife and arranged for the company to enter into lease arrangements with the director's family company on disadvantageous terms. The court held that the fact that the company is in liquidation is not a barrier to the court granting leave to an applicant who satisfied all the s 237(2) requirements:

> the shareholder satisfied the s 237(2)(a) requirement as there was evidence that the company's liquidator would not bring legal proceedings against the director for the alleged breaches of duty because the liquidator did not think the proceedings would succeed or that, having regard to the amounts involved, it would not be commercial to pursue the case;
> the shareholder satisfied the "good faith" requirement in s 237(2)(b). The court held that this required an applicant to show that they honestly believed that a good cause of action exists and has reasonable prospects of success. There is an absence of "good faith" if the applicant seeks to bring the action in the name of the company for a collateral purpose as would amount to an abuse of process;
> the shareholder satisfied the court that it was in the best interests of the company that leave be granted: s 237(2)(c). The court noted that as the company was being wound up and was insolvent, s 237(2)(c) required the court to be satisfied that the legal proceedings against the director would "enhance returns to creditors and promote the welfare of creditors". The court held that a successful case against the director would promote the creditors' interests and, in the circumstances of this particular company, must be regarded as in the best interests of the company; and
> the court held that there was a serious question to be tried for purposes of s 237(2)(d) and that the shareholder had given notice as required by s 237(2)(e). The court held that to establish the s 237(2)(d) requirement, an applicant has to show that there is at least a probability that the legal proceedings in the name of the company will succeed.

Section 237(3) assists a court in deciding whether or not it is in the best interests of the company that an applicant be granted leave for purposes of the s 237(2)(c) requirement. Section 237(3), which deals with the situation where the company's decision not to bring legal proceedings is made by its directors, creates a rebuttable presumption that granting leave is not in the best interests of the company in the following circumstances:

Section 237(3) assists a court in deciding whether or not it is in the best interests of the company that an applicant be granted leave.

> all directors who participated in the decision to bring, defend or settle proceedings made the decision in good faith for a proper purpose;
> the directors did not have a personal material interest in the decision;
> the directors informed themselves about the subject matter of the decision to the extent they reasonably believed to be appropriate; and
> the directors rationally believed the decision was in the best interests of the company. Such a belief is a rational one unless the belief is one that no reasonable person in the position of the directors would hold.

Section 241(1)(d) also assists the court in deciding whether or not to grant leave. That provision gives the court the power to appoint an independent person to investigate and report on the financial affairs of the company, the surrounding circumstances of the cause of action and the funds expended by all sides during the proceedings.

ratification by general meeting

[17.125] At common law, a shareholder could not bring a derivative action against directors if the directors' conduct was either ratified at a general meeting of shareholders, or was capable of being ratified at such a meeting. However, some breaches of duty were non-ratifiable and it was unclear when this was the case.

Section 239(1) overcomes the common law complexities by providing that ratification does not prevent a person from bringing proceedings on behalf of the company or applying for leave to do so.

Section 239(1) overcomes the common law complexities by providing that ratification does not prevent a person from bringing proceedings on behalf of the company or applying for leave to do so. The court may, however, take ratification into account in deciding what ultimate order it should make: s 239(2).

One of the main difficulties under the previous law was that company funds were generally not available to shareholders to finance the legal costs of their derivative actions. Section 242 gives the court a broad discretion to make any order it considers appropriate about the legal costs of the applicant, the company or any other party to the proceedings. Such orders can include an order requiring indemnification for costs.

section 1324 injunctions

The court has a discretion to grant an injunction restraining a person from engaging in conduct that contravenes the *Corporations Act*.

[17.130] Under s 1324(1), the court has a discretion to grant an injunction restraining a person from engaging in conduct that contravenes the *Corporations Act*. In addition, the court may, if it thinks it is desirable to do so, require that person to do any act or thing. Where an application is made under s 1324(1), the court may grant an interim injunction restraining particular conduct, before considering the application: s 1324(4). This means that an applicant may speedily obtain an order with the merits of the case to be decided upon at a later hearing.

In addition to granting an injunction under s 1324(1), the court may also order that the person acting in contravention of the *Corporations Act* pay damages to any other person: s 1324(10). In *Permanent Trustee Australia Ltd v Perpetual Trustee Co Ltd* (1995) 13 ACLC 66, the Supreme Court of New South Wales held that it could make a damages order under the predecessor of s 1324(10) even if the applicant had not applied for an injunction under s 1324(1).

contravention of Corporations Act

[17.135] Conduct that constitutes a "contravention" of the *Corporations Act* includes conduct that is regarded as a criminal offence under the *Corporations Act*. For example, as discussed in Chapter 7 above, a person who issues a disclosure document that contains a material statement that is misleading or deceptive contravenes s 728, which is a criminal offence. Section 1324 allows the court to grant an injunction to restrain the person from issuing the disclosure document in such circumstances.

Section 1324 also applies to a breach of the *Corporations Act* that is not a criminal offence. For example, as discussed in Chapter 8 above, a company may only reduce its capital if the reduction complies with the requirements in s 256B(1). If a company contravenes these requirements, the contravention does not affect the validity of the reduction and the company is not guilty of an offence: s 256D(2). Even though s 256D(2) specifies that the contravention of s 256B is not a criminal offence, s 1324 enables the court to restrain such conduct.

Section 1324 does not apply to conduct that merely contravenes a provision in a company's constitution or the replaceable rules. According to s 135(1) this is not regarded as a contravention of the *Corporations Act*, but may be remedied as a breach of contract under s 140(1).

A court may also grant an s 1324 injunction to restrain a contravention of a section of the *Corporations Act* that is a designated civil penalty provision. The designated civil penalty provisions include ss 180–183 (statutory duties of officers), s 588G (insolvent trading), s 208 (related party transactions) and the various sections that deal with share capital transactions. As discussed in Chapter 13.6 above, contravention of a civil penalty provision may have both civil and criminal consequences. Contravention may result in the imposition of civil penalty orders under s 1317G and a liability to pay compensation under s 1317H. Criminal proceedings may be brought under s 184.

who may apply?

[17.140] Only ASIC or a person whose interests have been affected by the conduct can apply to the court for an s 1324 injunction.

Only ASIC or a person whose interests have been affected by the conduct can apply to the court for an s 1324 injunction.

case note

The range of persons who may apply for an s 1324 injunction was considered in *Broken Hill Proprietary Co Ltd v Bell Resources Ltd* (1984) 2 ACLC 157. The Victorian Supreme Court held that a broad interpretation should be given consistent with the objects of the legislation when determining who could apply for an injunction under the predecessor of s 1324. It decided that the persons who could apply under s 1324(2)(b) need not show that personal rights of a proprietary or similar nature were or may be affected by the conduct. Further, they need not prove that they suffered any special injury arising from the contravention of the *Corporations Act*. However, applicants must establish that their interests go beyond the mere interests of members of the public.

Applying this broad interpretation, shareholders generally appear to have standing to apply for an s 1324 injunction to restrain contraventions of Ch 2D duties by directors and other officers. They have a greater interest in such contraventions than a mere member of the public. In effect, this would constitute proceedings being brought on behalf of a company similar to the procedure set out in Pt 2F.1A. However, in *Mesenberg v Cord Industrial Recruiters Pty Ltd* (1996) ACLC 519, the Supreme Court of New South Wales expressed strong doubts that s 1324 was intended to be used in this way. It held that because shareholders did not have standing to apply for a civil penalty order, only ASIC could apply for an s 1324 injunction to restrain contraventions of civil penalty provisions.

This approach was not followed in *Airpeak Pty Ltd v Jetstream Ltd* (1997) 15 ACLC 715. The Federal Court refused to restrict s 1324 in this way and did not follow the decision in *Mesenberg*. It approved the broad interpretation of *BHP v Bell Resources* and held that shareholders, as well as creditors, of a company had standing to apply for an s 1324 injunction to restrain breaches of duty by directors. Their interests could be affected by directors' contraventions of their duties. The court noted that, because it retained the ultimate discretion whether or not to grant an injunction, giving standing to shareholders and creditors would not result in an opening of the floodgates of actions against directors and cause disruption to the proper running companies.

A contravention of the *Corporations Act* is taken to affect the interests of a creditor or member of a company if:

> **the insolvency of the company is an element of the contravention; or**

> **the company contravenes the share buy-back, financial assistance or share capital reduction provisions contained in ss 257A, 260A and 256B, respectively: s 1324(1A).**

Where it is alleged that these provisions have been contravened by the company or other person, the onus is on the company or other person to prove that no contravention has occurred: s 1324(1B).

Section 1324B gives the court the power to order persons who contravened the following provisions to publish corrective advertisements at the person's own expense:

- managed investment scheme provisions of Ch 5C;
- continuous disclosure provisions of Ch 6CA;
- fundraising provisions of Ch 6D; and
- market misconduct provisions of Pt 7.10.

winding up

There are various grounds upon which the court may order the winding up of a solvent company on the application of a member.

[17.145] There are various grounds upon which the court may order the winding up of a solvent company on the application of a member.

It is a drastic step for a member to apply for a winding up of the company. It may have adverse results for the applicant as assets generally realise less than if they are sold as part of a going concern. This is especially the case if no ready buyer can be found for the assets of the company. The court will not make a winding up order under s 461(1)(e), (f), (g) or (k) if it is of the opinion that the applicants have some other available remedy or that they are acting unreasonably in seeking the winding up order instead of pursuing that other remedy: s 467(4). From the applicant's point of view, an order under s 233 is usually preferable because the courts have a wide discretion in the type of order they can make.

case note

In *Re Dalkeith Investments Pty Ltd* (1985) 3 ACLC 74, the facts of which are discussed above, para [17.70], a divorce between two major shareholders resulted in a breakdown in the mutual trust and confidence between members. As this was irreconcilable, the applicant shareholder was entitled to have the company wound up under what is now s 461(1)(k). However, the Supreme Court of Queensland held that a remedy under the equivalent of s 232 was less drastic and more appropriate in the circumstances. A winding up would have been prejudicial to the shareholders other than the applicant. The company was profitable and held considerable net assets and should not unnecessarily be brought to an end.

directors act in their own interests

The court may wind up a company if the directors have acted in their own interests rather than in the interests of the members as a whole, or in any other manner that is unfair or unjust to other members.

[17.150] Under s 461(1)(e), the court may wind up a company if the directors have acted in their own interests rather than in the interests of the members as a whole, or in any other manner that is unfair or unjust to other members.

There have been few cases dealing with this ground for winding up. The circumstances where s 461(1)(e) applies will normally also give a shareholder a remedy under s 232. They will also satisfy the ground for winding up under s 461(1)(k), the "just and equitable" ground. This is discussed below.

In *Re Cumberland Holdings Ltd* (1976) ACLR 361, Bowen CJ considered the meaning of a predecessor of s 461(1)(e). While his decision was subsequently reversed by the Privy Council, it did not disapprove his interpretation of the section. Bowen CJ put the following propositions in respect of that provision:

- the section applies where the board acts unanimously. It also applies where a majority of the directors act in their own interests or in the interests of one or more of them. Further, it may even apply where a single director is able to persuade the board to act in that director's personal interests.
- the words "affairs of the company" are extremely broad and include its business, capital structure, dividend policy, voting rights, consideration of takeover offers and any matters that are considered by the board; and
- directors may act in their "own interests" when they act in the interests of another company in which they may be directors or shareholders.

case note

In *Re William Brooks & Co Ltd* [1962] NSWR 142, the managing director of a prosperous company used his position as a director to acquire options to purchase shares that had been issued to the company's employees. This arrangement was entered into to enable him to control the majority of votes at a general meeting of members. The managing director also managed the company's business without consulting the other directors. Further, for a number of years he saw to it that the company paid extravagant bonuses to employees. These payments concealed the fact that the company was in fact very profitable and had the effect of depressing the market price of the shares on the stock exchange. The court held that in these circumstances the managing director had committed serious and persistent breaches of his fiduciary duty. As he acted in his own interests and in a manner that was unfair or unjust to members, the court ordered that the company be wound up under the predecessor to s 461(1)(e).

oppressive and unfair conduct

[17.155] Where the grounds for a remedy under s 232 are established, a member may also apply to have the company wound up under s 461(1)(f) and (g).

Where the grounds for a remedy under s 232 are established, a member may also apply to have the company wound up.

case note

In *Kokotovich Constructions Pty Ltd v Wallington* (1995) 13 ACLC 1113, the Court of Appeal of the Supreme Court of New South Wales ordered that a company be wound up under s 461(1)(f). The directors breached their fiduciary duties when they issued shares for the improper purpose of manipulating the voting power to the detriment of the minority shareholder. The court noted that even though winding up a successful and prosperous company was an extreme step, it was appropriate in this case because of the real risk of further oppressive conduct and the limited nature of the company's business activities.

just and equitable ground

[17.160] Under s 461(1)(k), the court may order the winding up of a company if it is of the opinion that this would be just and equitable. This ground has been interpreted very broadly so as to give the courts a very wide discretion as to when to order a winding up and has often been used as a means of resolving a situation where minority shareholders have been harshly treated by the controllers of a company. It appears to overlap with s 461(1)(e), (f) and (g) but goes further. It also overlaps with s 232. Any member has a right to apply for a winding up on these grounds even if the company is solvent and able to pay its debts.

The court may order the winding up of a company if it is of the opinion that this would be just and equitable.

The courts have wound up companies on the just and equitable ground in a number of different circumstances. These include situations where there is:

> a breakdown in the mutual trust and confidence of members;
> a deadlock;
> fraud, misconduct or oppression in the conduct and management of the company's affairs; or
> a failure of substratum.

The courts have wound up companies on the just and equitable ground in a number of different circumstances.

The just and equitable ground is, however, not confined to these categories.

It is just and equitable to wind up a company that is a "quasi partnership" if there has been a breakdown in the mutual trust and confidence that should exist among shareholders.

[17.165] breakdown of mutual trust and confidence. It is just and equitable to wind up a company that is a "quasi partnership" if there has been a breakdown in the mutual trust and confidence that should exist among shareholders. In the case of small companies that have evolved from partnerships or that operate in a similar manner to partnerships, it has been held just and equitable to wind up the company when the relationship between the "partners" breaks down.

The relationship may break down for a variety of reasons.

case note

For example, in *Lawrence v Lawrick Motors Ltd* (1948) 2 SA 1029 (WLD) a South African company was controlled by two families. The court held that the mutual trust and confidence between the directors broke down when one director committed adultery with the wife of the other. The court ordered that the company be wound up.

case note

In *Ebrahimi v Westbourne Galleries Ltd* [1973] AC 360, one "partner" attempted to "freeze out" the other from the management of the company's business. In that case Ebrahimi and Nazar had been partners in a rug business. They formed a company to take over this business, of which each was a director and each held 500 shares. Soon after, Nazar's son became a director and each of the two shareholders transferred 100 shares to him. The company made good profits, which were distributed as directors' remuneration. Disputes arose between Ebrahimi on the one hand and Nazar and his son on the other, who then passed an ordinary resolution at a general meeting to remove Ebrahimi from his position as director and excluded him from the conduct of the company's business.

The House of Lords upheld an order winding up the company on the just and equitable ground. The House of Lords held that even though the applicable *Companies Act* and articles may allow for a particular course of action, such as the removal of a director, where the company was in substance a "quasi-partnership" the majority shareholders had to act in a way that was consistent with the understanding the shareholders had at the time the company was formed. This understanding involved mutual confidence. It was appropriate in this case to order a winding up because this understanding had been repudiated. The minority shareholder was excluded from management of the affairs of the company and he lost his right to share in its profits.

Section 232 also applies in circumstances similar to *Ebrahimi's* case and provides for more appropriate remedies than the extreme step of winding up, especially where the company is solvent.

Other examples of conduct that indicate a breakdown of a quasi-partnership and justify winding up on just and equitable grounds are misuse of proceeds from the sale of company assets and exclusion of a director from access to the company's books: *Stapp v Surge Holdings Pty Ltd* (1999) 17 ACLC 896.

case note

The question of when a breakdown in confidence justifies winding up a company arose in *Carpenter v Carpenter Grazing Co Pty Ltd* (1986) 4 ACLC 18. A dispute involving share allotments was resolved by the court when an allotment was declared invalid as not being in the interests of the company as a whole. However, the court refused to wind up the company. Although the company was a small, family company, it was not a quasi-partnership as referred to in *Ebrahimi v Westbourne Galleries Ltd* [1973] AC 360. In the circumstances of *Carpenter's* case, the company was set up by a father in a way that conferred control of management on him and gave equity interest only to the children. This meant that the company was not analogous to a partnership, which presumes all partners have the right to participate in management. The fact that there had been a dispute over respective shareholdings that had since been resolved by the court did not in itself show an irretrievable breakdown of confidence or a deadlock between family members.

[17.170] deadlock. The just and equitable ground is established where the shareholders in a company are deadlocked to the extent that the company is unable to function properly. This is also analogous to the situation in partnership law where a deadlock or dispute between the partners results in an order that the partnership be dissolved. In such cases it is not necessary for the applicant to show that other members acted oppressively or unjustly. The courts will generally not interfere if the deadlock can be resolved under the articles.

The just and equitable ground is established where the shareholders in a company are deadlocked to the extent that the company is unable to function properly.

case note

Re Yenidje Tobacco Co Ltd [1916] 2 Ch 426 is an example of where a company was ordered to be wound up because there was a deadlock between the shareholders. Two people each carried on separate businesses and decided to amalgamate. For this purpose a company was formed with each person a director and equal shareholder. The company made considerable profits but the two members became bitterly hostile and were unable to communicate with each other. The articles did not provide for a casting vote. A provision referring disputes to arbitration had proved impractical in resolving continuous disputes.

Another alternative in the case of a deadlock is for the court to convene a general meeting where this is impracticable under the replaceable rules or constitution. In *Re Totex-Adon Pty Ltd* [1980] 1 NSWLR 605, a company had two shareholders, one of whom refused to attend meetings. The articles required a quorum of two. The court convened a general meeting under the equivalent of s 249G and ordered that the presence of one member would constitute a quorum.

[17.175] fraud, misconduct or oppression. The court may wind up a company on the just and equitable ground if there has been fraud, misconduct or oppression. This ground has been largely incorporated into s 232, which allows a wide range of remedies.

The court may wind up a company on the just and equitable ground if there has been fraud, misconduct or oppression.

case note

In *Loch v John Blackwood Ltd* [1924] AC 783, the Privy Council held that a small company be wound up because the directors showed a lack of probity or fair conduct in managing the affairs of the company. A strong indication of this was that the directors denied information regarding the company's affairs to the minority shareholders. This was done to enable the directors to acquire their shares at a low price.

This particular ground has been applied in those situations where directors or controlling shareholders have made unauthorised payments from company funds: *Re William Brooks & Co Ltd* [1962] NSWR 142. It has also been applied where the directors have breached their fiduciary duties. For example, in *Re Straw Products Ltd* [1942] VLR 222, the company was wound up on the just and equitable ground in circumstances where the breach of duty stemmed from a conflict of interests that enabled them to make undisclosed profits.

case note

In *ASC v AS Nominees Ltd* (1995) 13 ACLC 1822, the Federal Court ordered that a company that acted as trustee of several superannuation trusts be wound up under s 461(1)(k) on the application of the predecessor of ASIC. It held that there had been misconduct and mismanagement of the trust businesses. In particular, the directors had repeatedly made decisions on behalf of the trusts that advanced their own personal interests in breach of their fiduciary duties to avoid conflicts of interest. They engaged in misleading conduct and repeatedly breached the predecessor of s 251A by not arranging for appropriate minutes of decisions to be kept and may also have breached the equivalent of s 286 by failing to keep adequate financial records.

Another reason for winding up a company on the just and equitable ground is where it ceases to carry on the business for which it was formed. This is referred to as "failure of substratum".

[17.180] failure of substratum. Another reason for winding up a company on the just and equitable ground is where it ceases to carry on the business for which it was formed. This is referred to as "failure of substratum".

case note

In *Re Tivoli Freeholds Ltd* [1972] VR 445, a company was formed for the purposes of carrying on the business of theatre proprietor, conducting entertainment and other associated activities. Its main asset was land upon which theatres were built. The company came under the control of Industrial Equity Ltd which appointed its own nominees to the board of directors of Tivoli Freeholds Ltd. A fire severely damaged the buildings and the theatrical activities ceased. Tivoli Freeholds Ltd then sold the land with the approval of the general meeting. The board resolved to lend the surplus funds thus obtained to Industrial Equity Ltd, repayable at call. These funds were largely used to acquire shares in other public companies. A minority shareholder, who with supporters controlled 42 per cent of the company's shares, petitioned that the company be wound up by the court on the grounds of oppression and on the just and equitable ground. It was held that it was just and equitable that the company be wound up. This was because the company was acting entirely outside what could fairly be regarded as having been within the general intention and common understanding of the members when they became members. This was so, even though the new activities were not outside the scope of the objects clause in its constitution and therefore not ultra vires. In order to ascertain the commonly understood purposes of the company, it is necessary to determine the main or paramount object of the company. To do this, it is permissible to look beyond the objects clause to things such as a prospectus, the company's course of conduct, and even its name, in order to remove an ambiguity in the objects clause.

members' right to inspect books

[17.185] The right of members to inspect their company's books raises two distinct considerations. Such a right enhances the ability of shareholders to hold directors accountable because it gives them the means to enforce the members' remedies discussed above in this Chapter through access to company information and records. On the other hand, the members' right to inspect company books could infringe the legitimate interest of a company to prevent confidential or sensitive information becoming accessible to disgruntled shareholders. The statutory right of members to inspect books of the company attempts to strengthen the hand of shareholders whose rights at common law were limited.

at common law

[17.190] Prior to 1986, members did not have a clear right to inspect the books and records of a company. Any such right was a matter determined by the common law and the company's constitution. The replaceable rule in s 247D provides that directors or the company by resolution passed at a general meeting may authorise a member to inspect books of the company. "Books" are defined in s 9 to include financial reports, financial records and documents. Under this replaceable rule, members, other than directors, have no right of inspection except as provided by law or authorised by the directors or the general meeting.

At common law, the right of members to inspect books was limited to narrow circumstances. A member had to establish that inspection was necessary with reference to a particular dispute. The interest of the shareholder must be a "special interest" greater than that of other shareholders. Court rules provide for a discovery procedure where the parties gain access to documents from the other side relevant to the litigation. Once litigation has commenced, all parties to the proceedings have the right to require the other parties to produce relevant documents and answer specific questions dealing with the case. The rationale for this restrictive approach was that shareholders do not generally have the right to challenge the management decisions of directors.

statutory right

[17.195] The common law rights of a member to gain access to the books of a company have been expanded by s 247A. A member may apply to the court for an order authorising the member or another person to inspect books of the company. The court may only make such an order if it is satisfied that the member is acting in good faith and the inspection is to be made for a proper purpose: s 247A(1). The procedure under s 247A is not intended to bypass legal professional privilege and allow access to documents that are excluded from discovery in court proceedings. This discretionary power of the court was described as "remedial" and a provision of last resort: *Czerwinski v Syrena Royal Pty Ltd* (2000) 18 ACLC 337.

A member may apply to the court for an order authorising the member or another person to inspect books of the company.

The court has the discretion to restrict the books to which a shareholder is given access: *Majestic Resources NL v Caveat Pty Ltd* [2004] WASCA 201.

The court may authorise a person other than a member to inspect the books on behalf of a member. This enables a member to seek an order authorising a solicitor, auditor or other appropriate person to obtain certain information to assist the member in the conduct of litigation. A court order is required so as to prevent access to the books in circumstances where the member is not seeking information in the capacity of a member and this is to the detriment or inconvenience of the company. This could arise where the information sought is confidential or is to be used to further the personal interests of the member. The person authorised to inspect the books may make a copy unless the court orders otherwise: s 247A(2).

A person who is granted leave to bring proceedings on behalf of a company under s 237 also has the same rights as a member to inspect the company's books: s 247A(3)–(6). Persons other than members who may apply for leave under s 237 include former members, members of a related company and officers or former officers of the company: s 236(2).

In addition to an order authorising inspection of the company's books, the court may make any other orders it considers appropriate. Such orders may limit the use that may be made of information acquired during the inspection or the right to make copies of the books: s 247B.

A person who inspects the books on behalf of a member may only disclose information obtained during the inspection to the member or ASIC: s 247C.

In *Tinios v French Caledonia Travel Service Pty Ltd* (1994) 12 ACLC 622, a shareholder was able to nominate persons to inspect the company's books solely for the purpose of valuing the shares and not to assist in possible legal action.

The right of a member to apply to the court for an order authorising inspection of the company's books is in addition to a right of directors and former directors under s 198F to inspect the company's books for the purposes of legal proceedings. This is discussed in Chapter 15 above.

A member who applies for an inspection order must satisfy the court that they are acting in good faith and the inspection is for a proper purpose.

[17.200] good faith and proper purpose. A member who applies for an inspection order must satisfy the court that they are acting in good faith and the inspection is for a proper purpose. The question of what constitutes a "proper purpose" under s 247A and its predecessors has arisen in a number of cases.

case note

In *Re Humes Ltd* (1987) 5 ACLC 64, Unity APA, which held 36 per cent of Humes' capital, made a hostile takeover offer. Humes purchased a steel business, the consideration for which was a placement of shares to the vendor. The effect of this agreement was to dilute Unity APA's shareholding to 19 per cent. Unity applied for an order under the equivalent of s 247A authorising an accountant and lawyer to inspect and make copies of books relating to the acquisition of the steel business. Unity APA was concerned that the directors of Humes may have acted in breach of fiduciary duty and argued that access to the company's books was necessary to enable it to ascertain the motives of the directors. Humes argued against Unity APA being given access on the main ground that Unity APA was seeking information to assist its takeover bid and this was not a "proper purpose" within the meaning of s 247A(1).

The court granted the order allowing access. Unity APA may have sought information to assist its takeover offer but this was not its dominant purpose. In the view of Beach J, the dominant purpose was to ascertain whether the directors were in breach of duty and whether or not the Humes proposal should be opposed. Unity APA's suspicions regarding the proposed acquisition were well founded. The application for a right to inspect was not a simple challenge to a management decision as the proposal involved a significant restructuring and expansion of Humes' activities.

case note

On the other hand, in *Garina Pty Ltd v Action Holdings Ltd* (1989) 7 ACLC 962, it was held that the applicant was primarily concerned with seeking to facilitate a takeover bid. This purpose was not related to the applicant's interest in its capacity as a shareholder and the application for an order failed.

The right of a member to inspect books is limited to the books of the company of which they are a member. The right under s 247A does not extend to applications to inspect the books of subsidiaries or associated companies. However, in *Intercapital Holdings Ltd v MEH Ltd* (1988) 6 ACLC 1068, it was held that an application may be granted to inspect the books of a holding company where a subsidiary has entered into a transaction that may threaten the value of the shareholder's investment in the parent company.

duties of controlling members

At common law, there are certain duties owed by majority shareholders to the company that constitute restraints imposed on the general meeting of shareholders.

[17.205] At common law, there are certain duties owed by majority shareholders to the company that constitute restraints imposed on the general meeting of shareholders. In *Gambotto v WCP Ltd* (1995) 13 ACLC 342, the majority of the High Court considered that where a special resolution alters the constitution in a manner that gives rise to a conflict of interest or advantages, the special resolution is valid unless it is beyond any purpose contemplated by the articles or is oppressive. The meaning of "oppressive conduct" is discussed above, para [17.45]. Where the majority seek to expropriate the shares of a minority shareholder, this is outside the contemplated objects of the power to amend the company's constitution. Such a power cannot be exercised for the purpose of aggrandising the majority.

While these tests suggest that majority shareholders are under some duty to consider the interests of minority shareholders, the extent and application of this duty have posed difficult problems. The duties of majority shareholders, however, are quite different from those of directors. As discussed in Chapter 13 above, directors and certain other officers stand in a fiduciary position as regards the company. Their fiduciary obligation imposes clear duties on directors to consider the interests of their company ahead of their own interests. On the other hand, it is clearly recognised that shareholders have a proprietary interest in their shares that is similar to proprietary interests in any other property. This enables shareholders to exercise any voting rights attaching to their shares in their own self-interest: *North-West Transportation v Beatty* (1887) 12 App Cas 589. Shareholders, in contrast to directors, may even enter into a contract whereby they agree to exercise their voting rights in the future, in a particular way.

This right of shareholders to vote in their own interests extends to situations where a director seeks to exercise voting rights as a shareholder at a general meeting called to ratify her or his actions as a director which are in breach of duty: *Mills v Mills* (1938) 60 CLR 150. Thus where directors control general meetings, they are able to exercise voting rights as shareholders in their own interests. They are then able to have a resolution passed that exonerates them from breaches of duty as directors. However, this may constitute oppressive or unfair conduct and enable shareholders to obtain a remedy under s 232. In some cases, the *Corporations Act* prevents directors and their associates from voting their shares at shareholders' meetings. For example, under s 224 directors and other related parties of a public company are not permitted to vote at a shareholders' meeting that considers whether or not to approve the giving of financial benefits to them.

enforcement of members' personal rights

the rule in Foss v Harbottle

[17.210] The common law right of a member to bring a legal action in the name of a company to remedy an internal irregularity or a wrong committed against the company stemmed from the old rule in *Foss v Harbottle* and its exceptions. This rule was based on the philosophy that it was generally appropriate for disputes to be resolved in accordance with the constitution and vote of the majority. Courts were reluctant to interfere with these processes.

The common law right of a member to bring a legal action in the name of a company to remedy an internal irregularity or a wrong committed against the company stemmed from the old rule in *Foss v Harbottle* and its exceptions.

The common law rule in *Foss v Harbottle* (1843) 2 Hare 461; 67 ER 189 comprised two aspects:

> **the internal management rule; and**
> **the proper plaintiff rule.**

internal management rule

[17.215] The internal management rule was based on the courts' reluctance to interfere with internal irregularities that were capable of being ratified by ordinary resolution of a general meeting of members. This aspect of the rule in *Foss v Harbottle* was rationalised on the basis that it would be futile to allow minority members standing to bring legal actions against the company or its directors if the general meeting could afterwards ratify the irregularity.

The aim of the internal management rule was to prevent individual shareholders, who were disgruntled with the running of their company, bringing a multitude of actions that would have to be defended by the company or its directors. The rule recognised that in the affairs of companies, the will of the majority prevails.

Examples of internal irregularities contemplated by the rule are improper appointments of directors or improper conduct of general meetings such as a refusal to recognise the voting rights of a particular shareholder. Such irregularities may result in a member's personal rights being infringed. As discussed below, the enforcement of such rights fell within an exception to the rule in *Foss v Harbottle*.

The internal management rule is also subject to s 1322. Procedural irregularities are not invalidated unless the court finds that the irregularity has caused substantial injustice which may not otherwise be remedied by the court. This is discussed in Chapter 14 above. Further, as discussed in Chapter 13.7 above, the general meeting has wide powers to ratify breaches of directors' duties as well as other irregularities. Accordingly, the internal management rule also extends to such ratifications.

proper plaintiff rule

[17.220] The proper plaintiff rule recognises that a company is a separate legal entity. Where a wrong is done to the company, it is the proper plaintiff in any legal proceedings which seeks to remedy it. The proper plaintiff rule applies whether the wrong against the company is caused by the directors, the controlling members or outsiders. The *Corporations Act* provides for members to bring legal proceedings on behalf of a company under ss 233(1)(g) and 236. These provisions are discussed above, paras [17.95] and [17.115].

effect of rule

The rule in *Foss v Harbottle* placed a major obstacle in the way of minority shareholders.

[17.225] The rule in *Foss v Harbottle* placed a major obstacle in the way of minority shareholders. A company was unlikely to decide to bring an action against the majority shareholders, complaining of their breach of duty. The majority were also unlikely to bring an action complaining of an irregularity in the internal management of the company, where the irregularity worked to their advantage. Further, as it is usually within the powers of management of the board to determine whether to initiate legal proceedings on the company's behalf, directors were unlikely to take such action in respect of their own breaches of duty.

Generally, a company is only likely to initiate legal proceedings against its directors or controlling shareholders when a new group takes over control of the company or when the company goes into liquidation and the liquidator initiates the proceedings on the company's behalf.

The English courts have tended to be zealous in applying the rule in *Foss v Harbottle* with the result that minority members' actions are often blocked after lengthy hearings without the substantive issues being heard. The Australian courts were generally unwilling to hear protracted litigation on the issue of the standing of a minority shareholder under the rule in *Foss v Harbottle*. In contrast to the English cases, there were few, if any, Australian cases in which the rule in *Foss v Harbottle* was a central issue that prevented a plaintiff from proceeding with an action.

exceptions to the rule in Foss v Harbottle

There are a number of exceptions to the rule in *Foss v Harbottle*.

[17.230] There are a number of exceptions to the rule in *Foss v Harbottle*. If a member was able to establish standing under one of these exceptions to the rule, they were able to bring an action against the company, its directors or other members.

Under one category of exceptions, a member could complain of an infringement of personal rights as a member. Such rights could be conferred by the *Corporations Act* or the company's constitution. The rule in *Foss v Harbottle* did not prevent a member bringing a legal action against the company to enforce such rights and such actions may still be brought.

The right of a person at common law to bring proceedings on behalf of a company has been abolished.

Other exceptions to the rule in *Foss v Harbottle* enabled a member to bring a legal action in the name of the company to enforce a right of the company. This usually arose where the company's directors breached their duty to the detriment of the company, but because they controlled the company they would not cause the company to remedy the breach of duty. The right of a person at common law to bring proceedings on behalf of a company has been abolished: s 236(3). Proceedings brought on behalf of a company must now come under Pt 2F.1A. This is discussed above, para [17.115].

The exceptions to the rule in *Foss v Harbottle* are now only of significance in relation to the enforcement of personal rights by members in their capacity as members.

what are personal rights?

[17.235] Members' personal rights are enforceable in a variety of situations. Such rights could be conferred by the *Corporations Act* or the company's constitution.

Members' personal rights are enforceable in a variety of situations.

Corporations Act and constitution

[17.240] Personal rights may be conferred by the *Corporations Act*, the company's constitution or a separate contract. An example of personal rights conferred by the *Corporations Act* is provided by s 246D. This provision confers a right on holders of classes of shares to bring an action to prevent the majority from altering the constitution so as to vary class rights otherwise than in accordance with the procedure laid down in the *Corporations Act* or constitution. This is discussed in Chapter 8 above.

Personal rights may also be conferred on a member by the replaceable rules or constitution. In *Hickman v Kent or Romney Marsh Sheep-breeders' Assoc* [1915] 1 Ch 881, discussed in Chapter 4 above, it was held that a company's constitution may confer rights that are enforceable. These are constitutional provisions that confer rights on a member in her or his capacity as a member and include provisions in the articles that regulate the rights of members generally. By virtue of s 140, a company's constitution and any applicable replaceable rules have the effect of a contract between the company and each member and between a member and each other member. Where this is the case, a member has a personal right to oblige the company or other members to comply with the provisions of the constitution and any replaceable rules.

expropriation of shares

[17.245] Majority shareholders may use their voting power so as to deprive a member of her or his shares in the company. An expropriation of a member's property is a wrong that is committed against the minority member. One way shares can be expropriated is by modifying or repealing the company's constitution under s 136(2). However, the power to alter the constitution so as to allow for an expropriation of a member's shares is severely restricted. A member has a personal right to prevent the company altering its constitution to expropriate their shares if the expropriation is not for a proper purpose or is unfair.

A member has a personal right to prevent the company altering its constitution to expropriate their shares if the expropriation is not for a proper purpose or is unfair.

case note

In *Gambotto v WCP Ltd* (1995) 13 ACLC 342, it was held that a power to alter the constitution to expropriate shares of the minority can only be exercised for a proper purpose and must be fair in all the circumstances. The fact that the expropriation of minority shareholdings would result in taxation advantages and administrative benefits flowing to the majority shareholder if the company were to become a wholly owned subsidiary did not by itself constitute a proper purpose for the resolution altering the constitution.

An expropriation is for a proper purpose where it is reasonably considered that the continued shareholding of the minority is detrimental to the company and the interests of the existing shareholders generally. The expropriation must then be a reasonable means of eliminating or mitigating that detriment and not oppressive to the minority shareholders. Expropriation may be justified where a member competes with the company and where expropriation enables the company to comply with legislative requirements such as limits on foreign ownership.

An alteration to the constitution permitting an expropriation of shares must be fair in the circumstances. This involves fairness in the procedure by requiring full disclosure and valuation by an independent expert. It also requires the price offered for the shares to be fair.

case note

In *Grey Eisdell Timms v Combined Auctions Pty Ltd* (1995) 13 ACLC 965, the court considered the alteration of the company's constitution expropriating non-pawnbrokers' shares. It followed *Gambotto v WCP Ltd* and held that such expropriations would only be justified if the minority's continued shareholding would be detrimental to the company and expropriation was a reasonable means of eliminating this detriment. In the present case, the expropriation was not justified because the fact that significant numbers of current members were not pawnbrokers meant that the alteration was not needed to protect the company's business. Further, it was oppressive because it was a means of ensuring that the managing director obtained a controlling shareholding in the company.

The property of the minority that is expropriated may also be the voting rights attaching to a member's shares. The majority in such cases may commit a fraud on the minority even if it believes that to do so is in the best interests of the company: *Eastmanco (Kilner House) Ltd v Greater London Council* [1982] 1 All ER 437.

The principles stated in *Gambotto's* case are not applicable where the *Corporations Act* provides protection to minority shareholders and sets out prescribed procedures in cases such as selective reductions of capital or compulsory acquisitions: *Winpar Holdings Ltd v Goldfields Kalgoorlie Ltd* (2002) 20 ACLC 265. Reductions of capital are discussed in Chapter 8 above.

The *Corporations Act* specifically allows the shares of a minority to be expropriated in certain circumstances if the interests of minority shareholders are properly considered and proper compensation is paid. For example, for a person who has a full beneficial interest in at least 90 per cent of any class of securities in a company to compulsorily acquire the remaining securities in that class: s 664A(3). This compulsory acquisition procedure need not follow a takeover bid. An independent expert's report must be provided to minority securities holders setting out whether in the expert's opinion, the terms of the compulsory acquisition give a fair value for the securities and reasons for the opinion: s 667A(1). Court approval is required for the compulsory acquisition to proceed if 10 per cent of the minority securities holders object: ss 664E and 664F. A similar compulsory acquisition is permitted by an offeror who has acquired a relevant interest in over 90 per cent of a company's securities under a takeover: s 661A. Takeovers are discussed in Chapter 18 below.

voting rights

A member has a personal right to have their votes at general meetings counted.

[17.250] A member has a personal right to have their votes at general meetings counted.

case note

In *Pender v Lushington* (1877) 6 Ch D 70, a member's votes were disallowed. This resulted in the passing of a resolution for which he would not have voted had his votes been counted. The court upheld his right to bring an action and decided that he came within an exception to the rule in *Foss v Harbottle* because he was enforcing a personal right conferred on all members to have their votes recorded.

Where a general meeting attempts to pass an ordinary resolution where the *Corporations Act* or the company's constitution requires a special resolution, this could be a procedural irregularity that may be invalid if it causes a substantial injustice under s 1322(2).

conduct of meetings

[17.255] In *Efstathis v Greek Orthodox Community of St George* (1988) 6 ACLC 706, some members sought a declaration that a motion purporting to dissolve the council was invalid on the ground that proper notice had not been given. The motion was held to be invalid and the rule in *Foss v Harbottle* did not prevent the members receiving proper notice and bringing the action. They were seeking to enforce their rights as members to prevent the duly elected council being dismissed by an invalid action. This is similar to a member bringing an action to enforce personal rights under the constitution or replaceable rules to have an election of directors properly conducted.

improper share issue

[17.260] A shareholder has a personal right to bring an action where it is alleged that an issue of shares was made for an improper purpose: *Residues Treatment & Trading Co Ltd v Southern Resources Ltd* (1988) 6 ACLC 1160. King CJ of the Supreme Court of South Australia suggested that there was a clear trend in the cases to indicate that shareholders had a personal right, grounded upon equitable principles, to have the voting power of their shares undiminished by improper actions of directors.

A shareholder has a personal right to bring an action where it is alleged that an issue of shares was made for an improper purpose.

> **< A member's voting rights and the rights of participation which they provide in the decision making of the company are a fundamental attribute of membership and are rights which the member should be able to protect by legal action against improper diminution. The rule in *Foss v Harbottle* has no application where individual membership rights as opposed to corporate rights are involved. >**

ultra vires acts

[17.265] Individual shareholders could bring an action at common law complaining that the company was acting or intending to act on some matter that was ultra vires. In this sense, ultra vires refers not only to acts that were beyond the objects and powers set out in the memorandum but also to illegal acts of the company. As discussed in Chapter 4 above, a company has the legal capacity and powers of an individual and of a body corporate: s 124.

In the case of companies that have objects or restrictions on the exercise of powers set out in their constitutions, acts that are outside these objects or restrictions are treated in the same way as any other breaches of the company's constitution. Such acts may be relied upon in proceedings brought for breach of the s 140(1) contracts or under ss 232, 1324 and 461(1)(k). These actions are discussed above in this chapter. Where a director causes a company to act contrary to restrictions in its constitution, this may involve a breach of fiduciary duties by the director. This is discussed in Chapter 13 above.

A company may act ultra vires where it acts outside an objects clause stated in its constitution. Where a company's constitution does not contain an objects clause, the company cannot act ultra vires in this sense.

special majority

[17.270] As discussed earlier, the rule in *Foss v Harbottle* prevented a shareholder from bringing an action where the general meeting was able to ratify the misconduct or irregularity by ordinary resolution. Where this ratification required more than a simple majority and this was not obtained, a member could bring an action.

Under the *Corporations Act*, a company can only do certain things by special resolution of the general meeting. Section 9 defines a special resolution as a resolution passed by a majority of at least 75 per cent of the votes cast by members who are entitled to vote on the resolution. Section 136(2), for example, requires a special resolution to modify or repeal a company's constitution, and in some cases, the constitution itself may require that certain resolutions be passed by a 75 per cent or other majority.

This exception prevents a company from doing by bare majority that which the *Corporations Act* or constitution require to be done by special majority.

case note

For example, in *Edwards v Halliwell* [1950] 2 All ER 1064, alterations to the rules of a trade union required the agreement of at least two-thirds of the members. An attempt was made to change the rules regarding member contributions without a ballot of members. Two members brought an action against the executive committee and against the union itself, seeking a declaration that the alteration was invalid. The action was defended on the basis that the rule in *Foss v Harbottle* prevented the members from taking action. This defence was rejected when the court held that two of the exceptions to the rule applied. One of these was on the basis that the rules of the union provided for a two-thirds majority of members to approve an alteration to the table of contributions.

fraud on the minority

[17.275] A shareholder was entitled to sue at common law if the actions of the majority constituted a fraud on the minority. This exception to the rule in *Foss v Harbottle* was an application of a broader principle developed by the courts of equity which prevented the holders of various types of powers from exercising their powers improperly. In the company law context, the majority must use their voting power for a purpose contemplated by the replaceable rules or company's constitution and not oppressively. If the vote involves an expropriation of a minority member's shares, the vote must be for a proper purpose and fair in all the circumstances: *Gambotto v WCP Ltd* (1995) 13 ACLC 342. If the majority breach this duty, they are regarded as having committed a fraud on the minority.

"Fraud" in this sense has a broader meaning than under the law of torts where the term is used to connote deceitful or dishonest behaviour. "Fraud" in the context of "fraud on the minority" means an abuse of power whereby the majority secures an unfair gain at the expense of the minority. Despite the fact that the expression refers to the "minority", the injured party need not actually be the minority shareholders. The injured party may also be the company itself.

At common law, if the majority committed a fraud on the minority and the injured party was the company, the minority shareholders were permitted to bring a derivative action in the name of the company against the majority. This aspect of the fraud on the minority exception is no longer applicable because it has been abolished by s 236(3). Part 2F.1A, inserted by 1999 amendments, gives members a right to bring legal proceedings on behalf of the company with the leave of the Court. This is discussed above.

Where the minority are the injured parties, they have a personal right of action against both the majority and the company itself.

An essential element in a fraud on the minority case was proof that the persons who abused their power controlled the company. These persons need not actually be the majority shareholders in numerical terms. Rather, it applies to those who actually control the majority of votes at a general meeting.

The onus of showing an abuse of power is generally on the minority shareholder. Where the majority attempt to expropriate a minority member's shares, the onus shifts to the majority: *Gambotto v WCP Ltd* (1995) 13 ACLC 342.

personal and representative actions

[17.280] Personal and representative actions arise when the company deprives a member of a personal right. A personal action, as opposed to a representative action, is appropriate to enforce a right conferred on a member individually. A representative action is appropriate to enforce personal rights conferred on members generally. This is sometimes referred to as a "class action". In a representative action, a shareholder sues on behalf of her or himself and the other shareholders whose rights are being infringed. In such an action all the shareholders must have some common interest in the right being enforced. They have such an interest to enforce compliance with the replaceable rules or the company's constitution by virtue of the contract created by s 140(1). Thus, the rights conferred by the replaceable rules or the company's constitution may be enforced either as a personal or representative action.

An example of a case where a representative action was allowed is *Pender v Lushington* (1877) 6 Ch D 70. There the plaintiff brought a personal action as well as a representative action where a company attempted to deprive a member of his right to vote. Also in *Edwards v Halliwell* [1950] 2 All ER 1064, a member brought a representative action where a union tried to alter a table of contributions payable by members without the required two-thirds majority approval of members.

A shareholder's personal or representative action generally seeks an injunction to restrain a breach of the replaceable rules or company's constitution or a declaration that the actions contemplated by the company are invalid. The plaintiff normally cannot claim damages to enforce the s 140(1) contract created by the replaceable rules or the company's constitution because an injunction or declaration is usually the appropriate remedy.

pathways questions ...

The following questions dealing with members' remedies may best be answered by reading this chapter and considering the Internet resources on the Lipton-Herzberg Members' Remedies Pathway at http://www.lipton-herzberg.com.au/secure/pathways-chapter-17-members-remedies.html

1. Does the decision in *Gambotto*'s case properly balance the interests of majority and minority shareholders? Which provisions of the *Corporations Act* deal with expropriation of shares and how do these provisions attempt to balance the interests between majority and minority shareholders?
2. Why was the statutory derivative action introduced? Do you believe that it is successful in achieving its aims?
3. Why does CASAC's Report on Corporate Groups consider that non-assenting shareholders in partly-owned group companies are especially vulnerable? What are the major recommendations of the report to assist minority shareholders?

bibliography ...

Aherns, M "Incorporated Joint Ventures" in Austin, R P & Vann, R (eds). *The Law of Public Company Finance*. Lawbook Co, Sydney, 1986, Ch 17.

Baxt, R "Will Section 574 of the Companies Code Please Stand Up! (And will Section 1324 of the *Corporations Act* Follow Suit?)" (1989) 7 C & SLJ 388.

Boros, E "Compulsory Acquisition of Minority Shareholders—The Way Forward" (1998) 16 C & SLJ 279.

Bottomley, S "Shareholder Derivative Actions and Public Interest Suits: Two Versions of the Same Story" (1992) 15 UNSWLJ 127.

Colla, A "Eliminating Minority Shareholdings—Recent Developments" (2001) 19 C & SLJ 7.

de Vere Stevens, K B "Should we Toss Foss? Toward an Australian Statutory Derivative Action" (1997) 25 ABLR 127.

Duffy, M "Procedural Dilemmas for Contemporary Shareholder Remedies—Derivative Action or Class Action?" (2004) C & SLJ 69.

Fletcher, K "CLERP and Minority Shareholder Rights" (2001) 13 Aust Jnl of Corp Law 290.

Fridman, S "Ratification of Directors' Breaches" (1992) 10 C & SLJ 252.

Gillooly, M "Outside Shareholders in Corporate Groups" in Gillooly M (ed). *The Law Relating to Corporate Groups*. Federation Press, 1993, Ch 7.

Goldwasser, V "Shareholder Agreements: Potent Protection for Minorities in Closely Held Corporations" (1994) 22 ABLR 265.

Grave, D "Compulsory Share Acquisitions: Practical and Policy Considerations" (1994) 12 C & SLJ 240.

Hill, J "Protecting Minority Shareholders And Reasonable Expectations" (1992) 10 C & SLJ 86.

Kluver, J "Derivative Actions and the Rule in Foss v Harbottle: Do We Need a Statutory Remedy?" (1993) 11 C & SLJ 7.

Lipton, P "The New Statutory Derivative Action Proposals" (1995) 3 *Current Commercial Law* 14.

Lo, S "The Continuing Role of Equity in Restraining Majority Shareholder Power" (2004) 16 Aust Jnl of Corp Law 96.

McDonough, "Proposed New Statutory Derivative Action–Does it Go Far Enough?" (1996) 8 Bond LR 47.

McNee, S "The Just and Equitable Ground–A Remedy of Last Resort" (2001) 9 Insolv LJ 147.

Mayanja, J "Standing to Challenge the Implementation of Improper Defensive Measures" (1995) Aust Jnl of Corp Law 66.

Mitchell, V "The US Approach Towards the Acquisition of Minority Shares: Have We Anything to Learn?" (1996) 14 C & SLJ 283.

Mitchell, V "The High Court and Minority Shareholders" (1995) 7 Bond LR 58.

O'Donovan, J & O'Grady, G W "Company Deadlocks: Prevention and Cure" (1982) 1 C & SLJ 67.

Pentony, B "Majority Interests v Minority Interests: Achieving a Balance" (1995) 5 Aust Jnl of Corp Law 117.

Prince, P "Australia's Statutory Derivative Action—Using the New Zealand Experience" (2000) 18 C & SLJ 493.

Ramsay, I "Corporate Governance, Shareholder Litigation and the Prospects for a Statutory Derivative Action" (1992) 15 UNSWLJ 149.

Ramsay, I "Enforcement of Corporate Rights and Duties by Shareholders and the ASC: Evidence and Analysis" (1995) 23 ABLR 174.

Ramsay, I "An Empirical Study of the Use of the Oppression Remedy" (1999) 27 ABLR 23.

Schipani, C "Corporate Governance and Shareholder Remedies: The US Experience and Australia's Proposals for Reform" (1994) 6 Bond LR 28.

Shapira, G "The Hand that Giveth is the Hand that Taketh Away"—O'Neill v Phillips and Shareholder 'Legitimate Expectations'" (2000) 11 Aust Jnl of Corp Law 260.

Sirianos, S "Problems of Share Valuation under s 260 of the Corporations Law" (1995) 13 C & SLJ 88.

Stapleton, G P "Locus Standi of Shareholders to Enforce the Duty of Company Directors to Exercise the Share Issue Power for Proper Purposes" (1990) 8 C & SLJ 213.

Stapleton, G P "Use of the Oppression Provision in Listed Companies in Australia and United Kingdom" (1993) 67 ALJ 575.

Thai, L "How Popular Are Statutory Derivative Actions in Australia?: Comparisons With United States, Canada and New Zealand" (2002) 30 ABLR 118.

Whincop, M "Gambotto v WCP Ltd: An Economic Analysis of Alterations to Articles and Expropriation Articles" (1995) 23 ABLR 276.

Yeung, K "Disentangling the Tangled Skein: The Ratification Of Directors' Actions" (1992) 66 ALJ 343.

revision questions on the material in this chapter ...

- > Please see eQuiz at **http://www.thomson.com.au/academic** for multiple choice questions and answers.
- > For further corporations law links and material please refer to the Lipton-Herzberg website at **http://www.lipton-herzberg.com.au**

chapter eighteen

takeovers

key points ...

- The regulation of takeovers raises important economic and corporate governance issues. The takeover provisions of the *Corporations Act* seek to strike a balance between facilitating an informed and efficient market to determine the success or failure of a bid and protecting the interests of all target company shareholders.
- A general prohibition prevents a person from acquiring more than 20 per cent of the shares in a target company. The main exceptions to this prohibition arise where the bidder makes an off-market or market takeover bid or acquires up to three per cent of the shares in a six-month period.
- An off-market or market bid requires disclosure of information specified in the bidder's statement and target's statement in response.
- There is a compulsory acquisition procedure that enables a bidder to acquire outstanding shares after the 90 per cent threshold is exceeded. Similarly, the minority shareholders may require a bidder holding more than 90 per cent of shares to buy out their holdings.
- The liability provisions applicable to takeover documents are similar to those applicable to fundraising disclosure documents. Misleading and deceptive statements are prohibited and contravention is an offence and allows for recovery of loss or damage.
- Directors of target companies who adopt defensive strategies and tactics that aim to prevent hostile takeovers may breach their fiduciary duties.
- The Takeovers Panel is the main forum for resolving disputes that arise during a takeover bid. Its members are chosen for their commercial knowledge and experience. The Panel has wide powers where it believes unacceptable circumstances have occurred.

what is a takeover?

A takeover occurs when the target's shareholders sell sufficient shares to a bidder so as to give the bidder control of the voting power attaching to the target company's share capital.

[18.05] A takeover involves a change of control of a target company. This occurs when the target's shareholders sell sufficient shares to a bidder so as to give the bidder control of the voting power attaching to the target company's share capital. This will clearly be the case where a bidder acquires all or over 50 per cent of the voting shares in the target company. Effective control may also be achieved with a lesser shareholding, depending on the nature of the shareholding structure. In the case of large companies with thousands of shareholders, many may not actually vote at general meetings so that a shareholding well below 50 per cent may allow de facto control.

The consideration for an acquisition of shares sufficient to gain control of the target company is usually cash, but the consideration may comprise shares or debentures in the bidder company or a mixture of cash, shares and debentures.

sources of law

[18.10] Since takeovers essentially involve the purchase and sale of shares, the basis of the transaction is governed by the law of contract. In addition, Ch 6 of the *Corporations Act* sets out detailed rules regulating takeovers and is largely concerned with protecting shareholders of target companies. The policy objectives of the legislation are discussed below. Takeovers are also affected by other legislation such as Ch 7 of the *Corporations Act*, dealing with financial services and markets, the *Trade Practices Act 1974* (Cth) and the *Companies (Foreign Takeovers) Act 1972* (Cth).

Ch 6 of the *Corporations Act* sets out detailed rules regulating takeovers and is largely concerned with protecting shareholders of target companies.

The takeover provisions underwent a major rewrite in 1999. These amendments expanded the role of the Takeovers Panel and diminished the role of the court in resolving disputes arising during a takeover. The amendments adopted a simplified writing style and in several respects, introduced reforms aimed at removing unnecessary complexity and making the operation of the legislation more efficient so as not to unduly constrain takeover conduct.

policy issues

[18.15] Regulation of takeovers raises several contentious issues of policy and the takeover legislation must be seen in the context of the economic and social functions performed by takeovers and how they may affect target company shareholders.

The Explanatory Memorandum to the 1999 amending legislation considered that:

> < **takeovers are an essential element of a competitive business environment in that they allocate capital to its most productive uses by providing incentives for management to optimise performance. The concept of the equal opportunity principle whereby the premium for control is shared equally with all shareholders is to be retained as it contributes to investor confidence and market integrity.** >

Takeovers are an essential element of a competitive business environment in that they allocate capital to its most productive uses by providing incentives for management to optimise performance.

Takeovers provide a mechanism whereby company assets come under the control of a person, invariably a company, which believes it can utilise the assets in a more efficient way than was previously the case. The bidder for the target company's shares must generally be prepared to pay a price for the shares that exceeds the prevailing market price. This is because acquisitions of shares that can result in a change in control of the target are generally at a higher price than smaller, passive shareholdings. The payment of this "premium for control" will usually be justified only if the bidder is able to utilise the target company's assets more productively than the existing board of directors. This may occur because the bidder is a more efficient business manager or it may be in a related industry where efficiencies may arise through rationalisation of the bidder and target company's activities or economies of scale may arise.

In addition to these economic benefits directly arising from takeovers, the threat of a takeover may also provide a strong incentive to management to utilise their company's assets as efficiently as possible and to consider the interests of shareholders. The most vulnerable takeover targets are often asset-rich companies that generate relatively low profits. This results in a discounted market price for the company's shares relative to the value of its assets. Such companies also often pursue a conservative dividends policy which may cause shareholders to favourably consider takeover offers. Therefore, the threat of takeover often causes directors to react in a way designed to engender increased shareholder loyalty.

purposes of the takeovers provisions

The purposes of the takeovers provisions of Ch 6 of the *Corporations Act* are set out in s 602.

[18.20] The purposes of the takeovers provisions of Ch 6 of the *Corporations Act* are set out in s 602. They seek to ensure that:

> **the acquisition of control over voting shares in a listed company takes place in an efficient, competitive and informed market;**
> **the shareholders and directors of a target company:**
  - **know the identity of any person who proposes to acquire a substantial interest in the company;**
  - **have a reasonable time to consider the proposal; and**
  - **are given enough information to enable them to assess the merits of the proposal;**
> **as far as practicable, shareholders all have a reasonable and equal opportunity to participate in any benefits accruing to the holders through any proposal under which a person would acquire a substantial interest in the company; and**
> **an appropriate procedure is followed as a preliminary to compulsory acquisition of voting shares or other kinds of securities.**

The s 602 purposes also apply to acquisitions of control over:

> **voting shares in unlisted companies with more than 50 members;**
> **listed bodies other than companies; and**
> **voting interests in listed managed investment schemes. Listed managed investment schemes are treated as if they were listed companies: s 604. Managed investment schemes are discussed in Chapter 20 below.**

The purposes set out in s 602(b) and (c) adopt the principles identified by the Eggleston Committee in its *Second Interim Report* (1969). These principles have formed the basis of takeover regulation in Australia over the past 40 years. The equal opportunity principle contained in s 602(c) is seen as important because it contributes to investor confidence and market integrity.

role of ASIC

[18.25] ASIC has a particularly significant role in the operation of Ch 6. Its powers include obtaining information as to beneficial ownership of shares and exempting compliance with, or modifying the operation of, the legislation. It also releases policy statements, notices and practice notes setting out how it will interpret the legislation and exercise its discretions. *NCSC Policy Statements and Practice Notes* under the previous *Takeovers Code* remain operative until reviewed by ASIC.

The Takeovers Panel has the important power to make declarations of unacceptable circumstances. These powers are discussed below, para [18.240].

The general powers of ASIC are also applicable to takeovers and these are discussed in Chapter 21 below.

disclosure of ownership of shares

One of the purposes of the takeover provisions is to ensure that the identity of a person who proposes to acquire a substantial interest in a company be known to shareholders and directors.

[18.30] One of the purposes of the takeover provisions is to ensure that the identity of a person who proposes to acquire a substantial interest in a company be known to shareholders and directors: s 602(b)(i). This is partly implemented by the substantial holding provisions of Pt 6C.1 and the tracing beneficial ownership of shares provisions of Pt 6C.2 of the *Corporations Act*. These disclosure requirements also apply to holders of interests in listed registered managed investment schemes.

This is partly implemented by the substantial holding provisions of Pt 6C.1 and the tracing beneficial ownership of shares provisions of Pt 6C.2 of the *Corporations Act*.

The substantial holding provisions, Pt 6C.1, ss 671B and 671C, oblige shareholders who have relevant interests in not less than five per cent of the voting shares of a listed company to disclose to the company full particulars of their relevant interests in the shares. Disclosure of substantial holding information is often the first indication of an impending takeover bid. The definition of "relevant interest" is complex and is discussed below, para [18.50].

Part 6C.2 (ss 672A–672F) complements the substantial holding information provisions by enabling both the company and ASIC to obtain information as to the identity of persons who control or have a beneficial ownership in voting shares. The nature and extent of such interests and the identity of any other persons who have an interest must also be disclosed.

substantial holding provisions

[18.35] The purpose of the substantial holding provisions of Pt 6C.1 is to enable listed companies, and the market generally, to ascertain the identity of holders of large parcels of shares and the extent of their shareholdings. This is particularly important where a person is acquiring shares with the intention of launching a takeover bid. Disclosure that a person has acquired a substantial holding in a listed company is often the first indication that the company may be a potential takeover target. It may also be of interest to directors and shareholders to know if a particular shareholder is in a position to block special resolutions at general meetings.

A person who begins to have a substantial holding in a listed company must give prescribed information to the company and the ASX.

A person who begins to have a substantial holding in a listed company or listed registered managed investment scheme must give prescribed information to the company or responsible entity and the relevant market operator such as the ASX: s 671B(1). Information must also be given if the person ceases to have a substantial holding or there is a movement of at least one per cent in their holding or the person makes a takeover bid for securities of the company or scheme.

A person has a substantial holding if that person or their associates have relevant interests in five per cent or more of the total number of votes attached to voting shares.

"Substantial holding" is defined in s 9. Under that definition, a person has a substantial holding in a body corporate if that person or their associates have relevant interests in five per cent or more of the total number of votes attached to voting shares in a body corporate. A person also has a substantial holding if they have made a takeover bid for voting shares in a body and the bid period has started and not yet ended.

Details of the information required to be given is set out in s 671B(3).

Details of the information required to be given is set out in s 671B(3). They include:

> **details of relevant interest in voting shares;**
> **details of any relevant agreement through which a relevant interest in voting shares is acquired;**
> **the name and details of each associate who has a relevant interest (including the nature of the association); and**
> **the size and date of any movement in the holding of at least one per cent.**

This information must be given in the prescribed form and must be accompanied by a copy of any document setting out the terms of any relevant agreement or a statement setting out details of any relevant contract, scheme or arrangement: s 671B(4). The document or statement need not accompany the information if a holding was acquired or disposed of on a prescribed financial market: s 671B(5).

The required information must be given within two business days after the person became aware of the information.

The required information must be given within two business days after the person became aware of the information. If a takeover bid is made for voting shares or interests, the information must be given by 9.30 am on the next trading day of the relevant financial market after the person becomes aware of the information: s 671B(6).

A person who contravenes s 671B is liable to compensate a person who suffers loss or damage as a result of the contravention: s 671C(1). It is a defence under s 671C(2) if the person who contravened the section did so because of inadvertence or mistake or because of a lack of awareness of a relevant fact or occurrence. The defence does not apply to a mistake of law. Liability is joint and individual: s 671C(3).

tracing beneficial ownership

Part 6C.2 provides a mechanism for tracing the person who has the beneficial ownership of shares in a listed company. The aim of the Pt 6C.2 tracing provisions is to promote an informed market for shares in listed companies.

[18.40] Part 6C.2 provides a mechanism for tracing the person who has the beneficial ownership of shares in a listed company or interests in a listed managed investment scheme. The aim of the Pt 6C.2 tracing provisions is to promote an informed market for shares in listed companies and to prevent substantial transactions on an uninformed market: *Re North Broken Hill Holdings Ltd* (1986) 4 ACLC 131.

Part 6C.2 is not limited to companies involved in takeovers but is of general application: *Brunswick NL v Blossomtree Pty Ltd* (1992) 10 ACLC 658.

ASIC, the company itself or the responsible entity for a listed managed investment scheme may direct a registered shareholder or scheme member to disclose the information required by s 672B. A shareholder may also request ASIC to give such direction, in which case ASIC must exercise its power unless it considers that it would be unreasonable to do so: s 672A(2).

Where information is disclosed in response to a direction that another person has a relevant interest in any of the shares, that other person may also be directed to disclose information required by s 672B.

A person who is given a direction to make disclosure under s 672B must disclose the following:

- **full details of their own relevant interest and the circumstances that gave rise to that interest;**
- **details of other persons who have a relevant interest in any of the shares or interests and the nature and extent of the interest and how it arose; and**
- **persons who have given instructions about the acquisition or disposal of the shares or interests or voting rights or other matters in relation to them.**

A person does not need to comply with a direction given by a company or responsible entity if the person can prove that the giving of the direction is vexatious: s 672B(3). The direction to make disclosure imposes obligations on foreign corporations, even where performance would result in a breach of foreign law. In *ASC v Bank Leumi Le-Israel* (1996) 14 ACLC 1576, a Swiss company was obliged to disclose information under the predecessor of Pt 6C.2 even though to do so would infringe Swiss law protecting private and commercial confidences.

Disclosure must be made within two business days after a person receives a direction under s 672A: s 672B(2).

ASIC may pass on information received in response to a direction under s 672A to the company, responsible entity or the shareholder who requested ASIC to give the direction: s 672C.

A company or responsible entity is not taken to have notice of, or be put on inquiry as to, a person's right in relation to a share in the company or interest in a managed investment scheme: s 672E.

A person who contravenes s 672B is liable to compensate a person for any loss or damage arising from the contravention: s 672F(1). It is a defence to such proceedings if the person who contravened s 672B did so because of inadvertence or mistake or lack of awareness of a relevant fact or occurrence. This does not include a mistake of law: s 672F(2). Liability is joint and individual: s 672F(3).

prohibited acquisitions: s 606

twenty per cent threshold

[18.45] The takeovers provisions aim to regulate acquisitions of relevant interests in voting shares of a target company that have the potential to effect a change in its control. It does this by prohibiting any person from acquiring a relevant interest in voting shares above a threshold limit of 20 per cent of the shares in a target company. The threshold is set at 20 per cent by s 606(1)(c) on the assumption that persons who hold less than this percentage cannot control the affairs of a target company. To lower the threshold would extend the operation of the legislation to situations where a takeover may be a remote possibility and regulation would be inappropriate.

Section 606 is the key provision of the takeovers provisions. It sets out prohibitions on acquisitions of relevant interests in voting shares in a company that would increase a person's voting power in the company to more than the prescribed percentage of 20 per cent of the voting share capital: s 606(1)(c)(i). Acquisitions by a person who already possesses over 20 per cent but less than 90 per cent of voting shares are also prohibited: s 606(1)(c)(ii). Under s 606(2), a person is prohibited from acquiring a legal or equitable interest in securities if, because of the acquisition, another person acquires a relevant interest in issued voting shares and that person's voting power increases beyond the 20 per cent threshold.

Section 606 is the key provision of the takeovers provisions. It sets out prohibitions on acquisitions of relevant interests in voting shares in a company that would increase a person's voting power in the company to more than the prescribed percentage of 20 per cent of the voting share capital.

The prohibitions in s 606 are subject to a number of exceptions that are discussed below, para [18.65]. These exceptions permit regulated takeovers and certain other acquisitions that do not infringe the objectives of the takeover provisions.

The prohibitions in s 606 are subject to a number of exceptions.

relevant interest in securities

[18.50] The s 606 prohibitions refer to acquisitions of "a relevant interest" in issued voting shares. The term "relevant interest" is also a key component of the substantial holding information provisions and the tracing beneficial ownership provisions in Pts 6C.1 and 6C.2.

The term "relevant interest" has a complex definition. Section 608(1) sets out the basic rule. Situations that do not give rise to relevant interests are listed in s 609. The basic rule in s 608(1) provides that a person has a relevant interest in securities if they:

The term "relevant interest" has a complex definition. Section 608(1) sets out the basic rule.

> **are the holder of the securities; or**
> **have the power to exercise, or to control the exercise of, voting rights attached to the securities; or**
> **have the power to dispose of, or control the exercise of a power to dispose of, the securities.**

"Power or control" may be indirect or by means of a trust, agreement or practice, whether or not enforceable. It does not matter whether the power or control is express or implied, formal or informal or exercisable jointly with someone else. It need not be related to a particular security: s 608(2). A person is taken to have a relevant interest in securities that are held through an interposed body corporate in which the person's voting power is above 20 per cent: s 608(3).

The concept of relevant interests extends to situations where a person who already has a relevant interest enters into an agreement, gives or receives an enforceable right or grants or is granted an option with respect to the securities. The other party is also taken to have a relevant interest in the securities: s 608(8). The operation of s 608 may result in a body corporate having a relevant interest in its own securities: s 608(9).

associates

A person's voting power for the purposes of the s 606 prohibition comprises the aggregate votes of the person and associates taken as a percentage of the total votes in the body corporate.

[18.55] A person's voting power for the purposes of the s 606 prohibition comprises the aggregate votes of the person and associates taken as a percentage of the total votes in the body corporate: s 610. Section 12 defines the word "associate" in very wide and complex terms for purposes of the provisions dealing with takeovers, substantial holding information, tracing beneficial ownership and compulsory acquisitions and buyouts. For example, under s 12(2)(a) a body corporate (the second person) is regarded as an associate of another body corporate (the primary person) if the primary person either controls the second person or is controlled by the second person. The primary person and the second person are also associates if they act in concert in relation to the affairs of another body corporate: s 12(2)(c).

breach of prohibition

[18.60] A transaction is not invalid merely because it involves a contravention of s 606: s 607. However, contravention of the prohibitions in either s 606(1) or (2) is an offence of absolute liability: 606(4A). It is a defence to a prosecution for breach of s 606 if it is proved that the contravention was due to inadvertence, mistake or lack of awareness: s 606(5). This defence is necessary because the wide operation of s 606 may affect remote interests that have no implications for takeovers. Inadvertence or mistake does not include ignorance of a matter of law.

The s 606 prohibitions are supplemented by the broad discretionary powers of the Takeovers Panel to make declarations of unacceptable circumstances under s 657A. These declarations may be made where the policy of the *Corporations Act* has not been adhered to even though specific provisions have not been breached or a suspected breach may be difficult to prove. Declarations under s 657A are discussed below, para [18.245].

exemptions

[18.65] There are certain exemptions from the general prohibition in s 606 set out in s 611. For example, a person does not breach the section if an acquisition:

- resulted from acceptance of an offer under a takeover bid;
- results from an on-market transaction where the acquisition is by a takeover bidder during the bid period;
- was previously approved by a resolution of the general meeting of the target company;
- was by creeping takeover whereby the acquirer held voting power in the company of at least 19 per cent and no more than three per cent was acquired in the previous six months;
- occurred as a result of an allotment by the company to all shareholders on a pro rata basis; or
- resulted from a dividend reinvestment plan available to all shareholders.

These technical exemptions are based on the assumption that it would not assist the objectives of the takeovers legislation by requiring compliance in those situations.

takeover procedure

There are two types of takeover bids.

[18.70] There are two types of takeover bids:

- off-market bids (for quoted or unquoted securities); and
- market bids (only available for quoted securities).

These types of takeover are the main permissible methods by which a person may acquire a relevant interest in voting shares beyond the 20 per cent threshold in the target company. "Creeping takeovers" are also permitted under the exemptions to the s 606 prohibition. The procedures applicable to off-market and market bids are largely similar.

off-market bids

[18.75] An off-market bid is an offer to buy all or a specified proportion of all the securities in the bid class: s 618(1). All offers must be the same although they may include alternative forms of consideration of cash and securities: ss 619(1) and 621(1). Where the consideration is cash only, the price must be at least the highest price paid by the bidder or an associate for securities in the bid class in the four months prior to the date of the bid: s 621(4). Each offer must state that unless withdrawn, it will remain open until the end of the offer period: s 620(1)(c). The offer period must be of at least one month and up to 12 months: s 624. The offer must also state how and when the bidder is to satisfy their obligations: s 620(1)(d).

An off-market bid is an offer to buy all or a specified proportion of all the securities in the bid class.

Section 632 contains a diagram that illustrates the steps involved in an off-market bid.

market bids

[18.80] A market bid must relate to securities in a class of quoted securities (the bid class): s 617(3). An offer of securities under a market bid must be an offer to buy all the securities in the bid class: s 618(3). A market bid commences with an announcement of the bid to the relevant financial market. By their nature, market bids must be made for cash only: s 621(3). As with off-market bids, the amount of consideration must be at least equal to the maximum price that the bidder or an associate provided for the bid class security in the four-month period prior to the date of the bid: s 621(4). Market bids must be unconditional: s 625(1). The offer period also must last at least one month and not more than 12 months: s 624(1).

A market bid must relate to securities in a class of quoted securities (the bid class). An offer of securities under a market bid must be an offer to buy all the securities in the bid class.

Section 634 contains a diagram that illustrates the steps involved in a market bid.

bidder's statement

[18.85] A takeover bidder must prepare a bidder's statement disclosing the information prescribed by s 636. A copy of the bidder's statement (together with offer documents) must be lodged with ASIC and sent to the target and to the shareholders in the bid class. The information that must be disclosed in a bidder's statement is similar to the information that must be disclosed under the fundraising provisions.

A takeover bidder must prepare a bidder's statement disclosing the information prescribed by s 636.

The contents requirements of a bidder's statement are the same whether the bid is an off-market or market bid.

Information required under s 636 to be contained in a bidder's statement includes:

> **the identity of the bidder;**
> **details of the bidder's intentions regarding any changes to the target company's business, future employment of present employees and continuation of its business;**
> **details of how cash consideration will be paid;**
> **where consideration is in the form of securities, information required for a prospectus for an offer of those securities;**
> **price of purchases paid by bidder of securities in the bid class in the previous four months and any benefits given to induce a person to accept an offer under the bid;**
> **for an off-market bid, the bidder's voting power; and**

> **any other information that is material to the making of the decision by a holder of bid class securities whether to accept an offer under the bid.**

Under s 643, if a bidder becomes aware of:

> **a misleading or deceptive statement in the bidder's statement;**
> **an omission of required information; or**
> **a new circumstance that would have been required to be included had it arisen before the bidder's statement was lodged;**

the bidder must prepare a supplementary bidder's statement that remedies this defect where the defect is material from the point of view of a holder of bid class securities.

target's statement

The target's statement is the response of the target to the takeover bid and bidder's statement.

[18.90] The target's statement is the response of the target to the takeover bid and bidder's statement. Its contents are the same irrespective whether the takeover bid is an off-market or market bid.

A target's statement must include all the information that holders of bid class securities and their professional advisers would reasonably require to make an informed assessment whether to accept the offer under the bid: s 638(1). This information must be included to the extent to which it is reasonable for investors and their professional advisers to expect to find the information in the statement and only if the information is known to any of the directors of the target: s 638(1A).

A target's statement must contain a recommendation by each of the target's directors that the offers under the bid be accepted or not accepted and reasons for the recommendation: s 638(3).

A person whose statement is included in the target's statement must give consent to its inclusion: s 638(5).

An expert's report must accompany the target's statement if the bidder's voting power in the target is 30 per cent or greater or a director of the bidder is a director of the target: s 640(1). The expert's report must state whether, in the expert's opinion, the takeover offers are fair and reasonable and reasons for this opinion. Expert's reports are discussed below, para [18.170].

If a target becomes aware of:

> **a misleading or deceptive statement in the target's statement;**
> **an omission of required information; or**
> **a new circumstance that would have been required to be included had it arisen before the target's statement was lodged;**
> **a supplementary target's statement that remedies this defect must be prepared where the defect is material from the point of view of a holder of bid class securities: s 644.**

Section 648J requires a bidder and target to make clear sound recordings of all telephone calls made during the bid period to holders of security in the bid class.

telephone monitoring

[18.95] Section 648J requires a bidder and target to make clear sound recordings of all telephone calls made during the bid period to holders of security in the bid class or holders of securities which come into the bid class due to conversion or exercise of rights. This obligation applies to all telephone calls made for the purpose of discussing the takeover bid whether or not there was some other purpose for the telephone call as well. Recording telephone calls is not required if the call is made by holders of the securities to the bidder or target unless they were invited to make the call: s 648J(1A).

The purpose of s 648J is to ensure that there will be a record of conversation in cases where a bidder or target contacts holders of security during takeovers. This will enable the holder of the securities or ASIC to bring legal actions or enforcement actions that may arise from the statements made. In the absence of such recordings, it is usually difficult to prove what was stated.

variation of offers

[18.100] Generally, a bidder cannot vary a takeover offer except to increase the consideration or extend the offer period: ss 649A and 650A. ASIC may exercise its power under s 655A to exempt a person from a provision or modify the legislation to allow other variations.

withdrawal of offers

[18.105] Unaccepted offers under a takeover bid can only be withdrawn with the consent of ASIC or if an event specified in s 652C occurs and the bidder's voting power in the target is less than 50 per cent. The events mainly involve significant changes to the share capital or assets of the target or it becomes insolvent.

conditional offers

[18.110] Offers under a market bid must be unconditional: s 625(1). This is not the case with off-market bids which may be subject to conditions. However, certain types of conditions are not permitted. A bidder may wish to attach conditions to its offer so as to ensure that the takeover only proceeds in circumstances favourable to it. From the point of view of a target company's shareholders, conditions have the effect of creating uncertainty. They must commit themselves to selling but cannot be certain that the sale will be finalised because a conditional event may occur that permits the bidder to avoid completing the transaction. To protect the shareholders of a target company, the takeover provisions regulate conditions in off-market bids. Some types of conditions are prohibited while other types (defeating conditions) are permitted only if they obey certain requirements.

To protect the shareholders of a target company, the takeover provisions regulate conditions in off-market bids. Some types of conditions are prohibited while other types (defeating conditions) are permitted only if they obey certain requirements.

prohibited conditions

[18.115] The *Corporations Act* prohibits the following types of conditions in off-market bids:

> **maximum acceptance conditions: s 626. These provide that the offers will terminate if the number of securities for which the bidder receives acceptances exceeds a particular amount;**
> **discriminatory conditions: s 627. These allow the bidder to acquire securities from some but not all the people who accept the offers;**
> **a condition that payments or other benefits to officers of the target as compensation for loss of office be approved: s 628; and**
> **a defeating condition that depends on the bidder's opinion or belief or the occurrence of an event that is within the sole control of the bidder or an associate: s 629.**

defeating conditions

[18.120] The *Corporations Act* regulates "defeating conditions" in off-market takeover bids. A defeating condition is defined in s 9 and means a condition that entitles a bidder to rescind a takeover contract in the circumstances referred to in the condition or prevents a binding takeover contract from resulting from an acceptance of the offer unless or until the condition is fulfilled.

A defeating condition is only permitted where the offer specifies a date between 14 days and seven days before the end of the offer period, for giving a notice on the status of the condition:

s 630(1). In particular, the bidder must state whether the offers are free of the condition, whether the condition was fulfilled and the bidder's voting power in the target: s 630(3).

Notice of status of the condition must be given to:

> **the target; and**
> **for quoted bid class securities—the relevant market operator; or**
> **for unquoted bid class securities—ASIC.**

Occasionally, directors of a target company may enter into transactions or arrangements that are intended to trigger a defeating condition in the hope of destroying a hostile takeover bid.

case note

In *Re Pinnacle VRB Ltd (No 8)* (2001) 19 ACLC 1252, the Takeovers Panel set the following guidelines for directors of target companies in such circumstances. The Panel decided that in general, a transaction or conduct by a target board which has the effect of triggering a bid condition which is likely to lead to the defeat of the bid must be submitted to the target's shareholders for approval. This followed from s 602(c) which requires that shareholders have a reasonable and equal opportunity to participate in any benefits from the bid proposal. However, a target board cannot act to defeat or delay a takeover by entering into transactions of dubious benefit by the simple expedient of putting matters to shareholders. This may constitute a breach of director's duties or unacceptable circumstances. There could also be exceptional circumstances where shareholder approval would be unnecessary despite an action triggering a bid condition. For example, target directors may enter into a transaction which was clearly for the commercial advantage of the company and was so motivated. Shareholder approval would also be unnecessary, where a defeating condition was so far-reaching and constraining that they exceed what would be commercially reasonable in the circumstances with the result that perfectly legitimate transactions would trigger the bid condition.

partial takeovers

[18.125] Bidders may not always want to acquire all the shares of the target company but may seek to acquire only a sufficient proportion of the target company's shares to enable them to gain control. For example, bidders may seek to acquire only 51 per cent or perhaps a lesser percentage of shares. This type of bid is called a "partial takeover". From the bidder's point of view, a partial takeover presents an important advantage in that the bidder gains control of the target company while having to outlay an amount considerably less than would be the case with a full takeover for all the shares in a target.

Partial takeovers perform a legitimate economic function and may be beneficial to investors. They provide a means by which control of a target company's assets may pass to more efficient managers without the need to acquire all the shares. On the other hand, by their nature, partial bids may prevent target company shareholders having the opportunity to participate equally in the bid without coercion. Takeovers generally require a bidder to pay a premium for the privilege of control. The existence of this premium for control can be observed in the price increase of the target company's shares when a takeover occurs or is anticipated. A fundamental objective of takeover regulation is achievement of equality of opportunity between shareholders to share the premium for control. In a successful partial bid, the control premium will have been paid only to those shareholders who decided to accept the bid. This may place coercive pressure on shareholders to accept the partial bid because if they do not, they may miss out on participating in the premium for control. If the partial bid is successful, the share price of the target company will usually fall.

Partial takeovers are permitted, however they are regulated by the *Corporations Act*. A partial takeover can only occur by way of an off-market bid. This is because under a market bid, the bidder is obliged to take all securities in the bid class tendered by holders who accept the bid.

Partial takeovers are permitted, however they are regulated by the *Corporations Act*.

pro-rata and proportional bids

[18.130] Prior to 1986, partial takeover bidders could make either a pro-rata bid or a proportional bid for shares in a target company. In a pro-rata bid, the bidder offers to buy a specified percentage of the target company's shares. If the bidder receives acceptances for a greater number of shares than specified in the offer, each acceptance was pro-rated to the same proportion and the excess returned to shareholders. For example, if a bidder held 19 per cent of the target company's shares and wished to acquire in total a little over 50 per cent, it could bid for a further 35 per cent of the company's shares. If it received acceptances for 70 per cent of the shares, each acceptance would be pro-rated. The bidder would take half of each accepting shareholder's shares and the other half would be returned.

A proportional bid involves an offer for the same proportion of each shareholder's holding in the target company. For example, if the bidder holds 19 per cent of the target company's shares, it may bid for 50 per cent of every other shareholding. If the holders of all outstanding shares accept the offer, the bidder would end up holding 59.5 per cent of the total shares.

In practice, it would be unusual for all shareholders to accept a proportional bid. Some shareholders may oppose the bid while others may not be contactable or interested in responding. Therefore, in practice a bidder must pitch a proportional bid at such a level as it estimates will take into account non-acceptances in order to attain the shareholding it hopes to acquire. A pro-rata bid enables the bidder to aim directly at the desired level of acceptances and this indicates why pro-rata bids were more popular than proportional bids.

Pro-rata bids are prohibited. Partial takeovers may only take the form of proportional bids: s 618(1). Pro-rata bids were prohibited as a result of 1986 amendments because the government took the view that they exerted coercive pressure on shareholders and caused uncertainty as to the number of shares ultimately sold. The effect of the prohibition on pro-rata bids is that the uncertainty passes to bidders. This indicates that under the takeovers legislation considerations of equity or fairness as between shareholders are more important than potential cost savings for bidders and even general price efficiency.

Pro-rata bids are prohibited. Partial takeovers may only take the form of proportional bids.

Proportional bids do not exert the same degree of coercive pressure as is the case with pro-rata bids. A failure to accept a proportional bid does not result in an increased proportion of the premium for control passing to accepting shareholders. In addition, accepting shareholders have greater certainty as to the number of their shares that may be sold and are able to deal with the remainder.

shareholder approval of partial takeovers

The constitution of a company may provide for a requirement that shareholders approve of a partial takeover for securities of the company.

[18.135] The constitution of a company may provide for a requirement that shareholders approve of a partial takeover for securities of the company. Under s 648D(1)(a), the constitution may provide that registration of a transfer giving effect to a takeover contract for the bid is prohibited unless and until an approving resolution is passed. Such provisions are colloquially referred to as "shark repellents" because in effect a majority of a target's shareholders can prevent a partial takeover bid being successful even though the bidder may not want to acquire a majority of the shares.

Such provisions are colloquially referred to as "shark repellents".

A company's proportional takeover approval provisions generally cease to apply after three years: s 648G(1). The constitution may specify a lesser period. The company may renew the provisions in the same way as they were originally adopted.

compulsory acquisitions

[18.140] The *Corporations Act* has adopted the policy that where a bidder has acquired a large majority of shares in a company, it is entitled to the economic, administrative, taxation and other benefits of full ownership of the company. At the same time, the compulsory acquisition provisions also seek to protect the rights of minority shareholders from the potential dangers of being locked in.

A bidder who wishes to acquire all the securities of a target company may compulsorily acquire the securities of dissenting minority shareholders in the circumstances set out in Pt 6A.1. There is further power to compulsorily acquire securities at any time and not just after a takeover bid: s 664A(3). This is discussed in Chapter 17 above. The interests of minority shareholders to keep their shares are outweighed by the benefits accruing to the bidder. The necessary high acceptance levels are taken as indicating the fairness of the offers. In the light of the High Court's decision in *Gambotto v WCP Ltd* (1995) 13 ACLC 342, it is difficult to compulsorily acquire minority shareholdings outside the statutory procedures contained in ss 414, 661A and 664A. This case is discussed in Chapter 4 above.

ninety per cent threshold

A bidder may compulsorily acquire any securities in the bid class if the bidder and associates have relevant interests in at least 90 per cent of the bid class securities.

[18.145] A bidder, under a takeover bid, may compulsorily acquire any securities in the bid class if, during or at the end of the offer period, the bidder and associates have relevant interests in at least 90 per cent of the bid class securities and the bidder and associates have acquired at least 75 per cent of the securities that the bidder offered to acquire under the bid: s 661A(1)(b). The court may allow compulsory acquisition even if the thresholds have not been reached: s 661A(3).

notice

[18.150] In order to compulsorily acquire securities, a bidder must give a notice to holders of securities in the bid class informing them that the bidder is entitled to acquire their securities and their right to apply to the court for an order preventing the compulsory acquisition: s 661B(1). This notice must be lodged with ASIC and a copy given to each relevant market operator. Notice must be dispatched during the offer period or within one month after it ends. The notices cannot be withdrawn: s 661B(2).

terms of acquisition

[18.155] The terms of a compulsory acquisition must be the same as those under the takeover bid: s 661C.

preventing compulsory acquisition

The court may order that the securities not be compulsorily acquired if it is satisfied that the consideration is not fair value for the securities.

[18.160] The holder of securities covered by a compulsory acquisition notice may apply to the court for an order that the securities not be compulsorily acquired: s 661E. The application must generally be made within one month after the notice of acquisition was given. The court may order that the securities not be compulsorily acquired if it is satisfied that the consideration is not fair value for the securities: s 661E(2).

To ascertain what is fair value for securities, s 667C sets out how this is determined:

> **assess the value of the company as a whole;**

> **allocate that value among the classes of issued securities taking into account class rights and financial risk;**
> **allocate the value of each class on a pro-rata basis among securities of the class; and**
> **consider the price paid for the securities in that class over the previous six months.**

The onus is on the dissenting shareholder to establish that an offer is unfair. This is to be considered in relation to the general body of shareholders rather than whether it is fair to the particular shareholder.

The onus is on the dissenting shareholder to establish that an offer is unfair.

A high level of acceptances will generally indicate that an offer is fair. The court will be reluctant to impose its views of fairness in opposition to the attitude taken by the great majority of those who are directly concerned with the scheme. It is not sufficient for the dissenting shareholder to show that the offer is open to some criticism or could have been improved upon. A failure to comply with legislative requirements is relevant to the question of fairness.

The mere fact that a compulsory acquisition would make a company worth more to the majority shareholder than to a third party does not mean that the additional value should be wholly attributed to the minority shareholders: *Pauls Ltd v Dwyer* [2001] QSC 67. The amount of consideration offered is not the only matter to be examined. It may be relevant to consider the conduct of the bidder in the period prior to the making of the offer.

In considering the question whether a price is fair, the fact that it is considerably higher than the market price before the takeover bid is more significant than an expert's report stating that the offer price was unfair and did not reflect the target company's true value: *Elkington v Shell Australia Ltd* (1993) 11 ACLC 942.

compulsory buy-out

[18.165] A bidder and its associates who have relevant interests in at least 90 per cent of the bid class securities must offer to buy out the remaining holders of the securities: s 662A. Upon attaining 90 per cent, the bidder must give a notice to each holder of securities in the bid class. The notice must state that the bidder has exceeded the 90 per cent threshold, inform the holders of their right to be bought out and set out the terms on which the holder may be bought out: s 662B. The notice must be lodged with ASIC and given to each relevant market operator.

A bidder and its associates who have relevant interests in at least 90 per cent of the bid class securities must offer to buy out the remaining holders of the securities.

Within one month after this notice is given, the holder of securities may give written notice requiring the bidder to acquire the securities: s 662C(1). The notice by the holder gives rise to a contract between the holder and the bidder for the sale of the securities on the terms applicable before the end of the offer period: s 662C(2). The right to require the bidder to buy out securities also extends to the holders of securities that are convertible into bid class securities: s 663A.

These provisions enable minority shareholders holding any class of shares, option holders or convertible note holders to prevent themselves being locked in after control has overwhelmingly passed. The market price for the shares may fall to reflect the dominance of the major shareholder. The takeover offer may not have been addressed to them; however, their securities may be delisted because, for example, the target company's spread of shareholders is insufficient for the purposes of ASX Listing Rules.

experts' reports

[18.170] There are a number of provisions in the takeovers legislation and ASX Listing Rules that require the report of an independent expert so as to provide shareholders with information to enable them to assess the merits of a takeover proposal or proposed acquisition. Experts must have a "professional reputation" as required by the definition in s 9.

As discussed above, under s 640, a target's statement must be accompanied by an expert's report in cases where the bidder's voting power in the target is 30 per cent or more or where the bidder and target company have common directors. An expert's report is also required in situations of compulsory acquisitions and buy-outs: ss 663B, 664C and 665B. An expert may be liable for false and deceptive statements and omissions under ss 670A and 670B. This is further discussed below, para [18.205].

fair and reasonable

[18.175] Under s 640, the expert must report whether, in their opinion, the takeover offer is fair and reasonable with the reasons for that opinion. In the case of a compulsory acquisition or buy-out, an expert's report must state whether a fair value is proposed for the securities concerned: s 667A. In determining whether an offer or value is fair and reasonable, the expert should follow the guidelines set out in ASIC Policy Statement 75: *Independent Expert Reports to Shareholders*.

The concept of fair and reasonable is different to a recommendation as to whether or not an offer or proposal should be accepted. An offer is fair if the value of consideration is equal to or greater than the value of the securities concerned. An offer may be reasonable if, after considering significant factors, shareholders should accept the offer or proposal in the absence of a higher price. Some relevant considerations include the bidder's voting power in the target, market liquidity for the target's securities and the value to an alternative bidder.

To determine what is fair value, the expert should adopt the process set out in s 667C. This requires an assessment of the value of the company as a whole, an allocation of this value among the classes of issued securities and then a pro-rata allocation among those securities.

independence of expert

The expert who prepares the report is also required to set out details of the expert's business relationship with the bidder, the target company or their associates together with details of any financial or other interest the expert has with them that could be reasonably regarded as affecting the expert's ability to give an unbiased opinion.

[18.180] Under s 648A, the expert who prepares the report is also required to set out details of the expert's business relationship with the bidder, the target company or their associates together with details of any financial or other interest the expert has with them that could be reasonably regarded as affecting the expert's ability to give an unbiased opinion. The purpose of this is to enable shareholders in the target company, when reading the expert's opinion, to take into account any factor that may have influenced her or his independence.

The expert is not regarded as independent if the expert is an "associate" of the bidder or target within the meaning of ss 11 or 15. In addition, ASIC Practice Note 42: *Independence of Experts' Reports* states:

> < **PN 42.3. [ASIC] aims to ensure that an expert is independent of the party who commissions the expert's report ("the client") and its advisers and associates when assessing a proposal. The expert should be independent from the time that the client first approaches him or her to prepare an expert's report until the client publishes the final version of the report for its required purpose.** >

prohibited conduct

disposal of securities by bidder

The bidder must not dispose of any securities in the bid class during the bid period.

[18.185] The bidder must not dispose of any securities in the bid class during the bid period: s 654A(1). This prohibition does not apply if someone else who is not an associate of the bidder makes a takeover bid for securities in the bid class after the bidder's statement is given to the target. The bidder may then dispose of the securities after the offer is made or the consideration is improved: s 654A(2).

escalation agreements

[18.190] Prospective bidders are prohibited from entering into arrangements with selected shareholders whereby their shares are to be acquired in the six-month period before the bid is made with additional benefits attributable to the acquisition: s 622(1). Such an agreement is void to the extent of the benefit: s 622(3).

Prospective bidders are prohibited from entering into arrangements with selected shareholders whereby their shares are to be acquired in the six-month period before the bid is made with additional benefits attributable to the acquisition.

These arrangements are prohibited because they confer an advantage on some shareholders—usually large institutional investors. Such shareholders could dispose of their shares at a prevailing market price, knowing that when a takeover bid is later made, they will receive the benefit of any better price subsequently offered.

The effect of such arrangements is contrary to the principle that all shareholders have the opportunity to share in any premium for control.

collateral benefits

[18.195] A bidder is prohibited from giving a benefit to a person during the offer period if the benefit is likely to induce the person to accept the bid offer and is not offered to all holders of securities in the bid class: s 623. As with escalation agreements, this type of arrangement seeks to advantage some holders of securities over others.

A bidder is prohibited from giving a benefit to a person during the offer period if the benefit is likely to induce the person to accept the bid offer and is not offered to all holders of securities in the bid class.

public proposal of takeover bid

[18.200] A person who publicly proposes to make a takeover bid for securities must make offers for the securities within two months of the proposal. The terms of the bid must be the same or not substantially less favourable as those in the public proposal: s 631(1). It is an offence for a person to publicly propose to make a takeover bid if the person knows the bid will not be made or is reckless as to whether it will be made. It is also an offence if the person is reckless as to whether they will be able to fund their obligations under the bid if a substantial proportion of the offers under the bid are accepted: s 631(2). A person who enters into a transaction relating to securities in reliance on the public proposal for a takeover bid may recover any loss suffered as a result from the persons who contravened s 631: s 670E.

Defences to this liability may arise if the person was unaware of particular circumstances or if the circumstances changed: s 670F.

misleading or deceptive statements

[18.205] Chapter 6B of the *Corporations Act* contains the liability provisions for misleading and deceptive statements in relation to takeover activity. These provisions were rewritten as a result of 1999 amendments so as to make them consistent with the liability regime applicable to fundraising. Criminal liability is dealt with in s 670A(3), while civil liability is covered by s 670B.

section 670A prohibition

[18.210] Section 670A(1) applies to bidder's and target's statements, a takeover offer document and compulsory acquisition and buy-out notices. It provides that a person must not include a misleading or deceptive statement or make an omission of required information in these documents. This section also requires disclosure of any new circumstance in a bidder's or target's statement.

Section 670A(1) provides that a person must not include a misleading or deceptive statement or make an omission of required information.

A statement about a future matter such as a profit forecast or future act may be misleading if it is made without reasonable grounds: s 670A(2).

A contravention of s 670A(1) is an offence if the misleading or deceptive statement or omission is materially adverse from the point of view of the holder of securities to whom the document is given: s 670A(3).

A person who suffers loss or damage that results from a contravention of s 670A(1) may recover the amount of the loss or damage from the people referred to in s 670B. Civil liability may arise even if the person did not commit and was not involved in a contravention of s 670A(1).

who may be liable?

[18.215] People who may be liable under s 670B(1) for loss or damage include:

> **the bidder and its directors;**
> **the target and its directors;**
> **a person giving a compulsory acquisition or buy-out notice; and**
> **a person who consented to have a statement included in a takeover document or on which a statement made in the document is based. This includes experts.**

Directors are generally not liable if they can prove that they were not present when the resolution to adopt the document or statement was passed or they voted against the resolution. This defence is not available in relation to non-cash consideration bids and notices of variation of takeover offer.

notification of deficiencies

[18.220] The people who may be liable on a takeover or compulsory acquisition document under s 670B(1) must notify the issuer of the document as soon as possible after becoming aware of the misleading or deceptive statement or omission or that a material new circumstance has arisen: s 670C.

An expert is under corresponding obligations to notify the bidder and target where there has been a significant change affecting information included in the report accompanying a bidder's or target's statement: s 670C(2) and (3).

defences

[18.225] The defences set out in s 670D apply to both prosecutions for an offence under s 670A(3) and civil actions brought under s 670B. The defences include:

> **proof of lack of knowledge that a statement was misleading or deceptive or that there was an omission;**
> **proof of reasonable reliance on information given by someone else;**
> **withdrawal of consent by a person named in a document as making a statement; and**
> **a new circumstance has arisen of which the person was unaware.**

other liability

[18.230] Conduct in relation to takeover activity other than the content of takeover and compulsory acquisition documents is subject to s 1041H. This section prohibits misleading and deceptive conduct in relation to financial products or financial services and gives rise to civil liability. This is discussed above in Chapter 7.

Criminal liability is also imposed on an officer of a corporation who makes available or furnishes information that relates to the affairs of the corporation and to the knowledge of the officer is false or misleading: s 1309(1). This section encompasses information provided to a wide range of persons including other directors, the company auditor, members and debenture-holders. It also includes information provided to a stock exchange. This may arise during a takeover where a response is made by a company to a stock exchange query.

ASIC Policy Statement 25: *Takeovers—False and Misleading Statements* concluded that an offeror who states that the offer price will not be increased will generally be expected to honour this representation. A subsequent increase in the offer price may result in a misleading statement and attract civil liability.

ASIC powers

[18.235] ASIC has wide powers to exempt compliance with, and modify the operation of, the takeover provisions: s 655A. These discretionary powers are not intended to be used retrospectively where the *Corporations Act* has already been breached. Where a breach has occurred, application may be made to the Takeovers Panel or the court.

ASIC has wide powers to exempt compliance with, and modify the operation of, the takeover provisions.

In exercising its powers under s 655A, ASIC must take into account the underlying principles of the takeovers legislation as set out in s 602: s 655A(2).

The exemption may apply unconditionally or subject to specified conditions. ASIC may apply to the court for an order that a person comply with a condition: s 655A(4). ASIC is required to take reasonable steps to give each person whose interests are affected by an exemption or modification notice of the decision and of the person's right to have the decision reviewed by the Panel: s 655B(1).

In exercising its powers ASIC must take into account the underlying principles of the takeovers legislation as set out in s 602.

The Takeovers Panel may review a decision of ASIC to exempt or modify under s 655A: s 656A(1)(a). An application to the Panel may be made by any person whose interests are affected by the decision: s 656A(2).

Takeovers Panel

[18.240] The Takeovers Panel (formerly known as the Corporations and Securities Panel) was established under the *ASIC Act* with the powers and functions conferred on it under the *Corporations Act*. While its main functions are in relation to takeover bids, the Takeovers Panel's powers also apply to non-takeover situations such as rights issues, buy-backs, reductions of capital and other acquisitions of shares that may involve the control of a company or an acquisition of a substantial interest in a company.

The Lipton-Herzberg corporate law website site at **http://www.lipton-herzberg.com.au/corp-law-websites.html#Regulatory_bodies** has a link to the Takeovers Panel's website, which contains information about the Panel, its guidance notes, media releases, decisions and rules.

As a result of 1999 amendments, the Takeovers Panel takes the place of the courts as the main forum for resolving disputes arising from a takeover during the bid period: s 659AA. This was done so that takeover disputes could be resolved quickly and efficiently by a specialist body comprised of takeover experts attuned to the commercial realities and aware of market practices. It was thought that target companies in particular often resorted to the courts as a tactic to prevent or slow down a takeover bid.

The Takeovers Panel takes the place of the courts as the main forum for resolving disputes arising from a takeover during the bid period.

The Panel has the power to make declarations of unacceptable circumstances in relation to the affairs of a company: s 657A(1). If the Panel makes a declaration of unacceptable circumstances, s 657D gives it the power to make any order (including remedial orders) to protect the rights or interests of affected persons or ensure a bid proceeds as if the unacceptable circumstances had not occurred. Under s 9 remedial orders include orders that:

> restrain the exercise of voting or other rights attached to securities;
> restrain an acquisition of securities;
> direct a person to dispose or not dispose of securities;
> direct the payment of profits from a disposal of securities;
> vest securities in ASIC;
> direct a body corporate not to register a transfer of securities;
> cancel securities issued as consideration for offers under a takeover bid;
> cancel or declare voidable an agreement relating to a takeover bid or acquisition of securities;
> direct a person to disclose information to the holders of securities;
> direct a body corporate to amend its constitution; and
> direct a person to comply with a requirement of the legislation.

Before making an order, the Panel must give affected persons an opportunity to make submissions and it must be satisfied that the order would not unfairly prejudice any person: s 657D(1).

The Panel may make interim orders even if there is no declaration that circumstances are unacceptable or no application has been made for a declaration: s 657E. Interim orders may have effect for up to two months.

Section 657A(3) provides that in deciding whether or not to make a declaration of unacceptable circumstances the Panel must have regard to:

> the purposes of the takeover provisions as set out in s 602;
> the other provisions in Ch 6 of the *Corporations Act*;
> the Panel's rules made under s 658C; and
> any other matter it considers relevant.

The Panel must also take into account the actions of the directors of the target including actions that caused or contributed to the acquisition of shares not to proceed: s 657A(3). This indicates that defensive tactics and strategies may be considered by the Panel. In Takeovers Panel Guidance Note 4—*Remedies and Enforcement*, the Panel explains what outcomes it would attempt to achieve when making an order.

> **< [4.10] Generally when using a remedy the Panel will be seeking to achieve one or more of the following outcomes:**
> **/ getting a bid back on track;**
> **/ correcting any misinformation or omission and reversing any mischief to investors (including compensation) or the market; and**
> **/ establishing benchmarks and standards of corporate behaviour. >**

An application for a declaration or order by the Panel can be made by the bidder, target, ASIC or any other person whose interests are affected by the relevant circumstances: s 657C(2). The application must be brought within two months after the circumstances occurred or a longer period determined by the Panel: s 657C(3). The Panel must give each person to whom a proposed declaration relates, each party to the proceedings, and ASIC an opportunity to make submissions: s 657A(4). A declaration must be made within three months after the circumstances occur or one month after the application for the declaration was made. These time limits can only be extended by the court on application by the Panel: s 657B.

A party to proceedings in which the Panel made a decision or ASIC may apply to the Panel for a review of the decision: s 657EA. The court may also refer a decision of the Panel to it for review: s 657EB.

Orders of the Panel may be enforced by the court: s 657G. The Panel has power to make rules to clarify or supplement the operation of the takeovers legislation: s 658C. The rules must take account of the purposes of the legislation as set out in s 602. The court may give directions for compliance with a rule to a person who contravenes a rule and its directors.

unacceptable circumstances

[18.245] The ability to make a declaration of unacceptable circumstances under s 657A is one of the most important powers of the Takeovers Panel. The *Corporations Act* does not define the term "unacceptable circumstances". Section 657A directs the Panel to take into account the s 602 objectives and the detailed requirements of Chs 6, 6A, 6B and 6C of the *Corporations Act*. According to Takeovers Panel Guidance Note 1—*Unacceptable Circumstances*:

The ability to make a declaration of unacceptable circumstances is one of the most important powers of the Takeovers Panel.

> **[1.5] There is no definition of unacceptable circumstances in the Corporations Act. Instead, the Panel is directed to use section 602, Chapter 6 of the Act and the public interest as reference points to determine when circumstances are unacceptable. Parliament considered that black letter law would be insufficient to deal with all the possible circumstances that might defeat the policy of section 602. Accordingly, it empowered the Panel, as an expert body, to address the issues by considering whether circumstances are unacceptable in terms of those reference points.**
>
> **[1.14] The Panel is required to take the *public interest* into account when considering whether or not to make a declaration of unacceptable circumstances. *Public interest* is a difficult term to define. However, the Panel takes its significance to mean, for the Panel, that the Panel should not merely consider the commercial interests and convenience of the parties and their shareholders directly involved in a dispute before the Panel. Rather, the Panel should consider wider issues such as: what signals its decisions to make, or not make, a declaration of unacceptable circumstances in individual cases, will send to the market and the wider investing community.**

Guidance Note 1 identified the following types of unacceptable circumstances:

> **[1.16] The first broad category of unacceptable circumstances is where an efficient, competitive and informed market in the relevant securities is inhibited. Such circumstances may result from a false market, a deficiency of information, or the premature lockout of rival bids, among other things. Anything which leads to a false market in any securities affected by a bid or transaction may be in this category. Where there is a deficiency of information, the circumstances will often, but not always, also fall into the second category.**
>
> **[1.19] A second category of unacceptable circumstances is where holders do not have the *information* necessary to make an informed decision or are misled about the relevant transaction. The decision could be whether to accept a bid or whether to approve a transaction. The Panel treats misinformation or false information being given to the market the in the same way as a shortage of information, because the effects are likely to be similar and may be just as harmful.**
>
> **[1.23] A third category of unacceptable circumstances is where holders of voting shares or units do not have *reasonable* and *equal opportunities* to take part in *benefits* accruing to holders of shares or units in connection with a transaction effecting control.**
>
> **[1.25] A fourth category of unacceptable circumstances is where appropriate procedures are not followed leading up to compulsory acquisition of securities under Part 6A.1.**

defensive strategies and tactics

Directors of a target company often engage in various defensive strategies and tactics to frustrate hostile takeover bids.

[18.250] Directors of a target company often engage in various defensive strategies and tactics to frustrate hostile takeover bids. While the *Corporations Act* and the common law do not expressly prohibit the directors of a target company from engaging in such frustrating action, directors must, of course, comply with their fiduciary and statutory duties, particularly their duties to act in good faith, in the best interests of the company and for proper purposes.

In Guidance Note 12—*Frustrating Action*, the Takeovers Panel observed that action taken by a target company to frustrate a bid may give rise to unacceptable circumstances:

> < **Frustrating action may give rise to unacceptable circumstances if the particular circumstances offend the principles set out in sections 602 and 657A of the *Corporations Act*, even if it is otherwise legal or required for the proper performance of the directors' duties. In such a case, the Panel may prevent the target from proceeding with the frustrating action, unless it has first been approved at a general meeting of target shareholders, or the target has taken some other action to avoid unacceptable circumstances arising.** >

Defensive strategies and tactics were also examined in a report by the NCSC, "Defensive Schemes and the Duties of Directors", released in October 1986. This report outlined the common defensive schemes and examined whether the duties of directors may be breached in the implementation of the schemes. The NCSC report may be accessed on the Takeovers Panel website which is linked to Lipton-Herzberg Corporate Law Websites at **http://www.lipton-herzberg.com.au/corp-law-websites.html#Regulatory_bodies**

defensive tactics

[18.255] In examining various defensive schemes, the NCSC report distinguished between defensive tactics and defensive strategies. "Tactics" are measures adopted to combat a hostile bid that has been made or is thought imminent. "Strategies" are intended to discourage bids being made at all. The NCSC commented on the following common defensive tactics.

[18.260] branding the bid inadequate. This was found to be the most common defensive tactic. It may be of benefit to shareholders where the bid is ultimately raised or where shareholders are encouraged to reassess the value of their shares.

[18.265] criticising the bidder. Target company directors should ensure that their criticism does not involve a misleading statement in breach of s 670A.

[18.270] releasing favourable information. This may breach s 670A where it constitutes a misleading statement. The release of such information may have later adverse results for target company directors where shareholders' expectations are raised and these ultimately prove to be unfounded. This may increase the likelihood of a successful, later bid.

[18.275] bonus issues and higher dividends. The threat of takeover has often caused companies to declare greater dividends as a means of increasing shareholder loyalty. While this may not be for the long-term benefit of the company, it is a management decision that shareholders may take into account in their judgment of the directors. It is generally inappropriate for the courts or ASIC to interfere with such decisions.

[18.280] placements and "friendly" purchases. Once a bid has been made, ASX Listing Rules require shareholder approval for share placements. This restriction does not apply where a bid may be imminent. Friendly purchases may support or raise the share price or require the bidder to acquire a larger shareholding in order to gain control.

[18.285] "friendly" takeover. The target company directors may actively foster an auction in the face of a hostile bid or the first bid may attract a rival bidder which the directors regard as more attractive. This may be of benefit to shareholders, especially where they receive the offer of a higher price from a "white knight".

[18.290] appeal to employees or other interested groups. Employee shareholders are often very loyal to incumbent management. Employee share schemes may therefore constitute an effective defensive measure.

[18.295] institute legal proceedings. One of the most common and effective tactics was to bring proceedings before the courts or regulatory bodies such as the Australian Competition and Consumer Commission (ACCC). The 1999 amendments have substantially diminished the role of the courts during the takeover period while strengthening the role of the Takeovers Panel. This should result in less opportunity to delay a takeover bid by use of this tactic.

[18.300] asset redeployment. The purchase or sale of assets by a target company may cause a significant restructure of the target company. In particular, where a target company employs a "crown jewel" defence by selling assets that are especially attractive to a bidder, this may be detrimental to shareholders and a breach of duty by directors. The NCSC report concluded that it was difficult to determine the motives of directors who implement defensive tactics. However, it did not appear that shareholders were necessarily prejudiced by such tactics as the offer price was usually increased as a result. While defensive tactics were often initially successful in defeating a hostile takeover, later bids often proved successful.

defensive strategies

[18.305] Defensive strategies have been increasingly used by companies in an attempt to make themselves "takeover proof" or at least difficult to take over. A number of common strategies were examined in the NCSC report. These include:

[18.310] inter-company shareholdings. The development of such shareholding structures may arise for a number of valid reasons and it is difficult to determine whether they were established as defensive strategies. Inter-company shareholdings may be established to rationalise a market or to facilitate a greater degree of integration between the companies concerned. The structure may have evolved after a series of successful partial takeovers and has been retained for a number of reasons, which include tax benefits as well as making the group "takeover proof". In a number of cases, inter-company shareholdings have failed as a defensive strategy when one shareholder accepted a takeover offer. Some companies have entered into arrangements with other companies that share little or no commercial interests in common. Strategic shareholdings are acquired to prevent hostile takeovers of any of the participating companies.

[18.315] friendly placements. ASX Listing Rules restrict placements to less than five per cent of issued capital without shareholder approval in any two-month period. Placements may be made as part of a strategic relationship or to stabilise the share register. Placements to institutional investors are no longer as safe as was previously the case. Institutions have shown a greater willingness to sell strategic holdings to bidders in order to improve immediate returns.

[18.320] issue of convertible securities. The development of innovative securities that allow for conversion of debt into equity has enabled companies to utilise these securities for defensive purposes. Convertible notes and bonds, partly paid shares and options, enable investors to acquire ordinary shares at a future date. Under a defensive agreement, these securities may be issued on terms that they become convertible in the event of a takeover. This triggers an increase in voting capital in friendly hands with defensive implications against hostile takeovers.

[18.325] proportional takeover approval. The constitution of a company may provide that where offers are made under a proportional takeover bid, a resolution of shareholders approving the bid must be passed before related transfers are registered: s 648D. This type of provision is becoming more common.

powers of the court

[18.330] As discussed above, the Panel is the main forum for resolving disputes about a takeover bid until the bid period has ended. This is stated by s 659AA.

Prior to the end of the bid period, only ASIC or another public authority may commence court proceedings in relation to a takeover bid: s 659B(1). The court may stay proceedings that have already commenced until after the end of the bid period: s 659B(2).

case note

In *Glencore International AG v Takeovers Panel* [2005] FCA 1290, the court held that even though s 659B prohibited a party subject to Panel proceedings from seeking a court review of the Panel's decision, court proceedings were possible if the Panel made a jurisdictional error. In that case the Panel made a declaration of unacceptable circumstances in relation to Glencore's failure to disclose its acquisition of a substantial shareholding in a target company. One effect of Glencore's acquisition was that the takeover bidder would not be able to acquire 90 per cent of the shares in the target and then be able to compulsorily acquire the remaining shares.

The court held that in considering whether to make a declaration of unacceptable circumstances, the Panel is required to engage in a balancing exercise. It must weigh the object of protecting rights or interests of any person affected by the relevant circumstances against the prejudice to any person that would flow from the making of an order. In *Glencore's* case, the Panel made a jurisdictional error because it did not identify the particular interests or rights that were affected by the non-disclosure that were intended to be the subject of protection, in order to balance those rights and interests against the prejudice that would be suffered by Glencore.

The Panel may refer a question of law arising in proceedings before it to the court for decision: s 659A.

After the end of the bid period, the court may make certain orders where the Panel has refused to make a declaration under s 657A that particular conduct amounts to unacceptable circumstances: s 659C. If the court finds that the conduct contravenes the legislation, it may determine whether a person is guilty of an offence and impose a penalty. It may also order the person to pay money to another by way of damages, account of profits or pecuniary penalty. The court cannot make other kinds of remedial orders: s 659C(2).

other legislation

[18.335] The *Trade Practices Act 1974* (Cth) prohibits a corporation from acquiring shares or assets of a body corporate if the acquisition will have the effect of substantially lessening competition in a market: s 50.

An acquisition that has the effect of substantially lessening competition in breach of s 50 may be authorised by the ACCC. Authorisation will be given if the ACCC is satisfied that the acquisition will create a benefit to the public.

The *Foreign Takeovers Act 1975* (Cth) empowers the Federal Treasurer to prevent the acquisition by a foreign person of shares in an Australian company where the acquisition would result in control passing to the foreigner and this would be contrary to the national interest. A foreign corporation is defined as one in which 15 per cent of its voting capital is held by a foreigner or where two or more foreigners hold at least 40 per cent of the issued capital.

Certain industries are regulated by specific legislation that restricts the acquisition of shares in companies engaged in the industry, for example, the *Broadcasting and Television Act 1942* (Cth) seeks to prevent undesirable concentrations of ownership in the television and other media industries.

bibliography ...

Armson, E "Handing the Corporate Reins to Creditors: The Role of the Takeovers Panel in the Pasminco Administration" (2002) 25 UNSWLJ 651.

Armson, E "The Frustrating Action Policy: Shifting Power in the Takeover Context" (2003) 21 C & SLJ 487.

Austin, Justice R P "The Definition of 'Associate' in the Corporations Law" Uni of Melbourne, Centre for Corporate Law and Securities Regulation, Corporate Law Research Papers, **http://cclsr.law.unimelb.edu.au/research-papers/**

Bowden, R J "In Search of a Normative Takeover Code: Theory and Jurisdiction" (1998) 16 C & SLJ 516.

Calleja, N "The Takeovers Panel Process" Uni of Melbourne, Centre for Corporate Law and Securities Regulation, Corporate Law Research Papers, **http://cclsr.law.unimelb.edu.au/research-papers/**

Calleja, N "The Equality Principle and Prohibited Benefits in Takeovers" (1999) 27 ABLR 342.12

Calleja, N "Takeovers and Public Securities: The Panel's Reluctance to Declare Circumstances Unacceptable?" (2001) 19 C & SLJ 323.

Callum, C & Law, L "Soft Information Disclosure Requirements under the Corporations Law" (2001) 29 ABLR 149.

Colla, A "Schemes of Arrangement as an Alternative to Friendly Takeover Schemes: Recent Developments" (1998) 16 C & SLJ 365.

Colla, A "Eliminating Minority Shareholdings—Recent Developments" (2001) 19 C & SLJ 7.

Cross, R "The Takeovers Panel Three Years On: Should We Ever Go Back to the Courts?" (2003) 21 C & SLJ 367.

Crutchfield, P "The Requirement For Experts; Reports In Takeovers And Corporate Reconstruction" (1996) 14 C & SLJ 489.

Ding, A "An Interpretation of the Equality of Opportunity Principle in the Context of Benefits Prohibited under the Corporations Law" (2000) 18 C & SLJ 6.

Emma, A "The Australian takeovers panel: commercial body or quasi-court?" (2004) 28 *Melbourne University Law Review* 565.

Farrar, J "Joint Takeover Bids: Sidestepping the 20% Rule?" (1999) 17 C & SLJ 268.

Fridman, S "Super-Voting Shares: What's All the Fuss About?" (1995) 13 C & SLJ 31.
Garavaglia, M "Shark Repellants, Golden Parachutes, Crown Jewels and Imagination: Defending Against Hostile Takeovers in Australia and the United States" (1986) 14 ABLR 348.
Gething, M & Ould, K "The Wesfi Takeovers Panel Application: Lessons for the Future" (2000) 18 C & SLJ 351.
Goldwasser, V "Differential Voting Rights and the Super Share" (1995) 7 *Corporate and Business Law Journal* 203.
Goodman, S et al "ASIC Responds to Bidder Uncertainty over Judicial Interpretation of s 698 of the Corporations Law—Part 1; ASIC v Terra Industries—Part 2" (1999) 17 C & SLJ 325.
Hirst, S et al, "When will a Forecast be Required in Takeover Documents? Applying Relevance and Reliability" (2001) 19 C & SLJ 26.
Hirst, S & Law, L "CLERP and Takeover Disclosure Regulation" (1999) 17 C & SLJ 307.
Hopt, K "Takeover regulation in Europe—The battle for the 13th Directive on takeovers" (2002) 15 Aust Jnl of Corp Law 1.
Hughes, G "Compulsory Acquisition of Minority Shareholders' Interests—Still a Tyranny of the Majority?" (2000) 18 C & SLJ 197.
McCabe, B "The Roles and Responsibilities of Company Directors in a Takeover" (1994) 4 Aust Jnl of Corp Law 36.
Mannolini, J "The Reform of Takeovers Law—Beyond Simplification" (1996) 14 C & SLJ 471.
Mannolini, J & Rich, A "Break Fee Agreements in Takeovers" (2001) 19 C & SLJ 222.
Marson, E "The Australian Takeovers Panel and unfair prejudice to third parties" (2004) 16 Aust Jnl of Corp Law 187.
Mayanja, J "Reforming Australia's Takeover Defence Laws" (1999) 10 Aust Jnl of Corp Law 162.
Mayanja, J "The Equal Opportunity Principle in Australian Takeover Law and Practice: Time for Review" (2000) 12 Aust Jnl of Corp Law 1.
Mayanja, J "No-shop, No-talk and Break-up Fee Agreements in Merger & Takeover Transactions: The Case for a Fresh Regulatory Approach" (2002) 14 Aust Jnl of Corp Law 1.
Mayanja, J "A mandatory bid rule for Australia: an idea whose time has come" (2004) 16 Aust Jnl of Corp Law 205.
Mescher, B "Powers of the Takeovers Panel and their Effect upon ASIC and the Court" (2002) 76 ALJ 119.
Milne, S & Carr, F "Collateral Benefits—Do the CLERP Amendments Resolve the Dilemmas faced by Bidders?" (2002) 20 C & SLJ 477.
Morgan-Wicks, K "The New General Compulsory Acquisition Power: Re-Establishing the Minority's Right to an Independent Expert" (2001) 19 C & SLJ 349.
Noakes, D B "Takeover financing arrangements: An issuance of disclosure of market disturbance?" (2004) 22 C & SLJ 231.
Pathak, N "'Public to private' takeover bids" (2003) 21 C & SLJ 295.
Reichel, D & Dyer, B "Developments in break fees" (2004) 22 C & SLJ 439.
Rogers, J "Compulsory Acquisition under Pt 6A.2 and Its Implications for Minority Shareholders" (2003) 31 ABLR 97.
Rogers, J "Minimum Price Rule in Takeovers: Does the Minimum Price Rule Promote the Equal Opportunity Principle at the Expense of a More Efficient Market for Corporate Control" (2004) 22 C & SLJ 87.
Santow, Justice G "CLERPing the Panel" Uni of Melbourne, Centre for Corporate Law and Securities Regulation, Corporate Law Research Papers, **http://cclsr.law.unimelb.edu.au/research-papers/**
Steel, T "Defensive Tactics in Company Takeovers" (1986) 4 C & SLJ 30.
Thompson, C "Joint Takeover Bids: Where to Now after the ASIC v Yandel Decision in the Great Central Mines Takeover?" (1999) 17 C & SLJ 453.
von Nessen, P, Weeks, R & Hutson, J "Listed Property Trusts and Management Entrenchment:

Is Takeover Regulation Alone the Answer" (2003) 16 Aust Jnl of Corp Law 1.
Walsh, E "Judging the Takeover Panel" (2003) 20 C & SLJ 435.

revision questions on the material in this chapter ...

> Please see eQuiz at **http://www.thomson.com.au/academic** for multiple choice questions and answers.

chapter nineteen

financial services and markets

key points ...

- Chapter 7 of the *Corporations Act* regulates a wide range of financial products, financial services and financial markets under a single regulatory regime.
- The regulatory functions in relation to stock exchange share trading are shared by ASIC and the ASX. The operating rules of the ASX have statutory force.
- Financial services providers must be licensed and are under obligations to provide specified information, particularly to retail clients.
- Certain types of market misconduct are prohibited. These include insider trading, short selling, market manipulation, false trading and making false or misleading statements. The more serious types of market misconduct are designated as financial services civil penalty provisions and may result in the imposition of a pecuniary penalty and compensation order.

The *FSR Act* rewrote the *Corporations Act* provisions regulating financial services, products and markets.

The *FSR Act* was based upon the recommendations of the Wallis Report.

[19.05] The regulation of financial markets is necessary because, by their nature, financial products such as securities often do not have a readily ascertainable value as is often the case with tangible property. The value of securities depends on the financial position and the future prospects of the corporation that has issued them, or more particularly, the market's assessment of their value. For this reason, the legislation requires a certain degree of public disclosure of relevant information, the maintenance of proper markets in financial products, licensing requirements for financial service providers and various consumer protection provisions. The *Financial Services Reform Act 2001* (*FSR Act*) which was introduced in March 2002 rewrote the *Corporations Act* provisions regulating financial services, products and markets. This legislation completely revised Ch 7 of the *Corporations Act* as well as a large number of consequential amendments necessary to implement the *FSR Act*.

the Wallis Report

[19.10] The *FSR Act* was based upon the recommendations of the *Financial System Inquiry* (1997) (the Wallis Report) which undertook a comprehensive stocktake of the Australian financial system structure and regulation and considered the forces driving change and the key issues in regulatory reform.

The Wallis Report found that regulation of the financial system was carried out by a variety of regulatory bodies operating in a piecemeal way. This resulted in inefficiencies, inconsistencies and regulatory gaps which were not conducive to effective competition in financial markets. The regulation of various products depended upon the particular industry which provided the product rather than the nature of the product itself. With the development of new financial products such as derivatives, it was difficult to categorise such products to determine how they were regulated. The emphasis was on legal form rather than substance and investors often had difficulty in comparing the various products.

The Wallis Report recommended that a single licensing regime be established for sales, advice and dealings in relation to financial products, consistent and comparable financial product disclosure and a single authorisation system for financial market operation.

overview of the legislation

[19.15] Chapter 7 of the *Corporations Act,* containing most of the *FSR Act* amendments, regulates financial products, financial services and financial markets. The regulatory framework has wide application, regulating such matters as:

Chapter 7 of the *Corporations Act,* regulates financial products, financial services and financial markets.

> **securities;**
> **derivatives;**
> **general and life insurance;**
> **superannuation;**
> **deposit accounts; and**
> **means of payment facilities such as smart cards.**

Much of this regulation falls outside the scope of this book even though it is governed by the *Corporations Act.* This includes insurance contracts, life policies, superannuation interests and deposit-taking facilities. This chapter is primarily concerned with market dealings in shares and other securities on the ASX and the regulation of stockbrokers and related licensed investment advisers.

According to s 760A, the main objects of Ch 7 are to promote:

> **confident and informed decision making by consumers of financial products and services while facilitating efficiency, flexibility, and innovation in the provision of those products and services;**
> **fairness, honesty, and professionalism by those who provide financial services;**
> **fair, orderly and transparent markets for financial products; and**
> **the reduction of systemic risk and the provision of fair and effective services by clearing and settlement facilities.**

Financial service providers are regulated under a single licensing regime. There are various requirements which must be met in order to obtain a financial service provider's licence. These requirements are aimed at ensuring clients are protected as far as possible with additional obligations applicable where services are offered to retail clients.

Financial service providers are regulated under a single licensing regime.

Further protection for clients is afforded by various conduct and disclosure obligations such as provision of a Financial Services Guide, operation of a "know your client" requirement, maintenance of separation of funds held on a client's behalf and various reporting and accounting requirements.

Further protection for clients is afforded by various conduct and disclosure obligations.

Financial product disclosure is required throughout the life of a financial product—from its point of sale by means of a Product Disclosure Statement to ongoing disclosure and periodic reporting requirements.

A general prohibition applies to misleading and deceptive conduct in relation to dealings in financial products and provision of financial services. The market misconduct and insider trading provisions have been largely retained in their previous form, however, contravention of these provisions attracts the civil penalty provisions.

key concepts

[19.20] The three key elements of the regulatory system are:

> **financial product disclosure;**
> **licensing and conduct of financial services providers; and**
> **licensing of financial markets and clearing and settlement facilities.**

Two important concepts around which Ch 7 of the *Corporations Act* is based are the terms "financial products" and "financial services".

Thus the two important concepts around which Ch 7 of the *Corporations Act* is based are the terms "financial products" and "financial services".

financial products

The term "financial product" has a general definition as well as specific inclusions and exclusions.

[19.25] The term "financial product" has a general definition as well as specific inclusions and exclusions. Under the general definition contained in s 763A(1), a financial product is a facility through which, or through the acquisition of which, a person:

> **makes a financial investment;**
> **manages financial risk; or**
> **makes a non-cash payment.**

An investor makes a financial investment where money (a contribution) is given to a person to generate a financial return or other benefit for the investor and the investor does not have day to day control over the use of the contribution to generate the return or benefit: s 763B. "Making a financial investment" includes investing in shares, debentures and interests in managed investment schemes.

Managing financial risk is defined in s 763C and includes taking out insurance and hedging a liability by acquiring a futures contract or entering into a currency swap. "Non-cash payments" include cheque facilities and electronic payment systems: s 763D.

In determining whether a facility is a financial product, the intention or purpose of a particular person is not relevant. It is a financial product if it is of a kind through which people commonly make financial investments, manage risk or make non-cash payments: s 763A(2).

In addition to the general definition contained in s 763A(1), there are specific inclusions and exclusions. Under s 764A, inclusions include securities such as shares and debentures, an interest in a registered managed investment scheme, a derivative and various contracts of insurance. Various exclusions are listed in s 765A. In order to ensure that evolving financial products may be regulated without legislative amendment, the *Corporations Regulations* can specifically include or exclude products from being financial products: ss 764A(1)(m) and 765A(1)(y). ASIC may also exclude a facility: s 765A(2).

The most important financial products with which this book is concerned are securities and particularly shares. In Chapter 8 above, it was noted that a share is a chose in action. This means that a share is intangible property constituted by a bundle of rights and obligations which are legally enforceable. Other examples of choses in action that are types of financial products are debentures, government bonds and interests in a managed investment scheme. Collectively, all these come within the definition of "securities" under s 92(1).

financial services

[19.30] Chapter 7 of the *Corporations Act* focuses on the regulation of the provision of financial services and those who provide such services. Under s 766A, a person provides a financial service if they:

> **provide financial product advice (s 766B);**
> **deal in a financial product (s 766C);**
> **make a market for a financial product (s 766D);**
> **operate a registered managed investment scheme (managed investments are discussed in Chapter 20 below);**
> **provide a custodial or depository service (s 766E); or**
> **engage in conduct of a kind prescribed by regulations.**

A person who provides financial services must obtain a licence or other authorisation. This is discussed below, para [19.80]. There are various obligations which must be met in providing financial services, conducting a financial services business and making disclosure regarding financial products.

A person who provides financial services must obtain a licence or other authorisation.

Apart from Ch 7 of the *Corporations Act*, other provisions of the *Corporations Act* also regulate various matters concerning securities and other financial products. For example, Ch 6 of the *Corporations Act* regulates trading in shares during a takeover. Takeovers are discussed in Chapter 18 above. Chapter 6D of the *Corporations Act* regulates fundraising and is discussed in Chapter 7 above. In addition, Chs 2L and 5C regulate debentures and managed investment schemes. These are discussed in Chapters 11 and 20 of this book.

regulation of financial markets

[19.35] The *FSR Act* introduced reforms which aim to increase competition in the conduct of financial markets by encouraging new participants to operate competing markets and clearing and settlement facilities. Prior to 2002, a distinction was made in the legislation between securities and futures which were regulated in different parts of the *Corporations Act* so that securities exchanges could only deal with securities, and futures exchanges could only deal with futures. This distinction became increasingly problematic with the development of derivatives and other financial products which bore characteristics of each and could not be readily categorised.

The regime introduced by the *FSR Act* addressed these issues by introducing a single licensing regime for financial markets to replace the previous complex authorisation procedures. A suitably qualified market which meets the prescribed criteria can trade in any financial products including both securities and derivatives.

Several financial markets operate in Australia. The dominant and most important financial market is conducted by the ASX. Other financial markets include the SFE Corporation Ltd (the SFE), formerly called "the Sydney Futures Exchange", Newcastle Stock Exchange and Bendigo Stock Exchange.

role of ASIC

[19.40] ASIC is given wide powers to regulate financial markets and financial service providers. According to s 1(2) of the *ASIC Act*, ASIC must strive to maintain, facilitate and improve the performance of the financial system and the entities within that system, in the interests of commercial certainty, reducing business costs, and the efficiency and development of the economy. ASIC must also promote the confident and informed participation of investors and consumers in the financial system.

ASIC is given wide powers to regulate financial markets and financial service providers.

ASIC and the ASX have complementary roles in relation to the oversight of the market, clearing and settlement facilities offered by ASX, and the conduct of brokers and listed entities. Their respective roles and responsibilities are set out in a Memorandum of Understanding (MOU) which provides for referral to ASIC of cases of significant misconduct by listed entities and contraventions of ASX operating rules and the legislation. The MOU also provides for consultation between ASIC and ASX and the sharing of information so as to enhance the efficiency of market supervision.

ASIC has the following functions in relation to financial markets and financial service providers:

- **investigate and act against misconduct by listed companies, brokers and traders;**
- **monitor ASX Ltd as a listed company and monitor trading in its shares;**
- **advise the Treasurer about rule changes and whether to approve new markets;**
- **license financial service providers before they start operating;**
- **set standards for education, training and operations of financial service providers;**
- **investigate and act against misconduct by licensees; and**
- **record details of licensees and their representatives on a register.**

The objectives and powers of ASIC are discussed in Chapters 1 and 21 of this book.

role of stock exchanges

A stock exchange is a marketplace for the securities of corporations and governments.

[19.45] A stock exchange is a marketplace for the securities of corporations and governments. It provides the means by which securities, such as shares, debentures and bonds may be bought and sold. This market consists of two parts. The new issue, or primary market, is the market where new securities are issued by companies or government bodies. Once issued, these securities may then be bought and sold in the secondary market. These markets are interrelated.

One of the most important characteristics of a listed security is that its holder is generally able to sell it quite easily at the prevailing price. This is important from a company's point of view because if its shares and debentures are readily saleable it makes them more attractive to investors and it is easier for a company to raise capital. It is in the interests of the business community that securities be freely marketable and investors' confidence be retained.

In a broad sense, the stock exchanges provide a mechanism whereby available funds may be channelled into productive uses. The maintenance of proper, well-informed markets for securities enhances the prospects of available funds being attracted to efficient and profitable companies.

the ASX

The ASX conducts the main stock market in Australia.

[19.50] The ASX conducts the main stock market in Australia. The ASX was established in 1987 and effected a reorganisation of the major Australian stock exchanges into a single national stock exchange. The objectives of the ASX are stated in the Introduction to the Listing Rules as being to provide:

> **a fair and well-informed market for financial securities; and**
> **an internationally competitive market.**

The ASX website contains valuable information about the stock market and ASX listed companies and is linked to the Lipton-Herzberg Corporate Law Websites at **http://www.lipton-herzberg.com.au/corp-law-websites.html**

Trading in ASX listed securities is conducted electronically under the CHESS system. CHESS is discussed in Chapter 9 above.

The ASX demutualised and converted from a company limited by guarantee to a company limited by shares towards the end of 1998 and shares in the ASX were listed on its own exchange. Demutualisation occurred in order to enable the ASX to become more commercially focussed, flexible and responsive.

The ASX operates a number of financial markets apart from its market in securities.

The ASX operates a number of financial markets apart from its market in securities. It also operates markets in options, warrants and interest rate securities. A subsidiary, ASX Futures, operates a licensed derivatives market which competes with the SFE.

The major responsibilities of the ASX include:

> **surveillance of its markets;**
> **supervising market participants (stockbrokers);**
> **admitting entities to its official list; and**
> **monitoring and enforcing compliance by listed entities with its listing rules.**

There have been concerns expressed about the dual roles of the ASX as market supervisor and as a commercial entity listed on its own market. In response to these concerns, a subsidiary, ASX Supervisory Review Pty Ltd (ASXSR), was established with the roles of reviewing supervisory policy and procedures, providing assurance that the ASX complies with its supervisory responsibilities and overseeing supervision of listed entities where conflicts may arise because they are competitors of the ASX or commercial partners.

listing and operating rules

[19.55] Stock exchange operating rules cover two broad aspects. There are rules that govern the relationships between market participants (stockbrokers), their clients and the ASX. These rules were formerly known as "business rules". Other rules regulate entities whose securities are listed on the market. These are known as "listing rules".

Stock exchange operating rules cover two broad aspects. There are rules that govern the relationships between market participants (stockbrokers), their clients and the ASX. Other rules regulate entities whose securities are listed on the market. These are known as "listing rules".

Operating rules of a financial market are defined in s 761A to mean any rules, including listing rules, that are made by the market operator and that deal with the activities or conduct of the market or of persons in relation to the market. Section 761A also defines "listing rules" to mean any rules made by the operator of a market that deal with admitting entities to, or removing them from, the market's official list or deal with the activities or conduct of listed entities. The operating rules (other than listing rules) have effect as a contract under seal between the market licensee and each participant in the market and as between a participant and each other participant: s 793B.

An important way in which the ASX carries out its role of supervising the market is by requiring compliance with its listing rules. These rules seek to further the interests of listed entities by setting suitable standards of conduct, maintain investor protection and protect the reputation of the market. The listing rules are binding as a contract under which an entity is admitted to the Official List. Further, the listing rules are enforceable under the *Corporations Act*. This is discussed below.

The ASX carries out its role of supervising the market by requiring compliance with its listing rules.

The Introduction to the ASX Listing Rules states that they are rules that are "additional and complementary to companies' common law and statutory obligations". The rules impose strict requirements on companies, which, if not complied with, render them liable to removal from the official list.

The listing rules play an important role in the regulation of listed companies in Australia and have received judicial and legislative recognition.

Section 792D(1) requires a market licensee such as the ASX to provide such assistance to ASIC as ASIC reasonably requires for the performance of its functions. In addition, if a market licensee believes a person has committed, is committing or is about to commit a significant contravention of the market's operating rules or the *Corporations Act*, the market licensee must as soon as practicable notify ASIC in writing: s 792B(2)(c).

The ASX Listing Rules set out a number of prerequisites for admission to the official list. For example, listed companies must have at least 500 shareholders holding securities valued at least $2,000. Further, at least 25 per cent of the shareholders must not be related parties of the company. To gain admission, an entity must satisfy either the profit test in ASX Listing Rule 1.2 or the assets test in Listing Rule 1.3. To meet the profit test, an entity's aggregated profit from continuing operations for the last three full financial years must have been at least $1 million and consolidated profit from continuing operations for the 12 months prior to listing must have exceeded $400,000. To meet the assets test, an entity must have net tangible assets of at least $2 million after deducting the costs of fundraising, or a market capitalisation of at least $10 million. Further, under the assets test, less than half of the entity's total tangible assets must be cash or in a form readily convertible to cash.

The listing rules provide prerequisites for admission and continuation of listing. The continuing listing rules supplement the disclosure requirements of the *Corporations Act*. A company whose securities are listed on the ASX is regarded as a "listed disclosing entity": s 111AL.

Listed disclosing entities are required by Ch 6CA of the *Corporations Act* (ss 674–678) to comply with the ASX's continuous disclosure requirements. Listing Rule 3.1 requires a listed disclosing entity to immediately disclose to the ASX on a continuous basis, information that may have a material effect on the price or value of its securities. Under s 674(2), a listed disclosing entity commits an offence if it fails to notify the ASX of information that is not generally available and that a reasonable person would expect, if it were generally available, to have a material effect on the price or value of the entity's securities. This provision is also a civil penalty provision and where a declaration of contravention is made under s 1317E(1), orders may be made for payment of a pecuniary penalty, compensation or disqualification. Continuous disclosure is further discussed in Chapter 15 above and the civil penalty provisions are discussed in Chapter 13.6 above. The annual report of listed companies must contain prescribed information: Listing Rule 4.3. Voting rights of shareholders are regulated to ensure appropriate and equitable treatment: Listing Rule 6.1. Where a takeover offer has been made, target companies are prevented from engaging in certain defensive tactics. For example, share issues within three months of a takeover offer being made are restricted: Listing Rule 7.9.

The ASX website contains an ASX publication *How the Sharemarket Works*. It also sets out the Listing Rules and Guidance Notes. The ASX website is linked to the Lipton-Herzberg Corporate Law Websites at **http://www.lipton-herzberg.com.au/corp-law-websites.html**

applications for listing

[19.60] In line with the policy of allowing financial markets to be substantially self-regulating, they are given the discretion of accepting or rejecting applications for listing. This also applies to decisions whether or not to remove a company from listing. These discretions are part of the general duty of financial markets to maintain fair markets. It has been suggested, however, that where all statutory and listing requirements have been complied with in the making of an application for listing, the application must be properly considered and not arbitrarily refused.

The ASX website contains an ASX publication, *A Guide to Listing*. This is linked to the Lipton-Herzberg Corporate Law Websites at **http://www.lipton-herzberg.com.au/corp-law-websites.html**

enforcement of operating rules

The ASX's operating rules are given statutory force by s 793C.

[19.65] The ASX's operating rules are given statutory force by s 793C. This section enables an application to be made by ASIC, a market licensee or an aggrieved person, to the court for an order that the operating rules of the market be complied with or enforced. A holder of financial products of the entity that are tradable on the market is taken to be a person aggrieved by a failure to comply with the operating rules: s 793C(5).

Section 1101B enables the court to make a wide range of orders to ensure compliance with legislation, operating rules and other requirements relating to dealing in financial products, providing financial services or operating a licensed market. An application may be brought by ASIC, a market licensee or a person aggrieved by a contravention of the operating rules. In exercising its discretion, the court should consider the purpose of the legislation, which is to ensure that share acquisitions occur in an efficient, competitive and informed market. This will usually require the court to return all parties to the positions they were in before the share acquisitions occurred: *Gjergja v Cooper* (1986) 4 ACLC 359.

The court may also make orders that prevent unfair prejudice to vendors. In *NCSC v Monarch Petroleum NL* (1984) 2 ACLC 256, the NCSC successfully obtained orders under a predecessor of s 1101B to restrain a company from registering any transfers of shares and a declaration that certain transactions were void. This case arose when unknown persons circulated to the Perth Stock Exchange a forged letter purporting to be from the company, the effect of which was to increase the market price for its shares. This constituted a contravention of predecessors of ss 1041E and 1041F.

National Guarantee Fund

[19.70] A licensed market must have in place a scheme for compensation arrangements where the market participants provide financial services for retail clients and in doing so, accept money or other property from their clients. In the case of stock exchanges, compensation arrangements are made through the National Guarantee Fund (NGF). Other financial markets must have compensation arrangements approved in accordance with Div 3 of Pt 7.5.

The NGF is a compensation fund available to meet various types of claims made by clients of a stockbroker.

The NGF provides a compensation regime which is administered by the Securities Exchange Guarantee Corporation (SEGC) as the trustee of the NGF. SEGC is a subsidiary of the ASX although it operates autonomously. The NGF is a compensation fund available to meet various types of claims made by clients of a stockbroker which are set out in Div 4 of Pt 7.5 of the *Corporations Regulations*.

The types of claims which can be made include:

> completion of transactions entered into by a stockbroker which are required to be reported by a stockbroker to ASX (Subdiv 4.3);
> compensation for loss arising from unauthorised transfers of marketable securities by a stockbroker (Subdiv 4.7); and
> compensation for loss arising from the insolvency of a stockbroker to whom money or property was entrusted: Subdiv 4.9.

futures markets and the SFE

[19.75] Prior to the *FSR Act* amendments, trading in futures contracts was regulated in a self-contained part of the *Corporations Act*. This is no longer the case. Futures trading and futures markets are now regulated in the same way as share trading and stock markets. The main futures market in Australia is conducted by the SFE. The ASX also operates a futures market.

The main futures market in Australia is conducted by the SFE.

A futures contract is a type of derivative which is defined in s 761D. In *Sydney Futures Exchange Ltd v Australian Stock Exchange Ltd* (1995) 13 ACLC 369, Lockhart J described the nature of the futures market:

A futures contract is a type of derivative.

> **< A futures market is a market in which people buy and sell things for future delivery. A futures contract generally involves an agreement to buy and sell a specified quantity of something at a specified future delivery date. The price is the variable, determined competitively by "open outcry" on the trading floor or through a computer-based market place. Futures markets perform the economic function of managing the price risk associated with holding the underlying commodity or having a future requirement to hold it. The futures market is a risk transfer mechanism whereby those exposed to risks shift them to someone else; the other party may be someone with an opposite physical market risk or a speculator. By contrast, securities markets facilitate the purchase and sale of equities or debt instruments. A small proportion of futures contracts results in the commodity or financial instrument underlying the contract being in fact sold or bought by the parties to the contract in satisfaction of their obligations under that contract. However, the economic function of this delivery mechanism is to ensure that the contract price converges with that of the physical or cash market at maturity. This is essential to the efficiency of the futures market in its role of risk transfer and risk management mechanism. The delivery aspect of future contracts is not designed to make them alternative primary investment or securities vehicles. Futures markets along with options and other similar markets are often described as "derivative markets" in the sense that they are derived from the underlying instrument (for example, the cash securities market). >**

There are basically two types of users of the futures market: "hedgers" and "speculators". Hedgers typically deal in the physical commodity and use futures to manage price risks. Hedgers transfer risk to speculators. The futures market performs a price-setting function, allowing a hedger to know in advance the price at which they will buy or sell and to plan for known costs and returns. The futures market achieves its purpose of setting a price in advance by providing profits or losses that balance losses and gains in the physical market respectively. The SFE operates a market in a range of futures and options contracts:

> interest rate derivative products for trading and hedging short-, medium- and long-term fixed interest. These include 3- and 10-year bond futures and options as well as 90-day Australian and New Zealand bank bill futures and options;
> equities derivatives such as stock exchange index futures and options as well as share futures and options in selected top ASX listed companies;

> currency derivatives such as Australian/US dollar futures contracts; and
> commodities derivatives such as wool futures and electricity futures.

financial services licensees

Any person who carries on a financial services business in Australia must hold an Australian financial services licence.

[19.80] Any person who carries on a financial services business in Australia must hold an Australian financial services licence: s 911A(1). It is an offence for a person to hold out that they possess a licence when this is not the case: s 911C.

A financial services licensee must meet the general obligations set out in s 912A which include ensuring financial services are provided efficiently, honestly and fairly and in compliance with financial services laws. There are further obligations to ensure representatives of a financial services licensee are adequately trained and adequate risk management systems are in place. There are additional obligations set out in ss 912B–912F, including having arrangements in place to compensate retail clients for certain losses and notifying ASIC of breaches of these obligations.

A person may apply for a licence by lodging an application with ASIC. The application must include the information required by reg 7.6.03 of the *Corporations Regulations*. ASIC must grant the application if the requirements of s 913B are met. In particular, ASIC must be satisfied that there is no reason to believe that the applicant or the responsible officers of the applicant are not of good fame and character.

A financial services licensee may authorise a person to be a representative and provide financial services on its behalf by giving the person a written notice. Representatives may be authorised to provide all or some of the services covered in the principal's licence: s 916A. As a general rule, a financial services licensee is prohibited from acting as the authorised representative of another financial services licensee: 916D.

Financial services licensees are responsible for the conduct of their employees, directors and authorised representatives where financial services are provided on which a client could reasonably be expected to rely and on which the client relied in good faith: s 917A. Licensees are liable for any loss or damage suffered by a client as a result of the conduct of representatives: s 917E.

ASIC may ban a person from providing financial services on several grounds including a failure by the person to comply with the obligations set out in s 912A or where the person was convicted of fraud: s 920A(1). The banning order may be permanent or for a specified period and may be subject to conditions: s 920B. A banning order must be accompanied by a statement of reasons for the order: s 920F. A banning order can only be made after the person has been given an opportunity to appear at a private hearing and make submissions.

ASIC may also apply to the court for orders disqualifying a person against whom ASIC has made a permanent banning order. The disqualification order of the court may be subject to conditions or as the court considers appropriate: s 921A.

ASIC maintains a register of financial services licensees and authorised representatives which is available for public inspection without charge: ss 922A and 922B.

There are restrictions on the use of certain words and expressions by financial service providers which could create a misleading impression. It is an offence for a person to use the words "independent", "impartial" or "unbiased" or similar words unless the financial service provider does not receive commissions, volume bonuses or gifts or benefits from product issuers and there are no conflicts of interest which may reasonably be expected to influence the person: s 923A. It is also an offence for a person to describe themselves as a type of broker including a stockbroker unless authorised by ASIC by the conditions on their licence: s 923B.

Various protections are afforded to clients who enter into agreements with unlicensed financial service providers where the service provider should be licensed. The client may rescind the agreement (ss 925A–925D), the agreement is unenforceable against the client (s 925E) and the unlicensed person cannot recover commission from the client (s 925F). However, the client can recover any commission paid to the unlicensed person: s 925H. The client retains any other rights and remedies in addition to these statutory rights: s 925I.

financial services disclosure

[19.85] One of the main aims of Ch 7 of the *Corporations Act* is to ensure that consumers of financial products and services receive adequate information about those products and services. Important obligations are imposed on financial services licensees and authorised representatives to provide prescribed disclosure documents to retail clients. The main disclosure documents are the "Financial Services Guide" and "Statement of Advice". There are also further disclosure obligations which arise in particular circumstances.

Financial Services Guide (FSG)

when is an FSG required?

[19.90] A financial services licensee or authorised representative who provides a financial service to a retail client must give the client a Financial Services Guide (FSG): ss 941A and 941B. The requirement to provide an FSG aims to ensure that retail clients receive key information about the type of financial services they are being offered. An FSG is not required in the situations set out in s 941C.

A financial services licensee or authorised representative who provides a financial service to a retail client must give the client an FSG.

retail clients

[19.95] A distinction is made in the legislation between "retail" and "wholesale" clients. The purpose behind this distinction is that where financial services are provided to retail clients, licensees and representatives are required to provide greater disclosure and there are further protections and conduct requirements. A client is a wholesale client (and therefore not a retail client) where that person meets a wealth test or is a professional investor within the tests set out in s 761G(7).

prescribed contents of an FSG

[19.100] Sections 942B and 942C set out the prescribed contents of an FSG. These content requirements ensure that retail clients receive key information required to make informed decisions about whether to acquire the financial service that is offered, while at the same time providing flexibility for the industry in determining the level of information that should be included.

Sections 942B and 942C set out the prescribed contents of an FSG.

The level of information about a matter that is required to be specified in an FSG is such as a person would reasonably require for the purpose of making a decision whether to acquire financial services from the providing entity as a retail client: ss 942B(3) and 942C(3).

personal advice to retail clients

[19.105] Section 945A sets out a "know your client rule". Where personal advice is provided by a financial services licensee or their authorised representative to a retail client, they must have a reasonable basis for that advice and are required to ascertain the client's objectives and their financial situation and needs, investigate and consider the options available to the client and base the advice on that consideration and investigation: s 945A.

Section 945A sets out a "know your client rule".

"Personal advice" is defined in s 766B(3) as financial product advice that is given to a person in circumstances where the provider of advice has considered one or more of the person's objectives, financial situation and needs or that a reasonable person would expect the provider to have considered one or more of these matters.

Statement of Advice

Where a retail client is given personal advice, the provider must give the client a "Statement of Advice".

[19.110] Where a retail client is given personal advice, the provider must give the client a "Statement of Advice". The Statement of Advice may be the means by which advice is given, or a separate record of the advice: s 946A. The level of detail of information required in the Statement of Advice is that which a person would reasonably require for the purpose of making a decision whether to act on the advice provided: ss 947B(3) and 947C(3). There are specific content requirements contained in ss 947B(2) and 947C(2) including a statement setting out the advice, information about the basis on which the advice was given and any remuneration received or other factors which might reasonably be expected to be capable of influencing the advice provider in providing advice.

financial product disclosure

[19.115] Part 7.9 of the *Corporations Act* deals with disclosure throughout the life of a financial product from point of sale disclosure through to ongoing disclosure and periodic reporting requirements.

In general, the financial product disclosure requirements of Pt 7.9 apply to all financial products other than shares and debentures, and stocks or bonds issued or proposed to be issued by a government. In particular, the Pt 7.9 requirements apply to issues of interests in registered managed investment schemes. These are discussed in Chapter 20 below.

One of the main requirements of Pt 7.9 is the obligation to give retail clients a PDS at the point of sale of a financial product.

One of the main requirements of Pt 7.9 is the obligation to give retail clients a Product Disclosure Statement (PDS) at the point of sale of a financial product. The broad objective of this requirement is to provide consumers with sufficient information to make informed decisions in relation to the acquisition of financial products, including the ability to compare a range of products.

prohibited market misconduct

[19.120] There are various improper market practices which are prohibited because they create false markets for financial products such as securities and enable some persons to derive unfair advantages. The prohibited conduct falls into several categories and is independently regulated.

The prohibited market misconduct practices are:

> **short selling;**
> **market manipulation;**
> **false trading and market rigging;**
> **dissemination of information about illegal transactions;**
> **false or misleading statements; and**
> **misleading or deceptive conduct.**

short selling

Short selling is the practice of selling securities or other financial products when they are not owned by the seller at the time of the sale.

[19.125] Short selling in the context of financial markets is the practice of selling securities or other financial products when they are not owned by the seller at the time of the sale. Short sellers sell securities that they do not possess, at current prices, in the expectation that their price will fall. They hope to buy the securities, or cover their positions, before they are obliged to honour the contract of sale. Short selling therefore enables the seller to make a profit because of the time lag between entering the actual contract and its eventual settlement. It is usually practised in markets where prices fluctuate significantly or there is an expectation that prices will fall.

Short selling is not absolutely prohibited and may take place only in permitted circumstances.

Under s 1020B(2), a person can only sell securities and other products specified in s 1020B(1) if at the time of sale, the person has a presently exercisable and unconditional right to vest the products in the buyer or the person has reasonable grounds for believing they have such a right.

Under s 1020B(4)(e), securities that have been declared by the operator of a licensed market as being approved for short selling are outside the short selling prohibition, subject to certain safeguards. Under ASX Business Rules, "approved securities" in which short selling may be permitted require an issued capital of 50 million shares (excluding shares held by related companies) with a market capitalisation of $100 million. No more than 10 per cent of the approved security may be short sold at any one time. The business rules also provide for monitoring short sales by the stock exchange which has the right to prohibit such transactions where this is necessary to maintain an orderly market.

Securities that have been declared by the operator of a licensed market as being approved for short selling are outside the short selling prohibition.

There is an obligation on the seller to notify the financial services licensee acting as the broker, of short sales where these would be prohibited but for s 1020B(4)(b), (d) or (e): s 1020B(5). ASIC has a wide power under s 1020C to prohibit trading in securities and other specified products where it forms the opinion that it is necessary in order to protect investors who might suffer loss or is in the public interest. This is subject to revocation by the Minister.

Contravention of s 1020B is an offence.

market manipulation

A person is prohibited from taking part in or carrying out a transaction or transactions that have or are likely to have the effect of creating an artificial price for trading in financial products on a financial market.

[19.130] A person is prohibited from taking part in or carrying out a transaction or transactions that have or are likely to have the effect of creating an artificial price for trading in financial products on a financial market: s 1041A.

The Rae Committee found that groups of investors sometimes formed pools to which each contributed funds. Certain shares were then sold successively from one member of a pool to another in order to increase turnover and price and therefore give a misleading impression of the desirability of the shares. This would induce the public to buy the securities. The members of the pool then sold their shares at the increased price. This practice is now covered by s 1041A. This provision is designated as a financial services civil penalty provision: s 1317E(1). The consequences of a contravention of these provisions is discussed below, para [19.245].

false trading and market rigging

[19.135] A person is prohibited from doing or omitting to do something which has or is likely to have the effect of creating a false or misleading appearance of:

> **active trading; or**
> **the price for trading in financial products on a financial market: s 1041B(1).**

A person is taken to have created a false or misleading appearance of active trading if the person enters into transactions of acquisition or disposal that do not involve a change of beneficial ownership of the financial products. It may also arise where a person makes an offer to acquire or dispose of financial products at a specified price knowing that a matching transaction at substantially the same price will be made: s 1041B(2).

A person is also prohibited from entering into fictitious or artificial transactions if that results in an artificial price for trading in a financial product or causes the price to fluctuate: s 1041C.

A person is also prohibited from entering into fictitious or artificial transactions if that results in an artificial price for trading in a financial product or causes the price to fluctuate.

These provisions prohibit the practice of "churning". This involves the placing of buying and selling orders for shares with the object of artificially increasing the market turnover and price of those securities.

case note

In *ASC v Nomura International PLC* (1999) 17 ACLC 55, Nomura was a stock index arbitrageur. It sold large parcels of shares, which sparked a fall in share prices and the futures index. This allowed Nomura to repurchase, at a lower price, the futures contracts it had previously sold. It was held that the intention of the transactions was to self-trade at depressed prices that did not reflect the market but were unilaterally determined by Nomura and speculative profits were thereby gained. The court held that Nomura contravened a predecessor of s 1041B(1). It also contravened the misleading and deceptive conduct provisions now contained in s 1041H.

Sections 1041B(1) and 1041C(1) are designated as financial services civil penalty provisions: s 1317E(1). The consequences of a contravention of these provisions are discussed below, [19.245].

dissemination of information about illegal transactions

[19.140] A person is prohibited from disseminating any information that the trading price of a financial product will be affected by a transaction or conduct which constitutes a contravention of the market misconduct provisions where the person or an associate have entered into the transaction or engaged in the conduct or have received a benefit from disseminating the information: s 1041D. This provision is designated as a financial services civil penalty provision: s 1317E(1). The consequences of a contravention of these provisions is discussed below, para [19.245].

false or misleading statements

Section 1041E prohibits the making of false or misleading statements that are likely to induce persons to enter the market or to affect the price of financial products.

[19.145] Section 1041E prohibits the making of false or misleading statements that are likely to induce persons to enter the market or to affect the price of financial products. This section operates where the statement is knowingly made or made not caring if it is true or false. Section 1041F prohibits the making of false or reckless statements to induce another person to deal in financial products.

case note

In *NCSC v Monarch Petroleum NL* (1984) 2 ACLC 256, a copy of a letter purportedly sent by the Magnet group of companies to its shareholders was delivered to the Perth Stock Exchange. Parts of the letter were announced on the floors of all Australian stock exchanges. The announcements indicated that a possible takeover was imminent and the Magnet group would thereby acquire an interest in a valuable oil discovery. Share turnover rose on several stock exchanges after the announcement was made. The letter was subsequently found to be a forgery and share trading in the group was suspended. There was no suggestion that the Magnet group was involved or that the Perth Stock Exchange acted improperly. The Commission successfully applied under the predecessor of s 1114 for orders restraining the registration of transfers in connection with transactions made after the announcement. It also obtained an order declaring such contracts to be void. The granting of these orders required the Commission to establish that a person contravened the *Corporations Act* and in this case there had been a breach of the predecessors of ss 1041E and 1041F. This was despite the fact that the identity of the persons who breached the legislation was unknown.

case note

In *ASC v McLeod* (2000) 18 ACLC 424, a consulting geologist prepared a report for a mining company on the results of its exploration. The report claimed that based on samples, a particular annual profit would be made. In fact the exploration results did not bear this out and the sample was too small to draw such conclusions. The geologist contravened s 1041E as the likely effect of the statement would have been to induce a reader to purchase shares in the belief that the company had a basis for predicting the profitability of the venture.

dishonest conduct

[19.150] A person carrying on a financial services business must not engage in dishonest conduct in relation to a financial product or financial service: s 1041G. "Dishonest" is determined according to the standards of ordinary people.

misleading or deceptive conduct

[19.155] There is a general prohibition on a person engaging in conduct in relation to a financial product or a financial service that is misleading or deceptive or likely to mislead or deceive: s 1041H(1). Engaging in conduct in relation to a financial product is widely defined to include dealing, issuing, publishing a notice or making or evaluating an offer under a takeover bid: s 1041H(2). Actions for misleading or deceptive conduct in relation to financial services may be brought under s 12DA of the *ASIC Act* or s 1041H.

There is a general prohibition on a person engaging in conduct in relation to a financial product or a financial service that is misleading or deceptive or likely to mislead or deceive.

case note

In *GPG (Australia) Trading Pty Ltd v GIO Australia Holdings Ltd* [2001] FCA 1761, a shareholder of GPG brought actions against GIO and AMP Ltd, a substantial shareholder of GIO alleging that GIO and AMP engaged in misleading or deceptive conduct under the predecessor of s 1041H when the companies made a number of announcements to the market regarding the financial position of GIO. GPG claimed that GIO failed to disclose its knowledge of the likelihood of further losses and the need to increase provisions of which it had become aware through preliminary actuary reports. It was held that an announcement made by GIO was misleading and deceptive because reasonable readers such as investors would have assumed that there were no adverse changes since an earlier announcement which stated reserves were adequate to cover any uncertainties. GIO should have made reference to the actuary reports and the omission of this information was a cause, though not necessarily the sole or dominant cause, of GPG buying GIO shares and suffering losses when the share price fell. AMP was not liable as it had no duty to inform the market as to what it knew about GIO's financial position.

case note

In *National Exchange Pty Ltd v ASIC* [2004] FCAFC 90, the Full Court of the Federal Court held that an offer to purchase shares could be misleading even if the stated information was literally true. This would be the case when a primary statement is made which is later corrected or qualified but in an insufficiently prominent or conspicuous way. In that case, an offer to purchase shares in a particular company stated that the offer price was $2.00 and the market price was $1.90. In fact, the offer price was to be paid in 15 annual instalments and this was not made obvious to readers. The comparison of the offer price to the market price without reference to the terms of payment, made the comparison misleading and deceptive. This was deliberately done to mislead offerees and maximise uninformed acceptances.

Misleading and deceptive conduct in the context of takeover and fundraising documents and disclosure documents and statements under Pts 7.7 and 7.9 are excluded from the general prohibition under s 1041H as they are governed by their own separate liability regimes which contain applicable defences. These specialist disclosure regimes also operate to the exclusion of the State and Territory *Fair Trading Acts* which apply concurrently with the *Corporations Act* in other respects.

liability for contravention

[19.160] A person who contravenes ss 1041E (false or misleading statements), 1041F (inducing a person to deal), 1041G (dishonest conduct) or 1041H (misleading or deceptive conduct), commits an offence and a person who suffered loss or damage arising from the contravention may recover the amount of loss or damage by action against any person who was involved in the contravention whether or not there has been a conviction in respect of the contravention: s 1041I(1).

These provisions are not civil penalty provisions and hence civil pecuniary penalties cannot be imposed where they have been contravened. Where proceedings are brought under s 1041I, the court may relieve a publisher wholly or partly from liability if it appears to the court that the publisher received an advertisement in the ordinary course of their business and did not know and had no reason to believe that publication would amount to an offence: s 1044A(2).

insider trading

Insider trading is prohibited.

[19.165] Insider trading is prohibited under Div 3 of Pt 7.10 of the *Corporations Act*. Insider trading occurs where a person trades in shares or other financial products while in possession of price-sensitive information not generally available.

The insider trading provisions cover a wider range of financial products than shares. They also include derivatives, superannuation products and other financial products able to be traded on a financial market. These are referred to in the legislation as "division 3 financial products". The person with whom the "insider" dealt is also entitled to recover compensation and contraventions of the insider trading prohibitions attract the civil penalty provisions.

The continuous disclosure provisions of Ch 6CA (ss 674–678) of the *Corporations Act* complement the insider trading provisions. The continuous disclosure provisions require disclosing entities, such as listed companies, to disclose price-sensitive information that is not generally available: ss 674 and 675. Timely disclosure of such information reduces the opportunities for insider trading. The continuous disclosure requirements are discussed in Chapter 15 above.

why prohibit insider trading?

[19.170] In November 1989, The House of Representatives Committee on Legal and Constitutional Affairs ("the Griffiths Committee") published in its report, *Fair Shares for All: Insider Trading in Australia*, setting out various theories that have been put forward as a basis for prohibiting insider trading:

- fairness: market participants should have equal access to the relevant information from the company which issues the securities;
- fiduciary duty: a person who holds a position of trust should not make a personal profit from that position without the informed consent of the beneficiaries;
- economic efficiency: insider trading is damaging to the integrity of the financial market; and
- corporate injury: insider trading injures the company which issued the securities, the shareholders in the company and investors who deal with insiders.

The Griffiths Report noted that other theories defend the practice of insider trading but rejected these arguments.

> **Some commentators have suggested that regulation of insider trading is not necessary, as insider trading enhances the efficiency of the securities market through the faster dissemination of information. The Government's policy view is, however, that it is necessary to control insider trading to protect investors and make it attractive for them to provide funds to the issuers of securities, for the greater and more efficient development of Australia's resources. The effects of insider trading on investor confidence are regarded as outweighing any efficiencies arising from the faster dissemination of information which some commentators allege would accrue if insider trading were decriminalised.**

The Government's policy view is that it is necessary to control insider trading to protect investors and make it attractive for them to provide funds to the issuers of securities, for the greater and more efficient development of Australia's resources.

the insider trading prohibitions

[19.175] Section 1043A(1) contains the primary prohibitions against insider trading. Under s 1043A(1)(c), an insider must not apply for, acquire or dispose of, or enter into an agreement to apply for, acquire or dispose of, relevant "Division 3 financial products". Section 1042A defines "Division 3 financial products" to include securities, derivatives, managed investment products, superannuation products and any other financial products which are able to be traded on a financial market.

Section 1043A(1) contains the primary prohibitions against insider trading.

Section 1043A(1)(d) also specifies that an insider must not procure another person to apply for, acquire, or dispose of, or to enter into an agreement to apply for, acquire or dispose of, any securities or other Division 3 financial products. An insider is taken to "procure" the act or omission of another person if the insider incites, induces or encourages an act or omission by another person: s 1042F. These prohibitions apply whether the insider trades as principal or agent.

Section 1043A(2) prohibits an insider communicating or tipping inside information to another person. This prohibition applies only to financial products which are able to be traded on a financial market operated in Australia.

An insider must not, directly or indirectly, communicate the information, or cause the information to be communicated, to another person if the insider knows, or ought reasonably to know, that the other person would or would be likely to:

- **apply for, acquire or dispose of, or enter into an agreement to apply for, acquire or dispose of, any such tradable financial products; or**
- **procure a third person to apply for, acquire or dispose of, or enter into an agreement to apply for, acquire or dispose of, any such tradable financial securities.**

To establish a breach of s 1043A(2), it is not necessary to prove that there was an association or arrangement between the insider and the tippee with a view to dealing in the particular financial product. It is only necessary to show a communication of inside information to the tippee.

who is an insider?

[19.180] A person is an "insider" for purposes of the s 1043A prohibitions if:

> **the person possesses "inside information" (defined in s 1042A); and**
> **the insider knows or ought reasonably to know that the matters specified in the s 1042A definition of inside information are satisfied in relation to the information.**

The concept of inside information is further discussed below, para [19.185].

Despite the use of the word "insider", the s 1043A prohibitions do not focus on whether the person has a connection with a company.

It is important to note that despite the use of the word "insider", the s 1043A prohibitions do not focus on whether the person has a connection with a company. The insider trading prohibitions apply to anyone, whether they have a business or employment connection with a company or not. The prohibitions focus on the possession of inside information. For example, a person who overhears a conversation in a lift or on the street is regarded as an insider if that person knows, or ought to know, that the overheard conversation is inside information. As a result of the definition of "insider", the expression "insider trading" is not strictly correct because the legislation extends beyond persons who have a connection with the company concerned. It is more accurate to describe the insider trading provisions as dealing with the "misuse of non-public information".

case note

The operation of the insider trading prohibition in s 1043A(1) is illustrated in *R v Rivkin* [2003] NSWSC 447. In that case McGowan, was the CEO and major shareholder of Impulse Airlines. During 2000 and 2001 Impulse Airlines was involved in a price war with Qantas which had an adverse impact on both companies. Impulse Airlines suffered disastrous losses as a result. In addition, both Qantas' share price and profitability were significantly affected. At the end of April 2001, McGowan concluded confidential negotiations to sell his company's business to Qantas conditional on obtaining ACCC approval. A few days before the public announcement of the sale to Qantas, McGowan expressed interest in buying Rivkin's house. McGowan told Rivkin about the confidential Impulse Airlines and Qantas transaction because he wanted to make the house purchase conditional on the ACCC's approval. McGowan also advised Rivkin that he should not trade in Qantas shares. Within hours of Rivkin agreeing to the conditional sale of his house, Rivkin arranged for his family company to acquire 50,000 shares in Qantas for $2.78 per share. Rivkin sold the shares for $2.85 several days after the public announcement of the Impulse Airlines and Qantas transaction.

Rivkin was convicted of breaching the predecessor of s 1043A(1) and sentenced to nine months' periodic detention and fined $30,000. It was held that Rivkin was an insider in relation to Qantas and arranged for his company to acquire Qantas shares. The court was satisfied beyond reasonable doubt that Rivkin was an insider because he possessed information that was not generally available. This information was the confidential sale of Impulse Airlines' business to Qantas as well as McGowan's assertion that the ACCC approval would be forthcoming. The court was also satisfied that had the information been generally available, it might have a material effect on the price of Qantas' shares.

An insider can be an officer or employee of a company. A company may also be an insider. For example, under s 1042G a body corporate is taken to possess and know information which an officer possesses and which came into the officer's possession in the course of performance of their duties as such officer.

what is inside information?

[19.185] "Inside information" is defined in s 1042A as meaning information that:

> **is not generally available; and**
> **if it were generally available, a reasonable person would expect it to have a material effect on the price or value of particular Division 3 financial products.**

information not generally available

[19.190] To establish a contravention of the prohibitions in s 1043A, it is critical for the prosecution to prove that a person possessed information that is not generally available. Section 1042C explains when information is generally available.

To establish a contravention of s 1043A, it is critical for the prosecution to prove that a person possessed information that is not generally available.

Under s 1042C(1)(a), information is generally available if it consists of readily observable matter.

Information is generally available if it consists of readily observable matter.

case note

In *R v Firns* [2001] NSWCCA 191, the defendant's father was a director of a listed public company engaged in gold exploration in Papua New Guinea (PNG). A subsidiary of the company successfully challenged the validity of a government regulation in a PNG court which had restricted exploration rights. As a result of the court's decision, it could be expected that the company's share price would increase. The defendant purchased parcels of shares in the names of his wife and a friend after hearing of the outcome of the case. The ASX was notified of the court's decision three days later. The question arose whether the PNG court judgment was generally available before the ASX was notified. It was held that the judgment was readily observable and therefore generally available because it was available, understandable and accessible to a significant number of the public. Information may be readily observable even if no one observed it.

CAMAC, in its *Insider Trading Report* (November 2003), observed that the effect of *R v Firns* was that the "readily observable matter" test had the potential to cover information that could not, on any reasonable view, be described as being generally available to persons who commonly invest in relevant financial products. As a result, officers who become aware of readily observable matters affecting their company could obtain an unfair advantage by immediately trading in the company's shares even though the market has not been made aware of the information by means of a press release or continuous disclosure notice.

To overcome the undesirable consequences of *R v Firns*, a majority of CAMAC's members recommended that the definition of "readily observable matter" should be replaced. They proposed that information should only be regarded as readily observable if it was accessible to most persons who commonly invest in relevant financial products or consisted of deductions, conclusions or inferences made or drawn from such information.

Under s 1042C(1)(b), information that previously was not generally available becomes generally available if:

> **it has been made known in a manner that would, or would be likely to, bring it to the attention of persons who commonly invest in Division 3 financial products of a kind whose price might be affected by the information; and**
> **since it was so made known, a reasonable period for it to be disseminated among such persons has elapsed.**

Information referred to in s 1042C(1)(b) includes financial information in a company's annual report, corporate information contained in media releases and continuous disclosure announcements to the ASX.

Many listed companies have policies which specify when directors and other officers can trade in their company's shares. These are called "trading windows". Usually, such people are permitted to trade during a short period after the company has released its annual report. In most instances, trading during this period will not contravene the insider trading provisions because after an annual report is made public, price-sensitive information about the company's shares would become generally available. Instead of "trading windows", some listed companies have policies that prohibit their officers or employees trading its shares during specified periods of time immediately prior to the publication of their annual reports. These are called "black outs". The ASX corporate governance listing rule, Listing Rule 4.10, requires the annual report of a listed company to disclose the company's policy on the trading of its securities by directors and employees including the use of trading windows and black outs.

Information is also generally available if it consists of deductions, conclusions or inferences made or drawn from either or both of the types of information referred to in s 1042C(1)(a) and (b)(i).

Information does not become generally available for purposes of s 1042C(1)(b)(i) if it is merely released to a small sector of investors who commonly invest in the particular financial product. The information must be made known to a cross-section of the investors who commonly invest in the financial product. Further, s 1042C(1)(b)(ii) ensures that there is an embargo on trading by insiders who are aware of information prior to its release. They can trade only after a reasonable period for the dissemination of the information has elapsed.

Information is also generally available if it consists of deductions, conclusions or inferences made or drawn from either or both of the types of information referred to in s 1042C(1)(a) and (b)(i). This means that a financial analyst's deductions or conclusions about a company's financial position drawn from the company's published financial statements would not be regarded as inside information.

Information has a "material effect" only if the information would, or is likely to, influence persons who commonly acquire financial products in deciding whether or not to acquire or dispose of those financial products.

material effect on price

[19.195] Inside information must be such that if it were generally available, a reasonable person would expect it to have a material effect on the price or value of particular financial products. Information has a "material effect" only if the information would, or is likely to, influence persons who commonly acquire financial products in deciding whether or not to acquire or dispose of those financial products: s 1042D.

A person in possession of inside information is an insider only if that person knows, or ought reasonably to know, that the information is inside information.

possession of information

[19.200] A person in possession of inside information is an insider only if that person knows, or ought reasonably to know, that the information is inside information. The legislation provides an inclusive definition of the word "information". It includes matters of supposition and other matters that are insufficiently definite to warrant being made known to the public as well as matters relating to the intentions, or likely intentions, of a person: s 1042A.

A body corporate is deemed to possess any information that an officer of the body corporate possesses if the information came into their possession in the course of the performance of duties as such an officer.

A body corporate is deemed to possess any information that an officer of the body corporate possesses if the information came into their possession in the course of the performance of duties as such an officer: s 1042G.

It is curious that s 1042G deems a body corporate to possess information possessed by an officer only if that information came into the officer's possession in the course of the performance of that officer's duties as an officer. For example, if an officer acquires inside information on the golf course, knowing it to be inside information, and uses it to trade in financial products on the body corporate's behalf, the officer may contravene the prohibition against procuring trading in s 1043A(1)(d) and the prohibition against tipping in s 1043A(2). However, because of the operation of s 1042G(1)(a), the body corporate, which derived the financial benefit of the inside information and on whose behalf the officer traded, does not contravene the insider trading prohibitions.

As discussed above, to be categorised as an insider, s 1043A(1)(b) requires that the person knows or ought reasonably to know the information is inside information. If an officer of a body corporate knows any matter or thing because they are an officer of the body corporate, it is presumed that the body corporate knows that matter or thing: s 1042G(1)(b).

If an officer of a body corporate, in that capacity, is reckless as to a circumstance or result, it is presumed that the body corporate is reckless to that circumstance or result: s 1042G(1)(c).

The effect of s 1042G is that if an officer of a body corporate possesses inside information knowing it to be inside information, then both the officer and the body corporate are regarded as insiders and both are subject to the prohibitions in s 1043A. Section 1042H applies to partnerships and is similar in effect to s 1042G.

exceptions to the insider trading prohibitions

[19.205] There are numerous exceptions to the insider trading provisions set out in ss 1043B–1043J. Some of these exceptions alleviate unintended consequences of a strict application of the insider trading provisions such as the Chinese wall exception in s 1043F, and others facilitate acceptable commercial activity such as the underwriters and financial services licensees exceptions in ss 1043C and 1043K.

There are numerous exceptions to the insider trading provisions.

Chinese walls

[19.210] Under ss 1043A(1) and 1042G(1), if an officer of a body corporate possesses inside information, knowing it to be inside information, neither the officer nor their body corporate are permitted to trade in the financial products that are the subject of the inside information. Section 1043F provides an exception for bodies corporate and in certain circumstances permits them to trade in financial products notwithstanding that one or more officers possess inside information about the financial products.

A body corporate, whose officers possess inside information, may trade in financial products if it has a "Chinese wall" in place. A Chinese wall is an administrative arrangement that prevents information possessed by persons in one part of an organisation from being passed on to persons in other parts of the organisation.

A body corporate, whose officers possess inside information, may trade in financial products if it has a "Chinese wall" in place.

Section 1043G provides a similar "Chinese wall" exception for members of a partnership.

underwriters

[19.215] Underwriters and subunderwriters are persons, usually financial institutions, who for an underwriting fee, agree to acquire securities and other financial products issued by a body corporate that are not taken up by others. Further, underwriters and subunderwriters are often active in marketing the financial products. By entering into an underwriting agreement, the body corporate ensures the success of its issue. Usually, an underwriter will insist on obtaining information about the issuing body corporate and the proposed issue before it agrees to enter into an underwriting agreement.

If underwriters were subject to the insider trading provisions it would severely curtail the practice. For this reason, s 1043C(1) provides a blanket exemption from the primary prohibition for underwriters and subunderwriters in respect of applying for or acquiring securities or managed investment products under an underwriting or subunderwriting agreement as well as in respect of disposing of the securities or managed investment products. Further, s 1043C(2)(a) exempts persons from the tipping prohibition in s 1043A(2) where they communicate inside information about the securities or managed investment products solely for the purpose of procuring a person to enter into an underwriting or subunderwriting agreement. Underwriters are also exempt from the tipping prohibition where they communicate inside information solely for the purpose of procuring a person to either enter into a subunderwriting agreement or to apply for the securities or managed investment products: s 1043C(2)(b).

holders of financial services licences

[19.220] Section 1043K permits holders of financial services licences, such as stockbrokers and their representatives, to enter into transactions as agents of clients notwithstanding that the licensee or any representative possess inside information. In order to qualify for the exemption:

> **the licensee or representative ("the agent") must enter into the trading transaction under the specific instructions of a client ("the principal"); and**
> **the licensee must have a "Chinese wall" in operation which could reasonably be expected to ensure that at the time of the transaction, inside information in the possession of the licensee or of any representative was not communicated to the agent and that no advice with respect to the transaction was given to the principal or the agent by a person in possession of the information; and**
> **the information was not so communicated and no such advice was so given; and**
> **the principal is not an associate of the licensee or any representative.**

consequences of breaching prohibitions

A breach of the insider trading prohibitions is a criminal offence. The insider trading prohibitions are also designated financial services civil penalty provisions.

[19.225] A breach of the insider trading prohibitions is a criminal offence and the court may make a compensation order. The insider trading prohibitions are also designated financial services civil penalty provisions. These are discussed below at para [19.245].

criminal penalties

[19.230] A natural person who breaches the primary prohibitions in s 1043A(1) or the tipping prohibition in s 1043A(2) is guilty of a criminal offence punishable by a penalty of 2,000 penalty units ($220,000) or imprisonment for five years, or both: s 1311 and Sch 3. The maximum penalty for a body corporate guilty of breaching the insider trading prohibitions is $1.1 million: s 1312.

defences against criminal prosecution

[19.235] There are two defences available to a person prosecuted for an offence against s 1043A(1) or (2).

The s 1043M(2)(a) defence protects a diligent investor who relies on information that is "generally available" as defined in s 1042C(1)(b)(i). There is no liability if the information came into the possession of the accused solely as a result of the information having been made known in a manner that would, or would be likely to, bring it to the attention of persons who commonly invest in financial products of a kind whose price or value might be affected by the information. There is a corresponding defence in a prosecution for a breach of the tipping prohibition under s 1043A(2): s 1043M(3).

compensation liability

[19.240] Section 1043L sets out the situations when the court may make a compensation order under s 1317HA against an insider who contravenes the s 1043A prohibitions.

Under s 1043L(2), an insider who applied for or procured another person to apply for financial products is liable to pay compensation to the issuer of the products for any damage suffered by it. The amount of the compensation is the difference between the price of the financial product and the price at which they would have been likely to have been disposed of if the information had been generally available.

ASIC may, if it considers that it is in the public interest to do so, bring an action in the name of, and for the benefit of, the issuer of the financial product for the recovery of that compensation: s 1043L(6).

Where an insider acquired financial products from another person (the disposer) who did not possess the inside information, the disposer may recover compensation from the insider: s 1043L(3). The amount of the compensation is the difference between the price at which the financial products were acquired by the insider from the disposer and the likely price for which they would have been acquired if the information had been generally available.

In the case of a contravention of s 1043A that involves a disposal of financial products by an insider, s 1043L(4) enables the acquirer who did not possess the information to recover compensation from the insider. The amount of the compensation is the difference between the price at which the financial products were disposed of and the likely price for which they would have been disposed of if the information had been generally available.

Potentially, an insider may be liable for double the financial benefit gained by the contravention. This is because not only is the insider liable to either the acquirer or disposer of the financial products under s 1043L(3) or (4), but the insider is also liable under s 1043L(5) for the same amount to the issuer of the financial products traded by the insider. ASIC may, if it considers that it is in the public interest to do so, bring an action in the name of, and for the benefit of, the body corporate for the recovery of that loss: s 1043L(6).

Section 1043O gives the court additional powers to deal with insider trading. The s 1043O powers, which are similar to those available in cases of unacceptable conduct in takeovers, enable the court to make a variety of orders to ensure that insiders are denied any benefits from a contravention. The orders include:

> restraining the exercise of voting or other rights attached to financial products;
> restraining the acquisition or disposal or directing the disposal of financial products;
> vesting the financial products in ASIC; and
> cancelling an Australian financial services licence.

financial services civil penalty provisions

[19.245] The following provisions are designated as financial services civil penalty provisions:

> s 1041A (market manipulation);
> s 1041B(1) (creating a false appearance of active trading);
> s 1041C(1) (artificially maintaining market price);
> s 1041D (dissemination of information about illegal transactions);
> s 1043A(1) (insider trading); and
> s 1043A(2) (insider trading tipping).

The extension of the civil penalty provisions contained in Pt 9.4B to financial services contraventions aims to overcome the difficulty ASIC has had in successfully prosecuting offences arising from breaches of the provisions listed above. The criminal burden of proof—beyond reasonable doubt—applies to such prosecutions and it is difficult to prove elements of the offences beyond reasonable doubt as many elements refer to the defendant's state of mind. This has resulted in very few cases being brought alleging breaches of the market misconduct provisions despite considerable anecdotal evidence that such prohibited practices, especially insider trading, may often take place. The operation of the civil penalty provisions enables actions to be brought where the provisions are contravened and the requisite burden of proof is on the balance of probabilities.

Where the court is satisfied that a financial services civil penalty provision has been contravened, it must make a declaration of contravention. The court may make the following orders on the application of ASIC:

> a pecuniary penalty order where the contravention materially prejudices the interests of acquirers or disposers of the relevant financial products or the issuer of the relevant financial product or its members and the contravention is serious (s 1317G(1A)); or
> a compensation order where the person who has contravened a financial services civil

penalty provision compensates another person (including a corporation) for damage suffered by that person which resulted from the contravention. The damage suffered for the purposes of a compensation order includes profits made by any person resulting from the contravention: s 1317HA. The application for a compensation order may also be brought by the corporation and any other person who suffered damage as a result of the contravention: s 1317J(3A). A compensation order may be made regardless of whether a declaration of contravention in relation to the civil penalty provisions has been made.

case note

In *ASIC v Petsas* [2005] FCA 88, Finkelstein J considered what factors were relevant in determining appropriate civil penalties for insider trading which, if prosecuted as a criminal offence, would merit a term of imprisonment. These include:

(a) the cost to the offender of a term of imprisonment;
(b) the stigma of a criminal conviction, and the likely effects of a criminal conviction such as loss of employment opportunities and travel rights;
(c) the total harm caused by the offence, including the cost of apprehending, convicting and detaining the offender;
(d) the probability of detection and conviction; and
(e) the formula in s 4B of the *Crimes Act 1914* (Cth) which enables a sentencing judge to convert a person's prison sentence into a monetary penalty by multiplying the number of months in the term of imprisonment by five.

The civil penalty provisions are further discussed in Chapter 13.6 above.

bibliography ...

Aitken, M & Latimer, P "Principal Trading by Stockbrokers" (1995) 5 Aust Jnl of Corp Law 1.

Ali, P "Unbundling Credit Risk: the Nature and Regulation of Credit Derivatives" (2000) 11 JBFLP 73.

Ali, P "Mimicking Shares: The Nature and Regulation of Equity Swaps" (1999) 17 C & SLJ 436.

Ansell, S "The Regulation of Insider Trading in Derivatives" (1995) 13 C & SLJ 76.

Armson, E "Market Stabilisation in Australia" (1995) 13 C & SLJ 81.

Black, A "Regulating Market Manipulation: Sections 997–999 of the Corporations Law" (1996) 70 ALJ 987.

Bollen, R "Research Analysts and the Australian Insider Trading and Misleading or Deceptive Conduct Regimes" (2003) 21 C & SLJ 430.

Brown, P, Foo, M & Watson, I "Trading by Insiders in Australia: Evidence on the Profitability of Directors' Trades" (2003) 21 C & SLJ 231.

Chang, M, Hillman, R & Watson, I "Are corporate governance mechanisms effective in reducing insider trading profits?" (2005) 23 C & SLJ 165.

Ciro, T "Gambling Laws and Derivatives" (1999) 17 C & SLJ 171.

Ciro, T "Proposals for Regulatory Reform of Over the Counter Derivatives" (1997) 5 *Current Commercial Law* 23.

Ciro, T "Anti-speculation Laws and Financial Markets Regulation in Australia and the United States" (2002) 13 JBFLP 15.

Ciro, T "Trading in Financial Derivatives: Does it Increase Market Volatility and Systematic Risk?" (2004) 22 C & SLJ 23.

Donnan, F "Self-Regulation and the Demutualisation of the Australian Stock Exchange" (1999) 10 Aust Jnl of Corp Law 1.

Donnan, J "Debentures, Derivatives and Managed Investment Schemes—the Characterisation and Regulation of Investment Instruments" (2002) 13 JBFLP 28.

Freeman, M & Adams, M "Australian Insiders' Views on Insider Trading" (1999) 10 Aust Jnl of Corp Law 148.

Gengatharen, R "Regulatory Reform of the Australian Over the Counter Derivatives Market" (1998) 2 Southern Cross Uni LR 76.

Gething, M "Insider Trading Enforcement: Where We Are Now and Where Do We Go From Here" (1998) 16 C & SLJ 607.

Goldwasser, V "CLERP 6—Implications and Ramifications for the Regulation of Australian Financial Markets" (1999) 17 C & SLJ 206.

Goldwasser, V "The Enforcement Dilemma in Australian Securities Regulation" (1999) 27 ABLR 482.

Goldwasser, V "Market Rigging After Nomura" (1999) 17 C & SLJ 44.

Goldwasser, V "The Regulation of Stock Market Manipulation: A Blue Print for Reform" (1998) 9 Aust Jnl of Corp Law 109.

Goldwasser, V "Current Issues in the Internationalisation of Securities Markets" (1998) 16 C & SLJ 464.

Goldwasser, V "Short Selling Revisited: The Need for a New Direction" (1994) 12 C & SLJ 277.

Haly, A "Different Country, Different Rules? A Comparison of the Regulation of the Investment Industry in Australia and the United Kingdom" (2004) 16 Aust Jnl of Corp Law 124.

Hanrahan, P "The Proposed Suitability Requirement for On-Exchange Derivatives Markets: A Critical Analysis" (1997) 8 JBFLP 5.

House of Representatives Standing Committee on Legal and Constitutional Affairs. *Fair Shares for All: Insider Trading in Australia*. AGPS, October 1989.

Jacobs, A "Time is money: Insider trading from a globalization perspective" (2005) 23 C & SLJ 231.

Kingsford-Smith, D "Decentred Regulation in Online Investment" (2001) 19 C & SLJ 532.

Kingsford-Smith, D "Is 'Due Diligence' Dead? Financial Services and Products Disclosure under the Corporations Act" (2004) 22 C & SLJ 128.

Kwan, N "Is Australian Regulation of Short Selling too Restrictive in the International Market Place?" (1999) 6 *Current Commercial Law* 120.

Latimer, P "Legal Enforcement of Stock Exchange Rules" (1995) 7 Bond LR 1 and (1996) 8 Bond LR 210.

Lawrence, J "The Economics of Market Confidence: [Ac]Costing Securities Market Regulations" (2000) 18 C & SLJ 171.

Lewis, K "When is a Financial Product not a Financial Product?" (2004) 22 C & SLJ 103.

Magarey, D "Enforcement of the Listing Rules of the ASX" (1995) 13 C & SLJ 6.

Mann, M D "What Constitutes a Successful Securities Regulatory Regime" (1993) Aust Jnl of Corp Law 178.

Mannolini, J "Insider Trading–The Need for Conceptual Clarity" (1996) 14 C & SLJ 151.

Nuttall, P "Insider Trading in New Zealand: The Fletcher Challenge Report" (2000) 18 C & SLJ 521.

Rubenstein, S "The Regulation and Prosecution of Insider Trading in Australia: Towards Civil Penalty Sanctions for Insider Trading" (2002) 20 C & SLJ 89.

Ryland, M "Derivatives Regulation: The International Aspect" (1994) 5 Jnl of Banking & Finance 173.

Segal, J "Managing the Transition to the CyberWorld" (2001) 19 C & SLJ 519.

Semann, L, Freeman, M A & Adams, M "Is Insider Trading a Necessary Evil for Efficient Markets? An International Comparative Analysis" (1999) 17 C & SLJ 220.

Spender, P "The Legal Relationship Between the Australian Stock Exchange and Listed Companies" (1995) 13 C & SLJ 240.

Trichardt, A "Australian Green Shoes, Price Stabilisation and IPOs—Part 1" (2003) 21 C & SLJ 26.

Whincop, M "Towards a Property Rights and Market Microstructural Theory of Insider Trading Regulation—The Case of Primary Securities Markets Transactions" (1996) 7 JBFLP 212.

Zhen Qu, C "The Efficacy of Insider Trading Civil Liability Regime in the *Corporations Act*" (2002) 14 Aust Jnl of Corp Law 161.

revision questions on the material in this chapter ...

> Please see eQuiz at **http://www.thomson.com.au/academic** for multiple choice questions and answers.

> For further corporations law links and material please refer to the Lipton-Herzberg website at **http://www.lipton-herzberg.com.au**

chapter twenty

managed investments

key points ...

- A managed investment scheme is a scheme that involves people contributing funds to acquire an interest in a common enterprise. The pooled funds are invested to produce financial benefits for scheme members. A feature of managed investment schemes is that members do not have day-to-day control over the operation of the scheme.

- As a general rule, managed investment schemes that have more than 20 members must be registered by ASIC.

- Registered managed investment schemes must have a single responsible entity to hold scheme property on trust for members, operate the scheme and perform the functions conferred on it by the scheme's constitution and the *Corporations Act*. A responsible entity of a scheme must be a public company that holds a financial services licence authorising it to operate a managed investment scheme.

- All registered managed investment schemes must have a constitution whose provisions bind the scheme members and the responsible entity. A registered scheme must also have a compliance plan that explains how the responsible entity will ensure compliance with the scheme's constitution and the *Corporations Act*.

- If less than half the directors of the responsible entity are external directors, the responsible entity must establish an independent compliance committee to monitor the operation of the scheme and the adequacy of the compliance plan.

[20.05] The managed investment provisions stemmed from 1998 amendments which inserted a new framework—Ch 5C of the *Corporations Act* (ss 601EA–601QB)—into the *Corporations Act* for regulating collective investments, replacing the previous prescribed interest provisions. The changes implemented many of the recommendations by the Australian Law Reform Commission (ALRC) and Companies and Securities Advisory Committee (CASAC) 1995 report, *Collective Investments: Other People's Money*, as well as recommendations by the 1997 *Financial System Inquiry Final Report* (Wallis Committee Report).

Prior to 1998, the funds and assets of a prescribed investment scheme were vested in a trustee for prescribed interest holders with a management company responsible for the scheme's daily management. The main feature of the present regulatory framework is the replacement of the previous two-tier structure with a single responsible entity structure, operated and managed by an entity licensed by ASIC. It was thought that the previous two-tier structure for prescribed interests led to confusion about the respective responsibilities of the management company and the trustee for the conduct of a scheme's operations.

Prior to March 2002, the fundraising provisions of Ch 6D of the *Corporations Act* regulated the disclosure requirements associated with public issues of interests in managed investment schemes. As a result of amendments made by the *Financial Services Reform Act 2001*, interests in registered managed investment schemes are now included in the definition of "financial products". Part 7.9 now sets out the financial product disclosure requirements relating to the issue and sale of financial products such as interests in registered managed investment schemes. This is discussed in Chapter 19 above. The Pt 7.9 requirements are similar to the Ch 6D fundraising disclosure requirements.

what is a managed investment scheme?

[20.10] Section 9 defines the term "managed investment scheme" as a scheme with the following features:

Section 9 defines the term "managed investment scheme".

> **people contribute money or money's worth as consideration to acquire rights (interests) to benefits produced by the scheme;**
> **any of the contributions are to be pooled, or used in a common enterprise, to produce financial benefits, or benefits consisting of rights or interests in property, for the people (the members) who hold interests in the scheme; and**
> **members do not have day-to-day control over the operation of the scheme.**

The acquisition of units in unit trusts, such as cash management, property and equity trusts, are popular types of investments that come within the definition of a managed investment scheme. The money paid by investors for their units is pooled and invested in assets. In the case of cash management trusts, the pooled funds are invested in bank-accepted bills of exchange. In the case of property and equity trusts, the pooled funds are invested in income-producing real estate and shares, respectively. Some unit trusts are listed on the ASX and the units are traded in similar ways as shares in listed companies.

Units in unit trusts, such as cash management, property and equity trusts, are popular types of investments that come within the definition of a managed investment scheme.

A time-sharing scheme is specifically included in the s 9 definition of a managed investment scheme. Typically, time-sharing schemes involve the acquisition of the right to use a holiday apartment for a specified period of time during the year. Investments in some agricultural schemes may also be included in the definition. Examples of such schemes involve investors acquiring an interest in trees in a forest plantation, in ostriches on an ostrich farm and in race-horse syndicates. Investment in film syndicates may also come within the definition of a managed investment scheme.

A wide range of specific types of investments, such as a franchise, a regulated superannuation fund and a retirement village scheme, are excluded from the definition of a managed investment scheme. Investment in shares or debentures in a body corporate are also excluded.

Interests in registered managed investment schemes are referred in s 761A to as "managed investment products" and come within the s 764A definition of financial products. This means that the financial product disclosure requirements of Pt 7.9 of the *Corporations Act* apply to the issue and sale of such interests. These requirements are discussed in Chapter 19 above.

Interests in registered managed investment schemes are "managed investment products" and come within the s 764A definition of financial products.

registration

[20.15] As a general rule, the regulatory framework of Ch 5C of the *Corporations Act* applies only to managed investment schemes that are required to be registered with ASIC. Section 601ED sets out when a managed investment scheme must be registered.

Section 601ED sets out when a managed investment scheme must be registered.

Subject to certain exemptions, a managed investment scheme must be registered if it has more than 20 members or has been promoted by a person who is in the business of promoting such schemes, or is an associate of that person: s 601ED(1). Under s 601ED(2), a managed investment scheme does not have to be registered if all the issues of interests in the scheme that have been made would not have required the giving of a product disclosure statement under Div 2 of Pt 7.9 of the *Corporations Act* if the scheme had been registered when the issues were made. The requirement for product disclosure statements is discussed in Chapter 19 above. This means, for example, that managed investment schemes whose interests were offered to no more than 20 persons per 12 months and that did not raise $2 million or more do not have to be registered.

ASIC is responsible for registration of managed investment schemes.

ASIC is responsible for registration of managed investment schemes. A person who seeks to register a managed investment scheme must lodge an application with ASIC: s 601EA. The application must be accompanied by a copy of the scheme's constitution, the scheme's compliance plan and a statement signed by the responsible entity's directors certifying that those documents comply with relevant provisions. The application must also give details identifying the proposed responsible entity and the auditor of the scheme's compliance plan.

Section 601ED(5) makes it an offence for a person to operate a managed investment scheme that must be registered unless the scheme is registered. If s 601ED(5) is contravened, the court has a discretion to wind up the scheme on the application of ASIC, the scheme operator or a member of the scheme: s 601EE.

case note

In *ASIC v Chase Capital Management Pty Ltd* (2001) 19 ACLC 476, an investment club was operated in contravention of s 601ED(5) in that the scheme had not been registered. It was held that the exercise of the court's discretion to wind up the scheme involved similar considerations as a winding up of a company on the just and equitable ground under s 461(1)(k), discussed in Chapter 17 above. The court considered that it was in the public interest to wind up the scheme as there had been regular breaches of investor protection provisions, in particular, the offering of securities without a prospectus.

the responsible entity

[20.20] One of the main features of the managed investment regulatory framework is the requirement that registered schemes have a single responsible entity to perform the functions conferred on it by the scheme's constitution and the *Corporations Act*: s 601FB(1). The responsible entity is liable to scheme members for all aspects of the scheme's operation.

licensing

The responsible entity of a scheme must be a public company that holds an Australian financial services licence authorising it to operate a managed investment scheme.

[20.25] The responsible entity of a scheme must be a public company that holds an Australian financial services licence authorising it to operate a managed investment scheme: s 601FA. ASIC administers the licensing of responsible entities. An applicant for licensing will have to, among other things, satisfy ASIC that it is of good fame and character, has expertise to perform the duties associated with being a responsible entity and has available adequate resources (including financial, technological and human resources) to run the scheme competently: ss 912A(1) and 913B(3).

statutory duties

The responsible entity of a managed investment scheme is subject to a wide range of statutory duties.

[20.30] The responsible entity of a managed investment scheme is subject to a wide range of statutory duties under s 601FC. The duties include the duty:

- to act honestly (s 601FC(1)(a));
- to exercise the degree of care and diligence that a reasonable person would exercise if they were in the responsible entity's position (s 601FC(1)(b));
- to act in the best interests of members and, if there is a conflict between the members' interests and its own interests, give priority to the members' interests (s 601FC(1)(c));
- to treat members of the same class equally and all members fairly (s 601FC(1)(d)); and
- not to make improper use of scheme information: s 601FC(1)(e).

Sections 601FD and 601FE also impose a range of duties on the officers and employees of a responsible entity. These duties are subject to the civil penalty provisions discussed in Chapter 13.6 above and override any conflicting duty the officers and employees may have under Ch 2D of the *Corporations Act*.

Section 601MA gives members of a scheme the right to sue the responsible entity for any loss or damage due to its breach of any of the managed investment provisions of the *Corporations Act*.

related party transactions

Sections 601LA–601LE apply a modified version of the *Corporations Act* provisions dealing with financial benefits to related parties of public companies to responsible entities.

[20.35] Sections 601LA–601LE apply a modified version of the *Corporations Act* provisions dealing with financial benefits to related parties of public companies to responsible entities. The related party provisions are discussed in Chapter 13.3 above.

The object of the modified related party provisions is to protect the scheme property and the interests of members in the scheme property by requiring disclosure and member approval of financial benefits to the responsible entity or its related parties that could diminish or endanger scheme property or adversely affect the interests of members: s 601LB.

constitution

All registered managed investment schemes must have a constitution contained in a document that is legally enforceable as between the members and the responsible entity.

[20.40] All registered managed investment schemes must have a constitution contained in a document that is legally enforceable as between the members and the responsible entity: s 601GB. While the *Corporations Act* does not set out detailed contents requirements for the constitution, s 601GA specifies that it must make adequate provision for the following matters:

> **the consideration that is to be paid to acquire an interest in the scheme (s 601GA(1)(a));**
> **the investment powers of the responsible entity (s 601GA(1)(b));**
> **the method by which complaints made by members in relation to the scheme are dealt with (s 601GA(1)(c)); and**
> **the winding up of the scheme: s 601GA(1)(d).**

compliance plan and compliance committee

All registered managed investment schemes must have a compliance plan that sets out the measures that a responsible entity will apply in operating the scheme to ensure compliance with the scheme's constitution and the *Corporations Act*.

[20.45] All registered managed investment schemes must have a compliance plan that sets out the measures that a responsible entity will apply in operating the scheme to ensure compliance with the scheme's constitution and the *Corporations Act*. The responsible entity has a duty to ensure that the compliance plan meets the minimum contents requirements of s 601HA and to comply with the compliance plan: s 601FC(1)(g) and (h).

If less than half the directors of the responsible entity are external directors, the responsible entity is required to establish a compliance committee, the majority of whom must be independent of the responsible entity: s 601JA. A director is an external director if he or she has not been an executive officer, employee or in a designated relationship under s 601JA(2) within the past two years.

The function of the compliance committee is to monitor the operation of the scheme and the adequacy of the compliance plan. A compliance committee is not necessary if at least half the directors of the responsible entity are "external directors" who are independent of the responsible entity.

members' rights to withdraw

The constitution of a scheme must state whether or not members have a right to withdraw their investments from a scheme.

[20.50] The constitution of a scheme must state whether or not members have a right to withdraw their investments from a scheme: s 601GA(4). Withdrawals from a "liquid" scheme are not permitted unless the constitution permits it and the withdrawal is fair to all members: s 601KA. A scheme is liquid if its liquid assets account for 80 per cent of the value of the scheme property: s 601KA(4).

If the scheme is not liquid, ss 601KB–601KE impose restrictions on the right to withdraw. For example, under s 601KB(1), the responsible entity of a registered scheme that is not liquid may offer members an opportunity to withdraw to the extent that particular assets are available and able to be converted to money in time to satisfy withdrawal requests. The responsible entity must not satisfy withdrawal requests until the withdrawal offer period has closed. If the value of withdrawal requests exceeds the amount available for withdrawal, the requests must be met on a pro-rata basis in accordance with a formula: s 601KD.

scheme financial reports and audit

The financial reporting provisions of the *Corporations Act* also apply to registered managed investment schemes.

[20.55] The financial reporting provisions of the *Corporations Act*, discussed above in Chapter 15, also apply to registered managed investment schemes. For example, a registered scheme is required to:

> keep written financial records (s 286);
> prepare financial reports and have them audited (ss 295 and 301);
> send the financial reports and auditor's report to scheme members: s 314. The deadline for sending these reports to members is within three months after the end of the financial year (s 315(3));
> lodge the financial reports, directors' report and auditor's report with ASIC within three months after the end of the financial year (s 319); and
> lodge an annual return with ASIC within three months after the end of the financial year: s 345(2).

meetings of scheme members

Unlike public companies, managed investment schemes are not required to hold AGMs.

[20.60] Part 2G.4 of the *Corporations Act* contains provisions dealing with meetings of members of registered managed investment schemes. To a large extent, these provisions are based on the meeting provisions of public companies. These are discussed in Chapter 14 above. The main difference is that, unlike public companies, managed investment schemes are not required to hold AGMs.

winding up and deregistration

The *Corporations Act* contains separate provisions for the winding up and deregistration of managed investment schemes.

[20.65] The *Corporations Act* contains separate provisions for the winding up and deregistration of managed investment schemes.

A registered scheme may be wound up in the following circumstances:

> the constitution of a scheme may provide for the winding up of the scheme at a specified time or the happening of a specified event (s 601NA);
> the members of a registered scheme can call a meeting and pass an extraordinary resolution directing the responsible entity to wind up the scheme (s 601NB);

> the responsible entity can take steps to wind up a registered scheme if it considers that the purpose of the scheme has been or cannot be accomplished (s 601NC); and
> the court may direct the responsible entity to wind up the scheme if the court thinks it just and equitable to do so: s 601ND(1)(a). Court-directed winding up on the just and equitable ground may be made on the application of the responsible entity, a director of the responsible entity, a member of the scheme or ASIC. The court may also direct the responsible entity to wind up the scheme on the application of a judgment creditor where the creditor's execution of judgment has been returned unsatisfied: s 601ND(1)(b).

A registered scheme may be deregistered voluntarily or by ASIC. Voluntary deregistration is initiated when the responsible entity lodges a deregistration application with ASIC: s 601PA. Such an application may only be made if:

> the number of members of the scheme falls below 20 and all the members consent to the deregistration; or
> the registered scheme was not required to be registered and all the members consent to the deregistration; or
> the scheme ceases to be a managed investment scheme as defined in the *Corporations Act*.

Under s 601PB, ASIC may deregister a scheme if:

> the scheme's responsible entity, constitution or compliance plan does not satisfy the *Corporations Act* requirements; or
> the scheme's property is not clearly identified as such and is not held separately from the property of the responsible entity or property of other schemes; or
> the scheme is at least six months late lodging its annual return with ASIC and ASIC has no reason to believe that the scheme is being operated.

bibliography ...

Donnan, J "Debentures, Derivatives and Managed Investment Schemes—The Characterisation and Regulation of Investment Instruments" (2002) 13 JBFLP 28.
Hanrahan, P "Managed Investment Schemes: The Position of Directors under Chapter 5C of the Corporations Law" (1999) 17 C & SLJ 67.
Hanrahan, P "Responsible Entities: Reforming Manager Accountability in Public Unit Trusts" (1998) 16 C & SLJ 76.
Moodie, G & Ramsay, I "Compliance committees under the Managed Investments Act 1988 (Cth) (2005) 33 ABLR 167.
Ranero, F "Constitutional Amendments in Managed Investment Schemes" (1999) 11 Corp & Bus LJ 287.
Ranero, F "Managed Investment Schemes: The Responsible Entity's Duty to Act for a Proper Purpose" (1999) 17 C & SLJ 422.
Ventura, A "Implications of the Managed Investments Act on the Funds Management Industry" (1999) 17 C & SLJ 38.
Von Nessen, P "Securities Regulation for Interests in Managed Investment Schemes" (1999) 11 Aust Jnl of Corp Law 63.
Von Nessen, P "The Managed Investments Act—Difficulties in Transition" (2000) 11 JBFLP 165.

revision questions on the material in this chapter …

> Please see eQuiz at **http://www.thomson.com.au/academic** for multiple choice questions and answers.

chapter twenty-one

ASIC investigation powers

key points ...

> ASIC is a Commonwealth government authority set up by the *ASIC Act* and is the main government agency responsible for regulating Australia's companies and financial services, products and markets.

> ASIC has extensive powers to investigate suspected contraventions of the *Corporations Act* on its own initiative. It also has the power to investigate suspected contraventions of other laws that concern the management or affairs of companies or involve company or financial services fraud or dishonesty. The responsible Commonwealth Minister, the Treasurer, may also direct ASIC to investigate these matters where this is in the public interest.

> The *ASIC Act* gives ASIC wide information-gathering powers to facilitate its investigations. ASIC can examine any person if it believes that that person can provide information relevant to an ASIC investigation. An examinee must answer questions on oath and does not have the usual privilege against self-incrimination.

> ASIC has wide powers to inspect any books and records that the *Corporations Act* obliges companies to keep. It can also require people to produce such books and records.

> If, as a result of an investigation, ASIC believes that there is a contravention of the law it has the power to initiate prosecutions for criminal offences or apply for civil penalty orders. ASIC also has the power to apply to the court for the compulsory winding up of a company or the appointment of a receiver over company property.

[21.05] Provisions dealing with the investigation of the affairs of companies have been part of Australian companies' legislation since the mid-19th century. These investigatory provisions have been used as a means of discovering the true facts surrounding major corporate collapses as well as improper and illegal activities.

The investigatory and information-gathering powers of ASIC are largely set out in the *ASIC Act*.

The investigatory and information-gathering powers of ASIC are largely set out in the *ASIC Act*. However, as discussed in Chapter 25 below, ss 596A and 596B of the *Corporations Act* allow ASIC, among others, to apply to the court to summon a present or former officer for examination about a corporation's examinable affairs.

Section 11(1) of the *ASIC Act* provides that ASIC has such functions and powers as are conferred on it by or under the corporations legislation. Section 5(1) defines the term "corporations legislation" to mean the *ASIC Act* and the *Corporations Act*.

Section 12A gives ASIC certain functions and powers in relation to:

> **consumer protection in relation to financial services;**
> **insurance and superannuation; and**
> **monitoring and promoting market integrity and consumer protection in relation to the Australian financial system.**

ASIC's investigatory and information-gathering powers in relation to insurance and superannuation are beyond the scope of this book.

Section 12 permits the Minister to give ASIC written directions about policies it should pursue, or priorities it should follow, in performing or exercising any of its functions or powers. The Minister, however, is not permitted to give directions to ASIC about a particular case: s 12(3).

ASIC's Annual Reports summarise the outcomes of its investigations. The Annual Reports, published on ASIC's website, are linked to the Lipton-Herzberg Corporate Law Websites at **http://www.lipton-herzberg.com.au/corporate-law-websites.html**

ASIC's investigatory powers

[21.10] A number of provisions of the *ASIC Act* give ASIC investigatory powers. Section 13 of the *ASIC Act* gives ASIC broad powers to conduct investigations on its own initiative. Under s 13(1), ASIC may make such investigation as it thinks expedient for the administration of the corporations legislation where it has reason to suspect that there may have been committed:

> **a contravention of the corporations legislation; or**
> **a contravention of a Commonwealth or State law that either concerns the management or affairs of a body corporate or managed investment scheme or involves fraud or dishonesty and relates to a body corporate, a managed investment scheme or to financial products.**

Section 5(1) of the *ASIC Act* defines the expression "the corporations legislation" to mean the *Corporations Act* and the *ASIC Act*.

Before ASIC can begin an s 13(1) investigation it must have reason to suspect that a contravention of the corporations legislation or other law has occurred.

Before ASIC can begin an s 13(1) investigation it must have reason to suspect that a contravention of the corporations legislation or other law has occurred.

case note

In *Boys v ASC* (1998) 16 ACLC 298, it was held that the ASC (now called ASIC) was entitled to appoint a receiver and his legal adviser as consultants to assist the ASC in carrying out its investigation under s 13. This appointment was on the basis that their fees would be paid out of the company's assets and not by the ASC.

Section 13(2) of the *ASIC Act* gives ASIC investigatory powers in relation to unacceptable circumstances in takeovers. As discussed in Chapter 18 above, ASIC, amongst others, may apply to the Takeovers Panel for a declaration of unacceptable circumstances: s 657C(2). Under s 13(2) of the *ASIC Act*, where ASIC has reason to suspect that unacceptable circumstances have occurred it may make such investigation as it thinks expedient:

> **for the purposes of determining whether or not to make an application to the Takeovers Panel; or**
> **otherwise for the due administration of the corporations legislation.**

As discussed in Chapter 25 below, s 533 of the *Corporations Act* obliges liquidators to report certain matters to ASIC. These matters include Commonwealth or State offences that appear to have been committed by officers or members in relation to companies. Section 422 places similar reporting obligations on receivers. Pursuant to s 15 of the *ASIC Act*, ASIC, on receipt of such reports, has the power to investigate the matters to which liquidators' or receivers' reports relate for the purpose of determining whether or not a person ought to be prosecuted for an offence.

ASIC may investigate matters raised by liquidators' reports.

While the investigatory powers conferred by ss 13 and 15 are exercised on ASIC's initiative, the *ASIC Act* specifies that the relevant Minister (the Commonwealth Treasurer) can also direct ASIC to investigate certain matters where the Minister is of the opinion that such investigation is in the public interest: s 14(1). Section 14(2) lists a broad range of matters in respect of which the Minister may direct an ASIC investigation. These include:

> **an alleged or suspected contravention of the corporations legislation;**
> **an alleged or suspected contravention of a Commonwealth or State law that:**
  — **concerns the management or affairs of a body corporate; or**
  — **involves fraud or dishonesty and relates to a body corporate or financial products; or**
> **the establishment or conducting of a financial market.**

At the end of an investigation under either ss 13 or 15, ASIC may prepare a report about the investigation setting out its findings: s 17. Such reports must be prepared if the Minister so directs. ASIC has no discretion in respect of s 14 investigations. Preparation of a report at the end of such investigations is mandatory.

Section 16 enables ASIC to prepare interim reports where in the course of an investigation it forms the opinion that an interim report will assist the protection, preservation or prompt recovery of property where a serious contravention of the law has been committed. An interim report can also be prepared where ASIC is of the opinion that there is an urgent need for a law to be amended.

Copies of a report of investigations are distributed to the Minister who may then cause it to be published: s 18(1) and (4). Where a report relates to a serious contravention of the law, ASIC may also distribute copies to:

> **the Australian Federal Police;**
> **the National Crime Authority;**
> **the Director of Public Prosecutions; or**
> **a prescribed agency.**

information gathering

examination of persons

ASIC has wide powers to examine persons to gain information relevant to an investigation.

[21.15] ASIC has wide powers to examine persons where it suspects or believes, on reasonable grounds, that a person can give information relevant to a matter under investigation: s 19. The examination may be conducted by a Commissioner, a member of ASIC's staff or an inspector to whom the power has been delegated. At the examination, the examinee is required to give all reasonable assistance and answer questions on oath.

The notice requiring a person to attend an examination must state the general nature of the matter that is being investigated: *Johns v Connor* (1992) 10 ACLC 774. There is no need for the notice to identify the person suspected of a contravention: *Stockbridge v Ogilvie* (1993) 11 ACLC 645.

An examination is conducted in private: s 22. Section 23 gives an examinee the right to legal representation. During the examination the lawyer may address the inspector and question the examinee. It is an offence for any person to be present at an examination other than the examinee, the inspector, a Commissioner, an approved ASIC staff member or the examinee's lawyer.

An examinee does not have the usual privilege against self-incrimination. Under s 68(1)(a), a person cannot elect to refuse or fail to give information on the basis that the information might tend to incriminate them or make them liable to a penalty. However, an answer cannot be used against a person in criminal proceedings or other proceedings for the imposition of a penalty, if before answering the question, the person had claimed that the answer may tend to be incriminating: s 68(3).

Further, as a general rule an examinee is required to give information at an s 19 examination even if that information is subject to legal professional privilege: *Corporate Affairs Commission of New South Wales v Yuill* (1991) 9 ACLC 839. However, under s 69 a lawyer who is required to give information at an examination or is obliged to produce a book that is privileged is entitled to refuse to comply with that requirement unless the person on whose behalf the lawyer acts consents to the lawyer complying with the requirement. A lawyer who claims privilege must give ASIC a written notice identifying the name and address of the client. The lawyer must also give particulars that identify the documents or books that are subject to the privilege.

Subject to certain exceptions, statements made by an examinee during the course of an examination are generally admissible as evidence against any person in any proceedings: s 76. The exceptions include such matters as:

> **self-incrimination in criminal or penalty proceedings; and**
> **claims of legal professional privilege.**

Under s 25(1), ASIC may give a copy of a written record of the examination together with any related book to a person's lawyer, if the lawyer satisfies ASIC that the person is carrying on, or is contemplating in good faith, a proceeding in respect of the matter to which the examination related. ASIC may also supply any other person with similar records subject to such conditions (if any) as it thinks appropriate: s 25(3). Section 127(1) requires ASIC to protect from unauthorised use or disclosure any information given to it in confidence. Disclosure is permitted under s 127(4) if the ASIC chairman is satisfied that particular information will enable or assist:

> **CAMAC, the Takeover Panel, CALDB and other similar agencies to perform or exercise any of their functions or powers;**
> **the government or an agency of a State or Territory to perform a function or exercise a power; or**
> **a government or an agency of a foreign country to perform a function, or exercise a power, conferred by a law in force in that foreign country.**

case note

The relationship of ss 25(3) and 127(4) was considered by the High Court in *Johns v ASC* (1993) 11 ACLC 1021. One of the issues canvassed in that case was whether the ASC (the predecessor of ASIC), under those sections, validly provided a transcript of Johns' examination before an ASC officer to a Royal Commission in circumstances that allowed the information to be published generally. The High Court decided that the ASC's decision to disclose the transcripts to the Royal Commission was invalid in the circumstances. The predecessor of the *ASIC Act* gave the ASC limited authority to disclose information. Information obtained by the ASC in the course of an investigation may be used or disclosed for the purposes of the performance of any of the ASC's functions and for any of the purposes mentioned in s 127(2) or (4), but for no other purpose. While s 127(4)(b) authorised disclosure to the Royal Commission, the ASC should have imposed a condition restricting further disclosure by the Royal Commission to protect Johns' rights to confidentiality.

inspection of books

[21.20] Sections 28–39 of the *ASIC Act* deal with ASIC's powers to inspect books required to be kept by the corporations legislation. Section 5(1) defines "books" to include:

Sections 28–39 of the *ASIC Act* deal with ASIC's powers to inspect books required to be kept by the corporations legislation.

> **a register;**
> **financial reports or financial records however compiled, recorded or stored;**
> **a document;**
> **banker's books; and**
> **any other record of information.**

Section 29 authorises ASIC to inspect, without charge, any book required to be kept under the corporations legislation. Under s 28, ASIC is able to require production of any other books only:

> for the purposes of the performance or exercise of any of the functions or powers of ASIC under the corporations legislation;
> for the purposes of ensuring compliance with the corporations legislation;
> in relation to an alleged or suspected contravention of the corporations legislation or a law that involves fraud or dishonesty and relates to a body corporate or financial products; or
> for purposes of an investigation.

Apart from those books generally available, ASIC may gain access to specified books relating to the affairs of a body corporate by giving a notice to produce to the body or an eligible person: s 30. Under s 5(1), an "eligible person" is:

> a past or present officer of a body corporate; or
> a present or former employee, agent, banker, solicitor or auditor of a body corporate.

In *ASC v Lucas* (1992) 10 ACLC 888, it was held that s 30 permitted the ASC to gain access to an auditor's audit manual and quality control manual, and the file and working papers in relation to the management of the audit.

Sections 31 and 32A enable ASIC to give notices to produce specified books relating to financial products and services.

Sections 31 and 32A enable ASIC to give similar notices to produce specified books relating to financial products and services. If ASIC has reasonable grounds to suspect that there are books which have not been produced as required, it may obtain a search warrant and seize books found: ss 35 and 36.

Section 33 enables ASIC to give a person a written notice requiring the production to it of specified books that are in the person's possession and relate to the affairs of a body corporate. A bank's contractual obligation to keep its customers' affairs confidential is not a reasonable excuse for failing to comply with s 33: *ASC v Zarro* (1992) 10 ACLC 11.

A failure to comply with a notice given under s 33 is an offence, unless there was a reasonable excuse: s 63. This refers to physical or practical difficulties involved in the production of the books. It did not include an undertaking of confidentiality: *ASC v Ampolex Ltd* (1996) 14 ACLC 80.

disclosure of information about financial products

ASIC may obtain information without formal examination.

[21.25] Sections 40–48 of the *ASIC Act* deal with ASIC's power to quickly obtain information about financial products in situations where it is inappropriate to conduct a formal examination.

Section 41 permits ASIC to require:

> a person who carries on a financial services business to disclose the identity of parties to an acquisition or disposal of financial products and any instructions given in relation to that acquisition or disposal;
> any person to disclose whether they acquired or disposed of financial products as trustee for another and if so the identity of, and instructions given by, the beneficiary; and
> a person who operates a financial market to disclose the identities of the persons who acted in relation to an acquisition or disposal of financial products.

Section 40 restricts the s 41 powers of ASIC to require disclosure of information about financial products. It can exercise those powers only:

> for the purposes of the performance or exercise of any of ASIC's functions and powers;
> for the purposes of ensuring compliance with the corporations legislation;
> in relation to an alleged or suspected contravention of the corporations legislation; and
> for purposes of an investigation.

Section 43 also gives ASIC the power to require disclosure:

> from a director, secretary or executive officer of a body corporate, information that may have affected a dealing in financial products that has taken place; or
> from any person whom ASIC believes on reasonable grounds is capable of giving information about dealings in financial products; advice, an analysis or report given by a person who carries on a financial services business; the financial position of a financial services business carried on by a person giving such advice; or an audit or auditor's report.

Under s 43(1), the power to require disclosure in relation to financial products can be exercised only where ASIC considers that:

> it may be necessary to exercise its powers under s 794D to suspend trading in particular financial products;
> a contravention of certain provisions in relation to financial products, such as false trading and market rigging may have been committed;
> a contravention of Ch 6C (the substantial shareholder provisions or disclosure of relevant interest notices) may have been committed;
> a contravention of a Commonwealth law involving fraud or dishonesty in relation to financial products may have been committed; or
> unacceptable circumstances may have occurred during the course of a takeover.

consequences of investigations

[21.30] An ASIC investigation or report can have several consequences. Section 49 of the *ASIC Act* enables ASIC to initiate prosecutions for criminal offences where an investigation reveals contraventions of the law. As discussed below, ASIC may decide to initiate civil proceedings in the name of a company under s 50 of the *ASIC Act*.

An investigation can also lead to the winding up of a company. Section 461(1)(h) of the *Corporations Act* provides a ground for the compulsory winding up of a company where ASIC has stated in a report of an investigation that it is of the opinion:

> that the company cannot pay its debts and should be wound up; or
> it is in the interests of the public, the members or the creditors that the company should be wound up.

A person whom ASIC thinks appropriate may seek a remedy under s 232 where it has investigated matters connected with the affairs of a company: s 234(e). This is discussed in Chapter 17 above.

Where ASIC is carrying out an investigation of the acts or omissions of a person, it may apply to the court under s 1323 for a wide variety of orders designed to protect the interests of the creditors of the person under investigation. These orders include:

> prohibiting the person under investigation or any associate transferring assets out of Australia;
> prohibiting the person under investigation from leaving Australia without consent of the court; and
> appointing a receiver or trustee in respect of the property of the person under investigation. This is the most common order sought. Receivers are discussed in Chapter 23 below.

section 50 class actions

ASIC can initiate proceedings in the name of a company.

[21.35] Under s 50 of the *ASIC Act*, ASIC has broad powers to initiate certain civil proceedings in the name of a company where it appears as a result of an investigation or examination that it is in the public interest to do so. These proceedings are for the recovery of damages for fraud, negligence, default, breach of duty or other misconduct committed in connection with a matter to which the investigation or examination related.

ASIC can bring legal proceedings in the name of the company whether or not the company consents. ASIC may also bring an action in the name of a shareholder or creditor. In the case of a natural person, her or his consent must be given. Although ASIC is the active party in the litigation, any remedy obtained is for the benefit of the person in whose name the action is brought. Section 50 enables ASIC to commence proceedings against directors in the name of the company for breach of their fiduciary duties. It may also commence proceedings against a trustee for breach of trust: *Walsh v Permanent Trustee Australia Ltd* (1996) 14 ACLC 1443.

case note

In *ASC v Deloitte Touche Tohmatsu* (1996) 14 ACLC 1486, it was held that s 50 gives ASIC an extremely wide discretion to bring proceedings. ASIC is required to form a judgment as to the public interest in deciding whether or not proceedings should be brought. This is largely a question of fact and by its nature is not generally subject to review by the courts unless there is a failure to address the correct legal questions or the process of reasoning was manifestly unreasonable.

hearings

ASIC has the power to hold hearings.

[21.40] ASIC has the power to hold hearings for the purposes of the performance or exercise of any of its functions and powers: s 51 of the *ASIC Act*. Hearings cannot, however, be held for purposes of carrying out an investigation or for the purposes associated with applications for declarations of unacceptable conduct in takeovers. As discussed above, there are separate procedures for the examination of persons in such circumstances.

The *Corporations Act* requires ASIC to hold a hearing in certain situations. For example, s 739 allows ASIC to make a stop order where it is satisfied that a disclosure document contains a misleading or deceptive statement in contravention of s 728. Before making such an order, ASIC must hold a hearing and give any interested people a reasonable opportunity to make submissions on whether the order should be made: s 739(2).

ASIC has a discretion to decide whether to hold a hearing in public or private: s 52. In exercising its discretion, ASIC is required to have regard to a number of considerations such as the confidential nature or otherwise of the matters that may arise, as well as the public interest. A hearing must be held in private if this is required by the corporations legislation: s 54.

Members of ASIC have the power to summon persons to attend a hearing and give evidence or produce documents: s 58. Proceedings at hearings are conducted with as little formality and technicality, and with as much expedition, as requirements of national scheme laws and a proper consideration of the matters permit: s 59. At a hearing, ASIC is not bound by the formal rules of evidence but is required to observe the rules of natural justice. Rules of procedure applicable to courts do not apply to ASIC because it exercises an administrative function. ASIC can therefore reopen a hearing after receiving new evidence: *Boucher v ASC* (1996) 14 ACLC 999.

bibliography ...

Barnes, J "The Incidental Powers of the Australian Securities Commission" (1993) 21 ABLR 440.

Cameron, A "Enforcement, Getting the Regulatory Mix Right" (1994) 4 Aust Jnl of Corp Law 121.

duPlessis, J "Reverberations after HIH and Other Recent Australian Corporate Collapses" (2003) 15 Aust Jnl of Corp Law 225.

Healy, G & Eastwood, A "Legal professional privilege and the investigative powers of the Australian Securities and Investment Commission" (2005) 23 C & SLJ 375.

Kluver, J "ASC Investigations and Enforcement: Issues and Initiatives" (1992) 15 UNSWLJ 31.

Longo, J P "The Powers of Investigation of the Australian Securities Commission: Balancing the Interests of Persons and Companies Under Investigation with the Interests of the State" (1992) 10 C & SLJ 237.

McConvill, J "Australian Securities and Investments Commission's Proposed Power to Issue Infringement Notices: Another Slap in the Face to s 1324 of the Corporations Act or an Undermining of Corporate Civil Liberties?" (2003) 30 ABLR 36.

Middleton, T "Australian Securities Commission Investigations of Fiduciaries and Proceedings Against Constructive Trustees" (1998) 16 C & SLJ 16.

Middleton, T "The Production Under The ASC Law Of Documents Obtained By Discovery" (1997) 15 C & SLJ 96.

Middleton, T "ASIC's investigation and enforcement powers—current issues and suggested reforms" (2004) 22 C & SLJ 503.

Ramsay, I M "Enforcement of Corporate Rights and Duties by Shareholders and the ASC: Evidence and Analysis" (1995) 23 ABLR 174.

Richardson, D "Section 50 of the ASC Act 1989: White Knight or White Elephant?" (1994) 12 C & SLJ 418.

Senate Legal and Constitutional References Committee, Investigatory Powers of the ASC (June 1995).

von Nessen, P "The Section 1323 Power of the Australian Securities Commission: Its Operation and Shortcomings" (1996) 22 Mon LR 140.

revision questions on the material in this chapter ...

> Please see eQuiz at **http://www.thomson.com.au/academic** for multiple choice questions and answers.

> For further corporations law links and material please refer to the Lipton-Herzberg website at **http://www.lipton-herzberg.com.au**

chapter twenty-two

corporate insolvency

key points ...

- The main aim of corporate insolvency law is to provide a fair and orderly process for dealing with the financial affairs of insolvent companies.
- The *Corporations Act* provides for five main types of external administrations for insolvent companies; receiverships; voluntary administrations; deeds of company arrangement; liquidations (also called winding up); and schemes of arrangement.
- Receivership is a form of external administration that involves the appointment of an independent, registered insolvency practitioner called a "receiver". The role of a receiver appointed by a secured creditor is to take possession of the secured property, sell it and out of the proceeds, and repay the secured debt owed by the company.
- Voluntary administration involves the appointment of a registered, independent insolvency practitioner (called an "administrator") who takes complete control of an insolvent company for a relatively short period of time. The aims of the voluntary administration provisions of the *Corporations Act* are to maximise the chances of the company or its businesses remaining in existence and, if this is not possible, to achieve a better return to creditors than would result from an immediate winding up.
- A deed of company arrangement is one of the possible outcomes for a company that is put into voluntary administration. The aims of the voluntary administration scheme are largely achieved by deeds of company arrangement.
- Liquidation is a form of external administration that ultimately results in the company being deregistered and ceasing to exist as a legal entity. Liquidation is an orderly process under which the company's affairs are wound up, its property sold, debts owed to its creditors repaid and the surplus (if any) distributed among its shareholders.
- Schemes of arrangement for insolvent companies are a form of external administration that enables the rights and liabilities of shareholders and creditors to be reorganised under court supervision. The aim of a scheme of arrangement is to obtain a binding agreement that modifies, reorganises or alters the legal rights of creditors and shareholders.

[22.05] In its report, *Corporate Insolvency Laws: A Stocktake* (June 2004), the Parliamentary Joint Committee on Corporations and Financial Services (PJC) observed that while business failures often have negative outcomes, they may also have positive economic effects.

> **< A recent Productivity Commission study of business failures in Australia has underscored the fact that business exits are a natural and expected phenomenon associated with dynamic market economies. The study noted that although business exits, particularly failures, often involve negative outcomes, they have positive economic effects. Productivity growth is enhanced when inefficient and unprofitable businesses are replaced by efficient and profitable ones. Exits may be the result of longer-term structural changes that provide an opportunity for resources in the economy to be configured in new and better ways. The learning experience gained by entrepreneurs involved in exits will assist them in doing things differently next time around. >**

The PJC's report is linked to the Law Reform pages on the Lipton-Herzberg website at **http://www.lipton-herzberg.com.au/law_reform.htm#par**

Insolvency law has evolved over a long period of time to deal with insolvent debtors who are unable to pay debts owing to creditors. Debtors may be people or companies. While the general principles dealing with insolvent people and insolvent companies are broadly similar, different legislation applies in each case. Insolvent individuals are said to become "bankrupt" and are dealt with under the *Bankruptcy Act 1966* (Cth). Corporate insolvency is regulated by the external administration provisions of Ch 5 of the *Corporations Act* which provides for the following five types of insolvency regimes:

Corporate insolvency is regulated by the external administration provisions of Ch 5 of the *Corporations Act* which provides for five types of insolvency regimes.

> **receivership;**
> **voluntary administration;**
> **deed of company arrangement;**
> **liquidation (also called "winding up"); and**
> **scheme of arrangement.**

Table 22.1 sets out the number of insolvency appointments for each of the forms of external administration in 2003.

table 22.1 insolvency appointments: january–december 2003

Receiver appointed	90
Receiver manager appointed	533
Controller appointed (except receiver or managing controller)	157
Managing controller appointed (except receiver and manager)	1
Voluntary administrator appointed	2,874
Administrators of deed of company arrangement appointed	714
Court ordered (compulsory) winding up – liquidator appointed	3,253
Provisional winding up – provisional liquidator appointed	84
Creditors voluntary winding up – liquidator appointed	3,331
Scheme Administrator appointed	0

ASIC Insolvency Statistics

The features of these forms of external administration are summarised in this chapter and are discussed in detail in Chapters 23 to 25 of this book. It is a common feature of these different regimes that an independent and suitably qualified insolvency practitioner takes over the management of the insolvent company from its directors.

aims of insolvency law

[22.10] Insolvency law plays an important part in corporate regulation because it is inevitable that from time-to-time companies will fail, leaving unpaid debts. The consequences of insolvency may affect many parties including creditors, employees, taxation authorities, directors and customers. In some high-profile corporate collapses the interests of the general public have also been severely affected. Insolvency law attempts to balance the often competing interests of these various groups. While the various insolvency regimes sometimes have different objectives, it is helpful to identify the broad aims of insolvency law.

The Australian Law Reform Commission's *General Insolvency Inquiry* (1988) (Harmer Report) identified the following aims of insolvency law as the basis of its law reform proposals:

> **the fundamental purpose of an insolvency law was to provide a fair and orderly process for dealing with the financial affairs of insolvent individuals and companies;**
> **the insolvency law should provide mechanisms that enable both debtor and creditor to participate with the least possible delay and expense;**
> **an insolvency administration should be impartial, efficient and expeditious;**
> **the law should provide a convenient means of collecting or recovering property that should properly be applied toward payment of the debts and liabilities of an insolvent person;**
> **the principle of equal sharing between creditors should be retained and in some areas reinforced;**
> **the end result of an insolvency administration, particularly as it affects individuals should, with very limited exceptions, give effective relief or release from the financial liabilities and obligations of the insolvent;**
> **insolvency law should, as far as convenient and practical, support the commercial and economic processes of the community;**
> **as far as is possible and practical, insolvency laws should not conflict with the general law; and**
> **an insolvency law should enable ancillary assistance in the administration of an insolvency originating in a foreign country.**

The insolvency regime that will apply in a particular case generally depends upon the course of action taken by the creditors or directors of the insolvent company. A creditor may enforce rights conferred by contract or by operation of insolvency law. A secured creditor will often be able to exercise self-help by appointing a receiver under a power conferred by a debenture or other loan documentation. Creditors of an insolvent company will often initiate the winding up of the company while voluntary administrations are usually commenced by the directors of an insolvent company.

receivership

[22.15] Receivership is a form of external administration that involves the appointment of an independent, experienced insolvency practitioner called a "receiver". Where a receiver is appointed by a secured creditor of a company, the receiver's role is to take possession of secured property, sell it, and out of the proceeds repay the secured debt owed by the company.

The receiver's role is to take possession of secured property, sell it, and out of the proceeds repay the secured debt owed by the company.

While a receiver may be appointed in respect of the property of a partnership or an individual, receivership over a company's property is much more common. Receivership over property of a company is regulated by Pt 5.2 (ss 416–434) of the *Corporations Act*. Receivership is discussed in detail in Chapter 23 below.

The appointment of a receiver is not the only right conferred on secured creditors if a company defaults under its loan agreement. They also have the right to personally take possession of secured property. Secured creditors who do this are referred to as "mortgagees in possession". Alternatively, secured creditors may appoint an agent (called an "agent for a mortgagee in possession") to act on their behalf. As the role of an agent for the mortgagee in possession is very similar to that of a receiver, the *Corporations Act* regulates mortgagees in possession and their agents in the same way as receivers. Receivers and mortgagees in possession and their agents are all "controllers" as defined in s 9.

appointment by secured creditors

[22.20] A receiver may be appointed by secured creditors such as debenture-holders or by the court. In most cases, a company enters receivership when a secured creditor appoints a receiver to take control of property secured by a charge that the company has granted to the secured creditor. This is sometimes referred to as "a private appointment".

A secured creditor's right to appoint a receiver arises from the terms of the loan agreement or debenture. This agreement also specifies the property that is subject to the charge. Where the secured property includes the business of the company, the loan agreement also gives the receiver the power to manage the business. In such cases, the receiver is referred to as a "receiver and manager". According to ASIC insolvency statistics, 90 receivers and 533 receiver and managers were appointed during 2003.

A secured creditor's right to appoint a receiver and the specific charged property are set out in the loan agreement.

why would secured creditors appoint a receiver?

[22.25] One of the advantages of receivership for secured creditors is the speed with which it can be implemented. It is not necessary to obtain court approval for the appointment. Further, as receivers must be registered liquidators, they are experienced in managing insolvent companies.

The loan agreement, or debenture, specifies the circumstances in which a secured creditor may appoint a receiver or receiver and manager. In most cases, a receiver is appointed if the company has breached one or more of its obligations under the loan agreement, such as non-payment of interest or principal.

Default in payment is just one event that may trigger a secured creditor's right to appoint a receiver. For example, secured creditors are often given the right to appoint a receiver if the company's business is operating at a loss, ceases to operate or another creditor files an application to wind up the company.

appointment by the court

[22.30] The *Corporations Act* also gives the court the power to appoint a receiver. For example, under s 1323(1)(h) the court may appoint a receiver over the property of a person or a company that is the subject of an ASIC investigation of a suspected contravention of the *Corporations Act*. The purpose of such an appointment is generally limited to protect the interests of the company's creditors by preventing the company's property from being dissipated during the course of the investigation.

duties of receivers

[22.35] The role of a receiver appointed in respect of property secured by a fixed charge is to take possession of the property secured by the charge, sell it and repay the debt due to the secured creditor who appointed them. Any surplus after the sale of the property subject to the fixed charge goes back to the company.

On the other hand, where a receiver has been appointed in respect of property secured by a floating charge, s 433 specifies that before the secured creditor is repaid, proceeds from the sale of the secured property must first go to paying the debts owed to certain unsecured creditors who are given priority in a winding up. These include employee entitlements such as unpaid wages, superannuation contributions and leave entitlements.

A privately appointed receiver's main duties are to the secured creditor who appointed them.

While a privately appointed receiver's main duties are to the secured creditor who appointed them, they owe the debtor company a common law duty to exercise their powers in good faith and not to sacrifice its interests recklessly. In addition, under s 420A, receivers are required to exercise reasonable care in selling the secured property for not less than its market value. These duties recognise that there are other parties whose interests are affected by the insolvency of the debtor company. These include unsecured creditors and directors who have guaranteed the company's debts.

effect of receivership on the company and its directors

The appointment of a receiver does not affect the legal personality of the company.

[22.40] While receivership can have a significant effect on the company and the operation of its business, the appointment of a receiver does not affect the legal personality of the company. It continues to exist as a separate legal entity and remains the legal owner of its property.

The company's board of directors is severly restricted.

Receivership does not displace the company's board of directors. They remain in office but their ability to deal with the secured property is severely restricted. If a receiver and manager is appointed to take control of the company's business, the directors' management powers are superseded by the receiver and manager. Despite this, directors are still subject to their various fiduciary and statutory duties. For example, they must still comply with their obligations to ensure that the company prepares its annual financial reports even though the company's business is under the control of a receiver and manager.

effect of receivership on unsecured creditors

Unsecured creditors of a company in receivership do not lose their rights to take legal proceedings against the company for non-payment of their debts.

[22.45] In contrast to voluntary administration or liquidation, receivership does not result in a moratorium or stay on the commencement of legal proceedings against a company. Unsecured creditors of a company in receivership do not lose their rights to take legal proceedings against the company for non-payment of their debts. However, any rights they may have in respect of the secured property are subordinated to the secured creditor who appointed the receiver. Unsecured creditors may also apply to the court to wind up the company on the grounds of insolvency.

Receivership does not mean that pre-receivership contracts are automatically terminated. However, a receiver, as agent for the company, may decide to repudiate contracts if their continued performance is of no advantage to the conduct of the receivership. If a contract is repudiated, the company will be liable for damages to the other contracting party.

impact of voluntary administration and liquidation on receivership

[22.50] The commencement of voluntary administration has a significant impact on a secured creditor's ability to appoint a receiver. During voluntary administration there is a moratorium or stay of all legal proceedings against the company. This means that secured creditors cannot enforce charges by appointing a receiver over the company's property except with the administrator's or court's consent: s 440B. Secured creditors' rights to enforce charges and appoint a receiver resume after voluntary administration ends unless they have agreed to a deed of company arrangement.

The moratorium need not affect a secured creditor with a charge over the whole, or substantially the whole, of the property of a company. Under s 441A, such a secured creditor has the ability to enforce the charge within the "decision period" and personally take possession of the company's property or appoint a receiver. The "decision period" is defined in s 9 as being within 10 business days of the chargee being given notice of the administrator's appointment.

A company may be in liquidation and receivership at the same time. Creditors may apply to wind up a company on the ground of insolvency even though a receiver has been appointed by a secured creditor. Similarly, a secured creditor may appoint a receiver even though the company is being wound up. A liquidator's role is to look after the interests of unsecured creditors while the receiver represents the secured creditor who made the appointment.

While a receiver's right to take possession and sell the secured property continues despite the liquidation of the company, liquidation terminates the receiver's position as agent for the company and the receiver becomes personally liable for debts incurred in carrying on the company's business after the commencement of liquidation. A receiver may, however, continue to carry on the company's business with either the liquidator's consent or court approval: s 420C.

termination of receivership

[22.55] Receivership terminates when the receiver achieves the object of the appointment. This normally occurs when the secured property is sold and the debt due to the secured creditor is discharged and the debts of the receivership, such as the receiver's cost and fees, are paid. The receiver is obliged to account to the company for any surplus. If the company is not in liquidation, termination of receivership results in a resumption of the directors' control of the company's affairs.

Receivership usually terminates when the secured property is sold and the debt due to the secured creditor is discharged.

The court has the power to terminate a prolonged receivership that may impede an orderly winding up. Under s 434B, a liquidator of a company that is wound up in insolvency may apply to the court for an order that a receiver cease to act. The court may make such an order only if it is satisfied that the objectives for which the receiver was appointed have been largely achieved.

voluntary administration

[22.60] The voluntary administration scheme is regulated by the provisions of Pt 5.3A of the *Corporations Act*. There are two distinct phases of the voluntary administration scheme. The first phase begins with the appointment of a voluntary administrator. The second phase commences at the conclusion of a creditors' meeting that decides the company's future. Depending on the decision made by the creditors at this meeting, there is a smooth transition from voluntary administration to another form of external insolvency administration—liquidation or deed of company arrangement.

Even though the voluntary administration scheme commenced in 1993, it has become one of the most common types of insolvency administrations. According to ASIC insolvency statistics, there were 2,874 voluntary administrations in 2003. The voluntary administration scheme is discussed in detail in Chapter 24 below.

aim of voluntary administration

[22.65] The aim of the voluntary administration provisions of the *Corporations Act* is to maximise the chances of the company or its businesses remaining in existence and, if this is not possible, to achieve a better return to creditors than would result from an immediate winding up: s 435A.

The aim of the voluntary administration provisions of the *Corporations Act* is to maximise the chances of the company or its businesses remaining in existence and, if this is not possible, to achieve a better return to creditors than would result from an immediate winding up.

Voluntary administration involves the appointment of an experienced, independent insolvency practitioner (called an "administrator") who takes complete control of an insolvent company for a relatively short period of time. An administrator's task is to investigate the affairs of the company and to report on whether a compromise or arrangement can be negotiated that would be acceptable to the company and its creditors. Ultimately, however, the fate of the company is determined by its creditors who have the final say as to what should happen to the company after voluntary administration ends. Under s 439C, creditors can choose whether the:

> **company enters into a deed of company arrangement;**
> **company be wound up; or**
> **administration be terminated.**

Voluntary administration is intended to be a better form of administration for an insolvent company than liquidation or a scheme of arrangement under Pt 5.1 of the *Corporations Act*. The voluntary administration procedure is quick to implement and is a relatively cheap form of insolvency administration. It is designed to facilitate the negotiation of compromises or other arrangements with an insolvent company's creditors and to provide for a smooth transition to other types of insolvency administrations with the minimum of expensive court cases and formal creditor or shareholder meetings.

who initiates voluntary administration?

In most cases the decision to put a company into voluntary administration is made by a company's directors.

[22.70] In most cases the decision to put a company into voluntary administration is made by a company's directors and does not require approval of the shareholders, creditors or the court. Directors may appoint an administrator if they believe that the company is insolvent or is likely to become insolvent at some future time: s 436A(1). While it is relatively rare, a company may also be put into voluntary administration by its liquidator or a creditor who has a charge over the whole, or substantially the whole, of a company's property: ss 436B and 436C.

why would directors initiate voluntary administration?

Directors may decide to put their company into voluntary administration because of a number of legislative incentives.

[22.75] Directors are not forced to put a company into voluntary administration. If they do so, they lose their rights to run the company unless they have the administrator's written approval: s 437C. Directors may decide to put their company into voluntary administration for a number of reasons. They may choose to do so to achieve a better outcome for shareholders and creditors. They may also be encouraged to take early action because of a number of legislative incentives.

The insolvent trading provisions, discussed in Chapter 13.5 above, may encourage directors of companies in financial difficulties to appoint an administrator sooner, rather than later. Directors' personal liability to pay compensation for breaching s 588G arises only if their company goes into liquidation: s 588M. Directors may avoid personal liability if they put their company into voluntary administration and ensure that it executes a deed of company arrangement that is acceptable to creditors.

Even if a company is wound up, directors may avoid personal liability for contravening s 588G if, pursuant to s 588H(5), they can establish that they took all reasonable steps to prevent the company from incurring debts when there were reasonable grounds to suspect that it was insolvent. In determining whether the s 588H(5) defence has been proved, s 588H(6) directs the court to have regard to any action the director took with a view to appointing an administrator, when that action was taken, and the results of the action.

Placing an insolvent company in voluntary administration may also be an attractive option for directors who have personally guaranteed their company's debts. While the company is under voluntary administration, s 440J prevents creditors from enforcing the guarantee against the director. Section 440J also prevents creditors from enforcing guarantees of company debts provided by a director's spouse or other relatives.

Income tax legislation may also have the effect of prompting directors to put their company into voluntary administration at an early stage. The PAYG ("pay as you go") tax payment system requires employers to withhold tax attributable to employee wages and salaries and remit the withheld amounts to the Australian Taxation Office on a regular basis. Under ss 222ANA–222AQD of the *Income Tax Assessment Act 1936*, directors of a non-remitting company may be personally liable to pay an amount equal to the company's liability unless they come to an arrangement to ensure that the withheld amounts are remitted or ensure that the company goes into voluntary administration or liquidation.

duration of voluntary administration

[22.80] The *Corporations Act* ensures that a company is under voluntary administration for a relatively short period of time—three or four weeks. The effect of this is to put pressure on all parties concerned to make a decision about the company's future. Further, during voluntary administration there is a stay or moratorium on all claims against the company. The short duration of administration ensures that creditors, particularly secured creditors, are not unduly prejudiced by the moratorium.

Voluntary administration commences on the day an administrator is appointed: s 435C(1). One of the administrator's obligations is to call a meeting of the company's creditors to make a decision about the company's future. The date an administration ends depends on the time that meeting is held and the nature of the decision creditors make at that meeting.

The creditors' meeting to decide the company's future must be held within five days after the end of the "convening period": s 439A(2). The convening period is the period of 21 days beginning on the day administration begins: s 439A(5). The convening period is extended to 28 days if the administration begins in December or is less than 28 days before Good Friday. The convening period may also be extended by the court under either s 439A(6) or s 447A. The period of voluntary administration can also be extended if creditors decide to adjourn their meeting. However, the meeting cannot be adjourned for more than 60 days: s 439B(2).

At the creditors' meeting to decide the company's future, creditors have three alternatives: s 439C. They may resolve that the company execute a deed of company arrangement, the company be wound up or the administration should end.

Voluntary administration ends on the date of the creditors' meeting if the creditors resolve that the company should be wound up or if they decide to end the administration.

If creditors decide that the company execute a deed of company arrangement, the deed must be executed by both the company and the administrator within 21 days after the creditors' meeting and the administration then ends and the company becomes subject to the terms of the deed: s 444B(2). If the company fails to execute the deed within the 21-day period, the administration ends and the company is deemed to have entered into a creditors' voluntary winding up: s 446A(1).

role of the voluntary administrator

[22.85] Administrators take complete control of the company's affairs when they are appointed and directors lose their powers to manage even though they retain their office. Administrators must be registered liquidators: s 448B. This ensures that administrators are experienced insolvency practitioners. Administrators must also be independent of the company, its officers, creditors and the company's auditor: s 448C. From a creditor's perspective, an administrator's insolvency experience and independence is perceived to be one of the advantages of the voluntary administration scheme because often creditors have lost trust and confidence in the abilities of an insolvent company's directors to manage its business.

Administrators take complete control of the company's affairs when they are appointed.

One of the first tasks of an administrator is to convene a creditors' meeting within five business days of appointment: s 436E. At this meeting, creditors have the opportunity to remove the administrator appointed by the directors and appoint someone else as a replacement. At this meeting creditors may also decide whether to appoint a consultative committee of creditors to assist the administrator with matters relating to the administration.

The administrator must form an opinion as to whether it would be in the creditors' interests that the company enter into a deed of company arrangement, end the administration or wind up the company.

As soon as practicable after being appointed, the administrator must investigate the financial position and circumstances of the company: s 438A(a). The administrator must then form an opinion as to whether it would be in the creditors' interests that the company enter into a deed of company arrangement, end the administration or wind up the company: s 438A(b).

Administrators are required to convene a second creditors' meeting. At the second creditors' meeting, creditors are given the opportunity to decide the company's future.

One of the deficiencies of the voluntary administration scheme for large companies with complex businesses is the extremely short time limits imposed by the legislation for the completion of an administrator's investigations and report to creditors. Administrators are required to convene a second creditors' meeting within 21 days of the "convening period". At this meeting, creditors are given the opportunity to decide the company's future. To assist creditors in making their decision, s 439A(4)(a) requires the administrator to give creditors a report about the company's business, property, affairs and financial circumstances. As well as the administrator's recommendation about the future course for the company, the report must set out whether the administrator believes there are any voidable transactions that would be recoverable by a liquidator if the company were wound up. The administrator's report should also indicate whether directors breached their fiduciary or *Corporations Act* duties such as insolvent trading and the prospects of a liquidator recovering compensation from them.

effect of voluntary administration on creditors

While a company is under voluntary administration there is a moratorium or stay of all claims or legal proceedings against the company and guarantors of its debts.

[22.90] With some exceptions, while a company is under voluntary administration there is a moratorium or stay of all claims or legal proceedings against the company and guarantors of its debts: ss 440A–440J. This ensures that administrators have breathing space to carry out their task and prevents the piecemeal break up of the company's property by individual creditors that may undermine the company to the detriment of the majority of its creditors.

During voluntary administration, secured creditors cannot enforce charges over the company's property except with the administrator's or court's consent: s 440B. Secured creditors' rights to enforce charges resume after voluntary administration ends unless they have agreed to a deed of company arrangement. Similarly, owners or lessors cannot recover possession of leased property during administration: s 440C. Owners' and lessors' rights to repossess leased property resume after voluntary administration ends unless they have agreed to a deed of company arrangement.

A secured creditor with a charge over the whole, or substantially the whole, of the property of a company has the ability to enforce the charge within the "decision period" (s 441A) and personally take possession of the company's property or appoint a receiver. The "decision period" is defined in s 9 as being within 10 business days of the chargee being given notice of the administrator's appointment. There is little point in requiring a creditor with security over all of a company's property to be subject to the moratorium and wait until the normal end of voluntary administration before they can enforce their charge and take possession of the company's property.

deeds of company arrangement

[22.95] A deed of company arrangement is one of the possible outcomes for a company that is put into voluntary administration. The s 435A objects of the voluntary administration scheme—to save insolvent companies or their businesses or achieve a better return for their creditors than liquidation—are largely achieved by deeds of company arrangement. In 2003, 714 companies entered into a deed of company arrangement.

A company becomes subject to a deed of company arrangement in the following manner. As discussed above, one of the key tasks of a voluntary administrator is to report to creditors on whether it would be in their interests that the company executes a deed of company arrangement. Other interested parties, such as directors or major shareholders, may also propose deeds of company arrangement. If creditors vote in favour of a proposed company arrangement and the company and the voluntary administrator execute the deed, voluntary administration ends: s 435C(2)(a). The company's voluntary administrator becomes the administrator of the deed unless the creditors appoint someone else: s 444A(2).

types of deeds of company arrangement

[22.100] The *Corporations Act* is extremely flexible as to the terms of a deed of company arrangement so as to enable the arrangement to meet the particular needs and circumstances of the company and its various creditors. Typically, deeds of company arrangement may have the following features:

- **provision for a moratorium under which the company has additional time to pay debts incurred prior to the commencement of voluntary administration. The company, under the control of the deed administrator, is permitted to continue operating its business;**
- **provision for a compromise under which the creditors agree to accept payment of a lesser amount in final settlement of their debts;**
- **a combination of a moratorium and compromise with creditors; and**
- **an orderly sale of all the company's property over an agreed period of time.**

effect of deeds of company arrangement on creditors

[22.105] The moratorium that operates during voluntary administration terminates when a deed of company arrangement is executed. The creditors become subject to the provisions of the deed.

A deed of company arrangement binds all unsecured creditors.

A deed of company arrangement binds all unsecured creditors in relation to any claims that arose on or before the commencement of voluntary administration: s 444D(1). As a result, while the deed is in force, unsecured creditors are not permitted to apply to wind up the company or begin legal action to recover their debts without leave of the court: s 444E.

Secured creditors are in a better position. Their rights to enforce their security and take possession of, and sell, secured property resume with the end of the voluntary administration moratorium. With some exceptions, secured creditors are bound by a deed only if they voted in favour of the deed: s 444D(2). As a result, the terms of a deed must satisfy the needs of secured creditors if the company's continued use of secured property is crucial to the outcome of a deed. Similarly, owners and lessors of property are bound by a deed only if they voted in favour of the deed.

why would creditors agree to a deed of company administration?

[22.110] Under s 439C, the creditors, at the second creditors' meeting during voluntary administration, may resolve that the company execute a deed of company arrangement; that the company should be wound up or that administration should end. The voluntary administration scheme gives them the opportunity to make a cost benefit analysis and decide whether the company's liquidation or a deed of company arrangement produces a better outcome for them. This analysis will include an assessment of the likelihood of a liquidator increasing the amount of the company's assets available for distribution to creditors by successful proceedings against directors for breach of fiduciary or statutory duties such as insolvent trading.

In some cases, directors may be prepared to contribute to funds available for distribution to creditors in a deed of company arrangement from their own personal resources in order to avoid potentially higher claims against themselves if the company were liquidated. This is likely to be the case if, prior to the commencement of voluntary administration, directors have failed to prevent insolvent trading, have received unfair preferences or have breached their fiduciary duties by not taking creditors' interests into account. In addition, directors may be willing to contribute to a deed of company arrangement to regain control over the company's business or purchase some or all of its assets, perhaps for a higher price than would be paid by outsiders. Directors may be in a better position to utilise the company's carry forward tax losses than third party purchasers of the company's shares.

Creditors who supplied goods and services to a company prior to its voluntary administration may be induced to vote in favour of a deed if this results in the company continuing as a customer. Creditors may also vote in favour of a deed if they perceive that the company can trade its way out of financial trouble with more competent management provided by the deed administrator.

liquidation

Liquidation is a form of external administration that ultimately results in the company being deregistered and ceasing to exist as a legal entity.

[22.115] Liquidation (also called "winding up") is a form of external administration that ultimately results in the company being deregistered and ceasing to exist as a legal entity. Liquidation is an orderly process under which the company's affairs are wound up, its property sold, debts owed to its creditors repaid to the extent the value of the company's assets allow and the surplus (if any) distributed among its shareholders.

The *Corporations Act* recognises two modes of liquidation:

> **compulsory liquidation (by order of the court); and**
> **voluntary liquidation.**

There are two forms of voluntary liquidation:

> **members' voluntary winding up; and**
> **creditors' voluntary winding up.**

The common feature of all types of liquidations is the appointment of a qualified, independent insolvency practitioner as the liquidator.

The common feature of all types of liquidations is the appointment of a qualified, independent insolvency practitioner as the liquidator.

In this chapter we are concerned with winding up insolvent companies. Liquidation of such companies may take place in one of two ways. Creditors (or other eligible applicants, such as a director, ASIC or a shareholder) may force the company into liquidation by obtaining a court order to this effect. This is referred to as "compulsory liquidation" (or "compulsory winding up"). In a compulsory winding up, the court appoints the liquidator.

A creditors' voluntary winding up does not require court orders. It may be initiated in a number of ways. For example, a creditors' voluntary winding up is one of the possible outcomes of a voluntary administration: s 439A. In such cases, the voluntary administrator becomes the liquidator: s 446A. A members' voluntary winding up, initiated by a special resolution of the company's shareholders, converts to a creditors' voluntary winding up if the company is insolvent and the creditors have the right to replace the liquidator previously appointed by the shareholders: s 499.

According to the 2003 ASIC insolvency statistics, 3,253 liquidators were appointed pursuant to compulsory liquidations and 3,331 were appointed pursuant to creditors' voluntary windings up. Liquidation is discussed in detail in Chapter 25 below.

aims of liquidation

[22.120] There are three broad aims of the liquidation of insolvent companies. The liquidation provisions of the *Corporations Act* aim to ensure that:

There are three broad aims of the liquidation of insolvent companies.

> **creditors, particularly unsecured creditors, share equally and fairly in the distribution of an insolvent company's insufficient assets;**
> **hopelessly insolvent companies cease trading for the good of the wider business community; and**
> **there is an investigation into an insolvent company's affairs prior to the commencement of the winding up for the purpose of discovering the reasons for the insolvency.**

compulsory liquidation–winding up in insolvency

[22.125] The provisions of Pt 5.4, ss 459A–459T, of the *Corporations Act* regulate compulsory liquidation of an insolvent company. These provisions refer to liquidation in such circumstances as "winding up in insolvency" to emphasise the distinction between the compulsory winding up of solvent and insolvent companies. Compulsory liquidations of solvent companies usually involve disputes between members and are discussed in Chapter 17 above.

Section 459P lists the persons who may apply to the court for a winding up in insolvency. The eligible applicants include creditors, the company, a contributory, a director and ASIC. Winding up in insolvency is usually initiated by an unsecured creditor who has been unsuccessful in getting the company to pay a debt. While secured creditors may also apply to the court for a winding up order, this is rare because secured creditors are able to sell the property secured by a charge and repay their debt out of the proceeds.

Section 459P lists the persons who may apply to the court for a winding up in insolvency.

There are several stages to obtaining a compulsory winding up order. A creditor or other eligible applicant must file an application to wind up a company with the court and set a date for the application to be heard. An application for a winding up in insolvency must be determined within six months after it is made: s 459R. This gives sufficient time for the applicant to comply with other necessary requirements. These include serving a copy of the application on the company, lodging a copy of the application with ASIC and advertising the filing of the application in newspapers and government *Gazette*.

At the hearing of the application, the court must be satisfied that the company is insolvent before it will make an order to wind the company up in insolvency. A creditor may prove that a company is insolvent in a number of ways.

Section 459C(2) contains several circumstances in which the court may presume that a company is insolvent. These presumptions are designed to assist creditors to prove that a debtor company is insolvent for purposes of a winding up application. For example, a company is presumed to be insolvent if it has failed to comply with a statutory demand that the creditor served on the company: s 459C(2)(a). This is the most common way that creditors prove insolvency.

A company is presumed to be insolvent if it has failed to comply with a statutory demand that the creditor served on the company.

A statutory demand is a formal document signed by a creditor that specifies the amount of the debt (at least $2,000, "the statutory minimum") owed by the company. The statutory demand must require the company to pay the amount demanded within 21 days after the demand is served on it: s 459E. If the company fails to comply with the demand 21 days after it is served, it is presumed to be insolvent for purposes of the creditor's subsequent application for winding up in insolvency.

Some creditors serve statutory demands to blackmail debtor companies into paying genuinely disputed debts. Some debtor companies try to delay paying by asserting they have a dispute about the debt even though this has no genuine merit. The *Corporations Act* takes the view that a winding up hearing is not the appropriate forum for deciding the merits of disputed debts.

Section 459G allows a company to apply to the court for an order setting aside a statutory demand served on it. The company's application to set aside may only be made within 21 days after service of the statutory demand. Under s 459H, the court may set aside a statutory demand if it is satisfied that there is a genuine dispute about the existence or amount of the debt or that the company has an offsetting claim against the creditor. The court also has the power to vary the demand if the "substantiated amount" of the debt is equal to or greater than the $2,000 statutory minimum.

A creditor may also prove that a company is insolvent by providing evidence that a company is unable to pay its debts as and when they become due and payable: s 95A. This is often difficult to prove in practice because the conclusion that a company is insolvent requires an examination of its entire financial position and ought not to be drawn simply from evidence of a company's temporary lack of liquidity. Insolvency is proved by evidence of a company's inability to pay debts as they fall due from its cash resources or from selling or mortgaging its assets: *Sandell v Porter* (1966) 115 CLR 666.

creditors' voluntary winding up

A creditors' voluntary winding up does *not* involve court orders.

[22.130] Unlike a winding up in insolvency, putting a company into a creditors' voluntary winding up does *not* involve court orders. A company may enter into a creditors' voluntary winding up in a number of different ways.

The *Corporations Act* provides for a smooth transition from voluntary administration to a creditors' voluntary winding up.

The *Corporations Act* provides for a smooth transition from voluntary administration to a creditors' voluntary winding up. Under s 439C, creditors of a company under administration may resolve that the company be wound up. Creditors will pass such a resolution if they decide that a deed of company arrangement is not in their best interests. A company will also convert from being under administration to a creditors' voluntary winding up if it contravenes s 444B(2) by failing to execute a deed of company arrangement that was approved by its creditors: s 446A(1)(b). A company that is subject to a deed of company arrangement also converts to a creditors' voluntary winding up if its creditors pass a resolution terminating the deed and that the company be wound up: s 446A(1)(c).

A creditors' voluntary winding up may also stem from a members' voluntary winding up.

A creditors' voluntary winding up may also stem from a members' voluntary winding up. Where a shareholders' meeting is called to pass a special resolution to wind up the company under a member's voluntary winding up, its directors are required to provide the shareholders with a declaration of solvency: s 494. The company must call a creditors' meeting if the declaration of solvency is not provided or if the directors form the view that the company is unable to pay its debts. The creditors' meeting must be held either on the day of the shareholders' meeting or the next day: s 497. If shareholders pass the winding up resolution, it proceeds as a creditors' voluntary winding up and the creditors have the ultimate say as to who will be the liquidator. A members' voluntary winding up may also convert into a creditors' voluntary winding up if the liquidator appointed by the members forms the opinion that the company is insolvent even though the directors made a solvency declaration.

powers of a liquidator

When a company is placed in liquidation, the liquidator takes complete control of the company.

[22.135] When a company is placed in liquidation, the liquidator takes complete control of the company. Sections 477 and 506 give liquidators extensive powers. These include the ability to:

> **carry on the company's business so far as is necessary for the beneficial disposal or winding up of that business;**
> **sell all or any part of the company's property; and**
> **bring or defend legal proceedings in the name of the company.**

Liquidators are given extensive powers to access company books and obtain information from the officers and employees: ss 477(3), 483(1) and 530A. In addition, anyone who may be able to provide information and assistance about insolvent companies can be summoned by the court to attend an examination of an inquisitorial nature under ss 596A and 596B. Liquidators often initiate such examinations to:

- facilitate the recovery of property belonging to the company;
- discover whether the conduct of directors and officers led to its insolvency; and
- investigate possible causes of action against third parties.

effects of winding up on the company and on creditors

[22.140] Winding up has a significant impact on unsecured creditors. Prior to liquidation, every creditor is free to pursue their own legal action to enforce payment of their debts. This right is lost once liquidation commences. A creditor's pre-liquidation right to enforce their debts through legal action is replaced by an orderly, collective process that is controlled by the company's liquidator.

On winding up, a creditor's pre-liquidation right to enforce their debts through legal action is replaced by an orderly, collective process that is controlled by the company's liquidator.

table 22.2 effects of winding up on the company and on creditors

The company	Creditors
> A company continues to exist as a legal entity even though it has been placed into liquidation. > Liquidators take complete control of the company. > Directors lose their powers to manage the company's affairs: s 471A. > Shareholders lose their right to transfer shares and cannot pass resolutions at general meetings.	> Secured creditors are largely unaffected by the winding up of a debtor company. Creditors' rights to take possession and sell property secured by a charge are unaffected: s 471C. > Unsecured creditors must lodge a proof of debt and are entitled to a distribution only after secured creditors have been paid in full. > Unsecured creditors generally participate in distributions on the basis of receiving equal proportions of their debts.

division of assets

[22.145] One of the main tasks of a liquidator is to sell the company's property and divide the proceeds among the persons who are entitled. A fundamental principle of insolvency law is that creditors are paid first and then the surplus (if any) is divided among the company's shareholders.

A fundamental principle of insolvency law is that creditors are paid first and then the surplus (if any) is divided among the company's shareholders.

Creditors must prove their debts before they are entitled to share in the division of the company's assets. If there are sufficient funds available, a creditor whose proof of debt is admitted by the liquidator is repaid in full. Such repayments are referred to as "dividends". As a general rule, secured creditors are unaffected if the debtor company goes into liquidation and are not obliged to prove their debts. Secured creditors retain their rights to sell the secured property and repay themselves out of the proceeds.

All unsecured creditors with provable debts participate equally in the distribution of the company's assets on a winding up. If there are insufficient funds available to meet them all in full, they are paid proportionately.

The policy of the *Corporations Act* is that all unsecured creditors with provable debts participate equally in the distribution of the company's assets on a winding up. If there are insufficient funds available to meet them all in full, they are paid proportionately. This is called the "pari passu rule".

Certain unsecured debts are given preferential treatment and have priority in repayment ahead of all other unsecured debts.

Certain unsecured debts are given preferential treatment by ss 556–564 and have priority in repayment ahead of all other unsecured debts. While these statutory priorities detract from the pari passu rule, they are justified because they assist an orderly winding up and the general public acceptance of the fairness in recognising the special position of employees of an insolvent company.

Section 556 ranks various types of preferential debts in order of priority of repayment. If there are sufficient funds to pay preferential debts in the first rank, they are paid in full. If there is a surplus it is distributed to the next rank of preferential debts and so on. Where there are insufficient funds to pay all preferential debts within a particular rank, those creditors are repaid an equal proportionate amount.

recovery of pre-liquidation transactions

[22.150] Certain transactions between an insolvent company and other persons entered into before the commencement of winding up can have the effect of reducing the amount available for distribution to creditors when the company is wound up. Once appointed, a liquidator may apply to the court for orders making certain pre-liquidation transactions voidable and recover the value of any property lost as a result of the transaction for the benefit of the general body of unsecured creditors of the company.

A liquidator may apply to the court for orders making certain pre-liquidation transactions voidable and recover the value of any property lost.

Chapter 25 below discusses the various types of pre-liquidation transactions. In this chapter we only consider unfair preferences and uncommercial transactions.

Under s 588FA(1), a transaction that takes place prior to the commencement of winding up between a company and a creditor is an unfair preference if it results in the creditor receiving, in respect of a debt owed to the creditor, more than the creditor would receive in respect of the debt if the transaction were set aside and the creditor were to prove for the debt in a winding up. Repaying all or part of a debt due to an unsecured creditor is an example of an unfair preference. To the extent that an unsecured debt is repaid prior to liquidation, the creditor receives 100 per cent of the amount repaid. If the repayment did not occur and the company went into liquidation due to its insolvency, the unsecured creditor would have been entitled to share pari passu with other creditors of equal rank. As a result of being repaid prior to liquidation, the repaid unsecured creditor receives an advantage over the company's other unsecured creditors. This is contrary to the pari passu rule that provides for equal treatment of creditors in a winding up.

Under s 588FB(1), a transaction of the company that occurs prior to the commencement of winding up is an uncommercial transaction if it may be expected that a reasonable person in the company's circumstances would not have entered into the transaction. Examples of uncommercial transactions include gifts made by the company, sales of company property for less than market value and company purchases at more than market value. Section 588FB is designed to prevent pre-liquidation disposals of company property that result in the recipients receiving a gift or obtaining a bargain of such magnitude that cannot be explained by normal commercial practice.

Before a liquidator can avoid a transaction as an unfair preference or uncommercial transaction, the liquidator must satisfy the court that it was an insolvent transaction and a voidable transaction as defined in ss 588FC and 588FE, respectively. An unfair preference or uncommercial transaction is an insolvent transaction if it was entered into at a time when the company was insolvent or the company became insolvent because of entering the transaction. A company is insolvent if it is unable to pay its debts as and when they fall due: s 95A. The s 588E presumptions of insolvency assist a liquidator in proving that a company was insolvent for purposes of establishing that a transaction was an insolvent transaction.

An insolvent transaction is regarded as a voidable transaction if it was entered into during a certain period prior to the "relation-back day" as defined in s 9. In the case of a court-ordered winding up, the relation-back day is the date of filing the application for winding up with the court. Section 588FE sets different time periods prior to the relation-back day depending on whether the insolvent transaction is an unfair preference or uncommercial transaction.

An insolvent transaction that is an unfair preference is a voidable transaction if it was entered into either during the six months ending on the relation-back day or between the relation-back day and the day the winding up commenced: s 588FE(2). An insolvent transaction that is an uncommercial transaction is a voidable transaction if it was entered into during the two years ending on the relation-back day: s 588FE(3). If a "related entity" (defined in s 9) is party to an insolvent transaction, it is a voidable transaction if it was entered into during the four years ending on the relation-back day: s 588FE(4).

Under s 588FF, the court may make a variety of orders where it is satisfied that a transaction was a voidable transaction. For example, where the voidable transaction was an unfair preference, the court can order that the creditor refund the company money the creditor was paid under the transaction. A creditor who does this then stands in line with the other unsecured creditors and may prove for the debt in the winding up.

Section 588FG(2) protects persons who are parties to a voidable transaction. The court cannot make an s 588FF order prejudicing the rights or interests of a person who:

> **became a party to the voidable transaction in good faith; and**
> **had no reasonable grounds for suspecting that the company was insolvent; and**
> **provided valuable consideration under the transaction or changed their position in reliance on the transaction.**

schemes of arrangement

[22.155] The arrangement and reconstruction provisions of Pt 5.1, ss 410–415, of the *Corporations Act* regulate schemes of compromise or arrangement. Such schemes are a form of external administration that enables the rights and liabilities of shareholders and creditors of a company to be reorganised. The aim of a scheme of arrangement is to obtain a binding agreement that modifies, reorganises or alters the legal rights of creditors and shareholders.

The aim of a scheme of arrangement is to obtain a binding agreement that modifies, reorganises or alters the legal rights of creditors and shareholders.

There are several types of schemes of arrangement. A scheme may involve a moratorium or compromise of creditors' claims against a debtor company with the company being managed by an independent, insolvency practitioner as scheme administrator. A scheme may also provide for a "debt for equity swap" in which creditors take up shares in a debtor company. Schemes of arrangement are also used in a non-insolvency context to facilitate a merger between two or more companies. In this context, a scheme of arrangement may be used as an alternative to a takeover.

Setting up a scheme of arrangement is a complex, expensive and time-consuming process. The *Corporations Act* does not regulate the types of schemes that can be established. Instead, the legislation provides a mechanism for initiating a scheme, obtaining approval of the scheme and detailed procedural requirements for the duration of an approved scheme.

To a large extent, the voluntary administration provisions of Pt 5.3A of the *Corporations Act*, particularly those that deal with deeds of company arrangements, can achieve similar outcomes for insolvent companies and their creditors as moratorium and compromise schemes of arrangement. The voluntary administration is a far more popular means of dealing with companies in financial difficulties than schemes of arrangement because voluntary administration is swifter, cheaper and more flexible.

Initiating a scheme of arrangement is expensive because it requires an application to be made to the court for an order to convene meetings of shareholders and creditors. A draft explanatory statement that explains the effect of the proposal must be provided to the court and a copy given to the company's shareholders and creditors and ASIC. If the court is satisfied with the draft explanatory statement it will order that the various meetings be held. At these meetings, the various parties consider and vote on a proposed scheme. If the necessary shareholder and creditor approvals are obtained, there must be another court hearing to obtain formal court approval of the scheme. The court considers whether the proposed scheme is fair and equitable between the different classes of shareholders and creditors.

bibliography...

Annetta, V "Priority Rights in Insolvency—The Doctrinal Basis for Equity's Intervention" (1992) 20 ABLR 311.

Australian Law Reform Commission. "General Insolvency Inquiry" (1988) ALRC 45. Bennetts, K J "Dealing with Winding Up Applications Following the Appointment of an Administrator" (2000) 18 C & SLJ 41.

Brown, M "The Priority of the Expenses and Remuneration of an Administrator or Provisional Liquidator in the Winding-up of a Company" (1998) 9 JBFLP 127.

Darvas, P "Employees Rights and Entitlements and Insolvency: Regulatory Rationale, Legal Issues and Proposed Solutions" (1999) 17 C & SLJ 103.

Dean, M "International Insolvencies: The Difficulties, the Traditional Solution and the Ideal" (2001) 9 Insolv LJ 88.

Duns, J "'Insolvency': Problems of Concept, Definition and Proof" (2000) 28 ABLR 22.

Duthie, L "The Priority of Retrenchment Payments in Liquidation or Receivership" (1992) 20 ABLR 378.

Farrar, J "Corporate Group Insolvencies, Reform and the United States Experience" (2000) 8 Insolv LJ 148.

Glover, J & Duns, J "Insolvency Administrations at General Law: Fiduciary Obligations of Company Receivers, Voluntary Administrators and Liquidators" (2001) 9 Insolv LJ 130.

Gronow, M "Secured Creditors of Insolvent Companies: Do They Get Too Good a Deal?" (1993) 1 Insolv LJ 199.

Hamilton, G "An Insolvency Riddle: When is a Debt Which is Due Not a Debt Which is Due and Payable?" (1997) 5 Insolv LJ 78.

Hammond, C "Are Receivers and Administrators Liable for the Wages of Company Employees Retained after their Appointment?" (1997) 5 Insolv LJ 136.

Keay, A "The Unity of Insolvency Legislation: Time for a Re-think?" (1999) 7 Insolv LJ 4.

Keenan, P "Investigations by External Administrators" (1995) 13 C & SLJ 368.

Koeck, W J & Ramsay, I M "The Importance of Distinguishing between Different Categories of Creditors for the Purposes of Company Law" (1994) 12 C & SLJ 105.

Morrison, D "When is a Company Insolvent?" (2002) 10 Insolv LJ 4.

Noakes, D "Corporate Groups and the Duties of Directors: Protecting the Employee or the Insolvent Employer?" (2001) 29 ABLR 124.

Noakes, D "Dogs on the Wharves: Corporate Groups and the Waterfront Dispute" (1999) 11 Aust Jnl of Corp Law 27.

O'Donovan, J "The Effect of Liquidation upon Receivers' Agency and Powers" (1993) 11 C & SLJ 374.

O'Donovan, J "The Interactions of Winding Up and Receivership" (1979) 53 ALJ 264.

Omar, P J "Themes and movements in international insolvency law" (2004) 12 Insolv LJ 159.

Powers, L "Insolvency Law and Management: The Effect of the Liquidation on the Agency of a Receiver" (1999) 10 JBFLP 249.

Purcell, "The Contrasting Approach of Law and Accounting to the Defining of Solvency and Associated Directors' Declarations" (2002) 10 Insolv LJ 192.

Rheinhardt, G "The Availability of Tracing to the Insolvency Administrator—Is the Remedy Adequate?" (1996) 4 Insolv LJ 74.

Robinson, D "Remuneration of Corporate Insolvency Practitioners" (2000) 8 Insolv LJ 20.

Symes, C "Remuneration, Rent and 'Requisite' Costs: The 3 R's of Insolvency's Administrative Expense Priority" (2000) 11 Aust Jnl of Corp Law 149.

Symes, C "The Dawn of Green Corporate Insolvency Law: Environmental Accountability Creeping Over the Horizon" (1998) 9 Aust Jnl of Corp Law 64.

Taylor, T "Employee Entitlements in Corporate Insolvency Administrations" (2000) 8 Insolv LJ 32.

Thompson, D "Insolvency practitioner's costs: A tough new world?" (2005) 13 Insolv LJ 84.

Wyatt, A & Mason, R "Legal and Accounting Regulatory Framework for Corporate Groups: Implications for Insolvency in Group Operations" (1998) 16 C & SLJ 424.

revision questions on the material in this chapter ...

- Please see eQuiz at **http://www.thomson.com.au/academic** for multiple choice questions and answers.
- For further corporations law links and material please refer to the Lipton-Herzberg website at **http://www.lipton-herzberg.com.au**

chapter twenty-three

receivership

key points ...

- Receivership is a form of external administration that involves the appointment of an independent, experienced insolvency practitioner called a "receiver". The role of a receiver appointed by a secured creditor is to take possession of secured property, sell it and out of the proceeds, repay the secured debt owed by the company. Receivership is therefore an effective means whereby a secured creditor can enforce rights in relation to the debt without recourse to the courts.

- Where the secured property includes the business of a debtor company, the terms of a debenture or other secured loan agreement often gives a receiver wide powers to manage the business of the company. This is done in order to maximise the return to the secured creditor. Such a receiver is known as a "receiver and manager".

- The court may also appoint a receiver. Such appointments are usually where the secured assets are in jeopardy. A court-appointed receiver is usually appointed for specific purposes and for a limited duration.

- Receivers are given wide powers in carrying out their roles. An important power is to sell the company's secured property for the purpose of discharging the secured debt. Receivers owe certain common law duties to the debtor company to exercise this power in good faith. Receivers are included in the definition of "officer" and are therefore subject to the duties imposed on officers such as directors. Receivers are also under a statutory duty to take reasonable care in selling secured assets.

- Where a receiver is appointed over property secured by a floating charge, the receiver must repay certain unsecured debts ahead of the amount owed to the floating charge secured creditor. These include specified employee entitlements such as unpaid wages.

- Receivers are liable for certain debts incurred by them in the course of the receivership. This encourages persons to continue dealing with a company in receivership and enables the receiver to carry on the company's business. As an agent of the company, a receiver is entitled to be reimbursed by the company. A receiver will generally obtain an indemnity from the appointing creditor so as to be protected from personal liability.

receivers and controllers

Initiated by a secured creditor, receivership is a form of external administration a receiver.

[23.05] Receivership is a form of external administration that involves the appointment of an independent, experienced insolvency practitioner called a "receiver". The role of a receiver appointed by a secured creditor is to take possession of secured property, sell it and out of the proceeds, repay the secured debt owed by the company. Receivership is therefore an effective means whereby a secured creditor can enforce rights in relation to the debt without recourse to the courts.

Historically, receivership was an early method by which a creditor, such as a mortgagee, could safeguard their equitable interest in the secured property. The creditor could apply to the court for the appointment of a receiver to collect rent and profits and apply these to payment of the outstanding debt. Creditors later developed the practice of requesting the borrower to make the appointment, thereby avoiding the need to apply to the court. Creditors then began to insist that they be given the contractual the right to appoint a receiver and in order to better protect their securities, the receiver was given wide powers to manage the debtor's business and gain control over secured assets. It was generally provided in the loan agreement that the receiver was to be appointed as agent for the borrower in order to enable the creditor to avoid liability for the receiver's acts or omissions.

ASIC and the Insolvency Practitioners Association (IPA) publish an information sheet for creditors that gives an overview of receivership. This information sheet is available on the ASIC website and iis linked to the Lipton-Herzberg Corporate Insolvency Pathway at **http://www.lipton-herzberg.com.au/secure/pathways-corporate-insolvency.html**

receivership

[23.10] A company enters receivership when a receiver is appointed in respect of some or all of its property. Sections 416–434 contain provisions that apply when a company enters receivership or an agent for a mortgagee in possession takes control of its assets. These provisions, however, are not an exclusive statement of the law concerning the subject as certain aspects are left to the general law.

A company enters receivership when a receiver is appointed in respect of some or all of its property.

The *Corporations Act* does not define the term "receiver" comprehensively. At common law, a receiver is a person who is appointed to collect and receive the debts and other property belonging to another person. "Receivership" is not a term that applies exclusively to company law. A receiver can be appointed whenever an impartial person is required to collect and receive debts and other assets. For example, a receiver may be appointed to collect the assets of a partnership pending the resolution of disputes between the partners.

In Chapter 11 above, we saw that debenture trust deeds usually provide for the appointment of a receiver in the event that the company defaults in its obligations under the trust deed. In such cases, receivership is a method of enforcing a debenture. The receiver collects and sells the property secured by the debenture on behalf of the debenture-holders and distributes the proceeds to them. However, a receiver can be appointed in circumstances other than pursuant to a debenture. The circumstances when a receiver can be appointed are discussed below, para [23.35].

distinction between "receiver" and "receiver and manager"

[23.15] Both the *Corporations Act* and the general law distinguish between a "receiver" and a "receiver and manager". The distinction between these terms was explained in *Re Manchester & Milford Railway Co* (1880) 14 Ch D 645. Lord Jessel MR stated:

> **< "A receiver" is a term which was well known in the Court of Chancery, as meaning a person who receives rents or other income, paying ascertained outgoings, but who does not, if I may say so, manage the property in the sense of buying or selling or any thing of that kind ... If it was desired to continue the trade at all it was necessary to appoint a manager, or a receiver and manager as it was generally called. He could buy and sell and carry on the trade ... So that there was a well-drawn distinction between the two. The receiver merely took the income and paid necessary outgoings and the manager carried on the trade or business. >**

Both a receiver and a receiver manager of the property of a corporation are included in the s 9 definition of "officer". Under s 90, a receiver of the property of a body corporate is deemed to be also a manager of the corporation if that person manages the affairs or has power under the terms of the appointment to manage the affairs of the body corporate.

Both a receiver and a receiver manager of the property of a corporation are included in the s 9 definition of "officer".

It is usual for receivers to be appointed with wide management powers. Further, s 420 gives wide powers to all receivers, including the power to carry on the business of the corporation. For the purposes of Pt 5.2, ss 416–434 of the *Corporations Act*, a receiver in relation to property of a corporation includes a receiver and manager unless a contrary intention appears.

agents for mortgagees in possession

[23.20] Secured creditors have an alternative to receivership if a debtor company defaults under its loan agreement. They have the right to take possession of secured property personally and are referred to as "mortgagees in possession". Secured creditors may also appoint an agent (called an "agent for a mortgagee in possession") to act on their behalf.

In many respects, the roles of a receiver and agent for a mortgagee in possession are similar. As discussed below, the *Corporations Act* governs many aspects of the receiver's appointment, powers, liabilities and duties. Until the 1992 amendments, agents for the mortgagee in possession were largely unregulated by the legislation.

The practice of appointing an agent for a mortgagee in possession became common during the 1980s. The appointment of an agent for a mortgagee in possession, rather than a receiver to take control of a company's business, arose largely to enable secured creditors to avoid certain priorities including the priority of the Commissioner of Taxation under s 221P of the *Income Tax Assessment Act 1936* (Cth). This section gave the Commissioner of Taxation a priority for unpaid tax ahead of secured creditors if a trustee was appointed. "Trustee" was expressly defined to include a receiver but was held not to include a mortgagee in possession: *Deputy Commissioner of Taxation v General Credits Ltd* (1987) 5 ACLC 1103. This priority has now been abolished and an agent for the mortgagee in possession is now subject to the other priorities. These amendments have largely done away with the advantages of a mortgagee appointing an agent.

controllers

[23.25] Amendments made in 1992 ensured that mortgagees in possession and their agents are subject to the same duties and obligations as receivers. A number of important provisions formerly only applicable to receivers were amended so as to expand their operation to "controllers". Receivers, mortgagees in possession and their agents all are referred to as "controllers".

Receivers, mortgagees in possession and their agents all are referred to as "controllers".

Under s 9, a "controller" in relation to property of a corporation is:

- **a receiver, or receiver and manager, of that property; or**
- **anyone else who (whether or not as agent for the corporation) is in possession or has control of that property for the purpose of enforcing a charge.**

Some provisions apply only to "managing controllers". These are defined in s 9 as being receiver managers or other controllers who have the power to manage the corporation to which they are appointed in addition to merely taking possession of the charged property.

who may be a receiver?

[23.30] As a general rule, only a registered liquidator can be appointed as a receiver: s 418(1)(d). This requirement ensures that a receiver has certain minimum educational qualifications and experience. The registration of liquidators is discussed in Chapter 25 below. Only natural persons can become registered liquidators and hence receivers. However, certain authorised corporations, such as authorised trustee companies, may act as receivers, even though they are not registered liquidators: s 418(3).

As a general rule, only a registered liquidator can be appointed as a receiver.

Section 418(1) disqualifies certain persons from being appointed or acting as receiver of the property or part of the property of a corporation. The purpose of these disqualifications is to ensure that a receiver is independent of the company and its secured creditors. The disqualified persons are:

Certain persons are disqualified from being appointed or acting as a receiver.

> **a mortgagee of any property of the corporation;**
> **an auditor or officer of the corporation;**
> **an officer of any body corporate that is a mortgagee of any property of the corporation;**
> **an officer of a body corporate related to the corporation; or**
> **a person who has, at any time within the immediately preceding 12 months, been an officer or promoter of the corporation or of a related body corporate. ASIC may, if it thinks fit, waive this exclusion.**

Since s 9 defines an officer to include a person who is a receiver, the effect of s 418(1) is to disqualify a person who already acts as such in respect of part of the company's property from being appointed as receiver in respect of other property of the company. Section 418(2) overcomes this. Under that provision, an officer in s 418(1) does not include a person who is already a receiver.

appointment of a receiver

[23.35] A receiver or receiver and manager can be appointed in a number of ways, but is usually appointed by either secured creditors such as debenture-holders or by the court.

appointment by secured creditors

[23.40] It is usual for a debenture trust deed to provide for the appointment of a receiver or receiver and manager if the company defaults in its obligations under the debenture. Some secured loan agreements make similar provisions. The *Corporations Act* refers to the appointment of a receiver in such circumstances as an appointment under an instrument. The appointment of a receiver by debenture-holders is also referred to as a "private appointment" or an appointment "out of court".

A debenture trust deed usually gives debenture-holders or their trustee the power to appoint a receiver if the borrowing company defaults in paying any due instalment. Default in payment is not the only occurrence that triggers the right to appoint a receiver. Most debentures allow a receiver to be appointed in a wide variety of situations other than the company's default. For example, it is quite common for a trust deed to permit a receiver to be appointed if:

A debenture trust deed usually gives debenture-holders or their trustee the power to appoint a receiver if the borrowing company defaults.

> **the company ceases to carry on its business or is operating at a loss;**
> **any person files an application to wind up the company;**
> **the company reduces its capital; or**
> **the security is put at risk by a failure to maintain or insure it.**

In cases where large corporations become insolvent, it may be advantageous for the debenture-holder to appoint more than one receiver manager to act jointly and severally. The appointment of joint and several receivers must be specifically authorised by the debenture deed: *Velcrete Pty Ltd v Melson* (1995) 13 ACLC 799.

In *NZI Securities (Aust) Ltd v Poignand* (1994) 12 ACLC 550, the court stated that:

< a receiver is appointed when the document of appointment is handed to the receiver by a person having authority to appoint in circumstances in which it may fairly be said that he was appointing the receiver and where the receiver accepts the appointment. >

The formalities for the appointment of a receiver are governed by general law, which does not require the appointment to be under the company seal.

defective appointment

Secured creditors must comply strictly with the terms of the debenture when appointing a receiver.

[23.45] Secured creditors must comply strictly with the terms of the debenture when appointing a receiver. However, a secured creditor may misstate the grounds for appointment of a receiver but still make a valid appointment on other grounds that existed at the time of appointment. The secured creditor does not have to possess knowledge of these grounds at the time of appointment: *Retail Equity Pty Ltd v Custom Credit Corp Ltd* (1991) 9 ACLC 404. Where a receiver discovers a breach of the debenture, this may be relevant to justify the receiver's appointment: *Canberra Advance Bank Ltd v Benny* (1993) 11 ACLC 148.

If there is some defect in the appointment, a receiver who takes possession of the secured property may be liable in damages to the company as a trespasser. An appointment of a receiver may also be ineffective because of some defect in the debenture itself. For example, if the charge created by the debenture requires registration under s 262 and it is not registered, it is unenforceable as against the liquidator or administrator of the company: s 266.

Section 267 may affect the validity of the appointment of a receiver pursuant to a charge granted by a company in favour of its officers or their associates. Under that section, where a company creates a charge in favour of its officers or their associates and they purport to take a step in the enforcement of the charge within six months of its creation, the charge is void unless prior leave of the court is obtained to enforce it. The appointment of a receiver (or the entry into possession of the secured property) is regarded as "a step in the enforcement of the charge": s 267(2). A court may grant leave to enforce the charge if the company was solvent immediately after the creation of the charge and if it is just and equitable in the circumstances to do so.

declaration of validity of appointment

[23.50] Section 418A allows a receiver, a mortgagee who has entered into possession, the corporation or any of its creditors to apply to the court for an order declaring whether or not the appointment or the entry into possession was valid. The appointment or entering into of possession may be invalid either because the charge itself was invalid or the appointment or entering into possession was invalid under an otherwise valid charge.

relief where receiver improperly appointed

[23.55] Section 419(3) protects receivers and other controllers from being sued because of some defect in their appointment. That provision gives the court power to grant relief to an improperly appointed controller, if it is satisfied that when the person assumed control of the corporation's property there was a reasonable belief that the appointment was proper. Where this is the case the court may transfer liability for the improper appointment to the person who made the improper appointment.

Despite s 419(3), prudent receivers usually obtain an indemnity from the secured creditor to protect themselves from being personally liable as a consequence of a defective appointment or invalid debenture.

appointment by the court

ASIC application: s 1323

ASIC may apply to the court for the appointment of a receiver.

[23.60] Section 1323(1)(h) allows ASIC to apply to the court for the appointment of a receiver of the property of a person or a company in the following circumstances:

> **where an investigation is being carried out under the *ASIC Act* in relation to an act or omission by a person that constitutes an offence under the *Corporations Act*;**

- **where a prosecution has been instituted against a person for a contravention of the *Corporations Act*; or**
- **where a civil proceeding has been instituted against a person under the *Corporations Act*.**

The court may appoint the receiver if it considers it necessary or desirable to do so for the purpose of protecting the interests of any persons to whom the person or company may be liable. The appointment of a receiver under s 1323(1)(h) is a drastic step not to be taken lightly. The person seeking the remedy must show that the interests of the persons to whom the company is or may become liable require protection and a lesser remedy would be inadequate: *Beach Petroleum NL v Johnson* (1993) 11 ACLC 75.

Section 1323(1) also enables the court to make other orders apart from the appointment of a receiver. The purpose of the section is to freeze property of a person where there is an investigation being carried out by ASIC into conduct that contravenes or may contravene the *Corporations Act*. The freezing of the property is to benefit a person who may bring an action based on a breach of the legislation by providing property against which judgment may be enforced.

The powers of a receiver appointed under s 1323(1)(h) are limited to preventing a company from dealing with its property and do not extend to sales of assets and investigations to determine whether offences had been committed: *ASC v Aust-Home Investments Ltd* (1993) 11 ACLC 438. Section 1323 is discussed in Chapter 21 above.

where it is just and convenient

[23.65] A receiver or receiver and manager may also be appointed by a State or Territory Supreme Court pursuant to provisions in legislation governing the jurisdiction of such courts. For example, s 62 of the *Supreme Court Act 1958* (Vic), gives the court power to appoint a receiver where it appears to be "just and convenient" to do so. This enables the court to appoint a receiver on the application of a mortgagee if the company defaults in payment of the secured debt.

The court can also appoint a receiver where the secured property is in jeopardy, even though the company has not defaulted or the events that justify the appointment of a receiver by debenture-holders have not yet occurred. For example, the property may be in jeopardy if the company's unsecured creditors threaten liquidation proceedings. The court may also appoint a receiver when a company defaults under several debentures and it would be more convenient to have the one person acting in relation to all the debentures.

case note

In *Bond Brewing Holdings Ltd v National Australia Bank Ltd* (1990) 8 ACLC 330, it was held that that the court had no power to permit an unsecured creditor of a company in financial difficulties to apply for the appointment of a court-appointed receiver to manage the affairs of the company in the absence of consent or non-opposition from the company. Even where the company or a friendly creditor applies for such an appointment, it would not be made unless the court was satisfied that the substantial body of creditors supported it.

In most cases, the person appointed by order of the court is appointed as a receiver and manager. Because of the courts' general reluctance to interfere in the internal management of companies, the duration of a receiver's appointment is relatively short. The appointment is usually made for a specific purpose such as the sale of the company's business as a going concern, the investigation of the conduct of directors or to safeguard the company's assets.

The court has a discretion to extend the period of receivership even where the grounds upon which the appointment was made have gone. If there is a reasonable expectation that a claim will be made, it may be necessary to retain the security that the receivership gives until the claim is dealt with: *Corporate Affairs Commission v ASC Timber Pty Ltd* (1993) 11 ACLC 141. In this case, a receivership was extended for six months to allow a liquidator and the ASC reasonable time to make a claim.

Section 427 requires a person who obtains a court order for the appointment of a receiver or appoints a controller under powers contained in an instrument or for the purpose of enforcing a charge, to lodge a notice to this effect with ASIC within seven days of the order or appointment. Further, the fact that a controller has been appointed must also be advertised in the Government *Gazette* within 21 days after the appointment.

privately appointed and court-appointed receivers

[23.70] Privately appointed receiver/managers have different functions than court-appointed receiver/managers. In *Duffy v Super Centre Development Corp Ltd* [1967] 1 NSWR 382, Street J stated:

> **< There is some contrast to be borne in mind between the function of a privately appointed receiver and the function of a court-appointed receiver, and I use the word "receiver" as a compendious word encompassing a receiver and manager. To some extent the privately appointed receiver, particularly in current commercial practice, makes an effort to restore the financial prosperity of the company whose affairs he has been appointed to administer by a debenture-holder. A court-appointed receiver does not fill the same position. He is not so much what might be described as a company doctor, but rather his function is that of a company caretaker. His function is not so much to restore profitability. It is rather to preserve those assets of the company upon which its fortunes may be dependent, and to preserve its potentiality for earning profits in the future. >**

A court-appointed receiver/manager is regarded as an officer of the court. This is also the case with a liquidator appointed by order of the court. Court-appointed receiver managers are under more stringent duties than receivers appointed out of court. The duties of receivers are discussed below. Debentures usually provide for the appointment of a receiver or receiver and manager to avoid the legal costs associated with applications to the court for the appointment.

effect of appointment

The appointment of a privately appointed receiver does not affect the legal personality of the company, nor does it displace the board of directors.

[23.75] The appointment of a privately appointed receiver does not affect the legal personality of the company, nor does it displace the board of directors. The company continues to be the legal owner of the secured property even though a receiver is appointed and takes possession of that property. The appointment of a receiver and manager or other controller does, however, affect the ability of the directors to exercise their powers of management.

Despite the appointment of a receiver and manager or controller, the directors retain certain powers. They can still initiate legal proceedings in the name of the company under s 418A to challenge the validity of the appointment of the receiver or other controller.

case note

In *Deangrove Pty Ltd v Commonwealth Bank of Australia* [2001] FCA 173, it was held that where a company in receivership has a claim against the debenture-holder and the receiver declines to pursue the claim, the directors are entitled to initiate and maintain proceedings in the name of the company, provided the directors offer the company a satisfactory indemnity against the costs. The requirement for an indemnity against cost is designed to ensure that the interests of the debenture-holder are not prejudiced.

The ability of a company to continue its business will generally be greatly restricted after the appointment of a controller. The appointment itself will usually crystallise a floating charge so as to make it fixed. This revokes the power of the company to deal with its secured assets in the ordinary course of business. The directors retain greater residual powers only where the controller has control over part of the company's assets.

While a receiver manager may supersede the board, the directors are still subject to the duties imposed by the *Corporations Act*. For example, they are still responsible for the preparation and lodgment of financial reports.

powers of a receiver

source of receivers' powers

[23.80] Privately appointed receivers, receivers and managers and other controllers derive their powers from the debentures, charges or loan agreements under which they are appointed. Court-appointed receivers or receivers and managers have those powers granted to them by the court that appointed them.

Privately appointed receivers derive their powers from the debentures, charges or loan agreements under which they are appointed.

Section 420(2) gives certain specific powers to receivers in addition to those conferred upon them by the terms of the court order or instrument under which they were appointed. These powers are conferred for the purpose of enabling receivers to attain the objectives for which they were appointed. The inclusion of statutory powers alleviates many of the problems that may arise from poorly drafted debentures.

Section 420(2) gives certain specific powers to receivers in addition to those conferred upon them by the terms of the court order or instrument under which they were appointed.

Under s 420(2), a receiver's powers include the following:

> **to enter into possession and take control of property of the corporation;**
> **to lease, let or hire or dispose of property of the corporation;**
> **to borrow money on security of property of the corporation;**
> **to convert property of the corporation into money;**
> **to carry on any business of the corporation;**
> **to execute any document, bring or defend any proceedings or do any other act or thing in the name of and on behalf of the corporation; and**
> **to make an application for the winding up of the corporation in the name of the corporation.**

The courts interpret the power to carry on the company's business in a broad way so as to enable a receiver and manager to enter into any transactions that are advantageous to the company.

The powers listed in s 420(2) apply to both court- and privately appointed receivers unless the terms of the court order or instrument under which they were appointed specify otherwise. In addition, s 420(1) confers upon a receiver the power to do all things necessary or convenient to be done for or in connection with, or as incidental to, the attainment of the objectives for which the receiver was appointed.

power to sell assets secured by prior charge

[23.85] The Harmer Report noted that a problem that could arise where a receiver is appointed by a floating charge holder but another secured creditor holds a prior security over an important asset of the company. In such situations, the receiver is prevented from disposing of the assets of the company, particularly the business of the company as a going concern, at the most favourable price. This may be detrimental to achieving a beneficial realisation of the company's assets for all creditors and others such as guarantors of the company's debts. Section 420B now deals with this problem and balances the object of orderly dealing with the property of the company while protecting the interests of the prior secured creditor.

A "managing controller" of property of a corporation may apply to the court for an order authorising the sale of specified property despite the existence of a prior charge that has priority over the controller's charge: s 420B(1). The court may only make such an order if satisfied that the sale is in the best interests of the corporation and its creditors and will not unreasonably prejudice the rights or interests of the prior charge holder. The controller must have the power to sell the property apart from the existence of the prior charge and attempts must have been made to obtain the consent of the prior charge holder to the sale and this consent was not obtained: s 420B(2) and (3).

In considering the interests of the holder of the prior charge, the court may have regard to the effect on the proceeds of a sale whether the prior charged property was included or not: s 420B(4). This may involve a consideration of the difference in price between a sale of all assets as a going concern and the separate sales of assets excluding the disputed property. The court is not limited in the matters it may consider: s 420B(5).

The interests of the holder of a prior charge may be protected by the court allowing a sale of the prior charged property subject to conditions: s 420B(6). For example, all or part of the net proceeds of the sale may be applied in payment of specified amounts secured by the prior charge.

power to obtain information

A controller may obtain information from the company's officers and employees and inspect the company's books.

[23.90] Sections 429 and 430 assist a controller in exercising her or his power to get in the company's assets, by enabling her or him to obtain information from the company's officers and others. Fourteen days after a controller notifies the company of her or his appointment, the directors and secretary of the company are required to submit a report to the controller of the affairs of the company as at the date of her or his appointment: s 429. Within one month of receiving the report, the controller must lodge a copy with ASIC, together with any comments he or she may wish to make. The report and comments must also be sent to the trustee for debenture-holders.

Under s 430, a controller can also require reports to be submitted to them by other persons such as:

To assist the controller in carrying out the work, s 431 entitles them to inspect at any reasonable time any books of the corporation that relate to the secured property.

> **present or former officers;**
> **persons who took part in the formation of the company; and**
> **present or former employees.**

To assist the controller in carrying out the work, s 431 entitles them to inspect at any reasonable time any books of the corporation that relate to the secured property. Any person who refuses or fails to allow the receiver to inspect such books is guilty of an offence.

case note

In *Re Jet Corp of Australia Pty Ltd* (1985) 3 ACLC 216, the company's receivers applied for an order under the predecessor of s 431 compelling the auditors to make available photocopies of the company's records in their possession. It was held that the auditor's photocopies of the company's records belonged to the company. Further, even though the auditors had a lien over the documents and could therefore retain possession until their fees were paid, s 431 allowed the receiver to inspect them. This was so notwithstanding that the inspection would deprive the lien of its main value. Section 431 did not, however, enable the receivers to inspect audit notes that were not part of the original documents. These were intended to be confidential.

A receiver may be authorised by ASIC to apply to have a person examined under s 596A: *Whelan v ASC* (1993) 11 ACLC 1216. This right to conduct an examination may be useful in acquiring information about the company's assets or to assist an investigation into possible claims against the company's directors or auditor. Examinations are discussed in Chapter 25 below.

effect of liquidation on the powers of a receiver

[23.95] At common law, if a company is placed in liquidation after a receiver and manager is appointed the receiver's position as agent for the company ceases and the receiver becomes personally liable for debts incurred in carrying on the company's business: *Gosling v Gaskell* [1897] AC 575. However, the appointment of a liquidator does not greatly affect the receiver. The receiver continues to carry on the company's business as agent for the debenture-holder: *Mercantile Credits Ltd v Atkins (No 1)* (1985) 3 ACLC 485.

The appointment of a liquidator does not greatly affect the receiver and may carry on the corporation's business.

Section 420C modifies the common law. A receiver of property of a corporation that is being wound up may carry on and do whatever is necessary to carry on the corporation's business. The approval of the liquidator or the court must be obtained: s 420C(1). Where the receiver carries on the business of the corporation, the receiver does so as agent of the company: s 420C(3). This means that the receiver has a right of indemnity from the company's assets for expenses and liabilities incurred in carrying on the company's business.

From a creditor's point of view, a receiver is liable for debts and expenses incurred during the course of the receivership. However, this is without prejudice to any rights of indemnity that the receiver has: s 419(1). The consequences of a receiver being regarded as an agent under s 420C are that the receiver must look to the assets of the company or an indemnity from the appointing creditor to meet liabilities incurred in carrying on the business of the company. Such debts and liabilities are not costs and expenses of the winding up for the purposes of determining priorities among unsecured creditors under s 556(1): s 420C(4).

In addition to the power to carry on business, a receiver manager may also exercise other powers after winding up commences. A receiver can take possession of assets and may take legal action in the name of and on behalf of the company under the statutory power contained in s 420(2)(k). This power to take legal action continues after the commencement of winding up where the right to bring the action in relation to an asset or property of the company is charged to the appointor of the receiver. Even where a liquidator takes over the conduct of the legal action, a receiver may re-enter and resume control of the legal action if the cause of action is an asset secured by the debenture and there is no detriment to the liquidation: *SA Asset Management Corp v Sheahan* (1995) 13 ACLC 1135.

A receiver has a statutory power to make calls on shares where the charge is over uncalled capital.

A call can be made in the name of the corporation or in the name of the liquidator where a proper indemnity is given to the liquidator: s 420(2)(s).

A receiver is entitled to retain any documents relating to the secured property until the receivership ends even though the liquidator cannot carry out the winding up without them: *Re High Crest Motors Pty Ltd* [1978] VR 688. The effect of the decision in *Re High Crest Motors Pty Ltd* has largely been overcome by s 477(3). This gives the liquidator a statutory right to inspect and take copies of any books of the company even where they are in the possession of a receiver. The liquidator can also sell the secured property. However, any debts incurred by the receiver after the commencement of liquidation are no longer borne by the company, but by the receiver personally. The receiver's liability for contracts is discussed below, para [23.145]. A receiver manager may exercise the power of sale of charged assets conferred by the mortgage debenture despite the winding up of the company: *Re Landmark Corp Ltd* (1968) 88 WN (Pt 1) (NSW) 195.

A receiver may probably use the seal of the company under s 420(2)(n) even though the company is in liquidation. This is because while s 477(2)(d) empowers the liquidator to use a seal of the company, it does not give clear, exclusive use to the liquidator.

duties of receivers

common law duties

A privately appointed receiver and manager's primary duty is to the appointing secured creditors.

[23.100] A privately appointed receiver and manager's primary duty is to the appointing secured creditors. The receiver manager is obliged to take possession of the secured property, to manage the company's business and ultimately to sell the charged property for the purpose of discharging the secured debt. A receiver and manager also owes duties to the company, in respect of the appointment as its agent as well as to other secured creditors. Difficulties may arise where the interests of the secured creditor depart from the interests of the debtor company, its unsecured creditors or its members.

A receiver and manager also owes duties to the company in respect of the appointment as its agent as well as to other secured creditors.

A receiver and manager owes the same duties as a mortgagee to use their powers for the sole purpose of securing repayment of the moneys owing under the debenture and not for her or his own purposes. A receiver must also act in good faith: *Downsview Nominees Ltd v First City Corp Ltd* (1993) 11 ACLC 3101.

In *Expo International Pty Ltd v Chant* [1980] 2 NSWLR 820, Needham J considered the nature of the duties owed to the company. He stated:

> **< Those duties include the duty to exercise his powers in good faith (including a duty not to sacrifice the mortgagor's interests recklessly), to act strictly within and in accordance with the conditions of his appointment, to account to the mortgagor after the mortgagee's security has been discharged not only for the surplus assets but also for his conduct of the receivership. The latter duty, in my opinion, involves the duty to terminate the receivership by handing over the surplus assets to the mortgagor as soon as the interests of the mortgagee have been satisfied. I think the receiver would be acting outside his powers, or mala fide, if he failed to terminate the receivership because of some extraneous or collateral consideration ... There is, in my opinion, no warrant in the authorities for holding the receiver to be liable for loss caused by negligence. >**

case note

In *Cape v Redarb Pty Ltd (No 2)* (1992) 10 ACLC 1272, a receiver manager was appointed by the court to liquidate a solvent joint venture company and distribute the proceeds to the two shareholder directors. It was held that a court-appointed receiver manager had a duty to be fair and impartial. He owed a fiduciary duty to those interested in the property but was not an agent or trustee for those persons. In this respect, a court-appointed receiver and manager owes the same duty as a liquidator.

At common law, a receiver is required to exercise this power in good faith and not to sacrifice the company's interests recklessly. At common law, a receiver is only under a duty to act honestly and in a non-reckless manner. A receiver does not breach this duty if the receiver is merely negligent in the management of the company's business or the sale of the secured property.

At common law, a receiver is only under a duty to act honestly and in a non-reckless manner.

A receiver breaches their common law duty to act in good faith if they arrange for the sale of the secured property at a gross undervalue. Section 420A, discussed below, para [23.110], modifies a receiver's common law duty in relation to the sale of the secured property.

case note

In *Forsyth v Blundell* (1973) 129 CLR 477, a mortgagee advertised an auction to sell the secured property. It set a reserve price of $120,000, which was the amount owing under the mortgage. Prior to the auction a prospective bidder indicated interest in bidding up to $150,000. Despite this, the mortgagee entered into a contract to sell the property privately to another purchaser for $120,000. The High Court prevented the mortgagee from completing the sale. It held that the mortgagee had not acted in good faith and that he was either grossly careless or at least displayed a calculated indifference to the mortgagor's interests. A receiver is under a similar duty to act in good faith.

statutory duties

[23.105] Receivers and receiver managers are included in the definition of "officer" under s 9 and are consequently subject to the duties imposed by Ch 2D of the *Corporations Act*. The duties imposed on officers by Ch 2D are discussed in Chapter 13 above.

reasonable care in selling secured assets: s 420A

[23.110] The role of a receiver appointed in respect of property secured by a fixed charge is to take possession of the property secured by the charge, sell it and repay the debt due to the secured creditor who appointed them. Any surplus after the sale of the secured property goes back to the company. The sale price of secured property may cause tensions between the secured creditor on the one hand and the debtor company on the other. The secured creditor is mainly concerned to ensure that the sale price at least covers the secured debt plus the costs of selling. However, the debtor company will try to ensure that the secured property is sold for the highest price possible.

Section 420A imposes a specific duty on controllers in exercising a power of sale to take all reasonable care to sell property at not less than market value or for the best price that is reasonably obtainable, having regard to the existing circumstances when the property is sold. This duty does not limit the operation of Ch 2D.

Section 420A imposes a specific duty on controllers in exercising a power of sale to take all reasonable care to sell property at not less than market value.

Where there is any doubt as to the course of action a receiver ought to take, the receiver can apply to the court for directions: s 424. The power of the court to give directions is very wide and has covered a wide range of matters. However, the court will not make a commercial decision for receivers under s 424: *Deputy Commissioner of Taxation v Best & Less (Wollongong) Pty Ltd* (1992) 10 ACLC 520. The court also has a similar discretion to give directions to liquidators under s 479(3).

notification of appointment

A creditor who appoints a receiver is required to notify ASIC.

[23.115] A creditor who appoints a receiver is required to notify ASIC of the appointment within seven days after making the appointment: s 427(1)(a). The secured creditor must also notify the public of the appointment by publishing a notice in the *Gazette* within 21 days after making the appointment: s 427(1)(b).

A receiver is also required to notify the company.

A receiver or other controller is also required to notify the company and other relevant authorities of the appointment. A controller must forthwith serve a notice of the appointment on the company: s 429(2). A controller must also lodge a notice of their address with ASIC within 14 days: s 427(2). In addition, the *Income Tax Assessment Act 1936* (Cth), s 215, requires a receiver for debenture-holders to notify the Commissioner of Taxation of appointment within 14 days.

In order to publicise the fact that a receiver or other controller has been appointed, a statement to that effect must be set out after the company's name on all its public documents: s 428. These documents include the company's invoices, order forms and cheques.

financial records

Section 421 sets out a controller's duties with respect to bank accounts and financial records.

[23.120] Section 421 sets out a controller's duties with respect to bank accounts and financial records. Section 421(1)(a), (b) and (c) requires a controller to maintain a separate bank account for each corporation over which they have control and pay all money of a corporation into that account within three business days of coming under their control. Further, s 421(1)(d) requires a controller to keep such financial records as correctly record and explain all transactions entered into by them as controller. Directors, creditors or members of a corporation are entitled to inspect a controller's financial records unless the court orders otherwise: s 421(2).

Section 432 obliges a controller to prepare accounts including receipts and payments and an estimate of the total value of the property in respect of which they were appointed as controller. These accounts and estimates must be lodged with ASIC every six months during the course of the receivership and within one month after the controller ceases to act. ASIC may require a controller's accounts to be audited by a registered company auditor: s 432(2).

report about corporation's affairs

A managing controller of property of a corporation must prepare a report about the corporation's affairs.

[23.125] A managing controller of property of a corporation must prepare a report about the corporation's affairs: s 421A. This must be in the prescribed form and prepared within two months of appointment: s 421A(1) and (2). The report must be lodged with ASIC and the controller must advertise that it is available for inspection by any person: s 421A(3).

The managing controller may omit information from the copy of the report available for inspection if he or she is of the opinion that the particular information would seriously prejudice the corporation's interests or the achievement of the objectives for which the controller was appointed or acted: s 421A(4).

priority debts

A receiver appointed under a floating charge must pay certain debts ahead of the principal and interest due to the secured creditor.

[23.130] The most important duties of a privately appointed receiver are to sell the secured property and distribute the proceeds to the secured creditor. A receiver appointed under a floating charge must pay certain debts ahead of the principal and interest due to the secured creditor.

Section 433 governs the priority of payment of debts where a receiver or mortgagee in possession is appointed over property secured by a floating charge and the company is not in liquidation. It sets out the classes of debts that must be paid in priority to the debts of the floating charge creditor. Under s 433(3), receivers must pay, out of the property coming into their hands, the following debts or amounts in priority to any claim for principal or interest due to the floating charge creditor:

> first, any amount that in a winding up is payable in priority to unsecured debts pursuant to s 562. These are amounts received by the company under an insurance contract from its insurer in respect of the company's liability to third parties. This gives priority to injured employees covered by workers' compensation insurance;
> secondly, if an auditor of the company has applied to ASIC under s 329(6) for consent to resign as auditor and this consent has been refused, the reasonable fees and expenses of the auditor incurred from the date of refusal to the date of the receiver's appointment; and
> thirdly, any debt or amount that in a winding up is payable in priority to other unsecured debts pursuant to s 556(e), (g), (h) or s 560. This gives priority to amounts due to employees in respect of unpaid wages, unpaid amounts in respect of leave of absence, and retrenchment payments. Section 556 is discussed in Chapter 25 below.

Section 215 of the *Income Tax Assessment Act* obliges a receiver to notify the Commissioner of Taxation of their appointment. The Commissioner may then require the receiver to set aside an amount sufficient for the payment of income tax for which the company is or may be liable. Failure to comply with s 215 renders the receiver guilty of an offence. In addition, the receiver is personally liable to pay the tax to the extent of the value of the assets over which they have taken possession. Section 215, however, does not give the Commissioner a priority over secured creditors' debt in respect of income tax. The secured debts are paid first.

receiver's costs, expenses and fees

[23.135] Since a receiver and manager is usually appointed as agent of the company, it is responsible for payment of the receiver's remuneration, not the debenture-holders. Most debentures also specify the basis on which the remuneration is calculated. A receiver's remuneration can, however, be varied by the court under s 425, but only on the application of the company's liquidator or administrator or by ASIC. The receiver concerned may apply to the court for an order to vary or amend an order under s 425.

A debenture trust deed usually gives the receiver's remuneration priority over the debt due to the debenture-holders. In *Re Quarry & Foundry Engineering Pty Ltd* (1984) 2 ACLC 714, it was held that, notwithstanding the priorities set out in a predecessor of s 433, a receiver's right to the costs, expenses and fees of the receivership ranked ahead of the claims of the company's former employees for their holiday pay and long service leave entitlements. Section 433 only provides that employees rank ahead of the entitlement of the debenture-holder for payment of principal or interest in respect of the debenture.

report breaches of duty to ASIC

[23.140] Section 422 imposes a duty on a controller to report misconduct to ASIC. This is similar to the obligation imposed on liquidators by s 533. A receiver must make a report where it appears that:

Section 422 imposes a duty on a controller to report misconduct to ASIC.

> a company's present or former officers or members have been guilty of an offence in relation to it; or
> a person who took part in the formation, promotion, administration or winding up of the company may have misappropriated any of its money or property or may have been guilty of negligence, default, breach of duty or breach of trust in relation to it.

Where a controller makes such a report, s 534 gives ASIC power to investigate the matter. In order to protect controllers when reporting possible offences, s 426 provides them with qualified privilege in defamation proceedings in respect of any matter arising from the report.

liabilities of receivers

contracts

Under s 419(1), receivers may become personally liable for certain debts incurred by them in the course of the receivership.

[23.145] At common law, the appointment of a receiver as agent for the company meant that they were not personally liable to outsiders on any contracts made during the course of the receivership or control. However, under s 419(1), receivers may become personally liable for certain debts incurred by them in the course of the receivership. Where they incur such debts within the scope of their agency, they are, of course, entitled to be reimbursed by the company unless it has insufficient funds. For this reason, a prudent receiver usually obtains an indemnity from the debenture-holders to be protected from personal liability.

Section 419(1) does not extend to all debts incurred in the course of receivership. It only applies to debts for services rendered, goods purchased or property hired, leased, used or occupied. This does not include a debt for tax on income derived during the course of receivership, but does include wages of employees of the company. The Harmer Report proposed that the legislation be amended to make a controller liable for a contract or other transaction entered into or made by the corporation with the authority of the controller in the course of the receivership or control to the extent to which the corporation receives a benefit as a result of the contract or transaction.

A receiver was once not liable for contracts entered into by the company prior to the commencement of the receivership unless the receiver adopted those contracts. The Harmer Report considered it unfair to lessors that a receiver could permit a company to continue in possession of premises or goods under a lease without the receiver being liable for rental payments during the period while the receiver was in control. The lessor stood as an unsecured creditor.

Section 419A adopts the Harmer Report's recommendation. It applies where a corporation entered into a lease or similar agreement before the "control day" and continues after that day to use, occupy or be in possession of the leased property: s 419A(1). The "control day" is the day a receiver is appointed: s 9. It is also the day when a mortgagee or her or his agent first enters into possession or takes control of property for purposes of enforcing a charge.

Under s 419A(2), a controller is personally liable for the rent payable by the corporation. This liability commences seven days after the controller is appointed or enters into possession and continues as long as the corporation remains in possession or uses the property and the controller continues to act in her or his capacity. The seven-day period enables the controller to decide whether to continue the lease before becoming liable. The court may excuse the controller from liability where, for example, the controller was unaware of the existence of the lease during the seven days after appointment: s 419A(7). The controller is not taken to have adopted the lease agreement and, apart from payment of rent, is not liable for the performance of other terms of the agreement such as a covenant to repair in a lease: s 419A(8).

A receiver is also not personally liable for debts arising from contracts entered into by the company prior to the appointment that are completed during the course of the receivership. The creditor's right to payment of the unsecured debt is postponed until the receiver has discharged the debts of the debenture-holders and other preferred creditors.

A receiver and manager, being an agent of the company, may even repudiate contracts made prior to the commencement of receivership without incurring personal liability: *George Barker Ltd v Eynon* [1974] 1 WLR 462. In such cases, the outsider only has remedies as an unsecured creditor against the company for breach of contract. The receiver, however, is required to honour contracts if this is required to protect the goodwill of the company's business.

breach of duty

[23.150] As discussed above, a controller is regarded as an "officer" of the company for the purposes of the duties contained in Ch 2D of the *Corporations Act*. These duties are discussed in Chapter 13 above. If the controller is in breach of these duties, they may be liable under the civil penalty provisions. Despite the fact that receivers are subject to these statutory duties, there are very few instances where they have been sued for breach.

Since a controller takes part in the management of a company, they are also subject to ss 597 and 598. These provisions are discussed in Chapter 25 below. These provisions enable the court, on application by ASIC or a liquidator, to examine the conduct of a controller. If they are found guilty of fraud, negligence, default, breach of trust or breach of duty in relation to the company, the court may direct them to compensate the company for the loss or damage.

Section 423 specifically deals with breaches of duty by controllers. Under s 423(1), if it appears to the court or ASIC that a controller has not faithfully performed or observed the duties, the court or ASIC may inquire into the matter and the court may then take such actions as it thinks fit. Such an inquiry into a controller's conduct may also be initiated by a complaint made by any person to the court or ASIC.

Where a controller is guilty of misfeasance, neglect or omission, the court may order the receiver to make good any loss sustained by the corporation or such other order as it thinks fit: s 423(2).

Under s 1321, any person aggrieved by any act, omission or decision of, inter alia, a receiver or receiver and manager has a right to appeal to the court. The court may confirm, reverse or modify the act or decision, or remedy the omission and make such orders and give such directions as it thinks fit.

termination

[23.155] A receivership or controllership normally terminates when the receiver or controller achieves the objective of their appointment. That is, when the secured debt is discharged and the debts of the receivership or the controller are paid. The controller is obliged to end the receivership or cease to control property and account to the company or its liquidator for any surplus.

A receivership normally terminates when the secured debt is discharged and the debts of the receivership are paid.

Sometimes, a continuation of the receivership may impede an orderly winding up by a liquidator and add to the costs of the winding up. Section 434B enables a liquidator of a company wound up in insolvency to apply to the court for an order that a controller cease to act as a receiver or retain control of all or part of the property of a corporation: s 434B(1) and (4).

The court may only make such an order if it is satisfied that the objectives for which the controller was appointed or entered into possession have been achieved as far as is reasonably practicable: s 434B(2). The court must consider the interests of the corporation, the chargee who appointed the controller and the other creditors as well as any other relevant matter: s 434B(3).

An order under s 434B does not otherwise affect a charge on the property of a corporation. Nor does it limit any other power of the court to deal with controllers. For example, the court retains its powers under s 423.

A controller may be removed by the debenture-holder but not by the company, even though he or she is its agent. The right of a controller to resign will generally be set out in the mortgage debenture. In the absence of a contrary provision, a controller may be liable for breach of contract if resignation is premature.

The court may remove a controller in certain situations such as where he or she is not acting in the interests of the debenture-holders as a whole or is disqualified under s 418.

A controller may also be removed for misconduct. A corporation may apply to the court for an order that a controller cease to act as a receiver or give up possession or control of property of the corporation. The court must be satisfied that the controller has been guilty of misconduct in connection with performing or exercising any functions or powers as a controller: s 434A. As discussed above, a controller may also be removed where the purported appointment or entering into possession was declared by the court to be invalid under s 418A.

pathways questions ...

The following questions dealing with receivers may best be answered by reading this chapter and considering the Internet resources found on the Lipton-Herzberg Corporate Insolvency Pathway at **http://www.lipton-herzberg.com.au/secure/pathways-corporate-insolvency.html**

1. What were the main recommendations of the Harmer Report in relation to receivers and controllers? Which of these recommendations have been incorporated into the *Corporations Act*?

2. What are the differences and similarities between administration, liquidation and receivership?

3. Refer to the *Review of the Regulation of Corporate Insolvency Practitioners*. In what respects does the report recommend changing the duties and responsibilities of controllers?

bibliography ...

Agardy, P "Controllers' Duties on Sale: Section 420A of the Corporations Law" (1995) 3 Insolv LJ 182.

Aitken, N "The Receiver's Duty in Equity: The Impact of Statute and the Privy Council" (1993) 1 Insolv LJ 118.

Australian Law Reform Commission. "General Insolvency Inquiry" (1988) ALRC 45.

Badham, L A "Directors Versus Receivers: Control of Litigation on Behalf of Companies in Receivership" (1998) 16 C & SLJ 508.

Bennetts, K J "Payments by Receivers to Pre-appointment Unsecured Creditors—Are they Recoverable as Voidable Preferences?" (1993) 11 C & SLJ 327.

Christensen, L "A Receiver and Manager's Duties on Realisation of a Corporation's Assets" (1999) 6 E Law **http://www.murdoch.edu.au/elaw/issues/v6n3/christensen63nf.html**

Darvas, P "Employees Rights and Entitlements and Insolvency: Regulatory Rationale, Legal Issues and Proposed Solutions" (1999) 17 C & SLJ 103.

Duthie, L "The Priority of Retrenchment Payments in Liquidation or Receivership" (1992) 20 ABLR 378.

Glover, J & Duns, J "Insolvency Administrations at General Law: Fiduciary Obligations of Company Receivers, Voluntary Administrators and Liquidators" (2001) 9 Insolv LJ 130.

Hamilton, G "Provisions Which Avoid Charges Under the Corporations Law: The Effect on Secured Creditors and Receivers" (1998) 16 C & SLJ 333.

Hammond, C "Are Receivers and Administrators Liable for the Wages of Company Employees Retained after their Appointment?" (1997) 5 Insolv LJ 136.

McQuade, P "A Receiver's, Liquidator's and Provisional Liquidator's Claim to a Lien or Charge for Remuneration and Expenses" (1993) 1 Insolv LJ 199.

O'Brien, D "Receivers' Duties when Selling Assets" (2001) 9 Insolv LJ 180.

O'Donovan, J "Recent Developments Relating to Pre-Receivership Contracts" (2000) 18 C & SLJ 50.

O'Donovan, J "The Effect of Liquidation upon Receivers' Agency and Powers" (1993) 11 C & SLJ 374.

O'Donovan, J "The Appointment of a Company Receiver and Manager by the Court Pursuant to an Express Statutory Power" (1989) 7 C & SLJ 347.

Powers, L "Insolvency Law and Management: The Effect of the Liquidation on the Agency of a Receiver" (1999) 10 JBFLP 249.

Robinson, D "Remuneration of Corporate Insolvency Practitioners" (2000) 8 Insolv LJ 20.

Symes, C "Remuneration, Rent and 'Requisite' Costs: The 3 R's of Insolvency's Administrative Expense Priority" (2000) 11 Aust Jnl of Corp Law 149.

Taylor, T "Employee Entitlements in Corporate Insolvency Administrations" (2000) 8 Insolv LJ 32.

von Nessen, P "The Section 1323 Power of the Australian Securities Commission: Its Operation And Shortcomings" (1996) 22 Mon LR 140.

revision questions on the material in this chapter ...

- Please see eQuiz at **http://www.thomson.com.au/academic** for multiple choice questions and answers.
- For further corporations law links and material please refer to the Lipton-Herzberg website at **http://www.lipton-herzberg.com.au**

chapter twenty-four

voluntary administration

key points ...

- The voluntary administration procedure provides for the appointment of an administrator with power to take control of an insolvent company.
- The aim of voluntary administration is to maximise the chances of the company or its businesses remaining in existence. If this is not possible, voluntary administration aims to achieve a better return to creditors than would result from an immediate winding up.
- The administrator is usually appointed by resolution of the directors if they believe that the company is insolvent or likely to become insolvent. An administrator may also be appointed by a liquidator or chargee entitled to enforce a charge over the whole, or substantially the whole, of the company's assets.
- An administrator must convene two meetings of creditors. The purposes of the first meeting are to give creditors the opportunity to replace the administrator and to appoint a committee of creditors to assist the administrator. The second meeting is for the creditors to decide the company's future. The creditors may decide that the company execute a deed of company arrangement, the administration should end or the company be wound up.
- During voluntary administration a moratorium on claims against the company comes into effect. This enables administrators to carry out their role as creditors and certain others such as lessors are prevented from bringing actions to enforce their rights against the company or guarantees against the directors. The enforcement of such rights may be detrimental to the majority of creditors and may prevent the administrator from carrying on the business of the company in accordance with the objectives of the legislation.
- Where the administrator forms the opinion that it is in the creditors' interests to enter into a deed of company arrangement, a proposal is put to creditors who may resolve that the company enter into the deed. The terms of the deed may provide for debts to be compromised, payments to creditors to be delayed or paid in instalments, and priorities among creditors to be determined. If the creditors resolve that the company enter into a deed, it is binding on all unsecured creditors. Secured creditors are bound by the deed only if they have so agreed.
- Where it is appropriate to wind up the company, the administrator usually becomes the liquidator.

aims of voluntary administration

Voluntary administration involves the appointment of an administrator who takes complete control of an insolvent company.

[24.05] Voluntary administration involves the appointment of an administrator who takes complete control of an insolvent company for a relatively short period of time. An administrator must be a registered liquidator and is therefore an experienced, independent insolvency practitioner. The administrator's task is to investigate the affairs of the company and to report on whether a compromise or arrangement can be negotiated that would be acceptable to the company and its creditors. Ultimately, however, the fate of the company is determined by its creditors who have the final say as to what should happen to the company after voluntary administration ends.

The aims of the voluntary administration provisions of the *Corporations Act* are to maximise the chances of the company or its businesses remaining in existence and, if this is not possible, to achieve a better return to creditors than would result from an immediate winding up: s 435A.

The aims of the voluntary administration provisions of the *Corporations Act* are to maximise the chances of the company or its businesses remaining in existence and, if this is not possible, to achieve a better return to creditors than would result from an immediate winding up.

Voluntary administration is intended to be a better form of administration for an insolvent company than the other forms of external administration—liquidation or a scheme of arrangement under Pt 5.1 of the *Corporations Act*. The voluntary administration procedure is quick to implement and is a relatively cheap form of insolvency administration. It is designed to facilitate the negotiation of compromises or other arrangements with an insolvent company's creditors and to provide for a smooth transition to other types of insolvency administrations with the minimum of expensive court cases or formal creditor or shareholder meetings.

The voluntary administration provisions of Pt 5.3A stemmed from recommendations made by the Australian Law Reform Commission (ALRC) in its 1988 *General Insolvency Inquiry* (the Harmer Report) that the legislation should provide for a procedure that encouraged a creative approach to insolvency. The Harmer Report considered that the other forms of external insolvency administration were unsatisfactory in that they were expensive, inflexible and slow to implement,. Prior to the introduction of the current voluntary administrations provisions in 1992, companies occasionally went into liquidation notwithstanding that part of their businesses remained viable. This was often to the detriment of creditors, shareholders and employees. Further, the various insolvency administrations were not integrated.

The voluntary administration procedure has two phases. The first phase commences with the appointment of an administrator. The second phase commences at the conclusion of the creditors' meeting, at which decisions are made regarding the company's future.

The voluntary administration procedure in Pt 5.3A of the *Corporations Act* has two phases. Under s 435C, the first phase—voluntary administration—commences with the appointment of an independent, experienced insolvency accountant as administrator with powers to take control of the company's affairs while a moratorium on claims against the company comes into effect. The first phase of the voluntary administration procedure comes to an end and the second phase commences at the conclusion of the creditors' meeting, convened under s 439A, at which decisions are made regarding the company's future. Depending on what decision is made at this meeting, s 439C provides for a smooth transition from voluntary administration to one of the following three possible outcomes of voluntary administration:

> **a deed of company arrangement under which the company may have the opportunity of being restored to a viable financial state to the ultimate advantage of its creditors, shareholders and employees;**
> **winding up the company. If the creditors select this outcome, the winding up takes the form of a creditors' voluntary winding up with the administrator as company's liquidator; or**
> **voluntary administration terminates and control of the company is handed back to its directors and shareholders.**

The voluntary administration scheme has proved to be an extremely popular form of external administration for insolvent companies. While the Harmer Report anticipated that schemes of arrangement, discussed in Chapter 22 above, would continue to be used by large insolvent companies, this has not proved to be the case. The voluntary administration scheme has been utilised by numerous large listed companies as well as thousands of smaller companies.

Figure 24.1 below gives a diagrammatical overview of the voluntary administration procedure.

In 2003, CAMAC was asked to consider whether the voluntary administration procedure was the most appropriate means of facilitating the rehabilitation of large complex enterprises in financial difficulties. A company in serious financial difficulties is considered as rehabilitated if it succeeds in overcoming its problems and continues its business as a going concern.

In its report, *Rehabilitating Large and Complex Enterprises in Financial Difficulties* (October 2004), CAMAC identified the following five principles for effective rehabilitation procedures for large and complex enterprises:

> **the earlier a company responds to its financial difficulties, usually, the better its prospects of successful rehabilitation;**

> the prospect of a financially distressed company being rehabilitated may be improved if it can be encouraged to enter into discussions with its major creditors as early as possible on how best to rectify its financial position;
> a company may have a better prospect of successful recovery if it can obtain new loan or equity finance during the rehabilitation period;
> the procedural timetable needs to be sufficiently flexible to adjust to the needs of particular companies; and
> the process of rehabilitating a corporate group may be assisted if that group can be dealt with collectively, rather than on a company-by-company basis.

The Lipton-Herzberg Corporate Insolvency Pathway at **http://www.lipton-herzberg.com.au/secure/pathways-corporate-insolvency.html** has a link to the ALRC website which contains a summary of the Harmer Report recommendations. The Lipton-Herzberg Corporate Insolvency Pathway also has a link to a joint ASIC and Insolvency Practitioners Association (IPA) information sheet for creditors that gives an overview of voluntary administration. The CAMAC report, *Rehabilitating Large and Complex*

figure 24.1 overview of voluntary administration procedure

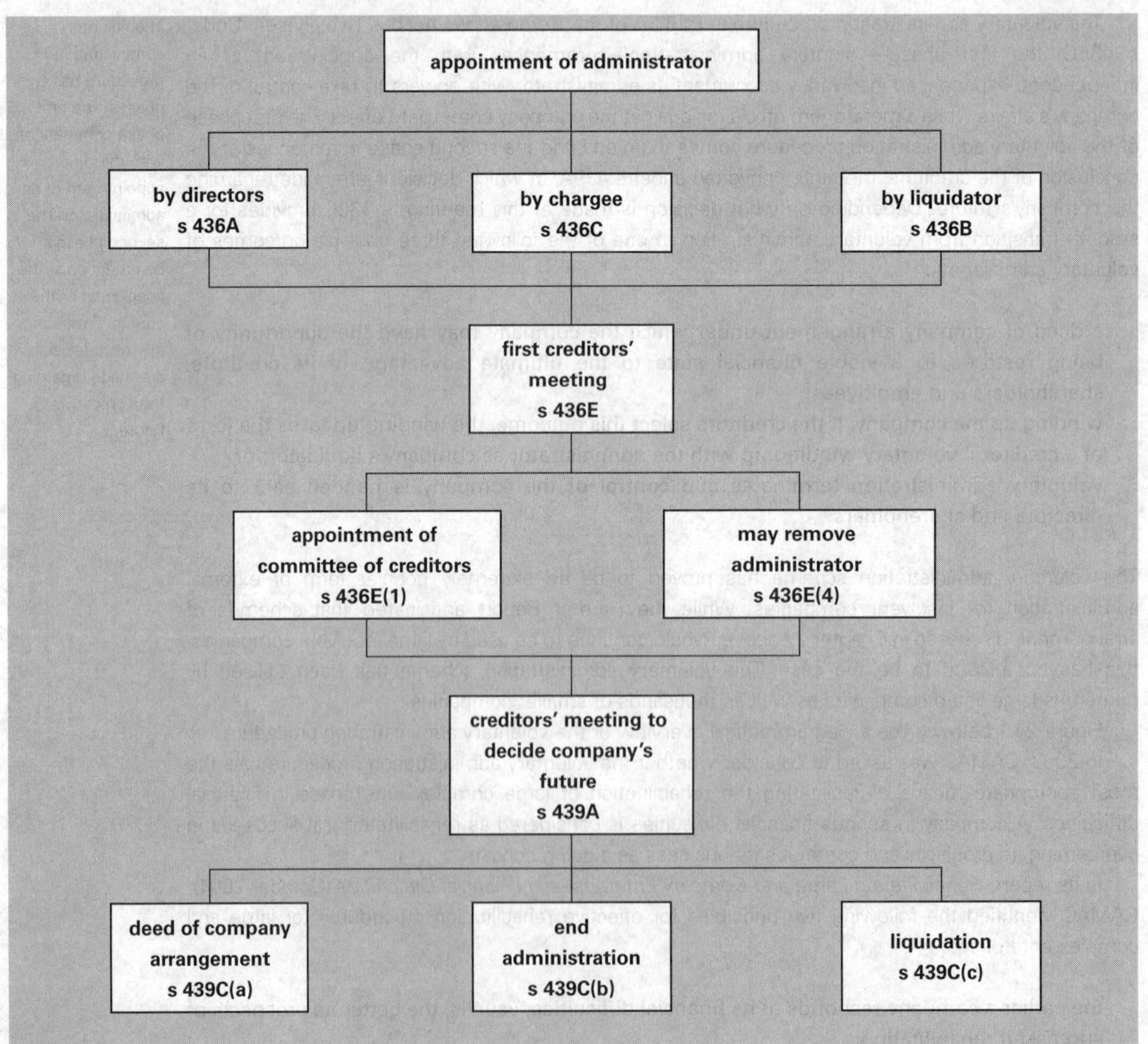

Enterprises in Financial Difficulties (October 2004)—referred to throughout this chapter as "the CAMAC report"—is available on CAMAC's website and is linked to the Lipton-Herzberg Law Reform site at **http://www.lipton-herzberg.com.au/law_reform.htm**

appointment of administrator

[24.10] A company can be put into voluntary administration quickly and with a minimum of expense. Voluntary administration of a company begins when an administrator is appointed: s 435C(1). Sections 436A, 436B and 436C specify who has the power to appoint an administrator.

A company can be put into voluntary administration quickly and with a minimum of expense.

In most cases, the decision to put a company into voluntary administration is made by a company's directors: s 436A. While it is relatively rare, a company may also be put into voluntary administration by its liquidator under s 436B or a creditor who has a charge over the whole, or substantially the whole, of a company's property: ss 436B and 436C.

In the case of large companies it may be convenient to appoint two or more persons as joint administrators. This is permitted by s 451A. Similarly, two or more persons may be appointed as administrators of a deed of company arrangement: s 451B.

In most cases, the decision to put a company into voluntary administration is made by a company's directors if they believe that the company is insolvent or is likely to become insolvent at some future time.

by directors

[24.15] As a general rule, the decision to appoint an administrator is made by the directors and does not require approval of the shareholders, creditors or the court. A resolution passed by a majority of a company's directors may appoint an administrator if they believe that the company is insolvent or is likely to become insolvent at some future time: s 436A(1). A failure to so resolve makes the appointment of an administrator invalid: *Wagner v International Health Promotions Pty Ltd* (1994) ACLC 986. A company is insolvent if it is unable to pay its debts as and when they fall due: s 95A. The meaning of insolvency is further discussed in Chapter 25 below.

The directors may appoint an administrator before the company actually becomes insolvent if they are of the opinion that the company is likely to become insolvent in the future. This enables financial difficulties to be identified promptly and treated.

In *Re Genasys II Pty Ltd* (1996) 14 ACLC 729, it was held that directors could appoint an administrator after the company was placed in receivership even though they had not obtained the receiver's consent. Once winding up has commenced, the directors lose their ability to appoint an administrator: s 436A(2).

Some submissions to the CAMAC report argued that directors should be able to begin an administration if there was "a reasonable prospect of insolvency" rather than the current "likely to become insolvent at some future time" test in s 436A(1). This would allow "an administration to be commenced where insolvency was possible, though not necessarily probable". Other submissions suggested that directors of a solvent company should also be able to invoke a rehabilitation procedure and gain protection from creditors whenever it had serious financial difficulties. This is similar to the US Chapter 11 Bankruptcy rehabilitation procedure. The CAMAC report rejected these suggestions. It did not think that there was "a clear case for introducing a debtor in possession regime based on Chapter 11 of the United States Bankruptcy Code." It also recommended retaining s 436A(1) in its present form.

Directors may decide to put their company into voluntary administration for a number of reasons. They may choose to do so to achieve a better outcome for shareholders and creditors. They may also be encouraged to take early action by the threat of the imposition of personal liability.

Directors are not forced to put a company into voluntary administration. If they do so, they lose their rights to run the company unless they have the administrator's written approval: s 437C. Directors may decide to put their company into voluntary administration for a number of reasons. They may choose to do so to achieve a better outcome for shareholders and creditors. They may also be encouraged to take early action by the threat of the imposition of personal liability.

The insolvent trading provisions, discussed in Chapter 13.5 above, may encourage directors of companies in financial difficulties to appoint an administrator sooner, rather than later. Directors' personal liability to pay compensation for breaching s 588G arises only if their company goes into liquidation: s 588M. Directors may avoid personal liability if they put their company into voluntary administration and ensure that it executes a deed of company arrangement that is acceptable to creditors.

Even if a company is wound up, directors may avoid personal liability for contravening s 588G if, pursuant to s 588H(5), they can establish that they took all reasonable steps to prevent the company from incurring debts when there were reasonable grounds to suspect that it was insolvent. In determining whether the s 588H(5) defence has been proved, s 588H(6) directs the court to have regard to any action the director took with a view to appointing an administrator, when that action was taken and the results of the action.

Placing an insolvent company in voluntary administration may also be an attractive option for directors who have personally guaranteed their company's debts. While the company is under voluntary administration, s 440J prevents creditors from enforcing the guarantee against the director. Section 440J also prevents creditors from enforcing guarantees of company debts provided by a director's spouse or other relative.

Income tax legislation may also have the effect of prompting directors to put their company into voluntary administration at an early stage. The PAYG ("pay as you go") system requires employers to withhold tax attributable to employee wages and salaries and remit the withheld amounts to the Australian Taxation Office on a regular basis. Under ss 222ANA–222AQD of the *Income Tax Assessment Act 1936*, directors of a non-remitting company may be personally liable to pay an amount equal to the company's liability unless they come to an arrangement to ensure that the withheld amounts are remitted or ensure that the company goes into voluntary administration or liquidation.

by liquidator

[24.20] A liquidator or provisional liquidator may appoint an administrator if they believe that the company is insolvent or is likely to become insolvent: s 436B(1). A liquidator may appoint her or himself as administrator with the leave of the court: s 436B(2). The courts will not ordinarily permit this because an administrator's independence may be compromised and the interests that a liquidator must protect may conflict with an administrator's duties: *Re Depsun Pty Ltd* (1994) 12 ACLC 482.

by chargee

[24.25] An administrator may also be appointed by a person who is entitled to enforce a charge over the whole, or substantially the whole, of a company's property. The charge must have become and remained enforceable: s 436C(1). The right of a chargee to appoint an administrator ceases once winding up has commenced: s 436C(2). Once an administrator has been appointed, a further appointment of an administrator cannot be made: s 436D.

The CAMAC report rejected the suggestion that other creditors, apart from those referred to in s 436C, should have the right to put a company into administration.

notification of appointment

[24.30] The appointment of an administrator must be publicised in several ways. The administrator must lodge with ASIC a notice of appointment within one day and cause this notice to be published in a national newspaper within three days: s 450A(1). Where a chargee appoints an administrator under s 436C, the chargee must give notice of the appointment to the company as soon as practicable: s 450A(2).

The administrator must also give written notice of the appointment to holders of charges over the whole, or substantially the whole, of the company's property: s 450A(3). As discussed below, such chargees have specific statutory protection during the moratorium period.

duration of administration

[24.35] Administration commences on the day an administrator is appointed: s 435C(1). The provisions of Pt 5.3A ensure a company is under voluntary administration for a relatively short period of time. The effect of this is to put pressure on all parties concerned to make a decision about the company's future. Further, as discussed below, paras [24.115]–[24.140], while a company is under administration, there is a stay or moratorium on all claims against the company. The short duration of administration means that creditors are not unduly prejudiced by the moratorium.

Administration commences on the day an administrator is appointed.

The short duration of administration means that creditors are not unduly prejudiced by the moratorium.

The date an administration ends depends on when the meeting of creditors that decides the company's future is held and the decision creditors make at that meeting. The meeting of creditors to determine the company's future must be held within five business days after the end of the "convening period": s 439A(2). The convening period is the period of 21 days beginning on the day when administration begins: s 439A(5). To avoid problems of creditors not being able to attend because of public holidays, the convening period is extended to 28 days if the administration begins in December or less than 28 days before Good Friday. The convening period may also be extended by the court under either s 439A(6) or s 447A. The period of voluntary administration can also be extended if creditors decide to adjourn their meeting. However, the meeting cannot be adjourned for more than 60 days: s 439B(2).

Administration ends on the date of the meeting if the creditors so resolve: s 439C(b). In such cases, the directors regain control of the company. Administration also ends on the date of the meeting if the creditors resolve that the company be wound up: s 439C(c).

Alternatively, the creditors may resolve that the company execute a deed of company arrangement: s 439C(a). In such cases, the deed must be executed by both the company and the administrator within 21 days after the creditors' meeting and the administration then ends and the company becomes subject to the terms of the deed: s 444B(2). If the company fails to execute the deed of company arrangement within the 21-day period, the administration ends and the company is deemed to have entered into a creditors' voluntary winding up: s 446A(1).

If the creditors fail to pass any resolution on the future of the company at the creditors' meeting, administration ends and the directors regain control of the company: s 439E(3)(e).

Section 447A(2) gives the court the power to end the administration if it is satisfied that the company is solvent or the administration provisions are being abused.

The CAMAC report considered that with minor modifications, the current time limits for the duration of voluntary administrations were sufficiently flexible to adjust to the needs of large and complex enterprises. The report recommended that the court should have a specific power to override the statutory timetable and to substitute a specific and comprehensive timetable for a particular administration. As discussed below, paras [24.75] and [24.80], the report also recommended incrementally increasing the period for holding the first and major meetings of creditors.

the administrator

who may be appointed?

[24.40] An administrator must be a registered liquidator. The qualification requirements of registered liquidators are set out in s 1282(3) and are discussed in Chapter 25 below. It is clear from s 448B that the legislation regarding the role of the administrator is sufficiently important and demanding so as to specify that the experience and available resources of a registered liquidator are necessary. It also enables a smooth transition to occur from administration to winding up in insolvency where this is appropriate. Usually in such a case, the administrator will continue to act as the liquidator of the company.

An administrator must be a registered liquidator.

The CAMAC report recommended that people other than registered liquidators should be permitted to be administrators if they had adequate expertise and experience in corporate rehabilitation.

An administrator must be independent of the company, its officers, creditors and auditor.

As is the case with a liquidator, an administrator must be independent of the company, its officers, creditors and auditor. A person who is connected with the company in these respects is disqualified from being appointed as an administrator of the company under s 448C without leave of the court. This section is based on s 532 which disqualifies connected persons from acting as liquidators. This is discussed in Chapter 25 below. A person is also disqualified from acting as an administrator if he or she is an insolvent under administration: s 448D.

Even though administrators are required to be independent, there is no requirement that they formally disclose material information about their professional, business or personal relationships with the company or its officers, members or creditors. In October 2005, the government announced a package of reforms to improve the operation of Australia's insolvency laws. It foreshadowed changing the *Corporations Act* to require administrators to provide creditors with a statement of independence prior to the first creditors' meeting. This would allow creditors to vote against the appointment of an administrator who was perceived to be too "friendly" to directors.

case note

In *Smarter Way (Aust) Pty Ltd v D'Aloia* (2000) 35 ACSR 595, the Victorian Supreme Court held that the appointment of an administrator was invalid because the appointor was in fact not a chargee. Byrne J commented on the need for administrators to be independent of the people who appointed them. He stated:

> < This was the engagement by the administrators of the solicitors retained by the appointing chargee. Let me say immediately and shortly that such a course is, in general, undesirable. An administrator has powers and functions which are conferred and imposed by Part 5.3A of the Law for the purposes set out in s 435A. It will often occur that the interests of the appointor, whether this be the board of directors of the company or a chargee, are or may be in conflict with the interests of the company's creditors or its members. The often burdensome duty of the administrator is to stand firmly and independently between these competing interests. In particular, it is important that the administrator not act and not appear to act merely at the bidding of the appointor to whom, it may be thought, they owe their employment as such. This may be of particular importance where the appointment is made by the directors who may wish to present a deed of company arrangement to the creditors with the support of the administrator's opinion in the s 439A(4) report. In such a case, the creditors are entitled to the independent opinion of the administrator as well as a full and accurate report of the matters specified in that section and in the regulations made under it. In principle, the creditors and members of the company are entitled to the same professional independence from an administrator appointed by a chargee. >

case note

In *Nambucca Investments Pty Ltd v Star* (1995) 13 ACLC 1814, Nambucca, which owned all the shares in four other companies, was placed in receivership. Nambucca's receiver and manager applied for leave to be appointed as administrator of the four companies. Leave was necessary because under s 448C(1)(b) he was a creditor of a related company, Nambucca. The Supreme Court of New South Wales refused to grant leave because there was at least an apprehension of conflict between the applicant's role as Nambucca's receiver and as the administrator of the four subsidiaries. As Nambucca's receiver, he was obliged to act in the interests of the secured creditor who appointed him, whereas an administrator must act in the interests of all creditors. There was also the prospect of the subsidiaries suing Nambucca for failing to prevent insolvent trading under s 588V.

A person cannot be appointed as an administrator unless that person has consented to the appointment and has not withdrawn that consent: s 448A.

investigation of company

[24.45] As soon as practicable after being appointed, the administrator must investigate the financial position and circumstances of the company: s 438A(a). On the basis of this investigation, the administrator must form an opinion as to which future course of action would be in the creditors' interests. The alternatives are whether the company and its creditors should enter into a deed of arrangement, end the administration or wind up the company: s 438A(b).

As soon as practicable after being appointed, the administrator must form an opinion as to which future course of action would be in the creditors' interests.

Because of the short time limits imposed by the legislation, an administrator is generally not required to carry out an investigation in the same detail as a liquidator: *Hagenvale Pty Ltd v Depela Pty Ltd* (1995) 13 ACLC 885. It is also unrealistic to require an administrator to use the compulsory powers of examination under ss 596A and 596B to investigate the company's affairs: *Deputy Commissioner of Taxation v Pddam Pty Ltd* (1996) 14 ACLC 659.

To enable the administrator to be properly informed, all the directors of the company must promptly hand over all books in their possession that relate to the company. If directors know where other books relating to the company are, their location must also be disclosed: s 438B(1). "Books" is defined in s 9 to include a register and any other record, accounts and documents.

The directors must also give to the administrator a statement about the company's business, property, affairs and financial circumstances within seven days after the administration begins: s 438B(2). The directors must also be available to provide such further information as the administrator reasonably requires. A failure to provide the required assistance under s 438B is an offence: s 438B(4).

Persons are not entitled, as against the administrator, to retain possession of books of the company or claim or enforce a lien on such books: s 438C(1). A secured creditor, however, may retain possession of books under a charge, but the administrator may inspect them and make copies: s 438C(2).

If, during the course of investigation of a company's affairs, it appears to the administrator that an officer or member of the company may have committed an offence, misapplied or retained property of the company or breached a duty to the company, the administrator must lodge a report about the matter and give assistance to ASIC: s 438D(1). The court may order an administrator to lodge such a report on the application of an interested person or of its own motion: s 438D(3).

The duty imposed on administrators under s 438D corresponds to similar duties to report which are imposed on receivers under s 422 and on liquidators under s 533.

powers

[24.50] In order to enable the functions of the administrator to be carried out properly, the legislation confers various powers on the administrator. The administrator has general powers under s 437A to take control of the company's business, property and affairs, carry on, terminate or dispose of the company's business or property and perform any function and exercise any power that the company and its officers could previously perform or exercise. In so acting, the administrator is taken to be acting as agent of the company: s 437B. No person other than the administrator may act as an officer of the company without the administrator's consent: s 437C(1).

The administrator has general powers to perform any function and exercise any power that the company and its officers could previously perform or exercise including the disposal of the company's business.

case note

In *Osborne Computer Corp Ltd v Airroad Distribution Pty Ltd* (1995) 13 ACLC 1129, the Supreme Court of New South Wales held that s 437A did not allow an administrator to destroy a third party's rights in property created before the administration. In particular, s 437A did not give the administrator the power to take control of computer components in the possession of a computer assembler where those components were subject to a pledge created prior to the commencement of administration.

The administrator is also given further additional powers under s 442A. The administrator may remove a director from office, appoint a person as a director, do anything in the company's name and on its behalf such as executing a document or bringing proceedings and whatever else is necessary for the purposes of the administration.

Where a company's property was subject to a floating charge and the charge crystallised on the appointment of the administrator or for some other reason, the administrator may deal with any of that property as if the charge were still a floating charge: s 442B. This provision enables an administrator to continue the company's business and deal with its assets despite the interest of the charge holder. Normally, the crystallisation of a floating charge results in the charge becoming fixed and this prevents the company dealing with the charged assets in the ordinary course of its business. This would effectively prevent the administrator from taking control of the company and proceeding with the administration. Section 442B restricts the rights of a debenture-holder secured by a floating charge so as to enable the company's business to be carried on during the administration.

The administrator may dispose of the business and property of the company without convening a general meeting of members: *Brash Holdings Ltd v Shafir* (1994) 12 ACLC 619. The administrator also has the power to terminate employment of company employees: *Australian Liquor, Hospitality & Miscellaneous Workers' Union v Terranora Lakes Country Club Ltd* (1996) 14 ACLC 1200.

In order to protect the interests of secured creditors and lessors and owners of property used by the company, the administrator is prevented from disposing of the charged or leased property: s 442C(1). This general prohibition aims to protect the interests of secured creditors and lessors during the time their rights of enforcement are suspended.

There are, however, three exceptions to the general rule contained in s 442C(2) that enable an administrator to dispose of such assets. A disposal of assets may occur in the ordinary course of the company's business. This allows an administrator to sell trading stock over which a charge is held. Assets may also be disposed of with the written consent of the chargee, owner or lessor or with the leave of the court. Such leave will only be given if the court is satisfied that arrangements have been made to adequately protect the interests of the chargee, owner or lessor: s 442C(3). The administrator's powers are subject to the rights of enforcement given to chargees, owners and lessors by ss 441A–441K: s 442D. These rights are discussed below, paras [24.145]–[24.170].

case note

In *Osborne Computer Corp Ltd v Riddell* (1995) 13 ACLC 1210, the Supreme Court of New South Wales gave an administrator leave under s 442C(3) to sell goods that were the subject of retention of title clauses provided the sales were in the ordinary course of business. The court noted that a sale of goods would not be in the ordinary course of business if it occurred after the owner demanded return of the goods or if the sale was made contrary to the terms of the contract for supply of the goods. The court also granted leave to sell goods subject to retention of title clauses where the sale was not in the ordinary course of business. In this case, leave was conditional on the cost of the goods being paid into a separate account.

The CAMAC report recommended that companies in a corporate group should be permitted to enter into a pooled administration. The effect of this would be that the assets and liabilities of the companies are pooled and that the creditors of all the companies would be treated as if they were creditors of one entity.

An administrator has qualified privilege in respect of statements made in the course of acting as the administrator: s 442E. This is similar to the qualified privilege of a liquidator under s 535. It aims to protect the administrator from defamation actions brought in respect of the contents of reports and other communications.

An administrator comes within the definition of "eligible applicant" in s 9. This enables an administrator to seek the issue of a summons for examination under ss 596A and 596B and enables an administrator to obtain information and conduct an examination in similar ways to a liquidator. The object of this power encompasses anything that may fairly be expected to advance the course of the administration and particularly the deed of company arrangement.

An administrator is deemed to be an officer of the company for the purposes of entitling a person dealing with the company to make the assumptions set out in s 129. These assumptions are discussed in Chapter 5 above. The outsider may assume that the administrator is acting within her or his functions and powers as administrator and is complying with the *Corporations Act*: s 442F(1).

liabilities and indemnity

personal liability

[24.55] The administrator is personally liable for debts incurred in the course of the administration for services rendered, goods bought or property leased or used: s 443A(1). This is despite any contrary agreement, although the administrator retains rights against the company or anyone else: s 443A(2). This liability on the part of the administrator is necessary to encourage third parties to do business with the company so as to enable it to trade out of difficulties.

case note

In *Molit (No 55) Pty Ltd v Lam Soon Australia Pty Ltd* (1996) 14 ACLC 1371, the Federal Court held that an administrator was not liable for damages caused by his removal of fixtures and fittings from leased premises. A liability for damages was not a debt for purposes of s 443A(1).

The administrator is also personally liable for the payment of rent on property leased before their appointment: s 443B. This liability only arises seven days after appointment, during which time the administrator can make a preliminary assessment of the financial position of the company and decide whether the continuation of the lease is the appropriate course. If the administrator decides not to continue the lease, no personal liability for rental payments is incurred.

The administrator is not liable for rental payments after a receiver of the property is appointed or the chargee or an agent takes steps to assume control of the property under the charge: s 443B(7). The court may also excuse the administrator from liability: s 443B(8).

An administrator comes within the s 9 definition of "officer" for purposes of the statutory duties in Pt 2D.1 of the *Corporations Act*.

case note

In *Re Heesh* (2000) 37 ACSR 198, Heesh unsuccessfully appealed against the decision by the Companies Auditors and Liquidators Disciplinary Board (CALDB) to suspend his registration as a registered liquidator. The suspension meant that he could not act as an administrator. Heesh and his partner had been appointed as joint administrators of a company, however, they agreed between themselves that Heesh would not take an active role. The CALDB suspended both Heesh and his partner. His partner's registration was suspended because he acted improperly in the administration. Heesh's registration was also suspended because he did nothing at all in the administration. The AAT held that Heesh had breached the statutory duty of care under the predecessor of s 180(1). An administrator cannot argue that they acted reasonably when the administrator did nothing at all, and in effect turned a blind eye to what their co-administrator was doing.

right of indemnity

The administrator is entitled to an indemnity out of the company's property for debts and remuneration.

[24.60] While the administrator may be personally liable for debts incurred in exercising powers during the administration, the administrator is entitled to an indemnity out of the company's property for these debts and for their remuneration: s 443D.

This right of indemnity has priority over all the company's unsecured debts and also generally the debts of the company secured by a floating charge over its property: s 443E(1). The indemnity does not take priority over fixed charges.

Where a floating charge has crystallised and has become a fixed charge prior to the beginning of the administration and the chargee has taken steps to enforce the charge, the right of indemnity of the administrator does not take priority over the chargee's debt unless agreed to by the chargee: s 443E(2). This indicates that where a receiver was appointed or the chargee or an agent entered into possession to enforce a floating charge before the beginning of the administration, it is treated as if it were always a fixed charge.

In a case where the floating charge crystallises after the beginning of the administration, as for example under s 441A, the administrator's right of indemnity takes priority over the chargee's debt only in relation to debts incurred or remuneration accruing before written notice of the action to enforce the charge was given to the administrator: s 443E(3).

The administrator's right of indemnity is secured by a lien on the company's property: s 443F(1). This lien has priority over a charge only in so far as the right of indemnity has priority over debts secured by the charge: s 443F(2).

The operation of ss 443E(3) and 443F(2) limits the statutory right of an administrator to an indemnity and lien in relation to debts incurred and remuneration after a receiver gives notice of appointment by a secured creditor. However, an administrator may still be entitled to a lien and remuneration for time spent exclusively on the realisation of assets on general equitable principles which are not displaced by Pt 5.3A. An equitable lien covers a wider range of liabilities than those referred to by s 443A(1): *Commonwealth Bank v Butterell* (1994) 12 ACLC 727.

remuneration

[24.65] The administrator is entitled to the remuneration fixed by a resolution of the company's creditors. If no remuneration is fixed, the administrator may apply to the court. The court may also review the remuneration fixed by the creditors: s 449E.

The CAMAC report recommended that administrators' remuneration should also be able to be approved by agreement between the administrator and a simple majority (by value) of the committee of creditors. Approval by the committee of creditors should be effective only until the major meeting or any other general meeting of creditors.

removal and replacement of administrator

[24.70] Once appointed, an administrator's appointment cannot be revoked: s 449A. This helps to ensure the independence of an administrator. The court may remove the administrator from office and appoint someone else on the application of ASIC or a creditor: s 449B. An order for removal of an administrator should only be made if it would be for the better conduct of the administration. It is not enough to show that a substantial or majority by value creditor wanted the administrator removed: *Network Exchange Pty Ltd v MIG International Communications Pty Ltd* (1994) 12 ACLC 594.

An administrator's appointment cannot be revoked and can only be removed by the court.

If the administrator of a company dies, becomes prohibited from continuing to act or resigns, someone else may be appointed by the directors, liquidator or chargee depending on who initiated the original appointment: s 449C. Where the office of administrator of a deed of company arrangement becomes similarly vacant, the court may order the appointment of a replacement: s 449D.

meetings of creditors

first creditors' meeting

[24.75] The administrator must convene a meeting of creditors within five business days of appointment: s 436E. The CAMAC report recommended that the time of convening the first creditors' meeting should be extended to within eight business days of the administrator's appointment.

The administrator must convene a first meeting of creditors within five business days of appointment.

The purpose of the meeting is to determine whether to appoint a committee of creditors and, if so, its composition: s 436E(1). The meeting may also pass a resolution to remove the administrator and appoint someone else as a replacement: s 436E(4).

Notice of the meeting must be given in writing to as many creditors as is reasonably practical and must be published in a newspaper: s 436E(3). Defects of a procedural nature such as failure to publish notice in a newspaper may be validated under s 1322(4) if the substantial requirements have been satisfied and no substantial injustice has been caused: *Re Vanfox Pty Ltd* (1994) 7 ACLC 357.

The functions of the committee of creditors are:

> **to consult with the administrator on matters relating to the administration; and**
> **to receive and consider reports by the administrator: s 436F(1).**

A committee cannot give directions to the administrator; however, it can compel the administrator to report on matters relating to the administration: s 436F(2) and (3).

Members of a committee of creditors must be creditors of the company or an attorney of a creditor under a general power of attorney or be authorised in writing by a creditor to be a member: s 436G.

meeting to decide the company's future

The administrator must convene a meeting of the company's creditors to decide the company's future within 21 days after the beginning of the administration.

time of the meeting

[24.80] The administrator must convene a meeting of the company's creditors within the convening period: s 439A(1). This is usually 21 days after the beginning of the administration: s 439A(5)(b). The CAMAC report recommended that the time for holding the major creditors' meeting should be extended to within 25 business days of the administrator's appointment. The convening period is automatically extended to 28 days if the administration begins in December or is less than 28 days before Good Friday: s 439A(5)(b).

The court may extend the convening period.

The court may extend the convening period: s 439A(6). In exercising its discretion, the court must consider the spirit of Pt 5.3A in not unduly extending administrations or encouraging applications for extensions. At the same time, the objects set out in s 435A are for an administration to maximise the chances of a company continuing in existence, or to ensure a better return to creditors than would result from an immediate winding up. This may require an extension of time, especially where no creditors are prejudiced: *Mann v Abruzzi Sports Club Ltd* (1994) 12 ACLC 137.

case note

In *Watson v Uniframes Ltd* (1995) 13 ACLC 609, the Federal Court held that it had no power to extend the time for convening the meeting under s 439A(6) unless the application for extension was made within the convening period. On the other hand, in *Re Greg Sewell Forgings Pty Ltd* (1995) 13 ACLC 1172, the Victorian Supreme Court held that the court had power under s 1322 to validate a meeting convened outside the period.

The meeting must be held within five days after the end of the convening period.

The meeting must be held within five days after the end of the convening period: s 439A(2).

Notice of the meeting must be given in writing to as many creditors as is reasonably practical and must be published in a national newspaper at least five business days before the meeting: s 439A(3).

case note

In *Re Ansett Australia Ltd and Mentha (No 3)* [2002] FCA 2, the administrators of the Ansett group of companies asserted that requiring them to comply with the written notice requirements of s 439A(3) would cause administrative difficulties and considerable expense as they would be required to notify over three million creditors. They sought court permission to place notice of the meeting and accompanying documentation on Ansett's websites and place large advertisements in two national and all capital city newspapers and provide a hotline for creditors to telephone to obtain copies of the documentation. The Federal Court held that "giving written notice" for purposes of s 439A(3) meant that a document had to be given to creditors. However, the court decided that notice by way of the Internet and newspapers would be appropriate and sufficient notice if creditors were told in the notice that the relevant documentation would be provided if they telephoned the administrator or downloaded it from the website.

A failure to give five days' notice of a creditors' meeting may be validated by the court under s 1322 where no material disadvantage has been caused to creditors: *Hagenvale Pty Ltd v Depela Pty Ltd* (1995) 13 ACLC 886.

adjournment

The meeting may be adjourned from time-to-time but not for more than 60 days.

[24.85] The meeting may be adjourned from time-to-time but not for more than 60 days: s 439B. The provision for adjournments encourages agreements to be negotiated because creditors may have various attitudes towards proposed steps that should be taken.

If a resolution on the future of the company has not been passed within 60 days, the administration comes to an end and control of the company reverts to the directors: s 435C(3)(e). This limit of 60 days may place pressure on some creditors to come to an agreement with other creditors rather than allow control of the company to return to the directors. The end of the administration also enables creditors to enforce their rights. Thus, secured creditors could exercise their security over the company's assets.

The court has power to order that the 60-day limit be exceeded.

The court has power under s 447A to order that the 60-day limit be exceeded where this is necessary to determine whether a deed of company arrangement could be successful and is not used as a delaying tactic against creditors. The court must consider whether it is in everyone's interest to have the administration continue rather than have the company wound up: *Cawthorn v Keira Constructions Pty Ltd* (1994) 12 ACLC 396.

case note

In *Re Taylor* (1995) 13 ACLC 313, a creditors' meeting was adjourned for 60 days under s 439B. Prior to the expiry of the 60-day period, the administrator applied to the court for extension. This was granted by the Supreme Court of New South Wales on the basis that the administrator had not been able to learn enough about the company's financial affairs to provide meaningful advice to creditors about their options. Further, creditors did not appear to be prejudiced by the extension.

information to be given to creditors

[24.90] Section 439A(4) sets out the information that must accompany the notice of the creditors' meeting and seeks to ensure that creditors are given sufficient information to make an informed decision about the company's future. Under that section, the notice must be accompanied by a copy of:

> the administrator's report about the company's business, property, affairs and financial circumstances (s 439A(4)(a));
> a statement setting out the administrator's opinion with reasons as to whether it is in the creditors' interests for the company to execute a deed of company arrangement, whether administration should come to an end or whether the company should be wound up (s 439A(4)(b)); and
> if a deed of company arrangement is proposed, a statement setting out the details of the deed must be provided: s 439A(4)(c).

case note

In *Deputy Commissioner of Taxation v Comcorp Australia Ltd* (1996) 14 ACLC 1616, the Federal Court held that the administrator could set out the s 439A(4) statements and report in one document. Further, the administrator's statement under s 439A(4)(b) must deal separately with each proposed course of action.

the administrator's report

The administrator must give creditors a report.

[24.95] Under s 439A(4)(a), the administrator must give creditors a report about the company's business, property, affairs and financial circumstances. According to the Federal Court in *Deputy Commissioner of Taxation v Comcorp Australia Ltd* (1996) 14 ACLC 1616, the information in an administrator's report need not be as extensive as is required for an explanatory statement for a scheme of arrangement under Pt 5.1A. However, it must contain sufficient information as can be reasonably expected to be material to creditors in all the circumstances.

Regulation 5.3A.02 of the *Corporations Regulations* sets out the prescribed information that must be contained in an administrator's report. This requires an administrator to specify whether there are any transactions that appear to be voidable transactions recoverable by a liquidator. Though it is not prescribed, an administrator should also indicate whether directors might be liable for insolvent trading should the company be placed in liquidation. Such information is relevant to creditors in assessing the relative merits of a winding up compared to entering a deed of company arrangement.

The Parliamentary Committee on Corporations and Financial Services (PJC) report, *Corporate Insolvency Laws: A Stocktake* (June 2004), recommended that the administrator's report to creditors should be required to include "any other matter material to the creditors' decision". The report also recommended that ASIC should publish a guidance note to assist administrators in this regard.

what decisions can creditors make?

The creditors' meeting may resolve that one of three steps be taken.

[24.100] At the creditors' meeting, the creditors may, under s 439C, resolve that one of three steps be taken:

> **the company execute a deed of company arrangement as specified in the resolution;**
> **the administration should end; or**
> **the company be wound up.**

voting at creditors' meetings

[24.105] The *Corporations Regulations* set out such matters as which creditors can vote and the required majorities necessary to pass resolutions at creditors' meetings.

Under reg 5.6.23(1), a creditor is entitled to vote only if:

> **their debt has been admitted wholly or in part by the administrator; and**
> **they have lodged with the administrator particulars of their claims or a formal proof of debt (if required).**

A creditor must not vote in respect of an unliquidated debt or claim or a contingent debt or claim: reg 5.6.23(2).

If a poll is demanded, a creditors' resolution is passed by a simple majority by number of creditors and value of debts owed.

Unless a poll is demanded, resolutions at creditors' meetings are passed by a simple majority of those present and voting in favour on a show of hands: reg 5.6.19. Under reg 5.6.21, if a poll is demanded, a creditors' resolution is passed by a simple majority by number of creditors and value of debts owed. If there is a deadlock between the majority in number and majority in value of creditors voting, the resolution is not passed. In cases of deadlock in the voting, the chair of a creditors' meeting (usually the administrator) has a casting vote and can vote either in favour of, or against the resolution: reg 5.6.21(4).

If creditors give an administrator general proxies with discretion on how to vote, the administrator is entitled to use those proxy votes to vote against a motion to remove the administrator: *Re Builders Associated Pty Ltd* [2001] NSWSC 626.

Occasionally, there may be concern that decisions made at creditors' meetings may be influenced by creditors who are either insiders or associated with insiders. Section 600A is designed to prevent such creditors from exercising an unfair influence over creditors' meetings.

Under s 600A(2), the court may, on the application of a creditor, set aside a resolution passed at a meeting of creditors. The court also has the power to order the reconvening of creditors' meetings and remove the voting rights of a "related creditor". A "related creditor" is a "related entity of the company" to whom a debt is owed: s 600A(3). Section 9 defines "related entity" in broad terms. It includes a director or member of the company and relatives of directors and members as well as related companies.

The court can only make an s 600A(2) order if the resolution was carried by the votes of related creditors and the resolution is contrary to the interests of the creditors as a whole or prejudices the interests of the creditors who voted against it: s 600A(1).

Section 600B gives the court the power to set aside or vary a resolution that is passed on the casting vote of the person who chaired the meeting. This enables the court to review decisions of the chairman.

case note

In *Cresvale Far East Ltd v Cresvale Securities Ltd* (2001) 19 ACLC 659, the administrator, who chaired a creditors' meeting, exercised a casting vote to defeat a resolution for his removal as administrator in circumstances where a majority of creditors by number voted against the resolution, but a majority of creditors in value voted in favour of the resolution. The court held that while there was no general rule that administrators should exercise their casting vote to prefer the view of the majority in value over the view of the majority in number, the court would take into account any large disproportion between the values of the debts of the numerical minority and the numerical majority. It was not appropriate for the administrator to use his casting vote in order to defeat a resolution for his removal, particularly in circumstances where the largest creditor in value had twice attempted to remove him from office.

effect of administration

[24.110] While a company is under administration, the administrator controls its business, property and affairs. The administrator may perform the functions or exercise the powers that the company or its officers could perform or exercise if the company were not under administration: s 437A.

While a company is under administration, the administrator controls its business, property and affairs and officers of the company lose their rights to exercise their powers as officers.

The administrator is taken to act as the company's agent: s 437B. This means that the administrator's actions bind the company generally.

While a company is under administration, officers of the company, excluding employees, lose their rights to exercise their powers as officers: s 437C(1). Officers, however, are not removed from office and may be allowed by the administrator to participate in management: s 437C(2). Members are excluded from any role during an administration: *Brash Holdings Ltd v Shafir* (1994) 12 ACLC 619.

Where a company is under administration, its property can only be dealt with by the administrator or with their written consent or by order of the court. Any other transaction or dealing is void: s 437D.

An officer who breaches s 437C by purporting to enter into a void transaction or dealing on the company's behalf or is in any other way knowingly concerned in, or party to, the transaction or dealing is guilty of an offence: s 437D(5). Where an officer is found guilty of breaching s 437D and the court is satisfied that the company or another person suffered loss or damage as a result, the court may order the officer to pay compensation, whether or not a penalty is imposed: s 437E(1).

The court may relieve an officer from liability to pay compensation under s 437E in the circumstances set out in s 1318. This section is discussed in Chapter 13.7 above, and provides that an officer may be relieved from liability where he or she acted honestly and ought fairly to be excused.

Once the administration of a company begins, any transfer of shares or alteration in the status of members is void except where the court otherwise orders: s 437F.

The acts and things done in good faith by an administrator are valid and effectual and are not liable to be set aside in a winding up of the company: s 451C. This means that payments made during an administration within six months of the commencement of winding up are not voidable as unfair preferences.

If a company is required to do some act within a particular period or before a particular time and this is prevented by the legislation, the period is extended or the time is deferred according to how long the act is prevented from being done by the legislation: s 451D. This extension or deferment of time applies to requirements of any law or under contracts. This provision acknowledges that Pt 5.3A may prejudice the rights of creditors in certain circumstances where a moratorium is imposed and so time does not run where a restraint on action results from the operation of the legislation. In *Milankov Nominees Pty Ltd v Roycol Ltd* (1994) 12 ACLC 734, the six-month period applicable to applications to wind up a company in insolvency was extended so as to exclude the period during which a company was under administration.

The company must set out in all its public documents and negotiable instruments the words "administrator appointed".

The company must set out in all its public documents and negotiable instruments the words "administrator appointed" or "subject to deed of company arrangement", as the case may be: s 450E. This requirement may be dispensed with by order of the court under s 447A: *Re Brashs Pty Ltd* (1995) 13 ACLC 110. A failure to give the required notice does not affect the validity of any act or omission, except so far as the court otherwise orders: s 450F.

moratorium on claims against the company and its directors

purpose of moratorium

[24.115] The administration process enables creditors to consider and vote on the future of the company. During the administration, the company is protected from actions that may be taken against it by individual creditors or others such as lessors. Such actions may undermine the position of the company to the detriment of a majority of creditors. For this reason, ss 440A–440J impose a moratorium or stay of proceedings against the company and guarantors of its debts.

A moratorium or stay of proceedings imposed against the company and guarantors of its debts.

stay of proceedings

[24.120] From the time of appointment of the administrator, a civil proceeding cannot be brought against the company or in relation to any of its property except with the administrator's written consent or the leave of the court: s 440D. This provision is an important protection for the company and gives the administrator and creditors breathing space to consider the appropriate course of action. This moratorium does not prevent criminal proceedings and certain prescribed proceedings being brought.

Section 440D does not stay an appeal by the company against a judgment obtained prior to the commencement of administration. The appeal is not a proceeding against a company for purposes of s 440D: *Uranna Pty Ltd v Tsang Chi Thug* (1997) 15 ACLC 443.

Where the court grants leave to proceed with an action under s 440D, this only authorises the prosecution of an action either against the company while it is under administration or against the administrator. After a deed of company arrangement is executed a further grant of leave is required under s 444E(3): *Roder Zelt Und Hallenkonstruktionen GmbH v Rosedown Park Pty Ltd* (1995) 13 ACLC 776.

In addition to the general stay of proceedings against the company, the legislation also restricts the rights of a judgment creditor to enforce a judgment against a company under administration: s 440F. This is also necessary to preserve the company's financial position during the administration.

Once a court officer such as a sheriff or registrar receives written notice of the fact that a company is under administration, the court officer cannot take further enforcement action and must hand over any property of the company in her or his possession to the administrator: s 440G. A person who buys property in good faith under a sale under a process of execution receives good title to the property: s 440G(8).

winding up cannot proceed

A company under administration cannot generally be wound up voluntarily.

[24.125] A company under administration cannot be wound up voluntarily except as provided under s 446A: s 440A(1). The court will adjourn an application for an order that a company be wound up and will not appoint a provisional liquidator if it is satisfied that it is in the interests of the creditors for the company to continue under administration rather than be wound up or have a provisional liquidator appointed: s 440A(2) and (3).

charges unenforceable

[24.130] During the administration of a company, a charge over the company's property cannot be enforced except with the administrator's written consent or with the leave of the court: s 440B. This general rule seeks to preserve the company's business and its continued existence by preventing an individual creditor from taking control of the company's assets by appointing a receiver or mortgagee in possession or agent and thereby preventing the administration from proceeding. Leave is not required under s 440B if the chargee had begun court proceedings to enforce the charge prior to the commencement of administration. However, leave to continue the proceedings is required under s 440D: *BBC Hardware Ltd v GT Homes Pty Ltd* (1997) 15 ACLC 431.

A charge over the company's property cannot be enforced except with the administrator's written consent or with the leave of the court.

A chargee can give notice to a company under the terms of a charge: s 441E. Although the chargee cannot enforce the charge during the administration because of s 440B, the giving of notice will allow for prompt enforcement as soon as the administration ends. Similarly, notice can also be given by a lessor or owner of property used by the company: s 441J.

Certain secured creditors and others are entitled to protection from the general moratorium rules and there are provisions that seek to balance the interests of particular creditors against the general objects of the legislation. These exceptions are discussed below, paras [24.145]–[24.170].

owners and lessors cannot recover property

[24.135] In addition to restrictions on chargees enforcing charges against the company's property, owners and lessors of property used by the company also cannot take possession or otherwise recover the property without the administrator's written consent or the leave of the court: s 440C. This proposed provision also aims to protect property that is necessary for the company's continued existence so that the administration can continue. If a company leases premises or equipment that are essential to its business, the lessor cannot recover the leased property as the administration would be severely disrupted. Similarly, unpaid vendors are unable to recover goods sold under retention of title clauses.

Owners and lessors of property used by the company cannot take possession or otherwise recover the property without the administrator's written consent or the leave of the court.

This general rule is subject to similar exceptions as apply to enable the enforcement of charges over the company's property. For example, a lessor who has already taken steps to repossess property before the appointment of the administrator can enforce rights under the lease: s 441F.

guarantor directors

[24.140] Directors often guarantee their company's debts to creditors. If directors' guarantees could be enforced by creditors, this would have the effect of discouraging directors from appointing an administrator as this would immediately trigger personal liability under the guarantee. The moratorium provisions therefore prevent a creditor enforcing a guarantee against a director, spouse or relative of a director in respect of a liability of the company: s 440J(1). This stay is subject to leave of the court or an order of the court to preserve the assets of the director during the administration or other order under s 1323: s 440J(2).

The moratorium provisions prevent a creditor enforcing a guarantee against a director, spouse or relative of a director in respect of a liability of the company.

Leave of the court under s 440J(1) will not be granted unless there is something more than the guarantor being denied the benefit of the guarantee. This is especially so where the administration would be impeded and implementation of the deed of company arrangement prejudiced: *Re Grenadier Constructions No 2 Pty Ltd* (1993) 12 ACLC 460.

Section 440J applies only to proceedings relating to enforcement of guarantees. It does not prevent a creditor from issuing a bankruptcy notice against a guarantor director: *Re Behan* (1995) 13 ACLC 1644.

exceptions to the moratorium provisions

[24.145] There are several sections that protect the rights of certain secured creditors and lessors of property to the company. These protections constitute exceptions to the general rules discussed above, which are aimed at enabling the company's business to continue in accordance with the objects of the legislation stated in s 435A.

charge over whole of company's property

A secured creditor that has a charge over the whole, or substantially the whole, of the property of a company under administration may enforce the charge within a "decision period".

[24.150] A secured creditor that has a charge over the whole, or substantially the whole, of the property of a company under administration may enforce the charge within a "decision period", defined in s 9 as being 10 business days after the chargee was given notice of the appointment of an administrator to the company: s 441A. The administrator must give notice of appointment to holders of charges over all or nearly all of the company's property under s 450A(3). The moratorium provisions that would otherwise prevent this enforcement, ss 437C, 437D and 440B, are specifically excluded: s 441A(3) and (4).

This exception recognises that a creditor holding a security over virtually the whole of the company's assets is entitled to be placed in a favoured position and be able to appoint a receiver. In such a case, the receiver is also capable of achieving an orderly administration by gaining control of virtually all of the company's assets.

One uncertainty with this exception is that the expression "substantially the whole" of the property of a company is not defined in the legislation. This may result in disputes where a secured creditor seeks to come within the exception and enforce rights independently of the administration.

secured creditor takes possession before commencement of administration

Where a charge is enforced by a receiver before the administrator was appointed. The charge may continue to be enforced after the administration has begun.

[24.155] Similar protection is afforded where a charge is enforced by a receiver or other person who has entered into possession or assumed control of the property of the company before the administrator was appointed. The charge may continue to be enforced after the administration has begun: s 441B. The moratorium provisions that would otherwise prevent this, ss 437C, 437D and 440B, are excluded: s 441B(2) and (3).

Where a secured creditor has started to exercise rights under a charge to sell property before the appointment of an administrator, the sale process may continue after the administration has begun. The moratorium provisions are again excluded: s 441B(1).

This exception recognises that where a secured creditor takes action before the directors appoint an administrator, the creditor should not be impeded by the administrator. This encourages directors to appoint an administrator before the company defaults under a charge over its assets.

enforcement of rights by owners and lessors before commencement of administration

[24.160] The enforcement of rights commenced before the beginning of the administration by the owner or lessor of property used by the company can also continue after the administrator has been appointed: s 441F. This is despite s 440C, which is discussed above.

perishable goods

[24.165] A creditor holding security over perishable goods may enforce a charge in relation to those goods despite the appointment of an administrator: s 441C. The general moratorium provisions do not apply because the creditor could be harshly affected by a delay.

leave of the court

[24.170] Certain of the exceptions to the moratorium provisions are subject to the power of the court. The court may order a chargee, receiver or other person to refrain from performing a function or exercising a power that would otherwise be permissible under s 441B(1): s 441D. The administrator may apply for such an order, which will only be made if the court is satisfied that the administrator proposes to act in a way that will adequately protect the chargee's interests. The power of the court under s 441D does not extend to limit the power of the holder of a charge over the whole, or substantially the whole, of the company's property under s 441A: s 441D(1).

Exceptions to the moratorium provisions are subject to the power of the court.

This power of the court is aimed at preventing a secured creditor from undermining the purpose of the administration where this is inappropriate. The creditor's interests may be capable of adequate safeguard within the administration procedure, which may ultimately benefit most other creditors.

The court may similarly order that an owner or lessor of property used by the company refrain from enforcing rights that would otherwise be enforceable under ss 441F and 441G: s 441H. The court must also be satisfied that the interests of the owner or lessor will be adequately protected.

deed of company arrangement

purpose of deed

[24.175] A deed of company arrangement is one of the possible outcomes for a company that is put into voluntary administration. The s 435A objects of the voluntary administration scheme—to save insolvent companies or their businesses or achieve a better return for their creditors than liquidation—are largely achieved by deeds of company arrangement.

The objects of the voluntary administration scheme are largely achieved by deeds of company arrangement.

A company becomes subject to a deed of company arrangement in the following manner. As discussed above, one of the key tasks of a voluntary administrator is to report to creditors on whether it would be in their interests that the company executes a deed of company arrangement. Other interested parties, such as directors or major shareholders, may also propose deeds of company arrangement. If creditors vote in favour of a proposed company arrangement and the company and the voluntary administrator execute the deed, voluntary administration ends: s 435C(2)(a). The company's voluntary administrator becomes the administrator of the deed unless the creditors appoint someone else: s 444A(2).

The information provided to creditors at the second creditors' meeting means that creditors have the opportunity to make a cost benefit analysis and decide whether the company's liquidation or a deed of company arrangement produces a better outcome for them. This analysis will include an assessment of the likelihood of a liquidator increasing the amount of the company's assets available for distribution to creditors by successful proceedings against directors for breach of fiduciary or statutory duties such as insolvent trading.

In some cases, directors may be prepared to contribute to funds available for distribution to creditors in a deed of company arrangement from their own personal resources in order to avoid potentially higher claims against themselves if the company were liquidated. This is likely to be the case if, prior to the commencement of voluntary administration, directors have failed to prevent insolvent trading, have received unfair preferences or have breached their fiduciary duties by not taking creditors' interests into account. In addition, directors may be willing to contribute to a deed of company arrangement to regain control over the company's business or purchase some or all of its assets perhaps for a higher price than would be paid by outsiders. Directors may be in a better position to utilise the company's carry forward tax losses than third party purchasers of the company's shares.

Creditors who supplied goods and services to a company prior to its voluntary administration may be induced to vote in favour of a deed if this results in the company continuing as a customer. Creditors may also vote in favour of a deed if they perceive that the company can trade its way out of financial trouble with more competent management provided by the deed administrator.

If the administrator proposes a deed of company arrangement, a statement setting out its details must be sent out to creditors with the notice of the creditors' meeting convened under s 439A.

terms of deed

The *Corporations Act* is extremely flexible as to the terms of a deed of company arrangement so as to enable the arrangement to meet the particular needs and circumstances of the company and its various creditors.

[24.180] The *Corporations Act* is extremely flexible as to the terms of a deed of company arrangement so as to enable the arrangement to meet the particular needs and circumstances of the company and its various creditors. Typically, deeds of company arrangement may have the following features:

- **provision for a moratorium under which the company has additional time to pay debts incurred prior to the commencement of voluntary administration. The company, under the control of the deed administrator, is permitted to continue operating its business;**
- **provision for a compromise under which the creditors agree to accept payment of a lesser amount in final settlement of their debts;**
- **a combination of a moratorium and compromise with creditors; and**
- **an orderly sale of all the company's property over an agreed period of time.**

case note

A deed of company arrangement may provide for differential treatment of creditors: *Lam Soon Australia Pty Ltd v Molit (No 55) Pty Ltd* (1996) 14 ACLC 1737. In this case, the deed of company arrangement proposed to close an unprofitable part of the company's business and continue a profitable part. The creditors connected to the profitable part of the company's business were likely to receive more than other creditors because they maintained a continuing relationship with the company.

If the company's creditors resolve that the company execute a deed of company arrangement they must appoint a person to be the deed administrator.

If the company's creditors resolve that the company execute a deed of company arrangement they must appoint a person to be the deed administrator: s 444A(2). This will usually be the initial administrator who is familiar with the circumstances of the company. The administrator must prepare the instrument setting out the terms of the deed: s 444A(3). There are certain requirements regarding the contents of the deed set out in s 444A(4). These include:

- the property of the company available to pay creditors' claims;
- the nature and duration of any moratorium period;
- the extent to which the company is released from its debts;
- any conditions for the deed to come into operation or to continue in operation;
- when the deed terminates;
- the priorities among creditors bound by the deed; and
- the day on or before which admissible claims must have arisen.

Unless expressly excluded, the property of the company available to pay creditors' claims includes compensation payable by a director to the company arising from a successful action brought by ASIC under the civil penalty provisions. The order for compensation does not have to be made before the deed of company arrangement is executed. It is sufficient that the asset, being the right to claim the compensation, exists at the time of distribution to creditors: *Elliott v Water Wheel Holdings Ltd* [2004] FCAFC 253.

Further prescribed provisions are taken to be included in the deed unless excluded: s 444A(5). These prescribed provisions are set out in the *Corporations Regulations* and provide for various matters such as the making of claims, priorities of claims, discharge of debts and appointment of a committee of inspection.

execution by creditors and company

[24.185] The company must execute the instrument that sets out the terms of the deed of company arrangement within 21 days after the meeting of creditors or such further time as the court allows: s 444B(2). The board of the company may by resolution authorise the execution of the instrument: s 444B(3).

The company must execute the deed of company arrangement within 21 days after the meeting of creditors or such further time as the court allows.

case note

In *MYT Engineering Pty Ltd v Mulcon Pty Ltd* (1999) 17 ACLC 861, the affixing of the company's seal to a deed of company arrangement was witnessed by a director who signed as both a director and secretary. While the board of directors had approved the execution of the instrument in this manner, it was contrary to the company's constitution, which required documents bearing the company's seal to be signed by a director, and countersigned by another director or secretary. The High Court held that the deed of company arrangement was validly executed notwithstanding that it was not signed in accordance with its constitution. The court noted that the fact that s 444B(2) referred to a company "executing an instrument" meant that a deed of company arrangement did not necessarily have to be executed as a deed. In this case the signature of the director authenticated the document. "It expressed, in visible terms, the company's assent to the arrangement." The administrator must also execute the deed: s 444B(5).

If a company fails to execute the deed within the prescribed time, it is deemed to have entered into a creditors' voluntary winding up.

If a company fails to execute the deed within the prescribed time, it is deemed to have entered into a creditors' voluntary winding up and the administrator is deemed to have been appointed as liquidator: s 446A(1). The transition into liquidation is discussed below.

Upon execution of the deed, the administration comes to an end under s 435C(2)(a) and the statutory moratorium in place during the administration is replaced by the provisions of the deed and certain statutory restrictions.

Upon execution of the deed, the administration comes to an end and the statutory moratorium in place during the administration is replaced by the provisions of the deed.

As soon as practicable after execution of a deed of company arrangement, the administrator must send notice of this to all creditors and cause this notice to be published in a national newspaper. A copy of the deed must be lodged with ASIC: s 450B.

effect of deed

[24.190] If a company's creditors resolve that the company execute a deed of company arrangement, creditors and others are bound by the deed even before it is executed: s 444C(1). They must not do anything inconsistent with the deed except with leave of the court.

unsecured creditors

A deed of company arrangement binds all unsecured creditors.

[24.195] A deed of company arrangement binds all unsecured creditors of the company so far as concerns claims arising on or before the day specified in the deed: s 444D(1).

case note

The meaning of "creditors" was considered in *Brash Holdings Ltd v Katile Pty Ltd* (1994) 12 ACLC 472. Companies in the Brashs group applied to the court under s 447A for a declaration that a deed of company arrangement was binding on current and contingent creditors. In particular, the administrators sought to bind lessors of premises rented by the companies in respect of future rent and outgoings that arose after the date specified in the deed. The Full Court of the Supreme Court of Victoria held that "creditors" extended beyond creditors whose claims arose on or before the date specified in the deed. It meant all creditors for the time being of the company as understood in the context of other references to "creditors" in Pt 5.3A and who are creditors for the purposes of a winding up under s 553. The reference to "claims arising on or before the day specified in the deed" is for the purpose of fixing a date as at which the existence of the claim is to be determined. It does not exclude future debts or claims and has similar effect to s 553 in relation to the "relevant date" in a winding up.

The Australian Taxation Office is also bound by a deed even though it was not a party to it: *Dexcam Australia Pty Ltd v Deputy Commissioner of Taxation* (2002) 20 ACLC 372.

Guarantors of a company's debts are regarded as contingent creditors and are therefore bound by a deed of company arrangement: *Re Zambena Pty Ltd* (1995) 13 ACLC 1020.

case note

In *Daydream Island International Resort Pty Ltd v Cushway Blackford & Assoc (Aust) Pty Ltd* (1995) 13 ACLC 82, a company had entered into a deed of company arrangement. The deed bound parties having a claim against the company being a debt or contingent debt or claim subsisting as at the date specified in the deed. The deed was held to be not binding on a defendant in separate negligence proceedings, which sought to join the company as a third party in these proceedings. The deed only referred to contingent claims that arose before the date specified in the deed. In this case, a claim for indemnity or contribution could only arise if the defendant was later found liable in negligence.

secured creditors

A secured creditor may realise or otherwise enforce or deal with the security unless that creditor has agreed to be bound by the deed or the court limits the rights of the secured creditor.

[24.200] A secured creditor may realise or otherwise enforce or deal with the security unless that creditor has agreed to be bound by the deed or the court limits the rights of the secured creditor under s 444F: s 444D(2). Such an order may only be made if the dealing with the security would have a material adverse effect on achieving the purposes of the deed and the creditor's interests will be adequately protected. The court may similarly order that an owner of property not take possession of it.

owners and lessors

[24.205] The owner or lessor of property used by the company may also enforce rights in relation to the property unless the owner has agreed to be bound by the deed or the court restricts the owner's rights: s 444D(3). The power of the court to limit the rights of secured creditors and lessors is discussed below.

The owner or lessor of property used by the company may enforce rights in relation to the property unless the owner has agreed to be bound by the deed or the court restricts the owner's rights.

prevention of winding up applications and other proceedings

[24.210] While the deed has effect, creditors and other persons bound by it are prevented from making an application for the winding up of the company, beginning or proceeding with an action against the company or in relation to its property or enforcing a court order against the company or its property: s 444E(1)–(3). These prohibitions are subject to the leave of the court.

While the deed has effect, creditors are prevented from making an application for the winding up of the company.

company and its officers

[24.215] A deed of company arrangement is binding upon the company, its officers and members and the deed's administrator: s 444G. The company is released from a debt only in so far as the deed provides for the release and the particular creditor is bound by the deed: s 444H. A deed of company arrangement cannot operate to discharge the personal debts of the company's directors. It can only discharge debts of the company: *Re Andersons Home Furnishing Co Pty Ltd* (1996) 14 ACLC 1710.

A deed of company arrangement is binding upon the company, its officers and members and the deed's administrator.

powers of the court to limit rights of secured creditors, owners and lessors

[24.220] Secured creditors and owners and lessors of property used by the company may enforce their rights after the deed comes into effect, except so far as they have agreed to be bound by the deed or the court orders under s 444F.

The court's power to limit the rights of secured creditors, owner and lessors is important in some circumstances to prevent a dissident, secured creditor or lessor from enforcing rights under a charge or lease where this would have a material adverse effect on achieving the purposes of the deed. This would be the case where the company is prevented from carrying on its business. On the other hand, the court will only make such an order if it is satisfied that the creditor's or lessor's interests will be adequately protected under the deed or the order: s 444F(3) and (5). This may involve paying out the creditor or granting further security over other assets owned by the company.

An application for such an order may only be made by the administrator of the company or the deed's administrator as the case may be: s 444F(7).

case note

In *J & B Records Ltd v Brashs Pty Ltd* (1995) 13 ACLC 458, Hodgson J considered that ss 444D, 444E and 444F were intended to set up a code relating to court proceedings in relation to claims arising before the date specified in the deed. This enables the court to control such proceedings either upon applications for leave under s 444E, or for orders limiting the rights of secured creditors or owners of property under s 444F. Hodgson J commented that this approach may encourage self-help and resort to enforcement outside the courts by secured creditors and owners of property. Such action will only be restrained by the courts if their interests are adequately protected.

case note

In *Hamilton v National Australia Bank Ltd* (1996) 14 ACLC 1202, the Federal Court under s 444F(2) ordered a bank, which held a second ranking change, not to deal with its security. There was no real prospect of the bank obtaining any better return than would be the case if the company were wound up. For this reason, the bank's interests were adequately protected by the order.

variation and termination of deed

Creditors of a company subject to a deed of company arrangement have the power to vary the terms of the deed. They may also have the power to terminate a deed and resolve that the company be wound up.

[24.225] Creditors of a company subject to a deed of company arrangement have the power to vary the terms of the deed: s 445A. They may also have the power to terminate a deed and resolve that the company be wound up: s 445E.

variation

[24.230] It is open to a meeting of creditors convened under s 445F to pass a resolution varying a deed as long as the notice of the meeting sets out the proposed variation: s 445A. This enables the company's creditors to vary a deed where circumstances have changed. Creditors who oppose a variation of the deed may apply to the court for an order cancelling the variation. The court has wide powers in dealing with such an application: s 445B.

termination

[24.235] A deed of company arrangement terminates when the court so orders under s 445D, the creditors pass a resolution to that effect in accordance with s 445E at a meeting convened under s 445F, or the deed specifies the circumstances in which it is to terminate and those circumstances exist: s 445C. The court may also order that the deed or a provision of it are void or invalid: s 445G.

The court may terminate a deed of company arrangement under s 445D in a variety of circumstances where the court is satisfied that:

> **information given to the administrator or creditors about the company's financial position was false or misleading and could reasonably be expected to have been material to creditors in deciding whether to vote in favour of the resolution that the company execute the deed;**
> **such information was contained in a report or statement sent to creditors with notice of the creditors' meeting under s 439A at which the resolution was passed;**
> **there was an omission from the report or statement that could reasonably have been expected to have been material to the creditors;**
> **there has been a material contravention of the deed by a person bound by it;**
> **the deed cannot be given effect without injustice or undue delay; or**
> **the deed should be terminated for some other reason.**

case note

In *Deputy Commissioner of Taxation v Woodings* (1995) 13 ACLC 469, it was suggested that a deed of company arrangement could be terminated in circumstances where creditors did not know of a director's previous involvements with insolvent companies and voting at the creditors' meeting was improperly influenced by offers to some creditors to pay their debts in full.

A meeting of creditors may be convened under s 445F to pass a resolution terminating the deed and, where the notice of meeting sets out a proposed resolution that the company be wound up, the creditors may also pass a resolution to this effect: s 445E.

The creditors' meeting to consider whether to terminate or vary the deed may be convened by the administrator of the deed and must be convened if so requested by creditors whose claims comprise no less than 10 per cent of all creditors' claims against the company: s 445F(1).

The meeting must be convened by at least five days' notice and the notice must set out the proposed resolutions: s 445F(2). Notice must be given to all creditors and published in a national newspaper where the creditors resolve to terminate the deed under s 445C(b). Notice must also be lodged and published where the company fails to execute a deed of company arrangement within the 21 days prescribed by s 444B(2): s 450C.

invalidation of deed

[24.240] The court may declare a deed of company arrangement to be void where it was entered into in contravention of the legislation: s 445G. The application for such an order may be made by the administrator, a member or creditor of the company or ASIC.

The court may make an order declaring the whole of the deed or a provision of it to be void or not void: s 445G(2). The court may declare the deed or a provision of it valid despite a contravention of the legislation, where it is satisfied that the legislation was substantially complied with and no injustice would result for anyone bound by the deed: s 445G(3). If the court declares a provision of the deed to be void, it may vary the deed only with the consent of the administrator: s 445G(4).

Where a deed is terminated or declared to be void, parties who previously acted in reliance upon the deed are not affected by the termination or avoidance: s 445H.

transition from administration to winding up

[24.245] The *Corporations Act* provides for a smooth transition from administration to winding up in insolvency. At various stages while a company is under voluntary administration or subject to a deed of company arrangement, the company's creditors may resolve that the company be wound up in insolvency. Such a resolution may be passed at the creditors' meeting convened under s 439A to decide the company's future and at a meeting convened under s 445F terminating a deed of company arrangement.

The *Corporations Act* provides for a smooth transition from administration to winding up in insolvency.

If creditors pass a resolution that the company be wound up in insolvency at either of these meetings, the company is deemed to have entered into a creditors' voluntary winding up and the administrator is deemed to have been appointed as liquidator: s 446A. The administrator is also taken to have been appointed as the liquidator where the company under administration fails to execute the instrument setting out the terms of the deed agreed upon by the creditors, within 21 days after the creditors' meeting in accordance with s 444B(2).

If creditors pass a resolution that the company be wound up in insolvency the company is deemed to have entered into a creditors' voluntary winding up and the administrator is deemed to have been appointed as liquidator.

As a result of 1997 amendments, where a deed of company arrangement provides for the company to continue to carry on business and it later goes into liquidation, debts incurred after commencement of the deed are provable in the winding up: s 553(1A). Creditors of the administrator are also entitled to priority under s 556(1)(a) but this does not apply where the administrator is not involved in the company carrying on business.

This winding up process may be halted by the court under s 482. An application to the court for such an order may be made by the company, the liquidator, a creditor or contributory. This order may be made where it can be established that the company is solvent. This would be unusual because the circumstances that led to the initial appointment of the administrator and the subsequent deemed appointment of the liquidator are usually indicative of insolvency.

powers of the court

The court has an important supervisory role to play in the administration process.

[24.250] The court has an important supervisory role to play in the administration process. It is also given wide powers so as to enable a balance to be struck between the interests of particular creditors whose rights are suspended and the objects of the legislation.

The court has a general power under s 447A to make such orders as it thinks appropriate about how the legislation is to operate in relation to a particular company. Such an order may be sought by a wide range of applicants including the company, a creditor, the administrator, ASIC or any other interested person.

Section 447A was described by the Full Court of the Supreme Court of Victoria in *Brash Holdings Ltd v Katile Pty Ltd* (1994) 12 ACLC 472 as:

> **< an unusual section, which evidently proceeds on the view that Pt 5.3A is inadequate in the provision which it otherwise makes for the new form of administration and that it is therefore necessary to enable gaps in the Part to be filled by the exercise by the court of wide powers to make such orders as it thinks appropriate about how the Part is to operate in relation to a particular company. It seems clear enough that s 447A(1) is intended to empower the court to make orders which alter what would otherwise be the operation of the Part in relation to a particular company. >**

This indicates that the discretion of the court under s 447A is not confined to gaps in the legislation but extends to altering what appear to be mandatory requirements. Hayne J, in *Re Brashs Pty Ltd* (1995) 13 ACLC 110, suggested that in appropriate circumstances, an order may be made dispensing with the requirement under s 450E(2) that a company set out the expression "subject to deed of company arrangement" in its public documents.

case note

The High Court in *Australasian Memory Pty Ltd v Brien* [2000] HCA 30 held that s 447A conferred a wide power on the court to make orders which had the effect of remedying irregularities by varying the statutory timetable for meetings of creditors. This was despite the existence of provision for the variation of meeting times contained in s 439A(6). Section 447A therefore permitted the making of orders which altered the way in which Pt 5.3A operated in relation to a particular company even where the company had gone into liquidation.

The court may order, under s 447A, that a resolution of creditors as to the future of the company under s 439C be set aside. An order may be made for winding up the company where this is in the public interest: *Deputy Commissioner of Taxation v Woodings* (1995) 13 ACLC 469.

The court may make an order protecting the interests of a company's creditors on the application of ASIC. It may make an order to protect an individual creditor's interests on the application of the creditor: s 447B.

This power of the court may be exercised before a deed of company arrangement is entered into. Section 447B may apply where a creditor has a reasonable claim to enable it to determine its rights and thereby take any appropriate action. In *Petrochemical Industries Ltd v Dempster Nominees Pty Ltd* (1995) 13 ACLC 103, a contingent creditor obtained an order under s 447B for the adjournment of the second creditors' meeting.

The court may declare whether or not the appointment of the administrator was valid: s 447C.

The administrator may apply to the court for directions about a matter connected with the administrator's functions and powers or the operation of the deed of company arrangement: s 447D.

The court may make an order as it thinks just where it is satisfied that the administrator has conducted the administration in a manner that is prejudicial to the interests of some or all of the company's creditors or members: s 447E(1). The court may also order that any vacancy in the office of administrator be filled: s 447D(2). An order involving the supervision of an administrator under s 447E may be sought by ASIC or a creditor or member of the company.

The court also has a general power under s 1322(4) to validate any act that has contravened the *Corporations Act*. The court shall not make such an order unless it is satisfied that no substantial injustice would be caused to any person: s 1322(6). In *Brien v Australasian Memory Pty Ltd* (1997) 15 ACLC 1359, it was held at first instance that s 1322(4) could be used to validate the appointment of a liquidator where the appointment was made at a creditors' meeting held outside the period required by s 439A(2).

pathways questions ...

The following questions dealing with voluntary administration may best be answered by reading this chapter and considering the Internet resources found on the Lipton-Herzberg Corporate Insolvency Pathway at http://www.lipton-herzberg.com.au/secure/pathways-corporate-insolvency.html

1. What were the main recommendations of the Harmer Report in relation to voluntary administration? Which of these recommendations have been incorporated into the *Corporations Act?*

2. What are the differences and similarities between administration, liquidation and receivership?

3. Refer to the CAMAC report, *Rehabilitating Large and Complex Enterprises in Financial Difficulties* (October 2004).
   (a) Compare the Australian voluntary administration scheme with its US and UK counterparts.
   (b) Is the voluntary administration scheme an appropriate method of rehabilitating large and complex enterprises?

bibliography ...

Agardy, P "Administrators, Trading and Risk" (2002) 10 Insolv LJ 164.

Agardy, P "Voluntary Administrators' Reports" (2001) 9 Insolv LJ 204.

Anderson, A "Decision-Making in a Voluntary Administration" (2004) 22 C & SLJ 163.

Anderson, C "Commencement of the Part 5.3A Procedure: Some Considerations from an economics and law perspective" (2001) 9 Insolv LJ 4.

Anderson, C "Finding the Background of Part 5.3A of the Corporations Law" (1999) 10 Aust Jnl of Corp Law 107.

Anderson, C & Morrison, D "Voluntary Administrations and Their Effect on the Use of Schemes of Arrangement" (1994) 2 Insolv LJ 195.

Anderson, C "Miracle workers for ambulance chasers? The role of administrators in the Part 5.3 process" (2004) 12 Insolv LJ 238.

Arboit, B "Discrimination of Creditors in a Deed of Company Arrangement" (1998) 10 Aust Insolv J 2.

Australian Law Reform Commission. *General Insolvency Inquiry* (1988) ALRC 45.

Bennetts, K J "Dealing with Winding Up Applications Following the Appointment of an Administrator" (2000) 18 C & SLJ 41.

Broderick, M "Demands on Directors/Guarantors of Companies in Voluntary Administration" (2001) 19 C & SLJ 46.

Brown, M "The Priority of the Expenses and Remuneration of an Administrator or Provisional Liquidator in the Winding-up of a Company" (1998) 9 JBFLP 127.

Collier, B "Uncertain Rights and Potential Liabilities: The Complex Position of Suppliers with Retention of Title Clauses and Administrators under Part 5.3A of the Corporations Law" (1998) 9 JBFLP 42.

Collins, R "When general powers become unconstitutional: s 447 A and the infringement of the separation of powers doctrine" (2004) 12 Insolv LJ 72.

CAMAC, *Rehabilitating Large and Complex Enterprises in Financial Difficulties.* Discussion Paper (September 2003) **http://www.camac.gov.au/camac/camac.nsf/byHeadline/PDF Discussion+Papers/**

Creelman, M & Collier, B "Problem for Creditors re Deed of Company Arrangement" (1995) 5 Aust Jnl of Corp Law 481.

Darvas, P "Employees' Rights and Entitlements and Insolvency: Regulatory Rationale, Legal Issues and Proposed Solutions" (1999) 17 C & SLJ 103.

Darvas, P "From the Outside Looking In: Employees and Voluntary Administration" (2001) 29 ABLR 409.

Donnenberg, V & Grant, J "Removing administrators and liquidators tainted by conflict, bias or bad practice" (2005) 13 Insolv LJ 133.

Forbes, D "Voluntary Administration: Remedies for the Lessor" (2002) 10 Insolv LJ 149.

Gidley, P "Administrator Reporting Persuant to Section 439A" (1999) 11 Aust Insolv J 17.

Glover, J & Duns, J "Insolvency Administrations at General Law: Fiduciary Obligations of Company Receivers, Voluntary Administrators and Liquidators" (2001) 9 Insolv LJ 130.

Griggs, L "Voluntary Administration and Ch 11 of the Bankruptcy Code (US)" (1994) 2 Insolv LJ 93.

Hamilton, G J "Deeds of Company Arrangement: The Prescribed Provisions" (1995) 3 Insolv LJ 67.

Hammond, C "The Relationship of Administrators to Company Employees: Issues Arising Under Part 5.3A of the Corporations Law" (1999) 7 Insolv LJ 74.

Harris, J & Gordon, B "Lost in transition: Sec 447A and the question of members' rights when a company transitions from voluntary administration to a creditor's voluntary liquidation" (2005) 13 Insolv LJ 96.

Herzberg, A "Why Are There So Few Insolvent Trading Cases?" (1998) 6 Insolv LJ 77.

Keay, A "Corporate Governance During Administration and Reconstruction Under Part 5.3A of the Corporations Law" (1997) C & SLJ 145.

Keay, A "Voluntary Administrations: The Convening and Conducting of Meetings" (1996) 4 Insolv LJ 9.

Keay, A "Court Involvement in Voluntary Administrations and Deeds of Company Arrangement: Powers, Problems and Prognoses" (1995) 13 C & SLJ 157.

Keay, A "Which Creditors are Bound by Deeds of Company Arrangement?" (1994) 2 Insolv LJ 147.

Kerr, D "Independence of Company Administrators Appointed Pursuant to Part 5.3A of the Corporations Law" (2000) 12 Aust Insolv J 4.

Madsen, A & Sherman, S "Protection of the Secured Creditor in the Voluntary Administration Regime" (1999) 10 JBFLP 318.

Merrett, R "Business Rehabilitation—Proposals for New Zealand" (2003) 11 Insolv LJ 233.

Noakes, D "Dogs on the Wharves: Corporate Groups and the Waterfront Dispute" (1999) 11 Aust Jnl of Corp Law 27.

O'Donovan, J "Which Claims are Admissible Under Deeds of Company Arrangement?" (1995) 69 ALJ 905.

O'Donovan, J "Voluntary Administration and Deeds of Company Arrangement under Pt 5.3A of the Corporations Law" (1994) 12 C & SLJ 71.

Purcell, J "A Public Policy Analysis of the Interaction between Insolvent Trading and Part 5.3A Administration" (2000) 8 Insolv LJ 202.

Robinson, D "Remuneration of Corporate Insolvency Practitioners" (2000) 8 Insolv LJ 20.

Robinson, W C "Statutory Moratorium on Proceedings Against a Company" (1996) 24 ABLR 429.

Routledge, J "Voluntary Administration and Commercial Morality: Aligning the Competing Interests" (1997) 5 Insolv LJ 125.

Routledge, J "An Exploratory Empirical Analysis of Part 5.3A of The Corporations Law" (1998) 16 C & SLJ 4.

Symes, C "Remuneration, Rent and 'Requisite' Costs: the 3 R's of Insolvency's Administrative Expense Priority" (2000) 11 Aust Jnl of Corp Law 149.

Taylor, T "Employee Entitlements in Corporate Insolvency Administrations" (2000) 8 Insolv LJ 32.

Walter, D J "The voluntary administrator's equitable lien: Nature, scope and priority" (2004) 12 Insolv LJ 150.

revision questions on the material in this chapter ...

> Please see eQuiz at **http://www.thomson.com.au/academic** for multiple choice questions and answers.

> For further corporations law links and material please refer to the Lipton-Herzberg website at **http://www.lipton-herzberg.com.au**

chapter twenty-five

liquidation

key points ...

- Liquidation (also called "winding up") is a formal process under which the affairs of a company are wound up, its assets collected and sold, its debts paid and the surplus (if any) distributed among its members.

- The *Corporations Act* recognises two modes of liquidation: compulsory liquidation and voluntary liquidation. The common feature of all liquidations is the appointment of a qualified, independent insolvency practitioner as the liquidator.

- A compulsory winding up is by order of the court on the application of a creditor or other eligible person. The liquidator is appointed by the court. A voluntary winding up is initiated by a special resolution of the members and does not involve a court application.
- There are a number of grounds for a compulsory liquidation but the most common is that the company is insolvent. Such compulsory liquidations are referred to as a "winding up in insolvency".
- Winding up in insolvency is usually initiated by a creditor and the winding up is ordered by the court. The most common way in which a creditor shows that a debtor company is insolvent is by a failure to comply with a statutory demand.
- A members' voluntary winding up occurs if the company is solvent and members appoint the liquidator. If the company is insolvent, the winding up becomes a creditors' voluntary winding up and the creditors may appoint the liquidator.
- A liquidator has wide powers as an agent of the company and under the *Corporations Act*. These powers are used for the purpose of winding up the company and distributing its assets.
- Liquidators owe duties similar to the duties of directors. They also owe further duties in relation to the winding up of the company. These include duties to collect, preserve and realise assets in the interests of creditors. Liquidators must also report breaches of the law to ASIC.
- The recovery of assets of the company includes legal actions brought against directors in breach of their duties or who engaged in insolvent trading. Liquidators may also take action to avoid certain transactions that took place before winding up commenced. They are of three main types: unfair preferences, uncommercial transactions and unfair loans.
- The liquidator is given the ability to avoid these antecedent transactions because they diminish the funds available to unsecured creditors or give a preference or advantage to a creditor over other creditors.
- The pari passu rule provides that, except for certain stated priorities, all unsecured creditors are ranked equally in the distribution of assets. Unsecured creditors who have priority include the liquidator and the costs of the winding up and, to some extent, employees.

[25.05] Liquidation (also called "winding up") is a form of external administration that ultimately results in the company being deregistered and ceasing to exist as a legal entity. Liquidation is a process under which the company's affairs are wound up, its property sold, debts owed to its creditors repaid to the extent possible and the surplus (if any) distributed among its shareholders. Until the liquidation is completed, the company remains in existence as a legal entity under the control of a liquidator who is a qualified, independent insolvency practitioner. The essential tasks of a liquidator are to sell the company's property and pay the debts of creditors. Any surplus after creditors are paid is distributed to shareholders. Deregistration is the final step in the liquidation of a company.

Liquidation is a process under which the company's affairs are wound up and it is ultimately deregistered.

The *Corporations Act* recognises two modes of liquidation—compulsory liquidation by order of the court and voluntary liquidation. There are two forms of voluntary liquidation—members' voluntary winding up and creditors' voluntary winding up. The common feature of all types of liquidations is the appointment of a liquidator.

A company is usually placed in liquidation is that it is insolvent.

The most common reason that a company may be placed in liquidation is that it is insolvent. This means that it is unable to pay its debts. In such cases, liquidation is the process whereby the company's assets are realised and distributed to creditors in payment of the debts due to them. Liquidation of insolvent companies is similar to bankruptcy of individuals. However, the terms "liquidation" and "winding up", must not be confused with "bankruptcy". In Australia the term "bankruptcy" only applies to individuals, whereas companies are wound up or liquidated. The bankruptcy laws are contained in the *Bankruptcy Act 1966* (Cth), whereas liquidation is governed by the *Corporations Act*.

There are three broad aims of the liquidation of insolvent companies.

There are three broad aims of the liquidation of insolvent companies. The liquidation provisions of the *Corporations Act* aim to ensure that:

> **creditors, particularly unsecured creditors, share equally and fairly in the distribution of an insolvent company's insufficient assets;**
> **hopelessly insolvent companies cease trading for the good of the wider business community; and**
> **there is an investigation into an insolvent company's affairs prior to the commencement of the winding up for the purpose of discovering the reasons for the insolvency.**

Insolvent companies may be placed in liquidation in one of two ways:

> **creditors (or other eligible applicants, such as a director, ASIC or a shareholder) may force the company into liquidation by obtaining a court order to this effect. This is referred to as compulsory liquidation or "winding up in insolvency"; or**
> **an insolvent company may also be placed into a creditors' voluntary winding up. Such a winding up does not require court orders and may come about in a number of ways. For example, as discussed in Chapter 24 above, a creditors' voluntary winding up is one of the possible outcomes of a voluntary administration: s 439A.**

While insolvency is the most common reason for winding up a company, it is not the only one. Solvent companies may also be wound up. For example, the members may decide to wind up their company so that they can realise their investment. As seen in Chapter 17 above, the court may also order a winding up to end oppression of members (s 232), or because it is just and equitable to do so: s 461(1)(k).

compulsory winding up in insolvency

[25.10] Part 5.4, ss 459A–459T, adopts the phrase "winding up in insolvency" to emphasise the distinction between the compulsory liquidation of solvent and insolvent companies. Compulsory liquidations of solvent companies usually involve disputes between members. This is discussed in Chapter 17 above.

Section 459A enables the court to order that an insolvent company be wound up in insolvency.

Section 459A enables the court to order that an insolvent company be wound up in insolvency on the application of a creditor or any one or more of the persons listed in s 459P(1). Section 459P is discussed below.

The *Corporations Act* also allows a court to order that a company be wound up in insolvency in other circumstances. Section 459B provides for a winding up in insolvency in the case of applications under three provisions of the *Corporations Act*. Under that section, the court may order a winding up in insolvency if it is satisfied that the company is insolvent where:

> **a member has made an application for a remedy under s 233, the oppression remedy;**
> **a person listed in s 459P has applied under s 462 for the winding up of a company on grounds other than insolvency; or**
> **ASIC has applied for a winding up under s 464 after having investigated a company's affairs and has concluded that the company is insolvent.**

applications for winding up

[25.15] Sections 459P–459T contain rules concerning the form of an application for winding up in insolvency and the notice that must be given of it. The aim of these sections is to narrow the scope for disputes about technicalities, thus facilitating the efficient disposal of the substantive issues.

permitted applicants

[25.20] Only the persons listed in s 459P are permitted to file an application for an order under s 459A that a company be wound up in insolvency. These persons are:

The persons listed in s 459P are permitted to file an application for an order under s 459A that a company be wound up in insolvency.

> the company;
> a creditor (even if the creditor is a secured creditor or is only a contingent or prospective creditor);
> a contributory;
> a director;
> a liquidator or provisional liquidator of the company;
> ASIC; and
> the Australian Prudential Regulation Authority.

creditors

[25.25] In the most usual case, the application is brought by a creditor. A person who is owed a debt by the company that is still unpaid at the date of the application for winding up is a creditor: *Re William Hockley Ltd* [1962] 1 WLR 555. A contingent or prospective creditor may also apply for a compulsory winding up: s 459P(1)(b). This enables creditors to apply for a winding up even though their debts are not immediately due and payable at the date of the application.

A "contingent creditor" is a person to whom a debt is owed, payment of which is only due on the occurrence of some future event that may or may not occur.

case note

For example, in *Community Development Pty Ltd v Engwirda Construction Co* (1969) 120 CLR 455, the High Court held that a builder whose debt only became payable on the outcome of arbitration proceedings was a contingent creditor and was therefore capable of filing a winding up application. This was so even though it was uncertain whether the builder would be successful in the arbitration.

case note

However, in *Roy Morgan Research Centre Pty Ltd v Wilson Market Research Pty Ltd* (1996) 14 ACLC 925, an applicant which had brought an action for unliquidated damages in which there was a dispute of substance was not a contingent creditor. It is not the role of the court hearing a winding up application to decide a disputed debt where the debt is disputed on substantial grounds. The applicant does not have standing as a creditor and is unable to gain standing by proving actual insolvency. The question of standing is important because of the serious consequences for a company of a winding up application.

A "prospective creditor" is a creditor to whom a debt is due but not immediately payable. For example, a person who sells goods on the basis of payment in 30 days after delivery is a prospective creditor of the buyer for the debt during the 30-day period.

The question of a person's standing as a creditor usually arises when the company disputes the existence of the debt. The question of disputed debts also arises in the context of determining whether a company is presumed to be unable to pay its debts or whether it may set aside a statutory demand made pursuant to s 459E. Disputed debts are discussed below, paras [25.95]–[25.105].

leave of court

[25.30] Certain of the persons named in s 459P(1) may apply for a winding up only if they first obtain leave of the court: s 459P(2). The court may give leave only if it is satisfied that there is a prima facie case that the company is insolvent: s 459P(3). The persons requiring prior leave are:

> **a contingent or prospective creditor;**
> **a contributory;**
> **a director; and**
> ASIC.

The reason for requiring contributories and directors to obtain leave of the court is to prevent mischievous and harmful applications.

abuse of process

[25.35] The court has a discretion whether to order that a company be wound up. It will not do so where the application is made for an improper purpose and is an abuse of process. In *Technomin Australia NL v Kollack Group Ltd* (1991) 9 ACLC 511, it was held that a contributory applied for the winding up of a company as a manoeuvre to assist the applicant in other litigation against the company. This was an attempt to obtain an improper advantage and the winding up proceedings were dismissed.

procedure

[25.40] An application for winding up must be advertised and gazetted under the applicable Court Rules. This serves as notice to the public that there is reason to suspect insolvency.

Section 459T permits an applicant to file a single application to wind up two or more companies in insolvency if they are joint debtors, whether or not they are partners.

Most creditors' applications for a winding up in insolvency rely on a company's failure to comply with a statutory demand.

Most creditors' applications for a winding up in insolvency rely on a company's failure to comply with a statutory demand that has been served on the company. Section 459Q deals specifically with such applications. It requires the application for winding up to set out particulars of service of the demand and of the company's failure to comply with it: s 459Q(a). A copy of the demand must be attached to the application: s 459Q(b)(i). If the court has varied the demand under s 459H(4), a copy of the court order must be attached to the application. Unless the debt is a judgment debt, the application must be accompanied by an affidavit verifying the debt and it must comply with the relevant court rules: s 459Q(c).

In order to ensure that an application contains up-to-date information about a company's insolvency, s 459R requires an application for a winding up in insolvency to be determined within six months of it being filed with the court. The court has power to extend the period within which an application must be determined if it is satisfied that special circumstances exist that justify an extension: s 459R(2). Applications not determined within the time limit specified by s 459R must be dismissed: s 459R(3).

Applicants must advertise that they have filed an application and also notify ASIC of this. Therefore, the fact that a winding up application has been filed becomes public knowledge before the court makes its decision. Winding up has serious consequences for the company, its members and creditors. The mere filing of an application can cause irreparable damage to the company. For example, a company may be refused credit, which could cause a liquidity crisis. In recognition of this, the court will not make an order winding up the company unless the applicant satisfies it that the company is insolvent. Even if this is established, the court still has discretionary powers to refuse the application.

Indeed, the court has power to grant an injunction to prevent the filing of an application as an abuse of process. The circumstances in which an injunction may be granted to restrain the filing of an application include:

- **when it appears that the applicant does not come within the class of persons permitted to apply under s 459P; and**
- **when it appears that the application on its face does not allege the existence of insolvency.**

Under the *Federal Court Rules* and the rules of the various Supreme Courts of States and Territories, an application for a compulsory winding up must be filed with the court together with supporting affidavits. Where the court grants the application and makes an order winding up the company, the winding up is taken to have commenced at the time stated by s 513A. This will usually be on the day the order was made. Winding up may also be taken to have commenced when a resolution was previously passed to voluntarily wind up the company, an administrator was appointed or a deed of company arrangement was executed.

what is insolvency?

[25.45] The consideration of whether a company is insolvent arises where an application is made to wind up a company in insolvency. This question also arises in relation to recovery of insolvent transactions which is discussed below, para [25.405]. Whether a company is insolvent also arises under the insolvent trading provision s 588G, discussed in Chapter 13.5.

Section 95A defines insolvency. Under s 95A(1), a person is solvent if the person is able to pay all their debts as and when they become due and payable. A person who cannot do this is insolvent: s 95A(2).

Section 95A defines insolvency. A person is solvent if the person is able to pay all their debts as and when they become due and payable. A person who cannot do this is insolvent.

This definition adopts a cash flow test rather than a balance sheet test of insolvency: *Melbase Corporation Pty Ltd v Segenhoe Ltd* (1995) 13 ACLC 823. The mere fact that assets exceed liabilities does not necessarily establish solvency. However, it is relevant to consider the extent of assets, the available credit and future events: *Leslie v Howship Holdings Pty Ltd* (1997) 15 ACLC 459. Indications of insolvency include the company's cheques being dishonoured or that it has a large number of unpaid debts, many of which are long overdue, and unsatisfied judgments. Insolvency can also be established by showing that the company has ceased trading, has no assets or that a receiver for debenture-holders has taken possession of all its assets.

Under s 459A, the court may order that an insolvent company be wound up in insolvency. In determining whether or not a company is solvent, the court may take into account the company's contingent and prospective liabilities: s 459D(1). This does not, however, limit the matters that may be considered: s 459D(2). Contingent and prospective liabilities have similar meanings as "contingent and prospective creditors" in s 459P(1)(b). This is discussed above, para [25.25].

In *Calzaturificio Zenith Pty Ltd v NSW Leather & Trading Co Pty Ltd* [1970] VR 605, Menhennit J considered the meaning of "an inability to pay debts". He stated:

> **< Merely to take a balance sheet which puts opposite each other book debts and creditor's liabilities as if they were to be equated is in my view, erroneous. It would be necessary to make an appropriate calculation to decide when the creditors had to be paid and when the debts were likely to be received in order to decide whether at any particular moment in time the company was or was not able to pay its debts as they fell due. >**

In *Sandell v Porter* (1966) 115 CLR 666, Barwick CJ stated:

Insolvency is more than a temporary lack of liquidity.

> **< The conclusion of insolvency ought to be clear from a consideration of the debtor's financial position in its entirety and generally speaking ought not to be drawn simply**

from evidence of a temporary lack of liquidity. It is the debtor's inability, utilising such cash resources as he has or can command through the use of his assets, to meet his debts as they fall due which indicates insolvency. >

A temporary lack of liquidity does not necessarily mean the company is unable to pay its debts. In *Downey v Aira Pty Ltd* (1996) 14 ACLC 1068, Ashley J said:

< It would be wrong to conclude that a company was insolvent on a given day only because on that day, or for some short period thereafter, the company was unable from readily available liquid assets to pay its debts as and when they fell due and payable. >

The distinction between a temporary lack of liquidity and insolvency was considered in *Re Timbatec Pty Ltd* (1974) 4 ALR 12. It was argued that the company was not insolvent at the relevant time as it would have had sufficient cash to pay its debts if it had time to sell plant and equipment used in carrying on its business. The court rejected the argument. Bowen CJ stated:

< The test as regards ready realisation of cash resources has regard, as I understand it, to the debtor who is conducting a business, and is applying his cash resources, and selling or mortgaging assets readily available to inflate those resources, while continuing his business. I do not take it to apply to a situation where the business is brought to a full stop, and either sale or mortgage can produce cash resources if it breaks up its business. >

Evidence of a company's insolvency is largely a question of fact to be decided as a matter of commercial reality in the light of all the circumstances.

Evidence of a company's insolvency is largely a question of fact to be decided as a matter of commercial reality in the light of all the circumstances. In *Southern Cross Interiors Pty Ltd v Deputy Commissioner of Taxation* (2001) 19 ACLC 1513, Palmer J considered that this included taking into account the reality that creditors will not always insist on payment strictly in accordance with contractual terms. However, for the purposes of the s 95A test, this does not mean that the debts are no longer payable on the contracted date and have become payable upon demand. In assessing insolvency, the court regards a debt as payable on the date specified in the contract unless there is proof of an express or implied agreement for an extension of time, there is a course of conduct giving rise to an estoppel preventing the creditor from relying on the stipulated time for payment or there is a well established and recognised practice in the particular industry or as between the company and its creditors generally that debts are generally payable after contract dates or only on demand. Where such assertions are made, it is for the debtor company to show satisfactory evidence.

In *Hamilton v BHP Steel Pty Ltd* (1995) 13 ACLC 1548, Young J took a more lenient approach and considered that commercial reality in the contemporary business environment should take account of the widespread practice of businesses delaying payments to creditors for as long as possible in order to minimise payment of interest to their bankers.

presumptions of insolvency

[25.50] In order to assist applicants to prove the existence of insolvency, the *Corporations Act* provides for several presumptions of insolvency, the most important being the statutory demand procedure.

Section 459C(2) sets out the circumstances in which the court may presume that a company is insolvent.

Section 459C(2) sets out the circumstances in which the court may presume that a company is insolvent. The s 459C(2) presumptions of insolvency apply unless the contrary is proved. If the presumptions do not apply, an applicant can, of course, prove insolvency using the s 95A test.

The presumptions of insolvency contained in s 588E do not apply for purposes of determining whether a company should be wound up in insolvency but are relevant for insolvent trading proceedings and the voidable antecedent transactions provisions.

The court must presume that the company is insolvent if any one of the events set out in s 459C(2) occurred during or after the three months ending on the day when the application was made:

> **the company failed to comply with a statutory demand;**
> **execution or other process issued on a judgment, decree or order of an Australian court in favour of a creditor was returned wholly or partly unsatisfied;**
> **a receiver of property of the company was appointed under a power contained in an instrument relating to a floating charge on such property;**
> **an order was made for the appointment of such a receiver for the purpose of enforcing such a charge;**
> **a person entered into possession, or assumed control, of the company's property for the purpose of enforcing a charge; or**
> **a person was appointed so to enter into possession or assume control (whether as agent for the chargee or for the company).**

statutory demands

[25.55] The most common way that creditors prove a company is insolvent is to show that it failed to comply with a statutory demand: s 459C(2)(a).

The most common way that creditors prove a company is insolvent is to show that it failed to comply with a statutory demand.

Section 459E allows a creditor to serve a demand on a company relating to a debt that is due and payable where the amount of the debt is at least the "statutory minimum". The "statutory minimum" is currently $2,000 or such other amount as is prescribed: s 9.

Under s 459E(2), the demand must:

> **specify the amount of the debt;**
> **require the company to pay the amount of the debt or secure or compound for that amount to the creditor's reasonable satisfaction within 21 days after the demand is served on the company;**
> **be in writing;**
> **be in the prescribed form (*Corporations Regulations*, Form 509H, Sch 2); and**
> **be signed by or on behalf of the creditor.**

Section 459F explains that a company is taken to have failed to comply with a statutory demand, for purposes of the presumption of insolvency, if, at the end of the period for compliance, the demand is still in effect and the company has not paid the amount demanded.

As a general rule, the period for compliance with a statutory demand is 21 days after the demand is served: s 459F(2)(b). If the company has applied to the court for an order to set aside a demand, the period for compliance ends seven days after the application is finally determined: s 459F(2)(a)(ii). At the hearing of an application to set aside a demand, the court has power to extend the period for compliance even further.

As a general rule, the period for compliance with a statutory demand is 21 days after the demand is served.

service

[25.60] Service must be personal service, meaning that the statutory demand must come to the notice of the person upon whom it is served. A statutory demand is served at the company's registered office. Service through a document exchange is not personal service and evidence must be provided that the notice was actually received within any relevant time period.

A statutory demand sent through the post is taken to have been delivered in the ordinary course of the post. This is generally two days: *Howship Holdings Pty Ltd v Leslie* (1996) 14 ACLC 1549. In *Cornick Pty Ltd v Brains Master Corporation* (1996) 14 ACLC 269, service was effected by placing a statutory demand under the door of the registered office. This was valid despite the premises no longer being occupied by the debtor and service occurring outside office hours. The same requirements for service also apply to an application to set aside a statutory demand under s 459G. This is discussed below.

verifying affidavit

A statutory demand must be accompanied by an affidavit that verifies that the debt is due and payable by the company.

[25.65] A statutory demand must be accompanied by an affidavit that verifies that the debt is due and payable by the company: s 459E(3). In *AZED Developments Pty Ltd v Frederick & Co Ltd* (1994) 12 ACLC 949, it was held that an s 459E(3) affidavit was required to verify the debt claimed in the sense of formally confirming that it is due and payable. The affidavit does not have to prove or demonstrate by evidence that the debt is due.

A verifying affidavit is not required if the debt demanded is a judgment debt. In *Victor Tunevitsch Pty Ltd v Farrow Mortgage Services Pty Ltd* (1994) 12 ACLC 963, the court set aside a statutory demand under s 459G because the creditor failed to serve a verifying affidavit on the company at the time of serving the demand.

The affidavit must be made by a person who could depose to their knowledge of the indebtedness of the company: s 459E(3)(b). In *Delta Beta Pty Ltd v Everhard Vissers* (1996) 14 ACLC 941, a statutory demand was set aside because the solicitor of the creditor made the affidavit based on hearsay assertions.

setting aside

A company may apply to the court for an order setting aside a statutory demand.

[25.70] Section 459G allows a company to apply to the court for an order setting aside a statutory demand that has been served on it. The application may only be made within 21 days after service of the statutory demand. The company must file a supporting affidavit with the court and serve copies of the application and the affidavit on the creditor.

A supporting affidavit under s 459G(3) must set out something that promotes the company's case to have the statutory demand set aside. It need not detail all the evidence that supports the existence of a genuine dispute but should set out material facts on which the applicant intends to rely: *Graywinter Properties Pty Ltd v Gas & Fuel Corporation Superannuation Fund* (1996) 14 ACLC 1703.

[25.75] extension of time for application. There was once a divergence of opinion between the courts of different States as to whether a company can obtain an extension of time for filing and serving an application to set aside a statutory demand. This inconsistency was resolved by the High Court in *David Grant & Co Pty Ltd v Westpac Banking Corporation* (1995) 13 ACLC 1572. The High Court held that the effect of the term "may only" in s 459G was to define the jurisdiction of the court by imposing a time requirement as an essential condition of the exercise of the discretion conferred by s 459G. A court does not have the power under s 1322(4) to authorise an extension under s 459G as this would deprive the word "only" of any effect.

A company served with a statutory demand may seek to set it aside because it contains a defect or for some other reason.

[25.80] defective demands. A company served with a statutory demand may seek to set it aside because it contains a defect or for some other reason: s 459J(1). The court will not set aside a statutory demand merely because of any other defect: s 459J(2). The word "defect" is defined in s 9 to include:

The court may set aside defective demands where it is satisfied that substantial injustice would be caused if the demand were not set aside, or that there is some other reason why the demand should be set aside.

> **an irregularity;**
> **a misstatement of an amount or total;**
> **a misdescription of a debt or other matter; and**
> **a misdescription of a person or entity.**

A statutory demand does not contain a defect merely because the company disputes the existence or amount of the debt demanded. Section 459H, discussed below, paras [25.95]–[25.105], deals with this situation.

Section 459J does not permit the court to set aside defective demands unless it is satisfied that substantial injustice would be caused if the demand were not set aside, or that there is some other reason why the demand should be set aside.

Solvency, in itself, does not constitute a reason to set aside a demand. The solvency of the company is to be determined in winding up proceedings and not while considering whether a demand should be set aside: *Chippendale Printing Co Pty Ltd v Deputy Commissioner of Taxation* (1995) 13 ACLC 229.

case note

In *Topfelt Pty Ltd v State Bank of New South Wales* (1994) 12 ACLC 15, the bank served a demand in which it required payment of a specified amount "together with interest from [a specified date] to date and continuing". The Federal Court held that the demand was defective in a number of respects and set it aside under s 459J on the grounds that the defects caused substantial injustice. It did not specify the applicable interest rate or a daily figure calculated by reference to the rate. The demand did not specify the amount of interest claimed at the date of the demand. A company that receives a statutory demand claiming interest should not have to make further inquiries to ascertain the amount of interest that the creditor claimed was payable.

A statutory demand that refers to multiple debts but fails to specify the individual amounts is defective and may cause substantial injustice if the debtor is able to identify and know the amount claimed to be owing only from its own information and records: *Delta Beta Pty Ltd v Everhard Vissers* (1996) 14 ACLC 941.

case note

In *Zhen Yun (Aust) Pty Ltd v State Bank of South Australia* (1994) 12 ACLC 521, a demand stated that a company owed a debt under a guarantee dated in November 1991 in respect of a loan facility agreement dated in August 1991. The verifying affidavit, however, referred to a guarantee dated November 1990 and a loan facility agreement dated January 1991. The court held that the demand contained a defect and set it aside. The failure to verify the demand as required by s 459E(3) constituted "some other reason why the demand should be set aside" for purposes of s 459J(1)(b).

case note

In *B & M Quality Constructions Pty Ltd v W G Brady Pty Ltd* (1994) 12 ACLC 970, it was held that a statutory demand contained a defect when it referred to the creditor as "W G Brady Pty Ltd", a non-existent company. The correct name of the creditor was W & J Brady Pty Ltd.

[25.85] effect of setting aside. Section 459K provides that a statutory demand has no effect where it has been set aside pursuant to an order under either s 459H or s 459J. It cannot be used as a basis for establishing the presumption of insolvency under s 459C.

restrictions on opposing winding up application

A company cannot, without leave of the court, oppose an application for winding up in insolvency that is based on its failure to comply with a statutory demand.

[25.90] Section 459S restricts a company, without leave of the court, from opposing an application for winding up in insolvency that is based on its failure to comply with a statutory demand. The purpose of the restriction is to penalise debtor companies who do not give early notice of all the issues they have with the statutory demand. A company is expected to put its claim that the demand is defective or that the debt is disputed at the time of contesting a statutory demand.

Under s 459S(1)(a), a company may not, without leave of the court, oppose an application on a ground that the company relied on for purposes of an application by it to set aside the demand. This prevents the same issues being litigated twice. Further, s 459S(1)(b) prevents a company, without leave of the court, opposing an application on a ground that the company could have relied on, but did not rely on, in an application to set aside a demand under s 459G. Section 459S(1)(b) applies whether or not the company made such an application.

A court must not grant leave under s 459S(1) unless it is satisfied that the ground for opposing the winding up application is material to proving that the company is solvent: s 459S(2). This reflects the public interest that solvent companies should not be put into liquidation with the resultant costs to be borne by the companies and their creditors.

disputed debts

[25.95] Some creditors serve statutory demands to blackmail debtor companies into paying genuinely disputed debts. Some debtor companies try to delay paying by asserting they have a dispute about the debt even though this has no genuine merit. A winding up hearing is not the appropriate forum for deciding the merits of disputed debts.

A winding up hearing is not the appropriate forum for deciding the merits of disputed debts.

As discussed above, under s 459G a company served with a statutory demand has 21 days to file and serve an application to set aside the demand. Section 459H sets out the requirements for setting aside a statutory demand where there is a genuine dispute concerning the amount claimed in the demand.

Section 459H sets out the requirements for setting aside a statutory demand where there is a genuine dispute concerning the amount claimed in the demand.

[25.100] the substantiated amount. A debtor company may dispute the amount demanded for a number of reasons. It may dispute either the existence or the amount of the debt. Alternatively, it may have an offsetting claim against the creditor. In either situation, s 459H requires the court to calculate the "substantiated amount".

If the substantiated amount is less than the statutory minimum of $2,000, s 459H(3) requires the court to set aside the demand. Winding up proceedings are not regarded as the appropriate forum for settling genuine disputes. It is more appropriate for the company and the creditor to resolve genuine disputes in separate litigation.

If the substantiated amount is at least the statutory minimum, then the court has a discretion under s 459H(4) to:

> **vary the demand; and**
> **declare the demand to have had effect, as so varied, as from when it was served on the company.**

If the court varies the demand to reduce the amount claimed, the company has seven days after the application under s 459G is finally determined to pay the amount: s 459F(2)(a)(ii). If the company fails to pay the varied amount, the varied demand forms the basis for a presumption of insolvency under s 459C.

The substantiated amount is defined in s 459H(2) as the "admitted total" less the "offsetting total". The "admitted total" is the total admitted amount of the debts to which the demand relates. If the court is satisfied that there is a genuine dispute between the company and the creditor about the existence of the debt, the admitted amount is nil: s 459H(5)(a). However, if there is a genuine dispute only about the amount of the debt, the admitted amount is so much of the debt as is not the subject of such a dispute: s 459H(5)(b). If the court is satisfied that the dispute is not genuine, the admitted amount equals the debt demanded.

The "offsetting total" is the total amount of the company's offsetting claims. An offsetting claim is a genuine claim that the company has against the creditor by way of counterclaim, set-off or cross-demand (even if it does not arise out of the same transaction or circumstances as the debt to which the demand relates): s 459H(5).

A cross-demand includes any claim for damages that is capable of quantification, including a claim for an unliquidated amount. However, it must be put forward in good faith and be more than a mere assertion in order to be genuine: *John Shearer Ltd v Gehl Co* (1996) 14 ACLC 147.

[25.105] genuine disputes. The debtor company has the onus of convincing the court that the dispute or offsetting claim is genuine. Something more than a mere assertion that a debt is not owed is required: *John Holland Construction & Engineering Pty Ltd v Kilpatrick Green Pty Ltd* (1994) 12 ACLC 716. Evidence of the dispute must be presented to the court. If the company does this, the court as a general rule will not examine the merits of the case or settle the dispute.

The debtor company has the onus of convincing the court that the dispute or offsetting claim is genuine.

According to Hayne J in *Mibor Investments Pty Ltd v Commonwealth Bank of Australia* (1993) 11 ACLC 1,062, the court is not required:

> **< to embark upon any extended inquiry in order to determine whether there is a genuine dispute between the parties and certainly will not attempt to weigh the merits of that dispute. All that the legislation requires is that the court conclude that there is a genuine dispute. >**

In *Spencer Constructions v G & M Aldridge* (1997) 15 ACLC 1001, the Full Federal Court held that a dispute was a "genuine dispute" under s 459H if it was bona fide and that the grounds for alleging the existence of a dispute were "real and not spurious, hypothetical, illusory or misconceived". The same considerations also apply in relation to a company's assertions that it has a counter-claim or set-off: *Edge Technology Pty Ltd v Lite-On Technology Corp* (2000) 18 ACLC 576.

Under the *Income Tax Assessment Act 1997* (Cth), a debtor company becomes liable for tax when the amount payable has been assessed, the assessment has been served on the taxpayer and the prescribed period has expired. The lodgment of an objection to the assessment does not constitute a genuine dispute for the purposes of s 459H: *Hoare Bros Pty Ltd v Deputy Commissioner of Taxation* (1996) 14 ACLC 394. Similarly, a pending appeal against a judgment debt also does not give rise to a genuine dispute: *Barclays Australia (Finance) Ltd v Mike Gaffikin Marine Pty Ltd* (1996) 14 ACLC 1367.

compulsory winding up on grounds other than insolvency

[25.110] The requirements for the winding up of a company by the court on grounds other than insolvency are contained in Pt 5.4A (ss 461–464). Section 461(1) sets out the grounds for the compulsory winding up of solvent companies. Only the persons listed in s 462(2) are permitted to apply for winding up on those grounds and have the onus of establishing that one of the s 461(1) grounds applies. Even if a ground is established, the court has a discretion whether or not to make the winding up order.

Section 461(1) sets out the grounds for the compulsory winding up of solvent companies.

Winding up is taken to commence at the time specified in s 513A. This will usually be on the day the order is made.

who may apply?

[25.115] Only the persons specified in s 462(2) can apply to the court to have a company compulsorily wound up on grounds other than insolvency. The persons who can apply to the court to have a company wound up on the grounds referred to in s 461(1) are:

> the company;
> a creditor (including a contingent or prospective creditor) of the company;
> a contributory;
> a liquidator appointed in a voluntary winding up;
> ASIC pursuant to s 464 (this is discussed in Chapter 21 above); or
> the Australian Prudential Regulation Authority (APRA).

Only the persons specified in s 462(2) can apply to the court to have a company compulsorily wound up on grounds other than insolvency. These include creditors and contributors.

the company

[25.120] Section 462(2)(a) permits the company to apply to have itself compulsorily wound up. An application by the company on any ground other than s 461(1)(a) must be approved by an ordinary resolution of the general meeting: *Re Woulfe & Son Pty Ltd* [1972] QWN 50. However, in *Re New England Agricultural Corp Ltd* (1982) 1 ACLC 557, the New South Wales Supreme Court held that the broad management powers usually conferred on the board of directors give them the necessary power to apply for a winding up on the company's behalf without the matter being considered by the general meeting. But unless there were exceptional circumstances, the court would decline to order the winding up of the company, unless the question had been submitted to the general meeting of shareholders and approved by it.

An application by a company for its compulsory winding up is quite rare. If the members wish to liquidate their company they usually do so by a voluntary winding up. A voluntary winding up does not involve a court hearing and so is cheaper. Further, in a members' voluntary winding up, the members appoint the liquidator and have greater supervisory powers over the conduct of the liquidation. On the other hand, a voluntary winding up can only be initiated by a special resolution that requires a three-quarters majority vote in favour, whereas an application by a company on any ground other than under s 461(1)(a) only requires an ordinary resolution.

In some circumstances, the members may desire to place the company into liquidation as quickly as possible. If this is the case, a compulsory winding up may be preferred over a members' voluntary winding up, because meetings at which ordinary resolutions are to be proposed require less notice than meetings at which it is proposed to pass special resolutions.

creditors

[25.125] The vast majority of applications for compulsory winding up are presented by creditors under s 459A, asserting that the company is insolvent. This is considered in detail above, paras [25.10]–[25.40]. Section 462(2)(b) permits a creditor, a contingent or a prospective creditor to apply for a compulsory winding up on grounds other than insolvency, as set out in s 461(1). However, this is unusual as creditors invariably seek to have a company wound up in insolvency. Where an application is brought to wind up the company on a ground other than insolvency, the court may order that it be wound up in insolvency: s 459B.

contributories

[25.130] A contributory may apply to have the company compulsorily wound up on any of the grounds referred to in s 461(1): s 462(2)(c). Section 9 defines a "contributory" to include:

> **a person liable as a member or past member to contribute to the property of the company if it is wound up;**
> **a holder of fully paid shares in a company; and**
> **a member of a no liability company.**

This definition of contributory, in the case of a company limited by shares, includes persons who at the commencement of the winding up, held either fully paid or partly paid shares, even though strictly speaking, only a holder of partly paid shares is liable to contribute an amount on the winding up. Not only must contributories hold the shares, their names must also be entered in the register of members. Membership is discussed in Chapter 9 above.

Under ss 515 and 522, past members may also be liable to contribute to the property of a company if they were members within one year of the commencement of winding up and the present members are unable to satisfy the full extent of their liabilities. Past members will not be liable for debts of the company incurred after they ceased to be members: s 520.

A deceased contributory's personal representative is, by virtue of s 528, also liable to contribute to the property of the company on a winding up. Accordingly, the personal representative is also included within the definition of "contributory" even though not registered as a member.

grounds for winding up

[25.135] Under s 461, the grounds for a compulsory winding up other than in insolvency are where:

> the company has by special resolution resolved that it be compulsorily wound up: s 461(1)(a). This ground is seldom relied upon in practice. The members generally choose a voluntary winding up;

> the company does not commence business within a year from its incorporation or suspends its business for a whole year: s 461(1)(c). This ground enables members to recover their investment in the company if it fails to commence business or ceases operation for the specified period. The court, exercising its discretionary powers, will generally dismiss an application on this ground if it is opposed by a majority of members and the company's inactivity is explained: *Re Metropolitan Railway Warehousing Co Ltd* (1867) 36 LJ Ch 827. This ground may also be relied upon when the company engages in a new business that is ultra vires its objects and ceases to carry on the business authorised by its main objects. In such cases, this ground may be coupled with the ground under s 461(1)(k) that it is just and equitable for the company to be wound up for failure of substratum: *Re Tivoli Freeholds Ltd* [1972] VR 445. This is discussed in Chapter 17 above;

> the company has no members;

> the directors have acted in the affairs of the company in their own interests rather than in the interests of the members as a whole, or in any other manner whatsoever that appears to be unfair or unjust to other members: s 461(1)(e). This ground is discussed in Chapter 17 above;

> affairs of the company are being conducted in a manner that is oppressive or unfairly prejudicial to, or unfairly discriminatory against, a member or members or in a manner that is contrary to the interests of the members as a whole: s 461(1)(f);

> an act or omission, or a proposed act or omission, by or on behalf of the company, or a resolution, or a proposed resolution, of a class of members of the company, which was or would be oppressive or unfairly prejudicial to, or unfairly discriminatory against, a member or members or was or would be contrary to the interests of the members as a whole: s 461(1)(g). Section 461(1)(f) and (g) corresponds with the wording of s 232. The only difference is that under s 461(1)(f) and (g) creditors and persons who are not members can apply for a winding up of the company, whereas s 234 specifies that only the persons listed may bring an application for a remedy under s 232;

> ASIC has stated in a report prepared pursuant to Div 1 of Pt 3 of the *ASIC Act* that it is of the opinion that a company should be wound up because it cannot pay its debts, or it is in the interests of the public, the shareholders or the creditors: s 461(1)(h). This ground is discussed in Chapter 21 above;

> an application is made by APRA and the court is of the opinion that it is in the interests of the public, the shareholders or the creditors that the company should be wound up: s 461(1)(j). This ground is outside the scope of this book; and

> the court is of the opinion that it is just and equitable that the company be wound up: s 461(1)(k). This ground is discussed in Chapter 17 above in the context of members' remedies. This ground may also be used where there has been misconduct and mismanagement to such a degree that it is in the public interest to ensure investor protection and enforce compliance with the legislation even though the company is not insolvent: *ASIC v ABC Fund Managers (No 2)* [2001] VSC 383.

voluntary winding up

There are two forms of voluntary winding up: members' voluntary winding up; and creditors' voluntary winding up.

[25.140] There are two forms of voluntary winding up:

> **members' voluntary winding up; and**
> **creditors' voluntary winding up.**

Sections 495 and 496 deal only with members' voluntary winding up and ss 497–500 deal with creditors' voluntary winding up. Sections 490–494 and 501–512 contain provisions applicable to both forms of voluntary winding up. The appropriate form of voluntary winding up depends upon whether the company is solvent or insolvent.

Unless the court grants leave, a company cannot resolve that it be wound up voluntarily if an application for its winding up in insolvency has been filed: s 490. Leave will only be granted if a voluntary winding up would be preferable from the point of view of saving costs or other reasons and does not disadvantage creditors.

members' voluntary winding up

[25.145] A members' voluntary winding up is initiated by special resolution of the company (s 491) and can only proceed if the company is solvent. A liquidator is then appointed by the members in general meeting: s 495.

Before a members' voluntary winding up can proceed, the directors must make a written declaration to the effect that they have made an inquiry into the affairs of the company and are of the opinion that it will be able to pay its debts in full within a period of 12 months after the commencement of the winding up: s 494(1). This declaration of solvency must have attached to it a statement of affairs of the company containing the information specified in s 494(2).

If the company is solvent and the directors intend making a declaration of solvency, it must be made and lodged with ASIC before the date on which the notices of the meeting at which the resolution for winding up is to be proposed are sent out: s 494(3). Directors are guilty of a criminal offence if they make a declaration of solvency without reasonable grounds: s 494(4).

If the members pass the necessary resolution to voluntarily wind up the company they appoint the liquidator, fix the liquidator's remuneration and have supervisory powers over the liquidator's conduct of the liquidation.

creditors' voluntary winding up

A creditors' voluntary winding up is only appropriate when the company is insolvent.

[25.150] A creditors' voluntary winding up is only appropriate when the company is insolvent. If this is the case, the creditors have a legitimate interest in the conduct of the liquidation. This is recognised by the *Corporations Act*, which permits the creditors to appoint the liquidator (ss 496(5) and 499(1)) and fix the liquidator's remuneration: s 499(3). Unlike a winding up in insolvency, putting a company into a creditors' voluntary winding up does not involve court proceedings.

The *Corporations Act* provides for a smooth transition from voluntary administration to a creditors' voluntary winding up. A company in voluntary administration may enter into a creditors' voluntary winding up in a number of different ways:

> **under s 439C, creditors may resolve that the company be wound up. Creditors will pass such a resolution if they decide that a deed of company arrangement is not in their best interests;**
> **if the company contravenes s 444B(2) by failing to execute a deed of company arrangement that was approved by its creditors (s 446A(1)(b)); or**

> **if creditors pass a resolution terminating the deed and that the company be wound up: s 446A(1)(c).**

A creditors' voluntary winding up may also stem from a members' voluntary winding up where:

> **the directors do not provide the shareholders with a declaration of solvency as required by s 494;**
> **the directors form the view that the company is unable to pay its debts; or**
> **the liquidator appointed by the members forms the opinion that the company is insolvent even though the directors made a solvency declaration.**

effect of winding up

creditors

[25.155] One of the major aims of the liquidation procedure is to provide for unsecured creditors to share equally in the distribution of the company's assets. As a result, unsecured creditors lose their usual right to individually bring legal proceedings to enforce payment of their debts after liquidation commences. The liquidator then acts for the body of unsecured creditors and has the power to bring legal proceedings to collectively enforce the creditors' rights.

The liquidator acts for the body of unsecured creditors and has the power to bring legal proceedings to collectively enforce the creditors' rights.

After the date of commencement of winding up, legal proceedings cannot be brought against the company without leave of the court: ss 471B and 500(2). Creditors cannot enforce any judgment or orders they have obtained (ss 468(4) and 500(1)) and any disposition of the company's property, other than those made by the liquidator, is void unless the court orders otherwise: s 468(1).

It is therefore important to determine the time of commencement of winding up. As a general rule, a compulsory winding up is taken to have begun or commenced on the day the court order was made: s 513A(e). However, in some situations a court ordered winding up is taken to have commenced before the court order was made. For example, if the company was under voluntary administration or subject to a deed of company arrangement that had not terminated before the court order, the winding up is taken to commence on the date the administration began: s 513A(b) and (d).

A voluntary winding up generally commences at the time of passing of the resolution for voluntary winding up: s 513B(e). If the company was under voluntary administration or subject to a deed of company arrangement that had not terminated before the resolution, the commencement of winding up is taken to be the day of appointment of the administrator: s 513B(b) and (d).

The position of secured creditors is different because under s 471, secured creditors retain the right to take possession and sell the secured property despite the fact that the debtor company's winding up has commenced. This enables secured creditors to appoint a receiver after commencement of winding up.

the company

[25.160] Even though a company continues to exist as a legal entity after winding up commences, it is prevented from carrying on its business after the winding up order except for the purpose of winding it up. Unlike bankruptcy of an individual, winding up does not mean that the company's property is automatically transferred to the liquidator. The company's property continues to belong to it, but its powers to deal with its property are severely restricted: s 468.

Even though a company continues to exist as a legal entity after winding up commences, it is prevented from carrying on its business after the winding up order except for the purpose of winding it up.

While a company is in the process of being wound up, all its public documents and negotiable instruments must have the words "in liquidation" set out after its name: s 541. Public documents include every:

> **business letter;**
> **statement of account;**

> **invoice; and**
> **order for goods or services.**

In both a winding up in insolvency and other compulsory winding up, the directors lose their powers to manage the company's affairs: s 471A. The company's affairs are controlled by its liquidator, whose powers and duties are discussed below.

With the commencement of winding up, members lose their rights to transfer shares. A company cannot pass special resolutions by its members.

With the commencement of winding up, members lose their rights to transfer shares, and nor can their rights be varied: s 468(1). A company cannot pass special resolutions by its members and therefore cannot change its name after winding up commences: *Re HDT Special Vehicles (Aust) Pty Ltd* (1991) 9 ACLC 1336. With the leave of the court under s 471B, a member may bring an action in the name of a company in liquidation. In *Eros Cinema Pty Ltd v Nassar* (1996) 14 ACLC 1374, a member was granted leave to bring actions for breach of duty against the liquidator and a director to whom the liquidator had sold the assets of the company at an alleged undervalue.

employees

[25.165] In the case of a compulsory winding up, publication of the winding up order serves as a notice of dismissal to the company employees: *Re General Rolling Stock Co* (1872) 7 Ch App 646. Where the liquidator wishes to continue their employment for a limited period, this dismissal notice may be waived: *Re English Joint Stock Bank* (1866) LR 3 Eq 203.

While the authorities are divided, it seems that a voluntary liquidation does not necessarily operate to dismiss the company's employees: *Re Matthew Bros Ltd* [1962] VR 262.

A company may be in liquidation and receivership at the same time.

receivers

[25.170] A company may be in liquidation and receivership at the same time. Creditors may apply to wind up a company on the ground of insolvency even though a receiver has been appointed by a secured creditor. Similarly, a secured creditor may appoint a receiver even though the company is being wound up. A liquidator's role is to look after the interests of unsecured creditors while the receiver represents the appointing secured creditor.

The receiver's power to take possession of, and sell, the secured property of the company is not affected by the liquidation.

The receiver's power to take possession of, and sell, the secured property of the company is not affected by the liquidation. Similarly, a receiver may bring a legal action in the name of the company where this is in relation to the charged property: *Gough's Garages Ltd v Pugsley* [1930] 1 KB 615. The effect of liquidation on a receiver is discussed in Chapter 23 above.

While a receiver's right to take possession and sell the secured property continues despite the liquidation of the company, liquidation terminates the receiver's position as agent for the company: *Visbord v Federal Commissioner of Taxation* (1943) 68 CLR 354. A receiver may, however, continue to carry on the company's business with either the liquidator's consent or court approval: s 420C.

In a compulsory winding up, an official liquidator is appointed by order of the court when it makes the order for winding up.

liquidators

appointment

[25.175] In a compulsory winding up, an official liquidator is appointed by order of the court when it makes the order for winding up: s 472. The selection of the particular liquidator is made by the appropriate officer of the court from a list of registered official liquidators. The applicant for winding up is required to obtain and file with the court the liquidator's consent to the appointment.

In a members' voluntary winding up, the liquidator is appointed by the members.

In a members' voluntary winding up, the liquidator is appointed by the members: s 495. The person must be a registered liquidator and is usually appointed at the meeting that places the company in voluntary liquidation. Prior to the appointment, the company must obtain the liquidator's consent in writing.

The method of appointment of a liquidator in a creditors' winding up depends on how the liquidation came about. When a creditors' winding up is established under s 496, the creditors' meeting may appoint a new liquidator in place of the person appointed by the members: s 496(5). If creditors do not nominate a liquidator, the person appointed by the members remains as liquidator of the company: s 496(8). In a creditors' voluntary winding up established under s 497, the members and the creditors may at their respective meetings nominate a person as liquidator. If different persons are nominated, the person nominated by the creditors is the liquidator. If no one is nominated by the creditors, the liquidator is the person nominated by the members: s 499.

In a creditors' voluntary winding up, the liquidator is usually appointed by the creditors.

In some cases, the court may appoint an additional liquidator to oversee a particular aspect of a liquidation. In *Re Spedley Securities Ltd* (1991) 9 ACLC 700, the existing liquidator had some commercial connections with a party involved in litigation with the company being wound up. An additional independent liquidator was appointed to conduct the litigation.

who may be appointed as a liquidator?

[25.180] A liquidator appointed by the court must be registered with ASIC as an official liquidator: s 532(8). ASIC may register natural persons who are registered liquidators and who apply for registration as official liquidators. Only some registered liquidators are also official liquidators.

A liquidator appointed by the court must be registered with ASIC as an official liquidator.

In both a members' and creditors' winding up, the appointed person must generally be a registered liquidator. However, in a members' voluntary winding up of a proprietary company, the liquidator need not be a registered liquidator: s 532(4). Persons become registered liquidators by satisfying the requirements of s 1282(2) or (3).

In both a members' and creditors' winding up, the liquidator must generally be registered.

Section 1282(2) sets out the qualifications of registered liquidators. A registered liquidator must:

> **be a member of the Institute of Chartered Accountants, CPA Australia or any other prescribed body;**
> **have qualified at a tertiary level in a course of study in accountancy of at least three years' duration and commercial law (including company law) studies of at least two years' duration; or**
> **have other qualifications and experience which are, in the opinion of ASIC, the equivalent of the above qualifications; and**
> **satisfy ASIC that experience has been gained in winding up companies, and that he or she is capable of performing the duties of a liquidator and is otherwise a fit and proper person to be registered as a liquidator. In Policy Statement 40: *Registration of Liquidators—Experience Criteria*, ASIC indicated that applicants for registration as liquidators require at least five years in public practice; at least three years' work in corporate insolvency under the supervision of an official liquidator and at least two years' supervision of corporate insolvency matters.**

Persons appointed under s 1282(2) remain registered liquidators for life or until their registration is cancelled by ASIC or the Companies Auditors and Liquidators Disciplinary Board (CALDB): s 1282(9).

Section 1282(3) permits ASIC to register a person as a liquidator of a specified body corporate. That person must satisfy ASIC that they have sufficient experience and ability, and are a fit and proper person to act as liquidator having regard to the nature of the property or business of the corporation and the interests of its creditors and contributories.

ASIC may refuse to register a person as a liquidator who is not a resident of Australia: s 1282(5).

Under s 1286, ASIC is required to establish and maintain a register of liquidators and official liquidators containing particulars of the persons registered as registered liquidators and official liquidators.

Registered liquidators must lodge and maintain an amount as security for the due performance of their duties with such sureties as ASIC requires: s 1284(1). This security may be applied to compensate persons who have suffered pecuniary loss arising from the liquidation.

Companies Auditors and Liquidators Disciplinary Board

CALDB is the authority that has the power to discipline auditors and liquidators by cancelling or suspending their registration.

[25.185] The Companies Auditors and Liquidators Disciplinary Board (CALDB) is the authority that has the power to discipline auditors and liquidators by cancelling or suspending their registration. The constitution of the CALDB and the procedures of its hearings are set out in Pt 11 of the *ASIC Act*. Its members consist of persons selected by the Minister from the nominations of the various professional accounting bodies.

Sections 1290–1298 of the *Corporations Act* deal with the cancellation and suspension of registration of auditors and liquidators. Under these provisions, the CALDB, on an application by ASIC, has the power to hold hearings to decide whether to cancel or suspend the registration of a liquidator: s 1294. Section 1292(2) and (3) sets out the grounds for cancellation. The grounds are that the liquidator:

> **has contravened s 1288. This provision requires liquidators to lodge triennial statements with ASIC;**
> **ceased to be an Australian resident;**
> **failed to carry out or perform adequately or properly the duties of a liquidator; or**
> **is otherwise not a fit and proper person to remain registered as a liquidator.**

The CALDB also has the power to reprimand and seek undertakings in addition to, or as an alternative to, cancellation or suspension of a liquidator's registration: s 1292(9). ASIC is also given wide discretionary power to cancel or suspend the registration of an official liquidator: s 1291.

persons disqualified from being liquidators

statutory grounds

Certain persons whose independence may be compromised are disqualified from acting as liquidators without leave of the court.

[25.190] Under s 532(2), certain persons are disqualified from acting as liquidators without leave of the court. Persons disqualified include:

> **persons who owe more than $5,000 to the company being wound up or a related corporation;**
> **creditors who are owed more than $5,000 by the company being wound up or a related body corporate; and**
> **officers or auditors of the company and their associates. The disqualification of officers does not apply to proprietary companies that are voluntarily wound up by their members.**

These disqualifications attempt to ensure that a company's liquidator is a person who is independent of the company, its officers, creditors or auditors.

case note

In *Re Capital Management Securities Ltd* (1986) 4 ACLC 157, a company was about to place itself under a members' voluntary winding up and applied for an order under the predecessor of s 532 for leave to appoint its auditor as liquidator. The company argued that his appointment would be convenient as he was familiar with the company's affairs, the company was solvent and the rights of third parties were not likely to be prejudiced. Despite this, the court refused leave. McLelland J held that the policy of the predecessor of s 532 of independence of liquidators should be applied unless there was some substantial ground for departing from it. Mere grounds of convenience and the improbability of wrongdoing were not the kinds of matters that would induce the court to depart from the legislative policy that a liquidator be entirely independent of the pre-liquidation activities of the company.

case note

In *Re Queensland Stations Pty Ltd* (1991) 9 ACLC 1341, Knight was appointed liquidator of three companies. He and Jessup were both partners in an accountancy practice. Jessup was also a partner in another firm that had acted for the solicitors of the companies in liquidation, had audited a trust account maintained by them and given advice. As these matters may have required investigation by the liquidator, Knight was removed as liquidator because his independence might be in question. He could be put in a position of having to review transactions on which his partner had given advice and which involved the trust account audited by his partner. It did not matter that the other partner had only slight involvement in the liquidations. A liquidator must be independent and must be seen to be independent.

An insolvent under administration is disqualified from acting as a liquidator: s 532(7). Persons who are disqualified from managing corporations under Pt 2D.6 cannot obtain registration as a liquidator: s 1282(4). These provisions are discussed in Chapter 12 above. Further, under s 1287(4), registered liquidators must provide ASIC with particulars of the circumstances by reason of which they became subject to an order under Pt 2D.6.

An insolvent under administration is disqualified from acting as a liquidator.

removal by court

[25.195] Under s 503, the court may remove a liquidator where cause is shown and appoint another liquidator. In exercising this power, the court must consider whether this would be for the general advantage of persons interested in the winding up. In *Re Biposo Pty Ltd* (1995) 13 ACLC 1271, the liquidators were ordered to be removed because the circumstances indicated that a reasonable bystander would consider that the liquidators were too close to the largest creditor and their impartiality may be impaired.

A liquidator is more likely to be removed during the early stages of a winding up rather than towards the end of the winding up.

conflicts of interest

[25.200] A person is disqualified from being appointed the liquidator of a particular company if there is a potential conflict between the person's private interests and the interests of the company.

A person is disqualified from being appointed the liquidator of a particular company if there is a potential conflict between the person's private interests and the interests of the company.

case note

In *Re National Safety Council of Australia* (1989) 7 ACLC 603, Ernst and Whinney were employed by the company to investigate and report on the accounting procedures, controls and records of the company. After the reports were completed and it became apparent that the company was hopelessly insolvent, its directors resolved to wind it up. The court appointed Humphris, the insolvency partner of Ernst and Whinney, first as provisional liquidator and later, liquidator of the company. Certain creditors appealed opposing Humphris' appointment.

The Supreme Court of Victoria granted the appeal and appointed another person as liquidator. The court held that Humphris faced a potential conflict of interest because as liquidator he would have to investigate whether the company might have a cause of action against Ernst and Whinney for failing to investigate the affairs of the company with due diligence and care.

powers of the liquidator

[25.205] In Chapters 5 and 12 above we saw that the board of directors and the general meeting of members are regarded as the two principal organs of a company. When a company is placed in liquidation, the liquidator replaces the board of directors as an organ of the company, and assumes all the powers of the board: s 471A.

The liquidator replaces the board of directors as an organ of the company and assumes all the powers of the board.

Because liquidators are also regarded as agents of the company, their actions bind the company. Like other agents, liquidators are generally not personally liable on contracts made on behalf of the company.

statutory powers

[25.210] Apart from the liquidator's powers as an agent of the company, the *Corporations Act* gives liquidators broad powers. In the case of a compulsory winding up, a liquidator has the powers granted by s 477. In addition, under s 488 and the rules and regulations of the *Corporations Act*, certain powers of the court are delegated to the liquidator.

The *Corporations Act* gives liquidators broad powers.

A liquidator's powers under s 477 include the following:

- to carry on the business of the company so far as is necessary for the beneficial disposal or winding up of that business;
- subject to the priorities set out in s 556, to pay any class of creditors in full;
- to make compromises with creditors and contributories with respect to their claims and liabilities;
- to bring or defend legal proceedings in the name of the company and to appoint a solicitor to assist him;
- to sell or otherwise dispose of all or any part of the company's property;
- to make calls;
- to sign documents on the company's behalf and use its common seal for that purpose;
- to appoint an agent to do any business that the liquidator is unable to do, or that it is unreasonable to expect the liquidator to do in person; and
- to do all such other things as are necessary for winding up the affairs of the company and distributing its property.

In the case of a voluntary winding up, s 506 authorises the liquidator to exercise any of the powers given by s 477 to a liquidator appointed in a winding up in insolvency or by the court.

sale of legal actions

[25.215] The power to sell part of the company's property includes the assignment of a chose in action such as a right to bring a legal action. This is a broad power vested in the liquidator and corresponds to an equivalent power conferred on the trustee in bankruptcy. It is not subject to the rules that prohibit trafficking in litigation known as "champerty and maintenance" because there is a public interest in ensuring that a company's assets are realised for the benefit of creditors: *Ultra Tune Australia Pty Ltd v UTSA Pty Ltd* (1996) 14 ACLC 1610.

The power to sell the company's property also includes a liquidator obtaining funding for a legal action from an insurer or other third party in return for payment of part of the proceeds of the legal action if it is successful. In such cases, the liquidator should act bona fide in the interests of the company and keep creditors fully informed and obtain their consent: *Re Movitor Pty Ltd* (1996) 14 ACLC 587.

supervision by court and creditors

[25.220] The s 477 powers may be exercised without prior approval of the court or creditors. Such approval is necessary only where a liquidator intends to compromise a debt due to the company exceeding $20,000 or where a liquidator intends to enter into a long-term commitment exceeding three months: s 477(2A) and (2B). The exercise by a liquidator of the powers in s 477 is subject to the control of the court: s 477(6). In exercising this control, the court looks to the interests of creditors: *Scarel Pty Ltd v City Loan and Credit Corp Pty Ltd (No 1)* (1988) 6 ACLC 213.

Liquidators exercise these powers by authority of the court, but s 479 requires them to have regard to any directions given by the creditors, contributories or by a committee of inspection comprising representatives of creditors and members. Liquidators are not, however, bound by these directions since s 479(4) allows them to use their own discretion in the management of the affairs and property of the company and distribution of its property.

Under s 488, a court-appointed liquidator is delegated powers as an officer of the court and is subject to its control with respect to:

> **holding and conducting meetings to ascertain the wishes of creditors and contributors;**
> **the paying, delivery, conveyance, surrender or transfer of money, property or books to the liquidator;**
> **adjusting the rights of contributories and distributing any surplus; and**
> **fixing a time within which debts and claims must be proved.**

application to court for directions

[25.225] Section 479(3) enables liquidators in a compulsory winding up to apply to the court for directions in relation to any particular matter arising under the winding up. The right to apply to the court for directions enables the liquidator to act in accordance with the directions without incurring liability to any of the persons whose interests may be affected.

Liquidators in a compulsory winding up may apply to the court for directions.

The court's power to give directions is limited to matters of general administration and the manner in which the liquidator should act and does not extend to deciding substantive questions against persons making proprietary claims. In some cases, the application for directions may be changed into proceedings for the determination of substantive rights; however, these are a different type of proceeding: *Re G B Nathan & Co Pty Ltd* (1991) 9 ACLC 1291. A liquidator is often required to make difficult commercial decisions and cannot seek directions of the court to determine such matters. A similar right of a liquidator to seek directions from the court in the case of a voluntary winding up is provided by s 511.

In addition, in the case of a voluntary winding up, s 511(1) enables the liquidator, or any contributory or creditor, to apply to the court to exercise all or any of the powers that the court might exercise in a compulsory liquidation. This is granted if the court is satisfied that the exercise of the power will be just and beneficial: s 511(2). In this way, a liquidator in a voluntary winding up may exercise the delegated powers of a liquidator appointed in a compulsory liquidation.

application to court to advantage certain creditors

Creditors who give financial assistance to a liquidator may receive a higher dividend.

[25.230] Section 564 provides an incentive to creditors to give financial assistance or indemnities to liquidators to pursue asset recovery proceedings or to protect or preserve property. Such proceedings may include the recovery of unfair preferences from particular creditors or proceedings against directors for insolvent trading under s 588G or breach of fiduciary duty.

If creditors provide such assistance, the liquidator may apply to the court for an order that the contributing creditors receive a higher dividend from the company's assets than they would otherwise be entitled. In exercising its discretion to determine how the funds should be distributed, the court takes into account considerations such as the amount of risk, the amount recovered and the proportion of debts of participating creditors: *Re Jacka Nominees Pty Ltd* (1996) 14 ACLC 633. The court will not make an order under s 564 where litigation by a liquidator is merely pending and the existence of property has not been established: *Bell Group Ltd v Westpac Banking Corporation* (1997) 15 ACLC 8.

access to books and information

A liquidator may apply to the court for orders requiring certain persons to hand over books and records.

[25.235] Under ss 483(1) and 500(3), a liquidator may apply to the court for orders requiring certain persons to hand over books and records to which the company is prima facie entitled. Such persons include the company's officers, bankers, receiver or agent. However, according to *Re High Crest Motors* (1978) 3 ACLR 564, these provisions do not oblige a receiver to hand over the company's books until the receivership is completed. It is only then that the company's prima facie entitlement arises. In some situations this may mean that a liquidator will not have information vital to challenging the validity of a charge or the receiver's appointment until it is too late.

To a large extent, the effect of the decision in *Re High Crest Motors* has been overcome by ss 477(3) and 1300(3). Section 477(3) gives liquidators a statutory right of access to company books. That provision entitles the liquidator to inspect any books of the company, even those held by the receiver or other person who has a lien over the company's books such as an accountant. A person who refuses to allow the liquidator to inspect the books is guilty of an offence. Under s 1300(3), the liquidator can make copies and take extracts. This power ensures that liquidators can quickly gain access to information for the purpose of determining whether legal proceedings should be brought in relation to transactions entered into by the company before the winding up.

Present and former officers of a company wound up in insolvency must help in the winding up.

Section 530A imposes a positive duty on present and former officers of a company wound up in insolvency to do everything they possibly can to help in the winding up. In particular, under s 530A(1)(a), as soon as practicable after a winding up order is made, each officer must deliver to the liquidator all the company's books in the officer's possession. If the officer knows the location of other company books, the officer must tell the liquidator where they are: s 530A(1)(b). An officer must provide information about the company and attend meetings of members or creditors: s 530A(2). In addition, under s 530A(5) an officer must, if required by the liquidator, divulge her or his residential and business addresses and keep the liquidator notified of changes of address.

A liquidator may apply to the court for a warrant to search for and seize property or books of the company.

Under s 530C, a liquidator may apply to the court for a warrant to search for and seize property or books of the company. The court may issue a warrant where it is satisfied that a person has removed or concealed the property or books. In *Cvitanovic v Kenna & Brown Pty Ltd* (1995) 13 ACLC 1654, it was held that the court would only order the issue of a warrant as a last resort after all other requests have been unsuccessful. Liquidators should not be encouraged to apply for warrants merely on the grounds of convenience. The court will generally impose conditions on the issue of a warrant. These conditions seek to balance the rights of the liquidator and the person whose premises are to be searched.

Liquidators may apply a variety of court orders to prevent officers and their related entities from absconding from Australia.

preventing absconding and removal of assets

[25.240] Sections 486A and 486B give liquidators the power to apply a variety of court orders to prevent officers and their related entities from absconding from Australia for the purpose of avoiding personal liability to the company. "Related entity" in relation to a body corporate is defined in s 9 to include a director, promoter, relative or de facto spouse of a director or promoter, a related body corporate and beneficiary of a trust of which the body corporate is a trustee.

Under s 486A(1) the court may, on the application of a liquidator or provisional liquidator, make any one or more of the following orders:

> **prohibiting an officer or related entity of the company from taking or sending money or other property out of Australia;**
> **appointing a receiver or trustee over the property of an officer or a related entity;**
> **requiring an officer or related entity to surrender to the court their passport and any other specified documents; and**
> **prohibiting an officer or a "related entity" from leaving Australia without the court's consent.**

A court may make an s 486A(1) order only if the company is being wound up in insolvency or otherwise by the court: s 486A(2)(a). The court must be satisfied that there is at least a prima facie case that the officer or related entity is or will become liable to pay money to the company or to account for property of the company: s 486A(2)(b). The court must also be satisfied that there is substantial evidence that the officer or related entity has concealed or removed money or other property, has tried or intends to do so, or has tried or intends to leave Australia: s 486A(2)(c). The court will only make such an order if it is necessary or desirable to protect the company's rights.

In addition to the s 486A orders, s 486B allows the court, on the application of a liquidator, provisional liquidator or ASIC, to issue a warrant for a person to be arrested and brought before it. An arrest warrant may be issued under s 486B(1)(b)(i) if the court is satisfied that the person is about to leave Australia in order to avoid paying money payable to the company, being examined about the company's affairs or complying with a court order. An arrest warrant may also be issued if the person has concealed or removed company property in order to prevent or delay the liquidator from taking possession or control: s 486B(1)(b)(ii). In addition, a person may be arrested and brought before the court if that person has destroyed, concealed or removed company books or is about to do so: s 486B(1)(b)(iii).

disclaimer

[25.245] A liquidator has the power to disclaim property of the company: s 568. The purpose behind the power of disclaimer is to relieve the company of an asset that is really a liability. Under s 568(1), a liquidator may disclaim property of the company that consists of:

A liquidator has the power to disclaim property of the company. The purpose behind the power of disclaimer is to relieve the company of an asset that is really a liability.

> **land burdened with onerous covenants;**
> **shares;**
> **property that is unsaleable or not readily saleable, or where the costs of realisation could reasonably be expected to exceed the proceeds;**
> **property that may give rise to a liability or other onerous obligation such as partly paid shares; or**
> **unprofitable contracts.**

The power to disclaim may be exercised in relation to property that is unsaleable or valueless and subject to rates or mortgage payments: *Re Middle Harbour Investments Ltd* (1976) 2 ACLR 226. Disclaimer also assists the liquidator to conduct the winding up in an orderly manner without undue delay.

case note

In *Re Nottingham General Cemetery Co* [1955] Ch 683, a company had been formed to establish and administer a cemetery. The company was obliged to maintain the cemetery and entered into contracts with purchasers which conferred a right to burial. The company became unable to maintain the cemetery and went into liquidation. The liquidator was able to disclaim the burial contracts in the interests of an orderly winding up.

Section 568D provides that a disclaimer has the effect of terminating the company's rights and liabilities in respect of the disclaimed property. The rights or liabilities of any other person are not affected by the disclaimer except so far as is necessary to release the company and its property from liability: s 568D(1). A person whose rights are affected by a disclaimer of property is taken to be a creditor of the company to the extent of any loss suffered and may prove such a loss as a debt in the winding up: s 568D(2).

The court may set aside the disclaimer and make further orders as it thinks appropriate: s 568B(2). A disclaimer may only be set aside if the court is satisfied that the disclaimer would cause prejudice to persons having interests in the property that are grossly out of proportion to the prejudice that setting aside the disclaimer would cause to the company's creditors: s 568B(3). Thus the court is required to balance the interests of owners of disclaimed property with the company's creditors. A disclaimer will only be set aside where the interests of the property owner are prejudiced to a considerable extent. Even then, the interests of other creditors must also be taken into account.

A person with an interest in disclaimed property may apply to the court for an order setting aside the disclaimer after it has taken effect: s 568E(1). Such an order will only be made if it was unreasonable to expect that the application should have been made before the disclaimer took effect: s 568E(2). The court will only set aside a disclaimer if it prejudices persons with an interest in the property to an extent that is grossly out of proportion to the prejudice caused to creditors if the disclaimer is set aside: s 568E(5).

duties of liquidators

general duties

[25.250] We noted earlier that a liquidator is regarded as an agent of the company. This agency relationship imposes upon the liquidator fiduciary duties and duties of care. These duties are similar to the duties imposed on directors of the company, discussed in Chapter 13 above. Indeed, s 9 includes a liquidator within the definition of "officer" for purposes of the duties and liabilities imposed by Ch 2D.1.

case note

In *Pace v Antlers Pty Ltd* (1998) 16 ACLC 261, a liquidator was held liable for breach of duty of care and skill. The liquidator breached this duty by failing to bring the company out of liquidation as soon as reasonably practicable when it had become solvent. This caused costs to be incurred in paying the liquidator and the liquidator failed to pay tax owing by the company with the result that penalty tax was imposed. Lindgren J of the Federal Court stated:

> < a liquidator must exhibit care (including diligence) and skill to an extent that is reasonable in all the circumstances. "All the circumstances" will include the facts that a liquidator is a person practicing a profession, that a liquidator holds himself or herself

out as having special qualifications, training and experience pertinent to the liquidators' role and function, and that a liquidator is paid for liquidation work. "All the circumstances" will also include the fact that some decisions and courses of action which a liquidator is called upon to consider will be of a business or commercial character, as to which competent liquidators acting with due care, but always without the benefit of hindsight, may have differences of opinion. >

While liquidators owe similar duties to other officers, the liquidator's obligations are, because of the nature of the position, wider and stricter than the duties imposed upon directors. In *Re Partridge* [1961] SR (NSW) 622, the court described the general duties imposed on a liquidator:

> **< Speaking generally, the liquidator's principal duties are to take possession of and protect the assets, to make lists of contributories, to have disputed cases adjudicated upon, to realise the assets and to apply the proceeds in due course of administration amongst the creditors and contributories. >**

The liquidator's principal duties are to take possession of and protect the assets, to make lists of contributories, to have disputed cases adjudicated upon, to realise the assets and to apply the proceeds in due course of administration amongst the creditors and contributories.

An official liquidator in a compulsory winding up has further duties as explained by Street J in *Re Allebart Pty Ltd* [1971] 1 NSWLR 24:

> **< A court winding up involves more than a mere realisation of the assets and distribution of proceeds. The official liquidator is an officer of the court, and as such he has public responsibilities to investigate past activities connected with the company, and, in appropriate cases, to initiate such further proceedings, civil or criminal, connected therewith as the circumstances may dictate. It is his duty to discover not only breaches of the *Companies Act*, but also conduct falling short of the requisite standards of commercial morality. In every instance the winding up of an insolvent company pursuant to an order of the court is attended with these obligations resting upon the official liquidator. >**

The official liquidator is an officer of the court, and as such has public responsibilities to investigate past activities connected with the company, and, in appropriate cases, to initiate such civil or criminal proceedings.

While s 479(4) permits liquidators to use their own discretion in the management of the affairs and property of the company and the distribution of its property, they are nevertheless under a statutory duty to exercise a reasonable degree of care and diligence: s 180. Section 181 imposes duties to act in good faith and for a proper purpose.

A liquidator is also required to act impartially in the conduct of the winding up and comply with the provisions of the *Corporations Act*. If difficulties arise, the liquidator is under a duty to seek the directions of the court: s 479(3).

case note

In *Commissioner for Corporate Affairs v Harvey* [1980] VR 669, a liquidator was found to have been in breach of his duties in a large number of respects. He failed to deposit the company's money in the liquidation trust account and to lodge accounts as required by provisions of the UCA. He dishonestly used the company's funds to make unauthorised payments to his firm. In some instances he used the company's funds for personal expenses unconnected with the liquidation. The court also found that Harvey delegated his powers to unsupervised employees and failed to seek the court's directions on controversial issues. He generally failed to act in the interests of the company, its contributories or creditors. The court ordered that Harvey make up the deficiency of two insolvent companies he was liquidating. Marks J explained the general duties of a liquidator appointed in a compulsory winding up in the following terms:

< The duties of the liquidator need to be clearly understood. Fundamentally, he must administer the estate strictly in accordance with the duties and obligations specifically imposed on him by the *Companies Act* and its rules. It is obvious that everything to be done in a competent administration is not and cannot be specifically prescribed. Preserving the assets, giving proper attention to the administration, acting with due despatch and ensuring adequate knowledge and understanding of the affairs of the companies are matters of commonsense. If there is a difficulty at any stage of the administration then it is the clear duty of the liquidator to inform the court and take directions.

An official liquidator is an officer of the court. In a compulsory winding up his office stems from appointment by the court. He is clearly not an employee of the court but the nature of the appointment makes him a representative of it. As Street J said in *Duffy v Super Centre Development Corp Ltd* [1967] 1 NSWR 382 at 383, the decisions the liquidator makes from time to time are in effect made under the authority of the court itself. The winding up is by the court which for the purposes the liquidator is. As such he is entrusted with the reputation of the court for impartial and proper despatch of duties. No lesser standard in that regard is to be expected of the liquidator than of a court or a judge.

When a winding up occurs, the financial outcome for creditors and contributories is dependent, among other things, on honest administration. It is the trust which those persons are obliged to place in the liquidator to preserve the assets and act faithfully and fairly that defines the weight of the duties owed and the strictness with which his conduct must be considered by the court.

The law in the circumstances regards such duties as fiduciary, although clearly it will not interfere with bona fide exercise of discretions that are not beyond the acts or omissions of a reasonable man. >

case note

In *Re Ah Toy* (1986) 4 ACLC 480, the Northern Territory Supreme Court considered whether a provisional liquidator was liable under the UCA equivalent of s 536 to make good losses caused by his negligent management of the liquidation. A partner of Price Waterhouse in the Northern Territory advised the company's shareholders that it should be placed in liquidation. The partner arranged for Ah Toy, an official liquidator, to be appointed as the company's provisional liquidator on the basis that Price Waterhouse did most of the work. The company was subsequently placed in liquidation and Ah Toy was nominated as its liquidator. Ah Toy accepted and appointed Price Waterhouse as his agent. Major decisions and most of the liquidation work was done without Ah Toy's involvement. The court held that Ah Toy did not have power to appoint Price Waterhouse as his agent in the way in which he had done. While provisions such as s 477(2)(k) permitted a liquidator to appoint agents, it did not authorise "wholesale delegation". Liquidators are appointed on the strength of their personal qualifications and are personally accountable for their work.

case note

In *Re Allebart Pty Ltd* [1971] 1 NSWLR 24, Street J commented on the interrelationship between the liquidator's duty to investigate the affairs of the company and the duty to act impartially. In that case, one of the creditors of an insolvent company in the process of compulsory winding up provided the liquidator with funds to investigate the conduct of the company's officers. Street J held that this was permitted since in some situations this money may be all a liquidator has available. However, a liquidator must ensure that their independence is not compromised.

specific duties of liquidators

[25.255] proper administration. One of the first tasks of a liquidator is to open a bank account, known as the "liquidator's general account", into which money received by the liquidator is deposited. A separate account is required for each company under liquidation. In the case of a compulsory liquidation, the court's order specifies the particular branch of a bank where the account is to be kept. A liquidator who merely deposits money received into his or her firm's general trust account breaches this duty: *Commissioner for Corporate Affairs v Harvey* [1980] VR 669. Liquidators must notify ASIC of their appointment within 14 days: s 537.

A liquidator is also under a duty to maintain a proper record of the winding up. Such records include:

A liquidator is under a duty to maintain a proper record of the winding up.

> **books recording minutes of meetings of contributories and creditors: s 531; and**
> **accounts in the prescribed form which must be prepared every six months and lodged with ASIC: s 539. These half-year accounts must show the liquidator's receipts and payments during the period and, in the case of the second and subsequent accounts, must also show the aggregate amount of receipts and payments during the whole period since the liquidator's appointment.**

[25.260] acquaintance with the company's affairs. In order for liquidators to collect and preserve the assets of the company, they are required to acquaint themselves with the affairs of the company. Their sources of information are the company's records, the company's officers and employees. In a compulsory liquidation, s 475(1) requires persons who were the directors and secretary at the time of the winding up order to submit a report to the liquidator in the prescribed form as to the affairs of the company. This report must be submitted not later than 14 days after the making of the winding up order. Under s 475(2),

Liquidators are required to acquaint themselves with the affairs of the company.

> **present or former officers,**
> **persons who have taken part in the formation of the company, and**
> **employees of the company,**

may also be required to supply information on the affairs of the company if requested by the liquidator.

Public examinations under ss 596A–596F and s 597 are commonly initiated by liquidators as a means of locating a company's assets and discovering information about transactions prior to the winding up. This is discussed below, paras [25.310]–[25.345].

[25.265] collect the company's assets. As soon as practicable after appointment, a liquidator is required to take into personal custody or control all the property to which the company is, or appears to be, entitled: s 474(1). In certain circumstances, the liquidator can take legal action to recover property that the company disposed of before the commencement of winding up. The liquidator may avoid certain antecedent transactions and dispositions made after the commencement of winding up.

A liquidator is required to take into personal custody or control, all the property of the company.

This is discussed below, paras [25.355]–[25.420]. In addition, the liquidator can take action on the company's behalf to recover property, profits or damages from directors or other officers who breached their duties to it prior to the commencement of winding up. The duties of directors and the company's remedies for breach of those duties are discussed in Chapter 13 above.

The company's assets also include the amounts that contributories are liable to contribute on a winding up. Under s 516, the holder of partly paid shares is liable to contribute the amount unpaid to the company when it is wound up. Persons who have ceased to be members within one year of the commencement of winding up are also liable to contribute to the property of the company where the existing members are unable to satisfy the full extent of their liabilities. However, past members are not liable for the company's debts incurred after they ceased to be members.

A liquidator is under a duty to preserve the company's assets until they can be realised.

[25.270] preserve assets. A liquidator is under a duty to preserve the company's assets until they can be realised. To achieve this end, a liquidator is permitted to carry on the business of the company: s 477(1)(a). This is especially important if this is the only means of preserving the goodwill of a company's business where the liquidator intends to sell the business as a going concern. The business can only be carried on for the purpose of a beneficial winding up and not with a view to its continuance: *Re Wreck Recovery & Salvage Co* (1880) 15 Ch D 353.

In order to preserve remaining assets, a liquidator may disclaim onerous contracts. This may include a lease under which rent is payable after the business of the company has ceased. Disclaimer is discussed above, para [25.245].

A liquidator is under a duty to sell the company's assets.

[25.275] sell assets. Because the purpose of a winding up is to distribute the company's assets to creditors and contributories, the liquidator is under a duty to sell the company's assets. To this end the liquidator is given powers to sell all the company's property and to execute documents in its name: s 477(2)(c) and (d). The liquidator, in exercising these powers, is under a duty to obtain the best possible price for the property. A company's property does not always have to be sold in a winding up. For example, the members may resolve to voluntarily wind up a solvent company for the sole purpose of dividing up its unrealised assets in specie among themselves.

Liquidators are under a duty to repay the company's debts and to distribute any surplus assets among contributories.

[25.280] distribute assets. Liquidators are under a duty to repay the company's debts and to distribute any surplus assets among contributories. A liquidator has a duty to invite proof of claims by advertising. Even if a claimant does not respond to an advertisement for claims, the liquidator is still under a duty to inquire into all claims of which he or she is aware: *Harry Goudias Pty Ltd v Port Adelaide Freezers Pty Ltd* (1992) 10 ACLC 499. These duties are considered below, para [25.440]–[25.465].

Liquidators are required to report to ASIC suspected criminal activity in relation to the company or breaches of duty.

[25.285] report breaches of the law. Liquidators are required to report to ASIC suspected criminal activity in relation to the company or breaches of duty: s 533(1). On receipt of an s 533 report, ASIC may decide to investigate the matters raised and launch prosecutions.

An s 533 report must be lodged if, in the course of winding up, it appears to the liquidator that:

> **a past or present officer, or a member or contributory, of the company may have been guilty of either a Commonwealth or State offence in relation to the company;**
> **a person who has taken part in the formation, promotion, administration, management or winding up of the company:**
- **may have misapplied or retained, or may have become liable or accountable for, any money or property of the company; or**
- **may have been guilty of any negligence, default, breach of duty or breach of trust in relation to the company; or**

> **the company may be unable to pay its unsecured creditors more than 50 cents in the dollar.**

The liquidators' duty to acquaint themselves with the company's affairs, requires them to carry out an investigation which inevitably involves time and expense. Because these expenses are ordinarily funded from the company's assets, liquidators face significant difficulties if the company has no assets. In such circumstances, liquidators will usually carry out only a superficial investigation and misconduct by directors and officers may not be detected and reported to ASIC. In October 2005, the government foreshadowed that one component of its corporate insolvency reform package would be the establishment of an assetless administration fund to finance liquidators' investigations in cases where it appears to ASIC that further investigation and reporting may lead to enforcement action. The government was of the view that an assetless administration fund would improve corporate conduct generally, improve returns for creditors and reduce the scope for phoenix activity. Phoenix companies are discussed in Chapter 13.5 above.

[25.290] effect deregistration. After the company's property has been realised and distributed to creditors and members, a liquidator may apply to the court for an order that they be released and that ASIC deregister the company: s 480. Within one month of ceasing to act as liquidator, the liquidator must lodge with ASIC an account of their conduct of the liquidation explaining how the company's property has been distributed: s 509. ASIC must deregister the company on order of the court or within three months of receiving the liquidator's return: s 601AC. Deregistration is discussed below, paras [25.520]–[25.545].

remedies for breach of duty

[25.295] The court is given power to remedy liquidators' breaches of duty under a number of different provisions.

Liquidators are within the s 9 definition of "officer" and breach their duties under Ch 2D of the *Corporations Act* if they fail to act in good faith in the best interests of the company, or fail to exercise their powers with reasonable care and diligence. The Ch 2D duties in ss 180–183 are civil penalty provisions so that officers who breach the sections may be liable to disqualification, imposition of a civil penalty, payment of compensation to the company or criminal liability. The civil penalty provisions are discussed in Chapter 13.6 above.

A liquidator may also be examined under ss 596A–596F and be liable under s 598. Examinations are discussed below. Section 536 deals with the supervision of liquidators by the court and ASIC. Section 536 provides that if:

> **it appears to the court or to ASIC that a liquidator has not faithfully performed duties or has not observed the requirements of the court or the *Corporations Act*; or**
> **a complaint is made by any person with respect to the conduct of a liquidator,**

the court or ASIC may inquire into the matter, and the court may take such action as it thinks fit.

If the company has suffered loss as a result of the liquidator's misfeasance, neglect or omission, the liquidator may be ordered to make good that loss.

provisional liquidators

[25.300] A provisional liquidator is an interim appointment pending the determination of a winding up application. The court has the power to appoint an official liquidator to be a provisional liquidator at any time after the filing of a winding up application and before the making of a winding up order: s 472(2).

A provisional liquidator is an interim appointment pending the determination of a winding up application.

The court will appoint a provisional liquidator if the assets of a company are in jeopardy. This may occur where the company's assets have either been, or are being, dealt with in a manner that is detrimental to creditors or members if the company is ultimately wound up. The role of the provisional liquidator is to prevent the company's assets being dissipated by its directors or shareholders after the filing of the winding up application and before the application is heard.

The court will appoint a provisional liquidator if the assets of a company are in jeopardy.

A member may seek the appointment of a provisional liquidator to safeguard assets where members are in dispute: *Alessi v The Original Australian Art Co Pty Ltd* (1989) 7 ACLC 595. The company may apply for the appointment of a provisional liquidator if the directors are not prepared to continue to manage the company and this may place its assets in jeopardy. Directors may be reluctant to continue to act because of the possibility of incurring liability for insolvent trading under s 588G.

A creditor may seek the appointment of a provisional liquidator where a company is continuing to trade at a loss or is incurring further liability.

A creditor may seek the appointment of a provisional liquidator where a company is continuing to trade at a loss or is incurring further liability. A provisional liquidator may be appointed to protect creditors by enforcing a contractual right of the company. In *Brimaud v Honeysett Instant Print Pty Ltd* (1988) 6 ACLC 942, a provisional liquidator was appointed where directors diverted assets of the company to another company in which they had an interest.

The court has a wide discretion in deciding whether or not to appoint a provisional liquidator. The court will consider the likelihood of the winding up application being ultimately successful: *Alessi v The Original Australian Art Co Pty Ltd* (1989) 7 ACLC 595. The appointment will only be made if it serves a purpose, otherwise the appointment would add to the costs of winding up: *Re T & L Trading (Aust) Pty Ltd* (1986) 10 ACLC 388.

Upon appointment, the provisional liquidator assumes control of the company's affairs and replaces the directors. The directors retain residual powers such as the power to oppose an application for a winding up order. The appointment results in a stay of proceedings against the company, except by leave of the court: s 471B.

A provisional liquidator may exercise such functions and powers as are conferred by the *Corporations Act*, court rules or the appointing order: s 472(3). The provisional liquidator is required to take control and custody of all the company's property: s 474(1). The main purpose behind this power is to maintain the status quo prior to the determination of the winding up application. The nature of this function means that generally a provisional liquidator will not have the power to sell assets or enter into long-term contracts. However, in some cases, it may be necessary to sell some assets quickly in order to best preserve all the assets: *Northbourne Developments Pty Ltd v Reiby Chambers Pty Ltd* (1989) 8 ACLC 39.

A provisional liquidator has certain statutory powers under s 472(4) and (5). These confer the powers to carry on the company's business and the powers of a liquidator under s 477(1)(d), (2) and (3). These powers include the power to initiate or defend legal proceedings in the name of the company, to sell or otherwise dispose of the company's assets, to act in the name of and on behalf of the company and to use the company's seal for these purposes. Provisional liquidators cannot exercise the power under s 477(2)(m), which empowers liquidators to do all such things as are necessary for winding up the affairs of the company and distributing its property. Such a power is inappropriate for provisional liquidators.

creditors' meetings

The court may direct the convening of creditors' meetings to ascertain their wishes in relation to the winding up of the company.

[25.305] There are numerous provisions in the *Corporations Act* that allow creditors' wishes to be taken into account in a winding up. For example, under s 547 the court may direct the convening of creditors' meetings to ascertain their wishes in relation to the winding up of the company.

Under the *Corporations Regulations*, unless a poll is demanded, resolutions at creditors' meetings are passed if a majority of those present and voting vote in favour on a show of hands: reg 5.6.19. Where a poll is demanded, a creditors' resolution is passed if a majority, in number and value of those present and voting, vote in favour of the resolution: reg 5.6.21. Under the *Corporations Regulations*, resolutions are passed by a simple majority in number of all creditors present and voting either in person, by proxy or by attorney. Two or more creditors are able to request that voting be by majority in number and value. If a vote according to majority in number and value results in deadlock, creditors are able to have the conflict resolved by either the court or the liquidator.

The Harmer Report was concerned that decisions made at creditors' meetings may be influenced by creditors who are either insiders or associated with insiders. Section 600A implements recommendations of the Harmer Report and aims to prevent such creditors from exercising an unfair influence over creditors' meetings.

Under s 600A(2) the court may, on the application of a creditor, set aside a resolution passed at a meeting of creditors. The court can only make an s 600A(2) order if the resolution was carried by the votes of related creditors and the resolution is contrary to the interests of the creditors as a whole or prejudices the interests of the creditors who voted against it: s 600A(1). A "related creditor" is a "related entity of the company" and a creditor to whom a debt is owed: s 600A(3). Section 9 defines "related entity" in broad terms. It includes a director or member of the company and relatives of directors and members as well as related companies.

The court also has the power to order the reconvening of creditors' meetings and remove the voting rights of a related creditor: s 600A(2).

Section 600B gives the court the power to set aside or vary a resolution that is passed on the casting vote of the person who chaired the meeting. This enables the court to review decisions of the chairman.

examinations

purpose

[25.310] Persons who may be able to provide information and assistance about insolvent companies can be summonsed by the court to attend an examination of an inquisitorial nature under ss 596A and 596B. The main purposes of such examinations are to facilitate the recovery of property belonging to the insolvent company, to discover whether conduct of the directors and officers of the company led to its insolvency and to investigate possible causes of action against third parties.

Persons who may be able to provide information and assistance about insolvent companies can be summonsed by the court to attend an examination of an inquisitorial nature.

Examinations are sometimes necessary to enable a liquidator to get in and maximise the assets of the company for the benefit of creditors. The liquidator comes to the company with little knowledge of its affairs and so is at a disadvantage in making informed decisions of a legal and commercial nature necessary to carry out the winding up. The legislation places the liquidator in a privileged position in order to redress this disadvantage. This privilege has been extended to allow other eligible applicants to conduct examinations.

Examinations can only be initiated when an eligible applicant applies for a summons under either s 596A or s 596B. "Eligible applicant" is defined in s 9 and includes ASIC, a liquidator or an administrator. It also includes any person authorised by ASIC to make an application for an examination.

examination of officers

[25.315] The *Corporations Act* distinguishes between examinations of an officer as defined in s 9 and examinations of other persons.

Under s 596A, if an eligible person applies for a summons to examine an officer about a corporation's examinable affairs, the court is obliged to grant the application without investigating the reasons why the application was made. "Examinable affairs" is broadly defined in s 9 to include the promotion, formation, management, administration or winding up of the corporation. Also included are the business affairs of a connected entity (defined in s 64B) in so far as these are relevant.

examination of non-officers

[25.320] Under s 596B, if an eligible person applies for a summons to examine people other than officers, the court must first be satisfied either that:

> **the person has taken part or been concerned in examinable affairs of the corporation and has been, or may have been, guilty of misconduct in relation to the corporation; or**

> **the person may be able to give information about the examinable affairs of the corporation.**

In this context, "examinable affairs" includes information concerning the prospect of successfully bringing a legal action. This information would assist a liquidator to estimate the value of the legal action and decide whether to bring it. Such information would include details of insurance policies entered into by the company, and insurers could be examined despite the lack of a direct connection with the company in liquidation: *Re Interchase Corporation Ltd* (1996) 14 ACLC 1674.

case note

In *Flanders v Beatty* (1995) 13 ACLC 529, the Appeal Division of the Supreme Court of Victoria held that an administrator of a company who was investigating whether the company had a good case against its auditor for breach of duty could require the auditor to produce his professional indemnity insurance policies at the examination.

Where an application is made under s 596B for the examination of a person other than an officer, an affidavit in support that complies with the court rules must be filed: s 596C. Affidavits are not available for public inspection unless the court orders otherwise.

provision of information

The summons to a person to be examined may require the examinee to produce specified books in their possession that relate to the corporation.

[25.325] The summons to a person to be examined under s 596A or 596B may require the examinee to produce specified books in their possession that relate to the corporation: s 596D(2).

Subject to some exceptions, notice that an examination is to be held must be given to the corporation's creditors and the liquidator or any other eligible applicant: s 596E. Creditors may take part in an examination and be represented by a lawyer. This is in addition to similar rights possessed by a liquidator, administrator or other eligible applicant and ASIC: s 597(5A).

The court may put or allow to be put such questions about the corporation or any of its "examinable affairs" as it thinks appropriate: s 597(5B). An examination is heard in public unless there are special circumstances: s 597(4). A person summoned under s 596A or s 596B contravenes s 597(6) if they fail to attend. Section 597(7) requires an examinee to answer all questions on oath or affirmation and produce books required by the summons. It is an offence to make false or misleading statements: s 597(11).

The court may direct a person to produce specified books in their possession that are relevant to the examination either at that person's examination or at the examination of any other person: s 597(9). This enables a liquidator to obtain production of books from third parties. A person directed to produce books at an examination must not, without reasonable excuse, refuse or fail to comply: s 597(10A).

A liquidator or other eligible applicant may require an examinable officer to supply an affidavit about a corporation's examinable affairs: s 597A. This requirement may be instead of or in addition to attendance at an examination. The affidavit must contain information as specified by the court: s 597A(2). Failure to comply constitutes an offence. Section 597A enables a liquidator to gather information more cheaply than by conducting an examination.

separate legal actions

[25.330] Where separate civil proceedings have already commenced, a liquidator may gain an advantage in these proceedings by examining a witness before the hearing has commenced. The examination might be conducted as a rehearsal or the credit of the witness may be attacked. Although the liquidator is given an advantage, he or she is entitled to gain information that enables the liquidation to proceed more effectively. A purpose of an examination and a requirement that an examinee produce books is the implementation of a "system of discovery" in order to determine whether legal actions should be brought against the examinee or others.

case note

In *Hongkong Bank of Australia v Murphy* (1992) 10 ACLC 1573, examinees applied to have orders for their examination and production of books set aside on the grounds that the applicant intended to use the information in other litigation already commenced against the examinees. The New South Wales Supreme Court refused to set aside the orders. Gleeson CJ stated:

> < Whilst the court will not permit a liquidator, or other eligible person, to abuse its process by using an examination solely for the purposes of obtaining a forensic advantage not available from ordinary pre-trial procedures, such as discovery or inspection, on the other hand, the possibility that a forensic advantage will be gained does not mean that the making of an order will not advance a purpose to be secured by the legislation. >

Where a liquidator gains a forensic advantage, this may constitute an abuse of process if it is the predominant purpose of the liquidator to gain such an advantage. In *Re Westmex Ltd* (1995) 13 ACLC 1070, an examination order was set aside in circumstances where litigation was well-advanced and the liquidator sought an examination in order to gain a tactical advantage in the litigation not available from ordinary pre-trial procedures.

case note

In *Hamilton v Oades* (1989) 7 ACLC 381, a director was charged with 19 criminal offences relating to the affairs of a company. He was examined prior to the committal proceedings. The High Court held that the examination could proceed. Mason CJ said:

> < Clearly the lengthy delay of an examination due to the pendency of criminal charges would be highly likely to frustrate the liquidator in the carrying out of his duties towards the company and the creditors by denying him the use of a major instrument in the tracing of assets. >

legal professional privilege

[25.335] A person may refuse to answer questions or produce books at an examination if they claim legal professional privilege. Legal professional privilege protects confidentiality between legal advisor and client. It is the client who is entitled to the benefit of the confidentiality.

A person may refuse to answer questions or produce books at an examination if they claim legal professional privilege.

case note

In *Re Transequity Ltd* (1992) 10 ACLC 95, a person was ordered to be examined and to produce certain books under the previous s 597. He argued that certain of the books were protected from production by legal professional privilege. It was held that s 597 did not exclude legal professional privilege.

Legal professional privilege may be asserted where the purpose of the documents was to provide legal advisers with information to assist in giving advice: *Hartogen Energy Ltd v Australian Gas Light Co* (1992) 10 ACLC 1324.

self-incrimination

A person being examined must answer questions even if the answer may be self-incriminating.

[25.340] A person being examined must answer questions even if the answer may be self-incriminating: s 597(12). However, provided the examinee claims privilege, incriminating answers are not admissible evidence in subsequent criminal proceedings or proceedings for the imposition of a penalty: s 597(12A). In *Spedley Securities Ltd v Bond Brewing Investments Pty Ltd* (1991) 9 ACLC 522, Cole J of the Supreme Court of New South Wales called for reform of s 597 so that directors and senior officers of companies that receive money from the public should not be able to claim privilege from incrimination when transactions of their companies were being examined. This suggestion has not been adopted.

powers of the court

[25.345] The court may give directions about an examination on several matters specified in s 596F:

> the matters to be inquired into;
> the procedure to be followed;
> who may be present when the examination is being held in private;
> whether a person may be excluded;
> access to records of the examination;
> whether publication or communication of information about the examination should be prohibited; and
> whether a document relating to and created at the examination should be destroyed.

case note

In *Re Emanuel Investments Pty Ltd* (1996) 14 ACLC 315, the court prevented employees of a company that was a creditor of the company in liquidation gaining access to transcripts of examinations in order to enable the liquidator to carry out his functions. This was because the purpose of an examination was to bring the examinee before the court without warning of the subjects with which the examination was concerned. This order was made despite the employer being a creditor and generally entitled to have access to transcripts under s 597(14A).

Where a person is summoned under ss 596A or 596B or is required to file an affidavit under s 597A and the court is satisfied that this is done without reasonable cause, the court may order that the person's costs be paid by the applicant or any person who took part in the examination: s 597B.

The court is given wide powers under s 598 to make such orders as it thinks appropriate, where it is satisfied that:

> a person is guilty of fraud, negligence, default, breach of trust or breach of duty in relation to a corporation; and
> the corporation also suffered loss or damage as a result of the fraud, negligence, default, breach of trust or breach of duty.

The orders include an order directing a person to pay money or transfer property to the corporation, or to pay compensation to the corporation for loss or damage suffered by it. While these remedies are ostensibly for the benefit of the company, if it is insolvent, they are in effect remedies that benefit its creditors because successful s 598 cases increase the company's assets available for distribution to creditors.

recovery of assets

[25.350] We referred earlier to the duty of liquidators to collect the assets of the company available for distribution to creditors and members. The assets available include all property owned by the company at the date of commencement of the winding up. In addition, the available assets also include:

> amounts due from contributories pursuant to ss 515–526;
> compensation or profits recovered from officers in breach of fiduciary duties or Ch 2D;
> amounts recovered from directors who breach the duty to prevent insolvent trading: s 588G. This is discussed in Chapter 13.5 above;
> amounts recovered from defaulting officers pursuant to s 598 following an examination. Examinations are discussed above; and
> amounts recovered from creditors of an insolvent company who were parties to voidable antecedent transactions.

void dispositions after commencement of winding up

[25.355] The powers of a company to deal with its property after winding up has commenced are limited by s 468(1). Under s 513A, winding up is generally taken to commence on the date of the winding up order. Section 468 declares such dispositions to be void unless the court otherwise orders.

A company cannot deal with its property after winding up has commenced without court approval.

As with voidable antecedent transactions discussed below, the aim of s 468 is to ensure that all creditors share in the assets equally and in accordance with priorities under the *Corporations Act*. It generally prevents disposals of assets after the winding up order is made other than those by the liquidator.

Disposition of property is given a wide meaning but requires "some change that takes out of the company at least the beneficial ownership in a corporate asset and passes it to someone else": *Re Loteka Pty Ltd* (1989) 7 ACLC 998. It includes a sale of company property, payments of money and forgoing of rights. It does not include the exercise of a power of sale by a holder of a fixed charge granted before the commencement of winding up. Nor does it include dispositions of property by a receiver in the course of the receivership: *Wiley v Commonwealth* (1996) 14 ACLC 863.

Certain dispositions are exempt under s 468(2):

> dispositions by a liquidator or provisional liquidator pursuant to the *Corporations Act*, rules of the court or order of the court. Similarly, disposals made in good faith by an administrator are also exempt; and
> payments made by an Australian bank out of the company's account before the order for its winding up.

The payment must be made in good faith and in the ordinary course of banking business. This protects banks that honour cheques drawn on the company's account in favour of a third party. Payments by a company into its overdraft account constitute a void disposition and are not exempt, although they may be validated by the court.

The court has a wide power to validate dispositions that would otherwise be void dispositions under s 468(3). The court may permit part or all of the company's business to be carried on and incidental acts to be done. The exercise of this discretion involves a balance of the interests of creditors that a rateable distribution occurs and the benefit to all creditors of an orderly winding up by allowing a company to continue to carry on its business in order to allow it to be sold as a going concern. This justifies the validation of payments to a creditor for the supply of goods after liquidation has commenced where the creditor acted in good faith, in the ordinary course of business or without knowledge of the winding up proceedings. This is particularly the case where the disposition enabled the company to carry on its business: *Prospect Electricity v Advanced Glass Technologies of Australia Pty Ltd* (1996) 14 ACLC 1721.

voidable antecedent transactions

Antecedent transactions between an insolvent company and other persons entered into before the commencement of winding up can have the effect of reducing the amount available for distribution to creditors when the company is wound up.

[25.360] Certain transactions between an insolvent company and other persons entered into before the commencement of winding up can have the effect of reducing the amount available for distribution to creditors when the company is wound up. These are referred to as "antecedent" transactions because they are entered into before the commencement of winding up.

The provisions of Div 2 of Pt 5.7B of the *Corporations Act* enable a liquidator to apply to the court for orders making such pre-liquidation transactions voidable and to recover the value of any property lost as a result of the transaction for the benefit of the general body of unsecured creditors of the company.

types of antecedent transactions

[25.365] Division 2 of Pt 5.7B (ss 588FA–588FJ) provides for the avoidance of a number of different types of antecedent transactions. These are:

> **unfair preferences (s 588FA);**
> **uncommercial transactions (s 588FB);**
> **unfair loans (s 588FD);**
> **unreasonable director-related transactions (s 588FDA);**
> **transactions for the purpose of defeating creditors (s 588FE(5));**
> **transactions that discharge a liability of guarantor related entities (s 588FH); and**
> **invalidation of floating charges: s 588FJ.**

As a general rule, the antecedent transactions provisions follow a similar pattern. In order for a liquidator to avoid a transaction, the liquidator must prove each of the following:

> **a particular transaction fits the *Corporations Act* definition (eg an unfair preference must satisfy the s 588FA definition);**
> **the company must have been insolvent at the time of entering into the transaction or became insolvent because of the transaction. This is an "insolvent transaction" as defined in s 588FC; and**
> **the insolvent transaction was entered into during a defined period before the winding up began. This is a "voidable transaction" as defined in s 588FE.**

"Transaction" is broadly defined in s 9 to include a disposition of property, creation of a charge, making a payment, giving a guarantee and releasing or incurring an obligation. It includes arrangements which produce legal consequences under either contract law or equitable estoppel which change the rights, liabilities or property of the debtor company: *Bartercard Ltd v Wily* (2001) 19 ACLC 1461. A transaction may consist of a series of events which are connected and discrete from other events. This may involve an order for supply of goods, delivery of the goods, delivery of an invoice, sending of a cheque and payment of the cheque: *Mann v Sangria Pty Ltd* (2001) 19 ACLC 696.

unfair preferences

[25.370] Under s 588FA(1), a transaction is an unfair preference given by a company to a creditor if, and only if:

> **the company and the creditor are parties to the transaction (even if someone else is also a party); and**

> **the transaction results in the creditor receiving, in respect of a debt that the company owes to the creditor, more than the creditor would receive in respect of the debt if the transaction were set aside and the creditor were to prove for the debt in a winding up of the company.**

A company repaying all or part of a debt due to an unsecured creditor is an example of an unfair preference. To the extent that an unsecured debt is repaid prior to liquidation, the creditor receives repayment in full. If the repayment did not occur and the company went into liquidation due to its insolvency, the unsecured creditor would have been entitled to share pari passu with other creditors of equal rank. As a result of being repaid prior to liquidation, the repaid unsecured creditor receives an advantage over the company's other unsecured creditors. This is contrary to the pari passu rule, discussed below, para [25.475], which provides for equal treatment of creditors in a winding up.

When deciding whether payment of a debt is an unfair preference, the courts look to the purpose of the payment in order to determine whether it has the effect of giving a creditor a preference, priority or advantage over other creditors. This requires considering the objective purpose of the whole transaction in a business sense in order to look to the ultimate effect of the transaction.

When deciding whether payment of a debt is an unfair preference, the courts look to the purpose of the payment in order to determine whether it has the effect of giving a creditor a preference, priority or advantage over other creditors.

case note

In *Airservices Australia v Ferrier* (1996) 14 ACLC 1403, the High Court held that the general course of dealings between the creditor and debtor before, during and after the six-month period prior to the commencement of winding up had to be considered. The business purpose and context of a payment had to be looked at in determining whether it gave the creditor a preference over other creditors. If the purpose is to induce the creditor to provide further goods, the payment is not a preference unless the payment exceeds the value of the goods acquired. If the sole purpose of the payment is to extinguish a debt, the payment is a preference. To have the effect of a preference, a payment must ultimately reduce the net value of the assets that were available to meet the claims of the other creditors. If, at the end of a series of transactions, the creditor has supplied goods of greater value than the payments made to it, the general body of creditors was not disadvantaged and the supplier would not have received a preference. There is an unfair preference only if the net effect of the series of transactions results in a creditor's position being improved.

case note

In *Re Emanuel (No 14) Pty Ltd* (1997) 24 ACSR 292, the Federal Court held that an unfair preference could also occur where a company arranges for a third party to pay a debt owed to a creditor of the company. While s 588FA(1)(a) requires both the company and the creditor to be parties to a transaction, a transaction could be made up of a composite of dealings and the company need not participate in all of these dealings. In *Re Emanuel (No 14) Pty Ltd*, the transaction consisted of two dealings. First, the company initiated an arrangement with the third party for it to pay the company's debt. The second dealing was the payment by the third party to the company's creditor. As the company was a party to the first dealing, the court held that s 588FA(1)(a) applied.

Transactions which constitute a running account are not taken to be unfair preferences.

Under s 588FA(3), transactions which constitute a running account are not taken to be unfair preferences. This covers situations where a particular transaction is one of a series of transactions forming an integral part of a continuing business relationship between a company and a creditor with the expectation that further debits and credits will be recorded. The particular transaction is not considered in isolation for purposes of determining whether that transaction is an unfair preference.

case note

In *Rothmans Exports Pty Ltd v Mistmorn Pty Ltd* (1994) 12 ACLC 936, Panasonic supplied goods on credit to a company. Between February and July 1993 the company made a series of payments to Panasonic, reducing its debt from approximately $105,000 at the beginning of the period to about $3,000 at the end of the period. The company was subsequently placed in liquidation. The Federal Court held that these payments were a series of transactions forming an integral part of a continuing business relationship between Panasonic and the company for purposes of s 588A(2). The net effect of the payments was to reduce the company's debt by about $102,000. Panasonic's receipt of these payments was an unfair preference because it resulted in Panasonic receiving more than it would have received in the winding up.

The court can make an order about an unfair preference if it is an "insolvent transaction" and a "voidable transaction".

The court can make an order about an unfair preference under s 588FF if it is an "insolvent transaction" as defined in s 588FC and a "voidable transaction" as defined in s 588FE.

A creditor who gives up the benefit of an unfair preference may prove for the debt in the winding up as if the transaction had not been entered into: s 588FI(3).

uncommercial transactions

A transaction is an "uncommercial transaction", if it may be expected that a reasonable person in the company's circumstances would not have entered into it.

[25.375] A transaction is an "uncommercial transaction", under s 588FB, if it may be expected that a reasonable person in the company's circumstances would not have entered into it having regard to:

> **the benefits (if any) to the company of entering into the transaction; and**
> **the detriment to the company of entering into the transaction; and**
> **the respective benefits to other parties to the transaction of entering into it; and**
> **any other relevant matter.**

Unlike an unfair preference, an uncommercial transaction does not have to involve a transaction between the company and one of its creditors. It can be entered into by the company and any other person.

According to the Explanatory Memorandum to the 1992 amending legislation that inserted the section, s 588FB is specifically aimed at preventing companies disposing of assets through transactions that result in the recipient, usually a director, relative or associated company, receiving a gift or obtaining a bargain of such magnitude that it could not be explained by normal commercial practice.

case note

In *Re Pacific Hardware Brokers (Qld) Pty Ltd* (1998) 15 ACLC 442, the sole director of an insolvent company used company funds to purchase an engagement ring for his fiancé. The court held that the use of the company's funds in these circumstances amounted to an uncommercial transaction under s 588FB and ordered that the director pay the company the ring's purchase price under s 588FF(1)(a).

case note

In *Demondrille Nominees Pty Ltd v Shirlaw* (1997) 15 ACLC 1716, a company owned by the directors of Cornelis Holdings Pty Ltd owed Demondrille $120,000. In order to pay this debt, Cornelis, a building company, entered into a contract to sell one of its home units to Demondrille for $180,000. The contract provided that Demondrille was deemed to have paid a $120,000 deposit. When Cornelis was wound up, its liquidator sought an order that the contract was void. The Federal Court held that the contract was an uncommercial transaction under s 588FB because there was no benefit to Cornelis in crediting Demondrille with the $120,000 deposit. The transaction entitled Demondrille to purchase a unit worth $180,000 at an undervalue.

case note

In *Lewis v Cook* (2000) 18 ACLC 490, a wholly-owned subsidiary forgave a debt due to it by its holding company. After the debt was forgiven both companies were placed in liquidation with different liquidators. The court held that the forgiveness was an uncommercial transaction. A reasonable person in the subsidiary's position would have been influenced not to forgive the debt for two reasons. First, there was a slight possibility that the holding company might succeed in recovering money from arbitration proceedings against third parties that would have enabled it to at least repay some of the loan. Secondly, there was the possibility of the holding company's liquidator taking action against its directors and other creditors to recover assets under the voidable antecedent transactions provisions of Pt 5.7B.

Before a liquidator can obtain a court order regarding an uncommercial transaction, the liquidator must show that the uncommercial transaction was also an insolvent transaction as defined in s 588FC and a voidable transaction as defined in s 588FE.

Amendments made in 2000 linked the uncommercial transaction provisions in s 588FB with the insolvent trading provisions in s 588G, discussed in Chapter 13.5 above. Under s 588G(1A), a company is regarded as incurring a debt by entering into an uncommercial transaction. This means that liquidators now have another means of recovering funds if a company enters into an uncommercial transaction. They may set aside an uncommercial transaction under s 588FF and recover funds from the other party to the transaction. Alternatively, a liquidator could recover compensation from directors for contravening s 588G. In addition, directors who arrange for their company to enter into an uncommercial transaction may also prejudice the interests of the company's creditors in breach their fiduciary and s 181 duties to act in good faith in the best interest of their company. These duties are discussed in Chapter 13.5 below.

unfair loans

Unfair loans committ a company to extortionate interest rates.

[25.380] Section 588FD ensures that the general body of an insolvent company's unsecured creditors is not prejudiced by a pre-liquidation loan agreement under which the company is committed to extortionate interest rates.

A loan to a company is unfair under s 588FD if the interest on the loan is, or the charges in relation to the loan are, extortionate. Section 588FD(2) lists several factors to be considered in determining whether interest or charges are extortionate. They are:

- the risk assumed by the lender;
- the value of any security in respect of the loan;
- the term of the loan;
- the schedule for payments of interest and charges and for repayments of principal;
- the amount of the loan; and
- any other relevant matter.

The Explanatory Memorandum to the 1992 amending legislation that inserted the section makes it clear that s 588FD:

> **< is not directed to loans which in hindsight may be judged as bad bargains but as transactions which are grossly unfair, so that in normal circumstances no reasonable company is likely to have entered into such a contract unless there were some further rationale such as where the agreement is a sham agreement intended to operate in circumstances of insolvency to confer an undue benefit on the lender. >**

unreasonable director-related transactions

Liquidators may reclaim unreasonable director-related transactions entered into by a company prior to its liquidation.

[25.385] Section 588FDA, inserted into the *Corporations Act* by the *Corporations Amendment (Repayment of Directors' Bonuses) Act 2003,* permits liquidators to reclaim unreasonable director-related transactions by companies prior to the company's liquidation. The provision was inserted as a result of public outrage over the circumstances surrounding the unexpected collapse of One.Tel, a large mobile phone company. A few months before the company's liquidation, its directors approved the payment of extremely large bonuses to One.Tel's two joint managing directors.

Under s 588FDA(1)(c), a transaction of a company is an "unreasonable director-related transaction" if it is made to a recipient and it may be expected that a reasonable person in the company's circumstances would not have entered into the transaction. The reasonableness of the transaction is determined with regard to the respective costs and benefits to the company, and benefits to the recipient, of entering into the transaction.

Section 588FDA(1) applies to a wide range of transactions including payments made by a company, dispositions of company property and issues of securities by the company. Recipients of these transactions include directors or their "close associates". Section 9 defines a close associate of a director to include a director's relatives and a relative of a director's spouse.

Under s 588FE(6A), an unreasonable director-related transaction is voidable if it was entered into or given effect to, within four years of the "relation-back day" (usually the date of commencement of the company's liquidation).

transactions to defeat creditors

A liquidator can avoid insolvent transactions entered into for the purpose of defeating, delaying or interfering with, the rights of any or all of its creditors on a winding up of the company.

[25.390] A liquidator can avoid insolvent transactions (defined in s 588FC) entered into at any time during 10 years prior to the relation-back day (usually the date of commencement of the company's liquidation) if the company became a party to the transaction for the purpose of defeating, delaying or interfering with, the rights of any or all of its creditors on a winding up of the company: s 588FE(5).

case note

In *Re Solfire Pty Ltd (No 1)* (1997) 25 ACSR 160, a company was involved in protracted litigation with two other companies. The directors formed the view that it was undesirable for the company to continue the litigation. They arranged for the company to withdraw from the proceedings and allowed the other two companies to enter judgment against it. Before judgment was entered against the company, the directors, who had previously lent large amounts to their company on an unsecured basis, arranged for the company to give them security in relation to their previously unsecured loans. They then entered into an agreement with the company under which the company repaid the loan and the directors paid out debts due to certain company creditors. The company then filed its own winding up application. The effect of this arrangement meant that the company was an "empty shell" with no assets to pay the two other companies when they entered judgment. The court held that the payment to the directors was voidable under s 588FE(5). The whole transaction was entered into as a strategy to defeat the company's judgment creditors.

transactions that discharge liability of guarantor related entities

[25.395] It is common business practice for a company's creditors to insist that its directors guarantee the company's debts. In order to escape personal liability under the guarantee, the director may see to it that such a creditor is repaid ahead of other creditors whose debts are not guaranteed. The effect of this is to give the directors an unfair preference as well as the creditor who received payment. Section 588FH deals with such situations and allows the liquidator to recover the value of a discharged personal liability under a guarantee from the guarantor director.

That section applies where a company entered into a transaction prior to its winding up that had the effect of discharging a liability (whether under a guarantee or otherwise) of a related entity of the company and the transaction was:

> **an insolvent transaction as defined in s 588FC; and**
> **a voidable transaction under s 588FE.**

The liquidator may recover an amount equal to the value of the liability that was discharged from the related entity: s 588FH(2).

"Related entity" is defined in s 9 to include a company's directors, members and their relatives. Section 588FH also applies where the guarantee or other liability is not entirely discharged.

case note

The operation of a predecessor of s 588FH was illustrated in *Matthews v Geraghty* (1986) 4 ACLC 727. A company had both a cheque account and a fully drawn advance account with the ANZ Bank. The directors were guarantors of the fully drawn advance account. In November 1985, the company deposited money into its cheque account and a few days later the bank transferred sufficient funds from this account to clear the amount owing on the fully drawn advance account. This transfer was effected pursuant to a "Letter of Set-Off" which the company had executed when the fully drawn advance account was first opened. When the company was placed in liquidation, its liquidator sought recovery of the amount transferred from the guarantor directors under the predecessor of s 588FH. It was held that the directors were liable to account for this amount to the liquidator. The transfer between the accounts had the effect of relieving the directors of their liability under the guarantee.

invalid floating charges

[25.400] Secured creditors are generally unaffected by the debtor company's liquidation. They are entitled to exercise their rights over the secured assets. To the extent of the value of the property secured, their debt is repaid.

Section 588FJ aims to prevent companies, on the verge of insolvency, securing past debts by granting floating charges over its assets in favour of particular creditors so as to remove those assets from the control of the liquidator.

Section 588FJ deals specifically with the situation where the security takes the form of a floating charge. The nature of a floating charge is discussed in Chapter 11 above.

This section aims to prevent companies, on the verge of insolvency, securing past debts by granting floating charges over its assets in favour of particular creditors so as to remove those assets from the control of the liquidator. It provides that a floating charge created within six months before the relation-back day is void against the company's liquidator unless it is proved that the company was solvent immediately after the charge was created: s 588FJ(1)–(3).

Section 588FJ(2) sets out circumstances where a floating charge will not be void. These include a charge that secures an advance paid to the company as consideration for the charge and interest on such an advance. A charge is also not void if it secures a liability under a guarantee or an amount payable for property or services supplied to the company.

insolvent transactions

Before a liquidator can avoid a transaction as an unfair preference or uncommercial transaction, the liquidator must establish that it was also an "insolvent transaction".

[25.405] Before a liquidator can avoid a transaction as an unfair preference or uncommercial transaction, the liquidator must establish that it was also an "insolvent transaction".

A transaction is an insolvent transaction under s 588FC if it is either an unfair preference or an uncommercial transaction and:

- **the transaction is entered into at a time when the company is insolvent; or**
- **the company becomes insolvent because of entering into the transaction.**

The word "insolvent" is defined in s 95A. A company is insolvent if it is unable to pay all its debts as and when they become due and payable. The meaning of insolvency is discussed above, para [25.45].

Section 588E assists a liquidator in proving the company was insolvent at the time when a transaction was entered into by allowing the liquidator to make certain presumptions of insolvency. These presumptions can be rebutted by proof to the contrary: s 588E(9). The liquidator may, under s 588E(3), presume that if the company was insolvent at a particular time during the 12 months ending on the relation-back day, the company was insolvent throughout that period. In addition, under s 588E(4), a company is presumed to be insolvent if it has contravened s 286 by failing to keep and retain adequate financial records.

voidable transactions

Insolvent transactions and unfair loans entered into during the applicable period prior to the relation-back day are "voidable transactions". Section 588FE sets different time periods depending on the type of transaction.

[25.410] Insolvent transactions and unfair loans entered into during the applicable period prior to the relation-back day are "voidable transactions". In the case of a court-ordered winding up, the relation-back day is usually the date of the application: s 9. Section 588FE sets different time periods depending on the type of transaction.

- **An unfair preference that is an insolvent transaction is voidable under s 588FE(2) if it was entered into during the six months ending on the relation-back day or between the relation-back day and the day the winding up began.**
- **An uncommercial transaction that is an insolvent transaction is voidable under s 588FE(3) if it was entered into during or after the two years ending on the relation-back day.**
- **An unreasonable director-related transaction is voidable under s 588FE(6A) if it was entered into during the four years ending on the relation-back day or between the relation-back day and the day the winding up began.**
- **An insolvent transaction for the purpose of defeating creditors is voidable under s 588FE(5) during the 10 years ending on the relation-back day.**
- **An unfair loan to the company is voidable under s 588FE(6) if it was made at any time before the winding up began.**

If a "related entity" of a company is a party to an insolvent transaction, whether the transaction is an unfair preference or an uncommercial transaction, a longer time period applies. Under s 588FE(4), such an insolvent transaction is voidable if it was entered into during or after the four years ending on the relation-back day. The definition of "related entity" is contained in s 9 and is discussed above, para [25.395].

If a "related entity" of a company is a party to an insolvent transaction, a longer time period applies.

court orders in relation to voidable transactions

[25.415] Pursuant to s 588FF(1), a company's liquidator may apply to the court for a variety of orders where a transaction is a voidable transaction as defined in s 588FE. Orders that can be made under s 588FF(1) include:

A company's liquidator may apply to the court for a variety of orders where a transaction is a voidable transaction.

> **requiring a person to pay to the company an amount that fairly represents the benefits that the person has received because of the transaction (s 588FF(1)(c));**
> **declaring an agreement to be void or an order varying an agreement (s 588FF(1)(h) and (i)); and**
> **releasing or discharging a debt incurred, or a security or guarantee given, by the company under or in connection with the transaction: s 588FF(1)(e). This is the most likely order in the case of an unfair loan.**

In the case of an unfair preference that involves the payment of an outstanding debt by the company to a creditor, the order most likely to be made is an order directing the creditor to pay to the company an amount equal to some or all of the money that the company has paid under the transaction: s 588FF(1)(a).

An application for an order under s 588FF(1) must generally be made within three years after the relation-back day. A liquidator may apply to the court within this three-year period for an extension of time: s 588FF(3). This provision seeks to prevent long delays in the commencement of proceedings involving voidable transactions and gives some protection to potential defendants from late claims. However, it also recognises that sometimes liquidators legitimately require further time to complete their investigations before being able to decide which transactions it is appropriate to pursue.

Section 588FI prevents the court from making an s 588FF order that prejudices a right or interest of a creditor who gives up the benefit of an unfair preference and puts the company in the same position as if the transaction had not been entered into. Such a creditor may prove for the debt in the winding up: s 588FI(3).

defences

[25.420] Section 588FG provides defences to persons who might otherwise be subject to s 588FF orders. Section 588FG(2) protects persons who are parties to voidable transactions other than unfair loans to the company. Section 588FG(1) prevents the court from making s 588FF orders prejudicing the right or interest of persons who are not parties to the transaction.

Section 588FG provides defences to persons who might otherwise be subject to antecedant transactions.

case note

In *Re Pacific Hardware Brokers (Qld) Pty Ltd* (1998) 15 ACLC 442, the sole director of a company used company funds to purchase an engagement ring for his fiancé. The liquidator claimed that the purchase was voidable as an insolvent transaction and uncommercial transaction and sought to recover the ring from the fiancé or the amount paid for it from the director. It was held that the fiancé was not a party to the transaction, received the ring in good faith and had no reasonable grounds for suspecting that the company was insolvent. As a result, s 588FG(1) prevented the court from making an order against her for the recovery of the ring under s 588FF. However, the court ordered the director to pay the company the amount paid for the ring under s 588FF(1)(a).

Section 588FG(1) prevents the court from making s 588FF orders prejudicing the right or interest of persons who are not parties to the transaction.

Under s 588FG(2), a court must not make an s 588FF order prejudicing the right or interest of a person if it is proved that:

- **the person became a party to the transaction in good faith (s 588FG(2)(a));**
- **at the time of becoming a party to the transaction, the person had no reasonable grounds for suspecting that the company was insolvent and a reasonable person in the person's circumstances would have no such grounds for so suspecting (s 588FG (2)(b)); and**
- **the person has provided valuable consideration under the transaction or has changed her or his position in reliance on the transaction: s 588FG(2)(c).**

The test of "good faith" in s 588FG(2)(a) is subjective and is satisfied if the creditor can prove that they did not believe that the company was insolvent or would become insolvent by paying the creditor.

In *Downey v Aira Pty Ltd* (1996) 14 ACLC 1068, Ashley J considered the operation of s 588FG. The test of "good faith" in s 588FG(2)(a) is subjective and is satisfied if the creditor can prove that they did not believe that the company was insolvent or would become insolvent by paying the creditor. An objective consideration of all the circumstances is applied to determine whether a person had no reasonable grounds for suspecting insolvency for purposes of the s 588FG(2)(b) defence: *Downey v Aira Pty Ltd* (1996) 14 ACLC 1068.

In itself, a request to a creditor to delay banking a cheque for a short while does not show that the creditor had become a party to the transaction in bad faith within s 588FG (2)(a). Nor does it deprive the creditor of a defence under s 588FG(2)(b) as it would not provide reasonable grounds for the creditor, or a reasonable person in the creditor's circumstances, to suspect that the company was insolvent: *Downey v Hartsteel Pty Ltd* (1996) 14 ACLC 1083.

In *Mann v Sangria Pty Ltd* (2001) 19 ACLC 696, the court held that a creditor would have reasonable grounds for suspecting that a debtor company was insolvent in the following circumstances:

- **inadequate explanations for non-payment by the debtor;**
- **reference to heavy financial involvement in an unrelated business as a reason for not paying;**
- **commencement of litigation for recovery of the debt;**
- **requests by the debtor for further time to pay;**
- **agreement to pay the debt by instalments over a two-year period;**
- **joining a director as guarantor for the debt and unsuccessfully seeking security; and**
- **the absence of transactions over a long period and arrangements for payment by post-dated cheque when transactions resumed.**

liability of directors to indemnify Commissioner of Taxation

If a liquidator obtains an s 588FF order against the Commissioner of Taxation each director of the company is liable to indemnify the Commissioner in respect of the loss arising from the s 588FF order.

[25.425] If a liquidator obtains an s 588FF order against the Commissioner of Taxation to recover a voidable transaction (such as an unfair preference), each director of the company at the time the payment was made to the Commissioner is liable to indemnify the Commissioner in respect of the loss arising from the s 588FF order: s 588FGA(2). The court may order that the directors pay the amount of the indemnity in the s 588FF proceedings brought against the Commissioner: s 588FGA(4).

The directors who are liable under s 588FGA have rights of recovery against the company and other directors as if the indemnity payment had arisen under a guarantee under which each director was jointly and severally liable: s 588FGA(5).

Directors have defences to these proceedings under s 588FGB. These defences are similar to the insolvent trading defences contained in s 588H:

- **the director had reasonable grounds to expect and did expect that the company was solvent and would remain so after the payment;**
- **the director reasonably believed that a competent and reliable person was responsible for providing adequate information that the company was solvent, this responsibility was being fulfilled and on the basis of this information, the director expected that the company was solvent and would remain so after the payment;**

- because of illness or other good reason, the director did not take part in management when the payment was made; or
- all reasonable steps were taken to prevent the company from making the payment or no such steps could have been taken. The types of steps which could be considered include any action taken with a view to appoint an administrator.

The insolvent trading defences are further discussed above in Chapter 13.5.

pooling

[25.430] The liquidation of an insolvent company that is part of a corporate group causes complex administrative problems, especially where other companies in the group are also in liquidation. As discussed in Chapter 2 above, limited liability and the separate entity concept means that the creditors of a particular group company in liquidation can only be paid their debts from the property of that company. As a general rule, such creditors cannot access the property of other group companies. Untangling the assets and liabilities of several insolvent group companies becomes extremely complex where their affairs have been intermingled prior to their respective liquidations.

The government foreshadowed the introduction of a statutory "pooling" mechanism as a component of its corporate insolvency reform package announced in October 2005. The pooling mechanism is designed to streamline the administration of complex group liquidations. The effect of pooling is that the companies in a group are not regarded as separate entities and they are wound up together as if they were one company.

The government foreshadowed the introduction of a statutory "pooling" mechanism. The effect of pooling is that the companies in a group are not regarded as separate entities and they are wound up together as if they were one company.

It is proposed to amend the *Corporations Act* to permit a liquidator to pool the unsecured assets and liabilities of two or more group companies in liquidation with the prior approval of all unsecured creditors of those companies. The court will also be given the power to make pooling orders for related companies in liquidation where their affairs have been intermingled. Secured creditors' rights will not be affected by pooling orders.

In deciding whether to make a pooling order, the court will be required to take into account:

- the extent to which the related company took part in the management of the company in liquidation;
- the conduct of the related company towards the creditors of the company in liquidation;
- the extent to which the circumstances giving rise to the liquidation are attributable to the actions of the related company; and
- the extent to which creditors of the companies in liquidation might be disadvantaged by the making of a pooling order.

employee entitlements

[25.435] Amendments made in 2000 inserted Pt 5.8A (ss 596AA–596AI) into the *Corporations Act* to protect the entitlements of a company's employees from agreements and transactions that are entered into with the intention of defeating the recovery of those entitlements: s 596AA(1).

Employees' entitlements are protected from attempts to restructure a group so as to ensure that an employer company in a group has no funds to meet employee entitlements despite related companies having substantial assets.

The Lipton-Herzberg Corporate Insolvency Pathway at **http://www.lipton-herzberg.com.au/secure/pathways-corporate-insolvency.html** has links to both the *Corporations Law Amendment (Employee Entitlements) Act 2000* and the Explanatory Memorandum to that Act, as well as commentaries on this legislation.

As discussed in Chapter 2 above, according to *Salomon v Salomon & Co* [1897] AC 22, the controllers of a company are not liable for the company's debts and obligations. This has significant implications for company groups. One company in a group is generally not responsible for the debts of other companies in the group. The amendments attempt to protect employees' entitlements from attempts to restructure a group so as to ensure that an employer company in a group has no funds to meet employee entitlements despite related companies having substantial assets.

case note

The problems facing employees' entitlements when groups are restructured were highlighted by the waterfront dispute in 1998 between Patrick Stevedores and the Maritime Union of Australia (MUA), the circumstances of which are described in *Maritime Union of Australia v Patrick Stevedores No 1 Pty Ltd* (1998) 27 ACSR 497. The amendments introduced in 2000 were largely brought about as a response to the waterfront dispute. The MUA alleged that the Patrick group of companies was restructured so as to facilitate the sacking of its waterside workers and their replacement with non-union employees. While the Patrick group argued that the main reason for the corporate restructure was administrative efficiency, it did not expressly deny that one of the reasons for the restructuring was to facilitate the sacking of its employees. This involved each employer company in the Patrick group selling its businesses to another company in the group, Patrick Stevedores Operations No 2 Pty Ltd (PSO2).

Another company in the group, Patrick Stevedores No 1 Pty Ltd (PS1), employed the waterside workers. PSO2 entered into a labour supply agreement with PS1 under which PS1 provided the labour for PSO2 to carry out its stevedoring business. The labour supply agreement, which was the only asset of PS1, could be terminated in the event of a strike or other industrial dispute. The PS1 employees took industrial action and PSO2 terminated the labour supply agreement. As a result of the termination of the labour supply agreement, PS1 had no funds to pay employees' wages and was placed in voluntary administration.

It is an offence for a person to enter into an agreement or transaction with the intention of either preventing the recovery of employees' entitlements or significantly reducing the amount of employees' entitlements.

It is an offence for a person to enter into an agreement or transaction with the intention of either preventing the recovery of employees' entitlements or significantly reducing the amount of employees' entitlements: s 596AB(1). In addition, if a person contravenes s 596AB by incurring a debt, the incurring of the debt is linked to s 588G.

Employee entitlements include wages, employer superannuation contributions, amounts due for employees' leave of absence and retrenchment payments: s 596AA(2).

As well as being guilty of a criminal offence, a person who contravenes s 596AB(1) is also liable to pay compensation if the company is being wound up and employees suffer loss or damage because of the contravention: s 596AC(1). The company's liquidator may initiate compensation claims and any amount recovered has priority under s 556(1)(e) to (h) and is regarded as a preferential debt that is owed to employees. Under s 596AC(3), employees may also sue for compensation if they have the liquidator's consent to do so, as required by s 596AF. Section 596AH allows employees to sue for compensation with prior court leave even if the liquidator does not consent. Their right to sue in such cases only arises three months after the liquidator is notified of the employees' intentions to sue.

division of assets

The creditors rank first, and then the surplus (if any) is distributed among the members.

[25.440] One of the tasks of a liquidator is to divide the company's property among those persons entitled to them. If the company is solvent, these persons are its creditors and members. The creditors are paid first, and then the surplus (if any) is distributed among the members. If the company is insolvent, only the creditors are entitled to share in its assets.

proofs of debts and claims

provable debts

[25.445] Creditors must prove their debts in order to have any entitlements. This enables the liquidator to ascertain what the liabilities of the company are in order to carry out the duty to discharge these liabilities under s 478(1)(a). The liquidator must decide whether to accept or reject a proof of debt.

Creditors must prove their debts in order to have any entitlements.

If there are sufficient funds, a creditor whose proof of debt is admitted is then entitled to be repaid. Such repayments are referred to as "dividends". If there are insufficient funds to pay all debts, creditors are paid a proportion of their debts.

A creditor whose proof of debt is admitted is entitled to be repaid. Such repayments are referred to as "dividends".

Not all debts are provable and hence are not repaid. Unprovable debts include debts that are unenforceable because they are based on illegal transactions or because of the operation of the Statute of Limitations. Claims in equity such as an entitlement to be subrogated rights against the company in liquidation may also not be provable or may be subject to equitable principles: *Re Trivan Pty Ltd* (1996) 14 ACLC 1654.

Not all debts are provable.

In *Re Media World Communications Ltd* [2005] FCA 51, Finkelstein J held that an investor who was misled into subscribing for shares in a company could not, while the investor retained those shares, prove for damages for fraud and misrepresentation against the company.

Prior to 1992 amendments, claims for damages for torts committed by an insolvent company were not provable in its winding up. The Harmer Report thought there was no justification for this and recommended that such claims should be admissible. This recommendation is adopted in s 553(1), which provides that in every winding up, all claims against the company (present or future, certain or contingent, ascertained or sounding only in damages) are admissible to proof against the company. Section 554A, discussed below, sets out a mechanism for determining the value of debts and claims of uncertain value. This includes claims for unliquidated damages in tort. Where the liquidator admits a debt or claim of uncertain value, the liquidator must make an estimate of value or refer the question to the court.

Debts owed by a company to its members in their capacity as members are not admissible to proof against the company unless the members have paid to the company or the liquidator all contributions they are liable to pay as members: s 553A. Unpaid dividends are regarded as debts owed to members in their capacity as members. Unpaid contributions on partly paid shares are an example of a member's liability to pay as a member. Even if members have paid all contributions they are liable to pay as members, debts a company owes to its members in their capacity of members are postponed until all debts due to non-member creditors are satisfied: s 563A.

Debts a company owes to its members in their capacity of members are postponed until all debts due to non-member creditors are satisfied.

case note

In *Sons of Gwalia Ltd v Margaretic* [2005] FCA 1305, Margaretic bought shares in Sons of Gwalia on the stock exchange. He claimed to have been misled into buying the shares because the company failed to comply with its continuous disclosure obligations in not disclosing its financial difficulties. Emmet J held that the shareholder had a provable debt in relation to his claim for damages against the company. This debt was not a debt owed to the shareholder in his capacity as shareholder for purposes of s 563A and therefore was not postponed until debts due to non-member creditors were satisfied.

As a general rule, unpaid penalties and fines imposed on a company by a court in respect of an offence against a law are not admissible to proof against an insolvent company: s 553B. The Explanatory Memorandum to the 1992 amendments took the view that it was illogical to penalise creditors for a wrong committed by an insolvent company. Section 553B(2) provides an exception to the general rule in respect of an amount payable under a pecuniary penalty order as defined in the *Proceeds of Crime Act 1987* (Cth).

set off of mutual debts

[25.450] A person may be both a debtor and creditor of a company. But for s 553C, the person would not be permitted to set off the amount that is due to the company against the amount the company owes to the person. Section 553C, which is modelled on s 86 of the *Bankruptcy Act*, provides that where there have been mutual credits, mutual debts, or other mutual dealings between an insolvent company that is being wound up and a person who wants to have a debt or claim admitted against the company, account is to be taken of what is due from one party to the other in respect of those mutual dealings. The sum due by one party can be set off against any sum due from the other party. Only the balance of the account is admissible to proof against the company, or is payable to the company, as the case may be.

quantification of debts

[25.455] Section 554 provides that the amount of a debt or claim of the company (including a debt for interest) is to be computed as at the relevant date. This is the date of the winding up order in the case of a court-ordered winding up. Sections 554A–554C set out rules for determining how specific types of debts and claims are to be calculated.

Section 554A provides a mechanism for estimating debts or claims of uncertain value. This includes claims for unliquidated damages for breach of contract or tort.

Section 554A provides a mechanism for estimating debts or claims of uncertain value. This includes claims for unliquidated damages for breach of contract or tort. Under s 554A(2), a liquidator must make an estimate of the value of a debt or claim of uncertain value or refer the question to the court. A person who is aggrieved by the liquidator's estimate may appeal to the court against the estimation: s 554A(3). If the liquidator refers an estimation question to the court or a person appeals against the liquidator's estimation, the court must either make its own estimate or determine a method to be applied by the liquidator in working out the value of the debt or claim: s 554A(4). The estimated or worked out value of the debt or claim is admissible to proof against the company: s 554A(8).

Under s 554B, the amount of a debt that is admissible to proof is reduced if, as at the relevant date, the debt was not payable by the company until after the relevant date. The amount of the reduction is the discount calculated in accordance with the regulations.

Section 554C deals with the conversion into Australian currency of foreign currency debts or claims. Where a company and a creditor have agreed on the basis for converting the amount of a debt or claim, the amount that is admissible to proof is the Australian currency equivalent of the foreign currency amount worked out as at the relevant date in accordance with the agreed method: s 554C(2). Where there is no agreed method of calculating the conversion, the amount of the debt or claim that is admissible to proof is the equivalent in Australian currency of the foreign currency, worked out by reference to the "opening carded on demand airmail buying rate" in relation to the foreign currency available at the Commonwealth Bank of Australia on the relevant date: s 554C(3).

secured creditors

[25.460] Sections 554D–554J deal with the rights of secured creditors in relation to proving debts. They give a creditor several choices. The secured creditor may either retain the security or give it up and prove in the winding up for the value of the debt. Alternatively, the secured creditor may retain the security and prove for the difference between the debt and the value of the security. This may occur where the debts exceed the value of the secured property. In such a case, the secured creditor ranks equally with the unsecured creditors.

procedure for proving debts

[25.465] The procedure for proving debts is governed by the *Corporations Regulations*. A liquidator fixes the time within which creditors must prove their debts. Notice must be given to the creditors of the time and the fixing of the time advertised. A debt or claim must be proved formally in accordance with the *Corporations Regulations* if this is required by the liquidator: s 553D(1). Section 553D(2)(b) also permits a liquidator to allow a creditor to prove for a debt or claim informally, subject to compliance with the requirements of the regulations relating to the informal proof of debts and claims. The liquidator can admit a debt without formal proof if satisfied that the debt is valid. If formal proof is required, the liquidator must notify the creditors and fix the final day for their receipt. The formal proof of debt contains particulars of the debt and is made on the prescribed form.

The liquidator must deal with a formal proof of debt within 28 days after receiving it or such further period as ASIC allows. If a proof of debt is rejected, the liquidator must notify the creditor within seven days, supplying the grounds for the rejection. Both a creditor and a contributory can appeal from the liquidator's decision to the court: s 1321.

priorities on payments of debts

secured and unsecured debts

[25.470] The policy of the *Corporations Act* is that unless otherwise provided, all provable debts rank equally and if there are insufficient funds available to meet them all in full, they are paid proportionately. The legislation distinguishes between secured and unsecured debts. A secured creditor need not prove the debt in a winding up and wait for payment with other unsecured creditors. Instead, on default, a secured creditor has the right to sell the secured property. Thus, to the extent of the amount realised, a secured creditor is unaffected by a winding up. In the case of companies, their secured creditors include debenture-holders who have fixed or floating charges over particular assets. This is discussed in Chapter 11 above.

A secured creditor need not prove the debt in a winding up, but has the right to sell the secured property.

the pari passu rule

[25.475] One of the most important principles of insolvency law is the general rule that all creditors participate equally in the distribution of a company's assets on the winding up of the company.

Prior to the commencement of winding up, however, each creditor is entitled to enforce any available legal rights. If a creditor obtains judgment against a debtor company, the judgment may be enforced against the company's assets to the full extent of the debt. Whatever assets are left are then available to the next judgment creditor and so on. Prior to liquidation, the abiding principle is one of "first in—best dressed". Eventually, later creditors may find that the assets of the debtor company have been exhausted and even though a judgment may have been obtained, there are no assets against which to enforce the judgment.

From the commencement of winding up, the scramble for recovery of debts by creditors ceases. It is replaced by the pari passu principle, which provides for an orderly distribution of the proceeds of assets to all unsecured creditors on an equal proportionate basis.

The pari passu principle which is set out in s 555, provides that except for certain priority payments, all debts proved in a winding up rank equally and, if the property of the company is insufficient to meet them in full, they shall be paid proportionately.

The pari passu principle provides that except for certain priority payments, all debts proved in a winding up rank equally and, if the property of the company is insufficient to meet them in full, they shall be paid proportionately.

This principle recognises that insolvency proceedings are of a collective nature. They aim to benefit the general body of creditors. Each creditor has lost the individual right to pursue separate remedies and must rely on the outcome of collective proceedings. It is then only reasonable that each creditor should have a fair interest in the insolvency proceedings.

As discussed below, among unsecured creditors, there are certain debts that are accorded preference over ordinary unsecured debts. These statutory priorities also detract from the pari passu principle; however, they are justified because they assist an orderly winding up for the benefit of all creditors or there is a general public acceptance of their fairness in recognising special interests such as that of employee creditors.

preferential debts

[25.480] Sections 556–564 rank the debts of particular classes of unsecured creditors in order of priority. The creditors with priority are known as "preferential creditors" and their debts referred to as

Unsecured creditors with priority are known as "preferential creditors" and their debts referred to as "preferential debts".

"preferential debts". The preferential creditors are themselves ranked in priority. The scheme of priorities is only relevant if the company is insolvent and there are insufficient funds to pay all unsecured creditors in full. Where this is the case, preferential creditors are paid in full before any amount is paid to the other unsecured creditors. If there is insufficient to meet the claims of all preferential creditors of a particular rank, they are paid proportionately.

The debts and claims that must be paid in priority to all other unsecured debts and claims are set out in order in s 556.

The debts and claims that must be paid in priority to all other unsecured debts and claims are set out in order in s 556:

> the expenses of recovering, preserving and realising the property of the company or carrying on its business. These rank first because all creditors have an interest in maximising the fund for distribution;
> the costs of the application for the winding up order. This expense is also incurred in the interests of all creditors as it initiates the winding up;
> various expenses that are also necessary for an orderly winding up. These include debts for which an administrator is entitled to be indemnified under s 443D(a), costs and expenses of the liquidator's report as to the company's affairs and the costs of an audit of the liquidator's accounts;
> the remuneration or fees for service of the liquidator or, if applicable, the administrator. These are referred to as "deferred expenses", which are defined in s 556(2). They are deferred for payment after the above liquidation expenses; and
> employee entitlements rank next. These recognise that employees are a class of unsecured creditors who ought to receive special priority. Section 556 limits the protection in the case of employees who are directors or relatives of directors. While employees receive priority for wages, superannuation contributions, amounts due in respect of injury compensation and other benefits under industrial awards, these are limited in the case of excluded employees who are defined in s 556(2) to include directors and their relatives. An employee who becomes a director is only excluded from the general employee priorities from the date of becoming a director. An excluded employee retains limited priority of $2,000 for wages and $1,500 for industrial award benefits but no priority for retrenchment payments: s 556(1A), (1B) and (1C).

As a general rule, liquidators have a lien over the assets in their hands for the costs and expenses of obtaining the assets and also for their remuneration. The right of lien does not extend to placing the liquidator in the position of a secured creditor with respect to all costs and expenses of the winding up where there are higher priority claims: *Re Biposo Pty Ltd (No 4)* (1996) 14 ACLC 78.

The claims of employees have priority over the rights of a chargee seeking to enforce a floating charge created by the company. Payment of employee debts can accordingly be made out of the proceeds of the charged property: s 561.

The effect of s 562 is to enable a person, who is a creditor of a company in respect of a claim for which the company is insured, to be paid from the insurance money received by the liquidator, in priority to other unsecured creditors. The money does not go into the general fund. This de facto statutory priority was enacted to overcome the decision in *Re Harrington Motor Co* [1928] Ch 105, which held that the creditor could not claim the proceeds of insurance but had to stand with other creditors.

priority of the Commissioner of Taxation

A company's debts to the Commonwealth government do not receive any special priority.

[25.485] A company's debts to the Commonwealth government do not receive any special priority. This means that amounts in respect of unpaid income tax rank as unsecured debts and are payable only if there is sufficient left over after all preferential debts have been paid.

A company that is liable to remit amounts such as employers' PAYG tax to the Commissioner of Taxation must either pay the required amounts or go into voluntary administration or liquidation. If these options are not taken up before the due date for payment, all directors become prima facie personally liable to a penalty equal to the outstanding amount of unremitted deductions. Directors who are made personally liable have a right of indemnity from the company and rights of contribution from other directors.

This personal liability of directors is subject to certain defences such as failing to take part in management because of illness or other good reason and all reasonable steps were taken to ensure that the company would pay the amount or go into liquidation.

Unremitted deductions are deemed to be debts for the purposes of the insolvent trading provisions: s 588G. This further forces directors to take steps to have the company enter voluntary administration or liquidation in order to avoid personal liability.

debt subordination

[25.490] The *Corporations Act* confers priority or de facto priority on various debts as discussed above. There are also three types of debts that are deferred until all other unsecured debts are paid in full:

> **payment of a debt to a member in the capacity of a member is postponed until all other debts are paid. This includes a claim for payment of a declared dividend (s 563A);**
> **a creditor who is paid an amount in respect of an admitted debt or claim is also entitled to interest at a prescribed rate for the period between the commencement of winding up and the date of payment: s 563B(1). The payment of interest is postponed until all debts and claims have been satisfied, other than debts owed to members as members of the company: s 563B(2). Where a debt is payable at a future date and has been discounted under s 554B, any interest accruing on the amount is not to be postponed (s 563B(3)); and**
> **where creditors agree among themselves that certain of them will be paid in priority to others if the debtor becomes insolvent, s 563C(1) recognises that such a debt subordination agreement is binding and prevails over the pari passu principle stated in s 555.**

Debt subordination agreements are binding only so far as any other creditor who is not a party to the debt subordination is not disadvantaged by the agreement. This is an adoption of existing case law: *Horne v Chester and Fein Property Development Pty Ltd* (1987) 6 ACLC 245.

division of surplus assets

[25.495] One of the final tasks in a winding up is the distribution of the surplus assets among the members. In a compulsory winding up, a liquidator is not entitled to distribute surplus assets without special leave of the court: s 488(2). There is no such requirement in a voluntary winding up.

Members are entitled to share in the distribution only after all the creditors have been paid in full. Unsecured debts due to members are paid only after all other unsecured debts are paid. The unsecured debts of members are referred to as "deferred debts". After these deferred debts are paid, the surplus assets remaining are distributed among the members.

Members are entitled to share in the distribution only after all the creditors have been paid in full.

The company's constitution usually sets out how the surplus is to be divided. In some cases, the shares are divided into different classes with different priorities as to repayment of capital and entitlements to participate in distributions of surplus assets. Unless otherwise specified, it is presumed that all classes rank equally and shareholders are entitled to repayment of both capital and any remainder, in proportion to the nominal value of their shares: *Re Wakefield Rolling Stock Co* [1892] 2 Ch 165. The same principle of equality applies if there is insufficient to repay the issued capital in full. The losses are shared in proportion to the par value of the shares unless the constitution provides to the contrary.

The company's constitution usually sets out how the surplus is to be divided.

winding up trustee companies

[25.500] In Chapter 3 above we discussed the growth in the popularity of the use of two dollar companies, which act as trustees of discretionary family trusts. The liquidation of trustee companies causes special problems for their creditors. Despite the fact that discretionary trusts have been popular since the early 1960s, the courts have only recently developed techniques for dealing with some of the problems that arise.

trustee's right of indemnity

Trustee companies are liable to trust creditors for debts incurred in operating the business of the trust. As a general rule, the only significant asset of trustee companies is their right to be indemnified from the trust's assets for debts and other liabilities properly incurred.

[25.505] Trustee companies are liable to trust creditors for debts incurred in operating the business of the trust. Trustee companies, however, rarely have significant amounts as issued capital from which to pay creditors. Further, they rarely derive income in their own right. Such income as they do earn is derived on behalf of the beneficiaries of the trust. As a general rule, the only significant asset of trustee companies is their right to be indemnified from the trust's assets for debts and other liabilities properly incurred. For this reason, the debts due to trust creditors can only be satisfied to the extent of the assets of the trust.

Under s 197, directors are personally liable to trust creditors where a trustee company incurs a liability and their company's right of indemnity is not available to satisfy those debts because they were incurred in breach of trust. In *Hanel v O'Neill* (2004) 22 ACLC 274, the court held that directors were personally liable under s 197 even if the trust has insufficient assets to indemnify the trustee. After this case, the *Corporation Amendment Act (No 1) 2005* amended s 197(1) by clarifying that it does not impose liability on a director merely because there are insufficient trust assets out of which the corporation can be indemnified.

Creditors of a corporate trustee also have the right to apply to wind up the company in insolvency: s 459A. If the court grants the application and appoints a liquidator, the liquidator can take control of the assets of the trust to satisfy the trustee company's right of indemnity. The liquidator has this power even where the trust deed provides for the appointment of another person as trustee in the event the company is wound up: *Re Indopal Pty Ltd* (1987) 5 ACLC 278.

priority of trustees' creditors

[25.510] One problem that arises concerns the priorities of the trust creditors of an insolvent trustee company. As discussed above, s 556 ranks the debts of certain preferential creditors in order of priority. The costs and expenses of winding up are given first priority. That section, however, does not address the position of trust creditors.

According to trust law, only trust creditors can be paid out of the assets of a trust. Trust assets cannot be used to pay the debts and liabilities of a trustee's personal creditors.

case note

In *Re Byrne Australia Pty Ltd (No 2)* [1981] 2 NSWLR 364, the Supreme Court of New South Wales held that this rule meant that the costs and expenses of a liquidator of a trustee company in voluntary liquidation cannot be paid out of trust assets. The liquidator was a personal creditor of the insolvent company in respect of the costs and expenses of winding up. One consequence of this conclusion is that no one is likely to agree to act as liquidator of an insolvent trustee company unless its creditors agreed to pay her or his costs and expenses. The court recognised this unsatisfactory state of affairs and suggested that the legislation be altered to specifically deal with the position of insolvent trustee companies.

case note

The conclusion in *Re Byrne Australia Pty Ltd (No 2)* was not followed by the Victorian Supreme Court in *Re Enhill Pty Ltd* [1983] VR 561, where the priority of a liquidator of an insolvent trustee company was considered. While the court agreed that the liquidator was not a trust creditor, it held that a trustee's right of indemnity was available for distribution to all its creditors, whether trust or personal creditors, and therefore the liquidation costs could be paid.

The decision in *Re Enhill Pty Ltd* can have adverse consequences for trust creditors of insolvent trustees who also have personal creditors and appears to be contrary to ordinary principles of trust law. It means that trust assets that should only be available for trust creditors must be shared with a trustee's other creditors.

priority of liquidator's costs and remuneration

[25.515] Section 556 gives the liquidator priority in relation to their expenses and professional fees. Several cases have considered whether the liquidator's priorities apply to the liquidator of a trustee company.

case note

In *Re Suco Gold Pty Ltd* (1983) 33 SASR 99, the Supreme Court of South Australia agreed that where a corporate trustee was insolvent, trust assets are only available to meet the debts and liabilities of creditors of the trust. These assets are not available for distribution to the trustee's general body of creditors. The liquidator, however, is in a special position and the liquidator's costs and expenses can be met out of trust assets.

case note

The *Suco Gold* approach was subsequently adopted by the New South Wales Supreme Court in *Re ADM Franchise Pty Ltd* (1983) 1 ACLC 987. In that case the company acted as trustee of a unit trust whose business was publishing *Australian Penthouse* magazine. The company did not undertake any activities on its own account and its paid up capital was $2. Its only other asset was its right to be indemnified out of trust assets for debts properly incurred by it in operating the publishing business.

The court held that the liquidator should apply the proceeds realised from the trust's assets in accordance with the priorities specified in s 556 and the costs and expenses of the winding up had first priority. The court noted that the decisions in *Re Suco Gold Pty Ltd* and *Re Enhill Pty Ltd* led to the same practical result in so far as the liquidator's priorities were concerned. However, the court decided that the judgments in *Re Suco Gold Pty Ltd* provided a more acceptable means of reaching that result.

Trustee companies, like all other companies, can be wound up for reasons other than insolvency. However, where a solvent trustee company is wound up there is considerable doubt whether the liquidator's costs and expenses can be met out of the assets of the trust.

Where a solvent trustee company is wound up there is considerable doubt whether the liquidator's costs and expenses can be met out of the assets of the trust.

case note

This situation arose in *Re Thomas Dawn Nominees Pty Ltd* (1984) 2 ACLC 459. The company acted as a trustee for two families, the O'Brien family and the Ward family. Another company, Eismeer Pty Ltd, owned and managed a ski lodge in Falls Creek. Thomas Dawn Nominees' only asset was its ownership of two parcels of shares in Eismeer. These shares were held by it on trust for each of the families, respectively. The shares entitled each family to occupy particular flats in the ski lodge. When Mr and Mrs O'Brien separated, Mrs O'Brien was granted an order winding up Thomas Dawn Nominees on the just and equitable ground. The liquidator wanted to sell the company's shares in Eismeer and apply the proceeds first in payment of the costs and expenses of the winding up and then, as the company had no other debts, divide the remainder between the two families.

The Victorian Supreme Court held that the trust assets, the shares in Eismeer, could not be used to pay the liquidation expenses. Beach J distinguished *Re Suco Gold Pty Ltd* and *Re Enhill Pty Ltd* on the basis that they dealt with the position of a liquidator of insolvent trustee companies with unpaid trust debts. In such situations the liquidation expenses are regarded as debts of the trustees incurred in discharging the duties of the trusts and are covered by the trustees' rights of indemnity. Thomas Dawn Nominees, however, was solvent. There were no debts due to trust creditors for which the company was liable. Consequently, it had no right to be indemnified out of trust assets for the liquidation costs and expenses. They were personal debts of the company and were not incurred by it in discharging the duties of trustee. This meant that the liquidator could not sell the Eismeer shares and apply the proceeds in paying the liquidation expenses. As a result of this decision, liquidators are unlikely to accept an appointment to act as liquidators of solvent trustee companies unless their shareholders or beneficiaries agree to pay all the costs of winding up.

deregistration

A company may be deregistered voluntarily by ASIC upon the application of eligible persons. Deregistration may also be initiated by ASIC.

[25.520] A company may be deregistered voluntarily by ASIC upon the application of eligible persons. Deregistration may also be initiated by ASIC.

voluntary deregistration

[25.525] Under s 601AA(1), the following persons are able to apply to ASIC for voluntary deregistration of a company:

> the company;
> a director or member of the company; and
> a liquidator of the company.

An application for voluntary deregistration can only be made if:

> all the members of the company agree;
> the company is not carrying on business;
> the company's assets are worth less than $1,000;
> the company has no outstanding liabilities and has paid all outstanding fees and penalties; and
> the company is not party to any legal proceedings.

If ASIC is not aware of any failure to comply with the above requirements, it must give notice of the proposed deregistration on the ASIC database and in the Commonwealth *Gazette*: s 601AA(4). ASIC may deregister the company when two months have passed since the *Gazette* notice. ASIC must give notice of the deregistration to the applicant: s 601AA(5).

ASIC-initiated deregistration

[25.530] ASIC may decide to deregister a company if the requirements of either s 601AB(1) or (2) are met.

Under s 601AB(1), ASIC may deregister a company if:

> **its annual return is at least six months late;**
> **the company has not lodged any other documents in the last 18 months; or**
> **ASIC has no reason to believe that the company is carrying on business.**

Under s 601AB(2), ASIC may also decide to deregister a company if it is being wound up and ASIC has reasonable grounds for believing that:

> **the liquidator is no longer acting;**
> **the company's affairs have been fully wound up and a return that the liquidator should have lodged is at least six months late; or**
> **the company's affairs have been fully wound up and it does not have enough property to pay the costs of obtaining a court order for deregistration.**

If ASIC decides to deregister a company, it must give notice of the proposed deregistration to the company, its directors and liquidator (if any): s 601AB(3). Notice of the proposed deregistration must also be given on the ASIC database and in the *Gazette*. This ensures that ASIC will not be able to deregister a company only because the company has forgotten to lodge necessary returns with ASIC.

ASIC may deregister the company when two months have passed since the publication of the *Gazette* notice. Once the company is deregistered, ASIC must give notice of the deregistration to the persons listed in s 601AB(3).

deregistration following amalgamation or winding up

[25.535] Section 601AC requires ASIC to deregister a company if the court orders the deregistration under:

> **s 413(1)(d) (reconstruction and amalgamation); or**
> **s 481(5)(b) (release of liquidator); or**
> **s 509(6) (liquidator's return following winding up).**

effect of deregistration

A company ceases to exist on deregistration and all its property vests in ASIC, which has all the powers of an owner.

[25.540] A company ceases to exist on deregistration and all its property vests in ASIC, which has all the powers of an owner: s 601AD. ASIC may dispose of or deal with the property as it sees fit and may apply any money it receives to defray expenses incurred by it: s 601AE(2). Section 601AF gives ASIC the power to fulfil any outstanding obligations of the company. This will bind the company as if it still existed.

Deregistration does not effect a person's pre-deregistration rights over the company's property which remain subject to all liabilities imposed on the property: s 601AE(3). These liabilities include a liability that is a charge or claim on the property or an obligation for rates, taxes or other charges imposed by a law. If the property was subject to a security, other interest or claim, ASIC takes the property subject to that security interest or claim: s 601AD(3). If the ASIC vested property was held by the company on trust, ASIC may continue to act as trustee or apply to the court for the appointment of a new trustee: s 601AE(1).

Under s 601AD(5), the directors of the company immediately before deregistration must keep the company's books for three years after the deregistration.

reinstatement

A deregistered company may be reinstated by ASIC if it is satisfied that the company should not have been deregistered. The court also has the power to order ASIC to reinstate a deregistered company if it is satisfied that it is just to do so.

[25.545] A deregistered company may be reinstated by ASIC if it is satisfied that the company should not have been deregistered: s 601AH(1). Under s 601AH(2), the court also has the power to order ASIC to reinstate a deregistered company if it is satisfied that it is just to do so.

The reinstatement application can be made by a person aggrieved by the deregistration or a former liquidator of the company. Persons aggrieved by a company's deregistration include persons with a proprietary or pecuniary interest in the reinstatement such as the company's creditors and other claimants.

case note

In *Krstevska v ACN 010 505 012* [2001] NSWSC 1093, a company was reinstated on the application of a former employee who had suffered injuries in the course of her employment. A workers' compensation claim was brought against the company and it was later discovered that the company had been deregistered. The reinstatement enabled the employee to continue with her legal proceedings against the company which was insured for such claims.

A company ceases to exist on deregistration, but this does not affect the liabilities of individuals or entities associated with the deregistered company prior to deregistration. The property of the company vests in ASIC on deregistration. The deregistered company's directors are under a statutory obligation to keep the company's books for three years after deregistration.

ASIC has the power to reinstate companies that have been inadvertently deregistered. This avoids the expense of a court application for reinstatement. ASIC exercises its reinstatement powers only where no dealings with the property of the company have been carried out which give rise to third party rights. Where third party rights have become involved, reinstatement requires a court application.

pathways questions . . .

The following questions dealing with liquidations may best be answered by reading this chapter and considering the Internet resources found on the Lipton-Herzberg Corporate Insolvency Pathway at http://www.lipton-herzberg.com.au/secure/pathways-corporate-insolvency.html

1. **What were the main recommendations of the Harmer Report with respect to company liquidations? Which of these recommendations have been incorporated into the *Corporations Act*?**

2. How will the proposals in the Corporate Insolvency Reform Package (October 2005) impact on liquidations?

3 Refer to the *Review of the Regulation of Corporate Insolvency Practitioners*.
   (a) Should the regulation of insolvency practitioners engaged in personal and corporate insolvency be further integrated or merged?
   (b) Should the distinction between official and registered liquidators be retained?
   (c) Is it sometimes appropriate for persons other than registered liquidators to act as administrators?
   (d) Should entry requirements for registered liquidators be changed? If so, how?
   (e) Should insolvency practitioners be subject to a code of conduct or prescribed ethical rules?
   (f) What recommendations were made in relation to fee-setting by insolvency practitioners? What problems were these recommendations seeking to address?
   (g) What provision should be made to remunerate practitioners dealing with companies without assets?

4. Explain how the *Corporations Law (Employee Entitlements) Act 2000* aims to protect the entitlements of a company's employees.

bibliography ...

Annetta, V "Priority Rights in Insolvency—The Doctrinal Basis for Equity's Intervention" (1992) 20 ABLR 311.

Atkins, S "Public policy: The Law's Guardian in the Clash between Insolvency and Maintenance in the Context of Litigation Funding Arrangements" (2004) 12 Insolv LJ 41.

Australian Law Reform Commission. "General Insolvency Inquiry". (1988) 45 ALRC.

Barlow, K "Voidable Preferences and the Running Account—The High Court Reconsiders" (1998) 26 ABLR 82.

Bennetts, K "Voidable Transactions: Consequences of Removing Avoidance Powers from the Liquidator and Vesting Them in the Court" (1994) 2 Insolv LJ 136.

Bennetts, K J "Dealing with Winding Up Applications Following the Appointment of an Administrator" (2000) 18 C & SLJ 41.

Bennetts, K J "Payments by Receivers to Pre-appointment Unsecured Creditors—Are They Recoverable as Voidable Preferences?" (1993) 11 C & SLJ 327.

Bennetts, K J "Unfair Dismissal Proceedings in Company Liquidation and Receivership" (1990) 8 C & SLJ 158.

Bourke, G "The Effectiveness in Australia of Contractual Debt Subordination Where the Debtor Becomes Insolvent" (1996) 7 JBFLP 107.

Broderick, M & Lenicka, M "Uncommercial Transactions—Corporate Governance for Insolvent Companies" (2004) 22 C & SLJ 7.

Campbell, C "An Examination of the Champertous Assignment of Bare Causes of Action" (1999) 27 ABLR 142.

Campo, R "The Protection of Employee Entitlements in the Event of Employer Insolvency: Australian Initiatives in the Light of International Models" (2000) 13 Aust J of Labour Law 236.

Caulfield, M & Baxter, A "Recovery of Company Assets from the Spouses or Associates of Delinquent Directors" (2002) 10 Insolv LJ 95.

Collier, B "Liquidators, Romalpa Clauses and Conversion of Goods: Robert A Conaghan (NZ) Ltd v A W Russell" (1995) 3 Insolv LJ 85.

Collier, B "The Power of a Company in Liquidation to Appoint an Attorney" (1993) 11 C & SLJ 49.

Darvas, P "Employees' Rights an Entitlements and Insolvency: Regulatory Rationale, Legal Issues and Proposed Solutions" (1999) 17 C & SLJ 103.

Dean, M "International Insolvencies: The Difficulties, the Traditional Solution and the Ideal" (2001) 9 Insolv LJ 88.

De Jong, L "The Corporations Act Approach to Uncommercial Transactions—Is It Working?" (2003) 11 Insolv LJ 199.

Donnenberg, V & Grant, J "Removing administrators and liquidators tainted by conflict, bias or bad practice" (2005) 13 Insolv LJ 133.

Duns, J "Winding Up Foreign Companies" (1999) 7 Insolv L J 38.

Duns, J "'Insolvency': Problems of Concept, Definition and Proof" (2000) 28 ABLR 22.

Duthie, L "The Priority of Retrenchment Payments in Liquidation or Receivership" (1992) 20 ABLR 378.

Edwards, R "Floating Charges and Preferences" (2000) 12 Aust Jnl of Corp Law 98.

Edwards, R "Void Dispositions by Companies and Bank Cheques" (2002) 14 Aust Jnl of Corp Law 149.

Farrar, J "Corporate Group Insolvencies, Reform and the United States Experience" (2000) 8 Insolv LJ 148.

Fisher, R "Preferences and Other Antecedent Transactions: Do Directors Owe a Duty to Creditors?" (1995) 8 *Corporate and Business Law Journal* 203.

Fryer-Smith, S "Voidable Transactions in Corporate Insolvency: The Constructive Trust Alternative" (1996) 4 Insolv LJ 34.

Glover, J & Duns, J "Insolvency Administrations at General Law: Fiduciary Obligations of Company Receivers, Voluntary Administrators and Liquidators" (2001) 9 Insolv LJ 130.

Gorman, K "Sidestepping the Statutory Demand: Is Solvency a Solution?" (2002) 10 Insolv LJ 239.

Gothard, P "Insurance Litigation Funding Agreements: Benefits and Potential Problems" (1999) 7 Insolv LJ 29.

Gronow, M "Secured Creditors of Insolvent Companies: Do They Get Too Good a Deal?" (1993) 1 Insolv LJ 199.

Gronow, M "Insolvent Corporate Groups and their Employees: The Case for Further Reform" (2003) 21 C & SLJ 188.

Hamilton, G "Are a Liquidator's Recoveries Available to the Company's Secured Creditors?" (2002) 20 C & SLJ 25.

Hamilton, G "Provisions Which Avoid Charges Under the Corporations Law: The Effect on Secured Creditors and Receivers" (1998) 16 C & SLJ 333.

Hamilton, G "An Insolvency Riddle: When is a Debt Which is Due Not a Debt Which is Due and Payable?" (1997) 5 Insolv LJ 78.

Hamilton, G J "Aspects of Official Liquidators' Personal Liability for Costs of Liquidation" (1989) 7 C & SLJ 263 and 301.

Hammond, C "Insolvent Companies and Employees: The Government's Year 2000 Solutions" (2000) 8 Insolv LJ 86.

Keay, A "Deregistration: The New End of the Road for Companies in Liquidation" (1999) 7 Insolv LJ 87.

Keay, A "The Unity of Insolvency Legislation: Time for a Re-think?" (1999) 7 Insolv LJ 4.

Keay, A "An Exposition of the Principles of Provisional Liquidation" (1998) 6 Insolv LJ 19.

Keay, A "Finding a Way Through the Maze that is the Law of Statutory Demands" (1998) 16 C & SLJ 122.

Keay, A "Liquidators' Avoidance of Uncommercial Transactions" (1996) 70 ALJ 390.

Keay, A "An Analysis of Unfair Preferences Under the New Avoidance Regime" (1996) 24 ABLR 39.

Keay, A "An Examination of Procedural Issues Relating to the Commencement of a Liquidator's Avoidance Action" (1996) 14 C & SLJ 78.

Keay, A "In Pursuit of the Rationale Behind the Avoidance of Pre-Liquidation Transactions" (1996) 18 Syd LR 55.

Keay, A "Preference Recoveries: Who is Entitled to Them?" (1996) 14 C & SLJ 442.

Keay, A "The Insolvency Factor in the Avoidance of Antecedent Transactions in Corporate Liquidations" (1995) 21 Mon LR 305.

Keay, A "Defending a Liquidator: Avoidance Action Commenced under Pt 5.7B of the Corporations Law" (1994) 5 Aust Jnl of Corp Law 17.

Keay, A "'Relation-back Day' and 'Related Entity': New Key Terms in Liquidations Law" (1994) 2 Insolv LJ 126.

Keenan, P "Investigations by External Administrators" (1995) 13 C & SLJ 368.

Koeck, W J & Ramsay, I M "The Importance of Distinguishing Between Different Categories of Creditors for the Purposes of Company Law" (1994) 12 C & SLJ 105.

Langton, R & Trotman, L "Sharing the Proceeds of Business Failure—Competition between Feudal and Democratic Principles in Liquidation of Australian Companies" (1999) 11 *Corporate and Business Law Journal* 263.

Lawrence, J "Are Directors Running Accounts in Breach of Their Duties" (1997) 8 Aust Jnl of Corp Law 200.

Lawrence, J "Keeping a Running Account on the Preference Laws" (1996) 4 Insolv LJ 171.

McPherson, B A "The Insolvent Trading Trust" in Finn, P D (ed). *Essays in Equity*. LawBook Co, Sydney, 1987, Ch 8.

McQuade, P "A Receiver's, Liquidator's and Provisional Liquidator's Claim to a Lien or Charge for Remuneration and Expenses" (1993) 1 Insolv LJ 199.

Maiden, S "Tensions between the Public and Private Purposes of Examinations under Pt 5.9 of the Corporations Act 2001 (Cth)" (2004) 12 Insolv LJ 28.

Martin, J "Distribution Complexities in the Winding Up of an Insurance Company in Australia" (2002) 10 Insolv LJ 80.

Mason, R "Choice of Law in Cross-border Insolvencies: Matters of Substance and Procedure" (2001) 9 Insolv LJ 69.

Mason, R "Cross-border Insolvency: Adoption of CLERP 8 as an Evolution of Australian Insolvency Law" (2003) 11 Insolv LJ 62.

Morrison, D & Anderson, C "Uncommercial Transactions—Development in the New Regime" (1999) 7 Insolv LJ 184.

Morrison, Rachel "Avoiding Inherent Uncertainties in Cross-Border Insolvency: Is the UNCITRAL Model Law the Answer?" (1999) QUT LJ 103.

Mourell, M & Willoughby, J "Disclaimers of Onerous Property Under s 568 of the Corporations Law" (1994) Aust Jnl of Corp Law 63.

Nash, L "Disclaimers by Liquidators—How Secure is your Guarantee?" (1997) 13 QUT LJ 82.

Noakes, D "Dogs on the Wharves: Corporate Groups and the Waterfront Dispute" (1999) 11 Aust Jnl Corp Law 27.

Noakes, D "Measuring the Impact of Strategic Insolvency on Employees" (2003) 11 Insolv LJ 91.

O'Brien, D "The Status of Optionholders and Redeemable Preference Shareholders in Compulsory Liquidations" (1996) 4 Insolv LJ 42.

O'Donovan, J "Voidable Dispositions and Undue Preferences: The Transition to the New Regime" (1994) 12 C & SLJ 7.

O'Donovan, J "Procedural Aspects of Recovering Voidable Preferences" (1993) 1 Insolv LJ 65.

Omar, P "Jurisdictional Criteria and Paradigms in International Insolvency Texts" (2004) 12 Insolv LJ 7.

Powers, L "Insolvency Law and Management: The Effect of the Liquidation on the Agency of a Receiver" (1999) 10 JBFLP 249.

Quo, S "Current Issues Affecting Secured Creditors: Whether Payments to Secured Creditors can be Recovered by Liquidators as Unfair Preferences" (2003) 11 Insolv LJ 117.

Quo, S "Legal practitioners and persons acting for those at risk of insolvency: In what circumstances will professional fees constitute unfair preferences?" (2005) 13 Insolv LJ 7.

Rheinhardt, G "The Availability of Tracing to the Insolvency Administrator—Is the Remedy Adequate?" (1996) 4 Insolv LJ 74.

Robinson, D "Remuneration of Corporate Insolvency Practitioners" (2000) 8 Insolv LJ 20.

Ross, M "Payments Made in the Ordinary Course of Business by an Insolvent Company" (2000) 8 Insolv LJ 157.

Stoney M "Applications to Set Aside Statutory Demands—Has Division 3 of Part 5.4 Achieved Its Stated Objectives?" (2000) 8 Insolv LJ 96

Symes, C "Remuneration, Rent and 'Requisite' Costs: The 3 R's of Insolvency's Administration Expense Priority" (2000) 11 Aust Jnl of Corp Law 149.

Symes, C "Do Not Dismiss the Employee as a Statutory Priority Creditor in Corporate Insolvency" (1998) 26 ABLR 450.

Symes, C "The Protection of Wages When Insolvency Strikes" (1998) 5 Insolv LJ 196.

Symes, C "The Dawn of Green Corporate Insolvency Law: Environmental Accountability Creeping Over the Horizon" (1998) 9 Aust Jnl of Corp Law 64.

Taylor, T "Employee Entitlements in Corporate Insolvency Administrations" (2000) 8 Insolv LJ 32.

Whelan, S "Administration of Insolvent Groups—The Present State of Pooling" (1998) 6 Insolv LJ 107.

Whelan, S & Zwier, L "Employee entitlements and corporate insolvency and reconstruction" Centre for Corporate Law & Securities Regulation, Corporate Law Research Papers Website **http://cclsr.law.unimelb.edu.au/research-papers/index.html**

Wyatt, A & Mason, R "Legal and Accounting Regulatory Framework for Corporate Groups: Implications for Insolvency in Group Operations" (1998) 16 C & SLJ 424.

Zumbo, F "The Liquidator's Power of Examination Under the Corporations Law: The State of Play" (1994) 12 C & SLJ 504.

revision questions on the material in this chapter . . .

> Please see eQuiz at **http://www.thomson.com.au/academic** for multiple choice questions and answers.

> For further corporations law links and material please refer to the Lipton-Herzberg website at **http://www.lipton-herzberg.com.au**

table of cases

Case	Paragraph
ACCC v ASIC [2000] NSWSC 316	[13.5.95]
ADM Franchise Pty Ltd, Re (1983) 1 ACLC 987	[25.515]
ANZ Executors & Trustee Co Ltd v Qintex Australia Ltd (1990) 8 ACLC 980	[13.5.10]
ASC v Ampolex Ltd (1996) 14 ACLC 80	[21.20]
ASC v AS Nominees Ltd (1995) 13 ACLC 1822	[17.175]
ASC v Aust-Home Investments Ltd (1993) 11 ACLC 438	[23.60]
ASC v Bank Leumi Le-Israel (1996) 14 ACLC 1576	[18.40]
ASC v Deloitte Touche Tohmatsu (1996) 14 ACLC 1486	[21.35]
ASC v Donovan (1998) 28 ACSR 583	[13.6.45]
ASC v Fairlie (1993) 11 ACLC 669	[15.25]
ASC v Lucas (1992) 10 ACLC 888	[21.20]
ASC v McLeod (2000) 18 ACLC 424	[19.145]
ASC v Marlborough Gold Mines Ltd (1993) 11 ACLC 370	[1.60]
ASC v Nomura International PLC (1999) 17 ACLC 55	[19.135]
ASC v Zarro (1992) 10 ACLC 11	[21.20]
ASIC v ABC Fund Managers (No 2) [2001] VSC 383	[25.135]
ASIC v Adler [2002] NSWSC 171	[8.270], [13.0.20], [13.2.05], [13.2.100], [13.3.10], [13.3.85], [13.4.30], [13.4.40], [13.4.50], [13.4.60] , [13.5.35], [13.6.45], [13.6.50]
ASIC v Adler [2002] NSWSC 483	[13.6.55]
ASIC v Adler [2003] NSWCA 131	[13.2.100], [13.3.50], [13.3.85]
ASIC v Adler (No 5) (2002) 20 ACLC 1146	[13.6.50]
ASIC v Adler (No 5) [2002] NSWSC 483	[13.7.25]
ASIC v Australian Investors Forum Pty Ltd (No 2) [2005] NSWSC 267	[7.25]
ASIC v Chase Capital Management Pty Ltd (2001) 19 ACLC 476	[20.15]
ASIC v Petsas [2005] FCA 88	[19.245]
ASIC v Plymin [2003] VSC 123	[13.5.55], [13.5.60], [13.5.70], [13.5.75], [13.5.90], [13.5.115], [13.6.40]
ASIC v Rich [2003] NSWSC 85	[12.30], [13.1.45], [13.4.20], [13.4.25], [13.4.35]
ASIC v Vines [2003] NSWSC 738	[13.4.15], [13.4.40]
ASIC v Vines [2003] NSWSC 1116	[13.4.40]
ASIC v Vizard [2005] FCA 1037	[13.3.135], [13.6.35]
AWA Ltd v Daniels (1992) 10 ACLC 933	[12.30], [13.4.30], [14.95]
AWA Ltd v Daniels (1992) 7 ACSR 759	[13.4.35], [13.4.55]
AZED Developments Pty Ltd v Frederick & Co Ltd (1994) 12 ACLC 949	[25.65]
Abalcheck Pty Ltd v Pullen (1990) 8 ACLC 1078	[11.110], [14.145]
Abeles v PA (Holdings) Pty Ltd (2000) 18 ACLC 867	[13.6.10]
Aberdeen Railway Co v Blaikie Bros (1854) 1 Macq 461	[13.3.05]
Adler v ASIC [2003] NSWCA 113	[13.4.30], [13.4.50]
Advance Bank Australia Ltd v FAI Insurances Ltd (1987) 5 ACLC 725	[13.2.85], [13.7.25]
Advance Bank Australia Ltd v Fleetwood Star Pty Ltd (1992) 10 ACLC 703	[5.140]
Aequitas v AEFC (2001) 19 ACLC 1006	[6.15], [6.25], [6.50]
Aerospatiale Societe Nationale Industrielle v Aerospatiale Helicopters Pty Ltd (1986) ATPR 40-700	[2.260]
Ah Toy, Re (1986) 4 ACLC 480	[25.250]
Airpeak Pty Ltd v Jetstream Ltd (1997) 15 ACLC 715	[17.140]
Airservices Australia v Ferrier (1996) 14 ACLC 1403	[25.370]

Mistmorn Pty Ltd v Yasseen (1996) 14 ACLC 1387	[13.4.40]
Molit (No 55) Pty Ltd v Lam Soon Australia Pty Ltd (1996) 14 ACLC 1371	[24.55]
Moodie v W & J Shepherd Ltd [1949] 2 All ER 1044	[9.115]
Mordecai v Mordecai (1988) 12 NSWLR 58	[13.3.110], [13.3.150]
Morgan v 45 Flers Avenue Pty Ltd (1987) 5 ACLC 222	[17.25], [17.45], [17.55]
Morley v Statewide Tobacco Services Ltd (1990) 8 ACLC 825	[13.5.85]
Morris v Kanssen [1946] AC 459	[5.120], [5.210]
Mount Edon Gold Mines (Aust) Ltd v Burmine Ltd (1994) 12 ACLC 185	[3.140]
Movitor Pty Ltd, Re (1996) 14 ACLC 587	[25.215]
Myers v Aquarell Pty Ltd [2000] VSC 429	[5.165]
NCSC v Monarch Petroleum NL (1984) 2 ACLC 256	[19.65], [19.145]
NRMA v Parker (1986) 4 ACLC 609	[14.40]
NRMA v Scandrett [2002] NSWSC 1123	[14.40]
NRMA Ltd v Snodgrass [2001] NSWSC 76	[4.75]
NZI Securities (Aust) Ltd v Poignand (1994) 12 ACLC 550	[23.40]
Nambucca Investments Pty Ltd v Star (1995) 13 ACLC 1814	[24.40]
National Australia Bank Ltd v Sparrow Green Pty Ltd (1999) 17 ACLC 1665	[5.130], [5.135]
National Education Advancement Programs Pty Ltd v Ashton (1996) 14 ACLC 30	[2.250]
National Exchange Pty Ltd v ASIC [2004] FCAFC 90	[9.40], [19.155]
National Safety Council of Australia, Re (1989) 7 ACLC 603	[25.200]
National Westminster Bank plc v Spectrum Plus Ltd [2005] UKHL 41	[11.75]
Network Exchange Pty Ltd v MIG International Communications Pty Ltd (1994) 12 ACLC 594	[24.70]
New England Agriculture Corp Ltd, Re (1982) 1 ACLC 557	[25.120]
New South Wales v Commonwealth (1990) 8 ACLC 120	[1.25], [1.45], [1.55]
New World Alliance Pty Ltd, Re (1994) 122 ALR 531	[13.5.35]
Newborne v Sensolid (Great Britain) Ltd [1954] 1 QB 45	[6.65]
Ngurli Ltd v McCann (1953) 90 CLR 425	[13.2.65]
Nicholas v Commr for Corporate Affairs (1987) 5 ACLC 673	[12.190]
Nicholson v Permakraft (NZ) Ltd [1985] 1 NZLR 172	[13.5.15]
Nilant v Shenton [2001] WASCA 421	[12.200]
Niord Pty Ltd v Adelaide Petroleum NL (1990) 8 ACLC 684	[9.100], [17.20]
North Broken Hill Holdings Ltd, Re (1886) 4 ACLC 131	[18.40]
North-West Transportation Co v Beatty (1887) 12 App Cas 589	[13.3.160], [17.35], [17.205]
Northbourne Developments Pty Ltd v Reiby Chambers Pty Ltd (1989) 8 ACLC 39	[25.300]
Northside Developments Pty Ltd v Registrar-General (1987) 5 ACLC 642	[12.260]
Northside Developments Pty Ltd v Registrar-General (1990) 8 ACLC 611	[5.10], [5.75], [5.125], [5.140], [5.180], [5.195], [5.200], [5.210]
Norvabron Pty Ltd, Re (1987) 5 ACLC 184	[17.25]
Nottingham General Cemetery Co, Re [1955] Ch 683	[25.145]
O'Brien v Walker (1982) 1 ACLC 59	[13.6.30]
195 Crown St Pty Ltd v Hoare [1969] 1 NSWR 193	[5.70]
Osborne Computer Corp Ltd v Airroad Distribution Pty Ltd (1995) 13 ACLC 1129	[24.50]
Osborne Computer Corp Ltd v Riddell (1995) 13 ACLC 1210	[24.50]
Overend & Gurney & Co v Gibb (1872) LR 56 HL 480	[13.4.10]
Overton Holdings Pty Ltd, Re (1984) 2 ACLC 777	[17.65], [17.95]

table of the Corporations Act

table of the Corporations Regulations

table of the Australian Securities and Investments Commission Act

table of codes

table of statutes

Commonwealth

Acts Interpretation Act 1901: [1.60]
s 15AA: [1.60]
s 15AB: [1.60]

Australian Securities Commission Act 1989: [1.40]

Bankruptcy Act 1966: [9.145], [22.05], [25.05]
s 86: [25.450]
Pt X: [9.120], [12.170]

Broadcasting and Television Act 1942: [18.335]

Companies Act 1961 (Uniform Companies Act): [1.30], [10.65]

Companies (Foreign Takeovers) Act 1972: [18.10]

Constitution
s 51(xx): [1.25], [1.45]
s 51(xxxvii): [1.60]

Corporate Law Economic Reform Program (Audit Reform and Corporate Disclosure) Act 2004: [1.130], [1.135], [1.145], [1.155], [1.170], [12.240], [13.6.45], [13.6.55], [13.6.85], [14.15], [14.75], [14.105], [15.65], [15.70], [15.90], [15.110], [15.140], [15.170], [16.20], [16.25], [16.45], [16.90], [16.115], [16.170], [16.180], [16.185]

Corporation Amendment Act (No 1) 2005: [3.200], [25.505]

Corporations Act 1989: [1.25], [1.40], [1.45], [1.50], [1.60]

Corporations Amendment (Repayment of Directors' Bonuses) Act 2003: [25.385]

Corporations Law: [1.50]

Corporations Law Amendment (Employee Entitlements) Act 2000: [13.5.140], [25.435]

Crimes Act 1914: [1.60]
s 4B: [5.55], [19.245]
s 173: [2.45]

Director of Public Prosecutions Act 1983: [1.60]

Federal Court Rules: [25.40]

Financial Services Reform Act 2001: [7.130], [19.05], [19.10], [19.15], [19.35], [19.75], [20.05]

Foreign Takeovers Act 1975: [18.335]

Income Tax Assessment Act 1936: [3.190]
s 215: [23.115], [23.130]
s 221P: [23.20]
s 222ANA-222AQD: [22.75], [24.15]

Income Tax Assessment Act 1997: [2.80], [25.105]
s 252: [2.340]

Insurance Contracts Act 1984
s 17: [2.45]

Life Insurance Act 1995: [11.40]

Proceeds of Crime Act 1987: [25.445]

Trade Practices Act 1974: [13.5.95], [16.180], [18.10], [18.335]
s 6(2): [16.180]
s 50: [18.335]
s 52: [2.260], [7.175], [16.180], [16.185]
s 52(1): [2.260]
s 75AZC(1)(g): [5.20]
s 82: [16.170], [16.180]

New South Wales

Associations Incorporation Act 1984: [3.20]

Law Reform (Miscellaneous Provisions) Act 1965
s 10: [16.165]

Minors (Property and Contracts) Act 1970: [9.55]

Victoria

Associations Incorporation Act 1981: [3.20]

Supreme Court Act 1958
s 62: [23.65]

Wrongs Act 1958
s 26: [16.165]

New Zealand

Workers' Compensation Act 1922: [2.45]

United Kingdom

Bubble Act 1719: [1.10], [1.15]

Companies Act 1862: [1.15], [2.40]

Merchant Shipping Act 1894
s 502: [5.10]

index